BRIDGING ENGLISH

Second Edition

Joseph O'Beirne Milner
Wake Forest University

Lucy Floyd Morcock Milner
Salem College
North Carolina Governor's School

Merrill,
an imprint of Prentice Hall
Upper Saddle River, New Jersey • *Columbus, Ohio*

Library of Congress Cataloging-in-Publication Data
Milner, Joseph O'Beirne
    Bridging English / Joseph O'Beirne Milner, Lucy Floyd Morcock
Milner. — 2nd ed.
      p. cm.
    Includes bibliographical references and index.
    ISBN 0-13-792946-3
    1. English language—Study and teaching (Secondary)   I. Milner,
Lucy Floyd Morcock.   II. Title.
LB1631.M455   1999
428'.0071'2—dc21   98-25239
                                           CIP

Cover art: ©Steven R. Schildbach
Editor: Bradley J. Potthoff
Production Editor: Sheryl Glicker Langner
Design Coordinator: Diane C. Lorenzo
Text Designer: Angela Foote
Cover Designer: Ceri Fitzgerald
Production Manager: Pamela D. Bennett
Electronic Text Management: Karen L. Bretz
Director of Marketing: Kevin Flanagan
Marketing Manager: Suzanne Stanton
Marketing Coordinator: Krista Groshong

This book was set in Garamond Book by Carlisle Communications, Ltd., and was
printed and bound by Banta Company. The cover was printed by Banta Company.

 ©1999, 1993 by Prentice-Hall, Inc.
Simon & Schuster/A Viacom Company
Upper Saddle River, New Jersey 07458

All photos by Cary Clifford

Printed in the United States of America

10 9 8 7 6 5 4 3 2 1

ISBN: 0-13-792946-3

Prentice-Hall International (UK) Limited, *London*
Prentice-Hall of Australia Pty. Limited, *Sydney*
Prentice-Hall of Canada, Inc., *Toronto*
Prentice-Hall Hispanoamericana, S. A., *Mexico*
Prentice-Hall of India Private Limited, *New Delhi*
Prentice-Hall of Japan, Inc., *Tokyo*
Simon & Schuster Asia Pte. Ltd., *Singapore*
Editora Prentice-Hall do Brasil, Ltda., *Rio de Janeiro*

for
Jonathan O'Beirne Milner
Benjamin Southwood Milner
Peter Cooper Milner

PREFACE

We wrote the first edition of *Bridging English* (1993) because we could not find a balanced, comprehensive English methods textbook whose theory was rigorous and whose practice was accessible and pertinent. Reviewers and users of our text have praised just those qualities we sought: comprehensiveness, theoretical soundness, practical usefulness. They found that it effectively moved readers from theories (learning, language, literacy) to classroom realities. One colleague and his class call our text *BE* because, as he explains, it captures all that his students need to know and be to launch them toward becoming able secondary English teachers. Its readers appear also drawn to its perspective which is student-centered, constructivist, developmental, inquiry based, and reflective. Many colleagues report that this is one textbook students do not sell back because they regard it not simply as a general introduction to English education, but as a reference and resource with which to begin their professional libraries.

We have revised the first edition of our text for two primary reasons: 1) to address new developments in the field of English education, and 2) to clarify, sharpen, and expand many of our original ideas. In this thorough revision, we have tried to retain and strengthen what has proven most valuable while we explained and vivified new ideas and methods.

STRENGTHS OF THE FIRST EDITION

In the first edition of *Bridging English,* we attempted to bridge many different shores: of self (as the reader prepares to move from the role of student to that of teacher), of instructional theories, of methods, of texts, of cultural expectations of English classrooms. With a consciousness of the quandaries of prospective teachers, we challenged readers to make personal connections between their previous experiences as students and their future expectations as teachers. Three Textual Features—Invitations to Reflection, Exercises, and Teaching Activities—engaged readers and invited them to reflect, to test, and to plan. Readers tell us that the text's breadth and balance "brought it all together"—their understanding and grasp of literature, language, and learning. We have retained many of the valued aspects of the first edition such as:

- the interplay of learning, language, and literary theory with best teaching practice
- the numerous sequences of instruction, teaching activities, and concrete examples of teachable texts that range from literary classics to works by minority and young adult writers, from print to non-print
- its balanced view of the debated pedagogical issues in the English Education field: grammar and writing instruction, cooperative learning, reader response based approaches to literature, multicultural literature, technology in the classroom, authentic assessment, and critical and cultural literacy
- its treatment of numerous vital, but sometimes overlooked subjects such as the history of the English language, ten schools of literary criticism, the canon wars' debate, oral language, nonfiction, media, and evaluation
- its authorial voice that filters and interprets its information and ideas through decades of teaching at the college and secondary levels

CHANGES IN THE SECOND EDITION

Like its predecessor, the second edition of *Bridging English* grows from our ongoing observations and reflections on English classrooms. We feel again a little like E. B. White, who explained of his writing that he just wanted to keep the minutes of his own meeting. In these intervening years, our meeting has continued and has opened many provocative developments in our field and in ourselves. With these changes in mind we update, amend, and enlarge our first edition. Our revisions include the following:

- In our largest reorganization, we describe the intermediate steps necessary to transform theory into practical classroom lessons by adding new sections to existing chapters and two new chapters on 1) writing and 2) planning lessons and units.
- We present graphic organizers in key chapters that provide visual maps of sequences of instructional approaches, methods of instruction, and teaching activities.
- We sharpen our focus and expand our treatment of many crucial issues.
    Constructivist Principles of Learning
    Approaches to Teaching Grammar and Writing
    Approaches to Teaching Literature
    Readers' Theater
    Portfolios
    Censorship
- We explore developments new to the field or to us, such as the following:
    A Reading Cycle (Enter, Explore, Extend)
    Christenbury and Kelly's Questioning Circle
    New Historical Criticism
    Dias's Research on Adolescent Poetry Readers
    Literature Circles
    Applebee's Conversation-Based Planning
    Authentic Assessment
- We include more descriptive research data that places our ideas and students' planning within a context of the actual practice in high schools today.
- We enlarge most of our lists of texts with new titles.
- To the insights of many veteran teachers included in the first edition, we add those of young teachers who read the first edition and are currently teaching.

As we have incorporated these changes, we have tried to avoid the decision made by an Austrian film company that wanted to remake Richard Rodgers and Oscar Hammerstein's 1965 classic, *The Sound of Music.* The Austrians knew that the original was too long and that they had to work within boundaries, so they decided to leave out the music. In our revisions, we have tried to trim old ideas in order to make way for new ones without leaving out the music.

NOTE TO TEACHERS

This edition of *Bridging English,* like the first, is designed for English methods courses that vary from state to state, from school to school, and from teacher to teacher. The chapters are self-sufficient and independent of one another and can be shifted around with no loss of coherence or momentum. Indeed in our own courses, each of us progresses through the text differently. One of us moves sequentially; the other begins with chapters 1, Envisioning English, and 11, Organizing Instruction, and then continues numerically from chapter 2. In those states and locales where literature-based instruction is paramount, chapters on drama, prose, and poetry can be interfaced with those sections of the writing and evaluation chapters focused on literature. In our examples of teaching prose fiction, we have tried to select either widely read novels or short stories that are often anthologized and are therefore either known or easily available to the reader. A list of those short texts that we most frequently reference and that we use as supplements to this textbook is on p. 85.

ACKNOWLEDGMENTS

Our second edition has benefited from the critiques and suggestions of reviewers who became valuable, if interior, counselors, critics, and supporters throughout this revision process: Hugh Agee, University of Georgia; Kathleen Benghiat, Cleveland State University; Linda Burns, Southeast Missouri State University; Helen Dale, University of Wisconsin-Eau Claire; Elise Ann Earthman, San Francisco State University; Bonnie Ericson, California State University-Northridge; Patricia P. Kelly, Virginia Tech; Deborah Wilson Overstreet, University of Wisconsin-Oshkosh; and Jane A. Zaharias, Cleveland State University. We continue to be indebted to other college and university English educators and secondary English teachers whose ideas and practices enlarge and strengthen our individual efforts and resolves. You will find many of their names within this textbook. Three abiding friends and gifted teachers, Becky Brown, Nancy Doda, and Julia Neenan, continuously enrich their students' lives, our lives, and so this book. Each embodies with unique intelligence and grace the finest ideals of a teacher: understanding that is scholarly, practical, and moral; a coherent pedagogical position that is clear-headed and creative; an insight into and compassion for students that keep them steadfast despite inevitable disappointments and frustrations; and a dedication to the common good of the young and of the community of those who teach them.

We are also grateful for what we have learned from teaching and observing our students. A number of them—undergraduate and masters students—contributed substantially to our revision process with their detailed critique of the first edition and their classroom demonstrations of its best ideas. Throughout this second edition, we scatter the creative teaching ideas of Deborah Alexander, Stella Beale, Mary Beth Braker, Meg Davis, Stuart Egan, Shelley Hale, Leslie Ann Huntley, Ashley Martin, and Michelle Utley. Cary Clifford, our former student, then an English teacher, now also a photographer, visited Texas and Virginia schools to capture new images of students and teachers at work. She brought the sensibilities of a teacher and the eyes of an artist to this creative project and, thus, the text is happily grounded in images of classroom actualities.

We are deeply indebted to the staff of the Education Department at Wake Forest University whose able skills and willing spirits helped move our manuscript through various awkward stages and into readable shape. We owe a special debt to Robin Hawkins, the department's administrative assistant, who deftly organized the work of student assistants and who knew long before we did how to make personal computers produce words—not only in straight lines, but in columns and graphic images as well. We are particularly grateful for the conscientious, intelligent, and cheerful labors of Karen Doub, who undertook tasks of word processing, reference checking, and permission requesting that she could never have imagined before this year and that she completed flawlessly. The surrounding support of other staff and colleagues greatly humanized the environment in which we labored.

At Merrill/Prentice Hall, our debts begin with Brad Potthoff, curriculum and instruction editor, who initiated this second edition and launched it with intelligent and sound advice. Mary Evangelista, his editorial assistant, gently prodded us through the first months of manuscript deadlines with an energy and sense that was steading. Genevieve D'Arcy brought literary and teaching experience to her discerning and gracious copy editing. She also brought invaluable resources of equanimity and judgment to face with us tight and unforgiving deadlines. This second edition has profited immeasurably from her touch. Lois Oster carefully prepared an index that greatly enhances readers' access to our book. Our deepest gratitude goes once again to our production editor, Sheryl Langner, whose perseverance, discriminating good sense, and insights worked to make this second edition better in every way. She adds to her deep knowledge, a generous humanity and even-tempered wit that represent the best imaginable virtues in one whose labors must constantly accommodate the diverse sensibilities and cranky timing of authors and production schedules. We cannot now imagine completing a book without her.

Finally, we are grateful to our three sons for all kinds of help, but mostly we are just grateful they are our sons. In the years since our first edition, each has chosen to become a high school teacher and has entered his own classroom in widely different circumstances and locales: ESL and social studies classrooms in the inner city schools of Houston, Texas; physics and geometry classrooms of rural King and Queen County, Virginia; and economics and politics classrooms of Winston-Salem, North Carolina. Each has experienced all of the challenges of beginning a teaching career, all of the occasions of uncertainty, enthusiasm, bewilderment, hope, self-doubt, and joy. Through them we have sharpened our empathy for and dedication to all those who take up this essential work. We once again dedicate this book to them and through them to beginning teachers everywhere.

CONTENTS

9 COMPELLING WRITING   263

10 ENABLING WRITING   295

11 ORGANIZING INSTRUCTION   343

12 PLANNING THE LESSON   388

1
ENVISIONING ENGLISH

There is no intellectual activity more American than quarreling about what education means, especially within the context of school. Americans rely on their schools, even more than on their courts, to express their vision of who they are.

Neil Postman

Blaise Pascal observed in the 17th century that "The last thing one knows when writing a book is what to put first." Most authors arrive at their subjects through years of experience, knowledge, and reflection. The larger and more complicated the subject, the more difficult the point of entry. English education is such a rich and various field that we could begin at any number of places:

- adolescent students
- secondary schools
- learning theory and research
- the study of language
- the study of literature
- the study of writing
- crucial issues in English education
- the profession of teaching

Each of these subjects makes sense as starting points in a text about teaching English. We delay each, however, until we have first queried you, the reader. We will alternate statement with query. By the end of this first chapter, you should understand why we consider the reader to be the most logical beginning.

INITIAL DEFINITIONS

John Dixon (1967) calls English teaching "a quicksilver among metals—mobile, living and elusive" (p. 1). What interests us initially is what teaching high school English means for you who stand as prospective teachers at the thresholds of your own English classrooms. Something has drawn you to this doorway. We imagine it was your student experiences in other English classrooms, experiences that were positive on some level, else you would not be about to enter this profession. Through the first of a series of Invitations to Reflection, we ask you to call to mind memories of former classrooms and connect them with teaching expectations for your own.

Invitation to Reflection 1–1

- Recall *one positive memory* of an English class.
- From what years of schooling (elementary, middle, secondary, or college) do your best memories arise?
- Recall a *cluster of positive memories* about your past English schooling. What language activities predominate in these memories? Reading? Talking? Listening? Writing?
- Do you recall an especially positive encounter with print or nonprint texts? Which one? With writing? Talking? Listening?
- Do you have memories of certain English teachers whom you would like to imitate as a teacher? Who were they and what did they do that inspired you?
- What memories do you have of unpleasant classroom events that you would hope to avoid in your teaching?
- Which of the following best describes the center of your interest in becoming a teacher? (Rank order them if you wish.)
  - Adolescent students
  - Print literature
  - Nonprint literature
  - Language (writing)
  - Language (speaking)
  - The act of teaching
  - The life of schools
  - Other (Explain)
- At this moment, how would you answer anyone who asked you, "Why do you want to become an English teacher?"

Your visitable past is our starting point and your seeable teaching future our destination. At present, your own experience with other teachers and learners probably provides your main source of ideas about and insights into teaching. You will draw on that experience as you encounter the theories and practices of other models of teaching. This book will serve partly to introduce you to some of these new ways to reflect on your past experience and imagine future actions. As a first step in that introduction, we invite you to join a central and persistent debate among English teachers. It concerns definition: What is English?

Invitation to Reflection 1–2

As a first approach to a definition, consider three descriptors of the discipline of English education:

- Communication Arts
- Language Arts
- English

The differences among them may seem innocuous enough, but each represents a very different understanding of the task we set for ourselves. Answer the following questions.

- Which descriptive term is the most comprehensive? The least?
- What does the term *communication arts* suggest to you that *language arts* does not? What powers of communication can you imagine outside of speaking, listening, reading, and writing? How important is the study of language to a communication arts curriculum? What is the role of literature in it? Is literature more than a vehicle for teaching other skills?
- Why might the term *language arts* be used at the elementary and middle school levels but not in high school? What term would be used in high school?
- Does the term *English* embrace literature *and* language in your mind? How, then, does it differ from *language arts*?
- Which of the three terms best describes the subject you aim to teach?

A BRIEF HISTORY

In this text we will follow current practice and refer to our discipline as *English,* but disagreements about how English is conceived as a discipline, how it is organized, and how it is taught persist. The teaching of reading and writing began in this country with its founding. The earliest settlers, with their vision of an informed citizenry free and competent enough to be self-governing, believed in teaching American children the rudiments of how to read and write. Learning occurred in homes or colonial "dame" schools organized by neighbors and taught by a designated community member. Even when communities had built school buildings, hired teachers, and purchased primers and grammar books, English instruction at all levels more resembled today's elementary school skills-and-drills instruction than our contemporary high schools' language and literature classes.

English as taught in today's schools is a young discipline that arose only toward the end of the nine-teenth century. Many different surveyors with differing interests and aims tried to establish its boundaries. Public and private school teachers and administrators, college professors, politicians, and the public—all were involved in drawing the lines of these boundaries. Questions of definition have been persistent and vexing from the moment of the founding of the National Council of Teachers of English (NCTE) in 1917. Each of the four subsequent decades saw an attempt to reconcile secondary English as "academic prepa-ration for college for the few" or "practical preparation for life for the many." Still at midcentury, Congress considered the English curriculum of its public schools a failed tradition. In 1962, the expanded National Defense Education Act's research and demonstration centers (dubbed "Project English") determined to re-form the field. In the summer of 1966, NCTE, the Modern Language Association (MLA), and the British National Association of Teachers of English (NATE) sponsored a groundbreaking invitational seminar at Dartmouth College (now known as the "Dartmouth Seminar") to consider common problems in the dis-cipline and to define English, both the subject and the way it should be taught. But the posing of the ques-tion itself caused trouble. Some wanted to ask, "What is the subject matter of English?" Others thought that what English is as an academic body of knowledge was subordinate to how English functions as a part of the lives of students and teachers. The proper question for them became "What do we want students and teachers to do?" Speculate on your own answers.

Invitation to Reflection 1–3

- Do you think the question "What is English?" can be answered in the same way as the questions "What is algebra?" "What is physics?" and "What is American history?" Are these questions interchangeable?
- Which of the following do you think is appropriate content for a high school course in English?
    - Language study (grammar)
    - Language skills
        - Writing
        - Speaking
        - Listening
        - Reading
    - Literature
        - Print (novels, short stories, poetry, drama)
        - Nonprint (film, music)
    - Communication skills
    - Students' own lives
    - Social/cultural life surrounding students
    - Other (Explain)
- If you don't define English in terms of content, how would you define what you think should actually happen in English classrooms? What would you want students to be doing?
- Language arts or English is basic to elementary and middle school education as well as a requirement of all four years of most high schools. Do you think it is prominent in the curriculum because of its specialized content? Or is it prominent because of its unique function of connecting different kinds of learning and experience?
- Do you think of teaching as the transmission of knowledge from teacher to student? If so, what is important to transmit? The great, humanist tradition of literature? Functional skills of reading, writing, talking, and listening? Personal understanding and enlightenment? Moral values? Other? (If so, what?)

Had those Dartmouth conferees scrutinized the English curricula of the 1950s and 1960s high schools we knew as students, they would have described classrooms divided at midyear into the primary content halves of English study: language and literature. In each semester, our teachers focused on distinct bodies of knowledge, but their general teaching strategies were similar in both. Teachers passed to the students their (presumably) superior understanding of literature or language (usually grammar) through lectures, whole-class discussions, drills, written exercises, quizzes, and occasional writing assignments. Once teachers had "covered" the subject, they tested students to see how well they had "learned" it. Questions about what went on in the classroom were questions of teacher technique, not learner action. The galvanizing center of the classroom was the teacher. Teachers determined content and agenda, and they guided, monitored, and evaluated student achievement. With conscientious industry, knowledge, conviction, and vision, they passed on the cultural heritage and the requisite language skills to read, write, and talk about it. You have probably experienced at least one such classroom in your schooling. What you will become is built on that legacy.

Invitation to Reflection 1–4

- Visualize yourself as a teacher in your own English classroom. Which of the five classroom arrangements shown in Figure 1-1 do you envision?
- Is the arrangement you chose the one that is most common in your own experience with school? What does this arrangement imply about the relationship between teacher and students?
- Who is most intellectually and physically active, the teacher or the student? Are they equally engaged?
- Which configuration would make you most comfortable as a teacher? Which would you have preferred as a student?
- In your imagined classroom, do you see yourself characteristically sitting, standing at a podium or desk, or walking about? If you see yourself sitting, are you at a teacher's desk, on an elevated chair, or at a student desk?
- Imagine that you want an alternative classroom design. Which would be your second choice of physical arrangement? Would those changes dictate changes in your teaching method?
- What precisely do you see you and your students doing in this classroom? Would your class design change if the assignment were, say, Native American narratives, loyalty in friendships, or slang in student writing? How would the physical design match the lesson design?
- Place each of the arrangements in Figure 1-1 on a continuum from the most student centered (students are active and often are independent agents and subjects of their own learning) to the most teacher centered (the students receive knowledge from the teacher).
- Who or what would you place at the center of your planning and practice?
  - Teacher
  - Student
  - Subject
  - Process

CORE BELIEFS

We believe that it is hard to define English apart from the ways it is taught in the classroom. We value definitions of English that match classroom actualities. The physical arrangements betray the teacher's assumptions; selection of instructional strategies and methods, materials, and texts expose the teacher's values and goals. The images and principles (implicit and explicit) of your former high school classrooms influence your image of your own future classroom. If you went directly to your own classroom without passing through an "English methods" course and text, you could link those formative images to available teacher resources—the steady proliferation of state and school district curriculum guidelines, inservice training workshops and institutes, professional meetings, and periodic and book literature—and generate enough teaching ideas to construct a year's worth of lesson plans. But effective teachers need more than busy classes; they need basic tenets, a core of beliefs about learning, language, and literature, to shape activity into engaging, purposive, and effective learning.

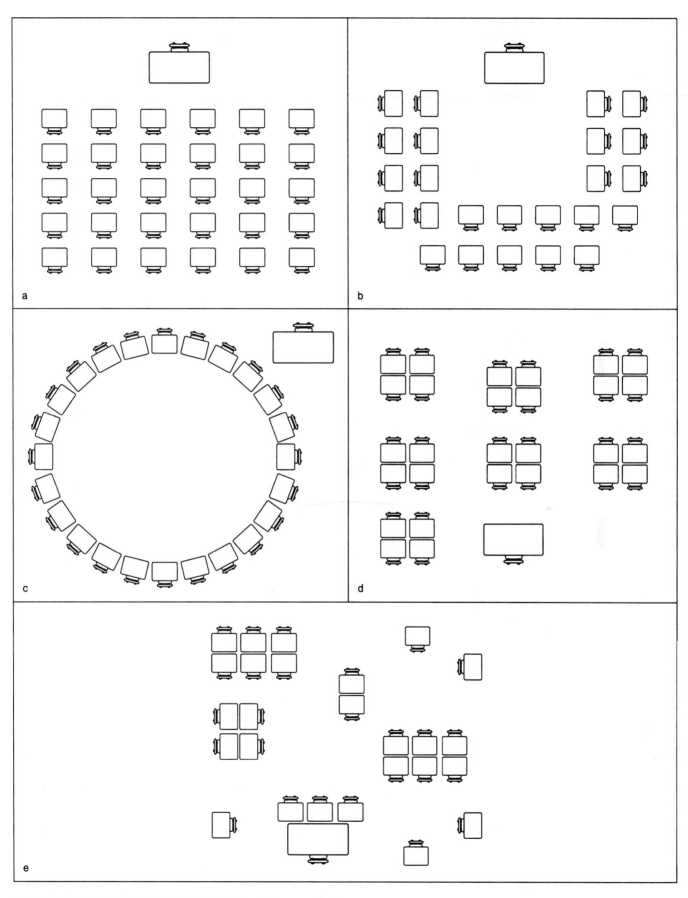

FIGURE 1–1 Five classroom designs

THE CRAZY QUILT OF ENGLISH

McEwan (1992) believes that a confusing "multitude of institutional and cultural demands" are placed on the English teacher (p. 102). Where there is no clear vision of the nature of the subject, the English classroom "becomes a storage closet of stray topics, a place to teach anything that does not fall clearly within the orbit of other areas of the school curriculum." He names a few of those areas of the curriculum that have "invaded" the English classroom without careful scrutiny or deliberate intent: "moral education, critical thinking skills, 'survival skills,' journalism, library research, and public speaking" (pp. 102–103). With no guiding principles, English teaching can become what McEwan calls "a patchwork" of instructional activities—a crazy quilt pieced together from the used materials of other projects without a pattern or design. While such a piece might be attractive hanging in a craft shop, it does not represent the best pattern from which to fashion learning.

IMPORTANCE OF CORE BELIEFS

Bridging English will be little more than a catalogue of teaching activities if it does not help you develop what philosopher R. S. Peters calls a "conceptual scheme." Such a scheme raises knowledge beyond "the level of a collection of disjointed facts" and enables us to "understand the 'reason why' of things." We call these "core beliefs"—foundational concepts that drive what we do in our classrooms. Elise Ann Earthman calls them "anchoring ideas." Others speak of "operating principles." Whatever you name these beliefs, they are central to who you will be, what you will do, and how you will regard your students. These beliefs will anchor your planning and teaching of a course, a unit, or a lesson with a logic and purposiveness that would be missing without them. Your teaching practice and your students' learning will be stronger, more focused, and more coherent with such an anchor.

We know of no other college or university courses that require students to absorb a subject, formulate a position on that subject, and then apply it to the extent that preteaching courses do. In these courses, something more is required than the usual coursework of attending class, reading texts, writing papers, and completing exams. Standard academic performance is not enough for an English methods course. Our English methods students are often startled by how quickly they must encounter a new field and perform effectively (and publicly!) in it. They enter methods courses with a mixture of personal history and expectations and some field experiences; they encounter new points of view and work to synthesize them with their prior knowledge; they leave to teach 100 or more adolescents each day. While premedicine, prelaw, preministry, and even prebusiness courses are usually followed by years of professional training and apprenticeships before students enter actively into their professions, English methods students take their final exams in methods one week and begin student teaching the next. We want this text to help prepare you for this work, both its theory and its practice. When you step into a classroom as a teacher, you are entering deep waters, but they are not uncharted. We turn now to consider some of those core beliefs that might guide and steady you.

CONFESSION

When we wrote the first edition of *Bridging English,* we envisioned bridging over several dimensions:

You as Student	to	You as Teacher
College/University Study	to	High School Teaching
Educational Theory	to	Classroom Practice
Positions Within the Field	to	Opposed Positions Within the Field

The first three bridges were easier to construct than the last. With the last one, we set about trying to do justice to multiple positions, and thus to bridge their differences with understanding. Of course, we realized that sometimes two positions are mutually exclusive. It is hard to believe in student-centered, constructivist education and be content to lecture for a class period about the use of dialect in Zora Neal Hurston's short stories, regardless of how clever your examples and graphics. If process writing is central to your writing project, you will not be comfortable selecting and assigning topics for an out-of-class essay to which you give grades A through F two weeks later, no matter how extensive and perceptive your marginal comments to students on their returned papers. If you believe in broadening the selection of literary texts, you will not teach only the novels and poems of British males, no matter how enthusiastic you are about William Wordsworth, Charles Dickens, and Thomas Hardy. If you are interested in bringing students to respond personally and feelingly to written works, you will not make traditional New Critical questions of form the centerpiece of your whole-class discussions. Despite such competing and irreconcilable positions, we tried in our first edition to present each fairly so that the reader could choose from the diverse perspectives within our field. We have been asked to be more direct about what we believe and practice.

We again try to distill clearly and memorably the best theories and practices in English education. Because others—theorists and practitioners with whom we both sympathize and differ—provide an essential context for our work, we attempt to present their ideas with as much sympathy and fair-mindedness as we hope they bring to ours. We want again to leave room for readers to move around in this text and get their own bearings. However, we will be clearer about our views this time around. We state straightforwardly that the decisions we make about how to run our own classrooms originate in the ideas about learning, language, and literature that you will meet in the next few pages of this chapter. However, as you may find in your own teaching, sometimes we find ourselves incapable of acting on our beliefs, we yield to the resistance of earlier training and of former habits, or we are coerced by particularly adverse circumstances into a strategy that we don't wholeheartedly endorse. In other words, our teaching is as active, constructivist, process oriented, and recursive as we suggest your students' learning be, and as prone to stray sometimes from our better judgments and our most conscientious resolves. We do, however, attempt to guide and evaluate our own practice from a coherent position about learning, language, and literature that grows from the traditional principles of learning that we first knew, but that now embraces alternatives to that tradition.

TRADITIONAL PRINCIPLES OF LEARNING

We begin with a description of a cluster of ideas about the ways students (and teachers) most effectively learn that operated in the schools that we knew as students, that our children attended several decades later, and that many children experience today. We describe four beliefs about learning and teaching that are at the heart of traditional schooling.

1. Learning involves a process of acquiring discrete pieces of information and certain observable skills.
2. The teacher's first responsibility is to transfer his or her knowledge to students; the students' primary responsibility is to receive and store that knowledge.
3. Learning can be measured by tests of the students' mastery of knowledge and skills.
4. The interactions between the teacher and the students are the primary focus of this process—from the teacher's organizing and sequencing the subject content, the teacher's clear and unambiguous explanation and illustration of that content and modeling of those skills, to the teacher's assessing students' ability to reproduce the specified knowledge and skills on paper-and-pencil tests or through other observable demonstrations.

Clearly, the teacher's role is at center stage in this traditional educational drama; students have essential, but supporting parts. This conception of education dominates the views of many school superintendents, school boards, principals, teachers, and students today. It influences the critiques of education that flow from family dining tables, editors' boardrooms, and politicians' podiums. In the modern era, challenges to it have been heard from the time of Jean Jacques Rousseau in France (1712–1778) and John Dewey (1859–1952) in the United States through the reforming decades of the 1960s and 1970s and into the more politically conservative decades of the 1980s and 1990s, with their countercalls back to tradition. Yet despite these constant and robust challenges, the traditional model persists in the daily rounds of schools everywhere, where teachers direct whole-class instruction to students who sit and listen, receive and absorb; administrators judge the success of classrooms by their silence; and the public evaluates schools by how well their students perform on nationally normed standardized tests. Because this traditional view is so pervasive and tenacious, all prospective and experienced teachers need to have a clear and distinct alternative in mind before attempting to resist or to jettison this model.

ALTERNATIVE BELIEFS ABOUT LEARNING

Three educators who have worked on school renewal projects for almost two decades have summarized a new set of underlying assumptions and principles about how students best learn in the main teaching fields: reading, writing, mathematics, science, and social studies. Figure 1–2 presents their summary as a useful glossary of concepts that you will encounter throughout this text and that we consider to be essential guides for teaching.

Student-centered, Active, Constructivist Learning. Zemelman, Daniels, and Hyde's ideas offer counterpoints to the traditionalist views. At the heart of the difference is a conception of learning as an active process of constructing meaning by taking in new information, connecting it to prior understandings, and then testing the new knowledge by applying it. Learning is not waiting for the revelation, but making it, not uncovering knowledge, but creating it. Learning is active and productive, not passive and receptive. Whereas "good students" were traditionally defined as being quiet and docile, their alternative counterparts are characterized as being engaged and questioning. Center stage is no

FIGURE 1–2
Zemelman, Daniels, and Hyde's underlying principles, assumptions, and theories of best practices

Child-centered. The best starting point for schooling is kids' real interests; all across the curriculum, investigating students' own questions should always take precedence over studying arbitrarily and distantly selected "content."

Experiential. Active, hands-on, concrete experience is the most powerful and natural form of learning. Students should be immersed in the most direct possible experience of the content of every subject.

Reflective. Balancing the immersion in direct experience must be opportunities for learners to look back, to reflect, to debrief, to abstract from their experiences what they have felt and thought and learned.

Authentic. Real, rich, complex ideas and materials are at the heart of the curriculum. Lessons or textbooks which water down, control, or over-simplify content ultimately disempower students.

Holistic. Children learn best when they encounter whole, real ideas, events, and materials in purposeful contexts, and not by studying sub parts isolated from actual use.

Social. Learning is always socially constructed and often interactional; teachers need to create classroom interactions which "scaffold" learning.

Collaborative. Cooperative learning activities tap the social power of learning better than competitive and individualistic approaches.

Democratic. The classroom is a model community; students learn what they live as citizens of the school.

Cognitive. The most powerful learning for children comes from developing true understanding of concepts and higher-order thinking associated with various fields of inquiry and self-monitoring of their thinking.

Developmental. Children grow through a series of definable but not rigid stages, and schooling should fit its activities to the developmental level of students.

Constructivist. Children do not just receive content; in a very real sense, they recreate and re-invent every cognitive system they encounter, including language, literacy, and mathematics.

Psycholinguistic. The process of young children's natural oral language acquisition provides our best model of complex human learning and, once learned, language itself becomes the primary tool for more learning, whatever the subject matter.

Challenging. Students learn best when faced with genuine challenges, choices and responsibility in their own learning.

SOURCE: Reprinted by permission of Steven Zemelman, Harvey Daniels, and Arthur Hyde. BEST PRACTICE: NEW STANDARDS FOR TEACHING AND LEARNING IN AMERICA'S SCHOOLS (Heinemann, A division of Reed Elsevier, Inc., Portsmouth, NH, 1993).

longer held by the teacher alone, but by the teacher and students in consort choosing the most fruitful and responsible route to learning.

Our observations and those of others (cognitive and developmental psychologists, among them) convince us that learning is not a lockstep process that all students begin and conclude together, some sprinting ahead, some keeping up, and others falling behind or faltering. We view learning as arising individually out of a particular learner's natural capacities, interests, and experiences and keeping stride with that person's developmental readiness. Strategies, activities, and texts should therefore be grounded in the actualities of the student's personal history and experience.

Enabling Structures.   Soviet psychologist Lev Vygotsky (1978) describes the dynamics of such learning. A child has a point (an "actual developmental level") at which he or she understands concepts and completes tasks without assistance from a more-knowing other. This same child also has a point (a "level of potential development") at which he or she can complete more complex tasks with the assistance of teachers or more expert peers. Between these two points lies the ground on which most school learning should take place. Vygotsky calls this the "zone of proximal development," and it is here that more- knowing others (teachers and/or expert peers) can influence and coach the student to move past what he or she presently knows and can do and move toward new learning that the student absorbs and calls upon without assistance. We often call the work a teacher sets up to enable a student to move into, within, and through this zone of proximal development *enabling structures.* Others call this work *scaffolding,* because just as carpenters use a scaffold to build a wall that will one day stand on its own, so teachers must develop supports for student learning that will eventually fall away and allow the learning to stand without assistance.

I-You-It.   James Moffett and Betty Jane Wagner (1976) envision another learning progression that begins with the individual and moves to the public: I-You-It.

I   Intellectual growth originates with personal experience. The child properly operates out of the egocentric center of the self.

You   Growth and maturity lead the child to reach out to others and begin to understand their perspectives.

It   As growth continues, the growing child can embrace more distant, less immediately personal experience and knowledge.

Effective instruction imitates that organic process by starting with the personal and slowly moving toward the public, by originating in experiential, personal centers of the self and moving toward more general, communal understandings and applications.

FIGURE 1–3
Applebee's model of
good, better, and best
writing programs

GOOD LESSON

There is an ordered variety of tasks for students to perform.
Assignments are clear and their purpose evident.
Students perform teacher-designated tasks.
Grades are used as the primary motivation.
When assigned, writing is used as a measure of student knowledge or performance.
The predominant teaching technique is teacher-led class discussion.

BETTER LESSON

Students are actively involved in teacher-designed tasks.
The teacher maintains a high level of student interest.
The teacher encourages a free flow of give and take.
The teacher incorporates student experiences into the lesson.
The predominant teaching technique is teacher-led class discussion—but student-led discussions are
     encouraged.
Students are prepared for writing assignments with prewriting activities such as audiovisual presentations or
     modeling.
There is a climate of trust between teacher and students.

BEST LESSON

Students assume an active role in their own learning.
The teacher encourages students to explore and discover and seldom dominates the class.
Students' own experiences are freely incorporated into class discussions.
Students are enthusiastic about their work.
Writing is viewed as a means of learning and emerges naturally out of other activities.

The Teacher's Role. The role of teacher changes with these alternative beliefs about learning. Rather than presenters, interpreters, regulators, and judges, teachers define themselves as facilitators, coaches, and fellow learners. Whereas traditional teachers more often aim instruction toward finished products and measure student achievement by them, their counterparts value the process as well as the products it produces. These teachers ask students not only to choose, sequence, and monitor their own learning, but also to participate in its evaluation. If learning is seen as a personal, dynamic, recursive act, it cannot be effectively encouraged nor fairly measured by periodic performance on tests and papers. Gardner (1983) has articulated and validated what many have observed: individuals express their intelligence with far greater diversity than that which is possible using only the verbal and logistical modes commonly valued and assessed in schools. Teachers must provide a range of opportunities for response so that students can construct their meanings and enlarge their strengths. Even in English classrooms devoted to using language logically and persuasively, the neglected intelligences (musical, spatial, kinesthetic, interpersonal, and intrapersonal) deserve recognition and expression. Being free to participate, these intelligences will enter the student's progress toward unfolding awareness and meaning.

Arthur Applebee, as director of the federally sponsored National Research Center on Literature Teaching and Learning, has provided reliable and nuanced pictures of writing and literature instruction in secondary schools in the United States during the last decades of the twentieth century. Applebee (1981) and his research team visited some 300 classrooms to observe what was taking place in writing instruction. Although the researchers' purpose was descriptive, they were experienced teachers and consequently began to form impressions of those classes that worked especially well. They were not interested in the lessons that failed, but in "the differences between lessons that gave the impression of a pleasant and effective teaching situation, and those in which that pleasant atmosphere of competence was transformed into something more exciting" (p. 104). Figure 1-3 provides a list of characteristics that the observers believe characterize good, better, and best lessons (pp. 104-105). Study the figure before you turn to our next Invitation to Reflection.

Invitation to Reflection 1–5

- Which of Applebee's three classroom models most resembles the writing instruction you received in high school English classes?
- As you read the descriptions of each, which class most attracted you as a student? As a teacher?
- Are you surprised at the researchers' evaluation of the three?

- Does Applebee's "best lesson" have more of the qualities valued by Zemelman, Daniels, and Hyde than the other two types of lessons do?
- Which of the following qualities do you see as being active in your favorite of the three?

Student-centered	Social	Constructivist
Experiential	Collaborative	Psycholinguistic
Reflective	Democratic	Challenging
Authentic	Cognitive	
Holistic	Developmental	

- Would traditional high school English classes (described in the preceding section) have been able to achieve Applebee's best rating? Why or why not?

Individualization, Interaction, Integration.   For decades, the three R's (Reading, wRiting, and aRithmetic) were regarded as the backbone of learning for the young. Moffett and Wagner (1976, 1992) suggest three essential I's as hallmarks of an effective language learning program (their equivalent of the three R's): Individualization, Interaction, and Integration. All three must be present in a classroom if students are to experience the full range and power of language.

Individualization	If learning language is personal, the process will vary from individual to individual. Teachers not only must acknowledge student differences of timing, interest, style, knowledge, and attitude, but also must set up structures that accommodate and encourage those differences. Teachers must give students practice in making their own choices of sequence, material, and activity. Classrooms should be so organized that individual differences can be honored and student uniqueness can be manifest.
Interaction	As students increase their sense and confidence of self, they often expand their desire to communicate. Interaction exploits that desire; it invites flexibility of classroom structure whereby students in pairs or small or large groups can join together in the varied and continuous social use of language. Students need many opportunities to talk, listen, and write to each other.
Integration	Finally, language learning must not be separated from other subjects or fields of knowledge, but must be integral to them. Language teachers need to promote authentic communication about issues active in their students' experience, whether from their homes, communities, other subjects, or other arts.

Moffet and Wagner discuss other principles for student-centered learning in the language arts classroom. We present these in Figure 1–4 as nine axioms and ask you to reflect on them.

Invitation to Reflection 1–6

- Check the axioms that operated in your high school English classrooms.
- With which of Moffett and Wagner's axioms do you most strongly agree?
- Which axiom do you question as theory? As practical for your classroom?
- Did you experience the bias they see against
  - oral language production?
  - writing production?
  - nonliterary content (texts or activities)?
- Was your instruction in language mainly presentations about language, rather than practice in using language?
- Were your English teachers more likely to teach you to avoid error, rather than to use error to learn?
- Two teachers notice numerous errors in subject-verb agreement in the speech and writing of their students. They set out to address the problem, but with quite different strategies. Which of the following two language lessons would Moffett and Wagner favor? Which more nearly puts "words on world," rather than "words on words"?

FIGURE 1–4
Moffett and Wagner's axioms for student-centered classrooms

1. Running a classroom cannot be like following a script. Panic comes from forgetting your lines and not being able to improvise. Trying to stick to a script causes more difficulty than playing by ear. But playing by ear works only when you have thought out well what you are about. (p. 2)
2. Despite our innovations [language arts] is still not four way. It is heavily biased against the productive activities of speaking and writing, against oral comprehension and composition, and against nonliterature. Not only does it favor receptive activities—in particular, reading and literature—but it fills the curriculum with information *about* language that cannot be justified in teaching speaking, listening, reading, and writing. (p. 17)
3. No evidence exists, either practical or scientific, that learning generalizations about language will improve speaking or writing. Experience shows that concepts and precepts fail to teach comprehension and composition . . . What [students] need is *practice* and *awareness*. The real problem is to think clearly and to say what one means . . . [C]hildren know how to comprehend and compose the word forms and word order of English before they come to school. (pp. 18–19)
4. Another form of the bias toward student intake is the tendency to convert the realistic use of language into information *about* language. This makes of language arts a history or science course. (p. 18)
5. You need not fear you have no subject and try to manufacture one by making kids read about writing and write about reading. Words on words strengthen nothing but doubts, because they merely shadow what you're trying to teach, which is words on world. The special province of the language teacher, and therefore the main definition of language arts, is communication consciousness. (p. 23)
6. Reading and writing can progress little further than the limits of their oral base. (p. 31)
7. Avoiding error is an inferior learning strategy to capitalizing on error. (p. 33)
8. Believing that lack of information or advice is the cause of comprehending and composing problems may be the greatest mistake of all language teaching. A reader failing to put together all the meaning cues of a text cannot be told what to do because he already *thinks* he is doing that. He is unaware of what he is omitting or how he is distorting or tuning out. (p. 34)
9. It is riskier *not* to change, to cling to proven failure. Furthermore, the kind of change proposed through this curriculum should be characterized as reactionary rather than radical. . . . Such innovations would in fact be a return to an early American tradition. It is a great irony that learning should have got so misshapen that the old tried-and-true methods appear new and risky while newer and failing methods are considered safe and traditional. (p. 45)

SOURCE: Moffett, James and Betty Jane Wagner, *Student-centered language arts and reading, K–13: A handbook for teachers* (2nd ed.). Copyright © 1976 by Houghton Mifflin Company. Adapted with permission.

SCENARIO 1: DISCUSSION: FISHBOWL, WHOLE CLASS, AND SMALL GROUP

The teacher selects four students to arrange their chairs in the center of the room and discuss the topic "Is it important to use correct grammar in speaking with others in this high school or in the community?" The remainder of the class sits in a circle around the "fishbowl," listening to the conversation and noting the differences of opinion. After the conversation has run for 4 or 5 minutes, the whole class joins in the discussion, using the original discussants' opinions as their points of reference. Following the whole-class discussion, the teacher presents some recent subject-verb agreement errors in the students' essays and in their conversations and asks the class to identify the problem in each. She asks individual students to consider how frequently they make these mistakes and then to list examples of their common or repeated errors. Individuals enumerate their lists within a small group. The small groups report their most common errors to the whole class. The teacher poses the question again, differently phrased, to the whole class: "Do you consider your errors in this construction to be a problem in your communication with others?"

SCENARIO 2: MINILECTURE AND WORKSHEET

On an overhead transparency, the teacher writes four sentences that have errors in subject-predicate agreement and, without locating the place of error, asks students to correct each sentence individually. Students volunteer their suggested corrections, and the whole class approves or disapproves. The teacher asks whether they notice something in common among all of the flawed sentences, gives a brief lecture on the problem, lists the most common errors made, and distributes a worksheet with 20 sentences containing examples of these problems. The students complete the sheets individually until the end of class.

- If you were a student, which of the two scenarios would you prefer? Moffett and Wagner aside, do you see any discernible difference between them?

FOUR PERSPECTIVES ON LANGUAGE LEARNING

Gere, Fairbanks, Howes, Roop, and Schaafsma (1992) observed teachers and students in middle or junior high school and high school classrooms and found four distinct perspectives on teaching English based on four quite different views of language. Their description provides a further clarification of the reasons for the diverse instructional choices that today's English teachers make—goals, strategies, activities, and texts. While most English teachers situate themselves primarily under one perspective, many borrow ideas and methods from all four. We present the premises and practices of each.

Language as Artifact.   Language is a cultural artifact to be understood and interpreted in order to open students to the richness of the human experience. Students should read to discover meaning and write to demonstrate their "ability to think clearly and well" (p. 87). Language study concentrates on its formal characteristics and often focuses on the formal rules of grammar or on "key grammatical concepts" (p. 91). Literature study employs the skills of intensive close reading of texts that are privileged by tradition and aesthetics. The text is paramount as an expression of the author's view of the human condition. Analysis is valued more highly than other approaches to literature and language. Evaluation of student knowledge is measured by a common standard.

Language as Development.   Language is a tool for cognitive and personal development. Cognitive and developmental psychologists suggest that all students can learn in school if a teacher (1) identifies a student's present developmental stage and proficiencies, (2) develops and sequences appropriate strategies to help the student acquire new skills, and (3) sets realistic goals for the student to meet. Teachers use cognitive structures and models (of their skills and others) to solve reading and writing problems. For instance, they might use prereading strategies to prepare students to comprehend literature and sentence-combining exercises to teach sentence variety and concept development. Texts are usually read to teach reading and writing skills, not to deepen interpretive insight or broaden aesthetic appreciation. Evaluation of measurable skills helps the student and teacher track progress.

Language as Expression.   Language provides a crucial means for exploring our own inner worlds and describing what we find there. Teachers center on the individual student and encourage student self-discovery and self-expression. In literature, teachers are interested not in analysis primarily, but in the student's personal response to the text. The writing of professional writers is not prized above student writing. Language study is integrated into reading and writing study; grammar and language rules are invoked not as the subjects of separate study, but as aids to expression. Writing instruction is more personal and expressive with students choosing their topics, experimenting with technique and form, and evaluating their own and their peers' work. Journal writing is common, and like other forms, is ungraded by the teacher. Process is emphasized over product.

Language as Social Construct.   Language is a social instrument by which we grow in critical understanding of the self and the world of which it is a part. Students are again at the center of the classroom, but teachers are more concerned with preparing them to be critical and committed "citizens in the political world" (p. 195). Consequently, students are more empowered to design their own learning in nontraditional ways. Teachers, interested in students' becoming more critical of the world around them, encourage a variety of classroom structures, some of which operate outside the walls of schools or the bindings of printed texts. For instance, community-based research projects may be undertaken by students working collaboratively to collect, interpret, and "publish" data. Professionally written texts and student-created texts are used to train students to question and examine their worlds and construct their own interpretations.

BELIEFS ABOUT LITERATURE LEARNING

Henry (1986) believes that "the supreme art of instruction in English" is "helping the self gain control of this peculiar medium called language" (p. 16). Language learning, however, is only a part of the modern English classroom. Purves (1986) does not share Henry's belief that "the study of English is primarily the reflexive use of language" (p. 43). He believes that "English has a content, the historical canons of literature and the historical facts of the language as it has evolved, thanks to the successive invasions of the British Isles and thanks to the successive conquests of the English around the world. There are English languages and English literatures" (p. 43). Even if one believes that the central content of English instruction is literature, the definition of what literature is desirable for the high school classroom is expanding to include diverse and previously silenced voices, those of women, African-Americans, Native Americans, Asian Americans, Hispanic Americans, and other non-Europeans. This expansion also embraces non-print literature and nontraditional genres. These expansionists do not regard literature as singular printed texts, but as a language act rightly connected to other expressive acts, visual, musical, and spatial. Thus, literature is more than a collection of formal literary elements (e.g., plot, character, theme, and symbol) to be analyzed objectively; it is a whole, expressive event to which readers respond subjectively. Their response is not mental only; it encompasses their whole experienced past at the moment of personal encounter with the text.

Our views of how to teach these expanding texts are also changing. For instance, many teachers now question whether the proper act for teachers is to drive students toward the author's meaning and the critics' interpretation; they value of equal or greater importance the reader's felt response to the text. These teachers do not treat texts as something "given" to be "received." They do not organize their classrooms around eliciting the individual student's virtuoso interpretation, but rather around soliciting the responses and interpretations of a community of readers.

In order to invite students into texts and to encourage students to stake personal claims there, teachers also employ a greater range of classroom organization and activity. Lecture and whole-class discussion, once the staples of English classrooms, now are joined by small-group, paired, and individual work. Writing becomes a more integral part of reading literature, not through traditional critical essays only, but through a variety of exploratory and expressive projects. Drama, music, and the visual arts enter to animate and extend literature study. Teachers are inviting students to participate in selecting classroom texts. Literature Circles allow students to read and discuss different texts within one class.

Most English teachers at some point in their careers will teach William Shakespeare's plays and poetry. Applebee (1993) found that, for grades 7–12, the three most anthologized plays were *Julius Caesar, Macbeth,* and *Romeo and Juliet,* and four of the most anthologized poems were Shakespeare's Sonnets 29, 30, 116, and 130 (pp. 233, 237–238). Please read Sonnet 116, "Let Me Not to the Marriage of True Minds," and then reflect on how you might approach it with your students.

Let Me Not to the Marriage of True Minds

Let me not to the marriage of true minds
Admit impediments. Love is not love
Which alters when it alteration finds.
Or bends with the remover to remove:
O, no! it is an ever-fixed mark,
That looks on tempests and is never shaken;
It is the star to every wandering bark,
Whose worth's unknown, although his height be taken.
Love's not Time's fool, though rosy lips and cheeks
Within his bending sickle's compass come;
Love alters not with his brief hours and weeks,
But bears it out even to the edge of doom.
    If this be error, and upon me proved,
    I never writ, nor no man ever loved.

William Shakespeare (1564–1616)

Invitation to Reflection 1–7

- Which of the following teaching ideas were typical of your English classes in high school or college?
- Which of the ideas interest you in thinking of your own?
- Which of the ideas meet the principles of learning, language learning, and literature learning just discussed?

WHOLE-CLASS DISCUSSION

1. What kind of sonnet is this, Italian, English, or Petrachian?
2. Does the meaning of the poem break into the standard three quatrains of the English sonnet? Does this form aid its sense? What is the effect of the final couplet on the ideas presented in the three quatrains? Does it provide a fitting conclusion?
3. Consider Shakespeare's use of metaphor. Name and locate the metaphors active in this poem.
4. Two important figures of speech are *metonymy* (in which one thing stands for another associated with it) and *synecdoche* (in which a part stands for a whole). Which figure does Shakespeare use when he refers to "rosy lips and cheeks"? To "bending sickle's compass"?

VIEWING FILM EXCERPT AND DISCUSSION

1. Describe the plot of the Jane Austen novel, *Sense and Sensibility*. View two excerpts from the Ang Lee movie *Sense and Sensibility* (1995), in which Sonnet 116 figures prominently: the first talk of the two young lovers, Marianne Dashwood and John Willoughby, and Marianne's lament for their lost love.
2. Discuss how the words of the poem fit the moments when they were used in the film. Are these moments intensified by Shakespeare's lines? Did the screenwriter (Emma Thompson) do justice to Shakespeare's meaning?

SMALL-GROUP AND INDIVIDUAL WORK: COMPARISON WITH CONTEMPORARY WORKS

1. Read two contemporary poems about love: John Frederick Nims's "Love Poem" and Anne Sexton's "The Farmer's Wife." Do these poems match your views and observations about love? Do they leave your ideas shaken? Enriched? Do they make you hopeful about the constancy of love?
2. If Shakespeare, Nims, and Sexton joined your group, would they agree on the nature of love? Which one holds the most idealistic view? Which are you drawn toward? With which of the three would you like to discuss any problems you have experienced with friendship and love? Does your life contain any examples that could illustrate their ideas of love?
3. Listen to the old folk ballad "Frankie and Johnny." How is the song's view of love and relationships different from or the same as those of the three poets? Does it jangle your earlier sense of love?
4. Free write for 5 minutes from this prompt: This discussion made me wonder about . . .

INDEPENDENT GROUP PROJECT

Choose one of the following assignments.

1. Your task is to find connections between Shakespeare's sonnet and the world you know. Connect the poem to your own life, to happenings in school or in the community, or to love stories you have seen or heard from others. The connection may be an illustration of or a rebuttal to Shakespeare's view of love. Present the connections you think most worth sharing to the rest of the class.
2. Your task is to develop a list of questions about Shakespeare's sonnet that you might want to discuss with the rest of the class. Don't worry too much about details. Try to help your classmates talk about the big ideas about love presented in the poem. Usually, the best discussions arise from your genuine reactions—thoughts and feelings—as you read. Connecting those to a story you have seen, heard, or experienced or quandaries about love you have known might also prompt an animated discussion.
3. Your task is to present the poem dramatically to the class. The purpose is to convey with your voices and staging an interpreted meaning to the audience. You can organize a choral reading or a mimed reading. You can use music, visual art, clips from movies or TV, and/or other connected poems in your production. Make certain each member of the group has a part in the presentation.

INDIVIDUAL DECISIONS

How are you to decide which of these beliefs deserve your acceptance and which will guide your teaching choices? One way to address these differences and arrive at reasoned conclusions is to look at a history of the profession. Several good resources are available for this purpose. (Applebee, 1974; Hook, 1980; Graff, 1987; special editions of the *English Journal*). Another way is to appeal to systematic theory—of learning, language, and literature. Another is to observe practice and to talk with experienced teachers. Another is to read about or conduct research. Yet another is to reflect on one's own experience. To which of those five sources would you most readily turn in attempting to answer the question of what we should teach in English classes? This text will touch on history, theory, practice, and research, but these are significant only to the extent that you exercise your own reflection on them. You stand at an intersection between these vital resources of the field and your own experience, as a student and now as a prospective teacher.

Grossman's study at Stanford (1990) of six beginning English teachers demonstrates the advantage of careful reflection on our purposes in teaching. Grossman found that the students who entered the profession without much consideration of what they were doing as teachers of English continued to transmit literary history, to engage largely in textual explication, and to assign their students language exercises that focused on correctness. Those who studied pedagogy and human development in their preparation for teaching taught quite differently. They aimed their students toward an active transaction with texts, gave them a sense of the connection between writing and reading and their daily lives, and engaged them in an exploration of language that centered on the variety of actual usage. Dixon (1967) captures that place of decision for all teachers, a vital place where the individual teacher asks "How will I teach my students?" "We come here to the border country between scholarship and the intuitive understandings of observant and sympathetic teachers. Ideally the one kind of evidence should feed the other" (p. 27).

CONCLUSION

Bridging English invites you over the threshold into many English classrooms. They are furnished differently, inhabited with a spectrum of individual teachers, visited by a multitude of different learners, and outfitted with textbooks, paperbacks, magazines, dictionaries, file cabinets, overhead projectors, posters, and personal computers. No one of them represents the one right room for you. We open these rooms so that you can gather ideas for designing your own. But just as a house requires a sure foundation for its strength and durability, your teaching requires foundational beliefs. We do not expect you to construct such a foundation instantaneously, but only to have begun that work, layering by idea, by practice, by reflection, by idea. You have time to build and to furnish; in fact, good teachers never stop.

You began this book with a visit to your past. In these first pages you have been invited to envision your future as a teacher, and, ideally, you will continue to re-vision your classroom throughout your teaching life. Blaise Pascal was right about the difficulty of knowing what to put first in a book. If you understand now why we focus our beginning on you, the reader. You have begun to grasp what is central to our core beliefs. As in our classrooms we try to put students at the center, so here we put you, the reader, first. We will continue to ask you to be an actor in this book, not simply its audience.

2

CENTERING ON LANGUAGE

The proper study of [humankind] is [human beings], and there is nothing so basic to our humanity as our language.

James Sledd

Linguist S. I. Hayakawa has speculated that if fish were to examine their lives scientifically, the last subject they would study is water. He maintains that we have come just as lately to the study of language. Like water to the fish, language so surrounds and encompasses us that we hardly recognize it as a field for study. We are unconscious that our language habits are at the heart of how we experience our world. Language does not just reflect a world view for its user; it creates that view. Thus, different languages construct different realities. Teachers and critics believe that our unconsciousness of the importance of language is worsened by the constant bombardment of our "language-polluted and language-deadened environment" (Nelson, 1991, p. 17). Nelson sees our students caught in "modern illiteracy," which "arises not from a paucity of language but from over-exposure to language" (p. 16). He quotes N. Scott Momaday's sensitive description of the destruction of the "magic of language" and its reduction to a "commodity." In *House Made of Dawn* (1966), Momaday explains that the dominant culture is "sated and insensitive" to language because "on every side . . . there are words by the millions, an unending succession of pamphlets and papers, letters and books, bills and bulletins, commentaries and conversations."

Reflection on language is basic to our field of English. As we noted in Chapter 1, in an article devoted to the question "What is the nature of English education?" Henry (1986) describes "the supreme art of instruction in English" as "helping the self gain control of this peculiar medium called language" (p. 16). In traditional elementary and secondary English classrooms, the study of language is usually confined to the study of grammar rules. It is often seen as remedial action against student errors of speech and writing. Many critics of schools appear not only to sanction this limited teaching but to ask for more. The cry "Back to the Basics!" arose in the 1970s, a time of societal shifts and lack of confidence in many institutions, but it continues to be heard several decades later as the populations of schools grow increasingly diverse. English teachers especially are called into this public admonition and reminded that student language needs to be standardized, homogenized, and corrected. Because reformers so often assume that the path to correct use is paved with rules of grammar, punctuation, and correct usage, the idea of language basics is often synonymous with teaching grammar.

As a prospective teacher, you need to articulate your position on the teaching of language, and to do so, you need a deepening understanding of the issues surrounding this instruction. We follow James Moffett's advice that English teachers should spend more time learning about language and less time having their students learn about language. We discuss theoretical positions and practical strategies for teaching grammar in Chapter 9, *Compelling Writing*, and Chapter 10, *Enabling Writing*. In this chapter, we introduce questions of language in the English classroom by considering five perspectives: (1) the story of language, (2) the study of language, (3) the linguistic, political, psychological, and practical debate over language instruction, (4) general strategies for teaching grammar and usage, and (5) specific activities to reawaken curiosity and delight in language. When you have finished, we hope that you and, in turn, your students might feel the affirmation and challenge in Ralph Waldo Emerson's words: "Language is a city, to the building of which every human being brought a stone."

Invitation to Reflection 2–1

The following questions will initiate our deliberations about language and language instruction.

- Are you interested in language because of its ability to help you to speak and write better or because you enjoy words, their sound and sense? Do you find more pleasure in written or spoken language?
- Does the historical and cultural evolution of language interest you? Do you regard language changes as natural or corrupt?
- How do you respond to variations from Standard English? Do you think of some forms of English as more socially prestigious than others? Do any forms stigmatize those who speak them?
- Have you ever noticed and thought about a child's acquisition of language? Do you regard language as learned or inherited?
- When you think of teaching language in an English class, do you think primarily of teaching grammar? Have you learned grammar indirectly through the experience of writing and speaking or directly through the learning and practice of grammatical rules? Do you feel confidence in your command of those rules? Do they help you in your speaking and writing?
- Is the study of language important to the study of literature? Is its primary importance to ensure that readers understand what a text literally says? Does it change or enrich that understanding?
- Do you imagine teaching language not for utilitarian reasons, but to awaken students to delight in its structure and meaning?

We will remind you often in the course of this book that there is some knowledge you will need to possess but not necessarily convey directly to your students. An understanding of the evolution of the English language might be such knowledge. We present in this chapter a brief overview of language evolution and linguistic history because we believe your English teaching must be grounded in the basic "stuff" of our discipline. (We also, frankly, consider this subject fascinating in and of itself.) The overview will have practical value as you consider what and how you will teach your students about language.

THE STORY OF THE ENGLISH LANGUAGE

Considering the dawn of oral and then written language stretches the imagination toward those early humans who used no speech, their later arrivals who developed utterance and painted signs to let their descendants know of this, and then those early creative and cooperative attempts to develop vocabulary with which to name, syntax with which to communicate, and alphabets with which to write words. Our first hints of these efforts at language were found in caves that date from about 30,000 years ago; however, the story of the English language begins much later. Many date its beginnings only within the last 1,500 years and recognize it as a great amalgam of many languages mixed by successive waves of invasion of and settlement on the British Isles. T. S. Eliot once remarked that English is the best language for a poet because it contains, for the poet's choice, the rhythms of many languages.

Although all languages stem from similar needs and purposes, they achieve their goals in quite a variety of ways. Apparently, no feature of grammar or syntax is necessary or universal. Some languages function satisfactorily without any fixed grammar, while others operate within amazingly complex rules. Some languages manage without vocabulary that English speakers regard as indispensable. Bryson (1990) notes, for instance, that "the Romans had no word for gray" and "Irish Gaelic possesses no equivalent of *yes* or *no*" (p. 35). The number of languages in the world today is usually placed at about 2,700. New languages continue to be born, usually as combinations of two or more languages, as others dwindle and vanish as their remaining speakers die.

THE UNIQUENESS OF ENGLISH

English, the language that concerns us here, was established as the dominant language in the United States only within the last 300 years. According to Smitherman (1990), the proclamations of the Continental Congress were printed in English, German, and French. In 1981, linguist and California Senator S. I. Hayakawa made the first proposal for an amendment to the Constitution declaring English the official language. At about the same time (1983), a pressure group called U.S. English formed to lobby state-by-state for recognition of English as the sole official language of the United States. The English-only movement continues to keep the issue alive and to embody the belief expressed by Hayakawa (1997) that "a very real move is afoot to split the U.S. into a bilingual and bicultural society" (p. 37). Not accidentally, perhaps, this merging of linguistic and political concerns originated in the 1980s, a decade when more immigrants came to the United States than in any other time of its history except for the peak immigration in the twentieth century's first decade.*

Despite these fears for our "mother tongue," English has grown to be not only our language, but also a global language. We summarize Bryson's (1990) views of the features that distinguish English from other languages:

- It is often said that what most immediately sets English apart from other languages is the richness of its vocabulary. *Webster's Third New International Dictionary* lists 450,000 words, and the revised *Oxford English Dictionary* has 615,000, but that is only part of the total. Technical and scientific terms would add millions more. Altogether, about 200,000 English words are in common use, more than in German (184,000) and far more than in French (100,000). The richness of the English vocabulary, and the wealth of available synonyms, means that English speakers can often draw shades of distinction unavailable to non-English speakers. (p. 13)
- A second commonly cited factor in setting English apart from other languages is its flexibility. This is particularly true of word ordering, where English speakers can roam with considerable freedom between passive and active senses. . . . English also has a distinctive capacity to extract maximum work from a word by making it do double duty as both noun and verb. The list of such versatile words is practically endless: *drink, fight, fire, sleep, run, fund, look, act, view, ape, silence, worship, copy, blame, comfort, bend, cut, reach, like, dislike,* and so on. (pp. 15–16)
- A third—and more contentious—supposed advantage of English is the relative simplicity of its spelling and pronunciation. For all its idiosyncrasies, English is said to have fewer of the awkward consonant clusters and singsong tonal variations that make other languages so difficult to master. (p. 16)
- [T]here are one or two small ways in which English has a demonstrable edge over other languages. For one thing its pronouns are largely, and mercifully, uninflected. (p. 18)
- In other languages, questions of familiarity can become . . . agonizing. A Korean has to choose between one of six verb suffixes to accord with the status of the person addressed. (p. 18)
- Above all, English is mercifully free of gender. . . . Not only have we discarded problems of gender with definite and indefinite articles, we have often discarded the articles themselves. (p. 18)
- English also has a commendable tendency toward conciseness, in contrast to many languages. (p. 19)
- But perhaps the single most notable characteristic of English—for better *and* worse—is its deceptive complexity. Nothing in English is ever quite what it seems. Take the simple word *what.* We use it every day—indeed, every few sentences. But imagine trying to explain to a foreigner what *what* means. . . . As native speakers, we seldom stop to think just how complicated and illogical English is. (p. 19)

We turn now to a brief history of English to suggest how it evolved as it did or, to borrow from Bryson's *Made in America,* "how it got that way."

---

*Bryson (1994) answers these fears of the corrosive impact of foreign speakers on our communal life: "A study by the Rand Corporation in 1985 found that 95 percent of the children of Mexican immigrants in America spoke English, and that half of these spoke *only* English. According to another survey, more than 90 percent of Hispanics, citizens and noncitizens alike, believe that residents of the United States should learn English. If history is anything to go by, then three things about America's immigrants are as certain today as they ever were: that they will learn English, that they will become Americans, and that the country will be stronger for it" (p. 364).

A BRIEF HISTORY

Even a brief history of the English language reflects rhythms of change and stability. The language originated in a historical migration, adapted continuously to other historical upheavals, and consolidated only recently into its present shape. Its development was, of course, continuous, but linguists usually divide its history into an Old English period (A.D. 450–1066), a Middle English period (1066–1500), and a Modern English period (1500 to the present). The English language began as a collection of Germanic dialects brought from the European continent to the British Isles by tribes who had no written language and consequently left no record. Scholars have painstakingly worked through linguistic comparisons to reconstruct its distinct origins and to verify that English, a relatively young language, is a member of a large Indo-European language family whose descendants once covered much of the globe.

Old English Period (450–1066).

The invading German tribes found a Celtic people recently abandoned by withdrawing Roman legions. The language of these sea raiders almost completely replaced the Celtic language but was itself influenced by St. Augustine's conversion of the English to Christianity in 597 and then by successive invasions from Scandinavia. In the course of this 600-year history, the language developed characteristic sounds, inflections, vocabulary, and word order.

Sound	The sound system apparently was like that of modern Dutch or German.
Inflection	Nouns, pronouns, articles, adjectives, verbs, and adverbs were inflected for gender, case, and number.
Vocabulary	The word stock was primarily Germanic. Of the few Celtic words that remained, most were place names such as *London* and *Avon*. The tribes brought a few Latin words from the Roman occupation; Christian conversion brought many more. Scandinavian invasions added vocabulary, but most importantly, they changed the third-person plural form of the personal pronoun with the addition of *th-* forms.
Word Order	The extensive use of inflections made word order extremely flexible.

During this period, Latin became the universal language for learned use. Late in the period, Alfred the Great (d. 899) struggled to make English (the vernacular) accepted for religious and governmental purposes.

Middle English Period (1066–1500).

With the invasion of the French in 1066, English became unacceptable for cultivated purposes, especially governmental administration. Latin retained its preeminent status and French became the vehicle for government, law, poetry, and history. It was the second language, after Latin, in developing universities. Because almost all writing in English ceased, there was no stabilizing force for the language. Consequently, change accelerated, foreign influences became more potent, and regional differences more pronounced.

Sound	The guttural sounds of German weakened and vowel distinctions blurred.
Inflection	Inflections lost their distinctness and later disappeared. Many linguists regard the loss of grammatical gender as one of the most important developments in the history of the English language.
Vocabulary	Latin borrowings grew and thousands of French words were added. French linguistic influence was almost entirely confined to vocabulary.
Word Order	With the loss of inflections, sentence word order became more rigid and auxiliary verbs became more common. Most sentences followed a subject-verb-complement pattern. Relationships were indicated by prepositions and other connecting words.

Chaucer, writing toward the end of this period, expressed his worry that with no authoritative standard of English, readers would not be able to understand his book. Its spelling ("myswrite") and pronunciation ("mysmetre") would be unfamiliar in this great "diversite" of language:

> And for ther is so gret diversite
> In Englissh and in writyng of oure tonge,
> So prey I God that non myswrite the,
> Ne the mysmetre for defaute of tonge.
> And red wherso thow be, or elles songe,
> That thow be understonde, God I biseche!

(Troilus and Criseyde, Book 5: 1793–1798)

Modern English Period (1500–present).   Near the beginning of this period, when the structure of English was changing and writers enjoyed greater grammatical freedom, Shakespeare took great advantage of this opportunity for verbal expansion. Modern English has since grown stable in its basic sounds, vocabulary, syntax, and semantics through diverse forces: the development of the printing press, the education of large numbers of people, the spread of English through the expansion of the British Empire, and its present adoption as the linguistic currency of international trade and diplomacy.

Sound	The Great Vowel Shift in the sixteenth and seventeenth centuries changed the pronunciation of many words.
Inflection	Inflections disappeared.
Vocabulary	English freely borrowed words from many languages. One of the most interesting developments was the second person pronoun. *Thou* (nominative), *thee* (objective), and *thy* and *thine* (possessive) gave way to *you* (nominative and objective) and *your* (possessive).
Word Order	Sentence word order became more firmly fixed. Present dialectical differences now tend to be in pronunciation or vocabulary.

Many regard American English as a dialect of British English whose sounds and grammar deviate very little from its source and whose primary difference is one of vocabulary. We Americans have put original English words to new uses, formed new compounds, and appropriated the words first of Native Americans and then of immigrant groups.

LANGUAGE CHANGE AND STABILITY

You can actively enter these questions of language change and stability through your own inquiry. Exercise 2-1 provides a look at what's happening right now to the past tense of five selected verbs.

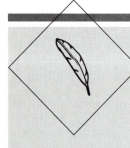

Exercise 2–1   Five Verbs

Decide on the past tense of each of the verbs listed. Then ask a group of 10 friends and classmates to tell you the past tense of each of them, and answer the questions that follow.

Present Tense	*Past Tense*
dive	_____
learn	_____
squeeze	_____
hang	_____
dream	_____

1. Can you immediately see a pattern to the responses?
2. Are both regular and irregular verb endings used?
3. Which are more prevalent?
4. How do you account for the concurrence of responses in some cases and the diversity of others?
5. If your respondents expressed ambiguity about *hang,* on what basis did most people decide on their preferred past tense? Meaning? Sound? Previous education?
6. Could an explanation involving preference based on meaning also be at work in our rules for *sit* and *set, lie* and *lay,* and *rise* and *raise*?
7. Most people in England say "learnt" as the past tense of *learn.* How many of your respondents did so? How do we regard people in America who say "learnt"?
8. Is there a trend in America toward regularity or irregularity that is registered in these samples?

These verbs were once strong, or irregular, verbs; their past tenses were formed not by adding the regular *-ed* ending, but by a change of spelling that often included a middle vowel shift (*hang* to *hung, squeeze* to *squose, dive* to *dove*) or an irregular ending (*learnt,* not *learned; dreamt,* not *dreamed*). In thinking about these changes, you will notice that there is a push toward regularizing such verbs. *Dived* is gaining strength every year, although the irregular form, *dove,* remains.

An interesting example of the interaction of change and stability in language is seen in what we will here refer to as *clichimiles.* We give examples in Exercise 2-2.

Exercise 2–2   Clichimiles

See how many of the similes you can complete using the common clichés of our culture. Ask 10 students and 10 nonstudents to complete these similes. Answer the questions that follow in light of your own and others' responses.

quick as a _____   crazy as a _____
dead as a _____   free as a _____
wild as a _____   late as a _____
sharp as a _____   fat as a _____
flat as a _____   happy as a _____

1. What does our name for these bits of language suggest about their character?
2. Why might these similes have frozen into clusters?
3. Which of the 10 seems most solidified, or certain? Why?
4. Which is least solidified? Why?
5. Does each of the 10 phrases have a correct answer?
6. What kind of society gave birth to these clusters?
7. In what sense have these clusters resisted change?
8. How have they been overcome by change?

Clichimiles have all frozen over time into clusters probably because they drew on common experiences for natural comparisons, were used repeatedly, and struck users and hearers as illuminating. They are a tribute to the culture that produced them, but as that homogeneous culture fades into a pluralistic society, they are heard and seen less and are therefore strongest in older readers of books and weakest in younger watchers and listeners of videos. That they once gained common currency is a testimony to language solidarity and to the relative slowness with which information was once transmitted. Their slow demise today is, paradoxically, a result both of the tremendous diversity in the American speech community and of the uniformity of language that the community receives through mass culture.

WHAT CREATES VARIATION

This dance of language—stability and change—produces many new words, pronunciations, and usages and, surprisingly, preserves others intact in isolated language communities throughout the English-speaking world.

Vocabulary.   In a cosmopolitan urban center, language is being created and modified every day by a rich blend of ethnic groups, a shifting set of social customs, and a variegated workplace. New words are coined and new meanings are found for old ones. The language of special groups adds vocabulary to the general fund at an accelerated rate. Physicists speak of "naked" and "clothed" singularity; rock groups move from "boss" to "bad" to "proper" in quick order. When the general culture catches up, the insiders shift to other terms that reinvigorate and reinforce their special worlds.

But in more isolated regions, the pace of change is less rapid. When an old-timer from the Appalachian mountains tells you he "holp" a stranger pull his car from a ditch, he's not mistaken or feebleminded. He is using the Old English form of the past participle of *help,* which still appears in the ancient carol "Holpen Are God's Folk So Dear." Peterson (1987) explains that the absence of the consonant sound /v/ in Old English might explain the use of "mighty" as an adverbial intensifier, as in "mighty good" rather than "very good." In Chaucer's Middle English, *right* was also used as an intensifier, as in "I awoke right early." Peterson describes the people of Appalachia as "a people whose linguistic heritage is rooted in orality and who have retained many of the older forms of usage" (p. 54). Similarly, the shrimper from the outer islands who still says "hit" for *it* is merely using a form of the pronoun that Shakespeare used in the beginning of the seventeenth century. It is perhaps mostly city dwellers who have reordered the King's English; the isolates are maintaining forms that were standard and proper long ago. Thus, these speakers from the less traveled paths of our world are not in error; they are keeping the faith much as some dedicated prescriptive grammarians might wish. They are maintaining standards. When their islands are bulldozed into beach condos and their mountains into ski slopes, the language of their children will change to fit the modern usage of the invading world. In the meantime, their failure to change or their extremely gradual change contributes to the diversity of the English language.

Pronunciation.   Pronunciation shifts make fascinating study, but they must be measured like the movement of glaciers, over long periods of time. Two Great Vowel Shifts are documented in the history of the English language, the first in Chaucer's day (1300–1450), the second in Shakespeare's (1550–1750). (The first shift is thought by many linguists to be the more dramatic; when they speak of a single Great Vowel Shift, it is usually to this one that they refer.) Vowels softened or shifted down so that endings that once rhymed no longer seem to do so, and word endings changed in pronunciation, for example, final *e* became silent. This shift can be observed in hymns and poems that date far back into English history. In fact, linguists think that this shift in pronunciation largely accounts for the inconsistency in the present English spellings of many words whose original fixed spellings were later changed to conform phonetically, while the earlier versions lingered in the written language. Other pronunciation differences originate in stress placement, not vowel sound, and distinguish, for example, the British gá-rage from the American ga-ráge, their con-tró-ver-sy from our cón-tro-ver-sy, and their la-bór-a-tor-y from our láb-o-ra-tor-y. In Old English, stress on the first syllable of two-syllable words was common and so can account for pronunciations such as gúi-tar and ré-ward in isolated areas of the United States.

Usage.   Similarly, time has its way with usage. Strong verbs such as *dive—dove* are weakening to *dive—dived.* Some teachers, on encountering an emerging form, think of the variant as wrong, because they do not see that it's really part of a larger usage shift; they cannot accept *dived,* but have little trouble with the almost fully shifted *dreamed.* In many cases, they will ignore or rationalize the shift from *hung* to *hanged* by explaining that a picture (inanimate object) is hung while a criminal (person) is hanged. Mykia Taylor sums up the ambiguity of this phenomenon nicely.

> *Sneak—Sneaked, Webster*
>
> Into our language, a new work snuck
> When I wasn't looking.
> Into the dictionary I puck
> To see what was cooking.
>
> All through the s's I suck and suck
> But it wasn't there.
> Whoever the new word "snuck" has spuck
> Had better beware.
>
> When the purists' vengeance on you have wruck
> I'll give no defenses.
> My joints may have cruck, my voice have squck,
> But I've stuck to my tenses.
>
> *Mykia Taylor*

Gender.   We know too that rules of grammar that were clear-cut 15 years ago are reversed today because of overriding gender concerns. The attempt to make our language inclusive of women and men necessarily situates us in awkward (and often reluctant) adjustments of language. But altering vocabulary, saying, for example, "police officers" rather than "policemen," is easier than changing entrenched grammatical pronoun forms. Thus, debate continues about which is preferred, as in the case, for example, of "everyone ate dinner and returned to his room" or "everyone ate dinner and returned to their rooms."

THE STUDY OF LANGUAGE: LINGUISTICS

Language has always been dynamic. In fact, many agree that the one universal linguistic fact is that all languages change. Scholars have long observed and speculated about the phenomenon of language; this study is called *linguistics.* Postman and Weingartner (1966) give this simple definition: "What is Linguistics? It is conducting oneself in a particular manner—a scientific manner—when studying language" (p. 16). This study can be divided into the different emphases and interests of linguists, but its earliest expression was in traditional scholarly grammar. The Greeks began to analyze the grammar of their language about 400 B.C., and Latin grammarians continued the method into the sixth century A.D. Medieval scholars carried on the tradition of studying classical Latin, as did Renaissance scholars. (Twentieth-century language scholars use this method to scrutinize the grammar of English to this day. Interestingly, four of the most noted are not native English speakers: the Danish linguist Jespersen, and the three Dutch linguists Poutsma, Kruisinga, and Visser.) Four distinct areas of linguistic study grew from these beginnings.

HISTORICAL LINGUISTICS

Some linguists study changes in language that occur over time in order to establish relationships among languages and trace their historical development. To such linguists as Jacob Grimm, an early historical linguist in the nineteenth century, we owe our early knowledge of the evolution of language. Today the field is so immense that, as linguist Raven I. McDavid Jr. (1985) acknowledges, even detailed histories of the language are "bound to be overviews" (p. 288). The field of comparative linguistics originated with eighteenth-century historical dialect studies, but its practitioners separated from historical linguists to compare language systems existing in different cultures at a given point in time.

DESCRIPTIVE LINGUISTICS

All linguistic study is basically descriptive, but the term itself has come to have a more precise meaning. Twentieth-century anthropologists such as Edward Sapir and phoneticians like Henry Higgins in *Pygmalion* made the description of written and spoken language more exact. Techniques of transcription have developed throughout the twentieth century and have allowed the collection of massive amounts of data about many aspects of different speech communities. For instance, a systematic investigation was undertaken in 1931 to collect data for a *Linguistic Atlas of the United States and Canada* that is not yet finished. Language is regarded by descriptive linguists as an artifact to be collected, explored, and catalogued; they see language as a matter of culture, habit, and convention, not as a matter of logic and correctness.

PSYCHOLOGICAL/SOCIOLOGICAL LINGUISTICS

A diverse and interdisciplinary group of linguists from various subspecialties in psychology, sociology, and even anthropology study the way language works in the lives of individuals and the larger society. They study language acquisition and linguistic behavior: the psychological/sociological mechanisms that produce them and the impact they have on users. Language is viewed by these linguists as an integral part of the individual and of group culture. Benjamin Lee Whorf studied the Hopi Indians of Arizona, for instance, and through that study formulated what is for us the most fascinating hypothesis in the field of linguistics: that the structure of one's language influences the way one perceives and understands one's world.

STRUCTURAL LINGUISTICS

Other twentieth-century linguists have stressed the structural aspect of language, its systematic form and internal organization. They have worked to describe and penetrate its deep structure, and they are interested in the particularity of a language and analyze each on its own terms. The academic study of language structures entered school grammars with Noam Chomsky's 1957 publication of *Syntactic Structures*. His transformational and generative grammar represents a different approach to language rules, not as consciously and systematically developed dogmas, but as patterns emerging unconsciously from the human mind.

Owen Thomas, in *Transformational Grammar and the Teacher of English* (1965), compares these four aspects of linguistics to the impulses that drive other academic fields of study:

Some linguists, for example, are interested in cataloguing and describing various features of languages, just as some botanists prefer to catalogue and describe plants. Other linguists are interested in the history of various languages and language families, just as some anthropologists are primarily interested in tracing the history of various families of mankind. Still other linguists are concerned with the interrelationships between language and society, or language and learning, or language and intelligence, just as sociologists, educational theorists, and psychologists are interested in similar questions. And finally, some few linguists are interested in general theories of language, just as some physicists are interested in theories that explain the operations of the universe. (pp. 3–4)

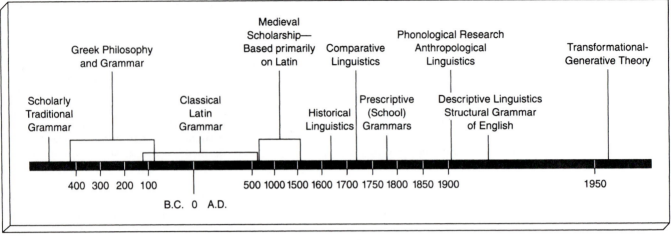

FIGURE 2–1 Methods of linguistic analysis

Figure 2-1 places these methods of linguistic analysis and description within a historic timeline.

This brief description is intended to suggest that linguists and grammarians have much to say that is of more than simply informational value. Their differing perspectives suggest the richness of language study; their differing conclusions guard us against dogmatic views of language. They open questions about the psychic and social effects of language; they prod us to consider how language is, to borrow a term from Postman (1995), a "world-maker" (p. 182). They also influence decisions that English teachers must make about what we teach about language. We now turn to consider language instruction and immediately we enter a contentious debate.

THE INSTRUCTIONAL DEBATE

Before we detail particular points of view in the instructional debate, we define two basic positions in this long-standing controversy: descriptive versus prescriptive grammar. Then we examine the arguments of four different perspectives in the debate over how to teach English: the linguistic, political, psychological or biological, and practical perspectives. Each takes a different tack on the question "Should we teach traditional English grammar to high school students?"*

DESCRIPTIVE OR PRESCRIPTIVE GRAMMAR

Linguists and grammarians distinguish themselves, in their reaction to language change, as either descriptive or prescriptive. Descriptive linguists look at the rich variety of new language and the attrition of older forms as a natural characteristic of any live language. Latin is more regular and tidy than languages such as English because no one is speaking it in the regular conversations of daily life. It remains "undefiled" by rock jargon or high-tech terminology. Descriptive linguists record the common tongue and watch dispassionately as many forces affect our language: status, access, new information, and cultural shifts. These linguists make some judgments about the efficacy and aesthetics of language, but largely they are permissive about what is brought into common discourse. They would agree with H. L. Mencken that "stability in language is synonymous with rigor mortis."

Prescriptive grammarians, on the other hand, resist "the never-ending process of linguistic change" (Postal, 1968, p. 114). Their resistance is based on the assumption that we are headed for a "breakdown in communication" unless they oppose change. Their implicit belief about human language is that it is "a fragile cultural invention, only with difficulty maintained in good working order" (p. 115). They might quote from the preface to Samuel Johnson's *Dictionary:* "Tongues, like gov-

---

*A more basic question might be "*Which* grammar do we teach?" For years, traditional grammar as formulated by eighteenth-century grammarians was unquestioned. Increasingly, it came under criticism as being unscientific, inappropriately Latinate in its origins, and too prescriptive. The new structural, transformational, and case grammars, which emerged in the 1930s and 1940s and began to appear in textbooks in the 1960s and 1970s, were judged to be promising but proved to be as unsuccessful as traditional grammar in making students language proficient (Tabbert, 1984, p. 41).

ernments have a natural tendency to degeneration; we have long preserved our constitution. Let us make some struggles for our language."

Definitions of Grammar.   Descriptivists usually define *grammar* as a physical phenomenon, a mechanism in the brain that forms and produces utterances. As Halpern (1997) explains, "To call any recorded utterance ungrammatical, given this sense of the term, is to make a strange, almost meaningless statement: it is like criticizing the way the stomach produces digestive juices" (p. 22). Prescriptivists define grammar quite differently, as "the mechanism embodied in books and teachers that decided whether what you've said was correctly said" (Halpern, 1997, p. 22). Given two such different viewpoints, it is no wonder that their debates are inconclusive and their "war," as Halpern calls it, is "a war that never ends."

Issues of Right and Wrong.   The different views of descriptivists and prescriptivists are often perceived by the general public and teachers as issues of right and wrong language, of judgmental and nonjudgmental standards of correctness. *Learnt,* for example, is not commonly seen as an ancient form of English kept intact in isolated rural areas, but as merely wrong or even bad language. Not only good people in the general community, but also many English teachers who hope to maintain standards view *learnt* as poor grammar and censor it in their students' talking and writing. Prescriptive grammarians, however, try to continue the use of archaic forms and exclude change. Postal (1968) uses as an example the "endless struggles" over the current use of *like* in instances in which an older generation would have used *as.* Many of these "language cops," as Robert MacNeil (1988) calls them, or "English Mafia," in Russell Baker's (1981) phrase, believe that a lack of mental capacity and a failure of will or discipline, rather than geography, history, or economics, are causes of this divergence from Standard English.

Such fears for the degeneration of the language and judgments of those who abuse it are so common that they seem natural to language itself. In fact, until the late Renaissance, this concern for correctness was quite rare; for a listener or reader to understand was enough. The sense that some usages and structures were more correct than others developed only gradually and culminated finally in the late-seventeenth and early-eighteenth centuries in the self-appointed arbiters of linguistic right and wrong. In 1697, Daniel Defoe called for an academy to judge questions of right and wrong usage, so that "it would be as criminal to coin words as money" (as quoted in McCrum, Cran, & MacNeil, 1986, p. 131). Jonathan Swift deplored the shortening of words, vogue words and phrases, and the chaos of English spelling. In 1712, he "proposed the only sure remedy against 'Manglings and Abbreviations' and against the innovations of 'illiterate Court Fops, half-witted Poets, and University Boys'—an English Academy" (as quoted in McCrum, Cran, & MacNeil, 1986, p. 132). Defoe and Swift had their counterparts in the United States, who, in the midst of the American Revolution, in 1780, called for an academy whose purpose, as John Adams wrote to the president of Congress, would be that of "refining, correcting, improving and ascertaining the English language" (as quoted in Bryson, 1990, p. 138). Much school time in the nineteenth and twentieth centuries was spent eradicating corruptions of language that prescriptive grammarians identified.

Correct English.   The spirit of these concerns for correctness can be seen in a periodical published in the United States between 1899 and 1950 called *Correct English.* Gould (1987) explains that, although the monthly publication resembled in some aspects *Reader's Digest, Saturday Review,* and *Writer's Digest,* its basic goal was to school its diverse readership "in the niceties of grammar, usage, diction, punctuation, and spelling. . . . The fundamental aim of *Correct English* was to edify its readers—more specifically, to help them know how to conduct themselves in proper (i.e., elite) society" (p. 22). Its founder and editor, Josephine Turck Baker, not only was "unabashed about equating 'correct' English with social class and intelligence," but she also was dogmatic about the standard of correctness and implicitly equated correct usage with law and incorrect usage with crime:

> *Correct English* is now becoming the final arbiter of that which is correct. . . . Under no circumstances does the editor express her private opinions, for when she indicates that which is correct her assertions are based, as in law, *upon the record.* . . . As in law, so it is in language, there must be a final arbiter. . . . [Therefore,] when the editor makes a statement as to the correctness or incorrectness of certain forms, the reader is fully aware that the statement is authoritative, and that *Correct English* is the final Court of Appeal. (as quoted in Gould, p. 24)

Josephine Turck Baker has her counterparts today. One of them, George Will, tells the story of a grammarian whom he regards as "one of civilization's friends." On his deathbed, the grammarian uttered these last words: "I am going to, or, I am about to, die. Either is correct."

Invitation to Reflection 2-2

Muinzer (1960, p. 26) put the situation this way:

Historically speaking, language is a tension between the old and the new, the linguistically conservative and the linguistically radical. Stated in human terms, the tension exists between society as the champion of conservatism and the individual as innovator and rebel. We may represent the conflict graphically as a tug-of-war between the two opposing forces:

Inertia	*Change*
traditional language	contemporary language
society	the individual

- Where do you find yourself in this tug-of-war? What kind of linguist do you feel yourself to be?
- In what ways might you borrow from both positions in your teaching?
- Would *descriptive* or *prescriptive* most likely represent the linguistic philosophy of English teachers you have known?

You may find yourself caught in the middle of this argument—you don't want to be permissive or casual about language use, but you also want to avoid being condescending and provincial. As you explore practical questions about language instruction, you may be torn between thinking that you need to draw the line against the barbarians at the gate and that the dynamic energy and life in language must not be overly restricted by rules. When we explore cultural pluralism in Chapter 6, Expanding Literacy, we will find the same dangers at each extreme: relativism, the loss of standards, and dogmatism, the rigidity of standards. Whatever your reaction might be to the question of what you teach about language, looking from a historical, cultural, or psychological distance at language gives you a sense of its complexity and its dynamism. Thoughtful and informed linguists rather than dogmatic "language cops" keep the vigor of the exploration alive. Peterson (1987), speaking of Appalachian language, suggests the most important consequence of such an approach: "Learning about the changes that have occurred in the English Language, and learning at what stages in the evolution of language Appalachia has lingered and why, is certainly preferable to merely being left with the impression that the people use a corrupted or substandard English, with ignorance their only reason for doing so" (p. 54).

THE LINGUISTIC DEBATE: CHANGE VERSUS STABILITY

If we believe that language is changing and that only dead languages will behave grammatically, we have to question the effects of teaching grammar. We may agree that language will continue to change and that social or psychological matters may override its stability, however, and still argue that we have an obligation to keep our students within the mainstream of standard language. Just because language is not absolutely frozen does not mean it is an unchecked flood.

Perera (1990) makes an argument for the preservation of Standard English: She questions how far variety in language can be extended before it becomes a new dialect or even another language. She wants to make room for both community and diversity. She praises the English language for providing the ever-more communicative and intermeshed world with an important common tongue. Yet she notes that North Americans say a garment "fit" last year while those from the United Kingdom say it "fitted." She believes that such usage differences are the spice of life. Our diversity becomes problematic only when it threatens the language community. Perera is saddened to think that we may meet the fate of the Portuguese and Brazilians, also separated by an ocean, but no longer sharing a language.

Postman, in *Teaching as a Conserving Activity* (1979b), celebrates digital language (letters and numbers) over pictorial information (nonsymbolic presentation) and argues for the effectiveness, economy, and aesthetic strength of Standard English. He does not regard all language forms as equally efficient and beautiful, but believes that Standard English has a power that should not be lost to any group of users.

MacNeil (1988) presents the counterargument: "What is hidden in all this is a simple fact: Our language is not the special private property of the language police, of grammarians, or teachers, or even great writers. The genius of English is that it has always been the tongue of the common person literate or not" (p. 18). MacNeil then quotes Walt Whitman, who wrote that American English is not "an abstract construction of dictionary-makers, but is something arising out of the work, needs, ties, joys, affections, tastes of long generations of humanity and has its basis broad and low, close to the ground "(p. 18).

Teachers who care about language and who also promote an education that liberates people will always be torn between the desires to maintain the order and beauty of language and to celebrate the energy and vitality of its ever-new creations. Shakespeare, for example, was ever the language smith; he coined more words than any writer before or since. Estimates are that he created 2,000 new words and countless phrases, such as "one fell swoop," "to be in a pickle," "vanish into thin air," "go down the primrose path," "flesh and blood," and "foul play." When in *Julius Caesar* he had Portia protest that Brutus kept her in "the suburbs of his pleasure," Shakespeare created the combination of *sub* and *urban*. Most people suspect *suburban* to be a twentieth-century word created by sociologists or city planners, but Shakespeare used it first as a poignant metaphor to describe the marginal place Portia feared she occupied in Brutus's life. According to Bryson (1990), Shakespeare used "17,677 words in his writings, of which at least one tenth had never been used before" (p. 76). This exploding vocabulary came in part from his use of nouns as verbs, adverbs, and adjectives. Clearly, teachers must balance their caution with openness: Only a dead language lies perfectly still.

THE POLITICAL DEBATE: CULTURAL DIVERSITY

The question of how to teach English is complicated by considerations other than language evolution. Language affects us in quite personal ways. The language we use carries messages to our hearers or readers about who we are. Their reaction to our words can have a significant impact on our sense of self, and on our social and economic achievements. Thus, the question of what we teach the young about language raises questions that are political as well as linguistic.

Respecting Diversity.   Smitherman (1990) estimates that 80–90% of African-Americans speak Black English. She believes that for too long teachers and textbooks considered speakers of Black English to have a language deficit. In 1974, the National Council of Teachers of English (NCTE) Conference on College Composition and Communication passed a strong resolution on African-American languages that clearly states the case for protecting the diversity of American English by respecting and accepting students' home language while they learn Standard English:

> We affirm the students' right to their own patterns and varieties of language—the dialects of their nurture or whatever dialects in which they find their own identity and style. Language scholars long ago denied that the myth of a standard American dialect has any validity. The claim that any one dialect is unacceptable amounts to an attempt of one social group to exert its dominance over another. Such a claim leads to false advice for speakers and writers, and immoral advice for humans. A nation proud of its diverse heritage and its cultural and racial variety will preserve its heritage of dialects. We affirm strongly that teachers must have the experiences and training that will enable them to respect diversity and uphold the right of students to their own language. (p. 1)

Labov (1973) presents detailed research findings that refute the idea that nonstandard Black English is an inferior language system that must be corrected and eradicated by English teachers. He enumerates some of the basic, but erroneous, assumptions that people make about nonstandard variants of Black English and the people who use them:

Verbality	Black nonstandard speakers use inferior monosyllabic language that lacks subtlety and elaboration.
Verbosity	Black nonstandard speakers are nonverbal; they do not use rich language forms.
Grammaticality	Black nonstandard speakers have no complete mature grammar from which to generate language.
Logicality	Black nonstandard speakers use illogical constructions such as negative concord ("you ain't goin' to no heaven"), negative inversion ("don't nobody know"), and the invariant *be* ("when they be sayin") (pp. 21–22).
Linguistic Environment	Black nonstandard speakers use a primitive, sloppy form of Standard English.

Clearly, these assumptions about speakers of Black English can be broadened to label and stigmatize any speaker or group of speakers. Aside from questions of racial prejudice, such assumptions are linguistically simplistic and naive.

The personal consequences of the failure to respect language diversity are movingly presented in Christensen's (1990) personal account of a teacher's attempts to teach Standard English to all her students. She recounts her own struggle with social class bias in an English classroom:

When I was in the ninth grade, Mrs. Delaney, my English teacher, wanted to demonstrate the correct and incorrect ways to pronounce the English language. She asked Helen Draper, whose father owned several clothing stores in town, to stand and say "lawyer." Then she asked me, whose father owned a bar, to stand and say "lawyer." Everyone burst into laughter at my pronunciation. What did Mrs. Delaney accomplish? Did she make me pronounce *lawyer* correctly? No. I say *attorney.* I never say *lawyer.* In fact, I've found substitutes for every word my tongue can't get around and for all the rules I can't remember. (p. 36)

Christensen goes on to explain other lessons she learned from Mrs. Delaney: "I learned early on that in our society language classifies me. Generosity, warmth, kindness, intelligence, good humor aren't enough—I need to speak correctly to make it. Mrs. Delaney taught me that the 'melting pot' was an illusion. The real version of the melting pot is that people of diverse backgrounds are mixed together, and when they come out, they're supposed to look like Vanna White and sound like Dan Rather" (p. 36). It took Christensen years to shake off the sense that she was ignorant and recognize that "grammar was an indication of class and cultural background in the United States and that there is a bias against people who do not use language 'correctly.' Even the terminology 'standard' and 'nonstandard' reflects that one is less than the other" (p. 36).

The inward toll on speakers who learn to censor their own speech is significant. Christensen (1990) explains that, for her, the "problem is that every time I pause, I stop the momentum of my thinking. I'm no longer pursuing content, no longer engaged in trying to persuade or entertain or clarify. . . . These side trips cost a lot of velocity in my logic" (p. 36). She senses the same discomfort in her students who are self-conscious about their words: "When more attention is paid to the *way* something is written or said than to *what* is said, students' words and thoughts become devalued. Students learn to be silent, to give as few words as possible for teacher criticism" (p. 37). In *The Color Purple* (1982), Alice Walker uses Celie as the spokesperson for those who struggle to learn the rules of Standard English. Celie reflects on Darlene's attempts to teach her how to talk:

Every time I say something the way I say it, she correct me until I say it some other way. Pretty soon it feel like I can't think. My mind run up on a thought, git confuse, run back and sort of lay down. . . . Look like to me only a fool would want you to talk in a way that feel peculiar to your mind. (pp. 193–194)

Standard and Nonstandard Language.   You might expect consensus on questions of language diversity from teachers and scholars who are sensitive to nonstandard dialects. In fact, they differ. Many African-Americans have been the strongest advocates for a strict adherence to the standard language system in speaking and in writing. They say that we do not have black language or dialect, but good language or bad language and that middle-class teachers, white and black, who do not carefully and rigorously correct the nonstandard language of their black students are patronizing and ultimately damaging. They believe that children who do not speak correctly will have little opportunity to advance in society. They believe that standard language facility is closely associated with social acceptance and economic opportunity.

Jones (1982) captures the dilemma of African-Americans who wish to remain true to their rich heritage and also thrive in a predominantly white culture:

James Baldwin once defended black English by saying it had added "vitality to the language," and even went so far as to label it a language in its own right, saying, "Language [i.e., Black English] is a political instrument" and a "vivid and crucial key to identity." But did Malcolm X urge blacks to take power in this country "any way y'all can"? Did Martin Luther King, Jr. say to blacks, "I has been to the mountaintop, and I done seed the Promised Land"? Toni Morrison, Alice Walker and James Baldwin did not achieve their eloquence, grace and stature by using only black English in their writing. Andrew Young, Tom Bradley and Barbara Jordan did not acquire political power by saying, "Y'all crazy if you ain't gon vote for me." They all have full command of standard English, and I don't think that knowledge takes away from their blackness or commitment to black people. . . .

I know from experience that it's important for black people, stripped of culture and heritage, to have something they can point to and say, "This is ours, *we* can comprehend it, *we* alone can speak it with a soulful flourish." I'd be lying if I said that the rhythms of my people caught up in "some serious rap" don't sound natural and right to me sometimes. But how heartwarming is it for those same brothers when they hit the pavement searching for employment? Studies have proven that the use of ethnic dialects decreases power in the marketplace. "I be" is acceptable on the corner, but not with the boss. (p. 7)

Shuy (1981) sees irony in the argument that we leave language alone while "one thing seems to remain constant: people go on judging or assessing each other because of their use of language" (p. 315). He wryly observes that those who argue for doing nothing about helping nonstandard speakers acquire standard English if they choose not to do so, "conduct those arguments in perfectly standard English. . . . I have yet to hear a black parent argue that we should not help his child learn standard English" (pp. 315–316).

Status and Stigma. Shuy (1982) argues that stigma or status can be conferred on speakers as they depart from the norms in three areas of speech: pronunciation, vocabulary, and usage.

Pronunciation. When you hear a person say fur-ni-′ture, what do you assume about the speaker? When a speaker says "ax" for *ask* what do you presume? On the other hand, if someone pronounces *about* so that it rhymes with *shoot*, or *yard* with a long *a* and no *r* sound, what do you think? In these cases, departures from standard pronunciation bring stigma to the first group and status to the second. The language of the second group is evaluated as socially prestigious and its members are thought to be Virginia tidewater aristocrats or New England intellectuals. In England, dialects indicate the class and social standing of a speaker far more than in the United States. In fact, George Bernard Shaw observed that "it is impossible for an Englishman to open his mouth without making some other Englishman despise him."

Vocabulary. When you hear a person say "griddle cakes," whereas you might say "pancakes," you might perk up your ears but are likely to regard the person as quaint rather than ignorant. In *Pygmalion*, George Bernard Shaw is concerned with the way language use can metamorphose a flower girl into a lady when she shifts her vocabulary and pronunciation from lower- to upper-class speech. In the *My Fair Lady* adaptation, at the Ascot races, Eliza Doolittle urges her losing horse to "Move your bloody arse!" and thus exposes her aristocratic pretense. If, on the other hand, she had referred to the horse's derriere, no one would have thought that anything was amiss. As this story illustrates, the use of any of the common Anglo-Saxon four-letter words shocks members of polite society, whereas the use of their antiseptic Latinate counterparts impresses them.

Usage. Pronunciation and vocabulary can earn stigma or status, but generally only to a moderate degree; the real social litmus test is found in usage. Usage comprises the choices made in the use of language: words, expressions, and syntax.

Walt Wolfram (1983) has comprised a list of superstandard (status), substandard (stigma), and standard usage levels that make this point well. Consider which usage level each utterance in the following trios reveals.

Wolfram's Usage Levels

1	2	3
It's mine, is it not?	I thought they was stupid.	He does not supposed to do that.
It's mine, ain't it?	I thought them stupid.	He is not to do that.
It's mine, isn't it?	I thought they were stupid.	He is not supposed to do that.

The standard usage goes unnoticed like a pleasant day, but people recognize the superstandard as the credential of high culture and view the substandard as unacceptable and part of a lesser world. Such trios of sub, super, and regular don't present themselves regularly, but judgments are nevertheless made along a continuum of acceptability. Exercise 2–3 exposes one such continuum.

Exercise 2–3 *Drawing the Line*

Read these sentences in order, and decide at what sentence you would draw the line between acceptable and unacceptable usage. Circle the problem areas you perceive in each sentence.

1. Jack's spontaneity often got in his way.
2. The drivers who failed to successfully complete the race were sent home.
3. Where is his car at?
4. Having leaped the chasm, a mere climb seemed easy.
5. Although we saw some bad spills, the race was different than the earlier ones.
6. He suggested that we might could meet on Wednesday.
7. None of the 163 students were finding their problems insoluble.
8. He never done any work in his life til now.
9. In spite of all that he did or failed to do.
10. Some the was home on and.

Most students, and even a majority of teachers, do not see sentence 1 as unacceptable; however, *The Harbrace Handbook* tells students that a pronoun's antecedent should be a noun but not a possessive form of the noun. Most people accept not only the first sentence, but also at least the next two sentences. Some go all the way to sentence 8 before drawing the line, but they won't accept *done* as a proper past tense of *did,* though it is widely used as such. For those who accept that renegade, sentence 9 is usually over the line, because it does not complete a thought. Most educated speakers, hearing this uttered, would know immediately that it is unacceptable, even if they might not be able to clearly say why. Linguists, while admitting that many of these sentences are not acceptable to the general public, would say that only the last is clearly not acceptable and nongrammatical; this collection of words would not be spoken by anyone who grew up hearing the basic subject-verb-object grammar of English. This final "sentence" makes an important distinction. *Usage* is defined as variations inside a general language system. For a language to be understood as a single system, it must have a set grammar that all users, even those who use variants and dialectical differences, recognize in other speakers of the same language.

The Holt Handbook (Kirszner & Mandell, 1986) refers to usage with other labels: "*informal* or *colloquial, slang, dialect* or *regional, vulgar, obsolete, archaic, rare, poetic,* and *foreign language*" (pp. 322–323). Usage within each category can stigmatize its user. That stigma disproves the old adage "Sticks and stones may break my bones, but words will never hurt me."

Compromise.   The situation with language is very much like what Israel Scheffler (1967) said about subatomic physics. In arguing with Thomas Kuhn and other indeterminists, who insisted that uncertainty and absolute certainty were the only kinds of knowledge it is possible to have about subatomic particles, Scheffler chose *fixity,* not *certainty.* Just because language change sometimes takes place at relatively rapid speeds does not mean that it is unclear what is mainstream or standard at a given time. We may even need to add an Einsteinian time/space relativity to our sense of language: At a certain place and time we can say with some authority what is standard or correct even as the general use of language shifts. If we are currently studying in New Zealand, we might well say we *learnt* a great deal, but when we return to America we need to report that what we *learned* about language was invigorating. Thus, we may need to develop, and to help students develop, a double standard: We should accept and celebrate language change on the grand level, but we should be able to accommodate to a standard when we are in or hope to enter a particular speech community. Teachers have a duty, then, to teach both an awareness of change and the ability to identify and accommodate to a standard. The following three strategies offer just such a middle path.

Stewart.   Stewart and colleagues (1964) developed a reading series that started readers in Black English and after two years of instruction made the shift to reading in Standard English. This series was supposed to be more effective than traditional series for African-American students because it allowed them to take on one major task at a time, rather than making them learn both to read and to master Standard English at the same time.

Smitherman.   Smitherman (1989) has developed a three-point language program that requires all students to switch to an entirely new code or second language. She bases her sense of the importance of this shift on research that closely associates cognitive development with acquisition of a second language. African-American students in Chicago schools who had been taught a second language in the elementary grades had otherwise unaccountable achievement gains in a number of other subject areas. Smitherman urges the code shift, then, not merely to meet the standard, but because multiplicity of language codes seems to enhance achievement across the board. She also wants to encourage majority speakers to be aware of the difficulty of shifting to a second language.

Christensen.   Christensen's (1990) classroom approach reminds us of the daily need for affirmation of the students' language, teaching some standard rules, and developing a critical consciousness about them. She affirms her "students' lives and language" as "unique and important" through the literature she selects, the history she teaches, and the use she makes of her students' own lives as "a content worthy of study" (p. 38). But she goes further to teach her students the rules of the dominant, standard language of our culture, what Jesse Jackson calls "cash language" (p. 37). She does not, for example, teach grammar to one of her students, Fred, as she was taught, through humiliation and textbook drills, but through reacting to the "text" of his own writing. She also teaches Fred the politics of language: "I teach Fred that language, like tracking, functions as part of a gatekeeping system in our country. Who gets managerial jobs, who works at banks and who works at fast food restaurants, who gets into what college and who gets into college at all are decisions linked to ability to use Standard English" (p. 39).

Thus, Christensen teaches her students the rules of Standard English, but she goes beyond the rules to teach a critical consciousness about them. "Asking my students to memorize the rules without asking *who* makes the rules, *who* enforces the rules, *who* benefits from the rules, *who* loses from the rules, *who* uses the rules to keep some in and keep others out legitimates a social system that devalues my students' knowledge and language. Teaching the rules without reflection also underscores that it's okay for others—'authorities'—to dictate something as fundamental and as personal as the way they speak. Further, the study of Standard English without critique encourages students to believe that if they fail, it is because they are not smart enough or didn't work hard enough. They learn to blame themselves" (p. 40).

Invitation to Reflection 2–3

Consider the various opinions you have heard expressed about moving nonstandard speakers to Standard English.

- Teachers seem caught between a rock and a hard place. Where do you align yourself between making students self-conscious about their nonstandard English and leaving them without a knowledge of Standard English?
- Do you think that most of the grammar taught in school is effective in moving students to Standard English in their writing and speaking?
- What activities come to mind when you think of teachers at work on this task?
- If you are not sure of the effectiveness of grammar instruction, where do you think its weaknesses may lie?
- Do you believe that this is a central or peripheral task for English teachers?

THE PSYCHOLOGICAL OR BIOLOGICAL DEBATE: LANGUAGE ACQUISITION

Understanding what linguists, psychologists, biologists, and educators know about language acquisition is central to our entering the debate over language instruction. When these researchers speak of language, they are not describing the etiquette of correct usage, but "the system of rules governing the formation of words and the abstract relationships among words which generates the syntax of a language" (Sanborn, 1986, p. 74). In other words, Sanborn continues, grammar is "an abstract set of rules describing what we do with the elements of language to make *meaningful* utterances, not necessarily correct utterances."

Research.   Researchers have concluded that most students have acquired a natural, thorough, and unconscious understanding of English grammar by the age of 5, when they normally enter school. They are competent to express meaning that they understand. They have achieved this competence not by learning the rules, but primarily by listening and responding. Furthermore, they achieved it in a sequence timed to their developmental maturity. Dorothea McCarthy first conducted research in the 1930s on the speech of children between 18 months and 4 years. She found, and subsequent researchers have validated, that the average vocabulary increased from 10 to 93 words in those years. At 18 months, half of these words were nouns; by 4 years, all parts of speech and most sentence forms found in adult speech were used (McCarthy, 1954).

Behaviorist B. F. Skinner (1957) explains that children are conditioned to speech by their interaction with their primary caregivers. Competence in speech is determined by how often the infant hears speech and how well the child is reinforced for it. In fact, if the child is reinforced strongly for talking, verbal expression becomes reinforcing in itself. Other researchers speculate that language acquisition is an innate feature of the human species. Noam Chomsky (1968) believes that this ability causes infants to attend to speech sounds in the early weeks of life and to begin to imitate those sounds and patterns throughout their infancy. Sanborn (1986) describes this process: "We're born with a language-learning system just as we are born with a digestive system; we 'know' what to do with words just as we 'know' what to do with food. Whether cognitive or visceral, the original response is innate" (p. 74).

Research on language acquisition also has explored the process in terms of the child's social context. Catherine Snow's work on mothers' speech suggests that language growth occurs as mother and child mutually seek a plane on which they can communicate (Ferguson, 1977). Mothers do speak in a special way to their children, but not to teach them syntax. Mothers adapt their own speech to the meanings of the child. Psychologists have catalogued and classified features of this baby talk or "motherese": a higher pitch than usual, fluctuations in intonation, simple and concrete vocabulary, and short sentences. Research in six languages found that these characteristics are true of the speech of almost all mothers (as well as fathers, other relatives, and strangers) in these speech communities (Ferguson, 1977). Snow's and Ferguson's research adds another dimension to Chomsky's innateness hypothesis. They see adults as skillfully adjusting their speech to the child's level of comprehension and the child as more active in language acquisition as he or she attempts to make meaning of the world. The child and the adult coordinate their communication, and their interest is not in syntax, but in meaning. They are motivated by more than imitation and reinforcement. Stern (1977) calls the nonverbal behaviors that begin within the first three months of life and develop into language the "dance" that forms the basis for the child's interactive life with others.

The acquisition of language begins, then, in infancy and continues by cognitive developmental sequence. Some researchers, such as biologist Eric Lenneberg (1967), see talking as a biological development as dependent on physical maturation as walking is. More agree that language learning becomes rapid when a child reaches a stage of development in which he or she can see the connection between words and objects or actions. Carol Chomsky (1969) and other researchers found that, although children enter kindergarten with a basic grammar structure intact, they are constantly adding nuances of language to their repertoire. Milner and Elrod (1986) observed that stress and other subtle communication features were not acquired by some students in their first 6 years of school.

It is important to understand that problems develop in language acquisition when stages are skipped and children are asked to operate at a stage developmentally beyond them. Further, difficulties arise when students are asked to grow conscious of what is for them an innate process. A story about W. C. Fields crystallizes the difficulty of making innate knowledge conscious: After reading an analysis of how he juggled, Fields could not juggle for 6 years.

Implications for Language Teaching.   These observations about language acquisition suggest certain principles for the teaching of language:

- Teachers should encourage language experiences that enable students to produce language and to receive language that is accessible yet challenging.
- Teachers should teach language in the context of making meaningful sense of the student's world.
- Teachers should realize that students are still acquiring language through the school years, even though they have mastered basic grammar by age 5.
- Teachers should not attempt to teach a consciousness of rules until the child has reached a level of abstraction that renders him or her capable of understanding them.

Sanborn (1986) summarizes these observations:

> Since students already know the grammar of their language unconsciously and since most of them cannot successfully take the steps of decentering and abstracting necessary to make the unconscious process conscious, I do not believe that we should attempt to teach grammar as early and as relentlessly as we do. It is valuable to understand the workings of one's own language but hardly necessary. Students who have not yet reached a level of formal operational thought or a level of ego development where they can step outside themselves should not be forced into grammar exercises that can have no meaning for them. (p. 77)

Sanborn does not dismiss grammar instruction entirely. The biological model indicates that "internal development may require an outside trigger" (p. 77). Students' readiness for that language trigger depends on their ability to think abstractly and to view language as a means of social interaction, not just as an extension of self. The timing of that readiness varies widely. But Sanborn thinks it most probably arrives in the final 2 years of high school and arises out of wide and constant language use.

THE PRACTICAL DEBATE: RESEARCH AND EXPERIENCE IN GRAMMAR INSTRUCTION

Practical questions remain in the debate over secondary language instruction, namely over the teaching of grammar. Given the evidence that this country's school teachers and students devote thousands of hours each year to grammar study, Wall (1971) asks questions about why students "have to know their grammar":

1. To pass grammar tests?
2. To "get into" college?
3. To be able to write?
4. To be successful?
5. To have an educated person's understanding of how language operates? (pp. 1127–1128)

She refutes each of the first four answers as (1) "immoral," (2) a "lie," (3) a "cliché of our culture," and (4) "another lie, unless one includes grammar knowledge in his definition of success" (p. 1128). She translates the fifth as meaning "Learn grammar because it is there," and she finds this just a bit more justifiable. She says; "We learn about the pupil, cornea, and retina of the eye in a science class because it is knowledge educated people should at some time know, too. But we do not teach the technical aspects of the eye in every grade from fifth through twelfth; nor does one 'have to know' his eye in order to appreciate either the miracle of a cornea transplant or what he sees" (p. 1128). Postman and Weingartner (1966) list and demolish other prominent claims on grammar's behalf. They use excerpts from the 1950 edition of the *Encyclopedia of Educational Research* to show that grammar does not (1) discipline the mind, (2) aid in the interpretation of literature, (3) improve writing and usage, (4) aid in the study of foreign languages, (5) improve reading, or (6) improve language behavior in general (pp. 63-74).

These third and sixth claims remain the most persistent, disputed, and tested rationales for grammar instruction. Much research has been done to measure the practical benefits of grammar instruction. These studies have been themselves the subjects of review and appraisal. The most noted critique, *Research in Written Composition,* by Braddock, Jones, and Schoen (1963), evaluated almost 70 years of research and reached a strong conclusion: "The teaching of formal grammar has a negligible or, because it displaces some instruction and practice in composition, even a harmful effect on improvement in writing" (pp. 37-38). More recently, Kolln's research (1981) concluded that the 1963 critique was severe in its claims of harm in grammar instruction. Many of the studies on which it was based did not meet today's research standards. Still, Kolln's study and those of others (Sherwin, 1969; Elley, Barham, Lamb, & Wyllie, 1979), while not concluding that formal grammar instruction is as harmful as Braddock et al. did, are not optimistic.

In the mid 1980s, Hillocks (1995) undertook a "meta-analysis," or "research synthesis," of 500 previously conducted experimental studies of writing instruction. He selected 60 studies that he considered to be well designed and compared their results. He divided these into four distinct "modes of instruction" and six "foci of instruction." We will discuss both in Chapter 10, *Enabling Writing.** For now, we summarize the dimension he calls the "focus of instruction," because its research bears on our practical question of grammar instruction. The "focus of instruction" refers to "the dominant content of instruction, for example, sentence combining, grammar, or the study of model pieces of writing" and so clarifies different approaches to grammar instruction in actual classrooms (p. 219). The six foci are (1) grammar (Teachers teach traditional grammar concepts such as parts of speech and parts of sentences, not prescriptions for correct usage.); (2) models (Teachers present concrete models of finished writing for students to understand and emulate.); (3) sentence combining (Teachers ask students to put phrases, clauses, and sentences together in certain ways.); (4) scales (Teachers ask students to apply criteria to judge their writing and guide their revising.); (5) inquiry (Activities are designed to present sets of data and "to help students develop skills or strategies for dealing with the data in order to say or write something about it" [Hillocks, 1986, p. 211].); (6) free writing (Students write whatever they wish in journals as a means to discover their own ideas and voices.). The results of Hillocks's research synthesis shed a more nuanced light on the question of teaching grammar in the context of writing. His study found that the two foci he terms *declarative* (his grammar and models categories) did not yield student gains (pp. 219-223). In fact, his data visually suggest that the students studying grammar lost ground; his analysis shows that they simply did not make any gains at all in contrast to students whose teachers used the other five approaches.

The question can still be posed, "Is grammar instruction useful in the study of language regardless of its uncertain impact on usage?" Glatthorn (1988) answers in the affirmative. He gives several "practical arguments for including grammar: most teachers think it is important; most administrators and parents want it emphasized; a knowledge of some grammatical terms helps teachers and students talk about writing and literature" (p. 49). He also asks "Why is it that science and math teachers never have to apologize for teaching the technical language of their disciplines?" (p. 49). John Wariner, a high school teacher whose *Handbook of English* has been a standard in the field since its first edition (1951), argues that the "chief usefulness of grammar is that it provides a convenient and indeed . . . indispensable set of terms to use in talking about language" (as quoted in Tabbert, 1984, p. 40).

Invitation to Reflection 2-4

Donovan (1990) conducted a survey that included all middle schools in three public school systems to determine language arts teachers' assumptions and practices about grammar instruction. Of those who responded to Donovan's study, 70% believed that mastering "grammatical terminology" was important for their students. She asked that they rank the following six reasons for teaching grammar. Based on your present thinking, rank these statements in terms of their relative importance.

_____ The more my students understand grammar, the better their writing will be.
_____ Students need to master English grammar as a preparation for studying a foreign language.

*Hillocks's four modes of instruction are (1) presentational (Teachers lecture and explain.); (2) natural process (Teachers encourage students to write about self-chosen topics, receive peer review, and make revisions.); (3) individualized (Instruction is accomplished through individualized writing conferences between teacher and student.); and (4) environmental (Student-led small-group discussions focus on problem solving using specific criteria for good writing.).

_____ The study of grammar will improve students' speech patterns.
_____ The study of grammar, like the study of mathematics, sharpens students' thinking skills.
_____ I want my students to do well on standardized tests.
_____ I personally find the study of language structures fascinating. (pp. 62–63)

The teachers ranked their reasons for teaching grammar in the order in which they are presented here.

LANGUAGE INSTRUCTION

We have discussed competing sides of the debate over language instruction. Let's assume that we can agree that *some* instruction in Standard English is desirable. The question of strategy then becomes paramount. Lindemann (1982) believes that students do not need to understand grammatical principles (as English teachers do) in order to be effective writers and speakers. She does think, however, that English teachers can do much to create in their students an awareness of their actual grammar usage and of the choices available between standard and nonstandard forms (p. 116).

LEVELS OF USAGE

So that instruction is apt and effective, the first thing teachers may need to determine is their students' levels of usage. If you can identify your students' language deficiencies, you can develop instructional plans that make sense in terms of the patterns that occur in your classroom. Students whose language is replete with departures from Standard English do not need intensive instruction on some of the niceties of language. To belabor split infinitives or preposition-ending sentences when other language deficiencies are enormous would be like working on punt-return defenses with football players who know little about blocking and tackling. Instruction needs to be pitched where it is most needed. The following list gives examples from three levels of usage.

Levels of Usage

1. Formal Differentiations (Distract)
   - Nominative/Objective selection: I/me; who/whom
   - Semantic content: good/well; may/can; to/too
   - Verbal misconstructions: dangling participles; split infinitives; prepositional closure
   - Usage variants: from/than; that/which
2. Usage Departures (Stigmatize)
   - Kernel rupture: he come; they helps
   - Semantic incongruity: she can't never; more better
   - Conjugational variant: he brung; she done; we knowed; they be
   - Reflexive excess: theyselves; John he did it
3. Communication Detractors (Confound)
   - Lame particles: that he left home. John and Sue at their houses
   - Dual deep structure: The shooting of the natives was terrible. Ginny and Bob were wrapped in a bandage.
   - Open referent: John saw Paul and told Tom he could fly home with him.
   - Hyperextension: He went with John who could come but we never knew how his cousin was on the park bench.

Teacher Stella Beale asked her students to locate their usage difficulties on this schema. She found that their questions and her explanations helped them identify their common errors and understand why they made them. More importantly, this minilesson defused their unease with grammatical correctness and eased grammatical tensions. Before, she reports, their grammatical blunders felt to them like undifferentiated sin. Afterwards, Beal and her students clarified the areas of real language need and directed their language study to the most serious departures from effective communication.

Middle school teacher Mitzie Renwick (1994) was so frustrated by the gap between grammar study and student usage that she significantly altered her classroom teaching strategies. Influenced by Lindemann, she became an astute observer and record keeper of her students' language use. She found the following to be the top five areas of misuse in her South Carolina middle school classrooms:

1. irregular verb forms*
2. *s, ed,* and *ing* endings
3. double negatives
4. pronoun usage
5. homophones

Understanding her students' real usage allowed her to design language lessons—with no reference to grammar jargon or grammar rules—that could help them recognize their mistakes and select an alternative construction.

STRATEGIES OF LANGUAGE INSTRUCTION

After you have identified students' levels of language usage, you need to examine a range of teaching approaches. The following list enumerates seven common strategies.

Strategies of Language Instruction

1. *Grammar Rules.* Make students aware of the basic rules of standard usage in our language system. Teach definitions of the parts of speech and more complex usage features such as gerunds and participles.
2. *Conjugation of Principal Verb Parts.* Have students memorize the proper forms of verbs and the pronoun subjects that accompany them, for example, *I bring, I brought, I will have brought,* and so on.
3. *Workbook/Software Drills.* Let students apply their knowledge of usage in fill-in-the-blank, multiple-choice, and other activities with electronic and paper texts.
4. *Sentence Diagramming.* Write sentences as schematic diagrams to represent the relationship of their component parts to one another.
5. *Writing Response.* Report problems in student writing by referring to grammatical rules or citing communication difficulties in commonsense language.
6. *Oral Transference.* Use pattern drills and other means of code consciousness to encourage students to switch to standard usage, first in oral work and then in writing.
7. *Acquisition/Attrition.* Encourage standard usage through extensive reading of fiction and nonfiction and oral interaction with users of Standard English.

Think about these seven strategies as a continuum. You can see that they move from the controlled and systematic to the natural and spontaneous, from the theoretical and abstract to the practical and concrete. They move, too, from work with writing to work with oral language. Finally, they move from distant to immediate connection to the everyday world. Some teachers would characterize them as moving from conservative to liberated.

Invitation to Reflection 2–5

Review the seven strategies of language instruction and answer these questions.

- Which strategy was used most often in your high school experience?
- Which approach seems to you most effective in enhancing student use of Standard English? Why?
- Which seems least effective? Why?
- Which two do you think would be most useful in combination? Why?

Figure 2-2 contains examples of instruction taken from actual classroom workbooks or worksheets.

- Define the instructional strategy or strategies embedded in each.
- Which activity do you consider the most useful for language instruction?
- In what ways would it be effective?
- Which do you believe to be the most ineffective activity?
- What do you perceive to be its basic fault?

*The most frequently misused verbs were *bring, ring, sing, think, drink, shrink, see, write, go, ride, do, run,* and *come.*

FIGURE 2–2
Sample classroom worksheets

1. Principle Parts

Three principal parts:	Present	Past	Past participle
	_____	_____	_____

Present Tense

I _____ We _____
You _____ You _____
He, she, it _____ They _____

Past Tense

I _____ We _____
You _____ You _____
He, she, it _____ They _____

Future Tense

I _____ We _____
You _____ You _____
He, she, it _____ They _____

Present Perfect Tense

I _____ We _____
You _____ You _____
He, she, it _____ They _____

Past Perfect Tense

I _____ We _____
You _____ You _____
He, she, it _____ They _____

2. *May* and *Can* and *Rise* and *Raise*

MAY AND CAN   MAY AND CAN   MAY AND CAN   MAY AND CAN

MAY refers to permission or to something that is possible. *Might* is another form of the word. There are no principal parts. MAY and MIGHT are used only as helping verbs. ex: May we go to the beach?   ex: Bundle up, you might catch cold!

CAN refers to ability. *Could* is another form of the verb. There are no principal parts. CAN and COULD are used as helping verbs.
ex: Karen can play the piano.   ex: We could see the oar.

RISE AND RAISE   RISE AND RAISE   RISE AND RAISE   RISE AND RAISE

RISE means to go upward.   ex: The elevator rises.
RAISE means to lift or to make something go up.   ex: Raise the volume on the stereo.

Present Tense	Past Tense	Past Participle
rise	rose	has risen
raise	raised	have raised

TURN YOUR PAPER OVER AND USE EACH FORM OF THE FOUR WORDS IN A SENTENCE. YOU SHOULD HAVE 10 (TEN) SENTENCES!!!

3. Concrete and Abstract Nouns

In each sentence, pick out the noun and identify it as being concrete or abstract. Tell how they are different.

1. The puppy has grown to twice the size since we bought it.
2. Time passes too quickly.
3. The coldness of the air made our noses feel funny.
4. The sound of the violin is sweet and mellow.
5. The power given off when the bomb exploded was outstanding.

Next to each noun, write *C* if it is a concrete noun, *A* if it is abstract.

1. Record _____
2. Light _____
3. Tire _____
4. Guitar _____
5. Softness _____

6. Cushion _____
7. Smell _____
8. Middle _____
9. Ashtray _____
10. Wetness _____

Write 6 sentences of your own; 3 using concrete nouns and 3 using abstract nouns.

I'm a concrete noun—everybody can see me, pick me up, etc.

I'm an abstract noun—I'm hard to describe to anybody!

4. Creative Adverbs

Directions:
Write a short story from the words listed below.

- You may use other words.
  - You may use the given words in any order or more than once.
    - But . . . *You Must Use All The Words Below.*

When you have finished the story, circle the adverbs.

NOTE: Remember that adverbs modify verbs, adjectives, or other adverbs. Adverbs answer the questions How? When? Where? and How Much?

awkwardly	beach	beyond	confused
friendly	happily	heavenly	here
inside	lonely	never	not
old	rock	shy	sister
slept	sometimes	song	stole
stranger	there	thought	told
too	upstairs	very	walked
water	wished	yesterday	

5. Time Line

Think of tense as a time line. We live in a narrow PRESENT. All that's behind us, our yesterdays, is PAST. All that lies ahead, our tomorrows, is FUTURE. Think of five or six verbs and place the appropriate form along the following time line. We give you two examples.

Yesterday BEHIND Past	*Today* NOW Present	*Tomorrow* AHEAD Future
was	am	will be
ran	run	will run

Basic Qualities in Language Instruction

You may ask of these five figures, "Does one provide better instruction than another?" "Are there any overarching principles of instruction that might guide us through all of the suggestions available in grammar texts, workbooks, the periodical literature, and the suggestions of experienced teachers?" The answer is yes. Neil Griffiths (1991), a primary educator from England, argues that schoolwork should always be practical, concrete, realistic, and purposeful. What he posits in every subject is very similar to what we call for in language instruction. He bases his views on sound developmental theory and a proven record in schools. Lucy Calkins (1986) reminds us that "English is a skill to be developed, not a content to be taught, and it is learned best through active and purposeful use" (p. 204). We would argue that whatever your approach to teaching, five basic qualities should characterize your instruction in language: that it be concrete, inductive, personal, developmental, and contextual.

Concrete.   Concreteness is a basic tenet of Piagetian and Montessorian instruction for young children. It is equally important as a starting point with adolescents, most of whom are not fully formally operational in their thinking. Just as the abstractions of mathematics (even simple ones such as addition and division) are understood through the teacher's use of concrete manipulatives, grammar's abstract concepts (such as nouns and participles) are understood best when they can be expressed in concrete ways. Grammar instruction should firmly ground the abstract rules and procedures in palpable matter. Putting a troop of silly clowns under, over, in, around, by, beside, into, and beyond a tiny automobile is a concrete way to teach prepositions. Describing their preposterous walk would be a concrete way to understand adverbs. Any time this is the first step in learning, the path is surer.

Inductive.   Closely related to the concrete is the inductive. Donovan (1990) encourages inductive discovery as one of her learning principles. She observes that the common approach of grammar texts is deduction: "definition of rule, example, practice." She contrasts that with the induction children use instinctively: "from the complex body of language which they hear, they construct their own set of rules" (p. 64). Thus, students explore how a sentence works to form meaning and discover in their deliberation that noun/subject and verb/predicate are the kernels of the English sentence. They examine pronouns, for example, and discern their role as substitutes, or scrutinize conjunctions as links between features of a sentence. They could inductively distinguish between abstract and concrete nouns and enumerate their common differences. Such instruction starts with the concrete objects or examples and moves to theories, generalizations, or rules that cover all instances. When students create their own rules out of an accumulation of instances, chances are better that they will understand the rules. What's more, they remember what they create. Their understanding of the language comes from inside out, so it is more deeply embedded than that which is merely appropriated from a textbook.

Personal.   Also related to the concrete is the personal. Language instruction that arises from personal experience will be more powerful for students in their adolescent years. They are eager to explore their own worlds, worlds set apart from those of family and adults. As with the movement from the concrete to the abstract, the move from the personal to the public will happen, but we must begin with what's close at hand. Such a beginning helps capture and hold student interest. S. I. Hayakawa, in the preface to *Language in Thought and Action* (1978), states the case succinctly: "Often when students who are bored with studying grammar and diagramming sentences become interested in the content and purposes of communication, their hostility to linguistic instruction vanishes, and problems of grammatical and syntactical propriety are solved in passing" (p. viii). Caccia (1991) notes his discovery as a teacher that "the only effective moment for introducing these distinctions comes in the midst of some breakdown that the students already care about" (p. 55).

Developmental.   To be consistent with a developmental strategy, we ought to abandon the practice of throwing all the rules of grammar at students from the moment the subject is first introduced, in the fifth or sixth grade, and of hammering away at them year after year. In the course of our own education, one of us was taught about run-on sentences at least seven times. He finally caught on, not because constant repetition drilled the concept into his head, but rather because he developed to a point at which he was able to understand what a sentence was and how a comma functioned. If we believe that the rules of handbook grammar should be taught to enable students to become competent speakers and writers of Standard English, then we should not expect those handbook rules to make sense before a student is in a position to understand the principles they exemplify. We would argue, for example, that it is probably pointless to try to teach seventh graders that nonrestrictive relative clauses must be set off by commas, if only because they may not yet be sophisticated enough to appreciate the logic of subsets or most of the rhetorical uses of nonrestrictive clauses.

Contextual.   The problem of selecting specific approaches is not unlike the war waged over reading instruction between phonics devotees and whole-language disciples. The first group calls for an analytical system of breaking down language so that, by mastering the pieces, students can begin decoding the language. In contrast, whole-language advocates believe that children have learned how to speak through natural interaction with their parents and siblings and that they also will learn to read if we present them with whole meanings (books), rather than analytical parts (words and sentences in primers). Similarly, some teachers believe that listening and reading will create the proper development of speaking and writing. This position was argued forcefully as early as 1898 by Samuel Thurber, a teacher at the Girls' Latin School in Boston. He wrote, "Language is acquired only by absorption from contact with an environment in which language is in perpetual use. Utterly futile is the attempt to give a child or youth language by making him learn something about language. No language is learned except as it performs the function of all speech— to convey thought—and this thought must be welcome, interesting and clear. There is no time in the high school course when language will be learned in any other way" (as quoted in Tchudi & Mitchell, 1989, p. 30).

Meyer, Youga, and Flint-Ferguson (1990) echo Thurber's position. They believe that the critical reason for the failure of traditional grammar instruction is that "it is given without any realistic *context*. . . . Language is often divorced from reading, literature, vocabulary, and spelling." They acknowledge that traditional grammar has been taught in conjunction with writing, but they believe even this link is suspect: "Instead of considering ways to provide a meaningful context for grammar, many teachers focus on making traditional kinds of grammar exercises interesting or cute. Magazines and publishers provide eye-catching charts, based on song lyrics or movies' titles, that are meant to stimulate interest in grammar. . . . Computerized versions of exercises with special effects are now readily available. These can perhaps sustain student interest for a little while, but unless this grammar instruction means something to the students, it, too, will fail to achieve lasting results" (p. 67). Meyer et al. (1990) make the following suggestions:

- Grammar should be part of an integrated curriculum which includes reading, literature, vocabulary, spelling, and writing and should not be taught as an isolated unit in a language-arts class.
- Grammar instruction should be concentrated on the proofreading stage of writing assignments. In the writing workshop approach championed by Nancie Atwell (1987), teachers base mini-lessons on the students' own writing, aiming "to be as relevant as possible to the whole group and what it needs," not letting these mini-lessons "become occasions for preaching abstract formulas and rules." (p. 148)

Newkirk, in *To Compose: Teaching Writing in High School and College* (1990), makes a similar point about grammar instruction. He advises that grammar should be taught in "small doses." "If grammar is to be taught it should be taught in mini-lessons of five to seven minutes at the beginning of some writing classes. The lesson should deal with an issue that relates to the writing that students are doing. . . . By relating grammar instruction to actual writing problems, the instruction has a better chance of sticking" (p. 306). Dixon (1967) makes the same point when he observes that "language is learnt in operation, not by dummy runs" (p. 13).

Invitation to Reflection 2–6

As you begin to imagine your specific approach to instruction, respond to the following 10 statements about language instruction. Write in the blanks provided your response to the following statements.
SA—Strongly Agree; MA—Mildly Agree; UN—Uncertain; MD—Mildly Disagree; SD—Strongly Disagree

_____ Being able to identify parts of speech and more complex grammatical construction is an important aid to developing speaking and writing skills.

_____ Speaking and writing are more effective ways to become a better communicator than is becoming conscious of various grammatical constructions.

_____ A basic, systematic approach to grammar rules seems to be the best guide for instruction in writing.

_____ If students cannot distinguish a gerund from a participle, they probably will not be able to use either of them correctly.

_____ The problem with students' language usage is that they are not taught the basics in English classrooms.

_____ Students do not need to know the parts of speech and the various kinds of phrases and clauses to write and speak well.

We suspend our discussion of teaching grammar at this point to resume it in Chapters 9, *Compelling Writing* and 10, *Enabling Writing,* where we will have the context that Newkirk recommends. We turn now to another approach to language, one with the broader goal of developing an interest in and a consciousness of language. Grammar or usage patterns may be a part of this, but we explore other approaches just now.

BROADENING LANGUAGE CONSCIOUSNESS

We learn to make generalizations about language based on our varied linguistic experiences. If we can broaden those experiences in English classes, we might deepen and enrich our students' consciousness. Such consciousness-raising exercises are neither in the literary tradition of language study nor in the tradition of grammar, rhetoric, and composition. Students who have been taught language essentially as literary analysis of others' linguistic virtuosity or as grammar drills may well look on language study as a dull and passive chore, rather than as an adventure of uncovering knowledge of the way language works. We would like to redirect them to an exploration of language—their own and that of a wider community. I. A. Richards (1938) observed that "the natural curiosity about how language works . . . struggles hard before it chokes." We want to breathe air into language study. To borrow from Robert MacNeil's account of his own childhood (1989), we want to make students "wordstruck."

Herbert Kohl describes such teaching in his *36 Children* (1967), an account of his experiences as a sixth-grade teacher in Harlem. One day in the midst of Kohl's frustration at not getting through to his class, one student shouted to another, "What's the matter, psyches, going to pieces again?" (p. 23). While the class broke up, Kohl lept on the word *psyches.* The students assumed it was spelled *s-i-k-e-s.* Kohl wrote the word on the board and told them the story of Psyche and Cupid. Not satisfied with the story, they wanted to know what happened to the history of the word. Not knowing the etymology and probably not willing to lose their interest, he asked them to think of all the English words that came from *cupid* and *psyche.*

Leaping ahead, Alvin shouted, "You mean words change? People didn't always speak this way? Then how come the reader says there's a right way to talk and a wrong way?"

"There's a right way now, and that only means that's how most people would like to talk now, and how people write now."

Charles jumped out of his desk and spoke for the first time during the year.

"You mean one day the way we talk—you know, with words like *cool* and *dig* and *sound*—may be all right?"

"Uh huh. Language is alive, it's always changing, only sometimes it changes so slowly that we can't tell." . . .

"Mr. Kohl, can't we study the language we're talking about instead of spelling and grammar? They won't be any good when language changes anyway." (p. 24)

Kohl reports that on that day he began what he called in his plan book "vocabulary" and "an enrichment activity," but what was actually "the study of language and myth, of the origins and histories of words, of their changing uses and functions in human life." His was not a continuous lesson, but "a fixed point in each week's work," a point that sustained and deepened his students' original excitement as they became "word-hungry and concept-hungry" (p. 25).

We believe that students at all grade levels and abilities can profit from such a heightened consciousness. Not all are ready to take the most abstract steps toward metalinguistic awareness, but all can be encouraged to enter a basic level of investigation. We want to foster in them a curiosity and interest in language study that will encourage them to continue to learn. In Tabbert's (1984) answer to the question "Why teach grammar?" we find motive for these final suggestions about language consciousness raising: "True literacy is more than the negative virtue of not making mistakes, and it cannot be attained primarily through analyzing sentences and memorizing rules" (p. 42).

DOUBLESPEAK

We introduce teaching ideas that promote this broadening with an issue our students consistently enjoy: doublespeak. In 1949, George Orwell published the novel *1984,* in which he described "Newspeak," a manipulation of language that sanitized any thoughts that opposed the principles espoused by the government. In 1972, the NCTE passed two resolutions concerned with the misuse of language in public discourse and its effect on public policy. Two years later, the council established a committee, the Committee on Public Doublespeak, to enforce those resolutions actively. The committee began in that year to publish a newsletter, now called the *Quarterly Review of Doublespeak,* which lists examples of doublespeak from government, business, and academia. The committee also awards an annual Doublespeak Award for persons or groups who use public language that is "deceptive, evasive, euphemistic, confusing, or self-contradictory" and has potential for "pernicious social or political consequences." In 1975, it established the Orwell Award for Distinguished Contribution to Honesty and Clarity in Public Language. In Chapter 8, we suggest ways to alert students to deceptive, manipulative language practices. Following are four of the most common kinds of doublespeak, as articulated by William Lutz, the Committee on Public Doublespeak chairman.

Euphemisms	Words or phases that soften unpleasant realities can be used to mislead or deceive, as when the phrase "unlawful or arbitrary deprivation of life" is substituted for "killing."
Jargon	The specialized language of members of a profession becomes doublespeak when used in addressing (and in fact, confusing) nonmembers. In its annual report to stockholders, an airline explained a three-million-dollar loss due to a plane crash as "the involuntary conversion of a 727."
Bureaucratese	A sheer volume of words or complicated syntax can be used to overwhelm audiences. One bureaucrat, testifying before a Senate committee, stated, "It is a tricky problem to find the particular calibration in timing that would be appropriate to stem the acceleration in risk premiums created by falling incomes without prematurely absorbing the decline in the inflation-generated premiums."
Inflated language	This language makes the ordinary seem extraordinary as when car mechanics are called "automotive internists," or electronics companies describe black-and-white television sets as units with "non-multicolor capability." (as summarized in Dorney, 1988, p. 50, our paragraphing)

Once students are sensitized to misuse of language in these and other ways, such as obfuscation and oversimplification, they can readily join in numerous data-gathering ventures. Examples surround them. Students can gather examples of doublespeak—words, phrases, slogans, and sentences—from advertising, public statements, and their private lives. Prime their interest with examples of your own. (The NCTE newsletter is a goldmine of detail.) The class in small or large groups can compare samples and analyze how they manipulate language to conceal or distort. The class might even wish to give its own Doublespeak Award. Humpty Dumpty rightly suggested the stakes in the use of language: power. In *Through the Looking Glass,* Carroll wrote:

"When I use a word," Humpty Dumpty said, in a rather scornful tone, "it means just what I choose it to mean—neither more nor less."
"The question is," said Alice, "whether you can make words mean so many different things."
"The question is," said Humpty Dumpty, "which is to be master—that's all."

Recognizing word manipulation will feel and be empowering to students. They may come to recognize the truth of C. J. Ducasse's observation "To speak of 'mere words' is much like speaking of 'mere dynamite.'"

FOUR LANGUAGE CONSCIOUSNESS-RAISING ACTIVITIES

We present the following Teaching Activities, our own and other teachers', to deepen students' true literacy. The clichimiles survey in Exercise 2–2 was one example of broadening language awareness. Such activities engage students in multiple dimensions of language, from etymology, dialect, idiom, and syntax to semantic context. We present the instructional purpose and strategy of each of these Teaching Activities in enough detail to illustrate our aim, but with the caution that they will need more specific enumeration for classroom use.

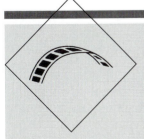

Teaching Activity 2–1   *Dialects on TV*

Perera (1990) has reported that the surest way to gain a consciousness of the standard is to inundate a classroom with examples of variants. It makes sense that one clarifies and more fully defines the other. When TV Cajun chef Justin Wilson says he likes the red wine because "it look more pretty" or explains "that is what I'm going to did," the regular comparative and the standard future are made more vivid for the interested listener. We recommend the following activity to raise that consciousness, but also to diminish the stigma attached to any one variant (in this case, dialects) examined alone.

Individual
- Select five characters from television whose speech is a clear departure from that of the mainstream characters who dominate sitcoms, soap operas, and dramatic productions.
- Tape or transcribe examples of departures (at least one each).

Small Group
- Read each others' samples aloud. Note any that are the same.
- Discuss the group members' samples:
  Are any expressions unfamiliar to you?
  Which expressions have you heard in the everyday talk around you?
  Do you regard any as archaic? Quaint?
  Do any stigmatize the speaker? If your examples come from written scripts, is the author using language to stereotype the characters?
  What language groups are represented in your group's examples?
- Choose your favorite examples to share with the whole class.

Whole Class
- Have each group leader read the groups' favorite examples of TV dialect.
- Discuss the conclusions drawn in each small group about the examples. Where do the groups' conclusions differ? Where do they concur?

Individual
- Free-write from the following prompt: I have gained the following new expressions and/or insights into dialect.

Teaching Activity 2–2   New Words of the Street

The language of the adolescent experience—rock music, high school, friendships, dating—provides a dynamic example of language change. Each generation coins words and idioms to secure its own separate identity and to differentiate itself from the adult world. The language of rock music, high school experiences, friendships, gyms, and special phenomena provides rich possibilities for investigation. (Our own students have usually been more interested in the idioms of other schools, near or distant, than in their own. They learned, for example, that in one local high school, "kicked to the curb" means to humiliate or put another person down; in another, 10 miles away, the term is "wasted.") Semantic comparisons vertically through time or horizontally by community can engage students in the shifting connotations of the vocabulary of their language.

Individual or Group Work
- Identify words or expressions used by your peers that appear to be unique to a specific activity.
- Ask others in locales or time periods different from yours how they would refer to the same activity.
- Compare the expressions of your own speech community with those of other communities or of years past.

Small Group
- List all original expressions and variants that group members have collected.
- As you consider your new expressions, do you find any that you would like to use? Why?

Whole Class
- Share the group findings.
- Create a lexicon of these expressions.

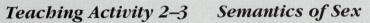

Teaching Activity 2–3   *Semantics of Sex*

Sociolinguists such as Tannen (1990) analyze everyday conversation and identify profoundly differ-ent ways in which men and women communicate. The following can be done individually or in small or large groups.

- Listen to samples of everyday talk and examine the speech of males and females. Do you discern differences of language and perception?
- Tape conversations at lunch tables or at any other public place where people are talking freely. Record radio talk shows or television interviews. Fictional characters from print or film provide excellent subjects. For instance, a comparison might begin with a look at the sentences of John and Lorraine, who alternate as narrators in Zindel's *The Pigman.*
- Gather examples of gender indicators, such as the suffixes *-ess* and *-ett,* and other gender-specific designations.
- Discuss where these distinctions are changing, where they are appropriate and necessary, and where they are offensive and detrimental.

Teaching Activity 2–4   *Stress Signals of Verbs and Nouns*

Stress is not recognized as a significant feature of the English language, whereas in the Chinese language, four different stress patterns on a syllable change the meaning of the sound symbol. In English, though at a much less obvious level, stress does have importance, as such words as *record* and *object* immedi-ately illustrate. When students are asked to identify the meaning of such words, they are unable to be pre-cise without hearing them used in a sentence. When the sentence is "We record the errors," they know that *record* is a verb meaning "to note," but when the sentence is "Play another Chuck Berry record" they know that *record* refers to a round disk. With ob jéct, students know that the verb is meant, and that ob-ject is the noun referring to a thing. In one-syllable words that work as both nouns and verbs, such as *hit,* a "success," and *hit,* "to strike," such stress differences are hard to detect, but they do exist.

- Work in groups of three or four to make lists of all of the words that you can recall for which the noun and verb differ in pronunciation by the use of stress.
- Compare your group lists and compile a class list.
- Collect newspaper and magazine headlines for examples of these confusions. Such confusions can have practical consequences. This exercise not only sharpens awareness of the importance of stress, but it invites playfulness and humor as well.
- Create your own ambiguous headlines.
- Gather a list of British pronunciations that are the same as American pronunciations except for stress.
- Note (record) some of these words and look for a stress pattern that separates the two versions of English or simply the pattern of noun and verb stress.
- Investigate the age at which children acquire such awareness of stress patterns. A simple oral test is to ask third-grade children and adults over 30 if they recognize different meanings by different stress. Is there a difference between the two groups in their understanding of the effect of stress on verbs and nouns?

WHITWORTH'S TESTED SUGGESTIONS

Whitworth (1991) suggests some excellent tested language activities based on the text and spirit of S. I. Hayakawa's classic *Language in Thought and Action* (1978). Whitworth divides his activities into "four traditional areas of general semantics: (1) language as a symbolic process; (2) the meaning of words in con-text; (3) referential [informative or factual] and emotive language; (4) relationships between language and thinking" (p. 50). He encourages teachers to allow students to "tinker with instructions" so that they can both envision more "fruitful ideas" and feel the pride and ownership in doing so. His list is arranged by pro-gressive steps for those with "low language skills to those with complex language talents" (pp. 50–54).

Language as a Symbolic Process

- Browse through Henry Dreyfuss's *Symbol Sourcebook: An Authoritative Guide to International Graphic Symbols* (1984). Discuss some of the unusual symbols such as hobo symbols, recreational signs, or semaphore signals. Or have students collect sporting symbols . . . and then have them create their own symbols for places and events around the school.
- Describe the body language of a person engaged in a telephone conversation that you cannot hear. Speculate on the gist of the content. What kinds of human behavior are displayed? Or tape a segment of a soap opera or sitcom. With the sound turned off, have students "read" the body language; then replay the tape with the sound on to verify student guesses.

Meaning of Words in Context

- Write a definition of *restaurant, theater,* or *cabin.* Compare the definitions to discover which attributes the group agrees upon and which are derived from personal experiences and biases.
- Research quotes from reviewers for inaccuracies and intentional misleading statements in movie ads or on the flipside of paperbacks, especially those highly praised ones with suspicious omissions by use of ellipses. For example, one newspaper movie ad reviewer's quote—"Magnificent! . . . Made me cry!"—sounds like a winner, but the reviewer really wrote: "How can a director turn such a magnificent novel into such a stinker of a movie? What they've done to it almost made me cry!" Once students get the idea, have them find really rotten reviews and turn them into positive statements with the use of ellipses.
- Tape class discussions or alert students to note situations where the meaning of the words comes not through direct context but indirectly through "reading between the lines" of the context. Examples: "I know this sounds stupid, but . . ." or "This is just off the top of my head . . ." The intent of these disclaimers is often to soften criticism if it should occur. How many of the following nonquestion questions have occurred in your classrooms: "Are we doing anything in here today?" "Is this movie any good?" "Is there extra credit in this class?" "Isn't this grammar stuff stupid?" Why are such nonquestions raised in class?

Referential (Informative/Factual) and Emotive Language

- After a basketball game with a rival town's team, compare the local newspaper's writeup of the game with that of the newspaper from the rival town. What language variations are found in the two stories?
- Create a computer database of euphemisms and circumlocutions found in television commercials or political campaigns. Divide the entries into *softeners,* those which remove the harsh edge of reality, and *impressors,* fancy words for ordinary facts. Or use William Lutz's (1989) categories: euphemism, jargon, gobbledygook, and inflated language.
- Play the old Bertrand Russell game of Conjugating the Irregular Verb (e.g., "I am fastidious; you are fussy; he is an old fuddyduddy" or the reverse: "He is broke; you are in debt; I am temporarily overextended") to show that although the basic meaning of the pivotal word remains the same, the value judgment changes. Bias often creeps into the language by our being very selective of words. The thesaurus often helps students to play the game effectively.

Relationships Between Language and Thinking (Analyzing, Synthesizing, Inferring, and Evaluating)

- Collect contradictory folk proverbs (such as "Two heads are better than one" and "Too many cooks spoil the broth" or "He who hesitates is lost" and "Look before you leap"). Can the contradictions be reconciled?
- Using the tabloids, present a series of articles that seemingly prove a generalization (e.g., children of movie stars are wild; the rich and powerful are really miserable). Show how the generalization may be faulty.

If you are sensitive to your students and alert to the universe of language in which they operate, you will devise other innovative activities. Figures 2–3, 2–4, and 2–5 are lessons on language submitted by three teachers in response to the *English Journal* roundtable query (Nelms, 1993) "What is your most successful lesson (or minilesson) on the nature of language and language study?" (p. 75); they catch our delight in exploring the linguistic sea around us. These three teachers have met what Thomas regards as a basic obligation of English teachers: "to keep language alive." Exercise 2–1 invites you to create your own language lesson.

FIGURE 2–3

G. D. Meyers's "Three Functions of Language"

To enhance understanding of the discrete but fluid nature of the three functions of language as defined by James Britton—transactional, expressive, and poetic—I present a lesson in which each student in the class receives one whole section of the local newspaper, a pushpin, and an unlined sheet of paper.

First, students are directed to scan their newspaper sections to find something which the rest of the class might want to know about. After five minutes of scanning, each student delivers a twenty-second *informative* news broadcast about some noteworthy item. Items range from serious current events to sports scores and show times.

After they have heard these news flashes, students freewrite for five minutes about what associations these broadcasts have aroused. These *expressive* journal reflections are kept private.

After the five-minute freewrite, students are directed to use their section of newspaper to write a "found poem." I model this by (1) finding words and phrases that catch my attention in my newspaper and cutting them out with a pushpin, (2) arranging and rearranging these words on a piece of paper in front of me, (3) gluing the words and phrases into lines of various lengths so that the finished product looks like a poem, and (4) taping my "found poem" to the chalkboard and reading it aloud with pronounced poetic inflection. Having witnessed this demonstration, students take to their own newspapers with their pushpins while I distribute glue sticks for preparation of the final productions.

Twenty minutes later, *poetic* pieces of writing have been composed, always to the astonishment of their student authors. After volunteers read their creations aloud, the lesson concludes with the disposing of newspapers, the collection of supplies and poems, and the beginning of a discussion of how we have experienced the unity of the three diverse functions of language.

SOURCE: From G. D. Meyers, Three Functions of Language. *English Journal, 82* (1), 75. Copyright 1993 by the National Council of Teachers of English. Reprinted with permission.

FIGURE 2–4

J. B. Meyers's "Where Do Words Come From?"

I tell students, "Choose a topic in which you are interested, and then list twenty-five words related to that topic." Working in pairs, students carry out this part of the task very quickly. "Food" or "eating" makes a productive topic, as does any sport. This year one group tried "sleeping," and some geometry lovers worked with "mathematics." A group of avid readers used "books."

The next part of the lesson requires dictionaries all around. I tell students that they are about to learn where their words came from. While my eighth graders are accustomed to looking up meanings of words, they have not previously dealt with word origins. We spend a few minutes studying the table of abbreviations for such languages as Old Norse and Medieval French and observing, from dictionary entries, that many words came through several stages en route from, say, Latin to English. Then I ask them to write down the language of earliest origin for each of their words.

At this point, somebody realizes that "football" is really two words, each with its own origin. And there's always at least one word per class with "origin unknown" in its dictionary entry. As the lists lengthen, somebody exclaims, "Most of our words came from Greek and Latin." This year's math words came exclusively from Greek and Latin. We speculate about the implications and reasons. We examine the oddities—some skiers included "mogul" and were surprised at the presence of a Mongolian word on a list where all the other terms were of European origin. Students become aware of languages they've not previously heard of and spot cognates of English words. They also realize what a hybrid language they themselves speak.

The last step is to make graphs. Students count the words in each origin category (I suggest lumping "Old French" and "Medieval French" together) and make bar graphs. This year some baseball fans from an advanced math group got out calculators and protractors and made a pie graph of the origins of their baseball terms. We post the graphs and lists on a wall.

The values of the lesson are

1. learning the variety of origins of English words
2. seeing the heavy debt the English language owes to Greek and Latin
3. seeing that a language is neither static nor isolated

SOURCE: From J. B. Meyers, Where Do Words Come From? *English Journal, 82* (1), 76. Copyright 1993 by the National Council of Teachers of English. Reprinted with permission.

FIGURE 2–5
Johnson's "The
Language of
Teenagers—Slang"

It was the mid 70s, early in my teaching career. I'll never forget the man—dressed impeccably in a business suit—who began his address to an auditorium full of adolescents, "Let's rap." I squirmed. They sniggered. And he—he went on with his speech, oblivious, I think, to the language *faux pas* he had made. In his well-meaning attempt to establish rapport with his audience, he borrowed from his teenage audience that which can never pass successfully from one group to another—slang.

Adolescents are the chief producers of slang in our culture. They own slang. This unique function of the adolescent to invent slang (that she will probably continue to use throughout her adulthood; my mother says "golly," and I say "so cool") is something that high-school kids may not consciously know.

To raise that consciousness, here is a simple, two-part activity that can easily be expanded if the teacher is looking for a longer unit:

1. In small groups of their own choosing, have students make lists of current slang expressions and their "definitions." (Examples: bad = good, chill out = calm down, face [v] = to top someone at something)
2. On the other side of each paper, ask students to imagine some slang expressions and their definitions for the year 2040. (Examples from my ninth-grade class two years ago: exxon = disaster; a velcro = a follower; to orbit = to flirt; ashed = put down royally; cogneato = smart and cool; hang it on the moon = get lost)

 Option a: Put at least one futuristic slang expression from each group on the bulletin board for a week or so. The other classes are bound to react with interest.
 Option b: Ask students to observe and/or interview someone at least twenty years their elder in order to compile a list of another generation's slang. Share the list verbally with the class.
 Option c: [Perhaps in conjunction with punctuating dialogue] Have students write a dialogue in which any two generations "swap" slang. Each generation uses slang from an era not its own. The result is always humorous.

The chief aim in these nonthreatening activities is to impress upon students their expertise when it comes to slang, an integral part of any language study. When literally everyone in the class can feel like an expert in English for at least one day, well, that's . . . fresh.

SOURCE: From J. Johnson, The Language of Teenagers—Slang. *English Journal, 82* (1), 76. Copyright 1993 by the National Council of Teachers of English. Reprinted with permission.

Exercise 2–4   *Language Phenomena*

Devise an exercise around one of the following language phenomena. Be specific enough so that a fellow student may use it as a teaching activity. Plan it either as a quick class-ending bit of word play or as an extended language lesson.

- Modals—Are there age, ethnic, or social class differences in the use of the modals *perhaps, could,* and *might?*
- Frozen clusters—What governs the order of such common clusters as *pell—mell, ding—dong, helter—skelter,* and *willy—nilly?* Can you name other pairs?
- Etymology—What are the word origins of common surnames, occupations, colors, animals, and natural phenomena? What are some common words that were originally proper nouns, for instance, *platonic, china,* and *quixotic?*
- Idioms—Listen to the idioms of everyday life. List common expressions. Do they group themselves by region, age, socioeconomic status, or educational level?
- Place names—Gather interesting place names in this country. Classify their origins: Are they the country's national history, local history, ancient history, mythology, or the Bible? Are any descriptive (Social Circle, GA)? A reflection of ideas (Providence, RI)?
- Shortenings—Consider the origins of words that are shortened forms of longer words, for example, *ad, curio (curiosity), fan (fanatic), hood,* and *mike.* Consider why words are seldom lengthened.
- Euphemisms—Recall euphemisms for human experiences, character types, occupations, and even profanity. List the words, for instance, that sportswriters use for *defeat.* Why do we use euphemisms? In what circumstances are they helpful? Harmful?

- Prefixes and Suffixes—Explore today's active English prefixes, such as *de-, dis-, ex-, mini-,* and *off-,* and suffixes, such as *-ize, -nk* (from the Russian), and *-wise.* Are the new words they create more expressive and precise than our existent word choices? Why do people create such words?
- Language Change—From 1914 to 1941, Monica Baldwin lived in a very secluded convent. When she emerged, she found astonishing changes and had difficulty understanding much of the new vocabulary. She describes her experiences in *I Leap over the Wall,* London: Hamish Hamilton, 1949. Imagine that you, like Monica Baldwin or Rip Van Winkle, fell asleep for decades (in, say, 1950, 1960, or even 1970) and awoke today. What language changes might you find?

CONCLUSION

We hope that this brief introduction to the history of our language, the present wars being fought over its usage, and future possibilities for raising student consciousness about it have helped you begin to develop ideas about what you would wish to teach your students. The reasons given in this chapter for studying language range from the most practical—developing grammatical tools for perfecting writing and speaking—to the most idealistic. Because the practical has probably been presented to you often in your own education, we close this chapter with two broader rationales. While Owen Thomas's (1965) argument is particularly directed towards the usefulness of transformational grammar, we feel that it has broad applicability:

> English is no less a living subject matter than physics and chemistry. And teachers of English have a definite obligation to theorize about their subject matter. They have an obligation to develop the details of grammatical theories and to test them against the reality of experience and intuition. They have an obligation to keep their subject alive. And in fulfilling their obligations, they must make use of all the information which scholars provide about their subject. In short, they have an obligation to teach "living English." (p. 17)

Finally, Bradford Arthur makes an eloquent justification for the humanistic, not just the functional, value of language study in *Teaching English to Speakers of English* (1973):

> The study of language need not be justified by its effect on learning academic skills. If man needs or desires to understand himself and other human beings and if education helps satisfy this need, then the study of language does not have to be an aid to reading or writing, or to anything else. Our ability to think, act, feel, and interact as human beings is bound up with our ability to speak to and understand each other. In learning about language, a student is learning about himself; no further justification is necessary. (p. 150)

3 DEVELOPING AN ORAL FOUNDATION

Talk underlies all subjects in school. . . . For talk enters into the whole range of human interaction, and drama builds, from that interaction and talk, images of human existence.

John Dixon

We begin this chapter with a paradox. We believe that oral, not textual, language is the foundation of the language arts. Children talk before they write and listen before they read. Cultures likewise start with oral history, which lasts centuries or millennia before alphabets and written messages appear. The written word still has not come to some societies; the fundamental communication tool, the spoken word, suffices. In many nineteenth-century English classrooms, oral addresses were prized above written compositions, as the organization of debating societies and the preeminence of valedictory speeches attest. The essay, which we value so highly today, was then regarded as a mere draft for the oral speech. Why, then, is oral language given so little instructional time or thoughtful attention in English classrooms? Why do many administrators consider silent classrooms to be effective and classrooms filled with talk to be suspect? Reading and writing are usually silent events. What place should talking and listening occupy in teaching English? Incidental only (from the teacher giving public directions to the students whispering private confidences)? Intentional? The first three sections of this chapter present both an assumption—English teachers should encourage active student talking and listening—and a response—conscious strategies for introducing oral activities into the classroom. These activities, Oral Language Exercises and Creative Drama, challenge passivity and stimulate movement, role-playing, and performance. We close the chapter with two sections which approach conventional drama through nonanalytic exercises like those in the preceding sections.

Invitation to Reflection 3–1

- In what context did most student talk occur in your own high school English classrooms: responses to teachers' questions, lesson-centered small-group discussions, or personal conversations?
- What was the usual direction? Teacher to student? Student to teacher? Student to student?

- What was the proportion of student talk to silence? Of student talk to teacher talk?
- In 1965, Flanders found that almost 70% of talk in the average classroom is done by teachers (p. 1). Does that figure seem accurate for your high school years? Too high? Too low?
- Why do you think oral language is seldom considered a serious part of the high school English curriculum?

CLASSROOM TALKING AND LISTENING

Consider the following common explanations given for the absence of instruction in oral language in secondary English classrooms.

- Talking and listening are natural acts. They do not need to be learned. Children learn them without adult help, so instructional time should be reserved for those skills and knowledge that must be taught, such as how to read and write. Lessons in talking and listening should occur outside of regular school hours.
- Talking and listening are too unwieldy to teach; we don't know how to help students learn much about this kind of language use. Teachers are challenged enough just preparing students to read and write without adding talking and listening.
- Talking and listening cannot be tested. We can't spend time on skills and ideas that are not worth a few items on schoolwide tests. What we're not accountable for is not our responsibility.

These explanations may sound reasonable, but can our understanding of language and learning lead us to better conclusions? Here are three counterpositions.

- Talking and listening in class develop students' abilities to clarify and understand the perceptions of others and themselves and to integrate the two in the individual process of making meaning. Attention must be paid to composing or producing meaning, rather than just receiving or discovering it.
- Talking and listening are the basic communication tools in most human lives. We are ever negotiating the workplace, relating to friends and family, and expressing ourselves to our intimates through these media.
- We must develop oral language skills because of their relationship to the highly tested skills of reading and writing. Britton, Burgess, Martin, McLeod, and Rosen (1975) explain this relationship in their seminal discussion of the development of writing abilities.

The relationship of talk to writing is central to the writing process. It is no longer necessary to justify classroom talk as a means to anything else; it is properly valued in its own right, but this doesn't detract from our conviction that good talk helps to encourage good writing. It is probable that of all the things teachers are now doing to make their pupils' approach to writing more stimulating, and the writing itself seem a more integral part of the manifold activities of the classroom, it is the encouragement of different kinds of talk which is the commonest and most productive factor. (p. 29)

These rationales alone (though we will uncover others) prompt us to suggest an expanded curriculum that deliberately includes talking and listening. Veteran teachers might still protest: "Talk? Why, I can't keep my students quiet! All they do is talk! What do you mean by talk? I have a battle royale each day suppressing it. I have trouble getting my homework assignments *said,* much less *heard.*" In fact, teachers often arrive at a common solution to this dilemma of highly vocal students alienated by school and insistent on supplanting it with their own talk: silent work by individual students at solitary desks. One of our most disheartening observations of the many high schools we visit is the silence in the classrooms. Although these schools appear to be controlled and orderly to some, to us they appear to be orally impoverished. Inside the classrooms, what talk we do hear is highly structured: Teachers give directions, students raise informational questions, and teachers answer. Often, even teacher-led discussions don't produce authentic animated talk. Too often the questions are serial: The teacher asks, a student answers, the teacher evaluates the answer and, with the ball back in his or her court, directs a question to another student. The discussion resembles recitation, not conversation. This chapter suggests an alternative: lively, purposive talk and alert, perceptive listening. Perhaps we can show school administrators that oral language can be taught and help test makers realize that it can even be evaluated.

CLASSROOMS IN THE U.S. AND ABROAD

The common assumption is that classrooms, English classrooms particularly, center around language and therefore naturally involve reading and writing and talking and listening; however, Goodlad's in-depth observation of over 1,000 American elementary and secondary school classrooms (1984) portrays the reality. Table 3–1 is the "snapshot" that Goodlad and his researchers took inside the secondary classrooms that they visited.

In sum, Goodlad found that the typical high school classroom is organized around either a teacher before a whole class lecturing and explaining or students at their desks working on individual assignments: "Three categories of student activity marked by passivity—written work, listening, and preparing for assignments—dominate . . . at all . . . levels of schooling" (p. 105). (Physical activity achieves as high a percentage as it does in high school only because of the arts, vocational, and physical education classes in the curriculum. The typical English class has considerably less than 17.5% active performance.)

In the United States, English teachers and educators are only beginning to formulate a rationale (why teach talking and listening), a subject (what kind of talking and listening to teach), and general instructional principles (how to teach them). In such unexplored territory, much uncertainty still exists. New Zealand elementary and secondary teachers have focused on oral language for some time and deliberately structure talking and listening into their curriculum along with other school subjects such as reading, math, science, and social studies. At Auckland's St. Thomas School, teachers have created oral genres that are diverse, differentiated, and defined in terms of age-appropriateness and complexity. They include Poem Reading, Question Posing, News Telling, Telephone Conversations, Introductions, Object Descriptions, Team Debates, Giving Instructions, and Jokes and Riddles, to which they devote 3 weeks of the three-term year. Listening Activities occur in all three terms. The last 3 weeks are devoted to Prepared Talks. The British National Curriculum requires that all students be provided with a third of their language instruction in talking and listening activities.

We know of no American equivalent to New Zealand's or Great Britain's deliberate approaches. In fact, most American high schools remove drama from the English classroom entirely, isolating it in a drama curriculum that concentrates on theater skills and showcases occasional student productions. Some secondary teachers, however, are experimenting with specific instructional activities to promote oral language development in the general English curriculum. These activities viewed alone may appear to be peripheral to the English classroom, as gimmicks, enrichments, or respites, but taken together, they are part of a general strategy that recognizes the essential importance of the oral language art.

FUNDAMENTAL ASSUMPTIONS

Our belief in the importance of active language production is based on a few fundamental assumptions about language and learning. Britton views talk as the sea upon which all other language activities

TABLE 3–1
Rank order of activities by probability of students being observed participating

Senior High Activity	Percent Probability of Observation at Any Given Moment
Listening to Explanations/Lectures	25.3
Practice/Performance—Physical	17.5
Written Work	15.1
Preparation for Assignments	12.8
Student Non-task Behavior—No Assignment	6.9
Taking Tests	5.8
Discussion	5.1
Practice/Performance—Verbal	4.5
Use of AV Equipment	2.8
Reading	1.9
Watching Demonstrations	1.6
Simulation/Role Play	0.1
Being Disciplined	0.1

SOURCE: From *A Place Called School: Prospects for the Future* (p. 107) by John I. Goodlad, 1984, New York: McGraw-Hill. Reprinted by permission.

ride. According to Barnes (1992), teachers claim that children who have learned to value talk in their learning

- are more likely to explore beyond facts, into situations, causes, and consequences;
- know more about the language in which knowledge is expressed;
- have a greater repertoire of learning strategies;
- have greater insight into the relationships between bits of information;
- have a greater understanding of how they acquire knowledge;
- have a better understanding of the possibility of multiple solutions to problems or questions; and
- have a greater understanding of why they are working within a particular area of knowledge.

Britton et al. (1975) articulate how talk more than any other variable operates to stimulate, integrate, and encourage other language competencies, in this case, writing.

> Talk is more expressive—the speaker is not obliged to keep himself in the background as he may be in writing; talk relies on an immediate link with listeners, usually a group or a whole class; the rapid exchanges of conversation allow many things to go on at once—exploration, clarification, shared interpretation, insight into differences of opinion, illustration and anecdote, explanation by gesture, expression of doubt; and if something is not clear you can go on until it is. (p. 29)

Britton et al. contend that one of the great values of talk is that it "permits the expression of tentative conclusions and opinions" (p. 30). It allows thought to incubate and be tried out.

Vygotsky (1962) wrote about this very connection between speech and thought. He believed that expressed speech begins in inarticulated, abbreviated inner speech; in order to say or write what we are thinking, we must elaborate upon that inner speech: "The structure of speech does not simply mirror the structure of thought: that is why words cannot be put on by thought like a ready-made garment. Thought undergoes many changes as it turns into speech. It does not merely find expression in speech; it finds its reality and form" (p. 126). Especially when a problem is at the boundary of our grasp, we are pushed to use our inner speech and to "talk our way through" difficulty.

Moffett and Wagner (1992) describe the internal process of an individual's talk as it meets the talk of other speakers:

> When talk teaches, the speakers are picking up ideas and developing them: substantiating, qualifying, and elaborating; building on, amending, and varying each other's sentences, statements, and images. All these are part of an external social process that each member of the group gradually internalizes as a personal thought process: he begins to think in the ways that the group talks. Not only does he take unto himself the vocabulary, usage, and syntax of others and synthesize new creations out of their various styles, points of view, and attitudes, he also structures his thinking into mental operations resembling those of the group interactions. Good discussions by groups build toward good thinking by individuals. (p. 75)

Our ideas about learning and language intersect in several foundational assumptions.

- Learning is social and is constructed by the action of learners in interaction with their environment or others who might be present in their written or oral words.
- Learning develops gradually over time according to a developmental sequence that moves from the simple to the complex, from the concrete to the abstract, from the private to the social.
- Learning, however, is not linear, moving in a straight line along a single dimension, but recursive, circling and repeating along complex dimensions.
- Language learning develops through a never-ending process, and that process, not the product of it, should be our instructional focus.

CLASSROOM ENVIRONMENTS FOR TALKING AND LISTENING

A significant objection to implementing these assumptions by increasing classroom talk is that too often, students are not focused and are not spending time on task but time on chat. Classrooms that provide personal freedom and communal ease because they value students' active oral participation are especially vulnerable to students' temptations for informal, discursive, small talk. Moreover, when many other classes are more formally structured and individualized, those conversations that are usually saved for hallways between classes and the cafeteria at lunch seem irrepressible in a more open classroom.

Listening receives even less instructional attention than talking does. In too many classrooms, "listening" simply means to be quiet and pay attention to the teacher. Such classrooms contain, as in the Simon and Garfunkel song "Sounds of Silence," "people hearing without listening." What we need to cultivate is active listening: attention, understanding, and response. Substantive talking is necessarily a reciprocal dance that reflects back what is heard, challenges it or extends it, shares observations and interpretations, and problem solves and brainstorms. At such a point two or more minds are actively engaged. As Sheldon Kopp explains in *If You Meet the Buddha on the Road, Kill Him* (1973), when we set out on our narrative journeys and begin to discover and tell our own stories, "there must be another there to listen."

In Chapter 11, Organizing Instruction, we discuss specific strategies for focusing classroom talk. Here we draw your attention to some general classroom features that promote meaningful talk and responsive listening. Teachers in such classrooms keep their focus on the student; they take seriously how the student responds and works to construct personal meaning. Where students feel valued, they are more inclined to risk talking. Where they confront matters that engage their ready attention, they are more likely to speak. Teachers, then, design classrooms that encourage this authentic talking: discussions involving the whole class, small groups, and pairs of students. They reason, quite simply, that if class time cannot be expanded, dividing into groups allows more students chances to talk. With the smaller units, listening is also more compelled and compelling. In such contexts, students can more actively sort out their thoughts. Moffett and Wagner (1992) believe that "because constant practice and good interaction are the best teachers of speaking and listening, talk in small groups should be a staple learning activity for all grades and allotted a large amount of time in the curriculum" (p. 74).

What of those increasing numbers of English-deficient or English-as-a-second-language students who may not easily achieve this fluency? As with proficient English speakers, the teacher's genuine, nonjudgmental interest in helping them find words that fit what they want to say should leave students with some sense of satisfied success. If talking is occurring in small groups, these students not only will have more chances to try out their emerging language, but they also will do so under less pressure and with the help of their peers.

In everyday classroom talk, teachers who trust in the importance of purposeful talk, should engage in it vigorously, most obviously leading whole-class and small-group discussion, but also greeting students, negotiating class business, giving directions, planning and executing projects, making decisions, brainstorming, introducing speakers, and parting from students. It is here, in routine dealings with our students, that we may have our greatest impact on language.

The National Council of Teachers of English (NCTE) International Assembly in 1985 drafted a statement that described the dimensions of classroom talk (Dillon & Hamilton, 1985). We adapt and abstract that statement. To enhance oral language use in their classrooms, teachers should attend to the following:

- Be aware of the distinction between "learning through talk" and "learning to use talk" and provide opportunities to increase fluency in both areas.
- Consider students' own ways of talking—idiolects, dialects, mother tongues—as linguistic resources that can enrich the language environment of the classroom.
- Involve students in a variety of class formats that encourage small-group discussions, dramatic improvisations, and conversations in order to discover the potential power of talk.
- Allow students to share their ideas with a variety of school audiences: different groupings of their peers, students of other ages, other adults in the school, visitors, parents, and others.
- Assist students in discovering what is valuable, powerful, and enjoyable in the way they use talk to explore ideas, to express and explain ideas, and to share a part of themselves.
- Ensure that students are provided the opportunity to regard listening as an active component of conversations and discussions, and to understand that participation does not mean holding the floor much of the time or ensuring that one's line of argument is carried along unmodified, any more than being a good listener means sitting quietly and passively out of the verbal arena.
- Encourage students to talk and to channel personal talk into more general concerns.

Let us say a final word about creating an environment for talking and listening. One of the most defining characteristics of typical classrooms, which was conveyed to Goodlad (1984) "loud and clear" by his data, was that "the emotional tone is neither harsh and punitive nor warm and joyful: it might be described most accurately as flat" (p. 108). Some days you *will* feel as flat as a cartoon coyote crushed by falling rocks (and the cause will seem to resemble just such a source). But your aim should be to create a more energized tone, one that expresses the enthusiasm of discovery and sharing, one that encourages talking and listening out of active interest and engagement.

ORAL LANGUAGE EXERCISES

We now present a range of oral activities, organized in the four-quadrant schema shown in Figure 3–1. Our structure provides a context and framework that support, encourage, and extend important oral language experiences. With it we can more easily visualize a range of possibilities for producing oral

FIGURE 3–1
Oral language exercise schema

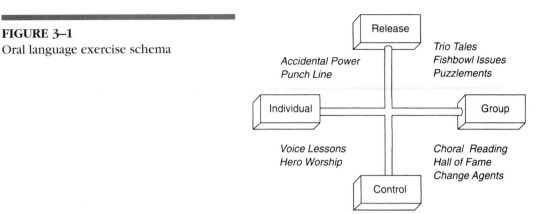

language (speaking) and for receiving it (listening). We can add and extend oral experiences from this base to promote language development and authentic talk. We understand that for every addition to the English classroom, there is a corresponding reduction. Many of these oral exercises will seem to be additive luxuries and therefore expendable when time is constricted. One way to include them without overburdening an overtaxed schedule or an incredulous administrator is to use them in conjunction with reading and writing instruction.

The horizontal axis of the schema extends from Individual to Group expressions, the vertical from Control to Release.

Individual   Students are involved in solitary production (monologue or storytelling). They may be speaking from a script (controlled) or spontaneously (released), but they are without a collaborating partner or group. In such solitude, personal creative talent, an authentic voice, and a singular syntax can emerge.

Group   Students work in collaboration that extends from pairs, to small groups, to large groups, to the whole class. Exercises can be more elaborate. Partners increase the need for talking and listening in advance of the presentation.

Control   Students are involved in scripted or heavily circumscribed talk. It is not personal, but it may nevertheless assume public authenticity.

Release   Students are spontaneous. Their language is not guarded or guided by anything other than their own sense of appropriateness.

TEN EXERCISES

We present activities in each of the four quadrants, from Individual Control to Individual Release, then to Group Control, and finally, to Group Release; that is, we move from the most structured and manageable teaching situation to the freest and most spontaneous. We will begin in the bottom left quadrant in imitation of students and teachers alike who often find comfort in starting in a controlled situation. Our movement through the four not only will introduce you to many language possibilities, but it also will draw on your openness to the spontaneous rather than the predictable, to energetic movement rather than stationary quiet, to moving from behind the teacher's desk into every corner of the classroom. Many teachers find protection and comfort in those desks or overhead projector stands, especially those who are, to quote Carol Fulton's teaching journal "strong introverts who generally prefer reading and especially writing to oral activities." These initial exercises allow you to grow as your students do. They also provide experiences in those of Gardner's multiple intelligences—spatial, bodily/kinesthetic, and musical—that are so often overlooked in English classrooms.

Voice Lessons.   In this exercise, you present a collection of first-person poems and ask students to select one for oral interpretation. The interests and abilities of the individuals in your class will influence your choices. Figure 3-2 provides a list of first-person poems that have been used successfully with a range of students. They are short, have accessible diction, and present concrete images, familiar situations, and rich voices. (Authorial dates are included not to emphasize the poet, but to aid your search.) We encourage you to begin a folder now of first-person poems expressing different cultural, ethnic, and racial perspectives that appeal to a wide range of ages and abilities, and to urge students to find poems on their own as well.

FIGURE 3–2
First-person poems

William Blake (1757–1827)	"A Poison Tree"
Robert Browning (1812–1889)	"Meeting at Night"
Emily Dickinson (1830–1886)	"I'm Nobody"
W. S. Gilbert (1836–1911)	"The Modern Major-General"
Thomas Hardy (1840–1928)	"The Man He Killed"
A. E. Housman (1859–1936)	"The Carpenter's Son"
William Butler Yeats (1865–1935)	"He Wishes for the Cloths of Heaven"
Paul Laurence Dunbar (1872–1906)	"The Debt"
Robert Frost (1874–1963)	"Stopping by Woods on a Snowy Evening"
Carl Sandburg (1878–1967)	"Grass"
Elinor Wylie (1885–1928)	"Let No Charitable Hope"
	"Pretty Words"
Rupert Brooke (1887–1915)	"The Soldier"
e. e. cummings (1894–1963)	"Next to of course God America"
Langston Hughes (1902–1967)	"Dream Boogie"
	"The Negro Speaks of Rivers"
Theodore Roethke (1908–1963)	"My Papa's Waltz"
Olga Cabral (1909–1997)	"Life and Death Among the Xerox People"
Robert Hayden (1913–1980)	"Those Winter Sundays"
Karl Shapiro (1913–)	"Autowreck"
William Stafford (1914–1993)	"Traveling Through the Dark"
	"Judgments"
Paul Larkin (1922–1985)	"A Study of Reading Habits"
Donald W. Baker (1923–)	"Formal Application"
Maya Angelou (1928–)	"Life Doesn't Frighten Me"
Peter LaFarge (1931–1965)	"Vision of a Past Warrior"
Alden Nowlan (1933–1983)	"Aunt Jane"
Imanu Amari Baraka (1934–)	"Rhythm Blues"
Audre Lorde (1934–)	"Hanging Fire"
	"Coal"
Alice Walker (1944–)	"Women"
	"For My Sister Molly Who in the Fifties"
Susan Mitchell (1944–)	"From the Journals of the Frog Prince"
Katharyn Machan Aal (1952–)	"Hazel Tells LaVerne"

The teacher's aim and the students' abilities determine whether students will read poems from a text, recite them from memory, or record them using sound and visual backgrounds. Recording the production can make this task even more comfortable for students who are shy in front of a class. The goal, whatever option is chosen, is to prompt students to use their voices to bring their poem alive. For many students, a prescribed and confined text makes public speech a bit easier. (This activity can be broadened to include literature other than poetry as well. A colleague of ours assigns tales from Chaucer's *Canterbury Tales* to each student to dramatize. We have asked students to read and present favorite children's picture books. Stella Beale has students read fairy tales.)

Learning about the flip side of talking—listening—is an important part of this exercise. Students, who are listeners as well as speakers, should be sensitized to the ways that volume, emphasis, tone, and other dimensions of the human voice can arouse interest, clarify ideas, and express emotion. Although this exercise is circumscribed by another's text, its opportunity for creative individual presentation and engaged listening is considerable.

Hero Worship.   This exercise involves asking students to read speeches and other documents that were conceived to be spoken and heard, not merely read. From a series of these, students extract short "sound bites" that capture the style and significance of the person who wrote them. When students find these words, assemble them in chronological order, and arrange them by emotional color or by themes, they often arrive at words that they "own." They gain more than powerful language for oral interpretation; they develop a personal identity with the source of its creative power. For instance, a dramatic sequence of Abraham Lincoln's words might start with the Lincoln-Douglas debates, move to the First Inaugural Address, include strong statements from his first term, highlight powerful segments from the Gettysburg Address, and conclude with words from the Emancipation Proclamation and the Second Inaugural Address. Martin Luther King, Jr.'s life might be rendered through excerpts beginning with his April 16, 1963 "Letter from Birmingham Jail," moving through his August 28, 1963 speech, "I Have a Dream," and his 1964 Nobel prize acceptance speech to his final April 3, 1968 speech in a Memphis church the night before his death, "I've Been to the Mountaintop." Maya Angelou's oral collage might begin with passages from *I Know Why the Caged Bird Sings,* move through poems such as "Life Doesn't Frighten Me" and conclude with lines from her 1992 inaugural poem, "On the Wings of the Morning."

In activities in the top quadrant, Individual Release, students continue to speak as individuals but to improvise their words. Students can easily convert the Hero Worship exercise to such a purpose by writing their own speeches as though they were real or imagined cultural heroes. Those speeches could be argumentative as in a debate with a political opponent, persuasive as in a rally speech by a social activist, conciliatory as in an opening statement at a summit conference, or expressive as in an acceptance speech at an awards ceremony. The students' task then becomes to seek out interesting subjects and to create speeches that develop naturally, are authentic in character, and respond to the given situation.

Accidental Power.   This exercise encourages improvisation within a structure. Dixon (1984) suggests that teachers provide a context from which students can generate language. He specifically recommends a point of crisis so that speakers will have an almost intrinsic linear direction, a narrative shape, and dramatic power that they would not otherwise possess. A simple classroom activity, then, asks students to tell a story of an acute embarrassment, an accident, a personal or family crisis, or an experience with a natural disaster. Dramatic exercises become more complicated and challenging when the speaker assumes the role of another. For instance, a student might imagine him- or herself as a president, a general, or a moral philosopher and hold a press conference in which student reporters fire questions as though a war had just been declared or an environmental emergency had just occurred. Students also might improvise any of the following roles:

- a reporter describing a natural disaster live
- a survivor of an earthquake who is still lodged in a damaged building
- a mother whose 3-year-old child is stuck in an abandoned well
- a Native American elder who must inform his community that the federal government has ordered them onto a reservation
- Hansel and Gretel being questioned by their police rescuers at the home of the witch
- Cinderella's stepsisters interviewed on a talk show the day of their sister's wedding to the prince

When listeners are engaged with an account of an accident or a moment of serious crisis, they can become helpful respondents. After the oral exercise, they can critique the speaker's use of critical detail, elaboration, foreshadowing, suspense building, and other elements simply by explaining when they were most moved—anxious, frightened, troubled, or relieved—or most confused.

Such structured oral improvisation in response to a crisis can also enliven, personalize, and dramatize literary study. Consider the impact of a spoken monologue by one of the five victims of the bridge collapse in Thornton Wilder's *The Bridge of San Luis Rey.* We think that such a dramatization might invite more entry into the characters' personal worlds than a more traditional analytical discussion would, even if it included a perceptive question such as "If this character had survived the fall, how might his or her life been changed?"

Punch Line.   As its name indicates, this exercise depends on humor. Because humor is fun, it often seems simple; in reality, however, it requires tremendous verbal skill. Ask students to recall an amusing story or elaborate on the skeleton of a joke. We encourage jokes embedded in a story, not one-liners. It is best that students begin by telling their stories to a partner or to two other students, because humor is best primed in a setting of ease and security that this more intimate arrangement encourages. Jokes and amusing stories, much like accident stories, depend on critical detail, elaboration, foreshadowing, and other oral language skills to be effective. The listeners critique the speaker based on their own genuine amusement. The pair or group can even rewrite or revise the humor, leave behind their intimate sanctuary, and try it on the entire class. The whole class provides an almost automatic evaluation with their response. Sometimes our students hold up scoring cards.

Choral Reading.   Group work lies on the other side of the central axis as groups of students talk, listen, or perform. The first Group Control activity, Choral Reading, engages students in the presentation of a previously scripted text. One of the most effective readings we have observed both in terms of student learning and audience reaction was a reading of the Declaration of Independence by a group of 25 students. The document itself, with its powerful and expressive arguments, was a charged vehicle for such a production, but the oral arrangements intensified its force. Students were assigned special lines and words so that their varied voices underscored critical ideas and language of the document. Spatial arrangements of the presenters, language tempo, modulation, emphasis, and the number of single or choral voices all contributed to the impact. The resources of a group create a more expansive range of possibilities for verbal and nonverbal communication. When performed on special occasions before an audience of parents or other students, this activity's effect and the learning involved are both heightened. Students sharpen their ability to project clearly, loudly, and expressively to an audience. Effective sources include fiction, poetry, drama, and nonfiction—wherever strong and vivid language is present.

The group Poetry Alive has a variety of programs that enliven poetry for students. This group publishes books that script poems for multiple voices and pose questions of interpretation and stage direction (Wolf, 1990). Group members also travel to perform themselves. Chapter 5, Reviving Poetry, presents an example of their work.

Terry Ley (1995) presents clear suggestions for preparing for Choral Reading:

1. Read through your poem once or twice. Discuss what the poem seems to be "about." Does the organization of the poem help you to understand it better? Then divide your poem into several natural parts. Stanza divisions may be helpful, but don't assume that they are the best divisions for an effective oral presentation of your poem.
2. Make solo, duet, and trio assignments for the parts that you identify.
3. Decide how readers of each part should use **volume, emphasis, speed, pause, and pitch** to communicate meaning. Use symbols to mark copies of the poem so that they become **scripts** for performing the poem.
4. Rehearse performing your poem once or twice, **revising the script** to improve it.
5. Enjoy performing your poem for the class!

Hall of Fame.   This exercise relies more heavily on student initiative. Encourage students to select two imposing or impressive statements made by a favorite president, public figure, or literary figure to weave into a group collage of voices. A presidential collage might include Abraham Lincoln's "Four score and seven years ago our fathers brought forth upon this continent . . ." as well as Harry S. Truman's "The buck stops here," and "If you can't stand the heat, get out of the kitchen." A collage of women's experiences of the War Between the States might include excerpts from the following.

Author	*Title*	*Genre*
Louisa May Alcott	*Hospital Sketches*	Novel
Mary Chesnut	*A Diary from Dixie*	Diary
Kate Cumming	*A Journal of Hospital Life in the Confederate Army of Tennessee*	Journal
Frances E. W. Harper	"The Slave Mother"	Poem
Harriet Jacobs	"The Loophole of Retreat" from *Incidents in the Life of a Slave-Girl*	Testimonial
Sojourner Truth	"Keeping the Thing Going While Things Are Stirring"	Speech

Group deliberation can determine the organizing principle among the quotes. They can be linked together by chronology, theme, personality, or some other unifying characteristic. The possibilities are as varied as the political, national, ethnic, ideological, and vocational differences that distinguish humankind. Costumes, props, music, and art may be used to recreate and vivify the world of each speaker.

Change Agents.   This exercise creates a pastiche of voices of senior citizens. Each student interviews a person of 70 years or older about his or her life. The interviewer might ask what has changed most since the person's childhood years, or what political event or personal crisis he or she remembers most vividly. Students listen carefully and record the essence of the interviewee's experience, noting memorable words or expressions. They return to their class or group and collaboratively decide how to arrange their acquired body of folk wisdom. We sometimes structure the pastiche by asking each student to speak for his or her informant twice: giving excerpted quotes first and then the name, the date of birth, and sometimes the place of birth. We also have staged this activity: Students represent their interviewees by dress or prop, some are seated, others kneel alone or in small clusters, some speak from their fixed positions, and others rise slowly to make their statements about change. A former student, Vanessa Davis, reports a similar assignment for her university women's studies class. Her professor has her students talk with mothers, grandmothers, and great-grandmothers about their experiences as women, for instance, how many children they had, whether they worked, and what they expected of marriage. Students then make comparisons across the age groups. Your students might designate such specific groups and shape those interviews into an oral social history.

Trio Tales.   Movement into the top right quadrant, Group Release, introduces full release into group language interaction through activities that structure spontaneous language. The Trio Tales exercise arranges such a structure for spontaneous talk. Three students collaborate on telling a short tale. Even though students are often inhibited by classmates and the school routine, they can more comfortably tell a tale with this structure. They choose one element from each of three columns to form the basic elements of their narrative. Following is an example of a chart that can be used to give students the germ of a story idea that they then develop. Because it is more natural for one person to spin a tale than three, the trio selects one member to tell the story.

Character	Locale	Resolution
1. Angel	School cafeteria	Elopement
2. Witch	Riverbank	Sprained toe
3. Sailor	Tugboat	Spasms of laughter
4. Amputee	Jail	Shutout
5. Grocer	Restroom	Rainstorm
6. Spy	Cemetery	Starvation
7. Hog	Dam	Inheritance
8. Emperor	Forest	Bigamy
9. Umpire	Library	Victory
10. Kangaroo	Picnic	Promotion
11. Spider	Space capsule	Upset stomach
12. Dolphin	Zoo	Suspension

One way to implement such a chart is to use each trio member's birthday month to create certain boundaries for the tale. Group members choose the word in each column that matches the number of each month. For instance, with our chart, a June-April-October group would tell a tale about a spy who is put in jail but winds up with a promotion. The tone is left up to the tellers; some stories will be light and humorous, some ironic, and others tragic. We sometimes intervene to influence tone by asking each group to flip a coin: heads, the tale is light; tails, it is serious. Our instructional purpose determines whether we ask students to speak from a manuscript, notes, or memory and whether their telling will be live or recorded. While one member of the group tells the tale, the whole class listens, critiques, and suggests improvements. We also use this exercise to conclude literature units by having students construct characters, locales, and resolutions from the texts they just read. Not only does this provide a good review, but also, it invariably amuses and makes students more comfortable and secure with their new learning.

Fishbowl Issues.   This exercise moves group work on spontaneous language production to a political or social arena. It focuses not only on talk, but also on listening. Groups of four or five students take seats in the middle of the classroom to discuss and debate timely political or social propositions. The other members of the class listen carefully and try to figure out where each of the discussants stands on the issue. When the teacher feels that the discussion has matured enough or been exhausted, or it has reached a predesignated time limit, discussion stops and the entire class tries to state the individuals' positions. If teachers anticipate topics and possible points of view, they can draw up position statements to promote this post-mortem. Students who are listeners remember or infer what each discussant said and use their own words to describe the position of each. The discussants do the same. The class then can compare descriptions, those of listeners and speakers, to determine the level of clarity in listening and speaking. Charts can be kept over the year in an oral language portfolio so students can mark their progress as listeners.

Classroom Setting. Basic to the success of Fishbowl Issues and other activities involving spontaneous utterance is a sense of classroom security and freedom. Trust might begin and build with small groups of five or so talking about serious topics that are of real interest to them without anyone's listening in or reporting out. Then listeners can be added. The teacher can even orchestrate a reliably animated discussion by mixing students who are strongly outspoken with those who are more careful, critical thinkers and likely to challenge spontaneous responses.

Topics. The selection of issues to discuss is, of course, crucial. A fine line in good topic selection lies between those that are too close, too much a part of students' most private worlds, and those that are too philosophical and too distant. We work toward student-generated ideas about issues to which they have authentic, personal responses, for instance, "Is rap a fad or is it here to stay?" or "Are adolescent females given more restricted messages about an ideal of physical beauty than adolescent males are?" We also prod students toward issues that they might not consider, but should, for instance, "Do you think human beings are presently more inhumane to each other than they have been before in recorded history?" During the study of literature, issues raised within the selections themselves can be distilled as questions, for instance, in Paul Zindel's *The Pigman,* "Does Mr. Pignatti exploit John and Lorraine because of his own loneliness?" In S. E. Hinton's *That Was Then, This is Now,* "Should Bryon have turned Mark in?"

We also collect timely newspaper and magazine articles and editorials on a given topic, for instance, ebonics or global warming, and distribute these to individuals. Each group discusses its point of view and selects a spokesperson for the fishbowl, who then enters the discussion with a more knowledgeable and nuanced position. This exercise demonstrates, without any teacher elaboration, how an interpretive community deepens individual perspectives.

FIGURE 3–3
Puzzlement
assignments

In small groups of four or five, solve the following problems in 20 minutes. You can move from one problem to another in any order you wish, but you must work as a group to solve the problems. You cannot assign individual tasks.

1. On a jetliner to Europe there are 9 boys, 5 American children, 9 men, 7 foreign boys, 14 Americans, 8 American males, and 5 foreign females. How many passengers are there on board? _____

2. Arrange the four pieces so as to fill in the block T below. Trace inside the T all sides of each of the four pieces so your answer can be checked.

3. Find the next number in this series:
   7, 12, 27, 72, 207, _____

4. Change *bean* to *soup* by changing only one letter on each line in turn. Each line must be a word.

    B E A N
    — — — —
    — — — —
    — — — —
    — — — —
    S O U P

Puzzlements.   This exercise offers the ultimate in spontaneous group language exploration because the teacher poses puzzles for a group of students and then lets the students work them out alone. Figure 3–3 is an example of several such prompts to authentic, unselfconscious verbal collaboration.

We have found these puzzles to be almost universally self-driving. The desire for cognitive closure makes most students want to find the solution. At the same time, the puzzles are difficult enough and sufficiently varied that most students will naturally seek the aid of others to come up with an answer. Because we are interested in their talk acquiring an authenticity and spontaneity often absent in class, we insist that the work be communal, not individual. Such talk, as noted by Barnes, Britton, and Torbe (1990), is marked by using language to discover, to collaborate, and to elaborate learning. It is rich, real, and purposeful. Students can record their language in such groups and can listen, for example, to hear whether they are really collaborating and building on one another's ideas, or whether they are merely trying to hold the floor and control the process. Sociolinguistic research, such as that done by Tannen (1984, 1990), has found that women and girls have an affiliative style that helps to accomplish tasks democratically, while men and boys are more likely to be directed by a leader, who works to keep the process under his control. Girls use conditional phrases such as "maybe we could" and "perhaps it might," while boys tend to speak with commands, such as "you get this" and "O.K., do that now." Students can listen to themselves and decide whether their talking follows generalizations about gender differences. They can listen, too, to understand whether they are using language as a way to discover meaning. If their group puzzle-solving discussions are recorded, students can listen to their own and other group's tapes later to see whether their talking matures over time.

Exercise 3–1   Reprise: Creating Your Own Oral Exercises

1. List first-person poems or children's books that would make effective Voice Lessons.
2. What historic or contemporary people have written or spoken words suitable for Hero Worship?
3. List ideas for possible crisis scenarios and characters for Accidental Powers activities. Imagine some of them as famous fictional characters reacting to actual historical crises.
4. Jot down the bare structure of three amusing stories or jokes that you might use for Punch Line.
5. What speeches or documents can you remember that might be effective for Choral Reading in excerpts or in their entirety?
6. List some persons whose words you would like to hear in a Hall of Fame collage. List them first by general focus, then by specific voice. Who would you choose if the title of the exercise were Hall of Shame?
7. What other groups can you imagine interviewing for an effective Change Agents activity? List five questions you might ask.
8. Create a chart similar to the one in the Trio Tales section for your own use.
9. If you were to return as a teacher in the high school from which you graduated, what questions might be of lively interest to your junior English students for Fishbowl Issues?
10. Describe any puzzles you know of that would be energizing to high school students. List the titles of puzzle books or other resources for puzzles or riddles.

Invitation to Reflection 3–2

On the basis of your reading about oral language exercises, how would you respond to colleagues Pam Godfrey and Rick Roberts?

- Fellow-teacher Pam Godfrey has shared a number of her successes and difficulties with you since you both arrived at Kennedy High School. She has had problems getting her ninth-grade students to write simple narratives and knows that you have been successful in this area. She thinks it may be because of your work in oral language development, work that is absent from her class. Can you explain any connection, and, if so, which approaches and/or activities would you suggest to her?
- Rick Roberts has been troubled that his 11th-grade students were not able to analyze issues arising from their study of American literature. For instance, before the class read F. Scott Fitzgerald's *The Great Gatsby,* he led a discussion of contemporary evidence of American materialism but found that his students were silent. He hears your lively discussions next door and asks you to help him imitate them in his own class. What might you suggest for him to do using oral language?

CREATIVE DRAMA

Simply defined, creative drama asks students to put original words and actions together in a dramatic situation. Other comparable terms—*dramatic play, creative dramatics, improvisation, children's theatre,* and *role-playing*—may lead to some confusion, but all describe the same type of activity. A pioneer and early theorist in the field, Winifred Ward (1930), in her struggle to have schools acknowledge the power of this new strategy, defined it crisply: "The term *creative dramatics* has grown up to distinguish this original dramatic work from the old formal study of ready-made plays" (p. 3). Since the 1930s, many have been drawn by the educative possibilities of creative dramatics and have elaborated on Ward's original work. We like the 1977 definition of the Children's Theatre Association of America:

> Creative drama is an improvisational, nonexhibitional, process-centered form of drama in which participants are guided by a leader to imagine, enact, and reflect upon human experiences. Although creative drama traditionally has been thought of in relation to children and young people, the process is appropriate to all ages. (as quoted in McCaslin, 1984, p. 9)

Creative drama occupies a place in the English classroom between oral language development and formal drama. Its association with the elementary language arts classrooms is well established, but many secondary English teachers feel uncomfortable about including it in their curriculum. It represents quite a departure from the "stand-up teaching" of the "talk and chalk" classroom. It frees students to imagine, think independently, develop their own ideas, and move closer to their emotions. It also challenges the teacher's traditional role.

THE TEACHER'S ROLE

In direct proportion to its freeing students to animated expression, creative drama loosens teachers' sense of predictable control. Although teachers can assume varying roles—of coach offering suggestions from the sidelines, of active participant in the drama, of equal partner with the student dramatists—all of these involve some of the same risks as those students take. Teachers, however, are more publicly on the line. Dixon (1967) sees drama's uniqueness in terms of its demand for concrete and direct action: " 'Drama' means doing, acting things out rather than working on them in abstract and in private. When possible it is the truest form of learning, for it puts knowledge and understanding to their test in action" (p. 43). Gardner's (1983) theory of multiple intelligences may also explain teacher reluctance. He observes that linguistic and logical/mathematical intelligences dominate school work; two of the other five, spatial and bodily/kinesthetic intelligences, dominate creative drama. Teachers may not deliberately suppress these intelligences, but neither are they comfortable with something relatively uncommon in English classrooms.

THE TEACHER'S CONTENT GOALS

Two purposes seem prominent in the plans of secondary teachers who use creative drama. First, it serves to teach important concepts in the curriculum. The American followers of English educator Dorothy Heathcote introduced creative drama as drama for learning. They have demonstrated how students might deeply and personally understand the religious life of the Incas or the principle of gravity by participating in their realistic portrayal. They use drama to impress important concepts into the memories of students, just as writing-to-learn proponents use writing. Under the spell-creating leadership of educator Betty Jane Wagner, we participated in a solemn dramatization of the Boston Tea Party; the personal learning was poignant and long lasting. We took on the identities of citizens in the Boston community, and when we were confronted with matters of revolution felt deeply conflicted. Heathcote (in Johnson & O'Neill, 1985) speaks of the differences between the kind of knowledge that comes from creative drama and that which comes from the traditional transfer of a "body of knowledge." She characterizes drama as leading to the "lively interest of the 'stirred' individual who has become 'involved in knowing' rather than just knowing by memory alone" (p. 29). Drama is a means to an end beyond itself.

Creative drama's second most often expressed purpose is to lead students into a deeper appreciation of formal drama written by playwrights for performance on the stage. Formal drama is subject to diverse interpretations and performances onstage, but the script has considerable authority over the actors, director, and audience. Creative drama is performed within some of the conventions of formalized drama, but it leaves a great deal to the players' spontaneous creation. Still, the two share common ground: They draw on the resources of language and action to put characters in motion before an audience. Playwrights and inventors of creative drama are bound by the same limitations and empowered by the same potentialities. The word *playwright* comes from an Anglo-Saxon word meaning "a workman or craftsman," as in *shipwright, wheelwright,* and *cartwright.* It is related to a past-tense form of *work, wrought,* not to the verb *write.* Young creative dramatists learn experientially the work or craft of drama: power of voice, movement, gesture, props, scenery, their relation to their characters' roles, and their effect on others.

THE TEACHER'S PROCESS GOALS

Dixon (1967) reminds us of the potential of creative drama to enhance the personal growth of students: "To help pupils encounter life as it is, the complexity of relationships in a group and dynamic situation, there is nothing more direct and simple that we can offer them than drama" (p. 38). We will discuss five important directions that personal growth may take via creative drama: language development, cooperative learning, risk taking, role-playing, and creativity.

Language Development.   In creative drama, students put language into simulated life situations. Words emerge in response to concrete settings and situations and in interaction with other characters. Language can come alive when students are projected into an authentic context. Furthermore, the collaborative requirements of many creative drama activities promote language through group planning, deliberation, negotiation, implementation, and assessment. Dixon (1967) observes that "drama, like talk, is learning through interaction" (p. 38). When teachers become personally involved in the drama, familiar classroom language roles are rearranged and new language potential is released.

Cooperative Learning.   This is the essential educational context for work in drama. Individuals are able to perform onstage only because of group efforts behind the scenes. Most of the creative drama activities that follow require cooperative work among actors, producers, stage managers, scriptwriters, and audiences. These cooperative acts often produce some of the most immediate and intense interactions between students in our classrooms. As O'Neill and Lambert (1982) observe, "Drama is essentially social and involves contact, communication and the negotiation of meaning" (p. 13). They explain some of the dimensions of this cooperation:

> Within the safe framework of the make-believe, individuals can see their ideas and suggestions accepted and used by the group. They can learn how to influence others; how to marshall effective arguments and present them appropriately; how to put themselves in other people's shoes. They can try out roles and receive immediate feedback. The group can become a powerful source of creative ideas and effective criticism. (p. 13)

Further, the public nature of drama enhances students' motivation.

Risk Taking.   Performance before an audience is daunting for many students. Even for normally dramatic extroverts, unscripted performance can be harrowing. Creative drama challenges students to feel and express emotions that, particularly during adolescence, are volatile but tightly controlled. It invites students to project themselves into other persons' perceptions, thoughts, and feelings in order to uncover surprises about themselves and their world. Students who would be reluctant to enter into a full dramatic production of *Macbeth* might more easily participate in less-structured creative drama activity. Because the words and gestures are spontaneous and audience expectations are subordinated, students more comfortably take on roles that demand complex and emotionally compelling responses. The risk then becomes focusing on the task at hand: expressing oneself through speech and movement within a public space.

Role-playing.   Empathizing or projecting oneself into the world of another is a natural consequence of the role-playing involved in creative drama. It requires students to open themselves to other experiences, to imagine themselves in difficult situations and so to enter others' personal perplexities. Creative drama projects often prompt students to research and explore unknown people or events. When students attempt to understand others—their histories, their characteristic behaviors, their motives, and their habits of relating or solving problems—they often receive sudden glimpses into other lives that challenge their existing assumptions and biases. In so doing, students can make significant advances toward genuine understanding of lives lived differently from their own. Young children play house to this effect. John and Lorraine dress up to take on the roles of Mr. and Mrs. Pignatti in Paul Zindel's *The Pigman,* and only then do they escape their teenage circumstances and kiss as mature lovers. Growth in understanding often results from this very challenge to customary perceptions and projection into new ways of thinking and feeling.

Creativity.   Philosopher Susanne Langer (1958) refers to the imagination as "probably the oldest mental trait that is typically human—older than discursive reason" (p. 6). Within varying degrees of constraint, creative drama can free that imagination and encourage it to encompass new, open possibilities and transformations. Students are active, not passive. They become participants, not spectators, at an event that draws on their physical, mental, social, and even emotional capacities. Creativity and playfulness are the essence of this activity. We ask students to unbridle their imaginations, to let the solid, "brute facts" world go for a moment, to suspend their self-conscious real selves, and to experience a moment of transforming play. Play allows students to move "from surge to stage," as Eugene Ionesco says in the *The Bald Soprano.*

All of these effects of creative drama are captured in philosopher George Santayana's remark that play is the most serious thing we do. But the play of creative drama has some structure, and, to enter it, students must be willing to accept certain rules.

RULES OF THE GAME

These rules of creative drama are not general and inflexible, but specific and fluid, depending on the particular activity of the moment. O'Neill and Lambert (1982) establish a few basic ground rules. Students must be willing to do the following:

- make-believe with regard to objects
- make-believe with regard to actions and situations
- adopt a role
- maintain the make-believe verbally
- interact with the rest of the group (pp. 1–12)

Even if students are willing, they may still be easily frustrated or remain shy and reluctant. Creative drama doesn't provide many hiding places for resistant students. It asks them to take risks and to act. Others can become giddy with unexpected freedom, unfamiliar assignments, and possible showmanship. Both the timid and the bold can defeat the enterprise. O'Neill and Lambert suggest building "certain safeguards into the work which can help to protect pupils against these risks":

- Establishing an atmosphere of trust and encouraging even the most limited contributions.
- Setting up work which has a clear focus and contains clearly defined tasks which are within the capacity of the class.
- Providing a model of appropriate behaviour and commitment, most effectively perhaps by taking a role within the drama.
- "Distancing" material which may prove embarrassing to the pupils by setting it within an analogous situation.
- Offering constant reminders that the pupils are working in an art form which will legitimately permit them to explore thoughts and feelings through the safety of an adopted role. (p. 149)

RESOURCES

Teachers also need to grow in their confidence in such activities. The following resources can stimulate and supplement the teacher's imagination.

Duke, Charles. 1974. *Creative Dramatics and English Teaching.* Urbana, IL: National Council of Teachers of English.

Johnson, Liz, and Cecily O'Neill. 1985. *Dorothy Heathcote: Collected Writings on Education and Drama.* London: Hutchinson.

McCaslin, Nellie, 1984. *Creative Drama in the Classroom.* Fourth Edition. New York: Longman.

O'Neill, Cecily, and Lambert, Alan. 1982. *Drama Structures: A Practical Handbook for Teachers.* Cheltenham, UK: Stanley Thornes.

Spolin, Viola. 1967. *Improvisation for the Theater.* Evanston, IL: Northwestern University Press.

ACTIVITIES

We suggest 13 specific activities that introduce creative drama into the English classroom. These activities range from having fixed structures to being almost wholly free.

Fixed   Students receive a simple set of words or gestures to enact that do not require rehearsal, prior talent, or an immensely risky display of self.

Free   Improvisation anchors the free end.

The sequence—from games, simple dramatic activities, and short improvisations to extended improvisations—provides students with increasingly more challenging tasks. After this accumulated experience, they are ready to undertake complex improvisations of their own devising.

Creative Drama: Fixed to Free Activities

Freeze-frames	Stationary body poses
Chaos Drama	Little snippets of a prescribed script
Mimetics	Mimicking a machine, a myth, or an archetypal pattern; acting out a myth or archetypal event
Faces, Hands, and Feet	Acting out words with a single focal point
So . . . So Drama	Dramatic interpretation of a script
Personified Poems	Acting out simple poems with gestures
Costume Drama	Costumed groups produce a brief play

Bag Act	Play devised out of the props placed in bag
Nonstop Triad	Two fast-talking antagonists and one arbitrator
When Worlds Collide	Elaboration of a fictive or historical event
Dramatic Monologue	Students create a character through staged monologue
Four Cs Improvisations	Drama that works out of Conflict between Characters in a Context to which there is a Conclusion or resolution
Intervention Drama	Dramatic interaction arising out of the interjection of strange characters into a normal situation

Freeze-frames.   This activity requires active imagination, but no action. Ask students to arrange themselves in the postures of sculptures, tableaux, monuments, still photographs, waxworks, or statues to illustrate various human situations and emotions. These body sculptures can be used simply as preparation for more ambitious creative drama. More specifically, they can vivify the structure of literature, human experience, and even ideas under discussion. They can be instantaneous or preplanned. They require little space and demand little acting experience. Imagine what can be added to a class discussion when the following freeze-frames are enacted.

- During a discussion of families, a group creates a tableau representing the traditional rural family of 1810, while another group presents a tableau of the contemporary urban family of 1990. (According to the U.S. Bureau of the Census, in 1810, 87% of the labor force was engaged in agriculture; by 1980, that figure had dropped to 3%.)
- While discussing Countee Cullen's poem "Incident," a group freezes in the posture of Baltimore citizens in the background and two children in the foreground just at the moment of insult and recognition.

Most students, if they work in groups, comfortably risk this bit of drama because no actions or words are required. However, they should be able to tell why they chose their particular poses and moments out of the range of possibilities inherent in the subject.

Chaos Drama.   In this activity, each member of the class draws a card that gives directions for a strange activity for that student alone to perform repeatedly. Following are a few representative performance cards that students can act out in class:

- Walk to the nearest window or door and pretend frantically to try to open it. After a 5-second attempt, cry out "Horrors! The air is streaming in on us!"
- Step up to a podium (or an imagined podium) and begin to recite the vowels with deep anger and great meaning in a loudspeaker voice.
- Skip slowly and gracefully about the room, stopping at any person who is not in motion around the room. Put both hands on this person's shoulders and say longingly, "It is so, so good to have you back home again."
- Crawl around the room stopping at every pair of feet you see. Push the person's left big toe with your right index finger and say "Now, doesn't that feel a lot better, Mr. Goodrich?"

Make up similarly chaotic acting assignments for the members of your class. When each student is assigned a role to play, the class is told to act out the individually assigned parts simultaneously in a dramatic, bold, loud, and unceasing fashion. Each student starts acting at the signal "Begin" and continues until the teacher says "Stop."

   The point of the performance is that individual craziness is acceptable, comfortable, and even liberating in a classroom in which every other individual is displaying equally bizarre behavior. Most students could not attempt the assigned dramatic task on stage alone. But in Chaos Drama, students have their words and their actions totally planned for them. All they need do is follow improbable directions. Although everything seems controlled, there is room for improvisation, and each student inevitably adds a special interpretative touch to whatever role is assigned. (We must mention the following caveats. If the noise threshold of your classroom is an issue, all utterances can be whispered or merely mouthed. If you use this exercise with an especially large, unruly, or excitable class, more than the drama may be chaotic.)

Mimetics.   A small step away from a full company of students acting out assigned words and gestures is a small group of students working in tandem to mimic a machine. Their bodies become the working parts or the elements in the machine process. In a drink machine, one student's feet might represent the selection pads, another student might represent the drink can, and three students, the machine itself. Other groups might mimic a revolving door, an egg beater, a washing machine, or a lawn mower. The entire body is used, not just the face, and machine noises replace words for dialogue. Students are put at ease on stage because no attention is focused upon them as ordinary persons. You also can ask students to act out a myth or archtypal pattern.

Faces, Hands, and Feet.   A further step toward an improvisational stage presence is concentration on a single element of the body's entire dramatic potential. A trio of students is asked to bare their toes and either recline with their feet exposed or sit at tables, head down, so that the feet can act in a normal foot posture. The three students are shown a card, which the other students cannot see, that contains a single word naming a human emotion or state of being. They must portray that word using only their feet. The student actors try to make their feet express such words as *anger, joy,* and *jealousy,* and the remaining students guess what the feet are suggesting. The acting job is, of course, a very tough one, but at the same time the risk is reduced by the wordless, physical, and psychological distancing. After the feet act out three or four words, the hands alone are placed above the tabletop and their owners receive a set of tougher words to act out, such as *anxiety, rage,* and *careful.* Because our hands are so fluent, they can successfully convey words that the feet struggle to express. Consciousness of the role of actor gradually develops in these students, still with little risk involved. The final step is to pass the acting job on to the faces, our body's most expressive actor. The eyes, the mouth, and all the other facial features work to act out difficult words, such as *savage, faithful,* and *bellicose.* Only the faces are allowed to appear, chins resting on a tabletop. Although to some, Faces, Hands, and Feet is only a warm-up exercise, it builds a sense of communicating ideas to an audience through bodily gestures on a stage. During a unit on Greek drama, Stella Beale used this activity to help students understand the difficulties that Greek actors, who wore masks, faced in expressing emotion without the use of facial expression. Not only did her Hands-Feet drama increase her students' understanding of the body's dramatic potential, but also, it served to build community in her classroom.

So . . . So Drama.   The ingredient left out of the creative drama activities that we have discussed so far is language. Language is the controlling ingredient of So . . . So Drama. As with a full-blown drama, a script provides students with a text to interpret through voice. Unlike most other dramatic texts, however, the script is so brief that students with poor memories or stage fright can comfortably take central roles. Pairs of students recite the lines as an exchange, given here in its entirety:

> So.
> So!
>
> It's up to you.
> Me?
>
> Please.
> Why?
>
> It's inevitable.
> That's what you think.
>
> No, really.
> I'll show you.

   The surprise and delight of the exercise, which turns mere recitation into a dramatic moment, is that voice interprets the words through volume, emphasis, inflection, speed, pauses, and pitch. For instance, students can decide to let the words convey the sorrow of a final parting, the anger of a violent encounter, or the ennui of an uneventful conversation. Whatever the choice of situation and tone, the student pairs must consider and dramatize the lines so that an audience of peers can readily guess what's afoot. To do this, they must envision how they would feel in such a situation in real life. Gestures, movements, costumes, and props can be used to complicate and enhance the performances. The great pay-off in this activity comes as different pairs presenting the same 10 lines create striking variations of tone, mood, character, and situation. No explication is needed to teach the effects of dramatic choice. To explore technique, a simple question is usually sufficient: "How did the pair create its effect?"

Personified Poems.   This activity, like So . . . So Drama, uses preselected words to provide student actors with a verbal structure to which they add their dramatic gestures. It also is like the first oral exercise, Voice Lessons, but with gestures. Students are given or asked to find short but memorable poems. One-person poems such as those in Figure 3–2 provide excellent texts. Those with pronounced rhyme and meter are easiest to commit to memory. Dialogue poems invite the interaction of two or more students. Figure 3–4 lists dialogue poems that we have used effectively. Some of these require a third voice as narrator, reading expository lines almost like an ancient Greek chorus. Another resource is a book written for children and focusing on common creatures: Paul Fleischman's *Joyful Noise: Poems for Two Voices.*

Costume Drama.   This activity depends almost entirely on the effect that special garb has on the group's imagination. We use Costume Drama both as literature review and as dramatic experience. We ask every student to come dressed as a character or significant object from literature that has been read

FIGURE 3–4
Dialogue poems

Anonymous	"Sir Patrick Spens"
	"Edward"
Thomas Nashe (1567–1601)	"A Litany in Time of Plague"
George Herbert (1593–1633)	"Love"
William Blake (1757–1827)	"The Clod and the Pebble"
Percy Bysshe Shelley (1792–1822)	"Ozymandias"
John Keats (1795–1821)	"La Belle Dame Sans Merci"
Robert Browning (1812–1889)	"My Last Duchess"
	"Meeting at Night"
	"Parting at Morning"
Lewis Carroll (1832–1898)	"Jabberwocky"
A. E. Housman (1859–1936)	"Terence, This Is Stupid Stuff"
	"Is My Team Ploughing?"
W. B. Yeats (1865–1939)	"For Anne Gregory"
Edwin Arlington Robinson (1869–1935)	"Mr. Flood's Party"
	"An Evangelist's Wife"
Paul Valery (1871–1945)	"Asides (Chanson a part)"
Robert Frost (1874–1963)	"Out, Out—"
	"The Death of the Hired Man"
	"Telephone"
John Crowe Ransom (1888–1974)	"Piazza Piece"
Countee Cullen (1903–1946)	"Incident"
W. H. Auden (1907–1973)	"O Where Are You Going?"
Karl Shapiro (1913–)	"Doctor, Doctor, A Little of Your Love"
Henry Reed (1914–1986)	"Naming of Parts"

in class. Each student offers a line from the story or a clue of some sort to enable others to identify the character or object. After we guess their identities (which makes an excellent review of the reading), we divide students into two groups and ask each to use the props to create a short play with a title, a narrator (if desired), central and supporting characters, action, and a climax.

Bag Act. This activity does not depend on prior reading, but on a set of three or four bags full of hats, odd shirts, shawls, festive material, gaudy beads, ties, and assorted objects found in attics and yard sales. As before, students allow the props to ignite their creative powers. You can, if you wish, guide them by offering a situation or conflict from which to work.

Nonstop Triad. Carter (personal communication, 1991) recommends this activity, which uses conflict with a twist to promote spontaneous drama. He assigns three students roles and a conflict situation. An authority figure has to try to arbitrate an intense conflict between two bitter adversaries: a policeman and two drivers in a major fender bender, say, or a principal and two students, one of whom has wronged the other. The only stage direction the teacher gives is that the conflict is a bitter one and this twist: The three participants should talk nonstop. Although they never cease talking, each is able to listen more than you might think. The triologue has produced for us amazingly authentic speech and inventive thinking. Improbable explanations and schemes arise frequently in these harried conversations. If the wild conversation is taped, groups can later transform it into a more traditional script as the core of a formal performance.

When Worlds Collide. This activity uses drama from the collision of two or three famous historic or fictional personages thrown together onstage without regard to normal historical constraints. Here we have character rather than conflict as the source of drama. Supply brief biographies, and ask students who have a pretty clear sense of these memorable persons to converse together in character. Imagine Moses, Sigmund Freud, and Helen Keller onstage responding to this simple prompt: "What do you think of women's contemporary roles?" Mere conversation gains dramatic scope and power. This transformation is particularly likely if the context also provides a particular, provocative setting, such as an infantry trench, a poolroom, or a union hall.

Dramatic Monologue. This activity provides an opportunity for the individual student to create and interpret a character first on paper and then through the telling of a story. Petrina McGowen (1997) explains the role of monologue in a traditional play: "To allow the audience some extra insight either into [character] or an[other] aspect of the play." McGowen sets tasks for her eighth-grade students that lead each to create a character (imagined, historic, or familiar) caught in the midst of a story. Each student must construct or select the following:

A list of emotions (at least three)
A list of physical attributes (at least three)
A setting
A conflict
A secret (Students do not allude to the secret; "it just helps deepen the structure" of the character.)
Simple props (hats, ties, scarves, and so on) that help bring the character to life.

After each student has visualized a character's attributes and imagined the character's story, the student tells the story to the class in the voice of the character. Students are not allowed to describe their characters' feelings or emotions, but must bring these traits to life through the situation, mannerisms, props, voice, and setting.

Four Cs Improvisation.   In this activity, students put character, conflict, context, and closure to work to achieve full dramatic effect. To initiate the improvisation, the teacher gives brief descriptions of specific characters, the conflict, and the context. With these three givens, students begin to construct a rising tension (complication), a moment of crisis and release (climax), and then the resolution (denouement). One of the most difficult things for students to achieve is satisfactorily clearing the stage, bringing the action to resolution and conclusion. They know that "and they lived happily ever after" does the job of closing fairy tales, but they are not quite as clear about how dramatic action ends. Student actors must do more than look lamely out at the audience and say, "That's all folks!" They have to anticipate and plan their drama so that the audience knows when to clap or when to expect the curtain to fall. Students can give the audience signals that the play has ended by talking in slow or fast motion, freezing at the moment the last line is uttered, or turning slowly 180 degrees away from the audience, but the test is that the audience knows by word and by deed that there is nothing more to say, that the play is complete. When students have become adept at dramatic closes, they will know it, because the audience's reactions will tell them so.

Intervention Drama.   Our final creative drama activity also satisfies all of the four Cs, but adds one new wrinkle. Students define the two Cs: character and context. Students are asked to define themselves as a group and then adopt separate identities as individuals in the group. They then put the group in motion in a concrete context, for example, an extended family at an out-of-doors reunion dinner. The teacher initiates a prompt for improvisation, not one that resolves a conflict, but incites one. In this example, the crew of an Andromedean spaceship comes unexpectedly upon the reunion. These intruders might be given distinguishing touches of costume or language, so that the original players can identify them and know they are not from Duluth or Topeka. The conflict appears to be inevitable, but if it is not, the Andromedeans should be sure to create one. The job is for the student family, who have worked on closure, to resolve the conflict and end the trauma. This activity can also become a starter for students actually scripting scenes or plays themselves.

A PROCESS OF RESPONSE AND CRITIQUE

Many oral language exercises and creative drama activities require no formal feedback from the audience (teacher or classmates), but at times, some form of response and even evaluation enrich and extend student learning. Deirdre Smith, a dancer and dance educator in New York City and at the North Carolina Governor's School, introduced us to a method of critical response developed by dancers Liz Lerman (1993) and Michelle Pearson (1997) as an alternative to the often-wounding critiques that dancers traditionally give to each other. We have found its six steps pertinent to any form of creative expression. We will discuss other methods for responding to students' written and oral work in later chapters on writing and evaluation. We include this process here as a helpful, nonthreatening way to respond to student drama. Although we see the logic in the sequence of steps suggested, we have also found practical wisdom in individual parts of it.

Following any performance, a facilitator sits by the artist/performer to field questions from the audience in a sequence of steps.

Step 1   **Affirmation**
             The facilitator solicits positive, affirmative responses from the audience with questions such as "What is working?" "What has meaning for you?" "What is unexpected?" "Cool?" "Invigorating?" "What was your favorite part?" "What should be definitely kept?" "What about this work 'brought you something special'?"

Step 2   **Artist as Questioner**
             The artist begins the dialogue by asking the questions, but often the facilitator must help the artist find the questions that are specific and essential. Usually, the facilitator steers away from general questions such as "What do you think?" and heads for the more particular questions, for instance, with creative drama, "Should the performers move to center stage at the conclusion?"

Step 3 **Responders As Questioners**

Next, the facilitator asks the artist whether he or she is willing to answer the responders' questions and, if so, asks the responders to frame their opinions in questions that are neutral, that do not themselves make critical suggestions or statements. For example, rather than telling the performer, "The dramatic monologue was diffuse and out of focus," the responder might rephrase that into a genuine question: "What was the most essential character trait you were trying to communicate and where is that most apparent in your monologue?" This rephrasing shifts the responder out of a superior position of authority and into a position as colleague and problem solver. In such a relationship, the artist is more likely to be open to what the other is saying than he or she would be in the face of an attack.

Step 4 **Opinion Time**

At this point in the process, when some greater distance from the performance and greater ease with the audience have been established, the artist may be ready to hear direct opinions. Thus, during this fourth stage, the responders can actively state opinions or offer suggestions, but first they must ask the artist whether he or she is interested in hearing an opinion about the specific issue that concerns them. For instance, a responder might say "I have an opinion about your timing. Do you want to hear it?" The artist can still control the situation by saying, yes, no, or not at this time.

In the final two steps, *Subject Matter Discussion* and *Working on the Work,* if the respondents and the artist are interested in continuing to talk, the discussion might broaden to the subject matter of the work. Sometimes the content of this discussion can be absorbed into any rewriting or reworking of the original.

SUMMARY

When students have completed these or similar dramatic activities, they will have worked their way into creative drama. They have started off in the relative comfort of given directions. They should by now have begun to feel more comfortable in a dramatic role and to experiment with what makes good drama. They have become more confident in their sense of their dramatic knowledge and skill. They have come to appreciate all of the body's potential for dramatic effects; they have seen how simple words such as *so* can be manipulated to change the dramatic meaning; they have felt the force of costumes to propel dramatic action; and they have sensed the shaping force of character, conflict (issues and themes), and context (places and settings). In the final stage they experimented with improvisation. Here they acquired a sense of the dramatic that taps their personal imagination and intellect, gives them stronger language arts skills, and prepares them for formal drama. Ideally, it has also provided delight.

Swartz (1988) provides a frame of reference to use for planning additional possibilities for drama in the classroom (p. 10).*

Classroom Possibilities in Drama

Sources	Components	Process	Grouping
picture book	games	discussing	individual
novel	mime	planning	pairs
poem	tableau	improvising	small groups
script	movement	role-playing	large group
short story	interviewing	problem solving	whole group
illustration	storytelling	decision making	audience
newspaper	choral speaking	questioning	
magazine	readers theatre	reflecting	
properties	illustrating	persuading	
film	designing	summarizing	
song	writing	imagining	
our own stories	researching	describing	
	ritual/ceremony	challenging	
	performing	recalling	
	play making	instructing	
		reporting	
		informing	
		evaluating	

*Adapted from *Dramathemes* by Larry Swartz. Reprinted with permission. Pembroke Publishers Limited, 528 Hood Road, Markham, Ontario L3R 3K9. Available in the U.S. from Heinemann Educational Books.

Teachers or students could almost treat these as a Planning Quartro Tale and randomly select the group size, the process, the components, and the sources with which to shape a dramatic activity for the class.

McCaslin (1984) provides a neat summary of the purposes and advantages of creative drama. She regards it "as a way of learning, a means of self-expression, a therapeutic technique, a social activity, or an art form. Children are helped to assume responsibility, accept group decisions, work together cooperatively, develop new interests, and—particularly in a classroom situation—seek new information. Drama is the most completely personal, as well as the most highly socialized, art form we have" (p. 22). Dixon (1967) summarizes the ways in which drama touches all four language arts for high school students:

- *improvising* talk appropriate to a vast range of situation and role;
- *listening and responding* in the fullest sense, while taking a role;
- *discussing* the approach to a theme, its possibilities, and finally the insights gained;
- *writing* scripts for one's own group;
- *reading,* learning and probing the meaning of a text—through private study, talk and enacting. (pp. 42–43)

Dixon also recognizes the classroom context in which creative drama finds its greatest potential, not in a teacher's sustained and conscious development of actors and producers of school plays, but in "an awareness among teachers of English of those moments in a lesson, or in a week's work, when what has been said or read moves naturally out to enactment with movement and gesture" (p. 42).

UNDERSTANDING DRAMA: TRANSFORMATION AND APPRECIATION

When students have used the full continuum of creative drama, they have accomplished much in terms of speaking and moving publicly, collaborating in groups, taking risks, and exercising empathy and creativity. What they begin to understand about formal drama is also of great importance. By the time they perform a 4 Cs Improvisation, they have seen essential elements of drama firsthand. They understand the nature of conflict and resolution for characters in a context. They begin to appreciate the expressive force of facial expression, gesture, and speech. They appreciate the power of objectifying human dilemmas in the spoken interaction of characters. With this felt or experienced conception of drama, they are better prepared to meet and greet formal drama.

Our focus shifts now toward the oral language of theatre. The learning goals of classroom talking, oral exercises, and creative drama remain, but we apply those in approaching the scripted drama of professional playwrights. Chapter 4, Responding to Literature, and Chapter 5, Reviving Poetry, suggest stages for reading any literary text and present numerous classroom activities for each stage. We discuss here classroom strategies that are especially apt for drama and that are active (not as dependent on teacher talk or whole-class discussion) and social (involving pairs and groups of students). These strategies have a common aim: to lift drama texts from page to stage and to lift students from passive spectators to active creators, performers, and appreciators. We set students in motion simply at first, with nondramatic texts for enactment, and then move to writing and performing student-created drama. With those moorings in place, we approach the plays of professional writers via dramatic activities that deepen students' appreciation of plot, character, theme, and form. Finally, we consider how any text can be approached through drama and can be more imaginatively and actively envisioned thereby.

READY-MADE PLAYS

Creative drama prepares students to translate simple stories into dialogue and narrative description into sets, props, and stage directions. A fine way to start their dramatic writing and performing is with material that has already been translated from story to dramatic form. Scholastic's *Literary Cavalcade* publishes easily accessible examples. This publication has transformed the works of such young adult novelists as Paul Zindel, Bette Greene, and S. E. Hinton, as well as such classic short story writers as Edgar Allen Poe and Arthur Conan Doyle, into short, engaging, easily readable drama for classroom use. *Literary Cavalcade* also publishes timely international dramas and screenplays, such as *A World Apart,* by South African playwright Shawn Slovo. Because this drama is concrete, immediate, and dynamic, it appeals to a wide range of students. Students who have not been energized by anything else in the traditional English classroom often respond to even uninspired dramatizations of these novels and short stories. Productions do not have to be elaborate. You can merely assign parts and ask students to read their roles from their desks. We have witnessed moving readers' theater performances on spare classroom stages, as well as costumed performances on classroom-adapted sets, with lines well rehearsed and even memorized. Both types of staged performances elicit students' lively interest. The simplicity and authenticity of characters speaking for themselves as they move and act on the stage draw these students nearer to fictive art than any silently read texts do. The brevity and simple language capture even unenthusiastic readers.

STUDENT-CREATED DRAMA

As both the audience and participants in these transformed dramas, students may come to understand how plays work and how they are transformed from fiction. That understanding will help them in the next step: initiating the transformation from text to theater themselves. We suggest that you begin slowly with brief scenes between pairs, progress to longer scenes with several players and perhaps a subplot, and culminate with two scenes that manage to move characters on and off stage, to link incidents, and to elaborate on the plot. Practice is required for this progress.

More ambitious dramatic transformations are outside the scope of this text. O'Neill and Lambert (1982), however, suggest specific strategies that teachers might use to establish a dramatic context and so give students a "stronger sense of purpose and motivation" (p. 25):

Provide a Starting Point for Inquiry	Groups prepare a short scene encapsulating their particular viewpoint on a chosen theme or topic, for example, emigrants, young offenders, a woman's place. (p. 25)
Provide Evidence and Information	Various aspects of a theme, life-style, or problem can be illustrated in a number of different scenes in order to build up a fuller picture of a particular way of life, for example, the differences between rich and poor in Victorian times. (p. 25)
Present an Alternative Reconstruction of Events	Each group shows a different version of the circumstances leading up to a situation in which events are open to interpretation, for example, what exactly happened when the child's bedroom was wrecked? (p. 26)
Provide Alternative Courses of Action	Groups illustrate a suitable solution to a problem with which they are concerned, for example, different versions of how the runaways can be reconciled with their parents. (p. 26)
Provide a Means of Reflection	Each group prepares a short scene or series of scenes summing up the most significant areas of their work on a particular theme, for example, the struggle of women for the vote. (p. 26)*

Once students negotiate these small steps, they are readier to construct a larger production. The resources for concrete and manageable ideas are the same as for oral interpretation and creative drama: poems, visual art, MTV videos, television commercials. Our students have also elaborated and staged narrative poems, ballads and poems such as Robert Browning's *My Last Duchess,* or Robert Frost's *Out, Out.* A more ambitious project is to transform short stories or novels into performances. We have found stories with strong but concentrated action, dramatic tension, and clearly developed characters are especially accessible to production, stories like Hernando Tellez's "Just Lather, That's All," Leo Tolstoy's "God Knows the Truth but Waits," Gabriel García Márquez's "The Very Old Man with Enormous Wings," or Zora Neale Hurston's "Snake" and "The Gilded Six Bits." Moving from those, a whole class might undertake a longer work, like vignettes from Sandra Cisneros' *The House on Mango Street.* One modest kind of staging is for a reader to read selected passages that others enact in tableau or pantomime.

The work of transformation can waken students to a clearer sense of the dramatic. Just as performing musicians become more acute and sympathetic listeners to music, so even amateur dramatists become more alert and responsive theatergoers. They can sense when characters are not well defined or when they are too predictable. They feel the presence of dramatic tension or the lack of it. They recognize whether or not a satisfactory resolution is achieved at the play's conclusion. (The four C's—character, conflict, context, closure—can be used as checklists to guide or critique the basic components of good drama.) Thus students learn through dramatizing much as writing-to-learn students expose what they know and don't know about science as they explain a crysalis. O'Neill and Lambert (1982) observe that although a guarantee of drama of "depth and integrity" is impossible, acts that produce it are most likely to occur at those points in the process when the class and teacher are working together spontaneously. Then students begin "to question, accept challenges, make decisions,

*Reproduced from *Drama Structures* © 1982 by kind permission of the authors, Cecily O'Neill and Alan Lambert, and publishers, Stanley Thornes (Publishers) Ltd.

realize implications, go beyond stereotypes and alter their perspectives. If the class is working with belief, commitment and integrity the pupils may even achieve the kind of change in understanding which is at the heart of educational drama" (pp. 27–28).

We have seen dramatization used successfully with English as a Second Language (ESL) students. Teachers ask small groups to select a favorite scene from a longer work, convert it to oral language, learn parts, and enact and videotape it. The whole class then assembles the scenes in chronological order. The performance gives motive to their work, yet the camera also places a distance between them and their audience. Converting scenes to written and then spoken speech in this way can bring the formal words to life.

By transforming texts, many students move toward a keener awareness and appreciation of drama. Other roads also lead to appreciation. The one we will travel continues to lead us to drama via the active engagement in plays, rather than the more passive reading and discussion of scripts. We frame suggested exercises in the context of the three dimensions of any drama:

Plot: What
Character: Who
Theme: Why

These three are more intricately meshed in drama than the four *W*s are in a newspaper report. But separating them helps many students understand plays more readily and explore drama more deeply. We don't explicate these three dimensions here, nor do we suggest that you do. We enumerate exercises whereby students might understand drama apart from classroom analysis of it. Figure 3–5 makes these suggestions more visible.

PLOT

The first question asked of any story is "What happened?" Before readers or viewers can appreciate character or theme, they must first comprehend the sequence of incidents and the causal connections between them.

Prereading.   One approach to plot centers on the play's first scene. We suggest that before students read or see an entire play, they see the first scene, act it out themselves, or hear it read by a group of strong readers. Then ask students to speculate on the possible middle and end that issue from this beginning. Not only are potential confusions cleared up at the outset, but also, curiosity is piqued and a sense of some dramatic conventions and continuities is sharpened.

FIGURE 3–5
Active exercises for
drama appreciation

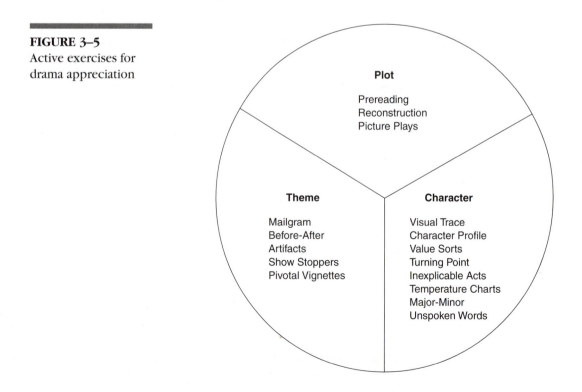

Reconstruction. One of the best entries into the play's action is to have pairs of students recount major events of the play to each other. The sequence might be

- In pairs, students construct a simple narrative by jotting down key words that capture the action, characters, and/or setting of major incidents.
- A pair of students tells the whole class their list's first five incidents at the play's beginning.
- Other pairs are asked to make an addition, a sequence change, or a correction.

With most classes, the invitation will evoke a hail of changes and rearrangements. This activity does not simply recount facts, but sorts out understanding, interpretation, and even criticism. After settling the beginning, a second pair can be asked to recount the middle, and a third the end. Everything, including the point at which they stop, gives clues to their sense of plot and structure.

We also have used two-page summaries to stimulate students' thinking about the plot. The class is divided into groups (one for each act) and asked to underline the event in their act's summary that seems most significant to understanding the play. When the small group reaches consensus, it informs the entire class. Then the whole class considers the one event whose omission would change the meaning of the play. Plot in this fashion comes to be more than a string of incidents. It is marked by relationships. The same groups can explore those relationships, and each group can link its scene to the act before and after it. The groups with the first and last acts, in linking the adjacent act, connect the acts at both ends of the play as well. When these underlined events are linked to the surrounding events, a clearer sense of the entire play's interrelated structure emerges. This is a simple beginning, and it lets the entire class start on a sure footing. Students move from comprehending events to perceiving significance in the events and finally to understanding the relationships among them.

Picture Plays. In addition to these two verbal methods of comprehending plot, we can capitalize on the playwright's use of visual and concrete image to depict character and conflict. The clues for what these props, scenery, gestures, stage movements, and stage positions mean are in the dialogue. Exploring students' physical presentations reveals how they as readers or viewers have picked up those clues. Students are asked to visualize the play and capture crucial moments in drawings, schematics, or props. Some depict groups of characters in sociograms; others bring in props such as a dagger for *Macbeth* and a unicorn for *The Glass Menagerie*. A more ambitious task is for individuals, pairs, or small groups to create a schematic of the events of the main plot or the defining incidents for the main character. Arriving at the play's plot through concrete objects or drawings often anchors and secures students' understanding. Interestingly, when students see other students' pictures and hear their explanations, they tend to reflect upon, and usually sharpen, their own sense of what happened. Here, too, we teachers gain a much surer understanding of what students have comprehended in the play.

Understanding plot, the most elementary dimension of the play, is essential to developing a deep understanding of the more complex notions about character, theme, and form that follow. The first step should be sure, but it also must be enlivening. It must build interest in the human, personal events at the heart of the dramatic story. It nudges students toward creating a vivid and precise performance in their minds' eyes.

CHARACTER

Character is what draws us to a play. We see an individual who "struts and frets his hour upon the stage"; he is concrete, alive, and among us—almost. The curtain between life and art is thin. Characters are like us. They are people, living out a crisis through action and spoken dialogue with each other. Even if the crisis or plot seems contrived and unconvincing, we can be diverted by the human beings involved in it. We are witnesses. In class discussion, we can focus our questions and our uncertainties on character, and generally, students will respond. But we also can focus, sharpen, and enlarge our responses to character through nonanalytical experiences. We recommend eight exercises that depart from the traditional formal analysis of character.

Visual Trace. Visual trace is a means of using videotape to trace the growth stages of a character.

Major Character. In Chapter 8, we describe an exercise involving the central character in the 1979 film *Norma Rae.* We excerpt a series of brief segments from the film and ask students to respond to each segment by noting the qualities of the central character as she changes in the course of the series. We also ask students to mark the most blatant change and the one that captures the most subtle shifts. Their response sheets become the concrete prompts to small-group, then whole-class discussion.

Character study based on familiar films always intrigues our students. We propose the same kind of analysis for staged drama. Select a play that is available on videotape. Ask students who have read or seen the play to choose and then analyze a set of six to eight taped excerpts that trace the movement of a character such as Antigone, Laura Wingfield, or Prince Hal. Small student groups select their set of steps in a character's development and submit their sequence to the entire class; the awareness that comes from watching and noting is also developed by the act of selecting. Both reception and production work are valuable.

Character Pairs. The analysis of a single character's development can be broadened to the scrutiny of two major characters. We ask students to isolate and watch the crucial interactions of pairs of characters as they relate to one another through the course of the play. Each scene in which they talk together can be taped and a growth chart used to examine the changes that transpire. For instance, we may sense shifts in the relationship between Tom and Amanda in *The Glass Menagerie,* but when we study their exchanges more intently, free of other characters and other plots, we can understand what has come of it, the subtle ways it changes. Through this piecing together, we drive more deeply toward understanding them as individuals and as family members.

Minor Characters. The kind of growth that is evident in a central figure is rarer in minor characters and is often perceptible in only small gradations of change. The distinction is useful here between characters who are static, or unchanged by the action in the play, and those who are dynamic, or develop as a result of the action. To help students gain a clearer sense of a lesser character in a play, ask individuals or small groups to select a minor character, chart his or her growth, and then present that character in a parade for the whole class. Students organize the parade in progression from the most one-dimensional and unchanging to the most intricate and dynamic.

Observers or Narrators. A playwright's spokesperson is not always present or evident, but students can be asked to search for that character who seems to present a consistent and collected perception of the unfolding events or to act as an outside observer of the play's action. The Stage Manager clearly serves this purpose in Thorton Wilder's *Our Town,* but characters such as York in Shakespeare's *Richard II* also present themselves through their words and placement in the drama as the voice of the playwright. York, for instance, is always present at the moments of crisis to comment omnisciently. Students can look for such authorial voices in other plays and videotape or record their key statements to look at how certain characters can serve to illuminate the meaning or theme of the play. Playing these recordings for the class provides a dramatic culmination.

Character Profile.   Writing character profiles is a simple way to involve students in the major players of a drama. Give each student two concrete measures of response to a character: (1) a list of five statements about a single character to be acknowledged as true or false, for example, "Amanda is more realistic than Tom." and "Hamlet does not love Ophelia"; and (2) an adjective list to be checked for descriptive terms that capture the character. Making your own specific checklist is best; a general list of feelings appears in Chapter 5. An alternative is to ask students simply to list characterizing adjectives. These can be explored in small groups or with the whole class. When students stake claims and clarify reactions through these simple responses, they are more likely to be engaged by discussion of the differing readings or viewings. A key to developing good exploratory conversations is to offer statements that address the ambiguities and uncertainties in plays.

Value Sorts.   Value sorts encourage students to consider the value systems of characters in a play and to compare them with their own. In this activity, which moves from individual to partnered to small-group work, students are asked to do the following:

- Select the characters that you consider to be the play's most admirable and least admirable.
- State three virtues and three vices of this polar pair, or select them from a list we provide.
- Discuss those values with a partner.
- Circle three of your worst character's values and invert each to see how closely those inverted values may lie to your own.

Where these conversations expose differences of literary and personal opinion, they gain energy and authenticity. This exploration of character can be connected more strongly to the text by asking students to cite specific lines, actions, or scenes to support their ideas. When students must hunt for evidence for their opinions, they give the text a deeper reading and acquire a more thoughtful interpretation of the play.

An alternative to the best-worst comparison is to ask students to rank a list of four or five characters drawn from one or several plays from most to least admired. When the stock of shared plays is limited, well-known film characters can work amid the play casts. Qualities are again enumerated for the most and least admired, and these rankings are discussed in small groups. We also find benefits in reporting these conclusions to other classes. Students enjoy hearing how other classes voted in these informal polls, and we like expanding their sense that literature is a subject of lively inquiry and speculation.

Turning Point.   Another way to measure growth and understand character is through the simple device of a time line that marks major events and crucial turning points. The teacher alone or, better, the class together constructs a plot time line, perhaps on a long roll of paper taped up for as much wall or bulletin board space as needed. Each student then marks the point on the time line at which the major character or characters make a turning point or engage in defining action. Next, students explain why these decisions or actions are formative. A nice benchmark is the freedom that existed before that point and the dwindling options available after it.

Inexplicable Acts.   Postman and Weingartner (1969) believe that the only questions that should be asked are those authentic ones for which the teacher has no ready answer. In this exercise, those are the *only* questions asked. First, ask students to keep a running list of actions and scenes that can't be satisfactorily explained, that leave them confused, or that might easily perplex others, for example,

> Why doesn't Hamlet kill Claudius?
> Is there method or madness in Hamlet's actions?
> Does Polonius deserve Hamlet's scorn?
> Is Polonius merely a meddlesome moralizer?

Then, poll students for a list of inexplicable acts and write them on the board, on the overhead projector, or on a sheet of paper. The class rates the list to find the top five most inexplicable scenes. Small groups or the entire class then attempts to find at least two plausible interpretations. A jigsaw arrangement of group discussion is excellent here: Give a question to each group to discuss, then, when time is called, each student goes to a new group composed of one member from each of the original groups and students discuss the answers to each of the questions. Students need to know that understanding character is never a settled business and that their same questions have puzzled audiences and critics for centuries, much as the persons in our own lives perplex us. They need to see that careful reflection can unravel some characters, and that others seem to become more perplexing upon careful examination. They need to see that thoughtful questions don't always have ready answers.

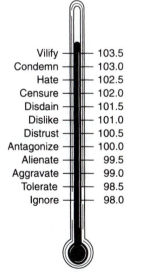

Vilify	103.5
Condemn	103.0
Hate	102.5
Censure	102.0
Disdain	101.5
Dislike	101.0
Distrust	100.5
Antagonize	100.0
Alienate	99.5
Aggravate	99.0
Tolerate	98.5
Ignore	98.0

Temperature Charts.   A helpful way to observe characters is in their relationships with one another. This is especially true when they are "mighty opposites," a protagonist, the chief character or contender, and an antagonist, a rival or opponent of the protagonist. Ask students to select two closely related characters and to locate contact points throughout the play when the two express their feelings for one another or respond to one another's actions or words. Their feelings for each other are likely to be synonymous, but occasionally they differ. With contact points established, ask individual students or groups to label each point according to the strength of feelings between the two. Students can create their own terms to characterize the attitudes or use a ready-made list similar to the scale of rising (negative) temperatures. For each of the agreed-upon contact points, the groups must come up with a temperature or term to define the positive or negative heat of the relationship. Differences are as instructive as agreements are; students begin to analyze characters more intently and to see their relationships more clearly.

Major-Minor.   This exercise lets students explore the parallels of two characters of unequal importance to a play. The major character's main actions throughout the play are listed on a time line; on a parallel line below it are those of a minor character. The study of the actions and feelings of minor characters at the important times of the play, as they compare to those of the major figures, is enlightening. This is particularly true of Shakespeare. We can see the craft of the playright at work with an unexpected clarity: Minor characters serve to create foils, character definition, tone, foreshadowing, and recurrent motifs.

Unspoken Words.   Our final entry into character asks students to use their imaginations to write soliloquies, asides, or dialogues that characters might have spoken. Imagining and then performing the inner thoughts of, for example, Laura Wingfield, Willie Loman, or Juliet opens students to insights into these characters that reveal and expand their depth of understanding.

Invitation to Reflection 3–3

1. Which of these approaches to character in drama appealed to you most for your own study? Why?
   - Visual Trace
   - Character Profile
   - Value Sorts
   - Turning Point
   - Inexplicable Acts
   - Temperature Charts
   - Major-Minor
   - Unspoken Words
2. Do you think that the exercise you chose would bring students closer to active response and interpretation of character in a play than a more traditional, whole-class, analytical discussion of the characters would?
3. Imagine yourself teaching students a play that you enjoy. If you think an analytical discussion would be a stronger approach to it, write the kinds of questions you might address to students. If you prefer one of the exercises here, consider how you would use it in a class.

THEME

Perceiving a play as action and character are the first steps to understanding dramatic art. But we must also invite students to see deeper significances or we shortchange them as students of both life and literature. We have to remember that such abstract, formal operational, thinking is not the natural province of most secondary students, who are largely caught up in concrete operational thinking. Thus, we need to nudge our students, using what Piaget called disequilibrium, to raise their thinking to the level of theme.

When we ask students to tell us what a play is about, their common response is to recite a list of significant incidents of plot. Few will understand these actions as embodying ideas. We need to work hard to help students see the abstractions that action encapsulates. We now explore ways that teachers encourage students to understand these broader meanings.

Mailgram.   One strategy for helping students develop their sense of the central thrust of a play is to compress the play's action into the 60 words of a mailgram. When they compact a play such as *Our Town* into these few words, the next step, deciding what those actions really mean, is a little easier to achieve. Groups can work to strip away excess until the major 60 words are found. The next step is finding one word, an abstraction such as *community, realization, fate,* or *transformation,* to stand for all of those actions. Once the groups have settled on a single abstraction, they can each post their single words and debate with the other groups the capacity of their choices to sum up the whole play. Those same groups, each having explained their single words, are more able to move from their general abstractions to single short sentences that further explain their words. These sentences can then be expanded to identify the center of meaning in the play. The conceptual movement is like an equation:

$$\text{concrete actions} = \text{single abstraction} = \text{abstract statement}$$

The transformation is less difficult when the steps are made more explicit. Those who deal best with concrete operations are more likely to make the shift to a general statement by using specific steps to get there. It is the shift from the concrete summary to the single abstract word that makes the entire process work. This activity can be easily varied. For example, during the study of Shakespeare's *The Tempest,* teacher Julia Neenan (personal communication, 1992) asked small groups of students to sum up the political platform for each of the play's contenders for leadership or power. The student groups distilled aphoristic phrases from those platforms to put on posters plugging their candidates.

Artifacts.   Another starting point is to use highly charged props or scenery to begin to articulate theme. We ask students to list three objects from a play that stand out as special and loaded with meaning beyond themselves. In *The Glass Menagerie,* for example, a student might list coffin, glass unicorn, and blue roses. When these have been selected, the three are translated into a word that captures the meaning behind each:

Object	Idea
coffin	death
glass unicorn	uniqueness
blue roses	unreality/imagination

The student then takes the transformed objects and tries to connect them in a sentence that captures the essence of the play. As with Mailgram, when an earlier distillation has occurred, the transformation takes place in a single word.

Show Stoppers.   Another approach that translates actions and objects to theme centers on the lines that we immediately know are significant upon reading them, those that catch us and perhaps urge us to write them down. A student's selection of a line suggests that it has power for him or her as a reader. Students select four they like best, then translate these powerful statements into encapsulations of a play's central ideas.

Pivotal Vignettes.   Focusing on significant, well-defined moments in the play can also help students make the leap to understanding theme. When these moments occur, we usually sense them; they possess a heightened intensity. If students can respond to and identify such moments, they are on their way to knowing what the play is about. The characters seem to be set up on stage as in a frieze, and students are asked to mimic these captured moments. Other students can walk around and reflect on such a moment just as they would an actual frieze. Rare teaching moments can occur as teachers help students puzzle over the meaning, much as good docents do with visitors to art galleries.

Before-After.   This exercise works not with one pivotal scene, but by comparing an early scene with a late scene in which a character is noticeably altered. Almost any character will work: Shakespeare's Macbeth, Richard II, or Lear; Ibsen's Torvald, Nora, or Hedda; or Williams's Amanda or Blanche. Students can focus on these stark contrasts and then complete the following:

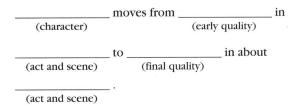

Students will find different words for character transformation, but that change process will probably lie near the center of the ideas that the playwright wishes to embody.

FORM

Form is even more distant and abstract than theme is, but for some it is the key to appreciation of drama and the learning toward which the preceding discussions of plot, character, and theme point. The oral exercises, creative drama, and active considerations of plays should have opened students to a sense of the play as a play with formal defining conventions. Other exercises also can help students learn to recognize form, which was not apparent to them as less sophisticated readers, audiences, or actors. The play's form is its art or its howness: what the playwright has done to shape the meaning of the story. Because considerations of form in the high school classroom always verge on the analytical and distanced, we take up questions of its teaching very carefully. Chapter 4, Responding to Literature, discusses the common pitfalls of formal discussions and suggests active ways to avoid those dangers.

STORY DRAMA

Dramatic activities can also allow students to enter the story worlds of prose and poetry, an entry sometimes narrowed to the vanishing point by traditional classroom discussions. Research studies such as those of Gambrell and Bales (1986) and Purcell-Gates (1991) suggest that lower-ability readers especially do not have strategies for imagining or visualizing fictive worlds. These less proficient readers regard reading as a passive act of decoding words and receiving meanings, not as the active envisioning of characters alive in imaginary worlds and so constructing meanings. They cannot arrive in what Bruner (1986) calls "the landscape of action," which the story triggers. Entering that landscape is a necessary prerequisite to arriving at "the landscape of consciousness," where the reader begins to entertain and envision the characters and "what those involved in the action know, think or feel, or do not know, think or feel" (p. 14).

In sorting out how to help his less engaged and proficient readers, Jeff Wilhelm (1997) asked the question "How might dramatic activity guide and support student efforts to fill textual gaps and to elaborate on and move around in textual worlds?" (p. 93). He turned to story drama activities in order "to evoke story worlds, to help them make inferences about characters and their situations, and thus find reading literature to be a rewarding experience" (p. 99). He drew on Heathcote's (1984) idea that in drama you "put yourself into other people's shoes and by using personal experience to help you to understand their point of view you may discover more than you knew when you started" (p. 44). We summarize some of the activities that Wilhelm used to invite students to put on the shoes of story characters and to walk around in them. He calls the first, Revolving Role Drama, the "staple" of the drama activity that he used daily.

Revolving Role Drama	Students are asked to assume the perspective of a character in the story, to "visualize the story world and enact movement and interaction within that world" (p. 100).
Dramatic Play	Students are given a prompt or a situation (that may or may not come from the story) and are asked to assume the role of a story character and enact what would naturally follow from such a stimulus, remaining consistent with the psychology of the character.
To Tell the Truth Game	Students play the parts of characters, other students interrogate them about their lives, and the class judges who has "most convincingly 'become' that character" (p. 101).
Newscast	Students produce a videotaped news show that involves "interviewing characters, reporting on their activities, and editorializing on particular actions and decisions" (pp. 100–101).
Two-sided Story	Students are asked "to act out a scene from their lives (real or projected) that in some way parallel[s] a scene from the book" (p. 108).

DRAMATIC APPROACHES TO SHAKESPEARE

When you hear that Shakespeare is being taught in an English class, you usually expect to find students conscientiously reading the text of his plays. This approach seems particularly proper to most of us, who have studied his great plays as literature to be read. English essayist and critic Charles Lamb, who had a clear understanding of literature and a particular love of Shakespeare, is said to have held the deep personal belief that these great plays should always be read, rather than seen on the stage. He approached them almost as poetry, which profits from careful scrutiny of its compressed sound and sense on the page. Some would say that a play that is read is almost a different genre from a play that is watched. Many teachers agree, arguing that the plays are too rich and complex to hurry over. The language and the deeper meaning of the play, they fear, will be lost on uninitiated or untrained student audiences. They believe that rather than killing drama, careful reading vitalizes it; savoring it over time yields deeper appreciation.

PERFORMING VERSUS READING SHAKESPEARE

In the last 15 to 20 years, we have seen this belief challenged. A strong contingent of English teachers have turned to the stage, not the page, to introduce students to Shakespeare. They contend that his plays, and those of other dramatists, were made for audiences to watch and hear in their full three-dimensional power; plays are aural and visual events, not read ones. These drama advocates would characterize the difference as analogous to studying a series of football downs in a playbook, rather than watching the athletes perform on the field. J. L. Styan (1965, 1980) and others observe that when students see a whole play enacted by a company of flesh-and-blood characters, it becomes "tangible and meaningful" rather than abstract and impenetrable. We know from Piaget and other psychologists and epistemologists that knowledge of wholeness helps us recognize parts better and that the sensory world is understood long before the symbolic word is. MacKail (1970) agrees, arguing that Shakespeare and almost all drama is meant for the stage, not the study; it is the stuff for actors; it is whole, not fragmented; it is sensory-rich, not abstract.

When students read a play over time, especially when that time extends over 3 or 4 weeks, they lose the power of the whole play, dramatic and unbroken. When we merely read it, we substitute verbal and symbolic code-cracking for primary contact with the characters in action on stage. The imaginations of professional directors can prompt this live process for less experienced audiences so that they can later become the directors of the scripts in their heads. For similar reasons, picture books come before words-only books. Encountering Shakespeare through performance rather than print is analogous to using manipulatives to help students understand math concepts rather than just teaching the abstractions of mathematics. We need to capitalize on those qualities that set plays apart as dramatic performances in front of an audience. We must approximate this performance condition in any way possible: to let students see it live if possible, in its entirety if possible, as unbroken and enveloping if possible. Videotape and film are the more common nonprint alternatives for introducing students to plays. We would argue, perhaps hyperbolically, that if you tried to create a scheme for destroying these great plays, it might well involve a too familiar classroom scenario—reading them slowly, over a few weeks' time, analyzing them piece by piece, and focusing on the form and context rather than the meaning and content.

This struggle between stage and page may be taken one step further to suggest that students not merely become the play's audience, but its actors as well. The move is from seeing to being the play. Muir (1984) has said that "to act any part is to understand." When we move to this performance extreme, we are using John Dewey's axiom that we learn what we do. Performance becomes interpretation, a visible "reading" of the play. The student who seriously acts and becomes Polonius onstage knows Polonius because he has entered his consciousness.

SEVEN SHAKESPEAREAN ACTIVITIES

We briefly explore here seven simple ways that you might help your students enact Shakespeare's plays, from ad-libbed vignettes to well-polished dramatizations of crucial scenes.

Beyond Memory. Brown (1981) suggests a simple approach that encourages students to understand Shakespeare's, or a more contemporary playwright's, works by standing inside the world of drama. He urges teachers to enlarge the assignment of memorized speeches from *Julius Caesar, Macbeth,* and *Hamlet.* He asks that we push students past memorizing the famous lines to performing the lines in dramatic fashion. Beyond mere memory, students work on the gestures, the posture, and the movement of their characters' bodies. When they reach deeply into their chosen lines, they will begin to see "the clues to performance that lie within the text" (p. 97). This deeper understanding pushes students to experiment with gestures and facial expressions as they master the text. A performance based on understanding can communicate a deep knowledge of the lines to the entire class. Brown goes on to say that he lets his students gain a sense of the dramatic by having the class read a Biblical text and then watch the same passage enacted as part of a miracle play. He argues that students come to a realization about drama that can be communicated in no other way.

Interestingly, this and other performance approaches mediate the controversy between stage and page. To work well on the stage, the text has to be given even greater attention than it normally receives in the traditional pedagogy of the classroom. The movement from reading to seeing to doing brings the process full circle.

Absorption Exchange. Hawkins (1984) and Halio (1977) take this performance approach a step further. Hawkins urges fellow teachers to have students rehearse speeches and even scenes in plays so that they develop a deeper sense of the dramatists' intentions and communicate that to classmates through both performance and reflection. Halio refines the process. He suggests that teachers ask groups of five to seven students to select a 15- to 20-minute scene from any play to perform for the class. The troupes are given sufficient time to develop a serious, well-wrought performance. They can choose to add simple scenery and costumes, but they are required to memorize their parts and must present their scene to a live audience. Here again, we get the double value of live performance absorbed by an audience and absorbed also, in the deepest sense of the word, by those who have performed. This depth of understanding can be explored and communicated when performing students talk about the textual discoveries each has made.

Language Shifts. O'Brian (1984) has developed a performance method that helps students attend to the language in Shakespeare's plays, especially the shifts from prose to poetry. She suggests that pairs of students work on a scene in which a shift occurs and discuss how to signal the shift and where the problems arise in this change. Students who perform these shift scenes become very much aware of what is going on metrically and so become more attuned to the structure as well as the meaning of the play.

Diverse Productions. Newlin (1984) recommends the combined use of the Royal Shakespeare Company's nine videotapes and live student performance. Ben Kingsley speaks in one of the excellent teaching tapes about a specific scene and then offers three distinct versions of the scene as his company performs it. The relationship between performance and interpretation becomes clear for students when they are faced with diverse renditions of the same scene. Similarly, student groups can perform the same monologues or dialogues, but with very different interpretations. In both instances, penetration of the text is more likely in the dramatic version of it than in a single reading or even viewing of the play.

Intense Scrutiny.   Swander (1984) suggests another approach to performance, in which two students are given 10 class days or more to develop a two-person scene of 25 to 50 lines. Before they produce it onstage, they give the other students in the class a copy of the text to study briefly. The students perform the scene and answer questions from their student audience. Students further internalize the drama by writing a short paper on their performance and the experience related to it. Not acting, but thinking about the play is central to this entire process. Understanding develops because the creators care, other students challenge, and they all reflect on the experience.

Concrete Details.   A dramatic routine suggested by Fuller (1989) is similar. His idea is simple: more rehearsal of fewer lines, rather than quicker reading of more lines. He urges teachers to choose a scene and make it become important to students. He believes that a diverse group of students will respond to this approach better than to lectures on Elizabethan times or discussions of imagery. He knows that the humanity of the live production is compelling to all students. He thinks students will come alive when they contend about concrete questions of dramatizing: where characters stand, who they look at, how they gesture, and what tone of voice they use. He allots less time than some of the other advocates of the performance approach, but he urges the teacher to coach students by stressing the following:

- observing closely
- analyzing action and effect
- asking strategic questions of actors
- listening carefully to their answers
- trying different ways to perform a scene
- reinforcing performances or challenging them

Students work in small groups to produce these scenes and then interact with their classmates to explore them more deeply.

Manikin Motion.   Brown (1981) suggests a final performance approach, which combines readers' theater and puppet drama. Students are not given time to memorize lines, but they practice reading for meaning and understanding. They use manikins with character labels or crudely defined dolls and move them about on the stage. The complication comes in asking another set of students to position the manikin characters according to their understanding of the lines being read for that character. The manikin movers are then challenged by students in the audience as to why a character looks in a particular direction, moves toward a certain character, or withdraws or moves in any specific way. Actions must be defended and explained.

These exercises build involvement, expand insight, and deepen understanding of this icon of English classrooms. They do not ask that you be a drama teacher to use them, but they do require more risks than do the traditional lecture or discussion of plays. You must be willing to rely on your imagination, your empathy, your invention, and your moving from behind a desk or lectern—in other words, rely on the same arts a dramatist uses. With practice, you will be ready to "take this show on the road" or, at least, confidently into class! Because of Shakespeare's presence in the high school curriculum, we will return to the Bard in Chapter 12, Planning the Lesson.

Invitation to Reflection 3–4

1. Your mentor teacher believes that careful explication of *Romeo and Juliet* is the only way to study Shakespeare in a rigorous fashion. What alternatives could you offer based on your own experience, your reading of this text, and the play itself?
2. How would you justify these alternatives to traditional instruction?
3. Your English department has a file of Shakespearean plays on videotape and strongly recommends your using them when you teach *Macbeth*. You have noticed that viewing whole plays from these dated productions invites students in other classes to sleep. What are alternative approaches that could satisfy the school's tradition of viewing whole plays and allow you to keep your students more active?

Conclusion

We have come quite a distance in this chapter, from taking our words seriously in ordinary classroom discourse to experiencing one of the English language's greatest wordsmiths, William Shakespeare, dramatically. In all five sections, the focus of teaching has remained the same: the student as active word user. The many exercises help students to find their own voices, to use the study of literature and language to release their words and ideas, not to bury them. Britton (1970) has fitting final words to remind us of the importance of bringing active talk into the classroom:

> Perhaps the most important general implication for teaching . . . is to note that anyone who succeeded in outlawing talk in the classroom would have outlawed life for the adolescent; the web of human relations must be spun in school as well as out. (p. 223)

4

RESPONDING TO LITERATURE

"At the center of the curriculum are not the works of literature ... but rather the mind as it meets the book, the response."

Alan Purves and Richard Beach

This chapter moves us from oral language to written text. In many English classrooms, after the roll is called, students settle into their desks and open their texts as predictably as some churchgoers settle into their pews and open their Bibles. *English* equals *literature*. Chapter 6 presents the historic reasons for literature's central position in the high school English classroom. For now, we address a more basic question: What do we have to learn from literature?

WHY READ LITERATURE?

We can begin to find an answer to this question in a common plea of children: "Tell me a story!" Young children, barely able themselves to form words into sentences, wait with eye-sparkling expectation to be told stories. Robert Coles (1989) names this urgent allurement in the title of his book, *The Call of Stories*. People heard and responded to this call long before they had written language to record their tales. Why do very young children and humans throughout history call for a story? To be entertained, to be instructed, to be enchanted, to be informed, to be thrilled, and to be comforted. Yet by the time we see children as adolescents, their zeal for stories has often diminished, sometimes to extinction. Literature holds no allure. Many approach classroom texts with leaden reluctance, as a burden to be borne until the bell rings. They do not read books outside of school. Their adult counterparts, too, more often turn on the television than open a book.

THE DEATH OF LITERATURE

Alvin Kernan reports in *The Death of Literature* (1990) that his university students now assume that they are more likely to find something in the way of truth on their computer screens than on the printed page. Kernan believes that we are presently undergoing a number of cultural shifts that affect reading: economic—in our marketplace economy, publishers no longer underwrite serious writers who don't sell; social—we are an entertainment-driven society in which entertainment is pitched to a mass audience; and technological—we are evolving from a print society to an electronic one. In a 1997 BBC interview, writer Cynthia Ozick lamented the "tyranny of accountants and computers" (Fraser,

1997). Independent booksellers are giving way to large national chains whose displays feature best-selling money earners, not writers like Cynthia Ozick, and whose coffee shops are better staffed than their book aisles. Sven Birkerts (1994) explains Kernan's assumptions about print and electronics: "The book dead-ends us in ourselves, whereas the screen is a sluice into the collective stratum, the place where all facts are known and all lore is encoded" (p. 188).

Some high school English departments are emphasizing practical language arts skills (technical preparatory programs, or School Tech), rather than literature in order to position their students to join this cultural stream. Yagelski (1994) explains that in this age of "inconceivable change," our emphasis on literature in high schools is "irrelevant to the challenges our students now face" (p. 31). He believes that we should remove literature from the center of our English curriculum and, if we must teach it, use it to "help students understand language and language use" (pp. 34–35). Yet by your reading this book aimed at the teaching of English, you give us cause to think that you too must be drawn to books, the traditional subject of English study. We English teachers can safely remain silent about many of our private delights, but the challenges to the English profession at present require us to articulate just why we think reading literature is important. You will need an answer for the question "what can literature teach us?"

THE LIFE OF LITERATURE

Birkerts launches one of the most eloquent answers to this question that we have read. The title of his collection of essays, *The Gutenberg Elegies* (1994), is telling. Birkerts would appear to lament the death of the printed page inaugurated by Johann Gutenberg's movable-type printing press. In fact, he calls us to recognize the loss we individually and collectively would suffer if literature died. He asks, "Is literature offering us less?" and answers "No." He continues, "Is it that what is offered is no longer deemed as vital to our well-being?" and implies "Perhaps" (p. 191): The climate of late modernity may have rendered us less able to appreciate literature's relevance, but literature "remains the unexcelled means of interior exploration and connection-making. . . . So long as there is a natural inclination toward independent self-hood, so long will literature be able to prove the reports of its death exaggerated" (p. 197). Literature is "a way of talking about important and difficult aspects of our universal experience" (p. 191).

Elliot Eisner's book *The Enlightened Eye* (1990) expands our view of what literature can teach, that is, the interior acts it prompts. He explains that literature can help the reader to do the following:

1. *Imagine new worlds.* To envision new possibilities; to create new visions
2. *Become seers.* To look into what we have never seen; to penetrate beyond what language tells; to flash into another domain; to unveil the familiar, or, as Coleridge said, "call to our attention that which we have neglected"
3. *Stabilize the evanescent.* To solidify the internal; to grasp the fleeting; to fasten the slippery thought
4. *Exchange our world with others.* To glimpse another's world and acknowledge that reality; to catch who we are and who we have been; to enlarge our receptive sensibility
5. *Rely on judgment without established criteria or standards.* To judge without received rules or predetermined interpretations
6. *See the universal in the particular.* To see the significance in the slight; to see metaphor's power
7. *Learn to play.* To prompt the spirit of playfulness, nimbleness, and gamesmanship; to refute Ciardi's observation "There is no poetry for the practical man."

Invitation to Reflection 4–1

- Name one piece of literature, long or short, that touched you deeply.
- Would you consider its effect on you, not the text itself, to be worth inviting high school students to experience?
- Does your reasoning match any of Birkerts's or Eisner's reasons for reading literature? Check those that apply.

_____ To explore one's interior life
_____ To make connections
_____ To talk about significant aspects of our universal experience
_____ To imagine new worlds
_____ To become seers

_____ To stabilize the evanescent
_____ To exchange our world with others
_____ To rely on judgment without established criteria or standards
_____ To see the universal in the particular
_____ To learn to play
_____ Your own reasons:

GOALS AND METHODS FOR TEACHING LITERATURE

If you can find your mooring for teaching literature in some of those reasons, you may be ready to consider our *goals for instruction* and our *methods* for meeting them. Alan Purves (1981) surveyed thousands of English teachers to answer this basic question: "What are your goals for teaching literature?" Table 4–1 lists his results for 9th- and 12th-grade teachers (p. 29).

The English teachers surveyed appear essentially to agree on their goals for teaching literature: Student self-understanding is first; critical and analytical skills are second. Yet their answers to a question about how they plan to accomplish those goals reveal significant differences. Teachers were asked to rate each of 17 questions that could be asked about a literary text. Invitation to Reflection 4–2 poses Purves's questions for you.

Invitation to Reflection 4–2

Alan Purves (1981) poses 17 questions that you might ask students about a piece of literature. Rank the importance of each on a 4-point scale from trivial (1) to very important (4).*

_____ 1. What literary devices did you notice in the work?

_____ 2. Is the work symbolic or allegorical? What is its theme?

_____ 3. How would you describe the language of the work?

_____ 4. What happened in the work? Who is narrating it? What is the setting?

_____ 5. How is technique related to what the work says?

_____ 6. What is the structure of the work? How is it organized?

_____ 7. Is the work well written? Does the form support the content? Is it well constructed?

_____ 8. How would you interpret the character of this person? What is the significance of the setting?

_____ 9. Did you find that any of these people are like people you know? Did anything like this ever happen to you?

_____ 10. Do any of the formal devices have any significance? What symbols do you find in the work?

_____ 11. What is the genre of the work? In what literary tradition is it?

_____ 12. Does this work describe the world as it is? Do you find the world like the way it is described in this work?

_____ 13. What is the author teaching us? What is the work criticizing?

_____ 14. What is the tone of the work?

_____ 15. What emotions or feelings does the work arouse in you?

_____ 16. Is this work about serious things? Is it significant literature?

_____ 17. Does the work succeed in getting you involved in its situation? Is it successful in arousing your emotions?

*From A. Purves, *Reading and Literature: American Achievement in International Perspective.* Copyright 1981 by the National Council of Teachers of English. Reprinted with permission.

TABLE 4–1
English teachers' rank order of goals of instruction

Goal	9th Grade	12th Grade
To improve the literary tastes of students	5	6
To teach students the history of their literature	8	8
To acquaint students with their literary and cultural heritage	5	4
To help students understand themselves and the human condition	1	1
To develop students' ability to discuss the variety of literary forms that are around them	7	7
To develop the critical faculties and analytic skills of students	2	2
To develop students' ability to use their language	3	3
To show students the ways by which language affects their response to events	4	5

SOURCE: From A. Purves, *Reading and Literature: American Achievement in International Perspective,* National Council of Teachers of English. Copyright 1981 by the National Council of Teachers of English. Reprinted with permission.

Purves found that teachers were more divided over the questions they would pose than the goals they had set. That division ran along a line that has been drawn and redrawn for decades between questions and classrooms that were text-centered and those that were reader-centered. English teachers have struggled between their sense of responsibility to the text and their responsibility to the students, their responsibility to matters of form and to matters of personal experience. That division is mirrored in a parallel line running between classrooms that are teacher-centered and those that are more student-centered. By joining our profession, you join these issues. In your classroom, will you focus either on exploring the text in all of its historical, biographical, cultural, psychological, thematic, and formal richness or on exploring students' responses to the text in all of the historical, biographical, social, and cultural richness of those students? Will you assume the role of knowledgeable interpreter of the text's riches or as facilitator of student discovery?

This chapter, like others, attempts to bridge these lines and do justice to the claims of text and reader, teacher and student. We present our bridge as

- a four-stage construct for reading literature—how we progress through a text
- innumerable teaching activities pertinent to each of these four stages
- a three-stage cycle for responding to literature in the classroom—how we study classroom texts

FOUR STAGES OF READING LITERATURE

The four Stages of Reading Literature are based on a conception of literature and on principles of personal and cognitive development. Our four-stage construct capitalizes on how people most naturally, effectively, and pleasurably read. Its general movement is from the concrete to the abstract, from the simple to the more complex, from a precritical immersion in the text to a critical perspective on it. In this construct, consideration of a literary work begins in personal response and grows more studied and complex.

As we chart the four stages, each stage builds on the work of the preceding stage and prepares for the next. Students move from their personal responses as readers of texts, to sharing and deepening those responses in the collective understanding of an interpretive community of other readers, to illuminating that understanding through formal analysis, and finally, for some, to synthesizing competing critical perspectives into their own interpretation. In actual practice, the movement is not rigidly sequential, but recursive. The stages overlap. Different readers—some proficient, some less able, some eagerly engaged in literary experience, some hardly able to decipher the words on the page—move at different speeds. The individual reader moves back and forth between response and analysis. Some never arrive at critical matters. Figure 4-1 schematizes these four stages in terms of the reader's purpose, primary task, distance from the text, and types of questions about the text. The figure is not linear nor circular—very much like our classrooms.

READER RESPONSE

All readers bring prior experience and knowledge of life and reading to any text. They are not blank tablets on which texts make unproblematic, predictable, definitive imprints. In the first stage, Reader Response, individual readers are face-to-face with the text. The center of our concern is with the reader's unmediated, felt response to the text. The author's world is not mediated by the intrusions of others—scholars or teachers. The teacher's role at this level is to remove scholarly, historical, critical baggage and to free students for their personal, unencumbered encounters with

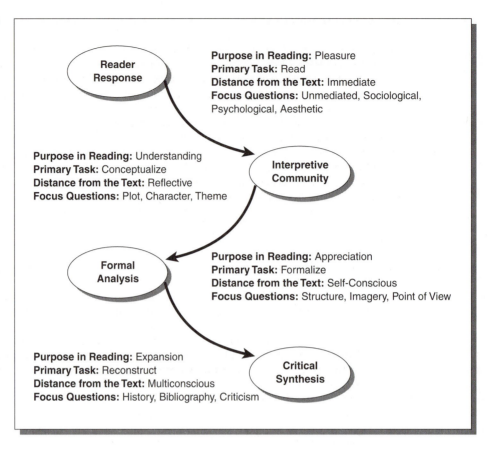

FIGURE 4–1
Four stages of reading literature

the text. Reader Response activities shift ownership for interpretation from teacher to student. They send the message immediately that studying literature is not a matter of a teacher's asking questions about a predetermined interpretation and students' scurrying to find the correct answer. As Rosenblatt stresses, texts—the words on the page—differ from "aesthetic experience"—the reader's "living through" the text by entertaining it, imagining it, and entering its life. The Reader Response stage is important for just this reason: Students must be restored or awakened, not to texts, but to themselves.

INTERPRETIVE COMMUNITY

When students have entered and responded to the world of the story or poem, they are ready to join a community of other readers. The Interpretive Community is Reader Response in chorus. The idea of students discussing ideas together and building on each others' ideas is not new, but the emphasis here remains on students' statements of their own responses and discovery of their own meanings. The chemistry for group work of such potential is delicate and builds over time, and with some students, not at all. But Langer (1995) paints the compelling picture we envision. She is watching a group just beginning to gel:

> After getting to know one another better, the openness, willingness to assume others' perspectives, and willingness to disagree and confront one another increased greatly, but always with sensitivity and support. These are the types of discussions that students should learn to engage in, where they have room to explore topics that touch their lives, to use the text, related literature, and the author's life, as well as one another's and their own. What a preparation for life, if students can learn to interact in a community where their ideas can stimulate new awarenesses and possibilities, and where the reading of literature can assume a profound role in their human as well as cognitive development. (p. 44)

A community of readers—whether they be pairs, small groups, or whole classes—profit from these shared reactions. The individual perspective broadens; new insights are aired; multiple perspectives are entertained; tentative hypotheses are tried. The ideal is that the classroom culture excludes no one, treats individual ideas kindly, accepts dispute, and aims to arrive at meaning together.

FORMAL ANALYSIS

In the third stage, Formal Analysis, students become more self-conscious explorers of the formal dimensions of the text, and they begin to reflect on the author's craft. For too long, literature study meant only an analysis of literary terminology and authorial craft. Thus, we move carefully here. Questions of form should be reached only after the earlier stages of enjoyment, engagement, and conceptualization have commenced. When students are so engaged, questions of literary knowledge, such as conventions and literary terminology, can arise naturally out of students' push to understand texts more fully. If they care about what they are reading, they often realize on their own or with a little prodding that understanding the craft of the author deepens understanding of the text. Students can appreciate literature in deeper, more nuanced, and more enduring ways. Their sense of craft and their observation of it in texts become part of their response to the next texts they read. (Some students may never move to this stage: Their level of abstraction is insufficient, their engagement with the text is too fragile, and their suspicion of literature as irrelevant is too strong.)

CRITICAL SYNTHESIS

Some students are ready to develop their own Critical Synthesis as they consider the text from the viewpoint of two or more schools of literary criticism. Even a simple understanding of historical, biographical, formalist, feminist, archetypal, or Freudian critical perspectives can make students more aware of the total possibilities of the text and the diverse ways in which a work might be understood. The challenge can energize literary discussion and can enable students to trust in their own imaginative responses. Although this stage may appear to be appropriate only for those students who are sophisticated readers, we have found it to be freeing and invigorating to students at all levels. The range of possible approaches to literature gives students a new sense of ownership over their own interpretations.

INSTRUCTIONAL STRATEGIES/TEACHING ACTIVITIES

In this chapter we elaborate on each stage of our construct and present examples of teaching methods that work well at each.* Some teachers work exclusively at one of these stages and some work exclusively at another. We believe that instruction is most comprehensive and effective when it encompasses all four. But the movement through them is not lockstep. In our own classrooms, we move back and forth between them with any given piece of literature, any group of students, any given day, and any moment in the term.

Because we teach literature as well as English education, we use our own book as a reference for teaching ideas that we forget to use in the crush of lesson preparations. The menu of those instructional strategies, presented in Table 4-2, helps us use this book efficiently. Each strategy is listed within one of the four reading stages, but they can move between these stages. We often use three or four in one classroom period. Block schedules beg for even more. We hope that this menu will be one of the most used pages of this book when you become a teacher in search of a change in plans.

READER RESPONSE

We begin with the most personal engagement with literature. The center of our concern is with the reader's unmediated, felt response to the text. Often, students in English classes approach pieces of literature as dry, isolated, academic events, disconnected from real life. We here introduce you to strategies that attempt to reconnect literature and life. They take what Rosenblatt (1978) considered the necessary first step of reading literature: paying close attention to what this particular group of words "stirs up within each reader" (p. 137). We believe that the cumulative effect of literature on the reader becomes progressively more powerful when students are open to making connections between their experiences and the text. The more we can open them to seeing these links, letting literature live actively in their imaginations, the stronger they become both as readers and as people.

---

*Even if you do not consciously adopt this approach, you should find specific strategies and teaching activities to be useful. We illustrate our strategies with a handful of stories frequently read in high school English classes and easily available to our readers. You can enter the exercises more productively if you have read the following: *Raymond's Run* (Toni Cade Bambara), *The Story of an Hour* (Kate Chopin), *A Rose for Emily* (William Faulkner), *The Sky is Gray* (Ernest Gaines), *The Ones Who Walk Away from Omelas* (Ursula K. LeGuin), *I Stand Here Ironing* (Tillie Olsen), *The Cask of Amontillado* (Edgar Allan Poe), *Just Lather, That's All* (Hernando Tellez), and *Harrison Bergeron* (Kurt Vonnegut, Jr.). Although our examples in Chapter 4 are drawn mostly from fiction, our suggestions apply also to poems and plays.

TABLE 4–2 Menu of instructional strategies: Responding to literature

Reader Response	Interpretive Community	Formal Analysis	Critical Synthesis
Personal Triggers	At the Point of Utterance	Teachable Moments	Small-group Questions
Suppositional Readers	Proximate Reading	Unpacking Conventions	Jigsaw Groups
Conceptual Readiness	Communal Judgments	Formal Discussion Questions	Role-Playing
Synergistic Texts	Defining Vignettes	The Questioning Circle	Oral Application
Personal Retrieval	Readers' Theater	Imaging Conventions	Body Sculptures
Associative Recollections	Assaying Characters	Intertextuality	Glossary
Evoked Response	Psychological Profiles	Contemporary Contrasts	Battle of the Book Critics
Dependent Authors	Venn Diagramming	Character Questions	
Imagine This		Students Write	
Polar Appraisals		Authors Speak	
Character Continuum			
Character Maps			
Focal Judgments			
Polar Response			
Verbal Scales			
Interrogative Reading			
Jump-starts			
Title Testing			

Reader Response, as we are defining it here, includes the generally accepted areas of association and emotions. But other kinds of responses are equally legitimate personal responses to the text. Readers, for example, might feel the following:

Emotion	*Response*
A personal association	"This story reminds me of how Uncle Fred treats Aunt Clara."
An instinct about character	"I don't believe she would act that way."
The clarification of an idea	"Yes, that's exactly how one feels."
A reading memory	"This seems like a fairy tale plot."
An aesthetic judgment	"That passage says so beautifully what I have long felt."
Cognitive dissonance	"I do not agree with this character's point of view."
A strong emotion	"I get all tense inside when I see someone treated like that."

Any narrower boundary privileges one kind of response while making pariahs of others. Although this first stage typically aims for students' independent reactions to a text, ones that are not controlled by teachers, we also know that some students need to be urged into response with approaches that are active without being controlling; if they are controlling, they are enemies of Reader Response.

PERSONAL TRIGGERS

These first four strategies are especially designed as beginning points of entry into texts. The basic intent of Personal Triggers is to connect students' personal experiences to the text. The basic strategy is to stir memory; to consider personal attitudes, beliefs, and values; and to revisit experiences or feelings that the text may echo. Many different activities—oral, written, individual, and group—might open these stirrings. We present three examples. The first two ask students to respond in their journals to carefully conceived prompts; the last one polls student opinion with a questionnaire.

Patricia Kelly and Robert Small (1993, personal communication) suggest the following prompt before ninth-graders read *Raymond's Run* by Toni Cade Bambara:

You probably meet new people often in your life—new neighbors, new kids in school, new teachers. When you meet a new person, how do you decide whether you like that person? When do you decide? What makes the difference for you between liking and not liking someone? In your Reader

Response Notebook write about meeting someone you quickly decided you liked a great deal. As you write, try to figure out how and why you decided you liked the person you chose to write about here.

Before Patricia Kelly (1992) has 10th-graders read "Words" by Sylvia Plath, she asks students to reflect in their journals about "a time when words hurt: When was it? What was the situation? Why do you remember it now? What did you learn?" (p. 85). Kelly's prompt can open sensitive subjects, so she protects students' privacy and encourages their honesty by asking them to reflect in the privacy of their journals. Before she reads the poem, she shares her own incident and invites their accounts as well—a constant point of reference in the subsequent discussion.

Mary Jo Schaars (1992) will not let her 11th-grade students "catch a glimpse" of Thoreau's *Walden* before she gives them a questionnaire that raises questions "about materialism, moral commitment, goals, lifestyle" (Schaars, 1992, p. 147). The questionnaire elicits honest self-examination with questions such as the following:

- If you didn't have to worry about making a lot of money what occupation would you choose? Why?
- When, during a routine day, do you find yourself happiest? Most bored?
- Do you believe you have too many, just enough, too few conveniences in your life? Explain, if necessary.

After students have examined their individual positions, the whole class discusses the issues raised before turning to discover how Thoreau might have answered similar questions.

The danger of even the most carefully constructed Personal Trigger activity is that it leads students toward a preconceived and narrow reading of the text. Its virtue is that it engages students and offers them some personal stake in what follows. More generally, it implies that the center of your concern is with the readers and that you expect literature to connect with them and they with literature.

SUPPOSITIONAL READERS

An effective entry into a text is to ask students to speculate about initial bits of information that are evident before they begin to read. With a novel, the job is easy. You can ask students to examine the book's cover, its chapter headings, and its layout and to speculate about what these visuals lead them to expect in their reading. Frequently read classics possess a mystique and oral tradition that you can tap by discussing questions such as "What have you heard about this book? Do you approach it with any prior knowledge or conception?" and "Have you read anything else by this author? What do you remember about that book that you might look for here?" Teaching Activity 4–1 poses questions about a short story, which does not have as many visual or contextual clues as a novel does.

Teaching Activity 4–1   Suppositional Prereading

Test the effectiveness of a Suppositional Readers activity by speculating on the questions as a student would. Do you think such an activity would enhance your connection with the text?

- Consider the story *Harrison Bergeron* by Kurt Vonnegut, Jr.
- Does the title or author's name set up any expectations in your mind? What can you possibly predict from such a small bit of information?
- List your suppositions drawn simply from the title and the author's name.
- If you drew a blank and did not know what to suppose, consider these questions:
  - What does the name in the title suggest? What assumptions do you make about a character named Harrison Bergeron?
  - What is the given name's relationship to the family name? Do they seem to go together?
  - Does his name seem stiff and formal or everyday? What do you make of that?
  - Do you recognize the author's name? Do you know of other fiction he has written? Can you describe a theme or style common to his other stories? Does your memory lead you to expectations for *Harrison Bergeron?*

If these questions prompt an additional reaction to the title and author of the story, add to your original supposition list. Test this list against your reading of Vonnegut's tale. You have very little advance information here, but you may be amazed at what this meager amount will yield.

- Now turn to the first sentence of *Harrison Bergeron* and consider where it might lead the whole text. If the title and author were hooks, the first line is bait: "The year was 2081, and everyone was finally equal."
- List what you suppose about the story from reading the first sentence.

Once again, we have seemingly little to go on, but once again we may know more than we think. Your suppositions will likely be driven by such information as the date, the final word *equal,* the adverb *finally,* the use of the word *everybody,* and larger issues such as the tone set by the language. You might also speculate about where the story is set and how you are supposed to feel about the described state of affairs: everybody being equal. Other features of the first sentence may cause you to speculate in other, more imaginative ways.

Suppositional Readers prompts students to bring to consciousness what normally occurs on an unconscious level, in nonverbal flashes and feelings. It invites students to become active participants with the text, not passive receivers of it. Through speculation about the title and author and then in suppositions about the first sentence, paragraph, and page, students become creative partners in reading the full story.

CONCEPTUAL READINESS

This prereading exercise moves toward the story's conceptual center by examining its main idea in other nonliterary texts. Studies have shown that prior exploration of a concept that is important in a text enriches the reader's response to that text (Hayes & Tierney, 1982). These concepts might appear in a Miss Manners' column or an excerpted news or sports interview, in lines of popular music or in a cartoon or painting. The idea is to draw out and articulate students' personal perceptions and, once primed, to connect them with what is relevant in the literary text. The best connections might not even be verbal, but may appear as echoes or resonances of images and thoughts experienced before.

In teaching *Harrison Bergeron,* we offer a short excerpt from John Stuart Mill's "On Liberty," an essay by conservative writer George F. Will selected from *The Pursuit of Happiness and Other Sobering Thoughts* (New York: Harper & Row, 1978), and John Lennon's song, *Imagine,* to help students focus on the central topic of Vonnegut's story: equality. We ask students to read and then compare these pieces; then we schematize the exercise on the sheet shown in Figure 4-2.

These comparisons can and should drive beyond an abstract discussion of ideas towards personal sharing and reflection on students' own experiences, values, and beliefs (see Venn Diagramming in the Interpretive Community section, pp. 105-106). When students have explored different views of the limits of freedom within democracy, they will be better prepared for *Harrison Bergeron.* Our experience is that the discussions of ideas in such pieces do not diminish the power of the fictive treatment, but open and reveal it more fully. One potential danger is that you will lead students toward conclusions that you have reached and away from a free discovery of their own. Making sure that the surrounding works have different biases, however, helps to avoid this pitfall. Figure 4-3 presents a list of texts and prereading texts that we use to produce this enriching effect.

SYNERGISTIC TEXTS

Clearly, the breadth of students' experiences—literary and otherwise—has a great impact on how they read a literary text. Synergistic Texts pairs texts that challenge each other's basic premises. The teacher uses the natural appeal of contentious positions to engage students and draw out and provoke their opinions. When related or contending texts collide, the act of reading becomes much more forceful and purposive.

Thus, we read *Harrison Bergeron* along with Ursula K. LeGuin's *The Ones Who Walked Away from Omelas.* LeGuin's story looks not at the power of gifted individuals restrained so that the wretched can be equal, but at one individual made wretched so that all others can enjoy pleasure and prosperity. We pair these stories and ask students to keep a basic question in mind as they read them: "How does LeGuin differ from Vonnegut on the question 'How can a society promote the greatest happiness for the greatest number of its people?'" Such a matchup can be created with any pair of stories that focus upon a shared concern. The combined power of both texts will be far greater than the individual impact of one. Figure 4-4 shows other examples of texts that we have successfully brought together.

FIGURE 4–2
Prereading *Harrison Bergeron*

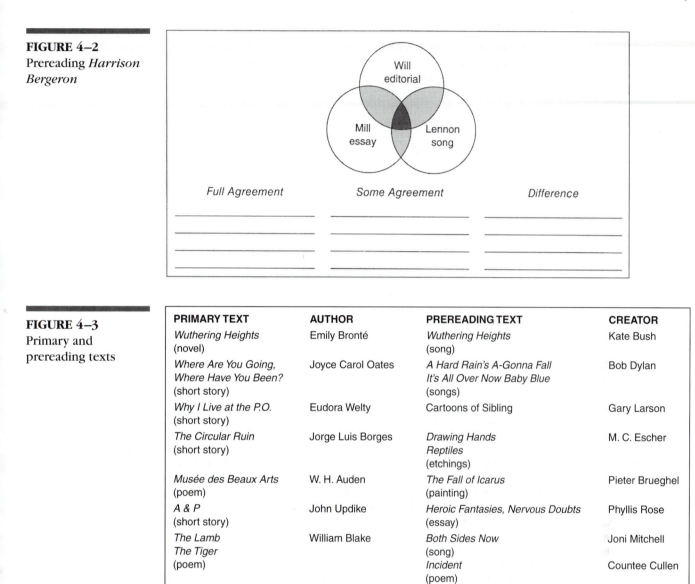

PRIMARY TEXT	AUTHOR	PREREADING TEXT	CREATOR
Wuthering Heights (novel)	Emily Brontë	*Wuthering Heights* (song)	Kate Bush
Where Are You Going, Where Have You Been? (short story)	Joyce Carol Oates	*A Hard Rain's A-Gonna Fall* *It's All Over Now Baby Blue* (songs)	Bob Dylan
Why I Live at the P.O. (short story)	Eudora Welty	Cartoons of Sibling	Gary Larson
The Circular Ruin (short story)	Jorge Luis Borges	*Drawing Hands* *Reptiles* (etchings)	M. C. Escher
Musée des Beaux Arts (poem)	W. H. Auden	*The Fall of Icarus* (painting)	Pieter Brueghel
A & P (short story)	John Updike	*Heroic Fantasies, Nervous Doubts* (essay)	Phyllis Rose
The Lamb *The Tiger* (poem)	William Blake	*Both Sides Now* (song) *Incident* (poem)	Joni Mitchell Countee Cullen

FIGURE 4–3
Primary and prereading texts

TEXT	AUTHOR	GENRE	CONNECTION
Their Eyes Were Watching God	Zora Neale Hurston	Novel	The growth of two heroines toward independence and self-assurance
The Color Purple	Alice Walker	Novel	
Angel Levine	Bernard Malamud	Short Story	The responses of individuals to the appearances of an angel
The Very Old Man with Enormous Wings	Gabriel García Márquez	Short Story	
The Occurrence at Owl Creek Bridge	Ambrose Bierce	Short Story	How individuals face their execution
The Secret Miracle	Jorge Luis Borges	Short Story	
Everyday Use	Alice Walker	Short Story	Struggle in the relationship of men and women
My Man Bovanne	Toni Cade Bambara	Short Story	

FIGURE 4–4
Synergistic texts

PERSONAL RETRIEVAL

In Personal Retrieval, immediately upon finishing a text, students are given the following instructions asking them to describe the story on a small response card: "After you have read the story, write two or three sentences about what you initially think is important about the story. Write as if you are telling someone who has not yet read the story. Do not simply list the story's events—describe what those events mean to you." With this exercise, the author's story in a sense becomes the student's story: The flats and the arches, the holes and the reiterations are the student's own formation. Every rendition is valid; neurons and dendrites fire across different synapses so that, as Donald Graves says about writing, everybody has a story to tell. This is an indirect way of uncovering immediate reactions in students. It opens what Peter Elbow calls "movies of the mind": the moving picture of their reactions, wonders, assumptions, and tentative interpretations. Students are not daunted by an expectation of a collected, finished, literary judgment. They are experts about their own felt responses. We find that limiting students to one small index card encourages succinctness in their writing. It also makes the writing task more inviting and less intimidating.

ASSOCIATIVE RECOLLECTIONS

Bleich (1975) believes that the reader's associations with the text are the "most complex but most useful form of expressing feelings about literature" because they reveal the pattern with which individual readers have organized "perception, affect, associations, [and] relationships" for themselves (p. 48). Associative Recollections prompts students to notice and harvest connections between their former experiences and texts. You might guide students in an exercise in this way:

- As you read, check moments in the story that feel familiar.
- When you complete the story, return to your checkpoints and dwell for a moment on past associations evoked by your recent reading.
- Record the associative recollections prompted by the two most powerful reference points in your journals or in free-writing. Begin each recollection with a phrase such as one of the following:
  This character/event reminds me of . . .
  The words here make me think of . . .
  This part touches a general memory chord, which is . . .
  This event awakens me to . . .
- In a small group, present your perception of the story's two most powerful reference points.
- Consider together such questions as "Do the same incidents touch others?" and "What is the emotional tone and content of the association for them?"
- Use the back of your cards to record any generalizations about your own or the group's recollections.

Appleman (1992) uses a Reader Response diagram to identify and connect the reader's characteristics and the text's qualities. Her directions are to "identify specific characteristics . . . that might affect the particular nature of [your] transaction with the novel." The following schematic borrows from the ideas of Appleman's students, who wrote in response to Judith Guest's *Ordinary People* (pp. 96–97):

Reader's Characteristics	*Ordinary People*
Parents' divorce: "Suddenly the family was ripped apart . . .	Realism: "People seemed like real life."
Relationship with parents: "Don't get along with my mom."	Characteristics of protagonist: "Thoughts were some that I've thought."
Thoughts of suicide: "The fact is I've thought about killing myself."	Setting: "You could relate it to our time."

Appleman explains that "this information helps to bring to the reader's consciousness the values, assumptions, and beliefs brought to the text; it also helps to inform the teacher of the factors that affect these students' responses to the text" (p. 96). Comparing the emotional impact of a story on oneself with its impact on other readers can deepen the reader's individual response and remind the group of the critical impact of former experience on reading a text.

EVOKED RESPONSE

In this activity, audiotaped passages are used as recorders of students' emotional reactions to a text. Here is a possible sequence with which to guide students:

- Read a story silently.
- Select a passage that especially touched you.
- Read the passage aloud into a tape recorder.
- Listen to your taped reading.
- Record on a card any emotion that surfaces in your voice. Use any of the following questions to help clarify what you hear in your personal reading:
  - What tone shifts can you discern in your oral reading of the passage? What do they reflect about your feelings? Are your feelings constant throughout or do they vary?

- Do certain incidents or characters in the passage carry a particularly powerful emotional load for you? How do you respond to these incidents or characters?
- What seems to be emotionally the most intense point in the passage?
- What moments of mixed emotion do you find in the passage? What might be a reason for this ambivalence?
- What is the emotional resolution of the passage (if one exists)?
- What is your most prominent emotional response to the passage as a whole—anger, sorrow, joy, fear, vexation, or amusement? Why?
- Review your cards and consider whether you have written of *feelings* about the text, or whether you have merely *explained* the text.
- Explain your choice of passage and response to a partner. Would you want to expand or alter your own reading after reviewing your explanation?
- Select one word that singularly captures your response.

DEPENDENT AUTHORS

You can promote students' subjective responses to the text through extending, elaborating, or revising the author's original work. Many teachers have realized the penetrating insights of students who imaginatively confront texts rather than analytically explicate them. Peter Adams (1987), who coined the phrase "dependent authorship," explains that one of the most compelling reasons for using this entry into the text is that students "can discover and explore elements of their response to the work that they could not grasp or articulate in any other way" (p. 121). They enlarge character, expand situations that are mentioned or implicit but undeveloped by the text, fill in gaps, and extend conclusions. Consider the following dependent or cocreative writing prompts as opportunities for students to assume the role of authors:

- Write interior monologues in the persona of a chosen character at a particular point in a story.
- Write dialogues between two or more characters.
- Add asides or subliminal thoughts to existing dialogue.
- Write an epilogue to the text.
- Write a continuation of a scene or the whole text.
- Imaginatively reconstruct a gap in the text.
- Write a dream for one of the main characters.
- Add another episode.
- Rewrite the ending.

Such prompts, whether they are completed as individual in-class exercises, homework assignments, or group projects, animate the original author's creation and the present students' insights into character as well. We ask students to imagine and perform the scene between Emily Grierson and Homer Barron on the fateful night in William Faulkner's *A Rose for Emily* when Homer died: "What did they say to one another before Emily made her decision to poison Homer?" Students' minidramas penetrate character and motive with far greater richness, depth, and empathy than their articulated responses to typical analytical questions such as the following, taken from an anthology of fiction:

- Who or what is the antagonist of the story? Why is it significant that Homer Barron is a construction foreman and a northerner?
- Explain how Emily's reasons for murdering Homer are related to her personal history and to the way she handled previous conflict.

Students in pairs, small groups, or whole classes can consider together whether their creative work as cocreators has given shape to aspects of the story that were implicit in it, but not overtly stated by it:

- Does the contemporary addition violate your sense of the characters and situations?
- Does it bring certain elements into clearer focus?
- Does it make you want to readdress certain other elements?
- Did you uncover richer insights than were immediately apparent, but that hover around the story's center, asking to be given form and substance?
- Does the original make it easier to write your additions?
- Does the original grant a richer significance to your work?
- If you departed from each other's sense of the text, where do the discrepancies lie?

Anderson and Rubano (1991) suggest several points to keep in mind while you lead this activity:

- The teacher's introduction to this exercise should stress that the writing must grow from the students' genuine curiosities about the text.

- Before students choose their writing project, they should list all the images they associate with the story. This will call up the significance for students, which will "inevitably find its way into the writing."
- Students should list and share the "writing possibilities that lie within and around the text." Then they choose one of real interest to them.
- Their writing is "not treated as a piece of writing to be revised and polished" (p. 58).

IMAGINE THIS

A first and almost instinctive response to reading a text is to reflect upon the actions, personalities, and motivations of its characters. We cannot believe that Iago can be so vicious with such flimsy cause; conversely, we are perplexed by Hamlet's failure to act on his own deep revulsion to the king. Readers have been puzzled for more than a century about Huck Finn's complicity with Tom Sawyer in harassing Jim at the Phelps's farm. The bond between boy and man, built on their many experiences on the river, make such a breach of Jim's faith almost inexplicable. Such concerns have perennially preoccupied initiates and seasoned readers and have produced both clarifying and tortured interpretations. Booth (1988) believes that books draw us toward answering simple first questions: "What happened?" "Just who are these characters?" "Why do I like or detest them, trust or mistrust them?" and "Who are the good guys and bad guys?"

An initial encounter with characters may occur through imaginative projection: interior monologues, dreams, encounters, dialogues, and dual diary entries. Consider using the following prompts to stimulate students to respond to and probe character:

- Write letters from one character to another in the same book or in different books.
- Keep journal or diary entries in the persona of a character.
- Make decorative suggestions for or bring in magazine pictures of how you imagine the houses and rooms of characters.
- Suggest a character's favorite songs or type of music. Play a selection.
- Write top-ten lists of characters' imagined attitudes, dislikes, and likes.
- Write yearbook entries for characters.
- Write a feature article for the local newspaper about a character.
- Write and deliver a speech in the persona of a character.
- Organize debates or panel discussions between characters on topics germane to the work or totally removed from it.
- Exchange gifts between characters in a text.
- Imagine a character from one book appearing at specific points in another book.
- Have a character visit a psychotherapist for a counseling session.
- Have characters go to family therapy together.
- Put characters on a talk show to discuss their struggles and dreams.
- Have a character apply for a job with a resume, interview, and follow-up letters.
- Write epitaphs for characters.

POLAR APPRAISALS

This exercise draws students into a reaction to characters by juxtaposing opposite characters and character traits and judging between them. You might lead this activity by asking students to do the following:

- Choose two opposing and imposing characters from the story being studied. They should be rounded and illuminate one another when juxtaposed. One you should admire; the other should trouble you.
- Recall three incidents or situations that most clearly show why you chose each character.
- Name two qualities or characteristics reflected in each character's reactions to each event.
- Look over the list of six qualities you have named for each character and narrow those down to what you consider to be the most essential character traits.
- Consider these questions: "Do these qualities of my best character reflect my own ideals or values?" "Which ones do I identify with and which ones do I not?"
- Take the traits of the worst character and describe an opposite for each. Do these opposing values match your sense of yourself?

Students may deepen this probe into character by comparing their lists of characters and qualities with those of other readers. If the same pair has been selected by both students, have them compare and discuss the chosen incidents and the qualities of the characters that they reveal.

CHARACTER CONTINUUM

This exercise clarifies the relationships of characters, one to another, by locating them on different continua. The continua might be a movement from bold to cautious, from good to evil, from just to tyrannical, or any other extremes represented in the work under study. Ask students to place characters' names on a line that represents movement from one extreme to the other. They may place the characters on the continuum without fully articulating what concept the two extremes represent. But having puzzled over which character belongs where, a concept that defines the continuum should begin to emerge. Good-to-bad, of course, can be such a starting point, but good or bad in what specific regard? Have students state a term or concept that guided their character placement.

The following Character Continuum is based on Ernest Gaines's *The Sky Is Gray,* a story with an assortment of strong characters: Mama, James, the Receptionist, the Storeowner, the Student, the Preacher, and the Café Man. This particular continuum is based on sensitivity; thus, James and the Receptionist are placed near the extremes.

Least   The Receptionist   The Preacher   Mama^3 James   Most
Considerate $\longleftarrow$ $\longrightarrow$ Considerate
       The Café Man   Mama^1 Mama^2 The Student   The Storeowner

When a character stubbornly resists being placed in one spot, as Mama does on the sensitivity continuum, assign the character two or three places with notations of 1, 2, and 3 to show the time order of their placement. Examine such characters to see whether they in fact change in their attitude and behavior, or whether we just gradually come to understand them better. Then explore the two most difficult characters to place on the continuum. You can extend this activity by directing students to work with other students as follows:

- In pairs, compare your placement of characters and your naming of the continuum.
- If your organizing concepts are the same, explore any specific differences in your responses to characters.
- If your continua are different, examine differences and similarities. Do you ultimately share the same general concept of character or do you have truly dissimilar views?
- Discuss with the whole class the impact these differences and similarities have on your basic understanding of the story.

Teacher Shelley Hale presents the Character Continuum differently. She asks one student to put a continuum on the board and explain his or her reasoning to the class. This student's opinions then become a springboard for discussion: "Who agrees with this?" "Who disagrees?" "Did anyone put someone else first or last?" Hale reports that everyone becomes involved because everyone has just completed his or her own continuum. She also uses this activity as a marker of student reaction throughout a long text. Students chart several continua as they read. At the end of their reading, students have multiple continua with which they can trace their changing reactions to characters.

CHARACTER MAPS

An even more visually complex way for students to probe characters is to map them according to their relationships with each other. The aim is not to make comparisons so much as to uncover strong relationships between characters and understand how those are webbed together to create a whole story. The maps can be drawn with a simple circle of characters or complex schematics. Figure 4–5 shows one student's Character Map for Alice Childress's *A Hero Ain't Nothin' but a Sandwich.*

Instructions to individual students or small groups might go something like this:

- List all the characters and place each within a circle.
- Connect the most obvious pairs or trios with lines. (Patricia Kelly [1993] uses colored markers to color code the "basic emotional relationships" in *A Doll House.* She asks students to choose the legend, for example, "green for jealousy, red for hatred, blue for love, yellow for distrust, or brown for dependency" [p. 132]).
- After a few such cliques are established, consider possible relationships between cliques so that all of the characters become visually connected in some fashion.
- Label them to characterize the kind of relationships between characters and groups. (If, for example, in *The Sky Is Gray,* the Student and the Preacher are set up in opposition, students need to find a label that represents the grounds of their antipathy. James, Mother, and the Storeowner who serves them lunch may have another relationship, one that may itself have a connection with the Preacher-Student relationship. The trio's relationship needs to be labeled, and the way in which the two sets are related may itself be labeled.)

FIGURE 4–5
Character map

A Hero Ain't Nothin' But a Sandwich

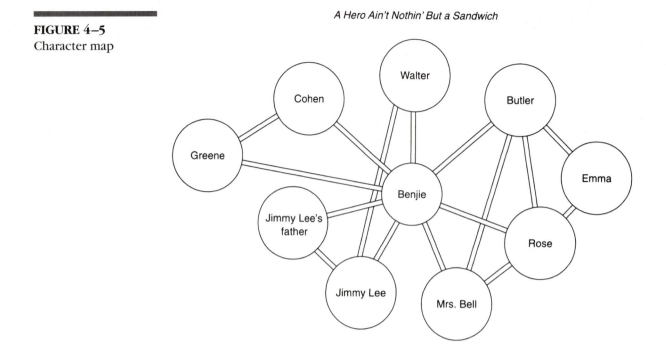

- Share your mapped arrays with the class. How do the different maps agree or disagree in their portrayals of these relationships? Do the diverse ways in which the characters relate to one another shed light on the story?

    Maps can also serve to clarify the reader's relationship to characters. Putting oneself at the center of a character map, a reader can draw lines to different characters and write his or her response to them at different vantage points in the reading of a text: Does the reader feel empathy for, distance from, or anger toward this character? For long works, the accumulation of graphs can prompt readers to reflect on their changed views of characters. Shelley Hale uses Character Maps to move a text even closer to students' selves. After they identify relationship connections, she asks students to talk or write about a relationship in their own lives that is similar to a relationship in the text. This establishes the text's connection with students' lives and gives students an opportunity to be the experts (on their own relationships). She then asks students to trace the progress of these "fellow characters" through the story, consider whether they admire or dislike the relationship's development or outcome, and write about what they would do in their own relationships to emulate or avoid that outcome.

FOCAL JUDGMENTS

In Focal Judgments, we elicit readers' judgments of the text, consciously using commonplace language, rather than literary terms, to prompt untutored responses. We ask readers to make their selection of the most important word, passage, and aspect of the text. Bleich (1975) first introduced us to this strategy to transform subjective reactions into what appear to be objective judgments. Without the paralyzing self-consciousness triggered by a request for literary, aesthetic discrimination, students more easily state their choices and then work from this vantage to explain their reasons. (Granted, the failure to read or to read carefully sometimes also begs to be exposed and explained.) That such judgment is personal clearly implies that no single word is the "correct" answer. What is important is the reader's subjective response and explanation of that response.

Most Important Word.   Selecting the crucial word for an entire work prompts students to think broadly about texts, especially short ones. The exercise might be written or oral; for us it is usually instantaneous in the midst of arriving at understanding.

Most Important Passage.   The focal point of this exercise continues to elicit personal and diverse judgments of a text. Students are asked to do the following:

- Read a story and note several passages of a sentence or two each that capture what you felt to be central to the text.
- Think the story through again and select the single most crucial passage.
- Reduce this passage to a three- or four-word phrase that captures the entire story.
- Compare your phrase with the work's title to see whether the two summon up the same meaning.

Most Important Aspect.   The term *aspect* is left intentionally vague to allow more free play in the reader's mind and so evoke the most natural response. Have students select, distill, and justify their choices.

Shelley Hale sometimes uses a version of Focal Judgments on her literature examinations. She chooses significant passages and asks students to answer five questions about the text:

- Who is speaking and to whom?
- What is the context (when and where does it occur)?
- Why is the passage important?
- How does the passage relate to central ideas or themes in the work?
- What does the passage remind you of in your own life experiences?

POLAR RESPONSE

One of the most effective means we know of engaging students in a text, Polar Response asks students merely to respond to a set of strong, declarative statements. The statements are all related to the text. They can be drawn from general observation, the words of others, or an interpretation of the text. The straightforward nature of the statements appeal to students—they require only a sudden, simple response. But although they invite quick, direct reaction, they can open rich possibilities for exploring because they raise points of uncertainty. They elicit and highlight honest differences of reader opinion. In turn, these differences can catalyze a deeper investigation of the text under study. They can be used at any point in that study. After students state their agreements and disagreements, we sometimes ask whether they think the author would agree with them. This shifts the argument beyond the class and invites students to project and to judge beyond their own points of view. Your directions to students might be as follows:

- Complete the survey.
- Put an X in front of the two statements you found most difficult to answer and write a brief explanation of your ambivalence.
- Review the remaining statements and circle the three about which you feel certain.
- In small discussion groups, explore areas of agreement and disagreement.
- Turn to the two statements that raised most controversy for members of your group and exchange ideas from your written explanations.
- As a whole class, discuss each group's essential agreements and disagreements.

The following statements pose both textual and related issues.

Title: *Ordinary People*
Author: Judith Guest
Teacher: Deborah Appleman (1992)

1. Most answers to problems lie within yourself.
2. Families that look perfect on the outside are not always perfect on the inside.

Title: *Where Are You Going, Where Have You Been?*
Author: Joyce Carol Oates
Teacher: Ed McNeal

1. People like Arnold Friend are prevalent in today's society.
2. Connie is wrong to let things get out of hand.
3. Most people, at first appearance, "judge a book by its cover."
4. Never trust strangers, even if they seem genuinely nice.
5. "Who isn't fascinated by evil?" (Marvin Gaye, 1985)
6. "Experience, which destroys innocence, also leads one back to it." (James Baldwin, 1962)
7. "It [rock music] is *the* youth culture and there is now no other countervailing nourishment for the spirit." (Allan Bloom, 1987)

Title: *The Chocolate War*
Author: Robert Cormier

1. You should always be an individual.
2. You should try to fit in after moving to a new place.
3. Small decisions can often greatly change your life.

VERBAL SCALES

A more nuanced kind of Polar Response asks students to rate the strength of their agreement or dis-agreement on a 5-4-3-2-1 (Likert-type) scale. Anderson and Rubano (1991) suggest using such a semantic differential or verbal scale throughout the reading of a text. For instance, they ask students to register their feelings after every stanza of Edwin Arlington Robinson's poem "Richard Cory" (pp. 31–32):

How do you feel toward Richard Cory?

Like	1	2	3	4	5	Dislike				
Admire	0	1	2	3	4	5	6	7	8	9	10

Anderson and Rubano observe that the scale not only elicits and clarifies an initial response, but also makes the final stanza's "turn" more obvious for students. They use such scales for longer works as well, for instance, charting Hamlet's psychological state on a sane-insane scale or the symbolic geography of Huck's journey downriver on a civilized-uncivilized scale. A final example that they use for Zora Neale Hurston's *Their Eyes Were Watching God* shows two ways to pose such questions to sharpen the reader's understanding of a central aspect of the story: Janie's "developing self-awareness and self-direction." Anderson and Rubano pose such scales repeatedly at particularly important points in the narrative (p. 33):

1

Who decides what Janie will do at this point in the story? (If it was completely the choice of the other person, circle 1; if it was completely Janie's choice, circle 7. Circling 4 means you think it was equally Janie's and the other person's choice.)

Other   1 2 3 4 5 6 7   Janie

2

At this point in the narrative, is Janie an active participant in the decision making, or a passive follower of the wishes of others?

Active   1 2 3 4 5 6 7   Passive

INTERROGATIVE READING

Since ancient times, philosophers have told us that education is not so much measured by the an-swers one receives as by the questions one raises. They have told us to question the answers rather than merely answer the questions. Many teachers affirm the advantage for themselves and their stu-dents of reading literature with pens or highlighters in hand, approaching the text interrogatively with questions to share with students. Research findings have confirmed this wisdom. Studies have shown that students instructed to answer questions about texts were not nearly so conversant with the text as those who were asked to develop their own questions (Palinscar & Brown, 1984). Furthermore, Christianbury (1994) reminds us of how using student-constructed questions for whole-class discussions, tests, and quizzes empowers students to "take charge of their learning" (p. 216).

To engender questions from students, we give them the following directions:

- Read a short work to get a total sense of it.
- Reread it, noting where interpretive uncertainty lies, where richness of insight leaps out, where startling connections are developed, or where sharp questions emerge.*

---

*Most public school districts rely on school-owned textbooks, and writing in them, even in pencil, is prohibited. An alternative is to have students write on separate sheets of paper or Post-it notes, noting their responses by page and line numbers.

- Look over the work a third time, searching these checkpoints. Were your questions resolved by the end? Do some puzzles still remain? Write phrases beside the checkpoints that you can later convert into full questions.
- Formulate questions from personal curiosity, perplexity, uncertainty, or from new discoveries and associations—in other words, from points in the story where insights are emerging but doubts remain.
- When you have written out several questions, pair up with a partner and select which queries to pose to the whole class. These questions can guide you:
  - Which of your partner's questions converge with your questions?
  - Do your partner's questions lead you to any ideas that you had not considered?
  - Do they deepen your insight into the work?
  - Do your individual questions follow any particular pattern, such as clarifying details of setting, character, or situation? Puzzling over language? Interpreting meaning?
- Revise your own questions based on the discussion.
- Share your best questions with the whole class.
- Consider the following: "Were many questions the same?" "Has question asking revealed insights that were not present before?" "Have you generated still more uncertainties about the work?"

JUMP STARTS

Myers (1988) has devised 20 reader response questions that invite students to react personally to texts. She constantly revises the questions to sharpen her attempts to elicit the students' "perceptions, feelings, and associations which result from the work" (p. 65). These questions are based on the text, but they give students room to expand their ideas. They involve students with the text so that students can't just angle to guess the teacher's opinion. These questions could be used as prompts for individual journal writing or free-writing, or as stimulants for whole-class or small-group discussions:

1. What character(s) was your favorite? Why?
2. What character(s) did you dislike? Why?
3. Does anyone in this work remind you of anyone you know? Explain.
4. Are you like any character in this work? Explain.
5. If you could be any character in this work, who would you be? Explain.
6. What quality(ies) of which character strikes you as a good characteristic to develop within yourself over the years? Why? How does the character demonstrate this quality?
7. Overall, what kind of a feeling did you have after reading a few paragraphs of this work? Midway? After finishing the work?
8. Do any incidents, ideas, or actions in this work remind you of your own life or something that happened to you? Explain.
9. Do you like this piece of work? Why or why not?
10. Are there any parts of this work that were confusing to you? Which parts? Why do you think you got confused?
11. Do you feel there is an opinion expressed by the author through this work? What is it? How do you know this? Do you agree? Why or why not?
12. Do you think the title of this work is appropriate? Is it significant? Explain. What do you think the title means?
13. Would you change the ending of this story in any way? Tell your ending. Why would you change it?
14. What kind of person do you feel the author is? What makes you feel this way?
15. How did this work make you feel? Explain.
16. Do you share any of the feelings of the characters in this work? Explain.
17. Sometimes works leave you with a feeling that there is more to tell. Did this work do this? What do you think might happen?
18. Would you like to read something else by this author? Why or why not?
19. What do you feel is the most important word, phrase, passage, or paragraph in this work? Explain why it is important.
20. If you were an English teacher, would you want to share this work with your students? Why or why not? (p. 65)

TITLE TESTING

As we walk through art galleries, whether we are looking at the works of vaguely familiar old masters or unknown modernists, our irresistible impulse is to check a work's creator and title. The artist's name sometimes sets the particular work within a context of biography, history, or artistic style. But the title has far more impact. It can re-form what we see; it directs our thinking and suggests a context that influences and even defines our sense of the work of art. With written texts, we are a little less aware of that telling effect because we always see the title before we read the whole text, and, for many of us, the words of the text are more leading than the line and color of a painting. But when we are stuck by or want better illumination of a text, the title is a natural place to focus our attention. We earlier discussed an exercise that asks students to speculate about the title *before* they read a text. Speculating about the title is an excellent strategy *after* reading as well. We often ask "What light is thrown on this piece by its title?" Teaching Activity 4-2 is a more extended consideration of the title of Raymond Carver's provocative short story about two young couples, "Neighbors."

Teaching Activity 4–2   *Title Testing Whole-class Discussion*

- After you have read Raymond Carver's *Neighbors,* think about Carver's title with as much mental playfulness, creativity, and speculation as possible.
- Write the word *neighbors* in the center of a circle and graph as many diverse connotations, suggestions, allusions, connections, and associations as you can. Figure 4-6 is an example of such a map.
- Consider: Which word best matches your speculation about the story? Do others work to enrich your understanding of the story?
- Invent story titles that you feel are better, more creative foci for the tale, such as *Invaders, Love Thy Neighbor,* or *Imagine.*
- Review the class suggestions and list several that seem to make good substitutes. Examine the power of the various titles to explain, compress, and focus the meaning of Carver's text. As a class, decide whether their effectiveness is greater or lesser than Carver's title.

or

- Create a short title of an editorial or philosophical essay that Carver might have written had he chosen nonfiction rather than fiction to capture his vision. Three suggestions, for instance, might be "Modern Decadence," "Homeowner's Insurance," and "Good Fences Make Good Neighbors."

Another provocative use of titles is to explain a title's history and to compare the effects of the final and earlier versions. For instance, Raymond Carver's working title for the brief short story *Popular Mechanics* was *Mine.* Ibsen entitled his play *A Doll House,* but contemporary productions call it *A Doll's House.* What is the difference between the two? What new light is shed by your comparison? Which do you prefer?

Flynn (1986) describes three approaches to reading a text: dominant, submissive, and interactive. A dominant reading is detached and resists involvement; a submissive reading is involved and resists detachment; an interactive reading has the capacity to be both involved and detached, and it is a way

FIGURE 4–6
Title Testing idea map

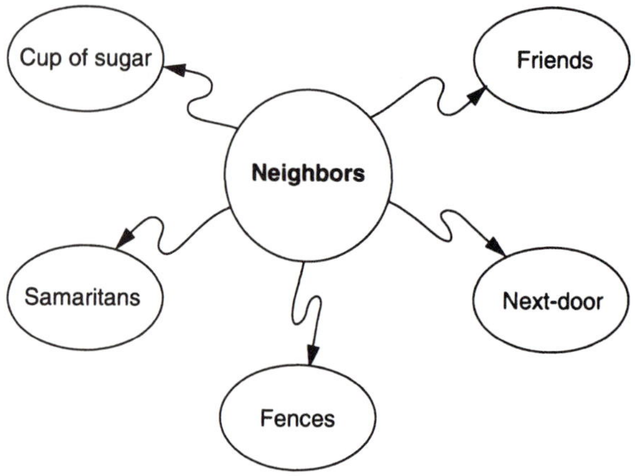

to a meaningful interaction with the text (pp. 267-271). We have designed each approach and teaching activity of Reader Response so that students might become interactive readers. The next step is to build on this individual involvement and response and enrich it by the shared work of a whole class community. We invite students into a collaborative kind of learning.

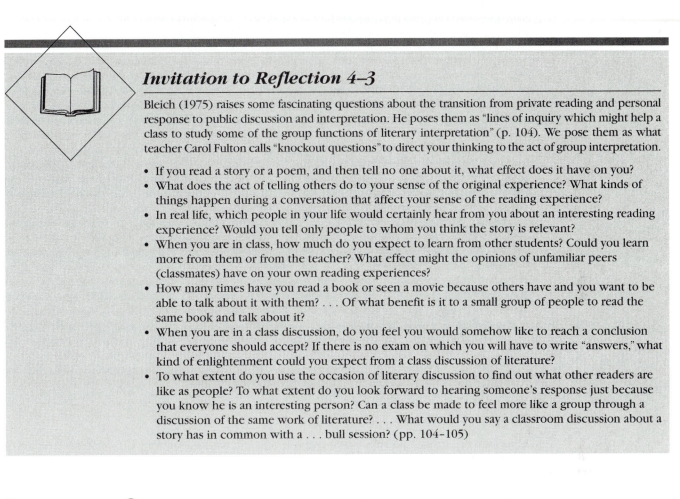

Invitation to Reflection 4–3

Bleich (1975) raises some fascinating questions about the transition from private reading and personal response to public discussion and interpretation. He poses them as "lines of inquiry which might help a class to study some of the group functions of literary interpretation" (p. 104). We pose them as what teacher Carol Fulton calls "knockout questions" to direct your thinking to the act of group interpretation.

- If you read a story or a poem, and then tell no one about it, what effect does it have on you?
- What does the act of telling others do to your sense of the original experience? What kinds of things happen during a conversation that affect your sense of the reading experience?
- In real life, which people in your life would certainly hear from you about an interesting reading experience? Would you tell only people to whom you think the story is relevant?
- When you are in class, how much do you expect to learn from other students? Could you learn more from them or from the teacher? What effect might the opinions of unfamiliar peers (classmates) have on your own reading experiences?
- How many times have you read a book or seen a movie because others have and you want to be able to talk about it with them? . . . Of what benefit is it to a small group of people to read the same book and talk about it?
- When you are in a class discussion, do you feel you would somehow like to reach a conclusion that everyone should accept? If there is no exam on which you will have to write "answers," what kind of enlightenment could you expect from a class discussion of literature?
- To what extent do you use the occasion of literary discussion to find out what other readers are like as people? To what extent do you look forward to hearing someone's response just because you know he is an interesting person? Can a class be made to feel more like a group through a discussion of the same work of literature? . . . What would you say a classroom discussion about a story has in common with a . . . bull session? (pp. 104-105)

INTERPRETIVE COMMUNITY

Classroom discussions of literature often appear to students to bludgeon texts into insensibility. For these students, it is murder to dissect literature. Here we turn to alternative ways for students to talk collectively about literature. In this stage of reading, students shape their personal responses to the text into interpretation through work within an Interpretative Community.* Reader Response was designed to prompt personal contact with the text and to prepare readers to take their responses into a larger community to be tested and sharpened. When students begin that communal sharing, the multiplicity of interpretations widens individual perspectives and unseats the idea that any one reading is the definitive reading. At this stage, students move to the company of others to explore their individual reactions, air their group differences, negotiate alternative perspectives, and enlarge their stakes in the text. Interpretive Community clarifies their visions, strengthens their confidence in their personal ability to respond to literature, and kindles their respect for others to do likewise. Bleich believes that "each reader's responses . . . will take on full significance only when they are brought together and tested against one another in a communal setting."

---

*Interpretive Community is a concept used differently by a number of different people (Bleich, 1975; Fish, 1980; Scholes, 1985). Fish uses the term to mean a set of attitudes or conventions shared by a particular community that influences or dominates the interpretive acts of any of its members. Meaning is shaped or determined for individuals by those dominant beliefs and practices of the reading community to which they belong. We use the term in this book more broadly to mean a formal or informal gathering of students in which each student's personal responses are elaborated, informed, and enlarged by interaction with others.

AT THE POINT OF UTTERANCE

Even before you invite student readers to bring their personal responses to the Interpretative Community, a helpful way to encourage inexperienced readers is for you, as the most experienced reader, to respond to a work with which *you* are unfamiliar. Students can be asked to make the selection. We have found that something short enough for a quick in-class reading works best. You can read the story or poem slowly, offering at natural breaks in the text partial responses: questions, puzzlements, predictions, and hypotheses. At these points, you should invite students to add their responses, feelings as well as interpretations, in an attempt to fill gaps, refine small points, and even offer radically different readings. In other words, you invite them into your own interpretive exploration without the usual teacher's resources of textbook manuals, critical reviews, university course notes, and years of reflection. Such an experience allows less sophisticated readers to see that even a very experienced reader must struggle with a text to begin to forge an understanding that is coherent, comprehensive, and satisfying. Iser (1980) delineates this internal process, not as smooth and continuous, but as one in which we readers "look forward, we look back, we decide, we change our decisions, we form expectations, we are shocked by their nonfulfillment, we question, we muse, we accept, we reject" (p. 62). At the conclusion, students can be invited to join the exploration. You may all agree that, although admirable, the reading was incomplete and the piece deserves further reflection.

This exercise has several effects. It demythologizes the notion that some people, namely teachers, have special interpretive gifts (almost genetic endowments) that most students can never match. It delivers a vital message to students to trust their intuitive responses. It may suggest too that the most satisfying and penetrating readings begin with individual subjective responses that are tempered by reflection and by the activity of the entire reading community. More than anything else, your students should get the message that the class cannot passively wait for the teacher to deliver the proper response to the text. Every member of the Interpretive Community—small groups or the whole class—is vital to the work of interpreting texts.

Students can profit from being invited into the activity you have just modeled: saying their responses aloud as they read a text. Arnold (1987) suggests a variation, "subtexting," in which students, in small groups or pairs, read a few lines of a play, pause, assume the character whose lines they are reading, and articulate that character's thoughts and feelings about the situation at hand.

PROXIMATE READING

In this activity, short, student-selected excerpts of a text are used to bring the subjective reading of individual students into the Interpretive Community. Students are given the following instructions:

- Select two important short passages from the text: the one that you consider to be the most important passage and one that foreshadows it.
- Write on a card the first one or two lines of each passage and the number of the page and line on which it begins and ends.
- Your teacher will collect all the cards, number them according to their proper order in the story, and redistribute them, two for each class member.
- Read your two passages aloud sequentially so that all cards taken together will form an approximate reading of the whole text.

In this last step, passages will likely be repeated and great gaps will appear, but those will both inform you of the power points in the text and offer another chance for the immediacy of the text to reach every reader. This exercise has some of the same effects as abbreviated ads that appear on television as fragments of longer ones: The full ad enters your mind even though you only see a partial showing of it. After the communal reading of the text, ask students to consider the following questions:

- What was the cumulative effect of the proximate reading of the text?
- What was the most important segment of the text for the community of readers?
- Why did so many select it?
- Were there any individual responses that diverged greatly from those of the majority of readers?
- What were other students' reasons for selecting other passages?
- Did other students choose the same or similar foreshadowing passages as you did?
- Did your general understanding of the text improve with this exercise?
- Did you find obvious differences in interpretation arising from the variety of the selected passages? If so, what were they?

Reconstructing the text in this manner and reviewing it with the help of such questions initiates talk about the text that opens it to the Interpretative Community and helps students open themselves to it as well.

COMMUNAL JUDGMENTS

In the Reader Response exercises, we suggested selection of the most important word, passage, and aspect to help individual readers focus and clarify their responses. In Focal Judgments, their choosing evolved naturally into communal discussions. Here we suggest questions that bring individual selections of the most important words, passages, and aspects into a fuller group consideration.

Most Important Word.
- Do your individual choices bunch together? Or are they spaced throughout the text?
- Are they attached to certain characters?
- Are they associated with special events?
- Can lines be drawn to suggest connections between the three or four most often selected words? What would these connections mean?
- Are they connected with the title? Like the title, do the selected words shed new light on the whole piece?
- Do we differ in our interpretations of the text?

We have found the following criteria useful in sorting out the strength of word selections. Use them to evaluate your group's choices.

strength of rationale
connection to important points of reference
versatility: explanatory power
comprehensiveness: breadth of understanding
ambiguity; multiplicity of meaning
appropriateness of tone

Most Important Passage.
- What passages are selected repeatedly?
- What gives those passages their import, their significance?
- Do the different selections suggest diverse readings?

Most Important Aspect.
The choice of most important aspect is difficult because the term *aspect* is not clearly defined. This very vagueness, uncomfortable for the teacher to wait out, often produces a great variety of responses. After students have chosen and before the group reviews the selections, discuss the following terms to see if any of them approximates what guided students' selections. The question is "What term feels closest to your definition of *aspect?*"

Theme	Setting
Situation	Character
Tone	Plot
Structure	Style

The following questions might guide discussion:

- Does the aspect comprise something central in the story?
- Do any of the aspects chosen suggest contradictory understandings of the story?

After the first time or two you use this activity to clarify and explore diverse responses, the class should begin to respond with an energizing sense of a variety of aspects. This exercise moves naturally into a discussion of formal issues.

DEFINING VIGNETTES

Bleich (1975) and Holland (1975) embrace the idea that literature sets in motion differing interior responses in the reader and that we should capitalize on those idiosyncratic readings. Defining Vignettes joins individual response to a group purpose. Students distill the essence of a longer text into a short, compact vignette. Teaching Activity 4-3 leads students from individual reading of a work, to imagining a crucial scene from it, to a final performance of that short scene.

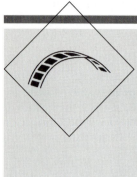

Teaching Activity 4–3   Defining Vignettes

Individual Work
- If you were filming this work, what four pictures or vignettes would you choose to capture the essential story?

Group Work
- As a group, study the individual selections and choose four vignettes to be the group's total sequence.
- In pairs, choose a vignette and develop a dramatic transformation of it, creating both dialogue and any narrator commentary needed.
- Reassemble as a group and appoint a script editor, a director, a prop manager, and a cast of characters to present the total sequence to the Interpretative Community.

Whole-class Work
- React to the variety of vignettes and the interpretations each seems to represent. If the work is one that has already been filmed (Flannery O'Connor's *The Displaced Person,* Ernest Gaines's *The Sky is Gray,* or James Joyce's *The Dead,* for instance), showing the professional version in class would allow students to compare their interpretation with another's.

READERS' THEATER

This activity approaches a text through performance rather than discussion. Patricia Kelly (1992) makes a strong case for class dramatization of poems or prose and dramatic passages as "a way into meaning." Here is how she set up her lesson in a 10th grade class whose students had enjoyed creative dramatics activities but were not experienced in Readers' Theater:

- In groups, prepare to "perform" selected sentences in order to project specified moods and emotions. (Five minutes.)
- As a whole class, guess the feeling being conveyed. (This exercise let groups cohere, performers grow less self-conscious, and the class grow accustomed to conveying "with the voice an interpreted meaning to an audience.")
- In groups, prepare a performance of a poem (in Kelly's case, Sylvia Plath's *Words*), namely, "wrestle with the meaning of the poem and how [you] might present that meaning to an audience." (Each group reads the same poem.)
- As a whole class, enjoy the Readers' Theater performance of each group.
- As a whole class, discuss the "readings." Consider: Why did you decide to present the poem as you did? (pp. 88–89)

This follow-up discussion was crucial. Kelly describes its impact:

> These whole-class discussions following Readers Theater presentations broaden students' understanding of the literary work because they hear the thinking that underlies different interpretations. The discussions are not a "reporting" of the group activity; neither are they like a class discussion of the poem. And therein lies their benefit. They are similar to an "expert" group approach because each group is an expert on its presentation, but the motivation is somewhat different. Each group wants the others, who have appreciated its rendering of the literary piece, to understand the uniqueness of its interpretation. Although they are teaching each other as "expert" groups do, students do not perceive the discussion in that way; they see it as an informal sharing. (pp. 89–90)

Several other benefits grew from this Readers' Theater: Less academic students could shine, both in their performances and in their "expert" perspectives on them; and students read the poem many times more than they would have in traditional discussions as they tried to understand its meaning, prepare their performances, perform, listen to other performances, and discuss! They may not have addressed some difficult images or lines, but they seem to have understood it "in a holistic way," a "sensing, emotional approach rather than an explicative one" (Kelly, 1992, p. 90).

ASSAYING CHARACTERS

Perhaps our most compelling entry into literature is to treat it as lived life. The best way to help students assess, or assay, characters is to have them treat these characters like family members, next-door neighbors, classmates, or other people they know. Many of the strategies already suggested invite students to entertain others imaginatively. Another strategy presents checklists of character traits and asks students to connect the attributes with a character. The most successful exercises are based on checklists devised for the specific pieces of literature that the class is reading. Your checklist might articulate traits that students could not themselves express and yet trigger recognition. The possible points of connection between character and descriptor are numerous:

- distinguishing personality traits of the character
- crucial, tragic flaws
- contrasting traits between characters
- strengths or weaknesses of character
- needful traits that are absent

Questions also prompt students to uncover the human mysteries of motivation, personality, and interaction. Direct questions can open students to perceive characters as real people, whether such questions are posed to individual students or to the entire Interpretive Community, and whether they are used as discussion or writing prompts.

Understanding the Central Person

1. What seems to drive this person to action?
2. What incidents tell us most about this person?
3. What acts affect your feelings about this person?
4. What are some basic character traits of this person?
5. What is the greatest weakness of this person?
6. How does this person relate to other people?
7. What is special or important about this person's moral or religious life?
8. How does this person change or mature?
9. What personal insights enlighten this person?
10. What question would you like to pose to this character?
11. Would you be friends with this person?
12. Does he or she share any values with you?
13. Would you enjoy spending an evening together? Where would you go?

Exploring the World of Characters

1. What other characters draw your special attention?
2. What do they tell us about the central figure?
3. What special relationships are formed by these less central people?
4. What groups of people are associated in your mind?
5. Do some of these people or groups represent values or ideas beyond themselves?
6. Do any characters provoke your distaste or disdain? Which ones?
7. Which character is most mysterious and hard to understand?
8. Which character could be most easily left out of this fictive world?
9. Do any of these other people seem to grow or change in the course of the story?
10. Does any character you don't know well play an important role?
11. Would you want to spend a Saturday or Sunday with any of them?

Imagining Characters in Our World

1. What serious matters could you talk about with this person?
2. What important values would you disagree about?
3. What would your parents think about this character?
4. What in our world would shock this character most?
5. What would make anyone know that this character doesn't fit in our world?
6. What social causes would this person support? To what charities would this person contribute?
7. What television program would be most appealing to this person?

Two final questions to ask of any discussion of characters might include the following:

- Have we done justice to the complexity of this person in the text?
- Has the text done justice to the world we know outside the text, that is, is the character believable?

Teaching Activity 4–4 was created by Patricia Kelly and Robert Small (1993, personal communication); it continues the class consideration of *Raymond's Run* begun as an individual prereading activity (see Personal Triggers in the Reader Response section of this chapter, pp. 86–87). It provides a visual assay of character.

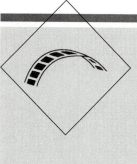

Teaching Activity 4–4   Assaying Character

By the end of the story you may have formed different impressions about Gretchen, Raymond, and Hazel from those you had at the beginning.

- Form groups of four.
- Your group should make three character sheets by writing each character's name at the top of a separate sheet of paper. Then draw a vertical line down the center of each of the three pages. Label one side "First Impressions" and the other side "Last Impressions."
- With members of your group, list all the things you know or feel about each of the characters at the beginning of the story and then your views of them at the end. Consult the story for specifics.
- For the whole-class sharing, have your group's "reporter" tell the other groups in turn an idea from your group's list of "First Impressions of Gretchen." If you hear good points offered by the other groups that are not on your group's list, add them. No information should be given twice.
- When all first impressions have been offered, begin telling ideas from your group's list of "Last Impressions of Gretchen" and add to your list in the same way. Follow the same procedure for the other two characters.
- Look at the class lists. Compare the first and last impressions of each character. Which character seemed to change most? Why do you think your perception changed?

PSYCHOLOGICAL PROFILES

One of the deepest appeals of fiction has always been, as Allen (1963) states, the opportunity it offers of knowing characters "with a far greater intimacy than we can ever know actual human beings," many of them becoming "more 'real' to us, more comprehensible, than all but one or two of all the living people we know personally" (p. 12).

Where readers want to probe further into character, the study of human behavior becomes useful. We have found the work of developmental psychology especially helpful for deepening insights into literature. Theorists such as Erik Erikson, Jane Loevinger, and Lawrence Kohlberg chart the stages in a whole human life cycle along dimensions of personality, ego development, and morality. Their constructs possess significant explanatory power in themselves, but they also present abundant means by which to understand fictional characters—their natures and their actions. Appendix A outlines three prominent psychological constructs: Erikson's stages of psychosocial development, Kohlberg's stages of moral development, and Loevinger's stages of ego development.

Erikson.   Erikson's psychosocial stages can help students comprehend a character such as Huck Finn, who seeks his identity in his river journey with Jim. Equally well defined is Laura in *The Glass Menagerie,* who is caught in the tension between a sensitive, intimate connection and a life in safe isolation. When students read Sophocles's *Antigone,* they can see characters who are in the midst of each of Erikson's focal crises of development. We ask students to consider individual or paired characters from literature in terms of their places on Erikson's life continuum and to place each of the characters at the proper stage in Erikson's hierarchy. Students consider whether each character has resolved the developmental stage well or poorly and explore the factors that influenced this resolution.

Kohlberg.   Kohlberg's theory of moral development provides students with another, perhaps even more helpful, means of understanding human behavior in fiction. Characters can be ranged along a clear moral continuum and are not limited by age in their progress; any character can reside at any stage of moral growth. Students can see Huck Finn inching toward Jim's higher level of moral reasoning when he is with him on the river, but they also watch him fall back when he takes on Tom's name and gets involved with Tom in abusive, lower-level actions at the Phelps's farm. If your students look again at *Antigone* in light of Kohlberg's stages, they might better understand and clarify Antigone's, Creon's, Ismene's, and Haemon's conflicts and choices. Teaching Activity 4–5 solicits students' reactions to moral questions posed by Hernando Tellez's *Just Lather, That's All,* the story of a revolutionary who tests the political position and will of a barber by extending his neck to the barber for a shave. Approaching the story in terms of Kohlberg's moral dimensions yields productive discussions of both the story and its ethical dimensions.

Loevinger. Loevinger enumerates six possible stages in the quest for identity formation (one of Erickson's stages): impulsive, self-protective, conformist, conscientious, autonomous, and integrated. Because one's development might be arrested at any of these six, they become resolutions as well as descriptions of personality. Adolescents struggle on just these grounds of self-definition and ego solidification; thus, Loevinger's concepts provide a compelling context through which they can explore young, middle-aged, and older characters as well as themselves.

Teaching Activity 4–5   Moral Choices

Read *Just Lather, That's All*. Decide what action the barber should take. Then select the amount of importance the barber should attach to each of the questions that follow when he is deciding what to do.

_____ He should kill him. _____ I'm not sure. _____ He should not kill him.

Importance: Great   Some   Little   No

_____ 1. Will I lose my effectiveness as a spy if I kill the lieutenant?

_____ 2. Can I get out of town before the murder is discovered?

_____ 3. Is it right to continue killing people to assert my political beliefs?

_____ 4. Is the lieutenant really planning to torture the newly captured prisoners?

_____ 5. Do I have any legal right to commit such a crime in the event of a U.N. settlement of the war?

_____ 6. Will the townspeople think me a coward if I fail to kill the lieutenant?

_____ 7. Are ideals ever worth killing for?

_____ 8. Should other, more well-trained guerrillas be asked to take on this difficult task?

_____ 9. Will my barber's shaving blade really kill the lieutenant?

_____ 10. Is the life of a grisly killer worth as much as that of any good man?

_____ 11. Whose army is most likely to be ultimately victorious?

From the list of considerations, select the four most important. Which stage of Kohlberg's moral development hierarchy does each represent?

Venn Diagramming

Neuropsychology has much to tell us about the brain's ways of processing reality. One insight pertinent to our work here is that the asymmetrical brain tends to process in two basic ways. At times it moves in; it focuses carefully upon one instance or event. At other times it stands back; its perceptual activity sprawls to include an entire field. In the study of literature, we might call the mind's work of focusing *analysis,* and its more distant viewing *synthesis.* If we want students to use all of their neurological potential in encountering texts, distant synthesis is needed as well as focused analysis.

Much of a student's experience in school focuses on reading one text at a time. Teachers may place that text in a historical context, set it among pieces of the same genre, or even treat it as a part of a thematic unit, but students typically analyze only one particular text, then move on to the next. Venn Diagramming, an approach from logic, uses the visual clarity of overlapping circles to compare and contrast texts, characters, events, or ideas within texts. Figure 4–7 is a model Venn diagram. When texts or elements within texts are charted in this visual way, their differences (white) and similarities (gray and black) become more apparent.

Instructions for a Venn Diagramming exercise might be as follows:

• Read Ursula K. LeGuin's *The Ones Who Walked Away from Omelas,* Hernando Tellez's *Just Lather, That's All,* and Kurt Vonnegut, Jr.'s *Harrison Bergeron.*
• Draw three overlapping circles. In the central portion (X), list issues with which all three writers are concerned. Do the same, in A, B, C, for the issues common to pairs of stories.

FIGURE 4–7
Venn diagram

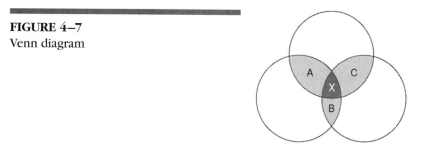

- Discuss: Are the issues of the individual stories made stronger by considering them together? Are issues of difference heightened?

The activities of the Interpretive Community present ideas about reading literature collectively in a classroom. They promote different angles of vision and attempt to free students from their routine ways of looking at a story. Crosman (1982) describes what happens in the communal enterprise: "We go on learning, after we have read a text, by sharing our interpretation with others, and by letting their interpretations enrich our own" (p. 214). If we enter into dialogue with others after our personal encounter, the text becomes richer, deeper, and larger. The Interpretive Community thus becomes a resource not only of ideas, but also of the processes by which ideas are formed and shaped.

FORMAL ANALYSIS

John Barth, comparing sex and storytelling, once said, "technique is not all there is, it's just all that we can talk about." We have seen in the first two sections of this chapter that we can talk of more than technique in talking about literature. In fact, students' journeys into literature could end at this point, midway through our four reading stages, and they would have touched the essential humanity of the fictive world. But Rosenblatt (1968) reminds us that "the literary work is not primarily a document in the history of language or society. . . . As a work of art, it offers a special kind of experience" (p. 278). That experience is rich with personal meaning, but with formal meaning as well. A technical focus alone would omit the personal and communal reading steps that are essential for strong engagement with the text, but a personal reading alone would omit much of the enrichment and delight of discovering the ways literature works and taking that knowledge to the next text. We believe that English teachers can address both the formal and the personal.

English teacher, critic, novelist, and religious apologist C. S. Lewis was caught in a similar debate of the 1950s and 1960s. He writes (1961) of his own quandary: Should one read poetry only to experience its private effect on you, the reader, or should you read it to fathom the poet's intent?

> The literary sometimes "use" poetry instead of "receiving" it. They differ from the unliterary because they know very well what they are doing . . . "Why," they ask, "should I turn from a real and present experience—what the poem means to me, what happens to me when I read it—to inquiries about the poet's intention or reconstructions, always uncertain, of what it may have meant to his contemporaries?" There seem to be two answers. One is that the poem in my head which I make from my mistranslations of Chaucer or misunderstandings of Donne may possibly not be so good as the work Chaucer or Donne actually made. Secondly, why not have both? After enjoying what I made of it, why not go back to the text, this time looking up the hard words, puzzling out the allusions, and discovering that some metrical delights in my first experience were due to my fortunate mispronunciations, and see whether I can enjoy the poet's poem, not necessarily instead of, but in addition to, my own one? If I am a man of genius and uninhibited by false modesty I may still think my poem the better of the two. But I could not have discovered this without knowing both. Often, both are well worth retaining. . . . It is rather like revisiting a beautiful place we knew in childhood. We appraise the landscape with an adult eye; we also revive the pleasures—often very different—which it produced when we were small children. (pp. 100–101)

Our interest in literature instruction is to work at having both the personal response (not in the least childish as we have described it) and the appreciation of form and its revelations. As Elise Ann Earthman (1997, personal communication) says, we need ways to "move students from an initial free encounter with a poem toward the analysis that comes after the poem matters to them . . . to something deeper and more considered." Formal considerations are part of that deepening: helping students to appreciate the craft of fiction, to understand how a work achieves its effects and, often, thereby its meaning.

In *How Does a Poem Mean?* (1959), John Ciardi distinguishes different approaches to the study of poetry. One is represented by Charles Dickens's teacher, Thomas Gradgrind, in his School of Hard Facts. After a student, "girl number twenty," had given a deeply felt definition of a horse based on her own experience of the living animal, Gradgrind turns to a boy for a proper definition.

> "Bitzer," said Thomas Gradgrind, "your definition of a horse."
>
> "Quadruped. Gramnivorous. Forty teeth, namely twenty-four grinders, four eye-teeth, and twelve incisive. Sheds coat in the spring; in marshy countries sheds hoofs too. Hoofs hard, but requiring to be shod with iron. Age known by marks in mouth." Thus (and much more) Bitzer.
>
> "Now girl number twenty," said Mr. Gradgrind, "you know what a horse is."
>
> *Hard Times*
> Charles Dickens

Ciardi describes a similar attempt at classification of literature by a "recent anthologist who wrote that the inspection of a poem should be as certain as a chemical analysis" (p. 665). Ciardi senses danger when "the language of classification" is used to define something that should be approached by "the language of experience." He wants to see the reader of poetry become "alive to it by natural process," as Dickens's girl was to the horse (p. 666). Too often, formal matters overwhelm the literature classroom and appear to be all that matters. They deepen our responses and our meaning making, but they do not substitute for it. They have a supportive, not the starring, role in this drama.

Basic to the effective teaching of literary knowledge is a teacher who is alive to literature. This third step, Formal Analysis, should originate in your own understanding of formal elements and their relationships as parts of a whole. Like painting, which has line, space, and color and physics, which has space, time, and mass, literature has its own basic elements. Understanding how the fundamental elements of literature work together can be as enriching to a reader as knowing proportion is to a painter (even an abstract expressionist) and statics is to an engineer. However, too often the study of literary concepts and terminology—character, setting, theme, and point of view—is the only approach to literature in the classroom. If they were left with such formal emphases only, painters would never paint, engineers would never construct bridges, and readers would never respond.

Ciardi tells a story of W. H. Auden that reiterates our hope for your approach to literature:

> W. H. Auden was once asked what advice he would give a young man who wished to become a poet. Auden replied that he would ask the young man why he wanted to write poetry. If the answer was "because I have something important to say," Auden would conclude that there was no hope for that young man as a poet. If on the other hand the answer was something like "because I like to hang around words and overhear them talking to one another," then that young man was at least interested in a fundamental part of the poetic process and there was hope for him. (p. 667)

Auden's advice to the prospective poet is the same as our advice to prospective teachers. Years of our reading and teaching have steadily increased our own pleasure in literature—its delights and riches. As Birkerts (1994) reminds us," reading changes across the trajectory of the reader's career" (p. 87). Yours will too, we hope. Your teaching will profit from that increase as you grow more confident about the way language and literature work. We encourage you to grow familiar with formal elements, play with them, and use them to deepen your own discoveries about how literature works. Do not rigidify them as definitions on their way to a final exam.

If these cautions sound convincing and straightforward, converting them into instructional practice is not. Often our recommendations to you feel uncomfortably simple, when our experience is far more complex. Refracting form through the lens of personal response and meaning making is one such struggle. Part of our personal dilemma originates in our own experience as students in New Criticism classrooms, where form was central. Unless we had accounted for all parts of a piece, we were not ready to leave it. Part is our own delight in discovering the way things work and in penetrating to a deeper knowledge as a result. Part may also be the distancing that formal discussions grant to literature that is emotionally demanding. We wonder whether, for others, part of the allure of form for reading literature is similar to the appeal of grammar for writing compositions. Form and grammar dress subjective events in objective garb. They make their subjects more manageable. *Hamlet* and *Macbeth* are less likely to threaten us or change us if we define soliloquies and scan iambic pentameters, rather than puzzle over Shakespeare's implication that life is more tragic than comic. For now, consider the knowledge of literary concepts and vocabulary as part of what allows us to clarify, deepen, and enlarge our initial responses to literature. Form can increase our thoughtfulness, understanding, and self-reliance as readers.

■■■■■■ TABLE 4–3 Questions of form

	Literature: Structure, Sound, and Sense — Lawrence Perrine	Bedford Introduction to Literature — Michael Meyer	The Harper Anthology of Fiction — Sylvan Barnet
Plot	Does the plot have unity? Are all the episodes relevant to the total meaning or effect of the story? Does each incident grow logically out of the preceding incident and lead naturally to the next? Is the ending happy, unhappy, or indeterminate? Is it fairly achieved?	What is the source and nature of the conflict for the protagonist? Was your major interest in the story based on what happens next or on some other concern? What does the title reveal now that you've finished the story?	Does the plot grow out of the characters or does it depend on chance or coincidence? Did something at first strike you as irrelevant that later you perceived as relevant? Do some parts continue to strike you as irrelevant? Does surprise play an important role or does foreshadowing?
Characters	What means does the author use to reveal character? Are the characters sufficiently dramatized? What use is made of character contrasts? Are the characters consistent in their actions? Adequately motivated? Plausible? Does the author successfully avoid stock characters?	Did your response to any characters change as you read? What do you think caused the change? Do any characters change and develop in the course of the story? How?	Which character chiefly engages your interest? Why? If a character changes, why and how does he or she change? Or did you change your attitude toward a character not because the character changes but because you came to know the character better? How has the author caused you to sympathize with certain characters, and how does your response contribute to your judgment of the conflict?
Setting	What contribution to the story is made by its setting? Is the setting essential, or could the story have happened anywhere?	Is the setting important in shaping your response? If it were changed, would your response to the story's action and meaning be significantly different?	Do you have a strong sense of the time and place? If so, how and at what points in the story has the author conveyed this sense? If you do not strongly feel the setting, do you think that the author should have made it more evident?
Point of View	What point of view does the story use? Is it consistent in its use of this point of view? If shifts are made, are they justified?	If it were told from a different point of view, how would your response to the story change? Would anything be lost?	Does the language help you to construct a picture of the narrator's attitude, strengths, and limitations? (Notice especially any figurative language and patterns of imagery.) How far can you trust the narrator? Why?
Tone		How does the author's use of language contribute to the tone of the story? Did it seem, for example, intense, relaxed, sentimental, nostalgic, humorous, angry, sad, or remote?	How would you characterize the author's tone? Whimsical? Bitter? Cold? Or what?
Style	What are the characteristics of the author's style? Are they appropriate to the nature of the story?	Do you think the style is consistent and appropriate throughout the story? Do all the characters use the same kind of language, or did you hear different voices?	How would you characterize the style? (You might begin by thinking about the vocabulary and the sentence structure. Are they fairly easy or rather difficult?) Is the style simple? Understated? Figurative? Or what, and why?
Theme	Does the theme reinforce or oppose popular notions of life? Does it furnish a new insight or refresh or deepen an old one?	Is the theme stated directly, or is it developed implicitly through the plot, characters, or some other element?	Suppose someone asked you to state the point—the theme—of the story. Could you? And if you could, would you say that the theme of a particular story reinforces values you hold, or does it to some degree challenge them? Or is the concept of a theme irrelevant to this story?
Symbol	Does the story make use of symbols? If so, do the symbols carry or merely reinforce the meaning of the story?	Did you notice any symbols in the story? Are they actions, characters, settings, objects, or words?	Do you feel that the writer wrote the story and then went back and stuck in the symbols? If you do have this feeling, which passages in the story seem stuck in?
General	Does the story offer chiefly escape or interpretation? How significant is the story's purpose? Does the story gain or lose on a second reading?	Do you think the story is worth reading more than once? Does the author's use of language bear close scrutiny so that you feel and experience more with each reading?	

SOURCE: Excerpts from *Literature: Structure, Sound, and Sense,* 4th ed. (1983), pp. 338–340 by Lawrence Perrine and Thomas R. Arp, copyright © 1983 by Harcourt Brace & Company, reprinted by permission of the publisher; M. Meyer, *Bedford Introduction to Literature,* 4th ed. (1996), pp. 259–261; S. Barnet, *The Harper Anthology of Fiction,* (1991), pp. 1250–1252. Reprinted by permission.

FIGURE 4–8
Rabinowitz's rules of notice

Peter J. Rabinowitz's book, *Before Reading: Narrative Conventions and the Politics of Interpretation* (1987) gives us a methodical and illuminating account of the "rules" which writers and readers use to shape a story. These "rules" are governed by culture, genre, and history, and are always open to change.

(a) **Rules of notice** help readers to establish which characters are important and which are minor; which details of plot are significant and which need only passing attention. Cues can be very simple, such as titles, typography, paragraphing. They can include more complex ideas such as the extra weighting given to the first or last sentence in a unit. Interruptions and deviations also attract notice, and Rabinowitz comments: "Different norms characterize different sets of narratives; what stands out as deviant, therefore, depends not only on social context but also on the intertextual grid against which the text is read" (70). In other words, readers will perceive different details as noteworthy if the text is seen as romance rather than mystery.

(b) **Rules of signification** assist in deciding how much and what kind of attention we pay to what we have decided to notice. They help us to establish the source of a particular sentence or idea: author, narrator, character (reliable or unreliable). They assist us in making ethical judgments about characters or situations, in working out the relationship of the particular fictional world to the real world, in establishing causes and effects. The author makes use of conventional cues to enable us to sort out how to attend to whatever we decide is important.

(c) **Rules of configuration** are used to help the reader fit the story together. These are the conventions which activate expectations—if certain elements appear in a certain arrangement, we expect a certain kind of outcome. Even if these expectations are confounded at the end of the story, they still play a role in how we approach the text. Rabinowitz suggests that "if too many of these activated expectations are ignored, readers may find the results dull or chaotic" (113). Rules of configuration vary according to genre, but Rabinowitz says there are two general "metarules" of configuration: "First it is appropriate to expect that *some*thing will happen. Second, it is appropriate to expect that not *any*thing can happen" (117).

(d) **Rules of coherence** are applied retrospectively, as the reader approaches the end of the text and attempts to make sense of it as a whole. "We assume, to begin with, that the work *is* coherent and that apparent flaws in its construction are intentional and meaning bearing" (147). We must come to terms with what has been left out and with what seems to be surplus or excessive, reshaping the story in our minds to make sense of what is given. Rules of coherence also involve the interpretation of patterns—both within the text and in relationship to other texts.

SOURCE: From M. Mackey, Lost in a Book: The Invisible Problems of a Learning Reader. *English Journal, 83* (1), 65–68. Copyright 1993 by the National Council of Teachers of English. Reprinted with permission.

they solidify into rules. Thereafter, they structure the way we enter and respond to fiction. Mackey (1993) has helpfully summarized Rabinowitz's rules; this summary is presented in Figure 4-8. These rules have helped us to notice and clarify our interpretive strategies. As they inform our reading, they inform the kinds of questions and responses that we make to literature in class. In this indirect way, we help students grow more confident of their interpretive strategies. These ideas do not need to be taught as terms to be learned, but as concepts to be applied as we discuss our responses to fiction.

THE QUESTIONING CIRCLE

Leila Christenbury and Patricia Kelly (1983), frustrated by the traditional questioning hierarchies (e.g., those of Bloom, Sanders, Taba, and Herber), developed their own schema, which more nearly matches the nonsequential, nonhierachical approach to literature in a reader response classroom and provides a useful guide to constructing questions. The look of it alone, Figure 4-9, suggests an approach to knowledge that is not linear, invariant, and hierarchical—one lower-level question giving way in an orderly progression to a slightly more challenging question, and all moving toward the most sophisticated, penetrating question of all. The three areas of their Questioning Circle stand alone, but they also overlap as pairs and trios, and their movement is circular. Christenbury and Kelly's definition of these three circles is as follows:

Matter	The subject under discussion (in this chapter, literary texts)
Personal Reality	The individual reader's experience, knowledge, feelings, and values that are brought to the reading of the text
External Reality	The "world": "the experience, history, and concepts of other peoples and cultures" (1983, p. 13).

Questions surrounding literary texts can address each of the three separate circles (white), as well as the intersections of two circles (gray) and the converging point (black) of all three. Christenbury and Kelly consider the central, dense point, where all the different ideas come together, to contain the "central, most important questions . . . whose answers provide the deepest consideration of

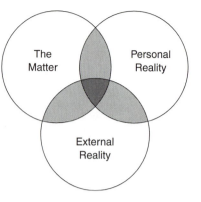

FIGURE 4–9

Christenbury and Kelly's Questioning Circle

SOURCE: From L. Christenbury & P. P. Kelly, *Questioning: A Path to Critical Thinking.* Copyright 1983 by the National Council of Teachers of English. Reprinted with permission.

the issue" (p. 14). They suggest that teachers write questions from each of the areas—white, gray, and black—but they prescribe no order for posing them. Unlike hierarchical taxonomies, the central question might easily arise at the first or in the middle or, more traditionally, at the last. (Chapter 11, Organizing Instruction, will return in more detail to the Questioning Circle.) For now, the Questioning Circle suggests a way for teachers to integrate the text, personal response, and the wider context of both. Sometimes that matter will be the formal conventions of the field. The following questions (Matter/Personal Reality/External Reality) that might be posed in a discussion of Mark Twain's use of language in *The Adventures of Huckleberry Finn* are examples of dense questions:

- How do you think contemporary minority readers might react to Mark Twain's references to African-Americans in his novel?
- Does Twain's implicit criticism of nineteenth-century racial prejudice and practice mitigate his use of such language?
- Should his novel be banned from public school curricula because of its language?

IMAGING CONVENTIONS

Literary conventions and terms can be profitably presented through the visual as well as the verbal. Clearly, those with spatial intelligence who think in images and pictures read "visual texts" more readily than they do verbal texts. Such students need to visualize, sketch ideas, and draw graphics. But all students respond to the freshness of drawings, graphics, cartoons, paintings, and photographs if only because of their novelty. We discuss the impact of linking poems, paintings, and photographs in Chapter 5, Reviving Poetry. Natural questions of authorial intent and choice rise from comparing the two types of media. Why did the painter emphasize certain elements? Why did the writer make a different choice? What is gained by these differences?

Cartoons are a staple bulletin board attraction in our contemporary literature classroom. We put ballooned questions in their midst to direct students' attention to different formal questions. Intertextuality is a natural issue because so many cartoonists take their inspiration and establish their context from preceding texts. Gary Larson, for instance, created two cartoons about writer's block in nineteenth-century American giants, Edgar Allan Poe and Herman Melville. Poe is puzzling over alternative titles—The Tell-Tale Kidney, The Tell-Tale Spleen, The Tell-Tale Duodenum, and Melville over first lines—Call me Bill, Call me Al, Call me Larry, Call me Warren. Students puzzle over the original inspirations, they enjoy the wit, they appropriate captions for their own cartoons, they play actively with the "tradition," they gain confidence in their own literary knowledge, and they exercise it.

Gary Larson provides endless perspectives on the effects of different angles of vision, or point of view. Illustrations of tone are abundant once you begin to search in single-frame cartoons and three-frame narratives. Techniques of characterization and plot development are evident in their extreme compression; they stand in bold (line) relief. We enter Eudora Welty's *Why I Live at the P.O.* via Gary Larson cartoons featuring the theme of sibling rivalry, albeit those of insects and fish. The conventions of romance, suspense, science fiction, and comedy are outlined succinctly in narrative cartoons. Although *The New Yorker* is our weekly staple for cartoons, we are also drawn to collections of cartoonists and have found the following especially literate in their frames of reference: Glen Baxter, Berke Breathed (Bloom County), Roz Chast, Jules Feiffer, Gary Larson, William Steig, and Bill Watterson (Calvin and Hobbes). Students become excellent collectors too.

We also use the visual as prompts for students' drawings. Character Continuum, Character Maps, and Venn Diagramming provide spatial means to respond to character, but they can be used to discuss issues of characterization as well. The questions they raise then become "As you look at this graph, what do you notice about the characters: Are they round or flat, dynamic or static? Have you ever read about such characters? Are they stock? Are they original? Whom do you regard as the protagonist? The antagonist?"

We also ask students to draw formal elements. Figure 4-10 is an example of one student's illustration of four character types commonly found in literature: round, flat, dynamic, and static. Students enjoy the exercise (even those who are inadept at drawing) and seeing other students' work. Their explanations of their illustrations involve them naturally in sorting out what they mean by the concept, how they understand it, and what they attempted to render. Other students' questions and responses engage the whole class in discussions of formal matters. The class bulletin boards crackle.

INTERTEXTUALITY

The notion of intertextuality is important to academics and scholars as they trace original sources and subsequent borrowings. One text may contain a mention of another, for instance, or a quotation from or citation of an earlier text. Less obviously, texts often build on character or situations in earlier pieces. One text may be a translation of another, an imitation, an adaptation, a satire, or a parody. Literary scholars emphasize that no writer writes without a consciousness of preceding texts.

Intertextuality is important for teachers for reasons beyond the enrichment of reading. The web of connections among texts can ensnare curiosity and release playfulness as well. In addition, as students read material that has been creatively reworked, questions naturally arise about why an author makes the decisions he or she does to change the material. Juxtaposing two texts nudges the curiosity naturally. The more texts students read, the more questions of form will bubble up and the more their knowledge of form will be activated and reinforced.

The term *intertextuality* refers not only to one author's references to another, but to the reader's use of other specific texts and the literary conventions of all texts to relate to the present text. Reading many texts becomes important to enlarge students' frames of reference, then. We often ask students to reflect back on how a character or a situation, say, is like something they have experienced before. Reading is also a part of their history. So we might ask, for instance, "Does this character remind you of a character you have encountered before?" As we build experiences of literature into their lives, they have more history to tap and more understanding to bring.

CONTEMPORARY CONTRASTS

Contemporary texts are especially useful in clarifying literary conventions. Many postmodern writers, particularly experimentalists and satirists, overturn our common expectations of literature to achieve their effects. Thus, after we read fables by Aesop (620–560 B.C.) and La Fontaine (1621–1695), we read some of the *Fables for Our Times* by James Thurber (1894–1961). The fable, one of the oldest written forms, achieves its effect by surprising the reader with its resolution, or moral. A moral is most effective when it both summarizes the action and advances the idea. Thurber adapts this fabulist tradition to comment on the mid-twentieth century. The incongruity of the old form put to sophisticated new purpose disarms our expectations and thereby throws fabulist conventions into clearer outline.

Thurber's *The Princess and the Tin Box* teaches about another set of literary conventions surrounding the romantic fairy tale. Thurber's Princess, "the prettiest princess in the world," forced to chose a husband from among five princes offering gifts, chooses the one with the most elaborate gift, rather than the humble prince with his small tin box filled with common crystallized minerals that he gathered along his way. The setting, the characters, and the situation are recognizable, but the surprise of her choice startles the reader into a recognition of the common expectations for fairy tale endings.

Here is a lesson that we use to lead students to consider the conventions of the fairy tale or two literary elements, point of view and authorial tone:

• Recall the story of the frog prince. Consider: What has always been your reaction to this story? Have you experienced another—and they lived happily ever after—kind of moment? Did you think of the frog as having been rescued from a cruel fate? Was it a triumphant story of goodness rewarded (the princess's) and evil overturned (the witch's)?

FIGURE 4–10 Student drawings of formal elements (Courtesy of Benjamin Milner)

- Read each of the following poems and, after each or after all three, consider: Does the (modern) poem change your point of view? Does it enlarge your sensibilities? Does it make you want to reevaluate the original? Does it spoil the enchantment? How does it leave you feeling?

Kathryn Machan Aal	*Hazel Tells LaVerne*
Susan Mitchell	*From the Journals of the Frog Prince*
Stevie Smith	*The Frog Prince*

- Consider: Which version attracts you most? Which kind of world would you rather inhabit: a world in which magic is present, good and evil are clearly defined and rewarded, and people live happily ever after or a world that uncovers romantic foolishness, is securely grounded in reality, and recognizes that happiness is tenuous?

CHARACTER QUESTIONS

We have seen that if we accept the Reader Response invitation to connect reader with the text, not any teaching strategies will do, not even those that appear to elicit vigorous reactions by students. Students readily adapt to the context that we as teachers set up. They become adept at operating within the ground rules we establish. Thus, if we pitch our discussion of form with questions such as "How does Jane Austen develop the character of Elizabeth Bennet in the context of the other females of her family?" students may be perfectly able to generate answers about the author's technique of characterization and even defend ideas with conviction and spirit. We expect more.

John Dixon and Leslie Stratta (1989) criticize the questions we pose about fictive characters in class discussion, writing assignments, homework, and examinations. Questions such as "How would you describe the character of Stella in Sue Ellen Bridger's *Home Before Dark* or identify the changes in her as the novel progresses?" carry "tacit assumptions" or suggestions that "somehow or other, definitive answers are possible. It is not how you imagine a character that counts; instead it is your ability to describe something already existing and defined" (p. 26). These kinds of questions register in the student a belief that they are "a passive mechanism to which texts do things and that all readers by rights should think the same" (p. 26). The consequence of these sorts of standard questions is to "give students the messages that 'the character' is something that must be talked about in an impersonal way and in summary terms. Characters become bundles of traits, of 'points you make' in 'your answer' to a question" (p. 27). Dixon and Stratta (1986) indict the way we discuss character in literature: It "blunts the edge of our perception of people. It treats the writing as a task, aimed at the production of a polished portrait, rather than an opportunity to search your own experience (or someone else's), reflect on it, and discover new meanings" (p. 57). These two educators (1989) have provided excellent guidelines with which teachers might scrutinize their practice so that the study of literary characters and characterization does not elicit an arid discussion of technique, but an imaginative engagement with the text.

1. Does the language of the assignment (or negotiated topic) indicate that the student is constructing a personal, imaginative experience, based on the printed text? Does it encourage students as they write to continue such imaginative work?
2. Does the topic or assignment allow the student to trace character(s) in action, to imagine people in relation to each other moment by moment? Is room left for narrative that comments and interprets from an imaginatively involved point of view?
3. Is there also an invitation to stand back and relate what happens in a specific scene (possibly chosen by students) to the way they now see the character in the action as a whole? Is there encouragement to keep any generalizations that emerge close to particularly telling moments in action?
4. Is there a further recognition that characters may be viewed as types (within a constructed social microcosm) as well as unique individuals? Is there room for an intelligent discussion of character as type? If so, are students aware enough of particulars to avoid overstereotyping and stock response?
5. Are there any opportunities for students who are at odds with the author and the way a character has been conceived? (p. 37)

STUDENTS WRITE

When students write fiction or drama or poetry, they face the same choices authors face. They address questions of form as practical matters, not as theoretical ones. After students have written their own stories, they are positioned to consider what they did. Consider, for instance, a Halloween unit on suspense stories that begins with several Edgar Allan Poe short stories and concludes with students' own tales of suspense. The writing assignment might be as follows:

- Write a suspense story to be read to the class on Halloween.
- Create a new tale or adapt one of Poe's stories by changing the point of view of the narrator.
- In pairs, read your stories to each other.
- Consider the narrator of your partner's stories:
  - Who is telling the story?
  - What is unique about the voice of the narrator?
  - Does the voice sound trustworthy and reliable to you?
  - What made you believe it? (How does it establish its reliability or authority?)
  - How does it compare to the voices of the characters presented in the story?
  - What is the relationship of the teller to the tale and its characters?
  - Does the teller's voice ever reach barriers or limits to the telling?
  - Does the point of view provide any clues to the story's meaning?
  - Does the point of view conceal or reveal the author's purpose?
  - What is the relationship of the teller to the listener?
  - What is the relationship of the teller to the tale and its characters?

AUTHORS SPEAK

Writers of literature are also inveterate writers about literature. We often use authors' words to make students conscious of craft. The words are often memorable, they have credibility coming from practicing writers, they often carry the punch of heightened language, and they make lively posters around the room. Some of our favorites follow.

Character	"It is also one of the most startling and effective devices in fiction to take characters out of one setting and put them in another, where different facets of their personality come to the fore." *Orson Scott Card*
	"Habits not only make the character more realistic, but also open up story possibilities—a change in pattern might show an important change in the character's life; other characters might take advantage of her habits; curiosity about or annoyance at a habit might lead to an interesting relationship between characters." *Orson Scott Card*
	"Remembering that of all these different ways of getting to know people—and therefore getting to know characters—the most powerful of them, the ones that make the strongest impression, are the first three: what the character does in the story, what his motives are, and what he has done in the past." *Orson Scott Card*
Dialogue	"Speech is what the characters do to each other. . . . Each piece of dialogue *must* be something happening.'" *Elizabeth Bowen*
	Writers should use dialogue with restraint, because dialogue forces the reader "to hear, to see, to supply the right tone and to fill in the background from what the characters say without any help from the author. . . . [Dialogue requires] the reader to do rather more than his share of the work of creation." *Virginia Woolf*
Idea	"There is no story written that has any value at all, however straightforward it looks and free from doubleness, double entendre, and duplicity and double play, that you'd value at all if it didn't have intimation of something more than itself." *Robert Frost*
Setting	"If a gun is hanging over the mantel in the opening scene, it had better go off by the last." *Anton Chekhov*
Symbol	"In good fiction, certain of the details will tend to accumulate meaning from the action of the story itself, and when that happens, they become symbolic in the way they work." *Flannery O'Connor*
	"You can't give a great symbol a 'meaning,' any more than you can give a cat a 'meaning.' Symbols are organic units of consciousness with a life of their own, and you can never explain them away, because their value is dynamic, emotional, belonging to the sense-consciousness of the body and soul, and not simply mental." *D. H. Lawrence*
Comedy	"The true test of comedy is that it shall awaken thoughtful laughter." *George Meredith*

A statement by the Committee on Response to Literature of the 1966 Dartmouth Conference (Squire, 1968) cautions against the negative consequences of strict or exclusive attention to formal analysis:

> Response is a word that reminds the teacher that the experience of art is a thing of our making, an activity in which we are our own interpretive artist. The dryness of schematic analysis of imagery,

symbols, myth, structural relations, et al. should be avoided passionately at school and often at college. *It is literature, not literary criticism,* which is the subject. (p. 26)

We would add that it is the *student responding* to literature that is our concern. Purves, Rogers, and Soter (1990) make the same point: "Literary terms can be used to scaffold and bolster responses, but not to build them" (p. 84). They also explain both the origin and dangers of formal language:

The critical language that developed came from people's need to classify and categorize their experiences. It came from the same impetus that has led to the elaborate classifications of plant and animal life. In one sense, education is the learning of these classificatory schemes, but too often the learning of the names of plants has replaced looking at them, smelling them, enjoying them. The same thing happened to the teaching of literature. (p. 57)

Formal analysis must be done within the clear context of readers responding and communities reflecting on texts. Remy de Gourmont's observation captures the academic attraction to formal labels and categories and reminds us of the need to resist it: "We live less and less and learn more and more. I have seen a man laughed at for examining a dead leaf attentively and with pleasure. No one would have laughed to hear a string of botanical terms muttered over it."

CRITICAL SYNTHESIS

With a secure grounding in reading that has become personally owned, communally interpreted, and formally considered, why now step into literary criticism? We, too, have asked this question and answer cautiously. Our observation of periodicals published for secondary English teachers is that different critical theories are implicit in many of the pedagogical designs and activities, but they usually remain tacit and applied, not defined and articulated as theory. These theories also represent a narrow range of approaches to literature, primarily formalist, archetypal, and reader response (Milner, 1986). Textbooks, especially those focusing on world, American, and English literature, give much prereading space to historical, biographical criticism and postreading apparatus to formalist and, increasingly, reader response questions. Applebee's (1993) national survey of literature instruction found that "the influence of specific types of literary theory also varied with grade level and track. New Criticism, in particular, was much more influential in the upper grades . . . and in college-preparatory classes" (p. 124). His results also "indicate that reader-response approaches are viewed as generally useful, across a wide range of grade levels and groups of students. . . . Teachers do not rate other approaches as having much influence on their instruction at all" (p. 124).

Different critical perspectives produce very different approaches to texts and generate very different questions about them. When critical theory remains relatively unexplained, students have difficulty developing a coherent framework for comprehending the field and individual pieces in it. One day they are queried—"What did the author intend?"—the next—"What does the literary history reveal?"—then—"What is the plot structure and how does it contribute to unity?"—and then—"How do you feel about this book?" No sooner is one critical perspective aired as central than another possibility arises to challenge it. Students are left with an isolated reaction to each literary event. They are often also left to wonder on what criteria literature is to be understood and judged and conclude that only the wise, learned, or especially gifted can know.

We proceed cautiously, however. Until students are comfortably and personally engaged and are confident of their own immediate and considered responses, they should not be asked to make their considerations more studied. If Formal Analysis is a stretch, Critical Synthesis will be a longer one. If students are curious, if critical questions arise about the ground rules for a good interpretation, and if students are moving to metacognitive perspectives, then perhaps the time is right.

Psychologists tell us that one of the characteristics of the young adolescent's intellect is metacognition, the ability to think about one's thinking. Many adolescents have moved beyond concrete-manipulatory stages of intellectual development and are capable of abstract reasoning. Piaget referred to this ability as reflective abstraction and did not believe that cognitive development could progress without it. Critical Synthesis invites students to that level of abstraction. If metacognition is thinking about thinking, metacriticism is thinking about criticism (in this case, of literature). Formal Analysis began such a standing outside and observing how the textual elements read as a whole and functioned as parts of a whole. Critical Synthesis takes a further step back from the text to look at the whole field of literary study. Not all students are ready, but those who can take this step discover a whole new way of seeing, a way that casts a clarifying light back on all that went before.

EARLY CRITICS AND 11 CRITICAL APPROACHES TO LITERATURE

The term *literary criticism* has multiple and diffuse meanings. Since the time of the early Greeks, literature has been attended by a parallel body of thought. In *The Mirror and the Lamp* (1953), M. H. Abrams distinguishes three possible foci for the critic: art, the artist, or the audience. In contemplating those three, critics have articulated elaborate theories about the way literature works, the way authors write, and the responses audiences or readers experience. Opinion differs about what portion of this is important for high school students to know. (Purves [1971] names the handful of those theories that college-bound high school students might be expected to know: "Aristotle's definition of tragedy, something of the system of genres, something of the new critical method" [p. 751].) Our approach introduces students to this parallel field simply and concretely (and waits hopefully to see if they ask for more.) Over time, clusters of critical approaches have formed around similar theories and techniques. We introduce 11 of the most prominent clusters or approaches, approaches that share common assumptions about texts and readers and about methods with which to read texts. These approaches originate in the earliest thinking about literature in the Western world and they animate current academic debates. We name these general approaches schools of literary criticism, and schematize our summary of them in Table 4-4.

We begin with a description of two of the earliest critics of literature, Plato and Aristotle, and then describe a few basic theoretical principles and characteristic techniques of each of these 11 schools. But each has many and varied practitioners. For a fuller explanation of these schools and related issues, we recommend several guides to literary theory and criticism that we have found useful:

> Groden, Michale and Martin Kreiswirth. (Eds.) *The Johns Hopkins Guide to Literary Theory and Criticism.* Baltimore: Johns Hopkins University Press, 1994.
> Magell, Frank N. (Ed.). *Critical Survey of Literary Theory.* Pasadena, CA: Salem Press, 1987.
> Makaryk, Irena R. (Ed.). *Encyclopedia of Contemporary Literary Theory: Approaches, Scholars, Terms.* Toronto: The University of Toronto Press, 1993.
> Peck, John, and Martin Coyle. (Eds.) *Literary Terms and Criticism.* London: The Macmillan Press, 1993.

We conclude Critical Synthesis with suggestions about how this knowledge might enter a classroom. We reiterate that much of what follows may remain background knowledge for you. (A clear understanding of the field will ground you more confidently in it and will protect you from being prey to literary assumptions and judgments that you cannot locate or name.) These theories may come into your classroom only indirectly and wordlessly. In your first years of high school teaching especially, this knowledge will more inform your practice than directly inform your students. If students encounter it directly, they should be invited into the "manifold possibilities" (McGuire, 1973, p. 3) that it opens, not into one or another dogmatic position. Figure 4-11 poses characteristic questions that each school of thought might ask of Tillie Olsen's short story "I Stand Here Ironing." We encourage you to consider these questions as you read the description of each school and observe whether your response and insight changes and deepens with each.

Early Critics: Plato and Aristotle.   We precede our survey with the story of these two seminal thinkers for three reasons:

1. Western literary criticism begins with them. They set down comprehensive and profound views of art.
2. Many contemporary positions are based on their thoughts or certain vestiges of them.
3. The argument between these two suggests that such reasoning about literature was taken seriously by eminent minds and that their conflict was understandable and inevitable. What we believe about literature is greatly influenced by what we believe about reality. In other words, Plato's and Aristotle's disagreement prepares students to appreciate a critical pluralism in which two minds equally intent on truth arrive at two different conclusions.

Plato faced a dilemma. He himself was a poet, but he had a critical view of poetry (or art). He believed that not only is art far removed from the truth, but also, it appeals to an inferior part of the hu-

TABLE 4-4
Prominent schools of literary criticism

Early Critics	Traditional	Textual	Psychological/ Sociological	Posttextual
Plato	Historical/Biographical	Formalist	Freudian	Deconstructivist
Aristotle	Moral/Philosophical	Rhetorical	Archetypal	Reader Response
			Feminist	New Historical
			Marxist	

SCHOOL OF LITERARY CRITICISM	QUESTIONS
Moral/Philosophical	• Whom should we judge most critically for Emily's plight: the social institutions during the American Depression, Emily's mother for her decisions, or Emily's father for his desertion?
Historical/Biographical	• What social and economic forces at work in the 1930s Depression could explain what caused Emily's father to leave and her mother to struggle? • Tillie Olsen was born in 1913 and lived through the poverty of working class families in the mining towns and farms of the West. Because she was raising children and struggling to make ends meet, she could not concentrate on writing until she was 40. Could these experiences have influenced this prize-winning story?
Formalist	• Who is the narrator? Do you consider the narrator reliable or unreliable? Does this point of view give the story unity? • Is this story anything more than a sociological or psychological case study or a list of personal difficulties? It violates many principles of short story writing as it summarizes 19 years of a person's life. What makes this story "literature"? (Pay special attention to its narration, its language, its structure, and its imagery.)
Rhetorical	• With which characters are you in greatest sympathy? • How did the author manipulate your feelings? • Did she "load the deck" for some and against others?
Freudian	• What particular events in Emily's life do you consider most influential in the development of her personality? • Could this story be a psychological case study? Does the pain and guilt of the mother influence the way she sees the world of her child? What is the effect of reading this story of self-blame and self-justification on you?
Archetypal	• This story has become a classic of the modern American short story. Do you find any mythical patterns here that would explain its lasting appeal? Could you identify the mother with one of the archetypal characters such as the Good Mother or Bad Mother, or the Heroine struggling on her personal journey through motherhood? • Would you have preferred that this story have more of a fairy tale ending, like *Cinderella,* in which she suddenly tries on the glass slipper, transcends her difficult childhood, and dances happily and wholly with the prince?
Marxist	• The mother clearly feels powerless to control her life and that of her daughter. Where do you lay blame for this, on the individual or the society of which she is a part? • What are the economic and social structures that create Emily's mother's terrible struggle? Does class have any bearing on her life?
Feminist	• What conclusions can we draw from the fact that the mother is never named? She seems to feel as though she had little control over her own or Emily's life. Why might that be so? • What role do the two fathers play in Emily's life? How do they fulfill the expected parenting roles for males at the time of the story? Which of the three adults, the fathers and the mother, would you judge most harshly as a parent?
Deconstructionist	• Do different members of the class have different interpretations of the narrator? Does her narrative contain contradictions that might lead to divergent interpretations? • Can you reconcile the narrator's exclamation—"She is so lovely. Why did you want me to come in at all? Why were you concerned? She will find her way."—with the last two paragraphs?
Reader Response	• Imagine an incident of behavior that might have caused the guidance counselor to call Emily's mother. Imagine Emily's reaction when she learned that the counselor had called home. Imagine how your mother would react to such a call. • Is there any incident or situation in your early life that you consider crucial in forming who you are? Have your parents ever spoken with regret about that time? • Did you feel more sympathy for Emily or her mother? What would be your advice to each?
New Historical	• Find images from newspapers, magazines, or films from the era of the Great Depression and World War II. Can you find any clues in them of the social pressures that surrounded Emily's family and shaped their actions? • There is more than one historic context for "I Stand Here Ironing." The history on which we focus is influenced by our present histories. The story was published in 1961. Do we read it differently from the way that readers of that cultural moment would?

FIGURE 4–11 The critics and Tillie Olsen's *I Stand Here Ironing*

man faculties, namely the passionate and fitful temper, not calm and wise reason. Thus, as a practical moralist, Plato concluded that poets must be banned from the ideal society—that proper environment for nurturing the good citizen—the Republic, because poets undermine the discipline that all citizens need to bring to their lives.

Aristotle answered Plato's objections. Aristotle believed that the best literature is that which best imitates the universal laws. Because of its universality, poetry is, in fact, superior to history. Furthermore, the artist, rather than being dominated by passion, is admirably in touch with the universals. And poetry, rather than harming its audience by inflaming the passions, gives benign and even therapeutic purgation to the passions.

The first two schools of literary criticism in our survey, Moral/Philosophical and Historical/Biographical, can be seen as outgrowths of this classical argument between Plato and Aristotle about the purpose, function, and disposition of literature. Traditional early approaches to the teaching of literature centered on literature as the vehicle for arriving at another, more serious, intellectual or moral field. It was not explored as a subject in itself, but for what it illustrated of history (the author's, the work's), of biography (the author's, the character's), or of moral virtues (implicit and explicit in the work itself). The function of literary study was thought to be to inform or to instruct.

Moral/Philosophical.   Standard American texts from well before the twentieth century—*The New England Primer* (c. 1686-1690), Webster's *Blue-Backed Speller* (1783), and McGuffey's *Readers* (c. 1836)—identify schooling with moral and religious instruction. In *Tradition and Reform in the Teaching of English: A History* (1974), Arthur N. Applebee states that these "early educational giants . . . provided a common background of culture and allusion, a common heritage for a nation too young to have any other" (p. 5). Although their explicit text was reading, their implicit text was personal and civic virtue. From grade schools to colleges, literature study served skills acquisition, but also moral instruction in what was good and virtuous. A nineteenth-century educator, William Riley Parker, observed that the typical professor of English at midcentury "was a doctor of divinity who spoke and wrote the mother tongue grammatically, had a general 'society knowledge' of the literature, and had not specialized in this or any other academic subject" (as quoted by Graff, 1987, p. 24). For instance, as Graff notes, "of the twelve professors of English appointed by the University of North Carolina between 1819 and 1885, nine were ministers" (p. 24).

The implicit assumption, then, of these scholars and critics is that literature is a secular scripture that needs to be explicated to the general public. Literature as an aesthetic or personal experience with claims to be taken seriously for its own intrinsic or its personally deepening sake would arouse in such teachers the same consternation that imaginative poetry awakened in Plato. For moral and philosophical critics, literature is the vehicle for arriving at more serious intellectual and moral matters. Texts are chosen to serve the ennobling agenda of the culture. Works that describe a more pedestrian, even debased, view of human affairs are not selected. Today's debate over cultural literacy has its roots in an old and admirable tradition. These critics ask "What picture of human experience does this text depict? What does it teach us about how to live our lives?"

Historical/Biographical.   Historical/Biographical critics and teachers regard a literary work chiefly, if not exclusively, as a reflection of its author's life and times, or the life and times of the characters in the work. Literary texts provide a different window into the past than any other sources do, and history can also provide clear windows into literature. In fact, often, history—of the author or of the times—shapes the work. For historicists, an enriched reading of a work depends on knowledge of what is happening in the world at the time the work was written: the intellectual currents, the artistic trends, the economic situation, the politics, and the writer's private life.

The history of our profession partly explains the tenacious hold of this point of view. English was attempting to establish itself as an independent academic department in colleges and universities in the second half of the nineteenth century. Graff (1987) reports that, particularly in the new American research universities, departmental status was purchased at the high price of making literature susceptible to "scientific observation and formulation" (p. 74). This resulted in historical literary scholarship, a search for sources and parallel references as an equivalent to the hard research being done in other departments. These early English departments tried to train readers just as others trained biologists.

We would not minimize the richness of such knowledge. With young students of literature, regardless of their age, the historical and biographical surroundings can envelop a text in greater meaning and the reader in greater confidence and certainty. The problem with this contextual approach is twofold: To begin with, it may overlook the work of art itself. Literary study becomes history, a record of the past, rather than something vital in the present. More significantly, such an approach, particularly in an academic setting with students who are initiates, can make responding to literature a privileged occupation, divorced from contact with the work itself. It reduces literature's potential for making meaningful sense in the life of the common reader.

Formalist.   In England and America in the 1920s and 1930s, the group of scholars, critics, and writers who made the first and most powerful challenge to the established Moral/Philosophical and Historical/Biographical traditions were called variously Agrarians, Fugitives, Formalists, and New Critics. These New Critics felt that any work of great art is an organic whole, united by its form, complete within itself, and written for itself alone. This organic form—that is, the necessary interrelationships of the parts of a literary work—animates and organizes it from within. So organized, a literary text becomes an autonomous or independent verbal artifact and can be scrutinized without regard for the traditional concerns of its historical, biographical, or cultural context. Instead, the primary concern of criticism is with unity—the kind of whole that the literary work forms or fails to form and the relation of the various parts to each other. The analysis of an individual text is complete only when everything in the work has been accounted for in terms of its overall form: How do the internal operations of the text—its language, images, tone, and so on—create intelligible structure and meaning? Are any of the elements in tension with each other? How are these resolved to produce a final unity? Cleanth Brooks summarizes: "There is surely a sense in which anyone must agree that a poem has a life of its own, and a sense in which it provides in itself the only criterion by which what it says can be judged."

Thus, the hallmark of a Formalist or New Critical approach is intensive, close reading of the text itself. The first question to be asked of literature is not *what* does the work mean, but *how* does it mean. Nothing external to the text is necessary to answer this. Archibald MacLeish's poem *Ars Poetica* begins, "A poem must not mean/But be. . . ." The Formalists' motto for poetry is "Trust the poem, not the poet." One of their principal proponents, Cleanth Brooks, made a famous declaration: "I have tried to read the poem, the *Horatian Ode,* not Andrew Marvell's mind." In an influential Formalist essay, "Technique as Discovery," Mark Schorer (1948) writes

> Modern criticism has shown us that to speak of content as such is not to speak of art at all, but of experience; and that it is only when we speak of the *achieved* content, the form, the work of art as a work of art, that we speak as critics. The difference between content, or experience, and achieved content, or art, is technique. (p. 67)

Different Formalist critics give different emphases to what is the central principle in all texts: tension, paradox, irony, or ambiguity. But all share a belief that close scrutiny of technique leads the reader to the discovery of the text's "statement" or its "insight into essential truth" (Brooks, 1947). New Critics trust that their criticism can lead them to "grasp the subject most thoroughly and deeply." Such insights are far more than opinions about literary taste or paraphrased statements of moral judgment.*

Rhetorical. Just as Plato's problems with imaginative literature invited Aristotle's response, so the Formalist position prompted a group of critics to differ. R. S. Crane and others at the University of Chicago were troubled by the Formalists' rejection of Historical/Biographical analysis, their assertion of subjective judgments as though they were objective, and their focus on poetry to the exclusion of prose and drama. Wayne Booth, in *The Rhetoric of Fiction* (1961), theorized that even if art is an autonomous, organic whole, as the New Critics believed, it is still not the world of experience. It is a conscious creation of an artist whom we must not forget or fail to notice. Despite the attempts at objectivity in art, authors can never excise themselves from their fiction. They can take on different disguises, but they are always there, attempting to persuade us. (*Rhetor,* the root of *rhetoric,* comes from Greek and Latin sources meaning "orator.") Just as we listen to orators with critical consciousness, we need also to scrutinize the implicit worldview or value system being expressed by an author through his or her work. Booth's intent was to examine "the art of communicating with readers—the rhetorical resources available to the writer of epic, novel or short story as he tries, consciously or unconsciously, to impose his fictional world upon the reader." Thus, the question is not "What is the organic unity of this piece?" but "What is the connection between the author and the creation?"

Paradoxically, Booth suggested that our critical consciousness would lead us to trust an artist more, if we trusted ourselves as readers as well. But we need to equip ourselves for our task. For a Rhetorical critic, the method is found in the Formalists' tools of close reading; however, Booth developed several new tools that are essential:

- The notion of an authorial "voice" or an "implied author" whose attitudes and perspectives the reader deduces from numerous elements of the text
- The separation of "reliable" and "unreliable" narrators in which the first is closest to the values of the "implied author" and the latter often deviates from it

Reading and interpretation need always to be conducted with a consciousness of a creator at work. Is the authorial voice reliable or unreliable? To what is it persuading us?

---

*The Formalist influence began to be disseminated beyond the concerns of academics and scholars to college students generally and then into the high schools, largely due to the impact of such respected college texts as Cleanth Brooks's and Robert Penn Warren's *Understanding Poetry* (1938) and *Understanding Fiction* (1943), John Ciardi's *How Does a Poem Mean?* (1959), and Laurence Perrine's *Sound and Sense* (1956) and *Story and Structure* (1959). These books and their subsequent revised editions were texts for generations of college students who began to teach and influence secondary English students in the early 1960s. Their techniques of close reading remain pervasive.

The first four schools of thought assume that literary texts possess an objective reality that readers, for all their different perspectives and biases, interrogate and appreciate. Twentieth-century critics of these schools appear to be the inheritors of nineteenth-century poet and cultural critic Matthew Arnold's "profound, almost reverential regard for literary works themselves" (Selden & Widdowson, 1993, p. 10). Arnold even proposed that religion and philosophy would be "replaced by poetry" in modern society. He was joined in this century by poet, dramatist, and critic T. S. Eliot and Cambridge academic and critic F. R. Leavis, who believed that great works of literature (called the "tradition") were the repositories or "vessels" in which humane and civilized values survive. They are our "weapons" in the battle of culture against barbarism. Yvor Winters viewed poetry as "moral statement"; Kenneth Burke regarded literature as "equipment for living." But even as these critics prized texts and disputed with each other as to the best approach to a text's vital life, other literary critics challenged their basic assumptions about literature: What is the nature of those texts? Ideas from the fields of linguistics, philosophy, psychology, sociology, anthropology, and even physics and economics reached the field of literature and yielded perspectives that opened entirely new ways of viewing it. We turn now to four of these perspectives drawn from the social sciences of psychology, sociology, and economics.

Freudian.   Critics who respect the theories of Sigmund Freud (1856–1939) have found in literature a perfect source for exploring the inaccessible world of the unconscious, that of writer, of character, and of reader. Freud believed that a literary work was to its author as dreams are to a dreamer: a rich source of insight into the psychology of the individual, a rich manifestation of unconscious desires, fears, and fantasies. In turn, characters themselves, in the hands of sensitive writers, give expression to the personality dynamics we are all heir to. Finally, readers' responses to literature reveal perspectives on their subjective experience.

High school students from vastly different backgrounds are usually prepared to name and appreciate basic Freudian insights because they have absorbed them unconsciously through our culture. An outline of some primary concepts awakens in students a latent understanding, even though the concepts have not been explicitly taught before. That outline generally includes the following:

- the levels of consciousness: conscious, preconscious, unconscious
- the theoretical structure of the psyche: the id, the ego, and the superego
- the influence of defense mechanisms on personality, especially those of repression, reaction formation, projection, rationalization, displacement, and regression
- the presence of certain key personality syndromes such as the Oedipus and Electra complexes
- the nature and interpretation of dreams

Our reading of literature has benefited from this animating sense of its latent and ambiguous meanings, as if it were no less alive and contradictory than the artist who created it. Freud himself used literature to show the applicability of his theory. (In a questionnaire on reading, he ranked the poems and plays of the following as the "most magnificent works" and the ones who provided his "best illustrations" of psychoanalytic theory: Homer, Sophocles, Goethe, and Shakespeare.) The analysis of the latent psychological content of language, characters, images, metaphors, and plots influenced readers through the work of early Freudian critics Ernest Jones (1879–1958), Otto Rank (1884–1939), and Ella Freeman Sharpe (1875–1947). Yet some psychoanalytical criticism reduces literature to a clinical case study of author, character, or readers. Ruthven (1979) sees the consequences of simplistic applications of Freudian theory: "any work of literature inspired by unconscious projections is likely to record little more than the spontaneous overflow of powerful neuroses" (p. 65). Such simplification greatly compromises literature's complexity and power. Psychological interpretation can easily become a superficial parlor game and Freudian literary criticism a silly search for sexual symbols. It deserves to be recognized for the provocative and rich insights it can yield.

Archetypal.   Archetypal criticism is based on insights dating back at least to Plato. For centuries, philosophers and theologians observed that identical characters, images, situations, and ideas occurred in the literature (particularly myths, religion, art, and folklore) of cultures widely separated by time and space. No explanations of cultural transmission or basic human nature could account for the repeated occurrence of just these universal human experiences. In the twentieth century, the hypotheses about the archetypes of the collective unconscious articulated by psychologist Carl Jung (1875–1961) have been enormously influential in the way we understand human history and in the way we read literature. These images, motifs, or patterns, shaped by the repeated experiences of our species and expressed in myths, religion, dreams, fantasies, art, and literature, reflect the deepest experiences and meanings of the human race. The archetypal critic examines literature in terms of these archetypes, reasoning that to recognize them puts us in touch with the deepest meaning of the text. The power of certain texts resides just here, in the presence of archetypes that resonate deeply within the reader.

FIGURE 4–12
Archetypes

IMAGES	CHARACTERS	MOTIFS/PATTERNS	LITERARY GENRE
Water: sea, rivers	The Earth-Mother	Creation	Spring: comedy
Sun: rising sun, setting sun	The Good Mother	Imitation	Summer: romance
Colors: red, green, blue, black, white	The Terrible Mother	The Hero's Journey	Fall: tragedy
Numbers: 3, 4, 7	The Soul Mate	The Quest/Journey/Search	Winter: irony
Garden	The Fatal Woman	Transformation	
Tree	The Old Man	(physical, spiritual, social)	
Desert	The Scapegoat	Prophecy and fulfillment	
Circle: manila, egg, yin yang	The Alter Ego	Immorality	
	The Serpent		

One of the fascinating pieces of twentieth-century cultural history is the falling out between Freud and his disciple Jung on a transatlantic trip to the United States in 1909. Students enjoy hearing the story and recognizing, as with Plato and Aristotle, the clash of powerful personalities and positions. Their original disagreement was due both to differences in theory and to Jung's dislike of Freud's reaction to disagreement. Their theoretical differences included the nature of the unconscious, the nature of the artist, and the responses of the reader to literature.

Freud believed that the unconscious is a blank tablet at birth on which imprints are made from one's earliest experiences. It becomes the repository of repressions and memories that cannot be recalled, but that influence personality and behavior; particularly for individuals who have had trouble in their psychosexual development, the unconscious can be troubling and destructive. Jung, on the other hand, believed that beyond our own personal conscious and unconscious is a more universal unconscious, the same for all members of the species. We inherit this collective memory of our past by being born human beings. The content of this collective unconscious consists essentially of archetypes or patterns formed by the repeated experiences of human beings during their entire history. Figure 4–12 is a schema of common archetypes. (The term has been traced to Plato; *arche* means "original" and *typos* means "form.") Jung adds to Freud's system of the psyche what he calls "a second psychic system of a collective, universal, and impersonal nature which is identical in all individuals. This collective unconscious does not develop individually but is inherited." Jung believed that being connected with these universal archetypes is health producing, while being unaware of them is destructive. He wrote, "It is only possible to live the fullest life when we are in harmony with these symbols (the archetypes of the collective unconscious); wisdom is a return to them."

Freud believed that art is produced out of neurosis that arises as an artist's conscious and unconscious struggle for expression. Jung held that art is created by an artist who possesses a special sensitivity to archetypal patterns and a gift for speaking in primordial images. He explains that "the work of the poet comes to meet the spiritual need of the society in which he lives." Although Freud, like Plato, was sensitive to literature and acknowledged that it can have a therapeutic effect on the audience by releasing mental tension, he also called art a "substitute gratification," "an illusion in contrast to reality," and "a narcotic" with which to escape reality or protect against unpleasant reality. Jung, on the other hand, thought of literature as enriching. In fact, he has helped explain the powerful impact that it can produce in the reader as its archetypes strike deep, primordial chords.

The danger in this critical approach is the same as that of the Freudian interpretation: When knowledge exterior to literature (even though it is intuited first and articulated later) becomes central to its interpretation, ordinary or inexperienced readers feel excluded and distrustful of their own responses. But the approach has been productive for high school students because the idea of archetypes is stirring and the archetypes themselves are easy to understand from one's own experience; this approach deepens and complicates their responses to texts.

Other perspectives from the field of psychology do not comprise schools of literary criticism that have systematic theories about art, the artist, and the audience, but many have provided rich practical insights into particular works of literature, their creators, and their readers. For instance, developmental theory such as that worked out by Erikson, Kohlberg, and Loevinger has been used to understand character definition, motivation, and growth (see Psychological Profiles in the Interpretive Community section, pp. 104–105). These constructs enrich the reader's understanding and appreciation of individual works. Furthermore, the writer's underlying assumptions or personal biases can be helpfully situated in the cycle of personality, moral, or ego development. While archetypal criticism flowered in the 1960s and 1970s, by the 1980s its greatest influence was felt in a new direction: Feminist criticism.

Feminist.   Feminist criticism arose in the 1960s from the sociopolitical movement that organized to name and combat the gender divisions that affect the legal, economic, and social lives of women. These modern Feminist critics drew on the liberatory energy and know-how of the social movements of that decade and on the insights of women who have spoken over the centuries about the subjugation of women. Simone de Beauvoir (1949) wrote that woman "is defined and differentiated with reference to man and not he with reference to her. . . . He is the Subject, he is the Absolute—she is the Other" (p. xvi). She continues: "The categories in which men think of the world are established *from their point of view, as absolute.* . . . A mystery for man, woman is considered to be mysterious in essence" (p. 257). Yet, as Jane Austen's heroine Anne Elliot says in *Persuasion* (1818), "Men have had every advantage of us in telling their story. Education has been theirs in so much higher a degree; the pen has been in their hands."

Feminist critics concur. They examine the image of women characters in texts written predominantly by men, the place of women writers in the canon, the differing responses of women and men to literature, and the differing ways that men and women use language. What constrictive roles did many of the conventions of fiction assign women, for instance, the fairy tale, the gothic tale, the romance? Did women characters ever have a leading role? Did any destiny present itself for female heroines other than securing a husband? Was the woman's existence always anchored in another person? Did she ever find an identity for herself not defined by attachment to a man? Did any women characters possess independent, active, original, expressive souls? Heilbrun (1979) says outright of American literature: "American male novelists have always been notoriously uninterested in female destiny" (p. 175).

They also raise questions about the different treatment of male and female writers. One example will suffice. Showalter (1971) describes the tumult over the author's identity when *Jane Eyre* was published. "Many critics bluntly admitted that they thought the book was a masterpiece if written by a man, shocking or disgusting if written by a woman" (p. 341). Ellmann (1968) summarizes: "Books by women are treated as though they themselves were women, and criticism embarks, at its happiest, upon an intellectual measuring of busts and hips" (p. 29).

Feminist critics regard most schools of literary criticism as expressing a predominantly male perspective. They are attempting to correct these imbalances and present a more balanced view. The practical exercise of their criticism employs tools from many disciplines: history, psychology, linguistics, anthropology, and sociology. Lynn (1990) reports that his university students take to Feminist criticism enthusiastically, perhaps, he reasons, because of its "simplicity"—they "need only read as a woman" (p. 268). But that perspective requires "the reader to dismantle or discard years of learned behavior" and the result is striking. The Feminist perspective "quickly turns out to have a profound effect on the reader and the text—an effect that hardly can avoid being political" (p. 268).

Marxist.   Marxist critics apply Marxist theory to literature, just as Freudian critics apply psychological theory. They, like the psychology-based critics, are critical of the New Critics for being too narrowly focused on literature as art rather than as a reflection of its social, cultural, and political milieu. They see art as a projection of social history. George Watson (1986) describes Marxist criticism as "inevitably historicist, and in a special sense, since it judges all contemporary literature in relation to its political effect, and all past literature in relation to its social setting" (p. 203). Thus, although Marxist critics overlap with Historical critics, the former's emphasis is on the social forces that shape the relations between people and within culture.

Marxist critics' differ from Historical or Biographical critics in the *use* of literature as well. Their interpretation attempts to expose the explicit and implicit assumptions of the writer and the times. They are especially concerned with issues of social and economic justice: Does the writer demonstrate a sensitivity toward the exploitation of the poor? Does the text support prevailing power relationships or challenge them? Meyer (1996) explains that Marxist critics "argue that criticism, like literature, is essentially political because it either challenges or supports economic oppression. Even if criticism attempts to ignore class conflicts, it is politicized, according to Marxists, because it supports the status quo" (p. 2013). They are scornful of New Critics, who make literature a precious and elitist aesthetic form, and of Historians, who treat art as important to the transmission of the general culture, and of psychological critics, with their emphasis on the individual rather than on the social context that defines the individual. They fear literature's role as an opiate, lulling readers away from their natural grievances and social judgments. Selden and Widdowson (1993) explain: "The critic must dismantle received notions of 'literature' and reveal their ideological role in shaping the subjectivity of readers. As a socialist the critic must 'expose the rhetorical structures by which non-socialist works produce politically undesirable effects' and also 'interpret such works where possible "against the grain," ' so that they work for socialism" (pp. 93–94). Literature possesses this potential for promoting a critical consciousness of culture, a first step toward liberating the reader.

Our high school seniors often come to us with the sort of working knowledge of Marx that they have of Freud. They like to interpret "against the grain" with his ideas. The challenge is to deepen their understanding of social theory, to call them to more than a parody of Marxist principles, and to push them toward the questions that matter to a Marxist critic: What does literature say about our culture—the writer's time, the book's time? What can literature be and do in our society?

As critics brought the ideas of these extraliterary fields into their readings of texts, other critics within the field brought other ideas. The first eight schools of literary criticism share a concern for mastering the text and opening its secrets. Three prominent critical schools that developed at the end of the twentieth century believe that their critical project is based on a fundamental error. These later critics do not accept the idea that texts have definitive meanings. Their theories and practices reflect another twentieth-century phenomenon: the relentless assault on objective certainty in every area of human life and learning.

Deconstructionist. Deconstruction is not generated by extraliterary psychological, political, or social theories, but by philosophical and linguistic theories. Deconstructionists, strongly influenced by French linguistic theory, believe in a social construction of reality. They believe that language has no absolute connection with anything outside itself. It is not a precise instrument. It can never express exactly what we intend it to mean. All language is metaphoric. The world provides us with a series of signs to be read that have nothing to do with truth or what's real. Language should be properly understood as an elaborate word game.

Because of the indeterminate nature of language and communication, we must relinquish the sense that we can arrive at a right or correct reading of any literary work. Texts have no fixed boundaries, no simple, solitary meanings. Whereas New Critics examine a text to arrive at a final, fixed reading of the work, Deconstructionists examine a text to expose it as indeterminant. If New Critics try through close reading to stabilize the meaning of a text, Deconstructionists aim through close reading to destabilize it. If New Critics try to account for all of the gaps and paradoxes in a text, Deconstructionists exploit those paradoxes to undermine our assumptions of a solitary interpretation. Hillis Miller divides readings of texts not into right or wrong, but into weak or strong. "Strong interpretations" are those that display creativity, cleverness, and ingenuity. No one interpretation is privileged above others. Lynn (1990) locates the value of Deconstructionist readings for his university students just here: "It encourages creativity" and, as a bonus, careful "scrutiny" of the text (p. 263).

Although the two schools have widely different purposes, Deconstruction and New Criticism share the same method of textual analysis: close reading. (Deconstructionists explain that the close reading of the New Critics just wasn't close enough! Others call Deconstructionists' techniques close reading with a vengeance.) But Deconstructionist scrutiny aims for the logical or rhetorical inconsistencies between the explicit and implicit meanings of words, images, characters, plot, and theme. Deconstructionists will also demonstrate how these confusions are disguised by the text. Jonathan Culler (1982) explains that "to deconstruct a discourse is to show how it undermines the philosophy it asserts, or the hierarchical oppositions on which it relies" (p. 86). Barbara Johnson (1980) describes the method as "the careful teasing out of warring forces of signification within the text itself" (p. 5). Steven Lynn (1990) enumerates a three-step process of deconstructive criticism:

1. a deconstructive reading must note which member of an opposition in a text appears to be privileged or dominant . . .
2. the reading shows how this hierarchy can be reversed with the text, how the apparent hierarchy is arbitrary or illusory . . .
3. a deconstructive reading places both structures in question, making the text ultimately ambiguous. (p. 263)

Reader Response. Reader Response is a term we have used to define the first stage of our four-stage approach to reading. It is also a term used more broadly to define a body of critical theory that centers on a concern of that first stage: What readers experience as they read a text. (Other terms are also used: reader theory, audience theory, and reception theory.) Bleich (1975) begins with this assumption: "The role of personality in response is the most fundamental fact of criticism" (p. 4). Reader Response critics all agree with several principles:

- The text has no literal meaning outside the reader's acting upon it. It is not ever a finished product with a fixed, "correct" meaning. Its meaning depends on the reader's activity.
- The reader actively constructs the meaning of a text, not simply discovers it there.
- The interest of a critic is on *how* the reader creates meaning and *what* influences that reading. As Meyer (1996) explains, "we get a reading of the reader" (p. 2017).
- The contexts that influence readings are personal and social and include the reader's past and present history, psychology, past experiences of literature, and knowledge of literary convention.

If the reader's response is central, it follows that these critics are not just interested in printed texts, but in texts from a variety of media—all stimuli for response. They have thus broken down the boundaries that separate literary study from other disciplines. Television soap operas and historical documents are legitimate texts for critical study. They have further challenged the evaluative standards with which readers and critics judge literary quality. Texts don't have unvarying literary status. The distinctions between escape and serious, popular and literary texts no longer apply. Radway (1984), for instance, criticizes traditional academic judgments of romance novels (just as others reassess westerns, spy novels, and mysteries). She explains that the cultural importance of those romances depends on the meaning ascribed to them by their readers, readers who approach texts with very different strategies of interpretation.

One technique of Reader Response that illustrates its major principles is to imagine how someone with an entirely different perspective would regard a text. Consider, for instance, how *Harrison Bergeron* would have been differently received had it been published in *The Village Voice* or *Pravda*. Meyer (1996) imagines *The Story of an Hour* read by readers of *Ms.* or *Good Housekeeping*. He asks, "What assumptions and beliefs would each magazine's readership be likely to bring to the story? How do you think the respective experiences and values of each magazine's readers would influence their readings?" (p. 2019). Appendix C provides a list of books about Reader Response as a critical approach and a pedagogical strategy.

New Historical.   New Historicists have used the notion of an indeterminant text to open another approach to texts: a study of what Selden and Widdowson (1993) call "the interconnections between the literature and the general culture" (p. 162). But they are not simply using literature to illustrate the events of the past or history to illuminate literature—the old Historical/Biographical approach. They view history as "narrated" stories about past events, but never as a stable and definitive entity that we can observe and ascertain with detached objectivity. We construct a view of history from previously written texts, but our vision is always partial, determined by the particular historical context of those authors and ourselves, the readers. The New Historicists explode the notion of texts as reflecting a unified and coherent world-view of their epoch. They offer new perspectives on traditional readings of the past.

Part of their technique is to enlarge the different kinds of texts that previous literary historians left to others. They refuse to consign literature to a precious aesthetic realm removed from other forms of cultural expression. For instance, they have opened what once was considered "popular" literature to serious scrutiny. They attempt to know the culture of a period in multiple dimensions: social, economic, political, and aesthetic. Jane Tompkins (1985) suggests, for example, that the nineteenth-century sentimental novel critiques American society with far more devastating insight than those written by the better-known literary giants such as Hawthorne and Melville.

The New Historicists present an array of procedures for reading texts. They begin with a rejection of the previous assumptions that literature is an autonomous entity and that the society mirrored by that literature is stable and coherent. Then they revisit literature and reinterpret the culture reflected there and how literature influences readers to yield to this culture. They have been ingenious in tracing what appear to be trivial anecdotes and passages to reveal the organizing beliefs and codes of whole societies. They are especially interested in exposing dominant ideologies and resistances to them. That delineation of power and of resistance to it, a kind of cultural dialectic, is a hallmark of New Historical criticism.

CLASSROOM STRATEGIES

Many students enjoy entering into discrete, systematic, self-contained systems. They like to see how the schools of thought grow from and relate to each other. They are animated by the points of difference among them. They readily understand the organizing principle of different schools of thought because they experience just such organization of politics by political parties and religion by denominations and sects. They enjoy standing outside the field and uncovering principles that have been implicit, but unstated in classroom discussions. The students who profit from this introduction seem to feel both relief and release. They discover a way to recognize, tolerate, and respect differences of literary interpretation. They can sample from this array to define their own unique approaches to literature.

We use the following strategies in a senior English class of motivated, college-bound students. We introduce the theories descriptively as natural openings in class discussion arise. Initial explanations are brief minilectures, more teacher-directed than most of the strategies of the first three stages of reading. As students begin to comprehend a position, we ask them to apply that perspective in their reading and interpretation. We move back and forth between brief explanation and extended illustration and application. As students ask questions or probe more deeply, we return to central ideas of each school of thought or to additional levels of complexity. We thus try to move students from their initial inklings to an articulation of basic principles and then an application of them. Here are specific activities that have worked with our students. They work best after students have become acquainted with at least four or five of the different schools of thought.

Small-group Questions. Students are assigned to small groups representing each of the schools of criticism and are asked to generate questions that a teacher of that school might pose to a class studying a designated text. These questions can form the basis of discussion for the whole class. They also can prompt a summary consideration of the usefulness of multiple critical points of view. Possible discussion prompts include the following:

• Which questions represent your characteristic approach to a short story?
• Which questions took you closest to an encounter with the text?
• Which yielded your deepest discovery of your own response? The author's position? The story's craft? The story's "insight into essential truth"?
• Were all of the questions text centered? Did any stir your thinking beyond the text?

Jigsaw Groups. Again, the class is divided into smaller groups, each representing a different school of criticism. Each group discusses a work from its particular critical perspective. At a signal, the groups reconstitute themselves, each new group comprised of representatives from a different original group. In this new group, each individual discusses the work being studied as the critic from the school of criticism that he or she represents. (Jigsaw groups are discussed in greater depth in Chapter 11, Organizing Instruction, pp. 359–360.)

Role-playing. Students are each asked to represent a critic from a particular school of criticism with consistency, depth, and enthusiasm during a whole-class or small-group discussion. Sometimes we ask them to play their roles incognito. The mysteries created are engaging. Oddly, while critical analysis would seem to distance readers from the text, readers actually seem sometimes to get closer because they have a conscious means for moving into it. We have found that discussions of literature fired by strong competing viewpoints do not grow more cerebral. Texts are transformed from something lifeless and inert into something that matters enough for people to discuss it seriously and passionately.

Oral Application. We pose sudden questions to our students that ask them to interpret a specific piece of literature from one of the perspectives that they have studied. For instance, in the midst of a discussion about *The Adventures of Huckleberry Finn*, we might ask "How is Twain characterizing all of these nineteenth-century women? What would a Feminist critic like to say to him? To us, his readers?"

Body Sculptures. In this approach, body sculptures are used to visualize the different schools of criticism based on Abrams's (1953) sense of each critic's focus. We assign four students roles: Art, Artist, Audience, and Critic. We ask them to arrange the critic in relative position to Abrams's other three foci according to the perspective of one critical approach. For instance, a Formalist critic would position Art in a central and prominent location, with Artist and Audience greatly removed. The critic would be gazing intently at Art. The Moral/Philosophical critic, on the other hand, would be aware of Art, but over Art would stand the Audience as the primary concern. This exercise does not offer altogether unambiguous groupings, but the act of working out the silent sculpture clarifies the process.

Glossary. Like many classroom projects, the emphasis of Glossary may appear to be on a tangible product—a list of schools of criticism and terms—but the emphasis is really on the process of creating the list. After basic schools of literary criticism are introduced and some seminal terms are generally defined, we sometimes ask students to create a glossary of the schools of literary criticism and literary terms that would be useful to have in one place. You might set up the project by giving students the following instructions:

• Join the whole class in selecting essential terms and schools of literary criticism.
• Select a partner or partners with whom you will define each school of criticism and term.
• Add to your definitions illustrations from print or visual literature.
• Join a committee and choose a role for the various tasks of publishing: graphic designers, editors, word processors, binders, printers, distributors, and archivists.

When students handle the items in their glossaries through all the stages of publishing, they have a more comfortable working knowledge of these challenging ideas. An additional pay-off comes for you in following years, as students compare their glossaries to those of prior classes.

Battle of the Book Critics.   This ambitious project culminates the smaller attempts at absorption and application. Students are divided into eleven schools of literary criticism and other classes are invited to come for a discussion of a selected piece of literature. Ranged in front of the visitors, students sit under banners that declare their perspectives. The teacher begins to lead a discussion of a short text with the uninitiated students. The student-critics gradually begin to make interpretive comments based on their particular points of view. The presence of an audience energizes them and encourages their more defined and contentious articulation of their points of view. The animated and competing viewpoints startle the audience into a lively examination of the text. This presentation never fails to generate strong responses in both performers and audience and a quickened awareness of the enlivening richness of literature.

A PLEA FOR PLURALISM

Academics debate whether to ask students to commit themselves totally to a single, consistent critical position or to employ and mix the methods and insights of different schools of thought. We favor the latter, pluralistic approach for ourselves, high school students, and their teachers—with one caveat. Critic and teacher Wayne Booth makes an important distinction in *Critical Understanding* (1979) between eclecticism and pluralism. He explains that eclectics "deliberately hack other critics' works into fragments, salvaging whatever proves useful" for their purposes (p. 21). He finds, though, that such ransacking does not do justice to the original positions and is often used in the service of an entrenched position. It appears to conform to the "dictionary sense" of "rejecting a single, unitary and exclusive interpretation, doctrine or method" (p. 346). But what appears to be open and inclusive might often just mask a rigid and monistic perspective. "In practice the attitude quickly resolves into a raiding of ruined edifices in search of bricks and straw useful in a preconceived building program" (p. 24). Such raiding or even borrowing keeps the reader unfocused, confused, and inconsistent and undermines the reading done and the conclusions drawn. Pluralists, on the other hand, "claim to embrace at least two enterprises in their full integrity, without reducing the two to one" (p. 21):

> Ideally, the pluralist will examine the question each critic has chosen to ask, the critical language he employs, and his characteristic way of seeking evidence and reasoning with it. He will have been forced into pluralism by his discovery that when he has taken at least two critics' reasoning with as much seriousness as they did themselves, more than one mode emerges intact, irrefutable, viable, and not reducible or totally translatable into some other, superior mode.
>
> In practice, he will expect that some controversies will lead to a both/and resolution rather than an either/or. Having learned in at least one case that, when conflicting conclusions were related back to their intellectual sources, sharply contrasting modes proved both sound and in no final sense contradictory, he suspects, and indeed works for, further experiences of the same harmonious kind. (pp. 27–28)

We saw just such a difference of basic assumptions and therefore critical conclusions with Plato and Aristotle, and with Freud and Jung. We hope that you have been emboldened by the discovery, not baffled by it. As John Stuart Mill, in *On Liberty* (1859, 1989) observed in the nineteenth century, "in an imperfect state of the human mind, the interests of truth require a diversity of opinions" (p. 51). Mill gives a further explanation of the advantages of pluralism: "the conflicting doctrines, instead of being one true and the other false, share the truth between them" (p. 45). Booth's (1979) way of approaching literature embodies our hope in presenting this multiplicity of perspectives: "It is more a way of living with variety than of subduing it. It thus begins in what might better be called an attitude than a critical position: methodological pluralism" (p. 3).

Exposure to schools of literary criticism need not make students narrow dogmatists with a single-minded approach to literature. If students move into one camp or another, it is only temporarily. The direction of their exposure to the 11 schools of criticism should ultimately drive them toward a personal synthesis. In the final sentence of *Critical Assumptions* (1979), Ruthven says, "the supreme critical act is not evaluation but recognition" (p. 202). We agree absolutely.

THE READING CYCLE: ENTER, EXPLORE, EXTEND

The reading cycle provides an easy benchmark for an individual's approach to the text as well as a class sharing of it. It is not so much theoretical as practical. We use it to plan our individual lessons, how we get into and out of a text. Its title alone suggests the driving direction. Colleagues refer to the same rhythm and movement with a title of prepositions: Into, Through, Beyond.

ENTER

Whether our students are capable readers who arrive at a text with rich expectations or less proficient readers who can barely decode the words or comprehend the story line, they are helped by activities that invite them into literature's house. Think of these activities as invitations across the threshold. Like invitations, they swing open a door, encourage the visitor, and welcome him or her enthusiastically inside. The more familiar the circumstances and the warmer and more considerate the greeting, the easier it is for the visitor to enter and feel at home. Invitations to enter into literary texts can take many forms. Many of the activities enumerated within the Reader Response and Interpretive Community reading stages have just the effect needed: They activate students' thoughts, experiences, and feelings about a subject present in the text that follows.

The first four strategies in Reader Response—Personal Triggers, Suppositional Readers, Conceptual Readiness, and Synergistic Texts—are especially designed to invite students to enter. They also might be called prereading activities or advance organizers or anticipatory sets, because all are designed to help students anticipate the text, connect with it, and prepare to integrate it with their previous experiences, both personal and cognitive. Unlike many advance organizers, however, they try to avoid the dangers of expository teaching with its reliance on spoken communication from a more knowledgeable teacher. Kelly (1992) cautions that prereading activities, even the most carefully designed, have the potential to push a discussion in a prescribed direction and thus "inhibit divergent thinking" (p. 87). We aim instead toward entering strategies that focus the lesson on students and elicit their responses. By aiming at the personal, these strategies attempt to make texts begin to matter to all the students in the class and then leave students free to respond.

EXPLORE

Once students are engaged, they are more confident, ready, and equipped to move through a work of literature. The bulk of this chapter has presented different means for exploration through all stages of response, interpretation, formal analysis, and critical synthesis. Wilhelm (1997) enumerates ten dimensions of response to narrative literature that present a strong skeletal notion of the content of what we call Explore. He is first concerned with students entering the story world, then showing interest in the story's action, relating to characters, seeing the story's world, elaborating on the story's world, connecting literature to life, considering significance, recognizing literary conventions, recognizing reading as a transaction, and evaluating an author and the self as reader. Appendix A of his *"You Gotta BE the Book"* provides a valuable outline of questions and activities for each of these dimensions (pp. 157-169).

EXTEND

If students have entered texts and explored them, they are ready to extend them. Wilhelm's notion of considering significance goes to this final point in the cycle. Literature opens a way of seeing, of understanding more than our individual experiences might yield, of making sense of our world, of transforming the daily, and of discovering the significance there. Extending means taking the ideas, urges, and preachments of the text into our daily worlds. Yagelski (1994) envisions just such a classroom that takes literature study beyond the traditional analysis and uses it to involve students in social, political, economic, and cultural questions. Thus, students might read Hemingway's *Fathers and Sons* to find what his story reveals "about the complexities of parent-child relationships" before they go on to write narratives about their own relationships with parents and to explore related issues of "gangs, teen fashions, school reform, drugs, music" (p. 35). Collaborative groups chose a project that involves both reading and writing. In one instance, students concerned about their city's juvenile curfew ordinance read the ordinance, wrote letters, followed public debates, went to computers for information, polled local opinion, and, finally, wrote a report to the school board. Moffett's insight might be a useful mantra here: "Words on Worlds."

CHOOSING STRATEGIES

Because we were raised and trained in classrooms different from those we choose for our students, we must constantly adjust and re-align our planning to the principles of the reading stages and the reading cycle that we have just presented. Scholes (1985) explains how such principles alter the traditional role of teachers. The job of teachers is "not to produce 'readings' for our students but to give them the tools for producing their own. . . . Our job is *not* to intimidate students with our own superior textual production: it is to show them the codes on which all textual production depends, and to encourage their own textual practice" (pp. 24-25).

McGonigal (1988) describes the consequences of traditional teaching that relies on the vicarious literary analysis of others. The student "can understand literature in a third person impersonal sort of way, but dependence on a critic or on *Cliffs Notes* only strengthens a student's belief that literature belongs to others, that literature is somehow written in a foreign language comprehensible only to teachers and critics and other strange anomalies of the third kind." On the other hand, when the reader's response becomes central, "wooden responses to literature give way to perceptions that literature, good literature, lives. But literature breathes and murmurs, cajoles and lambasts, laments and rejoices only when the reader makes it do so" (p. 66).

We find guidance once again from Louise Rosenblatt (1976), who provides a benchmark for our choosing just which strategies we will use in teaching literature. She cautions that we must

> be very careful to scrutinize all our procedures to be sure that we are not in actuality substituting other aims—things to do *about* literature—for the experience *of* literature. We can ask of every assignment or method or text, no matter what its short-term effectiveness: Does it get in the way of the live sense of literature? Does it make literature something to be regurgitated, analyzed, categorized, or is it a means toward making literature a more personally meaningful and self-disciplined activity? (p. 279.)

CONCLUSION

A crucial first step toward your becoming an effective teacher of literature is that you, the teacher, read gladly and openly and that you find delight, enrichment, and illumination in your reading. That is your best hope for introducing others to it. Only when you have found works that take "the top of your head off" will you be able to help others envision and know a similar experience. Then you and your students can begin to share those texts together, to work out interpretations through attention to the new collective understandings, to form, and to other critical insights. At the end of this process of responding to literature, perhaps you and they can arrive at some appreciative sense of the work and say with Rilke that "works of art are of infinite loveliness and with nothing to be so little reached as with criticism. Only love can grasp and hold and fairly judge them."

5 REVIVING POETRY

"A poem refreshes a world."
Wallace Stevens

Poetry is like nothing else we teach. In describing what a poem should do for its readers or hearers, T. S. Eliot used the verb "interrupt." Ntozake Shange (1978) points to the same effect:

> quite simply a poem should fill you up with something
> cd make you swoon, stop in yr tracks, change yr mind,
> or make it up, a poem shd happen to you like cold water or a kiss" (p. 57).

But high school students barely notice poetry; occasionally they will consent to a handshake with it, but rarely to a kiss. In fact, our students often bring strong biases to poems, and those biases are often more negative than positive. So we begin most classroom poetry encounters with many student resistances.

Yet nursery rhymes are the delight of childhood reading. The child is rare who does not respond to the rhythm and rhyme of the words with pleasure and even enchantment. How can we explain this dramatic decline? After all, music is at the heart of adolescence. What converts rhyme-loving young-sters and rhythm-loving youths into poetry-resisting students? To find an answer to this question, let's begin by considering the following:

- Could the individual's growth or the culture's general neglect of poetry account for the loss?
- Have teachers neglected the pleasure of sound and rhythm by reading poetry aloud too little?
- Have they taught more and more poetry that has little rhyme or meter to it?
- Have teachers and textbooks selected poems too unconnected from students' lives?
- Have they been slow to celebrate poetry beyond that certified by English textbooks?
- Have teachers overemphasized the formal aspects of poetry and marginalized personal response?
- Have they overwhelmed students' natural reactions to poetry by introducing their own analytical, even private, interpretations?
- Are teachers themselves wary of poetry? Do they read poetry out of choice?

Chapter 4, Responding to Literature, articulated four stages of reading literature that are as applicable to poetry as to prose. But poetry has unique properties, which therefore make a separate chapter both desirable and necessary. Before we discuss the way poems work for meaning making, we need first to engage students in the way poems work for pleasure. The initial teaching strategies and

TABLE 5–1
Reviving poetry

Finding Poetry	Forging Poetry	Reading and Listening to Poetry	Talking Poetry
Nonliterary Prose	Templates	Definition	Adolescent Readers
Music	Fixed Forms	Choice	Choosing Poems
Advertising	Limericks	Personal Response	Listening to Poems
Radiant Images	Sonnets	Enactment	Discussing Poems
Figurative Language	Haiku	Visualization	Poetry and Prose
Compressed Language	Cinquains and Diamantes	Synthesis	Poets Talk
Bumper Stickers	Folk Ballads		
Unexpected Places	Open Forms		
	Found Poems		
	Concrete Poetry		
	Wild Cards		
	Poetry Trap		
	Dictionary Magic		
	Magnetic Poetry		

activities that we present recognize the diverse reading and writing development, experience, and styles of students and attempt to respond to that diversity. These strategies also acknowledge poetry's playful pleasures and possible meanings. What follows invites students to a meeting with poetry; it bridges their personal worlds and poetry's world and opens their sense of the possibilities that lie within. Some students will never cross even these friendly thresholds, some will timidly move into the vestibule, and some will find themselves exploring the whole poetic house and, if not wanting to reside there, at least hoping to visit often. But we like at least to welcome all of our students to its door. Table 5-1 lists our welcoming moves.

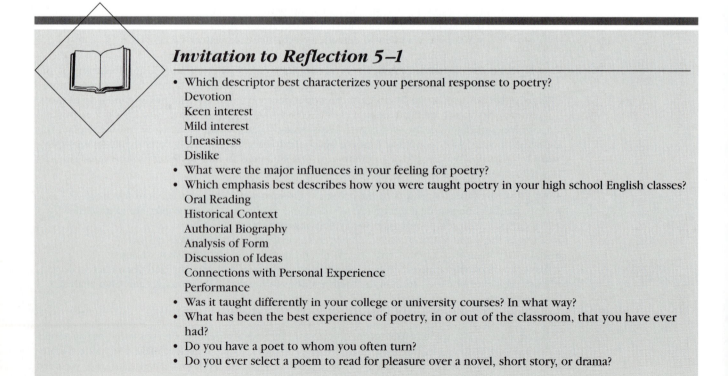

Invitation to Reflection 5–1

- Which descriptor best characterizes your personal response to poetry?
  Devotion
  Keen interest
  Mild interest
  Uneasiness
  Dislike
- What were the major influences in your feeling for poetry?
- Which emphasis best describes how you were taught poetry in your high school English classes?
  Oral Reading
  Historical Context
  Authorial Biography
  Analysis of Form
  Discussion of Ideas
  Connections with Personal Experience
  Performance
- Was it taught differently in your college or university courses? In what way?
- What has been the best experience of poetry, in or out of the classroom, that you have ever had?
- Do you have a poet to whom you often turn?
- Do you ever select a poem to read for pleasure over a novel, short story, or drama?

FINDING POETRY

We start this discussion at a place we have found to be an excellent beginning: letting students *find* poetry in the world around them. Poetry can be found in innumerable places if one knows how to look. Found poems begin as unintentional utterances discovered in such nonpoetic contexts as newspapers, advertisements, conversations, and product instructions. Found poetry has enjoyed a recent vogue, beginning with the publication of two anthologies, *Pioneers of Modern Poetry* (1967) and *Losers Weepers: An Anthology of Found Poems* (1969). But earlier practitioners such as William Carlos Williams have experimented with its power. His long poem *Paterson* quotes statistics and historical documents. In a letter, Williams says that prose can be a "laboratory" for poetry: "It throws up jewels which may be cleaned and grouped."

Finding poetry promises the delight experienced with most found treasures. And the poetic search and discovery involve all the language skills: listening, talking, reading, and writing. Our specific intentions in introducing students to found poetry are

- to awaken students to the everyday
- to expose in it unexpected realities and significances
- to discover how poetry uses words and images to startle us into an uncovering and recognition of meaning
- to move to more traditional forms of poetry with a new degree of attachment and understanding.

We discuss here poetry found in locations common to our everyday lives: nonliterary prose, music, advertising, bumper stickers, and even less expected places.

NONLITERARY PROSE

Devotees of found poetry make claims for it that take us to the heart of the questions "What is poetry?" "What distinguishes it from prose?" "How are the poet's perceptions and craft unique?" Lester, in the preface to *Search for the New Land: History of Subjective Experience* (1969) explains: "We are so accustomed to reading horror in each day's newspapers, the news columns bordered by ads, that we have become insensitive to that horror. By taking news articles and arranging them as poems, what was mere news in one context becomes the human experience it really is."

Gorrell (1989) enumerates a three-part lesson that begins with a found poem, *Parents,* by Julius Lester, and grows to an exploration of the nature and effects of poetry. That lesson will be explanation enough for our belief in the power of found poetry. Read, as Gorrell's students do, the following poem.

Parents

Linda failed to return home from a dance Friday night.
On Saturday
she admitted she had spent the night
with an Air Force Lieutenant.

The Aults decided on a punishment
that would "wake Linda up."
They ordered her
to shoot the dog
she had owned about two years.

On Sunday,
the Aults and
Linda
took the dog into the desert
near their home.
They
had the girl
dig a shallow grave.
Then

Mrs. Ault
grasped the dog between her hands and
Mr. Ault
gave
his daughter

a .22 caliber pistol
and told her
to shoot the dog.

Instead,
the girl
put the pistol
to her right temple
and shot herself.

The police said
there were no charges
that could be filed
against the parents
except possibly

cruelty
to
animals.

Julius Lester*

Students' shock and horror immediately provoke a discussion of the narrated events. And the class quickly arrives at an urgent question: "Did this really happen?" At this point Gorrell distributes the following article from the *New York Times* (1976, Feb. 7, p. 29):

Coed Kills Herself to Spare Pet Dog Doomed By father

PHOENIX, Ariz., Feb. 6 (AP)—Linda Marie Ault killed herself, policemen said today, rather than make her dog Beauty pay for her night with a married man.

"I killed her. I killed her. It's just like I killed her myself," a detective quoted her grief-stricken father as saying.

"I handed her the gun. I didn't think she would do anything like that."

The 21-year-old Arizona State University coed died in a hospital yesterday of a gunshot wound in the head. The police quoted her parents, Mr. and Mrs. Joseph Ault, as giving this account:

Linda failed to return home from a dance in Tempe Friday night. On Saturday she admitted she had spent the night with an Air Force Lieutenant.

The Aults decided on a punishment that would "wake Linda up." They ordered her to shoot the dog she had owned about two years.

On Saturday, the Aults and Linda took the dog into the desert near their home. They had the girl dig a shallow grave. Then Mrs. Ault grasped the dog between her hands, and Mr. Ault gave his daughter a .22-caliber pistol and told her to shoot the dog.

Instead, the girl put the pistol to her right temple and shot herself.

The police said there were no charges that could be filed against the parents except possibly cruelty to animals.

New York Times

As students sort out the differences in the two accounts, they naturally begin to consider why Lester left out certain details and then to speculate about the difference in news reporting and poetry writing. In a gradual, broadening progression, students work toward important definitions of the nature of poetry. Gorrell nudges them with her own perceptions. She writes: "I point out how the poem enabled us to 'be in Linda's shoes'—to experience the moment with all its choices and inexplicable emotional textures. I suggest that the poem, unlike the news article, enabled us to participate in the event. Lester skillfully leads us to place anger and blame. I stress that poetry should be evocative, empathetic, and experiential" (p. 32). She moves then to discuss how poetic language works to this end, not by the presence or absence of "meter, rhyme, stanzaic form, sound devices, and figurative language," but by its intensity, precision, and concision (p. 33).

Gorrell says that she concludes her first poetry class with "the most appropriate response to poetry—writing our own." She capitalizes on students' enthusiasm for the poem *Parents* with an assignment to find poetry that allows them to be "enthusiastic seekers having acquired a new sensibility—to feel and think poetically." Teaching Activity 5-1 presents two found poetry assignments: Gorrell's verbatim, with numbers added (p. 33), and an alternative version.

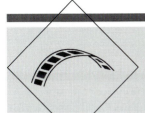

Teaching Activity 5–1   Found Poetry Writing

I

1. Search newspaper and magazine articles, editorials, textbooks, instruction manuals, catalogues, labels, personal and want ads, "notes left on paper bags"—any non-literary source—for hidden poetic potential.
2. Lift and isolate at least three consecutive lines from the text and arrange to expose new meanings.
3. Keep the words in the same order. Do not add words to change the original material.
4. You may add a title and space and break lines and words any way you wish to create new meanings or sound effects. Search for hidden ironies, puns, and incongruities. The result may be serious, shocking, ironic, sarcastic, clever, or humorous.
5. After you have written your poem, write it on a ditto master so that it may be duplicated for the class. Include a copy of the original source, including a complete citation. Have fun finding poetry in all the "wrong" places!

II

1. Find any prose sentence or passage (in a newspaper, magazine, catalogue, textbook, or advertising copy) that has "poetic potential."
2. Copy it into lines of poetry, placing what you consider the most interesting words at the ends of lines to give them greatest emphasis.
3. Strip out unnecessary, prosaic words.
4. Rearrange syntax, compress phrases, and repeat key words—anything but add words, the one rule in found poetry.
5. Repeat key words. Gather words to create a refrain.

Gorrell summarizes the effects of finding poetry in nonliterary expository prose, articulating the power that we, too, think it possesses for students:

> In sum, found poetry is an ideal tool or starting point for teaching poetic response. It lets students connect to what excites, outrages, inspires, and provokes them in the real world. It starts where they are, and lets them respond with passion. It provides a vehicle for attitudinal change—poetry is everywhere to be discovered. It makes students active observers and seekers developing their own poetic sensibilities. And last, it inspires students to write their own poems—the final and perhaps most important way of responding. (p. 34)

She demonstrates its potential for "enlightenment" as well as "sheer fun" in a poem a student mailed to her a year after her lesson on found poetry (p. 34):

Veteran
(*The Wall Street Journal,* October 27, 1987)

when the shooting comes
he (instinctively) dives
    for cover.
    as young men with machine guns
        run over his territory,

he scurries back
    to safety.
    (he has lived (so far))
he is wise
he feels no pain
he is hard.
he is not unscathed, he suffers
        "What psychologists call
          post-traumatic stress
           "disorders."

he has seen three young men die.
but that's what happens in war
And in life,
in the housing projects of Chicago.
For this veteran is
twelve years old.

Geoffrey Klingsporn

Jeff Morgan asked his high school sophomores to write poems based upon "a recent, actual event in the news." He collected these poems into a book, *Reality into Art: Selected Current Event Poetry by Watauga High School Sophomores: 1996,* and published it on the W.H.S. Web page. One of its poems, *The Trek,* by Andrew Tillman was later spotted by its subject, Borge Ousland, in Norway as he searched his name on the web. Ousland responded via e-mail to the poet.

The Trek
Borge Ousland did what no one else had done
He skied to the North Pole by Himself
And
He skied to the South Pole by himself without any Assistance
Then he tried to go across The White Wilderness the same way
But, also, he failed
"No
Matter"
Says he
He says,
"Skiing alone for so long gives you a different
Perspective
on
Life, you
Really understand what a small piece you are in
Nature's Greatness,"
His son painted his skis various colors so Ousland had
Something
To Concentrate on
While crossing a
White
Wilderness.

Andrew Tillman

MUSIC

Music provides another entry into poetic understanding and pleasure. We have mentioned that the sounds and rhythms of spoken language awaken children's earliest delight in poetry. Kennedy (1976) observes that "most poems are more memorable than most ordinary speech, and when music is combined with poetry the result is more memorable still" (p. 556). Songwriters, like poets, choose "words for sound as well as meaning," and use "the sound as a means of reinforcing meaning" (Perrine, 1983, p. 666). Teaching Activity 5-2 is designed to help students begin to make these connections between music and poetry.

Teaching Activity 5–2   Lyric Elements

Whole Class. Play a song that has printed lyrics available, selected by you, a student, or a group. Classic rock songs that have been instructionally effective for us include the Beatles *Eleanor Rigby,* Simon and Garfunkel's *Sounds of Silence,* Don McLean's *American Pie,* Leonard Cohen's *Suzanne,* Crosby, Stills and Nash's *Southern Cross,* Sting's *Fields of Gold* and *Fortress Around Your Heart,*

Natalie Merchant's *Carnival,* and the Dave Matthews Band's *Satellite.* These songs have lyrics that are rich, textured, nuanced, and challenging yet not overly elusive, and rhythms, meter, sounds, repetitions, and even rhyme that are kin to what is central to poetry.

Individuals. Ask students to look at and listen carefully to the lyrics two or three times. Ask them to ignore for a moment the music's content, then enumerate the lyrics' formal features and elements. Student lists will likely include such items as the following:

1. Two or more words repeat the same sound.
2. The words and music create a kind of beat or pulse that repeats with variations.
3. A few vivid, concrete objects or experiences are presented.
4. Unexpected comparisons are made.
5. Some words feel special; they seem to mean a lot.
6. Some phrases or lines are repeated at intervals.

Small Group. Have students listen to several student-selected songs, then examine sets of lyrics and determine whether those same elements are repeated in the additional songs.

Whole Class. Each group reports its conclusions. Ask students whether any of the musical elements that they have found resemble the terms they remember from earlier discussions of poetry.

Some students will need the teacher's prodding or direction to see the relation between music and poetry. But the preceding exercise usually prompts students to realize that they have rediscovered some of poetry's essential elements:

- Rhyme—Two or more words that sound the same are repeated.
- Meter—The words and music create a kind of beat or pulse, a rhythm.
- Images—Vivid and concrete objects and experiences are presented by an appeal to the senses.
- Figures—Unexpected comparisons are used.
- Symbols—Some words feel special; they seem to represent something beyond themselves.
- Refrain—Some phrases or whole sections that look alike are repeated.

You may wish to present additional songs whose sound and sense strike you and students as poetry. Many will need deliberate help in developing criteria for selecting lyrics that reflect some depth of observation or insight and some attention to the language that expresses it. Even when music is innovative, the lyrics may be banal and trite. If you and your students need other resources and have little time to search, you might look for the following references, older now and sometimes hard to find, but still containing original ideas and classic examples:

D. Pichaske, Ed.	*Beowulf to Beatles: Approaches to Poetry*	1972
D. Morse	*Grandfather Rock*	1972
Richard Goldstein, Ed.	*The Poetry of Rock*	1969
Stephanie Spinner, Ed.	*Rock Is Beautiful*	1970
Jonathan Eisen, Ed.	*The Age of Rock*	1969
Nancy Deane, Ed.	*Voices of Revelation*	1970

These books contain lyrics that the authors and editors believe deserve to be read as poetry, as well as examples of correspondences between "rock" poetry and "classroom" poetry. (Their copyright dates make us wonder whether the late 1960s and early 1970s were a time of greater open-mindedness about poetry than today is.) They make an aesthetic argument for accepting some rock music as narrative, dramatic, and lyric poetry of verbal grace and power. They also make a pedagogical argument: Approaching poetry through rock music demonstrates to the young that poetry is "not a thing far removed from the ordinary sphere of human experience, but a thing at the center of our lives" (Pichaske, 1972, p. xxvi).

Nowhere is the relationship between traditional elements of poetry and music more apparent than in rap, with its heavy reliance on cadence, rhythm, rhyme, and compression. The appeal of this music for the young affirms our sense of poetry's original pleasures. We have found students of all abilities absorbed by rap and deeply interested in playing it in class. One poem that neatly bridges the space between the poetry of class discussions and the rap of solitary headsets is Maya Angelou's *Harlem Hopscotch.* Imagine as you read the poem a classroom presentation in which two students read the poem aloud as one or two pantomime the action of this familiar game and one or two others mime the clapped rhythm of hopscotch bystanders.

Harlem Hopscotch

One foot down, then hop! It's hot.
  Good things for the ones that's got.
Another jump, now to the left.
  Everybody for hisself.

In the air, now both feet down.
  Since you black, don't stick around.
Food is gone, the rent is due,
  Curse and cry and then jump two.

All the people out of work,
  Hold for three, then twist and jerk.
Cross the line, they count you out.
  That's what hopping's all about.

Both feet flat, the game is done.
They think I lost. I think I won.

Maya Angelou

Music also can be linked as an accompaniment to poetry. Hutchinson and Suhor (1996) encourage students to make connections between words and music that animate each other. Their practical guidelines for a performance of these connections begin with questions of alternative sequences of poetry and music:

* Music begins, then poetry enters;
* Poetry first, music entering at appropriate point;
* Alternation of short poems and short musical vignettes;
* Short sections within a longer poem . . . with interspersed musical vignettes or phrases;
* Musical backdrop of one or more tunes for a string of short poems on a common theme. (pp. 80–81)

Sato (1995) uses a fifth alternative: She accompanies individual poems with music, selections such as *Nocturnal Sounds* by Kattie M. Cumbo, *Latest Latin Dance Craze* by Victor Hernandez Cruz, and *Piano Man* by Joyce Carol Thomas.

Music and poetry profit from being heard and read together. Many older English ballads began their lives as songs. Shakespeare scattered songs throughout his plays. Many of his contemporaries wrote original poems to fit existing tunes. Few of the melodies survive, but these survivors have power: Ben Jonson's *To Celia* (Drink to me only with thine eyes) and the anonymous Scottish ballad *Bonny Barbara Allan*. In the U. S., practically every school child knows the Kentucky mountain song *On Top of Old Smoky* and the ballad *Frankie and Johnny*. Modern composers have written powerful choral music based on poetry and poetic prose as well, following the example of Beethoven's choral finale to the ninth symphony based on Schiller's "Ode to Joy." The following are samples:

Benjamin Britten	*Hymn to St. Cecilia* (op. 27, 1942)	W. H. Auden
Frederic Rzewski	*De Profundis* (1992)	Oscar Wilde
Ralph Vaughn Williams	*Jerusalem*	William Blake

Whishaw (1994) used the linguistic variety in her classrooms to teach the music of poetry (and the rewards of collaboration with someone from another language family). During a poetry writing unit, she had her students write poems in their first language and then pair with a speaker of a different first language to translate the poem. Poet and translator read the original poem and its translation before the entire class. Whishaw asked students to listen for the music of the translation regardless of the words' meaning. Collom and Noethe (1994) suggest asking students who are acquainted with second languages to write poems that mix languages in the same poem in order to pick up the "sonorities" of language even when meaning is only barely grasped (pp. 158–159). (Modern poets Ezra Pound, T. S. Eliot, and Robert Lowell shuttled between languages, even ancient ones.)

ADVERTISING

We may not choose to listen to and read advertising as we do music, but we are nevertheless continuously bombarded by it. Because it is so pervasive and perceived as so ordinary, we seldom attend to it as a craft in its own right. But some of our most inventive minds are working in this field. Agencies, constricted by space (print media) or time (broadcast media), are forced to make words and images count so as not to waste their clients' money. If poets, as Emily Dickinson says, "tell all the truth but tell it slant," advertisers sell their truth but sell it "slant." Studying the carefully crafted language of advertising can serve poetic purposes. Advertisers use, among other techniques, three elements that are basic to poetry: radiant images, figurative language to compare unlike things, and compressed language.

Radiant Images.   A close scrutiny of advertising will heighten students' consciousness of the power of visual and verbal imagery to evoke a place, a person, a situation, or an idea. If students can understand the highly selective choices made by professional advertisers and the connections they make between objects and ideas, they may see and appreciate more readily these same careful selections made by poets. Students may also, by inference, understand the importance of using sharp, vivid images for the success of the commercial or poetic enterprise. One classic Coca-Cola TV ad has wholesome young people of great cultural diversity lighting up a European hillside with their brotherhood as evident as their bottles of Coke. The radiant connection is clinched by their melodiously singing "We'd like to teach the world to sing, in perfect harmony." Perrine (1983) observes that the poet seeks "concrete or image-bearing words in preference to abstract or non-image-bearing words" (p. 563). Holman (1980) describes the power of such images in literature: "The *image* is one of the distinctive elements of the 'language of art,' the means by which experience in its richness and emotional complexity is communicated. . . . The *image* is, therefore, a portion of the essence of the meaning of the literary work, not ever properly a mere decoration" (p. 223). Ezra Pound (1954) wrote that "it is better to present one image in a lifetime than to produce voluminous works" (p. 4). Advertising careers are made by creating just such singular imagery.

Figurative Language.   Observing advertising also can be instructive for introducing and playing with figurative language, specifically *metonymy,* the figure of speech in which a significant aspect or part of one thing is used to suggest its whole or something associated with it. Metonymy functions in poetry to make the abstract concrete. Similarly, metonymy is at work in most advertising as advertisers contrive for consumers to associate their product with a desirable outcome. Thus, if we wear a certain brand of basketball shoes, we can play like, or be, a superstar. A standard Christmas beer commercial assures viewers an experience of holiday cheer—even the old-fashioned, mythical cheer of horse-drawn, bell-jingling sleighs—if they drink a certain brew. As Scholes, Comley, and Ulmer (1988) suggest, these commercials aim to establish a "metonymic connection" between good times and their product, "hoping the viewer will accept a further metaphoric connection and finally a cause-and-effect connection: the beer *is* good and a *cause* of good times" (p. 122). The verbal imagery of poetry and the visual imagery of advertising transform abstractions into concrete sensuous or sensible objects.

Compressed Language.   Concision is important in both advertising and poetry. As with the poet's images and metaphor, the language of advertising must be concentrated. Readers, hearers, and viewers must have their attention arrested and quickly satisfied. Thus, advertisers, like poets, must be resourceful, and they must imaginatively choose their vocabulary. Korg (1966) explains that "in poetry, as in every art, the limitations of the medium provide the artist with his most exciting opportunities. Just as a sculptor may shape hard stone into the soft-looking curves of a body, or a painter may produce the effect of depth on a flat canvas, so a poet works with language to overcome its natural deficiencies. He does this not by using a special vocabulary of unusually high-powered words, but by using more or less ordinary words in special ways" (p. 22). The creators of billboards, magazine ads, and radio and TV spots are confined by space, time, and audience attention and therefore must carefully select their visual and verbal imagery. As Emerson said, "Poetry teaches the enormous force of a few words." Teachers can illustrate that same lesson through the contemporary medium of advertising, which in 1996 poured 175 billion dollars into a few words (Coen, 1997, p. 20).

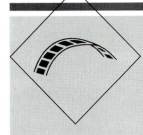

Teaching Activity 5–3   Advertising

Individuals	Bring print advertisements to class from any source (newspapers, magazines, broadsides, or fliers) or audio/video advertising (selected clips recorded from radio or TV).
Small Groups	Examine these ads. Select the ones that you consider to be the most effective in their use of vivid imagery and compressed and figurative language.
Whole Class	Present these selected ads to the whole class and explain why they are effective. Choose several class favorites.
Small Groups	Reconvene and attempt to improve the ad's appeal to this particular class. Words or images should be scrutinized and altered *if* they can be strengthened.
Whole Class	Each group presents the edited version or explains why the original ad cannot be improved.

BUMPER STICKERS

The world of bumper stickers is not very distant from that of advertising. Even more than advertisements, however, this single medium must rely almost exclusively on words to make its mark. And like poetry, the creators of bumper stickers often attempt to sell an idea rather than a tangible product. Gunslingers, choice protectors, and lovers of states and all sorts of creatures work to use a small space to deliver a strong message. Most of the qualities that distinguish ads are evident in bumper stickers, where words dominate. Many slogans reflect neither insight nor cleverness, but students can scavenge for really creative ones and examine the way in which the words are used—rich connotations, sharp images, imaginative juxtapositions, and ironies—to arrest our split-second vision. "America—Love It or Leave It" may not represent your idea of tolerance, patriotism, or respect for the individual, but this sticker was once so commonplace that we suspect its appeal is more than political. The language itself is appealing: its compression, alliteration, word and sound repetition, and approximate rhyme of *love* and *leave*. *America,* followed by the two visions balanced one against the other, is bold. "Give Peace a Chance" is another powerful slogan of just four words that comes from the other end of the political spectrum. Its power comes from its direct appeal, its compression, and the strong, concrete verb and nouns: *give, peace,* and *chance.* "Save the Baby Humans" is stark and direct also, but it draws its force from an ironic juxtaposition; it is a play on the original slogan "Save the Baby Seals." Anti-abortion advocates want a reader to be shocked into remembering the original version and realizing that the life of a baby human should be even more precious than that of a baby seal. The bumper sticker would not be as effective without the allusion. A similar bumper sticker, "Save the Whales," has been rendered ironically as "Nuke the Whales" and, more recently, as "Save the Males." One of our favorite bumper sticker parodies derives its punch from the original slogan "Preserve Your Right to Bear Arms." The parody has all of the poetic elements we've mentioned: concrete image, figurative (nonliteral) language, and compressed language: "Preserve Your Right to Arm Bears." In addition, this bumper sticker possesses one of poetry's most winsome qualities: playfulness.

Whatever the message may be, comparing bumper stickers with poetry can be useful in introducing students to the conscious selection of compressed, vivid language for a desired effect. Scrutiny of bumper stickers that fail can be equally instructive in uncovering the way words work. Students enjoy collecting and sharing the bumper stickers they see. Challenge students to both collect examples and make their own. Like ads, bumper stickers help students express the human predilection to play with language. (Visualize Whorled Peas.)

UNEXPECTED PLACES

We also suggest finding poetry in less expected poetic corners: children's books, student literary magazines, and other noncanonical sources. Easily accessible poems written for younger readers recall high school students to the world of poetry. High school teachers and librarians have long appreciated the appeal of Shel Silverstein's books *Where the Sidewalk Ends* and *The Light in the Attic* to attract and delight students. Table 5–2 lists 20 titles of accessible and appealing poems found in children's literature anthologies. They merely serve as exemplars of the resources available. They have reminded some of our most reluctant poetry readers of their childhood pleasure in verse. When these students enjoy and affirm these poems, they become more receptive to, comfortable with, and understanding of the poetry in their secondary and college texts. Julia Neenan asked her 10th graders to bring children's poetry to class to illustrate formal poetic elements. Their sharing brought them back to the origins of their experience of literature, and they realized that they knew and felt more than they thought they did.

One high school librarian points out that it is a discouraging but clear indication that students like a book when it is "ripped off" repeatedly. She cannot keep Mel Glenn's books on the shelves. He is a high school teacher who writes biographical poems and even attaches pictures of students. We include his titles in Table 5–3 with other anthologies that teachers and librarians have found bring even reluctant readers headlong into poetry.

A description by French author and artist Jean Cocteau (1969) of the nature of poetry's impact on the reader vividly explains our hope for the impact of found poetry on the student:

> Suddenly [in poetry], as if in a flash, we *see* the dog, the coach, the house for the first time. Shortly afterwards habit erases again this potent image. We pet the dog, we call the coach, we live in a house; we do not see them anymore. . . . Such is the role of poetry. It takes off the veil, in the full sense of the word. It reveals . . . the amazing things which surround us and which our senses usually register mechanically. (pp. 179–180)

Poet Marianne Moore calls this moment at which the mind apprehends "the lion's leap." We believe that we often underestimate poetry's appeal to young adults. Perhaps that is true because many have not received such cordial invitations to it.

	Author	**Poem**
TABLE 5–2 Poetry from children's anthologies	Anonymous	*Poor Brother*
	Richard Armour	*Money*
	Hilaire Belloc	*Henry King*
	Richard L. Callienne	*I Meant to Do My Work Today*
	Lewis Carroll	*The Crocodile*
	Arthur Hugh Clough	*"There is no God" The Wicked Saith*
	Ebenezer Elliot	*On Communists*
	Bret Harte	*At a Reading*
	Ralph Hodgson	*The Bells of Heaven*
	Maxine W. Kumin	*Sounds of Weeds*
	Vachel Lindsay	*The Moon's the North Wind's Cooky*
	John Masefield	*Sea Fever*
	E. L. Mayo	*The Mole*
	David McCord	*Books Fall Open*
	David McCord	*Cocoon*
	Theodore Roethke	*Praise to The End!*
	Shel Silverstein	*The Loser*
	Shel Silverstein	*Skinny*
	Karl Shapiro	*Manhole Covers*

TABLE 5–3 Noncanonical poetry anthologies	Arnold Adoff	*I Am the Darker Brother*	1968
		All the Colors of the Race	1982
	Steve Dunning, Edward Lueders, and Hugh Smith	*Reflections on a Gift of Watermelon Pickle*	1967, 1995*
	Mel Glenn	*Class Dismissed! High School Poems*	1982
		Class Dismissed II: More High School Poems	1986
		Back to Class	1988
		My Friend's Got This Problem, Mr. Chandler: High School Poems	1991
	Ruth Gordon	*Under All Silences: The Many Shades of Love*	1987
	Paul Janeczko	*Postcard Poems: A Collection of Poems for Sharing*	1979
		Don't Forget to Fly	1981
		Poetspeak: In Their Work About Their Work	1983
		Pocket Poems	1985
		Preposterous: Poems of Youth	1991
	Kenneth Koch	*Rose, Where Did You Get That Red?: Teaching Great Poetry to Children*	1973, 1990**
	Kenneth Koch and Kate Farrell	*Sleeping on the Wing: An Anthology of Modern Poetry with Essays on Reading and Writing*	1981**
		Talking to the Sun: An Illustrated Anthology of Poetry for Young People	1985**
	Myra Cohn Livington	*A Circle of Seasons*	1982
		There Was a Place and Other Poems	1988
	Frances McCullough	*Love Is Like the Lion's Tooth*	1984
	Jon Stallworthy	*A Book of Love Poetry*	1974

*About one-fourth of the material in the first edition has been cut and replaced with new poems.
**These valuable texts contain poems and suggestions for how to teach children, or, we would add, anyone, to read and write them.

Teaching Activity 5–4   Teaching Found Poetry

Whole Class

Have you ever read a newspaper account that caught your fancy and made you want to share it? Here's what Ursula K. LeGuin read from the Associated Press and what she did with it. Read the AP report and poem, first silently, then aloud.

Found Poem

However, Bruce Baird, Laguna Beach's chief lifeguard, doubts that sea lions could ever replace, or even really aid, his staff. "If you were someone from Ohio, and you were in the water having trouble and a sea lion approached you, well, it would require a whole lot more public education," he told the Orange County Register.

Paul Simon, for AP, 17 December 1984

If I am ever someone from Ohio
in the water having trouble
off a continent's west edge
and am translated to my element
by a sudden warm great animal
with sea-dark fur sleek shining
and the eyes of Shiva,
I hope to sink my troubles like a stone
and all uneducated ride
her inshore shouting with the foam
praises of the freedom to be saved.

Ursula K. LeGuin*

Small Group or Whole Class

- If you were drowning in the ocean, would the approach of a sea lion worsen your situation? Would it confound you?
- Which would you prefer reading, the news report or the poem?
- Did the AP account strike you as containing provocative material?
- What one line of the poem is most indebted to the news account? Which strays the furthest from it?
- What is the effect of arranging the newspaper account in lines? Is the meaning or language enhanced by this change?
- Does the arrangement of individual lines point out any particular image or meaning?
- Do any details take on additional depth?
- If you had written this poem, would you have published the source of the poem alongside the poem itself? What is the impact of reading the prose and poetry together?
- Do you consider the poet less creative because she found the poem outside of herself?

*From "Found Poem," copyright © 1986 by Ursula K. LeGuin; first appeared in *Buffalo Gals and Other Animal Presences;* reprinted by permission of the author and the author's agent, Virginia Kidd.

FORGING POETRY

Letting students make poetry is another essential step in promoting student engagement with and response to poetry. The word *poet* derives from the Greek *poietes,* which means "one who makes." (William Carlos Williams referred not to his *writing* a poem, but to his *making* a poem.) We are going to present specific poetry-writing suggestions that range from the more tightly controlled poetic forms to more open forms. Before we discuss specific activities, though, we want to present some general ideas about how to structure classrooms for poetry writing. The books of Georgia Heard* (1989) and Jack Collom and Sheryl Noethe (1994), poets and teachers themselves, have given us many sound and creative ideas about setting a stage and inspiring students to write poetry. Many of their suggestions are aimed at younger students, but they work for our high school students as well.

The physical arrangements of a room—its organization and furnishings—influence what goes on there, whether it be poetry writing, reading, listening, or discussing. Heard says she sometimes thinks that "the information about how to write a poem is less important than the atmosphere of the room. There are places that give me an excited urge to write, places that feel rich and warm, where time slows down and whatever I want to do is possible" (pp. 21–22). She goes on to render that visual environment for a classroom: "It's important that classrooms have this richness: books standing on the table, poems on large paper displayed all over, quotes by poets on the walls, kids writing everywhere, intently" (pp. 22–23).

With such a stage set, what are effective stage directions for poetry-writing projects that are spontaneous or calculated, brief interludes or class-long? Billings (1992) recalls an article in which Richard Hugo gave sage advice on how to approach poetry writing: "I remember three things from it: one, make them use lead pencils so that they are not in the slightest way encouraged to think of their early-draft words as permanent; two, tell them they had better have some favorite words and use them a lot, unless they are amazingly talented; and three, coax them to have 'the courage of their obsessions'" (p. 82). Heard has her own list of several things for teachers to remember as they begin to teach poetry writing:

- *Prepare the soil....*
- *Let students decide what they want to write about....*
- *Create an open, trusting environment.* When students are willing to write about what's really on their minds, their poetry is extraordinary. As a teacher I'm aware that every time I choose to listen instead of control, every time I encourage, and every honest self-revelation I'm brave enough to make bring the classroom closer to being the kind of environment where good poetry can flourish.
- *Spend enough time....*
- *You don't have to be the expert.* (pp. 34–35)

No matter how she begins, Heard "keeps in mind these lessons my own writing has taught me":

- *Poems start with a feeling, and an image is one powerful way to convey feeling....*
- *Poets write about what they can't help writing about....*
- *It's crucial not to censor, especially at the beginning.* (pp. 32–34)

Collom and Noethe are poets experienced in organizing poetry-writing sessions around a classroom hour. Their book (1994) is filled with effective poetry writing activities for that hour as well as general advice about leading these sessions. For instance, they suggest an organization of time that is divided equally between an introduction to the session, poetry writing, and oral reading of the new poems. They advise encouraging students to be playful with language, to experiment, to be concrete, and to allow significance to emerge naturally, not by reaching for the "Big Idea." They believe that teachers should "speak of the mechanics of poetry as naturally as you'd speak of fixing a broken shoelace." They think that teachers should insist that student writers reread their poems and revise them instantly while they are "still in the flow and feeling of the poem." They recommend that teachers not criticize student poetry when it is first read, but give praise that is genuine and concrete (pp. 1–9).

Appendix B contains other books that we have found useful for teaching poetry. We discuss here four strategies for encouraging poetry writing that moves from the most scripted to the most free: Templates, Fixed Forms, Open Forms, and Wild Cards.

TEMPLATES

A *template* is a mold or pattern from which a new object or idea is formed. Poetic templates provide a form into which students pour their own words. They are effective with young writers because they provide a structure that does not require what traditionally would be considered poetic utterance. Students can be engaged in careful word choice without the consciousness or intimidation of usual poetic elements such as meter and rhyme. And the template can begin with simple, structured patterns and later move to more complex, freer ones. The templates that follow are comfortable starters for students because they invite them to work from familiar material: themselves.

*All excerpts adapted by permission of Georgia Heard: FOR THE GOOD OF THE EARTH AND SUN: TEACHING POETRY (Heinemann, A division of Reed Elsevier Inc., Portsmouth, NH, 1989).

FIGURE 5–1
Bio-poems

Line 1: Your first name only	I am . . . (Use two words to describe yourself.)
Line 2: Four traits that describe you	I wonder . . . (What do you want to know about life?)
Line 3: Sibling of . . .	I hear . . . (What sounds do you hear in your mind?)
Line 4: Lover of . . . (three people or ideas)	I see . . . (What sights do you see with your mind's eye?)
Line 5: Who feels . . . (three items)	I want . . .
Line 6: Who needs . . . (three items)	I am . . . (Same as first line)
Line 7: Who gives . . . (three items)	I pretend . . . (What do you pretend to be or do?)
Line 8: Who fears . . . (three items)	I believe . . .
Line 9: Who would like to see . . . (three items)	I touch. . . (What do you reach out and touch—literally or figuratively?)
Line 10: Resident of (your city), (your road name),	I feel . . .
Line 11: Your last name only	I worry . . . (that . . . , about . . . , over . . . , when . . . , etc.)
	I cry.
	I am . . . (Same as first line)
	I understand . . . (What do you understand about life?)
	I say . . . (What do you have to say about this?)
	I dream . . .
	I am . . . (Same as first line)

The first templates result in a brief biography, called a *bio-poem,* and have been circulated for so many years that no one knows their precise origin. They have been effective for us with students of all abilities. Some students have already encountered them in junior high, but because they are undergoing such accelerated changes, they write fresh, new poems even though the templates remain constant. The two templates, as shown in Figure 5–1 consist of partially complete lines that students finish.*

Sears (1987) offers yet another pattern, which we adapt here, set up as an exercise that invites reflection and expression about oneself. Students pick one of the moods listed in Figure 5–2. They brainstorm ways that the mood does not feel, then brainstorm ways that the mood does feel. They cull from their lists to write a poem, using the following pattern:

1. Required Line (select your own mood)
2. An example of how your mood DOES NOT feel
3. Another example of how your mood DOES NOT feel
4. Another example of how your mood DOES NOT feel
5. Required Line (another way of describing the mood)
6. An example of how your mood DOES feel
7. Another example of how your mood DOES feel
8. Another example of how your mood DOES feel

The following student poem demonstrates the effect of Sears's template in guiding young writers to chose concrete images to carry specific feelings—important learnings at the heart of poetry.

> I'm mellow
>   Not a go lay in a sunny field
>   smoking a cigarette mellow
>   Not mellow enough to give a bum
>   all my money
>   Not mellow enough to sit on an
>   ocean yacht and drink lemonade
> But just a sit in the air conditioned
>   living room watching reruns mellow
>   Mellow like a nothing to do Saturday
>   morning
>   Mellow like watching your cork from
>   the banks of a cool country pond
>   A do what I want mellow that takes
>   no effort or planning.
>
>   *Jimmy O'Daniel*

*We ask anyone who knows the identity of the teachers who originated these two templates to write us care of the publisher. We will be happy to give full credit in subsequent editions of this book.

FIGURE 5–2
Feelings that people
have, but fail to
identify

Abandoned	Crushed	Frightened	Kicky	Piteous	Stingy
Adamant	Culpable	Frustrated	Kind	Pitying	Strange
Adequate		Full		Pleasing	Stuffed
Affectionate	Deceitful	Furious	Laconic	Pleased	Stunned
Agitated	Defeated		Lazy	Precarious	Stupefied
Agonized	Delighted	Glad	Lawful	Pressured	Stupid
Almighty	Desirous	Good	Left out	Pretty	Suffering
Ambivalent	Despairing	Gratified	Lifeless	Prim	Sure
Angry	Destructive	Greedy	Lonely	Prissy	Sympathetic
Annoyed	Determined	Grieved	Longing	Proud	
Anxious	Different	Groovy	Loving		Talkative
Apathetic	Diffident	Guilty	Low	Quarrelsome	Tempted
Astounded	Diminished	Gullible	Lucid		Tenacious
	Discontented			Raging	Tense
Bad	Distracted	Happy	Mad	Rapt	Tentative
Beautiful	Distraught	Hateful	Maudlin	Refreshed	Tenuous
Betrayed	Disturbed	Heavenly	Mean	Rejected	Terrible
Bitter	Divided	Helpful	Melancholy	Relaxed	Terrified
Blissful	Dominated	Helpless	Miffed	Relieved	Threatened
Bold	Dubious	High	Miserable	Remorseful	Thwarted
Bored		Homesick	Mystical	Restless	Tired
Brave	Eager	Honored		Reverent	Trapped
Burdened	Ecstatic	Horrible	Naughty	Rewarded	Troubled
	Electrified	Hurt	Nervous	Righteous	Turbulent
Calm	Empty	Hysterical	Nice		
Capable	Enchanted		Niggardly	Sad	Ugly
Captivated	Energetic	Ignored	Nutty	Sated	Uneasy
Challenged	Enervated	Immortal		Satisfied	Unsoiled
Charmed	Envious	Imposed on	Obnoxious	Scared	
Cheated	Evil	Impressed	Obsessed	Screwed up	Vehement
Cheerful	Exasperated	Infatuated	Odd	Servile	Violent
Childish	Excited	Infuriated	Opposed	Settled	Vital
Clever	Exhausted	Inspired	Outraged	Severe	Vivacious
Combative		Intimidated	Overwhelmed	Shocked	Vulnerable
Competitive	Fascinated	Isolated		Silly	
Condemned	Fawning		Pained	Skeptical	Weepy
Confused	Fearful	Jealous	Panicked	Sneaky	Wicked
Conspicuous	Flustered	Joyous	Parsimonious	Solemn	Wonderful
Contented	Foolish	Jumpy	Peaceful	Sorrowful	Worried
Contrite	Frantic		Persecuted	Spiteful	
Cruel	Free	Keen	Petrified	Startled	Zany

Templates can be more open, based on less restrictive patterns. We have found other poems to be effective templates. Each of the following has a distinctive structure or idea that invites adaptation:

Richard Armour	*Money*
Elizabeth Barrett Browning	*How Do I Love Thee?*
Adelaide Crapsey	*Triad*
Rudyard Kipling	*If*
Marcia Lee Masters	*April*
Harold Monro	*Overheard on a Salt Marsh*
Karl Shapiro	*Manhole Covers*
Stephen Spender	*What I Expected*
William Stafford	*Fifteen*
Wallace Stevens	*Thirteen Ways of Looking at a Blackbird*
William Carlos Williams	*This Is Just to Say*
William Carlos Williams	*So Much Depends*

We read the original poem and ask students to imitate it. The following is English teacher Lezlie Laws Couch's (1987) poetic confession. She mimics Williams's *This Is Just To Say* to reflect on why she changed her teaching method from a formalist to a response-based approach to poetry:

This Is Just To Say*
I'm sorry to have
guided you poorly

To have burdened you
with schemes and
trophes

And meter and form
Long before you
were ready

Forgive me
I didn't know
how to begin . . .

Lezlie Laws Couch

Rock music provides many templates that are provocative and have the additional appeals of being musical, rhythmical, and connected with the familiar and desirable in the worlds of our students. Lyrics that have worked well for us with students include Paul Simon's "These are the days of miracles and wonders . . . ," Billy Bragg's "I don't want to change the world, I'm not looking for New England, I'm just looking . . . ," and ". . . said the firefly to the hurricane, said the falling rain to the open plain." Students can add new verses or create new refrains using similar patterns.

Grossman (1991) presents broad but personal templates to her students with titles such as "When I Grow Up," "The Rooms We Live In/The Rooms We Leave Behind," and "I Am Not Who You Think I Am." Collom and Noethe (1994) enumerate many poetry-writing exercises based on loose templates. The exercise titles alone suggest a creative range of possibilities for patterned poems:

Acrostics	"Last Words" Poems
Acrostics from Phrases	List Poems
Chant Poems	"My Soul Is . . ." Poems
Declarations	Recipe Poems
Definition Poems	Spelling List Poems
Geometry Poems	"Things to Do" Poems
"Going Inside" Poems	Used to/But Now Poems

Harmston (1988) suggests a relatively open template and a method for encouraging spontaneous, not mechanical response. Figure 5–3 presents Harmston's lesson verbatim. Mary Beth Braker says that this page of *Bridging English* is particularly tattered because she uses Harmston's exercise with every level of students—general, college preparatory, and honors—several times a year (personal communication, 1997). She reports that she and her students are always amazed at the intimate, concise poetry this exercise sparks.

FIXED FORMS

Some students like to play with traditional fixed forms, patterns that strictly govern a whole poem. Adrienne Rich explains that writing within predetermined form was part of her early writing discipline: "like asbestos gloves, it allowed me to handle materials I couldn't pick up bare-handed." The limerick and sonnet are the most common fixed forms in English poetry. The haiku from Japan, the more obscure five-line cinquain and seven-line diamante from France, the folk ballad, and the ode are progressively freer fixed forms. Some of our students feel uncomfortably constrained by such arbitrary prescriptions and write grudging and mechanical verse. But others enjoy the constraints of composing within an established tradition. They even sometimes discover why these poetic conventions survived centuries; that is, they come to appreciate the relation between the structure and the thoughts or feelings. Perrine's (1983) explanation of the challenge of form for the serious poet is pertinent to students as well, even those who are reluctant writers and readers of poetry:

> The inferior poet, of course, is often defeated by that challenge: he will use unnecessary words to fill out his meter or inappropriate words for the sake of his rime. The good poet is inspired by the challenge: it will call forth ideas and images that might not otherwise have come. He will subdue his form rather than be subdued by it; he will make it do his will. There is no doubt that the presence of a net makes good tennis players more precise in their shots than they otherwise would be. And finally, there is in all form the pleasure of form itself. (p. 723)

---

*From Lezlie Laws Couch, "So Much Depends . . . On How You Begin: A Poetry Lesson," *English Journal,* November, 1987.

FIGURE 5–3
A lesson on
impromptu poetry

Sometimes an apparent constraint can serve to free the imagination. In this activity, students stretch their creativity and their understanding of metaphor as they write to beat the clock. With adaptation, this approach could be used at all grade levels.

I designate each row of students as a separate team and give each team a metaphor from the list below.

Sleep is a stone	Dreams are hollow logs
Belief is a doorway	Anger is a palace
Fear is cold water	People are windows
Evening is a crooked highway	Loneliness is an empty streambed
Parents are blankets	Love is a fountain
Friendship is a seesaw	Morning is a bridge
Summer is a sleepy turtle	Anger is a rope
Amazement is a mirror	Fear is a hummingbird
Jealousy is a razor	War is an old car

Working individually, students are to build and extend the metaphor by adding four additional lines. The result will be a five-line poem from each student.

In round one, students each have three minutes to complete a five-line poem. The students who finish their poems in the allotted time are asked to read them aloud. I comment briefly on interesting images and effective use of language in students' poems.

If students need help starting their poems, I suggest that they begin the second line with "that" or "when"; they can then develop answers to how, where, and why in the remaining lines. If some students are still having trouble developing poems quickly, they might simply describe the concrete object mentioned in the first line. The metaphorical connection established in the first line will be carried through the brief image students compose.

In round two, each row receives a new metaphor. This time, students have two minutes to complete a five-line poem. Again the students who complete poems read them aloud.

The third and final round proceeds in the same way, except that students have only one minute to complete their five-line poems.

As the time for writing is reduced, students have less time to plan what to write; with one minute of writing time, students end up jotting down whatever images or phrases spontaneously pop into mind. This may not create great poetry, but it does have a freeing effect, and the results sometimes contain fresh and original images.

Here is an example of a poem written for this activity.

> Belief is a doorway
> Opening, Closing
> Always thinking
> You have the truth
> But not really knowing

Teams with the most completed poems for each round may be recognized at the end of the activity. One appropriate way of rewarding students might be to let the winning team choose several poems by their favorite authors for the class to read and discuss.

SOURCE: From "Impromptu Poetry" by D. Harmston, 1988. In F. A. Kaufman (Ed.), *Ideas Plus: A Collection of Practical Teaching Ideas, Book Six.*

Ronald Gross (1967) produces found poetry from the prose of newspapers and traffic signs, yet his discovery of poetry in prose underscores Perrine's point: "As I worked with labels, tax forms, commercials, contracts, pin-up captions, obituaries, and the like, I soon found myself rediscovering all the traditional verse forms in found materials: ode, sonnet, epigram, haiku, free verse. Such finds made me realize that these forms are not mere artifices, but shapes that language naturally takes when carrying powerful thoughts and feelings."

Limericks.   The limerick is probably the most popular fixed form because of its association with playfulness and bawdiness. Its form demands only two end rhymes, and it has a catchy metric pattern that almost every secondary student knows; furthermore, its tone and content are almost exclusively irreverent and humorous, which students enjoy and relish. The limerick pattern is five anapestic lines (three syllables, two unaccented, one accented) that usually rhyme aabba, but it can be grasped almost instantaneously simply upon hearing it. Most limericks are anonymous, having passed into the oral tradition so readily that their authors went unnoticed. We have found that the name of a friend or one's school or town provides a good beginning for limericks. We have a friend who enjoys asking her seniors to write limericks after they read *Oedipus Rex*. Her students wrote the following two examples.

> There once was a king that was wise,
> who conquered a sphinx of great size.
> He went on a date,
> And met the wrong mate,
> And ended up losing his eyes.
>
> *Sally Wilson*

> There once was a king called Rex
> Upon whom the gods laid a Hex.
> He did a bad thing
> With mom had a fling
> And developed an awful complex.
>
> *Jonathan Milner*

Sonnets.   The sonnet has almost no rivals in English poetry for its popularity and durability. The English imported the form from Italy in the middle of the sixteenth century and almost immediately gave it their own rhyme scheme. Kennedy (1966) observes that "so great was the vogue for sonnets in England at the end of the sixteenth century that a gentleman courtier might have been thought a boor if he proved unable to write a decent sonnet when a lady demanded one" (p. 183). Sonnets are quite complex, but that very challenge may be what draws some students, just as it has many courtiers and poets, to them. Wordsworth captures that interest in the lines of his sonnet "Nuns Fret Not at Their Convents' Narrow Room":

> In sundry moods, 'twas pastime to be bound
> Within the sonnet's scanty plot of ground;
> Pleased if some souls (for such there needs must be)
> Who have felt the weight of too much liberty,
> Should find brief solace there, as I have found.
>
> *William Wordsworth*

The two forms of the sonnet provide students with some alternatives: the abrupt surprise of the English, or Shakespearean, form (with its three quatrains and concluding couplet) and the clear smoothness of the Italian, or Petrarchan, form (with its eight- and six-line division). In both forms, the divisions of the lines often correspond with divisions of thought. Many modern poets have revitalized the sonnet by writing variations of it. Maya Angelou's *Harlem Hopscotch,* presented earlier in this chapter, is one surprising variation. Part of the play for them, we might imagine, is the same for our students: putting an old form to immediate and everyday use. The following sonnet was written by high school senior Julie Dunlop and published in *Heritage* (Spring, 1991, p. 58), the James Madison High School (Vienna, Virginia) student literary magazine.

> *Resonance: An English Sonnet*
>
> A brightly colored patchwork offers me
> warm refuge from the chill of mountain air—
> I lie in Mother's childhood room and see
> out-dated photos—Mom with long, curled hair!
> The pale blue ceiling tempts me, and I think
> of wriggling through its cracks to find a bit
> of airborne thought and dreams to build a link,
> for that is how tomorrow's hopes are lit.
> Cold rain is spiking hard against the tin
> roof. I am reminded that we all
> are a part of life's sweet melodies (and din)—
> whose notes our sleepy, silent minds recall.
> The past is churning in a hoary brew
> just like a river when the rains are through.
>
> *Julie Dunlop*

Haiku.   The haiku is an attractive form for young writers because, we think, its structure is straightforward and manageable and the content calls for simple, stark, sensory images. In its Japanese origins, it consisted of three lines of five, seven, and five sounds (like English syllables) respectively; American practice has taken some liberties with these. The first line sets up a concrete image, usually from nature, and the subsequent lines juxtapose another image or "vortex" as Ezra Pound called it, on top of the original. The classic haiku moves from the concrete detail of a specific moment in the first line to that image's universal and spiritual implications in the last. Haiku depends on careful, precise observation and a sense of the meaning unleashed by the observed object. It possesses one of the virtues of poetry generally: An image can convey—in a flash—meaning beyond itself. An abstraction is understood through the senses. In effective haiku, the reader arrives at that suggested meaning with surprise and recognition. As with the limerick, a good introduction to writing haiku is reading haiku. Two good reference books are Cor Van Den Heuvel's (1986) *The Haiku Anthology* and William J. Higginson's (1989) *The Haiku Handbook: How to Write, Share, and Teach Haiku.*

Cinquains and Diamantes.

Heard (1989) calls the haiku and cinquain "the hamburger and hot dog of American poetry classrooms" (p. 96). The cinquain and a similar form, the diamante, are far more obscure than limericks, sonnets, and haiku, but they provide an accessible, somewhat flexible form for the student writer. Surprisingly perhaps, personal topics can be shaped with these forms. The familiar and personal material reduces the intimidation of the structure; the structure shapes the stuff of memory and reflection. Figure 5-4 outlines the two.

Folk Ballads.

The folk ballad is an inviting form because it is a simple narrative, not limited by either length or rhyme scheme. (Common four line rhyme schemes are abba, abab, or abcb in which only two lines rhyme.) Ciardi (1959) explains the nature of this oral, often musical, folk tradition, and enumerates its appeal to our students as readers and writers as well:

> It is easier to remember the high spots of an action than to remember all the connecting detail: so the folk ballad leaps from peak to peak of the story's action, skipping the incidentals. It is easier to remember an action than it is to keep straight the moral comment upon it: so the folk

FIGURE 5–4
Cinquain and diamante

CINQUAIN

title
describe   title
action   action   action
feeling   about   the   title
title

Line 1: A word for the title (two syllables)
Line 2: Two words to describe the title (four syllables)
Line 3: Three words to express action (six syllables)
Line 4: Four words to express feeling (eight syllables)
Line 5: The title again, or a word like it (two syllables)

DIAMANTE

noun
describing   describing
action   action   action
transition   nouns   or   phrase
action   action   action
describing   describing
noun

Line 1: noun
Line 2: two adjectives
Line 3: three participles
Line 4: four nouns or phrase
Line 5: three participles indicating change
Line 6: two adjectives
Line 7: contrasting noun

ballad tends to consist of action for its own sake, and to avoid moralization. It is easier obviously, to remember an effective image, phrase or detail than it is to remember an ordinary or ineffective one: so the folk ballad, its weak points weeded out, has become a treasury of a sort of poetry that English-speaking people have found unforgettable. Finally, the folk-mind is most likely to be attracted to larger rather than smaller kinds of action: so the folk ballad is full of tales of life and death—of tragic loves, of bloody betrayals, of heroic deeds; and so the action tends to be direct and uncomplicated by subtleties and minor motives. (p. 685)

You can invite students to write ballads from personal experience, from news stories, or from their own imaginations. The familiar form, the strong story line, the simple language, the repetition—all make this form accessible for the student writer. Although folk ballads are usually anonymous, Pete Seeger, Johnny Cash, Bob Dylan, Kenny Rogers, Joan Baez, Bruce Springsteen and many other modern songwriters compose and sing their own narrative versions of the traditional forms. The melody and rhythm of existing ballads may supply a musical template for students' compositions. (Many famous ballads are simply new lyrics composed to the tune of an old familiar melody.) Or, students can compose music for the ballads they write. As Hall (1987) predicts: "When a harrowing story is told in rhymed and delicate verses, the tension between form and content, story and music makes a dreadful energy" (p. 518). Here are some questions to be asked of ballads, anonymous, poet made or student made:

- What has happened here? Can you see why these events attract a balladeer?
- What are the feelings that rise from this action for the characters? For you, the reader?
- Could any of the stanzas be omitted? Do they build to a climax?
- Are important things implied, not stated? What is gained by what is *not* told?
- If there is repetition, what is its effect on you? Does it add to suspense or emotional intensity?
- How does music reinforce the tone?

Other Verse Formulas.   Many other established poetic designs provide patterns. Pantoums, rondels, sestinas, troilets, and villanelles are based on more complex patterns of rhyme, meter, and repetition. You might present one of these traditional patterns and examples to illustrate it or ask students to read an example and sum up the rules that govern it. For instance, Dylan Thomas wrote a poem to his aging father, *Do Not Go Gentle into That Good Night,* in the fixed form of the courtly French villanelle. After discovering the poetic rules, a good next question is: What does the poet gain by casting ideas and feelings in this fixed form? (A number of poems are entitled by their form and thus both demonstrate form and effect: Jean Passerat's "Villanelle," Elizabeth Bishop's *Sestina,* and Ezra Pound's *Sestina*).

Heard (1989) has distilled suggestions that give students a clear entry into the particulars of a given form. Her suggestions for a villanelle serve as models for effective teaching tips:

- Begin with a subject that's important, something crucial; then write the two rhyming lines that will repeat throughout the poem.
- It's easier if the two rhyming lines are big and open; if they're concrete, with specific images, it will be harder to keep hearing them again and again.
- After the two repeating lines are written, play around with the others; it's like working a puzzle. Patience and persistence pay off. (p. 95)

If stricter constraints frustrate students, they might respond to more open forms, those defined by intent and mood more than by stanzaic, metrical, and rhyming structure, such as the ode, lyric poem, and elegy. We have found the following references to be useful for other fixed forms:

Paul Fussell	*Poetic Meter and Poetic Form*	1979
Preminger, Warnke, and Hardison, Eds.	*Princeton Encyclopedia of Poetry and Poetics*	1965
Ron Padgett, Ed.	*The Teachers and Writers Handbook of Poetic Forms*	1987
Lewis Turco	*The Book of Forms: A Handbook of Poetics*	1968

Poetic Forms, hosted by Ron Padgett, consists of 10 30-minute audiocassette discussions of 10 basic poetic forms: free verse, haiku, ode, ballad, acrostic, list poem, sonnet, prose poem, villanelle, and blues poem. Each tape gives an informal definition and illustration of the particular form and lively advice about reading and writing poems in that genre. (The tapes can be ordered through Teachers and Writers Collaborative, 5 Union Square West, New York, NY 10003–3306.)

Hullet (1991 NCTE Idea Exchange) borrowed an idea from Grossman (1982) about a way to prompt her students to write an ode. An ode is constrained by conventions, although it is not as circumscribed by meter and rhyme as other forms are, as illustrated by *Ode to My Socks,* Figure 5-5. Teaching Activity 5-5 adapts Hullet's lesson, which employs this ode.

FIGURE 5-5
Ode to My Socks

Ode to My Socks

Maru Mori brought me
a pair
of socks
which she knitted herself
with her sheepherder's hands,
two socks as soft
as rabbits.
I slipped my feet
into them
as though into
two
cases
knitted
with threads of
twilight
and goatskin.
Violent socks,
my feet were
two fish made
of wool,
two long sharks
sea-blue, shot
through
by one golden thread
two immense blackbirds,
two cannons:
my feet
were honored
in this way
by
these
heavenly socks.
They were
so handsome
for the first time
my feet seemed to me
unacceptable
like two decrepit
firemen, firemen
unworthy
of that woven
fire,
of those glowing
socks.

Nevertheless
I resisted
the sharp temptation
to save them somewhere
as schoolboys
keep fireflies
as learned men
collect
sacred texts.
I resisted
the mad impulse
to put them
into a golden
cage
and each day give them
birdseed
and pieces of pink melon.
Like explorers
in the jungle who hand
over the very rare
green deer
to the spit
and eat it
with remorse,
I stretched out
my feet
and pulled on
the magnificent
socks
and then my shoes.
The moral
of my ode is this:
beauty is twice
beauty
and what is good is doubly
good
when it is a matter of two socks
made of wool
in winter.

Pablo Neruda
(*Translation by Robert Bly*)

Teaching Activity 5-5   Forging an Ode

Whole-class Minilecture. Explain that the topic of an ode is often serious and its tone formal. Odes tend to be more public than private. They often include lofty sentiments, spoken with dignity. They are longer than most lyric poems are. Common topics elevated enough for an ode are initiation, beauty, truth, freedom, love, the meaning of life, and death. One of the best-known odes in English literature is Wordsworth's *Ode: Intimations of Immortality.* Read a few of its familiar lines. Have students jot down topics that they consider to be of high seriousness that might be fit for an ode.

Whole-class Reading and Discussion

- What topics did you write down?
- Do they conform to the usual seriousness of odes?
- Listen now to Pablo Neruda's ode. (Have a student read *Ode to My Socks,* Figure 5-5. The student reader needs to be alerted in advance in order to provide an effective reading with the proper seriousness.)
- Did Neruda's poem fit your expectation of lofty sentiment and high poetic purpose?
- Does the language fit the way you talk about the socks you wear?
- What lines let you know the value of the socks to him?
- Does it seem a waste of good images and metaphors to go on so about socks?
- If you were Maru Mori, would you be pleased?
- Now that you know what an ode is, do you think that Neruda's title adds anything to his poem?
- Here is a letter that Neruda might have written to the knitter Maru Mori (Hall, 1987, p. 463). Which would you have preferred receiving: the poem or the letter?

Dear Maru Mori,
   Thank you ever so much for your kind gift of a pair of socks. They are very pretty. They are warm. They fit me perfectly. I will wear them all the time. Mrs. Neruda likes them too. Thank you again. Yours truly, Pablo Neruda

Individual. Choose your favorite article of clothing to write a poem about. Make a list or a cluster of the characteristics of this piece of clothing. (Show students the cluster of characteristics illustrated in Figure 5-6.) Include all of the information in the sample cluster and anything else you feel is important about it. Then select details that are especially striking. Use Neruda's poem as your model to write your own ode.

FIGURE 5–6
Cluster of characteristics

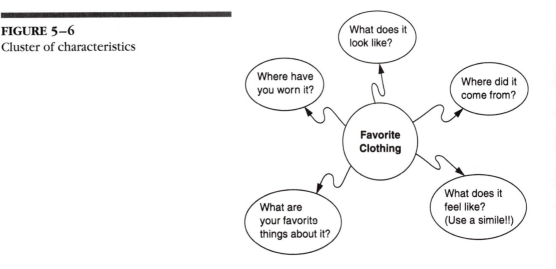

OPEN FORMS

Like templates or fixed forms, open forms invite students to play within constraints. Robert Frost defined freedom as "moving easy in harness." We have always thought that this perfectly defined poetry as well. Open forms provide a fairly easy harness, but they are not without restraints. They do not necessarily use traditional meter, rhyme, and stanzas, but they still rely on a heightened use of language—word choice, repetition, and rhythm—and line arrangement to achieve poetic effects. Frost distrusted open forms; he said, "writing free verse is like playing tennis with the net down." But many modern poets and earlier poets such as Walt Whitman played poetry quite effectively without the traditional nets.

Found Poems. The found poems discussed earlier are open poems. They rely on white space, line breaks, indentations, and repetitions as well as selected (intensified) words for their effect. An exercise that reveals the poet's purpose is to take any open poem and rewrite it into lines (even paragraphs) of running prose. Read it aloud, letting punctuation dictate pauses and stops. Then consider: What did the poet gain by arranging these words as poetry?

Concrete Poetry. Concrete poetry is arranged so that its words show visually what they render verbally. They are shape poems. They make designs out of the arrangements of letters and words. Elementary children delight in "picture poems," but such serious poets as George Herbert in the seventeenth century and e. e. cummings and John Hollander in the twentieth also have played with this form. Following is a modern poem for the eye, *Kitty and Bug.* As you read it, consider whether it is anything more than an ingenious exercise. Does the visual trimming of lines point out meaning? Does it mean less than meets the eye? Does it entertain eye and ear?

Kitty and Bug

```
          I           a
       cat        who
       coated   in   a
       dense shadow
       which I cast
       along myself
          absorb the
          light you
          gaze at me
          with can yet
          look at a king
          and not be seen
          to be seeing any
          more than himself
       a motionless seer
          sovereign of gray
       mirrored    invisibly
       in  the  seeing  glass
       of air Whatever I am
       seeing  is  part  of  me
       As  you  see  me  now  my
       vision   is   wrapped   in
       two  green  hypotheses
       darkness    blossoming
       in  two  unseen  eyes
       which pretend to be
          intent on a spot of                    bug
          upon
          the
          rug
       Who
       can
       see
          how
             eye
             can
       know
```

*John Hollander**

As you can see, what concrete poets try to achieve is an "eye pun." Poetry collections of concretists such as John Hollander, Richard Kostelantz, and Mary Ellen Solt give a range of examples, which provide a good starting point for students. Students should begin their own attempts at a concrete poem with a particular or tangible concrete image. This is an instance in which freedom of paper, time, and imagination is essential.

---

*From *Harp Lake,* copyright © 1988 by John Hollander; first appeared in the *New Yorker;* reprinted by permission of Alfred A. Knopf, Inc.

WILD CARDS

These strategies are freer and may attract students who are uncomfortable or annoyed by templates, fixed forms, and even open forms. They draw attention to poetry's playfulness and delight in words. The exercises discussed here are Poetry Trap, Dictionary Magic, and Magnetic Poetry.

Poetry Trap.   This exercise provides more structure than is imposed by the other forms, but that structure can be altered at will to meet your own goals and to interest your students. Our exercise was adapted from a Vassar College teacher involved in the Excellence in Teaching English Institute at Vassar. In this exercise, we use four fairly common poetic forms or tools: blank verse (unrhymed iambic pentameter—the best-known, repeated one-line pattern in English verse, which Shakespeare used for most portions of his plays), enjambment (a run-on line in which the sense of the line carries into the next line), internal rhyme (rhyme in which final-consonant sounds are the same, but vowel sounds differ, as in *rover* and *lover*) and slant rhyme. If students are unfamiliar with the terms, we define and illustrate them, although we are always most interested in their recognizing the devices and their function, not in labeling them. Oddly, in this exercise we ask students to move from words to meaning, rather than the usual sequence, from meaning to words. Student response to this has always been very positive; some complain about its rigidity at first, but that is the very source of creativity and interest for most. The trap of the title comes to suggest engagement, not imprisonment, in the playfulness of poetry making. Teaching Activity 5–6 shows a sample framework.

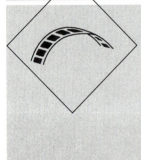

Teaching Activity 5–6   Poetry Trap

Individual Assignment.   Write a poem in blank verse using at least 13 of the following words. You must use at least three verbs, four nouns, and two adverbs. The blank verse should include one instance of enjambment, three internal rhymes, and two or more slant rhymes.

rent	whimper	apt
becalm	shunt	somber
tinge	spent	woefully
rancor	cudgel	throe
nor	already	shun
fleece	mince	trip
awful	meagerly	haze
spot	bubbly	vixen
balk	hoax	shore
gloat	nave	eagerly

Dictionary Magic.   The most adventurous of these divergent forms is Dictionary Magic. This exercise asks students to fill a form—a template, fixed form, or wild card—with words drawn randomly from the dictionary or preselected word banks. It is like formal verse without attention to the usual concern for meaning. Individual students or a group can assemble a verse in this way. It may appear to take poetic play headlong toward verbal chaos, but with some students it frees delight. The arbitrary construction is energizing, and the final production often invites a sense of wonder at its novel and surprising juxtapositions.

Magnetic Poetry.   Poet-musician Dave Kapell devised a method to help him through writer's block: He cut words from magazines and arranged them to form lyrics. Because he has allergies and his sneezing badly dislocated his songs, a roommate gave him magnets with which to secure his words. So successful was the project that Kapell developed and markets Magnetic Poetry Kits (Heller, 1996, p. 125). Each kit contains over 400 magnetized words and word fragments and, although they are most commonly seen on refrigerator doors, they also can work on classroom surfaces: stationary file cabinets, portable cookie sheets—any steel surface. Something in the play of words against surfaces, of words chosen and before you, of the words themselves, encourages poetic play by individuals, pairs, or groups. The popularity of Magnetic Poetry has led the 1990s president of the Academy of American Poets, Jonathan Galassi, to speculate that "America's youth is bored with the way technology tends to suppress the imagination" (p. 125). U.S. Poet Laureate Robert Hass calls Magnetic Poetry "one-man scrabble and the prize is insight" (p. 125).

Whether you are asking students to find or forge poetry, the goal is the same: From poetry play comes poetry ease, enjoyment, and understanding. Some students will continue to feel poetry's essential difference from our everyday prose and their everyday lives, but some may come to identify with Holden Caulfield's younger brother Allie in J. D. Salinger's *Catcher in the Rye*. Before he becomes ill with leukemia, 11-year-old Allie writes poems in his baseball mitt so he will have something to read while he waits in the outfield for fly balls.

READING POETRY

We believe in giving students the poetic license to find and create poetry, but also the poetic liberty to look at poetry in ways that are not strictly analytical. We present here six classroom strategies that engage students personally and experientially. We have drawn on the insights of Paulo Freire in naming this section Reading Poetry. Freire (1987) defines reading as the discovery of "the connections between the text and the context of the text" and also the connections of "the text/context with my context, the context of the reader." We welcome students into the text/context and personal context of the poems with our six strategies: Definition, Choice, Personal Response, Enactment, Visualization, and Synthesis.

DEFINITION

The first strategy camouflages as traditional analysis, but it is not. We start with a poem that does not have the look of serious poetry. A concrete poem, such as e. e. cummings's *1(a* is perfect:

E. E. Cummings*

The appearance alone of *1(a* prompts students to ask elemental questions:

- What is this? Is it a poem?
- What does it mean?
- Why does cummings arrange this on the page as he does?
- Has there been some terrible typo?
- Why doesn't he just write "a leaf falls"?
- Why not write the letters "loneliness" together?
- Is *1(a* more or less of a poem than *Tintern Abbey?*

Such questions engage students in the very act of defining the art form. By thinking at this level, some open themselves to a broader and more confident sense of what poetry can be and do. When students consider how an individual poem does or does not conform to their expectations of what a poem is, they may shake free from notions of poetry as remote, formal, and dismal. They may begin to discover for themselves the playfulness of poetry. They may enter the special kind of game poetry plays with language and experience—so different from our everyday use. They may discern that the stuff outside the parenthesis—"loneliness"—and that inside—"a leaf falls"—form the two basic components of a poem: the universal and the concrete. They may understand Edwin Arlington Robinson's observation: "Poetry has two outstanding characteristics. One is that it is undefinable. The other is that it is eventually unmistakable."

- What areas are still confusing to you?
- What feelings does the poem evoke for you?
- What meanings do you feel the poem is expressing?

Use freewriting (start writing and keep writing) for your process log. Do not be concerned if you have questions and uncertainties; simply try to identify them as specifically as you can. You are trying to describe HOW you read and understood as well as WHAT you read and understood. (pp. 59-60)

*Reprinted with permission of Kathleen Dudden Andrasick: *Opening Texts: Using Writing to Teach Literature* (Heinemann Educational Books, Portsmouth, NH, 1990).

Nelms (1988) recounts an incidental lesson that encourages just this personal response to poetry. She seized the moment of her students' early springtime restlessness and their pleas to have class out-of-doors. She had them go outside without talking or throwing Frisbees, read the poetry designated, and "take time to reflect in their quiet places, and then write in their journals for ten minutes before returning to class at the end of the hour" (p. 23). Then, in perfect synchronization with her lesson and her students' feelings, she saw them off by reading Wordsworth's *The Tables Turned*. We include the whole text here because Wordsworth's short poem contains our same warning about shutting the doors of perception.

The Tables Turned

Up! up! my Friend, quit your books;
Or surely you'll grow double:
Up! up! my Friend, and clear your looks;
Why all this toil and trouble?

The sun, above the mountain's head,
A freshening lustre mellow
Through all the long green fields has spread,
His first sweet evening yellow.

Books! 'tis a dull and endless strife:
Come, hear the woodland linnet,
How sweet his music! on my life,
There's more of wisdom in it.

And hark! how blithe the throstle sings!
He, too, is no mean preacher:
Come forth into the light of things,
Let nature be Your Teacher.

She has a world of ready wealth,
Our minds and hearts to bless—
Spontaneous wisdom breathed by health,
Truth breathed by cheerfulness.

One impulse from a vernal wood
May teach you more of man,
Of moral evil and of good,
Than all the sages can.

Sweet is the lore which Nature brings;
Our meddling intellect
Mis-shapes the beauteous forms of things:—
We murder to dissect.

Enough of Science and of Art;
Close up those barren leaves;
Come forth, and bring with you a heart
That watches and receives.

William Wordsworth

ENACTMENT

Enacting poems is another alternative to analysis. Chapter 3 presented many activities that use poems as the vehicle for drama. Narrative poems and ballads are clearly effective as drama, but practically all poems have a dramatic tension that students can enact. The following three activities move progressively away from the poem as written by the poet.

The first invites mimes and a narrator/reader to work as a team to present the poem. Frost's *Home Burial* works well for such staging. As one student reads the poem, two miming students, as the wife and husband, change places on stairs as the poem reveals their opposite but equal reactions to the death of their son. A more direct enactment stages the poem as a play with the words spoken in dialogue between two or three players. When a male and a female read Yeats's *For Anne Gregory* aloud or John Wakeman's *Love in Brooklyn,* the dramatic tension is palpable. Similarly, the serious disagreement between Booker T. Washington and W. E. B. Du Bois in Dudley Randall's *Booker T. and W. E. B.* comes vitally alive when spoken. In William Blake's *The Clod and the Pebble* and Ralph Waldo Emerson's *The Mountain and the Squirrel,* two opposing points of view are represented by inanimate objects. As you read the following, imagine staging it.

The Clod and the Pebble

"Love seeketh not Itself to please,
  Nor for itself hath any care,

But for another gives its ease,
And builds a heaven in Hell's despair."

So sang a little Clod of Clay,
Trodden with the cattle's feet;
But a Pebble of the brook
Warbled out these metres meet:

"Love seeketh only Self to please,
To bind another to its delight,
Joys in another's loss of ease,
And builds a Hell in Heaven's despite."

William Blake

The most indirect enactment of the poem is for students to script their interpretations as drama. Students could, for instance, write dialogue and action for the two infantrymen in Hardy's *The Man He Killed* as they faced each other in war and might have met in peace. Or, dialogue might accompany the work of the ants in Frost's *Departmental*. The conversations and actions of the characters in Brueghels' painting *The Fall of Icarus* could be enacted as someone reads W. H. Auden's *Musee des Beaux Arts*. A group, Poetry Alive! performs poetry in schools and encourages teachers to organize poetry performance in their classrooms. Their teacher's edition of Wolf's *Something Is Going to Happen: Poetry Performance for the Classroom* (1990) gives basic tips for poetry performance, 15 scripted poems, director's notes, and additional learning activities. Figure 5–8 is their scripting of Leigh Hunt's poem *The Glove and the Lions* and their questions to consider for staging it.

FIGURE 5–8
Script and questions for *The Glove and the Lions*

THE GLOVE AND THE LIONS
    BY LEIGH HUNT

Suggested cast:
voice 1: the lady
voice 2: the knight
voices 3, 4, & 6: the court
voice 5: the King

voice 1	The Glove and the Lions
voice 2	by Leigh Hunt
voice 3	King Francis was a hearty king,
voice 4	and loved a royal sport,
voice 3	And one day as his lions fought, sat looking at his court;
voice 5	The nobles filled the benches,
voice 6	with the ladies by their side,
voice 3	And 'mongst them sat the Count de Lorge, with one for whom he sighed:
voice 1	And truly 'twas a gallant thing to see that crowning show,
voice 2	Valor and love,
voice 1	and a king above,
voice 2	and the royal beasts below.
voice 5	Ramped and roared the lions,
voice 6	with horrid laughing jaws;
voice 1	They bit,
voice 2	they glared,
voice 3	gave blows like bears,
voice 4	a wind went with their paws;
voice 6	With wallowing might
voice 5	and stifled roar
voice 1	they rolled on one another,
voice 3	Till all the pit
voice 2	with sand and mane
voice 6	was in a thunderous smother;
voice 5	The bloody foam above the bars came whisking through the air;
voice 6	Said Francis then,
voice 5	"Faith, gentlemen, we're better here than there."

FIGURE 5–8
continued

voice 6	De Lorge's love o'er heard the King,
voice 2	a beauteous lively dame,
voice 1	With smiling lips
voice 4	and sharp bright eyes,
voice 3	which always seemed the same;
voice 6	She thought,
voice 1	the Count my lover is brave as brave can be;
	He surely would do wondrous things to show his love of me;
	King, ladies, lovers, all look on; the occasion is divine;
	I'll drop my glove to prove his love; great glory will be mine.
voice 3	She dropped her glove,
voice 6	to prove his love,
voice 4	then looked at him and smiled;
voice 3	He bowed,
voice 6	and in a moment leaped among the lions wild;
voice 2	The leap was quick, return was quick,
voices 4–6	he has regained his place,
voice 4	Then threw the glove,
voice 2	but not with love,
voice 1	right in the lady's face.
voice 5	"By heaven,"
voice 3	said Francis,
voice 5	"rightly done!"
voice 4	and he rose from where he sat;
voice 5	"no love,"
voice 3	quoth he,
voice 5	"but vanity, sets love a task like that."

QUESTIONS TO CONSIDER

Character
1) The characters in this poem are members of the King's court. How would they act? What mannerisms can you adopt to let your audience know that you are a member of royalty?

Setting
2) What is the setting of this poem? How could you arrange your stage area and use available props to communicate this setting to your audience?

Action
3) This is your chance to really ham it up. The action of this poem should be purposefully overdone. How could you portray the count's jump into the lion's pit?
4) Consider, at the appropriate moments, changing roles from court attendants to blood-thirsty lions. You don't necessarily have to get down on hands and knees to do this. What are some alternative ways of portraying a group of ferocious lions?

Meaning
5) While this poem is a lot of fun, it also offers us a lesson. What is this lesson? Can you think of any moments in your own life when you "set a task" like the woman in the poem? Has someone ever asked *you* to do something undesirable just to test your loyalty?

SOURCE: From *Something is Going to Happen: Poetry Alive!* by Allan Wolfe, 1970, 48, 49 & 50. Asheville, NC: IAMBIC Publications.

Whether the enactment remains bound by or freed from the text, the spatial and kinesthetic properties of drama work to enliven the poems; the concrete gesture lends expressive vitality to the read word. If drama is not possible, read or ask students to read the poems aloud with feeling, gesture, and emphasis. The ear can find delights of sound and sense that the eye misses. If you have fluent speakers of other languages, urge them to read non–English-language poems *not* in translation. (Discussions of the translated poems, if they are available, will also be enriched.) Table 5–4 contains a few of the poems that have been vitalized by our students' direct and indirect dramatization.

VISUALIZATION

Gardner reminds us of the prominent power of the visual or spatial in the intelligence of some people. Teachers who have appealed to the "eye's" intelligence in their classes say that the study of poetry can be enlivened and enhanced by the visual for all students. A simple guided exercise, Teaching Activity 5-8, can connect students with imagery by asking them to imagine through their senses and then write about their impressions.

TABLE 5–4 Poems for enactment	Jonathan Swift (1667–1745)	*A Description of the Morning*
	Percy Bysshe Shelley (1792–1822)	*Ozymandias*
	John Greenleaf Whittier(1807–1892)	*The Farewell: Of a Virginia Slave Mother to Her Daughters, Sold into Southern Bondage*
	Walt Whitman (1819–1892)	*A Noiseless Patient Spider*
	Matthew Arnold (1822–1888)	*The Last Word*
	Emily Dickinson (1830–1886)	*I'm Nobody! Who Are You?*
	Lewis Carroll (1832–1898)	*Jabberwocky*
	A. E. Housman (1859–1936)	*When I Was One-and-Twenty*
	James Weldon Johnson (1871–1938)	*Since You Went Away*
	Paul Laurence Dunbar (1872–1906)	*When Malindy Sings*
		We Wear the Mask
	Walter de la Mare (1873–1956)	*The Listeners*
	Robert Frost (1874–1963)	*Out, Out*
	Carl Sandburg (1878–1965)	*Chicago*
	D. H. Lawrence (1885–1930)	*Piano*
	Ezra Pound (1885–1972)	*The River-Merchant's Wife: A Letter*
	William Rose Benet (1886–1950)	*Stage Directions*
	Archibald MacLeish (1892–1948)	*The End of the World*
	Edna St. Vincent Millay (1892–1950)	*Oh, Oh, You Will Be Sorry for That Word*
	Robert Graves (1895–1985)	*Traveller's Curse After Misdirection*
	Arna Bontemps (1902–1973)	*A Black Man Talks of Reaping*
	Langston Hughes (1902–1967)	*Ballad of the Landlord*
		Harlem (A Dream Deferred)
		Minstrel Man
	Countee Cullen (1903–1946)	*From the Dark Tower*
		For a Lady I Know
	C. Day Lewis (1904–1972)	*Walking Away*
	Phyllis McGinley (1905–1978)	*Portrait of Girl with Comic Book*
	W. H. Auden (1907–1973)	*O What Is That Sound*
	Karl Shapiro (1913–)	*Autowreck*
	Mari Evans (1923–)	*And the Hotel Room Held Only Him*
	Maya Angelou (1928–)	*Africa*
		Prescience
	Marge Piercy (1936–)	*A Work of Artifice*
	Pat Mora (1942–)	*1910*
	William Hathaway (1944–)	*Oh, Oh*
	Alice Walker (1944–)	*Women*

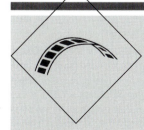

Teaching Activity 5–8   Guided Imagery

Whole Class

1. Imagine that you have lost your eyesight (or any of the senses).
2. Close your eyes and try to bring into your mind's vision some of the sights (sounds, smells, tastes, or touches) that you believe you will most miss.
3. Can you remember past experiences in which your vision (hearing, touch, etc.) was heightened? At such times, did you seem to sense everything more clearly and vividly?

4. Choose one sight (sound, etc.) that you would greatly miss.
5. Jot down ways you would describe it to others.

Individual

6. Gather your impressions into a poem. Focus on the sensory image that you selected in step 4. Use your impressions (step 3) and descriptions (step 5) to render this particular sense.

We can use art to prompt such visual imagining. We like to ask students to write poems inspired by photographs or paintings. Hollman (1989) explains the effects of taking her students to the library, giving them time to "re-experience the art books," and then quietly saying, "Find something in one of these that you're willing to spend some time with. I'm hoping a poem will come out of your time" (p. 24). The poems that emerged were remarkable: "These poems bristle with particulars, surprise the reader, focus on the moment rather than unarticulated longings or greeting card platitudes" (p. 27). She attempts to account for the success of the assignment and the poems it produced. Her reasoning is instructive:

> The art itself accounts for a lot. First, the writers' choices are generally powerful 'stuff,' and *they* choose it, to the extent it is reproduced in the library's collections. In these paintings, sculptures, or photographs, they encounter a piece of the world already shaped. Order has been imposed, details chosen; the undifferentiated landscapes of the world in which we see and feel have been particularized, composed, if you will. This frees the writer to confront the feeling, to enter the landscape, to concentrate on language to respond to or describe that world. The art, and perhaps the questions and talk which preceded the writing, seem to model a way of seeing, or organizing, experience so it can break out again in the poems. (p. 27)

Portraits, subject pieces, and landscapes provide excellent beginning points for many of our students: basic elements around which narrative, descriptive, or lyric poems can be imagined. (We have never encouraged epics!) If students are dubious, remind them that Stephen Crane based *The Red Badge of Courage* on Matthew Brady's pictures of the American Civil War. Show them the second edition of *Reflections on a Gift of Watermelon Pickle,* in which black-and-white photographs illustrate and vivify the poems on almost every third page. Pop art and abstract art also can stretch the imagination and invite students to see the world around them with fresh vision. We can ask students to create poems based on a given photograph or painting, or we can ask them to select art to match the poems they are reading. ESL teachers report that ESL students especially like using art as a prompt for writing or responding to literature. The visual allows a moment's pause from the verbal and supplies a common focus.

A final use of art for the study of poetry (or, of course, any literary genre) connects specific works of art with particular poems. Often, teachers bring in paintings that are contemporary to a text to illustrate the wider historical and cultural context in which the writer was working. Techniques of form and structure can become more comprehensible when those techniques are demonstrated in another media.

We also have used paintings that were the sources of poems to enrich our reading of the poem. The most striking examples are six poems based on Pieter Brueghel's *The Fall of Icarus:*

Dannie Abse	*Brueghel in Naples*
W. H. Auden	*Musée des Beaux Arts*
Edward Field	*Icarus*
Michael Hamburger	*Lines on Brueghel's Icarus*
Joseph Langland	*Fall of Icarus: Brueghel*
William Carlos Williams	*Landscape with the Fall of Icarus*

Poetry written in response to or as an interpretation of visual art is called *ekphrastic* poetry. Three other examples are X. J. Kennedy's *Nude Descending a Staircase,* based on Marcel Duchamp's modern painting, *Nude Descending A Staircase, No. 2;* William Carlos Williams's *The Great Figure,* based on his friend Charles Demuth's painting, *I Saw the Figure Five in Gold;* and Williams's *The Dance* based on Pieter Brueghel's *The Kermiss* (also called *Peasants Dancing*). (Williams has an entire volume inspired by Brueghel.) Brown (1992) corroborates the findings of Cage and Rosenfield (1989), who analyzed students' classroom reactions to ekphrastic poetry: "When the relationships between the poems and paintings are acknowledged, students' emotional and intellectual engagement with the texts is extended to new dimensions; the poem encompasses more and there is more to respond to simply because another art form is integrated into the literary text" (p. 44).

The following are useful books that link paintings and poems:

Voices in the Gallery	Dannie Abse and Joan Abse, Eds.	London: Tate Gallery, 1986
With a Poet's Eye	Pat Adams, Ed.	London: Tate Gallery, 1986
Double Vision:	M. Benton and P. Benton	London: Hodder & Stoughton, 1990
Reading Paintings . . .		
Reading Poems		

As Abse and Abse explain in their introduction, "The poet, through a personal vision and expression, brings to the subject a wider, sometimes entirely unexpected dimension, which in turn evokes new visual images" (pp. 11–12).

SYNTHESIS

Our final approach begins in a reading of several poems that converge in structure or idea. We ask students to listen to the individual poems and then listen for echoes among the poems. The following three poems are examples we use. We set them up with these words: "Enter the worlds of three insects, a mole, and a little caterpillar and the three poets who observe them. Can you find any similarities in these accounts? Do the lives of these creatures converge in any way?"

An August Midnight

I

A shaded lamp and a waving blind,
And the beat of a clock from a distant floor:
On this scene enter—winged, horned, and spined—
A longlegs, a moth, and a dumbledore;
While 'mid my page there idly stands
A sleepy fly, that rubs its hands . . .

II

Thus meet we five, in this still place,
At this point of time, at this point in space.
—My guests besmear my new-penned line,
Or bang at the lamp and fall supine.
"God's humblest, they!" I muse. Yet why?
They know Earth-secrets that know not I.

Thomas Hardy

The Mole

When the mole goes digging
He never meets a soul;
The stars are inattentive
To the motions of the mole.

He digs his frantic tunnel
Through chalk and clay and slime
His never-ending tunnel
A mouthful at a time.

Alone: no planet bothers
To tell him where to dig:
For moles are very little
And worlds are very big.

And when his tunnel ceases
The little mole lies stark,
And at his back is dimness
And at his head, the dark.

So to the mole all honor
And the labors of the mole,
With doubtfulness for tunnel
And ignorance for goal.

E. L. Mayo*

Cocoon

The little caterpillar creeps
Awhile before in silk it sleeps.

It sleeps awhile before it flies.
And flies awhile before it dies.
And that's the end of three good tries.

David McCord**

Students could, of course, analyze the structure and idea of each of these three poems individually and arrive at insights. A traditional classroom hour might center on just such careful, close scrutiny of single poems and not seem complete until all the details of that poem are accounted for. Our approach arrives at insight more broadly by asking students to suspend close reading and open themselves to the general impression that several poems make. A synthesizing approach requires no special knowledge or experience of poetry, just an open mind. Like analysis, it too uncovers meaning, but without intimidating the reader, particularly the poetically timid or resisting reader. One poem sounds a theme, subsequent poems repeat that theme and variations on it, and the cumulative effect is greater than one poem alone might achieve. The ideas take hold. After this approach is established, we ask the students to find poems that converge. To these three, they have, for example, brought the mouse under Robert Burns's plow in *The Mouse* and the worms under the battlefield in Thomas Hardy's *The Dynasts*. Table 5–5 lists groupings that we have used successfully.

TALKING POETRY

These ideas of finding and forging and reading poetry can stir students into caring about and responding to poetry in ways that the more traditional close reading of individual poems does not. After these initial encounters with poems, when poems matter to students and when they have a heightened sense of the way poems work, they can move toward considering and deepening their responses. As our discussion of schools of literary criticism (Chapter 4) suggested, New Criticism (Formalism) is no longer the predominant critical approach to literature, but it still has a mighty hold on the practice of English classrooms. If poetry is the class subject, poems are individual specimens to be analyzed, and the analysis is not complete until the poem's meaning has been explicated and its inner workings explained. High school and college classes on poetry are still dominated by teacher-directed lectures or discussions of poetic analysis. All of that meticulous accounting for meaning and meter can enrich our reading if we have grown to care about the poem. But we cannot assume that high school students do. We conclude this chapter by considering the question "What is the best way to talk about poetry together?"

ADOLESCENT READERS

Let's visit those text-bound and teacher-centered classrooms. Here is a common scenario:

- The poem is read, aloud or silently, one or perhaps several times.
- The teacher guides students through a series of questions about the poem, soliciting their reactions and interpretations.
- The students' challenge is not to make sense of the poem for themselves, but to figure out the predetermined answer that the teacher or any literary scholar generally expects.
- Finding students' initial, often fumbling answers inadequate, the teacher supplies the right answer (based often on years of reflection and research).

---

*From *Collected Poems,* "The Mole," by E. L. Mayo, 1981. Reprinted with the permission of The Ohio University Press/Swallow Press, Athens.

**From *One at a Time,* by David McCord. Copyright © 1949 by *The New Yorker.* By permission of Little Brown & Co.

TABLE 5–5
Poetry groups: duos, trios, quartets

African-American Experience

Imamu Amiri Baraka	*Rhythm Blues*
Countee Cullen	*Yet Do I Marvel*
Langston Hughes	*The Negro Speaks of Rivers*
Audre Lorde	*Coal*

Children and Fathers

Raymond Carver	*Photograph of My Father in His Twenty-Second Year*
Robert Hayden	*Those Winter Sundays*
James Reiss	*¿Habla Usted Español?*
Theodore Roethke	*My Papa's Waltz*

The Deaths of Insects

Karl Shapiro	*Interlude*
John Updike	*Mosquito*
John Hall Wheelock	*The Beetle in a Country Bathtub*

The Deaths of Mammals

Maxine Kumin	*Woodchucks*
William Stafford	*Traveling Through the Dark*
Richard Eberhart	*The Groundhog*

The Deaths of Other Living Things

Richard Lattimore	*The Crabs*
W. D. Snodgrass	*Lobsters in the Window*
Miller Williams	*The Caterpillar*

Dreams

Gwendolyn Brooks	*Kitchenette Building*
Langston Hughes	*A Dream Deferred*
William Butler Yeats	*He Wishes for the Cloths of Heaven*

Neighbors

Robert Frost	*Mending Wall*
A. R. Ammons	*Winter Saint*

The Sinking of the Titanic

Thomas Hardy	*The Convergence of the Twain*
David R. Slavitt	*Titanic*

Springtime

A. R. Ammons	*Eyesight*
e. e. cummings	*spring is like a perhaps hand*
William Wordsworth	*I Wandered Lonely as a Cloud*

• The teacher moves to the next question or to a neat summing up of the final interpretation.
• The teacher's inward suspicion is confirmed: These are immature or disinterested readers who don't like poetry and don't have a clue about how to unlock its riches.
• The students' inward self-doubt is confirmed: "Poetry is too remote or arcane for me ever to figure out. Only English teachers can make sense of it. Well, let them!"

Dias (1996) thinks an important first step to re-forming such a classroom is to understand the central question: "What happens in the transaction between adolescent readers and poems?" He believes not all students respond to poetry in the same way. He describes four patterns of response that are common in the high school classrooms he studied, shown in Figure 5-9. These are not static, inviolable patterns; they are changing and dynamic ones. As readers try to make sense of poetry, they develop working strategies based on what they can comfortably do and what they infer their teachers expect. Dias describes four of these strategic patterns (pp. 49–72), not as narrow categories with which to label and judge students, but as sympathetic attempts to understand what happens within adolescent readers when they encounter a poem. His description provides insight and holds implications for our approach to poetry in high school English classes.

Readers of any age might find themselves identified with one group more than another. An awareness of these types of readers holds important implications if we want students to become more responsive, independent, committed readers. Imagine the difficulties of a problem-solving reader who is confronted by fellow readers who are paraphrasers, thematizers, and allegorizers ready to dismiss many details of the text and to settle as quickly as possible on a solitary meaning,

	READER'S EXPECTATIONS	READING APPROACH	READER'S CLOSURE
Paraphrasers	To restate the text in one's own words will disclose meaning (usually one of several stock themes).	To work out meaning from the sentence or word level often directed by an impression based on the initial reading.	To close soon after a first or second retelling even if gaps appear. Sometimes to add a moral or lesson.
Thematizers	To find the simple theme—a statement or generalization about life—which underlies the poem.	To use any means available—a series of different probes—to arrive at a meaningful statement of theme.	To set the poem aside as soon as a satisfactory theme is discovered or to abandon the search if no coherent account emerges.
Allegorizers	To uncover the poem's extended statement about life—to work out the "equivalence between the poem and the real world."	To work from an initial feeling or intuition about the poem and align its details to that generalization.	To rest when a complete sense of the poem has developed even if there are gaps or flaws in this interpretation.
Problem Solvers	To explore several possibilities of meaning and connections to one's own experience.	To approach a poem as a complex artifact and so to try a variety of strategies to test tentative hypotheses.	To delay closure until difficult aspects of the poem can be accommodated. To realize that a poem continues to unfold its meaning.

FIGURE 5–9 Dias's four kinds of adolescent poetry readers

finish the reading, and move on. (Imagine that the thematizer were the teacher!) Rather than trying to reconstruct all students as problem solvers, Dias suggests various strategies so that students can develop confidence in their own individual resources as poetry readers and entertain alternative ways to read. Central to his reforms is the provision that teachers help students grow as independent readers.

The first three sections of this chapter aimed at setting students loose to find poetry, to write it, and to approach it without the teacher's analytic mediation. That push toward students' experience permeates talking about poetry as well. As poet Octavio Paz (1956) reminds us, "Now, the poem is just this: a possibility, something that is only animated by the contact with a reader or a listener. There is one note common to all poems, without which there would never be poetry: participation. Each time the reader truly relives the poem, he reaches a state that we can call poetic. The experience can take this form or that, but it is always a going beyond oneself, a breaking of the temporal walls, to be another" (p. 14).

CHOOSING POEMS

Selection of the poems for class is crucial. We have reiterated throughout this chapter that we often begin with short, contemporary poems. These have several advantages:

- The vocabulary and allusions are usually within the grasp of students, so the teacher does not have to become the more knowing expert and explainer.
- The poem's context is more likely known or accessible to students.
- The brevity reduces poetry anxiety and focuses attention on a manageable number of lines.
- Much contemporary poetry uses language, a subject, and a tone that are familiar to students and so breaks down stereotypes of poems as formal and elevated.
- Dias (1996) suggests that "students will come to realize that their own experiences are relevant to uncovering the experiences presented in the poem" (p. 85).

Heard (1989) explains another criteria for choosing: "I don't just pick poems that I think my students will like; I choose poems that I like, that I can share. If I read kids poems that don't interest me, it shows in my voice; I've had to take the time to search for words that satisfy us both" (p. 5). Reading a variety of poets also acknowledges diverse kinds of experience and craft. After choosing, prepare students to read a poem more than once. As Meyer (1996) says, "like a piece of music, a poem becomes more pleasurable with each encounter" (p. 607).

LISTENING TO POEMS

As we have discussed, poetry appeals to the eye and to the ear. The sounds of words—vowels, consonants, rhyme, alliteration, meter, and rhythm—create pleasure, produce effects, and contribute to meaning. Silent or prior reading may be necessary for longer poems. But if poems are shorter, reading aloud is important. In addition to the pleasure that the sounds bring, listening to poems can also uncover sense. Often, passages that have resisted understanding suddenly fall into place.

Lucy Calkins (1986) writes of prose: "It is listening that creates a magnetic force between writer and listener. The force of listening will draw words out; writers will find themselves saying things they didn't know they knew." How much more is listening important to poetry. Heard (1989) quotes Stanley Kunitz: "Above all, poetry is intended for the ear. It must be felt to be understood, and before it can be felt, it must be heard. Poets listen for their poems, and we, as readers, must listen in turn. If we listen hard enough, who knows—we too may break into dance, perhaps for grief, perhaps for joy" (p. 8).

The brown bat in Randall Jarrell's *The Bat Poet* (1963) says to himself, "The trouble isn't finding someone who will hear the poems. The trouble is finding someone who will truly listen." In our classrooms, our impatience to move to the next text and our uncertainty about students' genuine interest are the great enemies of oral reading and even silent rereading. We cajole ourselves with this reminder: "If you have done the work to create an environment in which students are enthusiastic about poems, trust what the sound will yield and trust the students to be willing to be still and listen."

We have found that audio resources animate poetry as well. Often, textbook publishers include in their teacher resources audiotapes of professional readers, even the poets themselves, reading poems. If you do not have your own resources, scour textbook rooms and ask other teachers about them. We have found the following sources helpful:

Moyers: The Power of the Word. *
PBS Video
1320 Braddock Place
Alexandria, VA 22314

The Academy of American Poets
584 Broadway
Suite 1208
New York, NY 10012

Poets' Audio Center
6925 Willow Street, NW
#201
Washington, DC 20091–0145

Modern Poetry Association
60 W. Walton Street
Chicago, IL 60610

DISCUSSING POEMS

If our aim is to encourage autonomous readers, small-group discussions hold clear advantages. They remove the teacher from the position of expert and transfer the responsibility for response and interpretation to the students. They also allow students to sort out their reactions without the fear of failure that whole-class, teacher-led discussions might invite. In this process, students are more likely to discover positions that differ from those they thought were self-evidently correct and to reconsider their original views. They also might be more likely to talk about the personal experiences that the poem evokes. In the freer pull and haul of a small group, students gain confidence in their responses. Whether you organize small-group or whole-class discussions, you will profit from the advice of other poets and teachers. We turn now to five of them.

Poets.   National and regional poets at New Jersey's East Brunswick High School Poetry Celebration (Lockward, 1994) gave sound suggestions to teachers:

Poets' Advice on What Not to Do with Poetry

- Do not explain the poem to students.
- Do not give tests on poetry.
- Do not be overly concerned with techniques.
- Do not approach a poem with historical matters.
- Do not impose the critics on students.

Poets' Advice on How to Teach Poetry

- Expose students to beautiful, powerful language.
- Allow time for multiple oral readings of a poem.
- Lead discussions that encourage a personal relationship with a poem.
- Teach contemporary poetry first and then go backwards in time.
- Teach poems you don't fully understand.
- Teach poems that are accessible to students.
- Allow students to sometimes choose their own poems.
- Provide opportunities for students to write poetry. (pp. 65–70)

*Bill Moyers's six-part videotape series. Tapes and teaching kits are also available.

Meyer.   We like an analogy that Meyer (1996) uses to introduce readers to poetry:

> Come to it, initially at least, the way you might listen to a song on the radio. You probably listen to a song several times before you hear it all, before you have a sense of how it works, where it's going, and how it gets there. You don't worry about analyzing a song when you listen to it, even though after repeated experiences with it you know and anticipate a favorite part and know, on some level, why it works for you. Give yourself a chance to respond to poetry. The hardest work has already been done by the poet, so all you need to do at the start is listen for the pleasure produced by the poet's arrangement of words. (p. 589)

Czury.   First comments or questions can set the tone and direction of the class. At the poetry celebration Lockward (1994) describes, poet Craig Czury suggested a number of questions that he would like readers and listeners to ask of his own poems:

- What does the poem remind you of?
- What did you think about while listening to it?
- Where did your mind go?
- Has anything been said in the poem to remind you of something in your life?
- What pictures did this poem give you? And what feelings do you get from those pictures?
- Does the poet bring up ideas you'd like to ask him or her about? Ideas you've often thought about yourself?
- How does the poem make you feel? And what has ever happened in your life that has left you with a similar feeling? (p. 67)

Golub.   Golub (1994) suggests an effective sequence for discussing poetry that allows students to be "responsible for their own meanings," rather than to be passive discoverers of "a predetermined meaning imposed on the poem by the teacher" (102). He suggests that a poem be introduced in this manner:

1. Read the poem aloud.
2. Ask students to "write down three questions they have about the poem."
3. Divide the class into small groups and instruct each group to answer the questions raised.
4. For the whole class, a recorder from each group summarizes the group's questions and conclusions.
5. The entire class adds its responses and interpretations. (p. 103)

Leggo.   Leggo (1991) asks students to respond to poetry by writing questions about individual poems. Then he and they decide whether or not to try to answer them. As he explains, "too many students grow up with the mistaken notion that all questions have answers. . . . The advantages of doing nothing with the questions are multiple: the poem remains open, the questions hint at tantalizing ideas and experiences and people and places to pursue, and the questioner remains open" (p. 60).

POETRY AND PROSE

As students grow more confident of their ability to recognize those elements often termed "poetic" in poetry, they profit from applying that understanding to prose. Mitchell (1995) uses found poems to teach imagery in novels. She has students reread parts of the novel with attention to those places that evoke vivid pictures in their minds. They then arrange them "poetically" on a page. She reports that students who might resist a discussion of the novelist's use of language willingly share their poems and respond to their classmates. One example from *The Red Badge of Courage* demonstrates the power of the lesson:

> The blue smoke-swallowed line
> curled and writhed
> like a snake stepped upon
> It swung its ends to and fro
> in an agony of fear and rage. (p. 67)

In Teaching Activity 5-9, we adapt the lesson of a teacher who asked students to find the poetry in a prose passage from John Steinbeck's story *Flight*.

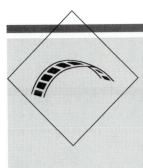

Teaching Activity 5–9   Tone Poems from Prose
John Steinbeck's Flight

- Select a page of prose.
- Choose 10 nouns, 10 verbs, 10 adjectives, and (if you wish) 5 adverbs. List these words in 4 columns.
- Look for unusual or powerful words. Search out words that particularly strike your fancy.
- (Teacher: make 4 columns, one for each of these parts of speech, on the board.)
- Individually select one or two of the most striking words from your list for the columns on the board. You are free to use any of these words along with your own list. You may also compare notes with a neighbor, "borrowing" any words that seem attractive.
- (Teacher: Hand out models of poems composed by other classes if they are available or ones you created using this model. Tip: It works best if you choose a model from a different source. Otherwise, the models can be limiting.)
- Keeping the models in mind, attempt your own "tone poems." You can combine the words on your lists in any fashion you choose. Look for unusual combinations and striking images.

This activity is little different from what William Butler Yeats did when he edited the *Oxford Book of Poetry* in the early twentieth century. He chose to begin the book by breaking a passage from Walter Pater's *The Renaissance,* on the *Mona Lisa,* into poetic lines.

Jeff Morgan asks his students to move from poetry to prose. His sophomores read *Parents* by Julius Lester and *Out, Out* by Robert Frost, and then they convert the poems into newspaper articles. Operating between the two writing modes teaches them more about the characteristics of each—poetic narrative and newspaper exposition—than considering one mode alone could.

Poems also provide links to prose that illumine and enrich both. Mitchell (1994) uses Mel Glenn's *Class Dismissed!* (1982) to introduce Paul Zindel's *The Pigman.* She reads aloud the poems *Dora Antonopolis, Rickie Miller, Benjamin Heywood, Jason Talmadge,* and *Faith Plotkin* and then discusses their common expression of alienation. Next, small groups list ways in which adolescents feel alienated at home or in school and sometimes create "a story, script, or poem that in some way illustrates alienation" (p. 79). Then the class turns to John and Lorraine better able to empathize with their distance from their families. (Teachers also find Mel Glenn's volumes to be excellent leads into the study of Edgar Lee Masters's *Spoon River Anthology.*) Zitlow (1995) reports on the poetry connections made by teachers and students to three young adult novels: Bette Greene's *Summer of My German Soldier* (ranging from Emily Dickinson's *I'm Nobody* to Myra Cohn Livingston's *The Secret*); Bruce Brooks's *The Moves Make the Man* (Arnold Adoff's *We are Talking About* and *Trilingual,* John Updike's *Ex-Basketball Player,* and Mel Glenn's *Neil Winningham*); and Gary Pausen's *Hatchet* (Jean Toomer's *Banking Coal* and Felice Holman's *Loneliness*). These connections were not simply to a central idea, but to the novels' settings, moods, situations, and characters. The students mirror "what proficient readers and writers do: make comparisons to prior reading, read a variety of literature and consider different points of view, make and defend interpretations and judgments, listen to the ideas of other readers" (p. 110). Some links are even more direct. Golub (1994) connects Ray Bradbury's short story, *There Will Come Soft Rains* and Sara Teasdale's poem *There Will Come Soft Rains.* We link Maya Angelou's *I Know Why the Caged Bird Sings* with Paul Laurence Dunbar's *Sympathy* ("I know what the caged bird feels, alas!").

You may also have students use poetry templates to describe fictional characters. Such imaginative play often uncovers deeper insights than students realize they possess. Two students of teacher Robert Hamm wrote this bio-poem about Dr. Heidegger of Nathaniel Hawthorne's *Dr. Heidegger's Experiment.*

> Doctor
> Eccentric, curious, singular, old
> Friend of Medbourne, Killigrew, Wycherly, Gascoigne,
> Lover of Sylvia, magic, a rose,
> Who feels isolated, alone, old,
> Who needs friendship, experimentation, love,
> Who gives medicine, free champagne, second chances,
> Who fears his own youth,

Who would like to see results, happiness, common sense,
Resident of Massachusetts,
Heidegger.

POETS TALK

One of the pleasures of teaching poetry is reading the prose reflections of poets on their art. The concision and playfulness, observation and insight that they bring to poetry makes for memorable prose as well. There are a number of quotes that we have found useful at serendipitous moments in our teaching. Some of our favorites follow.

W. H. Auden	"Poetry is memorable speech."
Samuel Coleridge	"That willing suspension of disbelief for the moment, which constitutes poetic faith."
	"I wish our clever young poets would remember my homely definitions of prose and poetry; that is, prose = words in their best order;—poetry = the *best* words in the best order."
Christopher Fry	"*Poetry* has the virtue of being able to say twice as much as prose in half the time, and the drawback, if you do not . . . give it your full attention, of seeming to say half as much in twice the time."
A. E. Housman	"Experience has taught me, when I am shaving of a morning, to keep watch over my thoughts, because, if a line of poetry strays into my memory, my skin bristles so that the razor ceases to act."
Maxine Kumin	"Poems are like lovers; you can forgive almost anything if the ending is good."
Percy Bysshe Shelley	"Poets are the unacknowledged legislators of the world."
Mark Twain	"The difference between the right word and the almost right word is like the difference between the lightning and the lightning bug."

Invitation to Reflection 5–2

Summerfield (1982) has drawn up a list of eight goals for teaching poetry, goals that join traditional analysis with alternative personal response. Check those goals with which you agree and add others that might govern your classroom.

_____ To provide an occasion for problem-solving talk between [and] among the pupils, collaboratively.

_____ To allow for a variety of reactions to the poem: to point the students reflectively, to their own "forms of life"—anger, uncertainty, confusion, skepticism—that the poem, the group-work and the questions aroused in them.

_____ To offer clues about the nature of interpretation.

_____ To point to various resonances within a single word.

_____ To invite pupils to reflect on their own experience, both directly and obliquely, so as to bring them into some implicit relationship with the poem.

_____ To ensure that talking about a text can come to be felt to be as "natural" as talking about people.

_____ To allow for that which is a feature of good personal relationships—namely, a near-symmetrical reciprocity and sharing between the members of the group.

_____ To learn to trust in the potential usefulness of relatively unrehearsed utterance.
(pp. 118-119)

CONCLUSION

We present these strategies to help our students enter and explore poetry and to extend it to their lives. As Meyer (1996) explains, "we read poems for emotional and intellectual discovery—to feel and experience something about the world and ourselves. The ideas in poetry—what can be paraphrased in prose—are important, but the real value of a poem consists in the words that work their magic by allowing us to feel, see, and be more than we were before" (p. 595). In many *English Journal* articles, teachers attest to their own faltering approaches to poetry that began in traditional formal analysis and moved, in despair, to experiments with experiencing poetry. One such teacher, Lott (1989), explains that she resorted to traditional approaches out of her own private delight in poetry and her unwillingness to risk the students' rejection of it. When she tried alternative strategies of "not teaching" poetry, she remembered "why I had wanted to be a teacher in the first place: to share what I love with those who are growing" (p. 68). She then draws an analogy that we like: She compares introducing her students to poetry with introducing her mother to her husband-to-be. "I didn't say to her, 'Look at the symmetry of his legs,' or 'Do you hear that special note in his voice?' Instead, I muttered, 'Mom, I want you to meet Gary,' and sat there petrified while she looked at him through her eyes and asked him her questions" (p. 68). And, she concludes, "analysis comes after recognition, and it rarely precedes love, maybe because we all have our own set of questions that we formulate only after something matters to us" (p. 68).

We hope that our four approaches to poetry—finding, forging, reading, and talking—provide you with ideas for just such an introduction for your students. Perhaps someday one of them may even bring to poetry feelings similar to those of Emily Dickinson:*

> If . . . it makes my whole body so cold
> no fire can warm me, I know that is poetry.

6

EXPANDING LITERACY

"The debate over the literary canon has taken on great importance because it embodies most of the key educational issues of our time: the knowledge that is most worth teaching, the teacher's role in fostering independent thinking, the extent to which schools will reproduce the social order or create a new, equitable order. . . ."

Anne Ruggles Gere, Colleen Fairbanks, Alan Howes, Laura Roop, and David Schaafsma

The last three chapters considered the process of teaching texts. This chapter focuses on the selection of those texts. As recently as 25 years ago, such a chapter might have concerned itself with an introduction to the great Western tradition of classic novels, short stories, plays, and poetry. In fact, as a young teacher, one of us lived constantly with a haunting sense that she had not read the classics and, more worrisomely, could not exactly identify them. No sooner would she read one "masterpiece" and become a bit more secure of the field than two more books would appear with claims of equal urgency to be read. Today, with an expanding canon, the young teacher has an even more daunting task. The battleground of text selection is one of the most contested in English education. We want to prepare you for the fray. We turn first to identify the "classics" and then defenders and challengers of this established canon.

THE CLASSICS

The term *classic* was originally used to designate the literature, art, and culture of ancient Greece and Rome, revered for centuries by scholars and educated people of Western cultures. It was then extended to include any piece of literature that by common consent was considered superior, that is, which achieved the high quality of Greek and Roman masterpieces. The term itself, according to Funk (1978), has a "slight touch of snobbery about it, for the roots of *classic* are in the Latin word *classicus,* which meant 'of the first rank' and was applied to the upper and better classes of Rome" (p. 309). Thus, before *classic* became used for everything from late-model cars to mass-produced hamburgers, it meant "to be in the first rank of literature." And what standards distinguish the first rank? Samuel Johnson gave the common answer: A masterpiece is a work that has stood the test of time. An aggregate of masterpieces has come to be assumed as the heritage of any educated person, a literary tradition to be passed from one generation to the next. That body of individual masterpieces is called the *canon.*

HISTORICAL ROOTS OF THE HIGH SCHOOL CANON

In his history of the teaching of English, Applebee (1974) examines an important question for the secondary English teacher: How did the high school literary canon evolve? He delineates the role of college entrance requirements in determining both that canon and, more importantly, English as a field of study in its own right. In fact, he sees these entrance requirements as the "moving force" of the rapid evolution from no formal instruction in literature in 1800, to its introduction into schools as a "handmaiden of other studies" by 1865, to its almost universal presence as an important study of its own by 1900 (p. 30).

In the late nineteenth century, college applicants were not assessed on the basis of SAT scores or common applications, but on entrance examinations constructed by each college. Colleges announced topics in advance and thus dictated the preparatory school's curriculum for the year. Literature first became established in the college entrance requirements as a vehicle for demonstrating competence in such non-literary fields as philology, rhetoric, and grammar. Applebee places a "real milestone" at Harvard's 1873-1874 requirements, in which literature was to be studied for the purpose of writing a short composition on a subject to be taken from "one of the following works: Shakespeare's *Tempest, Julius Caesar,* and *Merchant of Venice;* Goldsmith's *Vicar of Wakefield;* Scott's *Ivanhoe,* and *Lay of the Last Minstrel.* This requirement institutionalized the study of standard authors and set in motion a process which eventually forced English to consolidate its position within the schools" (p. 30).

As other colleges and universities set their own examinations and as these changed from year to year, preparatory schools were severely taxed. By the early 1890s, their call for uniform requirements produced regional, then national conferences and commissions whose work resulted in the clarification, unification, and validation of various aspects of English studies within American schools and colleges. The most influential of these bodies for the study of English, the conference commissioned by the nationally appointed Committee of Ten, gave their statement of the purpose of English studies in 1892:

> The main objects of the teaching of English in schools seem to be two: (1) to enable the pupil to understand the expressed thoughts of others and to give expression to thoughts of his own; and (2) to cultivate a taste for reading, to give the pupil some acquaintance with good literature, and to furnish him with the means of extending that acquaintance. (quoted in Applebee, 1974, p. 33)

Contained within this statement are central issues that remain sources of definition and debate more than 100 years later: the processes of English study as understanding, expression, and "appreciation" and the subject of English study as "good literature."

TEXTS IN THE HIGH SCHOOL CANON

In 1892, as now, works considered to be "good literature" were passed from one generation to the next, often by unspoken consensus. Over time, some works dropped from reading lists and classrooms as others were added. To orient you to what contemporary high school English teachers and educators consider to be "good literature," we mention several lists of the most frequently selected long works by anthologizers, teachers, and Advanced Placement test constructors. They will demonstrate the evolution from Harvard's 1873-1874 list.

Arthur N. Applebee's 1988–1989 Study.
In the late 1980s, Arthur N. Applebee (1993), director of the federally sponsored National Research Center on Literature Teaching and Learning, undertook four separate but interrelated studies designed to produce a comprehensive picture of the content and approaches to the teaching of literature in U.S. high schools.* The sample for the survey of required book-length works was large and diverse: public ($n = 322$), Catholic ($n = 80$), and independent ($n = 86$) schools with classes that were noncollege preparatory, college preparatory, and mixed-track, 7-12 grades, in urban, suburban, small-town, rural, and mixed communities. We list in Tables 6-1 and 6-2 his findings of the most frequently required books (grades 7-12) and authors (grades 9-12). In public school grades 9-12, 64.7% of these long works were novels, 25.5% were plays, 7% were nonfiction, and the remainder were collections of poems and short stories.

In Table 6-1, you will note that in these top 27, only two authors are women and none are minorities; four works are by Shakespeare, three are by Steinbeck, and two are by Dickens. Table 6-1 also compares 1988 titles with a 1963 study conducted by Anderson (1964). Only *Silas Marner* disappeared from the list (from being third on the list, taught in 76% of schools, to being taught only in 15%). Table 6-2 shows the data compiled by author. Because the ranks were based on the number of times a work by an author was taught, the figures reveal the magnitude of emphasis on the most popular authors. The majority of required texts were from the twentieth century (61% in public schools, for

*Several other comprehensive studies of the teaching of English have been conducted since the early 1960s. 1. Lynch and Evans (1963): 1961 content analysis of literature textbooks. 2. Anderson (1964): 1963 survey of the content of the literature curriculum. 3. Squire and Applebee (1966, 1968): 1962-1965 National Study of High School English Programs. 4. Applebee (1978): survey of teaching conditions for English teachers. 5. Applebee (1981, 1984): the National Study of Writing in the Secondary School.

TABLE 6–1

Titles of book-length works required in 30% or more of the public schools, grades 7–12

| Title | Author | Percent of Schools | |
		1988 (*n*=322)	1963 (*n*=222)
Romeo and Juliet	Shakespeare	90	14*
Macbeth	Shakespeare	81	90*
Huckleberry Finn	Twain	78	27*
To Kill a Mockingbird	Lee	74	8*
Julius Ceasar	Shakespeare	71	77
Pearl	Steinbeck	64	15*
Scarlet Letter	Hawthorne	62	32*
Of Mice and Men	Steinbeck	60	<5*
Lord of the Flies	Golding	56	<5*
Diary of a Young Girl	Frank	56	6*
Hamlet	Shakespeare	56	33*
Great Gatsby	Fitzgerald	54	<5*
Call of the Wild	London	51	8*
Animal Farm	Orwell	51	5*
Separate Peace	Knowles	48	<5*
Crucible	Miller	47	<5*
Red Badge of Courage	Crane	47	33*
Old Man and the Sea	Hemingway	46	12*
Our Town	Wilder	44	46
Great Expectations	Dickens	44	39
Tale of Two Cities	Dickens	41	33
Outsiders	Hinton	39	0*
Pigman	Zindel	38	0*
Death of a Salesman	Miller	36	5*
Tom Sawyer	Twain	32	10*
Miracle Worker	Gibson	32	<5*
Red Pony	Steinbeck	31	5*

SOURCE: From Applebee, A. N. *Literature in the Secondary School: Studies of Curriculum and Instruction in the United States.* NCTE, p. 71. Copyright © 1993 by the National Council of Teachers of English. Reprinted with permission.

*Percentage significantly different from 1988 sample, *p.* < .05.

TABLE 6–2

Ten most frequently required authors of book-length works, grades 9–12

| Author and Cumulative Percent of Titles Required | | | | | |
Public Schools (*n* = 322)		Catholic Schools (*n* = 80)		Independent Schools (*n* = 86)	
Shakespeare	364%	Shakespeare	358%	Shakespeare	334%
Steinbeck	150	Steinbeck	140	Steinbeck	101
Dickens	91	Dickens	108	Twain	76
Twain	90	Twain	96	Dickens	69
Miller	85	Miller	83	Miller	61
Orwell	70	Hemingway	76	Hawthorne	56
Lee	69	Sophocles	75	Fitzgerald	53
Hawthorne	67	Hawthrone	73	Sophocles	51
Hemingway	60	Lee	67	Homer	47
Fitzgerald	54	Orwell	66	Lee	47
Golding	54				

SOURCE: From Applebee, A. N. *Literature in the Secondary School: Studies of Curriculum and Instruction in the United States.* NCTE, p. 72. Copyright © 1993 by the National Council of Teachers of English. Reprinted with permission.

instance) of which texts written since 1960 were 12%. The results were almost identical for public, Catholic, and independent schools.

Applebee also examined the seven most commonly used literature anthologies (as cited by schools in his national survey). The 42 volumes with 1989 copyrights came from the following publishers: Harcourt Brace Jovanovich; Scott, Foresman and Company; Holt, Rinehart and Winston, Inc.; McDougal, Littell and Company; McGraw-Hill School Division; Prentice Hall; and Scribner Laidlaw (pp. 228-229). Table 6-3 lists the most frequently anthologized long fiction, excerpts from long fiction, and plays (p. 233).

Advanced Placement Lists: 1981–1996.   A list of titles that have been used on Advanced Placement (AP) literature exams between 1981 and 1996 appears in Appendix C. This list might be regarded as unrepresentative, produced by college and secondary teachers sensitive only to college-bound high school students far removed from the majority of secondary English classrooms. Still, while targeted for one segment of students, its influence reaches other segments as AP courses proliferate and as their courses of study affect book selection in nonacademic classes through teachers' talks with each other, their familiarity with selections, and the availability of texts. At the least, these titles represent the works that AP examiners consider what American colleges expect of the "educated student."

TABLE 6–3

Most frequently anthologized long fiction, excerpts from long fiction, and plays

Most Frequently Anthologized Long Fiction

Title	Author	Appearances						
		Total	7	8	9	10	US	UK
The Pearl	Steinbeck	7	0	1	0	6	0	0
Great Expectations	Dickens	5	0	0	5	0	0	0
The Call of the Wild	London	5	1	3	1	0	0	0
A Christmas Carol	Dickens	4	3	1	0	0	0	0

Most Frequently Anthologized Excerpts from Long Fiction

Title	Author	Appearances						
		Total	7	8	9	10	US	UK
Le Morte d'Arthur	Malory	7	0	0	0	4	0	7
Frankenstein	Shelley	6	0	0	0	0	0	6
Gulliver's Travels	Swift	6	0	0	0	0	0	6
A Journal of the Plague Year	Defoe	5	0	0	0	0	0	5
Moby Dick	Melville	4	0	0	0	0	4	0
The Adventures of Huckleberry Finn	Twain	4	0	0	0	0	4	0
The Adventures of Tom Sawyer	Twain	4	4	0	0	0	0	0

Most Frequently Anthologized Plays

Title	Author	Appearances						
		Total	7	8	9	10	US	UK
Julius Ceasar	Shakespeare	7	0	0	0	7	0	0
Macbeth	Shakespeare	7	0	0	0	0	0	7
Romeo and Juliet	Shakespeare	7	0	0	7	0	0	0
Our Town	Wilder	7	0	0	0	2	5	0
The Miracle Worker	Gibson	6	0	2	4	0	0	0
Pygmalion	Shaw	6	0	0	0	0	0	6
The Diary of Anne Frank	Goodrich and Hackett	6	0	5	0	1	0	0
Antigone	Sophocles	4	0	1	1	2	0	1

SOURCE: From Applebee, A. N. *Literature in the Secondary School: Studies of Curriculum and Instruction in the United States*. NCTE, p. 233. Copyright © 1993 by the National Council of Teachers of English. Reprinted with permission.

"Total" means number of series out of seven. This may be less than the sum of the individual grade levels.

unqualified in their reading of them. Indeed, parallel teaching materials, *Cliffs Notes,* and school traditions so surround the most commonly read "masterpieces" that they often become mystified for teacher and student alike and thus removed from the easy reach of novices. Nowhere is the danger of Brazilian educator Paolo Freire's "banking system" of education more dangerous than here.

Freire (1970) sees an analogy between education and banking in which education is "an act of depositing," the students are "the depositories," and the teacher is "the depositor." "Instead of communicating, the teacher issues communiqués and makes deposits which the students patiently receive, memorize, and repeat" (p. 58). Even though the students have become mere receivers, filers, and storers, teachers continue to "fill" students with "contents which are detached from reality, disconnected from the totality that engendered them and could give them significance" (p. 57). Ironically, "the more meekly the receptacles permit themselves to be filled, the better students they are" (p. 58). Teachers are vulnerable to this banking system. Because they themselves have been chastened and inspired by the weight of decades of critical analysis and interpretation of the classics passed on to them, they believe that their deposits of knowledge in the empty accounts of their students' minds are necessary and sufficient: This *is* education. And the most efficient banking method often appears to be the lecture.

RENEWING THE CANON

Canon defenders such as Bloom, Hirsch, and Bennett use it as a kind of secular scripture, a frame of reference that dogmatically affirms or denies certain expressions. They use the canon to wall off literature and culture into a protected preserve approached only by a narrow path, which they have marked. Poet, artist, scholar, and teacher Jack McMichael Martin (classroom presentation, 1991), explains the tradition in another way, as an inheritance handed down from one generation to another that has within it seeds of a message to those who follow. The seeds are fertile and have great power for growth, but they are only a beginning. These classic seeds are unfinished and wait for our use to flower. They are forerunners only, and tell us not to take their words as absolute, but to use them "to release the word not yet realized." They have the "fecund power" of the past responding to the present and preparing for the future. Hutchins's metaphor of the Great Conversation captures the same dynamic. Knowledge, when passed to another, does not remain immutable, but is modified, altered, and refined.

Martin (personal conversation, 1992) explains something about how the Conversation goes. He sees the author as "sender" and students as "receivers." The young are apprentice readers and their apprenticeship is active and toilsome. Martin sees reading as an attempt to "gain what the work has that is beyond oneself. This is the most active reading of all because it involves an imaginative leap beyond one's self-shackling urgencies and drives. Teachers must teach the young the virtue of contemplation, a listening for echoes and resonances within the integrity of the text. The strength of their reading is in the strength of their response to that which they are not and which surpasses them."

Postman (1995) adds a final frank and practical point about the dynamic of the canon:

> As to the legitimacy of canons, the word simply refers to agreed-upon examples of excellence in various genres of creativity. Any canon can be added to, modified, or even discarded if it no longer serves, in part or whole, as a model of excellence. This means that any canon is a living, dynamic instrument, and it is certainly not limited to those artists who are dead, and long dead. The long dead dominate for the obvious reason that their works have given pleasure and instruction to diverse people over long periods of time. They have earned, so to speak, their place. To the extent that teachers believe in the importance of conveying a sense of continuity in artistic creation, they must give respectful attention to the long dead. But, of course, teachers must not be reluctant to include models of excellence produced by living artists. (pp. 168–169)

THREE CHALLENGES TO THE CANON

Challenges to a canonical approach to literature—its content and its method—appear from several different directions. We turn first to three challengers from the fields of literary criticism and educational reform. You will recognize the first two, Deconstruction and Reader Response, from Chapter 4. The third, Critical Pedagogy, grows in part from a historical/sociological critique of culture and education.

DECONSTRUCTIONIST CHALLENGE

Deconstructionists quarrel with basic assumptions about definitions of greatness. We summarize their position briefly with an oft-told baseball anecdote:

> A seasoned umpire was behind home plate and a young hitter was at bat. The tension was high for the young player. He was sweating with every pitch. After a fast ball whizzed over the plate,

the umpire paused in his calling of balls and strikes. The hitter, puzzled, turned and said, "Well, what was it? A ball or a strike?" The umpire gazed directly at him and slowly said, "Sonny, it ain't nothin' 'til I call it."

The player assumes that balls and strikes are brute facts that enjoy an independent existence in the world. The umpire refuses to acquiesce to this common assumption of a world of preexisting facts that he must recognize and name. He understands that balls and strikes are not independent of his verbal actions. What we take to be real and indisputably there is the product of our way of thinking. Deconstructionists point out that the umpire is operating as they are: with a social construction of reality.

The traditional view was that nature exists outside of us and waits to be interrogated and described by our activity. The Deconstructionist view is that we are continually making and remaking our world. Those things that present themselves as inevitable and natural are, in fact, constructed. Nature and—even more—literature are products of human activity. Thus, to the question of whether, for example, Pat Conroy's *The Prince of Tides* is a masterpiece, popular fiction, or trash, Deconstructionists answer: "Sonny, it ain't nothin' 'til I call it."

Whereas before 1965, credentialed experts answered such questions definitively and, purportedly, with an unbiased appeal to objective criteria of greatness, today Deconstructionists contest the authority of anyone's making such literary value judgments. They assume that the text is re-created by every reader and are suspicious of anyone's making an authoritative claim of "classic." They have scrutinized and challenged the established masterpieces in traditional university curricula. They have shaken literary assumptions about greatness and have empowered readers to make their own interpretations. The following are two effects on the selection and teaching of texts:

- Deconstructionists look for the historical or political motives of canonization. For instance, they note that Shakespeare's place in the canon evades scrutiny because he has become a well-merchandised commodity and the profit motive sustains mistakes. They point out that Hawthorne was included in the canon because he had influential connections—he roomed with a future U.S. president at Bowdoin College—and had children devoted to preserving his memory; they persuaded the *Harvard Classics* editors to include his work in the first edition of the series, where he has been canonized ever since. Some call Deconstruction a "technique of trouble" as adherents undermine our certainty in the primacy of certain literary texts. It opens the curriculum to a variety of print and nonprint texts, including westerns, romance novels, and soap operas.
- Deconstructionists unsettle our confidence in the inherent and transcendent meaning of certain texts. They demonstrate, as Eagleton (1983) observes of Paul de Man, "that literary language constantly undermines its own meaning" (p. 145). We sometimes suspect that their inclusive selections are appealing because they are easy targets for the Deconstructionists' "ironic, uneasy business, an unsettling venture into the inner void of the text which lays bare the illusoriness of meaning, the impossibility of truth and the deceitful guiles of all discourse" (Eagleton, p. 146).

READER RESPONSE CHALLENGE

Reader Response is both a critical and pedagogical approach to literature that puts its emphasis on experience *through* literature, rather than experience *of* or *with* literature (see Chapter 4). Like Deconstruction, such an approach defines how any reader reads an individual text, but also how any teacher selects texts to be read. The classics present particular difficulties for teaching and selection. They have become so deified and mystified by the public, teachers, and even students that their reputations can interfere with the central focus—not the work itself, but the intimate personal response of the reader, what Rosenblatt (1978) calls "the web of feelings, sensations, images, ideas that he weaves between himself and the text" (p. 137). An established text can sink the reader beneath the weight of its title alone. It can too easily become an inert set of meanings waiting to be deciphered. Literature lives and is recreated by the reader's action upon it. Meaning is born in the transaction between the reader's active mind and the words of the text. Rosenblatt (1968) writes that "all the student's knowledge about literary history, about authors and periods and literary types, will be so much useless baggage if he has not been led primarily to seek in literature a vital personal experience" (p. 59).

Rosenblatt understood that her emphasis on the response in the reader would meet with much resistance and would require new teaching approaches to be realized. She believed (1968) that the primary role of teachers of literature "is to foster fruitful interactions—or, more precisely, transactions—between individual readers and individual literary works" (pp. 26-27). She further believed that "sound literary insight and esthetic judgment will never be taught by imposing from above notions of what works should ideally mean" (pp. 33-34). Instead, she suggested some principles for the sort of instruction that would arouse, challenge, refine, and enlarge the reader's response to literature:

FOURTH CHALLENGE: MULTICULTURAL LITERATURE

Women, people of color, and non-Europeans argue that the canonical texts have largely been written by white European males and thereby reflect a predominantly Eurocentric masculine consciousness. They note that the editors, the critics, and the academics who select and evaluate these texts have, until very recently, reflected the same cultural experience, yet their ultimate praise for works that they designate as classics is the accolade *universal.* Multicultural challengers remind us that these classics often do not, in fact, reflect universal experiences. They overlook significant intellectual, artistic, and social perspectives and contributions made by many diverse groups.

Applebee's (1993) research on the characteristics of anthologized authors validates those claims. Historically, the high school canon reflected "a mainstream Anglo-Saxon tradition," but in the last decades, anthologizers and teachers have tried to provide more balanced selections. In Grades 7–10 especially, 26–30% of the pieces contained in 1989 textbooks were written by women, and 18–22% were written by minority, nonwhite writers. The selections for the anthologies of national literature usually taught in grades 11 and 12, namely American and British literature, were less diverse. In the British literature texts, only 8% of the selections were written by women and 1% by minorities, even when these texts included Commonwealth writers. The American texts were somewhat more diverse: 24% of the pieces were written by women, and 16% by nonwhite minorities. When all of the selections of these texts were summed by national literary traditions, North American and United Kingdom writers accounted for 93% of the selections, European writers for 4%, and writers from other areas of the world just a smattering (pp. 93–96). The canon clearly needs to include texts by and about women, African-Americans, Native Americans, Hispanic Americans, Asian Americans, non-Europeans. Their experiences should not be excluded. Most multicultural challengers do not propose to trash the classics, but to open readers to a broader view, to a variety of perspectives.

WOMEN

In *A Room of One's Own* (1929), Virginia Woolf put the dilemma of women imaginatively. Wanting to explore the lives of women and finding so few remnants of women's lives in recorded history, she created several biographies herself. One of these imagined women is William Shakespeare's "wonderfully gifted sister," Judith. In relation to William, Judith "was as adventurous, as imaginative, as agog to see the world as he was. But she was not sent to school. She had no chance of learning grammar and logic, let alone of reading Horace and Virgil. She picked up a book now and then, one of her brother's perhaps, and read a few pages. But then her parents came in and told her to mend the stockings or mind the stew and not moon about with books and papers" (p. 49). Eventually Judith escapes to London, finds no place for herself in the theater, is pitied by an actor-manager, becomes pregnant with his child and, in "the heat and violence of the poet's heart when caught and tangled in a woman's body," kills herself (p. 50). The social role and political power of the ordinary Elizabethan woman were severely restricted; for the imaginative rebel like Judith, they were stultifying to talent and vision.

Women throughout history have left their written traces in the letters and journals of their assigned domestic sphere, but these were often discarded as ephemeral. In *Silences* (1978), Tillie Olsen gives a moving explanation and convincing evidence of the constricting impact of the traditional role of woman on her creative possibilities. She explains the literary achievement of a nineteenth-century writer, Rebecca Hardin Davis, who, after her excellent *Life in the Iron Mills* (1863), married and never thereafter wrote as well again; that decline "was the price for children, home, love" (p. 107). Maxine Greene (1988) suggests that "it was, most often, the infinity of small tasks, the time-consuming obligations of housework and child care that narrowed the spaces in which they could choose" (p. 60). Few could choose an education (women's education being more concerned with general learning and specific domestic arts) or a profession, or, if they wrote despite these odds, find a publisher or a public willing to take them seriously.

When they began to compose in the established genres—poems (Anne Bradstreet and Phillis Wheatley), essays (Mary Wollstonecraft), and novels (Jane Austen)—women met with the suspicion and rejection of critics, academics, and the public. Many became publishable only by assuming male pseudonyms. Woolf (1929) reflects on the bias against women's voices and women's concerns:

> It is obvious that the values of women differ very often from the values which have been made by the other sex; naturally, this is so. Yet it is the masculine values that prevail. Speaking crudely, football and sport are "important," the worship of fashion, the buying of clothes "trivial." And these values are inevitably transferred from life to fiction. This is an important book, the critic assumes, because it deals with war. This is an insignificant book because it deals with the feelings of women in a drawing room. (pp. 76–77)

If women's roles were constricted and their powers to choose and to act were limited, their power to understand themselves and to be understood were also compromised. Only at the end of the twentieth century did theorists begin to study and enunciate critical differences in the way women understand and respond to the world, differences that for centuries have simply been understood by a more dominant male perspective and accepted by women as being oddly female. These theorists have explored a distinct emotional, cognitive, linguistic, and moral development that grows from the particular historical, social, biological, and psychological experience of women. Donovan (1985) sees women's consciousness as being shaped by their roles in the domestic sphere and their biological and psychological experiences, particularly of birthing and nurturing children. These experiences distinguish the way women *know*—a knowing that is personal, private, intuitive, and subjective, rather than more public, rational, and objective. Carol Gilligan's *In a Different Voice* (1981) raises a serious challenge to the male emphasis on autonomy and principled decision making as the highest stages of moral development (Kohlberg) and as superior to the female value on the bonds of human connection. Gilligan differentiates between women's choices within the context of "mutuality and concern, of ongoing dialogue and conversation, of cooperation" and male choices within the framework of "competition" and gamesmanship (Greene, 1988, p. 84). Rather than focusing on their individual rights in human encounters, Gilligan believes that women are more prone to think in terms of responsibility to others. Many others point out that until recently, the range of the woman's sphere was severely limited to falling in love, getting married, and having children.

In this difference in experience lies the great motive for an expanding canon that embraces women. If we want our classrooms to be places in which students actively explore their own lives, the fictive lives they encounter need to reflect the full range of human experience, not just half of it. Particularly in adolescence, when the young are actively seeking to arrive at some self-definition, they need to be presented with accounts of the nature of their unique experiences and possible hopes. Barker (1989) recognizes that literature classes commonly approach that need in their young male students: "High school classics such as Miller's *Death of a Salesman,* Hemingway's Nick Adams stories, and Faulkner's "Bear" provide all sorts of opportunities for boys to make connections with their own lives—football, fishing and hunting, fathers and sons, and the like." Young women need the same provisions. "We always want our students to relate to what they're reading and bring their own experiences into discussions and essays; making sure that all students—girls included—are involved equally is not hard, but it requires conscious effort on the part of the teacher" (p. 42). Howe (1982) addresses the same issue: "Women must have a place in the curriculum that will allow them images of achievement and inspiration comparable to those the curriculum has generally afforded at least to white middle-class males" (p. 12).

Guilford (1985) reminds us of how literature might start to correct that constricting consciousness. She writes that in selecting literature for her classes around the "lives and problems of women," she wanted "stories to illustrate that women, like men, are sometimes major characters in the situations and problems of daily life. I also wanted stories that would identify some of the unique qualities that women represent" (p. 24). These expanded views serve our male, as well as our female, students. Segel (1986) concludes that literature is useful in a gender-divided society to reduce the alienation between men and women. She wonders whether men might become more understanding and easy with women "if they had imaginatively shared female experience through books, beginning in childhood. At the least, we must deplore the fact that many boys are missing out on one of fiction's greatest gifts, the chance to experience life from a perspective other than the one we were born to—in this case, from the female vantage point" (p. 183).

Appendix C presents a list of novels and collections of short stories written by women and other excluded authors. We have limited what could be a very long list by including only books that we or colleagues have taught to high school students and that do not appear prominently on other lists in this text. One of the vexing contradictions that we experienced as beginning teachers was not wanting to assign or suggest books that we had not read and yet not wanting our students to be limited by the limits of our own reading. (Those anxieties assert themselves here again as we compile these lists for you.) The problem eases in the course of a teaching career as the teacher has time to read more widely, profit from the suggestions of colleagues (in school or in professional resources), and gain confidence in introducing students to unknown texts. Teachers also learn pedagogical perspectives and organizational strategies for teaching longer works that do not require a teacher to be an authority on every work read or at the center of every discussion.

AFRICAN-AMERICANS

African-Americans also chafe under a canon that excludes their writers and ignores their unique cultural experience. Baker (1980) has observed that the men and women viewing the New World for the first time from the decks of the *Mayflower* saw a very different world from those seeing this same continent for the first time from the holds of a slave ship (p. 156). On their arduous and deadly passage into slavery and onto American soil, African men and women brought an oral tradition that spoke and sang of personal experience, religion, history, geography, and a long cultural heritage. The newly arrived African slaves were severed from ties to their former homelands—people, language, customs, and rituals—and were faced with a desperate challenge to survival. The slaveholding culture acted systematically to eradicate indigenous African values and practices, especially in the agricultural Deep South, where education was prohibited, families divided, and individuals cruelly exploited. Even when slavery was abolished, African-Americans continued for another century in narrowly defined, constricted, and stifling roles, living largely in the depressed and poverty-stricken South. Discrimination against ex-slaves and their progeny was sanctioned by "separate, but equal" laws and enforced by violence. African-Americans then began another defining exodus in search of unskilled and semiskilled employment in northeastern and midwestern urban industrial centers.

A written literature began even during the days when slaves were officially forbidden to read and write. The literature that followed gave voice to a unique and defining experience and it sprang from unique sources: an oral tradition, slave narratives, blues and spiritual music, jazz, signifying,* and African and African-American history. The black writer also wrote from a perspective of marginality, of the outsider looking in with a different perception of reality, unique historical and psychological experiences, and distinctive sociopolitical aims. James Baldwin sums up the content of those texts: "For a tradition expresses, after all, nothing more than the long and painful experience of a people; it comes out of the battle waged to maintain their integrity or, to put it more simply, out of their struggle to survive."

Theologian and philosopher Cornel West (1982) suggests two different perceptions of African-American history: African-Americans as "passive objects" of a history of continual political, economic, and cultural degradation and of "ceaseless attempts to undermine Afro-American self-esteem"; and African Americans as "active subjects" of a history of gallant persistence and struggle against "white paternalism," segregated capitalist opportunities, and "pervasive denigration" (pp. 69–70). Literature reflects both perspectives. West describes four traditions of thought and action that arose in response to that experience:

- One tradition claims a unique and exclusive African-American culture and personality that is exceptional because of its history and culture.
- A self-effacing tradition depends on assimilation with a white culture to break its cycle of political oppression and social and psychological pathology.
- A marginal tradition emphasizes the confinement and restriction of the African-American and therefore the need for individual rebellion and revolt.
- A humanist tradition provides a promising context for the study of African-American literature in our classrooms. West's description could be a statement of purpose for such inclusion:

  The humanist self-image of Afro-Americans is one neither of heroic superhumans untouched by the experience of oppression nor of pathetic subhumans devoid of a supportive culture. Rather, Afro-Americans are viewed as both meek and belligerent, kind and cruel, creative and dull—in short, as human beings. This tradition does not romanticize or reject Afro-American culture; instead, it accepts this culture for what it is, the expression of an oppressed human community imposing its distinctive form of order on an existential chaos, explaining its political predicament, preserving its self-respect, and projecting its own special hopes for the future (p. 85).

Both African-American students and their non–African-American counterparts need to be opened to what Cobb (1985) describes as "the communal wisdom of a culture, the survival strategies, hero-images, women-images, social ordering, and authority symbols that ultimately determine values" (p. 256). For African-American students, the need for inclusion is especially urgent:

  Growing up in a racist society which systematically conditions him to think negatively of his own racial group, the Black child develops a negative self-image. At school this negative self-image is further developed when he attends a class that is supposedly about general literature or American Literature and finds that the moral and social values, heroes, world view, and literary heritage of his own community are excluded. (Turner & Stanford, 1971, p. 6)

Gay (1988) has an even more specific prediction that contains within it the need for study of the African-American experience. "Demographic projections indicate that poor, urban, and racial minority students will increasingly dominate public schools in the next decade and well into the 21st century. . . . This new majority demands that schools seriously reassess and revise their policies, programs, and procedures to respond more effectively to its unique needs" (p. 328). Johnson (1990) observes that

---

Signifying is an indirect use of language not necessarily to exchange information or explanation, but simply to maintain connection with another in a hostile environment.

African-American youth live in a society and in a world in which the "happy ending" does not constitute a realistic model. Their realities must be represented, explored, and interpreted in the literature that they read. "Realistic" does not of necessity mean "bleak." It means only that the literature must be inclusive of a multitude of experiences. Fortunately, these include experiences of dreaming and imaging other realities, other worlds, and possibilities. (p. 2)

Our concern with the inclusion of African-American literature in the English class arises from our concern that students of all races be given the personal freedom of imagining different possibilities for themselves, an imagining that is at the heart of reading and writing literature.

Appendix C contains a list of works that provide such an introduction. We include them as a testament to the remarkable literary achievements of African-Americans and as starting points for those of you who are unfamiliar with this literature. We are indebted to many teachers for their suggestions of works that appeal to and are suitable for high school students, but especially to Mary Helen Washington (1991) and Angelene Reid (personal communication, 1992).

NATIVE AMERICANS

Historians estimate that when the Pilgrims landed at Plymouth Rock in 1620, 4 to 8 million people, with 500 distinct native cultures, each speaking its own language, were living in what is now the continental United States (Lincoln, 1983, p. 15). By the mid-twentieth century, that number was estimated to be eight or nine primary cultural groups. Lincoln (1983) explains:

About seven hundred thousand native Americans survive as full-bloods or "bloods," to use the reservation idiom, mixed-bloods whose parents derive from different tribes, and half-bloods or "breeds" with one non-Indian parent. Another half million or more blooded Indian people live as whites. Over half of the Indian population now lives off the fifty-three million acres of federal reservation lands. (p. 15)

No voices in our culture have been more severely silenced or more deserve to be heard than those of Native Americans. The history and culture of these first known Americans has been repressed and nearly destroyed by centuries of the dominant culture's blind misunderstanding, deliberate cruelty, and misguided attempts to "civilize" or "assimilate" Native Americans. When Native Americans have entered the dominant literature, they have been either romanticized or villainized. Bruchac (1987) writes, "From before Fenimore Cooper, the major presence of the American Indian in the writings of non-Indians has been as one of two opposed, yet complementary, incarnations: the murdering red skin and the noble savage" (p. x). Even those "objective" eighteenth- and nineteenth-century recorders of Native American narratives often distorted the accounts and made subjective moral observations about their subjects. White writers who were raised or worked among Native Americans and wrote of their experiences often judged these cultures naively and without sympathy.

Native Americans were usually seen by the European newcomers as being primitive. Velie (1979) explains that when "whites first came in contact with many tribes, the Indians had a Stone Age technology. . . . The whites equated civilization with level of technology, and therefore judged them as backward" (p. 4). In fact, their culture was rich and varied. Lincoln (1983) sees that variety reflected in the geographic origins of the different tribes: "forest, prairie, river, valley, seacoast, mountain, tundra, desert, and cliff-dwelling peoples. They have lived as farmers, food gatherers, fishermen, and hunters inseparable from the land" (p. 16). In this diversity, however, common traditions remain. Lincoln again enumerates: "Native American peoples acknowledge specific and common inheritance of the land. They celebrate ancestral ties. They share goods and responsibilities, observe natural balances in the world, and idealize a biological and spiritual principle of reciprocation. Personal concerns lead into communal matters" (p. 16).

Velie (1979) describes their literature as "an organic part of everyday life, not a thing apart to be enjoyed by a highly specialized class":

In former days, all members of an Indian tribe listened to tales, and in many tribes virtually everyone composed and sang songs. . . . [L]iterature was . . . functional. Myths and tales were educational tools that taught the younger generation the beliefs and history of the tribe. Many songs were good medicine; others were morale builders sung before battle. Songs were sung to increase the fertility of the fields, to assure a successful hunt, to gain power over a recalcitrant lover. Oratory played an important role in political decisions. . . . Ritual was a form of sacred drama filled with poetry, song, and dance; it acted out on earth events taking place in a more important realm. (p. 7)

As with most oral traditions, the centuries-old retelling honed those words, narratives, and perceptions to their essence. Until they came into contact with white settlers, Native Americans needed no written language. Their spoken voices embodied and transmitted the culture.

In the late nineteenth century, the U.S. government adopted policies toward Native Americans that had almost as devastating an effect on the culture as the periodic massacres had. In order to assimilate and civilize Native Americans, they systematically removed the young from their tribes, thereby separating them from the center of their material and spiritual existence, and sent them to boarding schools first in the East, then in states all over the union. Supporters of these schools argued that the children's native identities had to be suppressed and replaced with white values of hard work, ambition, and individualism. Most of the children returned to the reservation, or "back to the blanket" as it was called, but they returned feeling alienated from both worlds, victims of the white man's misguided, if well-meant, intentions. Larson (1978) describes this period (between 1880 and 1920) as "one of humiliation and defeat, above all one of hopelessness. The lessons of the recent past had taught them that the Native American was a dying breed—that survival (if one could call it that) could only be achieved by accepting the values of the white man's world" (p. 10). When the government reversed its policies in the 1930s, closed the schools, and urged Native Americans to reclaim their languages, the damage to Indian culture seemed irreversible.

In recent decades, however, attempts have been made to affirm Native American history and culture, not as anachronistic oddities, but as remarkable testaments of endurance and wisdom. Young writers who at one time may have had difficulty finding voices, publishers, or readers have been the beneficiaries of a changing history. Many Native Americans left the reservations during World War II and began to establish their separate identities; therefore, they were primed to respond to the political activism of the civil rights movement and the anti-Vietnam War protests of the 1960s and 1970s with their own counterparts. The National Youth Council (1960) and the American Indian Movement (1969) challenged the assumption that the Native Americans' demise was inevitable. Bruchac (1987) describes the reaction of Louis Oliver, a Creek Poet: "We were always taught in the schools that the Indian was doomed to be absorbed into the American melting pot and that all of our old ways were only memories. Before I met some younger American Indian writers, I was just like that old ground hog. I had crawled in my hole and just accepted that I was forgotten" (p. xi). Larson (1978) senses among the younger writers "the desire to articulate a new national awareness" (p. 12). A young Native American poet, Wendy Rose, explains that she was not raised to speak her native language, live on her lands, or know her native literary tradition, and so she is now engaged in discovering it. With a similar affirmation, a whole new generation of poets and writers have emerged to claim their identities and give written and visual expression to their experiences. Their flourishing has even been called a Renaissance. Others explain that, in fact, the "oral tradition has been central to every form of expression, and as Simon Ortiz argues, 'in that sense the literature has always been there; it just hasn't been written, with its more contemporary qualities and motives'" (Coltelli, 1990, p. 6).

As a simple matter of justice, we should make a place for Native American oral and written literature in English classrooms. We should acquaint our students with this deep and vital tradition that predated the one that European settlers brought and adapted. Stensland (1979) argues that "when the Pilgrims arrived in the New World, the Indians already had an oral tradition of storytelling and ceremony which integrated all of life" (p. 3). Furthermore, English teachers need to directly dispel the negative stereotypes that are products of both print and nonprint literature: the images of the noble red man, the warring savage, the drunkards and idlers, the murderous thieves, the reservation derelicts, the taciturn women, the passive victims, and the rootless drifters. Such stereotypes are tenacious, but one means of dispelling them is to read and discuss more accurate portrayals of three-dimensional individuals.

There are even deeper arguments for the inclusion of Native American literature. Stensland (1979) explains that "American Indians—with their spiritual oneness, their concept of the sacred hoop—have much to teach modern youth, many of whom find their own world dreary and materialistic. The Indian's problem of trying to live in two worlds also strikes a responsive chord in teenagers who are in search of self-realization" (p. 3). Teacher Cary Clifford sees Native American literature as possessed of the "magic quality" of a story told late at night around a campfire. Because it is not limited to the written word and is "lived literature" consisting of song and dance and oratory, it has the quality of individual action and communal participation, which draws students to it. She feels that for most secondary students, "leaving the classroom and coming into the natural world is an act of joy" and that they find a "natural bond with these people who told their stories under the stars and sang their prayers in the open dawn (personal communication, 1992)." Although some were hunters and others farmers, some wanderers and others cliff dwellers, they seem to share a spiritual sense of the oneness or roundness of life, a strong loyalty to the tribe (and most often to the family), a valuing of honesty, endurance, acuteness, and bravery, a sense of the earth and nature as ever-present and sacred.

Appendix C includes a list of literature written by Native Americans and by whites who seem to have done justice to the culture they sought to describe. The usual genre categories are restrictive for Native American literature, made up, as it is, of myth, legend, oratory, biography, autobiography, and history. The NCTE has published a very useful annotated bibliography, Anna Lee Stensland's

Literature by and About the American Indian (1979). Another early reference work is Arlene B. Hirschfelder's *American Indian and Eskimo Authors: A Comprehensive Bibliography* (1973).

HISPANIC AMERICANS

Hispanic Americans are the fastest growing minority in the country. Some census estimates predict that, by the early twenty-first century, one-fifth of our population will be Spanish speaking. An increasing number of immigrants and native Spanish speakers are entering our schools. These Hispanic Americans experience the difficulties of all latecomers in their struggle for economic security and cultural stability. One of the predicaments for a minority culture, especially one that is largely immigrant, is whether to reject its cultural history and personal memories in order to be assimilated into the dominant culture or whether to hold on to that heritage and risk standing on the outer boundaries of its new society.

Reading factual or fictional accounts of individuals bound by similar language, experience, and history is liberating for the young who are caught in such cultural perplexities. Richard Rodriguez's autobiography, *Hunger of Memory: The Education of Richard Rodriguez: An Autobiography* (1981), is a testament to just that dilemma. A bright youngster, Rodriguez's promise was identified early by teachers who conscientiously opened him to an awareness of intellectual and cultural possibilities, but in so doing, alienated him from his family and the culture that bore and sustained him; his parents were even discouraged from speaking their native language to him at home when he was a boy. Most of today's schools seem more sensitive about dividing students from their sources of identity and nurture, but still, the mainstream images are presented so continuously as the norm that minorities need to have their alternative perspectives affirmed. In Applebee's study of 1989 textbook anthologies for grades 7–12, only 2% of selections were by Hispanic writers (1993, p. 94).

Hispanic students are enriched in their understanding and deepened in their sense of themselves by reading Sandra Cisneros's novel *The House on Mango Street* (1989), a coming-of-age tale about a young Hispanic girl growing up in Chicago, or Nicholasa Mohr's novel *Nilda* (1973), the story of Nilda Ramirez, who lives in El Barrio of New York City and experiences the tensions of being urban, poor, and Spanish speaking. This kind of literature, reflecting honestly, perceptively, and unapologetically on their shared experiences, allows minorities and immigrants to envision life within a dominant culture without forsaking the customs and traditions of their origins.

Members of the dominant culture as well as other minority cultures also gain from learning about the experiences of Spanish Americans. It frees all from the restrictions of ethnocentric perspectives, exercises empathy, defeats stereotypes, and enlarges literature's boundaries. Oliver and Bane (1971) have said that the young "need the opportunity to project themselves in rich hypothetical worlds created by their own imagination or those of dramatic artists. More important, they need the opportunity to test out new forms of social order" (p. 270). Hispanic "social orders" are rendered in literature from three sources:

1. Hispanic writers born here, but torn between two cultures
2. Writers native to Mexico and countries of the Caribbean, Central America, and South America who have immigrated to the U.S. (whose works are translated for English readers)
3. Non-Hispanic writers who write with an understanding and appreciation of Hispanic culture.

Reading the works of these three groups has what Maxine Greene calls "emancipatory potential" for Hispanic and non-Hispanic students alike (1988, p. 131).

Appendix C includes fiction written by authors who are Hispanic American (born or having immigrated to the United States) and Latin American (born in and living in or writing about Mexico or countries in Central America and South America). Worthy of mention are two United States authors who are sympathetic to Spanish culture and highly teachable to high school students. Barbara Kingsolver, in her novels *The Bean Trees* (1988), *Animal Dreams* (1990), and *Pigs in Heaven* (1993), includes and affirms Hispanic characters and their dilemmas, not as isolated cultural oddities, but as integral to the variety and complexity of American life. When she was over 70 years old, Harriet Doerr wrote two novels about Americans living in small Mexican villages, *Stones for Ibarra* (1984) and *Consider This, Senora* (1994), that capture the sudden discoveries and insights that arrive when we leave the familiar expectations of home and open ourselves to the wisdom of a different culture.

ASIAN AMERICANS

Japanese American David Mura (1988) explains the gulf he sometimes feels between himself and white friends: "I point out to them that the images I grew up with in the media were all white, that the books I read in school—from Dick and Jane onwards—were about whites and later, about European civilization. I point out to them the way beauty is defined in our culture and how, under such definitions, slanted eyes, flat noses, and round faces just don't make it" (p. 137). Chinese American Amy Ling, born in Beijing, brought to America when she was 6 years old, and educated in American schools from first grade through a Ph.D. in comparative literature, describes the same experience: She never in her schooling encountered any Chinese American authors or characters except in a humiliating poem, Bret Harte's *Heathen Chinee.* When she first read Maxine Hong Kingston's autobiography, *A Woman Warrior,* and Nellie Wong's book of poems, *Dreams from Harrison Railroad Park,* she was "thunderstruck": "Here were people like me creating moving and artistic literature from our shared Chinese American experience. They expressed the struggle for personal balance that is the experience of every American of dual racial and cultural heritage, but, specifically, they wrote with pride and affirmation out of our common Chinese American back-ground" (1990, p. xi). Mura's experience leads him to conclude that "multiculturalism, for a member of a racial minority, is not simply tolerance, but an essential key to survival" (p. 141).

Amy Tan's novel *The Joy Luck Club* (1989), the intermeshed first-person stories of four Chinese im-migrant mothers and their American-born daughters, struck an imaginative nerve in the general American reading public. The story introduced the traditions and heritage of an Asian culture and the difficulties of assimilation for its first-generation children, alongside the recurrent dilemmas experi-enced by all human beings. If Asian Americans benefit from validating and enriching their experiences through works by and about other Asians, so mainstream readers also profit from a deepening under-standing of another culture and, by contrast, of their own. Applebee estimates that about 1.1% of the 1989 anthologies' selections are by Asian writers.

Other books, written in English by ethnic Asians and Eurasians and published in the United States for a general readership, that have had appreciative audiences and have been recommended to us for high school students include Jeanne Wakatsuki Houston and James D. Houston's autobiographical novel of Jeanne Wakatsuki's experience in a Japanese American internment camp during World War II, *Farewell to Manzanar* (1973); Maxine Hong Kingston's second book, *China Men* (winner of the 1981 Obie Award for Best New Play) and *M. Butterfly* (1988 Tony Award winner for Best New Dramatic Play); Carolyn Lau's po-etry collection, *Wode Shuofa* (1989 winner of an American Book Award from the Before Columbus Foundation); Frank Chin's short story collection *The Chinaman Pacific and Frisco Railroad Co.* (another 1989 American Book Award winner); Cynthia Kadohata's *The Floating World* (1989); Karen Tei Yamashita's *Through the Arc of the Rain Forest* (1990); John Okada's *No-No Boy* (1957, 1990); Lydia Minatoya's *Talking to High Monks in the Snow* (1991 winner of the PEN/Jarard Fund Award); Amy Tan's second novel, *The Kitchen God's Wife* (1991); Gish Jen's *Typical American* (1991); Chang-rae Lee's first novel (which many regard as the Asian immigrant's version of Ralph Ellison's *Invisible Man*) *Native Speaker* (1995). Monica Sone's *Nisei Daughter* (1979) and Yoshiko Uchida's *Journey to Topaz* (1971) are based on the authors' ex-periences in the Japanese American internment camps in California during World War II. Although this list includes mainly works by Chinese and Japanese Americans whose immigrant history is longest and most complex, immigrant groups from Korea and Southeast Asia can be expected to swell this number. A law teacher, Lan Cao, has published a fine first novel, *Monkey Bridge* (1997), the autobiographical account of the difficulties of the Vietnamese immigrant in the United States. Several anthologies, while old, provide good starting points for a search of Asian American works: Kai-yu Hsu's *Asian American Authors* (1972); Frank Chin, Jeffrey Paul Chan, Lawson Fusao Inada, and Shawn Hus Wong's *Aiiieeeee!: An Anthology of Asian-American Writers* (1975); and David Wand's *Asian American Heritage* (1974). For critical studies, see Elaine Kim's *Asian American Literature* (Philadelphia: Temple UP, 1982), Amy Ling's *Between Worlds: Women Writers of Chinese Ancestry* (New York: Pergamon Press, 1990), and Cynthia Wong's *Reading Asian American Literature* (Princeton: Princeton UP, 1993).

CANADIANS

Canadian literature reflects a unique cultural history and experience that United States' students and teachers profit from knowing. Gregory (1998) observes that "any reader interested in exploring world literature, learning more about other peoples and America's influence would be remiss not to read Canadian Lit." (p. 8). Canada is, after all, "America's largest trading partner, closest and friendliest neigh-bor" (p. 8). Canada's literature reflects the full scope of human experience set within a specific geog-raphy and history of frontier and settlement, rural and urban life, and Native American, English, and French languages and customs. We are most familiar with modern and contemporary English-speaking Canadian writers. We mention a few whose short stories, novels, and poems are rich resources in our classrooms. Several stories by Margaret Atwood, Mavis Gallant, and Alice Munro are staples; they never fail to engage students with their frank realism and astute insight. Munro's stories of adolescent life, such as *An Ounce of Cure* and *How I Met My Husband,* are centerpieces of units that we teach on friendship and love—issues of critical concern to high school students. We have recommended to avid and curious readers Robertson Davies's portrayal of Canadian life in the novels of *The Deptford Trilogy* and *The Cornish Trilogy.* Canadian teachers have extolled the success of teaching Margaret Lawrence's *A Jest of God* (1966), W. O. Mitchell's *Who Has Seen the Wind* (1947), and Mordecai Richler's *The*

Apprenticeship of Duddy Kravitz (1959) to high school students. In a Reading Circle choice, we have included Carol Shields's novel *The Stone Diaries* (1994) (winner of the 1995 Pulitzer Prize, the National Book Critics Circle Award, and the Governor General's Award of Canada), which portrays a completed life cycle that spans residence in Canada and the United States. The poems of Michael Ondaatje (known most recently as the author of the Booker Prize-winning novel *The English Patient*), Leonard Cohen, and Alden Nowlan are arresting. Canadian teachers have explained why Canadian literature is so rich in poems: More poetry than fiction is published in Canada. In all of the genres, Canadian writers have produced abundant literature that portrays all of the positive and problematic aspects of human life. This literature has a combination of the familiar and the foreign that intrigues and enriches those of us in the United States.

SOUTH AND CENTRAL AMERICANS

The South American writers that we teach—the prose of Isabel Allende (Chile), Jorge Luis Borges (Argentina), Gabriel García Márquez (Colombia), and Julio Cortazar (Argentina), and the poetry of Pablo Neruda (Chile) and Carlos Fuentes (Mexico)—reflect some of the same divisions of cultural identity that are so prevalent in Hispanic North Americans. Their lives and literature express a dual character based on the history of an indigenous population invaded and conquered by Europeans. Over centuries of cultural collisions and intermarriage, the questions arise for many: Who am I? What is my proper role? Fuentes (1992) speaks of that catastrophic encounter of two cultures when the Europeans came to Mexico and conquered and almost vanquished an Indian civilization with its own moral and imaginative universe. Although he acknowledges that the conquest was catastrophic, he does not regard it as sterile. From the merger of the European, the Indian, and the African came an Afro-Indo-Iberian new world that we can celebrate in the midst of economic disasters and cultural discontinuities. The European conquest interrupted the destiny of the indigenous civilization, but there is creative life in the tension between competing values and alternative possibilities. Many South and Central American writers give expression to this tension. Borges, one of the first Spanish American writers to achieve an international reputation, was preoccupied throughout his prose and poetry with just this constant striving for elusive, unknowable truth that is inevitably frustrated. He and his fellow countryman Cortazar often resort to games, riddles, and puzzles as a kind of reenactment of their personal and cultural labyrinths. Both men, Cortazar in *End of the Game and Other Stories* (1963) and Borges in *Labyrinths* (1962, English translation) wrote many short pieces, which students relish for their cleverness and insight. Nobel Prize winner, Gabriel García Márquez puzzles over the same important questions of meaning, but in an entirely different way. His longer novels, such as *One Hundred Years of Solitude* (1967, 1970, English translation), the novella *Chronicle of a Death Foretold* (1981), and his collections of short fiction, such as *Leaf Storm* (1972) and *No One Writes to the Colonel* (1961), present life in a small coastal town, Macondo, which draws our students almost unfailingly into it because of its realism and its magic. Finally, Isabel Allende, in *Two Words,* a story our students invariably choose in their top-10 lists of short fiction, imaginatively projects the power of language to answer the power of guns. She reminds us of the truth of Fuentes's affirmation of the imagination: We can only discover what we have first imagined.

NON-EUROPEANS

The political and social challenges to the canon extend beyond those American populations with interest in their gender, tribal, national, or ethnic heritages. The world's diverse peoples have left oral and written traditions that, from ancient times, have been rich with the variety of human experience. American students benefit from access to these divergent traditions. But world literature selections and courses, while becoming more common in high schools, still tend to center on the experiences of ancient Greece, Rome, and Israel, and Western and Eastern Europe. Applebee's (1993) estimates of the major anthologies, grades 7–12, tell the story of representation by authors from the following national traditions (p. 94):

North America	59.2%
United Kingdom	33.7%
Western Europe	3.6%
Russia and Eastern Europe	.8%
Africa	.8%
Central and South America	.5%
Asia	.6%
Other	.7%

The need is for greater inclusion, of, say, 1968 Japanese Nobel prize laureate Yasunari Kawabata's *Thousand Cranes* (1947, 1965) and *Snow Country* (1937, 1960); New Zealander (Maori) Keri Hulme's

The Bone People (1984, the 1985 Booker Prize recipient); Nigerian Chinua Achebe's *Things Fall Apart* (1967); Botswanan Bessie Head's *Maru* (1972, 1988); Egyptian Nobel prize laureate Naguib Mahfouz's *Midaq Alley* (1981); and South African 1991 Nobel prize laureate Nadine Gordimer's *July's People* (1981). (Additional suggestions are included in Appendix C.)

Alice Walker, in "Saving the Life That Is Your Own" from *In Search of Our Mothers' Gardens* (1983), talks about the impact of reading diverse literature on the artist and, we would add, on all of us. She writes that "the absence of models, in literature as in life . . . is an occupational hazard for the artist, simply because models in art, in behavior, in growth of spirit and intellect—even if rejected—enrich and enlarge one's view of existence" (p. 4). Students profit from knowing a great range of peoples. They move further toward a recognition that ours is not the only or even the best arrangement of institutions, ideas, and values. We put them in a position to grow and be challenged from a variety of perspectives, to open their cultural habits to scrutiny and their cultural understanding to a sense of wider possibility. Such study has the potential to develop our tolerance, enlarge our sensibilities, and deepen our appreciation of others and ourselves. We test the idea that to go deeply into the particular opens up the universal. Poet and essayist Kathleen Norris (1996) calls maturity "the slow process of the heart's awakening" (p. 80).

MULTICULTURAL LITERATURE IN THE CLASSROOM

This multicultural challenge for the high school English teacher is significant, and the resistances to it are many. Many English teachers have themselves been schooled in the Western European classics. These are the texts that they know and love as friends. In fact, teachers often enter the field with just this impulse: to share what has meant much to them. They want to introduce students to that which they love. The following are some of the difficulties that English teachers face:

- Selecting appropriate new texts requires teacher reading time. Many English teachers struggle constantly against the longing to read more and the guilt of not having time to do so. Opening the canon broadens the arena for the guilt of not having read enough considerably.
- Dilg (1995) presents a more subtle hesitancy arising from the awkwardness and tension of speaking of cultural differences in multicultural classrooms. She quotes Thomas Kochman (author of *Black and White Styles in Conflict*), who has noted that "as a culture we lack 'the public etiquette to talk about difference'" (p. 21). The result is that we avoid such uncomfortable conversations. The language alone with which we designate different groups is problematic because it is constantly changing. If we speak of groups different from our own, we are never sure what language is most acceptable to their members. Dilg uses as examples the uncertainty of the preference for "Chicanos" or "Mexican Americans" and the evolution of preference for "Negroes," "Blacks," "Afro-Americans," and "African-Americans" (p. 21). We don't have language or models for talking honestly in dialogue with others about differences of history, perspective, life experiences, expectations, and language.
- Dilg (1995) also points out that "multicultural classes embody the unresolved tensions of the larger culture" (p. 22). These emerge not only in students, but also in the teacher. Teachers who talk about groups different from their own run the risk of not understanding those groups, or, in assuming to do so, appearing to "speak from a position of hypocritical loftiness" (p. 23). To reach a balance is difficult.
- Even if teachers meet these personal obstacles to an expanding canon, practical school-based obstacles arise. Course syllabi, curriculum guides, critical resources, reading lists, textbooks, and school book rooms and libraries all stock the classics. The availability of noncanonical texts, especially in poor districts and those not served by community or neighboring college and university libraries, may be limited.
- Instructional time presents another problem. To introduce a new selection into your study is necessarily to omit another. Limited class time necessitates limited selection.
- Other teachers, administrators, and parents equate English with established literary traditions.

Each of these obstacles can be hurdled, but each requires patient, hopeful effort. You must have the conviction that we need to add the voices of women, African-Americans, Native Americans, Hispanic Americans, and Asian Americans, as well as other non-European national traditions to those of the classics. We describe here strategies to introduce this literature into your classroom that will open students to resistance to cultural stereotyping, sensitivity toward cultural difference, empathy for individual experiences, sympathy for common ground, and awareness of the shared narrative of the struggles and achievements of all humankind. They may encourage what Postman (1995) considers the purpose of public education: "to help the young transcend individual identity by finding inspiration in the story of humanity."

CLASSROOM ENVIRONMENT

On the simplest visual level, the classroom creates the stage for an openness to many cultures. If you display author pictures and biographies on bulletin boards and wall displays, the authors should be drawn from a variety of races, genders, and cultures. If you have images of cultural heroes or writers' quotes, they too should reflect diversity. Newspaper clips, maps of the world or of specific foreign countries, and cultural artifacts can open students to imagine other people, other places. Athanases, Christiano, and Lay (1995) affirm the value of the visual to "communicate to students that members of all groups are welcome, supported, and encouraged here" (p. 27).

Of course, creating a receptive classroom environment is far more complicated than hanging wall decorations. The arrangements of desks, the position of the teacher in the room, the openness of the students to respond to texts and work through them together, and the group tolerance, empathy, and curiosity all contribute to an environment that welcomes differences.

LITERATURE SELECTIONS

We need to select literature that sensitizes students to cultural differences, promotes empathy for others, and even opens points of connection. Because introducing new works into an already tight curriculum is difficult, the temptation is to remain with the tried-and-true anthologies described in this chapter. Barker (1989) explains the struggle: "The only problem is that if you start to get really serious about balancing your curriculum, it means dropping a man for every women you add. For me, that meant putting *Huckleberry Finn* aside to make room for stories by Sarah Orne Jewett, Charlotte Perkins Gilman, and Kate Chopin. These are tough decisions, and you have to be creative" (p. 39).

Selecting a high quality of literature from the array of multicultural possibilities multiplies the difficulty: Teachers don't have the usual sanctioned texts. The American Library Association (Hayden, 1992) recommends five broad guidelines for selecting multicultural literature for the classroom:

1. Look for a quality of reality that gives the reader a chance to experience something.
2. Try to determine the author's commitment to portray cultural groups accurately.
3. Avoid materials that sensationalize, enumerate unusual customs, or practice reversed stereotyping.
4. Be sensitive to emphasis on cultural differences at the expense of similarities.
5. Whenever possible, use the same critical criteria appropriate for all types of literature—distinctive language and appropriate dialogue, style, relevance and potential interest, clearcut plots, and believable characterizations. (p. vi)

Four multicultural anthologies that provide a range of shorter works appeared in the 1990s:

Braided Lives: An Anthology of Multicultural American Writing. Deborah Appleman and Margaret Reed, and the Minnesota Council of Teachers of English, Editors. 1991. St. Paul: The Minnesota Humanities Commission.
Hear My Voice: A Multicultural Anthology of Literature from the United States. Laurie King, Editor. 1994. New York: Addison-Wesley.
Responding to Literature: Multicultural Perspectives. Arthur N. Applebee and Judith A. Langer, Senior Consultants. 1993. Evanston, IL: McDougal, Littel.
Tapestry: A Multicultural Anthology. Alan C. Purves, General Editor. 1993. Paramus, NJ: Globe Book Company.

We also have found *The Gray Wolf Annual Five: Multicultural Literacy* (1985) to be a useful resource. It contains essays that answer the cries of cultural literacy by suggesting what *truly* literate persons need to know and by providing an alternative to Hirsch, Kett, and Trefil's famous list with its male and European bias. The *Gray Wolf* list includes the kinds of multicultural references absent from Hirsch's book and, too often, from our classrooms.

ALTERNATIVE ORGANIZATION

Jay (1991) offers an alternative to the traditional thematic or chronological divisions of American and English literature. He observes that "themes, like periods, derive from and are determined by a previously canonized set of texts and authors. The classic themes of American literature—the Virgin Land, the Frontier West, the Individual's conflict with society, the City versus the Country, Innocence versus Experience, Europe versus America, Dream versus Reality, and so on, simply make no sense when applied to marginalized texts and traditions" (p. 276). Jay suggests that we alter the usual division of seventeenth- through early nineteenth-century American literature into Colonization, Building a Nation, and New England Renaissance, and organize those divisions in terms of a minority, African-American experience. Our colleague Angelene Reid observes that for her, the 1920s is not the decade between World War I and the Depression; it's the Harlem Renaissance. Bigsby (1980) points out that as twentieth-century white writers became critical of oppressive, alien cities, their black counterparts were migrating to Harlem as a refuge of community and opportunity.

Jay (1991) makes another suggestion for instructional organization not around historical moments or even the conscious themes of a privileged, literate few, but around what he calls "problematics." These problematics represent the intersection of cultural events and modes of coping with them. Jay describes them as indicating "how and where the struggle for meaning *takes place*" (p. 277). He suggests raising the problematics and discussing texts that deal with them from different cultural perspectives. His own examples of problematics include "(1) origins, (2) power, (3) civilization, (4) tradition, (5) assimilation, (6) translation, (7) bodies, (8) literacy, and (9) borders" (p. 277).

Some high schools have cracked the canon by creating electives on minority writers. These have the advantage of focus and of not having to "bump" established classics as new works are added. We recognize the difficulties of adding to an already overtaxed curriculum, but we are still far more interested in integrating the study of diverse literature into the mainstream English course. That concern grows from practical motives (that is where most students are taught English), political belief (the experience of other genders and cultures is not something novel or exotic to be segregated from the culture's dominant experience), and personal conviction (such classroom integration exactly matches the necessary cultural struggle over gender roles and relationships). Writing by women, people of color, and people of different national traditions need not be regarded as incidental, isolated, and peculiar to one group. Instead, it needs to be affirmed and integrated into the experience of our diverse national and world culture, not as an anomaly, but as a rich, vital, and beautiful tradition.

PAIRING

We pair works by writers with diverse cultural perspectives. The pairings are especially effective when other elements remain constant, as in a similar genre, theme, or characters; the differences between the two writers' experiences and sensibilities become apparent and teach almost by themselves. Many students also find that they have more impressions to discuss when they compare and contrast two works, rather than talk of one alone. Figure 6–1 presents pairings of male and female authors that we and other teachers have used (Reid, 1992; Barker, 1989; Carlson, 1989; Lake, 1988; Moore, 1989; Hale, 1997).

MALE AUTHOR	TITLE	FEMALE AUTHOR	TITLE
Martin Luther King, Jr.	Letter from Birmingham Jail/I Have a Dream	Harper Lee	To Kill A Mockingbird
Henry D. Thoreau	Walden	Annie Dillard	Pilgrim at Tinker Creek
Richard Wright	Black Boy	Maya Angelou	I Know Why the Caged Bird Sings
James Baldwin	Go Tell It on the Mountain		
Walt Whitman	Song of Myself	Emily Dickinson	I'm Nobody!
	To a Locomotive in Winter		I Like to See it Lap the Miles
Mark Twain	The Adventures of Huckleberry Finn	Willa Cather	My Antonia
		Cynthia Voigt	Homecoming
Uri Orlev	Island on Bird Street	Anne Frank	Anne Frank: The Diary of a Young Girl
Scott O'Dell	The Island of the Blue Dolphins	Jean C. George	Julie of the Wolves
Edgar Allan Poe	The Black Cat	Charlotte Perkins Gilman	The Yellow Wallpaper
Thomas More	Utopia	Charlotte Perkins Gilman	Herland
Eli Wiesel	Night	Etty Hillesum	An Interrupted Life
James Baldwin	If Beale Street Could Talk	Ann Petry	The Street
Gordon Parks	The Leaning Tree	Mildred Taylor	Roll of Thunder, Hear My Cry
Alex Haley	Roots	Margaret Walker	Jubilee
August Wilson	Fences	Lorraine Hansberry	A Raisin in the Sun
Stephen Crane	The Red Badge of Courage	Grace King	Bayou L'Ombre
T. S. Eliot	The Wasteland	H. D. (Hilda Doolittle)	Trilogy (The Walls Do Not Fall)
John Steinbeck	The Grapes of Wrath	Willa Cather	O Pioneers!
		Harriette Arnow	The Dollmaker
Henry James	Daisy Miller	Edith Wharton	The Age of Innocence

FIGURE 6–1 Pairings of literature by men and women

As we do with women writers, we pair works by minority and majority writers that reflect contrasting experiences of the same phenomenon. Consider, for instance, comparing novels of initiation: Ralph Ellison's *Invisible Man*, Mark Twain's *The Adventures of Huckleberry Finn* or F. Scott Fitzgerald's *The Great Gatsby;* or of autobiography: Benjamin Franklin's *Autobiography* and Frederick Douglass's *Narrative of the Life of Frederick Douglass* or Harriet Jacobs's *Incidents in the Life of a Slave Girl.*

RESISTANT READING

Resistant Reading is a reading strategy that approaches texts with a heightened critical consciousness. We ask students to observe and uncover stereotypes of gender, race, ethnicity, and nationality in the texts they read. Toni Morrison (1992), in *Playing in the Dark: Whiteness and the Literary Imagination,* lists several rhetorical strategies used by writers to manipulate perceptions of African-Americans. These devices are equally effective in stereotyping other groups and the individuals within them. Students can be primed to look for these strategies in the texts they read.

1. *economy of stereotype*—physical and cultural descriptions of individuals and groups that are so brief as to render them caricatures with no unique distinctions between them;
2. *metonymic displacement*—where a single image, action, or object is used to represent an entire group of people—such as large lips or slanted eyelids to represent African Americans or Asian Americans;
3. *metaphysical condensation*—reducing a people's language, religious beliefs, and values to simplistic description—for example a multilingual Lakota Indian's speech might be reduced to "Ugh!" and "How";
4. *fetishization*—focusing attention on images or acts that evoke erotic desires or fears, such as miscengenation or cannibalism;
5. *dehistoricizing allegory*—describing groups as though they were somehow removed from a specific social, political, and historical moment. (pp. 67–69)

Direct questions can help uncover these stereotypes. For instance, if you read non African-American texts, pose questions such as the following:

- How are African-Americans portrayed?
- Does the author use stereotypes: lazy field hands, Black Mammy, Aunt Jemima, Uncle Tom, contemporary absent fathers, and menacing drug-addicted ghetto youths?
- Are the portraits two-dimensional?
- Are the African-Americans marginal to the main action?
- Could African-American characters be substituted for the main characters?
- As Wallace (1988) might ask, "Has Tonto walked away from the Lone Ranger yet? Has Rochester handed Benny his notice?" (p. 164).

Students also can look for counterexamples of stereotyping that demonstrate understanding and application of cultural pluralism.

For texts in which women are nonexistent, Barker (1989) has his students raise issues of gender. "What are the implications of Billy Budd's being described in feminine terms? . . . Could *A Separate Peace* have been written about a girls' school? Is the reason that girls give up swinging on "Birches" the same as it is for boys?" (p. 41).

Davis (1989) uses another type of resistance to intensify her students' insights into gender issues. She teaches such American classics as F. Scott Fitzgerald's *The Great Gatsby* and Arthur Miller's *Death of a Salesman,* but she uses "feminist scholars" in her interpretation rather than the "traditional explications" of male critics (p. 45). Barker (1989), in a "covert" attempt to create a "learning situation more responsive to the needs and interests of *all* students," focuses "discussion and writing topics on areas in which female students are authorities" (p. 39).

STUDENT ASSAYS

Like the Polar Responses discussed in Chapter 4, Student Assays can engage students before they read and discuss texts and can prime them for paying attention to stereotyping. Barker (1989) queries students by a variety of means to make them aware of their assumptions about gender. He takes quick votes. Could the situation in *The Yellow Wallpaper* happen today? He asks students to list the "qualities they perceive women and men expect from relationships" (p. 41). Lawrence (1995) prepares students for stories or novels that may have atypical gender roles by asking students to designate which gender is associated with particular activities, such as "washing clothes, doing dishes, vacuuming, mowing a lawn, cleaning out flower beds, fixing a bicycle, cleaning toilets, playing baseball, playing football, a career in ballet, a career in nursing, a career in engineering, etc." Then she asks them to write in response to this writing prompt: "Which of the above categories do you believe women should not be involved in? Why? Which of the above categories do you believe men should not be involved in? Why? Do you believe it is harder to be a male or female in our society today? Explain" (p. 82). Her list of activities could be used with other groups to spur students to consider their assumptions about the "other."

PERSPECTIVE TAKING

A number of different strategies can enlarge students' empathy for individuals and groups different from themselves. Many involve attempts to have students creatively project into the experiences and perspectives of another. Within another's world view, they can discover, first, differences and then, perhaps, similarities.

For a unit on Robert Cormier's *The Chocolate War* and William Golding's *Lord of the Flies,* Samuels (1993) suggests a prereading activity to tie the novels to the students' own experiences. Her plan for role-playing could help students project into the world of the "other" in any context. Samuels' suggestion goes like this:

> Have small groups role play a situation in which most of the students are part of the "in group" (they wear buttons that say "cool" or wear special hats) and one or two students are part of the "out-group." As we well know, middle and high school students are often organized in cliques or groups. The role play should involve some aspect of school life today. For example, the "in group" tries to convince the others to do something that is not acceptable according to the standard rules (i.e., cheating, wearing particular clothes, shunning a particular student, drinking alcohol, smoking, etc.). Discussion should follow on questions like the following:
>
> • What makes a group "in"? What makes a group "out"? How does the "in-group" in a school identify itself? Who identifies the "out-group"?
> • How does the "in-group" keep their power? What tools do they use to convince others to follow them?
> • Are "in-groups" good or bad for a school?
> • What are the "in-groups" at your school? What are the "out-groups" at your school? How can they each be identified?*

Higgins and Fowinkle (1993) suggest a dramatic activity that forces students into the perspectives of others:

• *Group Role-play:* (When all students have read the same novel and are working in groups.) "Role-playing is the taking on of another's position and psychological perspective to gain greater insight into a person's psyche. Have each person in your group choose a character in a novel and play out a scene (or several scenes). Each person should try to assume the character's position and perspective as much as possible."**

Lawrence (1995) gives a number of ideas to help students understand gender issues from the opposite perspective (p. 82). We list a few:

• *Collages.* She asks students to make a collage "of magazine pictures that shows how their gender is being encouraged to look and dress." She then asks them to write about "what the pictures tell females/males they should look like."
• *Adopting the opposite gender's point of view.* "Have students try writing a story from the point of view of the opposite gender about a very gendered issue such as being rejected in a dating relationship or asking someone out or getting ready for a big dance. Then ask them to write a reflective paper on which parts of the story were hard or easy to write and what they think they learned or realized about the opposite sex."
• *Collecting compliments.* "For a period of two weeks, ask students to collect compliments they hear or overhear from teachers, parents, peers. Categorize comments by gender and then look at what each gender is complimented on or appreciated for."

Athanasas does a similar thing when he asks students "to write narratives and poems from the points of view of people involved in current crises in the news and to role play characters from literary works

*From "The Beast Within: Using and Abusing Power in *Lord of the Flies, The Chocolate War,* and Other Readings." In J. F. Kaywell (Ed.), *Adolescent Literature as a Complement to the Classics* by B. C. Samuels, 1993, 200. Norwood, MA: Christopher-Gordon Publishers, Inc.

**From "*The Adventures of Huckleberry Finn,* Prejudice, and Adolescent Literature." In J. F. Kaywell (Ed.), *Adolescent Literature as a Complement to the Classics* by J. Higgins and J. Fowinkle, 1993, 47. Norwood, MA: Christopher-Gordon Publishers, Inc.

FIGURE 6–2
Statements associated
with feminist issues

How might each of the following statements be associated with feminist issues? Write briefly on each one, but choose one to explore your thinking in some depth.

1. [Ginny says] " . . . lately I have been trying to take care of myself. That's what women are most afraid of, you know. Being selfish. It's the ultimate sin." (p. 91)
2. "I am afraid, too," [Ginny] whispered in the darkness. "Hear me, Coralee Dickson, while you are curled like an animal in a hole away from sky and wind and sun. The demons that devour women are all the same." (p. 92)
3. "I just thought I'd reach the time when I didn't have to take care of nothing but me," Coralee said. "I want to have that feeling one day before I die." (p. 117)
4. "I thought that, too," Ginny said. "I married because of it. I did everything I was told because of it. But in the long run being safe meant being in prison. It took a long time, but I came out of it. I guess I thought for years somebody had to open the door for me. I was waiting for that. But the truth is, the door was locked from the inside. Nobody could open it but me." (p. 134)
5. [Leanna says] " . . . Travis wants us to get married. He says it will make college easier . . . He's got in his head how we'll have this cute little apartment instead of living in the dorm . . but I don't know. I was sort of looking forward to being with girls, talking and all like we're doing . . . I have to do things on my own sometimes." (p. 151)

involved in imaginary scenes. In these ways students voice and embody others' experiences" (Athanasas, Christiano, & Lay, 1995, p. 32).

Kelly (1993) suggests using passages from a text to prompt students to consider specific issues of gender or ethnicity. With Sue Ellen Bridger's novel *Permanent Connections,* she distributes the quotations in Figure 6–2 and asks students to write about each of these quotes, select one to explore more deeply before class discussion, and in a small group, discuss ideas and feelings stirred by the quotes they chose. Kelly explains that the small group creates a safe environment in which to encounter new, sometimes sensitive issues and to "formulate ideas and attitudes" (p. 136).

ENACTMENT

We have suggested the performance of role-play and visualization. We focus here on dramatically entering an oral tradition out of which the original texts were created. Native American literature lends itself to active reading or performance because so much of it was oral and ritualistic. If students have selected works appropriate to the communal circle, they should read them encircled by their fellow students, preferably out-of-doors, but at least on the floor of a classroom illumined perhaps by natural, not artificial light. Percussion instruments and flutes can add authenticity to the reading. Or, students may enact an event. For example, imagine what students might do with *The Deathsong of White Antelope.* Sanders and Peek (1973) describe the context of this deathsong: White Antelope of the Cheyenne tribe died at the 1864 Sand Creek Massacre "with the dignity expected of and befitting a war captain of some fifty years. With folded arms, he stood singing his death song as he was killed" (p. 285).

The Deathsong of White Antelope

Nothing lives long
except the earth
and the mountains.

Students may choose to enact what Lincoln (1983) calls the Navajo Night Chant (p. 47):

Navajo Night Chant

May it be beautiful before me.
May it be beautiful behind me.
May it be beautiful below me.
May it be beautiful above me.
May it be beautiful all around me.
In beauty it is finished.

The art and film of the places and peoples of any of these cultural groups extend the students' imaginative entry into other worlds. For instance, books have appeared of Native American art—paintings, architecture, pottery, weaving, silver, crafts, and photography: Adam's *Fritz Scholder Lithograms* (1975), Bedinger's *Indian Silver: Navajo and Pueblo Jewelers* (1973), Frank and Harlow's *Historic Pottery of the Pueblo Indians, 1600–1880* (1974), and Highwater's *Song from the Earth: American Indian Painting* (1976). Displaying or projecting these along with literature enhances and deepens the experience of both.

TACKLING STEREOTYPES

Multicultural literature is built on cultural differences and thus is often politically and culturally charged. The issues raised by this literature prompt envisioning and then understanding. This does not necessarily entail political debate; however, students' discoveries of the experiences of "the other" produce strong feelings. Dilg (1995) observes that fictional works by writers of color have a powerful impact on students that "makes them more complicated to address than are works with greater psychological or historical distance" (p. 24). Ideally, when political or cultural content enters your classroom, you will have built an ease and empathy within students and language for talking honestly about these issues.

Athanases, Christiano, and Lay (1995) face stereotyping head-on in our culture and in their students. They introduce texts (print and nonprint) that present stereotyping in overt and subtle ways, and they structure class activities that open these questions to student reflection and discussion. Christiano asks students in a unit of his U.S. literature/history class to examine their "impressions of racial and ethnic groups." A portion of this unit is described in Figure 6–3. He reports that "students moved from their personal experiences, often reactionary and purely emotional, to a consciousness of the widespread nature of racism in America. This deeper understanding of the larger social and political picture helped students begin to see the value of moving beyond divisiveness to unity among people of color and others interested in combating racism" (p. 30).

We confront serious questions about the dominant culture's treatment of Native Americans via the oratory and written correspondence between Native Americans and those who were negotiating their removal or demise. For example, Chief Joseph of the Nez Perce, in *An Indian's Views of Indian Affairs* written for the *North American Review* of April, 1879, eloquently explained his arduous and honorable attempt to save his tribe from encroachment, coercion, and destruction. These documents can be found in anthologies, then orated and debated. When students further assume the roles of Native Americans and whites, drama and intensity build.

Goebel (1995) has his students examine excerpts from the journals of Christopher Columbus with attention to the literary devices used to register his regard for the Native Americans whom he met on his arrival. Goebel's class uses Toni Morrison's list of rhetorical strategies as their guides. They also explore the accounts of these events in current junior high school and high school textbooks for racial and cultural bias and stereotyping. Finally, they return to fictional and poetical accounts of the same event to see whether these accounts give them greater access to the people who received Columbus. Michael Davis's young adult novel *Morning Girl* (1992) tells the story of one such family, both their daily lives before the Europeans arrived and their impressions of their arrival. Goebel reports the impact of reading this novel after reading the nonfiction accounts: "the reader can no longer take [Columbus's] words as objective truth, but rather as one perspective in a complex web of human interaction" (p. 48).

FIGURE 6–3
Christiano's unit that tackles stereotypes

In studying Latino culture and experiences, students read an excerpt from Piri Thomas's *Down These Mean Streets* (1967), poetry by Pat Mora (1985), historical texts, essays by Carlos Fuentes; and view a slide presentation of California Chicano murals and films such as *Nuestro Pueblo* (a 1991 documentary about Chicanos in Northern California) and the Hollywood feature film *Zoot Suit* (1991). In groups, students explore cultural assimilation and the phenomenon of feeling lost between two worlds.

To culminate this unit, students who identify themselves as Latinos answer questions that tap personal responses:

- How do your views of your ethnic identity differ from what you see as the general, popular impressions?
- What do you consider to be the most prevalent stereotypes about Latinos and to what extent do they accurately reflect the prevailing attitudes, behavior, and values of your culture?

Non-Latino students respond personally to questions such as these:

- When you hear the terms "Mexican," "Chicano," "Latino," or "Hispanic," what kind of image comes to mind?
- What is the source of this image (how did it form in your mind)?

While the first question asked of non-Latino students invites them to reveal whatever cultural notions they hold, however stereotypical, about Latinos, the second pushes them to examine how such notions developed. Students also answer questions such as these:

- What are some stereotypes you've come across having to do with Latinos?
- To what extent do you believe that these stereotypes have any truth to them?

Athanases, Christiano, and Lay (1995) state two questions as underlying their multiethnic classes. Their carefully designed teaching allows students to openly grapple with these tough issues.

- How can we understand or come to terms with differences within and between various groups such as those defined by race, culture, gender, or sexual orientation?
- How can these differences in identity expand rather than restrict the potential for human life and democratic possibilities? (p. 31)

FIFTH CHALLENGE: YOUNG ADULT FICTION

We turn now to literature that many would put at the opposite extreme from the classics: young adult fiction. The designation itself is of recent origin. It was once used to refer to slight, formulaic stories of adolescents turned out by sentimental hacks. Today it designates a body of work that not only centers on adolescent protagonists and is marketed for young audiences, but also possesses literary distinction. Until the publication of Louisa May Alcott's *Little Women* (1868), very little was written for adolescents in America. The young, when they graduated from school texts, read adult literature, classics and popular fiction. Indeed, until the late nineteenth century, the age divisions in the human life cycle were simple and direct: children and adults. Formerly, when children reached the ages of 14 or 15 and could begin to work and contribute to their families, they began to be considered adults. *Adolescence,* as a term used to describe an age of unique stages of cognitive, psychological, sexual, social, and even moral development set apart from both childhood and adult life is a relatively recent designation.

THE EXPANSION OF YOUNG ADULT FICTION

Literature featuring adolescents as protagonists grew in popularity at the end of the nineteenth and the beginning of the twentieth century. This literature was read by adults and the young alike, and it became noted primarily for its serialization and its sentimentality. As its writers moved toward greater realism at the mid-twentieth century and its publishers moved toward more specialized publishing and marketing efforts (spurred especially by the rise of paperbacks), it gathered to it an increasing number of quite talented authors and a corresponding number of interested young readers. Many of its writers did not consciously begin to write for the young. Donelson and Nilsen (1980) tell of Robert Cormier's initial reaction to becoming a "young adult" author: "shock followed by a month-long writer's block" (p. 6).

Some of these writers remain ambivalent about their being pigeonholed by publishers, booksellers, and librarians in this category. Others find that their adolescent characters can become involved with many of the same dilemmas as those faced by protagonists of classic literature, and they engage in other age-specific issues that are equally as life challenging. The adolescent reading audience is also distinguished by its hospitality to new ideas and to divergent styles. It is generous in its expectations of fiction. Many adolescents, of course, expect and demand certain predictable character types, plots, and ideas. (Nancy Drew and the Hardy Boys remain in print.) But many others have a tolerance and playfulness about literature and the time to read it. Writer S. E. Hinton speaks of the advantage in the adolescent reading audience: It is open to "all kinds of writing."

Robert Small (1992) enumerates characteristics unique to young adult novels that clearly explain their appeal:

- The main character is a teenager.   *Characteristics*
- Events and problems in the plot are related to teenagers.
- The main character is the center of the plot.
- Dialogue reflects teenage speech, including slang.
- The point of view presents an adolescent's interpretation of events and people.
- The teenage main character is usually perceptive, sensitive, intelligent, mature, and independent.
- The novel is short, rarely more than 200 pages.
- The actions and decisions of the main characters are major factors in the outcome of the conflict (pp. 282–283).

Gallo (1989) listed the results of a poll of past and present officers of NCTE's Assembly on Literature for Adolescents. Figure 6–4 lists the 18 young adult authors that they named as most important. Ted Hipple (1989) informally polled English teachers, English educators, and present and past officers of the same NCTE Assembly to "identify the ten adolescent novels they wanted all English teachers to know about" (p. 79). Figure 6–5 is that list in order of most popular choice to least. (The 11 titles for 10 places resulted from a tie.)

FIGURE 6–4

Important authors of young adult literature

S. E. Hinton	Judy Blume	Norma Klein
Paul Zindel	Sue Ellen Bridgers	Scott O'Dell
Richard Peck	Virginia Hamilton	Paula Danziger
Robert Cormier	Madeleine L'Engle	Norma Fox Mazer
M. E. Kerr	Robert Newton Peck	Paula Fox
Katherine Paterson	Robert Lipsyte	Zibby Oneal

FIGURE 6–5

Top 10 adolescent novels for English teachers to read

1.	*The Chocolate War*	Robert Cormier
2.	*The Outsiders*	S. E. Hinton
3.	*The Pigman*	Paul Zindel
4.	*Home Before Dark*	Sue Ellen Bridgers
5.	*A Day No Pigs Would Die*	Robert Newton Peck
6.	*All Together Now*	Sue Ellen Bridgers
7.	*The Moves Make the Man*	Bruce Brooks
8.	*Jacob Have I Loved*	Katherine Paterson
9.	*Words by Heart*	Ouida Sebestyen
10.	*Dicey's Song*	Cynthia Voight
11.	*Summer of My German Soldier*	Bette Greene

Many teachers welcome these well-crafted books. They say that these texts "make readers" of their students. They appeal to a wide gamut of reading interests. They reflect all of the genres of adult fiction: realism, romance, adventure, suspense, science fiction, fantasy, westerns, mysteries, historical fiction, utopias, and even horror. Students are clearly drawn toward the range of texts, from the mythological quests of fantasy to the excitement and thrill of suspense. Many of these genres attract a cult of devoted readers who haunt bookstores and libraries for new titles. Most importantly, as Rosenblatt (1983) understood, "Like the beginning reader, the adolescent needs to encounter literature for which he possesses the intellectual, emotional, and experiential equipment" (p. 26). "Books must be provided that hold out some link with the young reader's past and present occupations, anxieties, ambitions" (p. 72).

CONTENT

Since 1972, the staff of the University of Iowa's Books for Young Adults Program has annually polled 10th- through 12th-graders about their reading choices based on initial appeal and subsequent enjoyment. Consistently, the most popular books are those in the category of contemporary realism. The choices of these young readers, then, suggest an interest in their fictional counterparts involved in all of the perplexities and excitements of growing up. In his seminal two-volume work, *Adolescence* (1904), G. Stanley Hall reasons that adolescents' erratic emotional development coincides with their erratic physical growth. Young adult fiction centers on adolescent protagonists and therefore encompasses the experiences and feelings peculiar to the age: such overriding issues as personal identity, separation from family, identifications with groups, cliques, age mates of both sexes, and developing moral clarity and commitment. Formerly, boys' identity issues were tied to occupational choices and girls' to marriage choices. Those gender-specific benchmarks are no longer as predictable and straightforward. Both sexes are engaged in what Freud believed is the crucial resolution for mental health: one's ability to love and to work. And all of these issues are negotiated in the turbulent context of a fluid and changeable identity that engenders an overwhelming self-consciousness. For instance, the 15-year-old protagonist of Colin Neenan's sensitive and witty first novel, *In Your Dreams* (1995), is convinced he is hideously ugly and impossibly in love with his older brother's girlfriend. The words on a *Peanuts* poster that we saw on the wall of an English classroom exactly capture the feelings of this character and so many high school students: "As soon as I get up in the morning, I feel like I'm in over my head."

Books that reflect these experiences can reassure adolescents that they are not alone in being "over their heads" and that their clamor for emotional, intellectual, behavioral, and moral balance is normal. Many young adult novels deal with current, topical issues: child abuse; substance abuse; the turmoil of parental tensions, separation, and divorce; estrangement from families, friends, and community; confusions of sexual identity; running away; and date rape. These novels have a strong appeal for adolescents who are personally or vicariously caught up in similar traumas and tensions. Furthermore, the egocentrism so characteristic of adolescents can be challenged to include others. They can acknowledge and empathize with stories other than their own personal narratives of anxious hope and imagined glory. Adolescents often create imaginary audiences who watch and judge their appearance, behavior, and career; through reading young adult novels, they become the audience for others. There is reassurance and affirmation in such a role and a widening sense of possibility in the world.

Because students do personally engage with the fiction, they seem eager to share their responses to it, just as they commonly share their reactions to movies, sports events, and rock concerts. Small (1972) points to the balance of power that is common to secondary classrooms in which the teacher is perceived as authority and students as less knowing. He notes that teaching young adult literature changes that knowledge balance. Students become the more knowing in responding to the lives and situations of the adolescent protagonists. Small writes that "students can justifiably be said to speak from a greater authority than their teacher" (p. 226). Because this literature touches their authentic experiences, it engages students more actively and encourages the sharing of responses, feelings, ideas, and reactions—in short, the work of the interpretive community.

FORM

If teachers like the appeal and impact of this type of reading on their high school students, they also value its style. Teachers are glad of the expanded possibilities for the young to read writing that rises above the mediocrity of earlier juvenile literature and in fact often challenges the honesty and craft of adult fiction. Adolescent literature is usually easily accessible to students in its straightforward narrative, its recognizable characters, its uncomplicated syntax, and its approachable vocabulary. It is free of the obscurity and conscious incomprehensibility of many texts. Often those texts, so highly valued by critics and academics, appeal to a highly literate elite and in so doing exclude the uninitiated reader. Young adult writers, perhaps more conscious of their audiences, exercise care in making their fiction readable. Where they experiment, they do not exclude the reader from the possibility of comprehension. Thus, they capture the attention of the young and involve them in imagining fictive worlds. Students reading this fiction are likely to embark on Rosenblatt's (1978) transaction with the text: "The reader envisions the characters, participates in their uttered thoughts and emotions, and weaves the sequence of events into a plot" (p. 68). Students do so because these characters are struggling in the context of dilemmas they too are experiencing *and* because the prose invites the reader to comprehend it.

These works also allow teachers to teach form effectively—often better than with traditional classics. Students have a firmer grasp of the works and therefore more control over the material and more confidence in discerning the craft with which it is written. Small (1977) comments on this potential for formal analysis by analogy. He notes that we would not try to teach novices about the steam or internal combustion engine by taking them to visit a TVA generating plant or to inspect the most sophisticated car. Instead, a good teacher would start with a "simple steam engine, a one-cylinder engine, a working model, where each part was one of its kind and its functions clear. The junior novel is, for all purposes, that simple but working model of the adult or classic novel." For instance, students quickly understand such difficult concepts as irony in reading *The Chocolate War* (1974); multiple perspectives in *A Hero Ain't Nothin' but A Sandwich* (1973), or Tolkien's *The Lord of the Rings* (Trilogy) (1967); narrative voice in *The Pigman* (1968); and psychological complexity in *Home Before Dark* (1976).

APPEAL

Young adult fiction is appropriate for students at all reading levels. Grimes (1991) tries to find the special books that will lead reluctant readers of low or high ability to the "big breakthrough" to reading enjoyment. She describes this search for the "all-important breakthrough book" as "one of the reading teacher's most important contributions" (p. 45). And she finds these books in young adult fiction. She describes introducing some of her "toughest nonreaders" to a love of reading through Arthur Roth's "adventure-packed survival stories" *Trapped* (1983) and *Avalanche* (1989). She discusses the novels that led a snarling, problem-beset student to discover that other people have problems to which she could compare her own: Deborah Hautzig's *Second Star to the Right* (1982), Frank Deford's *Alex: The Life of a Child* (1983), Louis Lowry's *Find a Stranger, Say Goodbye* (1978), and Robyn Miller's *Robyn's Book* (1986). This same student explained that at first she had entered class hating to read; in fact, her deepest wish was "to pick up a book and throw it!" (p. 45).

Rakow (1991) is equally devoted to sharing young adult fiction with an entirely different student population: gifted students. She explains that teachers and parents often unwittingly deny these students valuable experiences and insights by insisting that they read the classics. She observes that teachers "frequently offer honors students fewer opportunities than their nongifted peers to explore through reading, writing, and discussion how modern literature addresses questions of growing up. Conditioned to seeking answers to questions and solutions to problems through books, these youngsters are cut off from a significant source of insight and support when they are discouraged (even forbidden?) from reading YA literature" (pp. 48–49). Rakow believes that "certain life experiences and developmental needs are shared by all students, and giftedness is not an inoculation against the pain and confusion of adolescence. Gifted teenagers . . . need young-adult books to help illuminate and validate their own experiences. They need books that can help them explore how others feel and function in the day-to-day teenage world in which they so often feel alien" (p. 48).

YOUNG ADULT FICTION AND THE CLASSICS

Other teachers use adolescent fiction as a bridge to adult fiction or the classics. Spencer (1989) brings young adult novels into her Advanced Placement classroom. Before teaching Jean Paul Sartre's *No Exit* and existentialist philosophy, she asks that her students read Chris Crutcher's *Running Loose* (1983) or his *The Crazy Horse Electric Game* (1987), or Norma Howe's *God, the Universe and Hot Fudge Sundaes* (1984). She regards these three novels as excellent catalysts for discussions of various aspects of existentialism with which Sartre is concerned: alienation, chaos, personal choice, and commitment. She reports her reasoning: "An advanced-placement student devours an adolescent novel in a single evening; change of pace, ease, and interest level provide new accessibility to the difficult, cold philosophy of existentialism" (p. 46). She further explains:

> Adolescent literature in an advance-placement classroom connects classics to the present. Even those students who read Nietzsche on their own find relevance and pleasure in sharing the lives of fellow teenagers Louie, Willie, or Alfie. If the purpose of a unit on philosophy in literature is to ask students to think more deeply about life, death, and their place in the universe, then this succeeds: perfunctory discussions dissipate. Personal, passionate, probing exchanges vitalize literary discourse. (p. 46)

Others have found connections between young adult fiction and the classics to be powerful. An *English Journal Booksearch* (March, 1989) asked the question, "What adolescent novel do you use to introduce students to a literary classic?" The responding teachers indicated that they used young adult fiction both before the classic, to "help readers make that leap of understanding," and after, to "clarify for young readers the meaning of more difficult selections" (p. 82). Figure 6-6 records these connections as well as those from other sources.

We have found two resources to be especially helpful in connecting young adult literature and the classics. These volumes are filled with ideas for thematic connections and detailed lesson plans for units of study:

Joan F. Kaywell, Editor. (1993). *Adolescent Literature as a Complement to the Classics.* Norwood, MA: Christopher-Gordon Publishers, Inc.

Sarah K. Herz with Donald R. Gallo. (1996). *From Hinton to Hamlet: Building Bridges Between Young Adult Literature and the Classics.* Westport, CT: Greenwood Press.

A list of recommended young adult works prepared in 1992 by high school librarian Sandy Benedict appears in Appendix C. She compiled this list of novels to strike a balance between literary merit and compelling subject matter. She included some genres, such as science fiction, that have great appeal to high school readers, especially males. Ted Hipple (1998) updates Benedict's recommendations with his speculations on the young adult novels that a potential survey of the best of the 1990s will include.

ADOLESCENT NOVEL	AUTHOR	PAIRED CLASSIC	AUTHOR
The Island	Gary Paulsen	*Walden*	Henry David Thoreau
		Civil Disobedience	
Z for Zachariah	Robert O'Brien	*Hiroshima*	John Hersey
Dove	Derek L. T. Gill	*The Odyssey*	Homer
The Wild Children	Felice Holman	*Animal Farm*	George Orwell
Bless the Beasts and Children	Glendon Swartour	*Lord of the Flies*	William Golding
Summer of My German Soldier	Bette Greene	*Anne Frank: The Diary of a Young Girl*	Anne Frank
The Chocolate War	Robert Cormier	*The Oxbow Incident*	Walter Van Tillburg Clark
The Witch of Blackbird Pond	Elizabeth George Speare	*The Scarlet Letter*	Nathaniel Hawthorne
The Homecoming[1]	Cynthia Voight	*The Odyssey*	Homer
		The Adventures of Huckleberry Finn	Mark Twain
A Hero Ain't Nothin' but a Sandwich[2]	Alice Childress	*As I Lay Dying*	William Faulkner
The Island of the Blue Dolphins[3]	Scott O'Dell	*Ninth Sketch* in *The Encantadas*	Herman Melville

[1]An idea from teacher and writer Julia Neenan and librarian and writer Colin Neenan.
[2]We have had able students who were fascinated by *As I Lay Dying;* however, we regard it as too difficult for most high school students.
[3]Sandy Benedict recommends the benefits of reading and comparing these two accounts of the same historical incident from two perspectives.

FIGURE 6–6 Adolescent novels as complements to the classics

Other resources for selection include annual awards and book lists chosen by school librarians, professors, and professional reviewers and published by the *School Library Journal* (a December award), *Booklist* (a January award), and the *American Library Association* (a Spring award). Appendix C also lists resources for those interested in learning more about young adult literature: journals, books (critical analysis, review, and bibliographies), and book awards.

SIXTH CHALLENGE: GENRE VARIETY

One consequence of the preceding challenges to the canon has been to open classrooms and criticism to a variety of literary genres once thought to belong solely to the realm of popular culture. One powerful assumption of traditional schooling about appropriate texts rests on a contrast between high and low culture. Chambers (1985) defines *high culture* as "cultivated tastes and formally imparted knowledge," which call for "particular moments of concentration, separated out from the run of daily life" (p. 5). Popular culture, on the other hand, "mobilizes the tactile, the incidental, the transitory, the visceral" and is not grasped by contemplation but by informal "distracted reception" (p. 5). Jameson (1983) sees the breakdown of the division between high and low culture as distressing to academics who have "traditionally had a vested interest in preserving a realm of high or elite culture against the surrounding environment of philistinism, of schlock and kitsch, of TV series and *Reader's Digest* culture, and in transmitting difficult and complex skills of reading, listening and seeing to its initiates" (p. 112). Kellner (1988) acknowledges the "unique pleasures and enticements" provided by traditional high culture, but believes that its enshrinement and canonization serve to exclude and marginalize "precisely those phenomena which most immediately engage most individuals in our society" (pp. 32–33).

For these critics, the canon is a device of exclusion, exclusion of students from their own experienced lives and exclusion of popular culture from serious scrutiny and discussion. Culture, they say, can also be defined as how people live, interact, and change. Rouse (1989) describes students in the classroom studying Shakespeare who feel perhaps "a sense of pious satisfaction for having done their duty before returning with a sigh of relief to their usual entertainments. Outwardly conforming, they inwardly resist the imposition of our cultural authority and the implied denigration of their own taste" (p. 87). Rouse believes that if we are to engage students in reading literature, we may have to relinquish our "promotion of 'art.'" He argues that we can do this "in good conscience" because the separation of high and popular culture is not necessarily "built into the nature of things." Shakespeare, after all, was the most popular dramatist of his own time and of nineteenth-century America. And, Rouse concludes, any work that will "engage the feelings and thoughts of young people, and help us shape the interior world by which they interpret their experience, is artful enough for our purpose, whether admired by the cognoscenti or not. The great themes are not found only in the great books" (pp. 87–88).

This redefinition of culture expands the English curriculum to genres that would have formerly been laughed out of school: detective stories, mysteries, romances, westerns, science fiction, fantasy, and even comics. (Interestingly, the university curriculum seems to have been most open to this diversity of forms.) Prodded by two of our former high school students for whom the popular genres of comics and science fiction were private passions and aware of the many other students who were closet aficionados of both, we have taken a closer look at these two. In Chapter 8, we discuss comics. Here we use the extensive reading and insights of Phillip Chester to describe science fiction and, in Appendix C, to list some prominent and well-regarded science fiction texts.

SCIENCE FICTION

We have long admired the work of some of science fiction's superstars, namely Isaac Asimov, Ray Bradbury, Arthur C. Clarke, and Kurt Vonnegut, Jr. We even sympathize with Vonnegut's lament about having his fiction labeled science fiction and thereafter being consigned to a folder in the back corner of some academic filing cabinet, even though he was dealing with all of the "mind-cracking" issues that "literary" writers were. Yet our scant reading in the genre is more than matched by the even scantier time we devote to it in our classrooms. We are not alone. Two Booksearch features in the *English Journal* asked readers to submit names of their favorite writers of mystery and science fiction (Nelms, 1993, pp. 83–85). Nelms, the editor, reports that they could hardly read all the mail about mystery writers and could publish only a fraction of the submissions, while they received a total of only six recommendations of science fiction writers. Those six named by high school and community-college English teachers and one public librarian were Isaac Asimov, Ray Bradbury, Arthur C. Clarke, Lois McMaster Bujold, Steven Lawhead, and Gene Wolfe. When we discovered in our midst someone with a passionate interest in science fiction, we asked him to write a justification for its inclusion in the English classroom. Here is Phillip Chester's statement about this genre (personal communication, 1997):

As we look into the seemingly endless future, we can't help but ask ourselves, 'What if . . .' What if aliens *have* landed on Earth? What if a Utopia *is* possible here on Earth? The limitless possibilities of these questions are dealt with in the genre of literature known as Science Fiction.

Although it is sometimes divided into subcategories such as hard sci-fi, old guard sci-fi, and literary sci-fi, all science fiction delves into possibilities and worlds that other literary genres may be incapable of exploring. Gardner Dozois, editor of *Asimov's Science Fiction,* observed that "all fiction is written to examine or illuminate some aspect of human existence . . . in science fiction the backdrop you work against is the size of the Universe." This means that there is a broader set of possibilities from which the author is able to draw to examine human experience.

Early science fiction, begun in the 1890s by H. G. Wells, taken up by Jules Verne, and continuing well into the mid-twentieth century, was basically "space opera." It was concerned more with characterization and less with the scientific explanations that allowed the characters to operate in their environment (*The Invisible Man* [1897], *Star Fox* [1965]). Although it was not written solely by academics, much of the early, and the best, mature science fiction was written by some of the premier scientists of the day: Asimov, Clarke, and Herbert. All of these men drew upon their knowledge of the world of science to enhance the world of science fiction.

As science fiction evolved, it came to balance characterization with technology. Descriptions of the technology provided an air of reality to the stories. With the change in focus came a change in the general mood of science fiction. Gone were the stories of the 1940s and 1950s in which the hero was almost always victorious and the story ended on a note of optimism (*Time and Again* [1951], *Point Ultimate* [1959]). Taking their place were darker, moodier stories whose protagonists might be anti-heroes instead of the basic heroes (*White Plague* [1982]) and whose pessimistic endings left the reader wondering what would happen to the characters (*In Death Ground* [1997]).

Several authors have offered science fiction fans an alternative to these darker stories. Harry Harrison's *Bill: The Galactic Hero* (1975) series and Douglas Adams's *Hitchhiker's Guide to the Galaxy* (1979) five-part trilogy draw the reader into the world of science fiction comedy. Although nothing is technically impossible in science fiction, the characters in these two series are placed in situations that could be considered odd or unlikely by many science fiction writers.

There are several outlets for budding science fiction writers. Two periodicals, *Asimov's Science Fiction* and *Science Fiction Age,* feature the work of both old and new science fiction writers. Many of the stories published in these magazines have gone on to receive the coveted Hugo or Nebula Awards presented by the Science Fiction Writers of America (SFWA) for the best novels, novellas, novelettes, and short stories of the year. Several of Science Fiction's greatest writers, Arthur C. Clarke for instance, began their fictional writing careers in this fashion.

While considered a lesser form of literature by some people, science fiction is capable of taking the reader into times and places that they had only dreamed of exploring: the distant future, the forgotten past, the farthest reaches of deep space, and the most intimate corners of the human mind.

Invitation to Reflection 6–4

- Think about the selections in your high school literature courses (anthologies and assigned longer works). What percent would you guess were written by writers who were

| Men | African-Americans | Hispanic Americans | Canadians |
| Women | Native Americans | Asian Americans | Non-Europeans |

- Have you ever had a course devoted to literature by a minority writer? Was it an elective?
- Can you imagine teaching this material differently from the way you were taught? How?
- Have you read any of the authors or texts listed in Figures 6–4, 6–5, and 6–6? Do you have any bias against teaching young adult fiction in the high school classroom? Why or why not?
- Do you consider accessibility of subject, setting, or character important enough for you to select young adult fiction rather than a classic?
- Would you ever consider one of the following genres as fit subjects for your high school class? Why or why not?

Science Fiction	Fantasy	Detective Stories
Romance	Horror	Spy Stories
Mysteries	Westerns	Comics

CENSORSHIP

An NCTE/IRA document that articulates the first national standard, "Students read a wide range of print and nonprint texts," goes on to ask, "What criteria should be used to select particular works for class-room study?" When those works fall within system-selected textbooks, the question is answered with reference to student ability, interest, and maturity and to curriculum sequence. When the work is supplemental to a basic text and teacher influenced or chosen, the questions raised are often shadowed by concerns about censorship.

Pressures mount on English teachers to select texts and instructional programs that are acceptable to all of a school's constituents. The media frequently report incidents of censorship and court cases that result from them. New and veteran teachers describe both external and internal attempts to censor what they teach: the superintendent's, principal's, department chair's, or their own self-censoring. Individual parents and collective pressure groups assume adversarial positions. Suhor (1997) names four types of typical protesters:

- Objects to particular passages or pages, oblivious to context or the overall theme of the work.
- Circulates photocopies of the offensive snippets or reads them aloud at public meetings.
- Has been given the opportunity to have his/her child read a substitute work, but insists on a total banning of the book.
- Assumes that the author, the teacher, and the school are endorsing the profanity, sexual activity, ethnic slurs, violence, or other offensive depictions in the work. (p. 26)

Suhor (1997) calls "violence, profanity, sexual content, and supernatural themes . . . the usual suspects" (p. 26).

Two examples will suffice to demonstrate the predicament for English teachers. Teacher Marion McAdoo Goldwasser (1997) was disciplined for choosing Clyde Edgerton's *The Floatplane Notebooks* (1988) for her two "unenthusiastic 'general' (low-level) eleventh grade" classes. Attacked by a radio evangelist for her choice, she was summoned before administrators, who withdrew the books and promised the vocal complainants that the book would not be taught again. The district expected Goldwasser to accept these compromises quietly, but she chose to fight. She asks, "Should professional opinion and judgment be cast aside whenever any individual voices complaints? And if so, where would the complaints stop?" (p. 35). She insisted that the complainants argue the merits of her choice through the procedures established. She came to regard herself and the novel's opponents as representing two opposing educational philosophies: "They believed school should teach facts, traditional conservative values, neat handwriting, and respect for teachers, who should fill students with the same knowledge the opponents themselves had received. I believed that students needed to be exposed to many and varied ideas, learn to analyze, synthesize and formulate their own opinions. Students needed facts to solve problems not as ends in themselves. Teachers helped students adapt to a changing world and gave them the tools to be effective thinkers and learners" (p. 41).

Cissy Lacks (1997) was disciplined because she had asked her 11th-grade language arts students to write a dramatic script in which they remembered the playwright August Wilson's advice "to write about things important to them and to write from authentic voices they heard in their lives" (p. 31). Not surprisingly, the scripts that they performed and taped to analyze dialogue contained profanity. The issue of censorship became clouded by other, clearer issues that administrators raised as less problematic grounds for their disciplinary action. Administrators shifted from concern over particular book selections and focused instead on Lacks's failing to follow district procedures. She was fired finally because she "supposedly disobeyed an appendix to a student discipline code, a Type II Behavior which includes a list of minor misbehaviors by a student to disrupt a class or show disrespect to a place" (p. 31).

The experiences of Goldwasser and Lacks read like cautionary tales. You might be ready to resolve to follow the old rule: When in doubt, leave it out. We present their stories to acknowledge the difficulty, not to paralyze you. Young teachers especially can become so terrified of offending someone that they choose only texts sanctioned by the tradition, the anthologizers, and years of safe teaching. Our culture does appear to be divided and acrimonious, and thus the teacher of the young is vulnerable to attack. We think you need to be aware that problems may arise, but equally that you have strategies to prevent censorship issues from arising and methods to handle complaints if they do. We mention three such strategies and then refer you to books about censorship that deal with these issues in more detail.

COMMUNITY STANDARDS

Most schools have experienced teachers and administrators who can orient you to the students and parents that your school serves. Even anecdotal accounts from wise practitioners can forewarn you of potential areas of sensitivity. Of course, even the safest materials and methods may trouble and offend someone, but you will at least know the cultural context in which you are working.

School Policies

Many schools have stated policies governing the selection of texts and even procedures to follow if one is challenged. Teacher Kenneth L. Zeeman (1997) and his entire English department, of which he was chair, were engaged in a fight over John Gardner's *Grendel* (1971) for 12th-grade students. He observes that the literature on censorship indicates "that censors most often win when there are no procedures for selection of materials and for curriculum design, or for reviewing the same when someone challenges them" (p. 48). He enumerates two of his English department's guards against censorship battles: "In addition to educational justification for the literature we taught, we had specific procedures for adopting new texts:

1. The teacher who introduced *Grendel* presented and defended it to her peers. During that defense she cited sound educational objectives supported by the book.
2. Her peers read the book and engaged in further discussion with her.
3. The department voted on the adoption.
4. The purchase request was reviewed by the district language arts supervisor and approved.
5. An alternate book was offered to students who, in consultation with parents and the teacher, found the book objectionable for justifiable reason. (p. 48)

These procedures didn't prevent the parental objections to *Grendel,* but they allowed Zeeman to demonstrate the good faith and considered judgment with which he and his teachers were operating.

Many teachers construct their own procedures. A common practice is to prepare a clear rationale for the texts you want to teach, give students choices of long works, send an annotated list of choices home to parents, and provide a phone number where parents can call and discuss choices with the teacher. This openness and willingness to communicate about students' learning can't prevent all fights, but it makes them less likely and equips you better to face them if they come.

Allies

Zeeman praises his department's defense against the censors, but he acknowledges that the resolution to the crisis was reached largely because of the support of his community. He and his teachers had long demonstrated their sensitivity and integrity in teaching the community's young. They were themselves moral people. Parents came forward in good faith to defend the teachers. He regards "parental and community involvement [as] the key to insuring that censors do not win" (p. 49).

Zeeman also was helped in his battle by turning to others for information, advice, and aid: NCTE, the Utah affiliate of NCTE, and People for the American Way. Teachers who find themselves under attack are not without support. People for the American Way (1995) observes that "when teachers or administrators are left to battle censorship groups on their own, the chances for the worst outcome increase dramatically. But when a community comes together and forms alliances that include parents, business leaders, clergy and educators, the censors are hard-pressed to prevail" (p. 11). People for the American Way maintains a toll-free censorship hotline and "offers a variety of technical and legal assistance" (p. 48). The NCTE provides help through SLATE (its intellectual freedom group) and the NCTE Committee on Censorship. Suhor (1997), an NCTE officer, explains that "in many cases . . . we can and do actively support teachers on matters like the literary quality, teachability, and general suitability of the challenged work, and also support their thoughtful use of controversial teaching methods, from journals to guided imagery, that are grounded in theory and research" (p. 28). The NCTE also publishes a number of free or inexpensive pamphlets and statements to aid teachers: *The Students' Right to Read; Guidelines for Dealing with Censorship of Nonprint Materials; Guidelines for Selection of Materials in English Language Arts Programs; Selection and Retention of Instructional Materials—What the Courts Have Said; Statement on Censorship and Professional Guidelines;* and *Common Ground.* Another resource is the American Library Association's *Newsletter on Intellectual Freedom.* Appendix C provides a list of other full-length treatments of censorship, especially those cases involving schools.

Censorship issues involve English teachers in more than political battles with parents and pressure groups (from the political right *and* left, according to the People for the American Way). Ken Donelson (1997) hints at the deeper range when he points out the powerful connection between literature study as meaning making and censorship issues (pp. 16–20). We would do well to consider deeper questions raised by censorship such as those posed by Noll (1994):

• What are our individual and collective responsibilities in advocating our students' intellectual freedom?
• In what ways do we support and silence our colleagues' freedom of expression?
• What are our beliefs about the roles and responsibilities of schools as institutions of a democratic society? (p. 64)

We leave this subject with the wise admonition of Charles Suhor (1997). We think he would caution us to choose our censorship battles wisely, but he would also charge us to "work with equal zest on the messy stuff, trudging inventively through the grounds that surprise and resist us" (p. 28).

EXPANDING THE TEACHING OF LITERATURE

Except for the section Multicultural Literature in the Classroom, this chapter has focused primarily on expanding literacy through expanding the choices of texts that are taught. Our next two sections present instructional strategies that expand the allowable ways we teach our chosen texts. We add these teaching activities to those presented in Chapters 3 (drama), 4 (fiction), and 5 (poetry). We will take most of our extended examples from those works that we designate as classics, but of course these activities represent good teaching practices for any literature. We organize our suggestions around five of Gardner's (1983) multiple intelligences, those most often overlooked in our verbal and logical/mathematical schooling: spatial, musical, bodily/kinesthetic, interpersonal, and intrapersonal (Table 6–4). Many of these ideas originate in the suggestions of classroom teachers presented at the annual NCTE convention's Concurrent Sessions and Idea Exchanges and in the *Ideas Plus* series, which compiles the best of those ideas.

RESPONSE CHART

Chapter 4 discussed the use of Verbal Scales to chart student reaction to literature. Kelly (1993) devised an assignment that elicits students' initial reactions to characters in a novel and then provides a continuing benchmark for their evolving impressions. Figure 6–7, her Response Chart, is based on Sue Ellen Bridger's *Permanent Connections* (1987). Kelly distributes a list of characters to whom the students respond in their Reader's Logs.

CHARACTER CIRCLE

Another visual presentation of characters that is especially helpful in long works in which characters and subplots multiply is a simple Character Circle. One of our student teachers, Lori Burrow, named this a Character Bull's-eye because it focuses students' attention on important characters and graphically indicates their distance from center. Students are given the following directions:

- Draw a circle in the center of a sheet of paper and write the name of the central character in that circle.
- Draw concentric circles around the center circle, one for each character connected to the central character. Write the name of the secondary character closest to the protagonist in the next-to-center circle. If two characters are equally close, put their names in the same circle.

TABLE 6–4 Expanding literacy through multiple intelligences

Multiple Intelligences	Teaching Activities	Thinking Process*	Instructional Strategies*	Teaching Activities* (examples)
Spatial	Response Chart Character Circle Story Quilt Mobile Guided Imagery	In images and pictures	See it, draw it, visualize it, color it, mind-map it	Visual presentations, art activities, imagination games, mind-mapping, metaphor, visualization, etc.
Musical	Song Search	Via rhythms and melodies	Sing it, rap it, listen to it	Superlearning, rapping, songs that teach
Bodily/Kinesthetic (Drama)	Impromptu Drama Reading Between the Lines Classroom Drama	Through somatic sensations	Build it, act it out, touch it, get a "gut feeling" of it, dance it	Hands-on learning, drama, dance, sports that teach, tactile activities, relaxation exercises, etc.
Interpersonal	Imitations of Life	By bouncing ideas off other people	Teach it, collaborate on it, interact with respect to it	Cooperative learning, peer tutoring, community involvement, social gatherings, simulations, etc.
Intrapersonal	Response Journal	Deeply inside of themselves	Connect it to your personal life, make choices with regard to it	Individualized instruction, independent study, options in course of study, self-esteem building, etc.

*Definitions of the Thinking Process, Instructional Strategies, and Teaching Activities from Thomas Armstrong (1994). *Multiple Intelligences in the Classroom*. Alexandria Association for Supervision and Curriculum Development. (pp. 27, 52).

As you are reading this novel, you will naturally have reactions toward characters, much as you do in real life when you meet new people. As you interact with new acquaintances on a regular basis, however, your views of them often change. At the points indicated in the novel, stop your reading and make decisions about how you feel about the characters. Give at least one reason why you have made your choice.

Chapters 1–15 Why?	like	1	2	3	4	dislike	no reaction
Chapters 16–30 Why?	like	1	2	3	4	dislike	no reaction

- Add character names, moving to those with increasingly distant relationships as you move from center.

STORY QUILT

Warstler (1997) and Whetstone (1997) introduced us to this visual and tactile activity to culminate the reading of a text. Their assignment follows:

> For the discussion of *My Name Is Asher Lev* we will be building a story quilt. Using the paper I provide, make a quilt square to represent the chapter assigned to you. Identify one quotation that seems to sum up the focus of the chapter and allow that to inspire the creation of your square. Each square must reveal artistically the idea you wish to convey. Think carefully which artistic medium will be most effective. In addition to the quotation (which must appear on the quilt), design a border that is appropriate for the novel. It may reflect the individual chapter you are using or the novel as a whole.

The selection of the quotation (similar to the activity in Focal Judgments) and the presentation through art are instructional enough, but the work in assembling it, the discussion while students work, and the display and scrutiny of the completed quilt carry perhaps the final educative payoff. Displaying the quilt can continue to evoke the work long after class discussions of it have ceased—a pleasing after-image.

MOBILE

Another visual project that can both sum up a book and leave it hanging is a Mobile of significant quotations from a text. Students individually or in groups select quotes, attach them to heavy paper, then to strings, then to wire (a coat hanger will do), and suspend them. We ask students to write a brief explanation of their choices—why they are important to students, why they are important to the entire text—and then have these available for others to read, in the manner of gallery fliers in an art museum. Images can be used along with quotes—either students' own visuals or clipped magazine art. Mobiles make an arresting public display of students' personal responses and of the book's heightened moments.

GUIDED IMAGERY

Through deliberate oral suggestions, students can be lead to imagine places, characters, or situations. In our impromptu and planned exercises of this sort, we usually ask students to close their eyes or we dim the classroom lights to focus the mind's eye on the images we suggest. Shuman and Wolfe (1990) use guided imagery to lead students through a hot summer's walk down a city street and then down a dusty country road in preparation for reading R. Baird Shuman's poem *Citykid*. Students enter the poem with heightened openness and energy having just visualized its setting and character imaginatively. Group work follows in which students create a visual design that illustrates the central dilemma for the boy in the poem.

Figure 6-8 is a more elaborate guided imagery assignment, without the eyes closed, created by Mary Abbott (1990). She carefully leads students into the spatial arrangements of a text. For students who think in images and pictures and who love to draw, design, or even doodle, Guided Imagery is a boon.

SONG SEARCH

We ask students to listen to music that reiterates the ideas or characters of a work of literature. For instance, teaching Edwin Arlington Robinson's *Mr. Flood's Party* or Seamus Heaney's *Mr. Bleaney* with the Beatles' *Eleanor Rigby* deepens the understanding of the loneliness of all three characters. We also employ music that captures tone, mood, or situation to set the stage for discussion, oral reading, or improvisation. (We don't always pause to listen, but have the music playing as students arrive and settle

FIGURE 6–8
Abbott's guided
imagery assignment

To Kill a Mockingbird is on our high school's core list and one of my favorite novels to teach. Last year, however, for the second year in a row, I was having trouble getting my general (below average) level 10th grade students "into the novel." The first chapter is especially difficult. Scout, the narrator, starts out discussing her family's history which seems long and detailed to low attention span students. She then goes into even further detail in describing her neighborhood as she remembered it as a child. These details are essential to the novel's setting and take on more importance as the story progresses. It finally occurred to me that my students just weren't imagining the "old neighborhood" described by Scout well enough.

Believing I had identified the problem, I thought perhaps I could create some sort of visual to help my students. So I re-read chapter one and started trying to map out Scout's neighborhood from what Harper Lee had written. Suddenly I noticed gaps in the description. That got me thinking, "how well could I remember my own childhood neighborhood?" Not too well, but certain things stood out just like they did to Scout, particularly those "crazy" people who became neighborhood legends and were the subject of many childhood rumors.

The next day, I passed out pieces of blank white paper to my students. I asked them to draw a map of the neighborhood they lived in when they were about six years old. I started out by drawing a portion of my old neighborhood on the board and describing some of the local characters. Some students said that they couldn't remember back that far and chose to draw their maps from the perspective of nine or ten years old, instead. The point was that the kids began to look back and think what their lives were like at another age and how they viewed it at that time.

After about 15 minutes of drawing, I asked students to hold up their maps and tell us about them. This turned out to be exceptionally fun! Many of the students in the class had known at least one other student as a small child, and the stories about the "old neighborhood" began to come out. Students who rarely spoke to each other suddenly were sharing experiences and remembering their past connections. Described were many boundaries—houses beyond which the children were not allowed to wander—just like with Jem and Scout. There were also the "scary" houses and the unusual "Boo Radley" type characters. In this discussion there was a lot of laughter as the students recalled their childhood fears and perspectives.

We finished up the hour by re-reading aloud the sections from chapter one in which Scout describes her childhood neighborhood and boundaries. We mapped out as much of her street as possible on the board and conducted many other activities to relate the novel to students' own lives, but I believe it was this particular activity that got our experiencing of this novel off to a good start.

NOTE: There were, of course, many differences between Scout's era and neighborhood life that children today experience (apartment complexes, etc.). Those comparisons added to the discussion and, for them, helped students understand the narrator's perspective.

in their places.) We angle to move in the course of a term from our selecting the music, to the students' initiating and bringing their own suggestions. Blanscet (1988) suggests an assignment that leads students to make connections between music and literature (Figure 6–9).

Impromptu Drama

We ask students to role-play characteristics of specific characters or the relationships between different characters, using their bodies in mime or nonverbal drama. We also ask them to use body sculptures to demonstrate personal traits of specific characters or critical relationships between characters at certain moments in the work. We often interrupt the flow of discussion and have students move into such postures according to their interpretation, as the whole class directs them, or as the author's words, read aloud, dictate. Because no words are spoken, this exercise is especially kind to less verbal students.

Reading Between the Lines

We have adapted an idea from Jeff Wilhelm (1998) for helping reluctant readers create the visual scripts that engaged and proficient readers habitually produce when they read. Wilhelm observed in many of his less-able readers what reading specialists have described: that these readers do not understand that the words in printed texts represent people, places, and things in action in the everyday world. They cannot visualize settings, imagine scenes, or empathize with characters. This contributes to and confounds their sense that school is dumb and reading is even dumber. Wilhelm asks students to dramatize scenes that do not exist in the written text in order to breathe life into characters and the difficulties they face. The teacher or an expressive reader reads the text to the class and stops at pivotal points to let students act out invented scenes. Each student is assigned to be a member of an A or B group, which are given temporary group roles throughout the exercise. Within the two groups, each student has a number. The pairs created from both groups (A 2 and B 2, for instance) dramatize the assigned vignette simultaneously with the other pairs. The students are active in imagining and speaking within character. Everyone has a part. No one faces the discomfort of a solo performance before the rest of the class. We have created the following "readings" for a short story, *The Fan Club,* adapted from a story by 15-year-old Rona Maynard that originally appeared in the magazine *Read* about Laura who is struggling to fit into a new group of students, to overcome her embarrassment in Algebra class, and to remain true to her childhood friend

FIGURE 6–9
Blanscet's Song Search

I begin by asking students if they can think of any songs whose words originated in literature.* Typically cited are Iron Maiden's version of "The Rime of the Ancient Mariner" and the Alan Parsons Project's album entitled "Tales of Mystery and Imagination—Edgar Allan Poe," the latter of which sets several of Poe's well-known stories to music. I then challenge each student to find a song that he or she likes and that has the same theme or idea as one of the literary works we have studied. (It's best to use this strategy during the latter part of the school year to ensure that students have a bank of literary works from which to draw.) To complete the assignment, I ask each student to prepare and turn in the following items:

1. a recording of the song on a cassette tape
2. the words of the song written out in stanza form (often found on the jacket sleeves of albums)
3. preliminary and final drafts of a short paper discussing (a) the main theme or idea in the song and the theme of the literary selection and how they relate; (b) the effect of the style of music on the theme; and (c) the reasons why the student chose the song and the literary selection
4. answers to these questions: May I share your paper and/or idea with other classes? Would you rather I did or did not use your name?

*Blanscet lists these especially effective student connections: the idea of premeditated murder in the Police's *Murder by Numbers* and Edgar Allan Poe's *The Cask of Amontillado* and the use of vignettes in Gordon Lightfoot's *The Wreck of the Edmond Fitzgerald* and Twain's *The Adventures of Huckleberry Finn*.

Rachel. The numbers correspond with stops in the story. Although we developed these dramatizations for less-proficient readers, we have used them with students in a range of grades and reading levels, and their responses have been universally engaged, energetic, and insightful.

1. **Laura Seeks Support**
   A. *Laura:* Tell how you felt about the algebra class, Mr. Knowles, and your "friends" after class on Friday.
   B. *Neutral Friend:* Listen to Laura and encourage her. But be sure to protect Diana and Terri and the back row crowd a bit too.
2. **Shopping Center Encounter**
   A. *Laura's Mother:* Ask about how Laura is doing at school, what's going wrong, why friends aren't stopping by the house lately.
   B. *Terri:* Try to let Laura's mom know that the algebra teacher was a creep for humiliating Laura.
3. **Granny's Bedroom**
   A. *Rachel:* Because you sense you are losing your friendship with Laura, you let your guard down with your grandmother, who seems to understand you better than your parents do.
   B. *Grandmother:* You listen to Rachel and try to make her understand that being young is always very tough.
4. **Ripping Knowles**
   A. *Laura's Mother:* You go to school to let Mr. Knowles know just how you feel about his humiliation of Laura.
   B. *Mr. Knowles:* You listen to Laura's mother without empathy and only reiterate that Laura's almost flunking algebra.
5. **Guardian Angels**
   A. *Laura:* You feel pretty unsure about your report and what Patti, Diana, and Steve are planning.
   B. *Guardian Angel:* (circle the room) You stop at each Laura and encourage her with a brief positive phrase. You circle once more and offer another word of support.
6. **Radio Talk Show**
   Interview Laura's English class on the question "What do you think of Laura's main point, that we are all prejudiced in quiet ways?"
7. **Vote with Your Feet**
   Move to the side of the room to show that
   Laura's Right ◄———————————————————► Laura's Wrong
8. **Laura's Alter Ego: Mixed Emotions**
   A. *Laura[1]*: What was your honest feeling when you saw the yellow index cards?
   B. *Laura[2]*: What do you think you should feel when you see the cards?
9. **Deep Letters**
   A. *Rachel:* Write a letter to Laura telling her how you are feeling about her now.
   B. *Laura:* Write a letter to Rachel trying to explain yourself.
10. **Best-phrases Poem**
    Underline your best phrases and read them antiphonally as a Laura-Rachel strophe/antistrophe or line up the phrases to make a poem.

CLASSROOM DRAMA

Dixon (1967) believes that drama provides a means of "doing, acting things out rather than working on them in abstract and in private" (p. 43). We do not suggest here drama as theater, the staged production of professionally written plays. The following three teachers have orchestrated elaborate dramatic lessons that require forethought and preparation, but not scripts with predetermined dialogue or stage directions. Coffin (1988) proposes a debate on some of Benjamin Franklin's aphorisms (Figure 6-10); Ditzian (1990) convenes a Child Custody Hearing (Figure 6-11); and Bickford (1991) calls a Town Meeting (Figure 6-12).

FIGURE 6–10
Coffin's microdebates of Benjamin Franklin's *Moral Perfection*

Pro—Prepare a short speech (only 1 1/2 minutes) developing one, possibly two, strong pro or affirmative arguments for Franklin's advice.
Con—Brainstorm and try to find telling arguments against Franklin's advice. Play devil's advocate! Have fun! You'll have to respond to what the affirmative speaker argues so anticipate what a pro speaker might say.

1. SILENCE
   Speak not but what may benefit others or yourself; avoid trifling conversation.
2. ORDER
   Let all your things have their places; let each part of your business have its time.
3. RESOLUTION
   Resolve to perform what you ought; perform without fail what you resolve.
4. INDUSTRY
   Lose no time; be always employed in something useful; cut off unnecessary actions.
5. SINCERITY
   Use no hurtful deceit; think innocently and justly, and, when you speak, speak accordingly.
6. MODERATION
   Avoid extremes; forbear resenting injuries so much as you think they deserve.

FIGURE 6–11
Ditzian's Child Custody Hearing: *Black Boy*

When I taught *Black Boy* by Richard Wright to sophomores in my American literature class at Marshall High School, I was amazed at the energy and sense of purpose with which my students threw themselves into reading a fairly long novel. At that time I was still operating on the model: read a piece of literature—write an analytical essay. My main thrust in writing instruction for these students was to get them to use evidence to support a thesis. My students had been responding so personally to this book, though, that I felt it would be inappropriate for them to remove themselves and dissect the work.

Rather than assigning a straight character analysis, I brought up the topic of parenthood in class. I asked my students what makes a good parent? What must a parent provide for a child? What makes a bad parent? We spent a whole period discussing these questions in depth. Everyone had plenty to say on the subject. The next day, I asked my students to form groups of four and gave each group the following memo, assigning each group a different character from the novel.

December 5, 1989
To: Investigative team
Re: Child custody hearing

The Department of Children and Family Services requests your expert investigation immediately. It has been brought to our attention that there is some question regarding the fitness of _____ (fill in character name) as guardian of the child of Richard Wright.

Your team has been given one week before the hearing into this matter to make regular visits to _____'s home and/or work place, and to assess his/her behavior in general and particularly as it relates to the child.

Be prepared to state your findings at a hearing Tuesday, December 13. At that time the court will also receive a written version of your assessment. It is of the utmost importance that your findings be based solidly on the evidence you gather. Judge _____, who will hear this case, will award custody of the aforementioned child based on the findings of your team.

Sincerely yours,
Maxine Assignment
D.C.F.S. Director

Groups were told earlier that they would share the work and the grade. When the court date arrived (actually, it took three days because we allowed courtroom observers to question the investigative teams after they had made their statement), we audiotaped the proceedings. All of a sudden my sophomores were using evidence to support an argument and doing it well. Aside from meeting my educational objective, this assignment allowed students the opportunity to respond personally to a novel.

FIGURE 6–12
Bickford's Town
Meeting

Huckleberry Finn is a good novel to assign for summer reading for students entering 9th-grade honors English. To encourage students to complete summer reading, I usually try to devise alternative methods of testing to determine that all students have read the novel assigned. Following is the evaluation method that I have found to be most successful with *Huckleberry Finn.*

I introduce the unit by telling the class about town meetings and their importance in the nineteenth century. Then I tell them that they will participate in a town meeting which might have taken place in St. Petersburg, Missouri, when Huck and Jim return after their "adventure." The town meeting is held to determine what should be done with Huck. Huck wants to be left to his own devices because he believes he has proved himself capable of surviving on his own. Aunt Sally wants to take him into her home to "civilize" him. Some other members of the town believe he should be sent to a school for wayward boys.

After this brief introduction, everyone in the class assumes a role of one of the characters from the novel who could be present at the meeting. We add characters so that everyone can participate. Of course, there must be a mayor, a sheriff, some constables, schoolteachers, store owners and clerks—even Pap might show up. (We do not really have proof that he is dead, and after all, this is a "fictional" assignment.)

Preparation for the town meeting involves having each student (1) develop a character sketch of his character and (2) write a letter to a friend explaining his or her opinion of what should be done with Huck. The character sketch must include physical and personality characteristics and must be written down in two well-developed paragraphs. Students who wish may draw their version of their particular character. The letters must be written in correct personal letter form. These two preparatory assignments give me an opportunity early in the year to assess students' writing abilities.

While the students are writing their character sketches and letters, we devote one day in class to studying the basics of parliamentary procedure. One of the constables "volunteers" to be the parliamentarian for the meeting.

On the day of the first town meeting (of course, this meeting cannot be completed in one session) students dress "in character." If possible we try to hold the meeting in the auditorium to get out of the classroom setting. The entire meeting is videotaped and made available for student purchase.

IMITATIONS OF LIFE

Here are several projects that prompt students to enter the texts imaginatively and to work cooperatively in pairs or small groups:

- Interview book characters or authors.
- Write letters to characters responding to their dilemmas, advising them, or criticizing their actions. Figure 6-13 is a note-writing exercise developed by Rogers (1990, pp. 12-13).
- Place characters in your high school annual and imagine their high school histories. Find an appropriate picture and caption it with lists of activities, awards, favorite quotes or subjects, characteristic expressions, plans for the future, superlatives, and teacher and classmate testimonials.
- Imagine how characters would respond to altered events in the text or to new phenomena that you imagine. The excerpts in Figure 6-14 are from an activity Belgard (1987) uses to provide a framework for such imagining.
- Write and illustrate a children's book that connects with the core text. Read it to a partner or small group with the animation you might bring to a listening child.
- Arrange a television talk show that substitutes writers or literary characters for the usual personalities. An amusing model for the satiric effects of such a juxtaposition is Woody Allen's piece *Impressionist Dentists,* which records imaginary letters from Vincent van Gogh that speak of molars, Novocain, and other dental matters.
- Stage a sort of Academy or Emmy Awards for Literature. Some of the categories might include the following:

Most Long-Winded Author	Most Romantic Heroine
Most Decisive Protagonist	Most Readable Novel
Most Chauvinistic Character	Most Astute Writer
Most Imaginative Author	Most Opaque Text
Most Personally Compelling Character	Most Likely to Succeed

(Simply imagining the categories for the rewards stirs divergent thinking and a proper playfulness with texts.)

RESPONSE JOURNALS

In preceding chapters, we have alluded to the benefits of Response Journals in studying literature and we will return to their advantages in the writing chapters. We want here to consider their use in reading longer works. Response Journals can provide opportunities to free-write about literature *before* any group discussion has occurred and opportunities for reflective writing *after* the students'

FIGURE 6–13
Roger's Half a Note

This is a completion exercise which requires students to make inferences and then develop an idea based on those inferences. In addition it gives students the opportunity to show their understanding of particular characters within a novel.

Write half of a note on the board or on an overhead projector.* Give students time to complete the note and to share their writing with the class.

```
To the most
Thanks so much for your
last week. It made me realize
without you. Life would be
I beg you to please
to upset you.
to the time when we'll
the problems we've had
                    All my
```

The first example is based on *The Crucible*, the second on *The Scarlet Letter*.

To the most outstanding witch-hunter around—Rev. Hale,
Thanks so much for your help getting the trials started last week. It made me realize how hard it would have been without you. Life would be still teeming with sin in Salem. I beg you to please help us condemn the rest of the witches, and we'll lock them up so they won't be around to upset you. I look forward to the time when we'll round up all the hateful witches and watch them die. It will solve the problems we've had in Salem.
    All my heartfelt thanks,
    Danforth

To the most beautiful and kindest woman I know—Hester,
Thanks so much for your words that were spoken to me last week. It made me realize how strong you are and how I would have faltered without you. Life would be nonexistent without you to hold me up secretly and quietly. I beg you to please forgive me, because I have so much guilt that I couldn't stand to upset you. I shall pray and wait until Judgment Day, to the time when we'll stand together as a family and take our punishment together. After that glorious day of freedom, the problems we've had will vanish and no more will we be judged.
    All my prayers and sorrow are for you,
    Arthur Dimmesdale

*This idea was developed with a colleague; the half-note itself is original.

FIGURE 6–14
Belgard's contemporary Huck Finn

Read each of the following statements and circle the letter that best completes the statement in terms of what you think would fit the character of Huck Finn. Be prepared to defend your answer with reasoning based on evidence from the book.

1. If someone approached Huck Finn with drugs, his reaction would be:
   A. he'd take them
   B. he'd refuse but not tell anyone
   C. he'd refuse and report the dealer
   D. he'd try to convince the dealer to give it up
2. If Huck got a traffic ticket, he'd probably:
   A. rip it up
   B. go to court and argue with the judge
   C. pay the fine
   D. leave town
3. On a typical date Huck would probably go:
   A. on a picnic
   B. to a rock concert
   C. to the movies
   D. to a museum

initial reactions have met and been informed by other students' responses. These-free writes should be private, protected pages that a student shares only voluntarily. They also provide memorable stops and points of reference in the course of reading a long work.

Many teachers assign Double-entry Journals. Students draw a line down a page and on the left side record passages (page numbers and whole lines or key words or phrases) that especially struck them (puzzled, disturbed, moved, or delighted them). On the right, students describe just how the passage affected them. Some teachers call this process note taking/note making. Students can even make subsequent notes as their views change and as hypotheses are proven or negated. They can share entries with the interpretive community and use them to track their gathering understanding. (These entries also can serve as a source book for story quilts, mobiles, and formal writing.)

Ericson (1993) recommends Literature Logs, in which students respond daily to any topic or question about the book provided by the teacher. Following are some of Ericson's prompts:

1. Describe one character's problem or a choice to be made. What advice do you have for the character?
2. Explain why you think a character is acting as he or she is.
3. Copy a provocative/interesting/important/enjoyable passage and comment on it.
4. From what you have read so far, make predictions about what could happen next, explaining the reasons for your predictions.
5. Explain why you would or would not like to have a particular character as a friend.
6. Explain why you would or would not like to have lived in the time and place of this novel.
7. Write questions about a part you had difficulty understanding. Choose one question and explore possible answers.
8. Examine the values of a character you like/dislike.
9. What real-life persons or events are you reminded of by characters or events in the story?
10. Reread your entries to date and discuss what your main reactions to this book seem to be so far.*

Ericson asks students to select entries to share in group discussions in order to hear the reaction of others. Once or twice a week, she skims the entries and writes *her* response to theirs in order "to encourage thoughtful reading and responding" (p. 6).

Roseboro (1994) gives the following specific prompts for texts by writers from cultural/ethnic minorities to enlarge students' sense of difference and similarity. She asks students to write about a half page after each reading.

*   It surprised me that . . .
*   Before I thought . . . ; now, I know . . .
*   When I read . . . , I began to understand . . .
*   This author writes (comment on style, subject matter, structure) . . .
*   What new information did you learn about the specific cultural/ethnic group?
*   Were any stereotypes demystified for you?
*   How similar/different to yours are the emotions expressed in this reading?
*   In what way is this story alike/different from those you usually read? (p. 15)

Finally, Schneider (1994) speaks of journaling as the most "significant change in her teaching" in the last decade (p. 88). Following is her description of how she organizes her journals and how they affect her students' reading of novels:

I have created a special kind of journal that keeps kids close to the readings, involves all students in thinking, and promotes frequent writing. The journals are just cheap notebooks with about thirty sheets of paper. Students create a cover page, an on-going table of contents, and a title page for each new section of the journal (when we start a new novel). Students' writing is of several kinds. "Thought pattern" questions, as Mina Shaughnessy called them, ask students to describe, explain, define, summarize, illustrate with examples, and compare and contrast. Open-ended questions ask students what they found most interesting or important in the reading. And creative-writing projects use something in the reading to fire students' imaginations. We may read aloud a dialogue which presents a conflict, and then students try their hands at showing conflict through dialogue. After reading Rosemary Sutcliff's *Dragonslayer,* students rewrite a scene from the monster's point of view. Often, at the end of the novel, I have students choose a character and have that character tell about a moment or event in the story. From these monologues, excellent poems can develop.

*From "Introducing *To Kill a Mockingbird* with Collaborative Group Reading of Related Young Adult Novels." In J. F. Kaywell (Ed.), *Adolescent Literature as a Complement to the Classics* by B. O. Ericson, 1993, 5–6. Norwood, MA: Christopher-Gordon Publishers, Inc.

Typically, students write at the beginning of class, and their responses are a fine way to initiate discussion. Some of the writings are taken through drafts, but many are one-shot responses. All drafts are kept in the journal, so the journal becomes a growing body of work, something students have to show for their work. (p. 88)

We turn now at the end of this chapter to questions of classroom strategy for teaching long works. Most of the works considered classic are lengthy, and that length creates special challenges. A few of the problems that arise for novels or any long work include the following:

- A novel represents a large reading commitment. In diverse classes, how can one novel appeal to the authentic interests and the reading abilities of many different students?
- If one novel is chosen and all students read in advance of classroom talk, the work can lose its compelling vitality by the time it is finally addressed. Your talk of it often ends up *summarizing,* rather than *experiencing* the novel. It has lost its fresh, living reality.
- If you talk about novels before they are finished, readers are at different points in their reading and therefore discussions are problematic. Fast readers can't use insight gained by completion; slower readers don't want the story spoiled by knowing its development prematurely.
- If the class is engaged in reading many different novels, coming together as a whole class dictates only the most general discussion and reduces the benefits (necessities for most of us) of working in an Interpretive Community.

We will discuss an approach to these problems that has revolutionized many English classrooms: Literature Circles.

LITERATURE CIRCLES

Reading/Literature Circles were originally designed to organize a whole class into small groups, often assigned by reading level or ability, to discuss the same teacher-assigned text and/or to plan a project about it. Assignment to specific groups, discussion or activity prompts, and project evaluation were provided by the teacher. Often the groups, once constituted, did not change in a school year. Some still use the term generally to mean any small-group, collaborative discussions of literature as distinct from whole-class teacher-led recitations and discussions. Literature Circles are increasingly associated, however, with small groups organized quite differently: They often are self-selected and each group reads and discusses a different student-selected text, rather than one teacher-selected text. Not only do students choose the book, often from a preselected menu of five or six choices, but also, they determine their pace and pursue their own discussion questions. The requirements are simple and straightforward: Write a given number of open-ended individual responses a week (which often become the basis for discussion later), and actively participate in group discussion and work. Students have great autonomy and responsibility. The teacher's role shifts from that of a performer on center stage where he or she presents, questions, assigns, and evaluates to that of a facilitator in the wings, where he or she

- models reading as active meaning making
- answers organizational questions and secures access to books
- plans prereading, during-reading, and postreading activities as needed
- observes and validates individual progress
- observes individual and group problems and introduces alternative reading strategies
- interacts with the group (usually as co-discussant, rarely as expert resource)
- sets realistic individual and group goals
- monitors classroom norms of civility and productivity so that students can focus productively, seriously, and even passionately on the work before them
- constructs evaluation instruments that match Literature Circle practice
- evaluates students' developing skills
- evaluates current Literature Circles and makes decisions about how and what to teach next

Evaluation is multiple: It includes self-evaluation of group work and a teacher-evaluation of a few responses, of group discussion contributions, and of a whole-group project.*

Teachers Cindy Whetstone and Debra Warstler (1997) distribute Literature Circle guidelines to students as they initiate this activity (Figure 6–15). They sometimes include a list of novels from which their students choose; oftentimes they leave choices more open. The actual work of the Literature Circle is suggested by Cindy Whetstone's handout (Figure 6–16). As you can see, much of the initiative for

*Zemelman, Daniels, and Hyde (1993) place Literature Circles within the NCTE's 1989 *New Policy Guidelines for Reading: Connecting Research and Practice* (pp. 21–44).

FIGURE 6–15
Whetstone's Literature
Circle guidelines

For the next several weeks we are going to be using a Literature Circle concept for the novels we have selected to read. I have designed groups consisting of 4–5 people who will be reading the same novel and sharing responses as they read. Each of you shares a responsibility in making this a rewarding activity. The following guidelines should help you get started:

Literature Circles are based on a "book club" philosophy. You have selected your own novel and are now responsible for deciding the reading/discussion schedule. Examine the calendar dates and divide the book into four sections. As a group, determine how far you will read for the first discussion day, the second, etc. Take into consideration the number of days in between each circle day so that you can all meet your deadlines. Agree that you will only discuss up to the page number you decide on; if you read ahead, be considerate of those who don't.

It is your responsibility to prepare for the discussions. Keep a journal as you read; this will give you something to draw on when you meet with the members of your group. Some suggestions for responses:

1. Short summaries to help you keep the plot line straight
2. Reactions to specific events, characters
3. Dialogue with the characters (talk to them)
4. Projections about future events
5. Connections to your own life—or the "real world"
6. Questions—these can stimulate discussion (What do you think about . . .)

At some point I will be collecting journal entries. This will tell me a great deal about your involvement in this activity.

Take advantage of class reading time. I value having a quiet time and place to be able to read; be sure that you are considerate of your classmates on these days.

My goal in this assignment is to give you an opportunity to read a piece of literature for enjoyment—but slow you down enough to allow for close reading. There's a difference in flying through a good book and truly becoming an involved reader. We're aiming for the latter.

At the end of this activity there will be an in-class writing and an extension project. It will be your choice whether you do a group project or work on an individual basis. Details for this will be given toward the end of our Literature Circle discussions.

SOURCE: From Literature Circles in One High School Classroom by Cindy Whetstone, April 11, 1997. Presentation at NCTE's Spring Conference, Charlotte, NC. Reprinted with permission.

FIGURE 6–16
Whetsone's Literature
Circle requirements

LIT. CIRCLES:

Will decide how much to read for each discussion.
Fill out form and return to Mrs. Whetstone.
Record schedule in the front of your novel.
If you have not purchased book, have it for Tuesday's class.
Check class calendar for schedule.

RESPONSE:

Have your response journal with you every day that you are reading in class.
Stop and respond as you read, not when you have finished an entire section.
Date each entry and record the page number/chapter.
Concentrate on characters and plot.
Ask questions, make predictions, record quotations that affect you, consider the theme you are exploring, and/or relate happenings to your own experience.

EVALUATION:

You will be evaluated each time there is a lit. circle discussion.
There will be a 25 point assessment for each of the 4 lit. circles.
The evaluation will include your journal response and your discussion in the group.
It is your responsibility to come to the group prepared. Do not be absent on lit. circle discussion days if at all possible.
You will be sitting in chairs for discussions. Bring your novel and your response journal with you.

GETTING STARTED:

Each person should share something from journal.
Include everyone in the group.
There should be no times when the conversation dies if everyone is participating.
A simple read around of journal responses is not a discussion.

SOURCE: From Literature Circles in One High School Classroom by Cindy Whetstone, April 11, 1997. Presentation at NCTE's Spring Conference, Charlotte, NC. Reprinted with permission.

discussion is the personal journal. In fact, Warstler gives her students this hint: "It might be worth your while to take some time and reflect on the discussions in your journal following the times that your circle meets; return to your journal when it's time to write the paper."

Nancy Johnson (1997) suggests other activities that nurture and guide response in small or large groups and that "encourage readers to respond other than 'academically.'" We mention three of her ideas.

Silent Dialogue—Each student lists one question about the literary selection at the top of a sheet of notebook paper. Have them select a question they'd like to pose during a discussion. Sitting in a circle, every student passes their question sheet to the reader on the right who reads the question silently, then writes a response. After a few minutes, students again pass the question to the readers on their right. Encourage students to read the question and each of the responses prior to writing their response.

Sketch to Stretch—After reading the literary selection, each student sketches what the selection means or what they made of the reading. Invite readers to experiment with interpretation through design, color, and shape rather than drawing an exact scene. In small groups, each reader shows his/her sketch while others say what they think the artist is trying to say. After each hypothesized interpretation the artist gets the last word. If there's time, each group can create a group sketch to share with the whole class.

Quaker Read—Readers first select a significant passage, line, phrase from their reading. Then, seated in a circle, giving no explanation or rationale, one student reads his/her passage aloud. In no particular order, another reader adds his/her passage and on and on. The key is to listen and consider how your passage connects to (or even contrasts with) the passage read. Remind students that lulls and pauses are okay as are repeated passages.*

A READER'S BILL OF RIGHTS

Frenchman Daniel Pennac has written a bestselling book, *Better Than Life* (1994), that addresses a paradox: How do children who find magic and pleasure in books read to them before school begins become indifferent and reluctant readers after they enter it? (We pondered a similar puzzle at the beginning of Chapter 5, Reviving Poetry.) In a succession of short chapters, Pennac evokes the problem and, quite surprisingly, offers remedies for home and school, parents and teachers. The force of his critique of schools is directed at practices that focus too much on comprehension and too little on pleasure and response. He quotes Flannery O'Conner: "If teachers are in the habit of approaching a story as if it were a research problem for which any answer is believable so long as it is not obvious, then I think students will never learn to enjoy fiction" (p. 46). He invites us to issue young readers invitations to read, grant them certain rights as readers, and then step back and mimic his own models, those "few adults who gave me the gift of reading," that is, who "let their books speak and never once asked if I had *understood*." He calls these rights and privileges a "Reader's Bill of Rights." Although we might not have drawn our bill of rights quite as Pennac does, his views provide a fitting close to a chapter concerned with fresh challenges to a tradition that, unexamined, might grow inert, but, examined and expanded, startles us with its new life.

1. The right not to read.
2. The right to skip pages.
3. The right to not finish.
4. The right to reread.
5. The right to read anything.
6. The right to escapism.
7. The right to read anywhere.
8. The right to browse.
9. The right to read out loud.
10. The right to not defend our tastes.

CONCLUSION

We have introduced the traditional classics and their modern challengers to take you into an important debate going on in our field and in our classrooms. All professions have their politically sensitive issues. The cries "Back to the Basics!" and "Expand the Canon" are two often heard in ours. The first assumes weaknesses in American students and the educational solutions for remedying them. It calls for invigorating doses of classics teaching in literature study. The second sees weakness in our traditional English subject matter and methodology and calls for an expansion of both. Our hope for you is this: that understanding the history, assumptions, and values of competing claims for the English classroom will enable you to select literary texts and teaching strategies on some confident ground between traditionalists and challengers. Applebee (1974) finds a meeting ground:

> Any definition of a literary heritage in terms of specific books or authors distorts the cultural significance of a literary tradition by failing to recognize that what the Great Books offer is a continuing dialogue on the moral and philosophical questions central to the culture itself. The usefulness of the heritage lies in the confrontation with these issues which it provides; any acquaintanceship which avoids the confrontation is both trivial and irrelevant. (p. 248)

Martin (personal conversation, 1991) also offers a vision that embraces both. He finds something indispensable in the continuum of reflected experience passed from one generation to another. He envisions this heritage as a baton passed from one runner to the next, necessary for both runners, happily offered, and eagerly grasped, in order to run the race. In his analogy, we not only receive a cultural inheritance, but we also act upon it by our own exertions. And the runner not only carries it on, but also carries it further and with energies that those who transmitted it could not have supplied.

So it is not Shakespeare who is universal, but what he reveals when we ask the right questions. The wrong question is "What value does *Hamlet* have?" *Hamlet* becomes valuable when we as teachers and students relate personally to it. The charge is not to enshrine the classics, nor to trash them, but to remain open to new and different perspectives and to relate personally to those we read. This shared past can call us to an awakening to present realities and future possibilities.

Jack McMichael Martin, a sculptor, artist, poet, and friend, has joined our attempts to articulate the ideas in this chapter over the last decade and, as is his nature, wrote a poem for this book. We close our chapter with it.

The Voices of These Masters

The voices of these masters
enjoin us to go farther

that is, to surpass them
and ourselves

we, who've taken their voices
into our own

as we must do,
we, their apprentices

to have done with them
and to go on.

That's their admonition
borne down the generations

on the wind that scatters them
and carries them to us.

Jack McMichael Martin

7

ASSAYING NONFICTION

"But fiction represents only a part of our literary legacy.... Nonfiction—with its stirring language, its compelling subject, and its impressive abilities to provoke thought and challenge beliefs—has shaped philosophies, societies, and individuals."

Richard Abrahamson and Betty Carter

Like young adult fiction, nonfiction has had to struggle to find a place in secondary English classrooms. Aidan Chamber, an English critic, defines traditional literature as the "Holy Three": fiction, poetry, and drama. Abrahamson and Carter (1991) document the rule of this triumvirate. They report that the most popular high school literature textbooks devote, on the average, 88% of their total content to fiction and that most "awards and prizes for both children's and young-adult literature" go to fiction (p. 52). Yet Ellis (1987) estimated that nonfiction accounts for at least 50% of the total reading done by high school students. Carter (1987) found that 49% of books checked out of the junior high libraries that were studied were nonfiction. On annual lists of titles recommended for young adult readers, such as those published by *School Library Journal* and the *English Journal*, 25–50% are nonfiction.

Despite what Purves and Monson (1972) call "a general tendency away from fiction to nonfiction" (p. 169) in the secondary school years, English faculty members, textbook publishers, and workshop organizers continue to operate as though fiction is the overwhelming choice of high school readers. High school literature and writing textbooks are apt indicators. In the genre and thematic anthologies of the first high school years, nonfiction occupies a spot, but a decidedly narrow one compared to fiction. Texts organized by geographic identity (American, British, and world literature), scatter a few nonfiction entries among the predominant fiction and poetry selections. Teachers, particularly those in schools with compressed block schedules and/or end-of-term standardized exams, report to us that "covering" literature is difficult enough, and that nonfiction textbook selections are the ones they usually omit.

Nonfiction has traditionally been chosen for a more functional purpose in writing textbooks: to display a variety of rhetorical models for students to emulate. As student writing has grown more personal, expressive, and informal, however, even the formal nonfiction models have become less pertinent. The very idea of a model is less valued as students try to find their own unique voices. In sum, nonfiction has an established, if modest, place in the English curriculum: a quiet accompaniment to fiction, poetry, and student compositions. But often, in the accelerating pace of a school year, the position of nonfiction in English classrooms fades past seeing.

Invitation to Reflection 7–1

- Do you remember reading nonfiction in secondary English classes? If so, list any names of nonfiction authors or pieces that you recall.
- Do you tend to make a distinction in the books that you read between "literature" and "nonliterature"? If so, how do you make the distinction?
- When you select reading material out of choice, not assignment, what percentage of your choices are fiction? Nonfiction?
- Where do you most frequently encounter nonfiction?

Newspapers	Magazines	Letters
Books	Anthologies	Other

- When you write for school or out-of-school purposes, what genre do you most frequently use, fiction or nonfiction?
- Which genre, fiction or nonfiction, best serves the following purposes?

Enjoyment	Insight
Information	Inspiration

- Have you been in classes, high school or university, that assume that fiction deserves a more serious reading than nonfiction does?
- Have you read nonfiction whose language or style struck you as powerful, that is, whose subject was measurably enhanced by the power of its presentation?
- If so, can you name a few titles or authors?

WHY TEACH NONFICTION?

The strongest reason for teaching nonfiction is pragmatic and has already been introduced: It comprises a significant portion of what students actually read. We should capitalize on the reading that naturally interests students; to ignore these texts is to miss an opportunity. Omitting nonfiction from our classroom notice and discussion mystifies their chosen texts. The student may reason "Is my reading not worth a teacher's notice? If it does not deserve teacher scrutiny, does it deserve my critical attention? Should I keep my reading a private, guilty pleasure, removed from public attention?" We need to openly acknowledge, address, and validate students' reading choices. We need to encourage students to approach nonfiction with the same comprehending, responsive, and critical minds that they bring to fiction.

Another justification for teaching nonfiction is simply that the boundaries between it and fiction are becoming increasingly indistinct. The New Journalism, or journalistic fiction, has done much to dim those lines. Today, such novels as Truman Capote's *In Cold Blood* (1965) and Norman Mailer's *Armies of the Night* (1968) and *The Executioner's Song* (1979), as well as essays, are based on real people and events and are written with the novelist's attention to voice, character, narrative, and conflict. Tom Wicker, a political editorialist, wrote a fine novel of the Civil War, *Unto This Hour* (1984), and Tom Wolfe, a social critic of wit and insight, wrote the highly acclaimed comedic novel *The Bonfire of the Vanities* (1987). Maimon, Nodine, and O'Connor (1989) believe that "we live in an age of 'blurred genres'" (p. xx). In fact, many of the techniques that students use to analyze and interpret literature apply to nonfiction as well. These can be taught via nonfiction as readily as fiction. Welcoming nonfiction into the English classroom enlarges our definition of reading to encompass the act itself, not just particular acts of "high literature."

Invitation to Reflection 7–2

When 300 English teachers were asked to recommend 10 adolescent and 10 adult novels as "worthy of young adult reading," the following nonfiction titles appeared on the fiction survey (Donelson & Nilsen, 1980, p. 342). Read the titles that follow. Would you make the same mistakes?

Piers Paul Read	*Alive*	1974
James Herriot	*All Creatures Great and Small*	1972

Robin Graham	*Dove*	1972
Peter Maas	*Serpico*	1973
Doris Lund	*Eric*	1974
Alvin Toffler	*Future Shock*	1970
Maya Angelou	*I Know Why the Caged Bird Sings*	1969
Dee Brown	*Bury My Heart at Wounded Knee*	1970
Claude Brown	*Manchild in the Promised Land*	1965
Eldridge Cleaver	*Soul on Ice*	1968
John H. Griffin	*Black Like Me*	1961
Carlos Castaneda	*Journey to Ixtlan*	1972
Vincent Bugliosi and Curt Gentry	*Helter Skelter*	1974
Studs Terkel	*Working*	1974
Pat Conroy	*The Water Is Wide*	1972
Henry David Thoreau	*Walden*	1854
Eliot Wigginton	*Foxfire* (the series)	1972
N. Scott Momaday	*The Way to Rainy Mountain*	1962
Lorraine Hansberry	*A Raisin in the Sun*	1959
Annie Dillard	*Pilgrim at Tinker Creek*	1974

A third reason for teaching nonfiction flows from those challenges to the canon—Deconstructionist, Reader Response, political, social, and aesthetic critiques of the tradition—discussed in Chapter 6. It is the contention of these postmodernist critics that any sharp distinction between "good texts" (which tend to be fiction) and "bad texts" is an arbitrary distinction—a human construct based more on cultural/historical/political norms than on objective standards of excellence. Scholes, in *Textual Power* (1985), explains that university English departments have divided the field into two categories: "literature and non-literature" and "mark those texts labeled literature as good or important and dismiss those non-literary texts as beneath our notice. . . . The proper consumption of literature we call 'interpretation,' and the teaching of this skill, like the displaying of it in academic papers, articles, and books, is our greatest glory" (p. 5).

By contrast, the consumption of "nonliterature" is called "reading," and is left to elementary and secondary English teachers. Scholes believes that the bias against the serious study of "nonliterature" is based on the perception that it is "grounded in the realities of existence, where it is produced in response to personal or socio-economic imperatives and therefore justifies itself functionally. By its very usefulness, its non-literariness, it eludes our grasp. It can be read but not interpreted, because it supposedly lacks those secret-hidden-deeper meanings so dear to our pedagogic hearts." (p. 6). Scholes asserts that "all texts have secret-hidden-deeper meanings, and none more so than the supposedly obvious and straightforward productions of journalists, historians, and philosophers. . . . And who is to say that Locke or Gibbon is less valuable than Dryden or Gray?" (p. 8).

Annie Dillard (1988) makes the case that in the two prior centuries, fiction writers struggled to have their work regarded as nonfiction in order to maintain respectability:

In the eighteenth and nineteenth centuries, some literary folk considered fiction ipso facto trash. Serious writers tried to weasel out of that genre. Fielding originally titled Tom Jones "The History of a Foundling," to lend it the artistic dignity that nonfiction alone was then thought to possess. Melville's Typee, a work of pretty outrageous fiction, masqueraded as fact in its day; so did Omoo. Poe published The Narrative of A. Gordon Pym as nonfiction. Twain's first title for his novel was "Huck Finn's Autobiography"—to distinguish it from a mere romance, and thereby to plead for serious reading. (p. xiii)

Increasingly in the twentieth century, the reverse is true. Writers consider fiction the more "intellectually respectable" and fudge on the genre "as if fiction were not descriptive but honorific, as if fiction didn't mean fabrication but artfulness" (p. xiv). Thus, writers today call their "closely autobiographical narratives fiction": Henry Roth's *Call It Sleep* (1934), James Agee's *A Death in the Family* (1957), Norman MacLean's *A River Runs Through It* (1976), Stratis Haviaras's *When the Tree Sings* (1979), J. G. Ballard's *Empire of the Sun* (1984), Harriet Doerr's *Stones for Ibarra* (1984) (p. xiv). Dillard's point is obvious enough: If the standard of good literature is as plastic as to have almost completely reversed itself in the past centuries, why discredit nonfiction today?

Abrahamson and Carter (1991) suggest a final rationale for nonfiction in the classroom. They argue that nonfiction has the potential to provide some young readers with a vital personal encounter with a text that is unavailable to them in fiction:

While a general love of literature may be shared by many individuals, the realization of that passion is always intensely personal. It begins when readers encounter an author whose theme, or subject, or language speaks directly to them, when they experience a moment of self-realization, or discover a piece of themselves in a particular work, or see ideas and actions they hope to emulate. For many teenagers, fiction introduces these incipient responses. But for just as many, non-fiction triggers the same reactions. (pp. 53-54)

Abrahamson and Carter reason that we cannot "afford to prescribe their responses by deciding for them" that fiction leads to an enlarged aesthetic response and nonfiction to a narrowed transactional one. We must present students with a wide and free choice of texts so that they, sampling among them, can decide for themselves. We should not be dogmatic about the relative importance of one type of text as opposed to another. No one can be sure for someone else—especially those as young and varied as today's high school students—just where the most telling and eloquent voices may be heard.

Teaching Activity 7-1 surveys student experience and opinion as a prelude to a nonfiction unit or selection.

Teaching Activity 7–1   The Place of Nonfiction

Individual
On a piece of paper, respond to the following statements by writing a number 1 (wholeheartedly agree) through 10 (strongly disagree).

1. The term *literature* designates nonfiction as well as fiction.
2. In my literature classes, we read more fiction than nonfiction.
3. I have read fiction pieces that have made a strong impact on me.
4. I have read nonfiction pieces that have made a strong impact on me.
5. Fiction deserves a more careful reading than nonfiction does.
6. The language of fiction is more impressive than that of nonfiction.
7. The books that I like to reread tend to be fiction.
8. The books that I like to reread tend to be nonfiction.
9. If I could chose, in English class I would prefer to read nonfiction over fiction.

Small Group
Sum your responses to each item. Are there any strong agreements among you? Any strong disagreements? Under numbered columns on the board, list the magnitude of your group's response. Look at Donelson and Nilsen's 1980 survey of teacher mistakes (Invitation to Reflection 7-2). Do you know these titles? Are you confused about any of them?

Whole Class
On the basis of the survey, what is the class's preference for reading? Do English classes typically satisfy that preference? Why would English classes have a prejudice toward fiction? Does the survey suggest any change that needs to be made in the selection of class texts?

NONFICTION GENRES IN THE CLASSROOM

Nonfiction printed genres have burgeoned to include essays, diaries, journals, reviews, memoirs, letters, autobiographies, biographies, aphorisms, lists, interviews, epigrams, dictionaries, proverbs, testimonials, and speeches. If we add nonprint genres, the list grows longer. Each of these has a power of purpose, subject, and language peculiar to it. Examination of a few will illustrate how their study can enliven and enrich the English classroom.

ESSAYS

We turn first to the essay, the most frequently anthologized nonfiction genre for high school readers. The genre is far more flexible and expansive than its formal name connotes. When French philosopher Michel de Montaigne (1533-1592) retired from active life, he devoted himself to reflection and began to collect and publish both the aphorisms popular in his day and an explanation of his reasoning about them. He is considered the first modern essayist, and he established characteristics for the essay that still distinguish it today: personal, informal, and intimate. Its root word means "to attempt," and essays are just that—attempts to merely address issues, not attempts to fully cover issues as treatises do.

Since the time of Montaigne, essays have become such a popular means of expressing an opinion that anyone interested in looking for good essays finds an appetizing variety. In the eighteenth century, essays took such a public turn in England that one can rummage through a wealth of terse and pithy pieces about the day ranging in authorship from Joseph Addison (1672-1719) to Sir Richard Steele (1672-1729). In the nineteenth century, essayists such as Charles Lamb (1775-1834), William Hazlitt (1778-1830), Thomas De Quincey (1785-1859), Thomas Carlyle (1795-1881), Thomas Macaulay (1800-1859), and John Ruskin (1819-1900) ruminated more on their personal experiences than on public life in a form that was as relaxed as it was lengthy. In the United States, two of our earliest literary forbearers, Emerson and Thoreau, were essentially essayists. Even Washington Irving, Edgar Allan Poe, and Mark Twain contributed significantly to the genre. Essayists from the early part of this century included English wits such as G. K. Chesterton (1874-1936) and Hilare Belloc (1870-1953) and U.S. writers such as William Dean Howells (1837-1920) and H. L. Mencken (1880-1956).

Dillard (1988) explains that the "essayist does what we do with our lives; the essayist thinks about actual things" (xvii). Yet today, some consider the essay a bit stilted and old-fashioned. They prefer the article—a piece that is usually informative, timely, impersonal, and more concerned with covering the subject matter than with style. The essay, by contrast, possesses a more consciously literary style and offers a more personal distillation of and reflection on the complexity of the subject at hand. Atwan (1988) suggests a reason for this bias against the essay: Despite the radical changes in other forms of twentieth-century literature, essayists "broke no new ground; . . . resisted no rules; . . . violated no conventions" (p. i). Yet the essay's status is changing. Its place is more assured in literary quarterlies and general magazines. Serious writers are exploring its imaginative and narrative possibilities—pushing its border with fiction and poetry. Such publishing houses as the Oxford University Press and W. W. Norton publish essay anthologies. Collections of individual writers occasionally appear, for instance, Sven Birkerts' *The Gutenberg Elegies* (1994) and Barbara Kingsolver's *High Tide in Tucson: Essays from Now or Never* (1995). The collection *The Best American Essays* began to be published annually in 1986 and has a guest writer-editor each year whose introductions provide a running commentary on the state of the literary essay. Writers of proven fictive and poetic ability turn more and more to writing essays: Louise Erdrich, William Gass, Elizabeth Hardwick, Jamaica Kincaid, James A. McPherson, Joyce Carol Oates, Cynthia Ozick, Robert Stone, and John Updike.

At a time when teachers are moving to alternatives to the textbook, magazines provide a rich source of nonfiction. Nelms (1990) explains: "More and more of us are questioning the expenditure of instructional materials budgets on traditional textbooks. We see the advantages of a magazine format: timelines, flexibility, diversity, and appealing design. Classroom sets of magazines saved over a long period of time provide a smorgasbord of selections for repeated use" (p. 77). Figure 7-1 lists a few of the periodicals in which essays of substance and style often appear.

In addition to these literary magazines, English teachers have long used magazines written specifically for students, such as *Scholastic Magazines' Voice, Sprint, Action, Scope,* and *Literary Cavalcade; U.S. Express,* written for ESL students in grades 6-10; and *Writing!, Merlyn's Pen, Challenge,* and *International Readers' Newsletter.*

Essays in the English Classroom. Essays can serve to generate ideas for writing and discussion. Essayists often deal with the present issues that engage our attention. And, as Dillard reasons (1988), "in some ways the essay can deal in both events and ideas better than the short story can, because the essayist—unlike the poet—may introduce the plain, unadorned thought without the contrived entrances of long-winded characters who mouth discourses" (p. xvi). Nonfiction can address ideas directly without weaving them indirectly through narrative and character.

One approach to an essay or any passage of prose is called a Quaker Reading. Teacher Katie Moulder adds questions and discussion to the Quaker Read of Chapter 6 (Johnson, 1997). She has students

FIGURE 7–1
Periodicals that
publish literary essays

The American Scholar	Encounter	Northwest Review
The American West	Esquire	The Paris Review
Antioch Review	The Georgia Review	The Partisan Review
Antaeus	Harper's Magazine	The Sewanee Review
The Atlantic	Hudson Review	Shenandoah
Audubon	Kenyon Review	Spectator Magazine
Civilization	Natural History	Village Voice
Community Review	The New Yorker	The Virginia Quarterly Review
DoubleTake	North American Review	Witness

read a passage aloud with the understanding that if anyone in the class has any question about the words or ideas, that person will interrupt and pose his or her question. Students often have to practice interrupting and publicly acknowledging confusion. In time, though, readers approach seriously and deliberately this chance for shared working through a passage. They often discover that they are voicing the queries of others. Progress can be slow, but also active and enlivening. The class arrives at the conclusion with a deeper understanding.

We often choose essays to sound themes preparatory to encountering them in literary texts. (Correspondences can also occur in style, narrative technique, character development, and tone.) One of the most delightful essays in our repertoire is Phyllis Rose's (1984) "Heroic Fantasies, Nervous Doubts." It strikes a deep chord in students. The title alone indicates the connection with human experience and fiction: our uncertainties about ourselves in the midst of our stubborn hopes. We have even found essays such as Russell Baker's "Schlemiel" (1980) that imaginatively respond to literature, in this case to Woody Allen's short story "The Kugelmass Episode" (1977). We also pair essays together, such as Virginia Woolf's "Death of a Moth" and Annie Dillard's "Transfiguration," both triggered by the observation of the dying of a moth.

BIOGRAPHIES

Our earliest independent and happy reading was of little orange-backed biographies written for children. We never got over our delight. Biographies serve the same goal we expect of imaginative literature—that we stretch ourselves, travel from our narrow personal perspectives, and enter into the lives of others with empathy and broadened sympathy. A well-written biography possesses the same virtue as well-crafted fiction: It renders a person who is recognizable, but distinct and individual. For high school students just starting out on their own life careers, biographies can provide useful views into different lives and offer compelling alternative visions for a life. Biographies can trace the formative people, events, and places in a subject's life. They can track significant changes, recurring patterns, or repeated themes over time. They shed retrospective light on crucial moments in a life. They can illuminate the private experience of public acts. Biographers can discern the wholeness of a completed life history. They offer the comforting solidity of that completed cycle. Encountering the lives of others illuminates not only those lives, but also our own. When a biography focuses on the life of a writer whose works are being studied, it also suffuses those texts with a richer light. Thus, biography is an ideal companion to fiction reading and reflective writing.

Standard biographies present historic figures, significant for their contributions to literary and civic life. Donelson and Nilsen's annual pick of adolescent literature for the *English Journal* usually includes one or two works of nonfiction. Recently, they have recommended the following biographies:

> *Columbus and the World Around Him* (1990), Milton Meltzer
> *Eleanor Roosevelt: A Life of Discovery* (1993), Russell Freedman
> *Abigail Adams: Witness to a Revolution* (1995), Natalie S. Bober

We also find excellent biographies in shorter form. Lytton Strachey's *Eminent Victorians* (1918) is an early example that still reads easily, although students might miss his iconoclastic treatment of the Victorian heroes and heroines of his day. Phyllis Rose's *Parallel Lives: Five Victorian Marriages* (1983) and Howard Gardner's *Leading Minds: Anatomy of Leadership* (1995) are examples of collections of shorter biographies that are accessible to high school students. We also turn to the Internet for either a detailed biography or the resources with which to piece together a portrait ourselves.

Biography in Five English Classrooms.   As you read the teaching activities that follow, notice the variety of creative ways in which these teachers approach biographies, some as a subgenre worth studying for itself alone, some as a biographical enrichment to literary study, some as an approach to particular stories or to the general elements of fiction, and some as a way to learn skills.

Johnson (1986) introduces his biography unit by having students read short biographies. He then asks students to write or speak about their subjects in response to his informal, spontaneous questions: Would the subject "make a good friend"? Were there times when the subject was "not courageous"? He says that these prompts "lead the students into thinking of these biographical figures as real people—people they might know, like, or sometimes dislike" (p. 27). He then asks students to write short stories in which they meet their subjects and answer the following questions: "How do your lives interact? Are you close friends? Rivals?" (p. 27). Johnson concludes by having each class member write a three- to five-page biography of a classmate, whom he assigns and whom they must interview.

Bowen (1991) encourages her students to try a variety of forms for expressing their insight into their subjects: "dialogues, poems, and newspaper articles. Obituaries, songs, and letters also work" (p. 53). For instance, one of her students, interested in Eric Clapton, took on his persona and wrote a letter to

Clapton's friend and fellow musician Muddy Waters. Bowen asks her students to keep what Romano (1987) calls "research journals" (which note "details as well as impressions") and to write in them a "dozen questions they would ask their subjects if they were to meet them" (Bowen, 1991, p. 54). She checks their journals often and adds her own questions. As they write their larger biographies, she also uses small in-class assignments to encourage their creative thinking about biography's multiple possibilities:

- Free write for ten minutes as though you were the subject.
- Make a list of twenty-five important things in the subject's life (titles, objects, people, etc.).
- Choose a date in the subject's life and write a diary entry.
- Write a dialogue between the subject and someone else.
- Answer these "quiz" questions—What is the subject's favorite leisure activity, favorite place, most regretted incident, best assets (personality and physical), and the like?
- Write a letter from a friend of the subject or from yourself.
- Write a descriptive paragraph about the subject.
- Using the strongest words and images from one of the previous assignments, develop poetic phrases and write a couple of lines of verse. (p. 54)

Wahlenmayer (1991) also found in students' genuine questions an alternative to the deadly biography reports that used to haunt her classroom. She lists on the board questions that they would like to ask their chosen subjects, combines them, deletes duplicates and highly specific ones, and uses the remaining questions as the core of a 10-question oral interview. The students' assignment is to select a subject and become so familiar with that person that they can talk of his or her life "comfortably and in some detail" (p. 56). An interviewer (the teacher or one of the students) picks 10 of the following questions at random, plus an additional 2 submitted by students:

1. Why would someone want to write a book about you?
2. What was the place where you grew up like?
3. How much of your life is covered by this book?
4. Tell me something important about your parents.
5. How did you prepare for what you became famous for?
6. What was the happiest period in your life?
7. What is the most difficult situation you ever faced?
8. Describe yourself emotionally.
9. Tell me about a turning point in your life.
10. Tell me about your family since you've been an adult.
11. Do you have any idiosyncrasies or trademarks?
12. What was the source of your motivation to accomplish what you did?
13. Tell me something about yourself that's not commonly known.
14. What part has romance played in your life?
15. How do you like to spend your free time?
16. Who was a very influential person in your life?
17. Explain whether your fame has brought you happiness or unhappiness.
18. How do you feel you were portrayed in this book?
19. What is something you'd like to be remembered for?
20. Was the time you lived in important to what you did?
21. Describe your death.
22. Tell me more about that. (p. 55)

Hogarty (1991) conceived of an audacious activity that set students up as IRS auditors. He gathered as many different IRS forms as he could find and asked his students to fill out forms for imaginary persons who might exist. Other students audited them and wrote the biographies and autobiographies of these characters. In his more direct approach to biography, Hogarty does not try to distinguish fiction from nonfiction. He uses excerpts from Gore Vidal's historical fiction *Burr* (1988), for instance, to "provide a marvelous counterpoint to the typical history text treatment of that figure" (p. 58). Further, he uses William Carlos Williams's (1956) essay about Aaron Burr, "The Virtue of History," because "it is definitely nonfiction and obviously literature" (p. 58). He also links Vidal's historical fiction and Carl Sandburg's biography to textbook accounts of Abraham Lincoln. His students appear to be able to operate comfortably between what purports to be fiction and nonfiction. They see, for example, what historical fiction can do to compensate for the "squeezing out of the man" that occurs in many history textbooks. They ponder the discovery that "Wolfe's astronauts in *The Right Stuff* (1979) lived different lives from those portrayed in many newspapers and magazines of their time. Why? What gives?" (p. 58).

Mitchell (1996) uses biographies as she would literature. While at one time she approached the genre unenthusiastically, with a focus on the "facts of a person's life," she now organizes her biography lessons around the traditional "elements of literature":

Setting	Students "create a visual representation of the places the character lived or visited and . . . indicate . . . the importance of each place" (p. 75).
Plot	Students create a "time line illustrating what they perceive to be the most important actions and events in the character's life and represent them with words or pictures" (p. 75).
Characterization	Students discuss "which characters came to life for them, which . . . they would like to meet, and which actions of characters seemed hardest to understand." She elicits the same responses to biographical characters as she does for fictional ones. Students "write letters to them, find poems the character would like, and create conversations with them" (p. 75).
Theme	Students discuss the recurring issues of their subjects' lives, the common problems they confronted, what they learned from their struggles. The class sometimes creates a word collage from individual students' suggestions of what the most persistent issues or themes were.
Point of View	Students consider how the perspective on the subject would have changed "had the book been written by the subject's parents or friends or even an enemy" (p. 75). Students test that hypothesis by writing brief character sketches of themselves, one written by someone unsympathetic and another by someone sympathetic toward them.

Teaching Activity 7–2 suggests questions that you might pose to students to make connections among biography, history, and fiction. Although the emphasis is on analytical questions, this activity could culminate in the freer expressions of art, music, drama, or creative writing. The questions can be used for whole texts or selected excerpts, for oral or written work, and with individuals, small groups, or the whole class.

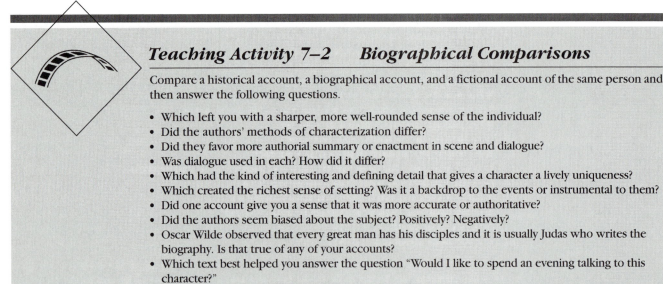

Teaching Activity 7–2   Biographical Comparisons

Compare a historical account, a biographical account, and a fictional account of the same person and then answer the following questions.

- Which left you with a sharper, more well-rounded sense of the individual?
- Did the authors' methods of characterization differ?
- Did they favor more authorial summary or enactment in scene and dialogue?
- Was dialogue used in each? How did it differ?
- Which had the kind of interesting and defining detail that gives a character a lively uniqueness?
- Which created the richest sense of setting? Was it a backdrop to the events or instrumental to them?
- Did one account give you a sense that it was more accurate or authoritative?
- Did the authors seem biased about the subject? Positively? Negatively?
- Oscar Wilde observed that every great man has his disciples and it is usually Judas who writes the biography. Is that true of any of your accounts?
- Which text best helped you answer the question "Would I like to spend an evening talking to this character?"
- Which text did you enjoy the most?
- From which did you learn the most?

AUTOBIOGRAPHIES AND MEMOIRS

Autobiographies, like biographies, take us into the lives of others, but at closer, more intimate range. We are eyewitnesses to actual events; we are introduced to real people. Often, in the course of our reading, we develop a partnership with the narrator-subject as we receive the self-disclosure and willing confidences that are so hard won in our everyday friendships. Like knowing a mystery's successful conclusion before we begin reading, we read with the trust that struggles have been overcome and order has been achieved. Autobiography, then—this immediate and compelling genre—often snags the adolescent's natural curiosity about the lives of others and offers the reassurance that childhood and youth, particularly, can be negotiated and life commenced successfully.

Autobiography has other attractions. It provides models for high school students involved in their own personal writing. Much of what we do with language and literature in the English class is designed to encourage students to explore and compose their own lives. In his introduction to the 1983 edition of *Dandelion Wine*, Ray Bradbury discusses a secret that allows his ideas to flow, a secret that taps the vein of autobiography. It is the source of both autobiography and of students' personal writing. He says that from age 24 through 36, he would let his mind wander through his childhood "hoping to come across some old half-burnt firecracker, a rusted toy, or a fragment of a letter written to myself in some young year hoping to contact the older person I became to remind him of his past, his life, his people, his joys, and his drenching sorrows" (p. viii).

We have found another form of autobiography to be even more popular: Memoirs do not attempt to comprehend a whole life, but to reflect on and render only a portion of that life. Zinsser (1987) distinguishes between autobiographies and memoirs along just these lines: "Unlike autobiography, which moves in a dutiful line from birth to fame, omitting nothing significant, memoir assumes the life and ignores most of it. The writer of a memoir takes us back to a corner of his or her life that was un-usually vivid or intense—childhood, for instance—or that was framed by unique events. By narrowing the lens, the writer achieves a focus that isn't possible in autobiography; memoir is a window into a life" (p. 21). Dillard (1995) calls the memoir "a powerfully fixed point of view" (p. ix). In a useful collection, *Modern American Memoirs,* editors Dillard and Conley excerpt passages from 31 classic modern American autobiographies to capture the memoirist's fixed viewpoint. Dillard explains that these writers celebrate, as Charles Wright does in his poem, "all the various things that lock our wrists to the past."

Zora Neale Hurston's *Dust Tracks on a Road: An Autobiography* (1942), Thomas Merton's *The Seven Storey Mountain* (1948), Mary McCarthy's *Memories of a Catholic Girlhood* (1957), Margaret Mead's *Blackberry Winter* (1972), Harry Crews's *Childhood, The Biography of a Place* (1978), and Russell Baker's *Growing Up* (1983) are examples of moving autobiography, "the gradual unfolding of a life in all of its remembered particulars." John Updike wrote a more focused memoir, *Self-Consciousness: Memoirs* (1989), in which he candidly and sensitively takes us inside the boy and youth, troubled by psoriasis, stuttering, dentists, and Vietnam, who became one of our finest novel-ists. *Angela's Ashes* (1996) is Frank McCourt's remarkable account of growing up Irish, Catholic, and poor in Limerick, Ireland. Jill Ker Conway's two books, *The Road from Coorain* (1989) and *True North* (1994), present lucid but lyrical accounts of her life as she moved from the Australian outback on a sheep station, to provincial post-World War II Sydney, to graduate school at Harvard University, to an academic appointment at the University of Toronto, and then to the first female presidency at Smith College. Conway has also edited two anthologies of autobiographical writing by other women: *Written by Herself: Autobiographies of American Women: An Anthology* (1992) and *Written by Herself Volume II: Women's Memoirs from Britain, Africa, Asia, and the United States* (1996). These shorter fragments of lives have the appeal of brevity for student readers. Helen Keller, at age 22, wrote a classic account of her struggle to overcome blindness and deafness: *The Story of My Life* (1902). Another classic memoir is that of Black Elk, *Black Elk Speaks* (1932, 1988). John Neihardt records (with some changes, we now realize) Black Elk's vital account of the Lakota's customs and world views both before and after the tribe was forced onto reservations. *Making Waves: An Anthology of Writings by and About Asian American Women* (1989) contains memoirs (as well as poems, fiction, and essays) organized around such themes as immigration, war, work, and generations. In *Facing Mount Kenya* (1962), Jomo Kenyatta begins the account of his remarkable life with his an-cestors, the Gikuyu, how they became oppressed, and how he, their son, became the first president of an independent Kenya. The last emperor of China, Aisin-Gioro P'U Yi, wrote his autobiography, *From Emperor to Citizen* (1960), detailing his life from emperor at age 3 under a regent, to isolated life in the walled Forbidden City, to a citizen deposed by the Chinese Nationalists, to observer of com-munist rule under Mao Zedong. Mark Mathabane wrote *Kaffir Boy* (1986), whose subtitle tells it all: *The True Story of a Black Youth's Coming of Age in Apartheid South Africa.* In *When Heaven and Earth Changed Places: A Vietnamese Woman's Journey from War to Peace* (1990), Le Ly Hayslip writes movingly of her traditional Buddhist childhood in a Vietnamese farming family, the nightmare of war begun when she was 12, her decision to fight as a Viet Cong, her struggle to survive in Saigon, her marriage to an American, and her return to Vietnam as a Vietnamese American. Nilsen and Donelson chose an autobiography for their annual adolescent honor lists: *Black Ice* (1991) by Lorene Cary, in which Cary describes her experience as a student from West Philadelphia sent on a scholar-ship to a prestigious prep school in New Hampshire.

Not surprisingly, many writers have written autobiographies of their lives (sometimes veiling these as fiction) and memoirs of brief segments of their lives. We especially like James Thurber's

FIGURE 7–2
Autobiographies

I Dream a World (1989)	Brian Lanker
Bloods: An Oral History of the Vietnam War by Black Veterans (1984)	Wallace Terry
Voices from the Future: Our Children Tell us About Violence in America (1993)	Susan Goodwillie, Ed.
Freedom's Children: Young Civil Rights Activists Tell Their Own Stories (1993)	Ellen Levine
Warriors Don't Cry (1994)	Melba Pattillo Beals
Lives on the Boundary: The Struggles and Achievements of America's Underprepared (1989)	Mike Rose
The Hunger of Memory: The Education of Richard Rodriguez (1981)	Richard Rodriguez

My Life and Hard Times (1933), Eudora Welty's *One Writer's Beginnings* (1984), and Reynolds Price's *Clear Pictures: First Loves, First Guides* (1988). Interviews of authors often appear in educational magazines: *Language Arts, Instructor, Learning,* and *Creative Classroom.* Barbara Kiefer has compiled some of these in *Getting to Know You—Profiles of Children's Authors Featured in Language Arts* (1991). Eve Shelnutt has edited the writing memoirs of living male and female writers: *The Confidence Woman: 26 Women Writers at Work* (1991) and *My Poor Elephant: 27 Male Writers at Work* (1992). Linda Gray Sexton has written about life with her mother, poet Anne Sexton in *Searching for Mercy Street: My Journey Back to My Mother, Anne Sexton* (1994). These volumes shed an autobiographical light on active authors that will humanize their works for students and personalize the career of writing. Kai Erikson edited *Encounters* (1989), a brief series of 18 portraits, each of an encounter with a literary figure written by another literary figure. For instance, John Hersey was secretary to Sinclair Lewis and describes him as someone who "could no more stop telling stories than he could stop his hair growing."

Figure 7–2 lists other autobiographical pieces that deal with issues vital to today's students.

Holocaust Literature.   Some of the most compelling memoirs of our time are those of the Holocaust survivors. One survivor, Elie Wiesel, eloquently explains the need to give witness to these catastrophic events. In our teaching of this tragic moment in history, we rely primarily on letters, diaries, and memoirs, although we supplement with historical accounts and with fiction, drama, and poetry. *Anne Frank: Diary of a Young Girl* (1952) is well known by many students coming into high school. Another diary was kept during these same years by Anne's adult counterpart, 27-year-old Etty Hillesum. That diary, *An Interrupted Life: The Diaries of Etty Hillesum, 1941–1943* (1983), and Hillesum's subsequent letters from the last deportation center before Auschwitz, *Letters from Westerbork* (1986), are absorbing. So too are Primo Levi's accounts of his 10 months in Auschwitz, *Survival in Auschwitz* (1959) and *The Drowned and the Saved* (1986) and Elie Wiesel's memoir *Night* (1960). A more recent memoir by Robert O. Fisch, a Minnesota pediatrician and visual artist, *Light from the Yellow Star: A Lesson of Love from the Holocaust* (1994, Minneapolis: Frederick Weisman Art Museum of the University of Minnesota) combines his art (on the cover and each page of text), quotations from the gravestones of the memorial concentration camp cemetery in Budapest where his father is buried, and his personal narrative. Fisch opens his memoir with words which capture both our motive and our challenge in teaching this literature. "I have been thinking for quite a long time whether any medium is appropriate to describe the scope of the tragedy of the Holocaust. How can sorrow, suffering, and atrocities of this magnitude be expressed?" Gorrell (1997) describes in detail how she and her high school juniors read and learned from Fisch's memoir.

In addition to the gripping first person accounts of nonfiction are autobiographical poems, art, stories, and novels. Excellent bibliographies are available on Holocaust nonfiction and fiction for adolescent readers. The Internet has multiple sites with annotated references. We have found *A Teacher's Guide to the Holocaust* from the University of South Florida especially helpful. Kaywell (1993) has an excellent annotated list of general reference sources and specific books for young adults (pp. 13–35). The U.S. Holocaust Memorial Museum publishes a teaching resource with instructional guidelines and a detailed bibliography called *Teaching about the Holocaust: A Resource Book for Educators* (no publication date given).

Memoirs in One English Classroom.   Gillespie (1991) uses memoirs to prompt students to write their own memoirs, to allow each to become, as Zinsser says, "the editor of his own life" (p. 24). Gillespie introduces memoirs with a brief overview and reads aloud the first few paragraphs of each book. She also reminds students of Calkins's observation that "what appears to be an ordinary event can be meaningful" (pp. 48–49). She uses Romano's ideas of "percolating" as students select a viable personal topic by saving ideas from their own lives, events that upon reflection might reveal something important. She also has them read the memoirs of others as they write their own. Her list (p. 50) includes the following works:

I Know Why the Caged Bird Sings (1970)	Maya Angelou
A Girl from Yamhill: A Memoir (1988)	Beverly Clearly
An American Childhood (1987)	Annie Dillard
Homesick: My Own Story (1982)	Jean Fritz
China Homecoming (1985)	Jean Fritz
The Endless Steppe (1968)	Esther Hautzig
ME ME ME ME ME: NOT A Novel (1983)	M. E. Kerr
The Woman Warrior: Memoirs of a Girlhood Among Ghosts (1976)	Maxine Hong Kingston
Little by Little (1987)	Jean Little
West with the Night (1983)	Beryl Markham
Blue Remembered Hills (1983)	Rosemary Sutcliff
One Writer's Beginnings (1984)	Eudora Welty

Autobiographies and memoirs raise speculative questions about how we write about ourselves as well: What can people tell about me from reading what I write? How much do I want my reader to know? What writing techniques do I use or not use to expose or conceal myself in my writing?

TESTIMONIALS

Carey-Webb (1991) defines testimonials as "edited oral narratives collected from people who by their circumstances cannot write about their own experiences firsthand" (p. 44). Many of the narratives of African-American slaves, Native Americans, Holocaust victims, and survivors of natural catastrophes, airplane crashes, shipwrecks, and dam collapses come to us through testimonials. The breadth and variety of their human experiences and the immediacy of their presentations often make compelling reading. Librarians report that one of the most popular nonfiction books for high school students (on *The New York Times* best-seller list for 7 months) was Piers Paul Read's account of the Uruguayan airplane crash in which only 16 of 46 passengers (most of whom were members of a rugby team) survived. *Alive: The Story of the Andes Survivors* (1974) is based on Read's interviews with survivors, their families and friends, and rescuers.

Carey-Webb describes *I Rigoberta Menchu* (1984), the story of a courageous Guatemalan Indian woman told to a French anthropologist, as one of the "most moving books I have ever read" (p. 44). He sees such testimonials as a "sort of Third World 'autobiography' that brings to the center the experience of the unlettered, marginalized, and oppressed. They are ideal texts in which students and teachers alike attempt to hear the voice of the voiceless, investigate cultural and social differences, and raise questions about what it means to be 'culturally literate'" (p. 44). Carey-Webb's annotated list of these compelling nonfiction testimonials includes the following (adapted from pp. 45–46):

Life Among the Piutes: Their Wrongs and Claims (1969)	Sarah Winnemucca Hopkins	Encounter between the Piutes and nineteenth-century white settlers in Nevada, Oregon, and Washington
Let Me Speak! Testimony of Domitila, A Woman of the Bolivian Mines (1978)	Domitila Barrios de Chungara and Moema Viezzer	Wife of a Bolivian miner witnesses the labor organization of some of Bolivia's poorest
The Testimony of Steve Biko (1978)	Steve Biko	Testimony in the most legal sense
Rachel and Her Children (1988)	Jonathan Kozol	Homeless families in New York describe their lives
Fire from the Mountain (1985)	Omar Cabezas	A Sandinista guerilla tells his story of revolution and struggle

Testimonials in the English Classroom.   Whole- or small-class discussions can focus on the subject of the testimonial with the same kinds of questions that we ask of fiction.

Character	Did you like the subject? Could you identify with the subject? Did you know enough to understand and predict how he or she met difficulty? Would you like to have known more? What details helped you empathize most? Find sentences that you think are especially important in revealing the central character. Did you know enough about other minor characters? Were they well-enough developed to become individuals? Did your regard for any of the characters change as you read?
Setting	Was the setting important to the action? What details helped create the sense of place for you? Did you have enough details? How did it affect your reaction to the story?
Plot	Did the narrative hold your attention? How did the writer create reader interest and suspense? Did you find the events predictable? Where were you surprised? Was your main interest in the testimonial on the subject or on what happened? Did the testimonials reach a satisfactory conclusion?
Point of View	What was the effect on you of how the story was told? Would you have reacted differently had it been told by an objective observer? Would you have liked it better had someone shaped the events and characters of the testimonial into fiction?
Significance	Did the story seem worth telling? Does it add to your understanding of human experience? What ideas came to you as you read it? When you had concluded it? Would you recommend it to others?

Testimony by its nature raises excellent speculative questions for personal writing or discussion:

- What would you consider to be the most difficult crisis the subject describes?
- What do you think you would have done in such a situation? Would you have acted differently?
- What is the greatest fear you have ever known or the gravest crisis you have ever faced?
- Is it easy for you to accept help from others? Would you accept help in a crisis?
- With whom would you like to face a crisis in your own life?
- Would you rather face a sudden, severe crisis or multiple smaller difficulties that linger over time?
- Do you admire or censure how the subject acted in his or her crisis?
- What is your "worst nightmare"?

Students can use testimonials as spurs to record oral histories of those around them who have endured traumatic events. Veterans, survivors, and ordinary people who experience car accidents, urban unrest, rural disasters, tornadoes, and floods live in most communities and are often willing interviewees. (Almost everyone is willing to tell a story in response to the question "What was the most challenging personal catastrophe you ever experienced?") The individual testimonies can be transcribed and written as character sketches, dialogues, or short biographies. A collage of testimonials with photographs or music can become a project for the whole class. Reading the testimonials of others also can provide scripts for Readers' Theater (Chapter 4) or situations for an Accidental Power exercise (Chapter 3).

DIARIES AND JOURNALS

Diaries and journals are two other nonfiction sources infrequently studied in English classrooms, but they are well-worth studying. They can provide glimpses into lived lives that novels only aspire to. More than autobiographies, which are written at some reflective distance, and testimonials, which usually are spoken accounts to others, diaries and journals take us to immediate experience. They also are a particularly important resource for access to the experiences of those who, like most women, have lived in the domestic, rather than the public sphere. Whether kept during a lifetime or through a significant segment of personal or world history, diaries guard their writers against perishable events, impressions, and reflections. *Diary* (from the Latin *diarium,* meaning "daily allowance") connotes a greater privacy, while *journal* (from the Latin *diurnalem,* meaning "daily," and the Old French *journal,* also meaning "daily") suggests a greater public importance; both however, seek to preserve the rapid passage of experience before it sinks into oblivion. Anne Morrow Lindbergh (1971) provides another motive:

> My diaries were written primarily, I think, not to preserve the experience but to savor it, to make it even more real, more visible and palpable, than in actual life. For in our family an experience was not finished, not truly experienced, unless written down or shared with another. (p. xvi)

Students are surprised by the variety and sheer number of published and manuscript diaries kept over the centuries and are more surprised still to discover their gripping interest. They often will have encountered the two best-known English diarists: Samuel Pepys (1633–1703), known for his accounts of major seventeenth-century events, and James Boswell (1740–1795), remembered for his picture of monumental eighteenth-century genius Samuel Johnson. They bear immeasurably valuable witness to public and private history. But others, such as the Rev. John Wesley, Dorothy Wordsworth, Elizabeth Barrett Browning, Charles Darwin, Queen Victoria, and Virginia Woolf, kept daily records of their lives that offer candid glimpses of exterior and interior events. We mentioned as memoirs what were originally journals written by Anne Frank and Etty Hillesum. A remarkable diary was kept in Brazil by Carolina Maria de Jesus (1913–1977). She lived a life of wrenching poverty, had only 2 years of formal education, wrote on notebooks she found in the garbage, and struggled to support herself and her three children by selling scrap paper and metal that she had collected. A reporter found out about her diaries by chance and had them published serially in the newspaper and then later as a book entitled *Child of the Dark* (1962), which became the best-selling book in Brazilian history. Anne Morrow Lindbergh's diaries and letters chronicle her childhood, her youth, her meeting with Charles Lindbergh, her participation in aviation history, and the tragic loss of her first child: *Bring Me a Unicorn* (1971) and *Hour of Gold, Hour of Lead* (1973). She explains that she was encouraged to write an autobiography of her life and times, but instead went to her diaries. Her adolescent diaries cause her particular embarrassment because they are often "self-conscious and self-centered, immature and sentimental." But, she writes (1971), "if one eliminates adolescence from life and records, how much is suppressed: youth, hope, dreams, impractical ideals, falling in love with countless 'not impossible He's,' gaiety that spurs up for no reason, despair that is gone the next morning, and a foretaste of the inevitable tragedies of life along with one's early confused attempts to understand or meet them" (p. xxv). Lindbergh's justification for using her diaries to tell her story is ample testimony to the power of such personal writing.

Diaries and journals are valuable to the English classroom as records of actual events played out in history and literature and as personal testaments to the whole range of human experience. Their immediacy and rare self-disclosure can bedazzle our critical faculties and leave us simply to savor the individual before us and share favorite passages. Like biographies, autobiographies, and testimonials, however, they can be approached with the same questions we raise about literature, especially those surrounding character. Prompts for discussion or writing might include the following:

- This entry exactly described something that I have experienced myself: . . .
- I felt most pain at this entry, because . . .
- I was most uncomfortable at this point because . . .
- If I could enter this life as the subject, I would want to experience this day . . .
- If I could travel with the subject to one time and place, it would be . . .
- If I could ask the subject one question, it would be . . .
- If I could give the subject one bit of advice, it would be . . .
- I envy the subject this one thing: . . .
- I would like to change this one episode or event: . . .

Diaries and journals can also validate, encourage, and model the journal-keeping instincts and possibilities that we value for our students.

LETTERS

Although they are written to an audience, the language of letters, by Dittmer's (1991) account, is "perhaps the closest to natural speech and represents that casual spontaneity we associate with conversation, which makes letters a good form of writing to use with reluctant writers and beginning writers" (p. 24). Even though we delight in writing and receiving letters and treasure the published letters of others, we taught literature for 25 years before we talked formally about letter writing. Mail is so common in our lives, letters so rare. The two get confused. Letters are often treated as impersonal massproduced announcements or as personal ephemera. We want students to pay attention to the possibilities in letter writing. We assume that most of our students are or will be writers and receivers of letters. We ask them to attend to the unexpected richness of language put to everyday use. We want them to discover what American writer Thomas Bailey Aldrich felt: "There's a singular and perpetual charm in a letter."

Teaching Activity 7–3 illustrates our linking of this private writing to the experiences of students. We have used this activity successfully with high school students of all ages and abilities. You will observe that it teaches more than insight into letters by linking letter writing to the private writing of students as well as to the literary letters of others.

Teaching Activity 7–3   Letter Writing

We begin our lesson with caution. We are aware of the danger of drawing attention to something that is very personal and, we hope, spontaneous. We don't want to spoil the natural and introduce self-consciousness and contrivance. But we try to demonstrate that the promise outweighs the danger. Following this disclaimer, we ask students to complete the following survey. While we ask them to commit their responses to paper, we assure them that we will use those responses for discussion only with their permission.

Letter-writing Survey

 1. Do you ever write notes in class to other classmates?
 2. If so, why? If you will see the person later, why take the risk? What drives you to write notes?
 3. How many letters have you received in the last month? From whom have you heard?
 4. How many letters have you written in the last month? Are you writing to anyone out of town or do you write letters to those you could just as easily call?
 5. What prompts you to write letters? Is the motive like your motive for writing notes? Do you see them as anything more than an occasion to pass along information?
 6. What other kind of writing do you do that is not assigned by a teacher?
 7. Which is more important to you, a letter written to you from someone you know and value or a well-written story by an accomplished writer?
 8. What do you think is the most common form of writing for the average adult?
 9. Think for a moment about any of your adult friends or family. What occasions prompt them to put a pen or pencil to paper?
10. Have you ever seen sections of your English textbooks devoted to the writing of letters?
11. Do teachers ever discuss letters as an important form of writing?
12. What does your work in class lead you to conclude is the premier genre of writing? Novels? Short stories? Poems? Personal memoirs? Diaries? Journals? Letters?

We discuss the written answers to these personal questions with the whole group. With the class sensitized and conscious of letter writing, we move to the students' own writing. Here is the sequence of our in-class assignments and our instructions.

1. Note to a Classmate

a. Begin by writing a note to a partner, a note about anything that's on your mind at this moment, the kind of note you might write in any given school day. Be candid. A public reading of your note will be undertaken only with your approval.
b. Now send your note, read your correspondent's note, and respond on the back. Return the note to its origin.
c. Talk as a class about what just happened. If I were to spy on your note writing and say "All right, Leah, is that something you'd like to share with the class?" would you be embarrassed? Is your communication that confidential? What delights you in writing the note? In receiving it? What kind of message does it contain? What was the best note you ever remember receiving in a class? If you are not a note-passer, have you ever envied those who are?

2. Postcard to Your Family

a. Shift your location from the classroom to home. Imagine that your family is away for 2 weeks and you find a postcard from them in the mailbox. Here is what it says:

> Everything is going well. The food is good. The company is enjoyable.
> I wish you were here. I want to hear from you. Please write.

b. Write a postcard responding to this request.
c. Exchange cards with another student and talk together about what you've each written to your family.
d. How do these cards differ from notes written to a classmate? Which interested you more? In which was the writer the most spontaneous? Which had the greater specificity? Substance? Imagination?
e. Would any of you read your postcards to the class? If you were the family member reading this account, would you have additional questions that you'd like to ask of the writer?

f. Cartoonist Gary Larson has a number of cartoons featuring letters. (We distribute several *Far Side* cartoons involving letter writing between animal families and friends.) Do you notice anything in these cartoons that reminds you of your experiences with letters?

3. Letters to a Friend

a. Imagine now that a friend, rather than your family, is away. Write a letter or postcard back to that friend.

b. Don't share this correspondence. Is there any difference between it and what you wrote to your family? If so, what?

c. Consider this observation of Arthur Schopenhauer: "If you want to discover your true opinion of anybody, observe the impression made on you by the first sight of a letter from him."

4. Published Letters

Read the excerpt from a seventeenth-century letter of Madame de Sevigne (1626–1696) (Figure 7–3). She was writing to her daughter about a royal house party during which a disconsolate cook took surprising action. (Many other letters, of course, would serve for this activity.)

a. Does Madame de Sevigne describe the scene sufficiently for you to imagine it? Can you imagine a cook or restaurant owner in our day becoming equally as distraught as Vatel over the food and the service? How were Vatel's circumstances different from ours today? Have you ever been so publicly embarrassed or privately guilt-stricken for letting someone down that you despaired? Are you surprised by the reaction of the court to his death?

b. Imagine that you are a friend of Vatel and that you observe his misery on this night and want to write something that will comfort and calm him. Write that note.

c. A contemporary of Madame de Sevigne once said, "When you have read one of Madame de Sevigne's letters you feel a slight pang, because you have one less to read." Can you see in this excerpt why she was valued by her contemporaries?

d. Does this letter interest you, more than three centuries after it was written? Does it provide any insight of value to you? What impresses you about it?

e. Model Madame de Sevigne by describing an event or situation in your recent life. Can you imagine what someone in 300 years might make of what you are describing?

We go on to read and discuss a variety of published letters. They include a range of writers—Lord Chesterfield, Abraham Lincoln, Emily Dickinson, George Eliot, Rainer Maria Rilke, Anne Morrow Lindbergh, H. L. Mencken, Etty Hillesum, Flannery O'Connor, and Leslie Marmon Silko—and of letter types—anecdotal, reflective, satiric, humorous, and literary. Our approach to these letters varies. Often we give groups a number of letters and ask them to select those that they want to share with the whole class. Discussion easily follows the groups' oral reading. Questions that readily open discussion include the following: Had you received this letter, how would you have responded? Have you ever gotten such a letter? Does it make you want to write back?

The published exchange of letters between correspondents adds the dimension of a dialogue. Reading the give-and-take between two minds resembles eavesdropping (which may account for the power of these collections). For instance, some of our students have been entranced by a slim volume of letters between the poets Leslie Marmon Silko and James Wright, *The Strength and Delicacy of Lace* (1986). Our students have also been intrigued with fictional letters. C. S. Lewis wrote a robust batch, *The Screwtape Letters* (1959), between an older devil, Screwtape, and his apprentice nephew, a fledgling devil, Wormwood, to present a theological argument about the nature of the human struggle between good and evil.

5. Letters to the Teacher

The unit concludes with student letters to the teacher in which they explore their reaction to the unit. (If the easy spontaneity of the other activities is threatened by this final letter, we would advise against this assignment.)

Many teachers find letters engaging as focuses of study in themselves and as supplements to other units of study. Dittmer (1991) suggests a letter writing assignment that he says has produced some of the best writing he has received from students. He asks them "to write a letter in which they confirm or reestablish a relationship. They can write to someone real or imaginary, living or dead, animal or human, and if appropriate, they should consider sending it to the party to whom it is written" (pp. 21–22). Teachers report the popularity of a collection of letters from American soldiers, *Dear America: Letters Home from Vietnam* (1985). The letters range from the tragic to the humorous, from the bitter to the

FIGURE 7–3
Madame de Sevigne's letter

Paris, Sunday, April 26, 1671

This is Sunday, April 26th, and this letter will not go out till Wednesday; but it is not so much a letter as a narrative that I have just learned from Moreuil, of what passed at Chantilly with regard to poor Vatel. I wrote to you last Friday that he had stabbed himself—these are the particulars of the affair: The king arrived there on Thursday night; the walk, and the collation, which was served in a place set apart for the purpose, and strewed with jonquils, were just as they should be. Supper was served, but there was no roast meat at one or two of the tables, on account of Vatel's having been obliged to provide several dinners more than were expected. This affected his spirits, and he was heard to say, several times: "I have lost my honor! I can not bear this disgrace!" "My head is quite bewildered," said he to Gourville. "I have not had a wink of sleep these twelve nights; I wish you would assist me in giving orders." Gourville did all he could to comfort and assist him; but the failure of the roast meat (which, however, did not happen at the king's table, but at some of the other twenty-five), was always uppermost with him. Gourville mentioned it to the prince, who went directly to Vatel's apartment, and said to him: "Every thing is extremely well conducted, Vatel; nothing could be more admirable than his majesty's supper." "Your highness's goodness," replied he, "overwhelms me; I am sensible that there was a deficiency of roast meat at two tables." "Not at all," said the prince; "do not perplex yourself, and all will go well." Midnight came: the fireworks did not succeed, they were covered with a thick cloud; they cost sixteen thousand francs. At four o'clock in the morning Vatel went round and found every body asleep; he met one of the under-purveyors, who was just come in with only two loads of fish. "What!" said he, "is this all?" "Yes, sir," said the man, not knowing that Vatel had dispatched other people to all the sea-ports around. Vatel waited for some time; the other purveyors did not arrive; his head grew distracted; he thought there was no more fish to be had. He flew to Gourville: "Sir," said he, "I can not outlive this disgrace." Gourville laughed at him. Vatel, however, went to his apartment, and setting the hilt of his sword against the door, after two ineffectual attempts, succeeded in the third in forcing his sword through his heart. At that instant the carriers arrived with the fish; Vatel was inquired after to distribute it. They ran to his apartment, knocked at the door, but received no answer, upon which they broke it open, and found him weltering in his blood. A messenger was immediately dispatched to acquaint the prince with what had happened, who was like a man in despair. The duke wept, for his Burgundy journey depended upon Vatel. The prince related the whole affair to his majesty with an expression of great concern; it was considered as the consequence of too nice a sense of honor; some blamed, others praised him for his courage. The king said he had put off this excursion for more than five years, because he was aware that it would be attended with infinite trouble, and told the prince that he ought to have had but two tables, and not have been at the expense of so many, and declared he would never suffer him to do so again; but all this was too late for poor Vatel. However, Gourville attempted to supply the loss of Vatel, which he did in great measure. The dinner was elegant, the collation was the same. They supped, they walked, they hunted; all was perfumed with jonquils, all was enchantment. Yesterday, which was Saturday, the same entertainments were renewed, and in the evening the king set out for Liancourt, where he had ordered a *medianoche;* he is to stay there three days. This is what Moreuil has told me, hoping I should acquaint you with it. I wash my hands of the rest, for I know nothing about it. M. D'Hacqueville, who was present at the scene, will, no doubt, give you a faithful account of all that passed; but, because his hand-writing is not quite so legible as mine, I write too; if I am circumstantial, it is because, on such an occasion, I should like circumstantiality myself.

patriotic. One teacher reports that they give students "a perspective not available in traditional history textbooks" (Shaw, 1991, p. 25). Shaw intensified the class reading with a film by the same title (from Home Box Office), which provides a visual backdrop against which many actors read hundreds of letters. Another enterprising teacher (Perrin, 1991) used his junk mail to teach lessons about analyzing audience, searching for "poetic" language, identifying persuasion, analyzing meaning through close reading, developing vocabulary, and writing synopses (pp. 30–32). We have used letters both to clinch discussions and to provide a more public audience for writing. At the end of an integrated unit on war poetry and persuasive writing, during which students research and position themselves on a current topic, we ask them to present their strongest ideas in letters to the local newspaper editor. We know teachers who use letters for another motive: informing and communicating with parents. They ask students to write periodic letters home about what they are experiencing in English.

MISCELLANEOUS NONFICTION BOOKS

Many full-length nonfiction books fall within the categories of biographies, autobiographies, memoirs, testimonials, and published diaries, but the array of other categories extends from Bruce Catton's histories of the American Civil War to David Macaulay's illustrated books, such as *Cathedral* (1973), *Motel of the Mysteries* (1979), and *The Way Things Work* (1988). Abrahamson and Carter (1987) describe their attending a convention where adolescent nonfiction reading interests were being discussed and observing that the librarians in the audience were nodding knowingly, while the English teachers looked bewildered (p. 104). Librarians, who respond to student queries and check out their book selections, often know more about the reading habits of students than those of us in English classrooms surrounded by novels, poems, and plays. From librarians we have heard the strongest appeals to address the students' desire to know how to survive in this world and their eagerness to read those books that give

FIGURE 7–4
Teachers' choices:
books of nonfiction

Hiroshima (1946)	John Hersey
A Night to Remember (1955)	Walter Lord
The Dog Who Wouldn't Be (1957)	Farley Mowat
Night (1960)	Elie Wiesel
Travels with Charley (1962)	John Steinbeck
Ishi: Last of His Tribe (1964)	Theodora Kroeber
Growing Up Female in America: Ten Lives (1971)	Eve Merriam, Ed.
The Hiding Place (1971)	Corrie ten Boom
Gone for a Soldier: The Civil War Memoirs of Alfred Bellard (1975)	David Herbert Donald, Ed.
Dove (1978)	Robin Lee Graham
First Person Rural (1978)	Noel Perrin
A Walk Across America (1979)	Peter Jenkins
Queen Eleanor: Independent Spirit of the Medieval World (1983)	Polly Schoyer Brooks
From Russia to USSR: A Narrative and Documentary History (1985)	Janet G. Vaillant and John Richards II
One Writer's Beginnings (1985)	Eudora Welty
Under the Eye of the Clock (1987)	Christopher Nolan

them clues. They point to the popularity of informational books on topics of importance to them, such as the relationships between men and women, families, music, sports, work, college admissions, suicide, and drugs. Popular titles themselves reflect those interests: Richard Moll's *The Public Ivys* (1985), Clifford J. Caine's *How to Get into College* (1985), and Torey Hayden's *One Child* (1980).

An *English Journal* "Booksearch," in 1984 and another in 1990 asked its readers: "What books of nonfiction narrative have you found useful in the classroom?" As shown in Figure 7–4, teachers suggested books that take the reader through centuries, from the second and third Crusades, to the American Civil War, to the twentieth-century Russian Revolution, the sinking of the *Titanic,* the Holocaust, and Hiroshima, and on a post-Vietnam walking tour of the United States. The editors of the *English Journal* wrote that in "nonfiction we see how events shape people's lives, and we learn about our own" through "narratives of lives and events as intriguing as any work of fiction" (1990a, p. 91). Nilsen and Donelson have put three books of history on their annual adolescent literature honor list: *The Long Road to Gettysburg* (1992) by Jim Murphy, *Unconditional Surrender: U. S. Grant and the Civil War* (1994) by Albert Marrin, and *When Plague Strikes: The Black Death, Smallpox, AIDS* (1995) by James Cross Giblin.

These merely suggest the range of titles and subjects available, but they are enough, we hope, to validate reading that you too may have enjoyed and to encourage you to consider it for your classrooms. The appearance of good new books is constant. Nonfiction often has a shorter shelf life than fiction does, but that should not discourage you or your students from recognizing and holding onto quality when you find it. Listed in Table 7–1 are nonfiction titles popular with adolescent readers and a suggestion about the subject matter that contributes to their appeal.

Of course, no externally provided list of texts will be as good as the ones that individual teachers make through wide reading and sensitive awareness of the students before them. We would encourage you to start immediately to collect nonfiction pieces of any length that attract you because of their interest as stories, their grace of expression, or their keenness of insight. We read anything we can find, long or short works, by writers such as the following:

Sven Birkerts (culture critic and essayist)	Gerald Johnson (journalist)
Freeman Dyson (physicist)	Primo Levi (chemist)
Roger Ebert (movie reviewer)	C. S. Lewis (medieval scholar)
Loren Eiseley (scientist)	Margaret Mead (anthropologist)
Adam Gopnik (essayist)	H. L. Mencken (social critic and writer)
Meg Greenfield (editorialist)	V. S. Naipaul (writer)
Stephen Hawking (astronomer)	Lewis Thomas (medical doctor)
Carolyn G. Heilbrun (literature critic)	Barbara Tuchman (historian)
Etty Hillesum (diarist)	E. B. White (journalist and author)

If reading full-length works is not feasible, we encourage you to use excerpts from longer books. Some feel that such borrowing violates the original source. Certainly an argument can be made that the intention and force of the original is compromised. But our concern for what the text provokes for the student overrides these reservations. Indeed, high school students often can enter the writer's world more easily with a short piece than with one that stretches the limits of their reading time. We cull and save newspaper articles and editorials, books of aphorisms, lines of biographies, paragraphs of history, phrases from published letters, captions of cartoons, and single words that strike us as *right* anywhere we find them. We encourage our students to be their own savorers as well.

TABLE 7–1
Popular nonfiction
books

Title	Author	Subject
Zen and the Art of Motorcycle Maintenance: An Inquiry into Values (1974)	Robert M. Pirsig	How to negotiate a problematic world
Dove (1972)	Robin Graham	Endurance and survival of a school dropout who sails around the world
Adrift: Seventy-Six Days Lost at Sea (1986)	Steven Callahan	Story of survival on a 5-foot rubber raft in the Atlantic
Blood Games: A True Account of Family Murder (1991)	Jerry Bledsoe	Story of a family murder in North Carolina
Cruel Doubt (1991)	Joe McGinniss	Story of a family murder in North Carolina
Helter Skelter (1974)	Vincent Bugliosi and Curt Genry	Account of the murders committed in California by members of the Manson "family"
All Creatures Great and Small (1972) *All Things Bright and Beautiful* (1974) *All Things Wise and Wonderful* (1977) *The Lord God Made Them All* (1981)	James Herriot	The ordinary events in the life of a country veterinarian in Yorkshire, England
Working: People Talk About What They Do All Day and How They Feel About What They Do (1974)	Studs Terkel	Interviews of working people
Never Cry Wolf (1963)	Farley Mowat	Description of the work of a naturalist with the Canadian Wildlife Service among the wolves of the Canadian tundra

NEWSPAPERS

Nelms (1990) explains that "magazine and newspaper columnists can help wake up our students; columns bring them into the world of current events and issues, and challenge them to observe and reflect on the world around them" (p. 79). Students experience the pleasure of an inward "so someone else has felt that." These columns create the effect of having "us look at life and at ourselves as we live it" (p. 79). Mitchell (1996) observes that newspapers naturally appeal to students and are filled with a variety of types of writing. She asks students to examine newspapers in order to review and connect ideas in the literature the class has been discussing. Before she arrives with the papers, she lists with students what they have read, viewed, discussed, and written in the two preceding weeks. She brings enough copies of her daily newspaper so that each student can look for articles about "any issues or ideas we have touched on in the last two weeks" (p. 78).

We like to bring editorials from the morning paper to class because their recognizable and compelling subjects engage students. The editorialists' observations often pull students toward insights that they would not entertain on their own and toward the power of language to express those insights. The *English Journal's* "Booksearch" feature (1990b, pp. 79–82) asked readers what magazine column or syndicated newspaper column and columnists that they had found to be effective in their classrooms. The readers discussed columnists Erma Bombeck, D. L. Stewart, Dave Barry, Mike Royko, Bill Stokes, Anna Quindlen, William Safire, and Bob Greene. We add to that list some of our favorites, influenced of course by the choices of our local paper's editors: Russel Baker, Meg Greenfield, Ellen Goodman, Donald Kaul, George Will, William Buckley, and Molly Ivins. We also like to collect several editorials on a single issue. Divergent positions and deepening perspectives enlarge students' views. Because differences of opinion attract student enjoyment of a good fight, these editorials provide natural prompts for engaged thinking. They also can model a rarity in our civic life: honest disagreement about an issue that doesn't resort to the personal. One assignment that grows from these comparisons asks students in pairs to construct a pro and con editorial page on a selected issue.

The columns mentioned by *English Journal* readers were "First Person" in *Cyclist Magazine,* "Metropolitan Diary" in the *New York Times,* and "The Talk of the Town" in *The New Yorker.*

Nonfiction in the Fiction Classroom

We have described links that we make between fiction and nonfiction, links of subject matter and style. We also use the following nonfiction models indirectly in responding to fiction:

1. *letters* of advice, counsel, condolence, and outrage to characters, to authors, and between characters and authors
2. *interviews* of characters or authors by students or other characters and authors
3. *dialogues* between characters from different books
4. *epitaphs* of characters
5. *journal or diary entries* of characters
6. selecting what might be the favorite *proverbs* or *maxims* of characters
7. selecting *aphorisms* that could be drawn from having read a piece of literature
8. using Ambrose Bierce's *The Devil's Dictionary* as an example from which to write *definitions* of qualities as the book's author or characters might write them
9. imaginative *speeches:*
   - Mae Tuck of *Tuck Everlasting* being the keynote speaker at the national convention of the American Association of Retired Persons (AARP)
   - Huck Finn, testifying before a Congressional Committee on runaways
   - Stella Willis of *Home Before Dark* explaining to her guidance counselors why she chooses to live alone, apart from her family
   - Ishi from *Ishi: Last of His Tribe* talking to a group of anthropologists
10. *lists* of characters or authors studied in categories of the class's own making. Easy models for categories are the superlative sections (Best Athlete, Most Likely to Succeed, and so on) of many high school yearbooks. Imagine such a section in Trinity High of *The Chocolate War.* Top-ten lists can rank categories of all sorts from Top-ten Best Characters (Most Like to Spend a Vacation With, Most One-dimensional, Most Like Me) to Top-ten selections of literature studied.
11. *newspaper articles* about an event in a work, a *feature story* about a character, an *editorial* about an idea, and an *obituary* of a character

Conclusion

In sum, nonfiction can be a valuable resource in any lesson at any time. Like devotees of the "Holy Three," many of our high school students (often those most partial to English) at first devalue nonfiction as a poor kinsperson of fiction and consider our use of it to be "a holding pattern" until we land again with serious literature. Simply on the level of language, however, it provides invaluable lessons. Language is set apart from imaginative story and character, and thus it can sometimes be scrutinized more directly and its power perceived more keenly than in literary analysis. Considering style apart from literary genre springs students free from literary categories and biases. It provides a more generic demonstration of how the skillful presentation of any subject can dramatically increase its power. Enthusiasm about individual words, the way phrases are put together, how sentences work, how an argument moves, how an image crystallizes, how a caption functions—all enthusiasms over nonfiction— can teach a great deal about the pure play and potential of language. Then students do not so easily mistake carefully crafted language as isolated only in a pristine enclave called "literature," written by rare geniuses, and accessible primarily to "elected" scholars and critics. Rather, the skillful use of language surrounds us and can surprise those with the confidence and openness to recognize it, even in our morning newspaper and magazine cartoons.

Students often ask English teachers for recommendations of good books. We believe that teachers need to base their answers not on a sorting operation of their personal library shelves, but on taking stock of the individuals before them. For the first years of teaching, one of us was often made miserable by the very question she should have welcomed, because she was never sure that the stock of novels that she had read would appeal just to this or that student. Only when she began to trust her pleasures in nonfiction (and the necessity to recommend books she had not actually read) did she have a wide enough inventory from which to pull promising titles.

We believe that high school English teachers should take nonfiction into their teaching. The divisions between literature and "nonliterature" are imposed on students by texts and teachers, and they harm both those who love literature and those who feel it to be alien. Embracing both without disparaging one and extolling another frees students to appreciate what the printed word brings to their lives wherever they find it. Nonfiction may even bring some to a discovery that eluded them in the more traditional genres of fiction, poetry, and drama.

8 MAKING MEDIA MATTER

A major new medium changes the structure of discourse; it does so by encouraging certain uses of the intellect, by favoring certain definitions of intelligence and wisdom, and by demanding a certain kind of content—in a phrase, by creating new forms of truth-telling.

Neil Postman

Sven Burkerts (1995) believes that the book world is in its death throes. The fast-paced world of media will soon bury books as we know them. Is Burkerts overreacting? Are English teachers overlooking something essential and enlivening? Oscar Wilde offers his view of the new media of his day with a quip: "There is much to be said in favor of modern journalism. By giving us the opinions of the uneducated, it keeps us in touch with the ignorance of the community." Wilde's disregard for the media and the general public may, in some sense, be valid, but we don't want students to disengage from the world entirely.

The word *media* is so common in contemporary life that we use it freely without precisely understanding its meaning. To arrive at a working definition of the term, we must start by thinking of as many media forms as possible. When we enumerate the different media—compact disc player, VCR, telephone, slide projector, television, bumper sticker, radio, FAX, overhead projector, e-mail, newspaper, CD ROM, and billboard—a definition begins to emerge. Can you see a central purpose in these disparate forms?

Invitation to Reflection 8–1

Before reading this chapter, answer these questions about media in the classroom:

• Have media other than books ever been a part of the English instruction you have known as a student?
• If so, how were they used:
  To enrich the study of written texts?
  To vivify a lesson?
  To examine each media as a separate form of popular art?
  To explore the impact of media on our culture?
  To prompt writing?

- Which of these media would you find most inviting and promising for classroom study?
  Television
  Film
  Magazines
  Newspapers
  Radio
  Comics
  Art (painting, prints, photographs, sculpture)
- Would you make a distinction in this list between forms of media for mass, often commercial consumption and those with a rarer, more artful purpose? Which on the list would you consider "high" culture and which "popular" culture?
- Do your own personal interests and style suggest media approaches that ought or ought not to be undertaken?
- Do you think that the study of media itself is
  relevant to English classrooms?
  important in understanding our culture?
  important in understanding ourselves?
  a capitulation to mass culture?

How would you answer these questions about media in your personal life? (They may be questions that you will want to pose with your students.)

- Do you consider the media in your life to be a source of entertainment? Education? Liberation?
- Which of the following technical means of access to media do you frequently rely on in your daily life?
  Television
  VCR
  Tape recorder
  Radio
  CD player
  Movie theater
- To what media form do you turn in your leisure time? Would you seek that resource before talking with a friend, writing in a journal, or reading a book?
- When you are alone, how often do you fill the silence with music or TV: 25%, 50%, 75%, or 100% of the time?
- Does television or film influence your assumptions and aspirations about your life?
- Do you think that you are influenced in your desires by advertising?
- Through what source do you get your information about the news of the world?
- Do you consider some media less biased, more straightforward, and more objective than others?
- When you go on a trip, do you feel frustrated if you do not have a camera with you to record your experience?
- If you have ever been at a stadium or coliseum with a wide screen, have you ever found yourself watching the screen as well as the event before you?
- Do you know anyone (perhaps even yourself) for whom some media form is more real than lived life?

Figure 8-1 is a graphic representation of media's classroom possibilities. Let us make sense of this graphic organizer. We start at the foundation level with the concrete *Products* of media: student-created productions (Mimic) and professional creations (Entertain). We then move to the upper level of *Process* where students consider how the various media work (Examine) and how they influence us (Expose). The graphic can thus be sliced horizontally with a lower foundation of concrete *Products* and an upper realm of abstractions or ideas about the *Process* of media.

The media graphic also can be sliced vertically into Compose on the left side and Comprehend on the right side. The left side of the lower level contains teaching ideas that invite students to create productions based on the media models that surround them. We call this *Mimic* because students imitate or copy the forms developed by others. The right side of the lower level employs the powerful appeal of media to bring its carefully constructed language, sound, and images to the classroom. For instance, multiple versions of the opening scenes of *Macbeth* on CD-ROM, Beatles' music that nicely parallels Edward Arlington Robinson's poetry, and videotapes of America's 10 best commercials all invite students to *Entertain* the artful craft of verbal, visual, and auditory images. The left and right

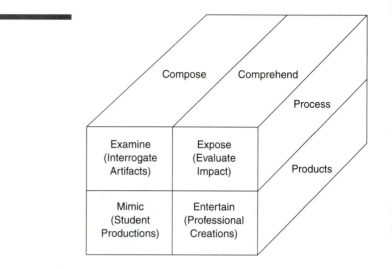

FIGURE 8–1
Media literacy

sides of the upper level are ways of exploring the *Process* of media. The left side is more interactive and constructive because when students *Examine* the media, they make their own analysis of the process of media and its impact on the culture. Students might look at the target audience of the various ads on television to determine how special groups are being targeted, or they might consider the difference between the top-ten pop hits of 1977 and 1997. On the right side, students would become aware of both the negative and positive impact of the various media. We want to *Expose* students to media's impact through ideas presented by the teacher, assigned articles, and materials that students find on their own.

Each of the four possibilities can stake a strong claim for being used in the English classroom. Your choices will be based on a number of variables: you, your students, your resources, and your environment. As you consider the teaching possibilities in these four approaches to media, consider Susan Sontag's warning in *Against Interpretation* (1967):

> Ours is a culture based on excess, on overproduction; the result is a steady loss of sharpness in our sensory experience. All the conditions of modern life—its material plenitude, its sheer crowd-edness—conjoin to dull our sensory faculties. What is important now is to recover our senses. We must learn to see more, to hear more, to feel more. (pp. 13–14)

We believe that all four approaches need to be a part of an English teacher's repertoire to help us awaken our students. But we want to begin with those that lie at the foundational level because they are the most useful in developing language awareness in our students.

MIMIC: STUDENTS AS PRODUCERS

The initial approach to media offers students a chance to create and produce TV programs, newspapers, magazines, cartoons, comics, drawings, and photographs. We are not suggesting that English teachers mimic highly technical and ambitious media productions in their regular English classrooms. What we suggest more modestly involves students in media production in the service of language enrichment. Our objective will be to harness the power that the visual and the auditory dimensions of media bring to the spoken and written word.

This kind of media production has a natural appeal: It appropriates for the classroom a cultural phenomenon that is familiar, persuasive, and powerful in the lives of most students. They know the context almost intuitively and thus they can quickly understand and manipulate media for a variety of purposes. Beyond its natural appeal, though, asking students to be producers invites them to be active language users. Thompson (1988) summarizes the power of this expressive use: "Perhaps the best way to be an active learner and to exercise all mental abilities is through *expression*—actually producing videos rather than watching television, for instance. The formulation of an expression demands very complex mental activity, in which all the impressions that have been gathered . . . are utilized . . ." (p. 49). Students then are putting "words on world," as Moffett and Wagner counsel. They are acting, not passively receiving. An analogy can be drawn: Reading is to writing as viewing is to producing. Reading and viewing are essential for our enrichment, but to move to the act of writing or producing is to appropriate what we have received for our own purposes. Using media as a structure for production gives a natural push toward students' lively interaction with their worlds.

FIGURE 8–2
Media activities

Language Arts Skills	12 Classroom Activities											
	Juxtaworlds	Madison Avenue	Rock Review	Piggyback Pop	Jacketeering	Rock Market	Anchor People	Crisis Interview	Pilot Making	Class Magazine	Classy Comics	Bumper Stickers
Playing with words												
Discerning an audience												
Recognizing a dramatic context												
Developing a character												
Compressing language												
Selecting richly connotative words and images												
Combining the unexpected												
Selecting and organizing material												
Sequencing ideas												
Shaping an argument												
Summarizing												
Creating and producing a piece												
Manipulating methods of persuasion												
Comprehending a position												
Choosing appropriate language for a context												
Exercising the imagination												
Posing questions												

We include an example of the kind of "learning by experience" that media production opens up. Teacher Teresa Regina (1988) gives a nice example of the learning effects of composing a TV show, in this case a sports report:

> It gave the opportunity to introduce style and format of presentation. Indeed, a review of the football season, which had not been very eventful, would have been boring if recounted game by game. However, as students became more familiar and comfortable with editing, they saw that segments could be selected from the season and placed to music. Those who spent much time on the project found sequences with similar actions or camera positions and enhanced the sound tracks by inserting interviews or players' comments. (p. 50)

She goes on to explain what the composing of a production revealed to students: "As words and sentences are placed in an order and in a particular form to reveal style and tone, so sound and visual images must be ordered. The process of selection, of deciding what is to be included or excluded, continues throughout the production process. If composing involves talking, reading, writing, thinking, and communicating, then video production is composing in a most exciting and creative way" (p. 52). Asking students to engage in those acts of composition deepens their awareness of the similar acts of professionals in any media.

Figure 8–2 presents 12 activities that ask students to produce media events. We intend these activities to function as more than an abbreviated cookbook. They do have ingredients and directions for student productions, but they are intended primarily to prompt your creative ideas, to provide examples of varied possibilities for production, and to illustrate the range of language experiences that are possible through production projects. We think that they may carry our message better than an extended explanation of the potential of media to stimulate language play and production in the classroom. Each prompts students to borrow from a format that is well known to them to produce a facsimile in the classroom. We will enumerate each activity in broad outline and suggest uses to which it may be put. Figure 8–2 presents in its left column language arts skills that many of the activities promote. We have not checked just which skills might possibly be learned in each activity. We invite you to consider those connections and to note others.

JUXTAWORLDS

Students are asked to juxtapose the words and images of poetry with the images of advertising and thereby to create an original piece. Students may work in groups or as individuals. They are asked to set single lines, a group of lines, or an entire short poem to the advertising images. Thus, their original pieces will be presented to the class as either the visual ads of television with poetry voiced over the original script or the print ads of magazines or newspapers with the oral accompaniment of poetry.

The commercial images of advertising reflect the sophisticated work of professional advertising people and photographers. They are usually targeted toward a specific audience with the single-minded aim of persuading that audience to buy a product. Consequently, the ads are usually short, vivid, carefully focused and paced, richly connotative, original, and memorable. The quality of these commercial images can be profitably discussed during this project. Their success can be measured with some of the same standards with which the images and impact of poetry are assessed.

An interesting side effect of this exercise is that the words of the poetry and the power and vitality of its imagery can be reinforced every time its newly juxtaposed commercial ad appears on the screen or in print. For example, Walt Whitman's "Song of Myself" can be set to the Chevrolet ad, "The Heartbeat of America." The melody and images of the song may come to evoke Whitman's words as well as Chevy cars. Or, in a more somber example, the ironic juxtaposition of Wilfred Owen's anti-war poetry with the army's "Be All That You Can Be," might make it difficult to hear that advertisement uncritically.

This exercise can enrich, enliven, and clinch the study of a single poet or poem, a number of poets or poems in a unit, or selected poets or poems from a whole term.

MADISON AVENUE

In this activity, students are challenged to use their imaginations and their skill with words and actions to create a new product and develop a 30-second commercial for television. The imagination demanded to create a new product is paralleled by that needed to develop the advertisement that will market it. Students complete this activity best in stages. A successful approach that we have used follows.

1. Teams of seven or eight students are given a plastic soft-drink bottle, a plain paper box, or a squat cylindrical packet and asked to come up with a new product.
2. After each of the teams has come up with its product, students use crayons and paper to create a label for the container.
3. The group then develops the action and script for a 30-second commercial with actors, product, jingle, and announcer.
4. The groups each take turns in a room where their creations are videotaped.
5. The teams' ads are presented to a panel of advertising professionals for review and comment or to another class, which ranks the ads using a set of criteria developed by the original class.

ROCK REVIEW

Rock music is one of the most powerful media for adolescents, and its capacity to promote language can be demonstrated by a number of projects. One approach is to let trios assume studio production responsibility for a local rock station; they must create a script for a 2-hour broadcast. (Students more devoted to country, classical, or classic rock music could organize competing programming.) A series of 15 to 20 hot recordings with 30 seconds or less of commentary for each is the goal for the 10 or so groups in the class. The productions are judged on the basis of their selections, the sequence they form, and the language that is used to promote them. All members of the audience (teacher and students) critique it. (Each group is allowed to play only one song during its "broadcast.") If the class is energized by the project, students might collapse the best scripts and present them to a local station.

PIGGYBACK POP

Another approach to the domain of rock music is to add lyrics to existing songs. A song such as John Lennon's "Imagine" promotes imaginings of additional lines or verses. In Lennon's song, the first verse deals with religion, the second with politics, the third with economics, and the last is a coda, or conclusion. A new fourth stanza could be added to extend Lennon's basic philosophy by imagining that which is not, but ought to be in the world we know: education, friendship, or peace. (To provide interest and clearer thinking, dissenting students could write a satirical set of stanzas that stand Lennon's ideas on their head.)

JACKETEERING

Another approach to the medium of music is to ask students to draw up a list of 40 or 50 titles of what they consider to be the best music being played today. Small groups of students are then given the list and asked to categorize the music by its thematic center. Some songs defy categorization, of course, and these can be discarded or assigned to a miscellaneous category. The groups are then responsible for selecting two or more of the categories they developed to create a thematic album of 15 to 20 songs. The students create a title for the album and a jacket cover that explains the special collection and comments on each of the songs in it.

ROCK MARKET

Just as a pilot TV show tries to anticipate trends and project a marketable theme for a soap or sit-com, this project asks students to locate an audience, develop a core idea or thrust for a song, and create lyrics that make sense for that context. The selection of an audience should be somewhat specific at first, for example, pop, rock, blues, country, progressive, rap, or heavy metal. That selection will rule out certain themes and encourage others. Can you imagine, for instance, the Beatles singing a Willie Nelson ballad? Once a few general themes are considered (students working alone or in large groups can do this), a set of lyrics needs to be written. To help ideas flow, the class could be asked to list 8 to 10 words that would likely be associated with each of the musical categories. Each group then tries to use two or three of these as key words in its lyrics. Putting words together with feeling and sense is the goal.

ANCHOR PEOPLE

Another direction to take with television is spawned by the slightly more serious world of news broadcasting. Consider a current story of national or international urgency. If a class is large, two stories might be used, with half the students being given the first and the other half the second. Each of these groups is in turn divided into as many groups of four as possible. Each of the quartets takes its story and, in pairs, fashions a strong liberal or vigorous conservative bias into a 40-second news story. Each pair writes its script and creates stick-figure visuals that punctuate the script. Then the two pairs actually produce a videotape of that 40-second slot for an evening news program. The other students critique the news spots after they have viewed them. They might even continue in a television idiom by expressing their reactions in a point-counterpoint or news talk-show format.

CRISIS INTERVIEW

This is one of the most reliably successful pieces of media mimicry. The interview should be recorded on audiotape or even videotape if students dress for it and create a proper backdrop and props. The focus should be on language, however, not on the physical objects. A designated reporter interviews onlookers at the scene of a catastrophe or an unusual event. The questions and responses of all participants are spontaneous. Here are scenarios that have worked for us:

- Tourists at the scene of a hot-air balloon crash at the rim of the Grand Canyon
- Chicago firefighters at the site of a conflagration caused, it seems, by a gas explosion at a restaurant
- A trio of pedestrians at the foot of Radio City Music Hall, where an unidentified woman threatens suicide on a ledge 16 floors up
- A group of rodeo clowns who have just discovered that an unidentified novice has entered the bull-riding contest on a dare
- The community and family of the boy killed in Robert Frost's "Out, Out," or of Richard Cory in Edwin Arlington Robinson's "Richard Cory," or of Emily Grierson in William Faulkner's "A Rose for Emily"

The special nature of each place and crisis event makes it easy for the reporter to ask strong questions. Because these are well-defined crises, the respondents find it very easy to build spontaneously a shared story, and the language that flows from the vignette is almost always authentic and bold. Students do not plan it; it just moves. Because students are projecting into a critical life event, the language matures to meet the expectations of that particular situation. The episode is recorded on tape, and thus, it can be easily transcribed into a dramatic scene with directions and rewritten as a radio play. After reshaping it, another group can rehearse and finally perform it. Students can then compare the original and the revised versions to decide which is most powerful, most true.

PILOT MAKING

Students know a great deal more about soaps and sit-coms than about Chaucer and Dickens. Their literacy in the media world can help them create a pilot for a new dramatic series that might introduce them to elements essential to the study of a story, elements, say, of character, dramatic conflict, and plot. The students' task is not actually to make the pilot, but to create the general format for the entire project.

- We ask students working in pairs or as larger teams to come up with a set of two or three characters who are delineated in such a way that conflict naturally occurs between and among them.
- A context for their relationship must be established as well: the kitchen of an exclusive restaurant, the office of an elementary school, or a life-guard station at the beach. A novel situation that is uncommon in the popular media is preferable.
- Students are asked to imagine the nature of possible conflicts that would arise from *these* characters in *this* setting.
- When character, context, and conflict are formulated, all the ingredients to generate drama are available; what we don't know is the conclusion. The shape of the conflict between the characters will shift for each episode and will demand episodic conclusions or resolutions. Each team is responsible for summarizing a set of four episodes that spell out specific conflicts and resolutions, as well as for creating a final climactic conclusion.

If you have used the combined power of cooperation (the groups at work learning together) and competition (each group's sense that others are equally engaged in this work), you may wish to select the most promising by popular response, just as networks do. When a pilot is selected from those presented, the class might set out to develop the dialogue for a few of the shows and could even get into the production with props and costumes. This final development of the dialogue can offer the crucial test of its effectiveness. Whether or not you take the pilot into production, students learn a great deal about turning daily language into dramatic dialogue. More importantly perhaps, their sense of how character, conflict, and context work together will be a nice step toward better understanding fiction as well as drama.

CLASS MAGAZINE

Ask students to create their own class magazine, a one-time commemorative issue designed to express something fundamental about the class's experience, spirit, or nature. Working in small groups, have students brainstorm about the nature of the magazine: What would be most expressive of the class: a news magazine, a literary magazine, a tabloid, a human interest magazine, or a wildlife publication? The range is wide. Each group selects the most promising idea and writes up an outline of its format. The whole class hears each group's suggestion and votes on the class choice. Serious production roles, assignments, schedules, and necessary materials are decided with a student chair and the groups collaborating together. The production activities are done by individuals, small groups, and the whole class. When the magazine is "published," each student is asked to select two nonclass members, perhaps parents, to read and respond to it. That "public" response can be combined with the students' assessment for evaluation.

CLASSY COMICS

Ask students to render any narrative literature as frames of a comic strip with dialogue bubbled in. No painterly skill is needed; stick figures will do. The simplifying of plot, character, and language is the essence of the exercise. The visual delight for the class is the secondary side effect. Another graphic play with literature or language is to use professionally drawn comics or cartoons and juxtapose students' words or captions with them. When the additions are relevant to class studies, the benefits of the exercise are greater. We bring cartoons of our own to class and let students cut them up or add their words over them. Our sons' chunky *Far Side* calendar pads, along with our *New Yorker* magazines and newspaper cartoons, have been rifled like this for years.

BUMPER STICKERS

The bumper sticker, like the billboard, provides a quick message. The drivers who see the message usually glimpse it for a limited time. The medium thus dictates certain characteristics such as brevity, cleverness, and a logocentric style. Show students facsimiles of some classic stickers and discuss what makes these examples effective. Then challenge students to produce equally good ones that address current issues. Ask students to come up with a political issue such as antismoking legislation and to work in small groups to create bumper stickers that support or attack the issue. The wordplay and compression central to success in this medium make it a very nice connector to poetry. This activity also can be used as the beginning point or as a clincher in exploring topics that will be used for extended debate and discussion and in expository and persuasive essays.

Invitation to Reflection 8–2

- Have you ever been involved in these kinds of projects in English classes?
- Which of the 12 was most immediately appealing to you?
- Which was least appealing?
- Can you imagine actually initiating such an activity with a class?
- Do you believe that having students produce media would teach a student anything about media that a discussion would not?
- Because some of these projects are uncommon in traditional classes, to achieve them demands energy, vision, and toughness. If you think such production is promising, what can you imagine are the obstacles to trying them?
- How could you overcome these obstacles?

ENTERTAIN: STUDENTS AS LISTENERS AND VIEWERS

Invitation to Reflection 8–3

- Do you associate visual images and musical sounds with the study of literature or language?
- What classroom media experiences have you had that touched your work as a reader or writer?
- Are those experiences especially vivid?
- Did you ever experience dramatic enactments of the plays being studied in your English classes? Did you ever view film adaptations of novels or short stories?
- If so, did you respond differently to seeing or hearing them than to reading them?
- Have you ever used still pictures to augment your texts?
- Do you ever find correspondences between music you hear and literature you read?
- Would you be more likely to introduce a literary character or theme by discussion or by a picture?
- Would you more likely prompt writing by verbal explanation, pictures, or music?

When we focus our attention on the bottom right quadrant of Figure 8–1, students turn from composing to comprehending CDs, videos, film, and other media that bring vivid sounds and sights to the classroom. Before we discuss using professional media productions in the classroom, we want to establish some general guidelines for the best use of two of the most prominent forms, music and film. We believe that the use of both is enhanced by careful selection and incorporation of excerpts—seldom whole pieces—of film (or videotape) or long pieces of music. Fehlman (1987) calls excerpting brief passages of film "quoting films" (p. 84). He is convinced that films provide rich texts that prompt lively

FIGURE 8–3
Nathanson's
guidelines for using
videotape

1. The videotape segment, after motivating discussion and direct teaching, is from ten to twenty minutes in length, not a full-period component.
2. The videotape segment is used to develop appreciation by providing rapid plot exposition when covering a difficult or complex work such as a Shakespearean play.
3. Students have already read or previewed the material which is covered by the videotape segment.
4. A directed reading/writing question precedes the viewing of a particular video segment; discussion of that question follows viewing.
5. The aim of the lesson is not "to watch a videotape."
6. All students have a clear instructional purpose in watching the video segment, not passive viewing or time-killing. The objective in viewing is product or task oriented.
7. Active viewing is checked by the teacher via a writing assignment, worksheet, small-group activity, or other evaluative means.
8. As a meaningful homework assignment, students are urged to compare, contrast, evaluate, or perform some critical thinking or writing task related to the videotape lesson.
9. Careful summary notes are provided by the teacher so that absentees can still grasp the essence of the videotape lesson, or obtain a sense of continuity.
10. New and unfamiliar material is not introduced by the videotape; introductory, technical, or background material related to the unit of study may be provided via videotape.
11. The teacher reduces the light in the room for greater visibility; however, a dark room is not necessary; lit rooms may actually be preferred for outlining or other note-taking activities done while the video segment is on.
12. Videotape, as opposed to audiotape, versions are used because seeing and hearing are more appropriate to the lesson than simple audiotape.
13. Consecutive class periods are not devoted to the showing of a videotape; serialized viewing is not teaching.
14. Videotape is not a daily lesson component nor a one-time special event. It is effective if used frequently, used to present material which is to be tested later, and elevated to an importance equal to that of print material.
15. Video segments have been carefully previewed and screened for potentially offensive or controversial material, technically poor copies, and other problems.
16. Video segments have been carefully cued to minimize loss of instructional time from fast-forwarding or rewinding.
17. Sufficient time has been built into the lesson for student questions and comments following the viewing experience. Viewing does not end at the bell, the lesson does.
18. Teachers make clear their expectations concerning student viewing behavior; respect, politeness, and courtesy are stressed before, during, and after the viewing experience.
19. During the viewing the teacher circulates and actively supervises the class, answers individual students' questions, and insures task-orientation.
20. The teacher avoids sending unintentional—but destructive—double messages through performing clerical tasks during the viewing session.

SOURCE: From Steven Nathanson, "Guidelines for Using Videotape: A Checklist for Educators," *English Journal,* March 1992. Reprinted by permission.

interpretation because these texts and their language are familiar to students. But film is traditionally brought into the English classroom through viewing entire adaptations of the classics, usually after the original is read. "Often the film is shown without explanation (a mere 'treat,' to see an audio visual representation of what was written). The follow-up to viewing consists of criticizing the film for not being faithful to the original" (p. 86). Fehlman believes that a more productive exercise is to select particular film segments that augment specific points of classroom discussion.

Nathanson (1992, pp. 88–89) elaborates the productive classroom use of film in a list of 20 guidelines for viewing videotapes (Figure 8–3). Kearns (1997) recommends several texts for analyzing and teaching film:

Boggs, Joseph M. 1985. *The Art of Watching Films.* Palo Alto, CA: Mayfield.
Bone, Jan and Ron Johnson. 1991. *Understanding the Film: An Introduction to Film Appreciation.* Lincolnwood, IL: National Textbook Company.
Perkins, V. F. 1993. *Film as Film: Understanding and Judging Movies.* New York: Da Capo.
Resch, Kenneth E. and Vicki D. Schicker. 1992. *Using Film in the High School Curriculum—A Practical Guide for Teachers and Librarians.* Jefferson, NC: McFarland and Company.
Watson, Robert. 1990. *Film and Television in Education: An Aesthetic Approach to the Moving Image.* Bristol, PA: The Farmer Press.

We turn now to consider media in our English classrooms as a means of studying literature and developing film literacy.

STUDYING LITERATURE: FILM

The study of "electronic texts" opens the study of literature in several directions. The most traditional use of media for literary study is in the comparative analysis of classics and their film adaptations. Many plays, novels, and short stories have been dramatized in excellent productions. The shared experience of watching these in class can greatly intensify students' experience of reading them. The emotional charge of having been engaged by the drama heightens viewer/listener response. Films of plays, using the original medium of the *spoken* word, restore power that is lost in reading. Furthermore, older plays, most notably Shakespeare's, can be made more comprehensible with speech that clarifies inflection and pronunciation, and with gestures, props, and setting. Veidemanis (1988) explains that the best purpose of such comparisons "is not to elevate one medium over another or even to win consensus. Rather, the goal is for students to come away more secure in articulating their own judgments and responses and fortified to continue the imaginative performance of classic literature on their own" (p. 57).

Films promote an imaginative involvement with literature with many of the same strategies found in a reader response approach. Films promote students' visual participation and emotional involvement in the text, their filling gaps in the text, and their appreciating multiple interpretations of it. Griffin (1989) explains that he teaches Shakespeare on video because he finds that "unless our students visualize a play as they read, the words can seem disembodied and devoid of meaning" (p. 43). He describes the ways in which videos complement the literary text:

- Videotapes can help students perceive the atmosphere of a play.
- Videotapes can help students understand the subtext of a scene. . . those ideas and feelings not stated directly in the dialogue but implied by the way characters look, move, and talk to each other.
- Videotapes can help students see that the same scene can be validly interpreted in different ways. At the very heart of the reader-response approach to literary works is the premise that they can be interpreted by various readers, actors, and directors in different ways. One way to encourage students to experiment with different interpretative possibilities for the same text is to show them how it has been interpreted in different productions. (p. 42)

Fowler and Pesante (1989) demonstrate the power of multiple interpretations of texts by having their students view the same scene performed by different actors. For instance, the same scene from at least five productions of *Hamlet* and *Jane Eyre* (available in many video stores) can be shown and students asked to respond to the different versions: How do they differ? Does the difference alter your interpretations of character or idea? Do you have a preference? Does that preference correspond with any bias you bring to the works?

> *Hamlet.* 1948. Dir. Lawrence Olivier. With Lawrence Olivier, Jean Simmons, and Felix Aylmer.
> 1969. Dir. Tony Richardson. With Nicol Williamson, Gordon Jackson, Anthony Hopkins, and Judy Parfitt.
> 1980. Dir. Rodney Bennett. With Derek Jacobi, Claire Bloom, and Eric Porter.
> 1990. Dir. Franco Zeffirelli. With Mel Gibson and Glenn Close.
> 1997. Dir. Kenneth Branagh. With Kenneth Branagh, Julie Christie, and Kate Winslet.
>
> *Jane Eyre.* 1944. Dir. Orson Welles. With Orson Welles and Joan Fontaine.
> 1952. Westinghouse Studio, made for TV. With Katherine Bard and Kevin McCarthy.
> 1971. Dir. Delbert Mann. With George C. Scott, Susannah York, and Jack Hawkins.
> 1983. Dir. Julian Aymes. With Zelah Clark and Timothy Dalton.
> 1997. Arts & Entertainment Production. With Samantha Morton and Ciaran Hinds.

Fowler and Picante then ask their students to read specific scenes in class and draw on their own interpretations for their reading. They even talk through the interpretive possibilities: "For example, would you really play Polonius as a fool as he makes one of the most memorable speeches, his advice to Laertes?" (p. 28).

Fehlman (1987) suggests another use of segments from adapted films: to view "additions to or alterations of the original" and to reflect on what is gained and what is lost. Changes are necessarily made as print is converted to film, but Fehlman observes that some of these, "rather than undercutting the original, expand ideas inherent in it" (p. 86). Fowler and Pesante (1989) believe that such imaginative projections allow students "to interact in more provocative ways not only with contemporary texts (including television programs, commercials, comic books, music, movies) but also with classics and myths" (p. 28). They have their students read Tom Stoppard's contemporary play, *Rosencrantz and Guildenstern Are Dead,* after *Hamlet,* not as an example of existential or absurdist theater, but to enlarge *Hamlet* and invite students to play with the original text. They report that what "initially engages students is how Stoppard creates an entirely new work, using two characters who, in the students' earlier reading of *Hamlet,* were seen simply as Hamlet's friends" (29). Student speculation on that reversal of perspectives, as Rosencrantz and Guildenstern move to the foreground and Hamlet shifts to the background, brings them to question the gaps in any author's text and the important and imaginative role of the reader in filling them. These teachers capitalize on students' reflections by asking them to do for *Hamlet* what Stoppard did, that is, to fill gaps in *Hamlet* creatively. They give as examples of students' writing a short piece of dialogue between Gertrude and Claudius in their bedroom, a dialogue between Hamlet and Ophelia before the death of the king, a description of the gravedigger and his wife at home, and an essay on Hamlet and the jester when Hamlet was young (pp. 29–30).

Fehlman (1987) uses film quotes in yet another way: "to contemporize literary classics by demonstrating similarities in themes, especially those expressed in parallel scenes from book to film" (p. 85). There are several provocative illustrations of his strategy: "after my class reads Conrad's "The Secret Sharer," I have used a scene from Hitchcock's *Strangers on a Train,* in which Bruno first announces to Guy that they share the guilt of Miriam's death. Both narratives deal with shared identities: thus, they can be discussed together, one helping to clarify or verify the message in the other" (p. 85). Other connections he makes are in the keeping of dead bodies in Faulkner's "A Rose for Emily" and Hitchcock's *Psycho;* the singular pursuit of a compelling and alien phenomenon in *Alien, Jaws,* and *Moby Dick;* and the gathering of travelers in the opening scene of John Ford's *Stagecoach* and Chaucer's *Canterbury Tales* (pp. 85–86).

Similarly, we have used clips from the 1974 *Monty Python and the Holy Grail* to teach aspects of the medieval concept of chivalry. Basic assumptions about royalty can be hilariously grasped in a sequence in which King Arthur talks with members of an anachronistic medieval communist collective. The exploration of the causes of chivalry's decline, for instance, can be capped by a viewing of the entrenchment of the two knights who duel until one has lost both arms and legs yet is still challenging the other.

Film can vivify many literary units as extensions or recapitulations of setting, character, plot, tone, and idea. We ended a unit on diaries, memoirs, short stories, and poems of the Holocaust with a 1988 French film, *Au Revoir les Enfants,* based on writer-director Louis Malle's childhood memories. Set in 1944 in a Catholic boarding school in Nazi-occupied France, the film centers on the friendship between two bright adolescents, one a Jewish student. Our students' understanding of the subtleties of the film was much deepened by their prior reading. The dimensions of the Holocaust's horrific tragedy were personalized in the character of the Jewish schoolboy and his classmates, and thus left an imprint that summed and held all the suffering we had met.

Excerpted clips abound for a unit on satire: for instance, scenes from Woody Allen's 1973 *Sleeper* (filled with satirical scenes of 1970s American life) and Robert Townsend's 1987 *Hollywood Shuffle* (a personal protest against black movie stereotypes). Students readily understand satire's critical laughter in *Sleeper* when the Allen character is asked to identify 1970s relics such as Howard Cosell: "When people committed great crimes, they were forced to watch that." In *Hollywood Shuffle,* a black actor's school trains African-American aspirants with impeccable British accents to speak as field slaves and muggers.

Finally, film contributes to the study of literature as what Fehlman (1987) calls a "textbook" for teaching literary technique and craft. Students, drawn to the compelling and immediate visual and auditory drama of this "film text," transfer an understanding of the technique of the director to an appreciation of the craft of the author of a "printed text" (p. 84). Directors achieve with picture and sound what authors must achieve solely with words. When students begin to think analytically about technique, they must consider the tools of the craft in order to articulate their insights. Fehlman observes that "[m]ost all literary terminology is applicable to film, so narrative terms like 'setting' and 'conflict,' along with more poetic terms like 'imagery' and 'figures of speech,' can be identified, defined within a film segment, either directly or as an offshoot of the discussion of the film as text itself" (p. 84). Nathanson (1992) reminds us of how music videos are also helpful in analyzing poetic imagery. He asks students to match the visual images with "the lyrical and musical text of a rock video!" (p. 89).

In one successful classroom exercise, we use clips from the 1979 film *Norma Rae* to explore how authors or directors lead us to their perspective through carefully selected detail (visual imagery, evocative music, and spoken dialogue). We use the list and the sequence shown in Figure 8-4. The ideal setup is to tape the selected parts onto a second tape so that you do not have to hold students through the awkward fast-forwarding process. We have used this exercise with individual students, small groups, and the whole class. On one side of a sheet of paper we list the nine sequences with blank lines following each. The directions, shown in Figure 8-5, are on the reverse side.

STUDYING LITERATURE: MUSIC

Music, as well as film, enriches literary study. We have linked music and literature already in this text. We make that connection here again with a story we teach. Joyce Carol Oates's chilling "Where Are You Going, Where Have You Been?" has the influence of mass culture on adolescents at its heart.

FIGURE 8–4
Norma Rae film clips

Sequence	VCR setting	Duration
1. Theme song	013-094	2 minutes, 30 seconds
2. Setting	095-115	1 minute
3. Noise, Mamma	116-173	2 minutes, 18 seconds
4. Organizer and millhand/father	174-219	2 minutes
5. Bulletin board	220-265	2 minutes
6. Norma Rae joins union	265-284	50 seconds
7. Letter and fight	284-330	2 minutes
8. Letter and the law	330-396	3 minutes, 10 seconds
9. Fired	396-472	4 minutes

FIGURE 8–5
Two ways to view
Norma Rae

FOCUS:
A. Record (using numbers to guide you) your sense of each scene by writing about
   a) dominant images, sounds, and feelings of the scene
   b) what Norma Rae is feeling and thinking about her world
   c) what the director wants us to think and feel about the world of a textile worker

SPRAWL:
A. Write a short response to the entire film clip. Pay particular attention to the important shifts in Norma Rae's development as a worker and as a person.
B. Write a brief comparison of the consciousness the artist-director is hoping to develop in his audience. Pay particular attention to the ways he elicits the audience's sympathies.

Connie, its 15-year-old protagonist, is deeply absorbed in the lyrics of the popular songs of her culture; they form the basis of her best and deepest hopes, but they badly deceive her. The fulfillment of the idol promised in her songs turns out to be a threatening sham, probably a rapist, perhaps a killer.* Centrally important in suffusing the story with additional meaning and import is noting the story's dedication ("For Bob Dylan"), tracking the title back to its musical source, "It's All Over Now, Baby Blue," or to another Dylan song, "A Hard Rain's A Gonna Fall," listening to the songs, and tracing their imagery to Oates's story. The refrain in "A Hard Rain's A Gonna Fall" is "Where are you going, my blue-eyed son? Where are you going, my handsome young one?" Possible questions to be raised include the following:

- How is Oates's story an answer to the question posed in its title? What happens to Connie?
- Which is more horrific, the story's or the song's vision?
- If you had written a story in response to Dylan's vision, what kind of plot and characters would you have imagined?
- Although Oates clearly worked imaginatively on her material, she said in an interview that the "story came to me more or less in a piece" after reading a story about a killer in a Southwestern state and thinking about old legends and songs about death and "the maiden." Write your own newspaper account of the events in Oates's story.

One of our students, Susan Quinn, was so interested in the interactive effects of music and literature that she began to collect correspondences between them. We list several of those connections as well as those of other students who followed her, as examples that you might introduce into the classroom and of connective work that your students might undertake.

Beneath the Wheel, Herman Hesse	"The Wall," Pink Floyd
The Stranger, Albert Camus	"Killing an Arab," The Cure
Their Eyes Were Watching God, Zora Neal Hurston	"Crossroads," Tracy Chapman
Richard Cory, Edward Arlington Robinson	"Richard Cory," Simon and Garfunkel
Romeo and Juliet, William Shakespeare	"Romeo and Juliet," The Indigo Girls
To the Lighthouse, Virginia Woolf	"Virginia Woolf," The Indigo Girls
What Are Years?, Marianne Moore	"The Sound of Silence," Simon and Garfunkel
The Glass Menagerie, Tennessee Williams	"Father and Son," Cat Stevens
Wuthering Heights, Thomas Hardy	"Wuthering Heights," Kate Bush
A Raisin in the Sun, Lorraine Hansberry	"For Emily. Wherever I May Find Her," Simon and Garfunkel

*A made-for-TV movie, "Smooth Talk," is based on this story and appears to have captured its characters, plot, and cumulative tension. Thus, it vivifies the story, but for several telling details. A discussion of the differences of the story and movie intensifies appreciation of both.

STUDYING LITERATURE: PAINTINGS, PRINTS, AND PHOTOGRAPHS

In our chapters on teaching literature, we discussed the enhancing possibilities in the still visual imagery of paintings, prints, and photographs. We have found visual print media to be instructionally powerful as enrichment, clarifier, clincher, and extender of literature.

We discussed how the study of W. H. Auden's "Musée des Beaux Arts" is greatly intensified by showing the painting that inspired it, Pieter Brueghel the Elder's sixteenth-century painting *The Fall of Icarus.* Writer Jorge Luis Borges acknowledges a particular indebtedness to art: "To a painting by Watts, done in 1896, I owe 'The House of Asterion' and the character of its sad protagonist." That painting, *The Minotaur,* from the Tate Gallery in London, invites viewers, as Borges does readers, to redirect their sympathies toward the lonely, isolated creature so commonly reviled in myth, story, and picture. (Many other sculptures and paintings, such as Maggi Hambling's 1986–1987 *Minotaur Surprised While Eating,* present the conventional view of the minotaur as rapacious monster and thereby provide a perfect contrast to Watts's and Borges's imaginative reversal.) After the riddle of the story is solved, our students move with sympathy into the minotaur's perceptions and unconscious suffering. Examining the painting reinforces that surprising view, as well as the imagination of both artists to conceive it.

Many M. C. Escher prints are perfect visual foils for Borges's verbal games, riddles, and puzzles. Both the Dutch artist and the Argentinean writer concern themselves with the creative and enigmatic interplay between the logic of everyday realities and of infinite possibilities. The fiction of Raymond Carver and the paintings of Edward Hopper present the same stark, hauntingly similar perspectives on human experience through different media. The motives and art of each of these four creative artists become far more accessible when they are examined together.

We also teach short stories with cartoons. In Eudora Welty's 1941 short story "Why I Live at the P.O.," for instance, the jealousy and resentment of the narrator, Sister, towards her younger sister Stella-Rhondo is basic to the story's plot, characters, and idea. Four Gary Larson cartoons of insect and fish siblings locked in jealous and acrimonious domestic combat invite students to both laugh at and take seriously this common and corrosive experience. The visual art used to teach literature, however, need not be titled, professional images found in museums or books. We have used students' own searches and selections of faces in periodicals as springboards for discussions of characters in literature.

Jane Marshall (1992) believes that the visual world can open students to literature because the visual world dominates her students' lives. She discusses Jules Prown's (1982) three-step methodology for analyzing the visual dimensions of artifacts: description, deduction, and speculation. Beginning with close observation of the concrete anchors students' responses; moving to inferences about a particular piece based on other general principles extends those responses; and ending in creative reflection about it drives viewers toward new insight. Prown also helpfully categorizes visual objects from the portentous (museum masterpieces) to the pedestrian (Brillo boxes):

Portentous				**Pedestrian**	
Art	Diversions (books, performances)	Adornments	Modifications	Applied Arts	Devices (vehicles, machines)

By using Prown's analytical steps, Marshall moves her students from exploring paintings, to films, to photographs, and to television (from the arty to the everyday). Students claim jokingly that she has ruined their enjoyment of films: "I can't go to the theater and just let it happen. I notice everything." She knowingly concurs; that was her hope.

STUDYING LITERATURE: COMICS

Few forms of writing are taken less seriously than comic books; however, comic books have grown up, and many have turned from the simple superhero versus supervillain to more complex plots, characters, dialogue, and ideas. Many of them are even regarded by some as literature. Some comic books, published as "graphic novels," work from a complex sense of philosophy, history, and current events, as well as possible futures.

Teachers have long appreciated the seductive appeal of comic books, with their vivid pictures, limited verbal descriptions, sparse dialogue, strong plots, and predictable, almost formulaic ideas. In fact, in our high school generation, classic comics were as much an anathema to English teachers as *Cliffs Notes* often are today. But even traditional comics have been allies of teachers concerned with engaging reluctant, limited, or ESL readers with printed texts. This new generation of comic books has drawn more English teachers to it because the pictorial appeal remains but with far richer narrative, character, and theme. Students become engrossed in the graphic story and emerge from it with characters well-worth pondering and ideas well-worth discussion. Admittedly, many teachers see these pictorial stories as points of entry on the way to mature nonpictorial literature, the kind of progress expected as children move from simple, illustrated nursery rhymes toward robustly pictureless college poetry anthologies. Comic book pundits would like to see even that snobbery erased and the pictures in comic books viewed as exciting enhancements to good literature, not cover-ups for poor writing. One such devotee, our former student Matt Wood, directed our attention to several. In the following paragraphs, he and we describe them as an introduction to this genre.

Among the earliest of the "serious" graphic novels is *The Watchman* by Alan Moore. It is a book about a world that is changed by the existence of "superheroes," most of whom are merely men in masks. Some are noble of heart, strong of arm, and empty of thought, but others are characters who can be taken seriously. In addition to superheroes, Moore explores the minds of a diverse range of ordinary people: frightened little men and grandiose dreamers. He enters the mind of a frustrated New York City detective, as well as a lonely newspaperman and an exasperated psychologist. It is a book that looks at a world on the edge of the end and the ways that people cope with the fact that they may soon die.

Alan Moore has also written a 10-part miniseries, *V for Vendetta,* set in a totalitarian society that springs up in England after World War III. The hero, a man called "V," decides that England would be better off with no government. He proceeds to dismantle the existing government and attempts to usher in an age of voluntary, rather than imposed, order. Whether he succeeds or not is not revealed to the reader, nor is it important. Moore's depiction of a complacent society, a government's power, and an individual's responsibility go to the heart of the important political issues of our time. V is a philosophical man, but his most important belief is that the time for education, the time for knowledge, and the time for freedom is now and forever. Dangerous as they are, they must never be repressed. The author appears to share those beliefs and to write his books for an audience that might be persuaded otherwise.

Several comic books have historical resonances. One such book is Art Spiegelman's graphic novel *Maus: A Survivor's Tale.* This book does to the Nazi Holocaust what Orwell's *Animal Farm* did to the Russian revolution. It is the personal account of a survivor of the Holocaust, and the reader re-experiences the horrors of Nazi Germany, but not through human characters: All the characters are animals. Neil Gaiman's *The Sandman* is an ongoing series of comic books that touch upon history through the main character Morphers, the Lord of Dreams, who has existed for as long as dreams have, and will not disappear until they do. Often, the book touches upon history that he has altered. One of the story lines, entitled "Distant Mirrors" deals entirely with the effect that he has had on the shaping of the world. For instance, Morphers appears in a conversation with Augustus Caesar that determined the fate of Rome, and in action that contributes to Robespierre's fall in the French Revolution. Other stories involve Morphers's meetings with William Shakespeare and the deal he makes with the great playwright. The story "A Midsummer Night's Dream" details the first production of that play—before Oberon and Titania and thousands of the other denizens of Faeries.

Other comic books worthy of mention include Steve Gerber's *Foolkiller,* which takes a difficult look at our society and its problems; *Classics Illustrated,* which makes graphic, faithful versions of many classic stories; Guy Davis's *Baker Street,* which details the adventures of Sharon Ford, a modern-day detective modeled after Sherlock Holmes; and Scott Beadestadt's *Trollords,* a book with silly characters and serious themes.

Comic strips, too, are extremely popular with adolescents and deal with the basic issues of our time. Comics such as *Dilbert* and *Bloom County* offer relevant social commentary. They appeal to adolescents because of their cynical look at the established order. Black's (1997) study of comics found that students responded to them more positively than to short stories and were able to deal with them in a more sophisticated fashion in their writing.

Our discussion of the challenge to the canon has presented the argument for a breakdown of these divisions between high and low culture. Never has that breakdown been more apparent than in the open admission of comic books into the English classroom. We suggest that you take a look at them before you close your door to their benefits.

DEVELOPING FILM LITERACY

A number of teachers apply film to the teaching of literature; a smaller number believe that film should be taught for itself alone. Even if film were an inferior art form composed only for commercial entertainment, some teachers would feel that it still warranted attention because of its importance to youth. Gallagher (1988) observes that it "is not entirely coincidental that videocassettes resemble, in shape and heft, books, nor that, despite their sometimes sleazy and usually tacky atmosphere, videotape rental outlets function very much like the commercial lending libraries of old. The fact is that film and literature, particularly in terms of narrativity, share a great deal. Clearly, today's students are 'reading' films at the rate English teachers have always wished they would read books." (p. 59). This high interest in film among the young argues for some attention to it. It attracts students and thus holds within itself a lively motive for study. More importantly, students often view film uncritically. The same claims for making students critical readers, alert and awake to the printed text, apply to this "filmed text" in which they are absorbed. Instructional attempts should be to enhance students' viewing and to make it more selective, not, as sometimes happens, to spoil their viewing through analysis and to make it more self-conscious.

Teaching film per se has claims for study that rest with the medium itself. An expanding canon validates such study; the creative collaborative work from directors and screenwriters to actors and actresses provides rich material and justifies close critical attention. William Arrowsmith (1985), a renowned classicist, believes that if Sophocles were alive today, he would be making films. The technology of VCRs, like CDs, with their digital precision and their ability to fast-forward, rewind, pause, and stop, facilitates their study. Teachers can make easily programmed sequences of character development, imagery, and structure. Gallagher (1988) predicts that the "new technology, because it permits and so encourages a concentration on the 'micro-skills' of visual analysis, will bring the study of film and of literature closer together. Film segments can now be analyzed in all their detail and not just for the overall impression they create" (p. 58). He goes on to suggest that "we need to give students the names, and so the ability to speak critically, of those devices whose basic use they already comprehend but about whose structure and formal operations they remain ignorant" (p. 59).

Griffin (1989, pp. 40–41) enumerates some of the vocabulary of film, the range of "theatrical, cinematic, and film signs" that a study of videos introduces to students (Figure 8–6). Gallagher (1988) mentions another motive for the learning of film vocabulary (roughly parallel to learning the vocabulary of fictional elements and devices):

> We might also note that there is a growing reciprocity between film and modern literature, not only in that about half of American films are derived from some literary source or other, or even that some modern authors (like Norman Mailer) are involved in filmmaking, but also in that a number of authors—Joan Didion is a particularly striking example—have been strongly influenced on a *structural level* by the motion picture. Film devices like jump cuts, lap dissolves, fades, and track-ins are part of contemporary 'signifying practices' and are regularly approximated in much contemporary literature, particularly fiction. (p. 59)

Teasley and Wilder (1997) have developed some extremely useful and insightful ideas for using film in English classes. For example, they focus students' initial perceptions as they watch the first 10 minutes of the film *Pathfinder* with questions that link what they have seen and heard to a deepening understanding of how setting, character, and theme merge. Then they show five clips of poignant

---

FIGURE 8–6
Signs pertinent to film study

THEATRICAL AND CINEMATIC SIGNS

Body: the actor's voice, facial expression, physical gestures, bodily posture, physical movement, size and shape, make-up, hairstyle

Costume: its color, texture, weight, cut

Space: its size and shape and its relationship to the auditorium

Set: whether realistic or symbolic; how related to movements of the actors; the colors, shapes, textures, and weights of all its stage properties

Lighting: whether obtrusive or supportive only, warm or cold, sharp or gentle, bland or emotional

FILM SIGNS

Shot types: whether long, medium, close-up, or deep focus

Camera angles: whether bird's eye, high, eye-level, low or oblique

Lighting: whether high key, high contrast, or low key

Color: whether cool or warm, advancing or retreating

Frame areas: whether pictorial elements are located at the center, top, bottom, or on the edge of the frame

Composition: how pictorial elements such as contrast, weight, line, planes, and proxemic patterns are used

Camera movement: whether pan or tilt shots, dolly or tracking shots, use of zoom lens

Editing: how shots are used to establish a scene, how they are joined into sequences through cuts, dissolves, and wipes

Sound: how the sound track, including music, is used to underscore, parallel, or counterpoint an image or scene

moments in the film and ask another set of questions about the meaning of what students have watched. This punctuation of watching with questions keeps their interpretive minds wide awake as they soak up the vital sounds and sense before them. The process is intended to lead students toward habits of active viewing of the films that are so important in their lives. Teasley and Wilder suggest a list of six questions that can be used with any film:

1. What changes did you notice in the film as you watched? What changes did you notice in your feelings or opinions as you watched?
2. Go back over your viewing guides looking at your "visual images" and "sounds" notations. Do you notice any patterns emerging? (For example, do you see the same images again and again? Do you hear musical phrases or lines of dialogue repeated?) What do you think the director was trying to communicate by using these patterns?
3. Make a list of all the things that this film is about.
4. Make a list of all the conflicts you have seen in this film.
5. What characters, incidents, or objects in this film remind you of other stories you have read or movies you have seen?
6. In your opinion, is this film neutral, or does it clearly take a position on a particular issue? (p. 65)

Like the questions in their viewing guide, Teasley and Wilder's six questions prompt students to view with depth of thought as well as feeling. To these methodological suggestions they have compiled a list of 100 films (Appendix D) that are extremely effective with adolescents (1996).

Burmester (1983) summarizes the history of film instruction in American classrooms after McLuhan gave "respectability" to mass-media study: "There was a brief 'golden era' in the late 1960s and early 1970s when it appeared that film and television courses might find a permanent niche in the schools, but 'back to basics' and budget problems put an end to such optimism" (pp. 95–96). At present, most film study occupies a tight place in an already overtaxed study of the printed word. But some curricula have electives. Franza (1984) describes one he offered called The Art of Film. His course goals articulate a thoughtful and balanced regard for an art form often overwhelmed by glamour and hype; his aim is "(1) taking no movie for granted, (2) being aware of the collaborative effort in filmmaking, (3) focusing attention on directors rather than on actors and actresses, (4) knowing a bit about the history of movies, (5) realizing that other people make movies besides Americans, (6) knowing some of the technical aspects of moviemaking, and (7) being aware that movies are conscious, carefully planned, creative and expensive undertakings" (p. 40). Whether we integrate the study of film into the regular English literature and language course or teach it as an elective, Franza (1984) reminds us of our basic motive. He quotes what Joseph Conrad said of his purpose in his novels: "My task, above all, is to make you *see*." (p. 40). That should be our purpose also in the study of film.

LOCATING MATERIALS

We have found nothing so helpful in locating media materials as experience coupled with awareness. As we grow more familiar with that which we teach, we search more efficiently and freely for relevant collateral material. We ransack libraries, art museums, periodicals, television listings, and advertisements for media that connect, enrich, and extend the language and literature we teach. Students themselves, when alerted, can enter the search. The next-immediate source of materials after your own experience is your school, municipal, or nearest accessible college or university library. Departments of media are becoming common in all types of libraries.

In Appendix D, we suggest some general resources for you as a beginning teacher left to your own solitary search. These resources can provide access to film, TV programming, radio drama, and books on tape. Ongoing rapid developments in media make a list of specific sources quickly dated; this list, however, of names and addresses of periodicals can acquaint you with upcoming live events and the range of nonprint productions from verbatim reading and acting of novels and plays to interviews, analyses, and documentaries. The list also includes the names of distributors of film, videotape, and recorded books, as well as several video series that we have used in whole or part with great success.

EXAMINE: STUDENTS AS ANTHROPOLOGISTS AND LITERARY CRITICS

To examine media is to look at media in terms of how they work to wield such influence over our lives. In this quadrant, we ask students to behave as archeologists or anthropologists digging carefully through these cultural phenomena in order to understand more specifically how they touch us. Then we suggest ways in which skills of literary analysis are also useful tools for examining media not as artifact, but as art.

Interested students might enrich their understanding of how TV works and how it affects the viewer or hearer by reading the results of demographic studies. At the University of Pennsylvania's

Invitation to Reflection 8–4

- What is your hunch about the heavy TV watchers in America (those, that is, who watch over 4 hours a day)? Are they males or females? Young, middle-aged, or old? College educated or not? Low-, medium-, or high-income level? Urban or nonurban?
- Do you receive news any differently from TV, newspapers, or periodicals? Which is more likely to satisfy the need for logical, sequential analysis?
- Do you assume that national news coverage on TV is unbiased? Liberal? Conservative?
- Do you think of TV news more as information or entertainment?
- Does advertising more often inform you or persuade you?
- Do you often encounter print or nonprint advertising with no pictures, just words?
- Do the soap operas present a picture of American culture with which you are familiar in your own life?
- Do you ever interrogate the lyrics of popular music?
- Can you imagine using your critical tools of literary analysis on mass-media forms such as TV or film?

Annenberg School of Communications, Gerbner, Gross, Morgan, and Signorielli have conducted meticulous research on prime-time TV viewers each year since 1967. Table 8–1 provides a demographic picture of TV viewing in America using data for 1977, 1978, and 1980 (Gerbner, 1982).

If you were using this professionally polled data with students, you might ask them to notice especially where the greatest discrepancies lie, for instance, in the educational level of medium and heavy viewers: Does this lead you to wonder what attracts this disproportionate number of women, non–college-educated, and lower-income viewers? And what picture of life do they see?

These researchers' delineation of prime time's skewed picture of social life in America is instructive also. Even though this research was conducted two decades ago, we excerpt parts of it to reveal how professional media watchers draw conclusions. We would use such an analysis after asking students for their interpretation of data.

> The world of prime time as seen by the average viewer is animated by vivid and intimate portrayals of over three hundred major characters a week, mostly stock dramatic types, and their weekly rounds of dramatic activities.
>
> Conventional and "normal" though that world may appear, it is in fact far from the reality of anything but consumer values and social power. The curve of consumer spending, unlike that of income, bulges with middle-class status as well as middle age. Despite the fact that nearly half of the national income goes to the top fifth of the real population, the myth of middle class as the all-American norm dominates the world of television. Nearly seven out of every ten television characters appear in the "middle-middle" of a five-way classification system. Most of them are professionals and managers. Blue-collar and service work occupies 67 percent of all Americans but only 10 percent of television characters. These features of the world of prime-time television should cultivate a middle-class or "average" income self-designation among viewers.
>
> Men outnumber women at least three to one. Most women attend to men or home (and appliances) and are younger (but age faster) than the men they meet. Underrepresentation in the world of television suggests the cultivation of viewers' acceptance of more limited life chances for women, a more limited range of activities, and more rigidly stereotyped images than for men.
>
> Young people (under eighteen) comprise one-third and older people (over sixty-five) one-fifth of their true proportion in the population. Blacks on television represent three-fourths and Hispanics one-third of their share of the U.S. population, and a disproportionate number are minor rather than major characters. . . . Weigel, Loomis, and Soja (1980) show that although blacks appear in many programs and commercials, they seldom appear with whites, and actually interact with whites in only about 2 percent of total human appearance time. The prominent and stable overrepresentation of well-to-do white males in the prime of life dominates prime time. Television's general demography bears greater resemblance to the facts of consumer spending than to the U.S. Census (Gerbner, Gross, Signorielli, & Morgan 1980; Gerbner & Signorielli, 1979). . .
>
> But threats abound. Crime in prime time is at least ten times as rampant as in the real world. An average of five to six acts of overt physical violence per hour involves over half of all major characters. Yet pain, suffering, and medical help rarely follow this mayhem. (pp. 443–445)

TABLE 8–1
Relationship between
amount of television
viewing and
demographic variables

		Television viewing*		
		Light %	Medium %	Heavy %
Sex				
	Male	50	46	37
	Female	50	54	63
Age				
	18–29	24	24	31
	30–54	51	46	34
	55+	25	30	36
Education				
	No college	54	67	82
	Some college	46	33	18
Income				
	Low	31	33	49
	Medium	35	37	33
	High	35	30	18
Region				
	Urban	45	43	43
	Non-Urban	55	57	57

SOURCE: Adapted from G. Gerbner, L. Gross, M. Morgan, and N. Signorielli (1982), Charting the mainstream: Television's contributions to political orientations. From *Journal of Communication, 32*(2), 100–127. Copyright © 1982, *Journal of Communication,* Oxford University Press, Inc. Used with permission.

*TV viewing: light = 0–1 hours per day; medium = 2–3 hours per day; heavy = over 4 hours per day.

These researchers do not suggest causal relationships between prime-time content and viewer attitudes, but they do find correlations. For instance, among TV viewers versus their non–TV-watching counterparts, the study found the following:

- "stronger prejudices about women and old people" (p. 445)
- heightened "perceptions of danger and risk" (p. 445)
- "an exaggerated sense of mistrust, vulnerability, and insecurity" (p. 445)
- susceptibility to "simplistic appeals to law and order" (p. 412)

Such an analysis of this commonplace phenomenon holds natural interest for most students and serves as a model of critical perception. It can also be a precursor to their own data gathering and interpretation.

Morris (1989) explains her design for moving her students from being "couch potatoes" to "informed critics." She asks them to "practice three kinds of analysis in [her] classes: (1) individual detailed logs of text, (2) group dialogue about TV programming, and (3) researched essays documenting and interpreting details of television programs" (p. 35). Her first step is "to ask students to keep their own individual written logs of program content. I describe these viewing/writing homework assignments as being similar to anthropologists' field notes." (p. 35). She moves toward speculation only after these concrete details are gathered and recorded. She says that students learn that "intellectually sound and worthwhile criticism depends upon the employment of accurate language and documentation" (p. 36). Their discussion is based on reading aloud from their logs.

Morris cites studies that "indicate that alarmingly high numbers of regular television watchers believe TV content is primarily transmission of unmediated and direct imagery, when, in reality, television production results from selection, arrangement, and emphasis of countless textual elements by authors for specific purposes and from their own viewpoints" (p. 39). Because television content is so familiar to students, Morris feels that she must help them "acquire sufficient distance" to form discriminating responses to different kinds of programming, to the producers', directors', and actor's choices, and to the cinematic influences on viewer reactions. She believes that asking students to exercise their critical abilities through television analysis helps them develop "analytical methods that further their thoughtful interpretations" (p. 40). She also poses provocative questions to her students to help "break their habits of casual acceptance of texts and, instead, think anew about meanings of television's messages: How is society and people's roles in it being portrayed? What values, attitudes, and conceptions of pleasure does this program promote? What responses might this program elicit from viewers who are watching from differing situations and circumstances than your own?" (p. 41).

Another teacher, Lorraine Lewis (1984), involved students in "visual research and observation" (p. 52). Her assignment was less structured than Morris's. She did not tell students what to look for;

rather, they were to observe the topic area and draw conclusions about the nature of the media" (p. 52). Here is a list of her topics:

- advertising and audience appeal in specialized magazines
- objectivity and news magazines
- broadcasting time in relation to commercials and content
- lyrics as social statements
- ways to interest teens in news shows
- how children, teens, women, minorities, the elderly, and social classes are portrayed in news broadcasting and programming
- point of view in news writing
- liberal vs. conservative media recognition
- rescheduling weekly TV programming to increase ratings
- emotion and advertising as shown in the slogans for brand name products
- the future of cable (p. 52)

Her classes did discuss the implications of their observations, but they also demonstrated their eye-opening insights by becoming "media manipulation experts" themselves. They wrote biased news stories, stereotypical macho or sultry or all-American commercials, and satirical cartoons; and, for their final evaluation, they divided into three groups and produced "a television show that would elicit specific emotions. They also had to include two commercials appropriate to their target audience, radio 'spots' announcing the show's premiere, and ads prepared for newspapers and magazines urging readers to watch" (p. 53).

Teacher Margo Sorenson (1989) describes several journal-writing prompts that set up her classroom activities for using television to develop critical viewing and writing. The first is a prewriting assignment to introduce the unit.

- How does TV influence your life?
- Write about your favorite and least favorite commercials, listing your reasons for your opinion. Remember to consider viewpoint and tone in your reasons.
- Watch two TV programs. List the main characters, their major actions during the show, and what other types of people are shown on the program. List what you like about the show.
- Does TV control people, or do people control TV? (pp. 42-45)

For other ideas about instruction that examines media, Thoman (1998) gives a detailed "guided tour" through resources for teaching media literacy. We name just a few major references:

Considine, David. 1994. *Visual Messages: Integrating Imagery into Instruction*. Libraries Unlimited.
Davies, John. 1997. *Educating Students in a Media-Saturated Culture*. Technomic Publishing.
Masterman, Len. 1989. *Teaching the Media*. Routledge.
Worsnop, Chris. 1994. *Screening Images: Ideas for Media Education*. Wright Communication.

Invitation to Reflection 8–5

- What media do you consider to be the proper subjects for critical (social science) study in the English classroom?
- What media would you be most interested in exploring?
- How would you design research with a class of 30 heterogeneously grouped ninth graders? Write out an abbreviated assignment that would initiate their out-of-class work.

We turn now to exercises that examine television news, advertising, and soap operas. We hope that they suggest possibilities for learning and incite you to try them. As you read about these classroom activities, take note of those that appeal to you as being most feasible and most productive.

EXAMINING THE NEWS

We suggest six ways to involve students in examining the news.

1. Make a quantitative study of television newscast and news talk-show roles: weather reporters, news reporters, news commentators, sportscasters, and talk-show hosts. Small groups of students select and focus on several different subjects, watch those subjects intently, and

compare the subjects' body language and voices. Training the eye to see the subtleties of TV behavior is good preparation for a closer and more critical observation of the messages being conveyed. The questions that follow the observations and drive them toward some meaning might include the following:

- Do these mannerisms seem spontaneous or contrived?
- Are these the mannerisms of everyday life?
- What is the image being conveyed to the viewer?
- Does it inspire confidence or skepticism, seriousness or amusement?
- Does it heighten drama or move at the calmer pace of lived life?
- What is the implicit, nonverbal message in the mannerisms?
- Do you trust this person?
- If you could ask the person any question, personal or professional, what would you ask?

2. Replicate the kind of study done by a New York group, Fairness and Accuracy in Reporting (FAIR), and log in several weeks of the guest lists of several Sunday news interview shows, such as CBS's *Face the Nation,* NBC's *Meet the Press,* and ABC's *This Week.* What kind of racial, sexual, and political representation is present?

3. Log in the pictures of world leaders and politicians that appear over a designated span (at least 6 months) on the covers of news magazines such as *Newsweek* and *Time.* Chart the racial, sexual, and political point of view that each represents.

4. List *all* pictures of individuals on these magazines' covers. What are the proportions of famous to ordinary persons; of individuals from entertainment, business, politics, art, academia, and religion; and of world and United States citizens?

5. Explore this question: Is the mass media an adequate source of public information?

Small-group Assignment: In a 30-minute segment of a national news program, monitor the minutes and seconds given over to

- reporting of national events
- reporting of international events
- reporting of legislative deliberations
- investigative reporting
- in-depth news analysis, commentary, and discussion
- interviews
- unrestricted questioning of public officials
- debates
- human interest stories

After you have gathered your data, consider the data's implications. Do the national networks provide us with the kind of news coverage that gives us accurate, unbiased information with which to know our world and live responsibly in it? Where does news reporting verge on entertainment?

Whole-class Activity: Small groups report and discuss their findings and their conclusions. This information might be discussed generally or used as background for classroom debates or panel discussions that revolve around these questions: Do our mass media provide us with an adequate source of information? Do our national media bias our perceptions of the world around us?

Individual Writing Projects: This data gathering, speculation, and discussion leads, we hope, to individual students' arriving at personal judgments. Ask students, as a clincher for this work (and possibly the evaluation of it), to articulate their judgments in forms of their own choosing: letters to the editor, editorials, satires, or parodies of the network news shows.

6. Have students use the form shown in Figure 8–7 to scrutinize the lead news story carried by each of the major networks on the same evening's news. Each of three groups could be assigned to watch one of the presentations of the major story and to enumerate very specific features and details that will allow them to make cross-network comparisons.

EXAMINING ADVERTISING

Here are five ways to take a new look at advertisements.

1. Have students bring in print or video ads by which they would like our culture to be known and, conversely, ads that are embarrassing. After students have presented their selections, list on the board those qualities of which they are proud and those of which they are critical. Do they

Observations	Networks			
	ABC	**CBS**	**NBC**	**CNN**
Total length of time				
Anchor frame time				
Correspondent time				
Visual variety				
Coloring language				
Inflectional bias				
Balance of opinion				
Depth of background information				
Other				
Shift time				

disagree? (We have asked students to arrange these visual images and words into bulletin board collages or "box collages," which we suspend as mobiles from the ceiling.)

2. Have students log in the ads for a whole segment of programming. We asked students to record each of the ads during a Superbowl and then to arrange them by type. They reported that the project, as shown in Table 8-2, became more exciting than the football game. They formed a new awareness of the extent of advertising time (in comparison to game time), of the values and predispositions of those whom advertisers targeted, and of the values that the advertisers wished to impose on them. Questions that might be posed by such a list include the following:
   - How are these advertisers appealing to the viewer: through rational analysis, emotional persuasion, or subliminal suggestion?
   - Of what social class, race, or sex are most of the subjects of the advertisements?
   - What image of American culture is presented?
   - Do any ads represent products or services that fill genuine human needs, or only manufactured needs?
   - Do they employ the idiom of our culture in their pitch?
   - Are there any hidden messages about American life in our advertising? What are they?
   Another strategy that explores the propaganda techniques of advertising is to find ads of the same product marketed to different audiences.
3. Political advertisements pose other important issues. Have students view political ads and answer these questions: What is the visual image behind the words that the candidate is selling to the

Advertisements	Total Number	Percentage of Total
Network Previews	11	13.75
Other	10	12.50
Car	9	11.25
Insurance	6	7.50
Alcohol	6	7.50
Shipping	6	7.50
Local (Miscellaneous)	5	6.25
Personal Hygiene	4	5.00
Medical	4	5.00
Soft Drink	3	3.75
Telephone	3	3.75
Fast-food	3	3.75
Financial	3	3.75
Computer	2	2.50
Food	2	2.50
Airlines	2	2.50
Tires	1	1.25
Total	**80**	**100.00**

public? Are these characteristics and the words uttered related to the office being sought? Do they appeal to reason? Emotion? Logic? Fears?

4. Sorenson (1989) describes a unit on advertising that examines how advertisers analyze their audiences and persuade them through emotional appeals and statistical manipulations. As a culminating event, she asks students to write and perform an advertisement and the class audience to analyze its methods of persuasion. The following is her checklist of emotional appeals.

Patriotism	Motherhood
Affections (love, hate, friendship)	Fear
Security	Self-preservation
Personal honor	Preservation of society
Family life	Ego (social prestige, recognition, well-being)
Better life for the future	Better life for your children
Fair play	Progress
Power	

5. Postman (1985) observes that commercial messages "defuse the import of the news, in fact render it largely banal. . . . We have become so accustomed to its discontinuities that we are no longer struck dumb, as any sane person would be, by a newscaster who having just reported that a nuclear war is inevitable goes on to say that he will be right back after this word from Burger King. . . . One can hardly overestimate the damage that such juxtapositions do to our sense of the world as a serious place" (pp. 104–105). He especially worries about the impact on youthful viewers who look to TV for clues about "how to respond to the world" (p. 105). Ask students to watch TV news and record the juxtapositions between the emotional tone and content of news and commercials. After the whole class compares notes and their own emotional reactions, discuss Postman's proposition: Do these juxtapositions teach the young that the difficulties of our world are "not to be taken seriously or responded to sanely" (p. 105)?

SCRUBBING THE SOAPS

Burmester (1983) uses a feature on soap operas from a PBS series, *Media Probes,* to prompt students to examine the daily and prime-time soap operas. His students "contrast the life shown on the soaps with their own lives" and with the communal life of this country (p. 96). They speak of soap operas as mirrors, "perhaps distorted, funhouse mirrors, but mirrors nonetheless," of "our hidden selves" (p. 96). We suggest that students work again from their own gathering of data. Use the follow-up discussion and writing questions listed here, or develop your own.

- Did these characters and their stories seem believable?
- If they distorted life as you observe and experience it, describe the distortion.
- Does the life on these soaps seem more vivid or heightened than your own?
- Is there a range of characters that reflect different social classes and ethnic, racial, and age groups?
- Was there anyone your age? Could you identify with that person's life situation?
- Could you affirm the implicit values and overt behavior of these characters?
- Have you ever known a "soapaholic"?
- Burmester says that "the media are makers of myths and molders of opinion" (p. 96). Do the soap operas bear out his observation?

A final examination of media might use the tools of literary analysis for media analysis. Each media form has its own elements, conventions, and standards. Literary analysis sensitizes students to the author's intent and technique. This same sort of critical consciousness can be applied to the creators of media and their persuasive strategies, which Vance Packard (1957) called the "hidden persuaders," that are practiced on us, the viewers and listeners. Some of the analytic tools that can transfer comfortably from printed text to media text include point of view, setting, characters, style, plot, and tone. These can be used, for example, to penetrate TV drama. Consider, for instance, a show's plot: Is it formulaic or imaginative, focused on strong physical action or more psychological? Are the characters stereotyped or original? Flat or round? Dynamic or static? Does the point of view (the camera's eye) focus on one character with frequent close-ups or is its angle of vision usually long shots of many? Is the tone of the show upbeat? Melodramatic? Somber? Does the whole show break with tradition in this genre, or is it conventional? Genre distinctions such as the following can provide useful frames of reference for analysis as well: drama, realism, tragedy, comedy, melodrama, serials, westerns, crime and detective stories, musicals, fantasy, action, family and children films, documentaries, romance, special-effects films, silent films, and social-issues films. Evaluative questions about the quality of a show mirror those critical questions that we asked of literature in Chapter 4.

EXAMINING MEDIA AS ARTIFACT AND ART: MAGAZINE ANALYSIS

A teacher (whose name did not survive this handout's long use) set up guidelines for magazine analysis that combine several of these anthropological and literary approaches to media. The directions can guide the work of individuals or small groups of students. You will need three to five successive issues of a magazine in order to fully analyze the magazine.

Part One: Design.   Analyze the design of the magazine, section by section, and include cover specification, color usage, column design (it may differ from section to section), type styles, headline styles, graphics, photography, and special effects. Be sure to look for anything that unifies the magazine as a whole, such as logos or catch phrases. Also, be sure to look for things that unify the individual sections.

Part Two: Content.   Analyze the content of the magazine. Include feature and/or news coverage as well as any regular features, such as editorials, letters, and reviews. Based on the content you find, whom do you perceive the audience of this magazine to be? What is the magazine's purpose?

Part Three: Business.   Who is the publisher of this magazine? What other major publications does this publisher publish? Who is the editor of this publication? Find out who advertises in the magazine regularly and what the advertising rates are. (Include classified advertising rates, if applicable.) What are subscription rates and what is this magazine's circulation? (Often, there is an 800 number listed in the masthead. If not, locate the publisher and dial the 800 information number to see if there is a number for this publication. If not, you will have to drop a postcard or letter in the mail as soon as possible.)

Part Four: Politics/Philosophy.   What is the ethical stance, political perspective, and world view expressed in this magazine? Who would be its presidential choice, what is its view on controversial issues, and how does it picture women, men, and family?

EXAMINING MEDIA AS ARTIFACT AND ART: STUDENT PUBLIC SERVICE ANNOUNCEMENTS

This activity bridges this examination of media as artifact and art and the exploiting of media in student productions. Have students take a cause such as DWI legislation and devise a public service announcement that will be broadcast in each of five different media: television, billboards, radio, magazines, and bumper stickers. Students should shape their announcements to the requirements of the form. After students present their announcements, the whole-class discussion might move to clarify the basic characteristics of each of the five media and the technique required for communicating effectively in each.

EXAMINING MEDIA AS ARTIFACT AND ART: VIEWING STYLES

Our emphasis in exploring the media of television may have seemed negatively biased. Formerly a high school English teacher and now a television researcher, Patricia Gillard (1994) reminds us of a very different story. In her research on television with children and adolescents, she says that she "tapped a reservoir of energy and enjoyment and a desire to share their TV experience. Perhaps they are surprised that an adult is interested. They 'love' TV. They know it well and celebrate it in the playground, but keep it to themselves around disapproving adults" (p. 82). Gillard believes that TV viewing is not the same for all adolescents and that teachers need to appreciate those differences before they disparage the viewing habits of their students. She summarizes some of the differences that were revealed in her own research. (She uses the term *children* to designate an age group spanning from elementary through high school years.)

- The more TV is on, the more likely children are to engage in other activities as they view. This suggests that children adapt to their TV environment. How they view may be the most important aspect of TV viewing, because it differentiates between children in the ways that they 'see' and therefore, presumably, what they learn from what they see.
- A definition of TV viewing as watching particular *programs,* rather than a continuing activity taking place with other events, assumes a particular style of viewing which is typical of families who structure their time and generally have more leisure options.
- This pattern is probably typical of many teachers as well. The view that TV is an inferior use of leisure time and that other media such as books are superior, is associated with this particular program-related definition of television.

- Families where TV is a major source of leisure and where it is switched on for much of the time are less likely to perceive the need for 'control.' On the other hand, viewing is more likely to be a shared activity and a part of being 'at home.'
- Where TV is a major source of leisure there is likely to be less difference between what adults and children view.
- In families where women work away from the household, alternative ways of dealing with TV will usually be adopted, such as discussion with children of program content, and deliberate co-viewing with children. (p. 79)

Teachers need to be sensitive to the family context in which students watch TV before criticizing it. Gillard reiterates our sense of the importance of locating students' experience and of building our instruction from that. She reminds us too of the probable error in assuming that their experience is like ours. Thus, she gives four cautionary "don'ts" to teachers before they begin to discuss television media:

- measure the time spent viewing TV with the purpose of encouraging students to 'reduce' it.
- list programs viewed by students and exhort students to watch 'better' programs
- set television viewing in opposition to other 'preferred' uses of leisure time such as reading
- prohibit students from doing homework in front of TV

She does not ask that we be noncritical of television, just that we don't impose our biases and thus silence and shame students about their own and their family's daily habits. The chances of students thinking critically are much greater if they are not defending themselves from the first. Then, both teacher and student might be open to explore and discover in television that which is creative and vital and that which is stultifying and false.

EXPOSE: STUDENTS AS SOCIAL CRITICS

In this quadrant, we are not engaged in helping students examine the nature of media; we are exposing its impact on the culture. As we begin to look at the possibilities in our classrooms, we want to understand and articulate the power of media in our lives. Aronowitz (1977) maintains that "in the last half of the twentieth century, the degree to which mass audience culture has colonized the social space available to the ordinary person for reading, discussion, and critical thought must be counted as the major event of social history in our time" (p. 468). Can you imagine a day in your life without those media that we have come to regard as necessities? Media have so pervaded our lives that we are barely conscious of their impact. Raymond Williams (1980) observes that viewers have grown so accustomed to receiving one-way "talking-head" content from television speakers who cannot be interrogated and images that cannot be slowed down that they do not even ask questions about it. Salomon and Leigh (1984) observe that past experience and TV's unchallenging programming lead viewers to expect to exercise little mental effort in processing television content and so to put little into it.

Postman (1979a) argues that we must actively resist turning our youth over to the "entertainment media: television, film, records, radio," and that we must actively resist them in the classroom. He enumerates four media "biases which are in special need of opposition by the schools" because they disregard or undermine essential skills, values, and behaviors that schools should promote in the young: The media are (1) "attention-centered," with their main goals being to capture and hold their audience's attention, (2) entertaining and so must not be too "demanding or disturbing" or they will lose their audience, (3) image-centered and so work against sustained thought or language development, and (4) narrative, rather than expository, and so make "the systematic presentation and development of ideas" alien to students. Postman suggests counterbalancing strategies with which these seductions might be resisted: "This would imply that the schools stress, for example, subjects that require students to understand and express themselves in words; that require them to pay attention even when they are not being entertained; that require them to evaluate and criticize ideas; that demand concentration and a confrontation with complexity."

Postman's emphasis here is on reinforcing teachers' confidence in a curriculum that is "sharply differentiated from other cultural institutions such as movie theaters, rock concert sites or playgrounds." Other educators join his struggle and suggest the focused study of media as another strategy. Aronowitz (1977) believes that media study is necessary, but difficult; it asks students to run in the face of accepted realities:

The teacher must persuade students of the significance of the study before the study will be meaningful to them. The objects of mass-cultural perception, particularly rock music and television, are so close that achieving critical distance from them requires even more intellectual and emotional effort than literature or math, which are sufficiently distanced by their historical character and academic legitimacy to make them easier to study. Mass-cultural forms have colonized the leisure time activities of youth so completely that giving up, through analysis, the pleasure one gets from them may be painful . . . Having successfully demystified media content and seen how certain forms such as popular music provide only spurious satisfaction, students are still left to face daily life. (p. 470)

Despite these resistances, Aronowitz suggests that an examination of media be undertaken to free and exercise critical thinking. He believes that teachers must first be willing to examine media as a legitimate subject "in order to criticize and transcend it—or to discover whether genuine expressive forms are repressed within it" (p. 469). We have, in this chapter, presented concrete exercises that do that. Now, we summarize some of the most common and persuasive critiques of television, film, and musical recordings.

CORRUPTS CULTURAL MORALITY

One of the most common complaints in the popular press is that the media have corrupted our morality with its graphic portrayals of violence and sex. Social and behavioral scientists in laboratory and real-life studies have discredited some of the most inflammatory charges and the anecdotal evidence of copycat crimes and seriously harmful antisocial acts. But some researchers (Milgram & Lance, 1973) have convincingly demonstrated a correlation between the viewing of violent programming and aggressive behavior. Many social critics identify that corruption as more than provoking violent behavior, as also deadening sensitivity to real-life suffering and violence. Because violent programming dulls the reaction to the experience of the media itself, media must escalate violence to assure the same degree of viewer interest and excitement.

FALSIFIES EXPECTATIONS OF LIFE

Many social critics identify media's impact as even more subtle and pervasive. Neil Postman in *Teaching as a Conserving Activity* (1979b), claims that the media now serve as "a surrogate for reality." He gives the amusing example of a popular hospital-set TV drama of the 1960s, *Marcus Welby, M.D.* Not only did Robert Young, the actor who played Marcus Welby, receive more than 5,000 letters a week seeking his medical advice, but also, the American Medical Association actually invited him to one of its annual conventions as the keynote speaker. Postman acknowledges that long before the "electronic revolution," reading played a significant role in encouraging a fantasy life, and that many nineteenth-century novel readers probably found more pleasure among fictional characters and places than with the people and situations of their actual lives. But today the power and frequency of experiencing life removed from actuality, life filtered through a technological screen, is tenfold.

We read with our students the poem "Reel One" by Adrien Stoutenburg, which speaks of the same sort of impact in film. After a young couple watch an action-packed, Technicolor movie "like life, but better" in which "the screen shook with fire," they walk home through falling snow, which, disappointingly, isn't "blue in the drifts" and is so silent that the "sound track" seems dead. The young people are startled when life turns out so differently from the controlled and heightened projection on the screen. Can you see the handicapping of the young's ability to face their real lives: You expect, don't you, that "reel two," the flesh-and-blood experience of the two moviegoers, will seem diminished? They have no sound track, no camera selecting the important scenes, and no ability to see, interpret, and validate their own lives for themselves.

REINFORCES PASSIVITY

Many other social critics join Postman in his alarm at the media's encouragement of passivity and the attendant retreat of reason. Aronowitz (1977) characterizes the impact of media on students: "Most students go through their classes as if in a dream. They are bemused by daily interaction as if it were the unreality. Many of them live for the spectacle of the television show, the rock concert, the record party, and other mass-cultural activities. The spectacle appears as the real world in which they wake up and participate in the process of living; their nonmedia life is the fiction" (p. 469).

Bloom (1987), although he is quite different from Aronowitz in his general critique of the culture, observes a similar phenomenon in the effects of rock music on the young. In *The Closing of the American Mind,* Bloom writes of this music:

It is *the* youth culture and. . . . there is now no other countervailing nourishment for the spirit. . . .
It makes conversation impossible, so that much of friendship must be without the shared speech

that Aristotle asserts is the essence of friendship and the only true common ground. With rock, illusions of shared feelings, bodily contact and grunted formulas, which are supposed to contain so much meaning beyond speech, are the basis of association. None of this contradicts going about the business of life, attending classes and doing the assignments for them. But the meaningful inner life is with the music. (p. 75)

UNDERMINES CRITICAL REASONING CAPACITY

For Aronowitz (1977), this absorption in media assaults "the capacity to engage in critical thought as a meaningful form of social discourse" (p. 463). He believes that TV, film, and photography have restricted "the capacity of persons to make inferences, to offer arguments, to develop explanations of social events that may counter those that are considered authoritative" (p. 468). He locates the educational crisis today not in the decline of the skills that the "Back to the Basics" movement addresses, but in this loss of critical thinking. This numbing of reasoning is exacerbated by the one-way communication of the media. Individuals are the passive recipients of messages to which they have no power to respond. Sorenson (1989) sees English teachers as embattled with a piece of "talking furniture— the television set" (p. 42). Postman (1985) cites the effects of our movement from a print-based to a television-based culture: "We are getting sillier by the minute" (p. 24).

Postman believes that schools are the last bastion of processing the world through letters and numbers; that is, we are a part of the Gutenberg galaxy now being threatened by a technological galaxy. When we read a book's print, he argues, we are forced to distance ourselves from the reality it represents; we must transform letters to words and words to mental pictures. We are three steps from reality:

(word)	(idea)	(thing itself)

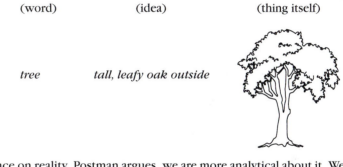

tree   *tall, leafy oak outside*

With some distance on reality, Postman argues, we are more analytical about it. We cannot be so easily manipulated when we are three steps removed. Graphic processing is not the same; it is immediate and stirs us in a way that Postman says is akin to magic or religious rites. We are not allowed any distance from the reality it presents. We are moved to action or internal response with very little or no reflection. In a sense, the analysis, objectivity, and progress (or decline) that print brought us in the sixteenth century are now being foreclosed by the lack of mentality ushered in by the visual media.

PROMOTES CONSUMERISM

Beyond stunting the mind and dulling the imagination, critics point to another impact of the media on our lives: It manufactures false needs that obscure authentic ones. The vast media system we live under manipulates our needs and persuades us to become uncritical buyers of an endless supply of commodities. Citizens step onto a treadmill of consumption, are never quite satisfied with the life promised by purchase, and so purchase more in an endless cycle of phony promises and disappointed hopes. Kellner (1988) observes that "[a]ds work in part by generating dissatisfaction and by offering images of transformation, of a 'new you'" (p. 43). Kellner traces the geometric expansion of advertising expenditures from 1950 (about $6.5 billion a year), to 1970 ($40 billion a year), to 1980 ($56 billion) to 1988 ($102 billion). (In Chapter 5, we reported that in 1996, advertisers spent $175 billion.) "When one considers that an equal amount of money is spent on design, packaging, marketing, and product display, one grasps that a prodigious amount of money is expended on advertising and marketing. For instance, only eight cents of the cosmetics sales dollar goes to pay for ingredients; the rest goes to packaging, promotion, and marketing" (p. 48). Individuals are being bombarded by sponsors intent on enticing them to buy. It is no wonder that they cannot distinguish between needs and wants, between the genuine and the spurious, and between the important and the trivial.

Exercise 8–1 invites you to evaluate your own understanding of these five critiques of media.

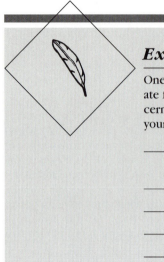

Exercise 8–1   Media Consequences

One way to explore media is with an interest in exposing their power over the culture. We enumerate five consequences of that power. Rate the strength of your concern for each from 5 (most concerned) to 1 (not concerned). Then check which of these critiques you would consider bringing into your classroom.

_____ Mass media corrupt the morality of the culture with tolerance for violence, sexism, and stereotyping of minorities.

_____ Mass media falsify life and set up unrealistic expectations for life.

_____ Mass media reinforce a passive reception of life, rather than active engagement in life.

_____ Mass media undermine the capacity for critical thought and for analytic and synthetic reasoning.

_____ Mass media promote consumerism, not self-reflection and self-discovery.

We have summarized the critical perspectives on media in order for you to grasp the position of many social critics. If you choose to teach this material to your students, you will be attempting to shake students awake to a part of their culture that is so intertwined in their lives that they are hardly conscious of its impact. We would not recommend, however, that you teach by polemic, but rather by their inquiry into their own experience of media. Their "text" surrounds them. In 1964, McLuhan spoke prophetically of the importance of such exploration for the purpose of exposing media: "Just as we now try to control atom-bomb fallout, so we will one day try to control media fallout. Education will become recognized as civil defense against media fallout" (p. 305).

CONCLUSION

We have suggested four ways in which the secondary teacher might use media in the classroom. We think that all students need to confront these powerful phenomena as more than means of entertainment and information. Students need to understand media more critically, to appreciate them with greater subtlety, to be warned of dangers, and to be encouraged in the enjoyment of potential delights. Whether your perception of the classroom study and use of media is positive, negative, or neutral, you must make decisions about how to employ them in your classroom. We believe that we can appropriate media's power to deepen our students' experiences, to enliven their study, and to energize their language production. The possible roles are challenging, but well within our students' range: producers, listeners and viewers, anthropologists and literary critics, and social critics.

9

COMPELLING WRITING

While speech is the medium of home and neighbourhood interaction, writing is largely or completely the medium of the school, and the child whose school writing is stultified has little else to draw on.... A sense of the social system of writing has so inhibited and overawed many teachers that they have never given a pupil the feeling that what he writes is his own.

John Dixon

In no area of English teaching is there more theorizing, experimenting, and researching than in writing pedagogy. And in no area are English teachers more vulnerable to the public's recent outcry about the failure of schools to teach elementary skills and the simplistic solution to return to the "basics." Shuman (1985) explains that "because one's use of language, whether spoken or written, is much more public usually than one's use of a subject like mathematics, the secondary school English curriculum has been criticized more than most for not teaching students basic skills" (p. 324). Often, laypersons who look at English classrooms as deficient point to the failure of students to learn the structure of the language (grammar), the mechanics of expression (spelling and punctuation), and appropriate usage (conventions of correctness). Those within the profession criticize writing instruction for stymying the expressive and communicative needs to write and encouraging, instead, the dull and lifeless language of many school classrooms. Macrorie (1970) has named this "phony, pretentious" language "Engfish." Mayher (1990) characterizes the common experience of "being taught writing as a kind of civil defense preparedness drill that most of us had in school: something we might have to use in some future emergency, but of no real consequence to our current lives" (p. 227).

Elbow (1973) believes that "the ability to write is unusually mysterious to most people" (p. 12). He observes that our lives are full of mastering difficult tasks, but "few of them seem so acutely unrelated to effort or talent" (p. 12). Various explanations are given for this inscrutable mystery: Writing is a special faculty or a force of inspiration or a capacity for "having something to say." Elbow captures our basic misconception about the process of writing in a parable:

> Once there was a land where people felt helpless about trying to touch the floor without bending their knees. Most of them couldn't do it because the accepted doctrine about touching the floor was that you did it by stretching upwards as high as you could. They were confused about the relationship between up and down. The more they tried to touch the floor, reaching up, the more they couldn't do it. But a few people learned accidentally to touch the floor: if they didn't think too much about it they could do it whenever they wanted. But they couldn't explain it to other people because whatever they said didn't make sense. The reaching-up idea of how to

touch the floor was so ingrained that even they thought they were reaching up, but in some special way. Also there were a few teachers who got good results: not by telling people how to do it, since that always made things worse, but by getting people to do certain exercises such as tying your shoes without sitting down and shaking your hands around at the same time. (pp. 13–14)

Teachers, both experienced and new, feel that teaching writing is as mysterious as writing itself. This chapter introduces several foundational theories and strategies of writing instruction and teaching activities for helping students enter it, teaching activities that are more than exercises in which students take out paper and shake their hands around. In Chapter 10 we become even more specific about classroom practice. Before we begin to discuss the teaching of writing, however, we would like for you to look inward for a moment to consider the assumptions about writing instruction that you bring to this chapter.

Invitation to Reflection 9–1

WRITING ASSUMPTIONS AND PROCEDURES SURVEY

Write D (disagree) or A (agree) before each statement in the survey.

_____ 1. In teaching writing, correctness and organization should be emphasized more than the clarity and substance of thought.

_____ 2. Grammatical conventions (including punctuation and spelling) should be emphasized only in the final edited version of a piece of writing.

_____ 3. Usage problems such as noun-verb agreement should be corrected through workbook exercises to instill the rules of grammar.

_____ 4. Students should be asked to write about their own experience, and to develop their own ideas about what they wish to write.

_____ 5. Writing is best generated by assigning topics on which students can write well.

_____ 6. Most of a student's writing time should be spent in the initial writing and proofreading of a paper.

_____ 7. Students are of little help in responding to other students' work.

_____ 8. Teachers should grade everything that students write.

_____ 9. Students should spend as much time in creative, expressive writing as in analytical, expository writing.

_____ 10. Grammar instruction is essential to the writing progress of secondary students.

This chapter presents a circular pattern of five interlocking writing constructs, shown in Figure 9–1, that encompass a total approach to writing in the English classroom. Each of the five constructs provides answers to basic questions about the teaching of writing. We define each construct briefly before illustrating them with specific writing activities.

Developmental Tasks. Here we note the cognitive tools that student writers must command to accomplish successively more difficult composing tasks. The construct answers the question "*How* do students think when they write in different discourse modes?" We focus on the kind of thinking required to write in increasingly complex discourse modes.

Process Model. Here we discuss the process used to write. The construct answers the question "*When* should each step in the process be taken?" We focus on a sequence of extended steps that enrich, deepen, and polish a piece of writing.

Writing Workshop. Here we examine a style of instruction in which students are given a great deal of independence and responsibility as they work on their writing. The construct answers the question "*Where* are different writing tasks completed?" Teachers such as Nancie Atwell restructure their classrooms so that they no longer resemble the once-familiar row-by-row teacher-centered arrangement,

FIGURE 9–1
Five writing constructs

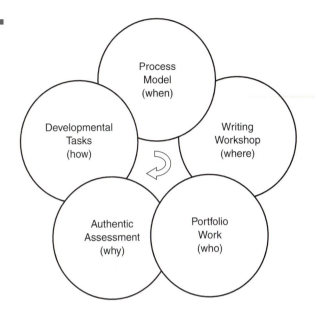

but rather look like an artist's studio or a newspaper office where everyone is working alone or in teams on different projects.

Portfolio Work. Here we show how students rather than teachers can take responsibility for producing, maintaining, revising, sorting, evaluating, and reflecting on their own writing. The construct answers the question *"Who* is responsible for writing in the classroom?" This reversal of roles makes portfolio work a new and profitable development.

Authentic Assessment. Here we explore new ways in which teachers assign and evaluate writing to meet the communication needs of the everyday world. The construct answers the question *"Why* is a piece of writing deemed good?" Writing that is authentic moves out of the cloistered classroom and into the real world of authentic daily tasks and normal work-force expectations. Because these authentic tasks are accompanied by rigorous real-world criteria for assessment, they set a standard that ties them closely to the first link in our circle, the cognitive tools for writing. In this chapter, we discuss each of these five circles—their assumptions, their classroom practice, and teaching activities appropriate to each—and we suggest their overlapping connections.

DEVELOPMENTAL TASKS

One of the best known and most influential challenges to the primacy of classical writing constructs has come from James Britton and his research team from the British Schools Council Project. Britton, Burgess, Martin, McLeod, and Rosen (1975) acknowledge their indebtedness to Piaget and Vygotsky as they define the use of language. Like Piaget and Vygotsky, they see words as a means of expressing thoughts that are prior to language. Unlike classical rhetoricians, they do not assume that the function of those words will always be to achieve a certain purpose.

HOW LANGUAGE FUNCTIONS: PURPOSE AND AUDIENCE

Britton et al. describe three categories of how language functions:

Transactional	language used to "get things done: to inform, to advise or persuade or instruct people"
Expressive	language used to think "aloud on paper," to "record and explore the writer's feelings, mood, opinions, preoccupations of the moment"
Poetic	language used to create "phonetic, syntactic, lexical and semantic" patterns depending on the requirements of the writing (pp. 88–90)

The user, audience, and purpose are interrelated in one of two basic ways: Writers can assume the role of participants, as they carry out transactional purposes with an audience, or of spectators, as they employ language to render "real or imagined" experience "without seeking outcomes in the actual world," (pp. 79–80). The spectator role is more detached from immediate experience. Transactional language requires the user to be a participant; poetic language puts the user in a spectator role. When language is used for an expressive function, the user might be either participant or spectator. Thus, in written discourse, writers are situated differently depending on their function and their relation to the subject.

To complete this picture of the act of writing, Britton et al. explain that writing also differs according to its audience; they maintain "that one important dimension of development in writing ability is the growth of a sense of audience, the growth of the ability to make adjustments and choices in writing which take account of the audience for whom the writing is intended. This accommodation may be coarse or fine, highly calculated or totally intuitive, diffused through the text or explicit at particular points in it." (p. 58). Teachers have traditionally initiated the writing task and "nominated" themselves as the audience. Furthermore, the teacher is not simply a one-person audience, but also "the sole arbiter, appraiser, grader and judge of the performance" (p. 64). Thus, school writing has required students to make elaborate judgments about satisfying the teacher's demands as audience, rather than the students' ideas as writers. Applebee's (1981) observations, interviews, and surveys of American secondary school writing also found that the most common audience for student writers was the teacher as examiner (pp. 46–58).

The implications of Britton et al.'s observations for writing instruction are clear. If language use originates in an expressive impulse for forming meaning, and if the making of meaning remains central to English classrooms, opportunities for expressive writing should be frequent. Yet Britton et al. found in their examination of British high school seniors that 84% of the writing was transactional, less than 7% was poetic, and less than 4% was expressive (with 5% distributed among additional and miscellaneous categories) (p. 165). Britton et al. propose that we alter this emphasis: In the early stages of writing, children write a form of "written-down expressive speech. . . . As their writing and reading progress side by side, they will move from this starting point to . . . broadly differentiated kinds of writing" (p. 10). Moffett, in *Teaching the Universe of Discourse* (1968), observes this same movement from egocentric communication to public discourse. He believes that our instruction should also progress through a sequence of writing tasks from the familiar and personal to the more distant and impersonal. Moffett's *Active Voice* (1992) for teachers and his coedited anthologies of student writing have encouraged and permitted teachers and students to value writing assignments that would once have been considered nonacademic. This and other texts invite students to write at different levels of discourse, to move from the personal writing of inner speech to monologues, dialogues, and narrative before reaching the formal essay. When the developmental ideas about language of Britton, Dixon, and Moffett are coupled with Piaget's concept of intellectual development from infancy to adolescence, a new model of writing instruction emerges.

WRITING STAGES

Piaget's observations and speculations suggest a fruitful way to understand how a developing mind structures knowledge in that period from infancy to late adolescence. Piaget described four stages of cognitive development through which he believed all people move in the same succession (Figure 9-2). Each stage is distinguished from the next by certain "operations" that the individual masters, new ways of seeing the world and thinking about what happens in it. We build from one stage to the next, as capacities consolidated in one stage give way to and are synthesized into the maturing of the next stage. These four stages have been questioned and studied since Piaget first conceptualized them, but they have been confirmed as being sequential (higher stages always emerging out of lower ones), invariant (regressing or moving out of sequence does not occur), and universal (valid in all cultures).

Piaget's cognitive development theory can be linked to writing to form three postulates that serve as the foundation for a developmental writing construct:

1. Writing is built on talking and listening, both of which grow out of thinking.
2. If thinking is the basis of talking and writing, it follows that writing would have developmental stages built on or parallel to those of cognitive development.
3. Writing tasks or stages that require more complex, abstract procedures would follow.

The instructional conclusion from this theory is developmental. Teachers should locate a student's stage or level of writing comfort and ability and try to move him or her to higher stages, whether this movement occurs within a class, over a year, or through the entire K–12 curriculum.

FIGURE 9–2
Piaget's cognitive
stages

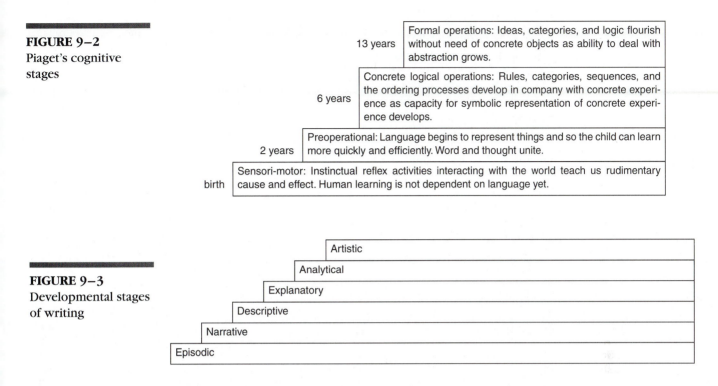

FIGURE 9–3
Developmental stages
of writing

DEVELOPMENTAL SEQUENCE

We begin our discussion by describing a six-stage developmental writing sequence, which is illustrated in Figure 9–3. We find these six stages to be useful as a scaffold or organizing principle for instruction and long-range planning. They will be most beneficial as a general sequencing device, not as an invariant order. Writing at each of the six stages requires progressively greater cognitive complexity and competence. Students need control of the cognitive skills required of one stage to write at the next higher one. Preceding stages will be revisited as new ones are entered. Growth within each of the last five stages will be ongoing.

Two complementary Piagetian concepts will be important in helping your students move through these stages: *decalage,* the complete mastery of a new cognitive capacity, and *disequilibrium,* the lack of balance resulting from being poised between two cognitive capacities. Piaget observed that children move into the concrete operational stage and master its tasks one at a time until all are under control. Similarly, students must undertake each writing stage so that they feel certainty and comfort in that stage before rushing on to the next. Students who are beginning to understand a higher stage of thought become less satisfied with working only at the former stage. They are off balance, caught between two worlds. When students are off balance, they signal that they can begin to move to another stage. Teachers must walk a fine line with their students. They need to allow students to work at each stage until they are very comfortable with it, but they also must nudge students into disequilibrium so they can move to the next higher stage. The six-stage developmental sequence is represented much as is Piaget's stair steps of cognitive development.

Episodic (Nonsequential).   Episodic writing is usually the first produced by children and probably is seldom encountered in secondary schools. An amazing percentage of children entering school believe that they can write, even though their essentially episodic writing may not be easily understood by others. Giacobbe (1982) and others merely give children writing materials and tell them that they are expected to write in their books. Teachers in Wiltshire Schools in England have their preschool children write initially, then record what the children tell them their writing says. Thus, the teachers enter the communication process with their students. Later, that which seemed scrambled, mazelike, and impossible to read becomes more communicable. Children mimic the shapes of adult letters if only imperfectly and begin to appropriate the standard noun-verb-object syntax that characterizes simple oral and written communication.

Narrative (Temporal Events).   A philosophical comic once said that "time is Mother Nature's way of not letting everything happen at once." Stories use time to do that. Narration is the simplest form of writing, and children who first shape their words tell stories. Most of them use the structure of their daily lives. Giacobbe (1982) calls these "bed-to-bed stories": "I woke up this morning, put on my jeans and ate some runny eggs for breakfast. Then I went with Uncle Fonzo to the Farmers' Market where we saw some gooses and . . . My stomach was hurting so much from Uncle Fonzo's yellow candy chickens that I could hardly get to sleep at night." The child merely has to recall the correct order of events to tell a story. When adult friends gather or families reunite, stories are often the discourse that connects them. They do not generally turn to analysis; it is a more complex cognitive process, and it brings more distance to the language at hand.

Narration is a simple and natural form, and teachers can evoke it, enliven it, and empower it. Chapter 3 provided prompts for oral stories, including the Accidental Power, Trio Tales, Four *C*s Improvisation, and Intervention Drama exercises. Look at the elliptical bed-to-bed story and consider what could be done to encourage the storyteller to create an interesting story. Consider how a teacher can help students shape a better story. What would be the effect of a teacher who circled the crisis event, the stomachache from Uncle Fonzo's yellow chickens, and asked students to look for any earlier event that should be emphasized so that the reader could recognize the cause of the stomachache? Sophisticated narratives that involve dialogue, varied and complicated characters, and a rich and ingenious plot with narrative suspense can be developed by young students.

Descriptive (Spatial Sweep).   Description leaves sequential, chronological order behind. Students must impose their own order on the world around them. The palpable external world keeps the descriptive task in the concrete operational range. The difficulty for writers is choosing and following an ordering device for their description. This task touches on abstraction itself: going from near to far, significant to trivial, or large to small. Teaching Activity 9–1 presents two writing activities that together can help students develop the perception, precision, and perspective needed for excellent description.

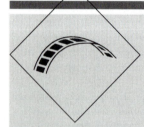

Teaching Activity 9–1   Descriptive Exercises

The Small Shell Game
Find 8 to 10 small conch shells that closely resemble each other and discreetly number each shell on its inner fold. Divide the class into teams of two or three students (one team per shell). Ask each team to write a precise description of its particular shell and give it an exotic place-name as a title for its description (the Auckland Shell, for example). Record the name and number on a master list and distribute each of the descriptions to a team other than the one that wrote it. Display the conch shells and have each team study all of the shells using the description in hand. Each team then must decide which of the numbered shells is being described. Consult the master list to see which team descriptions are apt enough to enable readers to identify their shells. The descriptions are thus given reality testing; precision and perception pay off.

Cultural Artifacts
Ask students to look at the sheet of penny heads shown in Figure 9–4 and select the one that most closely resembles the actual coin. Having warmed up with the commonplace penny, ask students to extract a single square cheese cracker from a pack of snack crackers, examine it more closely than they have examined pennies all their lives, and write a one-page detailed description of this ordinary artifact. This exercise involves solitary exploration in which an individual's careful attention to detail will lead to exacting writing.

Explanatory (Temporal-Spatial).   When students move into the explanatory mode of discourse, they are still dealing with physical objects and sequences, but they are working with the two at once. Narration and description deal only with one; two makes the task tougher. In addition, the sequence is not remembered from past experience, as in temporal narration, but must be established by the composer to produce an intelligible system. Studies have shown that explanation is a difficult task for elementary children because they can't see a whole system made up of disparate parts (Milner & Elrod, 1986). Writing explanations will help develop this systematic thinking. We have found that the best assignments avoid systems or procedures that are familiar to

Penny Wise

FIGURE 9–4
Penny wise

the reader. It is better to ask students to develop explanations that can be tested by the performance of an uninformed apprentice. The articulation of the new requires clarity and precision, hallmarks of good explanatory discourse, or the apprentice will fail. Teaching Activity 9–2 is an example of such an assignment.

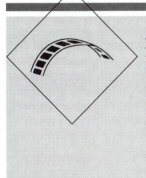

Teaching Activity 9–2   *Explanatory Exercise*

Game Plan

Ask groups of four students to create a new board game based on characters and events of a book that they have read. The game should have a board with pieces, moves, tokens, complications, obstacles, and ways to win. Bring the games and directions to class and let groups try to play them. The games need to be creative and fun, but the explanation must be quite precise and complete to allow the game to be played. After the games have been played, the creators should rewrite their explanations so as to ensure that any new players will play the game correctly. A simpler task requires a group of students to explain in writing how to play the card game Hearts. A group of students who do not know the rules begins to play the game while another group whose members know the game serve as monitors to see how well the rules are understood.

Analytical (Categorical-Logical).   This mode of discourse parallels the formal operational ability to depart altogether from the concrete world of space and time, the everyday familiarity of persons, places, and things. In analysis, students explore topics categorically and build arguments logically. Abstractions provide the structure at this level of discourse. The difficulty is that teachers often ask students to approach a complex analytical problem when students have not arrived at a cognitive stage at which they can do so with ease. Few average ninth graders are ready to analyze Shakespeare's use of irony in *Romeo and Juliet*. If we expect them to have success at such a task, we must teach the kind of thinking that lies at the foundation of analysis from the very earliest years in school. Wiltshire's primary teachers prepare 6-year-old students by asking them to place baskets or buttons in separate piles and then label each pile. Concrete objects are thus turned into abstract concepts. Teaching Activity 9–3 encourages analytical thinking using the concrete objects that are part of a shipwreck (Kahn, 1984).

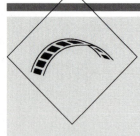

Teaching Activity 9–3   Analytical Exercise

Survival Dilemma

A ship is sinking and you have managed to board a lifeboat with 12 other people. Most of the people were not able to reach the cabins to get warm clothing, so they are in street clothes. One woman is in a bathing suit. The ship is in the North Atlantic, and the temperature is near freezing, with strong winds and high waves. The lifeboat is an open wooden craft with no motor, so it must be rowed. You may have to spend several days at sea, depending on when the boat is spotted. The ocean is very foggy with low, heavy clouds. The boat is dangerously overloaded, and in order to keep safely afloat you *must* remove 60 pounds of weight. You must decide which items you will remove. For safety reasons, you cannot suspend any items from the lifeboat. You cannot remove any of the people. You must choose from among these items:

- three wet suits, each 5 lbs.
- a 2-gallon container full of water, 15 lbs.
- four wool blankets, each 2 lbs.
- a large S.O.S. flag, 3 lbs.
- 30 cans of tuna fish (flip tops), each 1 lb.
- eight oars, each 5 lbs.
- first-aid kit, 10 lbs.
- five slicker raincoats with hoods, each 2 lbs.
- battery-operated signal light, 8 lbs.
- two buckets for bailing, each 3 lbs.

We ask students to make thoughtful individual decisions about which 60 pounds are to be tossed overboard before we ask groups of five to agree on the best solution to the problem. Each student writes a paragraph listing and justifying his or her choices; each group selects the best and combines them into a single document. When all groups have had enough time to collaborate, we call on one group to list the items selected to be jettisoned and their reasons for tossing them. We then invite other groups to challenge this group's selections and offer better lists. These exchanges usually lead us to question what these expendable items represent beyond themselves. Categories of items begin to emerge: oars and flag used like a sail represent movement or mobility; tuna and water represent sustenance; signal light and flag represent communication; and oars, wet suits, and blankets represent protection.

This classification facilitates discussion. And as the categories are refined and ordered, material and motive for writing develop. (Studies at the University of Chicago [Hillocks, 1986] have examined the power of such activities in developing prewriting skills, which are the building blocks for good analytical writing.) Exercises such as these, which pique analytical reasoning and give it a concrete and engaging context, energize thinking and therefore writing.

Artistic (Concrete Universal).   Most of us do not expect to nurture professional artists in our classrooms, but we can help free students to give expression to their own creative impulses. Our suggestions on Right Writing later in Chapter 10 will elaborate this encouragement of the artistic. For now, one of the most obvious ways to shape student ideas and experiences is to center on the metaphorical or analogical. Teaching Activity 9–4 introduces a natural way to enter into this world by asking students to write parables. Parables and fables are often thought to be more simple and moralistic than artistic. Their very directness, however, can encourage young writers to a simple shaping of their own deeply held convictions.

In addition to parables and fables, other, more elusive kinds of stories can be attempted by students. Some of the suggestions in the Apprentice Writing section of Chapter 10 are helpful in creating this sixth step of developmental writing in which the events of a story represent (symbolize) more than themselves.

Teaching Activity 9–4   *Artistic Exercise*

Parables

Explain to students that a parable, or fable, is a story that relates a series of concrete events that suggests an abstract moral lesson that means more than the mere description of those events. Ask students in groups of four or five to recall the details of the African fable "The Tortoise and the Hare" and the Biblical parable of the talents (provide texts if needed). Have students individually write on note cards what each story means and as a group compare interpretations. Then discuss the similarities in how the two work as stories, and how they are different from ordinary narratives. Having explored these two well-known tales, students read "The Parable of the Lord's House" and write down what the story means.

The Parable of the Lord's House

A young boy passed through his years of tender ease in a household of safekeeping where all about him seemed good and sure. Many was the time he was told of a fine lord's house to which he must make a journey. Its riches and splendor were often made known to him. So it seemed quite well to him that he should journey to that house some day.

And indeed one day he set forth on his journey and the road was long but the path was soft; and the ease of rest and the bounty of his sustenance made the journey seem no longer than the twinkling of an eye. And when he came upon the house of the lord, his eyes were pleased, for it appeared as his father had said—its riches and splendor seemed more than could be told.

He dwelt there in that house which his father had spoken of so often, and it seemed as if he were almost dwelling there as his father and not as he himself. And while he was dwelling in that house he was coming of age. And his feet began to wander on paths that led away from the lord's fine house. And on some days he would journey forth and sojourn for a night or more before returning to the lord's house. And on those days away from the house, he began to rest his eyes on many a strange sight and his ears heard many a troubling tale. And at times he would forget that he had traveled forth from the lord's house and would stay many a night away before awaking to the vision of the lord's house of which his father had spoken. And he would rise and journey to that house again. But the way was never easy as it had once been in his youth.

Then on one of his sojourns away from the lord's house, he came upon a wise man who knew the paths upon which he had wandered and who knew the lands which lay beyond those paths. And this wise man explained many new things to the youth which made his head spin with zeal. He told him that the lord's house from which he had wandered was not a house at all but only a facade which fooled his senses. Such counsel was so strong that the youth continued to dwell in the land of the wise man for many a day and explore its many paths and tangled ways.

After dwelling in that land for so long a time the aging youth felt a strong power begin to grow in his heart which made him want to return to the lord's house. So he set forth on a curious, labored journey which brought him to that house. And when he gazed upon it his heart felt full. It seemed good and just as he remembered it from his father's words. But as he drew closer upon that house the loathsome thought came to him that what he saw was merely what his father had taught him to see. And though he felt good he did not feel at peace. For his mind troubled him all the more.

Discuss various readings of this parable and then consider whether it works as the previous ones do. Once students have examined the three parables in their groups and have determined some of their basic features, have each group try to create a parable, one that uses characters (people or animals), events, and objects to represent truths or ideals that lie beyond these ordinary matters. Use the following questions to see how well students have developed their parables.

1. Does the story make sense as a simple story?
2. Does the story have a simple meaning that most readers could recognize?
3. Do characters, objects and events clearly represent something beyond themselves?
4. Do the characters have characteristics that reinforce the idea of the story?
5. Do all of the events fit together to work toward a unified meaning of the story?

When you have checked out the workings of each group's parable, have the students read it to other groups and let them first judge it by these same standards and then write down its simple message.

The National Assessment of Educational Programs' (NAEP) *Writing Framework and Specifications* (1998) reinforces the concept of writing stages built on cognitive tasks in its designation of three major genres of writing (narrative, informative, and persuasive) and by its brief explanation of the increasing "cognitive complexity" of the sequences: "Each writing assignment may also be categorized according to the major form of reasoning required." This is an important confirmation, because we believe that the cognitive tasks underlying writing vary greatly and that a teacher's awareness of their range and relationship to different genres of writing provide crucial knowledge for understanding students and their writing progress.

Invitation to Reflection 9–2

- Which writing purpose does most of your present writing serve: transactional, expressive, or poetic?
- Who is its audience?
- Does a developmental construct correspond to what you know of the stages of cognitive development or what you have observed of children and young people?
- In your elementary and middle school experience, at what stage did most writing instruction occur?
- In your high school experience, at what stage did most writing instruction occur?
- As you read the descriptions and the teaching activities associated with each of the six stages, which stage seemed most left out of the writing instruction you have experienced? Which most appealed to you?
- Can you imagine how these stages could be sequenced in a high school writing program? Would one have greater emphasis over another? If so, which? Do any seem peripheral to what you consider appropriate for high school students?

PROCESS MODEL

Although the term *process* is often overused or too loosely used, its name explains itself. It means "becoming," not "being." It focuses on change and growth. It acknowledges the struggle involved in any authentic and thoughtful writing, whether for 13-year-old students or mature writers. It urges teachers to honor that struggle by encouraging students to think of writing as an extended process, one that lasts longer than a 55-minute classroom assignment. It acknowledges that for even the best writers there is an extended period of time in which writing changes shape from prewriting to writing to rewriting. For some extremely able writers, this extended process can take place in their heads. Mozart, for example, is said to have composed music by just writing it down perfectly the first time, "as if," according to Leonard Bernstein, "it were phoned in from God." Some literary geniuses struggle to write like that, but most of us struggle to catch our thoughts, then write and rewrite. We revise even a simple memo three or four times. For most students it helps to segment these separable parts of the writing process, although they are by nature recursive. We will enumerate a set of steps in the process, but first we present some basic assumptions that are the foundation for these steps.

BASIC ASSUMPTIONS

A process approach to writing puts many of the theories discussed in this chapter into a practical classroom operation. Eight assumptions are basic to it.

- The writer is an autonomous self-starter who has a need to explore meaning and to communicate.
- Writing is an extended process that includes prewriting, writing, and rewriting (revising and editing).
- All modes of written discourse are equally respected.
- Students are expected to write and are given responsibility for shaping their own writing.
- Conferencing with student writers is a basic feature of instruction.

- Student writers need many readers to respond to their work.
- Ownership of writing begins with selecting a topic and extends to giving writing a public platform.
- Writing is a whole process whose parts are not easily divisible, but are recursive one with another.

We explore these one at a time.

1. *The writer is an autonomous self-starter who has a need to explore meaning and to communicate.* The writing process approach reflects a deep-seated belief in the nature of humans as communicators and writing as a basic means of satisfying this need. Assigning topics, then, only perverts the direction of that natural motion. Phrases such as "everybody has a story to tell" and "no more writers' welfare" suggest that all students have something to say and that teacher-suggested topics lead to dependence and misdirection. That is why, Graves (1983b) argues, students who have become dependent insist "Write it on the board, Teach." They begin to believe that they have nothing to say. Conversely, he also found (1983b) that teachers who make the least assignments receive the most writing. This assumption also means that writing serves multiple purposes—learning, play, self-discovery, and more—and that these purposes direct the way the writing works.

2. *Writing is an extended process that includes prewriting, writing, and rewriting (revising and editing).* The idea that such a thing as the writing process can be reduced to a neat formula, be laminated, placed on a classroom wall, and carefully imitated is antithetical to the complexity and mystery of good writing. Many good lists have emerged, but none is definitive. Some simplify writing to the three foundational stages of prewriting, writing, and revising. Others say that no list is complete without the idea of publication at the end of the process. Still others want to add at least peer review and editing as discrete steps in the process. We offer the following list as a clarification of important steps in this approach, but with the caution that any list can be reductive or cumbersome and, in the attempt to clarify, can turn what should be a natural process into an unnatural act.

Extended Writing Process

- Inventing: brainstorming, listing, webbing, and nonstop writing to discover ideas for writing
- Arranging: looping together the best ideas into patterns and structures that make sense
- Drafting: writing at top speed so that composing can try to keep pace with thinking
- Uniting: rereading a draft all at once to see how it can be made to move forward in a purposeful way
- Proofreading: reading a paper slowly after some time has elapsed since drafting to find the mistakes
- Peer reviewing: partnering to get an outsider's view of the writing
- Revising: reviewing the writing to see if it does what it was intended to do and reshaping it to do just that
- Editing: reading of the writing by a more mature writer so that important help can be offered
- Refinishing: using the help of an editor to revise and proof so that the writing best meets the writer's hopes
- Evaluating: assessing the worth and status of the writing by the writer and/or teacher
- Publishing: putting the writing forward in the world so that it can reach its fullest audience

3. *All modes of written discourse are equally respected.* The idea that school writing takes only one shape (analytical, expository writing) is too narrow a view of writing. Graves (1983b) honors narrative in talking about "stories to tell" and Murray (1977) makes a convincing case for student narratives' exhibiting all of the composing skills developed by any other mode of discourse.

4. *Students are expected to write and are given responsibility for shaping their own writing.* Primary teachers give first-grade students writing books and ask them to write in them. Writing process teachers give older students portfolios and ask them to keep in them samples of their own work that show changes through a series of drafts. This strategy carries important messages: The direction of a piece of writing is set by the writer's taking into account advice from many sources, and some writing in all of its stages is valuable enough to keep. Writing grows out of students' insights and feelings and matures when they feel full responsibility for its final shape.

5. *Conferencing with student writers is a basic feature of instruction.* The teacher who teaches best reads students' writing with great attention and shows deep respect for the writer. Conferencing means listening carefully to a student's intention in the writing, reading the draft itself, questioning the student about the next step, and offering suggestions. It means finding out what students are discovering that they want to say and helping them reflect on effective ways of

saying it. Conferences are often brief and speculative rather than lengthy and directive. In *A Writer Teaches Writing* (1985), Murray offers practical suggestions for organizing and conducting student conferences (pp. 147–186).

6. *Student writers need many readers to respond to their work.* If teachers are the only people who read their students' writing, students feel that their words are not touching the real world. They learn to write to the teacher's tastes and beliefs. They need more opinions about their work than any one person can offer. They need to see that a story judged as confusing by a teacher may be judged as both confusing and uninteresting, or as coherent and engaging, by another reader. Furthermore, if students are active writers, teachers cannot read everything they write. Multiple readers aid the composing process and allow teachers to give careful attention to the best work, writing that students "own" because they have labored over it.

  Many means of promoting multiple readers are available. Four that have proven useful for us are Monitor Conferences, Inductive Centers, Read/Write Groups, and Limited Partnerships. Each of these has a slightly different configuration, purpose, and procedure. In Monitor Conferences, the entire class will look at one paper and respond to its achievements or its problems, at depth or on the surface. Inductive Centers use an overhead projector or hard copies of a number of pieces of student writing to compare features and to consider what works and what does not. When seven opening sentences are seen side-by-side, an inductive sense of which one seems most effective may emerge in the group. Read/Write Groups work like the Monitor Conference except with a much smaller number of students. If continuity and trust have developed within the group, the writers and respondents can explore their writing with greater ease and effectiveness because their insights are shared only within the small group. The Limited Partnership is a less broad venture. Pairs of students read each other's work over time, talk about the growth steps they see, and even keep informal charts on what is developing in their partners' writing.

7. *Ownership of writing begins with selecting a topic and extends to giving writing a public platform.* Two ideas are key here. First, when students write out of their own choices, ownership is under way from the start. It then must be maintained by the way writing is handled. The student should stay in charge of the piece—turn it over to us for our help, but retain primary concern and involvement with it. We honor students' work and encourage their honoring it in the way we question them sincerely, recommend alternatives, suggest other readers, and reveal our own honest quandaries about the piece. Second, this encouragement is a careful process that continues until the work is published in some form. The student has worked all along with the intent of releasing the writing, of allowing it to be read and responded to by a variety of readers. This public platform has compelled more risk and investment in the early and middle stages of the process, and now it can reward that effort.

8. *Writing is a whole process whose parts are not easily divisible, but are recursive one with another.* The idea that there may be 3 or 11 steps in the writing process is not as important as the deep commitment to the idea that those steps are not discretely set apart, but are naturally recursive. A rocking back and sliding forward are always at work. Writers plan as they revise and revise while they write. While a word is checked for its spelling, an unintended strong right turn in the thrust of the piece may present itself. Writing proceeds, but new plans race ahead, and some of those are revised in turn.

FURTHER DEFINITION

Some of what this approach is all about can be best seen by comparing it with the more traditional product approach that it has replaced (Figure 9-5).

  The eight process assumptions, together with these simple points of comparison, help define this new approach, but a fuller exploration of the steps in the writing process, the act of responding to students' writing, and the kinds of questions that promote revision will help you use the process approach effectively in your classes. We offered a brief explanation of the steps in the writing process as we discussed eight assumptions of the process approach. We believe that elaboration of the writing process is important enough to present Murray's more complete and somewhat different understanding of it as rendered by Giacobbe (1982) in Figure 9-6.

  Most teachers have found that the process approach is valuable, but their students have sometimes balked at shifting to an entirely new way to write and to be evaluated. Vickie Martin, a former student of ours and now a practicing teacher, decided to reward her students for their move to a new approach by using the grading system shown in Figure 9-7 (personal communication, 1997).

FIGURE 9–5
Two writing
approaches

Product Approach	Process Approach
1. Topics are assigned.	1. Writing is self-initiated: everybody has a story to tell.
2. Expository essays are the staple of school writing.	2. All modes of writing are respected equally.
3. Grammar study, handbook rules, and exercises lead to good writing.	3. Prewriting, writing, and rewriting produce good writing.
4. Good writing is based on models and formal guidelines.	4. Meaning precedes and determines questions of form.
5. Teachers are the single audience for student writing.	5. Writing should be read like literature by a diverse audience.
6. Teacher-corrected papers are central to the teaching effort.	6. Conferencing with students and organizing other readers is central to the teaching effort.

FIGURE 9–6
Giacobbe's adaptation
of Murray's view of
the writing process

PREWRITING

1. *Collect.* Writers know effective writing requires an abundant inventory of specific, accurate information. The information is collected through reading, interviewing, observing, remembering.
2. *Connect.* Meaning begins to be discovered as pieces of information connect and evolve into patterns of potential meaning. The writer plays with the relationships between pieces of information to discover as many patterns of meaning as possible.
3. *Rehearse.* In the mind and on paper, the writer follows language toward meaning. The writer will rehearse titles, leads, partial drafts, sections of a potential piece of writing to discover the voice and the form which lead to meaning and which communicate that meaning.

WRITING

4. *Draft.* The writer completes a discovery draft, usually written as fast as possible, often without notes, to find out what the writer knows and does not know, what works and does not work. The writer is particularly interested in what works, since most effective writing is built from extending and reinforcing the positive elements in a piece of writing.

REWRITING

5. *Develop.* The writer explores the subject by developing each point through definition, description and, especially, documentation which shows as well as tells the writer, and then the reader, what the piece of writing means. The writer usually has to add information to understand the potential meaning of the drafts and often has to restructure them.
6. *Clarify.* The writer anticipates and answers all the reader's questions. At this stage the writer cuts everything which is unnecessary and often adds those spontaneous touches we call style. They produce the illusion of easy writing which means easy reading.
7. *Edit.* The writer goes over the piece line by line, often reading aloud, to make sure that each word, each mark of punctuation, each space between words contributes to the effectiveness of the piece of writing. The writer uses the most simple words appropriate to the meaning, writes primarily with verbs and nouns, respects the subject-verb-object sentence, builds paragraphs which carry a full load of meaning to the reader and continues to use specific, accurate information as the raw materials of vigorous, effective writing. The writer avoids any break with the customs of spelling and language which do not clarify meaning.

The Teacher's Role

The part of the process that Murray has been most helpful with is the careful way he talks about a teacher's role and the ways a teacher responds to student writing. We include his ideas in the following list, adapted by Giacobbe (1982):

- *Motivation.* I assume everyone wants to understand his or her own life, to make meaning out of experience, to share this meaning.
- *Assumptions.* All of my students have the potential to write something worth writing. They come to me with experience, language, and the human need to use language to order, evaluate, and communicate experience.
- *Method.* I teach a process of using language to discover meaning in experience. My students do not necessarily learn any specific form or how to respond to any specific writing task. They learn a discipline of thinking in writing which they can apply whenever they need it.
- *Discipline.* Writing is one of the most exciting things I do, yet I avoid it unless forced by external or internal deadlines to write. I do not think this should be so, but it is, and I assume my students are like me.

FIGURE 9–7
Martin's grading
matrix

Name _____   Period _____

The Writing Process

Step								
Zero Drafting (selection of topic, recording all thoughts)	5 pts.							
Student/Teacher Conference #1 (focus on content, develop context)	10 pts.							
First Draft (first and best effort at communicating content to a reader)	10 pts.							
Peer Review (identify best part of paper and why; find places where communication to reader is not clear and why)	15 pts.							
Second Draft (based on peer review; correct problems in communication—aim at clarity, unity, coherence)	15 pts.							
Student/Teacher Conference #2 (editing goal—spelling, punctuation, usage, grammar)	10 pts.							
Self/Partner Review (analyze your paper; make corrections which you perceive necessary; attend to unity, coherence, clarity)	10 pts.							
Release Draft (including editing goal—skill mastered, footnoted for teacher)	25 pts.							
Total	100 pts.							

- *Ethos.* Writing is a craft before it is an art. All writing is experimental, and therefore the writing course must be failure-centered, or at least failure-accepting, for trial and error is the process of discovery through which subject, form, and language are found.
- *Content.* I have no content to teach in the writing course, nothing to say in advance of writing. I am a coach who attempts to help each student develop the student's own subject and own voice.
- *Energy.* My student's papers provide the energy upon which the course runs. They motivate the students to write and me to teach.
- *Relationship.* My students teach me how to teach writing. In the conference I listen to what they say about their own writing and help them hear what they are saying.
- *Attitude.* I am a mirror in which the student will see his or her own potential, but the mirror image I project must be honest. I cannot reflect a potential in which I do not believe.
- *Goal.* I am a success when I am unnecessary. My goal is to underteach. I try not to teach my students what they already know or what they do not need to know at this particular moment. It is my responsibility to create a climate in which my students can teach themselves.

Murray sees teaching writing as a matter of responding to student writing. In responsive teaching, the student acts and the teacher reacts. The range of reaction is extensive and diverse because an individual teacher is responding to an individual student, and the student in turn is passing through an ever-changing process of discovery through writing. Here is a closer look at the steps of response that Murray encourages:

The Student Writes: Do not respond until there is at least a primitive text—lists, notes, drafts, attempts at writing. Instruction given prior to writing may limit or interfere with the student's writing.

The Student Responds to the Text or to the Experience of Producing It: The student must learn to evaluate a draft to produce a more effective draft. The teacher must know what the writer thinks of the draft to know how to read it because the teacher's job is to help the writer make increasingly effective evaluations of the evolving draft.

The Teacher Listens to the Student's Response to the Text and Watches How It Is Presented: The student teaches the teacher the subject matter of the text and the process by which the text was produced. In teaching the teacher the students teach themselves.

The Teacher Reads or Listens to the Text from the Student's Perspective: What the student thinks of the text is the starting point for learning and teaching. The teacher will understand where the student is in the writing process if the teacher frequently experiences the process of writing.

The Teacher Responds to the Student's Response: The teacher attempts to give the minimal response which will help the writer produce increasingly effective drafts. The teaching is most successful when the teacher helps the student realize what the student has just learned, first the learning and then the teaching.

Murray's suggestions make it clear that the writing process needs to be extended and that the student needs to be given ownership of the writing. The teacher follows as the student leads.

We now offer a list of questions that help students look at their writing in such a way that they can bring a fresh mind to its revision (Giacobbe, 1982):

- Do I have accurate information?
- Do I have enough information to satisfy the reader?
- Do I have so much information I will confuse the reader?
- Is there a pattern of meaning in the information?
- Does each piece of information lead towards that meaning?
- Is the meaning worth communicating?
- Are the reader's questions answered when they will be asked?
- Is the most important information emphasized?
- Would the information be better presented in a different genre?
- Is each part of the piece of writing developed effectively?
- Do the parts of the piece of writing add up to a pleasing and effective whole?
- Does each paragraph carry a digestible amount of information to the reader?
- Does each sentence carry information or its meaning to the reader?
- Does each phrase and each word, especially verbs and nouns, clarify information or its meaning for the reader?
- Does the entire piece of writing have a consistent and appropriate voice?
- Have I been honest?

With questions like these, students are urged to extend the process and deepen the content of their writing.

Having worked through these theories and more specific pedagogical suggestions, you may have begun to articulate more precisely some of your own basic beliefs about writing.

Invitation to Reflection 9–3

Our basic assumptions about writing are presented in the following list. Check those that you would claim as being important to you, altering and expanding them to match your own vision. Add two or more additional assumptions of your own.

_____ *Holistic not Partial.* All writing should be communication in the real world. Workbook dummy runs don't make sense to students. Contrived assignments don't ring true in their world.

_____ *Organic not Formulaic.* All writing takes some form, but form should follow meaning. Communication should lead; rules and methods should follow.

_____ *Inclusive not Exclusive.* Writing should move across many modes of discourse and touch many dimensions of life. Analysis of literature is important, but it is only a small segment of the whole writing continuum.

_____ *Developmental not Static.* Writers grow as they develop through many stages of life. Teachers need to be aware of those developmental paths and praise their students for the growth they see.

_____ *Foundational not Isolationist.* Writing is built on the foundation of thinking. It should be integrated into a full language curriculum in which students move from thinking to speaking to writing and in which reading is seen as reciprocal to writing.

WRITING WORKSHOPS

Writing workshops are not new in secondary classrooms, but there is a revolutionary quality to this approach to writing. The furniture and the pedagogy have been rearranged so that the classroom has lost its center or focal point—the teacher. The question *where* is answered by the many and varied places in which students are doing their work. The writing workshop was first clearly defined and illustrated by Nancie Atwell's *In the Middle*. Graves tells *In the Middle* readers that "Atwell has no method, rather, she provides a full immersion approach to reading and writing." His statement is meant to praise her for her integrity and depth, for moving beyond recipes and formulas, but Atwell's book is profoundly a methods book. She takes readers step-by-step through a 150-page manual for constructing a writing workshop. Numerous elementary and secondary teachers have adapted and transformed her approach. We will use other sources to help round out the story of this phenomenon, but more often than not, Atwell's ideas will dominate our description of this compelling approach.

ANTECEDENTS

When an idea such as writing workshops enters the world of English with such force, we want to know where it came from and why it is so appealing. Moffett and Wagner (1992) declare flatly that a workshop is "a group of students working together to augment the writing process." They clearly locate the antecedent for writing workshops in pedagogy. Graves tells us too that process writing does not lend itself to students sitting in neat rows. Bromley (1998) argues similarly that the workshop approach is a popular teaching technique partly because the writing process does not lend itself to whole-class, teacher-led methods. Because the steps in the writing process are elongated, the places where students happen to be at any one time both mentally and physically are numerous and unpredictable. When topics are assigned and students write to prompts without much or any time to plan before they write and revise after they write, there is little need for anything other than a traditional arrangement of desks.

It is important to realize too that workshops grew in the nurturing soil of middle-grade classrooms that were being redefined as less cozy than elementary classrooms but less demanding than high school classrooms. Middle-school leaders developed a rationale for less push and stress than high schools placed on students, so with less ground-covering to accomplish, writing and other subjects had time to move at a slower pace. Atwell (1987) admits that a more personal and psychological need prompted such a change, "I saw through my defenses to the truth. I didn't know how to share responsibility with my students (p. 11)." Graves suggests an additional reason for the shift toward a new writing environment, "As teachers, we need to free ourselves for effective observation and participation in all phases of the writing process (p. 12)."

WRITING WORKSHOP PRINCIPLES

To understand and put into practice the workshop approach, we need to start with a set of principles that, for Atwell, undergird this new way to teach writing:

- Writers need regular chunks of time.
- Writers need their own topics.
- Writers need response.
- Writers learn mechanics in context.
- Young writers need to know adults who write.
- Writers need to read.
- Writing teachers need to take responsibility for their knowledge and teaching.

You can see from these principles that the class is decentered in more than its physical arrangement. The work and the responsibility for writing shifts from the teacher to the students. Writing time is given primacy and thus is expanded lavishly so that deliberate rather than harried, trivial writing can be undertaken. Atwell reports that her students' newly found devotion to writing, "comes from the freedom to choose and the time to exercise that freedom" (p. 21). About her second principle, choice, she says, "all the strong feelings and raging enthusiasms of adolescents get directed toward ends that are meaningful because students choose them (p. 43)." She offers equally compelling reasons for all of her principles and, although she does not say it directly, her final principle challenges teachers to seek the same credibility and autonomy she offers her students in the writing workshop through their own professional growth. Teachers cannot know what to do with their classes unless they keep up with best practice and current research. But even more importantly, teachers cannot know writing unless they write, and they cannot know teaching unless they find ways to observe their students and examine what works and what does not.

Atwell's seven principles lead inexorably into a variety of very specific teaching acts: helping writers discover topics; learning how to talk to students about writing in helpful, sensitive ways; showing them how to confer with one another productively; helping students control mechanics and conventions; and offering ways to make students' work reach beyond the classroom walls. The shifts in the classroom landscape and in the locus of control define the workshop approach to writing, but because this is such a departure from what most of us have experienced, the entire procedure needs to be clearly explained. Whether writing workshops are adopted for upper elementary classes, as Gail Tompkins (1996) suggests, or for grades K–12, as Moffett and Wagner (1992) suggest, the format is similar. Writing workshops have many unique features, but all must have four basic components:

- Mini Lessons
- Writing Workshop Proper
- Group Share
- Status of the Class Conference

FOUR COMPONENTS

The Writing Workshop Proper (that is, the specific class time of intense individual writing) is a place for students to work full-tilt on their own writing with increasingly greater independence. Teachers usually allocate a large part of class time for serious writing. It provides them a chance to step back and watch students at work and then move in closer for one-on-one conferences. The Group Share provides a time for the entire class to respond to a few students' writing. The freedom and learning by doing of the Writing Workshop Proper and Group Share are balanced by the whole-class direct instruction of the Mini Lessons and by the accountability and structure provided by the Status of the Class Conference. The Workshop Proper and Group Share occupy most of the class time even when block scheduling is used. Only 5 to 10 minutes should be used for the Mini Lesson; it needs to be brief and focused. As Atwell warns us, "one skill or issue at a time (p. 56)." The Status of the Class Conference is even more abbreviated (2 or 3 minutes) and is a kind of pulse-taking roll call. This brief outline of the four components of the Writing Workshop sounds simple enough, but each needs to be explained a bit further.

Mini Lessons. Mini Lessons offer both direct instruction on procedures in the workshop and techniques on writing itself. The procedural guides to the workshop can range from models for how to confer to where various writing materials can be found. Atwell's list of writing techniques includes ways to develop leads, strategies for revision, methods for editing, and various crafts that shape writing. Tompkins (1998) offers her own list of ideas that should be considered as topics for minilessons (pp. 562–564):

- Teach the stages of the writing process.
- Teach writing workshop procedure.
- Identify new topics.
- Explain a writing workshop schedule.
- Explain and model conferences.
- Demonstrate group share process.

Mini Lessons should not be developed without regard to the classroom context; they should be the result of particular needs and gaps detected in the students' writing during the Writing Workshop. Even those short sessions should not be filled with teacher talk; they are most effective when techniques and strategies are demonstrated.

Writing Workshop Proper. The Writing Workshop should consume most of the period; it lasts at least 30 minutes or more so that students can become seriously engaged in their writing and so that you will have time to confer briefly with most of your students during that intense working period. Some teachers fear this new and apparently loose structure, but Atwell responds, "it is a tight ship . . . but a different kind of ship (p. 56)." Brock and Mirtz (1994) believe that three axioms provide the structure for that ship: Keep it real, provide time, and provide reflection. Giacobbe (1983) lists similar ingredients that will be explained in some detail because they are crucial for successful workshops: time, ownership, and response. Each of these three must be given serious attention.

Time. Time is needed to consider and reconsider what students have written. When teachers use most of a day's time for writing, students see that it is valued. The time also must be used to confer with students and to keep track of where students are in their latest projects. This time is needed for students to get serious writing under way. Graves says that 3 hours a week is a minimum allotment.

The more time students are given to write, he argues, and the more often they are given an extended period of time in which to write, the more students will have something to write about. Regular, frequent, writing time helps writers grow. There is no instant writing—not even in our quick-fix culture.

Ownership. Ownership is vital for adolescents who are caught between childish dependence and mature autonomy. They need to claim things as their own partly because they choose them. Atwell (1987) says that she made a huge change when she carted "her stuff" home and allowed students to make the class their room. She told them, "This is your room. That's your bulletin board. Feel free to fill it up (p. 63)." Many materials for writing must be present to make writing work, but when all of this material is explained and located and students have free access to it, that too becomes theirs. When students are involved in decision making, experimentation, and independence in their writing, a sense of ownership rides in on that tide. Because students in this workshop environment do not wait for teachers to prompt them at every step in their writing, they naturally develop a deep feeling that the work is truly their own.

Response. Response is another vital ingredient. Fernan (1993) believes that the focus on reflection through feedback is what truly distinguishes writing workshops. Teachers, peers, and adults provide this for students, but the coaching, conferring, and consulting affirmed by Moffett and Wagner are very different from the pushing, prompting, and prodding that students experience in more traditional classrooms. Teachers are not, however, thought to be useless because they are not the apparent driving force: "Students need teachers who will help them discover the meaning they don't yet know (p. 68)." When students are set in motion and writing is going well, teachers use workshop time for one-on-one conferences that are unavailable to teachers whose classes are not engaged in extended periods of writing. The conferences provide an opportunity for what Murray describes as a time for students to teach the teacher about their writing.

Because conferences are so important to the success of writing workshops, we suggest guidelines that Atwell (1986) has found to work very effectively:

- Keep conferences short.
- See as many writers as possible.
- Go to the students so you can control conference length.
- Make eye contact with the writers.
- Don't tell writers what should be in their writing.
- Build on what writers know and have done.
- Resist making judgments about the writing.
- In questioning students, ask about something you're curious about.

Questions play an important role in conference success. Atwell names her favorite open-ended questions: "What are you up to here?" and "How's it coming? Any problems?" Susan Sowers has some problem-centered prompts that she finds very useful: "Tell me more about that"; "I don't understand that."; and "Read it to me again." A few of her more pointed and also most effective questions provide a better sense of just how a brief conference might work:

- What's the most important thing you're trying to say?
- What's your favorite part? How can you build on it?
- How could you find out more about your topic?
- Is all this information important to your reader? What parts don't you need?
- Why is this significant to you?
- Does this lead bring your reader right into the piece?
- What do you want your reader to know or feel at the end of your piece? Does this conclusion do it?

Moffett and Wagner (1992) offer an equally powerful list of prompts that students use to make small workshop groups effective places to rethink and revise writing (pp. 204–5):

Title	Withhold the title of your writing and ask group members to try their hands at one.
Describe	Ask group members to describe the main point of the writing.
Ask	Ask questions about uncertainties in the piece.
Author	The writer asks about specific areas of concern in the piece.
What If	The group considers the effect of changes from key words to main ideas.

Whether you use questions, problem-related statements, or prompts, the key to excellent practice is that responses to writing begin with the writer's meaning.

We offer this extended explanation of the Writing Workshop because so many instructional departures are one-dimensionalized and trivialized by popular renditions of them. These lead only to dumbed-down approaches that are ineffectual or to misinterpretations that are counterproductive.

Group Share.   The central idea of Group Share is that everyone stops work and gathers at the center of the classroom, where two or three students read their writing and receive responses from the other student writers. It is best when the two pieces have some relationship to each other, for example, how the writers used leads or how they generated body and texture for their topics. Sometimes, every writer may be asked to read a lead or a close so that a general sense of what might work best in those techniques can emerge. Megyeri (1996) believes that Group Share is extremely important, so she offers a set of useful rules:

- The speaker must not begin reading until the listeners are ready.
- If any parts are especially entertaining, the speaker should wait for the audience to finish reacting.
- The speaker needs to make eye contact often, as people like to be read *to*, not *at*.
- The reading rate must be slower than in conversation. Listeners need time to process and absorb what the reader is saying.
- The presenter needs to speak in a voice loud enough to reach every corner of the room.
- The speaker should use facial expressions: smile, frown, gasp, show surprise, anger, suspense, etc.
- Reading aloud is a performing art, and the reader must bring some sense of enthusiasm and energy to the work. (pp. 73-76)

Atwell believes that two things are always accomplished by these plenary sessions: They "bring closure to the workshop" and "allow you and other students to find out what writers in the workshops are up to" (p. 85). This forum (along with the Status of the Class Conference) brings accountability to the entire enterprise that makes you and your students feel more comfortable and purposeful. The simple rules are that everyone but the reader puts down his or her paper, listens carefully, watches the face of the reader, and comments after the reader finishes if comments are sought. This segment of the Writing Workshop is extremely important to the success of the entire process because rules like these breed courtesy and respect for writing.

Status of the Class Conference.   The other task for you as you move about the room observing or conferring is to fill out the days' Status of the Class Chart. It is the key to the organization and ongoing progress of your students' writing. It must be simple enough that you can complete it during the writing workshop. A simple model like the one shown in Figure 9-8 helps solve organizational problems. Whatever the shape of your chart, you must remember that it is the essential means for keeping you and your students aware of students' progress and knowing how to help them direct their efforts purposely. The conference takes very little time but is an essential organizational device for the writing workshop approach.

PHYSICAL ARRANGEMENTS AND WORKSHOP PROCEDURES

The physical arrangement and materials of a workshop are not superficial matters; they have a great impact on the workshop's ongoing effectiveness. A variety of floor plans are possible, but most proponents agree that things flow smoothly when the workshop provides the following:

- Counter space for materials
- Stack trays, one for each class for writing ready to be edited and writing to be photocopied

FIGURE 9–8
Status of the class chart

Names	Dates								
	4-1	4-2	4-3	4-4	4-7	4-8	4-9	4-10	4-11
Adam	5,6	7	7	8	8	8	8	8,9	9
Brittany	1	2	3	3,4	3,4	4	4,5	6	6,7
Emily	8,9	9	1	2	2,3	4	4,5	6,7	7,8
Joshua	9	6	8	8	8	9,1	1	2,3	3
Phillip	8,9	9	9	9	9	1	1	1,2	3,4
Sara	1,2	2	2,4	5,6	8	9,1	1,2	2,3	3,4,5
Troy	4	4	4,5	5,6	6,7	7,8	8	9,1	1,2,3

Code:
1 = Invent   4 = Proof   7 = Edit
2 = Draft   5 = Peer   8 = Print
3 = Confer   6 = Revise   9 = Publish

- File cabinet, one drawer per class for portfolios
- Quiet zone corner table: no talking, students' backs to class
- Center decks: to write and confer
- Conference corner: away from quiet zone
- Group sharing area: carpeted or comfortable sitting area

Inside this workshop space where writers are on their own and call their own shots, there are simple rules that allow students to produce their best work as they write alongside and with one another:

- Don't erase; strike through.
- Use one side of paper only.
- Save everything.
- Date and label everything.
- Speak quietly.
- Work really hard.

Some of these may seem innocuous, but each has a purpose that relates to students' seeing themselves as being a part of a place where writing is valued and seeing themselves as developing writers.

Block (1997) believes that the rules that guide students during a writing workshop need to be focused on developing student independence. She finds four rules indispensable in creating this attitude (p. 42):

- No one interrupts individual conferences.
- Student team leaders resolve team needs and put them in writing for them to be addressed at next workshop.
- Students assess their own work at close of workshop each day.
- All other students continue to work in groups or alone while teacher is at conference with other students.

These guidelines not only control the noise level and promote on-task behavior, but they also contribute to students' reflecting on their writing and thus are doubly valuable.

A final procedure that all practitioners agree upon is the need to begin the first writing workshop with a "topic search activity." There are many ways to accomplish this. Giacobbe offers a simple but successful one: In pairs, one student tells a story to his or her partner in 2 minutes and then listens to the partner's story. Somewhere in those two tales lies a topic for those students to write about.

The Writing Workshop is not a panacea. Serious questions about it have been raised: Is it overbearing and lopsided? Is it unfocused and flaky? Is it hostile to analytical writing? For each of these questions, thoughtful and evenhanded answers have been provided. You may have already proffered some of these; others are answered by workable compromises that do not undermine the Writing Workshop's integrity. Writing Workshops' track record includes high test scores, students who become devoted and skilled writers, and students who read and write for pleasure in ways they never did previously. Moffett and Wagner (1992) offer a summative assessment of the natural power of the Writing Workshop, "When a workshop works well, everyone's personal performance improves, and individuals learn from it how to function well independently" (p. 202).

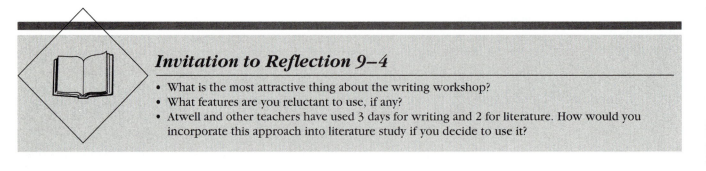

Invitation to Reflection 9–4

- What is the most attractive thing about the writing workshop?
- What features are you reluctant to use, if any?
- Atwell and other teachers have used 3 days for writing and 2 for literature. How would you incorporate this approach into literature study if you decide to use it?

PORTFOLIO WORK

The process approach and the writing workshop lead almost inextricably to portfolios. The three pedagogues emerged over time in that sequence because each naturally requires the next to fulfill its possibilities. They follow one another as the night follows the day. When teachers begin to elongate the actual process of students' writing and then rearrange the room and loosen the lock-step schedule of writing, the necessity for portfolios becomes apparent. Ironically, because the use of portfolios can be so readily simplified and cause almost no departure from more traditional forms of writing instruction, it is easily adopted and adapted. Thus, it is much more popular than the pedagogues that spawned it and that are not so easily reduced to fairly simplistic look-alike versions of the most thoroughgoing practice. In spite of the ease of counterfeiting portfolios in simplistic ways, true versions are evolving in secondary classrooms everywhere.

Portfolios make explicit what the process approach and writing workshops only imply: Students, not teachers, are now in charge of writing. When that responsibility shifts, teachers are free to teach, not grade papers. In support of this transfer of responsibility and what it might mean for teachers, Murphy and Smith (1992) call for writing teachers to put aside their overbearing work ethic that forces them to respond to every piece of student writing and let their students take some measure of responsibility for the quality and appraisal of their work. A legitimate part of the popularity of this approach may thus be the relief from the paper load it provides.

Elbow (1994) defines portfolios in terms of student capabilities. He believes that the portfolio is an invitation: "Can you show us your best work so we can see what you know and what you can do—not just what you do not know and cannot do?" (p. 16). The portfolio is defined by Kneeshaw (1992) as a vehicle for measuring the "cumulative success of individuals over time." He offers more specificity by saying that it is writing conceived as "living pieces" that are of three basic kinds: working drafts, holding drafts, and final drafts. Sorting out their own writing gives students the responsibility of self assessment and, thus, the realization of those pieces that need a great deal more effort, those that seem hopeless, and those that seem well composed. When these pieces are assembled and are kept over time, they "offer teachers a focused observation tool" that allows teachers, students, and parents to "monitor accomplishments." Applebee (1994) finds that they offer an opportunity for teachers and students to represent a broader spectrum of performance than can ever be sampled in an examination situation (p. 44). Schools are realizing more than ever that the student-parent portfolio conference during open-house nights is one of the best drawing cards for parent involvement. Some schools that were once lucky to attract 60 parents to a PTA meeting now regularly draw 300 or more because of these conferences. Some of this success is due to the developmental nature of the approach to students' academic achievement. It is more concerned with what steps (for example, spelling growth, use of proper punctuation in dialogue, control of voice, and use of tone) students have taken from month to month or semester to semester than with students' scores on achievement tests that are used to compare one student with another.

It is important to understand the pedagogical shifts associated with using portfolios, but we also need to explain what distinguishes the true portfolio from a simple manila folder that some teachers call a portfolio. Purves, Jordan, Peltz, and Gordon (1997) cite characteristics or principles that define a portfolio:

- A portfolio is meant to present the student to the outside world.
- A portfolio should seek to reflect the breadth of the student's accomplishments.
- A portfolio should justify the courses or curriculum a student has undertaken.
- A portfolio should be the responsibility of the student.
- A portfolio has a rhetorical purpose: to inform or persuade.
- Creating a portfolio is formative evaluation; the portfolio, summative evaluation.
- The portfolio has nothing to do with state or national assessment.

A number of other educators define the portfolio in various ways, but three characteristics seem to be universal in best practice:

- Portfolios emphasize writing in a wide variety of genres and tasks.
- Portfolios provide the means for treating writing as works in progress.
- Portfolios focus attention on students' responsibility for assessing and refining their writing.

VARIETY OF CONTENTS

In celebrating portfolios, Bromley (1998) makes it clear that students need to make choices about what writing they select for their portfolios, but she is equally adamant about the variety of content that should be included. The entries should be multidimensional; she wants to see skills checklists, learning logs, self-assessment pieces, creative writing, letters, poetry, reports, and a number of other kinds of writing. Morrow (1997) also insists on a wide range of writing but adds the need for other kinds of evidence of ongoing performance in class. Her list includes observation checklists, daily performance samples, anecdotal notes, audiotapes, teacher-made tests, and standardized tests. Her concept of the portfolio brings personal artifacts and external evidence together for student, parent, and teacher to gain a full-bodied sense of performance. Other teachers promote the inclusion of a variety of discourse modes so that narrative descriptive writing and analytical pieces all have a niche in the total collection. Some portfolio advocates urge students over the course of a year or over a span of 2 or 3 years to use each of the traditional modes of discourse, from narrative to exposition to poetry. When they move through such a range of writing, their strengths and weaknesses in each can be seen in terms of a developmental pattern. Porter and Cleband (1995) offer a list that is very inclusive: journal entries, bookmarks, written conversations, multiclass book responses, "sketch to stretch" visual entries, reflections on discussions, and photographs of students at work writing. Purves et al. (1995) argue that two portfolios are needed: one they call a "working portfolio," which is all-inclusive, and the other a presentation portfolio, where form and content come together. This compromise allows the process to be kept alive instead of falling into a product-oriented trap. The compromise may itself be a trap because of the separation of the process from what ends up as the final product. Much that is valuable is lost between the cracks. Porter and Cleband (1995) found after a time that they had been too directive and controlling about the kinds of writing that needed to be included in portfolios:

> We told the students to put into their portfolios their first through final drafts of all pieces of writing they had completed. We also asked students to display their journal entries or other responses to literature from each novel read during the semester. Finally, we prepared a series of questions about each draft of writing and about the responses to literature from each book . . . it became apparent that we had been too directive, not only about the items that should go into the portfolio, but also about what should be said about each item. (p. 8)

Luce-Kapler (1996) reports the same resistance to control:

> The students had similar feelings about the writing process. They wanted the opportunity to explore their fictional worlds without being given a road map. Some students didn't want any guidance for the writing process while others appreciated suggestions in the way an adventuresome traveler would welcome an occasional road sign. (p. 47)

Raines (1996) adds strength to this argument in her ethnographic essay built on the metaphor of a house becoming a home. She finds that transformation occurs when writers sense that a portfolio has, in fact, become comfortable and they have a sense of ownership of what belongs there. Other teachers have contended that if they do not require a variety of writing in the portfolio, students will write only stories and will never extend their range of writing capability. A fine line must be walked between demand and expectation.

WORKS IN PROGRESS

The second defining characteristic of portfolios is that they ensure that a piece of writing is seen as a work in progress, and that the process is extended beyond assigning, writing, and correcting. Mondock (1997) suggests a three-step procedure that ensures that writing is ongoing, and that students capture all of their work and push their best writing forward toward completion. The three steps are part of what Mondock calls the "story behind" the writing. Each step is composed of questions that call for a return to the work as writing in progress. The first set comes after the first draft of a piece of writing and focuses on the prewriting process.

Step 1 Questions

- What is your focus/purpose of writing?
- Are you satisfied with your topic and ideas so far?
- Is there anything that you need to change to make your topic/focus/purpose clearer or more interesting for the reader?

Students answer the three questions on an index card and then use the comments to revise the work in progress. The next set of questions asks for extension once again.

Step 2 Questions

- What significant changes are you going to make or have you made in your piece to improve the focus?
- Could anything still be improved through revisions?
- Are you satisfied with your piece to date?

When the writing is complete, a third set of questions is used to reconsider the writing, even though it is a finished piece.

Step 3 Questions

- Are you satisfied with your final piece?
- What did you like about your piece that you think will appeal to your reader?
- How could you improve your piece if you write about this topic again?
- How did the class respond to your writing and publishing? (pp. 61–62)

Although nothing more will be done to this piece of writing, students think of it as ongoing: The idea emerges that writing is completed but never perfect.

Mondock poses such questions to push students to think further about the writing at hand, but it is students' attitude toward returning to the writing that makes it an ongoing process. In time, those questions and thoughts about additional work on the writing should be internalized for students; they will no longer need to be prompted by teachers. There is a zone of proximal development at work here in which the added support of the teacher's enabling structure prompts students to do more than they might have without the thoughtful intervention.

STUDENT RESPONSIBILITY

The portfolio clearly nudges writers (and teachers) into accepting a wide range of writing and to understanding writing as an ongoing process. Portfolios promote those two characteristics beyond what might occur if only the process approach and writing workshops existed. But the third characteristic of portfolios adds a dimension to writing that is truly unique and would not exist without them: They carry students far beyond what could be expected in their writing without that final concept. As Graves and Sunstein argue, "If we want to help them become independent learners, then we *must* nurture self-evaluation of writing" (p. 60). Portfolios offer a panoramic view of writing performance rather than a snapshot; they offer an entire time line rather than a mere time capsule. A student who is troubled with vocabulary choices early in the year may use his or her portfolio to understand how that problem is being solved or remedies that may need to be taken. A student who almost always writes narratives can use the portfolio to gain awareness of the repetition and narrowness of his or her writing. Similarly, students who are making progress in handling troublesome connections or in developing a rich voice can be given that same kind of awareness by thoughtful use of portfolios. Mondock (1997) believes that portfolios that contain the total record "accumulate more evidence of student growth than may be possible from the final product." A small key to students' thoughtful and accurate scan of their own work is a simple date stamp that Raines (1995) requires all of her students to use on every piece of writing in their portfolios. Porter and Cleband (1995) put it succinctly: "reflection made possible by portfolios allows learners to see changes and development over time" (p. 48). Mondock (1997) affirms the reflection process of portfolios and what comes of it:

> By reflecting regularly on their portfolios, students soon realize that they have not simply collected evidence from the process but that this evidence is first-hand feedback for their self-directed improvement in future efforts. In this way, the students put their collections to work to serve as a guide or goal for improvement of the process, and ultimately for the final product. Thus, a higher-quality process leads to a higher-quality product. (p. 59)

Raines (1995) supports this same line of reasoning and draws from it three important qualities that a portfolio contributes to students' writing growth and learning:

- Portfolios help to extend the amount of time that students spend in practicing authentic writing.
- Portfolios provide important evidence of students' evolving learning experiences and useful information about the unique literacy development of each student in our classes.
- Portfolios encourage and nurture collegial relationships between students and teachers.

Robbins et al. (1994) prompt this reflection through a required essay in which students respond to seven issues that call on them to carefully think through their writing and the procedures that prompted their writing:

- What you selected and why.
- What you learned about writing these pieces and how.
- Improvement, strengths and weaknesses in your writing.
- Piece of writing that best represents your work and why.
- Aspects of the class or particular assignments that were most helpful in your writing.
- Types of assignments that you would like to do more of.
- Assignments that you particularly disliked and why. (p. 74)

screened off from the performer. Assessment is more direct and thus more authentic and valuable. Resnick (1987) believes that we need to move to a totally new way of assessing students' work that is central to the New Standards Project. Whereas certain disciplines' standards might appear to be a bit vague or fuzzy (Milner, 1997), the process that Resnick offers for assessing performance has a very hard edge to it. In the assessment she envisions, real-world tasks are assigned and then assessed by clearly delineated criteria that are defined by a six-level rubric. When this kind of assessment is in place, the testing tail will truly wag the instructional dog, and for once that will be proper because the tests will be a measure of real writing ability.

STATE-INITIATED PERFORMANCE-BASED ASSESSMENT

Virginia was one of the first states to develop a rubric for writing assessment, though it did not link class practice to the process. The Virginia Literacy Testing committee established five domains for assessment that are weighted in favor of composing features rather than conventions:

> *Composing:* Building a message for the reader.
> *Style*: Shaping the message to engage or affect the reader.
> *Sentence Formation:* How the sentences are made.
> *Usage:* How the paper sounds.
> *Mechanics:* How the paper looks.

The five domains are not as well defined as best practice would require, but the state's Domains and Definitions, Figure 9-9, attempts to offer specificity within each domain.

Along with the indicators in the five domains, there is a lengthy clarification of the five domains for teachers. The three-paragraph statement says, for example, that style is the second-most important domain and includes "appropriate vocabulary selection, sentence variety, voice and tone." The domains are each "evaluated holistically" according to the "extent to which the features appear to be under the control of the writer." The rubric for control, Figure 9-10 has four levels. These do not offer definitions of what control entails, but we must remember that Popham (1997) has warned us that more complex rubrics can become too mentally taxing for teachers to want to use them in their classrooms (p. 23). Another problem with the Virginia model is that the writing task is not necessarily one that has been practiced by students through the year.

Some proponents of authentic assessment believe that there are problems in multidomain rubrics, and thus, they have developed a simpler assessment rubric that ranges from a high of 9 to a low of 1. The top papers (8-9) are well defined (Figure 9-11), while the low papers (2) are described by negative comments (Figure 9-12): This rubric is simpler than some, but it does not take into account performance that is strong in one area and weak in another. Duke and Sanehez (1994), working in Pennsylvania, were aware of the insufficiency of these two options and helped develop the Pennsylvania State Assessment System to help students develop a 6-point rubric that has five domains, or traits, with a "range of quality within each trait" (p. 50). Their assessment rubric, Figure 9-13, takes five major fea-

FIGURE 9–9
State of Virginia's domains and definitions

COMPOSING: (C) WEIGHTED ×3

- Central idea
- Elaboration
- Unity
- Organization

STYLE: (S) WEIGHTED ×2

- Vivid vocabulary
- Selected information
- Sentence variety
- Tone
- Voice

SENTENCE FORMATION: (F) WEIGHTED ×1

- Completeness
- Non-enjambment
- Expansion through standard coordination and modifiers
- Embedding through standard subordination and modifier
- Standard word order

USAGE: (U) WEIGHTED ×1

- Standard inflections
- Agreement
- Word meaning
- Conventions

MECHANICS: (M) WEIGHTED ×1

- Capitalization
- Punctuation
- Formatting
- Spelling

FIGURE 9–10
Rubric for control

Consistent Control

4 =   The writer demonstrates consistent, though not necessarily perfect, control of almost all the domain's features.

Reasonable Control

3 =   The writer demonstrates reasonable, but not consistent, control of most of the domain's features, indicating some weakness in the domain.

Inconsistent Control

2 =   The writer demonstrates enough inconsistent control of several features to indicate significant weakness in the domain.

Little or No Control

1 =   The writer demonstrates little or no control on most of the domain's features.

FIGURE 9–11
Rubric for top papers
(8-9)

- Developed a good introduction.
- Maintained an appropriate point of view throughout the paper.
- Employed precise, apt, or evocative descriptive vocabulary.
- Did not shift in tense or person.
- Organized ideas effectively and provided an introduction, some closure, and an orderly progression from one idea to another.
- Varied sentence structure and length.
- Used effectively the conventions of written English—spelling, usage, sentence structure, capitalization, punctuation.
- Used at least three examples with specific supporting details.
- Used at least three of five senses.
- Wrote legibly.

FIGURE 9–12
Rubric for low papers
(2)

- Has no sense of organization.
- Shifts constantly in tense and person.
- Shows little or no development of ideas; lacks any focus on specific and related details.
- Distorts, misreads, or ignores the topic.
- Contains disjointed sentences, lacks sense of sentence progression and variety, and contains many sentence errors.
- Shows serious faults in handling the conventions of written English to the extent of impeding a reader's understanding.
- Has no discussion of the five senses.
- Handwriting cannot be read easily.

tures into account. While their rubric solves some serious problems, two still exist. There are only three distinct scores for each domain, and the rubric is not specific to the mode of discourse assessed.

California is another state that has sought to construct an authentic assessment model. Dudley (1997) reports that as early as 1987, English teachers in her state began to develop the California Learning Assessment System (CLAS). The teachers, by dint of their own efforts, selected the types of writing, the prompts, and the assessment criteria that would help teachers throughout the state participate in authentic assessment of writing. In addition, she shows the sequence in which the California teachers determined the writing types to be included in the portfolio:

> The assessment was introduced with a few writing types at the eighth-grade level in 1987. Over the next few years, two other grade levels were added, one in high school, which eventually became tenth grade, and one in elementary school at grade four. When fully implemented, the test encompassed eight writing types at grade eight (Problem Solution, Firsthand Biography, Story, Report of Information, Evaluation, Autobiographical Incident, Observational Writing, and Speculation about Cause and Effects) and eight at grade ten (the last five grade eight types plus Controversial Issue, Interpretation, and Reflective Essay). Four broader, more developmentally appropriate types were introduced at grade four (Expressive, Informative, Narrative, and Persuasive). (p. 15)

The teachers added reading to CLAS, but the politics of division entered the fray and in 1994, Governor Wilson ended the project with his veto of funding.

Focus

6/5
- establishes and keeps a clear purpose
- maintains a clear purpose most of the time
- shows clarity and originality of ideas

4/3
- maintains a clear purpose most of the time
- varies occasionally in keeping a single point of view
- ideas are generally clear but not especially original

2/1
- shows uncertainty about task and audience
- has no clear sense of purpose
- has difficulty in holding a single point of view or role
- lacks clarity or originality of ideas

Content

6/5
- shows sophisticated thinking and ideas
- provides well developed examples and explanations related to topic and purpose
- selects information appropriate for audience and situation

4/3
- presents ideas somewhat lacking in sophistication
- provides examples and details related to the topic but they may be uneven in development
- selects information appropriate for audience and situation

2/1
- presents under-developed and unsophisticated ideas
- provides examples and details as listings without development and not always relevant to topic and purpose
- shows little awareness of the audience's needs

Organization

6/5
- maintains a logical order/sequence
- focuses on one subject in each paragraph
- provides logical transitions within sentences and between paragraphs
- offers a clear introduction and conclusion that frame the topic under discussion

4/3
- maintains a reasonable order/sequence
- focuses most of the time on one subject per paragraph
- provides logical transitions within sentences and paragraphs but is not always consistent in their use
- offers an adequate introduction and conclusion but without much clarity or originality

2/1
- displays inconsistent order/sequence
- exhibits difficulty in maintaining focus on one idea in a paragraph

- shows inconsistency in use of transitions within sentences and paragraphs
- offers little in the way of a controlled introduction and conclusion

Style

6/5
- shows precise language use
- exhibits effective word choice that suggests originality and a sophisticated vocabulary
- offers a consistent voice and tone appropriate for the topic, purpose, and audience
- demonstrates control over variety of sentence structure, types, and length

4/3
- shows fairly precise language use
- exhibits appropriate word choice
- offers somewhat inconsistent tone and voice or selects voice and tone inappropriate for audience and purpose
- demonstrates control over basic sentence structure but appears uncertain about variety, types, and length

2/1
- shows little precision in language use
- exhibits little originality in word choice and some choices may be inappropriate
- offers an inconsistent voice and/or inappropriate voice/tone
- shows little control over sentence structure, variety, types, and length

Conventions

6/5
- exhibits few if any errors in spelling, punctuation and capitalization
- demonstrates control of appropriate forms of usage—pronoun reference, subject/verb agreement, etc.
- displays a control of sentence completeness (absence of run-ons and unnecessary fragments)

4/3
- exhibits a number of repetitive errors in spelling, punctuation, and capitalization but not severe enough to interfere significantly with reader's understanding
- shows inconsistency in appropriate choice of usage
- displays inconsistency in control of sentence completeness

2/1
- exhibits repetitive and frequent errors in spelling, punctuation, and capitalization that interfere with the reader's understanding
- shows inconsistency in choice of appropriate usage
- displays lack of understanding of sentence completeness

FIGURE 9–13 Pennsylvania State Assessment System rubric

Because education reform networks are so intimately related (McCollum-Clark, 1995) it is not a coincidence that performance-based learning promoted by the New Standards Project has become a priority initiative for states that have strong connections with the education reform movement and that they would adopt strong assessment measures from the cutting edge of the field. North Carolina's work on authentic assessment has been led by its Education Standards and Accountability Commission, established by Governor Hunt, former Chair of the National Board for Professional Teaching Standards. The commission has given tremendous support to assessment by sponsoring workshops in population centers across the state where teachers have worked with national consultants such as Grant Wiggins to develop their skills in creating strong assessment criteria and precise rubrics that will guide other teachers in establishing the assessment tools that will prod writing instruction in this new direction.

North Carolina's assessment plan was well supported at first. It flourished. Two salient features of its approach to instruction and assessment set it apart: It creates tasks for students to perform that are quite similar to tasks in the workplace and the real world, and the levels of performance are defined by performance rubrics that are clear and well understood by students. Both of these features are found in an exemplary training document developed by the Education Standards and Assessment Commission for practitioners' workshops.

One of North Carolina's performance-based standards in writing is a real-world writing task that could be undertaken by a president, a prophet, or any thoughtful person: the memoir (Milner, 1998).

The task places students inside the real-world context of a memoir submitted to a magazine that will be judged by its editor on the basis of three criteria: It must be engaging, clear, and insightful. The content standard of the task is spelled out in a succinct paragraph for teachers:

> Content Standard: writes for extended periods of time; writes imaginative and personal narratives that have a coherent, logical, and organized structure; writes imaginative narratives with sufficient, related detail that revolve around an event and have a resolution; expresses main idea and supporting detail in descriptive writing; edits written work for errors in sentence formation, usage, mechanics, and spelling. (p. 41)

The interest in control of conventions such as spelling, punctuation, and usage is present, but other, more complex dimensions of writing are highlighted as well. The assignment itself is directed to the student and spells out much more than a simple topic:

> *Cricket* magazine is collecting memoirs of students to include in a special spring edition of the magazine. It will focus on memorable moments in their lives. They have sent out a call for submissions. You decide to submit. The editor of *Cricket* has indicated that the submissions must relate to one memory, and will be judged on how *engaging, clear,* and *insightful* they are. In judging how clear the memoir is, the editor will be looking at *main idea, supporting details, organization,* and *coherence.* (p. 41)

The assignment also promotes a real-world demand for revision in that it includes a note to the writer warning that the editor will return the submission with editorial marks that need attention: "After you make your submission, the editor writes back expressing enthusiasm for your work but suggesting revisions. With the confidence of a 'soon-to-be-published' author you complete the rework and submit it again" (p. 41).

TIED TO DAILY INSTRUCTION

The instructions for the teachers reinforce the authentic nature of the task. The total context for the assignment ratchets up the real-world nature of the task and prepares the way for assessment that will be authentic because it is similar to that practiced in the everyday world and is based on writing instruction that takes place in the classroom daily. And to enhance that authentic attitude, teachers are reminded "you must remember that during the completion of this task, you are an assessor, not an instructor/coach. What you are interested in is finding out what the students can do independently." Smede (1993) believes that the opportunity to practice the tasks in class and the specificity of the tasks promote both fairness and student participation: "Part of assessing student work fairly according to the beliefs of performance gurus is to let them know exactly what you expect before they begin. In essence, this is just a part of good teaching" (p. 21). During instructional time, teachers help students understand "what a memoir is," which is, in this case, defined "as a piece of writing that is personal, has action, contains a 'lesson' learned (or insight made) in the situation remembered, and is written in the first person." Along with this definition, the student writers are given multiple examples of memoirs to study and, by induction, bring into their own repertoire of writing genres. Teachers show their students how the three criteria—being engaging, clear, and insightful—and their rubrics will be used to assess their writing and encourage them to look for and discuss these qualities in the exemplary memoirs. As a final instructional task, teachers assign a shared class memory that all students later turn into their own memoirs. These are collected in a book and sent home so that parents become a real audience for their children's writing. The cycle of definition, induction, publication, and reflection is imprinted on these students so that the final assessment of their ability to write a memoir will be a fair test of a real-world skill that is used to perform an authentic task.

CONSTRUCTING RUBRICS

The most revolutionary step in this writing and assessment cycle is the use of the scoring rubric. Dudley (1997) speaks about what these are and what they mean for instruction: "We were seeing the scoring guide not only as an assessment tool but as a set of coherently and precisely articulated expectations that were grounded in classroom reality and that would help us to be better teachers when we returned to our classrooms on Monday morning. So as a scoring guide developed, there was a constant revision process, until we felt it reflected not only what many students had achieved, but what more, with good instruction, could be expected to be achieved" (p. 17). Burch (1997) adds to this an unintended positive consequence for students when they develop rubrics: "Working together to construct the rubric helps students accommodate their strengths as learners and creates a more democratic classroom by engaging them in the process for assessing their work" (p. 56). For each of the criteria that students use

FIGURE 9–14
Rubric for clear
writing

> 6. The communication is usually clear. Language is sophisticated and precise, the work is thoroughly and logically developed, and the message or meaning is unambiguous. The work reveals an unusual control over form and content in the service of intention.
> 5. The communication is clear. Language is apt and precise, the work reveals a well-thought-through message or meaning, and good control over how to convey it best.
> 4. The communication is mostly clear. Language is apt but not always sufficiently precise. There are some instances of ambiguity, vagueness, or otherwise hard-to-discern meanings (especially concerning the more subtle or complex ideas). The work suggests, however, a thought-through message or meaning.
> 3. The communication is somewhat clear. Language may be inadequate, not always apt or up to the demands of the task. There are major instances of ambiguity, vagueness, or otherwise hard-to-discern meanings throughout. Key ideas are insufficiently developed or explained. The work is insufficient to communicate the message or meaning effectively AND/OR the work suggests an insufficiently worked-through intended message or meaning.
> 2. The communication is unclear. There are many places where intended messages or meanings cannot be discerned. Language may be too imprecise, inappropriate, or immature to convey the intended message AND/OR the work suggests an insufficiently thought-through message or meaning.
> 1. The communication is difficult if not impossible to decipher. OR there is no evidence in the work of an intended or deliberate message or meaning. (pp. 42–43)

as standards for evaluation, there is a set of performance rubrics that includes six well-specified definitions of criteria accomplishment. For the first criterion, the CLASS (1996) rubric for clear writing (Milner, 1998) shown in Figure 9-14, lists six levels of performance. The levels are very neatly delineated so that each represents greater performance of the criterion of being clear as the rubric level ascends from 1 to 6. The shift from "no evidence . . . of an intended message or meaning" (level 1) to "The work is insufficient to communicate the message or meaning" (level 3) to "The work reveals a well-thought-through message or meaning" (level 5) offers assessors a refined way to classify the performance level of the memoir. The level attained not only allows teachers to come up with a qualitative score, but also tells the student writer just where the problem or proficiency lies in his or her piece. Language use, likewise, which helps define clarity, shifts from "imprecise" (level 2) to some instances of "ambiguity, vagueness" (level 4) to "sophisticated and precise" (level 6).

The rubric for insight, which is an even tougher criterion to define by a six-level rubric, is shown in Figure 9-15. The features that define the six levels of the rubric are perceptive, lessons learned, impact, and originality. Each of these features is more evident in the writing as the rubric rises from "blah" to "wow!"

Writers who perform best when this kind of authentic assessment is used are the ones who engage the instruction most completely, comprehend the criteria, and fulfill them best when producing their memoirs. Because the writing tasks are like those of daily life and are assessed using clear-cut criteria, students begin to view writing less as a mystery and more as a job that they can perform. This does not mean that writing becomes mechanical and arid, but that it advances to new levels of excellence.

Burch (1997) reports on how an individual class developed a very useful two-tiered portfolio that awarded 40% credit for the quantity of its contents and 60% credit for its quality as determined by a rubric that the students and teacher established. The two-tiered portfolio is presented in Figure 9-16.

NAEP FRAMEWORK

The National Assessment for Educational Progress's (NAEP) belief in the power of rubrics is manifest in the process of rubric construction suggested in its *Writing Framework and Specifications* (1998) and presented in Figure 9-17. In addition, the publication offers a set of useful guides for developing rubrics to promote better writing through authentic assessment, Figure 9-18. Both NAEP contributions make it more likely that such new means of assessment will be adopted by states, districts and individual teachers.

Whether they are the collective effort of an association of English teachers, the initiative of a state governor, the suggestion by a respected national testing body, or the good work and good will of a single teacher, rubrics for assessment can be created that are similar to everyday writing tasks used in class, are cooperatively established, and provide fair, well-defined measures of incremental success. This is a difficult, time-consuming, and sometimes politically dangerous next step to take, but it seems to link the circle together inexorably. It is a compelling approach to writing. Most states, of course, will not encourage such teacher-developed assessment systems like the one California teachers created, nor will they fund training for assessment as did North Carolina for a time. Most of the strength of this new movement will have to emerge from the bottom up.

FIGURE 9–15
Rubric for insight

6. The memoir is unusually perceptive. The writing contains keen insights of discovery or self-discovery beyond the particulars of the episode(s) but thoughtfully and ably derived from them. The writing has great impact: significant lessons have been learned and shared through reflection and writing, insights that speak to readers, not just the writer.

5. The memoir is perceptive. The writing contains insights beyond the particulars of the episode(s), but thoughtfully and ably derived from them. The writing has impact: lessons have been learned and shared through reflection and writing.

4. The memoir contains thoughtful reflections beyond what is recalled and described, but the message is somewhat obvious or restricted. The writing has somewhat limited impact. Lessons have been learned and/or offered, though they may speak more to the writer than the readers (due to weaknesses in drawing insights from the memories or limits in the richness of what has been recalled).

3. The memoir contains reflections beyond what is recalled and described, but the message is somewhat obvious, restricted, ambiguous, or unwarranted. The message amounts to little more than a restatement of the facts OR involves leaps to conclusions somewhat unwarranted by the facts presented. Lessons may well have been learned and/or shared, but the exact nature or importance of the lessons remains somewhat unclear.

2. The memoir does not go much beyond recall OR the writer jumps to a simplistic conclusion that may or may not be warranted by the facts presented. The lack of warranted insight may be due to EITHER a lack of rich detail in the memoir AND/OR an inability to draw thoughtful conclusions from experience.

1. The writing does not amount to a memoir, containing merely facts and descriptions without any apparent meaning or value to the writer (as revealed by the absence of deliberate reflection or meaning-making). (p. 43)

FIGURE 9–16
Two-tiered portfolio

A. Contents of Portfolio
(60% of portfolio grade)
Writing (40) Points

_____ 1. _____[Name of piece]_____
_____ 2. _____[Name of piece]_____
_____ 3. _____[Name of piece]_____
_____ 4. _____[Name of piece]_____

Metawriting/Reflection (15 points)

_____ 1. _____[Name of piece]_____
_____ 2. _____[Name of piece]_____
_____ 3. _____[Name of piece]_____

Peer Writing (5 points)

_____ 1. _____[Name of piece]_____
_____ 2. _____[Name of piece]_____

Writer's Choice
(up to 5 extra points: not required)

_____ 1. _____[Name of piece]_____
_____ 2. _____[Name of piece]_____

B. Quality of Portfolio
(40% of portfolio grade)
You must allot 3–12 points to each criterion, for a total of 40 points. Write your allotments in the bracketed spaces.

_____ 1. Voice—distinctness of style, creative   [   ]
    expression and arrangement, personality
_____ 2. Organization—logical, orderly arrangement,   [   ]
    ease of movement within portfolio
_____ 3. Reflection—thoughtfulness, awareness of self   [   ]
    and teacher in metawriting
_____ 4. Development—fullness of contents, full   [   ]
    explanations, adequate detail
_____ 5. Mechanical and Usage—spelling, punctuation,   [   ]
_____   word choice, usage

Contents points (   ) + Qualities points (   ) = Total score (   )
Comments about the portfolio (p. 57)

FIGURE 9–17
Suggested process for rubric construction

- Convene a group of writing experts and classroom teachers to discuss the nature of the assessment (e.g., number and nature of tasks, time allowed).
- Read a wide sampling of field test papers, looking for special characteristics of the *students* contained in the sample as these characteristics will influence the level of complexity in the information specified by the rubric. Also, look through the student responses to get an idea of the *diversity of responses and levels of achievement* to identify the characteristics and content that should be included in the rubric.
- Consider the level of discriminations necessary for the purpose of the test. Consider the length of time the student has had available to respond to the task.
- Read all the papers and divide them into piles that demonstrate the characteristics of writing that are described in the rubric for each score point.
- Write descriptors for each pile of papers. Consider what characteristics distinguish the top papers from the lowest levels. Then, assess what categories these characteristics fall into. In assessing writing, for example, the categories of most rubrics fall into purpose, audience, idea development/support, organization/structure, sentence structure, and word choice, voice, and mechanics.
- Write rough drafts of descriptors for each score point.
- Consider the rubric to be a "draft in process" until after the field test results have been evaluated. (p. 58)

FIGURE 9–18
General characteristics of writing by mode

NARRATIVE

Understands the narrative purpose.
Develops character.
Maintains focus.
Has satisfying resolution.
Has appropriate ordering of events.
Gives attention to audience when appropriate to the prompt.
Uses elaboration and details.
Handles direct and indirect discourse.
Demonstrates control of mechanics.

INFORMATIVE

Understands the informative purpose.
Has clear and complete information.
Conveys messages, instructions, and/or ideas.
Uses sufficient detail.
Uses coherent and logical organization.
Shows efficient relationships between and among ideas.
Gives attention to audience.
Fulfills the demands of the task.
Uses language level appropriate to the topic and voice desired by the writing.
Demonstrates control of mechanics.

PERSUASIVE

Understands the persuasive purpose.
Takes and retains a position.
Supports and develops a position through examples, details, statistics, and supporting evidence.
Has coherent and logical organization.
Gives attention to audience.
Uses language level appropriate to the topic and voice desired by the writing.
Demonstrates control of mechanics. (pp. 58–59)

CONCLUSION

These five constructs are linked together in such a way that they continuously reform the circle; each one naturally leads to the next. They are affirmed by best practice and current research but have varying degrees of acceptability and status in today's secondary schools. The process approach is almost old hat, while portfolios are becoming highly acclaimed in reform-centered schools. Writing workshops are much rarer but still are attractive curriculum models for teachers who like challenges. Atwell's new edition of *In the Middle* (1998) has taken some moderating stands on ownership and other critical positions that will make her approach easier to adopt. Authentic assessment still has tremendous support from important reform sources, but its complexity is inherently problematic, so the vote is not yet in on that promising approach. The developmental model is traditional in the modes of discourse it includes, while it is somewhat radical in relating those modes to the thinking process. The five constructs work together as a dynamic cumulative model for writing instruction. In 3 or 4 years the tale will be told; we will probably see these constructs as fixtures rather than cutting-edge pedagogy. They may, in fact, become so commonplace that innovative teachers will begin to develop new constructs in the ever evolving attempt to teach writing.

10 ENABLING WRITING

It's the head-to-page trip that is so frightening and difficult for writers. Acting as coaches of writing, teachers can assist students by helping them understand the strategies they are using and suggesting others they might use, by raising questions and more questions as the text emerges, and by encouraging and supporting student decision-making throughout the growth of the piece.

Dan Kirby, Tom Liner, and Ruth Vinz

In Chapter 9 we looked carefully at a set of five compelling approaches to writing that are most prominent in current research and best practice. They create a comprehensive picture of writing instruction, but they may not speak directly to the everyday issues of teachers who want to build their writing programs on the critical needs for good writing. For this reason, we offer a number of successful writing strategies that we believe provide enabling structures. They do not control student writing in a step-by-step fashion, but they provide a structure of support, or scaffolding, that Vygotsky and others propose, because they help learners achieve maximum performance within the zone of proximal development. The enabling structures we offer address four critical needs in student's writing.

FOUR BASIC NEEDS

SUBSTANCE

Substance, or content, is the fundamental need. To get writing started, we must help students find the subject of their thoughts and bring that thinking to consciousness on paper. Fluency is what is wanted. We hope to find ways to let students express themselves. We need to know how to offer an invitation to writing that is provocative and genuine. We need to construct enabling structures that nudge students beyond their starting points. We need to call on students to express themselves and explore their experiences through writing. Substance is richest and flows most easily when students write about what they know best and when it follows thinking and talking.

SKILLS

Skills are naturally acquired, but they are also consciously mastered. They come about because students are absorbing them all along *and* because teachers are helping students gain consciousness of them. Vocabulary, spelling, and punctuation are some of the basic skills that students must master to write well, and students value these skills most when they care about what they are writing. These skills become much more complex as writing itself becomes more complicated. Usage, which is called grammar by most people, describes the way words relate to one another. Its basic components are the relationships between major features such as the subject and predicate of a sentence: *she runs; they run.* Similar but less crucial relationships are those between pronouns and their referents: *He is the man whom you seek; Mary said that it was her book.* Relationships in form are least noticeable: splitting infinitives and using prepositions at ends of sentences are mildly unacceptable. Style can sometimes override relationship and social concern can outweigh form: *Everyone ate their dinner.*

STRUCTURE

Structure is the architecture of composing. It is the macro form rather than the micro level of design and relationship. We know that form and organization should arise from the content at hand, but we also try to provide some organizing structures to help students mold and shape their content. We fail them when we insist on only one way to organize writing: Metaphors and graphic patterns can inform organization as well as a five-paragraph theme or a comparison-contrast paper can. Coherence has to do with making the sentences and paragraphs fit together. Connectors and other function words (*and, but, therefore*) provide complex ways to direct, redirect, and calibrate the directions of a writer's thinking.

STYLE

Style is the most subtle element. It is founded on all of the other four elements, but it goes far beyond them. It can be created by the vocabulary of the writer, through the variety and aptness of its use, by the inventive use of images and actions that represent something beyond themselves, and by metaphors, symbols, and extended figures of speech. Style's most sophisticated language dimensions are related to syntax: the arrangement of words. The maturity of syntax and the ability to juxtapose stark simple utterances and lengthy complex ones are central here. Voice is even more difficult to cultivate and nourish. Murray (1985) explains its crucial importance in writing: "Voice allows the reader to hear an individual human being speak from the page. . . . Voice is the quality, more than any other, that allows us to recognize exceptional potential in a beginning writer; voice is the quality, more than any other, that allows us to recognize excellent writing. . . . Voice gives the text individuality, energy, concern" (p. 21).

Each of the writing strategies we recommend has the power to meet some or all of these four critical needs. The chart in Figure 10–1 indicates the 16 strategies that we suggest and a measure of their effectiveness in meeting each of the four critical needs.

FIGURE 10–1
Basic needs matrix

● Profound Effect   O Moderate Effect   ○ Slight Effect

	Substance	Skills	Structure	Style
Collaborative Writing	●	O	O	O
Environmental Journalism	●	O	O	○
Right Writing	●	○	○	●
Journal Writing	●	○	○	●
Write to Learn	●	O	O	○
Code Switching	○	●	O	○
Pedagogical Grammar	○	●	O	O
Vocabuspell	○	●	○	●
Mediated Instruction	O	●	●	O
New Research	●	O	●	○
Elemental Variation	O	○	●	O
Lit. Write	●	O	○	●
Sentence Combining	O	○	O	●
Dependent Authors	●	○	O	●
Apprentice Writing	●	O	O	●
Practical Stylist	O	O	○	●

COLLABORATIVE WRITING

When students aren't able to start writing, one of the most successful ways to bypass that block is to turn to collaboration. Very little research has been done on writer's block, but Rose (1984) finds that the best explanation is a psychological resistance to putting anything on the table that might be embarrassing. Minninger, Goodman and others are cited by Rose as researchers who believe that the child in the writer has a block because of a fear of meeting disapproval (pp. 13-15). When students work together, their talk can be used to produce a confidence and a fluency in their writing that they do not possess when working alone. In the early grades, three students taking turns at a computer keyboard can work wonders. Halting utterances can become extended narratives. Uncertain individual thoughts gather assurance as they are aired and refined in a small group of peers. When a trio of secondary students compose a bizarre story using a list of items from three columns labeled *Character, Conflict,* and *Conclusion,* the same collaborative power is unleashed. The social fun derived from such interaction makes the language flow.

What Vygotsky tells us about the social construction of language helps us see how language is unlocked in a social situation. We observed children with language deficits who were almost mute when faced with solo language exercises but came alive with language when they interrupted their "work" to play games such as Red Rover at recess. We know, too, that the most repeated research finding about effective writing strategies is that talk promotes writing best. Dale (1997) thinks of the collaborative process as coauthoring and lists a set of eight activities, Figure 10-2, that work well when students write in groups. Each of these ideas calls on group members to think for themselves, talk about their differences of opinion, analyze the problem or phenomenon together, and compose a forceful position statement that has a real and well-defined audience. Dale says that the advantage of the topics and procedures is their strong appeal to students. They deal with contemporary issues that fully engage adolescents' political and social interests. Because most secondary students are moving toward formal operational thinking, they are intellectually and psychologically ready to measure the realities of the world around them against the ideals that they are formulating in their minds. *Is* versus *Ought* is the ground they occupy. That is why parents and adults who are seemingly inured to the unsettling facts of daily life are often alien to them. Adolescent literature works so well with them, in part because it focuses on the tension between being a dependent child and an independent

FIGURE 10–2
Coauthoring activities

- Write a letter to a school official which defines a problem that you think exists in this school.
  - Propose a solution.
  - Detail the feasibility of that solution.
  - Ask members of another group to edit the draft.
- Write a questionnaire and survey classmates about an issue that you know your classmates are talking about.
  - Conduct short interviews.
  - Characterize the views at your school.
- Name your generation.
  - Support your stance.
  - Draw from the experiences of all members of the group.
  - Protest the labeling of your generation as Generation X.
- Think of a trend in society.
  - Combine your experiences.
  - Explore the underlying causes.
  - Explain why this trend exists.
- Satirize a phenomenon in society.
  - Choose a specific subject.
  - Show what is mildly to very irritating.
- Analyze a particular advertisement.
  - Describe the ad's script and visual message.
  - Investigate the product or the target audience for the ad.
  - Analyze the ad for its underlying social message.
- As a group, analyze a movie you view together.
  - See a recently released film.
  - Discuss the movie.
  - Compose a movie review.
- Use a political cartoon as a visual prompt.
  - Bring to class political cartoons.
  - Objectively describe the cartoon in one or more paragraphs.
  - Write a description of the cartoon using slanted language.
  - Present these short papers orally to the class. (p. 63–65)

adult. Adolescence is a self-searching and self-defining time that makes students ripe for teaching, especially the kind of teaching that provides them with the opportunity for intellectual dissent.

COGNITIVE CONFLICT

Dale's report on the research on cognitive conflict is compelling (p. 23):

1. Cognitive conflict occurs with the recognition that one's ideas are different from another person's or are incompatible with new information (Daiute & Dalton, 1988).
2. Students in groups restructure their thoughts by comparing new information with information previously acquired and modify or replace existing concepts or attitudes if that seems necessary (Webb, 1982).
3. Some cognitive conflict is an inevitable part of the process of collaborative writing because students must negotiate differences of opinion in order to arrive at consensus (Dale, 1994b).
4. A number of studies find that cognitive conflict is a vital component of successful collaborative writing (Burnett, 1994a; Daiute & Dalton, 1988; Dale, 1994b).
5. A strong correlation occurs between the quality of written work and the amount of substantive engagement in the collaborative writing group (Burnett 1994a).
6. Cognitive conflict is one of the most important factors in separating a model group of writers from a typical or problem group (Dale, 1994b).

VERBALIZATION

All of the research that Dale (1997) cites about verbalizing in groups and writing together also speaks clearly about its effectiveness. Four findings about verbalization are especially provocative and appropriate to the kind of writing we suggest here (p. 26):

1. Verbalizing is the best factor behind the success of collaborative learning in all its forms (Brown & Palincsar, 1989; Cagne & Smith, 1962; Johnson & Johnson, 1985).
2. Verbalizing about what they're learning helps students comprehend fully and the more explaining a student does, the more benefits that student receives (Cohen, 1994).
3. Requiring verbalization forces students to think of reasons for the choices they make as they think through a problem or issue (Cagne & Smith, 1962).
4. The social context allows students to think out loud, which, in turn, provides an opportunity to think not only about the ideas involved, but also about writing itself (Daiute & Dalton, 1993; Dale, 1994b).

BENEFITS OF COLLABORATION

Dale (1997) concludes that the general benefits of collaborating are very powerful:

- it socializes the writing process
- it shifts the responsibility for good writing to students
- it helps students see each other as resources not competitors
- it removes the loneliness of writing
- it encourages cognitive growth
- it helps students plan more (pp. 55–56)

All of the benefits that Dale lists are significant, but one that has additional punch is that working in teams is so commonplace in the work world that students need solid preparation for working together rather than alone. Goodman (1980) introduced collaborative writing to teachers from 10 city school systems from California to Mississippi at the Excellence in Teaching English Institute. He arranged the outstanding teachers into teams that responded to a Request for Proposal for a bi-plane by completing an extended written proposal. His exercise demanded the same kind of group discussion and decision making of teachers before writing their proposals that Dale calls for in her text. The proposals they completed as teams were full of strong writing because of the rigorous discussion that led to the writing. They were matched against a real-world activity almost 100 years old, the Wright Brothers' submission to the patent office as they worked on the dunes at Kitty Hawk to manufacture a vehicle that would provide sustained flight.

Gillis (1994) developed a collaborative writing plan that emerged as "young writers [were] paired with writers in the community outside the school" (p. 64). They wrote at first about life at their school but began "to experiment with a range of writing" (p. 64). The group discussion and decision making that take place before writing in Dale's project is absent here. But the knowledge that a real partner who shares your interests is reading what you write and is thinking over your ideas creates some of the same reflection and cognitive dissonance that is generated by group writing. We have entered into a similar project with our students and those at Peking University, and Dilworth (1976) and Pope (1998) also have created partnered writing experiences of this same sort. Each project has proven such collaboration to be a very effective way to initiate writing and to provide forward steps in skills, structure, and even style, because students are learning so much from each other.

ENVIRONMENTAL JOURNALISM

This approach to writing has deep roots in the life of the community that surrounds the English classroom. Mining the local environment for lively information is an approach conceived and given notoriety by Eliot Wigginton (1985) through his *Foxfire* books. In the midst of his attempts to solve common classroom problems, he hit on the idea of setting his students loose to explore their native ground, the North Georgia community of Rabun Gap. What Wigginton found was that he had shifted the responsibility for writing from the teacher to the students and so had changed his classroom from a place where he presided to one where all worked together as in a workshop. English teachers from urban centers to small coastal towns, from elementary schools to colleges, from classrooms of gifted students to those of slow learners, have tried his strategy and found similar success. Three features of the *Foxfire* writing model are constant: student control and responsibility for the project, student interaction with the community, and student publication of their journalistic research. The community provides both resources and reasons for writing. Outstanding examples of environmental journalism have been created even in settings that seemed to possess minimal allure and support. Brunwin, for example, brought his own brand of this approach from England to a sixth-grade class, which collectively wrote a historical novel about nineteenth-century gold mining in their small town of Concord, North Carolina.

FOXFIRE'S LESSONS

Students learn at least five important lessons from this writing model. They represent sequential stages of discovery for those engaged in such projects, a chain reaction that drives the process toward strong writing:

- Awareness of writing's public nature
- Understanding of requisite detail
- Sense of community
- Investment of self in writing
- Desire to develop a rich, well-finished product

Public Nature.   The public nature of environmental, or cultural, journalism awakens students to the realization that writing can be located in a concrete world of real people and consequential events. Students base their writing on material from their known worlds and return that writing to the world by publishing it for the public. That public audience may be the class, the school, the school administration, or the community at large. Students begin to feel that the written word is more than an insular academic exercise, read and evaluated by one reader only. Writing concerns itself with a concrete reality in the world beyond the classroom and elicits the attention of the same people who read the local paper or a national magazine.

Requisite Detail.   Writing based on oral histories drives the writer toward specific and detailed content. The available material is as rich as the student's genuine interest and curiosity. With sensitive and probing questions, anecdotes of community history and folklore open onto a more personal and nuanced history. Student journalists may even begin to realize the intrinsic interest in the material to others and their responsibility to the person interviewed. The challenge then becomes to distill the personal account into a cogent and effective form.

Sense of Community.   Because of their natural ties with their subjects in the community, students often feel more invested in their own communal history. As they publish their findings to that community, a cycle develops. Students discover an interest in people and events that they once did not know or notice, and they find a way to express that interest. The broader community, through the interviews and the publication of them, intensifies its interest in the work of the school. This interest prompts students to take themselves and their work more seriously.

Self-investment.   When students know their past, care about the people who are the repositories of that past, and tender it in the present, they write with a greater certainty of purpose. As they engage in the actualities of real lives and invest themselves in the project, writers develop a personal stake. The product of environmental journalism grows from individual and collective sources, but it has a good chance of being personally *owned* by each contributor to it.

Left Hemisphere	Right Hemisphere
Parts (Sign)	*Connectedness (Design)*
explanation	word images, rhythm
clarity	recurring pattern
sequence	metaphor

Rico identifies the artistic, Design Mind, as the "stepchild" of schools. She believes that through simple processes, she can bring most students in her classrooms into contact with the right hemispheric wholeness found in the writing of children and poets. Her major working tool comes from an associational linking of ideas and images in a roadmap-like design she calls *clustering*. She claims that clustering can help students write with greater ease and authenticity because it works toward wholeness. The fragmented use of grammar, the frustration of mechanics, and the isolation of most vocabulary study are all the products of left hemisphere-dominated approaches. She believes that the two must work in harmony, but that the right hemisphere's looking for connections and patterns must be allowed to work freely and work first. Without both minds at work, writing will fail, but writers must turn off the nagging Sign Mind at some point in the process or it will wholly quell the Design Mind.

RICO CLUSTERS

Rico's book of exercises (1983) propels students toward whole-mind writing. Two exercises—clustering of words alone and clustering with art—suggest her approach. In the first, she sets the Design Mind free by asking students to focus on a kernel word, such as *popcorn* or *revenge* (it can be concrete or abstract), and then begin to allow associations to rise out of the focal point. Figure 10-3 records the associations that arose when one of us played with *popcorn*. The Design Mind has run free here. (It's run amuck, you might say, but that would be your Sign Mind talking.) Rapid responses are important. Rico promises that the process "unfolds from a center like ripples." She does say that it is most important that the process begin with a word at the center of a blank page. She recommends doodling or darkening lines if the free association process slows down. The artistic play relaxes you and lets you exhaust the mind's store momentarily. When the process is completed, Rico says you'll sense what the mind maps tell you to write. Glance at the cluster a few seconds and then write away. No stopping. The mental footwork has charted a course that you cannot know, but that will lead to something.

An even more productive technique of clustering juxtaposes the process with evocative art such as that of Cezanne, Giacometti, Klee, van Gogh, Turner, Rembrandt, or Whistler. Very recent works from a local art gallery can have the same power. In this exercise, Rico tells students to let the Design Mind pore over the work of art until a dominant impression is formed. With a painting such as Goya's *The Third of May, 1808,* that impression might be fear, death, tyranny, or even darkness. Her instructions are to relax and let the eyes play over the painting. After scanning it, students take the feeling or dominant impression and use it as the nucleus from which they generate a cluster of images. She tells them to look at the central word and return with it to scan the picture. Then, after a short period, a sense of what to write about will emerge. At this point, she has students write nonstop for 8 to 10 minutes. Rico reports that some of the very best results she has had were from a class of tough, nonverbal ninth graders. The Right Writing approach makes the unthinkable happen.

OTHER PATHS

Dellinger (1982) offers another extremely effective way to reach the Design Mind through the use of photographs of striking people. In the Prospector and the Child activity, each student is given a photo of an old prospector or a sad child (or any other dissimilar and provocative pair). Working with a partner, each student writes a monologue as if he or she were the child or the prospector. Students paired as prospector and child read their monologues to each other. They talk about how they see the characters in the monologues. Then, as a team, they write a dialogue in which they find a common ground and speak to each other. After they read the dialogue, they plan a story line for a vignette in which the two talk in the context of the events of a story. Finally, the students read the story and discuss their sense of what it is about. They explore ideas, the characters, and the tone. Then each student writes an essay that locates something universal or public in the relationship of the pair: loneliness, differing views of time between the very old and the very young, or healing grief. Thus, students move from monologue to dialogue to story to essay. Student-selected photographs of interesting characters provide a similar structure for writing.

Wood (1985), an informed but healthily skeptical neuropsychologist, believes that much of what has been drawn from the hard research in his field has been overextended by the popularizers and practitioners. He argues that our basic tendencies toward either flight or fight are the only ones we can count on as the consequence of bilateral asymmetry. Wood characterizes those whose cognitive style is to sprawl as "cowboys"; those who focus and pinpoint are caricatured as "librarians." Those

FIGURE 10–3
Focal point associations

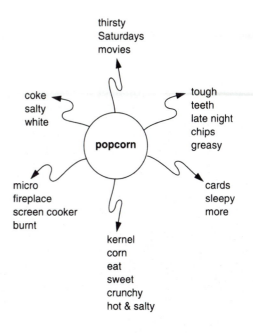

who sprawl see the big picture. Those who focus move in close to the reality at hand, dwelling on detail. Wood pictures the coordination of these brains as the left hand (right-hemisphere cowboy) holding the nail and the right hand (left-hemisphere librarian) placing a well-aimed blow to its head.

We can find a pedagogical analogy here and apply it to interpretation and writing about literature. We will use as our example Shakespeare's Sonnet 116 (page 13, Chapter 1). You may have looked at this poem through the lens of imagery, structure, persona, metrics, or other analytical frames. You may be unaware of these tools and still have made use of them. When you examined the poem, you may have noted the metaphors of time and space that compare love to exploration and hazard; you may have been struck by the prohibitionary *not* and *never;* you may have been conscious of the writer-lover who understates in each venue. The nature of the examination appears to be to look to the particular, the discrete. Focus upon detail often seems the essential task when we analyze literature for a writing assignment.

Henry (1974) presents an alternative in his brief but explosive book *Teaching Reading as Concept Development.* His idea is to look big instead of small in reading literature. Rather than explore only Shakespeare's sonnet, he uses it and two other poems that circle roughly the same topic: love. He selects also W. B. Yeats's "For Anne Gregory" and Anne Sexton's "The Farmer's Wife." Exercise 10–2 demonstrates his method of exploration.

Exercise 10–2   *Right-brain Poetic Analysis*

Consider these three poems as a unit. Henry's Venn diagram may be helpful as you explore what is common to two (*A, B,* or *C*) and what is central to all (*X*).

Let Me Not   For Anne Gregory

A

X

B   C

The Farmer's Wife

Common ground among the poems might emerge through questions such as the following:

- Do you find any aspect of love upon which all three poets agree (X)?
- Do any two poets perceive common qualities in the love relationships between men and women (A, B, or C)?
- Which poets appear to have more realistic views of love? Which have more idealized views?
- Are any cynical?
- Which view of love appeals most to you? Why?
- Do you sense a dialogue in any of these? Whom is the narrator addressing?
- Imagine all of the narrators gathered together. What would you say to them together and as individuals?
- Which of the other two narrators would Sexton choose for her husband?
- Which poem would you send to a beloved? Why do you make that choice?

We suggested other groups of two, three, and four poems in Chapter 5 (Table 5-6). We believe that this shift to the right side of the mind provokes rich and plentiful new insights. Seeing three visions at once can clarify all three. Shelly Hale was taken with this idea in her student teaching and developed other trios. She suggests the following grouping around marriage.

Adrienne Rich, "Aunt Jennifer's Tigers"
Ezra Pound, "The River-Merchant's Wife: A Letter"
e. e. cummings, "if there are any heavens my mother will (all by herself) have"

How many times can you recall discussing literature using such a synthetic method? We believe this shift to the right side provokes rich and plentiful new insights. Seeing three visions at once can clarify all three.

Left-Right Continuum

A last writing strategy centered on neuropsychological insights moves students from writing about concrete objects to using symbolic texts (Milner, 1976). It takes another look at the power of sequence and progression in writing. In hemispheric terms, this strategy invites students first to use graphic and concrete experiential materials (those that appeal to the global imagination and intuition), and then to use those most clearly associated with verbal texts (those materials that are processed linearly, analytically, and logically).

Far Left	Near Left	Center Left	Center Right	Near Right	Far Right
Short Fiction	Dramatic Verse	Dramatic Performance	Film, TV	Visual Arts	Cultural Artifacts

Cultural Artifacts.   Writing in this sequence begins at the far right with seeing. Just as the artist is said to paint with the eye, not the hand, the new writer can be urged to look more closely, to write with the eye. Prime cultural artifacts (such as cheese crackers) can be set before the student to respond to with visual acuity and then verbal precision. When such a limited visual space is established, response is intensified. Such graphic certainty builds a reportorial confidence that infuses the student's writing. Most students know that their eyes are as sharp as anyone else's and that they do not have to make any ingenious interpretation beyond their range of vision.

Visual Arts.   Visual arts lie at the near-right position, so the global process is still primary. Mere fact is still dominant; ideas and generalizations take a back seat to sensorial experience. The object can still be processed immediately; the mind goes from line, shape, and color directly to meaning. Students who have not studied or even seen Harnett's work before can catalog many of the tricks the artist has massed to convey the sense of reality in his canvas.

Film and Television.   Film and television, at center right, possess visual immediacy but also a verbal element, which is left-brained. Not surprisingly, these are the media that are most compelling to most adolescents. Students easily respond to the visual intensity, yet because of the verbal "intrusion," this medium stands as a halfway house in the move from right (visual) to left (verbal).

Dramatic Performance.   The kinship between dramatic performance, at center left, and film and television, at center right, is obvious from their positions alone. It is, however, close kin to textual literature as well, for it is often read as well as seen. But it is distinct from literature, not only because it is intended for production, but also because there is no authorial intermediary who diminishes the "reality" or compounds the complexity. Thus, its right-brained essence makes it precede all textual forms in a composition continuum.

Dramatic Verse.   At near left, perhaps surprisingly, comes what we call dramatic verse. This readable poetry, which adds voices and action located in particular time and space, comes before fiction because it is more immediate and intense. Students can respond to a reasonable and provocative poem almost as they might to a work of visual art; it stands before them all at once. In all poetry, the spatial quality is more significant than it is in fiction. But because most poetry is highly condensed, intense, and intellectual, it requires left-brain processing and thus resides near the extreme edge of the continuum.

Short Fiction.   Fiction, on the far left, requires full left-hemisphere attention, but it can be used to promote writing that ignores formal matters at first—writing that attends primarily to emotional response and meaning. The Aristotelian premise of beginning with one's emotive response to the work does much to keep that focus. Centering on what Fowler (1981) refers to as "faith issues" (essential questions related to one's world view) or using developmental constructs such as those of Kohlberg or Erikson urges the writer to respond initially in terms of character and theme rather than more formally. When writers do write about formal concerns, they should be urged to consider these in relation to personal response and meaning. It is then that they occupy the whole of the continuum.

With this hemispheric strategy, we need neither eschew literature nor wholly adore it. Both the visual and the literal can be used at the appropriate juncture. We need merely to locate our students' places on the continuum and then offer the appropriate materials from which their writing may most freely and powerfully flow.

JOURNAL WRITING

Fader and McNeil, in *Hooked on Books: Program and Proof* (1968), describe how daily journals were used at the Maxey Training School in Michigan and resulted in students' becoming freer about expressing themselves, discovering that they had more to say, and developing confidence in their ability to do so. What was novel in the 1960s has become a growing educational phenomenon: journal writing. Other terms are used almost synonymously: *diaries, commonplace books, writing notebooks, daybooks,* and *thinkbooks.* Journals have become almost as popular in biology and math classrooms as they have in English classrooms. One side of this popularity is that a common student complaint has become "I have to keep a journal in four of my five classes!" Why have journals become so popular with teachers? They may appear to be faddish, but their use is based on sound pedagogical principles.

The research of Britton et al., described in *The Development of Writing Ability, 11–18* (1975), analyzed writing in all subject areas in British secondary schools where extended writing occurred. Two

---

Exercise 10–3   Purposes for Journal Writing

- What additional types of journals have you heard of being used or can imagine using?
- Which of these journal types best serve students' *personal* uses? Which best serve *pedagogical* aims?
- Consider the following list of possible purposes to be served by journal writing. Which seem important and useful? Why?
  - to make connections between personal experience and the class material at hand
  - to recapitulate the course material through identifying what has been learned, what is confusing, and what needs further study
  - to assess learning
  - to collect observations, responses, and data
  - to practice writing
  - to experiment with voice
  - to examine the self
  - to clarify values
  - to have an ungraded forum for writing
  - to provide information on the student's feelings and understanding
  - to be a repository for writing ideas and materials
  - to have a chronological record of student thought and opinion during a term
  - to have prompts for classroom discussion

writing dimensions that Britton and his colleagues describe in detail have import for journal writing: the relation of the writer to the audience, and the purpose of writing.

The NCTE has formulated guidelines for journal writing in most school settings that provide concrete, practical suggestions for their positive and efficient use. It suggests that students write in loose-leaf notebooks so that they can submit only the pertinent pages and keep more personal entries private. It also recommends that every time students write in class, teachers "do something active and deliberate with what they have written. For example, have volunteers read whole entries aloud, have everyone read one sentence to the whole class, have partners share one passage with each other, etc. (In each case, students who don't like what they have written should have the right to pass.) Sharing the writing in this manner gives credibility to a non-graded assignment" (quoted in Newkirk, 1990, p. 276). The NCTE also suggests that in lieu of qualitative grading, teachers should quantitatively count student journals in some way, perhaps "a certain number of points, a plus added to a grade, or an in-class resource for taking tests" (p. 276). The guidelines advise teachers not to write a response to each entry, but to skim and respond to selected entries. The NCTE's final proposal is that at the end of a term, teachers "ask students to put in (a) page numbers, (b) a title for each entry, (c) a table of contents, and (d) an evaluative conclusion. This synthesizing activity requires journal writers to treat their documents seriously and to review what they have written over a whole term of study" (p. 276).

The promises of freedom, confidentiality, and respect all enhance the possibility of students' moving toward deeply probing journals. These three conditions are worth brief explanation.

FREEDOM

Freedom is what drives students toward depth, because when they trust that constraints and possible disapproval are removed, they may write about what truly matters. What matters is what creates good writing.

CONFIDENTIALITY

If students know that we guarantee their right to privacy, they may feel an even greater sense of freedom and may risk writing about private thoughts and feelings. We are not trying to become confessors or counselors, but as educators, we might agree with Socrates that the unexamined life is not worth living and that self-knowledge is both curative and painful. A further word about confidentiality involves the paradox of students who want total privacy with their thoughts and perceptions but, at the same time, a trusted, sensitive other who knows these inner thoughts. Some teachers resolve this paradox by allowing secret journals, ones that remain unread by any but themselves. An alternative to private journals is "flopped" journals, in which students review their writing and select pieces that they especially want another to read. As trust grows and confidentiality is maintained, students sometimes ask that these flopped pages be unfurled.

RESPECT

Freedom and confidentiality have a powerful bearing on the way students use journals; they are almost contractual assumptions. Respect, that sense of positive regard and esteem that a student feels from a teacher, goes further. A sense of the teacher's regard originates in the whole-class interactions, but all other encounters deepen and validate it. The teacher strives for an unconditional acceptance and a valuing of the student. Respect means a prizing of the student with no thought of evaluating or selecting only those features that appear to be good and dismissing those that seem bad. The teacher's response can approach in the classroom what Rogers (1957) believes to be the necessary conditions for therapeutic change in the counseling encounter: genuineness, empathy, and a high level of positive regard. Journal writing removes many of the barriers between students and teachers, namely, barriers of teacher-dominated assignments and grading. At that moment, it is important that the two, writer and reader, shake hands heartily; but the regard must be genuine. If it is simply a strategy with which to manipulate the student, it will be hard to sustain and its discovery will be harmful.

We conclude this section with specific suggestions for journal assignments that suggest the diversity and complexity of this approach. They address two dilemmas in journal writing: how to encourage greater depth of reflection, and how to encourage experimentation and risk taking without compromising spontaneity.

Intense structures such as that developed by Progoff (1975) have been designed to promote a deep level of self-understanding. Nelson (1991) asks students to write their thoughts in two major territories: the subconscious world of dreams and fantasies (kept in a pink notebook) and the conscious world of observation and insight (kept in a yellow notebook). The two worlds are separate, but they can be fused by reading the pink and then the yellow. From the juxtaposition, students create a new journal (a blue one) and a new reality.

The choices presented in Teaching Activity 10-1 shake students from journal writing that has become too pat and invariant. For instance, a student who is always aloof and distant might be drawn toward more personal writing when dreams, aphorisms, encomiums, myths, and introspections are ordered up by fate or by date. For the sentimental writer, polemics, sarcasms, critiques, and sophistries may turn the tide. The swift rotation from mode to mode and form to form is enlivening and, once sustained for a time, can lead to exploration and discovery for a young writer.

Teaching Activity 10–1   *Experimental Writing Logs*

Have students make log entries three times a week during time assigned in class or as homework. Suggest a specific question, or ask students to free-write. As a departure from explanatory prose forms, suggest that students experiment with one of the following forms. Collect the logs periodically every 4 or 5 weeks. Respond to, but do not grade, the work.

1. Dreams	16. Fantasies
2. Satires	17. Sarcasms
3. Aphorisms	18. Axioms
4. Reviews	19. Critiques
5. Conceits	20. Analogies
6. Essays	21. Editorials
7. Polemics	22. Diatribes
8. Encomiums	23. Panegyrics
9. Fables	24. Parables
10. Allegories	25. Myths
11. Lyrics	26. Verbosities
12. Analyses	27. Epiphanies
13. Meditations	28. Introspections
14. Narrations	29. Yarns
15. Commercials	30. Sophistries

Specific prompts for journal writing arise out of many different purposes. Probst's Reader Response questions posed in Chapter 4 could be used as points for reflection about literature under study, for instance. The following general writing topics are selected from those Neenan (1989) found to be provocative with her students.

- Write a letter to yourself or someone with whom you would like to talk but can't (because they're dead, they're too far away, you're not on speaking terms, you just can't communicate, etc.).
- Describe a time when you felt afraid. How did you deal with that fear? What was the outcome?
- Imagine what it would be like to be a member of the opposite sex.
- List the people who have been most influential in shaping your life. Choose one person and describe the way he or she has influenced your life.
- Write a letter to God.
- Cite an instance when you have been disappointed about something. Why were you disappointed? How did you show your disappointment? Was there anything you could have done to change the situation? Explain. Who or what disappoints you the most? Why? How?
- A man from another planet visits us. He knows our language but not our customs. Explain baseball, television, a holiday, a dance, or a video game.
- What will humans be like in 2,000 years? How will the human body have evolved to cope with that world?
- You awaken one morning and find you have turned into an animal. You have the same mind but a different body. What animal are you? Describe your day.
- What are the five most important things a parent can teach children? Explain.
- Describe a situation when you felt isolated and alone, separated from others. What other feelings emerged? What really caused you to feel this way? What did you observe about yourself?
- What cruelty have you seen or experienced? How did you feel about it? Are children more cruel than adults?

- What are five ways you personally exercise control or power over people or situations? Describe how you feel when this happens. Evaluate your method of control and tell whether it is negative or positive. How? Consider how you feel when others exercise control over you; also consider how you feel when you are in control of yourself. What feels best? Why?
- Write a letter to a possession telling why it is so important.
- Write a letter to a future child of yours. Explain how life is now . . . things you have been through . . . lessons you have learned . . . dreams you have for the child . . . where you are in your life right now.
- Write a letter to yourself today as though you were eighty. (pp. 7-12)

For some students, school writing has been so tedious and arid that reaching into the personal dimensions of emotion and imagination is the only way to remove the block to writing. Somewhere in these journaling suggestions lies a new pathway for writing for those students.

WRITE TO LEARN

When a history or biology teacher becomes interested in writing across the curriculum, that zeal is likely spurred by a desire to have all students write better: fewer errors, better organization, more style. At a time when teachers see all too many errors and all too few writing virtues, such enthusiasm is understandable. What they champion is *learning to write,* but what is even more important in schools is *writing to learn.* If you turn the concept around and think of writing as a tool for stronger and clearer thinking (Langer & Applebee, 1987), you can see that it is a powerful instrument for instruction in all subject areas. And because it is an instrument that will improve achievement in all subjects, it is easier to sell to all of your colleagues in history and biology. Figure 10-4 summarizes five of the NCTE Commission on Composition's assumptions about the connections between language and thought that have clear applications here. Such assumptions suggest why writing is as relevant to a science class as it is to an English class. If math teachers can be shown how to make use of writing to help their students solidify and expand their grasp of basic or sophisticated math concepts, they will listen to your ideas and employ writing in their classes. But if you ask them to take on the job of making students write better, all but a few will politely disengage from the conversation. They may ask what you've done lately for numeracy if you ask them to help with literacy. Tierney (1990), Griffiths (1991), Fulwiler and Young (1982), and others have demonstrated countless ways to make learning deep and long-lasting through the use of writing. We offer two of their ways to use writing as a tool for learning: one from basic math, and one from Advanced Placement biology.

MATH AND SCIENCE

Griffiths uses tiles to help students understand mathematical patterns and sequences. The teacher asks his students how many square tiles will be needed to surround a central tile if another tile is added. The students are asked to think about the problem and write down their answers. Some are confused; some challenge him about what he means by *surround* (he encourages that kind of care with words); others quickly figure the answer to be two. He then asks them how many tiles would be needed to surround the central tiles if a third tile were added. At this point he asks them to explain their answers. Some give simple answers, such as that it is two more because one has been added; some see it visually as slipping in the center a new tile, whose top and bottom edges are all that need to be surrounded; some few see it as a mathematical pattern and explain it in those terms. He uses their writing to provide a picture of their thinking so that he can identify problems and students can profit from a comparison of their thinking with their peers'.

In his AP biology class, Tierney uses writing in a different way but to the same purpose: to increase understanding. He says that he never lectures more than 8 minutes because more would be lost on his

FIGURE 10–4
Assumptions about language and thought

1. When people *articulate connections* between new information and what they already know, they learn and understand that new information better (Bruner, 1966).
2. When people *think and figure things out,* they do so in symbol systems commonly called languages, which are most often verbal but may also be mathematical, musical, visual, and so on (Vygotsky, 1962).
3. When people *learn,* they use all of the language modes—reading, writing, speaking, and listening; each mode helps people learn in a unique way (Emig, 1977).
4. When people *write* about new information and ideas—in addition to reading, talking, and listening—they learn and understand them better (Britton et al., 1975).
5. When people *care* about what they write and see connections to their own lives, they both learn and write better (Moffett, 1968).

students. Instead, he uses writing. During a lecture, he asks each student to take notes on the left-hand page of a spiral-bound notebook. After he has completed his brief explanation and the page is filled, he asks each student to divide the right-hand page into a top and bottom half. On the top half he asks students to put into their own words what they have just learned. Then he asks them to divide the lower half into two equal right and left sides. The left side is to be used to answer the question "So what?" and the right side is to be used to sketch out a diagram or figural representation of the concept just encountered. Figure 10–5 shows what the whole spread looks like in a physics lesson on volume and mass. Using all four steps to capture concepts takes longer than the traditional lecture and note taking method does. Less ground can be covered. But Tierney's (1974) research and that of others shows that although the traditional method of lecture and note taking develops performance equal to that developed by Tierney's methods at end-of-course testing, the results 2 and 3 years later are significantly greater for those who use Tierney's methods of writing to learn.

Writing to predict what will happen in experiments, writing to capture very accurate observations, writing to define abstractions such as angles, writing to connect course concepts with personal experience, writing to express tentative understanding of a poem, writing to capture the conversation of a small group exploring why port cities are laid out differently from river cities, and writing to explain what the saying "a rolling stone gathers no moss" means and what the language intends—all of these uses of writing enhance learning and solidify concepts for your students. Books by the leaders in the field provide examples you can use with your colleagues to lead them toward a kind of teaching whose results are manifest in student performance and student attitude. Mitchell (1996) offers a superb list of interesting writing tasks that support learning. We report five of her best suggestions. You can use them to build a larger repertoire of your own.

1. Making Connections to One's Own Life: Students work to find ways that material and concepts in their classes relate to their own lives.
   - What three geometric shapes have had a direct influence on your life today?
   - Who have you met in history that you want to be like?
   - What would your life be like if calcium were absent from all foods?
2. Making Judgments/Evaluating Concepts: Students use higher-level thinking skills as they draw on content knowledge to come to conclusions.
   - Which character seems to have the worst self-concept?
   - Which planet, aside from Earth, seems to you to be superior?
   - Are high heels a physics nightmare?

FIGURE 10–5
Tierney notebook

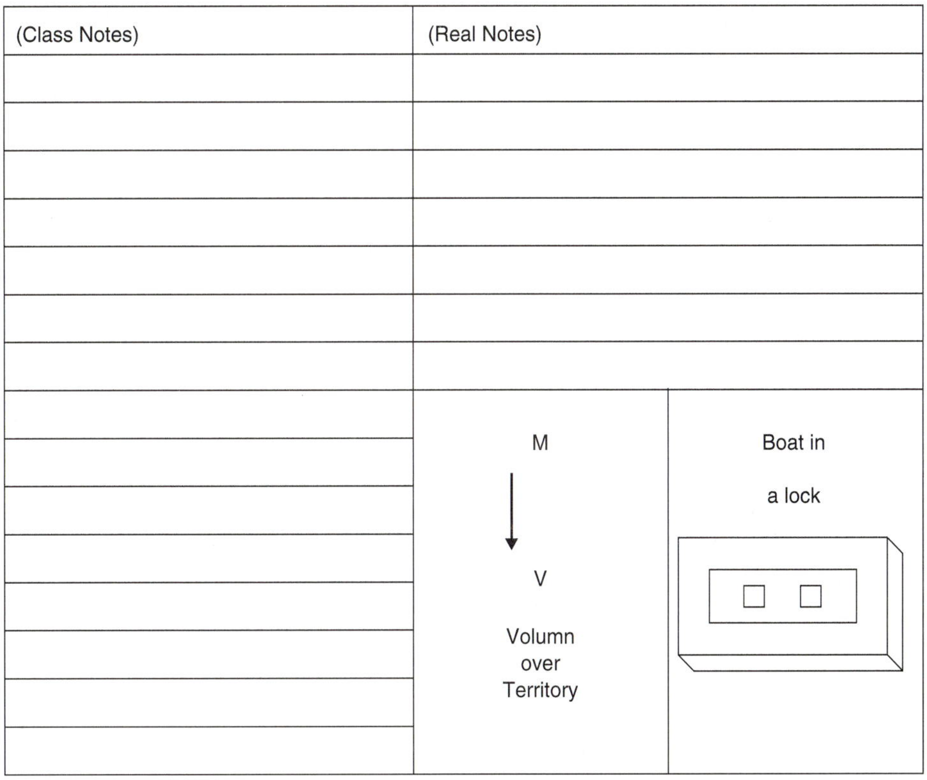

FIGURE 10–6
Write to solve

1. The captain of a Dutch cargo vessel was concerned that the water level in the canal lock was too low for his heavily loaded vessel. He was not sure what to do when the lock commandant, who spoke a language he did not understand, tried to offer a solution. A young deckhand finally came up to suggest a solution: Toss the two extremely heavy but worthless lead cylinders overboard. Should the captain follow the suggestion? If he does, will the water in the lock rise, remain the same, or fall? Explain your answer in a clear written statement.
   Use two baking tins, two batteries, water, and a pencil to test your previous thoughtful response. Be sure that the larger tin is almost 3/4 full when you start your experiment. Write your new explanation of what will happen if your experiment proved something different from what you wrote previously.
2. On a jetliner to Europe, there are 9 boys, 5 American children, 9 men, 7 Canadian boys, 14 Americans, 8 American males, and 5 Canadian females. How many passengers are there on board?
   Explain in writing the thinking that allowed you to find that answer.
3. Find the next number in this series: 7, 12, 27, 72, 207, ____.
   Explain in writing how anyone can find that answer.
4. Three baskets sit on a high ledge with signs over them that correctly mark their contents: Apples, Pears, Mixed. A clever child mixes up the signs so that none of the signs correctly indicates what is actually in the basket below. The orchard owner decides to make a game of it by allowing you to reach into one of the baskets above you and, without being able to see what is in the basket, pick out one piece of fruit. The challenge is that if you then can put all the signs over the correct baskets, you can have all three baskets without charge. Explain in writing how you might beat the orchard owner at this game.

3. What If . . . ?: Students figure out how the absence of something would have an impact on something else.
   • What if we had no moon?
   • What if your heart had only three chambers instead of four?
   • What if the liquid on the surface of Earth were methyl instead of water?
4. Awards: Students create awards based on any criterion the class or teacher develops.
   • In science, students could nominate lab experiments that were the most exciting or the most demanding.
   • In math, students could give awards to most important formula.
   • In foreign languages, students could give awards to the least desirable grammatical concept or favorite verb.
5. Three Words: Students choose three words that best describe an era, chapter, or any other concept and explain why they chose those words.
   • What three words describe the problems in the American diet?
   • What three words best describe the Bill of Rights?
   • What three words best describe the mossy stage of a climax community?

DIFFICULT PROBLEMS

The fact that we sometimes talk our way through difficult problems illustrates the power of writing to learn. The basic idea in all of the problems posed in Figure 10-6 is to use writing to deepen the way your students conceptualize what they are learning. Each of the tasks assigned is difficult and encourages talking and writing to learn. In writing to learn, you may find yourself working with colleagues in other disciplines, and this will have the unexpected benefit of helping you integrate the power of the full curriculum into your teaching of English. You also will find that, although you are selling writing across the curriculum as a way to help students learn, they also will learn to write because they are writing about things that they come to understand deeply. Everyone ends up a winner.

CODE SWITCHING

As an English teacher, you are likely to have some variation of the following experience: You have been having an easy and fluent conversation with a stranger in a comfortable social setting. Suddenly he or she asks, "Well, what do you do?" You answer innocently, "I teach English." The stranger blanches and immediately exclaims self-consciously, "Oh. I'd better watch what I say. I never was good at grammar." Both of you then lapse into embarrassed silence. This stranger assumes that you are a traditional grammarian with a long list of do's and don'ts. S. I. Hayakawa (1950) notes that most English teachers have "felt the need to publicly split an infinitive or two in order to dispel that anxiety."

Have you heard these rules for "good" English before?

• Don't use double negatives.
• Never end a sentence with a preposition.

- Don't use *ain't.*
- Don't split infinitives.
- Don't start a sentence with a conjunction (*and, but, or*).

When you hear the following, do you have the urge to correct the speaker or writer?

- My friend be at the mall.
- You played good tonight.
- I don't have none.
- That teacher don't know what she's talking about.
- Everybody has a right to their opinion.
- It's me. I'm home.

The field of sociolinguistics provides an approach to writing instruction that addresses the issue that concerns many English teachers and an ever larger segment of our population: that of determining "good" and "bad" grammar. Many teachers, and the public at large, want young people to speak and write inside the bounds of standard usage. They see current usage as a corruption of norms of educated language, and the teacher's charge is to teach students Standard English. As we discussed in Chapter 2, among many educators, linguists, and public figures, there is a counterargument. This group reasons that students have a right to their own language and the dignity that accrues to that language. Their underlying assumption is that language has no fixed and permanent rules because it is constantly changing. The criterion for judging usage is not "Is it correct?" but "Does it work in the context in which it is used?"

PROGRAM REQUIREMENTS

Chapter 2 mentioned Smitherman's (1989) three standards that all strong and pluralistic language programs should embody:

- All teachers should know enough about linguistics to understand that all languages are equally effective in communicating ideas.
- All students should have their own variants from the standard affirmed while they are given an opportunity to learn the standard or mainstream language.
- All students should be required to learn a second language (e.g., Spanish, Chinese, or German) from their first years in school through graduation.

Smitherman believes that second-language learning is extremely important to the cognitive development of all students; those who are Standard English users will better understand the complexity of language and the variety of languages. Furthermore, she argues, they will struggle with the same challenge posed for non-Standard English users who are asked to acquire a second language. Both groups will share the common ground of an acquired language. Her program affirms non-Standard English usage on practical and psychological grounds while acknowledging the need for using Standard English in a culture in which it is the dominant language. Smitherman's standards also offer a theoretical context for a four-step plan developed by Elifson (1977) for the Atlanta Public Schools and employees of Coca-Cola.

Like Smitherman, Elifson's first step requires that teachers who adopt this program be well informed about the nature of the English language, its variability, and its changes over time. They must then make students understand that all language systems work equally well, though somewhat differently. They must affirm the language of all students and encourage or permit them to use that language with confidence and energy. This step must be treated seriously and handled deliberately. Varied methods should be used, for instance, a study of concrete instances of variability (sampling, polling, and interpreting the results). It is important too to discuss freely the value of pluralism and of a standard language system. The rewards and losses for those who do and do not have the ability to use Standard English should be explored. Elifson sees three important realities that must be established:

- All language users switch dialects to fit the setting in which the language is being used.
- All languages are equally effective in transmitting ideas.
- Standard language helps to open the paths of opportunity for all students, and inability to switch to the standard code in certain settings penalizes students who cannot switch codes.

With this framework of attitudes in place, students can elect to move toward possession of a second language system or dialect. They can embrace rewards of this language learning without having to disown their first language.

SWITCHING PRINCIPLES

Elifson sets up four principles to guide the process of code switching. Each is important and integral to the next:

- Select target areas in which to work.
- Make the transition to Standard English in oral, not written, language first.
- Move from wholly controlled language drills to ones that allow spontaneity of student language.
- Develop the ability to switch codes by creating exercises wherein students can develop consciousness of their language.

Unless attention is given to a few points at which the differences between the nonstandard and standard are most notable, students will be frustrated by the size and difficulty of the task. (In setting up a program of this type at a local high school, we used student papers as our source for sentences that departed from Standard English.) Because oral language is our most fundamental language, basic code switches can be made most readily and most lastingly if they are begun at the oral level. If students begin to talk in the standard code, their writing will likely follow suit. The reverse is not true.

PROGRAM OUTLINE

The program begins with rather strict controls on the oral productions of students. Students hear a sentence read that was written with nonstandard usage, for example, *Rony ate a whole nother dinner.* Students then repeat the sentence by "correcting" it to standard usage by guidelines provided by the teacher. Gradually, the language under scrutiny moves from short memorized parts in plays, to planned and recorded speeches, and finally to almost wholly spontaneous talk. Control for the analysis, critique, and change also moves from teacher to student. The progression of Elifson's activities is as follows:

- Pattern drills
- Short memorized dramas
- Planned speeches
- Unmemorized planned skits
- Planned oral speeches
- Controlled discussion
- Role-playing
- Impromptu speeches

For the program to work, though, consciousness must develop. If language change and variability are explored with openness and without judgment, language has a chance to take on interest for students. If, however, it is treated in an entirely prescriptive way, as rules to be mastered, a healthy consciousness of language may well be stymied and experimentation with it will be stifled. Students are left with no interest, desire, or method for exploring their own language. Rather, they become self-conscious and silenced in the presence of those they consider to be "grammarians."

These four principles—target areas are well selected, transitions are oral, control is released, and consciousness of language is developed—undergird the work of the class. In our teaching we have adapted Elifson's progression. We laid the groundwork in discussions of language change and variability, discussed honestly the power of all languages to communicate, explored the value of code switching, and then began a regimen of 5-minute pattern drills. Each day began with a short drill based on 10 sentences in the target area such as the following:

1. Braden come home last night.
2. Willy run fast.
3. Mozelle done eat.
4. Jack and Fred they can't stay tonight.
5. Sally bes mad at me.
6. Wanda ain't going with us.
7. Felisha ain't got none.
8. We might could find some.

A sample week of lessons is presented in Figure 10-7. Through this series of 5 days, each student works in the target area, moves from oral to written language, works with controlled and then somewhat more spontaneous language, and develops self-consciousness by the repetition, the emphasis, and the markings. The short version of this program used in our schools proved to be remarkably effective in a period of weeks. It resulted not only in control of standard features, but also in a greater confidence

FIGURE 10–7
Pattern drill

Monday. The teacher gives each student a list of 10 Standard English sentences with the target area underlined. The teacher has the same sentences but the target areas are nonstandard expressions. The teacher says the same faulty sentence and students respond by saying the sentence emphasizing the underlined standard form.

Tuesday. The teacher reads the same faulty sentence and the students respond using a new sheet with the 10 standard English sentences, but without the targeted area marked. Again they respond by emphasizing the area of correction.

Wednesday. The students have no sheet, but respond to the faulty sentence emphasizing the correct usage as they have on the first 2 days.

Thursday. The students have a sheet with the nonstandard feature underlined and are asked to write the sentence correctly above the faulty one.

Friday. On the final day, the students have the same sheet, but with unmarked nonstandard sentences. They write standard versions above the nonstandard sentences.

in writing. While the success of such programs has been remarkable, the need to approach them with care is imperative.

PEDAGOGICAL GRAMMAR

Grammar instruction has been a nonsubject for a number of years now. The prescriptive grammarian was a kind of Wicked Witch of the West for English. The vendetta against grammar is fairly well substantiated: disdain for detached workbook drill-and-skill work, realization that the structure of Latin grammar was incompatible with our Germanic language, high regard for constructivist learning, and displacement of correctness as the centerpiece of writing. These and many other reasons caused grammar to be given increasingly less attention in secondary classrooms. Recently, research has revisited the question, and extensive books have been written that call for reconsideration of our appraisal of grammar instruction, especially when it is taught in the context of writing. Some of the distance that has been traveled can be measured by the shifts that have taken place in writing instruction. English educators of several decades ago favored Elbow's position, stated in his book *Writing Without Teachers* (1973), while those of recent decades do not go that far. Two leaders in the field, Donald Murray and Donald Graves, for instance, agree that teaching means responding to writing and describe the teacher as a mirror to the student. Both celebrate teacher-initiated conferences and believe that teachers must learn to ask Rogerian questions to become effective. Atwell's *In the Middle* grows out of Murray's and Graves's approaches, and, like them, she focuses on independence and ownership. But because she was a middle-school teacher, she is aware of the teacher's responsibility as well and thus carves out a system that always provides a small segment of time for mini-lessons devoted to direct instruction. The lessons are drawn from the writing needs of her students, but they are presented as direct instruction, often to the entire class. This escalation definitely does not mean the return of the daunting traditional grammarian, but rather the emergence of contextualized grammar instruction like that proposed by Weaver (1996). This moderating position is not unlike what some political analysts describe as the "radical center" of the Clinton years. The work of three or four pedagogical linguists has gone even further toward direct instruction. Noguchi and others have earned a good bit of attention because they believe that "correctness" is not central but needs to be given due consideration. They also agree that some of the problems caused by teaching grammar out of context can be dispelled, and that writing and language consciousness can be brought together.

CONTEXTUALIZED GRAMMAR

Weaver (1996) has been writing about grammar for many years, but when she put aside this focus to teach other courses in writing pedagogy she began to see how to bring process writing and grammar together. She has serious questions about formal grammar instruction but recognizes that contextualized grammar instruction, connected to students' writing, is essential. She takes a strong constructivist stance and challenges the idea of a prepackaged curriculum like that she associates with Madeline Hunter's goals and objectives model. Weaver shows that the Hunter model moves from objectives to instruction to assessment and does not take into account students' daily performance in shaping objectives or instruction. Traditional approaches to grammar make this very mistake. Weaver has compiled a thought-provoking list of reasons why teachers, in spite of research findings, continue to teach formal grammar. It is drawn from research and her own suppositions:

1. They are not aware of the research.
2. They do not believe the research.

3. They believe that grammar is interesting.
4. They assume that writers need to know about grammar to write effectively.
5. They believe students can read/write well because they know grammar.
6. They find it easier to assign exercises and grade them.
7. They believe that grammar study does no harm.
8. They are required to do so by the school.
9. They fear students might miss out on something for which they will be held accountable.
10. They bow to pressure from parents.
11. They believe that the writing of some students will benefit.
12. They do not realize that grammatical concepts can be applied without formal study.

Weaver praises Atwell's approach, because Atwell designs her language instruction using notes from her own informal assessment of her students' writing. She takes this strong stand to help teachers use their new knowledge as "a starting point for experimenting with other approaches to teaching those aspects of grammar that are most relevant to writing" (p. 25). She believes that "students can learn and apply many grammatical concepts without learning to analyze and label the parts of speech and various other grammatical constructions" (p. 25). She urges teachers to give up the role they have been too often trained for—to look for errors—and find new ways to help students with their writing. She believes that "students mainly need to be guided in learning and applying certain grammatical concepts as they revise and edit their writing" (p. xi).

To this end, she argues that we should teach only the relevant aspects of grammar, teach these within the context of writing, minimize terminology, emphasize those elements useful in helping students make sentences more effective, and target those aspects of grammar that are helpful in editing sentences for conventional mechanics. Weaver offers a useful list of specific alternatives to formal grammar that range from schoolwide changes to new ways of teaching language in the classroom:

- Restrict the teaching of grammar as a system to elective classes
- Promote the acquisition and use of grammatical constructions through reading
- Minimize the use of grammatical terminology and maximize the use of examples
- Emphasize the production of effective sentences rather than their analysis
- Teach not only "correct" punctuation but effective punctuation
- Lead students in discussing and investigating questions of usage

The first three alternatives seem to serve as pacifiers to an unconventional audience; the last three are more proactive and lead to a specific list of objectives that outline a precise plan for contextual grammar instruction. Five of her key concepts offer "a minimum of grammar for maximum benefits" (p. 143):

- Teaching concepts of subject, verb, sentence, clause, phrase, and related concepts for editing
- Teaching style through sentence combining and sentence generating
- Teaching sentence sense and style through the manipulation of syntactic elements
- Teaching the power of dialects and dialects of power
- Teaching punctuation and mechanics for convention, clarity, and style

This outline of objectives leads naturally to an extended set of classroom lessons in which grammar is integrated into the context of writing instruction. Most are useful and interesting because they are inductively taught and bear down on the most serious usage problems that students face. We hope that the following listing of a few useful lessons will prompt you to go to Weaver's book to check out the details:

- Understanding Subjects and Verbs and the Concept of Clause
- Understanding Basic Subject-Verb Agreement
- Understanding Independent and Dependent Clauses and the Concept of Fragment
- Eliminating Run-on sentences and Grammar Splices (pp. 188–203).

COMPREHENSIVE GRAMMAR

While Weaver argues for a contextualized approach, other voices have argued for a pedagogical grammar that is easily understood by students but is nevertheless comprehensive. One of the most impressive of them is Noguchi's (1995). He offers three reasons given for the "failure of formal grammar instruction to improve writing" (p. 21):

- Grammar is not adequately learned.
- Grammar is not transferred to writing situations.
- Grammar is not transferable to writing.

FIGURE 10–8
Hairston's levels of
grammatical problems

STATUS MARKING

- Nonstandard verb forms in past or past participle: *brung* instead of *brought; had went* instead of *had gone.*
- Lack of subject-verb agreement: *We was* instead of *We were; Jones don't think it's acceptable* instead of *Jones doesn't think it's acceptable.*
- Objective pronoun as subject: *Him and Richard were the last ones hired.*

VERY SERIOUS

- Sentence fragment
- Nonparallelism
- Faulty adverb forms: *He treats his men bad.*

SERIOUS

- Dangling modifiers
- *I* as an objective pronoun.
- Tense switching

MODERATELY SERIOUS

- Lack of commas to set off an appositive.
- Failure to distinguish between *among* and *between.*
- Comma splices

MINOR OR UNIMPORTANT

- Use of a qualifier before *unique: That is the most unique city.*
- Writing *different than* instead of *different from.*
- Omission of the apostrophe in the contraction *it's.*

Each reason, if true, would be progressively more catastrophic to Noguchi's position. The first is merely the fault of the teacher; Noguchi believes that we can do better. The second is the fault of the student, but good teachers can help them do better. The third is devastating because it accepts the idea that the learning *cannot be* transferred to writing: Good teachers, good students, good luck—nothing can help. Noguchi uses the majority of his text (1995) to fight that third battle. To begin that battle, he cites a study by Hairston (1981) in which 101 professionals classified the grammatical or usage problems contained in 65 sentences from the most grievous, "status marking," to the most "minor or unimportant" (p. 24). Figure 10-8 lists the five categories and three examples of problems identified at each of those levels.

Hairston closes his remarks about the study with a word of warning. "We cannot afford to let students leave our classrooms thinking that surface features of discourse do not matter. They do" (p. 799). Seeing the task implied by Hairston's study, Noguchi begins to show teachers a way to construct a logical and relatively simple grammar. He does this by showing us that students have an "unconscious underlying knowledge" (p. 45) of language that cannot be articulated but can be brought to consciousness with good instruction. He argues that sentence combining depends upon it and that we can do the same for other aspects of writing instruction. He starts with a lesson entitled "Underlying Knowledge of the Subject," which allows students "to locate the subject of a sentence easily" (p. 46). He helps them do this by turning basic statements into questions by adding tags: *Jim and Sal can ride our horses* becomes *Jim and Sal can ride our horses, can't they?* Six-year-olds can make this transformation, and when they do, you need only ask what *they* represents to enable them to find the subject. "Underlying Knowledge of the Main Verb" tries to do the same job on the predicate. Noguchi locates this second key element also with a substitution rule. From these two fairly simple building blocks, Noguchi moves on to "Underlying Knowledge of a Sentence," which depends on knowledge of the two earlier lessons. Having worked up to this level, he turns to more complicated items such as the "Presentence Modifier" (p. 58). He believes that this newly developed knowledge of such basic categories "comprises a fundamental set for identifying and correcting many high frequency and sometimes highly stigmatizing kinds of errors."

Despite having vanquished so many stubborn obstacles, Noguchi is not willing to rest. He goes on to develop similar means for attacking run-ons and comma splices using what he calls "five native speaker abilities":

1. The ability to distinguish a grammatical sentence from an ungrammatical one: e.g., *The cook put the soup on the stove* versus *The cook put the soup* or *Cook the put soup the on stove the.*
2. The ability to produce and understand an infinite number of new sentences of potentially infinite length: e.g., *Jack went home, and he fixed himself a sandwich, and he cleaned his room, and he turned on his stereo, and . . .*

3. The ability to recognize ambiguous sentences: e.g., *My mother hates boring guests* (i.e., "My mother hates to bore guests" or "My mother hates guests who are boring").

4. The ability to recognize synonymous sentences: e.g., *Alice and Tom washed the car* versus *The car was washed by Alice and Tom.*

5. The ability to recognize the internal structure of sentences: e.g., *Julia is eager to help* versus *Julia is easy to help.* (In the first sentence, Julia does the helping; in the second sentence, someone helps Julia.) (pp. 65–66)

Finally, Noguchi systematizes this underlying grammatical knowledge to form a comprehensive framework. All of it works well and is accessible to almost any student. He also cites numerous studies that indicate the effectiveness of this knowledge as it carries over into writing. His approach does not take care of the motivational and fluency problems we must solve in the early stages of the writing process, but it does offer a possible solution for dealing with surface errors. These usage problems are not major concerns in most good writers' minds but do need attention before writing meets the public eye. The excitement of enabling structures and the power of acquisition can overcome many of the problems Noguchi labors to solve, but for many writers in many situations, they do not have the environmental help or the extended time to let acquisition do its powerful work toward correction.

Another System.   Hunter (1996) is in Noguchi's camp although his *Sentence Sense* has not received as much attention. His *English Journal* article on his students' experimental study reports how his formal grammar concepts were put into play. He takes issue with McCleary (1995), who searches for a "pedagogical grammar" but believes that most of the recent improvements on traditional grammar are "too technical to use in teaching" (p. 2). Hunter believes that his approach is simple enough to use and points to Stubbs's success with it in her New Jersey classroom. Hunter also focuses some of his attention on the misrepresentations of older research studies that reported little or no writing success from using formal grammar. Weaver and Noguchi contend with the results as well, though each from a different perspective. But Hunter returns to pedagogical grammar's effectiveness and cites Stubbs (1995), who reports that the Hunter approach successfully teaches that "the verb is the hub of the English sentence" and that inexact definitions in current use need to be replaced with "strategies that are easy, familiar and fun" (p. vii). Hunter briefly outlines some of his key pedagogical concepts: the use of mnemonic devices, "metacognitive self-questioning techniques," "The Test" for identifying nouns, "ingrained, intuitive grammar" to find verbs, and "tools to identify syntactical errors" (pp. 105–106). Hunter concludes by claiming that his grammar addresses the need for simplicity, which is necessary for any new grammar to help with writing: "Its simplicity is testified to by the fact that slightly learning disabled seventh graders have learned it sufficiently well to be able to apply it to their writing" (p. 107).

At a recent NCTE conference, we fell into conversation with a thoughtful young teacher whose quandary perfectly represents the competing positions in this ongoing debate. She had read Noguchi's *Grammar and the Teaching of Writing* and was just getting ready to dive into Weaver's *Teaching Grammar in Context.* She found Nagochi's approach appealing and believed that it had potential applicability in her classroom. His system did not seem too complex to be useful. But even though her school wants to put greater emphasis on grammar, she has not yet put the more direct kind of instruction into play in her class. She had heard of Weaver's book and liked the idea that it offers a way for grammatical conventions to be taught inside the context of her students' writing. Her basic problem was that she was so busy teaching that she was hard pressed to take the time to apply one of the approaches in her classroom. That is the dilemma that most secondary teachers face. They are revisiting the grammar question and see the positive features of both approaches to the issue.

EJ's Views.   The December 1996 issue of the *English Journal* (*EJ's Views*) was devoted to articles concerned with grammar instruction that highlight the Weaver-Noguchi split. The essays ranged from those by well-known and respected debunkers of formal grammar instruction as linguistic manners of the privileged, such as James Sledd (1996), to those who point out the flaws in research that discredits grammar instruction, such as Anthony Hunter (1996). They included the views of young classroom teachers such as John Skretta (1996), who believes that students "do not see the validity of explicit instruction in grammar" (p. 65) and that "grammatical knowledge is best acquired as all language is: naturally and authentically" (p. 66), and the responses of experienced teachers such as Brenda Petruzzella (1996), who interviewed 25 English teachers and found that "researchers and classroom teachers often have different *definitions* of grammar or grammar instruction" (p. 69). The issue of grammar instruction is once again open to scrutiny, and that is better than mindless affirmation of the time-honored practice of teaching formal grammar or endless sniping at any grammar instruction through less-than-rigorous studies. The crucial test that we have always used to test the necessity of grammar is the writing ability of a young woman who had absolutely no formal grammar instruction because her father raised her in the wilds of Colorado. She spoke and wrote exceptionally well and did so without grammar tutoring. She used the powers of acquisition through reading and listening to her father talk to develop a solid competence. The question that we must ponder in spite of this test case is how we complement the work of acquisition with constructivist learning and even direct instruction. Where does the teacher intervene and how directly? We all have to answer this question to see if and how we use such instruction to support good writing.

VOCABUSPELL

Writing skills that promote organization, development, and coherence are essential to the deep structure of a piece of writing—surface features seem far less grand and conventional and sometimes get left out of the equation of good writing. We know, however, from the Hairston (1981) study of usage that a preponderance of professionals who read the sentences in her survey were troubled by problems with just such surface features. Vocabulary and spelling are two such surface features that significantly enhances or diminishes writing. Both can be improved by good teaching in a number of ways that we suggest here.

VOCABULARY GROWTH

Vocabulary instruction in secondary English classes has been only slightly more informed than spelling instruction. Only the public's ire over low SAT scores has prompted serious work in this area of the secondary English curriculum. The impetus, however, has been largely toward a one-dimensional approach to vocabulary strength, which may divert English teachers from better ways to improve the vocabulary of adolescents.

Basically, the growth of students' vocabulary can be seen as a natural process that continues as they move through all of the school years. We know too, however, that the growth depends on the students' environment: It can flourish or wither. The 6-year-old brings as many as 6,000 words to school that are clearly not the result of direct parental instruction (de Villeas & de Villeas, 1978); rather, they are gleaned from the word world that surrounds them. We know too that voracious readers gather the strongest vocabularies. But unlike spelling, for which words and letters need to be seen, vocabulary can be drawn from a wider environment. Spelling is restricted to the print world; vocabulary includes both the oral and print worlds. Thus, although readers develop strong vocabularies, students who live in talk-rich environments in which new words are used repeatedly in lively and enticing discourse will also grow robust vocabularies. The consciousness awakened by seeing words in print may give some edge to the readers, but such listeners are also likely to have strong vocabularies. And this same consciousness that reading develops (seeing words in print) enables secondary students to respond more to informed vocabulary instruction; they are developing a new consciousness of themselves and of language during these years that was not afforded to them in earlier years.

Our basic question is, then, "How shall we best contribute to this natural process during the secondary school years?" We know that our contribution to the natural process will not be large as a percentage of total vocabulary, but it can be important. We know too that what Moffett and Wagner say about reception and production of language (discussed in Chapter 1) applies here too. Your students will have a reception or decoding vocabulary that differs from their production or encoding vocabulary: One they understand only partially; the other they feel free to use. What they risk in one situation they won't risk in another. Our job, as with sentence combining, is to help them move the larger reception vocabulary over to production so that they will risk using newly incorporated words to empower their utterances, private and public, oral and written. The following four strategies that we suggest for vocabulary development grow out of this belief.

Acquisition.   The span from acquisition to semantics moves from unconscious collection to playfulness with language. The acquisition position is dependent on three important conduits for new language: texts, talk, and television. While written words are the only way to acquire spelling power, the two other modes can be engaged to propel vocabulary growth. And because we believe that meaning precedes form, we also believe that when students find new words they want to use, they more readily incorporate words whose message is important to them. Thus, you should try to enlist the power of all three modes to help your students find words that attract them. It is important to think in the broadest terms in considering texts. Books ranging from William Steig's and E. B. White's rich children's literature to bizarre microfiction such as that found in the collection *Sudden Fiction* and E. Annie Proulx's *The Shipping News* are loaded depositories. Because poetry is semantically rich, new words are plentiful there, as they are in any compressed language. You can urge your students to read insurance policies, bonds, users' manuals, and guarantees to see if this mundane world of print does not also yield word dividends.

Text print is important, for it may imprint vocabulary more deeply than the other two modes, but the other two conduits are livelier sources for most students, so attachment is strong when they too are used. To make acquisition most available for your students, oral interaction is essential. This can include the fascinating world of television talk shows, where guests, hosts, and callers provide a potpourri of language, but it is probably best that your students glean vocabulary from talk with each other and with people outside the classroom. The process of acquiring new vocabulary is natural, but you can promote the natural process by the opportunities you provide students to confront new and engaging language. The list of people who can provide that enrichment is endless, but four likely providers are elders, specialists, creators, and outsiders. The best class formats are probably like those presented in Chapter 3, and others that make sense to you and engage your students with these people and their language. Elders have a rare language by dint of time spent with it and a different set of experiences and circumstances. Even their special vocalization makes their language memorable. Specialists obviously must speak with some general, popular language terms, but their specialties as doctors, pilots, or electronic engineers make new language inevitable. Creators, with their inventive styles, will likely use creative language, and outsiders such as libertarians, Amish folk, sports heroes, and other fascinating people who don't conform make fine language bearers.

Television, film, and other modes in which words and pictures are combined offer your students many occasions to encounter new language. This is especially true when the material is less narrative and more analytical. *Nova, 60 Minutes, Larry King Live, Wheel of Fortune,* and many other shows have goldmines of new words in them. But film adaptations of books also work well, as do the animated zany Dr. Seuss stories, especially when they are faithful to the author's language.

Morphology.   This is a more abstract process, but you can move your students to a consciousness of some of the core features of the language around them and they will then be more sensitive to it, understand it, and adopt it. It is true that many students do not do as well with parts as with wholes, but if this approach were productive with no more than 25% of your students, it would still be worthwhile. The idea is to work with two primary techniques and two basic elements to expand students' vocabulary. The two basic elements are roots and stems. If you give your students a sense of words' antecedents in classical language, they are given a key that unlocks many verbal treasure chests, for instance, the root words *pose, geo, scribe,* and *bio* are basic language features that refer to the hard reality of the nouns and verbs *lead, earth, write,* and *life.* If your students can transpose what they can guess into clear and useful knowledge, they take command of a sizeable list of words. It won't be sheer memory work. With this logical root knowledge, as well as knowledge of stems, they can begin a growing list of words. The stems are not central, as are the roots, but they are the inflections or redirections on words, which, along with roots, create the semantic load of the word at hand. Prefixes and suffixes, the two stem types, are almost never interchangeable. Understanding the word *interchangeable* itself is a perfect example of morphological knowledge, with its double stem on either side of the root *change.*

Two primary techniques that are useful parts of this analytical process are analogies and context clues. Students unconsciously use these two techniques from birth to soak up language, but they can be made explicit, like the use of morphology, to further activate this process. Students can be taught to use analogies and parallels to see what words likely mean. These can cut across cultures or can reside in the same language. By the same token, students can look at the context to predict what a word may mean. Such prediction works increasingly well when students see the same words in different contexts, because the contexts let them rule out some guesses and bolster others. These techniques and their features of analysis are bits of prior knowledge that your students possess and that you can bring to consciousness to help them develop their vocabularies more effectively.

Immersion.   This is a simple technique of being dunked into a new culture so that language is acquired and mastered as a means of survival, of getting through the day. It is like the acquisition strategy, but with an added dose of consciousness and even mastery to ensure that students come in contact with words.

Word Dots. This may be an approach that some of your students have already developed on their own, but most students need to be prompted to do this. You merely ask your students to keep a pocket dictionary with them at all times so that they can place a dot in front of every new word that they hear or see, whether it is on TV or in a book. You can ask small groups to take a few minutes each week to compare notes from their dictionaries or ask the whole class for spectacular words that they've dotted during the past 7 days. You can ask them to make a bimonthly checkup whereby they make a count of dots over a specified 10 pages to see which student or group has the most collected.

Class Webster. This is a delegated approach to word collection in which you appoint or students elect a word-hawk from the class who is to keep a list of all of the new words that pop up, in class or out of

FIGURE 10–9
Semantic awareness

1. Etymology: finding the origins of words and phrases (*dope, stole my thunder, kitty-corner,* and *becoming*)
2. Hobble de Hoy: creating multiple fanciful or realistic definitions of words that have dropped out of the language since the 1933 edition of the OED (*yamph, gumple-foisted, tic-polonga*)
3. Doublespeak: listing examples of euphemistic pleasantries and obfuscating bureaucratic language and discussing their intent as insidious or salutary (*passed on, sorties, misspoke*)
4. Jargon: exploring the language of special groups and its necessity or pretension (*throughout, spin doctor, burnout*)
5. Limpids: investigating bland basal verbs and their loss of power, and offering helpful replacements (*do, have, eat, run*)
6. Place names: explaining the unusual names of towns, rivers, and other geographic entities (*Paris, Texas; Buffalo, New York; Mt. Rushmore*)
7. Superchargers: examining hyperbolic journalistic language to replace it with neutral and opposing language (*rabble, crowd, throng*)
8. Synontinuums: creating lists of almost-equivalent words that students put on their own continuums (*happy-glad-joyous-ecstatic-peaceful-content*)
9. Faces-Hands-Feet: acting out words with one of these three parts of the body for classmates to guess (*bellicose, anxiety, jealous*)
10. Slanguage: noting language that has passed from unacceptable slang to public parlance (*bounds, snooze, narc*)
11. Amphibonyms: locating words that are spelled the same but that shift from verbs to nouns when the stress moves forward or the vowel lengthens (*record, permit, bow, lives*)
12. Technese: noticing language that has invaded our daily lives by way of the high-tech world (*interface, leverage, fax, deplane*)

it. This is a communal approach in that it is a collective list, one that all students contribute to and one that is the same for all students. The advantage is that all or parts of the list can be used by students as they write group stories or wacky Lazlo letters to unsuspecting public dignitaries (Novella, 1977, 1992), or make some other interesting use of the word collection. The disadvantage is that it is not a list made by individual students. A compromise that works is to let groups of five or six appoint their own word-hawk to collect a slightly different set of words.

Semantics.   The semantic strategy is a potpourri of ideas tied together by the basic notion that words represent meaning beyond themselves and that meaning is, after all, what is most attractive about words. With this in mind, we present in Figure 10–9 a sample of semantic descriptors that generate and create consciousness about words. (See Chapter 2 for more discussion of this idea.)

We believe that students who become engaged in looking at language in these challenging and interesting ways will, with your help, noticeably increase their vocabulary and, more importantly, their interest in gleaning and using new language in their everyday discourse. We believe that each of the five strategies makes sense; but what makes the most sense is the use of the entire set of strategies. Eclecticism is not a fault when the strategies are not mutually exclusive or contradictory, but reinforcing.

SPELLING POWER

You probably remember having weekly spelling tests in elementary school. You may feel that spelling lessons are the stuff of elementary schooling, but researchers suggest that they are also appropriate for high school. Beers and Henderson (1977) observe that children have invariant patterns of spelling development, which over many years form knowledge about orthography. Reed (1986) concurs with the idea of growth stages and shows that most young spellers make mistakes in similar patterns. Hodges (1982), aware of the intellectual dimensions of spelling, argues that learning to spell is a lengthy developmental process that begins in childhood and continues into adulthood. It is clearly more than mere rote learning. In fact, the complexity of the rules makes it a task better undertaken in later grades by students with more mature intellectual capacities. Hodges illustrates the complexity of the rules and the multiplicity of their exceptions by referring to a computer program that was built on the basic phonem-graphem correspondences but still had only a 50% accuracy rate in spelling a list of 17,000 words.

Some secondary teachers have felt, too, that the strengths of the process approach to writing have carried with them in some cases not merely the appropriate postponement, but the unhealthy neglect of spelling and other conventional features in writing instruction. Some of this neglectful attitude is reflected in an educator's quip that "an idiot can tell a genius that he has made a spelling mistake." But it is also true that students' serious efforts and deep thoughts can be overlooked when spelling errors mar their papers. Graves (1983a) speaks of broader consequences when he says that students who have spelling problems "feel information poor." Thus, teachers need to offer help to remove that self-doubt in their writing.

The use of 20-word spelling lists is not the best way to develop effective instruction in spelling in the elementary or secondary grades. We suggest three basic strategies for teaching spelling, which take account of your students' mental maturity and their social development. Each of the three strategies is increasingly more abstract and context free. One may work with some students and another may work with other students. A balance of the three will probably produce the best results.

Acquisition.   Those teachers who approach spelling through the acquisition path are aware of the spelling stages discovered by Reed (1986) and others and are conscious of the fact that they need to pitch their instruction to run parallel with the natural learning progression. Chomsky (1969), as a developmentalist, talks of children's inventive spelling and delineates some of the shifts that Hodges notes in their spelling maturity. Graves (1983a) notes five stages that teachers need to recognize as students mature. This recognition is important, for without prior knowledge, teachers do not understand the growth process of their students; they merely see random error, which they ascribe to failure of will or intellect. But beyond recognition, you will need to think of ways to prompt secondary students to move along those developmental paths so as to present themselves most forcefully to their public, their readers. The simple answer, of course, is that you encourage your students to read. Most students who read voraciously are able spellers. Reading here is broadly defined. Stories are good, but *The Book of Lists, Spin* or *Redbook* magazine, or the backside of a Cheerios box may be just as effective. The more your students see words in print, the more likely they are to begin to assimilate the correct spellings of those words.

Hodges (1982) suggests four kinds of activities that will help secondary students become more proficient spellers as they process words in context more self-consciously.

- *Exploring Word Forms and Letter Constraints.* Helping students focus on common letter patterns as when they compete to see who can use the top row on the typewriter to form the most words
- *Seeing Relationships Between and Among Words.* Looking for relationships between and among the way words are formed and searching for endless lists of words derived from roots such as *scribe* and *pose*
- *Discovering How New Words Enter the Language.* Helping students see how words enter our language by grammatical and meaning changes, structural modification, new ideas, and borrowings
- *Examining Dictionaries, Proofreading, and Meaning.* Raising consciousness through a focus on dictionaries, proofreading, and meaning

Mastery.   The second basic strategy for spelling power is in some sense the opposite of the developmental or assimilation approach of acquisition. It works to gain mastery of carefully selected sets of words over an extended period of time. The methods of mastery take only slightly different paths:

- *Make Word.* Students in groups of three are given a set of three to six letters (the same set for each group) and to try to make a list of words from them.
- *Mangled Monsters.* Students master lists of 50 or 100 spelling monsters—words that are difficult for most secondary students.
- *Sense Loading.* Students use as many senses as possible to process new words into a mental file.

Rules.   The third basic strategy for spelling instruction is rule centered. It is related to Hodges's sense of patterns, but it is clearly learned rather than acquired. It differs, too, from mastery, which is whole-word centered, because the rule approach breaks down the formation of words into a small set of highly complex rules or a large set of fairly simple ones.

The use of such complex systems makes no sense in the early grades, so this strategy is most effective as students move into the later secondary grades, where formal systems are a bit easier for them. At that age your students can learn a small set of complex rules that cover almost all cases:

> final *e*
> variations on *ie*
> suffixes (*ly, able, ing*)
> plurals
> possessives

Students can learn the three basic rules relating to final *e* without much trouble, and the *ie* rules are not overly difficult but for the exceptions. Your students could stop with that accomplishment and have gained much ground; that is not a minor step. The rules for plurals are difficult, but because plurals are often the troublemakers in students' spelling problems, learning them is worth the effort. The same can be said for the possessives, so you will need to match your students' wills with the gains they are likely to derive.

McAlexander, Dobie, and Gregg (1992) in *Beyond the "SP" Label* demonstrate a number of ways to help struggling spellers. They shift the focus from sheer memorization of rules to use of a range of cues to learn and remember correct forms. They explain how to analyze student writing for error patterns that are the result of auditory, visual, and other miscues. They provide a list of guidelines for diagnosis and a simplified list of 24 spelling rules that will help correct student miscues. As an aid to removing those miscues, they offer a set of activities to strengthen visual and auditory skills.

MEDIATED INSTRUCTION

Fearn and Farnan's *Writing Effectively* (1990) addresses the fundamentals of writing. Although they acknowledge that a balanced writing program is composed of several aspects, they limit their attention to the basic conventions of writing but make it clear that correctness is only one of three parts. They place all instruction inside the context of whole pieces of writing, "but the unit is always a sentence" (p. 6). This context gives them great control of what they want students to master. Noguchi and other grammarians do not shy away from a decontextualized method of teaching a topic or a feature that they believe is crucial to writing success but would be taught inefficiently in the much larger and uncontrolled context of students' writing. Fearn and Farnan believe that teachers must develop a systematic approach to the host of major writing problems suffered by a majority of students; they fear that incidental or spontaneous teaching directed to the problems that happen to appear in students' writing will not solve the problem. They opt for a kind of instruction that they believe will achieve maximum effectiveness in minimal time. The use of minilessons in Atwell's Writing Workshop works along these lines, even though her topics arise out of her students' writing.

MIDDLE GROUND

Maximum efficiency is not the top priority for mediated instruction, but it is a pedagogy by which the teacher controls the structure rather than the content of learning. Moreover, the sequence of the structure is planned out by the teacher. Mediated instruction's most respected proponent is George Hillocks, who, with his able graduate students, has been offering exacting teaching strategies for a number of decades. If you want to know about prewriting, descriptive writing, or a number of other features of writing, you need only look to their studies. Hillocks is so capable that he is often one of four or five researchers cited in national publications focused on writing (NAEP, 1988). His work can be seen as antagonistic to strict constructivists because he is unwilling to let instruction arise spontaneously. For this and other reasons, he often takes swipes at what he senses to be the vagaries of process writing, and because of his talent and track record, he often goes against the grain of prevailing trends in writing.

Hillock's *Research on Written Composition* (1986) has been a landmark in the field, but he has recently updated his research, broadened his pedagogy, and raised further questions about process writing. He seems to have positioned his work (as we do) between two unacceptable extremes: the traditional presentational teacher who explains everything in a lecture or relies on workbook drills and the strict constructivists who rely on the hope that students will discover everything for themselves. He believes that traditionalists will fail because "the abstract rules and formulas of such teaching exclude the self" (p. 23), yet he is not willing to abandon some form of direct instruction. He uses a simple rite-of-passage incident as an analogy to the failures of these extremes and his own success:

> Consider learning how to use the clutch on a standard transmission. My dad's explanation, by itself, would have done little good. His explanation, combined with my trying (and stalling the car fairly frequently) and his coaching, finally did the trick by the end of our second session. On the other hand, had he chosen simply to demonstrate, I would have been in trouble. It would have taken a long time to perceive exactly what the relationships of the pedals had to be. (p. 122)

Explanation and demonstration are insufficient; only learning by doing together with careful coaching will get the job done. Hillocks says that his scrupulous planning and exacting arrangements for student interaction brings about the desired results. He hopes (as do we) that his scaffolding is working students through Vygotsky's zone of proximal development. He calls his pedagogy "environmental instruction" because its successes are due to the arrangements he crafts. He acknowledges that his book is an attempt at "integrating these diverse theories" (p. 39) and he believes that his theory for teaching composition will "draw upon knowledge from a variety of sources" (p. 41) and can overcome the paradigm split between the positivists and the constructivists. He speaks of bridging apparent polarities. He offers an example from his graduate education: One of his English professors, after many hours of lecture on *Paradise Lost,* during which he told students what they "*should* make of Milton's work," asked them what they "*did* make of it" (p. 54). Hillocks says of his professor,

> Diekhiff changed the learning environment radically. He refused the despot's throne and took instead the role of learned and emphatic counselor. He allowed our ideas, no matter how poorly conceived, to become a legitimate part of the conversation about *Paradise Lost.* In doing that, he allowed us an important degree of control over classroom events as our ideas became the focus of discussion. At the same time, this counselor retained control. We were still dealing with the themes and structures of Milton's work. (p. 56)

Hillocks's next-to-last sentence's final word, *control,* and its referent *dealing with the themes and structures,* is what places his approach in special territory.

HILLOCKS'S LESSON

Hillocks offers a sample lesson that he developed to promote the ability "to make interpretations that required support and explanation" (p. 202). He found 100-year-old ads in the *Chicago Tribune* and a Sears Roebuck catalog that promoted the cure for a wide range of health problems. His intent was to promote "inquiry and argument" (p. 202). Hillocks and his graduate students meticulously planned how groups would be composed and the direction for their activity but Hillocks adds that a significant part of this kind of teaching is "that the teacher has reconsidered certain variables and decided to change the plan" (p. 202). He lists four important principles of sequencing in his plan that are essential for an activity to work effectively (pp. 180–82):

> *Fun.* Enjoying work at the early stages is necessary as a way to establish interest
> *Building.* Using earlier simple knowledge to create more complex understanding later
> *Integration.* Pulling standard activities together to engage and complete gateway activities
> *Independence.* Learning to use appropriate and fruitful strategies at the students' discretion

The following sequence for personal narrative, which Hillocks and his team used in a Chicago school for 22 days, illuminates these principles:

1. *Initial writing sample.* Students write about an experience that is important to them.
2. *Examples of personal narrative.* Students talk about examples by professionals and other students.
3. *Idea sheets.* Students write a few sentences about their own experiences.
4. *Introduction to using specific detail.* Students describe shells in teacher-led session.
5. *Details about people and places.* Teacher-led talk about an interesting drawing or photograph of a person in action or in a mood.
6. *Describing sounds.* Teacher-led talk about recording or various sounds.
7. *Writing about bodily sensations.* Students write briefly about what they feel.
8. *Writing about the "dumpster scenario."* Students write what they see, hear, and feel as the ominous man approaches.
9. *Pantomime of characters in emotional states.* Students write details for an audience who did not see the person.
10. *Invention of dialogue.* Students talk about two of three examples of dialogue from professional and student pieces.
11. *Individual work on dialogue from idea sheet scenario.* Students read aloud to groups for feedback and revision.
12. *Punctuation of dialogue.* Teacher demonstrates simplest form on overhead: speaker, verb of saying, quotation.
13. *Workshop.* Students select an incident to develop from their idea sheets, to work on drafting, and to revise.
14. *Class publication.* Students choose which pieces to include.
15. *Final writing sample.* Students compare first and final writing. (pp. 178–179)

Much more can be learned from Hillocks's complex and provocative strategy. It truly breaks new ground and avoids the difficulties of the insufficient options of those on either side of his centrist position.

ANOTHER RIGOROUS WAY

Collins and Collins (1996) take the same centrist position as they describe "strategic instruction for struggling writers." They offer four clear steps for such writers that help them gain strength and independence:

- Identifying a strategy
- Introducing and modeling it
- Helping students use it
- Repeating practice to achieve independence

Collins and Collins explain their position clearly: "The strategic writing approach asks teachers to add instruction in procedural knowledge to their work with writers, especially procedural knowledge in the form of self-regulatory strategies, ways of thinking about writing which help students control the writing process by setting goals and monitoring progress toward achieving them" (p. 55). They use goal setting, double-entry note taking, read-think-summarize-interpret revising strategies, and heavy-line marking of students' writing for analysis (p. 56). They help students understand the sense of sentences by carefully looking at ways of connecting referents and strengthening coherence. Other educators are turning to this kind of intensive work with students in order to develop a rigor and power in their writing that is sometimes missed in other approaches.

NEW RESEARCH

If you consider the proper role of the research paper in the English classroom, you may pause to ask the prior question: Should it have any place at all? It requires careful research, in fact, to locate articles in the *English Journal* advocating traditional research papers. Many secondary English programs either drop the requirement or turn all but the mechanics over to other subject areas. Even its marginal place in the English curriculum is denied by Taylor (1965) and others, who argue that secondary "students are not equipped to carry on meaningful literary research" and that "reasonably correct and creative writing—the goal of instruction in composition—cannot be developed by teaching students to regurgitate the thoughts of others" (p. 126). Even more critically, Stevenson (1972) sees these long papers as "a rite of passage" that is in fact "an exercise in deception" because of the woeful lack of emphasis on primary materials (p. 1030).

In spite of this ample qualification of the research paper, its credentials as an instrument of instruction are defensible if its essential shape rather than its superficial form is kept in view. Its role in encouraging critical thinking and the close examination of fact is compatible with the instructional design of any English classroom. Schroeder (1966) offers a slightly different focus in defining the two components of the research paper as "library research techniques and intellectual investigation of a subject" (p. 898). He goes on to break down the development of the necessary skills into a 4-year continuum: 9th-grade library skills, 10th-grade paraphrasing and documentation, 11th-grade controlled research, and 12th-grade topic restriction and free research. Others have suggested an intensive 6-week period of instruction on the conventional research paper to address such matters as limiting the topic, taking an argumentative stance, and learning the art of documentation. Some have suggested more unconventional research strategies such as audiocassettes and mixed-media presentations as possible alternatives to the traditional format. These appear to be manipulations of the surface or the form rather than suggestions of research papers that differ at a more essential level. We suggest the following six models for the research paper that we believe differ in kind and might be appropriate for secondary English students.

CONTROLLED SOURCES RESEARCH

This approach has been one of the most popular in English classrooms, for it allows the teacher to thoroughly survey the source material and ensures that all students come in contact with a wide range of usable materials. This approach makes use of such texts as the Norton Critical Edition of *Moby Dick*, which contains raw historical material (letters, analogues, sources, reviews, and criticism), and more narrow casebooks such as the Merrill text of "A Rose for Emily" and Macmillan's *Huck Finn and His Critics*, which contain critical essays without the other historical paraphernalia. Because these texts can be expensive, many teachers have turned to teacher-made casebooks as an alternative within this general format. No matter which of these you employ, your students will encounter the disadvantage of failing to get involved in original research. On the other hand, they will learn how to extract, evaluate, and synthesize materials, which may be more essential research components for secondary students to engage in initially.

TEXTUAL ANALYSIS

This approach offers students the opportunity to locate and carefully examine a definable body of writing so as to extract differentiations, comparisons, or progressions within that corpus of material. Such dissections can be performed on both literary material (for instance, a short story collection such as Malamud's *The Magic Barrel,* selected poetry of the Harlem Renaissance, or the fiction of *Redbook* magazine) and nonliterary material (for instance, Franklin Roosevelt's inaugural addresses, four standard American dictionaries, George Will's editorials, or Elton John's lyrics). The emphasis is on primary materials and students' ability to assess them. This analytical approach allows students' interests to be expressed in the research they select and yet makes it possible for students in all but the most isolated locales to engage in the *search* part of research.

HISTORICAL SYNTHESIS

This approach demands an even more complete range of source materials, but it allows students to uncover both primary and secondary sources as a means of arriving at an informed answer to a given question. Students might, for example, be asked to investigate the details (who, when, where, how, and why) of an isolatable event in history, such as the death of Hitler. They might be asked as well to make use of varying kinds of sources and to become involved in evaluating the reliability of those sources. Even when they work with a limited supply of sources, students have the chance to be confronted by the researcher's most essential tasks: locating, evaluating, and synthesizing material.

CONTEMPORARY ISSUES RESEARCH

This kind of research offers students even more engaging subject matter to investigate, but it also broadens the scope of the research, thus decreasing teacher awareness of the material under consideration and placing greater demands on students in locating source material. Students involved in research of this kind might be found probing such local problems as zoning, child abuse, or allocation of funds by the school board. They use interviews, examination of records, questionnaires, and other research tools to gather their data. Other teachers might prefer more general research problems such as no-fault insurance, gun laws, or gender discrimination in the workplace. Students are involved in consulting governmental reports, current periodicals, and recently published books, as well as other source materials. Both kinds of research consume much time and energy, but the payoff in enthusiasm and understanding of the research process is sizeable.

SCHOLARLY RESEARCH

This approach offers an alternative for more advanced students. It is the most traditional and earns the most prestige in some settings because it seems to be the most pure, original kind of quest. Its free, uncontrolled search for relationships, connections, analogues, and influences can be directed toward both nonliterary and literary topics. Moreover, because this kind of research activity demands a more comprehensive library and a greater measure of sophistication than can be generally expected, some teachers save students' time and energy by offering them lists of possible productive investigations. This short-circuits some of the originality but also greatly reduces anxiety and frustration. A topic such as the influence of Eugene Zamaitin's *We* on George Orwell's *1984* offers solid potential and at the same time much room for student initiative.

FABULOUS ANALYSIS

Romano's *Writing with Passion: Life Stories, Multiple Genres* (1995) created this category if it did not already exist. His much-acclaimed multigenre research paper is a kind of search-and-analysis process that ignites secondary students when no other work in this area will: "Its amalgam of poetry, prose, drama and nonfiction capitalizes on the cognitive benefits of each genre, and, most importantly, recognizes that there are many ways to see the world" (Bencich, 1996, p. 92). Romano says that his method is ever-changing—evolving through constant negotiation with his students: "The multi-genre research paper was born out of my own literacy pursuits, the dynamic connection between my students' needs and development and my own wonder and delight with literature and writing" (p. 128). His method is described painstakingly in *Writing with Passion,* but it is basically a class production in which a fictive character's artifacts from a wide range of genres (thus the name) are brought together to flesh out the details of that life. A favorite gift from a dying grandfather, a program from a rock concert, notes from a biology class with telling romantic doodles, a fragment from a speech of a radical politician, a letter from an angry brother, three well-worn children's books, and divorce papers from his first marriage are assembled, annotated, and analyzed by individuals or small groups to bring together a kind of analytical biography. The energy generated from both imaginative and analytical thinking and writing makes this a powerful winner.

As a student-teacher, Karen Haymes developed an extended writing-and-research project for five small groups of six or seven students. Each group developed the life story of a fictive character who grew up in their city years earlier. The biographical research included materials from five major periods of the character's life: childhood innocence, adolescent struggles, early adult adjustments, mid-life achievements, and aging reflection. Like Romano's students, Haymes's were asked to build the story around artifacts from their character's life. The finalé was not so much a paper, though there was one, but a kind of dramatic production that centered on a table that featured all of the critical artifacts with carefully composed legends that explained each artifact and its place in the character's life.

Brunwin's work with class-developed historical research is similar to Romano's process, but it uses real historical events and artifacts to produce a historical novel. His students follow the trail of an incident that occurred nearly 100 years ago. He shows his students how to seek details from their city's or region's past, attack in small groups the stubborn historical record, and as an entire class develop not a research paper but a historical novel. Lively and credible stories of gold mining, extortion, and illegal ventures by offshore island pirates have come of such class projects, and the research and analysis that the project demands are every bit as solid as those provided by less exciting tasks.

Cameron (1994) suggests a number of effective ways to use superheroes from television and comics to promote writing. One that could be adapted for imaginative but careful research involves concepts about the hero drawn from Joseph Campbell's *The Power of Myth* (1988). Students begin by listing all of the superheroes that they follow and then work at Cameron's list of Campbell's powerful attributes of mythic heroes:

1. A hero gives his or her life to something bigger than oneself, to some higher end.
2. A hero performs a courageous act either physical or spiritual.
3. A hero is usually someone from whom something has been taken or who feels there's something lacking in the normal experience available or permitted to members of his society.
4. A hero embarks on a series of adventures to recover what is lost or to discover some life-giving information.
5. The hero usually moves out of the known, conventional safety of his own life to undertake the journey.
6. The hero undergoes trials and tests to see if he has the courage, the knowledge and the capacity to survive.
7. A hero has to achieve something.
8. A hero's journey usually consists of a departure, a fulfillment, and a return. (p. 92)

Using this authoritative list of heroic qualities, students select a set of six superheroes and analyze them. After researching each of the six superheroes' words, thoughts, deeds, and the wonders attributed to them, students can develop a careful analysis using all of the rigorous paraphernalia of a bonafide research paper.

All of these approaches to the research paper may prove to be both suitable and effective preparation for your students, but none of them alleviates the dreaded burden of writing the paper itself. As you consider this reality, you may decide to use an alternative. Ask your students to create a chart that will be used to develop a class discussion that will capture the basic ingredients of locating data and synthesizing it to develop a thesis. The basic categories of information (who, when, where, how, and why) may be used as column headings; list below these the source materials that provide information in each category. The discussion can start with students presenting their findings to small groups and creating a synthesis. The findings of each group can be compared, with the teacher urging students to look carefully at each source and scrutinize the inferences developed by each of the groups. With a few hours' work out of class and an intensive hour's work together, a group of students may discover more about the nature of research than many others do in days of writing and hours of teacher time evaluating long papers. This is an alternative worth considering.

ELEMENTAL VARIATION

Winterowd argues, and the research supports him, that we can help students expand their consciousness of what he calls the full rhetorical context. Following is a distillation of the six elements that he identifies as being fundamental to rhetoric.

WHO *Persona*	WHAT *Topic*	WHERE *Medium*	WHY *Purpose*	HOW *Tone*	WHOM *Audience*
Congressman	Frogs	Bumper Sticker	Election	Sarcasm	Senior Citizens
Accident Victim	Nepotism	Radio Spot	Conversion	Precision	Ministerial Association
Murderer's Mother	Creationism	Public Letter	Excuse	Pity	Little League Managers
Inventor	Elevators	Editorial	Congratulations	Elation	Right-to-Lifers
No. 1 Draftee	Popcorn	Poem	Praise	Pride	Chamber of Commerce
Retiring Miner	Ambition	Mediation	Compromise	Chastisement	Beloved Uncle

FIGURE 10–10 Milner's rhetorical topology

Element	*Interrogative*	*Definition*
Persona	Who?	The voice that allows the reader to hear an individual human being speak from the page.
Topic	What?	The subject of the piece.
Medium	Where?	The form through which the writing is achieved.
Purpose	Why?	The author's intention in writing.
Tone	How?	The flavor of the piece.
Audience	Whom?	Those who will read or listen to the piece. (pp. 66–69)

Each of the elements is important to writing, and their complex union brings the writer to new levels of writing maturity. We use a game, Rhetorical Topology, Figure 10–10, so that students can experience the effect of Winterowd's powerful scheme without having to remember the intricacies of his textbook definitions. Notice also that the medium, or form, of the composition departs from the usual rhetorical forms of school writing.

TOPOLOGY PROCEDURES

Students in a typical classroom are divided into groups of six. Each member of the group is assigned an element and a die is rolled to select one of the six choices within each element. For instance, if the first student (WHO) rolls a 4, the persona is an inventor; if the second (WHAT) rolls a 5, the topic is popcorn; and so on until all group members have explicit rhetorical definitions. Individual group members write in the full rhetorical context of their group within a set amount of time, read their papers within the small group to each other, respond, and even select one or two to read to the whole class.

If the writing assignment seems too difficult with all six elements, begin with three or four of them. The choices in the matrix can easily be tailored to the ability level of the students you teach. Abstract and concrete entities can both be used, as they are here. A different matrix also can be composed by students. A matrix of literary characters, settings, titles, authors, and periods generates interest, imagination, and energy. The topology encourages the free and expansive play of the mind with the literature. For instance, personas for a writing assignment after a unit study of modern American drama might include Amanda Wingfield, Laura Wingfield, Willy Loman, Stanley Kowalski, Emily Gibbs, and the Stage Manager. The possibilities for audience after a unit on Greek and Roman myths and legends might be Zeus, Aphrodite, Hercules, Theseus, the Medusa, and Atalanta. Students become collaborators in the creative enterprise of literature as they extend these characters imaginatively. Becky Brown used Rhetorical Topology, but she substituted fixed, though provocative, writing configurations. One of her best evoked the response shown in Figure 10–11. Common to these suggestions is our sense that the use of Rhetorical Topology reinforces the complexity of writing and inspires both creative expansion of texts and creative iteration of other concepts under study.

EVALUATION

Mastery of the topology can be evaluated fairly straightforwardly. Portfolios of writing activities over a quarter or a semester should be kept to measure growth in consciousness of the five elements other than topic. Students can look at their own work or that of other students and measure the effectiveness of a piece of writing by seeing how faithfully each of the six elements is handled in the piece. A person from an outside group (or the teacher) can look at the paper and try to locate which of the choices under each element was the one selected by the roll of the die. At a more advanced level, the reader could try to name the six pieces of the configuration. If all are located, able writing has begun. In a known configuration, each of the elements might be rated on a 4-point scale (excellent, good, fair, weak) so that scores can range from 16 to 4. Exercise 10–4 gives you an opportunity to evaluate the idea of Rhetorical Topology, and to construct your own.

FIGURE 10–11
Brown's literary topology

Topic	Speaker	Audience	Tone	Purpose	Medium
"Royal Rumble"	Beowulf, Arthur, and others	National TV viewers	Intimidating	To entertain	Pro wrestling match

Announcer: In this corner, the legendary Celtic hero and world champion King Arthur. And in this corner, the challenging hero from the wild wastes of Scandinavia, Beowulf! Gentlemen, the fight is without armor and to the death or at least severe bodily mutilation! Begin!

Arthur: You're nothin! man! The Intercontinental Belt is mine, man; I've got all the Knights of the Round Table on my side, and all you've got is that little punk, Wiglaf.

Beowulf: Yeah, just send in your knights to fight for you the way you always do. You never even got off your butt to find the Holy Grail; you just sent your knights out to do it! It didn't matter when I was king, man! I still went out to fight.

Arthur: Yeah, well if you're such a big hero, how come you never had a woman?

Beowulf: What?! All you even had was Gwynevere, who was sleepin' around anyway! You're dead!

Wiglaf: Come on you punk Catholic king. You ain't nothin' man! I'm right witcha, Beowulf.

Arthur: That's it, man! Lancelot, Palomides, Tristram, get in there and show him what the Round Table boyz can do.

(Beowulf trashes all three of the knights, and he tosses them out of the ring.)

Beowulf: (pointing) All right, man, I want YOU!

Arthur: (He runs in and puts Beowulf in the Cranium Crunch.) Right makes might, you punk Scandinavian!

Wiglaf: I'm right by ya, Beowulf! (Wiglaf takes Arthur down in a figure-four leg lock and breaks Arthur's legs.)

Beowulf: This right makes might, dude! (Beowulf delivers a right cross that crunches Arthur's mandible.)

Announcer: It's over, baby! Arthur has tried to let his knights do the work as usual. But Beowulf comes out on top because whereas Arthur leads by claim to kingship, Beowulf leads by example. Beowulf is the stronger warrior and leader of men! That's it, folks, I'm outta here.

Exercise 10–4   Rhetorical Topology

1. What has been the typical emphasis in English writing assignments that you had in high school and college? (Circle all that apply.)
   a. Topic
   b. Purpose
   c. Persona
   d. Medium
   e. Tone
   f. Audience
2. After reading Winterowd's theory and our application, which elements in the full rhetorical context seem to you important enough to include in making writing assignments?
   a. Topic
   b. Purpose
   c. Persona
   d. Medium
   e. Tone
   f. Audience
3. Which one(s) seem to you not important enough to articulate and assign to your students?
   a. Topic
   b. Purpose
   c. Persona
   d. Medium
   e. Tone
   f. Audience

4. Now fill in the following matrix as a final writing project in a comparative study of two literary works or two literary periods. State your general subject and fill in the 36 blanks.

Rhetorical Topology

	WHO *Persona*	WHAT *Topic*	WHERE *Medium*	WHY *Purpose*	HOW *Tone*	WHOM *Audience*
1.	_____	_____	_____	_____	_____	_____
2.	_____	_____	_____	_____	_____	_____
3.	_____	_____	_____	_____	_____	_____
4.	_____	_____	_____	_____	_____	_____
5.	_____	_____	_____	_____	_____	_____
6.	_____	_____	_____	_____	_____	_____

LIT. WRITE

Writing about literature is the oldest and yet possibly the newest writing strategy in the field. It was the staple of secondary English classrooms until the early 1970s. Literature was what students wrote about then. Applebee (1993) notes that "Historically the relationship between writing instruction and literature has always been a close one" (p. 155). Now, states such as California are turning back to literature as the focal point of an integrated curriculum in which all of the modes of discourse are unified into a seamless cloth of instruction. Applebee's (1993) research shows that 73.8% of writing in public schools is about literature (p. 161) and that 75.2% of English teachers report that writing about literature is their primary approach to composition (p. 167). He praises Kathleen Andrasick for showing us how to use process writing to teach literature (p. 1). Newkirk calls her book *Opening Texts* (1990) "a conservative book" yet an "innovative book" (p. xii) in that it retains the rigor of the "critical tradition" and the reality quotient of the reader-friendly journaling response approach. She shows us how to urge students to turn their initial exploratory responses into elaborated pieces of analysis that have none of the formulaic emptiness of five-paragraph themes. The combination she produces is extremely useful. Andrasick shows us ways to help students "change and/or enlarge the angle of vision" to become a "critical reader," one who is "able to distance self from text" (p. 5) without killing the initial personal contact with it. She shows us how to help students "recognize and *value* their personal connections and initial readings" (p. 6). She creates this recognition through students' writing and talking. After the initial contact and explanation, she nudges students toward imitating, transforming, and acquiring texts so that they become adept at the following tasks:

- Enjoying literature on levels beyond simple comprehension of narrative line
- Exploring literature for questions and insights interesting to them
- Composing meanings from texts
- Knowing how they understand literature and expand the repertoire of ways they compose meanings from texts
- Making connections between and among texts
- Learning to trust their responses and critical assessments

OPENING A TEXT

Andrasick teaches us how to see the different ways in which students read and annotate texts as a prelude to true collaboration, in which the crucial mental event in growth "is abandonment of a position we hold" (p. 22). Her objective, procedure, and evaluation for teaching an understanding of imagery in *The Red Badge of Courage* make her method clear:

Objective	Students should learn to question a repeated image for patterns and emerging meanings.
Procedure	Students will trace a particular image through a novel; they will work in groups to validate and extend their findings. They will analyze and report to the class the

significance of any patterns they notice. They will repeat the process independently, using a new image, in papers they will share with the class.

Evaluate   Students discuss an image not covered by class work in a final unit essay. (p. 24)

Andrasick also shows us how a 7-day unit would unfold using some of the objectives and procedures that she outlines:

Day 1   Yes-I-read-the-book writing and discussion review of the literal level of the work: characters, statements, setting.
Day 2   Discussion of Henry's shattered expectations using written reports by groups and class discussion of round and flat character changes.
Day 3   Discussion of how Jim Conklin and Henry change.
Day 4   Defining naturalism using passages.
Days 5 and 6   Group work in imagery, reports to class and discussion on how imagery works.
Day 7   Wrap-up discussion. (pp. 24–25)

Andrasick shows us how she prompts students to plunge deeply into the first day's topic, Henry's expectations. She begins with a quote from critic R. W. Stallman (1976): "Everything goes awry; nothing turns out as Henry had expected" (p. 201). She asks her students to "identify and define Henry's expectations about war, himself and his behavior and briefly detail how they go awry" (p. 26). She lets them think, search, and write for 20 minutes and then asks them to read their lists, which she uses to forge a discussion. In that exchange, she participates only by asking for clarification and prompting students to make connections; at the same time, she creates a graphic representation of their points to use later.

Andrasick uses two process writing strategies to deepen insights for writing about literature: Dialog Journals, and Process Logs. The Dialog Journal is a double-entry journal in which students first enter jottings, excerpts, and brief summaries of the text on the left page of their journals and on the opposite page respond with their interpretation and feelings about them. The second step is rereading their entries and writing on another page as many questions as they can generate about their responses. They use the other side of the second page to group questions, answer them, and locate areas of central importance for general inquiry. Students use the questions in a general class discussion, then elaborate a central question for their personal investigation and use all of their journal entries to compose their responses.

Andrasick uses Process Logs to help students "identify the analytical strategies they use with particular texts" (p. 59). The Process Log helps students explore a poem by asking them to respond to questions such as the following:

- What did you understand, feel, think after your first reading?
- What questions did you have?
- What words/phrases were confusing?
- What words/phrases seemed to have particular importance?
- As you read the poem a second time, marking it, what insights did you have?
- What areas are still confusing to you?
- What meanings do you feel the poem is expressing? (p. 60)

She emphasizes that she is asking her students to describe *how* they read and understand as well as *what* they read and understand. She ends the section on Process Logs by reminding us that "we are not teaching skills but awareness of the thinking process." The two formats that she urges "show us how we can teach students to use language to distance themselves from their perceptions, feeling and thoughts about a text" (p. 67) and thus produce fresh insights and strong writing.

Even though some teachers, school districts, and states are returning to literature as a focal point of an integrated curriculum, most teaching is not so seamless. Literature can still serve well as a vehicle for writing, which in turn can deepen and clarify insight. Stephen Young, a student-teacher, developed a character exploration chart, Figure 10–12, that he used to push his students toward a more rigorous look at focal scenes in *The Glass Menagerie*. He asked each group to produce one of the selected scenes while the audience absorbed them and then entered careful notes on the chart to capture the connections between the text and the gestures, and between the words and the characters' feelings. Students entered their own responses in the final blocks and then used their "lab reports" to develop pieces of writing that captured their own ambiguous responses to the scenes. Such strategies can help students use the vital quality of stage or page to explore their understanding of and felt responses to them. Literature should never occupy the dominant place in writing it once held, but its usefulness as a vehicle for writing should not be ignored.

FIGURE 10–12
Focal scenes, *The
Glass Menagerie*

	Laura		Amanda		Tom	
	Text	Performance	Text	Performance	Text	Performance
Focal Scene						
	Words	Feelings	Words	Feelings	Words	Feelings
Exterior and Interior						
	Empathy	Scorn	Empathy	Scorn	Empathy	Scorn
Your Feelings						

SENTENCE COMBINING

Sentence combining is a pedagogical strategy that gained popularity in the 1970s as an alternative to the rigid, ineffective categories of traditional grammar. It was the pedagogical outcome of generative, or transformational, grammar, which broke from traditional grammar in the middle of the twentieth century. As mentioned in Chapter 2, the study of English grammar began in the eighteenth century and used Latin grammatical principles as the criteria on which the English language was judged, even though significant aspects of the two languages are dissimilar. The function of the traditional grammarian was to articulate the formal rules governing language and to protect the language from misuse and decay.

Beginning in the nineteenth century, linguists began a more scientific investigation of the language, which resulted in a "structural grammar" that identified parts of speech by function and sentences by their structural characteristics. For instance, Latin is an inflected language that expresses grammatical relationships by a system of word endings. The basic grammatical principal in modern English is the position of the word in a syntactic structure, that is, word order. The most prominent structural study of the language to date is Charles Fries's *The Structure of English* (1954).

At about the time that structural grammar was moving into classroom textbooks, another system for understanding the English language was developing. This system, generative (or transformational) grammar, moved from describing syntactic structures to understanding the deeper structure that produced them. By delineating the mental processes underlying the transformation, which could produce an infinite and varied number of sentences from a few basic structures, these grammarians sought to explain the intricacies of language.

Noam Chomsky's *Syntactic Structures* (1957) gave the most prominent description of the formal structures of the English language as something we acquire or absorb without training: All sentences originate as simple declarations or "kernels," which comprise the "deep structure" of those sentences. The basic kernel is S-V-O: Rain (Subject) pelts (Verb) sidewalks (Object). Various transformations of these kernels, through negatives, appositives, and possessives, for instance, produce more complex "surface structures." The basic task for generative or transformational grammar was to articulate the rules by which the basic kernel sentences can be transformed into all the possible sentences of English. Roberts, for example, in *Patterns of English* (1956), distilled from the English language a set of 20 basic sentences.

English teachers have been faced with an uncomfortable question: Which grammar should we teach, traditional or generative? Many teachers and educators, reluctant to be drawn into a grammarians' war, found much traditional grammar clear and useful, yet discerned possibilities for writing instruction in generative grammar. Linguistic research (Chomsky, 1968) suggested that students at a certain stage of maturity (about fifth grade) have acquired a comprehension template for complex sentences by merely having heard them repeatedly. Syntactic complexity is known at first, but not used, much as vocabulary is understood before it is used in speech or writing. These teachers believed that students might be taught to use a wide repertoire of sentence structures imprinted on their templates to improve the syntactic maturity of their writing. Sentence combining was the classroom application of these new grammatical insights. Although its original popularity has declined, it remains an effective teaching strategy for encouraging syntactic growth. It invites students to *build,* rather than *repair* sentences.

Christensen (1967) experimented with students generating strong sentences from basic sentence structures. Mellon (1969) suggested rules for transforming two or three simple sentences and then combining them into one sentence. Strong (1973) and O'Hare (1975) simplified the process by dropping the rules and merely asking students to combine sets of kernels to form new, complex sentences; this relies on students' deep acquisition of language.

STRONG KERNELS

"Motorcycle Pack," shown here, is a typical set of Strong's (1973) kernels, that individuals or groups can combine by adding coordinating and subordinating structures or by embedding modifiers.

Strong's Kernels: Motorcycle Pack

1. We could hear them coming.
2. They were way off in the distance.
3. They were winding down the road.
4. The road was through the mountains.
5. The road was east of town.

6. The sound made us think of power saws.
7. But the sound was more sustained.
8. The sound was deeper.
9. The sound got louder.

10. The first one broke into view.
11. He was at the edge of town.
12. The edge is where the brush is thick.
13. The brush was full of shadows.

14. The others swarmed behind him.
15. The others rapped their pipes.
16. The others brought the noise.
17. The noise was like a wave.

18. The leader geared down.
19. The gearing down was at the grocery store.
20. The leader set the pace.
21. The pace was swaggering.
22. The pace was through the middle of town.
23. The leader did not glance to the side.
24. The leader did not acknowledge the people.
25. The people watched from the sidewalk.

26. The leader personified seriousness.
27. The leader personified bravado.
28. The seriousness was leather.
29. The bravado was chrome.

30. The others stared at his back.
31. The others tried to imitate him.
32. The others tried their best.

33. He lifted his right hand.
34. The lifting was at the highway.
35. The highway belonged to the state.
36. The highway intersected Main Street.

37. The pack leaned to the right.
38. The pack followed him.
39. The pack accelerated toward the road.
40. The road was open.

41. Exhaust ripped the air.
42. The exhaust was from motorcycles.
43. The exhaust was like an insult.
44. The air healed.
45. The healing took all day.

FIGURE 10–13
Two perspectives

DAVE GRATTON (ASSISTANT PRINCIPAL)

Ronnie Morris is nothing but trouble. I feel sorry for him. He has gotten in with the wrong crowd. He is abusive to the teachers here at our school; he comes to class high, and just last Friday he openly threatened me. He said he'd kill me. I was a bit worried but not too much. I get threatened a lot. You see, the principal and I decided the only disciplinary action left was to expel Ronnie. We have tried many different punishments such as in-school and out-of-school suspension, reports, etc. Nothing works. As the assistant principal, it is my duty to administer these various punishments. A great job, huh? I know the kid doesn't like me but hey, he ain't exactly my favorite person either. So, we kicked him out and good riddance. He was a bad apple. Today is Monday and the day has been fairly calm, I am on bus duty and am getting on to some boys who are horse playing. It is then that I feel a terrible pain shoot through my shoulder and hear a shot simultaneously. I've been shot. I hear laughter, sick laughter, and I know it's Ronnie Morris who has shot me. He made good his threat. I don't move for fear he'll shoot again and then another shot and then I lose consciousness.

MR. TEEDER (PRINCIPAL)

If all days were like yesterday, I would have to retire from principalship. A terrible tragedy occurred that could have easily been prevented by communication and self-control. I have tried my best to be a good principal—to be objective, fair but follow through with my decisions. My assistant principal was shot today. Yes shot! The young man who fired the gun turned it on himself, the gun failed to fire at first, and despite the pleading of his friends, he tried again . . . and this time succeeded in taking his own life.

His mother was in my office, discussing his suspension with me at the time of his death. He was suspended from English for insubordination and then cursing at the teacher and other students in the classroom. We had come to a decision pertaining to the work he would miss. I think he could have graduated on time if he had stuck it out. Why? Why? How could he take his life? He was not a totally bad kid. He had friends and family who loved him, even if they weren't always present in his life. I'm concerned about how this will affect the student body. Some professional counselors will be on campus tomorrow.

FIGURE 10–14
Cameron's
superordinate
intervention

1. What superhero or hero could have helped a character? For instance, could any of the heroes have prevented Malcolm X from becoming involved in petty criminal activities?
2. If you could add a hero or superhero to the story just read, which one would you add? What would you like that hero to accomplish or change in the story?
3. Which hero would a character most admire? Explain. OR Which heroic characteristics would a specific character like Jay Gatsby from *The Great Gatsby* most want?
4. After reading several short stories or a novel, create a HELP WANTED poster advertisement for the kind of person most needed in the story. Cut a picture from a magazine showing a person who represents the heroic qualities you are seeking.
5. Who would specific characters have as their heroes/heroines? Describe the characteristics they would pick and why these are important to them. (p. 93)

FIGURE 10–15
Walker's planners

1. Describe the problem in at least 50 words, including why they feel it is significant;
2. Propose a specific solution to the problem in one to three sentences;
3. List three print and/or human resources that would give useful information for designing and implementing the plan, explaining why each would be helpful;
4. List in complete statements at least five specific steps they would take to implement the plan in the order the tasks should be accomplished; and
5. Write an explanation of at least 100 words to tell how Emerson and/or Thoreau would view their proposed plan, basing their explanation on what they know about Transcendentalism from the readings and citing at least two supporting quotes.

Although she does not work inside an original work as closely as Dixon does, Walker (1997) borrows from authentic assessment to have students become Dependent Authors. She uses authentic assessment's basic axiom that school writing must look like writing in the real world to connect with Thoreau's "Civil Disobedience" and other essays. As town planners or members of citizens' groups, students carefully construct a plan or proposal that puts an author's ideas into action or resists them. Walker's five requirements, presented in Figure 10-15, are exact and demanding, yet they allow students to extend the author's ideas in realistic fashion. As a part of the plan, students engage in Walker's process.

Dixon uses the powerful antiwar poem "Dulce et Decorum Est" by Wilfred Owen to show how an earnest and sensitive student could produce only a faltering essay that is unable to articulate the terror of the gas attack for the individual soldier or the universal sickness of war. Dixon (1984) argues that a narrative that another student wrote about a retreating terror-struck infantryman was poignant and deeply sensitive to both the plight of the individual soldier and the horror of such warfare as it brutalized humanity. When he presented the two writing pieces to a group of Michigan teachers, the narrative was so much more compelling that they began to realize how effective this Dependent Authors strategy could be. Many teachers were convinced of the insight and particular understanding of Owen's poem in the narrative piece. Some concluded that they would try Dependent Authors a good part of the time; others said that they would sometimes allow students a choice of the two forms; and still others said that they would consider using Dependent Authors as a step toward better expository writing. Such conversions suggest that Dixon's idea has merit.

APPRENTICE WRITING

Many professional writers attribute their writing abilities to cutting their composing teeth on the works of the masters; as aspiring writers, they painstakingly copied the masters' work until something of their genius seeped through. Formerly, classic models were basic to instruction in rhetoric. Although textbooks often continue this approach through collecting model essays, it has lost credibility in today's classrooms. For some, however, the rationale remains: Writers learn their craft by striving to meet standards set by reading good models. In *The Anxiety of Influence* (1973), Bloom argues that unconscious apprenticeships are always served in the lives of great writers. Some of that same process can be useful for all writers, not just those who want to make writing their craft. In the realms of style and content, models can give uncertain students training wheels that keep their forward motion from faltering. More importantly, modeling can help students to evolve their own original voices. We present four steps that can be taken in this apprenticeship. Each step is more difficult and takes more effort and independence than the preceding one. The individual imagination must be kept alive at each stage or the process will sink into tedious, stupefying, and even harmful work.

COPYING (DUPLICATING EXACT TEXTS)

When children hear parents read a bedtime story over and over, they seem almost able to read it themselves. They have so absorbed the tale that its rhythms and sounds become embedded in their memories. Researchers tell us that children learn much about reading from this repetition. Secondary students might learn much about writing with just such attention to and reproduction of the words of others. (You will find as you teach the same works over time that certain lines, phrases, and words insinuate themselves into your thoughts and speech.) The following three exercises suggest a close attention to key words, phrases, and sentences and a heightened repetition of them. The purpose is to acquaint students with the power of another's writing and to encourage their identification and ownership of that language. They first reproduce the original and then impose their own interpretation, verbal or visual, on it.

Little Snippets.   Each student selects prized phrases from a favorite writer, copies those snippets onto posterboard, and surrounds the words with related visual images. These collages can be presented to the class visually as students recite the snippets from memory or from carefully rehearsed reading. The emphasis here is on the words. The visual imagery and spoken words together deepen a student's proprietary identification with the author's consciousness and expressiveness.

Listen In.   The teacher divides students into Listen In groups of four or five each. The teacher then finds a well-recorded selection from a professional writer and has students listen to it several times. They listen a final time while reading the written text and highlight four or five of its most memorable lines. These they practice and record for the other students in their Listen In group. The group listens to the individual tapes and talks about what makes the lines have such punch for them. This exercise combines writing with the more fundamental skills of listening and speaking.

Write Out and Draw In.   Students combine art with writing in this exercise. They each choose and transcribe a personally meaningful poem or prose extract. We find that short passages work best. Students then paint, draw, or paste together a picture or collage that rises from their reading of literature. We are asking students to connect to the words of the artist. Not all students feel artistically capable, but as long as care is given to both the transmission of the poet's words to paper and the creation or selection of the accompanying artwork, the power of the process is secure. Figure 10–16 is an example of one such personal connection between the imaginations of two students, Cary Clifford and Benjamin Milner, and lines from Wallace Stevens.

FIGURE 10–16
Copying (duplicating
exact texts)*

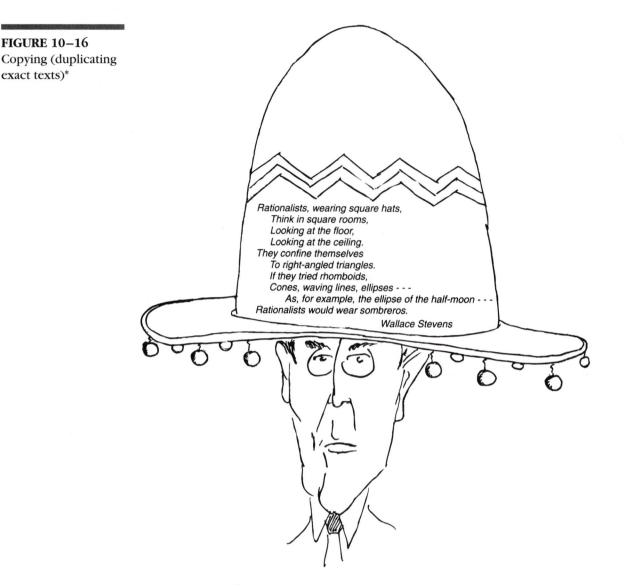

Rationalists, wearing square hats,
  Think in square rooms,
  Looking at the floor,
  Looking at the ceiling.
They confine themselves
  To right-angled triangles.
  If they tried rhomboids,
  Cones, waving lines, ellipses - - -
    As, for example, the ellipse of the half-moon - - -
Rationalists would wear sombreros.

Wallace Stevens

PARAPHRASING (TRANSLATING PASSAGES)

Paraphrasing moves in a new direction. We are trying to help students believe in themselves as writers, as people with something to say to others. We know that we all have something to say; Graves (1983b) convinces us that everybody has a story to tell. Unfortunately, not all of our students believe this. Many of them have little faith in themselves as communicators. Three exercises follow that invite original writing by providing a preformed structure. The teacher furnishes the form to free students to find their own meaning. Our examples are taken from poetry, but other forms can work as well: aphorisms, famous passages from speeches, and even bumper stickers or advertising slogans.

Translation.   Translation prompts students to rewrite poetry in their own words. The process may seem reductive, but students who have little self-confidence often create written prose statements that are penetrating and satisfying to themselves. After each student develops a working paraphrase of a poem, groups of three students read their translations to one another, comparing their prose with the poem's original meaning and with its greater economy of words.

Official Plagiarism.   Such paraphrasing can take place after students have developed a feel for the use of another writer's words. They can select a poem already studied in class and restate or reorder it with their own words. Students give their poems titles and display them under their own names, with the original poet's name and the poem's real title on the back. (To add interest and reward for the paraphrasing authors, class members might read the poems closely and identify the sources of

*Poem from COLLECTED POEMS by Wallace Stevens, Copyright 1923 and renewed 1951 by Wallace Stevens. Reprinted by permission of Alfred A. Knopf, Inc.

FIGURE 10–17
Once template

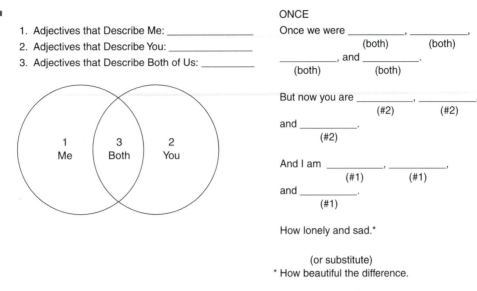

1. Adjectives that Describe Me: _____
2. Adjectives that Describe You: _____
3. Adjectives that Describe Both of Us: _____

ONCE

Once we were _____, _____,
                    (both)   (both)
_____, and _____.
  (both)   (both)

But now you are _____, _____,
                         (#2)   (#2)
and _____.
      (#2)

And I am _____, _____,
                (#1)   (#1)
and _____.
      (#1)

How lonely and sad.*

(or substitute)
* How beautiful the difference.

the new titles.) This appropriation leads students to trust themselves a bit more. They can trust the original author's structure and thereby gain trust in their own words.

Humpty Dumpty.   This activity reverses the writing process and can be fun and instructive. In this activity, the deep structure or paraphrased meaning of four poems is given to students, who are asked to put the poems back into their original configuration or into the best arrangement of words that they can create. When they have recomposed the poems, students compare their word choice with that of the original poets. (They can be awarded points for every original word they recompose.) Or, students can work in collaborative writing groups of four to compose one of the poems using the best work of each participant.

In all of these instances, writing masters have become what John-Steiner (1987) calls "distant teachers" (p. 37). Paraphrase is not done in the old, reductive attempt to pinion literature into a simple declarative statement. Rather, it is used to help students see how the stylist carefully shapes meaning with special arrangements of words and to release students to trust their own voices to carry their own insights.

MODELING (EMPLOYING A TEMPLATE)

Modeling evokes student writing while allowing students to borrow form and pattern from master word crafters. All elementary teachers make use of this in some fashion, but the process can be equally successful for secondary students. Brooks (1973), in her essay, "Mimesis: Grammar and the Echoing Voice," proposes carefully composed exercises that encourage her students to find their own unique styles and to learn specific grammatical points by using what she calls "persona paraphrase." She asks students to give conscious attention to the professional writer's medium and to use that writer's words to discover their own voice and style. She uses established writers to free young writers to the possibilities of writing for their own purposes. In a similar effort, in Chapter 5 we discussed using single poems or fixed poetic forms as templates from which students can develop their own poems.

Building Conceits.   This model develops a piece of writing around one powerful comparison, as the poet Karl Shapiro does in "Manhole Covers." Lines such as "Mayan calendar stones" and "like medals struck by a great Kahn," make us transform the everyday object into a larger-than-life artifact from an exotic world. Students can use this model to build poems of their own from a conceit. Rather than just telling them to come up with a comparison, you can give them a method for coining such metaphoric constructions. We ask students to think of a mundane object such as a hammer or a slide, then list attributes such as shape, size, use, color, and material; from that list, they try to shape an extended conceit.

Once Template.   This simple template uses two interlocking Venn-like circles to list the qualities of the writer and a close friend (Figure 10–17). The first circle serves as a place to list distinct qualities of the writer; the second circle contains the qualities of the friend. In the space where the two intersect, the shared qualities are listed, though there may not be as many as there are differentiating qualities. The template provides slots where the listed qualities, both shared ones and dissimilar ones, can be used so that the polarities work off one another. Then the writer is offered a large choice: Does the mix of unshared and shared qualities ensure a deepened relationship or does it cause the pair to be

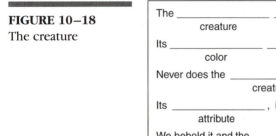

FIGURE 10–18
The creature

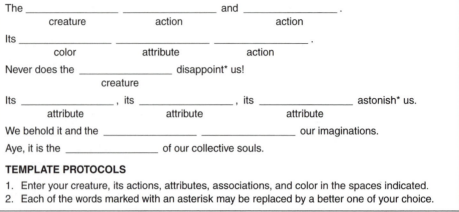

split asunder? The writer decides and can use the template to capture a fond relationship or a forlorn situation. The student can use two friends to provide some distance on the relationship; this is a matter of how disclosive and vulnerable the writer wants to be.

The Creature.   This template is not so personal; it encourages students to use their eyes to write well. The enabling structure that releases this poetic writing is a nature study. Students visit a zoo or an aquarium or merely set out to watch a creature in nature closely: a dimpled spider, a buzzing fly, a beetle trapped in a bathtub, a harmless snake in the grass, or a twitching wren. Students watch this creature carefully and record as would a naturalist its attributes, actions, colors, habits, and dwelling. Then they use the template, Figure 10–18, to slot in the features they like best and add in the qualities and metaphysical appellations made possible by their choices for the poem. Although the template is fairly tight and may seem to constrain the autonomy and creativity of writers, most students experience a good feeling when their animal springs to life and takes on a significance that did not previously seem inherent in the creature.

Avoid.   This prose template is very simple yet perverse in its structuring strictures. It is a challenging, problem-solving kind of assignment that appeals to students who never fail to take on brain teasers. The challenge is to construct a story with absolutely no letter *e* in it. *A Void* by George Perac did just that. Here are a few sentences from his book: "Incurably insomniac, Anton Vowl turns on a light. According to his watch, it's only 12:20. With a loud and languorous sigh, Vowl sits up, picks up his whodunit and idly scans a paragraph or two . . ." Ask your students to take on Perac's challenge. If students believe they are writing to avoid the *e* landmine, the problem of length becomes instead a teacher limitation to overcome. The longer and more clever the avoidance of the letter *e,* the more satisfied the writer. Because *e* is the most-used letter in the English language, its avoidance is most difficult; easier letters can be chosen for the class, or each student can choose his or her own avoided letter—it could be, for example, the initial letter of his or her last name.

IMITATING (MIMICKING THE MASTERS)

This final stage of stylizing cuts the student free of copying, paraphrasing, and using models. Students remain on a leash of sorts, but a long one. We ask them to make their own decisions in mimicking a master. They have to have both a sensitive consciousness of another's style and the ability to play with an imitation. The following three exercises demonstrate this method.

Public Parody.   In this initial activity, students write and tape-record the verbal style of a well-known public figure. These recordings are played, and students are asked to note their impressions of the voice and syntax, the vocabulary and the rhythm. Students then determine which aspect is nearer the defining center of that person's public utterances.

Literary Caricatures.   From this pure parody, students may move to caricaturing literary figures whom they have studied and whose styles are distinctive, such as Edgar Allan Poe, Emily Dickinson, Ernest Hemingway, Langston Hughes, or William Faulkner. These written pieces might be exaggerated so as to overuse characteristic styles. They are half-fun and half-serious. Other students can try to guess each caricature. From the exaggeration of these extreme characterizations, students can turn to more serious imitations of childhood favorites such as William Steig, Dr. Seuss, and Maurice Sendak. These writers are supposedly simpler and, more importantly, are more removed from students' present reading menu. To capture Sendak in an unpublished chapter of *Where The Wild Things Are* takes great effort, but teaches much about that writer's craft.

Emulate Masters.   Ask students to read such writers as C. S. Lewis, John Updike, Alice Walker, Eudora Welty, and E. B. White to soak up their styles. When they read, reread, and listen to them on tape when possible, they absorb their styles. Choosing from a diverse stylistic range will provide appeal to a wide array of students. Those who can absorb them deeply can begin to note their tricks and slowly appropriate them in their own writing.

We must never forget that we are trying to invite students into genuine literary activity—writing comfortably and frequently for their own purposes and reading confidently and frequently from the vast array of written texts. Modeling masters was once the primary means of teaching rhetoric. We have moved to understand the importance of many other modes, but we can still profit from acquainting our students with the successful craft of others and with validating an apprenticeship to them. The success of any apprenticeship is in its releasing the learner from imitation to independent craft.

Invitation to Reflection 10–1

Have you ever yourself experienced writing instruction by copying, paraphrasing, modeling, or imitating? These four instructional modes are arranged on a continuum from most model-dependent to least model-dependent. Write under each one titles, authors, or passages that you believe have distinctive styles worthy of imitation.

Copying ⟶ Paraphrasing ⟶ Modeling ⟶ Imitating

PRACTICAL STYLIST

Style is elusive and, as we pointed out earlier, very difficult to teach. We believe books on style do exist that are worth looking at; their good ideas can help your students work at this goal. Copying texts is the way many of the finest writers began. Some writers, such as Abraham Lincoln, who were limited to the few books they could find, may have developed into master stylists because they repeatedly read exceptionally crafted texts such as the Bible. We believe, however, that exposure to a number of fine writers and excellent texts that explain the secrets of the craft of writing is the best way to help writers develop mature and idiosyncratic styles that make reading their writing a pleasure.

THREE STYLE BOOKS

Williams's *Style: Toward Clarity and Grace* (1990) is a complex work of a thoughtful linguist. His thinking is as comprehensive as any in this limited but important field. He says that he wants to go beyond the mere "high-mindedness" about style that is typical of standard works; he argues that his book "explains how to achieve those ends" (p. ix). Williams deals carefully with seven central features of style: clarity, cohesion, emphasis, concision, length, elegance, and usage. He shows the consequences of bad writing (too many prepositions; complex, unfamiliar concepts at the beginning of sentences; and negative verbs used to describe benefits), offers illustrations of their negative impact, and explains how to correct them. He speaks insightfully about metaphors. He shows how they can add elegance and power to writing but how, if they are ineptly posed, they can confuse a reader and undermine the writer's intent. In his usage chapter, he sanctions the split infinitive and shows cases in which that construction can clarify meaning and provide more direct communication. He also clarifies the use of *shall* and *will* and how turning to *will,* though it may be unconventional, adds the force of intent to writing. His book is full of instruction for more clarity and grace in everyday writing.

Romano's *Writing with Passion* (1995) is famous for its chapter on "The Multi-Genre Research Paper," but his chapter on "Breaking the Rules with Style" is certainly worth reading. In that chapter he (like Williams) teaches writers to intentionally break the conventions of writing as a way to establish a style and a voice that are both noticeable and attractive. He honors unmentionables such as fragments and extended, involuted sentences. The brash brevity of the former and the droll, desultory nature of the latter break the rules of length at either extreme. Humorists Donald Karl, H. L. Mencken, and Dave Barry all use unsanctioned brevity to great effect. Other stylists use repeated phrases or even seemingly redundant passages to capture their readers. Romano tells us, too, how to build a recognizable voice with labyrinthine catalogs, spelling aberrations, double discordant voices, and verbal collages. He uses the glories and peculiarities of literature to demonstrate the way stylists violate the norm in beautiful and clever ways to entrap the reader. His *Writing with Passion* makes learning new ways to encourage bolder style in student writing a treat.

Collette and Johnson's *Common Ground* is not as familiar as the other two are. It is not the work of a linguist or an English educator; however, it is rich with detail and stout with insight. It is replete with thorough explanations and apt demonstrations. The opening chapter appropriately is titled "Reaching the Reader." Details, analogies, and anecdotes are some of the authors' hooks. In discussing anecdotes, they show the need for a balance of uniqueness and typicality; bright ideas like these are commonsensical yet fresh. The authors discuss Howard Nemerov's essay "On Metaphor," which offers the jewel "if you want to see the invisible world, look at the visible one" (p. 18). They show us how to exercise our metaphoric powers by making a passage "metaphorically richer by working on the verbs" (p. 22). They show writers how to search for metaphors to explain, not express, a feeling or emotion to someone else. Their other chapters pore over such specific matters as finding a common ground via humor, setting, and special perspectives—it becomes clear that such comic wordsmiths as Woody Allen, Stephen Wright, and Paula Poundstone must have learned such lessons somewhere to achieve their delightful way of getting us to move into their worlds. The authors further show writers, in the chapter on "Movement," how to achieve focus or energy, how to make "paths," and how to "move through the whole." In a highly stylistic chapter on "Discourse," they, like Romano, show us how to go about "changing the rules" (p. 140) and then move on to finely articulated chapters on "Roles and Relations" and "Voice, World and Authority." In the latter, they show how cadence in prose can be recognized and then developed (pp. 224-234) and how to mix and shift voices (pp. 241-248). All of this is done with economy, straight talk, and verve. It is not a methods book but it is full of methodology. It is worth any teacher's time; its lessons are so lively. One thing more: It may be seen as a creative writing primer, but the lessons of style are not confined by genre or discourse mode. Style is totally transferable across all genres.

OTHERS

In your search for books about style, be sure you also look back at Strunk and White's *The Elements of Style*. Remember, though, that they are more prescriptive than demonstrative, and positive suggestions mean more to writers than warnings do. The authors also can be a bit overbearing, as when they say no to the passive voice. Loren Eisly's *The Invisible Pyramid* and writing by other fine authors make use of that voice powerfully and beautifully. We merely need to avoid passive voice as a way of obfuscating responsibility.

Macrorie's *Uptaught* also has a somewhat caustic tone to it, but it can jolt us in the right direction occasionally. Murray's *A Winter Teacher's Writing* is useful, as is Welty's *One Writer's Beginnings* and other such books by fine writers that reflect in useful ways on their craft. The *Penn/Faulkner* audiocassettes, which feature contemporary writers speaking briefly yet at times eloquently about beginnings, places, and characters, can be very useful as a way to urge students toward deeper understanding of style. A wealth of material is available for building writing, and when young writers start to care about style, you know they are moving in free flight.

CONCLUSION

In Chapter 9 we looked at five major approaches to writing and suggested a structure for bringing these approaches together. In this chapter, we offered a broad array of instructional strategies that fulfill critical needs in writing. These are not wedded to a single ideology but are affirmed in current research and best practice. It seems a fitting point of closure to report some confirming appraisals that have appeared in broad educational journals, expansive scholarly texts, and respected and widely circulated documents.

A broad review of accepted writing practice in *Educational Leadership* (1987) reported the research of Hillocks and his associates, who looked at six important writing strategies. They found that grammar instruction had little or no positive effect on writing and that free-writing was only slightly more effective as an instructional strategy. The use of models was more effective but was not as powerful when used exclusively. Sentence combining was very effective, twice as useful as the free-writing approach. Generally, Hillocks found that carefully planned and systematic writing strategies were most effective. Attitude and good feeling were necessary, but they were not sufficient.

Another report that gives us a general sense of what is most important in writing is Zemelman, Daniels, and Hyde's *Best Practice: New Standards for Teaching and Learning in American Schools* (1993). They present eight practices in writing that are endorsed in the standards:

• Teachers must help students find real purposes to write.
• Students need to take ownership and responsibility.
• Effective writing programs involve the complete writing process.

- Teachers can help students draft and revise.
- Grammar and mechanics are best learned in the context of actual writing.
- Students need real audiences and a classroom context of shared learning.
- Writing should extend throughout the curriculum.
- Effective teachers use evaluation constructively and efficiently.

We believe that the strategies we presented in Chapter 9 and in this chapter cover these standards sufficiently to help your teaching of writing meet or exceed those standards.

Perhaps more convincing is the report produced by William Bennett's Department of Education, *What Works* (1986), and *What Matters Most* (1985), produced by the Commission on Teachers and American Future. They both report that the writing process is the essential ingredient for effective writing. Success comes when teachers develop a sequence that includes prewriting, writing, and revising. The reports also note that when writing programs extend across the curriculum, students' performance is much improved.

The findings of the National Assessment for Educational Programs (NAEP) have great credibility. The goals and achievement levels for writing published in the NAEP's *Writing Framework and Specialization: 1998* are worth comparing with what we have outlined in these two chapters on writing to see whether we are speaking to those national standards. The NAEP's five goals are terribly broad:

- Students should write for a variety of purposes: narrative, informative, and persuasive.
- Students should write on a variety of tasks and for many different audiences.
- Students should write from a variety of stimulus materials and within various time constraints.
- Students should generate, draft, revise, and edit ideas and forms expressed in their writing.
- Students should display effective choices in the organization of their writing. They should include detail to illustrate and elaborate their ideas, and use appropriate conventions of written English. (p. 27)

The NAEP's Writing Achievements (Basic, Proficient, Advanced) for grades 8 and 12 are more precise and thus give us a good sense of the mark our students must achieve. These are presented in Figure 10-19.

FIGURE 10–19
Writing achievements

PRELIMINARY ACHIEVEMENT LEVEL DESCRIPTIONS FOR GRADE 8 WRITING

These achievement levels are proposed for first drafts, not final or polished student writing, that are generated within limited time constraints in a large-scale assessment environment.

BASIC

Students performing at the basic level should be able to:
- Demonstrate appropriate response to the task in form, content, and language.
- Maintain a consistent focus.
- Respond appropriately to the task.
- Use supporting detail.
- Demonstrate sufficient command of spelling, grammar, punctuation, and capitalization to communicate to the reader.

PROFICIENT

Students performing at the proficient level should be able to:
- Create an effective response to the task in form, content, and language.
- Express analytical, critical, and/or creative thinking.
- Demonstrate an awareness of the purpose and intended audience.
- Have logical and observable organization appropriate to the task.
- Show effective use of transitional elements.
- Use sufficient elaboration to clarify and enhance the central idea.
- Use language (e.g., variety of word choice and sentence structure) appropriate to the task.
- Have few errors in spelling, grammar, punctuation, and capitalization that interfere with communication.

ADVANCED

Students performing at the advanced level should be able to:
- Create an effective and elaborated response to the task in form, content, and language.
- Express analytical, critical, and/or creative thinking.
- Have well-crafted, cohesive organization appropriate to the task.
- Show sophisticated use of transitional elements.
- Use varied and elaborated supporting details in appropriate, extended response.
- Begin to develop a personal style or voice.
- Demonstrate precise and varied use of language.
- Use a variety of strategies such as analogies, illustrations, examples, anecdotes, and figurative language.
- Enhance meaning through control of spelling, grammar, punctuation, and capitalization.

FIGURE 10–19
Continued

PRELIMINARY ACHIEVEMENT LEVEL DESCRIPTIONS FOR GRADE 12 WRITING

These achievement levels are proposed for first drafts, not final or polished student writing, that are generated within limited time constraints in a large-scale assessment environment.

BASIC

Students performing at the basic level should be able to:
- Demonstrate appropriate response to the task in form, content, and language.
- Demonstrate reflection and insight and evidence of analytical, critical, or evaluative thinking.
- Show evidence of conscious organization.
- Use supporting details.
- Reveal developing personal style or voice.
- Demonstrate sufficient command of spelling, grammar, punctuation, and capitalization to communicate to the reader.

PROFICIENT

Students performing at the proficient level should be able to:
- Create an effective response to the task in form, content, and language.
- Demonstrate reflection and insight and evidence of analytical, critical, or evaluative thinking.
- Use convincing elaboration and development to clarify and enhance the central idea.
- Have logical and observable organization appropriate to the task.
- Show effective use of transitional elements.
- Reveal personal style or voice.
- Use language appropriate to the task and intended audience.
- Have few errors in spelling, grammar, punctuation, and capitalization that interfere with communication.

ADVANCED

Students performing at the advanced level should be able to:
- Create an effective and elaborated response to the task in form, content, and language.
- Show maturity and sophistication in analytical, critical, creative thinking.
- Have well-crafted, cohesive organization appropriate to the task.
- Show sophisticated use of transitional elements.
- Use illustrative and varied supportive details.
- Use rich, compelling language.
- Show evidence of a personal style or voice.
- Display a variety of strategies such as anecdotes, repetition and literary devices to support and develop ideas.
- Enhance meaning through control of spelling, grammar, punctuation, and capitalization (pp. 53–57).

Teaching writing is one of the English teacher's essential charges. Nowhere does the dual sense of teaching as art and craft seem more pertinent. In the course of these two chapters, we trust that you have found some theories and strategies around which you can begin to practice the craft. We hope too that you have felt some connection with the art that is also necessary for teaching writing. Teacher Bill Stifler provides a fitting close for the chapter as he muses on the art, and on the teaching.

On Writing

I've tried to think what I could tell you,
about the way words feel, the sound
they make when they touch, the way
words fight you, fall flat, clattering
like pans to a kitchen floor or the slap
of a tire limping, only you know all
this, and I wonder if there's anything
I could tell you, or tell myself,
because words make their own way,
play by their own rules, and all we do,
if we're lucky, is find them.

Bill Stifler

11
ORGANIZING INSTRUCTION

A good conversation is neither a fight nor a contest. Circular in form, cooperative in manner, and constructive in intent, it is an interchange of ideas by those who see themselves not as adversaries but as human beings come together to talk and listen and learn from one another.

Jane Roland Martin

Some say that tests drive the curriculum. Some say that texts drive the curriculum. The verb *drive* is apt. *Curriculum* comes from the Latin word *curro,* which means "run" and, we have been told, originally meant a race course. It is easy to imagine our students racing around on just such a circular course. With 13 circuits, most of them have finished their scholastic race. Our concern here is how their 9th, 10th, 11th, and 12th laps are organized. You may have begun to wonder how the many ideas and activities you have met in this text might be molded into effective instruction. How can they be gathered into a coherent answer to the question "What shall I do on Tuesday?" Some steps need to be taken between your being a student in a methods classroom and your becoming a teacher in your own English classroom. This chapter will help you bridge that gap between what you know and are learning about sound and creative theory and practice and how to summon and shape that knowledge into effective learning for students. We introduce four basic approaches to instruction; we consider how computers can enter that instruction; and finally, we propose planning models for shaping instruction into units, weeks, and daily lessons. Many general methods courses cover similar material, but we find that these approaches and models hold a different light when illuminated by our discipline.

FOUR APPROACHES TO INSTRUCTION

In Chapter 4 we introduced you to Mr. Gradgrind's School of Hard Facts in Charles Dickens's *Hard Times.* It was clearly a place of rigid questions and certain answers. It tolerated no ambiguity; if a student felt any, the teacher was sure to correct it. How would you imagine the desks were arranged in Gradgrind's school? Where was the teacher situated in his classrooms? As we asked in Chapter 1, what assumptions about learning are manifest in such arrangements?

McLuhan has made us aware that the medium is the message. Our organization of physical space and time in English classrooms reflects basic assumptions about our students, ourselves as teachers, and the learning enterprise that joins us. The various classroom configurations that we considered in Chapter 1 correspond with four basic learning approaches, four fundamental ways in which classrooms and the learning there are organized. They also embody basic assumptions about the way learning *should* occur.

The four most basic teaching approaches to high school classes are lecture, whole-class discussion, group work, and individual work. Each of these four has an educational history, an established practice, and a logic of its own. Each makes a legitimate claim for our consideration. But one or more may collide with ideas you have about learning. Certain ideas about learning are incompatible with certain approaches. Before we investigate these irreducible collisions, we describe each approach. Figures 11–1 through 11–4 present an array of four organizational possibilities: student desks, teacher's desk, possible interactions between students, and possible paths of the teacher's movement through the classroom. (They differ from the figures of Chapter 1 because of the attempt to represent those dynamics.) In general ways, each of the four classrooms corresponds to each of the four approaches.

Invitation to Reflection 11–1

We asked variations of these questions in Chapter 1. Your answers may have begun to alter since then.

Lecture	Group Work
Whole-class Discussion	Individual Work

- Which of the four strategies comes to your mind first when you think of an English classroom?
- Which of the four was most common in your own high school English class? In college?
- Think back to three of your favorite teachers. Which did they use?
- Look at Figures 11–1 through 11–4. Which resembles the arrangement of those favorite teachers? Did the room setup suggest anything about the teachers' approaches to learning and teaching?
- In which of the four classroom arrangements pictured do you feel most at home?
- Which would you employ today in planning an introductory lesson to non–college-bound 11th graders studying the theme The American Dream?
- Which would you choose in teaching an individual poem to average 10th grade students?
- Which would you choose for a lesson ending in a unit on persuasive writing?
- Consider how you might combine several strategies and desk arrangements within one class period on any of these subjects.

As we have noted, Goodlad (1984) found that the dominant organizational pattern in American high school classrooms was that of a teacher lecturing or explaining to a whole class (Figure 11–1). That teacher was central to "determining the activities, as well as the tone, of the classroom" (p. 123). The students "generally engage[d] in a rather narrow range of classroom activities—listening to teachers, writing answers to questions, and taking tests and quizzes" (p. 124). Applebee (1993) found almost a decade later that the technique that had a "heavy emphasis" in high school literature classes was "whole-class discussion of texts read by all students" (p. 136). Does such activity sound engaging for students? Goodlad's study found that "large percentages of the students we surveyed appeared to be

FIGURE 11–1
Lecture

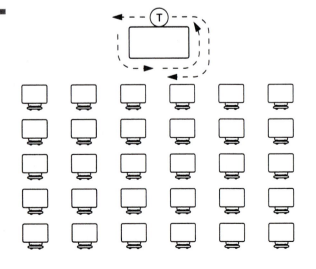

FIGURE 11–2
Whole-class discussion

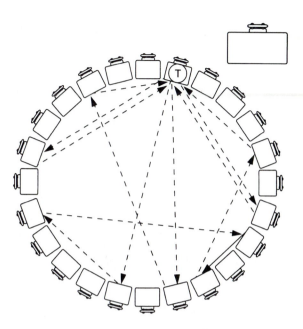

FIGURE 11–3
Group work

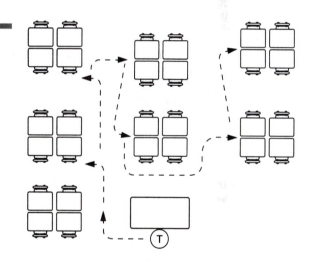

FIGURE 11–4
Individual work

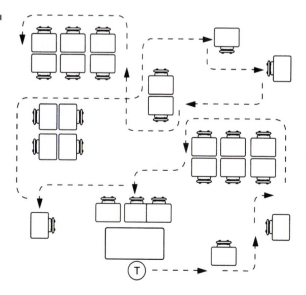

TABLE 11–1
Four teaching approaches

Approach	Types/Strategies	Styles/Features
Lecture	Total Partial Kernel Interactive	Holistic Linear Contentious Dualistic
Whole-class Discussion	The Questioning Circle	
Group Work	Task/Project Inquiry/Exploration Jigsaw Fishbowl Buzz Groups Simulation	Size Stability Selection Structure Self-consciousness
Individual Work	Independent Study Workshop/Conference Individualized Instruction	

passively content with classroom life. In general, they felt positive about both peers and teachers" (p. 124). Indeed, students are socialized to this classroom organization by the end of the early elementary grades (p. 123).

We encourage you to enter our general definitions and concrete elaborations of each of four organizational approaches, Table 11-1, with openness to its possibilities. Often, teachers select one of these, stick with it, and never shift to another. You will probably find one that is most congenial to you and that you regard as most effective with your students, and you may favor it in your choices of instruction. As with reading, though, your classroom organization will change over the course of your career. (After decades of teaching, we still alter our plans each new year.) We elaborate each strategy and enunciate its unique claims so that your choices are enlarged and you don't fall into a habit of using only one. In the hands of able teachers, each strategy can be energizing for student learning. You should be open to the potential for each and for choosing different strategies to meet different needs. Variables that will influence your decision of instructional strategy include the following:

- the developmental level of students
- the dynamics of the group of students in your class
- the nature of the subject to be taught
- the nature of the work you hope students will accomplish
- the strategies used in preceding and following lessons
- the physical possibilities and limitations of your classroom
- the resources of your school and community
- the time of the school and calendar year

LECTURE

As Goodlad has documented, lecture is the most common form of instruction in American high schools, and it is the mode that the general public usually visualizes when it thinks of a classroom. Many colleges and universities still refer to teachers as lecturers. Figure 11-1 shows the typical physical arrangements: the teacher is at the front and center of the classroom; the students face that center, backs to each other, in orderly rows; if the teacher moves, the movement is primarily up front around the desk, lectern, or overhead projector. This approach is based on the notion that knowledge flows from a knowledgeable teacher to less-knowledgeable students. Freire's (1970) analogy (discussed earlier) of teachers filling meek "receptacles" contains within it the visual image of a teacher raised above the students to facilitate ease of pouring.

FOUR TYPES OF LECTURE

If the transmission of knowledge is of primary importance and if lecturing is an efficient way for learners to master new knowledge, it makes sense for the class to be so arranged. We believe that Freire's banking model for passing on knowledge is neither primary nor efficient. But that is not the only kind of lecture, and some kinds fall within our bias toward more active, student-centered, constructivist classrooms. We describe four types that differ according to structure, duration, intent, and student

Lecture Type	Structure	Timing	Intent	Student Role	Example
Total	Organized, structured (usually prewritten) talk that covers a prescribed body of knowledge	Entire class period	To cover content of lesson	To receive, transcribe, and remember	The differences between the English Romantic poets and their predecessors
Partial	Preorganized presentation of small discrete portions of knowledge	A limited part of a period. Could occur more than once after students have responded.	To prime students to apply the concepts presented	To apply and illustrate	Four central qualities of the Romantic poets, which students illustrate in a rereading of several poems
Kernel	Shorter, more pithy and contentious presentation. Tries to go to the core of the lesson. Can resemble a feisty polemic.	Can occur at any time as a prompt or stimulant for a lesson	To generate response and to challenge	To rebut and defend. Stake a pro or con position.	The Romantics were caught in a losing battle against the change from a rural, agrarian culture to an urban, industrial society in the early nineteenth century. Their poetry has little to say to us today.
Interactive	Presentation of knowledge that originates in asking students questions or answering theirs	Can last an entire period or some portion. Sometimes impromptu.	To engage students and to convey knowledge	To listen actively and to interact	Responses to student questions about four poems

TABLE 11–2 Four lecture types

role: total, partial, kernel, and interactive. They progress from a prepared lecture that dominates an entire period to teacher-talk in response to questions students ask that lasts until those questions are answered satisfactorily. Students also move progressively from being silent receivers to being more active questioners. The center of knowledge shifts from the teacher as knower to the student as generator of knowledge. The likeness between these types is only that each is a form of teacher-talk. Their differences are more pronounced than their similarities. Table 11–2 schematizes these four.

We have had teachers who could detail the differences between the Romantic poets and their predecessors, outline the social and historical changes between the two, enumerate divergent styles and themes, illustrate those differences with textual references, finish, and gracefully summarize the hour's lesson just as the bell rang. The grimmest foreshadowing of such a *total lecture* is the appearance on a raised podium of sheets of paper yellowed at the edges. The *partial lecture* and the *kernel lecture* both employ a legendary benchmark of public speakers and preachers for how long an interested audience can attend: 20 minutes. Many feel that the attention spans of today's adolescents, raised as they were with television's staccato movement and time, are even more limited. These briefer lectures respect those limits. Finally, we have witnessed such energetic, able authorities as James Britton and Buckminster Fuller build their presentations around student or audience questions in stunning *interactive lectures*. They remain the center of knowledge, but students are engaged in prompting and shaping their presentations through questions. We have seen educational reformer John Holt rise to give a lecture and say simply: "I don't give talks anymore. I'll be happy to answer any questions." A more student-centered use of the form invites students themselves to become centers of knowledge about a particular subject and then to answer questions posed by fellow classmates. Such an assignment uses an interactive lecture, but establishes a new center of knowledge: the student.

FOUR RHETORICAL STYLES

Teachers who make the choice of using lectures to effect student learning still have other decisions to make. We will call these choices *rhetorical styles*. The Greek origin of the word *rhetoric, rhetor* (orator), reminds us of the ancients' lively interest in the art of speaking and writing effectively and persuasively. Teachers have at their disposal all of the rhetorical methods described since the time of Aristotle. They can appeal to reason (called Argument) and emotion (called Persuasion) with Analysis,

Definition, Classification, Illustration, Comparison, and Contrast. Whether a lecture is total, partial, kernel, or interactive, it can draw on these individual strategies. We mention here four more general organizing principles for a lecture:

Holistic Analysis	This organization takes a subject and divides it into its constituent parts to create an understanding of that subject.
Linear Explication	This organization does not break down the general into its component parts, but sets forth a subject by examining it sequentially item by item.
Contentious Construction	This organization articulates contending positions and invites students to support or attack them.
Dualistic Resolution	This organization develops two opposing positions, but works to show how both are persuasive. It invites students to understand ambiguity and see situations as often too complex for an either-or resolution.

A traditional total lecture is associated with the thorough coverage of a subject and is often organized by Holistic Analysis or Linear Explication. But Holistic Analysis could also be used in the kind of minilessons suggested by Calkins (1986) and Atwell (1987) for a writing workshop. If, for instance, problems have arisen about what students should do with their completed work, the teacher might break down the necessary steps that a writer must take to be published. Contentious Construction and Dualistic Resolution are less frequently used, but they can be quick energizers to classroom talk that prods the conversation further along and presents, like written texts, new ideas or information to which students can respond and on which they can work. For instance, to initiate small group discussions of texts, we present three contending responses to a short story and ask students to choose which they find most persuasive. Or, in talking with students about Frost's "Mending Wall," we might present Montgomery's (1962) view that the poem could as easily be praising walls and recognizing the need for separation as criticizing walls and artificial boundaries. The only time we are comfortable with lectures in our own classrooms is when they are very brief, present new concepts or knowledge, and immediately invite students to test or apply these new ideas. On the rare occasions that we use any form of lecture, we also like to have visuals or manipulatives to hook students' interest, participation, and understanding.

LECTURE'S CRITICS

Despite its predominance in classrooms for decades, critics have criticized the lecture strategy on theoretical and practical grounds for years. Dixon (1967) writes of the "agreed concern" of the Dartmouth Conference to substitute the "round table" for the "disappearing dais" (p. 34). Howard Gardner (Birk, 1996, p. 7) believes that the lecture favors students with linguistic intelligence. They are best suited to "translate" or "convert" the lecturer's words into understanding, while others with different intelligences and learning styles suffer. Pragmatists worry that even those who can comprehend and take in the content of a lecture will rapidly lose what they heard. Constructivists believe that the lecture removes the locus for meaning making from the student. Even if lecturers attempt to connect their content with student knowledge and experience, few students can inwardly make their own connections. Lectures are far removed from what reformers value in an active, experiential, inductive, hands-on learning environment. When teachers use lectures, often they become stuck in the role of lecturer.

Often, criticism focuses on the worst practices of lecture, usually those of the total lecture. We have found little research about the amount of time devoted to lecture in United States high school classrooms, and no research that acknowledges a variety of lecture types. We are wary of teacher self-report. In fact, as lecturing has become suspect—even vilified—many teachers say that they do not lecture (in a local university, only 25% said that they lecture), while students report that lecture is the predominant classroom activity (in that same university, students reported that 75% of their teachers lecture). We do know of teacher-talk that is effective, however, and want to say a word in its defense.

LECTURE'S BEST EXEMPLARS

A legendary American lecturer is philosopher and psychologist William James, whom generations of Harvard students characterized as brilliantly spellbinding in the classroom. He employed the full range of vivid and animated expression, energetic and unconventional gesture, and spontaneous and idiosyncratic blackboard use, but he seems to be remembered most for the originality of his responses to student questions and challenges. Barzun's (1983) description of his daily use of students' responses to "bring forth a new perception, a new formulation" (p. 278) makes us assume that he used at least interactive lecture in portions of his classes. James, writing for teachers, calls for "the kind of teaching that respects freedom and compulsion, individuality and the claims of common reason and common action" (p. 280). His own classroom reflected his willingness to encounter and engage his students, even though he began with lecture. In fact, he defined an uneducated person as "one who is nonplused by all but the most habitual situations," whereas the educated person is one who can "extricate himself from circumstances in which he never was placed before" (p. 282). James himself, even when he described his annual September "trepidation" of returning to the classroom with his mind a "blank" (p. 277), opened himself to the novel and unexpected from his students. This is not the picture that critics present of a wooden lecturer. Granted, many regard James as a genius, with a rare intellectual vitality, a comprehensive grasp of his subject, and an intuitive sense of the students before him, but those hallmarks of the gifted lecturer can be embodied in those who are not geniuses.

Closer at hand, a Wake Forest University colleague of ours, Edwin Wilson, is almost universally mentioned by his former students as their most outstanding teacher ever. He relies in the classroom almost totally on lecture (and outside of the classroom, although he is also the provost, he schedules one-hour private interviews with each of his students). Former students often recount hearing the echoes of his speech in describing the English Romantics years later. His example alone would require us to be generous about the educational possibilities of lecture, although we think he communicates human spirit as much as literary knowledge. And every school has distinguished lecturers. History teacher John Giles at our sons' former high school grows so animated in his occasional lectures that he leaps onto his desk to emphasize points. We borrow a familiar logical argument from William James: "If you wish to upset the law that all crows are black, you must not seek to show that no crows are; it is enough if you prove one single crow to be white." Our own white crow is Edwin Wilson.

Thus, the image of the student as passive container simply waiting to be filled by the teacher is not always fair to the dynamics between the two. Lecturers and lectures vary. The selection of what kind and when are open to broad choice. We recommend that you make careful choices so that you can throw out the bathwater and save the baby.

Invitation to Reflection 11–2

- Which is the most common form of lecture that you have experienced as a student?
  - Total
  - Partial
  - Kernel
  - Interactive
- Name a lecturer whom you consider to be excellent. What qualities distinguish that person's style?
- Have you ever known a teacher to take a strong position on a subject in order to prompt your response?
- Timpson and Tobin (1982) speak of lecturing as a kind of performance whose success can be enhanced by several behaviors. Read their tips and check those that your experience would confirm.
  - Moving around the room rather than remaining rooted
  - Modulating and varying voice
  - Using cuing devices to focus attention (key terms on the blackboard, gestures, pictures, charts)
  - Pausing for reflective silence and emphasis
- What percentage of your time as a teacher could you imagine spending on lecture?
  - 5%
  - 10%
  - 25%
  - 50%
  - 75%
  - 100%

WHOLE-CLASS DISCUSSION

The classroom in Figure 11–2 mirrors the second teaching approach, whole-class discussion, at its most democratic.* The teacher claims no head or center position. All are actively involved, sharing equally in the process of exploring and learning. (Sometimes such a configuration only camouflages as being democratic, but is, in fact, just a different seating arrangement for a lecture. Teachers may pose questions, but the answers sought and expected are predetermined. Gradgrind, in a circle of desks, lectures seated.) In practice, the democracy of discussions varies, but a shared aim persists: to focus students on a common subject and involve them more actively in the construction of their own learning. In most English classrooms, the teacher's place is not exactly that of the other learners. The teacher most often selects the text or idea under consideration, and guides, shapes, and prompts the conversation. But student response is central. In discussions, because teachers' roles are neither that of the purveyor of knowledge nor that of equal participant with the students, they walk a tightrope. Too much leaning toward one side or the other can create a mishap.

CLASSROOM DISCUSSION DEFINED

In a respected general methods text, Grambs and Carr (1991) state what a discussion is not:

- Discussion is *not* recitation.
- Discussion is *not* just talking by people who know little and care less about the subject being discussed.
- Discussion is *not* a debate in which different factions try to win.
- Discussion is *not* a chance for two or three students to show off their verbal acrobatics.
- Discussion is *not* a bull session, where individuals exchange prejudices or feelings. (p. 92)

A keen young observer of classrooms, Benjamin Milner, adds, with feeling,

- Discussion is *not* a discursive sharing of personal and irrelevant anecdotes.

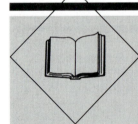

Invitation to Reflection 11–3

As you walk into any high school, you see many clusters of students engaged in talk, gathering outside the building before the school day begins, clumped around lockers and in corridors between classes, in cafeterias at lunch, and at school events after hours. As you pass those students, you hear them talking together with energy. Imagine that scene and consider what assumptions you make about their talk.

- Would you assume that they are involved in a "discussion"?
- What is the difference in their informal talks together outside of class and what you normally mean by a discussion in class?

These students disperse into different classes, and in one English class, a teacher makes the following assignment: "Read the short story 'I Stand Here Ironing' by Tillie Olsen and be prepared to discuss it in class tomorrow." Consider your assumptions about tomorrow's "discussion."

- What would you expect it to be like? A disguised lecture on the story? An active exchange of ideas with all (teacher and students) exploring the story together?
- Who would have the greater share of classroom talk, students or the teacher?
- Would students move beyond the boundaries of the questions to explore new ground on their own?
- Would students be allowed to introduce their speculative questions or observations outside of a response to the teacher's questions?
- Would the teacher's questions be aimed at leading students to a single reading of the story, the same for everyone?

*Discussion can of course occur in small groups or between pairs. For the sake of clarity, we focus in this section on the dynamics of a whole class engaged in discussion.

Discussion as an instructional approach is based on some important assumptions about learning. Socrates modeled education as vigorous, active dialogue between novices and more-knowing others. Rousseau's ideal model of education was of one child and one adult in face-to-face work. William James, in the nineteenth and early twentieth century, demonstrated how dynamic dialogue could occur within a whole classroom of students. Vygotsky (1978) and Bruner (1986), later in the twentieth century, speculated about and tested the hypothesis that education grows from the social interactions of a learner with others, not in isolation: We help each other construct meaning. Martin (1983) captures the impulse and drive of this social interaction at its best:

> As individuals we have to assimilate our experiences and build them into our continuing picture of the world; as social beings we need to legitimize the world picture we are continuously constructing and maintaining. So we hold out to others—in talk—our observations, discoveries, reflections, opinions, attitudes and values; and the responses we receive in the course of these conversations profoundly affect both the world picture we are creating and our view of ourselves. (p. 6)

WHOLE-CLASS DISCUSSION PRACTICED

Martin explains why we converse with others in any setting. Classroom talk shares these motives, but differs from the informal conversations that we engage in everywhere else. Several practical distinctions hold tremendously important implications for the way teachers organize their classroom conversations.

Turn-taking Discussions. Whole-class discussions often resemble this simple pattern: Teacher asks, students answer, the floor returns to the teacher (who can choose how long to keep it), and the cycle begins again. Seldom do students respond to each other's answers or pose questions themselves of other students. They appear to try to come up with the one acceptable answer and then wait for the teacher to pose the next question. If they do interact with their peers, they often go through the teacher as a dispatcher of turns. Students' raising their hands and the teacher's recognizing the person who next holds the floor typify these arrangements.

Beach and Marshall (1991) explain that a three-part sequence of this turn-taking—teacher question, student response, teacher evaluation—is the most frequently observed pattern in classrooms. Cazden (1988) calls this pattern IRE: The teacher *I*nitiates the questions, the students *R*espond, and the teacher *E*valuates (p. 29). This sequence encourages serial questioning in which a teacher queries one student and receives a response, then goes to the next, and repeats the exercise to all those who are willing or forced. The last part of this three-part sequence, teacher evaluation, is the part missing in normal conversation. In classrooms, it might be a "Very interesting, Angela" or a simple murmur, "Hmmmmm," and head shake, but most teachers feel that some immediate feedback is necessary. (On many teacher evaluation instruments, instructional feedback is one of the principle items.) This last part returns the floor to the teacher, who is then "positioned to ask another question—either following up on the student's response . . . or turning to a slightly different agenda" (Beach & Marshall, p. 54).

Pseudoquestions. Beach and Marshall (1991) also note the presence in many classrooms of questions posed for which the questioner already has an answer in mind. These pseudoquestions create a different dynamic from that of ordinary conversations in which questions are normally asked in order to obtain information. Their effect is profound. They establish the teacher as the more-knowing one, with privileged knowledge and a privileged classroom position, and the students as seekers after the teacher's insights. The teacher is the fielder of questions; the students are the answerers. In such a setting, students rarely initiate their own speculative questions. They might ask for information or clarification, but seldom do they enter the interpretive enterprise. In this context, we might better understand the common scenario of the student question following the teacher's inspired reading of a poem: "Will this be on the test?" Clearly, the student is a spectator of the teacher's performance and asks one of the few subject-related questions available to him or her.

Schaffer (1989) describes a breakthrough insight she gained about discussions: "If there are certain points we want students to know . . . we should tell them. We should not use it as a discussion item, because the point is not really open for discussion" (p. 40).

Student Responses. We have mentioned how these two patterns of whole-class discussion foster assumptions about the role of students as cogs within the wheel turned by the teacher's energy. Something more subtle also develops. Language and literature students, in inverse proportion to their regard for the teacher's superior knowledge and response, devalue their own. Rather than growing through discussion to expand, enrich, and qualify their original responses, they cast them off as ignorant and naive. They substitute, or replace, their earlier responses with the new. Not only does this fail to integrate new learning with old, to build on the ground of one's own knowledge and understandings, but also, it fails to teach a strategy for developing one's own knowledge. It is a model of appropriation, not of learning.

Teacher Assumptions.   In their role of leader of class discussions, it is easy for teachers to deceive themselves about the true nature of class dynamics, especially if those discussions are lively, with several students engaged in strong and active answers. At that moment, a teacher is so busy fielding questions, doing justice to responses, asking follow-up questions, evaluating responses, and connecting them to what was said earlier, that he or she assumes or hopes that the 25 other students are as engaged. The reality may be significantly different. Especially when able talkers take responsibility, the passivity of the less-able increases. So many high school students are masters of the polite appearance of listening that the teacher, deceived, forges on.

ALTERNATIVES ATTEMPTED

The usual protocols of whole-class discussion leave the teacher in clear control of the classroom. To relinquish that control is anxiety producing for most teachers, but especially for young teachers who have few alternative teacher models, who struggle to define and claim their own roles as teachers, and who might be evaluated by administrators who mistakenly equate silent classes with good classes. We must lay careful foundations and, layer by layer, build toward alternative discussion patterns. Certain principles and skills require time to develop. Too many teachers turn away from alternative arrangements because their one or two experiments meet with failure. Discussions happen within the total ethos of the classroom, of the classroom in the school, of the school in the community, and of the community in the national norms of what teaching and learning mean.

General Strategies.   Smagorinsky and Fly (1994) provide suggestions for general changes that teachers can make in the way that they conduct whole-class discussions. Their suggestions originate in their interest in small-group work, why it sometimes produces authentic explorations and other times stiff, unproductive work—a kind of fill-in-the-blank approach to the subject. They examined the classroom talk of 10th-grade students in two settings: a teacher-led discussion and a small-group discussion of two coming-of-age stories. They concluded that what happened in the whole-class setting was essential in enabling students to develop the ability "to talk on their own" (p. 55). They regard small-group work as "an extension of the continuum of discussions enacted during the school year" (p. 58). Four discussion-leading techniques facilitated first, whole-class, then small-group interactions:

1. prompting students to generate a contextual framework to guide interpretation;
2. prompting students to elaborate their responses;
3. building on student contributions to generate questions; and
4. making the process of analysis explicit. (p. 55)

In the first, when teachers prompted students to create their own strategies, students possessed a framework for interpreting literature or analyzing writing that stood independently. The teacher's modeling an interpretive strategy did not result in students' being able to apply the technique on their own. In the researchers' transcription of a class discussion of one of the stories, Figure 11–5, the teacher prods students to develop a "conceptual context through which to interpret the literary character's experience" (p. 56). These strategies might include Rabinowitz's (1987) "rules of notice" (discussed in Chapter 4, Responding to Literature), not presented as abstract principles, of course, but embodied in the questions posed to students. Secondly, Smagorinsky and Fly recommend that teachers resist the temptation to elaborate students' responses for them, rather than prompting students' own elaboration. Teachers should relinquish their talk to students' attempts at understanding, even when those are fumbling. Teachers also need to generate questions from the flow of conversation, not from a preconceived list. Nystrand and Gamoran (1991) call this kind of question posing *uptake*. When students' comments generate a follow-up question or a request for expansion of an answer, students learn to take themselves more seriously, to probe more deeply into their responses, to anticipate a way to push themselves to greater insight, and to elaborate responses and defend their views. Finally, Smagorinsky and Fly found that discussions grow richer and more productive when teachers call attention to common strategies for reading literature or writing effectively. They might build on their own interpretive activity: wondering aloud, searching for evidence, making generalizations, and checking them with subsequent reading. These are not the fancy acrobatics of New Critical scholars, but the necessary work of competent and interested readers made explicit.

FIGURE 11–5
Strategies for
discussion

Patsy: He thought it was so mature to, well, he was eating grapes and staying up late with, he was eating grapes and grape seeds and staying up late and watching TV without his mother's approval.

Teacher: OK, eating grapes and seeds and a couple of other examples. He was staying up late.

Patsy: Yeah.

Teacher: And he was also . . .

Patsy: Watching TV.

Teacher: And watching TV when told not to. And these fall into the category of what?

Patsy: Huh?

Teacher: These all have something in common.

Patsy: Well, disobeying.

Teacher: OK. He was disobeying his mother. All right. Now what can you do with this? In other words, what are you trying to tell us by bringing up these points?

Patsy: That he thought he was mature by disobeying his mother. He thought it made him a more mature person and older by doing things he wasn't supposed to do.

Teacher: Thought he was mature through these acts. OK, and what does Patsy think? Do you agree with it?

Patsy: What? No.

Teacher: Why not?

Patsy: He was just showing how immature he is by doing that.

Teacher: And what criterion of a definition of maturity are you using to make this judgment? Why is this, you are saying that this is, in fact, immature even though he thought he was mature. That is what you are saying, right?

Patsy: Yes.

Teacher: Why? You are saying he is immature because of something and that *because* is your definition. And what is it about your definition that allows you to make this judgment? (p. 56)

SOURCE: From P. Smagorinsky and P. K. Fly, "A New Perspective on Why Small Groups Do and Don't Work." *English Journal, 83* (3), 54, 58. Reprinted by permission.

Dixon (1967) describes more generally a teacher's role in facilitating and extending a discussion: "Here a teacher can help by noticing and reinforcing potential change in the level or direction of the discussion, summing up an attitude perhaps, making an issue quite explicit, or calling for an instance when generalizing seems to have lost touch with reality. Learning to do so, without disturbing the tentative informal exploration that good talk becomes, is a matter of awareness and tact" (pp. 34–35) and, we add, experience. These techniques are examples of the broader strategy, which we discussed earlier, called *scaffolding:* a temporary structure of learning techniques or strategies that support and strengthen a growing learner and that can be gradually withdrawn as students become more proficient and, finally, independent.

Specific Attempts. Two experienced English teachers provide cogent pictures of the traditional teacher-controlled approach to whole-class discussions, their growing dissatisfaction with it, their desire to reach more students, and their development of an alternative. The *English Journal* posed this question for its readers: "What has been the most significant change in your approach to teaching since 1987?" The answers of Robert Perrin (1994) and David Noskin (1994) testify to how one can move away from teachers' turn-taking discussions to student-initiated conversations.

Perrin (1994) describes his established ritual for discussion: "Start with five-by-seven index cards; write ten to fifteen questions, carefully crafted and sequentially ordered; conduct class by asking the questions in order" (p. 89). This pattern worked for most students, but Perrin realized that the questions were too "*me* centered." "Students felt little responsibility for their own learning; instead, they knew I would lead them through the essays, poems, plays, or novels—highlighting what *I* thought was important" (p. 89). Perrin changed his routine by asking students to "write two questions about the assigned essay on three-by-five index cards—any questions, so long as the questions were 'real' and related, at least in some way, to the reading" (p. 89). He fought back guilt—his preparation was rereading the text—and anxiety—what if students didn't write questions or the written questions were "odd." But, in fact, his students were excited and his discussions became invigorating. "*They* determined what we talked about; *they* found out what they wanted to know; *they* were responsible for directing their learning" (p. 89).

Like Perrin, Noskin (1994) once thought he understood the ingredients for an "ordered, involved, informative, and well-paced" discussion: "involving the majority of students, asking for a balance of lower and higher level questions, and providing sufficient wait time for students to generate answers" (p. 89). Today, he would describe those discussions differently, as "rehearsed, passive, unintellectual, and mechanical" (p. 89). Rather than effective discussions, he now describes them as "pseudodiscussion[s]" in which he controlled "the intellectual climate through a series of teacher-generated questions, in which all communication was channeled through me" (p. 89). This new understanding, that he calls the most significant change in his teaching, requires new arrangements.

First, the students must take ownership of the discussion. This can be accomplished by appointing discussion leaders, having students come to class ready to share one question, commenting and sharing significant passages from the previous night's reading, or asking students to share their ideas with one or two others and then choosing one of those ideas to bring to the entire class. I also realize that my role has to be that of a *facilitator.* I might begin by asking a student to share a puzzlement or reaction to a piece of literature. Other times, I might use a favorite passage or idea, but the discussion must quickly become theirs. I can encourage, clarify, mediate, and participate as long as I do not dominate. Finally, I have learned that an effective discussion is more aptly perceived as a conversation. (p. 89)

He acknowledges the need for setting guidelines for behavior as the year begins that establish "a semblance of order and genuine mutual respect" and encourage "an open and nonthreatening exchange of ideas" (p. 89). Now in Noskin's classes when students express ideas, other students respond directly to them. "In the past, my students were responding to me. Now they are talking to one another" (p. 89).

QUESTIONS RAISED

Like Noskin and Perrin, for some of us, the central act of preparation each night is to write out questions for the next day's discussion. Even when our classroom organization embraces other approaches, we can't feel completely comfortable about going into class without an outline of some essential questions. The margins of every novel or short story that we read, and most poems, remain littered with questions. This habit has its benefits: a ready means of response to texts and an encapsulation of personal wonders about them. It joins our private acts of reading with the public sharing of perplexities and pleasures with others. We continue to think that question writing is solemn work. Aristotle ("Metaphysics II") wrote "Those who wish to succeed must ask the right preliminary questions." Nash and Shiman (1974), observed that "questioning is perhaps the central skill in the teaching-learning experience" (p. 38). Bruner (1983), reflecting on his lifetime of teaching, writes "I had no question in my mind (nor do I now) that teaching is a form of dialogue, an extension of dialogue. Dialogue is organized around questions" (p. 191). Dewey (1933) was equally unequivocal about the importance of questions: "What's in a question, you ask? Everything. It is the way of evoking stimulating response or stultifying inquiry. It is, in essence, the very core of teaching" (p. 266). Yet questions differ, and not any question will do. (Dickens had Gradgrind pose the question about the horse in a chapter entitled "Murdering the Innocents.")

The Questioning Circle.   Handbooks have been written about question posing. We have scattered such advice throughout this book. In Chapter 4, Responding to Literature, we presented a model for developing questions conceived by Christenbury and Kelly (1983) that works at the intersection of three circles: the subject's, the student's, and the world's (Figure 4-9). Christenbury and Kelly (1983), teachers, scholars, and researchers themselves, explain their model as an alternative to the usual "sequential and hierarchical schemata" for developing questions (p. 12). "While each circle represents a different domain of cognition, the circles overlap—as does knowledge—and are not ordered" (p. 13). The goal of the questioner is to prepare questions in each of the circles, white, shaded, and dense, and to draw on those components as the right timing presents itself during discussion. The order in which questions are posed is flexible; thus, the discussion "builds on a variety of perspectives" (p. 17). Figure 11-6 contains questions that Christenbury and Kelly wrote to illustrate each of the three areas. They probe one single, but significant incident in *The Adventures of Huckleberry Finn.*

Getting Started.   The first question posed can set the stage for all that follows. Many fine starting points have been suggested in other chapters. We want to suggest a few for classes engaged in literature study, because it is here that many of us have the strongest pull toward traditional close reading. Once you have begun close analysis of texts, breaking off is hard to do.

Broad Questions. A broad approach to questions takes as its starting point one particular and significant question about a subject. For instance, if the class has completed Shakespeare's *Julius Caesar,* the one question might be any of the following:

- What makes Brutus ready for a conspiracy?
- How do the two marriages differ?
- How do political altruism and personal gain vie as motivational forces in the play?
- What weaknesses and strengths of the common people are presented?

Here are other strong questions that in some sense sum up a work or idea:

- In Faulkner's *A Rose For Emily,* what in Emily's past helps explain why she might rather cohabit with a corpse than continue occasionally seeing a live man?
- Why does Hamlet fail to act?
- Why does Twain let Huck behave as he does at the Phelps's farm?

FIGURE 11–6
Christenbury and
Kelly's questioning
circle

WHITE QUESTIONS

The Matter: What does Huck say when he decides not to turn Jim in to the authorities?
Personal Reality: When would you support a friend when everyone else thought he or she was wrong?
External Reality: What was the responsibility of persons finding runaway slaves?

SHADED QUESTIONS

The Matter/Personal Reality: In what situations might someone be less than willing to take the consequences for his or her actions?
Personal Reality/External Reality: Given the social and political circumstances, to what extent would you have done as Huck did?
The Matter/External Reality: What were the issues during that time which caused both Huck's and Jim's actions to be viewed as wrong?

DENSE QUESTIONS

The Matter/Personal Reality/External Reality: When is it right to go against the social and/or political structures of the time as Huck did when he refused to turn Jim in to the authorities? (p. 16)

SOURCE: From L. Christenbury and P. P. Kelly, *Questioning: A Path to Critical Thinking.* National Council of Teachers of English. Reprinted by permission.

- How much change and nonstandard usage can be accepted without the threat of linguistic chaos?
- Who was the most unrealistic member of the family in Williams's *The Glass Menagerie?*

The teacher's task becomes to listen, to think, and to encourage, react, and build on student responses, not to plan for or try to remember the next question in a sequence, and certainly not to try to account for all the details of the play. If students consider the big questions, try out hypotheses, add support for their positions, and select telling details of the text that was read or the ideas that were studied, teachers often find that the essence of a text has been discussed and what has been aired will be memorable.

Titles and Conclusions. Two kinds of these comprehensive questions focus on the title and on the nagging questions that readers often take away from a text's conclusion. Thus, we might ask the following questions:

- How does Joyce Carol Oates's short story title "Where Are You Going, Where Have You Been?" sum up Connie's tragedy?
- What is the rich paradox in Richard Wright's title *Native Son?*
- Was Sammy's quitting the A&P a foolish or a noble gesture in Updike's "A & P"?

Significant Questions. Many questioning hierarchies recommend beginning with lower-level questions and moving toward the culminating higher-order ones. Christenbury and Kelly (1983) suggest a reversal: Starting with the most significant questions. In their Questioning Circle, those are the questions at which the matter, personal reality, and external reality intersect. These questions can arise at any time in a discussion—a radical enough suggestion. Alternating dense with white or shaded questions causes, as they explain, "the complex and central dense questions to be answered with added perception, knowledge and understanding" (p. 14). Starting with the dense question and keeping it as the discussion's focus can also stir student interest, generate questions from the shaded and white areas, keep the conversation moving around a central rivet, and, at the end, account for the most important responses to a subject that would have evolved had separate questions been posed. Riveting.

Teacher Perplexity. Sometimes an honest admission of perplexity initiates productive discussions. A teacher can simply tell the class that the text or the writing dilemma is a mystery or is confusing and that he or she needs students' help in figuring it out. When the classroom enterprise is focused on inquiry and exploration and when trust and respect between teacher and students have built over time, such vulnerability can unleash strong efforts from students.

Other Questioning Strategies. Schaffer (1989) uses student-written questions as the basis for her discussions. Three of her seven postulates for teachers in assigning and "fielding" these questions reiterate ideas that we presented earlier and extend them.

- Our discussion questions must be important to our students.
- We must allow enough "wait time" for reflection before we call on students to speak.*
- The students who speak the least may need this sort of activity the most. (p. 40–42)

*Research studies show that when a teacher pauses after a question to wait for student response, the students give better answers (Rowe, 1974; Tobin, 1987). Yet Tobin (1987) also found that teachers typically wait only one second for student response before they start talking. (Other estimates are even lower.)

TABLE 11–3
Probst's reader
response questions
for literature
discussions

Focus	Questions
First reaction	What is your first reaction or response to the text? Describe or explain it briefly.
Feelings	What feelings did the text awaken in you? What emotions did you feel as you read the text?
Perceptions	What did you see happening in the text? Paraphrase it—retell the major events briefly.
Visual images	What image was called to mind by the text? Describe it briefly.
Associations	What memory does the text call to mind—of people, places, events, sights, smells, or even of something more ambiguous, perhaps feelings or attitudes?
Thoughts, ideas	What idea or thought was suggested by the text? Explain it briefly.
Selection of textual elements	Upon what, in the text, did you focus most intently as you read—what word, phrase, image, idea?
Judgments of importance	What is the most important word in the text? What is the most important phrase in the text? What is the most important aspect of the text?
Identification of problems	What is the most difficult word in the text? What is there in the text or in your reading that you have the most trouble understanding?
Author	What sort of person do you imagine the author of this text to be?
Patterns of response	How did you respond to the text—emotionally or intellectually? Did you feel involved with the text, or distant from it?
Other readings	How did your reading of the text differ from that of your discussion partner (or the others in your group)? In what ways were they similar?
Evolution of your reading	How did your understanding of the text or your feelings about it change as you talked?
Evaluations	Do you think the text is a good one—why, or why not?
Literary associations	Does this text call to mind any other literary work (poem, play, film, story—any genre)? If it does, what is the work and what is the connection you see between the two?
Writing	If you were to be asked to write about your reading of this text, upon what would you focus? Would you write about some association or memory, some aspect of the text itself, about the author, or about some other matter?
Other readers	What did you observe about your discussion partner (or the others in your group) as the talk progressed? (pp. 35–36)

SOURCE: From Robert E. Probst, "Dialogue with a text," *English Journal,* January, 1988. National Council of Teachers of English. Reprinted by permission.

Probst (1988b) poses both questions and a strategy for using them that encourage a "loose and flexible" pattern of discussion that still drives toward the reader's personal engagement with the text (p. 35). He suggests that teachers select questions from the list shown in Table 11-3 that are suitable for their students, the time available, and the text being read. They should be reworded, written on small pages of a booklet (if not bound, then stapled or clipped together), and given to small groups of students to prompt and guide their discussion. (He omits the Focus column in his booklets.) A young teacher, Mary Beth Braker, has explained to us that she keeps a copy of these reader response questions "taped to my podium, my desk, and my lesson plan book. These questions serve as a constant reminder to me of what I want my classroom question and discussion sessions to do—to bond my young adult readers to a text personally and intimately; to guide them in using the skills they already possess— first reactions, associations, visual images—to connect with a literary text. My most successful moments in the classroom have involved adaptations of these questions."

MIDRASH

An image from early Jewish community life captures our ideal for discussion in English classes, whether with a whole class or a small group. Midrash was a way of interpreting Jewish texts in which a group inquired, speculated, puzzled over, and teased out meaning. Often the participants filled gaps in the text. Always they examined words and debated their import. Bill Moyers (1997) calls midrash "an assault on silence." Elie Wiesel, Primo Levi, and other survivors have written of the famous midrash in Auschwitz in which God was put on trial. We value the image for the process it recalls and for the seriousness, openness, and expectation of those engaged in it.

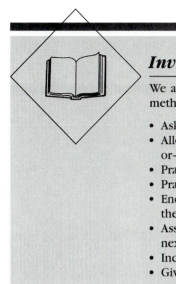

Invitation to Reflection 11–4

We abstract tips to encourage student-initiated questions from Grambs and Carr's (1991) general methods text. Check those that strike you as promising. Add others.

- Asking students what questions they need answered before a lesson continues
- Allowing students to answer one another's questions, intervening only to redirect questions or—in absolute necessity—to say that an answer is inadequate
- Praising students for acknowledging the need for help
- Praising questions that show intellectual curiosity
- Encouraging students to maintain in a special part of their notebooks questions that arise when they read or engage in problem solving activities
- Assigning, periodically, a specific student to ask two or three questions at the beginning of the next class which raise significant issues for class discussion
- Includ[ing] students' questions in quizzes and tests
- Giving students extra points on quizzes and tests for providing additional, good questions (p. 91)

GROUP WORK

A group-centered approach to learning is like the discussion approach in many ways: The teacher is not the sole provider of knowledge; students actively participate in their learning; learning revolves around genuine inquiry and evolves out of interaction. But group-centered work is defined by a crucial difference: The teacher sets students on a more independent course so that group discoveries are made without the direct intervention of the teacher. Teachers provide a structure for learning and assistance with that learning, but their roles change. Students have a greater share of the classroom's talk space and more individual responsibility for the learning experience. More than whole-class or even individual approaches, the group or collaborative approach allows students to generate ideas, use language (listening and talking especially), learn from each other, teach each other, and recognize that their thoughts and experiences are valuable and essential to new learning.

COLLABORATIVE LEARNING

Collaborative learning should not be regarded as another gimmick to manipulate students into learning what we, their teachers, think is good for them. It is a transforming approach based on carefully formulated and researched assumptions about language and learning. It assumes that students' acts of talking, listening, writing, and reading are fundamental to their development; it acknowledges that if these all must be funneled through the teacher in a classroom of 20 to 30 other learners, their quantity is necessarily limited; therefore, it recognizes that group collaboration is essential for frequent opportunities to use language. It frees these communicative acts. The teacher's removal from a central place becomes like uncorking a bottle. Students' interactions and responses to each other flow more freely and confidently.

Collaborative learning invites students to explore ideas, to wrestle with new information, and to make sense of changing experience. It encourages genuine conversation that flows naturally from one to the other. Collaborative learning takes students seriously and asks that they take each other seriously and direct their talking and listening to each other. Barnes, Britton, and Torbe's (1990) studies of talking to learn show the powerful advances that are made because of authentic talk that emerges when students learn together. In such a context, they can try out half-formed ideas and make tentative suggestions as they help each other move toward deepening understanding. James Britton (1986) calls this constructing of shared meaning "leap frogging" (p. 120). Bruffee (1984) defines the purpose this way: "Our task must involve engaging students in conversation among themselves at as many points in both the writing and the reading process as possible" (p. 642).

A TEACHER ADOPTS COLLABORATIVE LEARNING

Bayer (1990) provides a clear picture of her interactive sense of learning and the need to provide a classroom setting for its use. She names three major language and learning principles that guided her teaching:

- Students have to make connections between new ideas discussed in class and their prior knowledge.
- Students can use language to help them make these connections, that is, they can use language as a tool of learning.
- Students' language and thinking competencies develop with regular use in meaningful problem-solving tasks. (p. 7)

What Bayer realized was that she lacked a context in which those three principles could be achieved. Vygotsky, Bruner, and others provided one. Individuals do not construct knowledge in a vacuum. If learning occurs in a social context, it is not an individual act. Initially, a more-knowledgeable other guides a learner's activity; gradually, as the two share in problem solving, they become more equal; the learner begins to take initiative with the other critiquing and guiding; and finally, the learner is able enough to take control and the other becomes a supportive audience. Thus, Bayer's fourth language and learning principle becomes

- Learners need opportunities to work collaboratively under expert guidance and with more knowledgeable peers within an apprenticeship process; novice learners increasingly assume more responsibility for their own learning. (p. 11)

Parker and Goodkin (1987) explain that if there is "no social interaction with others who offer us an expanded range of alternative viewpoints, no new viewpoints to incorporate into our thinking, [there can be] no intellectual development" (p. 38). Vygotsky (1978) is more succinct: "Human learning presupposes a specific social nature and a process by which children grow into the intellectual life of those around them" (p. 88).

This question, however, always arises when novice learners are dependent on the help of peers: Who is providing the more-expert knowledge for these peer teachers? That is a serious question and should not be dismissed. One of Seneca's observations has survived two millennia and provides perhaps a partial answer: When you teach you learn twice.

Invitation to Reflection 11–5

Other gains are also achieved through collaborative learning that are good in themselves and instrumental to learning. Check those that strike you as persuasive reasons for this approach and add others.

- Reduces the threat of whole-class lecture or discussion
- Enhances the motivation to learn
- Cultivates student curiosity and involvement
- Stimulates genuine peer interaction
- Instigates shared problem solving within the whole group
- Reduces the sense of alienation students feel in the chasm between their school life and their "real" life
- Invites students to move beyond their egocentrism and interact with others
- Develops students' confidence in themselves as learners
- Improves their attitude toward the subject at hand
- Gives opportunities for quiet and shy students to participate
- Allows for spontaneous exploratory talk, not rehearsed, self-conscious talk
- Develops a sense of audience and what is appropriate for different audiences
- Develops confidence in presenting to a larger group because of the opportunity to sort out ideas first with a smaller group

PRACTICAL STEPS TOWARD COLLABORATIVE LEARNING

Suppose that collaborative learning is in place. The teacher has established a framework and a content. Students have been empowered to give order and direction to that work. The teacher still faces additional challenges. Group discussion of ideas or texts is not the customary discourse of most high school students. Earlier in this chapter we discussed Smagorinsky and Fly's (1994) insights about ways in which the discourse of whole-class discussions can positively influence the work of small groups. But will those acts be enough to change the level of discourse if it is habitually less serious, focused, and purposeful in other areas of school life? If teachers are not directly involved, how can they be sure that the group discourse moves beyond the discursive conversations that are typical of the time between classes and after school hours?

Moffett and Wagner (1992) add to Smagorinsky and Fly's advice for shaping collaborative learning into educative moments:

- create a "relaxed but concentrated" climate for conversation
- adopt a "warm and friendly but not saccharine" tone
- in every way, reflect a genuine valuing of what students say "well beyond polite conversation."

They conclude that "the art of conversing is at once a profound social and cognitive activity, based on real respect, not etiquette" (p. 80). We consider conversation to be an art of hearing as well as talking. We must listen to others' description of reality as we hope they listen to ours. In classrooms, teachers can listen attentively and respond actively and spontaneously; they can validate the serious responses of others; they can make connections between old and new knowledge. They can nudge students toward habits of questioning, self-disclosure, sensitivity, and tact. This is not to say that the work of groups is always earnest and intense. Part of the importance of the group is that it brings natural language use to the classroom. With the young, this brings humor and wit as well as serious inquiry. Use the range.

Finally, teachers must resist the notion that small group work is not real teaching, that it's a teacher's holiday. (Invariably, when our student-teachers learn that we will be visiting them on a day they've scheduled group work, they request that we come when they are "really teaching.") The teacher's preparation for small groups is significant (just as their facilitating it is). Teachers must be carefully organized, ready to tolerate talk, confusion, and surprises, energized for authentic conversation, and, mainly, willing to step down from the controlling center of the classroom.

COMMON GROUP DESIGNS

The actual work of a group can be organized in a number of ways, but two common arrangements for the English classroom are the task or project setup and the inquiry or exploration setup. These provide defined starting points—group goals, organization, and process—for incorporating collaborative learning into your classroom.

Task or Project.   In a task or project design, the teacher, alone or in consultation with students, assigns specific work or activities to the members of the group. The group functions like a committee, with common goals and individual responsibilities. Group completion of the assigned task depends on the solitary work of individuals first and then the collaborative work of combining these isolated pieces into a whole. For example, as a prereading activity for John Steinbeck's *The Grapes of Wrath,* a teacher might ask groups to create a collage (visual, recorded, or oral) from 1930s Depression images that each member gathers. The assignment and task structure predispose the group to making good use of every member's thinking. Task groups, though, tend to require teacher motivation, even materials gathering, and monitoring. They are a good step toward introducing students to the group process because they build on a process that many have experienced (in student clubs, for instance), have specific assignments, and build group work from individual effort. This task approach is parallel to the movement from the first to the second stage of Four Stages of Reading Literature: Readers respond personally before moving to the sharing of the interpretative community.

Inquiry or Exploration.   The inquiry or exploration group is less structured. The teacher gives a group of students a more general purpose, a finite amount of time for achieving it, and much flexibility about the process of doing so. Whether students are discussing explicit questions or the most general—What is going on here?—they are working together to arrive at the most satisfying conclusions they can. In English classes, this type of group is used to explore texts, both authors' and students'. In our chapters on language, literature, and writing, we often suggested small-group discussions. Those would generally fall within inquiry purposes. One important message in the assignment is that students do not have to depend on or validate their responses to the subject through their teacher's. The learning accomplished by the group itself is sufficient.

Other Group Designs.   Task and inquiry groups are the two broadest types of group designs. The following group designs are variations on these two with other goals, structures, and outcomes.

Jigsaw Groups. We first learned of this stratagem from Forrestal (1990). Students are assigned a task in an original home group. Once the task is complete, individual discussants move to a different interchange or sharing group, so that each interchange group has a report of what each of the home

FIGURE 11–7
Jigsaw questions
about *Antigone*

> You are responsible for the following from the collaborative learning activity on *Antigone:*
>
> 1. You should be able to argue that Antigone is the tragic hero of the play, understanding what tragic hero means, according to Aristotle.
> 2. You should be able to argue that Creon is the tragic hero.
> 3. You should understand Aristotle's concept of tragedy and be able to apply it to the play and contemporary drama.
> 4. You should be able to list the five types of conflicts, to define them, and to apply them to the play and other dramas. You should be able to say which is most important in this play.
> 5. You should be able to identify, understand, and discuss the significance of selected metaphors and mythological references in the play.
> 6. You should understand the role of Teiresias in the play and be able to explain how the scene in which he appears suggests important facts about the Greek's religious beliefs. You should also be able to explain the symbolism behind some of his specific characteristics—e.g., that he is blind.

groups has accomplished. That is the great strength of this process: Each group member is responsible for transmitting the learning of its home group. Neenan (personal communication, 1992) organized discussion questions (Figure 11-7) for jigsaw groups of 10th-graders studying Sophocles's *Antigone.* She explained that she cannot be vague about her expectations. Students need to be able to give clear and distinct answers to the question "What am I expected to know by the end?" Because a student's peers are held accountable for what the group learns, students must understand and teach well to their second group. She said of this lesson that her students were so energized that she could have left the room and her absence would never have been noticed. She felt that her students learned in a period and a half what by another strategy would have taken 3 days.

Fishbowl. We described a Fishbowl group in Chapter 1 and Chapter 3. We remind you again of this strategy: Four or five discussants talk together about a specific topic in the center of a ring formed by the rest of their classmates sitting outside the inner circle, listening. Granted, the small-group discussion is public, yet it still shares the qualities of a more private small group. After the discussants have concluded their talk, the listeners can respond in discussion with the whole class or in small groups. Teacher Jonathan Milner used this strategy often with his average ninth graders who had mixed language proficiencies. The students within the inner circle liked being on center stage. Their talk became more authentic and directed to classmates, not to the teacher. He reports that the listeners were often bursting to talk and would ply the discussants with questions or rebuttals when time was called. His ESL students liked listening without the worry of their being required to talk.

Buzz Groups. A variation on the inquiry group, a buzz group is focused, student managed, problem centered, and time limited. The name itself suggests the activity of working bees. That is the goal. Often, we name topics and let students quickly gather according to the topic of their choice and spend a designated amount of time sorting out their views before they report back to the whole class. The subjects for these quick discussions are typically immediate and topical. Teacher Benjamin Milner posts declarative position statements on different walls in the room and asks students to move to the statement with which they agree. When all students have chosen a place, the groups so formed (regardless of their size) work out fuller, more persuasive positions to present to the class.

Simulation (Role-playing). In Chapters 4 and 6, we discussed the use of simulations in the study of literature. The method is the same here—to invite students into an imaginative situation in which they construct and enact a role different from their own or solve an imaginary dilemma—but it is undertaken in a group. For instance, the survival dilemma discussed in Chapter 9, p. 270, lends itself to the problem solving of a small number of students. Each is more likely to become immersed in the activity, to adopt a personal perspective, and to arrive at decisions seriously. Simulations provide powerful opportunities for solving problems and for applying knowledge. After we have discussed schools of literary criticism with our 12th grade students, we divide the students into small groups to answer the question "If critics of only four schools of literary criticism could survive, which four schools would you choose to inform our view of literature?"

FIVE GROUP FEATURES

Groups, whatever their purpose and design, have five important features that teachers must consider carefully in composing them: size, stability, selection, structure, and self-consciousness.

Size.   The sizes of groups should vary to accommodate the task that they are to undertake.

Large groups (five or six students)	When students work on sizable projects in class over long periods of time
Small groups (three or four students)	When more intimate matters are primary

Johnson (1990) recommends that no collaborative learning group have more than four students. He observes, in fact, that the great mistake in traditional classrooms is to make groups too big. Book and Galvin (1975) place the ideal group size at five students.

Stability.   English teachers who use groups consistently usually vary the composition of their groups. All students come to know each other, and neither cliques nor dysfunctional groups form. Change vitalizes group interaction and strengthens one group advantage: Students come to know each other more personally. If the group composition remains constant, however, real depth of personal sharing and communal exploration can develop between students who work together over long periods of time.

Selection.   Placing students in groups can be done by the teacher, the students, or random chance.

Teacher Assignment	At times, teachers want to constitute groups with a range of varying ability levels or cognitive styles or to distribute other variables evenly (such as a mix of male and female students). Some teachers knowingly form groups to separate friends or to contain potential troublemakers.
Arbitrary Assignment	Random features such as birth month or height can be used to determine groups. (The sense of fate is often more pleasing to students than our decisions or even the students' own preferences.)
Self-assignment	Individual students might privately record their preferred topic or task or even select two other students with whom to work. Another variation of self-assignment is to give individual students time before entering a group to begin or complete individual tasks as an entrance requirement.

Structure.   As we have implied, one of the great hazards for students who are inexperienced with groups is aimlessness. Group work can seem indistinguishable from lunch chat. A strategy that encourages active involvement of all members of a group is to assign a specific role to each member, for instance, that of leader or group facilitator, researcher, recorder, writer, reporter, compromiser, or standard setter. Each role has specific duties and responsibilities, and the roles are complementary to each other. Students profit from the opportunity to take on a wide spectrum of functions or offices.

Most groups need a leader or facilitator to keep the group on task, to help it be both cohesive and productive. The designated leader can be teacher appointed or group selected. (You can practice a subtle form of leadership designation by putting a set of questions or directions in front of a student whom you hope will take on that role.) The leader can rotate or remain fixed until the completion of the work. We value a democratic leadership and observe that group members are more responsive, involved, and satisfied when they feel that they have influence on group decisions.

Self-consciousness.   Some teachers work deliberately to introduce and orient students to the collaborative skills necessary for group effectiveness: how decisions are made, how typical group roles function, the educational problems and pitfalls of the group process, and the potential advantages of the process. Some teachers feel that this self-consciousness paralyzes groups and compromises their success. Those who use it feel that it makes students more motivated, more directed, and more confident of their work. It helps the group maintain its status as educative and helps prevent it from slipping into chat. We find that some evaluation of group process is important for student accountability and our planning. If students don't have this metacognitive view of the process, the evaluation itself alerts them. Figure 11–8 is an example of such a form.

FORMING, STORMING, NORMING, AND PERFORMING

Even if the classroom climate is well prepared and your specific group assignments are well developed, the groups themselves will not necessarily be ready to work productively together. In their work with small groups in writing workshops, Brooke, Mirtz, and Evans (1994) found predictable challenges for students in those groups: (1) questions of handling "established patterns of interaction (and literacy)

Criterion	Very Ineffective	Somewhat Ineffective	Not Sure	Somewhat Effective	Very Effective

Team Name _____

Your Name _____

Your Group's Responsibility _____

Directions: Rate your own group work by circling one of the numbers in the scale (from 1 to 5) that best measures your response to the questions stated at the left. Answer Question 10 on a separate sheet.

Criterion	Very Ineffective	Somewhat Ineffective	Not Sure	Somewhat Effective	Very Effective
1. How would you rate the effectiveness of your group?	1	2	3	4	5
2. How effective was the assignment in getting you interested in the subject and in guiding your work?	1	2	3	4	5
3. How effectively did your group work together by the conclusion of your assignment?	1	2	3	4	5
4. How well did all the group members participate?	1	2	3	4	5
5. How well did democracy work in your group? Did the members take equal responsibility for the group's work?	1	2	3	4	5
6. How effective was the group in considering the ideas that you contributed?	1	2	3	4	5
7. How effective was the leader in encouraging everyone to talk and work together?	1	2	3	4	5
8. How effective were you in encouraging others to speak or to become involved?	1	2	3	4	5
9. How effective was the group's attitude toward the work?	1	2	3	4	5
10. What did you learn from this experience? Could you have accomplished the same results in whole-class or individual work?					

FIGURE 11–8 Small-group evaluation form

they bring with them . . . especially their established ways of managing public and private discourse; (2) the problem of diversity and individual differences, of the fact that other people (in the group, in the class) seem to be operating in ways that make little sense or directly challenge the ways in which they act; and (3) the problem of educational context," how this experience relates to previous school experiences or how it makes sense in this classroom at this moment (pp. 37–38). They refer to group theorists (Tuckman, 1965; Rothwell, 1992) who claim that all groups must move through stages in which the group members negotiate among themselves how they will function. Even though their task is assigned by someone outside, the group must sort out group dynamics for themselves. Brooke et al. name three stages after a group has formed:

Storming   The storming stage is characterized by clashes of individual agendas, as the group struggles to work out for itself a set of regular procedures and roles for its members.

Norming   The norming stage occurs as the group moves out of storming into the establishment of standard procedures and roles.

Performing   The performing stage occurs once the norms have been established and the group falls into a pattern of performing according to the procedures and roles it has created. (1994, p. 51)

Brooke et al. advise anticipating these stages as a possible progression, not a necessary one. No schema can represent the idiosyncrasies and complexities of individual group processes.

We conclude our description of the power of this approach with the words of a teacher who uses collaborative learning with a challenging group of students. Day Kennon (personal communication, 1992) teaches developmental reading to young disadvantaged mothers so that they can pass a community-college entrance examination and be placed in college-level work. In such a setting, she and three other colleagues might be expected to use a basic skills-and-drills approach; instead, however, they choose collaborative learning. Here is Kennon's account of how it works for her:

> For my first class I tell students that our goal is to develop effective reading and clear thinking skills. I think reading is a critical interpretive process. To be a critical reader, one must understand language (the semantics), interpret the author's purpose and tone, evaluate and apply the ideas, and perhaps identify a solution.
>
> I firmly believe that the atmosphere of the learning situation is one of the most important factors in developing analytical thinking skills. Students who feel they are within a community open to sharing ideas really do respond more openly and willingly. The response in itself motivates them to a distinctive level in the thinking process. Whenever I have asked students what they have found to be the most helpful element in their learning process in my class, the consensus constantly has been "we learn best from each other—from talking it out in a group, from discussion with the class, with a partner, with the teacher." The sharing with their classmates seems to involve and stimulate them to their highest potential for creative thinking. Verbalizing their own ideas to a listening, responsive party not only helps them generate language and reflection, but it also encourages them to synthesize thought content, context, and mood.
>
> The teacher's role in this is knowing how to ask the appropriate questions and having a rapport with the students (enabling that "sharing community" to happen). Students with low self-esteem or those who do not feel their contribution to be important often feel inhibited in their critical and creative thinking processes. Such students are motivated to interact only when they feel secure enough to share in the trial and error process of "talking an idea through." Speaking their thoughts about what they have heard—discussing and debating these with others—helps them consolidate what they learn. It helps them to process what they have read in light of their own background knowledge—but also a shared world view.
>
> I enjoy seeing the growing trust and interaction of a class as the semester unfolds. Some of the students, though they may not realize it, become responsible for each other's learning. They spontaneously help each other understand mistakes or fallacies in their thinking. They become motivators to each other. Some actually cheer the efforts made at presentations. They help one another as they explore different points of view and try to think more clearly and logically. Even in the lecture format, they are more interactive than in a traditional classroom. And as students grow into "owning" the program of study in their class, I grow more confident that what they have learned through their active participation will remain with them because it is both collectively and individually their own.

Clearly, effective group work does not happen accidentally or haphazardly; it develops from organization, confidence, and patience from the teacher and practice by the students. If collaborative learning succeeds, the rewards are significant. McClure (1990) concludes that collaborative learning "is the most direct means of initiating [students] into participation in the active shaping of knowledge and meaning for themselves" (p. 66).

INDIVIDUAL WORK

An individual approach to learning might conjure images of silent monks at work in solitary cells. In fact, individual work in the high school classroom at its best more closely resembles a newsroom; a journalism class working to produce a biweekly student newspaper offers a recognizable model for this mode of instruction. Students are working on different tasks as often as they are on the same assignment. Some may work in pairs (covering sports news) or large groups (analyzing an opinion poll), while others may work alone (writing feature articles). Central to this model is releasing students to choose and pursue their own projects. The teacher sets up the circumstances but then steps back off of center stage to assume roles as material gatherer, coach, consultant, and rerouter. Primarily, the teacher observes and encourages the students' self-reliance and self-confidence as learners in their own right. Individualizing instruction requires great energy and full attention from the teacher in organizing projects and in being fully present for students during these projects. Like group instruction, individual instruction pushes us toward students in one-on-one, personal encounters. Individual teaching strategies can provide many openings for us to join students in the "great conversation." But it transfers choice and responsibility to students for their work of "goal-setting, record-keeping, monitoring, evaluation" (Zemelman, Daniels, & Hyde, 1993, p. 5). Individual learning opportunities take many forms, but three formats are most common: independent study, workshop/conference, and individualized instruction.

INDEPENDENT STUDY

McNees (1977) calls independent study the "purest form of individualization" (p. 32). Students select and work solely on independent projects, and the teacher acts as a resource. Selection of a focus is critical. Students may select topics from a list of areas of investigation, in consultation with the teacher. (Our conferences with students on selection of independent-study topics have been highly useful in our uncovering individual interests and passions, and in their clarifying and validating these.) The age, experience, and ability of students will determine their readiness for such independent work.

McNees's study of English independent-study programs found four elements to be important to their structure:

Self-direction	students are given much freedom in selecting and directing their own English study;
Interrelationship of fields	students may relate English study to other disciplines;
Flexible scheduling	students have schedules which allow them time outside the English classroom to conduct independent study;
Freedom of movement	students are permitted to move from one area to another in the school (school library, English resource center, etc.) and outside of the school (community library, resource center, etc.) to work on particular study projects. (p. 32)

We add two additional elements that we consider to be essential:

Checklists of steps	students have before them certain steps to be accomplished (in detail or general as the student requires);
Periodic conferences	students meet at intervals with study groups and/or the teacher.

The discussion that takes place during these conferences is essential to students' developing ideas as they are explored in a social cycle of explanation, reaction, and response. Students also can be assisted by mentors who are experts in the field of study. Students may even serve "internships" with these mentors and learn firsthand from their expertise.

Traditionally, students reported the results of independent study in extended papers. Recent thinking encourages a greater diversity of end products. Certain cognitive styles and subjects of investigation are often better represented by other media.

WORKSHOP/CONFERENCE

The workshop/conference classroom puts students on independent paths for extended periods of time, but the work is classroom based and group dependent. Writing workshops such as those proposed by Graves (1983a) and Atwell (1987) have students work alone on their individual composition products, but with peers and teachers at all stages of the composing process. (An initial motive of the writing workshop was to provide a responsive audience for students' incipient ideas and tangible productions through every phase of writing, an audience that no one teacher could be for all students.) The size of each reading/responding peer group is small, usually from three to five. Its duration is varied: Some form for a single project; others persist together for an entire term. A workshop classroom organizes itself around the individual, the responding/reading peer group, teacher conferences, and whole-class mini-lessons. Although all of the students are working on personal projects, a basic working structure ties them together. Thus, some students may be working at word processors, others at tables in reading or editing groups, and others at desks in short conferences with the teacher. On entering the room, an observer might think that things are in disarray: The configuration and activity resemble those of an editorial room more than those of a classroom. But the structure of the work, the "discipline of the discipline," binds students to purposive and productive activity.

INDIVIDUALIZED INSTRUCTION

Individualized instruction can take many forms, but essentially it invites students to work independently on a project whose timing, process, and even product they choose. This self-paced work may provide the basic structure of instruction in a class, or it may be supplemental and scheduled for outside-of-class and occasional in-class work. In the 1970s, individualized instruction (sometimes called programmed instruction) grew in popularity in elementary and secondary schools and even in universities as teachers prepared handouts, publishers wrote and packaged modules, and computer programs took students step-by-step through the mastery of a given subject. Students worked on small, sequential tasks, had immediate and corrective feedback (especially in the computer models), mastered a discrete segment of content, and demonstrated their new knowledge on measurable, objective scales. When students had achieved competence in a specific learning task, they moved to the next. The preponderance of high school English classes are now organized around whole-class discussion, but individualized instruction still has legitimate claims as an option that we should consider.

Appendix F contains an example of individualized instruction developed by Meiers (1990) for 2 and 3 weeks. This plan allows students to work alone on a large-scale but well-structured task. The activity starts with a newspaper article that especially interests students and follows through on the interest area with many other genres: poems, cartoons, technical articles, letters, and pieces of personal writing. Meiers provides forms for daily checks of student progress and the criteria for evaluation.

If such individualized learning looks like a holiday for the teacher, it deceives. In fact, if it is teacher constructed, it requires careful attention to individual needs, abilities, and interests; creative instructional activities; meticulous organization and structure; and attentive feedback for each student. Like independent study and workshops, individualized instruction relies on students' conversations with the teacher and with peers. It does however, have benefits that compensate for these challenges: It addresses individual differences in ability and interests, it allows individuals to meet with academic success in their work, and it gives the teacher an opportunity to work closely with individual students.

As heterogeneous mixed-track classrooms proliferate (they have been the staple in many poor and rural districts all along), individualized learning offers a strategy for dealing with the diversity and range among students in one class. Different texts can be chosen, and different projects can be undertaken by students who need enrichment or remediation, those who are able in the first two stages of the reading cycle (Reader Response and Interpretive Community) but could not profitably move to the last two (Formal Analysis and Critical Synthesis). Two of Applebee's findings that disappoint us are that students in nonacademic and mixed tracks are less likely to be asked challenging questions than their college-preparatory counterparts, and that when students are grouped heterogeneously, teachers tend to make few adjustments to those changed circumstances. We don't suggest that individualized instruction allows you to "dumb-down" your expectations, but that it provides an approach that lets you acknowledge differences and guide students toward a deepening understanding of literature and writing from whatever place they start.

Each of these three formats for individual work puts students on their own to pursue their own learning with a more self-chosen focus and pace. Some are explicitly structured and short-term; others are open and long-term. Each has potential power for organizing classrooms to meet the varying cognitive styles and abilities, multiple intelligences, and interests of its students and for equipping them to become independent, able, life-long learners.

LAYERING THE FOUR APPROACHES

These four approaches of lecture, whole-class discussion, group work, and individual work comprehend the usual possibilities of teacher-learner organization within an English classroom. William James remarks in his *Principles of Psychology* that habits develop a dynamism of their own. Teachers often adopt approaches to instruction and styles of teaching early in their careers and elaborate those through the lifetime of their teaching. The four approaches are most effective if no single one of them is the steady diet of a class. Many variables influence a teacher's choice of approach: student styles, class size and duration, class dynamics, subject matter, and teaching objectives. We need to open ourselves to imagining a variety in our classrooms, and to layering the four approaches within any one lesson. Teaching Activity 11–1 is an example of mixing several approaches.

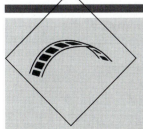

Teaching Activity 11–1   Layering the Four Approaches

Mode I: Lecture (Kernel)
The teacher explains that Ivor Winters called Frost a "spiritual drifter." The teacher asks students to write down what they think Winters might have meant by that and to guess what kind of beliefs Winters might have held as a critic. The teacher then tells the class that Winters was a Neo-Marxist critic and that he attacked Frost for seeming to be a liberal but taking no stand on causes that were important. He says that Frost always posed more questions than answers and that Frost always left the reader confused rather than certain about a moral solution. The teacher reads "Mending Walls" to show Frost's lack of full commitment to destroy such walls.

Mode II: Individualized Instruction

The teacher asks each student to read Frost's "The Lockless Door," select the best interpretation provided, and find four specific pieces of the text to corroborate that reading.

Mode III: Group Work (Task)

The teacher asks students to discuss in groups the various interpretations selected by individuals and the texts to support them, select the best possible interpretation from a list provided, and develop solid reasons to defend it.

Model IV: Discussion (Focused)

The teacher asks a group to offer its best interpretation of the poem, asks whether any other group has a different one, and lets the different groups engage one another in a full exploration of the text.

Model V: Individualized Instruction

The discussion closes with students writing an answer to the question "Do you agree with Winter's assessment of Frost based on the two Frost poems you read? If your lasting reaction to these poems is confusion, do you learn anything by it?"

INQUIRY LEARNING AND LEARNING CENTERS

Two other instructional strategies provide rich learning opportunities within classrooms. They can employ combinations of each of the four basic approaches to instruction, but they structure them uniquely. We begin with inquiry learning because it is the broader strategy. As a perspective and attitude toward learning, it is as foundational to our teaching as the ideas that cluster around constructivist, student-centered classrooms. In an inquiry classroom, teachers and students join each other in asking, questioning, pondering, and as Orlich, et al. (1990) explain, posing "the question that every Nobel Prize winner has asked: I wonder what would happen if . . . ?" (p. 278). We describe it here as it would operate within classrooms.

INQUIRY LEARNING

Inquiry learning is embodied in our country in the work of Jerome Bruner at Harvard and his colleagues who developed Man: A Course of Study (MACOS). In the early 1960s, a number of university and public school scholars and teachers gathered to consider a new curriculum. They were open to any approach that would rouse students to think about important, elemental questions. The National Science Foundation funded the project and joined its planners to create a course of study that would act as a model for other schools. The planners (predominately social scientists and historians) decided on a curriculum of three courses, one each for elementary, middle, and high school, organized around three central queries:

- What is uniquely human about human beings?
- How did they get that way?
- How could they be made more so? (Bruner, 1983, p. 191)

Although the distribution of this initiative was compromised by conservative political opposition, it is still used in many private and independent-minded public schools with a wealth of materials with which students ponder these questions. It makes tangible the inquiry method.

The inquiry method asks students to look at the facts of language and life around them in order to frame generalizations. It is based on the belief that facts are the stuff from which sound solutions are found and theories built. It is grounded in a foundation of questioning. Inquiry or discovery learning opens the scientific method for students: raising questions, posing a problem, generating hypotheses, testing those hypotheses, and drawing conclusions. Students can be taught to question genuinely, to observe openly, and to explore areas of inquiry confidently. They can initiate lifelong inquiry. Freire (1970) reminds us again that students must learn not only to read "the word," but also, to read the "world" (pp. 75–77). We will locate inquiry first in classrooms focused on language or literature.

Language.   Inquiry can be a powerful tool for creating language consciousness, perhaps the most important step in developing our students' language. Students can become engaged with the vitality of language when they begin to see its shape and behavior in ways other than that provided by the study of grammar.

Inquiry about words casts students in the role of linguists. The stuff of descriptive linguistic study is the "language of the street"—Main Street to Wall Street—which makes no community too small or insignificant to sample. For instance, students can investigate the geographic dispersion of language in their area (rural or metropolitan) by taking vocabulary or pronunciation samples from six or so distinct communities in the area. (Chapter 2 enumerated examples of these kinds of student research projects.) When a class of 20 or more student-linguists takes to the street, an amazing amount of information (well over 1,000 discrete usage samples) can be amassed by that one class, and exciting explanations and generalizations can be derived from the wealth of data. Students usually become bemused by their own uncertainty of preferred usage and even a little disturbed about that uncertainty.

Literature. Inquiry into literature takes single texts or extensive groups of texts as the facts from which to develop generalizations. In this book, we have cast the literature-learning enterprise in the spirit of exploration; therefore, we know we are not inaugurating something novel in the next three activities. We reiterate this kind of learning to emphasize that quality of inquiry within them.

Native American Literature. A short project in a literature unit on Native American writers (or any other group) illustrates the method. We encourage students to read brief selected works of a few Native American writers and then write an introduction to this literature, rather than read an expert's ready-made list of their literary or cultural qualities. The expert's list would obviously be better informed. But if students draw up their own lists and then test and possibly revise them after a full study of Native American writers, they will become more careful and skillful readers and more confident scholars themselves. If the expert finds qualities A, B, and C in an introductory essay, students will likely find them too, but they will not then look at the works as thoughtfully, nor discover D.

The Far Side. The "graphic literature" of *The Far Side* cartoons offers an easily accessible tool for inquiry and generalization. If students look at a self-selected or teacher-selected set of six cartoons, they might begin to ponder such questions as the following:

- What is human life like?
- How are animals and humans depicted?
- How are the norms of our society depicted?
- What does the extensive use of animals and their facial expressions tell us?

Students will begin to ask their own questions to form generalizations. Then, if a final cartoon unknown to the class is introduced, students can examine it to test their generalizations about Larson's work. Building generalizations from art or graphics draws on students' delight in wit and their natural interest in things graphic.

Emily Dickinson's Poetry. Teaching Activity 11-2 demonstrates inquiry into the poems of Emily Dickinson. This approach allows students to develop a more independent, personal judgment of a work, an independence that enables them to read other writers and trust their own reactions and interpretations without the intervention of the teacher.

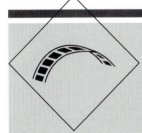

Teaching Activity 11–2   *Exploring Emily Dickinson*

Individual Work

Read four poems by Emily Dickinson.* Create three basic axioms about ideas important to and style characteristic of the poet.

1

"Hope" is the thing with feathers—
That perches in the soul—
And sings the tune without the words—
And never stops—at all—

And sweetest—in the Gale—is heard—
And sore must be the storm—
That could abash the little Bird
That kept so many warm—

I've heard it in the chillest land—
And on the strangest Sea—
Yet, never, in Extremity,
It asked a crumb—of me.

2

"Faith" is a fine invention
For Gentlemen who see—
But Microscopes are prudent
In an Emergency.

*Reprinted by permission of the publishers and the Trustees of Amherst College from *The Poems of Emily Dickinson*, Thomas H. Johnson, Ed., Cambridge, MA: The Belknap Press of Harvard University Press, Copyright © 1951, 1955, 1979, 1983 by the President and fellows of Harvard College.

3

Immortal is an ample word
When what we need is by
But when it leaves us for a time
'Tis a necessity.

Of Heaven above the firmest proof
We fundamental know
Except for its marauding Hand
It had been Heaven below.

4

I never saw a Moor—
I never saw the Sea—
Yet know I how the Heather looks
And what a Billow be.

I never spoke with God
Nor visited in Heaven—
Yet certain am I of the spot
As if the Checks were given

Small-group Work

Compare each member's generalizations and decide on a set of three to offer from the group to the whole class.

Whole-class Work

Discuss the groups' insights. Examine a fifth Dickinson poem,

5

Apparently with no surprise
To any happy Flower
The Frost beheads it at its play—
In accidental power—

The blonde Assassin passes on—
The Sun proceeds unmoved
To measure off another Day
For an Approving God.

Does this poem confirm or refute your generalizations?

Public Opinion.   Extending the boundaries of inquiry beyond classrooms and texts rouses students to those speech acts central to English instruction: thinking, talking, listening, and writing. It sends students out again, as in Chapters 2 and 8, to gather data as anthropologists and researchers. The generalizations made from these data engage students in questioning and ground the class in an added measure of reality. For instance, we ask students to survey the habits of their fellow students or to leave the confines of the school grounds to test the habits of adults. Students create a list of questions that pique their curiosity. Again, the best questions are those that are of genuine interest to students; for students who are passive and declare an absence of curiosity, the exercise is especially important. It reminds them of the possibility of questioning, a small rear-guard action in the continuous battle against passivity. Here are questions, for instance, of individual habits or taste.

- How many hours do you spend reading each week?
- How many personal letters do you write each week?
- What is your favorite TV commercial? Magazine ad? Billboard ad?
- What do you consider the best and worst comic strip?
- Who do you consider the most biased TV reporter or newspaper editorialist?

The experience of investigation calls on the individual qualities of sensitivity, tact, clarity, listening, fair-mindedness, and penetration, and on collaborative skills. The next step is to make some generalizations that rise out of the data and speculate as to why these seem to be true. Perhaps the final step, after the information has been gathered and the generalizations have been made, is for students to write about what they have come to believe.

Inquiry learning in the public domain is a challenge to traditional practice; it reminds us that the subject matter of English does not have to be limited to written texts or even to walled classrooms. Resources of natural inquiry lie outside school buildings. Students *can* leave the narrow confines of the classroom to locate fact and opinion in the lives of people and in the events surrounding school. This interaction with the open world is valuable in its challenge to students to attend to the actualities of their lives, rather than to accede to the "given." Asking students to question the social context in which they live invites them to think more carefully and critically and to test their capacities for individual interpretations of their worlds.

LEARNING CENTERS OR STATIONS

The idea of classroom learning centers or stations arose from the world of primary education and grew out of an interest in having students construct their own learning, at their own pace, in their own style. Learning centers or stations structure learning and make it more active and experiential. Sometimes they make learning more social and collaborative; at other times, they make it more personal and reflective. They also manage scarce materials and equipment (for instance, tape recorders, CD players, personal computers, and books) economically. Like group and individual work, learning centers promote independence by offering students their choice of subject, of learning approach, and of learning pace at a distance from the teacher. They also allow teachers to have one-on-one time with students.

Definition.   Debate over the exact name of this instructional strategy—learning stations or learning centers—brings us to its organization. Stations are commonly defined in the professional literature as being more permanent classroom fixtures than centers are. Thus, a classroom may have reading, writing, listening, talking, drama, art, and computer stations. In such stationary arrangements, a sign or banner typically hangs over the station to mark its boundaries and define its use. Teachers dispatch students to these stations in a variety of ways:

- Students may move freely to these stations when they have time, need, and interest
- Students sign up for scheduled times
- Students work at the stations as individuals or in groups

Centers represent places in the classroom marked out for work that is more temporary and specific to the present learning, such as projects that might last only a few days or a week. Typically, all students work concurrently at multiple centers.

Both permanent learning stations and temporary learning centers possess an immensely enticing energy for learners because they allow freedom of movement. Students may still meander listlessly through a classroom, but the movement alone usually prompts them to wake up and be more active. (At a time when a large and diverse population of students live in family structures that allow them to control a sizable portion of their daily lives, tight control over their movements in class feels all the more restrictive.) Secondary school environments are often highly structured and learning centers provide a chance to move freely and act independently. They are particularly welcome in schools that have 90-minute block scheduling.

We must match our expectations for these permanent stations or temporary centers to the physical constraints of most classrooms. A permanent reading station, for instance, may simply be a revolving paperback rack in a corner; a permanent art station may be a grouping of pictures run up the entire wall, a four-sided box mobile of pictures hung from the ceiling, and a collection of art and graphic books on a desk underneath. With increased funding for educational technology, word processors or computers represent an increasingly predictable classroom station for writing and research. Permanent stations might also demarcate locales for writing (in which there are folders, portfolios, writing materials, dictionaries, thesauruses, and grammar handbooks) and for reading (in which there are folders, books, dust jackets, bookmarks, author pictures, and author biographies). A temporary center for a week-long study of Hispanic American Literature may be in boxes in the corner that are hastily reconfigured on desks between classes of freshmen and junior English. The reality, especially for young teachers, may be even more severe. If you do not have your own permanent classroom, centers may have to be flexible, mobile, and pushed on a cart.

Organization.   Organizing multiple temporary centers is a taxing challenge. Decisions regarding the learning activities at each center require the same calibration that we use in balancing the needs of the students and the subject. Those decisions will be influenced by other strategic choices that you make.

Student Choice	The teacher structures the array of centers, but inside that scheme, students elect the order of their work and the centers that interest them most. Typically, students select a designated number of centers and omit the ones that least appeal to them. (Certain key centers can be designated as necessary for everyone to experience.)
Station Variety	The teacher, recognizing the diversity of student interest, style, and ability, constructs centers to provide a range of content and learning processes. These centers should be creative and unpredictable. A good benchmark for

the development of centers is to have a mixture of the four language modes—speaking, listening, writing, and reading—and of the learning styles of multiple intelligences.

Interaction   The teacher must choose whether students can choose to work in pairs, in small groups, or individually. Some centers should be designed to make interaction with another necessary.

Once these basic decisions are made, the teacher has to construct cards or posters that define the learning expected at each center. These instructions must be especially clear and articulate so that students can be self-sufficient and purposive. They can be printed on posters or cards, programmed into a computer, or recorded on a video- or audiotape, but they must be designed to set the students on a specific course of action. The teacher must be clear about the outcome of each center as well. Students must understand what they are expected to know by the end. The kind of evaluation for the centers also needs to be articulated clearly. Will it be self-evaluation, peer evaluation, or cumulative? And how will students record their progress—through written records, check sheets, or maps, and will these be stored in writing folders or turned in to the teacher? When all of these decisions are made, teachers must assemble the materials (books, magazines, newspapers, paper, pens, folders, technical equipment, and supplies) necessary for their implementation.

Example of Learning Stations.   Imagining the physical arrangement of a classroom into stations will be difficult for those who have never experienced stations, but for them such a visualization is especially important. Secondary classrooms are not commonly arranged with stations, so we have few models to help us envision this as a realistic alternative. Also, stations require ambitious organization and a sturdy tolerance of confusion. In other words, attempts to set up stations meet with resistances. As a consequence, working in conjunction with other teachers is especially helpful.

Here is an example of stations used in a class's brief study of biography: One station invited students to explore biography through rock music, listening to the Beatles' "Eleanor Rigby," for instance; another to write descriptions of a selected portrait from a folder of art and magazine photographs; another to interview an American Association of Retired Persons (AARP) member; and another to respond to a reading of one of three selected passages of autobiography. We present concrete and elaborate examples of three sample learning centers in Appendix F: one textual, the exploration of a literary text (usually a novel or a set of works by a single writer, in this case Mark Twain's *The Adventures of Huckleberry Finn*); and two topical, the investigation of the topics of utopias and family.

Invitation to Reflection 11–6

- Do you remember learning stations or centers in your school career? If so, are these memories from elementary, middle, or secondary school classrooms?
- Have you ever had a college or university class that was taught in this way?
- If you experienced them in elementary school, was a teacher present at the work site? If so, was your experience of a reading group or math group?
- Draw a classroom with four walls and a door. Imagine the luxury of arranging a classroom of learning stations that can be devoted to one class of students. Select a general focus, think about possible activities, draw the stations and their furnishings, and label each with a title. In a legend, you might enumerate the materials you will need. Remember to draw in the constants of a room: a file for folders, dictionaries and books, a teacher's desk, and perhaps a master wall chart of learning stations and student names.

COMPUTERS AND ENGLISH

Instructional technology took the early form of the teaching machine and audiocassette tutorials. The computer has so increased the instructional possibilities of technology that those two now look like biplanes compared to today's supersonic jets. Computers are only tools, but they are very powerful tools that have completely captured the American imagination. We should neither overlook nor overstate their possibility in the classroom. We must nevertheless understand what Monroe (1993) has noted about their limits: "A computer is an information processor dependent on the user's ability to put information into it and then transfer that information in a meaningful way" (p. 3). The electronic cutting edge is awash with sizzling computer uses that we should understand in terms of those limitations.

CUTTING EDGE

New worlds are unfolding very quickly. Some of the offerings are merely bells and whistles that cost great sums of money. Others truly provide something we can find nowhere else, and many of these are congruent with a constructivist kind of learning rather than a more traditional presentational approach. Some of the visions of electronic English that Jody and Saccardi (1996) offer can tantalize us:

- distance learning, with an instructor teaching students at multiple sites via two-way video and audio;
- online research that accesses the best of libraries and news sources everywhere;
- home/school communication that allows home tutoring and homework hotlines, and encourages parent involvement;
- video teleconferences that link students in town meetings by video, telephone, and fax;
- collaborative learning projects where students from different cultures create joint projects or learn foreign languages from each other by two-way video;
- video field trips via live television to places as remote as outer space and under the sea; and
- interactive television shows, like quiz programs, that can involve viewers in the action.

Hypertext novels are another intriguing new development: "Reading hypertext fiction is an associative process, unlike the linear act of reading a conventional text, in which the reader processes pages sequentially. Instead, the reader selects unnumbered hypertext 'pages' on the screen, sometimes randomly, sometimes by choosing one pathway or another, or by selecting from options within the text. Each 'reading' differs from a previous sequencing of blocks of text" (Jody & Saccardi, p. 69). Robert Coover (1993), a hypertext kind of novelist before his time, speaks of Stuart Moulthrop's *Victory Garden* as a kind of desultory travel: "the reader moves about in the story as though trying to remember it, the narrative having lost its temporality by slipping whole into the past, becoming there a kind of obscure geography to be explored" (p. 10). These nonlinear electronic books are even more elastic than were the original children's books whose paper text could be read in any sequence one pleased. And, over time, the electronic version will become less expensive.

Project Gutenberg is another way in which books' special qualities are preserved while the benefits of the electronic revolution are exploited. The Gutenberg Project began in 1971 at the University of Illinois when Michael Hart was given 100 million dollars to collect the great books of our civilization as electronic texts (e-books). (The U.S. Constitution and Shakespeare's works were some of the first to be inscribed.) The project's plan was to have over 100 million users by 2001. Electronic books are now available that are lightweight and look like old-fashioned books. When they are opened, a screenlike page is revealed that seems to turn just like an ordinary page. The advantage is multiple texts in one light computer. One e-book held in the hand is the equivalent of carrying a shelf of 20 or more books. We have worked on a personalized English anthology that will include only those texts that English departments select for their classes. A simple next step is the purchase of e-texts that not only are packaged to fit one teacher's course requirements, but also could easily be revised into new arrangements.

Holden (1994) offers a word of caution about this jump into e-texts: "The printing press gave us something far more valuable than information. It gave us reading. Slow, quiet, introspective, character-building reading. The DEM (digital electronic media) has made information available on the 'information highway' at nearly the speed of light, which can certainly enhance our knowledge; but maybe we should rebuild some back roads" (p. 70).

We await the common presence of these electronic possibilities in English classrooms, but even now there is much we can do with computers. Technology continues to change so rapidly that lists of computer resources that are at the cutting edge of today's instruction will be replaced by the time this book arrives in bookstores. Thus, we explain the two primary uses of the computer in the English classroom, as tutor and tool, and use only a few examples of today's software programs to illustrate those uses.

COMPUTERS AS TUTORS: COMPUTER-ASSISTED INSTRUCTION

Computer-assisted instruction (CAI) enhances student learning through programs that act as prompts for drill and practice, tutoring, and simulation.

Drill and Practice.   Lucking and Stallard (1988), CAI advocates, admit that drill-and-practice software dominates the market (p. 70). They list over 100 software sources for grammar learning and reinforcement—noun-verb agreement, pronoun referents, verb tenses, and misplaced modifiers. They characterize many of these as "essentially electronic workbooks" (p. 60). But sometimes this sort of intensive, focused, student-specific instruction is needed. Most English educators believe that nonstandard usage is best addressed as it surfaces in student writing, but some students can benefit from direct instruction, and computers can provide that assistance. We offer a brief list of software programs in English for this form of direct instruction:

Grammar Mechanics	Mindscapes, Inc.	1988
Sensible Grammar	Sensible Solutions	1989
Author, Author	Methods and Solutions	1990
Grammar Games	Davidson	1995

Tutoring.   Schwartz and Vockell (1988) differentiate tutorials from this first level of CAI software in that tutorials provide more than drills; they offer students full explanations of the governing rules, examples of convention departures, and then a chance to apply these new concepts. Tutorial software has complex programs that offer further explanation and a second chance for application when students need additional help. They offer feedback and multiple branches of instruction to meet students' individual capacities. A few recent ones seem effective for writing:

Student Writing Center	Learning Company	1994
Multimedia Workshop	Davidson	1995
Storybook Weaver Deluxe	MEEC	1996
Creativity Center	Learning Company	1996

A highly sophisticated CAI that acts as a tutor and broadens possibilities for literature study is interactive video (requiring a VCR, a monitor, a computer, and a laser disc). *Labyrinth,* for example, gives students information about *Macbeth.* They can see the text of the opening scene of the play and then the Orson Wells and Ralph Richardson versions and compare the interpretations of the two directors. The computer also can locate all of the scenes in which Macbeth speaks after having been with Lady Macbeth, for example, or those in which clothes are mentioned, or those in which the word *heir* is mentioned. The computer program leads students into the work and prompts them to make discoveries that even mature scholars are unable to make intuitively or through painstaking reading and rereading of the play. Columbia University Press recently released a *Macbeth* and a *Romeo and Juliet* laser disk that present multiple performances of key scenes, commentary on various scenes by the actors, a brief visual synopsis of the play's five acts, paraphrases and glosses on archaic terms, videotapes of settings in Scotland and Italy, and background material on boys in girls' roles in Shakespeare. (These treasures are presently available for Windows and Macintosh.) Coronet's laser disk of *Macbeth, Julius Caesar, Romeo and Juliet* and *Hamlet* have high-quality visuals (others are somewhat jerky and have low resolution) and explications of some scenes in these plays that are richer and treat the themes of the play with greater depth than most do.

Simulation.   The imaginative interaction of simulations may make them the most effective form of CAI. These programs set up a context in which to operate. An example drawn from science illustrates the setup: *Operation: Frog* (Scholastic) simulates a zoology lab and leads students through a step-by-step decision-making dissection of a frog. English simulations involve the language acts of writing, reading, and speaking. The object of *Grammar Examiner* (Design Ware), for instance, is to move from the rank of cub reporter to editor-in-chief. It has an additional touch of reality in that it can work with canned or real student writing. *Grammar Quest* (Scott, Foresman) and *Secret Language* (Scott, Foresman) are simulations that focus on parts of speech and are adaptable to specific grade levels. (Some simulations place too high a premium on speed as a part of the competition and, in so doing, diminish the quality of instruction.)

Powerful Attributes.   Computer-assisted instruction has several distinct and powerful instructional characteristics. It is self-contained and sets the student free from the teacher into a self-sufficient world. The student may have procedural questions for the teacher about operating the computer, but even those can be answered by a more knowledgeable partner. Conventional instruction gives a limited amount of time for a project and often asks all students to perform the same task at the same time. CAI allows students to proceed at their own pace and master the material before moving to the next task. Learning speeds vary. With programmed instruction, slower learners do not proceed at the faster pace to keep everyone together, and speedy learners do not need to lag behind for those who are slower. All can move at their appropriate speeds and neither extreme is frustrated. CAI also provides the opportunity for incremental learning. Discrete bits of information are learned; complex ideas are reduced to manageable steps that students can learn at their own rate. One of CAI's most powerful advantages is that it provides immediate and continuous feedback to the learner. With this facility, the learner is able to know immediately whether or not the answer is correct. Often, the program will allow the student to move on to new material when a high percentage of the answers in a segment is correct. If the percentage is not high enough, some programs review the concepts to be learned in different language with new examples. The advantage of these characteristics are apparent:

- The individual needs of each learner are targeted and addressed.
- Students become self-directing and self-paced in their learning.
- Competition among students diminishes.
- Cooperative learning occurs as students tutor and assist each other.
- Teachers are released from skills and drills exercises and freed for conferences with students.
- The teacher role becomes one of encourager and facilitator, not evaluator and judge.
- Many programs provide effective enticement and motivation for work that might otherwise be considered dull.

Evaluation.   Despite these advantages, the use of computers in English instruction has strong critics. They believe that CAI is too mechanized, too unresponsive to the student who sits before the machine, too reductive of the higher cognitive levels of synthesis and evaluation, and too compromising of the teacher's role as more than a manager of electronics. You will need to determine for yourself whether the benefits outweigh the risks. If you have the resources, Dunfey (1989) recommends criteria that English teachers should use to evaluate what software works best:

- Is the program interesting to you?
- Does the thinking that the program requires seem worthwhile?
- Is the emphasis on thinking rather than on repetitive practice?
- Does the program involve two or more students at a time?
- Does the program introduce an activity or thought that is different from that provided by books or paper and pencil?
- Does the program allow the user to customize material?
- Can the program be used many times by a student and remain interesting and worthwhile?
- Does the program allow time for reflection?
- Does satisfaction in using the program come from the content itself? (p. 21)

COMPUTERS AS TOOLS: COMPUTER-MANAGED INSTRUCTION

Computer-managed instruction helps teachers with the management of learning assistance for the following three major instructional concerns.

- Word-processing: to help at all levels of the writing process: prewriting, writing, and rewriting
- Databases: to store compositions, lists, ideas, research, teacher evaluation, teacher comments, syllabi, study guidelines, and group assignments
- Networking: to connect with other individuals and institutions over shared inquiry and materials (print and multimedia)

Word Processing.   Word processing provides a tool to help students move through all stages of the writing process. As writers compose, word processors allow them to free-write comfortably and then revise, organize, and edit these ideas easily. If organization takes shape in the act of composing, the writer can easily shift sentences as well as paragraphs. In nonelectronic writing, the student's attempt to correct all of the surface errors can be so arduous that this becomes the focus of the revision process. With a word processor, students have access to spelling, grammar, and style checkers and they are freer to undertake deep-structure revision. Sentences can be revised, and paragraphs can be rearranged. Even a new vision of the topic can be developed without as much pain as with paper and pen. Students can print their hard copies, edit them a final time using spelling and usage checkers, get a word count, and immediately make revisions. The finished look that many printers produce is a further spur to composition.

Beals (1998) evaluated the impact on student writing of *Editor,* a program designed by the Modern Language Association, that he considered "the most sophisticated grammar and style checker available to students and scholars" (p. 67). Its creators, Elaine and John Thiesmeyer, claim that it is the "electronic descendant" of Strunk and White's *Elements of Style.* They are clear about its scope: "Neither *Editor* nor any other computer program can help significantly with weaknesses in a text stemming from poor ideas. Ideas, coherence, logic, argumentative strategy—these are the bone and muscle of good writing. . . . *Editor's* business is writing's flesh—vocabulary, usage, mechanics, style" (Thiesmeyer & Thiesmeyer, 1990, p. 11). Beals agrees that *Editor* can address problems with surface structure, but that it has a basic limitation: "its inability to improve the deep structure below the surface structure" (p. 68). He acknowledges that its identification of structural problems and a student's correction of such errors "can make a significant improvement in the quality of the piece" (p. 68), but it cannot substitute for teacher interaction with student writers—"both nurturing and critiquing—throughout the writing process" (p. 72).

Word processors can be tools for writing in other ways as well. They aid writing because they tend to quell impulsiveness, an enemy of good writing generally and rewriting particularly (Milner & Richman, 1983). Revision also can be encouraged by putting student writing on the lab network, a PC viewer, or overhead projector so that students can suggest changes. Students learn that even for the best writers, revision is necessary, doable, and effective.

Composing Process Software.   In addition to word processors, students can use composing process software as a tool for writing. Composing software helps students work on various writing tasks: organization, development, coherence, and other matters more sophisticated than meeting the conventions of spelling, punctuation, and usage. *Right Writer* (Decision Ware, Inc.) is a good example of this kind of software. During rewriting, it can help develop rhetorical power through its capacity to proofread and even analyze style. It can search out passive voice construction, colloquial language, ambiguous phrases, misused subordinate clauses, and other sophisticated matters of rhetoric. It can even analyze a piece of writing in terms of jargon, strength, description, and readability indexes (Lucking & Stallard, 1988, p. 65). Other software, such as *Grammatik* (Want Electronic Publishing) and *Ghost Writer* (MEEC), are somewhat less sophisticated but provide revision or proofreading aids.

Other programs help writers at the prewriting stage to become more creative. *Writer's Helper* (Conduit) offers ways to develop new ideas and gather up insights for writing. It uses "crazy contrasts," "trees" (associations), and "three ways of seeing" (multiple perspectives) as aids to discovery for students. Lucking and Stallard (1988) observe that because *Writer's Helper* and other software programs of this kind "require students to think about their chosen topic either in a very linear fashion or, in some cases, in very creative ways . . . they assume some of the responsibilities teachers of writing always have and they do so by requiring a response from each individual student" (p. 62). *Quill* (D. C. Heath) even moves students from prewriting to drafting to revision. Lucking and Stallard believe that these new kinds of "composition software" will likely change how youngsters view the purpose and value of writing. A further step in this same direction, *Fiction Writing* (The Software Teacher) helps students get plots moving, prompts them to develop characters, and shows them when they need to subordinate lesser incidents in a piece of writing.

Klem and Moran (1991) offer a careful review of the research on computer-assisted writing. In their survey, they focused on five basic composing areas. In each of the five they found a glimmer of hope, but in four of these areas of investigation they concluded that the results were either neutral or problematic. We distill the findings in these four areas of computer-assisted writing:

Revision	"Student writers did less revising on screen than they would have on paper" (p. 135).
Planning	Writers do not get a global view that is helpful; it "draws the writer's attention to the 'planning' of smaller units of the text" (p. 137).
Invention	It produces "no difference either in the quality of the writing or the quantity of ideas" (p. 139).
Proofreading	The three best programs for textual analysis are in agreement with the suggestions of teachers only between 2% and 6% of the time (p. 141), and the results are "more likely to confuse than to help" (p. 141).

Because computer capabilities and applications change rapidly, Moran's current regard for his earlier research is important. Moran (personal communication, 1997) believes that these findings haven't changed as much as has the larger question surrounding computers: access. He sees a gulf widening between students who have $3,000 "pencils" at their disposal and those who have only the 5¢ variety in hand.

Databases.   Students can create their own individual computer files of ideas, resources, journals, writing projects, grades, tests, and reading interest inventories. They can also pool databases with students in the same or other classes. This information can then be reorganized and retrieved for a variety of purposes.

Networking.   Networks are arising from many sources and have the power to connect students with a wealth of personal and material resources. Klem and Moran's research on their fifth topic, networking, is much more optimistic. Networking, they argue, creates an opportunity for positive collaboration and produces a redistribution of power, one tilting toward the student. They find e-mail "intrinsically motivating," (p. 142) in that it promotes more risk taking than face-to-face communication does (p. 142). Some English teachers believe that the Internet offers the best resources for their own growth in English. They regard networking for either pedagogical or discipline knowledge as the best way to reach quickly and widely for knowledge. The Internet is a vast, electronic terrain that can yield both amazing treasures and very pedestrian dross. The search can be frustrating because unassisted surfing can lead to endless dead ends and finds that seem auspicious at first but eventually yield little or nothing. Search engines are the answer here. *Yahoo, Magellan, Excite, AltaVista, Internet Sleuth, InfoSeek Guide, Explorer,* and *Webcrawler*—just to name a few—are amazing time savers. You can use these to type in key words or phrases that the search engine will use to scan the Internet for all of the Websites that match your interest. All of the search engines just mentioned are effective; you may prefer one that is more or less inclusive, one that sorts one way or another, or one that is either more sophisticated or more user friendly. Excellent Websites for teachers such as the following can be found without search engines:

Library of Congress: www.loc.gove
National Museum of American Art: www.lamaa.sl.edu
William Faulkner in Oxford: www.mcsr.olemiss.edu
NCTE: www.ncte.com
Project Guttenberg: www.promo.net/pg/
Classroom Connect: www.classroom.net
Bethany Guide to John Keats: www.fufu.edu

Some of these addresses may change, but most remain stable and will help you find rich repositories of information.

In a 1997 *English Journal* article, Knowles (1997) lists many other Internet resources for the English teacher. For instance, she explains how to gain access to Web pages for authors such as Jane Austen, Emily Dickinson, T. S. Eliot, Nathaniel Hawthorne, Seamus Heaney, Franz Kafka, William Shakespeare, and Virginia Woolf. She enumerates specific subject addresses where the teacher can locate, for instance, a selection of syllabi for African-American literature, an archive of women authors' writing, and another of literature about the environment. The Camelot Project is an example of the rich resources available. Sponsored by the University of Rochester, it has a database of Arthurian texts, bibliographies, images, and links to other medieval texts. Knowles also includes a short bibliography of books that might be useful for the English teacher, such as Harley Hahn's and Rick Stout's *The Internet Complete Reference* (1996, Berkeley, CA: Osborne, McGraw-Hill) and Elizabeth Miller's *The Internet Resource Directory for K-12 Teachers and Librarians, 1995/1996* (1994, Englewood, CO: Libraries Unlimited).

Michelle Utley, a computer-nimble young teacher, reports that she was able to find information about the Harlem Renaissance on the Internet that allowed her to teach a unit on African-American writers that would have been impossible otherwise. For Zora Neale Hurston and Langston Hughes, she found a trove of bibliographic information, edited texts, literary history, teaching ideas, and art and sculpture related to these noted artists. She also utilized electronic media to let groups design a Web page as a tribute to an author, design a multimedia project using a program similar to Power Point, use networking to affect better peer editing, and use the Internet to communicate with other classes around the world.

Teachers typically have better access to the Internet, word processors, and tools for multimedia presentations than they do to up-to-date computer programs for language arts. In addition, when they do have a chance to book the computer lab, it is usually for only 1 or 2 days, so the time pressure is too great for sustained work. Statistics show that the ratio of students to computers in U.S. schools fell from 92 students per computer in 1983–84 to 7 students per computer in 1996–97, but that number is still too large for serious sustained work with a full class. The drop from 92 to 12 in 1992–93 was remarkable, but in the following 5 years the number of students per computer dropped only from 12 to 7. We seem to have hit a ceiling beyond which huge expenditures will be needed to move to ratios that are truly productive (Education Hotline, 1997).

Many computer-specific periodicals and resource books update software continually. The *English Journal* has a column that regularly reviews new programs and computer strategies. We have found Lucking and Stallard's (1988) list of 100 software companies (pp. 181–189) and Schwartz and Vokell's (1988) list of software for English (pp. 228–238) to be very helpful sources. More recently, books by Hawisher and Selfe (1991), Monroe (1993), and Jody and Saccardi (1996) offer both resources and teaching strategies. Busy English teachers have the same limitations for covering the field of software as they do for covering the field of literature. Once you have located what is available and previewed possible choices, criteria for selection such as those provided by Dunfey (1989) can guide you. Madden (1989) has his own philosophical and pragmatic criteria, which also provide a fine guide for selection of programs:

- They are easy to operate.
- They encourage personal response and reflection.
- They require writing.
- They allow students to revise their responses.
- They emphasize process before product.
- They are consistent with the philosophy and objectives stressed in the classroom.
- They allow students to print a hard copy of their work or save their work as a test file for transfer to a word processing program. (pp. 231–232)

WISE APPLICATIONS

Monroe (1995) believes in computers but he also believes that technology must serve the English curriculum. He affirms, for example, Stephen Marcus's simple approach to drafting that is possible only with computers. Marcus asks students to turn down the contrast control on the monitor and begin "invisible writing." Because students have no way to correct the surface errors, they continue to write at or near the pace of their minds. Monroe cites Wresch's *The English Classrooms in the Computer Age: Thirty Lesson Plans* (1991)—the volume in which Marcus's idea appears—as a source for powerful and unique uses of computers in the English classroom. Monroe's book, too, is full of ideas for new ways of composing with computers. "Electric Read-Around" involves students writing in a computer lab. One student writes, then moves over three stations, and another student takes a seat at the vacated computer. That student reads the first student's text for 5 or 10 minutes and enters comments in a different font right on the screen. The process continues through four or more 10-minute cycles until the original writer returns to the computer to find a set of honest and detailed comments on his or her text. Monroe also shows the power of computers to teach students to use difficult constructions such as appositives. Students change the font on identified appositive phrases to boldface in a set of five sentences and afterwards imitate the model by constructing five additional sentences containing appositives (pp. 16–18).

Monroe offers two other simple but effective ways that students can use computers to write well. A Writing Wall gives students' writing a wider audience and more varied critical responses. Students print out their best writing and place it on a dedicated wall where other students are able to read it and respond. Monroe's response sheet poses two requests that provoke simple responses that are left for each writer:

1. What do you consider the one particular strength of this piece? Be specific, and use examples to support what you say.
2. Recopy one sentence you find especially well written. (p. 24)

Everyone who completes the response sheet is given credit, so good grades as well as good will produce responses. A word processor is not necessary for this lesson, but it makes the display more standardized and readable and makes any necessary rewriting easier.

Split-screen imitations is another computer use Monroe finds effective. He urges students to imitate a brief passage or a few lines from a fine writer. His assignment is explicit:

Each student chooses one passage from a selection of three or four passages. The assignment is to create an almost literal imitation of the original passage. If you insert hard returns between the sentences in the lesson file, then students can enter their work between the lines of the original passage in a different typeface, deleting the original text when they are finished. (p. 24)

Monroe finds that this process helps students develop a sense and use of stylistic elements such as "rhythm, assonance, complexities of syntax, or imagery" (p. 24). He argues that it is "one of the best ways for students to get a feel for how diction, organization or dialect affect a writer's communication purpose."

SEISMIC QUALMS

In spite of the problems of access, we see computers in great numbers in our schools. We know that they are often misused, purchased with a top-down mentality, and provided without the training to make application wiser. Viadero (1997) reports that only 3% of the nation's schools integrate computers into all aspects of their educational programs. Only 12% were placed in the high-tech, or wise users, category. Even where the technology is lushest, 57% of eighth-grade math students, who should be wise users, never or almost never use computers at school to learn. Only about 12% of these students report using computers daily (Edwards, 1997). In *Release 2.0,* Dyson (1997) argues that economies of scale make computers powerful tools for business and industry but not for schools, where the work is mind-to-mind and does not gain efficiency when it is scaled up. Milder qualms have been expressed by Viadero (1997), who opposes "massive investments in educational technology" (p. 6): *Quality Education Data* reports that U.S. schools spent 5.2 billion dollars on technology in 1997. According to Viadero (1997), researchers acknowledge that even with this outlay of funding, the way students and teachers use computers is often rudimentary, and significant gains in student achievement have not materialized.

OVERRIDING HOPES

Wiske (1997) believes that this misuse of funds can be reversed if educational leaders "put the education piece first." She further believes that "they have to figure out how to use technology in the face of a well-conceived education agenda" (p. 3). Thoughtful studies such as the extended piece by Hannafin and Land (1997) argue that technology will in fact breed reform, that computers and other electronic media have a way of disrupting traditional teaching, empowering students and decentering knowledge: "They afford opportunities to seek rather than comply, to experiment rather than to accept, to evaluate rather than to accumulate, and to interpret rather than to adopt" (p. 175). We have witnessed computer applications and interactive classes with the Globe Theater in London that produced a heightened concern for the context of Shakespeare plays, rather than engagement with the text itself. The examination of Edmund Hall's histories of the costumes of the Old Globe preoccupied the students because that was the focus of the teacher. We know of other classes in which constructivist principles are honored, but they can be subverted by misapplication of the computer.

GUIDELINES FOR GOOD USE

Whatever we find on this visionary electronic landscape must be evaluated with the critical test: What is its value as a tool to learn? Here are some simple rules that Wiske (1997) suggests we use in such an evaluation:

1. **Don't expect change overnight.** Technology does not have a magical ability to turn things around overnight. Instead, plan for the long haul.
2. **Start Small.** Keeping the focus on specific learning needs, such as middle schoolers' writing skills or early literacy programs, is essential.
2. **Pay attention to equity.** Students attending schools with a high number of poor and minority students have less access to Internet connections, multimedia computers, CD-ROMs, videodisc technology, computer networks, and satellite technology than those attending other schools.
4. **Make teacher needs a top priority.** School administrators need to pay attention to the barriers that can prevent teachers from using technology effectively. If a teacher has to compete with students for computer time, for example, he or she is less likely to make technology part of their everyday plans. (p. 3)

As English teachers work with computers more, the bulk of the pure gimmicks and misapplied actions will be replaced by more thoughtful and more inventive ways to use these electronic tools. Harrington-Lueker (1997) sees a natural progression that evolves toward best practice.

An entry stage, in which teachers struggled to master the nuts and bolts of using computers

An adoption stage, in which teachers began using computer-based activities daily, but primarily for drill and practice

An adaptation stage, in which teachers typically used computers as a way to increase student productivity (students could write better and faster using a word processor than they could by hand, for example)

An appropriation stage, in which teachers abandoned their effort to simply computerize traditional practices

An invention stage, where teachers began experimenting with new instructional patterns, such as interdisciplinary and project-based instruction or team teaching (p. 4)

We can muster hope, too, by looking at the results of the U.S. Office of Technology Assessment report on the basic use of technology in teaching from 1982 to 1994 (Table 11-4). The years have brought slow yet steady progress. The same government document reports on both the potential and the barriers of technology use in our classrooms (Figure 11-9). The barriers are not insignificant, but the great potential urges us to find ways to remove them.

TABLE 11–4
Instructional use of computers, 1982–1994

Year	Teachers Were Told To:	Rationale
1982	Teach students to program in BASIC.	It's the language that comes with your computer.
1984	Teach students to program in LOGO.	Teach students to think, not just program.
1986	Teach with integrated drill-and-practice systems.	Individualize instruction and increase test scores.
1988	Teach word processing.	Use computers as tools like adults do.
1990	Teach with curriculum-specific tools (e.g., history databases, science simulators, data probes).	Integrate the computers with the existing curriculum.
1992	Teach multimedia hypertext programming.	Change the curriculum—students learn best by creating products for an audience.
1994	Teach with Internet telecommunications.	Let students be part of the real world.

FIGURE 11–9
Technology in the classroom: The potential and the barriers

THE POTENTIAL	THE BARRIERS
Changing teaching and learning.	Lack of teacher time to experiment with new technologies, share experiences, plan lessons using technology, and attend technology courses or meetings.
Assisting with daily tasks, including preparing lesson plans, tracking student progress, and communicating with parents and colleagues.	Access to equipment.
Enhancing professional development, including use of on-line resources for informal educational opportunities.	Vision or rationale for technology use. Current assessment practices: Standardized tests may not reflect what students learn with technology, and teachers are held immediately accountable for changes that take time to show results.
Preparing new teachers.	

Perhaps the most encouraging hope for computers comes from a learning-styles expert's comments about their forerunners. Sternberg (1997) believes that calculators and word processors have changed what intelligence is because they have refined the conceptual and problem-solving abilities necessary to operate them. The *English Journal* provides us with a cartoon that sums up the issue in enigmatic fashion: A room is full of monkeys at their keyboards with *zzz*'s and other scribbling on their monitors, but the foreground composer has his hand poised on the keyboard and his monitor reads:

That = question
To be or not to be that is the ques

PLANNING INSTRUCTION

Provoking, challenging, and engaging activities are what students remember about good teachers. What students may not know consciously, but do know intuitively, is that a master teacher welds these activities into a thoughtful sequence of instruction, one that makes the interesting pieces all the more powerful as they work together. Research has shown that teachers who develop long-range plans are those seen as most able by their students (Zimpher, 1988).

For you to put these four basic approaches to their best use, you need to consider ideas about planning. Teachers are regularly engaged in four basic types: yearly, unit, weekly, and daily planning. (Occasionally, they also are asked to deliberate over school- or systemwide curriculum planning, but this is rare for young teachers.) Each type of planning is important for effective instruction, and each needs to be worked out within the context of your own abilities, your students' needs, and your sense of how learning best occurs. Owen (1991) likens teaching to composing and sees planning as "similar to pre-writing, the stage of the writing process which precedes the first draft" (p. 57). She sees the planning process as "a rehearsal in which the teacher prepares for teaching," as Murray (1980) says, "in the mind and on the page" (p. 62). Every teaching day compels this sort of rehearsal, but Clark and Yinger (1979) report that many teachers identify their most important planning as unit planning. Because unit plans contain implications for weekly planning, and weekly for daily—as Morine-Dershimer (1990) calls them, a "nesting" of one inside another— we will begin with unit planning.

Unit Planning

Teachers commonly define a unit as a series of lessons or experiences related to one central topic. Its length varies, but units are seldom less than two weeks or more than nine. High school English classes are usually organized around units of literature or language. Some school systems, schools, and teachers even divide the year neatly so that one semester is devoted to literature and the other to language. Very often, writing instruction and literary study are integrated. Literature serves as a prompt for writing; writing serves to teach and evaluate literature.

Focused on Integrated Units

Both literary study and writing instruction lend themselves to one of two kinds of organization: integrated, in which the two mesh and reinforce each other, or focused, in which literature is central for a period and then writing instruction assumes prominence. We have seen and experienced difficulties in the focused approach. Of course, when teaching is text centered, teachers do have the advantage of moving crisply from one text to another. Units are clearly distinguished from each other. As one "subject" area is mastered, say the theme of Human Hopes and Dreams, the class moves to the next, Composing the Paragraph. The organization is simplified and students are focused. Tests and evaluation are concentrated and the measures of achievement are precise and straightforward. The problem we see in such focus is that each unit suffers from not being approached by the full power of all four language arts.

This book has offered specific strategies and general approaches to teaching English that move back and forth among the four language arts: reading, writing, talking, and listening. Integration, being key to our instructional strategies, is basic to our organizational strategies as well. We have continuously suggested the advantage of variety and diversity of strategies and approaches, and the integrated approach provides just that. We have repeatedly proposed that instruction address the multiple intelligences and learning styles of students, and an integrated approach has a chance of meeting those student differences. We also have placed the student at the center of our planning—not the text, or the curriculum guideline, or even the teacher. The integrated approach offers more possibilities to focus on students and to plan the curriculum around them. Even if book and material shortages circumscribe planning and make focusing on literature or language in turn imperative, teachers can integrate instruction in every day's learning.

A primary decision for your unit planning is choosing which of four current planning models to follow: content-based, objectives-based, process-based, and what we will call conversation-based models. (These also influence daily planning.) The first is the most common in the practice of teachers, the second is the most popular in the minds of many educators, and the third and fourth are the newest and the truest to a student-centered curriculum. Taylor's research (1970) found that experienced teachers seldom plan according to the curriculum expert's models of good procedure. Morine-Dershimer (1990) elaborates: "Rather than beginning by stating instructional objectives, and then selecting and organizing instructional activities to meet those objectives . . . secondary teachers focus almost exclusively on content and preparation of an interesting presentation" (pp. 27-28). We will focus first, then, on unit planning based on content.

Content-Based Model

Goodlad and his colleagues (1984) found that in the American high schools they visited, English/language arts "formed the backbone of the curriculum" and "occupied more . . . teachers at the secondary level (combining both junior and senior high schools) than any other subject" (pp. 204-205). More specifically, "in English, there was still a substantial emphasis on the basics of grammar and composition—punctuation, capitalization, sentence structure, paragraph organization, word analysis, parts of speech. . . . The most commonly offered courses in English at the high school level were those combining mechanics with some literature, courses only in literature, and courses in grammar and composition—in that order. These formed the core of the required English in our high schools. Beyond this core were electives in journalism, speech, and creative writing" (p. 205). Applebee's (1993) study broke down the time allocation to different components of representative public school English classes: literature, 48.3%; writing, 26.8%; language, 15.4%; speech, 6.9%; and other, 3.2% (p. 35). Because of the interrelated activities in speech, writing, language, and literature, another survey question yielded a higher estimate of literature-related class work, 78.3%.

Literature. Whether you will be working with a curriculum in which literature predominates or is integrated with language instruction, its study often revolves around divisions set by textbooks. Consequently, a look at the literature programs of six major textbooks can ground planning in actual practice. Applebee's (1993) survey found that the most typical course of study is organized around genres in grades 7–10, American literature in grade 11, and British literature in grade 12. World literature is increasingly being offered at either grade 10 or 12. Particularly in poor districts and schools, these textbooks comprise all the literature that will be taught. Whatever the organizing principle of these books—genre, theme, or chronology of national literatures—each has advantages and disadvantages.

Genre. Genre study splits the year into units of poetry, drama, fiction (short stories and novels), and occasionally nonfiction, usually biography or essays. Often, within these general categories, stories are arranged by elements of fiction or poetry, such as plot, character, point of view, imagery, or figures of speech. Many states have begun standardized tests of just this literary terminology and so have given a rationale for a genre approach. This organizational arrangement directs attention to form and the more aesthetic dimensions of literature, which is poor timing in the developmental progress of students. The arrangement by elements also further distances literature as whole works and carries the false implication that particular works have one element primarily or only and that by knowing the element, we have read the work. Moffet has a kinder word for this organization. He advises us that if we must teach something in an anthology, we should teach genre. It is the freest of teacher dogma and prejudice. The lesson can't suddenly jump into history, nor into a thematic ax to grind.

Theme. Thematic organization of the curriculum has had periods of both acceptance and disrepute. Major texts for a time were providing alternative tables of contents so that teachers who wanted to approach the text thematically could have a ready-made guide. Thematic study gains favor with those who want to relate literature to the lives of their students, or to explore compelling ideas, or to instill the best ideas in a culture, or to use literature as cautionary tales. Thematic study was a stronger phenomenon in the 1960s and 1970s than it was in the 1980s and 1990s. (Perhaps the back-to-basics movement discouraged it.) Fewer textbooks are arranged by thematic content these days. But some signs of regeneration of interest in theme or topic are appearing in the trend toward integration or whole language in the elementary grades. Teachers in American elementary schools who work by topics or themes (an established tradition in British and New Zealand schools) are increasingly enthusiastic, and their students' performance on tests has been as strong or stronger than that of students in traditionally taught classes. One explanation for this achievement may lie in research-based reports that the power of graphic, connective memory (triggered by topic or thematic organization) is far greater than rote memory (O'Keefe & Nadel, 1990).

Chronology. Anthologies used in 11th and 12th grades typically focus on national literature, and the units are set up chronologically by periods. These texts generally include a three- or four-page introduction to each period of literary history. The various sections of the chapter present authors of the period, who are usually introduced with some biographical material, a part of which often ties a figure to the intellectual, cultural, or political history of the period. These anthologies (and often parallel reading in novels) determine the sequence and scope of study. The danger of the chronological approach is that the exactitude of dates, titles, and other historical generalizations can become a terrific temptation for teachers and students alike. The course easily begins to emphasize "knowledge of" the national literature and history. This approach can so concentrate on the literary history that a study of Shakespeare's England, Dickinson's Amherst, or Hughes's Harlem can take the place of a full encounter with the texts.

In the 1960s, Lynch and Evans (1963), two literary scholars, called for teachers to abandon the chronological approach. Applebee (1997) explains that the American literature course entered U.S. high schools after World War I in reaction to the national fervor of the era and the growth of the field of American studies in universities. As it became institutionalized, it became a "chronological survey of works by major Americans (*not* of major works by Americans, thus adding many relatively minor works to the syllabus)" (p. 27). As the course further evolved, it lost the power of patriotism with its legends of national destiny, its "myths of the frontier and the American Spirit," and turned instead toward "the internal character of works" (p. 27). Applebee sums up the results of this "disarray": American Literature courses "spend too much time on works that students don't like and lack a real tradition of conversation into which students can enter" (p. 27).

On the other hand, apologists explain that the chronological approach helps students see connections between texts and authors and culture. Students can participate in what T. S. Eliot calls the tradition. They can make connections themselves, between, say, the romances of Nathaniel Hawthorne and Flannery O'Connor, rather than have them explained by the teacher. Intertextuality can be a serendipitous affair and create a sense of literature unfolding.

Grammar and Composition.   The third most common classroom structure that Goodlad found in secondary school English classes is organized around units of grammar and composition. Chapters 9 and 10 presented multiple strategies for teaching writing, and many of these strategies could comprise effective individual units. But there are assumptions about organizing writing instruction more basic than questions of strategy. Traditional classrooms presented writing and grammar instruction as they did literature, as a body of knowledge (grammar or rhetorical rules) to be comprehended and mastered. A process/workshop approach is organized out of quite different assumptions and in a far different structure. One of the central structural differences is that whole groups, small collaborative groups, partners, and individual students working at solitary tasks are on center stage, not the teacher.

Invitation to Reflection 11–7

- How were your 4 years of high school English organized?

9th _____	1. Literature and grammar/composition
10th _____	2. Literature
11th _____	3. Grammar/composition
12th _____	

- Was your language study essentially grammar, composition, or both?
- How was literature study organized?

9th _____	1. Genre
10th _____	2. Theme
11th _____	3. Chronology
12th _____	4. Other

- Which organizational plan did you find most beneficial?

OBJECTIVES-BASED MODEL

Planning by objectives is based on a "rational approach" to curriculum planning proposed by Tyler (1975). Although his claims for the original formulation were modest, as Kliebard (1970) has observed, they have almost attained the status of "revealed doctrine" (p. 256). Kliebard explains that Tyler's rationale revolves around four central questions:

1. What educational purposes should the school seek to attain?
2. What educational experiences can be provided that are likely to attain these purposes?
3. How can these educational experiences be effectively organized?
4. How can we determine whether these purposes are being attained?

The work of Bloom and his group of university examiners in the 1950s gave shape to Tyler's model. They attempted to devise a means to talk more precisely about possible student educational outcomes in three domains: cognitive, affective, and psychomotor. Educators have especially used cognitive and psychomotor objectives to identify the outcomes of education in observable, measurable, terminal student behavior. They believed, and some subsequent research has validated, that a teacher's clear statement of a lesson's specific learning objectives is instrumental to student achievement. Such learning objectives

- define the desirable directions for growth to occur,
- provide a guide for the choice of learning experiences, and
- provide a basis for evaluation.

We borrow here from a well-respected general methods text by Grambs and Carr (1991) to enumerate the six component parts of planning by objectives that must be addressed in this model:

1. Scope—how much content is to be covered? (And consequently, how much time is required?)
2. Sequence—in what order are the elements of the content to be studied?
3. Objectives—what learnings are to be achieved?
4. Learning activities—in what day-to-day experiences will students engage that will allow them to achieve the objectives?

5. Materials—what things will teachers and students need to examine and use to complete the learning activities?
6. Evaluation—(a) how successfully did the teacher perform? and (b) how successfully did the students perform? (pp. 138–139)

Proponents of education by objectives list these advantages in its favor:

- It establishes a sense of control and order.
- It originates in the observations of specialists and experts who generated hypotheses about education and tested them.
- It is based on learning theory, educational psychology, and research about best practice.
- It has overtones of both a scientific and an engineering model.
- It provides a model, for the inexperienced teacher especially, that is systematic and inclusive. It presents an image of education under control, guided by authorities who know what is best for students.
- It corrects for a teacher's random choices in planning and aimless drift in teaching.

In sum, observation has defined and research has demonstrated the correct approach to educating the young, and skillful technicians have constructed efficient plans and devices for achieving it. Education by objectives even has within its system a way of testing the hypotheses because it lays heavy stress on measurable behaviors that can be readily evaluated.

Despite these claims, critics consider this approach seriously flawed for the following reasons:

- It overlooks the individual learner whom it purports to teach.
- It does not allow for variation among individuals.
- It separates persons from their behavior.
- It ignores the cultural context of learners in its attention to the intellectual context.
- It fails to attend to the whole person.
- It caps the possibilities of learning as though there were clearly definable limits.
- It reduces the possibilities of serendipitous discovery within the classroom.
- It overlooks learning outcomes that cannot be stated in easily measurable terms.
- It is based on a scientific model, not an artistic one.

Particularly in our field of English, the objectives that many teachers most value—appreciation, valuing, discovering, and understanding—are suspect. The whole realm of subjective response to literature resists the narrowing statement of objectives with verbs describing observable actions or products that can be measured: *identify, list, compute, locate, explain,* and *analyze.* Some of those intellectual acts should be a part of an English class, but not the exclusive work done there.

PROCESS-BASED MODEL

Cain (1989), in her work with preservice teachers, found the "rational means-end" planning model developed on the Tyler rationale inadequate. It produced in her students "unit plans characteristic of the old-world instructional routine . . . giving the reading assignments for homework, discussing the questions at the end of the text, taking the quiz" (p. 5). She wondered, "Why not construct a planning model that would help preservice teachers think creatively about their 'worldmaking,' about their educational designs? Why not help them see more clearly that they are creating an educational environment, a new classroom culture, instead of just objectives that need to be met and tested?" (p. 6). She went to research on planning and creativity and to writing-to-learn theory for ideas for a "creative planning model," which she articulated and tested. Her design imagines teachers to be like architects, sculptors, and other creative people who must consider many design variables in creatively thinking about their projects. These variables remain active points of consideration for the teacher through three planning stages: preplanning, planning, and postplanning. Cain's planning model, Figure 11–10, includes the three planning stages, design variables that are active in each, and design evaluation questions.

Preplanning.   Writing process theory suggests that writers do not begin with their thesis statements first because that diminishes their thinking. Similarly, teachers do not begin with a statement of measurable behavioral objectives as they compose a unit or they limit their thinking.

Planning.   In traditional expository writing, when the thesis statement is established, the writer's task is simply to elaborate and neatly conclude that thesis. In unit planning by objectives, a similar pattern often occurs: The objectives are established, the enabling activities are planned, and the unit is summed up. No recursive reworking is necessary. The whole paper or unit is neatly concluded. Cain has no such straightforward blueprint, but rather the mental activities necessary for envisioning one's unit of instruction.

FIGURE 11–10
Cain's process-based
planning

PREPLANNING	PLANNING	POSTPLANNING
Brainstorming	Organizing	Experimenting and testing by teaching
Researching	Sequencing	Evaluating
Collecting	Visualizing	Reorganizing
Generating	Integrating	Internalizing
Collaborating	Designing	Storing away
		Creating sound methods

DESIGN VARIABLES

1. Physical characteristics of classrooms and ideas for their use.
2. Other available school space and ideas for its use.
3. Number of students.
4. Number of periods.
5. Pupil characteristics.
6. Philosophy of education.
7. Theories of learning.
8. Learning activities.
9. Curriculum and resource materials.
10. School objectives and/or standards of learning.
11. Current social events that may impact on classroom content or activities.
12. Evaluation procedures.
13. Classroom management strategies (example: quick way to break students into small groups).
14. Executive management strategies (example: way to collect information about authors).
15. Personal teaching refinements (example: want to use more metaphors to illustrate ideas).
16. Professional goals (example: want to publish article on experimental method).
17. Goals for making instructional environment beneficial and stimulating for students.

EVALUATION OF EDUCATION DESIGN

Does form follow function?
Is the total educational design beneficial and stimulating for students? (p. 8)

SOURCE: From Beatrice N. Cain, "With Worldmaking, Planning Models Matter," *English Education,* February 1989. Reprinted by permission of National Council of Teachers of English.

Postplanning.   Cain's model, like the writing process, keeps the teacher reexamining and refining the unit. In her study, the young teacher using the creative planning model kept a journal of her thoughts, and they reflect a consciousness of what the students needed and how she was meeting their needs. "The creative planner created a learning community that eventually became what she hoped it would be: a place where teacher and students could learn and grow together." Her concerns always seemed to be related to the question "Is the plan well suited for my group of students?" whereas the rational means-end planner's concerns were with whether "the objectives she established for the unit would be met by the students" (p. 23).

CONVERSATION-BASED MODEL

Research undertaken and conclusions drawn by Applebee (1996, 1997) have ramifications for planning. Applebee (1997) and his team of researchers collected case studies of elementary, junior high, and high school teachers designated as "expert" in order to investigate teachers' decisions about "what to teach and when" (p. 26). They examined the tacit assumptions that influenced teachers' decisions, the classroom results of those decisions, and the curriculum that evolved from them. They were especially interested in "the kinds of choices that led to teachers and students experiencing a sense of coherence and continuity in the curriculum" (p. 26). The results of the study caused Applebee to propose a rethinking of the language arts curriculum in terms not of content or objectives, but of students engaged in sustained and interrelated conversation. (The idea has echoes of Jay's [1991] proposal for organizing instruction around a "problematic," discussed in Chapter 6, Expanding Literacy, pp. 191–192.)

Applebee's model reconciles the opposed positions of traditionalists (Hirsh, Bloom, and Bennett) and reformers (Freire, Giroux, and Levine) by recognizing the tradition as "knowledge-in-action." As we learn to participate in these traditions, to draw from them "alternative and complementary ways of knowing and doing," we gain the knowledge and confidence to "reject or to change them" (p. 26). The teachers studied clearly worked to reconcile two different frames of reference: constructivist, integrative, reader centered; and traditional text centered. These teachers engaged students in exploring the different "voices" of others in print and nonprint texts in order to enter conversations with and about them. The conversations were crucial. As the researchers observed classrooms across grade levels, they distilled a view of the most effective curricula, "that is, of those that were most successful in providing a sense of continuity and coherence, maintaining student interest and engagement, and helping students enter into culturally significant domains of conversation" (p. 29). Applebee's (1997, pp. 29–30) four touchstones, or principles, for planning an effective curriculum follow:

Quality	It must be built around episodes of high quality.
Quantity	It requires an appropriate breadth of materials to sustain it.
Relatedness	It must have interrelated parts.
Manner	It must gear instruction to helping students enter into the curricular conversation.

At this point, you might think that you hear a strange ringing in your ears, as though E. D. Hirsh is peacefully planning a curriculum with Louise Rosenblatt. Their different perspectives represent the conflict that we see Applebee bridging, a bridgehead he has gained because he observed classroom teachers struggling with and reconciling these very issues. He uses one teacher, Tony Harrison, as an example. Harrison inherited an established 10th-grade American literature survey course that had evolved into five units, each anchored by a novel:

The Scarlet Letter (Puritan literature)
Billy Budd (Transcendentalism)
The Red Badge of Courage (the Civil War)
The Adventures of Huckleberry Finn (Realism, we imagine, but later eliminated because of controversy)
The Great Gatsby (Modern literature)

Although the English department's concern for multiculturalism had caused revisions—*I Know Why the Caged Bird Sings* had replaced *Billy Budd,* Twain had been dropped, and a Native American literature unit now introduced the course—Harrison inherited this still-traditional shape and approached it with the skills of textual analysis refined by the New Critics. As Harrison adjusted to additional selections, he found that he had less and less time for discussion, so he reorganized the course around a focus: the clash of cultures. Applebee explains that "initially this was simply a new template within which he continued to emphasize textual analysis, but gradually the template began to influence the questions that he and the students asked, and Harrison began to think of the course as an exploration of the question, 'Who chooses the canon?'" (p. 28). These changes caused a fundamental shift in the way Harrison thought of the curriculum. He now saw it not as helping students "solve the puzzle of the text" (with himself as the final verifier of the "appropriate solutions"), but as "helping students participate in a set of living conversations" (p. 28). Texts became appropriate or interesting, not in and of themselves, but because of the questions they engendered and the kinds of discussions they generated. Harrison broadened his instructional approach from a primary reliance on whole-class discussion to "'lead' the class toward a shared set of understandings" to those that would allow "room to explore multiple interpretations and diverse points of view" (pp. 28–29).

Applebee's work points to new ways to envision the English curriculum and to plan for that restructuring. It defines a central and coherent domain for all language arts. It helps us unite issues of curriculum (content) and instruction (process). He suggests several concrete steps for members of the profession to take in such a shift:

- to develop examples of domains for conversation that will be appropriate at different grade levels, domains whose topics and experiences will be sufficiently compelling to engage students in extended curricular conversations . . .
- to develop a rich repertoire of appropriate topics that teachers and departments can adapt to fit their local circumstances . . .
- to demonstrate its effects on students' learning . . .
- [to] learn from the disappointments that also always occur amidst the complexities of schools and classrooms. (pp. 30–31)

GROUNDING UNIT PLANNING IN STUDENTS

We want to conclude this section on unit planning by suggesting other means of grounding your planning in student interests and abilities. As Cain's research demonstrates, if we are concerned with "designing new versions of classroom life" and with the individual's making meaningful sense of our classes, we get a head start if we plan with them in mind: their styles, their interests, and our perception of their academic and social needs. We can even engage them directly in the process, surveying their ideas, responding to their suggestions, and conferring with them about the next step. Taking students into active, rather than indirect, decision making is most effective when the students are older and have confidence in the group process. Above all, we can pay attention and listen to students.

Furthermore, we can plan for students by leaving the unit fluid, with enough flexibility to accommodate the unexpected. Cox (1991) explains how that flexibility works on a daily, quarterly, and yearly basis: "I cannot plan my daily lessons too far in advance. My quarterly and yearly plans give me general ideas for weeks; I set aside tentative dates for projects and assignments, but in doing so, I always make myself aware of the need for fluidity, informing my students from the beginning of the quarter that those dates may change" (p. 35). This flexible openness, while rewarding, has its price. Coon (1991) summarizes the dilemma exactly:

> I struggle constantly to strike a balance between planning carefully structured assignments and allowing room for my students—and me—to follow a promising idea wherever it leads us. Both sides of this balance contain pitfalls. With too rigid a structure, I find that students only go through the motions, giving superficial responses and not involving themselves in their work. With too much latitude, some will respond with excellent work while others wander off course in directions that aren't as productive as I would like. (p. 28)

Owen (1991) reports on a ninth-grade teacher for whom "teaching is like writing, a constant pull between freedom and structure" (p. 57). Despite the struggles of this tension, keeping the focus on students makes the tension necessary and worthwhile.

These considerations in planning, no matter how carefully weighed and implemented, can still produce a unit that has flaws. Your planning and execution of a unit should always allow for evaluation of that unit. If you are observant and critical, you will discover ways to restructure your lessons as you go along. But at its conclusion, you can reflect with the greater insight that a completed event discloses. The analogy between planning and writing again can be helpful. Cox (1991) uses that analogy and finds that if "teaching resembles writing [then] planning is the prewriting stage where attention must be given to the connections among the teacher/writer, students/audience, and the needs and goals of the two. It is also recursive, involving revision not only after an initial delivery of a lesson but also during the act of teaching itself. In fact, planning for the present always requires looking back to the previous year and being ready to adjust ideas to past experience" (p. 33). We would suggest that you begin with fresh plans for any new group of students in order to be true to their unique abilities and interests. But you can profit from your past units, if you use them retrospectively as field tests.

WEEKLY PLANNING

Weekly planning is not as strategic to your instructional decisions as unit and lesson plans are, but it is not without its importance. In fact, although a week is an arbitrary, though clearly marked block of instructional time, in many schools administrators require teachers to submit weekly lesson plans each Friday afternoon. Students often mark their school time by weeks. In many schools, specific days of the week are designated for different subject tests (for instance, all math tests are on Tuesday, science on Wednesday, and English on Thursday). Assemblies, pep rallies, and altered class schedules are often predictably scheduled by days of the week. Many teachers anticipate student affect and behavior around weekly rhythms beginning with dazed Mondays and ending with distracted Fridays. Thus, calibrating your instruction around a weekly calendar has some merit.

Another form of calibration that touches your instructional effectiveness even more is using a weekly calendar to chart the nature and variety of your instruction. Figure 11-11 displays graphically the kind of blueprint that can help you ensure variety in your classroom. Plan and monitor each day's lesson by checking which of the four language arts or Gardner's multiple intelligences will be engaged by your work. Other variables can be substituted or added, such as the four teaching approaches introduced earlier.

DAILY PLANNING

Young teachers put most of their energies into daily planning. Daily lesson plans are important for any teacher, but especially for the new teacher who is moving into unfamiliar territory. Lesson plans serve as organizational tools, as guides for managing new procedures, new subject matter, and unknown interactions with students, and as security. The four alternative models discussed for unit planning—content, objectives, process, and conversation based—are alternatives for daily planning as well. Common practice is for experienced teachers to organize their lessons around content. Clark and Elmore (1981) found that experienced teachers in their daily planning "rely heavily on curriculum guides and textbook materials to determine the content and pace of their lessons" (p. 28). A model of teaching and planning based on Tyler's model has captured the imagination of educators and the public so strongly that it is now used in many school systems to evaluate teacher effectiveness. This model

Days of the Week	Four Language Arts				Gardner's Multiple Intelligences					
	Reading	Writing	Listening	Talking	Logical/Mathematical	Musical	Spatial	Kinesthetic	Interpersonal	Intrapersonal
Monday										
Tuesday										
Wednesday										
Thursday										
Friday										

NOTE: Talking is a language art and is also part of Gardner's schema (Linguistic), and is thus placed under both headings.

FIGURE 11–11 Weekly planning guide

is related to the instructional process called mastery learning. According to Guskey's (1985) definition, mastery learning "involves organizing instruction, providing students with regular feedback on their learning progress, giving guidance and direction to help students correct their individual learning difficulties, and providing extra challenges for students who have mastered the material." Process-centered and conversation-centered planning models such as Cain's (1989) and Applebee's (1997) have not become pervasive.

A content-based model, then, appears to be the one most used by teachers; an objectives-based model is most extolled by school administrators. We will turn in Chapter 12, Planning the Lesson, to a discussion about some of the everyday quandaries that teachers face as they plan and execute lessons, quandaries that lead us to test the usefulness of all four alternatives once again within the imperatives of daily planning.

CURRICULUM PLANNING

Many teachers are called upon to help formulate broad curriculum goals and objectives for their schools, their school districts, or even their states. Although these advisory and collaborative assignments seldom go to new teachers, they too are affected by this planning. They absorb the implicit assumptions of curriculum planners and teach within the structure set by their decisions. And, they may one day be asked to think about the broader context in which they teach. For that reason, we mention a few issues to alert the novice teacher.

As a beginning teacher, you will be amazed by and preoccupied with learning about the protocols of your school—attendance forms, hall passes, and copying schedules—but you will adjust to the daily routines of any school soon enough. You will probably simultaneously crave specific ideas and suggestions to keep your head above water in your classroom. The shock of the sudden immersion in daily, weekly, unit, and yearly planning will claim your attention and energies. When some of the urgency of the newness begins to settle, then you will be ready to look around you and take stock. You can become more aware of the contexts in which you teach, both the explicit expectations of the educational establishment and what has been called the hidden curriculum: beliefs, mores, norms, and values that, though not articulated directly, communicate themselves to students through both course content and the social arrangements of school and classroom. Then you can begin to observe the wider context of the student and community culture. Curriculum planning becomes unrealistic if it is not anchored in such a framework; it seems random if it is not seen in a context.

As you become aware of your individual classroom as a part of a wider educational and cultural world, you will want to remain open to thinking creatively about your classroom possibilities. Curriculum planning is more than a problem-solving process. It calls for a critical re-examination or re-evaluation of what you consider to be worth teaching. Doing it with others is creative. If teachers share their individual hopes, aims, and struggles, rather than compare pros and cons of educational "objectives" and grind out solutions, the result is likely to be wiser, more rich with diverse meanings, and more commensurate with the complexity of human lives. What is required, then, is openness, imagination, inquiry, intellectual rigor, aesthetic sensitivity, and creative freethinking. The paradigm that often exists for curriculum planning is mechanistic and controlling—What are our objectives? How will we implement them? How will we measure their achievement?—and rooted in a cluster of assumptions that are hard to understand and recognize. Purpel (1989) encourages us to "squeeze as much humanity and sanity as can be found in existing arrangements" and then to think creatively of alternatives (p. 140).

Invitation to Reflection 11–8

You observe that in your school teachers tend to be either tellers or askers (lecturers or questioners). You would like to try some new instructional approaches and you begin with organizing learning stations around an American literature unit on the American Dream. (Your stations resemble the topical *Utopia* stations presented in Appendix F. They require individual and group work.) At first, many students, unused to individual work or group responsibility, ask you questions and talk with their classmates, but only about subjects other than the American dream. Most are cheerful enough, but unfocused. Your top-achieving students keep rolling their eyes and looking restless. By the second day, teachers are beginning to notice a greater noise and movement level in your classroom. On the third day, you notice that one of your least-motivated students has his head down on the desk and one of your most-conscientious students asks to be excused to see another teacher about a make-up test. On the fourth day, as several students move aimlessly from station to station to "just tell Jody something," you cannot overcome your rising uncertainty and conclude that you will have to change your plans. What can you do to preserve your interest in collaborative learning and individual student direction and responsibility and your hope for energized and purposeful work?

CONCLUSION

As a teacher, you will draw from the options presented in this chapter for organizing your instruction. When students arrive in your class, they will enter the day's learning through lecture, discussion, group work, or individual work. Within those four approaches, you have many choices open to you. In his introduction to *Tom Jones,* Fielding asks, "Where . . . lies the difference between the food of the nobleman and the porter, if both are at dinner on the same ox or calf, but in the seasoning, the dressing, the garnishing, and the setting forth? The one provokes and incites the most languid appetite, and the other turns and palls that which is the sharpest and keenest." Fielding appears to believe that the subject is not as important as its presentation. That might be said for teaching as well. Our presentation makes much of the difference.

12
PLANNING
THE LESSON

One of the commonplaces of any profession is the need to exercise judgment in the presence of the unexpected and the uncertain. Experience occurs when design and chance collide. This happens every time a lesson plan encounters a child. We wouldn't need professionals otherwise; they are professionals who reason and intuit, decide and discern.

                  Lee Schulman

Most of our readers are in the unusual position of having to put the suggestions of a textbook into immediate practice. *Bridging English* is both an academic text and a practical guidebook. Thus far we have presented many theories, general approaches, specific methods, and texts (print and nonprint) that critically influence what goes on in English classrooms. But a gap falls between discussing why, how, and what to teach and actually teaching students. We want to fill that gap by articulating the intermediate steps that we and others take to transform theories about English teaching into practice. Beginning teachers need to be able to conceptualize their purposes in teaching, but also to implement those ideas in classroom teaching that is energetic and confident. We want young teachers to talk as teachers and act as teachers. At some time in their schooling careers, most prospective teachers have been good students and willingly followed at least a few teachers whom they admired. You are about to become a classroom leader for others.

We turn first to ideas about planning the lesson. We then consider constant structures and concerns that influence the classroom stage on which those lessons will be enacted: everyday but critical concerns such as student involvement, assignments, and classroom management. Finally, we conclude this chapter with general suggestions about how to organize units of instruction and an exercise that challenges you to consider plans for two specific units, one on the theme of happiness, the other on Shakespeare—a subject that practically every English teacher will one day teach.

LESSON PLANNING

Our former student, now a teacher, Stella Beale, describes her anxieties as a student teacher and in so doing explains the need to consider practical suggestions for planning that will help the reader shape the ideas of *Bridging English* into a lesson (personal communication, 1997):

> I was about three weeks into my student teaching. It was 2:00 in the morning, and the hard knot of anxiety which had been centered in the pit of my stomach rose to my throat. Choking back tears, I cried out to no one in particular: "I don't have anything to do tomorrow!" Hastily, I threw something together—some wisp of a plan, and stumbled to the bedroom.

Several weeks later, at a dinner organized by my methods teacher, I somewhat hesitantly asked a first-year teacher and former graduate of the master's program at Wake Forest, "How do you plan?"

I'd been teaching for over a month and I still didn't feel confident about my ability to plan effective lessons. I was just beginning a unit centered around *Grimms' Fairy Tales,* but I could no more tell you what would happen tomorrow in the classroom than I could predict the weather. It wasn't that I didn't have any ideas. In fact, quite the opposite was true. I had thousands of ideas, and no effective method for translating these ideas into 50-minute lessons. My wise friend didn't chastise or scorn me; instead she offered me a simple solution.

"Go home," she said, "and write down all of your ideas. Don't monitor your writing, just get it all down on paper. When you've finished, take one of those ideas and, on a separate sheet of paper, write as much as you possibly can about that particular concept. Do the same for all of your ideas. Each sheet of paper represents one lesson." Her idea was simple but effective. And, as time passed, I combined her technique with other hints and strategies. I realize today that there are many effective ways to plan and that there is no need to adopt one indiscriminately. I have stopped looking for a recipe or formula for planning; I have not, however, stopped searching out the experience of other, more experienced teachers; I have not stopped asking: "How do *you* plan?"

Invitation to Reflection 12–1

- Have you been responsible for planning lessons or programs in your school life?
- Have you ever known the kind of blind panic that Stella Beale describes?
- What strategies have you developed to resolve that panic and approach planning productively?
- As you observe experienced teachers, do they appear to plan from curriculum guides, from their former lesson plans, from the ideas of others, from electronic sources, or from sudden inspiration?
- When do they appear to plan? At school? At home? During planning periods? The night before?
- What seems of paramount importance in their planning? Individual classes of students? Content that must be covered? Curriculum concerns from outside their own classrooms? The expediency of their personal circumstances?
- Do they write out their plans in detail, in a jotted outline, in notes in the text, or not at all?

Hawkey (1995) observes that "teachers must integrate public and personal knowledge in the complex task of learning to teach" (p. 176). To learn any complex and difficult human activity, we must draw heavily on the experience of those who know it better. Lesson plans occupy a central place in the daily lives of teachers, from the experienced to the novitiate. They are especially important for new teachers in order for them to enter classrooms with ease and launch lessons energetically and confidently. In considering how to plan a lesson, we turn first to schemas that teachers, educational psychologists, and teacher educators have designed to help us plan. We begin with two of the most commonly recommended schemes.

BEHAVIORAL GOALS AND OBJECTIVES

Many educators identify the central mission of schools with mastery learning and the central means of attaining that learning with the implementation of goals and objectives. Goals (the general aims or purposes of the curriculum) are generally stated in terms of broad concepts, such as *understand* and *appreciate,* and objectives (the desired changes of students' thoughts, actions, or feelings as a result of a particular lesson) are stated in terms of measurable outcomes of instruction, such as *enumerate* or *recognize.* The work of Madeline Hunter (1976) has had a great impact on the development of a model for mastery learning. She describes her model (1989) as a "teacher decision-making model" that employs "research-based, cause-effect relationships between teaching and learning . . . to escalate all students' achievement" (p. 16). The decisions center around what the teacher's goals are for instruction, what knowledge or skills students need to learn to achieve these goals, and how the teacher can facilitate that achievement. She outlines three planning questions that a skilled teacher must address.

- What will these students be able to do as a result of their time today, or at the end of several days (not daze) in this class?
- What information or skills will students need to achieve that goal?
- How will the teacher artistically use research and intuition to make students' satisfactory achievement more probable? (p. 16)

She recommends that teachers answer these questions by "task analysis," which "enables the teacher to identify knowledge, skills, and processes that can accelerate or, if not present, inhibit learning" (p. 16).

The Six-step Lesson Plan.   Hunter's model has given rise to a lesson structure, widely called a Six-step Lesson Plan, that embodies rational decision making and problem solving. Such a step-by-step process appeals to our sense of deliberate organization and good order. It establishes the teacher's authority clearly and firmly. It is more and more widely used by school systems to govern teachers' instruction and evaluate teachers' effectiveness. Our colleague, Leah McCoy, has distilled the six steps of this model.

1. *Objective(s)*—The objective of a lesson is a statement informing the student what he or she will be able to do by the end of the instruction.
2. *Focus/Review*—The anticipatory set consists of those activities that prepare the student for learning by
   - focusing the student's attention
   - providing a very brief practice on previously achieved and related learning
   - developing a readiness for the instruction that will follow.
3. *Teacher Input*—The dissemination of new information and activities necessary to achieve the stated objective. It may include modeling or demonstrating of the acceptable finished product or process, and checking for understanding (often by oral questioning) as the lesson progresses.
4. *Guided Practice*—The close monitoring and direction of the student by the instructor as the student practices the task for the first time.
5. *Independent Practice*—Continued practice of the task by the student without the instructor's monitoring and guidance.
6. *Closure*—The conclusion of the lesson, which reviews and reinforces the major points of the lesson and helps students to organize their knowledge.

The Six-step Lesson Plan not only sets this agenda, but also prompts the teacher to assemble all of the necessary components for the plan: objectives, subject matter, instructional activities, materials, evaluation instruments, time estimates, and assignment schedules. Other miscellaneous materials for noninstructional classroom business might also be noted, such as library notices, special announcements, or papers for return.

This model has as many detractors as defenders, but we present it because at this date in American education, we think you need to be familiar with it. It may be an ally at first, particularly if it is not applied too rigidly. It will give you a frame of reference for broad planning—What will be the overall outcome of the lessons?—for intermediate planning—What do these students need to learn to achieve them?—and for specific planning—What activities will facilitate students' learning this knowledge and these skills? It is straightforward and orderly in the midst of the many initial ambiguities and uncertainties of student teaching. Just as a driver's manual is essential for the beginning driver and a dictionary and grammar are necessary for the learner of a foreign language, so too can a Six-step Lesson Plan provide direction for the beginning teacher. It codifies some classroom strategies that experienced teachers do instinctively. We know teachers who simplify it into a formula: Presentation, Practice, Production. It gives the hope that even something as complex as teaching can be mastered and its uncertainties subdued if we approach it as a logical chain of cause and effect. We present it, finally, because administrators often use it as their rubric for teacher evaluation.

The Six-step Lesson Plan's Critics.   Despite the fact that many educators consider Hunter's behavioral-objectives approach to lesson planning to be the quintessential model, many others think that the model has drawbacks. Among its harshest critics are more experienced teachers. They believe that it confines their knowledge of students and the field and limits their creative designs for class time time. When it is used as a rigid model from which teachers cannot deviate, it punishes teacher creativity and spontaneity, the very hallmarks of teaching that we celebrate. Milner's (1991) research revealed the consequences of its 3-year use in the classrooms of one school system: a 50% decline in suppositional questions asked by teachers in each year of the study. Many teachers, particularly in a field such as English that values the subjective and personally felt response, feel that it doesn't fit their subject. It is reductive to what they are trying to teach and restrictive to their styles of doing so.

Hunter (1989) whose work is closely identified with this narrow rigidity, is clearly answering those critics when she writes her own rebuttal in an article for the *English Journal:* "There is no one best way to learn; it varies with content, situation, and learner" (p. 16). She explains that "teaching is surely an art, but it is based on science, as are all arts. Using that science separates the competent from the incompetent teacher. Translating the science into artistic performance identifies the virtuoso" (p. 17).

HIERARCHICAL SCHEMATA

There are other planning schemata that follow an articulated, though more flexible, design. These models revolve around classification schemes that establish teachers' expectations for student learning and their choices of activities and texts for meeting their expectations. These schemata often complement planning that is essentially driven by content. For instance, if a teacher is teaching a short story unit, he or she might use Harold Herber's (1970) schemata and design activities that move from establishing literal comprehension of the text, to eliciting interpretive comprehension, and finally to applying that comprehension.

Bloom's Taxonomy of Educational Objectives.   The most influential of these schemata is that developed by Benjamin Bloom in his taxonomy of educational objectives for the cognitive domain (1956). We have discussed this taxonomy elsewhere. It enters planning to guide teachers in identifying the skills and abilities that they want to elicit from their students and in selecting appropriate texts and activities that allow a student to work at a particular level. Bloom is a frequent accompaniment to a goals-and-objectives approach to teaching. He offers a guide to a sequential progression of learning from the most basic cognitive level—knowing—to the most challenging—evaluating. His taxonomy is frequently cited as the ultimate heuristic that enables teachers to determine whether they have included a reasonable range of skills and abilities in their plans. Classifying objectives according to the taxonomic divisions provides teachers with a clear question: "Have I included opportunities for a student to progress through all the six levels of the hierarchy: to know, to comprehend, to apply, to analyze, to synthesize, and to evaluate?" If the answer is no, teachers can adjust their plans to ensure that a range of skills and abilities are developed. Bloom devotees believe that his taxonomy is especially important as a reminder to include the higher-order objectives in lessons that can too easily focus on the more basic levels of knowledge and comprehension. It assures that no crucial level will be inadvertently omitted.

Bloom's Critics.   Many English educators consider Bloom's taxonomy inappropriate for the English classroom. The natural progression from one level to another does not match the realities of classroom life. The cognitive levels are mixed as students in a discussion of a short story, say, move back and forth between questions of plot (knowledge) and connections with another story (synthesizing), among interpretation of character (comprehension), a comparison of that character with another fictional character or with an actual friend (synthesis), and a return to plot for clarification. Such an interweaving of levels in a discussion would be defeated by an imposed set of questions moving from "low" to "high." An authentic conversation does not move in such order, and to impose it compromises the authenticity. These divisions in the teacher's train of thought can be diverting to the spontaneous questions (teacher's and students') that should ideally arise from an animated discussion. A high consciousness of Bloom's taxonomy also can directly or subtly undermine the teacher's attempts to encourage greater student autonomy. It sets up the notion, despite its denial, that some questions are of a "higher order" and some questions are "inferior" and that the teacher holds the key for identifying each. Also, despite disclaimers, Bloom's hierarchy can rigidify the work of the class and reduce the flexibility to pursue unforeseen directions suggested by student interest or contributions.

CREATIVE-PROCESS DESIGN

One of the reasons for the inadequacy of most schemata for planning is that the process itself is complicated and their simplicity doesn't match the reality. The Six-step Lesson Plan implies that we arrive at lessons through an objective progression, an entirely logical chain of events. Cognitive taxonomies make teaching appear to be almost scientific in the classification and application of objectives and skills. Lois Weiner (1997) cautions that "most formulas for solving teacher problems reduce the challenging, creative decision-making of lesson planning to a banal, anti-intellectual endeavor. Just as importantly, the formulas frequently don't accomplish their ostensible purpose because classrooms and teaching are too unpredictable for one-size-fits-all solutions" (p. 78). Not only will each of your classes be different (whether or not they share course name and number), but also, a single class's dynamics might shift from day to day. Cain's proposal of a creative planning model comes nearer to the complex dance of many variables that planning appears to be for Weiner and certainly is for us. In Chapter 11, we likened Cain's model to the writing process with its preplanning, planning, and postplanning, and the teacher-planner to a creative designer, not an industrial engineer.

    In Cain's model, the actual written lesson plans should be only the tip of the planning iceberg. They follow much internal work that can occur at any place, at any time. Preplanning teaching ideas and rehearsals can be recorded in notes jotted in a lesson plan book, questions noted in the margins

require writing skills to complete successfully. One student brought her his only writing of the term—a perfectly written business letter to a mail order catalog to order a fake I.D.

Individualization, Interaction, and Integration.

Lois Weiner (1997), in distilling what she learned about planning in over 20 years in high school English classrooms, names two formulas for developing effective lesson plans. Both originate in the work of two experienced and creative educators, James Moffett and Betty Jane Wagner (1992), and are basic to what we do in English classrooms. In the first chapter we discussed Moffett and Wagner's three *I*'s: Individualization, Interaction, and Integration. These educators believe that all three must be present in order for students to "master the full power and range of language" (p. 78). Although the three *I*'s no longer represent completely novel ideas, Weiner believes that the formula helps prospective teachers recall that "*all* are essential" (p. 78).

Individualization calls for students to construct their own individual meaning from the activities in which we engage them. This *I* reminds us to plan lessons that "deepen the individual's desire and ability to communicate" (p. 79). Remembering the *I* of Interaction "reminds us to consciously apply our understanding of students so that instruction exploits the desire to communicate, rather than attempting to suppress it" (p. 78). She notes what anyone who has stood for an instant before an adolescent audience knows feelingly, that "students usually have a great deal to say to one another, but frequently the conversation doesn't focus on the teacher's instructional goals." Integration requires planning lessons that tap "the entire range of skills and forms in communicating and receiving messages" (p. 78). For Integration to occur, any lesson must meet these two requirements:

1. At some point students should be listening, speaking, reading, and writing.
2. The product or process should involve authentic communication that taps life outside the classroom. (p. 78)

Weiner's student teachers critique their lesson plans for the presence of these three *I*'s and, with this formula, can spot and correct problems. For instance, one student, frustrated with the response to her carefully designed poetry unit, applied the formula and realized that all three *I*'s were absent; "That night she generated an entirely different approach: students would bring in poems of their choosing and read them to the class. On copies of the poems, students marked literary terms they had studied with color-coding schemes. The poems were then put on the bulletin board for classmates to read and inspect for accuracy of coding" (p. 79).

Four Modes of Classroom Organization.

In his Interaction series (1973—now out of print), Moffett divided activities into roughly the same organizational possibilities that we do in Chapter 11: whole group, small group, pairs, and solo. Weiner articulates for her students the circumstances that favor the use of each (p. 79):

Whole Group	When the same information must be communicated to every member of the class, for example "instructions for projects" or "discussions of classroom rules"
Small Groups	"When students need the maximum interaction they can get, to exchange ideas and clarify their thinking"
Pairs	When "practice and drill" profits from a partner and when students share something that is "too personal" to communicate to more than one other person
Solo	When students are involved in tasks of assessment or individual writing or reading for which solitude is preferable (Writing and reading could, of course, be done in one of the other three arrangements.)

Weiner's recapitulation of the four basic modes of instruction also reminds her prospective teachers of the possibility of instructional variety and cautions them against relying too heavily on one mode in their teaching.

Sequence, Variety, and Flexibility.

You should gauge your sequencing of activities by your students' interests, abilities, and learning styles. Some students thrive on varied activities and pace within a class period; others are jangled by such animation. When students are willing, resist the predictable patterns. Most students profit by the surprise and energy created by variety. We estimate and note the probable duration of each activity in a given lesson. That timing provides a realistic gauge and a temporal structure, but we remain open to the serendipitous possibilities that may arise. We try to tailor our plans to the particular students in a particular class and to the given class size and allow that class of students to determine our progress. When planning time is limited and three classes are studying the same subject, we are drawn to the economy of sharing one "preparation" among them. But we try to resist squeezing all students into the same mold. We want *what* we bring to class to match *who* we find there. We don't want to force the closure of a lesson for one group because another worked at a different rate. Because all of these differences confound and complicate planning, we note what each class has accomplished while the memory is fresh. Given the urgencies of your time constraints, however, when preparation time is terribly squeezed and keeping classes together becomes necessary, we believe that it is better to omit activities to synchronize classes than to herd students mechanically through lessons.

First-year teacher Stella Beale addresses this need for flexibility (personal communication, 1997): "I frequently have to remind myself not to be so rigid. Once I have a plan in mind and on paper, I often find myself unable to relinquish control in the classroom. I find myself unwilling to risk going in a new direction. Plans should not be written in stone. Planning is important, but once inside the classroom, the students, not the plans should be central. I struggle to allow myself to follow the students' lead, to perceive and seize the teachable moments, to referee instead of control discussion, and to let discussions have their own evolution."

John Dixon (1967) believes that a unitary rather than a fragmented approach to English "permits the flow from a prepared activity to one relatively unforeseen" (p. 33). He does not reject careful pre-planning, but he cautions against the kind of abstract planning of curriculum guides and textbooks that organize class activities around different foci, moving for instance, from a lesson about talk, to another about drama, to others about writing, each completed in turn. Dixon envisions a variety of activities in English classrooms unified by a focus on some "theme or aspect of human experience" around which all work centers (p. 33). Other learning, while important, is secondary to "effecting insight into experience" (p. 33). His example of planning with this focus in mind illustrates how issues of sequence, variety, and flexibility intersect:

> A teacher who is planning flexibly needs to consider beforehand *many* possible avenues that his pupils may discover in the course of a lesson, so that whichever catches their enthusiasm he is aware of its possibilities. The more active the part pupils are given, the more difficult to predict all that they will find and uncover: thus the need for a flexible teaching strategy rather than rigid lesson plans, and for teachers confidently able to move with a class for instance from reading *My Childhood* to discussing old people they know or to acting encounters of youth and age. (p. 33)

A Common Danger.   Britzman (1991), in a book about learning to teach called *Practice Makes Practice,* discusses a common fear of new teachers: that they do not "know enough" about literature, methodology, and theory. He believes that this fear arises from a cultural myth about the "teacher as expert" and from a conception of the knowledge taught as "a set of discrete and isolated units to be acquired" (p. 228). A common planning error of young teachers grows from this very fear. In preparing to teach literature, they rely too much on their research into the literary interpretation of the texts that they are teaching. They expect to teach in the same way as many of their college professors taught them: through whole-class lecture or discussion that formally analyzes literature. They have not experienced a reader response approach to literature themselves, so they rely on finding the "correct" interpretation from the critical books and articles of academics and scholars. Finally, they assume that everything they studied in their preparation needs to be somehow passed on to their students. You can avoid some of these difficulties if you concentrate on the question that Cain (1989) discusses: How can I create a learning community in which I and my students learn together? Then turn to frame the kinds of questions you would genuinely like to explore with your students.

Writing Out the Lesson.   When you are ready to commit your ideas for the daily lesson plan to paper, we suggest that you write down your outline for the day. Such an outline is far more than numbers of textbook pages or titles of selections to be covered. It is detailed with classroom organization and the actual questions that you will use in whole-class or small-group discussions or the precise tasks that you will ask small groups to complete. You do not have to worry about form or neatness. What you are preparing is a personal script for the day. You will depart from it, of course. Teaching is improvisational. But you will depart more confidently if you have a framework from which to work.

One of our repeated surprises is the impact of written instructions that we distribute to students for any task that requires independent or small-group work, particularly work that is nuanced or multilayered. With rare exceptions, our students like to hold directions or assignments in their hands, to mull over them, to question them, and to write on them. A printed assignment seems to possess an imprimatur that dignifies the task and intensifies students' work in tackling it. We are not recommending that all assignments be distributed in writing. We use paper sparingly and strategically, recycle always, and cut assignment sheets into halves or fourths to preserve paper. Many schools do not have funding for such handouts. But when they do and when we judge the moment to be opportune, we carefully prepare sheets in the confidence that they will appreciably increase the effectiveness of the assignment and student work.

Advantages. Clearly, the work of the English class is enhanced when students read and write before coming to class. The enhancement is more than simply not having to devote class time to individual work and thus being able to read, write, or collaborate more. Out-of-class work provides private, relatively chosen moments when students can respond and create alone. Such work has the power to develop those independent, committed habits of reading and writing for which we aim. The private moment sometimes yields a kind of autonomous, personal response that collective work cannot.

Advance Organizers. One important spur to homework or any long-term project is an advance organizer. Advance organizers anticipate the new material or ideas that the student will encounter and prepare the student for that newness. They put the anticipated work in a frame of reference or a context. Mayer's (1979) study demonstrated that "when learners have clearly established goals and when they can organize information around key concepts, they retain more of what they learn" (p. 168). Advance organizers also arouse curiosity and pique interest in the work to come. They are particularly effective when they tie the assignment to personal experience or to prior reading, for example, a personal question that will be central to the text; a group reading of the first paragraphs of a story followed by the question "What do you think will happen next?"; or a photograph or picture that touches on the character, setting, or situation to come followed by the question "What comes into your mind when you see these images?"

Teacher Response to Homework. Two uses to which homework should never be put are punishment and busywork. Whatever your motive in making an assignment, if the work is worth student effort, it deserves the teacher's or the class's attention. You have many ways to respond to student work, but you should respond in some way. We tell our students "Use up everything: Nothing goes unheard or unread."

Block Scheduling.

For classes of any length, a variety of activities within any one period keeps you and your students alert and energized. That variety is an absolute necessity with the 90-minute classes of block scheduling. Proponents of block scheduling like the concentration that a few subjects offer students, rather than the scattered focus over five or six subjects. They also applaud the opportunity to extend lessons over a long span of concentrated time so that students can immerse themselves in a subject deeply, rather than losing impetus and time with numerous stop-and-start classes. Block scheduling has created a challenge to teacher planning, however. Some teachers have been slow to adjust and merely extend their customary 50-minute classes to 60 or 65 minutes and leave the remainder of the time for working on homework assignments. Many other teachers have felt a compression of total course time and have responded with panic over coverage of material. They believe that they must teach with great efficiency in this abbreviated time and thus make lessons less student centered and more text and teacher driven. Much that is gradual, gracious, and spontaneous falls before the need for speed and efficiency.

We recognize in these new circumstances a need for careful planning more than controlled planning. We present many ideas for one or more lessons on satire in Exercise 12–2. Use these ideas to practice planning for a 90-minute lesson.

Exercise 12–2   Satire: Planing a 90-Minute Lesson

Plan a 90-minute lesson for 11th-graders on satire. Use some of the following ideas about satire and create some of your own. Because of the length of the period, using varied modes of instruction will be important. We suggest that you place an estimated time beside each activity. As you work or when you have finished, evaluate your plans according to Moffett and Wagner's three *I*'s and Moffett's four modes of classroom organization. Consider Dixon's perspective (1967). Can you construct this lesson so that the notion of satire becomes secondary to a primary focus on insight into human experience? What question could you raise to start the sort of conversation Applebee (1997) encourages?

Individual	*Writing*	Write definitions of satire.
Small Group	*Talking*	Read individual definitions and revise the ideas into one best definition.
Whole Class	*Talking*	Discuss the groups' definitions and write a class definition on the board.
Individual	*Thinking*	Examine four teacher-selected cartoons to determine which of the four is satiric.
Individual	*Reading*	Bring in examples of satiric cartoons or editorials from magazines and newspapers.

Pairs	*Talking*	Select your favorite satires from those brought and present to the class.
Whole Class	*Talking*	Discuss reactions to pieces and determine whether or not this piece is satiric. (Your students will probably discover that satire has no one solitary identification. Opinions differ.)
Whole Class	*Listening*	To identify satiric tone, listen to three examples of satire: brief excerpts from Ambrose Bierce (*The Devil's Dictionary*), H. L. Mencken, and Woody Allen.
Whole Class	*Viewing*	Watch film excerpts from Monty Python's *In Search of the Holy Grail*
	Talking	What is being satirized? What makes us laugh?
Individual	*Writing*	Respond to this prompt: What is this excerpt satirizing? *Tip:* Use concrete details from the film to explain and elaborate your ideas.
Pairs	*Writing*	Write a satiric letter to the editor of your school or community paper criticizing something about the school.
Individual	*Writing*	Complete this prompt: I do/do not enjoy satire because . . .

Paper Load.   Debating each night whether to evaluate and respond to papers or plan for the next day's lesson is rugged, dispiriting work. It is often tempting to let the planning go as you grade paper after paper hoping to get to the bottom of the stack and satisfy students who are clamoring for your return of their essays or tests. They assume, as you might come to, that the plans will take care of themselves. Resist that assumption. When faced with the choice, we recommend that you plan the next day's lesson. The burden of evaluation can grow heavy and sink you in anxious gloom, but a worse gloom descends when you and your students are dissatisfied with your lesson. (Alternatives to teacher-graded papers are discussed in other parts of this book.)

Advice from Experienced Teachers.   One of the difficulties of planning as a new teacher is knowing where to turn for advice about such a complex activity as teaching. Many friends and family members will willingly share their impressions and opinions of you and your students, but you may wonder how you can approach experienced teachers who understand your situation better. In his first year of teaching, our son Benjamin, a physics and math teacher, commuted with three others—an English teacher, a PE teacher, and a counselor—on a 45-minute drive to a remote high school in tidewater Virginia. He was first shocked, then shaken, then devastated by the school culture and his inability to influence his students to want to learn or even to attend. On certain days, quite apart from his difficulty in making simple instructions heard, he could not even be heard in asking students to quiet down. He regarded the problems first as his weakness, and then as his failure. What was as disheartening as his daily classroom struggles was the nonsupport of the faculty members to whom he turned for help. When he began to articulate his perplexities and misery and ask for advice of the colleagues in his carpool, he met often with, "Well, he doesn't act that way in my class" or "No, I've never had any problems like that." His gloom deepened as his resources for help narrowed.

Often, approaching experienced teachers for advice is difficult: They are busy, competent professionals; they have developed effective techniques of classroom management; they have gained reputations that students anticipate and respect; and they have increasingly taught highly motivated and older students and have forgotten the quandaries of the beginning teacher. Their competence alone can intimidate the novice who is pained by his or her sense of insufficiency. Turning to professional literature can be just as disheartening. Journal articles, for instance, are usually written by those who have succeeded with some technique or strategy. If these articles admit to frustration and failure, they are failures overcome. Understandably, stories of triumph are the norm. Jason Farr (1997) sought consolation in the narratives of teachers in the professional literature and met the same sort of success stories that were at odds with what he was experiencing. He confesses that they "seemed utterly out of my reach. I was dealing with students for whom realistic expectations might involve merely coming to class most of the time" (p. 107). Ben Nelms (1992), a past editor of the *English Journal,* reflected on the predominance of such idealism in the journal and acknowledged that "such stories do not always convey the uncertainty, the ambivalence, the apprehension, the misgivings that are a normal, even necessary, part of every teacher's life" (p. 43).

We agree with Farr that what is needed is "a balanced picture of our profession: quite high-minded goals, perhaps, but tempered by realistic expectations" (p. 108). He concurs with Robert Inchausti (1993) that the stories of teachers are crucial to the professional development of beginning teachers. Yet, as Inchausti says, "Most teachers, I found, seldom admit to the psychological horrors in their classrooms or to misgivings about their teaching skills to anyone but a few trusted souls" (p. 26). For this reason, Farr values Mike Rose's (1989) *Lives on the Boundary: A Moving Account of the Struggles and Achievements of America's Educationally Underprepared.* Rose and Inchausti acknowledge that a balance is needed—not of arriving at "some bland middle ground, but of affirming extremes of success and failure that teaching truly presents" (p. 108). All teachers—experienced and new—must work toward this honesty. If you have no one at present who can help you, you do have a resource in your own reflections, which we now address.

Learning by Mistakes.   Janet Allen (1995) believes that the real success stories often come after struggle and even failure. "We never really learn anything without experiencing unsettled thoughts. If that is true, I no longer have to wonder why this year of almost constant disequilibrium was the most significant learning experience in my life" (p. 154). New teachers will of course make mistakes. No one should expect to master a profession of such complexity quickly. Student teaching and the first several years of teaching that follow are a period of apprenticeship and formation. Our colleague Bob Evans's most frequent admonition to his prospective science teachers is this: "It will take 2 to 3 years for you to become the teacher you envision for yourself. You are starting on a long road and you should be patient with yourself as you move down it. You are not going to become the excellent teacher you want to be quickly." He assists his students in meeting their difficulties directly and honestly. He asks them to enumerate daily the good things they did in any period of the day. He insists that they also restrict the time they worry about the things that did not go well. He helps them train themselves to separate the good times from the bad. He advises students to worry only during a defined time. (He recommends that they let their worries surface as they exercise so that they can burn off their negative emotions. When they finish exercising, they are to quit worrying.) Then they can address the question "What can I do tomorrow to be better?"

Student judgments of the teacher also must be resisted. Students often assume that good teachers are born with special endowments and sort teachers accordingly. They can be especially tough on new teachers. You might begin to accept their valuation. Resist it. It won't do you or them justice. Hawley (1979) exactly captures the difficulties of teachers' daily public performances:

> Human beings generally dread the prospect of speaking authoritatively before a group. The dread is greatest when the group being addressed is not particularly receptive or welcoming, when they do not anticipate being pleased. Teachers play to tougher houses than actors do. They also play to them in more intimate settings, and the scheduled run is generally long regardless of the reviews. An actor, often with reason, may blame a flat performance on his material. Teachers are less able to do this; it is rarely Euclid's or Melville's fault that a class has fallen flat. Teachers move among their audiences, address them, converse with them. Any inattention, boredom, hostility is clearly visible before them. Because there are normally no co-stars or supporting players, the experience of teaching imperfectly is essentially a private matter. And again, because failure is by nature humiliating, we tend to keep it to ourselves. (p. 597)

We still have teaching experiences that leave us with a terrible sense of desolation and insecurity. All our confidence in ourselves as teachers capable of teaching these students totters. At those times, we regard teaching as the best school for humility that we know of. But even these blunders or failures can be used for profit if we work on understanding what they teach us about ourselves. In time their impact is blunted. Sometimes we can and do function as teachers with wonderfully little to go on, without all that we at first believed indispensable, in the knowledge that this is a profession dedicated to change and growth in ourselves as well as our students.

CREATIVE PLANNING WITH THE TEXT

Our text is dedicated to the proposition that what teachers do in classrooms should center on their perceptions of the students before them. Thus, any curriculum begins with an estimate of the students. Characteristically, texts, especially textbooks, provide an organizing structure. Often, schools or school systems have written curriculum guides or tacit curriculum expectations, which accompany textbooks to shape what individual teachers do in the classrooms. But extending instruction beyond what is found in even the most creative texts and most solid teacher handbooks promises richer experiences than simply using the texts alone. We suggest two ways in which you might impose your order (and ardor) on traditional texts. We then summarize other suggestions that are scattered throughout this text.

Turned Tables.   Turned Tables is a simple way to recreate the text by revising its table of contents or altering its sequence. If the text is arranged chronologically, the simplest revision is to move through it in reverse order. (In Chapter 5, we discussed how starting with a contemporary idiom and era that students know experientially can engage them initially in a more confident understanding of the historical and cultural context.) Chronologically organized texts can be rearranged by genres. Sonnets, for instance, can be extracted from the Renaissance, the Romantic period, and the twentieth century and studied together. Thematic topics can be regrouped historically in units on a history of ideas. A look at the yearning for individual freedom or liberties can be traced chronologically in the American experience through the works of Thomas Jefferson, Sojourner Truth, Kate Chopin, W. E. B. Dubois, Langston Hughes, and the adolescents before you. Your best rearrangements and additions will be based on your perceptions of students' needs and styles and even on your collaboration with them on how they would like to structure the course. In such classes, the text will be uncovered, not merely covered.

Immediate Texts.   Immediate Texts are those that you can print on the board or hand out on a sheet of paper to evoke an immediate response. E. E. Cummings's *1(a* is just such a poem: It is brief, arresting, and engaging. (Concrete poetry often encourages students to play detective with the scant figures they see on the board before them. Its visual qualities urge students to play verbally. It seems less official, and it is less important that meanings be just right.) The short-short story has almost the same effect. It is so brief that it can be read in a minute and responded to immediately. One anthologist calls it "sudden fiction," and it does have that effect of startling with its condensed brevity. Beyond their specific virtues, Immediate Texts gain emotional power from being something shared by students in one sitting. Our aim in searching for short, compressed pieces is to engage students and enlarge an idea under discussion (for instance, a philosophical or social question, a matter of form, or a characteristic of an author, period, or literary convention). Often our aim is to enrich, but it can also be to enliven. Table 12–1 lists other means by which teachers both can make their imprint on certain givens that are mandated and can be responsive to the individual learners before them. We gather them from throughout the text.

We hope that, having considered planning issues, you now have a more certain sense of how to go about setting up a classroom lesson. But there is something more that warrants our return to it, a context for individual lessons within a wider unit of study.

TABLE 12–1
Extending learning beyond the text

Strategy	Description	Chapter Location
Transformed Texts	Take a simple poem or short story and put it into a new dramatic form	3—Oral 5—Poetry
Literary Surprises	Read children's literature as oral reading or as accessible works for analysis of theme and form	5—Poetry
Home Stories	Invite parents to class to read and explore their favorite writing, poem, story, letter, or editorial, or ask students to read their parents' selections	14—Professional
Feature Film	Watch full-length or selected segments of films (adaptations of classic literary works or original films)	3—Oral 8—Media
Literary Listening	Listen to recordings of short stories, poems, or selected parts of novels read by the authors or actors	4—Fiction 8—Media
Art Watch	Use art as a prompt for writing; explore its connections to literary texts, authors, and periods	4—Fiction 5—Poetry
Musical Methods	Find and listen to music as an extension of ideas, a prompt for writing, an illustration of literary periods, an illumination of literary works, or a connection with students' experiences	4—Fiction 5—Poetry 8—Media
Thinking Heads	Periodically work on creative problem solving to isolate and focus upon the process of students' thinking	3—Oral

UNIT PLANNING

Many prospective teachers feel more comfortable with planning an individual lesson than with shaping lessons into whole units. Research shows that what separates able teachers from excellent teachers is the latter's ability to develop long-range plans. Teachers who design their work for a semester or a year usually build with unit plans. Lessons do not stand alone. They work in consort with other lessons on a shared topic. As we discussed in Chapter 11, traditionally, the organizing principle for upper-level high school English classes has been literature by genre or chronology. (Some English teachers become history teachers in practice because they fall into the habit of teaching lists of works and dates, focusing on literary periods and emphasizing the context of literature rather than the literature itself. Genre study likewise can end up as a study of the formal elements of literature at the expense of engaging the ideas and feelings found in texts.) Elementary and middle school teachers have long recognized the power of another planning principle; they organize their units of study around a theme. Many high school teachers are turning to themes, as Tony Harrison did (Chapter 11), because themes draw students into more engaged and authentic participation in study. A growing number of teachers and some school districts are turning to thematic units because they also encourage an integrated curriculum. We suggest a few guidelines to help you produce strong and effective thematic units.

TOPIC SELECTION AND QUALITY CONTROL

Topic selection controls all that you plan, just as a thesis sentence controls a well-composed essay. A strong unifying idea is essential. We favor topics that raise broad questions, that matter to your particular students, and that are versatile and open a rich store of literature and language arts on which to draw. Once a topic is selected, it will serve as a lens by which to focus and control all of the activities selected for the unit. Selecting those activities is a second important dimension of planning. To make sure that instruction is excellent, we suggest four standards that should govern topic selection and activities development.

Significance and Pertinence.   The first and most important standard is selecting a topic that has both pertinence and significance. We distinguish pertinence from relevance. *Relevance* generally means that adolescents are naturally attracted to the idea. *Pertinence* means that the topic is connected to the students' interests, although that connection may not be immediately obvious. Significance tugs us in the other direction; it requires that a topic not only be personally attractive but also be in some sense important. This is a tough standard, but it will help you avoid the opposing pitfalls of banal fluff and academic disconnection.

Diversity.   The second standard of diversity reminds the planner to shape the activities selected so that multiple intelligences and multiple learning styles are engaged. In addition, the four language modes—talking, listening, writing, and reading—should all be used.

Balance and Challenge.   The third standard is dependent upon the teacher's view of learning. When teachers work to establish a balanced and accepting approach to the topic, students feel free to explore. Challenge is essential as a way of asking students to examine their basic assumptions and leave their minds open to new possibilities; however, teachers who badger their students into accepting their own positions on issues are not teaching, but preaching. Author bell hooks (1998), who does not shy away from tough issues, says that teaching must involve a "radical openness" that balances, for example, a classic novel with a work by Toni Morrison. We are all biased and can never achieve a fully neutral classroom, but we need to consider how openly we approach each topic that we encounter. Patricia Grace's "Butterflies" illustrates this point briefly and beautifully. In it a young farm girl in New Zealand is sent off to school by her adoring grandparents, who stay home to tend their fields of cabbages. When she leaves for school, her grandfather reminds her to "Listen to your teacher, do what she say." When the young girl returns home that afternoon, her grandfather asks her about her day. She softly replies that she wrote in her book and sadly reports that when her teacher saw that she had written "We killed all of the butterflies," the teacher told her, "No one would want to hurt butterflies. They are beautiful creatures; they visit all of the pretty flowers." Her grandfather listens to her report and after a pause says, "I reckon she buys her cabbages at the supermarket, and that's why." The teacher has a narrow view of life that sees butterflies only as beautiful creatures. She cannot imagine that any of her students might see them as life-threatening pests. Similarly, we teachers cannot be aware of all of our misconceptions or narrow ways of understanding, but we can make sure that we make room for all reasonable and civil perspectives in our classrooms.

Depth and Discovery.   The fourth standard is to make sure that a unit moves to increasing depth and to a sense of discovery. Students need to move from a naïve, uninformed, and simplistic sense of a topic to one that takes them beyond their starting point. It must start with their own personal experiences and ideas, but it should move them far beyond those by consistently challenging them to rethink old assumptions and explore new possibilities.

STEPS OF UNIT DEVELOPMENT

A third dimension of unit building involves the process of generating the basic ideas and activities that will, when finally assembled, create a sound unit that will engage students and help them to grow. The three steps in this process are similar to writing a paper in that one starts with a barrage of ideas that loosely gather around a central proposition and ends up with a well-organized and tightly sequenced set of activities that constitute 2 weeks of instruction. It also resembles the creative-process design that we recommended for daily lesson planning.

Brainstorm.   The first step is to brainstorm for as many ideas as you can come up with in a brief period of time. Scribble these hastily on a piece of paper or at the board if a number of teachers are working together. Self-adhesive notes are helpful in group planning because they allow everyone to work individually but to post their ideas for use by the groups. Group and self-criticism are important, but if they come too early, they can stymie the production of strong ideas. Piggybacking on your initial wild ideas or those of others is what is important here, not subjecting them to premature scrutiny.

Cull and Expand.   The second step is two directional. Good ideas need to be expanded; unproductive ones must be culled. In this step, you might circle all of the activities that seem truly promising and consider ways in which they can be expanded. Elaboration and intricacy of structure almost always enrich learning. Rearranging our mindsets helps us open up so many new ideas that it needs to be mentioned as an isolated step in the total process. Here we think of ways to explore a unit topic, such as happiness, by opening up the concept in three specific ways. The first of these is to consider synonymous concepts that broaden and deepen the original topic. For instance, happiness might be reframed as joy, peace, contentment, or bliss. Working with contentment rather than happiness may automatically deepen the exploration. Likewise, an inversion of the concept may widen and deepen students' understanding of the general concept of happiness. Dickinson's "Success is counted sweetest by those who ne'er succeed" is a poignant articulation of what the inversion of the concept can do to make a unit's activities stronger and more challenging. A third way to deepen the topic is to make sure that the egocentric circle is broken so as to take in ever-wider perspectives. Looking at the views of people well beyond the age of students, asking the opinions of citizens of different socioeconomic status, and taking the role of other ethnic groups can also add greater depth and challenge to the unit.

Arrange.   Once the many different kinds of activities have been developed, the third step involves arranging them so that those that are most obvious and natural are used at first and those that are culminating and call for reflection occur at the end of the unit. In the middle, you will need strong activities that look toward the deeper ones at the end and create a smooth and solid transition from the beginning steps.

Using this sequence, our students developed the unit on happiness in Exercise 12–3. It is not polished, but it has some excellent ideas. We ask that you shape these ideas and extend them with your knowledge. Envision using them in a class during student teaching.

Exercise 12–3   Developing a Unit: Happiness

Read the following sketch of a 10-day unit on happiness. What would you add? Subtract? Alter? This proposal does not have an evaluation component. How would you evaluate student work on this unit?

Day 1 Introduction

I. *General Expectations.* Brainstorm with students about what they think happiness is (using connective words, word etymologies, and so on).

II. *Introduce the Topic.* Explain what the focus of the unit is; give some specific details and pique their interest.

III. *American Dream.* What does society say "happiness" is? Break up into small groups. How does Hollywood paint happiness? Name one television show or one movie as an example of your view. What words from our brainstorming exercise does Hollywood's picture include? What is the "American dream"? Is it equally accessible to everyone? For what groups has obtaining it been more difficult? Why?

IV. *Journal Assignment.* What does happiness mean to you?

V. *Long-term Assignment.* Interview someone who is 50 years old or older, and have the person describe the experience that gave him or her the most happiness. The assignment is due on the 9th day of the unit.

Day 2 Paintings

I. Look at the reproductions of the paintings *Ecstasy* by Max Parrish, *The Kiss* by Klimt, *Water Lilies* by Monet, and assorted paintings by Matisse. Draw or color with markers where you find happiness or describe the happiness in one of the paintings.

Day 3 Media

I. Watch Robin Williams and/or Steven Wright.

II. Break into small groups. Write a short stand-up routine about happiness or how comedy affects parts of life. Volunteers perform stand-up routines.

III. Watch a clip from the television show *Good Times.* Discuss the irony in the title of the show. Does an accumulation of wealth make one happy? Can happiness occur without reference to wealth?

IV. Watch the final wedding scene and a bantering scene between Beatrice and Benedict from *Much Ado About Nothing.* Discuss what seems to be Shakespeare's idea of happiness throughout the play.

Day 4 Music: Blues

I. Have blues music playing as students enter the classroom. Write down three feelings evoked by blues. Hand out lyrics to two songs. Play the songs, read the lyrics, and discuss them.

II. *Assignment.* Bring in written lyrics and a cassette or CD of a love song for the next day.

Day 5 Song Lyrics

I. Look at the written lyrics of several of the students' love songs. Discuss the relationship between the song lyricist and a poet. How does the lyricist use rhythm, words, and sounds (like a poet) to convey a message? Why does music evoke such strong feelings and memories?

Day 6 Poetry

I. Compare and contrast Wordsworth's "Surprised by Joy" and Keats' "Ode to Melancholy." Are both happiness and melancholy worthy of being poeticized? How is sadness a part of happiness and vice versa?

II. Read "We Wear the Mask" by Paul Laurence Dunbar. What emotions do we try to hide in order to put up a facade to the outside world? How and why do we hide these emotions?

III. Draw a mask expressing an emotion you would like to show to the outside world. On the back of this mask write the emotion you are attempting to hide and why and under what conditions you would hide this emotion.

Day 7 Stories

I. Read "Max the Dread Dog" aloud to the class. Talk about dreams and how dreams relate to happiness. Was Max's happiness fixed to his dream? Were the Stravinskys happy? How about Max's best friend?

II. Talk about how children's stories/fairy tales always seem to end with "And they lived happily ever after." Is that realistic? Why or why not? Are the endings of most stories happy?

III. Read Aesop's fable about the man, his son, and the donkey. Discuss how we go out of our way to make other people happy. How do we sometimes forsake our own happiness to ensure others' happiness?

IV. Read aloud Chaucer's "Wife of Bath's Tale" from *The Canterbury Tales*. What would make the Wife of Bath happy? Would finding the perfect mate make her happy? What characteristics would the perfect mate for you have? If you found this person, would he or she make you happy? Can you be happy without this person?

V. Talk about how sometimes the thing we think would make us the happiest is unattainable. Write in your journal about what would make you happiest. Would you still strive for it if others said it was unattainable?

Day 8 Festivals and Holidays

I. Decorate the room in the style of holidays and festivals from different cultures (Easter, Christmas, Hanukkah, Kwanzaa, and so on).

II. Read Rosetti's "The Birthday." Discuss, in pairs, their most memorable birthday (good or bad). Ask for volunteers to discuss their birthday memories.

III. Look at clips of a production of *A Midsummer Night's Dream* and May Day celebrations. Discuss holidays that allow for activities and behaviors not ordinarily allowed.

Day 9 Interviews

I. Share interviews in small groups. Write a snippet (from 1-3 sentences) expressing the interviewee's feelings and perceptions during this happy event.

II. Perform this snippet, in character. The teacher is the audience. This dramatic presentation may even be videotaped and viewed later by students to critique their performances.

III. *Reminder:* Complete journal entries and interviews.

Day 10 Conclusion

I. Reread your journal entry on happiness from the first day of the unit. Write a response to that entry about how your perception of happiness has changed. What part of this happiness unit altered your perceptions about happiness the most? What was the most meaningful activity?

II. Devise a list for the classroom of 50 things that make this period happy.

FIGURE 12–1
Unit for upper-level
high school students:
The Stranger

Billy Joel	"The Stranger"	popular song
Robert Heinlein	*Stranger in a Strange Land*	science fiction
Albert Camus	*The Stranger*	existentialist novel
Joseph Conrad	"Amy Foster" or *Lord Jim*	modern fiction
New Testament	Parable of the Good Samaritan	parable
Old Testament	Psalm 146	psalm poetry
Mary Shelley	*Frankenstein*	quasi-science fiction
Selection(s) from the work of anthropologist Mary Douglas or historian of religion Mircea Eliade		

We include as a final demonstration of a thematic unit selections suggested by Cooke (1989) for high school seniors. His unit on strangers moves students from the known to the barely grasped with a rich variety of texts, Figure 12-1. In addition to Cooke's suggestions, the short film *Neighbors*, Spike Lee's *Do the Right Thing*, Frost's "Mending Wall," Hinton's *The Outsiders*, and Seidman's *Lifeline* interview, could be used in the unit. Such a journey is what we intend for our students.

CONCLUSION

Planning daily lessons and extended units is both hard and joyous work. If teachers remain alert and attentive to their students and to developments in the field, planning will remain active and challenging. Like so much of teaching, though, as you become more experienced, its challenges appear less formidable. At present, you will often be pulled in many competing directions. You will negotiate between two poles: between a keen awareness of the personal needs of your students and the demands of textbooks, curriculum guides, English departments, and other teachers; between a desire for a classroom environment that grants students space in which to think independently and respond authentically and one that possesses an order in which a whole class can work productively and creatively; between the establishment of your own authority and your belief in students' autonomy; between finding energy and time to plan lessons and finding the time to treat yourself kindly; between the calls of expediency and creativity, of safety and risk. These pulls are still active in our teaching careers. Sometimes, although we want a definitive solution, that is, we want to pitch ourselves in one direction or another, we take solace in Virginia Woolf's words in *To the Lighthouse,* "The great revelation had never come. The great revelation perhaps never did come. Instead there were little daily miracles, illuminations, matches struck unexpectedly in the dark."

13
EVALUATING
LEARNING

*Evaluation should not dictate,
distort, or displace what it
measures.*

      *James Moffett and
Betty Jane Wagner*

Tchudi and Mitchell (1989) observe that "grades have so permeated the school system that everyone has become addicted to their use" (p. 384). Purves, Rogers, and Soter (1990) report that the "United States has been called test mad" (p. 161). In this chapter we are concerned with evaluating the learning of students within individual classrooms, classrooms that operate within a wider cultural context permeated with grading.

Laypersons and educators alike can be heard deploring the decline of American education. They desperately point to lower test scores as proof that we are losing ground in a competition with other countries or with our own former educational achievement. Perhaps this sentiment explains the popularity of two films, *Stand and Deliver* (1988) and *Lean on Me* (1989), inspirational stories of academic betterment that reflect the hegemony of tests in our culture. Both are accounts of real teachers and principals struggling with troubled, mostly minority high schools. The success of these schools and the students and teachers within them is measured by student achievement on statewide proficiency and college placement exams. The viewer, exhilarated by the novel stratagems of Hispanic teacher Jaime Escalante and the authoritarian tactics of African-American principal Joe Clark, may applaud the dramatic turnarounds of both schools without questioning the final measure of the achievement: test scores. These films attest to the cultural confidence placed in scores on one or another assessment instrument. Concern reaches from the worries of parents, who have legitimate anxieties about their children's college admission requirements, to the reputations of local, state, and national educational entities.

Despite the increasing clamor over competencies and deficiencies as measured by testing instruments, the number of journal articles and books addressing assessment in English classrooms is far outstripped by those addressing issues of language and literature instruction. Research tells us much more about instruction than about evaluation. The connection between what we teach and how we evaluate is seldom made. But the two are intimately associated and no methods text would be complete without inviting you to think about evaluation very carefully.

Invitation to Reflection 13–1

- List at least three adjectives that capture your attitude toward evaluation and the grading process.
- Recall one positive and one negative experience that formed your attitudes about evaluation and grading.
- How is evaluation in English different from that process in other subjects?
- Would you distinguish grading from evaluation? How?

GRADING AND EVALUATION

Many terms are used almost synonymously in talking about evaluation: *measurement, assessment, appraisal, grading,* and *testing.* Although some prospective teachers will have taken courses on evaluation, many will not have. We will define these general terms, then, both to inform those who are less familiar with this material and to establish and clarify our usage for those who are more familiar with it. The most important distinction is that between evaluation and grading. Figure 13–1 demonstrates our sense of that crucial difference of purpose.

The distinction between grading and evaluation is fundamental. Grading looks at specific work at a discrete moment in order to assign a mark to it. Evaluating, with a more student-centered developmental perspective, considers the relationship of students' performance to their earlier efforts and future possibilities. Grading tends to compartmentalize, label, rate, and rank students, while evaluation tends to engage students in a continuing process of self-assessment and growth. Grading often serves adults in their needs to assign students to groups, classes, grade levels, or colleges, or to inform parents, administrators, or school systems. Evaluation primarily serves students because it focuses on the students' growth and learning.

Grading is so endemic to our culture that we can hardly conceive that it has not always been a part of education. In the United States, grading was introduced at Yale University in the 1760s and spread slowly. A 100-point scale began in the 1830s and letter grades in the 1880s. The growth of universities and their desire to admit qualified applicants occurred simultaneously with the expansion of public school education. As grades became instrumental to higher education, they began to influence all schooling, finally becoming inseparable from the learning enterprise. Although elementary schools put up occasional resistances, for the most part our institutional arrangements supported and legitimated grading, and it seemed inextricable from those arrangements. But grading came under attack by reformers of the 1960s such as John Holt (1967, 1969): It removed all intrinsic value from the process of learning; it absorbed too much instructional time and energy; it was biased against minorities; and it dictated too many educational decisions. Holt (1969) summarizes: "At best, testing does more harm than good; at worst, it hinders, distorts, and corrupts the learning process" (p. 53). Kirschenbaum, Napier, and Simon's *Wad-Ja-Get?: The Grading Game in American Education* (1971) satirized the grading process as equivalent to a government inspector's role in the beef industry. They considered such labels alien to the education process, undermining the self-esteem of students for the sake of a consumer mindset. But grading still had its defenders. The idea that grades are extrinsic to the learning process does not necessarily mean that they are toxic to it. Measuring one student's performance against others and themselves with concrete and unequivocal marks can present a realistic gauge of how well the student is doing and to what kind of life work he or she might aspire. It provides reality testing for students who must enter a competitive culture. It also can motivate students to a higher level of achievement.

The lines are typically drawn in sharp ways: The evaluators seem naive to the graders; the graders seem brutal to the evaluators. Grading defenders often resort to a final argument: Grading is so interwoven with schooling that a wholesale abandonment of the process is impossible. The debate often breaks down at this point; strong critics of grading leave no leeway for those who must work within the present schooling system.

Some compromise is essential for the classroom teacher working in the context of these strong competing positions. Nothing you decide about your teaching will have more immediate impact on your daily action in class and your interaction with your students than how you evaluate. We have found that grading is the common expectation of parents, students, and administrators when they speak of evaluation. Consequently, if you do not sharpen your own perspective, you might

FIGURE 13–1
Evaluation versus grading

EVALUATION	GRADING
Happens anytime self- or group reflection about learning occurs.	Happens at discrete moments usually of oral or written production.
Measures a developmental process.	Measures a concrete product.
Is integral to instruction.	Occurs after instruction.
Offers a qualitative explanation of value judgments.	Offers a quantitative enumeration of value of individual performance.
Is experienced as a supportive learning activity.	Is often experienced as a judgmental activity.
Attempts to engage students' process of self-assessment.	Informs students about the teacher's perception of progress.
Reinforces students as active agents in this process.	Reinforces students as passive receivers of the teacher's marks.
Can involve teacher and student collaboration.	Is essentially teacher directed.

FIGURE 13–2
Relationships among common terms used in evaluation

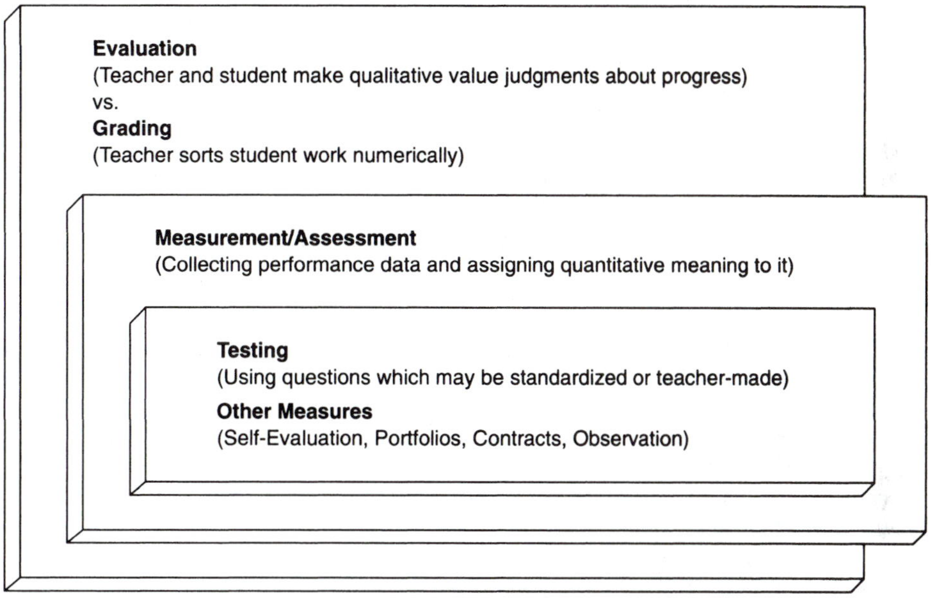

Evaluation
(Teacher and student make qualitative value judgments about progress)
vs.
Grading
(Teacher sorts student work numerically)

Measurement/Assessment
(Collecting performance data and assigning quantitative meaning to it)

Testing
(Using questions which may be standardized or teacher-made)
Other Measures
(Self-Evaluation, Portfolios, Contracts, Observation)

be coerced into treating evaluation as a sorting operation inflicted by the teacher on the hapless student. Grading is such a routine part of instruction that it is taken for granted and thus goes unchallenged. We want you to formulate your own position along this continuum from evaluation to grading. We encourage you at the outset to remember other principles of teaching that you have begun to construct and to try to envision evaluation that is consistent with those deepest aims. Remember, too, the different learning styles of students and different learning possibilities and how evaluation acknowledges that variety. We think that some form of evaluation is central to our concern with the aims of English instruction. This chapter should help you decide what form.

DEFINITION OF TERMS

Figure 13-2 schematizes the relationship between evaluation and grading and other terms commonly used in psychometric parlance. As you can see, measurements can be used for evaluation, for grading, or for the purposes of diagnosis or description that do not involve a judgment. Measurement instruments include far more than the traditional tests or exams. Each of the following is increasingly used to measure student progress and performance: self-evaluation instruments, portfolios, contracts, and teacher observations. Appraisal is used at times to mean either evaluation or measurement. It carries connotations of the value or worth of its subject, the sort of estimation a jeweler makes about the quality of a gem.

PURPOSES OF EVALUATION

Assessment instruments are constructed to serve many different purposes. We list here those most prominent in English classrooms.

Descriptive   To describe the present status of students on any chosen variable. Example: A beginning-of-the-year worksheet to show how accurately students use semicolons or a survey of their attitudes toward reading.

Diagnostic   To determine the strengths or weaknesses of a student in a specific area in order to make instructional decisions for the student. Example: A beginning-of-the-year test on knowledge of five formal elements of fiction (setting, plot, characters, point of view, and tone).

Formative   To monitor student progress in small increments during a term. Example: Periodic checks in the writing process during the early stages of prewriting, the first draft, and rewriting.

Summative   To measure mastery of a body of knowledge at the end of a unit or grading period. Example: A comprehensive test over all key texts and concepts in a 6-week unit on literature and life on the American frontier.

A final important purpose of standardized tests, as opposed to teacher-made classroom tests, is prediction. Many of the tests taken for college/university admission requirements, such as the Scholastic Aptitude Test (SAT) and the American College Test (ACT), are used to predict the future performance of students and their likelihood of success. They often are taken to be absolute measures of ability, but the more modest interpretation is more accurate: They predict only. The use of such predictive tests for diagnostic, descriptive, formative, or summative purposes threatens the integrity of these tests and, more importantly, the students who take them. Gardner (1984) articulates that harm in terms of the original intent and subsequent misuse of another kind of test, intelligence tests: "Decisions made about 80 years ago in France by Alfred Binet, who was interested in predicting who would fail in school, and later by a few Army testers in the United States in World War I, now exercise a tyrannical hold on who is labeled as bright or not bright. These labels affect both people's conceptions of themselves and the life options available to them" (p. 22).

Invitation to Reflection 13–2

- Before you continue reading, try to identify the basic purpose for the following kinds of assessments used in English classrooms.
  1. Descriptive
  2. Diagnostic
  3. Formative
  4. Summative

  _____ Open-book quiz on the use of metaphor during a poetry unit

  _____ Department-made worksheet on knowledge of Greek and Roman mythology

  _____ Creative dramatization of one god or goddess studied in a classical mythology unit

  _____ Collage capturing the feeling of the time and culture of an independently read novel

  _____ Beginning-of-the-year in-class writing assignment

  _____ Essay exam on the question "Trace the awakening consciousness of characters in the short stories read in this unit on *Discovery of the Self*"

- Which of the four purposes motivated most of the assessments you remember in your high school English classes?
- Have you ever been in a class in which only summative evaluation was used? Did you feel that provided a fair reflection of your work? Did it help you learn something about yourself as a learner?
- Have you ever had your SAT or ACT scores used as final statements of your ability and worth, rather than as indicators of possible college performance?

LEARNING POSSIBILITIES TO BE MEASURED

Recognizing one's principal purpose in evaluation is essential. An awareness of the range of learning variables is also important to sound evaluation.

Bloom's Taxonomy. As we have discussed, a group of university examiners, Bloom et al. (1956), attempted to systematize the possible educational objectives for student behavior. Although they divided objectives into three domains, cognitive, affective (attitudes, interests, and values), and psychomotor, the cognitive objectives have received the most attention. Figure 13–3 lists the six major categories in Bloom's cognitive domain. Notice that they are arranged in a hierarchy of behavior (or objectives) from simple to complex. As with other stage theories, work at Bloom's higher levels of understanding depends on completing preceding stages. Thus, without knowledge of the short stories of Edgar Allan Poe, no analysis of his Gothic technique can occur, nor a comparison of his fiction to contemporary horror movies, nor judgments of the value of the macabre as a form of entertainment or enrichment.

In earlier chapters we noted the dangers of a rigid application of Bloom's taxonomy to instruction. However, a general consciousness of these different levels of cognition can be useful as a gauge to evaluation strategies. In evaluation, for instance, if you are interested in determining whether your students have read an assigned chapter in Amy Tan's *The Joy Luck Club,* you might administer a short-answer quiz. If, on the other hand, your class discussions of the novel have built from comprehension toward a final consideration of the difficulties in the relationships between immigrant parents and their first generation Asian American children, you would not evaluate learning by a true/false exam. Your awareness of the variety of cognitive levels that you might prime should guide choices about appropriate evaluation. Table 13–1 schematizes those different levels in possible evaluative questions of Shakespeare's *Romeo and Juliet.*

Gardner's Intelligences. Gardner (1983) examined evidence from a large and diverse group of resources and isolated seven ways in which human intelligence is expressed. (In the late 1990s he began to articulate additional intelligences.) Preceding chapters stressed the importance of a range of instructional strategies that enable students to exercise those diverse intelligences. Evaluation needs to provide those same alternative means of expression. Linguistic and logical/mathematical intelligences are the two favored by traditional and alternative English testing. For students whose strengths lie in other intelligences, other options validate those competencies. For students whose best abilities are linguistic and logical/mathematical, alternatives provide new possibilities for self-discovery and self-expression. And when evaluation strategies encourage collaboration, students can benefit from the differing intelligences of others.

We borrow from Peter Smagorinsky's (1991, p. 2) helpful distillation of Gardner's ideas to define his first seven intelligences.

Linguistic	A sensitivity to the sounds, rhythms, and meanings of words, and to the different functions of language
Logical/Mathematical	A sensitivity to and ability to discern logical or numerical patterns, with the ability to follow or generate long chains of reasoning
Musical	The ability to produce and appreciate rhythm, pitch and timbre, or an ability to appreciate the forms of musical expression
Spatial	The ability to perceive the visual-spatial world accurately and perform transformations on one's perceptions
Bodily/Kinesthetic	The use of the body to solve problems or fashion a product

FIGURE 13–3
Bloom's taxonomy of cognitive educational objectives

1. *Knowledge:* the ability to recognize or recall previously learned information and processes. Knowledge is usually defined more broadly; here it merely involves remembering information.
2. *Comprehension:* the ability to understand what is being communicated, but at a basic level. The student knows the meaning of information or ideas, but may not necessarily be able to relate it or apply it to other material or see its implications.
3. *Application:* the ability to use learned knowledge in particular and concrete situations. The student can apply rules, principles, and concepts in new and appropriate contexts.
4. *Analysis:* the ability to break down information into its component parts.
5. *Synthesis:* the ability to put together elements or parts so as to form a whole. The student arranges and combines pieces to form a pattern or structure that was not clearly evident before.
6. *Evaluation:* the ability to judge the value of materials, methods, or ideas for a given purpose. This represents the highest level of intellectual functioning and is difficult for even the brightest students.

Level of Objective	Teacher Questions	Typical Questioning Verbs Used
Knowledge	Name the two feuding families.	*Define, draw, repeat, record, recall, recite, recognize, identify, write,* describe, label, list, name*
Comprehension	Describe the consequences of their hatred on the relationship of Romeo and Juliet.	*Classify, compare, contrast, describe, discuss, interpret, translate,* explain, give examples, summarize*
Application	How is the predicament of Romeo and Juliet similar to other thwarted romances you know of personally or in other literature?	*Apply, calculate, complete, demonstrate, illustrate, practice, solve, use,* predict, show*
Analysis	Human experience: Why do we feel Romeo's and Juliet's deaths more keenly than Mercutio's and Tybalt's? Literary: Why does Shakespeare open the play with Romeo's infatuation with Rosaline? How does Shakespeare use other characters to underscore the tension surrounding Romeo and Juliet?	*Analyze, classify, discuss, divide, explain, infer, inspect, separate, sort,* diagram, outline*
Synthesis	What is the effect on the audience of all of these contending characters and events? How do they affect our sense of the tragedy? If you could view either *Romeo and Juliet* or *West Side Story*, which would you prefer? Why?	*Arrange, combine, construct, create, design, develop, generalize, organize, plan, predict, prepare,* categorize, compile, rearrange, revise*
Evaluation	Are Romeo and Juliet equally mature in their love for each other? If not, how do they differ? Does Shakespeare's dramatic reflection on human experience have value for our lives almost 400 years later?	*Appraise, assess, critique, estimate, evaluate, grade, judge, rank, rate, recommend, test, value,* justify, interpret*

*Guerin and Maier (1983, pp. 63–64) listed these verbs by cognitive levels in a table on which ours is loosely based.

Interpersonal	The ability to discern and respond appropriately to the moods, temperaments, motivations, and desires of other people
Intrapersonal	The ability to achieve self-knowledge, demonstrated in its highest form by the great ascetics, such as the Buddha, but also achieved by highly reflective individuals who have achieved great personal insight

Table 13-2 enumerates strategies that express five of Gardner's seven intelligences in evaluation. These suggestions can be a part of formative or summative evaluation; they can be used as primary evaluative procedures, as adjuncts, or as alternative choices. They are posed as directions to students who are engaged in reading and responding to literature.

Hemisphericity.   Chapter 10, Enabling Writing, presented Rico's (1983) chart of the talents of the two hemispheres of the brain. The following example is another version drawn from Moffett and Wagner (1976), who credit Ornstein (1972).

Left Hemisphere	*Right Hemisphere*
Intellectual	Intuitive
Analytic	Synthetic
Linear	Holistic
Verbal	Nonverbal
Sequential	Simultaneous
Temporal	Spatial
Digital	Analogical
Explicit	Implicit
Literal	Metaphorical

	Intelligence	Strategy
TABLE 13–2 Evaluation and testing via Gardner's multiple intelligences	Linguistic Logical/Mathematical	(See "Evaluating Knowledge and Response to Literature" and "Evaluating Writing" later in this chapter for a discussion of these first two intelligences).
	Musical	Select music or write lyrics for a song that expresses the mood or situation of a piece of literature (poetry, fiction, or drama), or that elaborates a theme. Neenan (personal communication, 1992) has students compile a series of pop songs to reflect stages of a character's growth. Assemble or compose soundtracks for a found or student-scripted play.
	Spatial	Diagram settings or character relationships. Present photographs or pictures that suggest characters. Create sets, props, and staging for poems, dramatic monologues, and plays.
	Bodily/Kinesthetic	Perform dance or mime that expresses ideas or feelings from literature studied. Arrange tableaus or body sculptures that capture the essence of a literary piece or a central episode, situation, or theme.
	Interpersonal	Collaborate on projects anywhere from productions to artistic displays that distill the most important insights from a single or a group of literary pieces. Conduct interviews with persons whose experiences touch the subject at hand and write these up as dialogues, character sketches, dramatic monologues, or productions. Work with another individual or small group to write essays and tests jointly.
	Intrapersonal	Reflect on literature or write out of personal experience. Take these inward acts seriously.

A sensitivity to the features of both hemispheres is important to your instruction and evaluation. Students should be evaluated in work other than that which is characterized as left-brain, school-honored work. For instance, students can reflect on poetry with art that they create or with art masterpieces that they select. They can match a literary period with its music. They can discuss a novel by imagining themselves to be a character in it and composing letters, diary entries, lists of gifts for other characters, New Year's resolutions, and a scrapbook. If learners are asked to transfer impulses from one hemisphere of the brain to the other, they are in touch with a far greater range of responding capacities than is traditional. The dominant side within school and our culture is the left side. Postman (1979b) believes that schools should serve as a kind of corrective to the one-sidedness of everyday life. But whenever there are cuts in school budgets, you can usually expect music, art, and drama teachers to receive the first pink slips. The challenge to the teacher is to keep the right half of our students' brains awake in both teaching and assessment.

Dynamic and Contextual Views of the Mind. Psychologists are exploring other models of thinking and learning that focus on the mind not as a passive storage container, nor as a solitary machine working independently, nor as a composite of smaller parts each doing an isolated task. They have tried to determine the "kinds of basic processes that underlie intelligent performance" (Resnick, 1976, p. 4). Because developmental psychologists have entered this inquiry, they have brought ideas from Piaget's theory of cognitive development to it. Resnick and Glaser (1976) reflect that influence in their "concern for transitions in cognitive competence" and particularly in the "acquisition of new competence" without the influence of direct instruction (p. 6). They define intelligence as "the ability to acquire new abilities under less than optimal environmental conditions, conditions where the appropriate solution routines are not directly prompted or specifically taught" (p. 228). They envision a more complicated model of the mind's weaving back and forth in a dialectic between basic skills and higher-order thinking (a kind of interplay between Bloom's cognitive levels).

Ebel (1982) sees the interdependence of knowledge, thought, and performance and the insufficiency of one without the other. We must acquire knowledge about which to think; but without thinking, such knowledge remains inert and useless. He observes that "Acquiring knowledge and learning how to think thus would seem to be identical goals. One simply cannot assimilate knowledge without knowing how to think, and assimilated knowledge is the kind most worth having. A mind stuffed with memorized facts possesses very little useful knowledge" (p. 269). Beyond assimilated knowledge, Ebel posits performance as that which applies this knowledge to related tasks. Performance is knowledge in action. Myers (1991) conceives of thinking as embedded within situations and subjects. He sees knowledge as so decontextualized (existing in a vacuum) that we do not ask it to make sense of the world. Vygotsky (1978) adds a social context to our understanding of how we construct knowledge. Persons do not learn in isolation but help each other to make meaning. He reasons that learning occurs as a dynamic dialectic in which the expert (a more knowledgeable other) guides the learner (or novice) toward insight, to problem solving, and finally to initiatives that demonstrate learning.

These dynamic and contextual conceptions of the mind contain implications for evaluation. They, even more than Bloom's taxonomy, recommend evaluation that looks at using knowledge, rather than having knowledge. Evaluation methods should include opportunities for further growth. Furthermore, evaluation should reflect the social situation in which students know and learn. Thus, it should assess students working in groups, not in isolation, and the process of their work, not the final product. Exercise 13-1 prompts you to apply these four different perspectives on learning to the process of evaluation.

Exercise 13–1   Using the Models to Outline an Evaluation Strategy

With one of these four models in mind, construct an outline of an evaluation strategy for a familiar work of literature.

1. Bloom's Taxonomy of Cognitive Objects
   Knowledge
   Comprehension
   Application
   Analysis
   Synthesis
   Evaluation
2. Gardner's Multiple Intelligences
   Linguistic
   Logical/Mathematical
   Musical
   Spatial
   Bodily/Kinesthetic
   Interpersonal
   Intrapersonal
3. Hemisphericity: Left/Right
4. Dynamic and Contextual Views of the Mind

ALTERNATIVE METHODS OF EVALUATION

Later in this chapter we discuss traditional evaluation with some specificity. We assume that you are experienced with its general outline. Traditional assessment approaches are largely teacher controlled. Just as teachers determine the curriculum and present it, they test students' mastery of it. Students have little or no choice. Standards are set and met; homework assignments, class reports, writing assignments, quizzes, and tests determine whether or not the student has mastered the essential curriculum. Individual exceptions and departures have little place in this heavily prescribed, closed system. We suggest here four alternative strategies that may help you bridge the hazards of grading for students and the imperative to do so from students, parents, principals, and administrators. Each of these—self-evaluation, portfolios, contracts, and observation—can serve the purposes of evaluation or grading. They direct us toward patterns of evaluation that respect and encourage the individuality and autonomy of the student.

SELF-EVALUATION

Because we are concerned with the independent development of students, we believe that encouraging them to evaluate themselves should be an essential aim of English teachers. Whether it becomes the exclusive form of evaluation in your classroom or an adjunct to the primary teacher-based evaluation, student self-evaluation should have some place. Students need opportunities to assess their work habits, learning strategies, progress, achievements, and areas to be improved. Because schooling has traditionally located evaluation outside of the student—in the teacher, the parent, the school, and the school district—students have learned to depend on others for identification of their weaknesses or confirmation of their achievements. We need to relocate some of that responsibility.

The benefits of student self-evaluation include the following:

- It more solidly anchors evaluation within the individual as opposed to making it a series of impersonal verdicts handed down by outsiders.
- Educational goals and individual progress become clearer to the student and are more personally owned.
- Processes of learning become more important than the products.
- Students "gain an authority in the classroom otherwise reserved for the teacher" (Schwartz, 1991, p. 72). Their self-esteem rises simply through their empowerment.
- Students can sometimes identify areas of strength or weakness that the teacher might not observe.
- The importance of grades can be mediated by shifting focus to the student's self-perceived progress.

A classroom shift to even modest forms of self-evaluation works against strong prevailing student and parent expectations and thus presents a challenge. An experienced teacher, Schwartz (1991), describes moving to a new school and trying to change traditional practices in a classroom in which the teacher controlled grading and evaluation with teacher-made reading quizzes, cumulative tests, and assigned writing topics. In incremental steps he began to ask students to assess their own learning. His midyear exam reflected that refocusing. He posed the question "In what central area of your writing have you made most substantial progress?" (p. 69). He asked that they write a two-part essay, the first a "summary of central strengths and weaknesses," and the second "an in-depth analysis of one central area of their writing" (p. 69). His summation of the rewards of the project included a more subtle consequence of it: "By having to synthesize patterns in their work over time . . . they are gaining additional practice in how to read literature. . . . Most important, by identifying strengths and weaknesses, and by taking control over their own processes, students are becoming more independent learners, always the most important goal of my classes" (p. 72).

Self-evaluation can be instituted throughout the year and can be weighted differently in an overall evaluative scheme. In an *English Journal* "Roundtable" discussion (November, 1989), secondary and middle school teachers shared their initiatives to involve students in the evaluation of their own work. Figure 13–4 reproduces some of those responses. Other forms of self-evaluation that can be made a part of the English classroom are self-assessment inventories, learning logs, student-maintained records, and teacher-parent-student conferences.

Self-Assessment Inventories.   Inventories of student attitudes, prior reading, preferences, reading and writing habits, and interests can be administered at any time in a term

- to sensitize yourself to your students
- to aid instructional planning
- to promote student self-analysis
- to gather baseline data with which to assess the gains of study
- to measure progress or the attainment of established goals

Figure 13–5 is a self-assessment inventory that we administered during a 6-week literature course for eighth and ninth graders. We had just completed a 2-week study on the topic The Wisdom of Fables

FIGURE 13–4
Teacher initiatives to promote student self-evaluation

TECHNIQUE	DESCRIPTION
Student-generated Rubrics	Students working in small groups with anonymous sample drafts establish five standards by which a paper is to be graded and the weight of each of them. The whole class agrees on the criteria and they guide the revision and evaluation process of compositions, posters, speeches. (Kathleen T. Choi)
Weekly Peer Evaluation	Each Friday the class circles the desks to read a journal assignment made on Monday. After each reader, every person comments on the writing, at first via sentence opening teacher prompts, but progressively from suggestions the listeners initiate. Readers make notes and submit a revision for teacher evaluation. (Phyllis Parypinski)
Tell Me a Story	With each finished piece of writing, students turn in a "process log," which tells the story of their composition. "Because process logs emphasize the most important reader—the writer—they can produce richly revealing biographies of the writing process" (p. 76). (Susan Kimball and Susan Grotewold)
Learning from the Process	Disappointed with an essay exam, the teacher discussed the problem with students, set up grading criteria, assigned points, and weighted possible responses. Students got their tests, evaluated them and defended points they think they deserved. In class, two students read and evaluated each test. The three scores were averaged. (Marilyn Cole Wenzel)

FIGURE 13–5
James Thurber's
Fables for Our Time:
self-evaluation

Please evaluate your work this week during the study of James Thurber's fables. Circle the number that best describes your work.

5—Strongly Agree	4—Agree	3—Neither Agree nor Disagree	2—Disagree		1—Strongly Disagree

POSITIVE BEHAVIORS

I listened actively to the class discussions.	5	4	3	2	1
I was prompt in focusing on the work at the beginning of class.	5	4	3	2	1
I completed homework assignments.	5	4	3	2	1
I tried to enter into the class conversations about Thurber's fables by either offering my interpretations or listening to others.	5	4	3	2	1
When my mind wandered, I tried to bring it back to the literature.	5	4	3	2	1
I was open to new ways of approaching this literature.	5	4	3	2	1
I participated in the oral reading.	5	4	3	2	1
I did not distract others from learning.	5	4	3	2	1
I did not introduce unrelated topics.	5	4	3	2	1
I did not use class time for private chats with friends.	5	4	3	2	1
I contributed constructively to small-group work.	5	4	3	2	1
If my family had been silent witnesses to this week's English classes, they would probably have been quite proud of my work.	5	4	3	2	1

Total Self-evaluation Score _____

Extra Points (one each for your serious response to the following questions) _____
What are the two most important learnings for you in this week's study?
If you were the teacher, what fable(s) would you omit from study? Why?
If this unit on The Wisdom of Fables had been eliminated, what would be lost?
Describe one thing you did well in English class this week.

Total Points _____

that concluded with selections from James Thurber's *Fables for Our Times*. Because much student and teacher effort had been spent in adjusting to new classroom expectations and arrangements, we felt that such a self-evaluation would reinforce and clarify our expectations and would prompt student reflection on theirs. Because students were primed for end-of-unit tests and were accustomed to taking them seriously, we assumed that they would apply themselves to what *looked like a test.* It had exactly the effect that we had hoped, as students, in the heightened moment of self-scrutiny, paused to take stock of themselves, to ask penetrating questions of our intentions, and then to settle more solidly into our new routines and purposes.

We also use inventories on the first day of new courses to survey student reading and writing preferences or experiences from which we construct a tentative course agenda. Our classroom inventories usually have the side effect of alerting students to our interest in their personal experiences. This seems to promote individual reflection, excitement about the subject, and group sharing.

Learning Logs.   Learning logs differ from journals by focusing on students' reflections on their own learning. Entry topics can be student or teacher generated. We list here specific sample prompts that focus on different aspects of learning.

Learning Styles

- Do you prefer to study alone or with a group?
- What do you do first when you are assigned an out-of-class essay?
- What kinds of questions do you most enjoy considering?
- When you do not understand something in class, what do you do?
- If you think the teacher is incorrect, what do you do?

Strengths or Weaknesses

- Describe one thing you do well (need to improve) in this class.
- If you could strengthen one thing about your work in English, what would it be?
- Tell a story about something you have done in class this year of which you are proud (or embarrassed).

End of Unit

- What are the two most important things that you learned in this unit?
- What topics, if any, would you wish to pursue?
- What did you find confusing?
- What skills or concepts do you wish to improve?
- If you were the teacher, what would you omit in the unit? Add?

Purpose

- If this class were eliminated from this school, what would be lost?

A Finished Piece of One's Own Writing

- How did your idea for this piece originate?
- Why did you choose this form?
- What new techniques did you try?
- What problems cropped up and how did you solve them?
- Which lines or sections do you consider the best? Which still don't satisfy you?
- What surprises came during your writing?
- How does this work compare to previous writing you've done?
- What did you learn in the process? (This last list is adapted from Kimball and Grotewold, 1989, p. 76.)

Student-maintained Records.   Students can be encouraged to do their own recordkeeping. The purposes of such recordkeeping are multiple: to gather in a central place (student folders, for instance) a summary look at goals and performance; to encourage students to take responsibility for their own work; to provide an opportunity for them to revisit that work as they log it in; to prompt students to reflect on their past learning, their progress, and their next plans; and to free the teacher from this time-consuming task. The simplest log is merely a list of all the novels (or plays, stories, or poems) read during a term; writing and oral productions may be documented as well. The particular purposes to which you and your students put such records will determine their exact shape. This process holds greatest potential when learning goals are clearly articulated and progress in achieving them is conscientiously recorded.

Teacher-Parent-Student Conferences.   We tend to envision the parent-teacher conference as a meeting of adults to resolve a student's classroom problems, often with "last resort" connotations. But if we refashion this image as a productive collaboration of all parties—parent, teacher, and student—we might disengage the punitive implications of these conferences and find something more potent. Try to imagine the conference as a natural extension of a student's self-evaluation in which his or her input is sought and valued. The experience becomes a joint discussion about an individual's learning—strengths and weaknesses—rather than what may seem to the student to be a conspiracy of fault-finding adults. Anthony, Johnson, Mickelson and Preece (1991) delineate how to conduct such a conference for younger school children (pp. 161–174), but their scheme can apply to secondary school students as well. They remind us that with careful planning, students can be asked to share the responsibility for describing and interpreting for parents their classroom performance. All three parties can then discuss the setting of new goals and tasks. (Our final chapter discusses other strategies for engaging parents in the work of the classroom.)

PORTFOLIOS

Portfolios have been common in fields other than English education for centuries. Whether they are documents carried by ministers of state, financial papers of investors, or paintings of artists, portfolios represent a comprehensive collection of somebody's hard work. The educational portfolio is no different: It is a gathering of student work in an ongoing, dynamic process.

Although their contents and purposes will differ from classroom to classroom, educational portfolios have a common origin. We explained in Chapter 9 how they are the natural consequence of a process approach to learning that focuses on the development of individual students—how they learn—not on the end results of that learning. Educators want their instructional and assessment practices to be commensurate with that basic approach. If the emphasis in writing instruction, for example, is not on final products but on how students compose, traditional assessments based on finished compositions are inadequate. If, in literature instruction, the concern is with developing breadth of reading or depth of response, multiple-choice exams or even traditional essay questions limit the student's demonstration of learning. For the sensitive teacher, these situations beg for an opportunity to sift through a portfolio and witness the evolution of a student's grapplings. Portfolio assessment has been common in English schools for some time, but has come only recently to the United States. Teachers here have begun to experiment with it because portfolios promise to match new instructional perspectives: to do greater justice to the student as a growing learner and to the teacher as collaborator, not examiner.

Writing Portfolios.   Some teachers include all of a student's writing in the writing portfolio. Other teachers prefer to keep the bulk of student writing in writing folders and use portfolios for selected pieces. Each group establishes different criteria for the portfolio's contents. Common criteria are as follows:

- A specified number (usually three or four) of pieces representing the student's best writing.
- One best piece of writing with all of the stages of composition represented: drafting, review, revision, editing, final piece.
- Best pieces chosen to represent different writing modes: exposition, persuasion, narration, description, argumentation, expression.
- A number of best pieces chosen from the term and one in-class composition written without feedback or revision.
- A number of best pieces chosen by the student and one selected by the teacher.
- Pieces that demonstrate the student's "best work as well as any experiments . . . attempted in order to extend and diversify . . . (the) portfolio" (Graves, 1991, p. 168).

In addition to this collection of student writing, other contents might include the following:

- A statement of the writer's personal goals and/or the class goals for the period covered by the portfolio.
- An introduction to the portfolio to provide a context for the reader.
- A cover sheet for every piece that reflects on the writing process and acknowledges any help received.
- A writing checklist devised by the teacher or, better, by the teacher and student in concert.
- Writing learning logs or writing process checklists.
- A rationale for selection of a best piece or all of the pieces chosen.

Figure 13–6 is an actual portfolio assignment sheet in *Portfolio News* (1990). It instructs students in their selection of a best writing sample.

Herter (1991) regards portfolios as the most powerful form of writing assessment because they can "involve students in assessing the development of their writing skills by inviting self-reflection and encouraging students to assume control over their writing" (p. 90). She argues for this approach as the most thorough way to promote students' knowledge about their own writing. She sees portfolios as the recorded history of the semester's learning.

Reading Portfolios.   Graves (1991), in describing the literate classroom for younger students, suggests that reading portfolios "require a broader interpretation than writing portfolios. The objectives for reading portfolios are similar, to show both range and depth. But in the reading portfolio, the child will include favorite books, authors, and characters. It should also contain evidence that the child is experimenting with various kinds of reading. . . . The key element in the reading portfolio is the opportunity it affords the child to demonstrate good thinking about books, especially books that have had a significant impact in the child's life" (p. 170). Secondary reading portfolios should include the following elements:

- An introduction to the contents of the portfolio with a statement about what the student has learned as reflected in the portfolio pieces
- Lists of novels, stories, drama, and poems read; favorite characters, authors, settings, fictive events, and ideas
- Written compositions about literature
- Journal, "quick-write," or other brief personal reflections on reading literature
- Plain or annotated lists of collateral reading about literature
- Clippings of book reviews or biographies of favorite authors
- Glossaries of vocabulary learned from reading or terms learned and demonstrated in reading
- Evidence of intertextual correspondences
- Descriptions of epiphanies while reading

Duration.   Time lengths for reading or writing portfolios vary from a unit, to a term, to a year, to a school career depending on the purposes of the portfolios and the nature of the students. Older, more mature students seem more able than younger ones to profit from work collected over extended periods.

FIGURE 13–6
San Dieguito Union
High School District
portfolio instructions

In selecting this best writing, you will be thinking of reasons why it is better than other pieces. Part of the requirement for putting this item in your portfolio is that you explain, in writing, your reasons for selecting it. Such an explanation for a choice or decision is called a *rationale*.

Directions: In order to make it clear to others why you have chosen this piece, it may be helpful if you include in your rationale the following:

1. *Identify* what's being evaluated (title of your paper).
2. State clearly your *opinion* about the paper.
3. Explain what *standards* (criteria) you used when selecting this paper as better than all your other writing.
4. Show how this paper meets those standards by pointing out *examples* in your paper of what makes it your best. Be *specific*. You are *explaining* your choice so a reader will understand the *reasons* why you chose this paper. (p. 4)

SOURCE: From *Portfolio News* (1990). Encinitas, CA: Portfolio Assessment Clearing House. *1*(2)

Evaluation Strategies.   If portfolios are used for assessment across grade levels, the process and product remain unfinished. One of the most promising features of portfolios is this sense of a dynamic ongoing cycle. In many schools, portfolio grading is done by teams of teachers. Elbow and Belanoff (1986) report that "the only way to bring a bit of trustworthiness to grading is to get teachers negotiating together in a community to make some collaborative judgments. That the portfolio promotes collaboration and works against isolation may be, in the end, its main advantage" (p. 338).

Krest (1990) uses portfolios not only to promote writing production and progress, but also to encourage risk-taking explorations on papers that will not be graded traditionally. She assigns two grades on her portfolios:

1. A "portfolio grade," which reflects the amount of revision, risk taking, and changing they do on *all* papers
2. A "paper grade," which reflects the outcome of *one* final product (p. 31)

Her rubric for evaluating student papers is as follows:

High order concerns (HOCs)	focus, development, organization, and voice
Middle order concerns (MOCs)	style, sentence structure, and sentence variety
Low order concerns (LOCs)	spelling, punctuation, and usage (p. 31)

A great advantage of Krest's strategy is that the teacher can adapt the system to the personal needs of students and to the broader aims of an individual classroom. The teacher weighs the portfolio grade and final paper grades differently, depending on the circumstance. Krest enumerates four consequences of adopting portfolios in her writing workshop classes:

- I lightened my paper load.
- I began spending most of each semester coaching rather than grading students.
- I began looking forward to grading students' papers (at least I became excited about how an idea or revision turned out).
- Most important, I watched as previously unmotivated writers became motivated to work for a grade they desired and at the same time to improve their writing. (p. 29)

Other teachers make other claims for the consequences of portfolio assessment. Portfolios

- encourage students to become conscious, reflective, independent, and responsible learners
- promote students as self-evaluators
- document growth over time and sequence that growth
- individualize student instruction
- provide a collection of writing of which students are proud
- make students "more aware of their experiments and their specialties" (Graves, 1991, p. 169)

This focus on the developing student, whether reader or writer, places portfolio assessment outside of the norm-referenced tradition of sorting and distributing individuals along a normal distribution curve. Elbow and Belanoff (1986) observe that "the portfolio process . . . assumes that the ideal end product is a population of students who have all finally passed because they have all been given enough time and help to do what we ask of them" (p. 337). It also promises to diminish the separation between learning and evaluation.

Assessment Tips.   Here are a few practical suggestions to aid portfolio assessment:

- Determine intervals for collection, selection, and submission and then announce them clearly.
- Vary the suggested contents of the portfolio to reflect your instructional aims.
- Keep the entire portfolio in the classroom (except for removal of single pieces).
- Date everything that goes into the portfolio.
- Give all responsibility for keeping track of the portfolio to the students.

CONTRACTS

Contract assessment invites students to establish an independent course of study in collaboration with the teacher and to determine their grades by choosing the amount and quality of their work. As with legal agreements between people or parties, educational contracts involve negotiation and agreement. Although the teacher maintains important control in initiating the contract and establishing its terms, individual students gain choice and responsibility for their work.

Most contracts begin with a teacher presenting work options for the entire class. For both specific and broader choices, the criteria by which they will be judged should be clearly enumerated. Ideally, the teacher confers with each student individually about how to structure his or her learning and to assess outcomes. A vital collaboration between teacher and student girds the autonomous nature of the contract. The teacher helps each student set realistic goals (while pushing those goals beyond the most obvious boundaries) and then works with the student during the process to unravel snarls, suggest additional resources, and encourage follow-through. Anthony, Johnson, Mickelson, and Preece (1991) believe that contracts should offer students an opportunity to revise work for resubmission that fails the requirements of the contract. When the teacher has supported and facilitated all stages of the contract, grading should be straightforward and without surprises.

Contract work can be time intensive for the creative and attentive teacher; thus, we recommend scheduling it strategically. Often, contracts make ideal vehicles for culminating a unit of work. Figure 13–7 is a sample contract used as a concluding event in a unit on short fiction. We have used contracts with the study of other genres, literary themes, literary periods, and even literary conventions (such as satire and metaphor). Some have been open; others present a range of possible options. We negotiate this contract with college-bound juniors after whole-class study of a number of short stories and their authors. We plan it as a unit-concluding event to allow students to pursue personal interests and to express their discoveries in idiosyncratic ways. It makes use of knowledge gained with the whole class, then extends and personalizes that knowledge. The amount of work to be done is the most natural place for grade demarcations ("You must do this for a *C,* more for a *B,* and even more for an *A.*), but the teacher must relentlessly advocate for the good quality of that work regardless of the quantity.

Contract assessment attempts to engage students in sharing evaluation decisions and in making grades secondary to the work achieved. But contracts can sometimes drive students to gun for grades alone: they can become preoccupied with productivity, not learning. The role of the teacher is crucial in keeping the focus on the progress of students' work. Simply asking questions of process and content, rather than number of contract items achieved, can redirect students to their own learning.

OBSERVATION

Observation can serve many purposes: description, placement, instruction, evaluation, and reporting. It is an integral part of teaching. If we remain alert and sensitive to our students, we can push our understanding of them beyond the cues of their written or oral work. The interest in human experience that draws many to the study and teaching of English explains why English teachers are often excellent intuitive observers. We encourage you to focus this intuition with sharpened consciousness, perhaps even systematizing your observations. We envision observations for evaluation as augmenting other strategies. When they are systematized and documented, they possess great explanatory power. We discuss here a few common means of observation that are useful in English classrooms.

Anecdotal Records.   These consist of records of unanticipated student behavior or events. Our colleague Becky Brown prepares a separate notebook page for each of her students at the beginning of the school year. Each day after school, she records memorable anecdotes of individual students. She uses these primarily to prepare her letters of recommendation for students, but we suggest that you use the technique also to clarify and solidify your impressions of a student and to illustrate your sense of the student during conferences.

FIGURE 13–7
Short-fiction contract

I _____ contract to complete the following assignments by
 (student's name)

_____ .
      (date)

                                        _____
                                             (Author)

I will:

1. Read _____ short stories by my author.
2. Read _____ pages of biographical material about my author.
3. Read _____ essays about my author's fiction.
4. Record in my journal my thoughts and feelings as I
    a. read the stories.
    b. read the author's biography.
    c. read the literary criticism.
5. Submit a bibliography of my reading.
6. Find another person who has read works by my author, conduct an interview about his or her responses to those readings, and write a report of that meeting.
7. Research and list available public resources (school and public libraries, bookstores) for my author's stories.

I will choose any _____ of the following, but one must be a written account for the teacher and my reading group and another an oral or visual presentation for the whole class:

1. Compare narrators, techniques, or ideas in my author's stories in a three-page response paper.
2. Write an imitation or a parody of my author's style.
3. Compare or contrast my author with another author whose works we read in class.
4. Find nonfictional material (editorials, news or human interest stories, cartoons, music, comic strips, TV programs, movies) that remind me of my author's stories (character, theme, setting, tone) and present those correspondences imaginatively.
5. Dress as my author or a character and deliver a 4-minute monologue about other characters and arrange music to accompany it.
6. Create a visual impression (collage, illustration) that would entice my classmates to read my author's works.

For the above work I will be awarded a grade of _____

_____   _____
Student's name   Date

_____   _____
Teacher's name   Date

Participation Charts.   Such charts list behaviors in a group context. These can be elaborate— "What kinds of questions are raised by students? What are characteristic responses to discussion?"— or simply counts of how often a student speaks. Because of the teacher's time constraints, they will often be done intuitively. We have tallied participation most often to answer questions about students who are quiet and seldom speak. Such students are easy to lose in a classroom of their more vocal peers. Sometimes we can sense cliques building or antagonisms growing; participation charts help clarify our feelings and guide our strategy for negotiating them.

Checklists.   Checklists record the presence or absence of individual behaviors or attitudes. These can be made by you, an outside observer, or by students. Checklists can be lists of expected behaviors or of actual behaviors. Figure 13-8 is a list of questions that Probst (1988a) suggests as a way of monitoring student progress.

Rating Scales.   Checklists also record frequency or quality. These can involve error counts made in writing or the number of pages completed in reading. They are especially important when performance is essential to evaluation, as in the selection and individual reading of novels or poems for a term.

Chronologs.   A chronolog is a detailed report of a student that records all that the observer sees and hears during a specified learning event. Such reports can be only infrequently attempted by the classroom teacher, but they can provide comprehensive data from which to draw conclusions. When we have had serious difficulties with students, having a colleague come and quietly keep a chronolog has helped us form keener impressions and take more positive remedial steps than would have been possible otherwise.

FIGURE 13–8
Questions about
student progress

1. Does the student seem willing to express responses to a work, or is she cautious and constrained?
2. Does the student ever change her mind, or is she intransigent?
3. Does the student participate in discussions, listening to others, considering ideas offered, and presenting her own thoughts?
4. Does the student distinguish between the thoughts and feelings she brings to a literary work and those that can be reasonably attributed to the text?
5. Is the student able to distinguish between fact, inference, and opinion in the reading of a literary work?
6. Is the student able to relate the literary work to other human experience, especially her own—that is, can she generalize and abstract?
7. Does the student accept the responsibility for making meaning out of the literature and the discussions? Or does she depend on others to tell her what works mean?
8. Does the student perceive differences and similarities in the visions offered by different literary works, or is she unaware of the subtleties?

To record our observations of students more easily, we might recast our list of questions as dichotomous pairs. The first question, for example, might simply be:

open .... closed

Others might be:

speaks willingly .... speaks reluctantly
enjoys the reading .... dislikes the reading
relates work to self... remains distant
listens to others .... refuses to hear other ideas
rational .... emotional

Locating students on each continuum may give the teacher useful information about their habits and inclinations. (p. 228)

SOURCE: From Robert Probst, *Response and analysis: Teaching literature in junior and senior high school*. Portsmouth, NH: Boynton/Cook.

Whether you rely on informal observation or try to incorporate formal observation into your evaluative plan, these principles can help guide you. Observation

-   should not intrude or disrupt instruction.
-   should "take place in authentic situations—those that are part of normal instruction" (Anthony et al., 1991, p. 30).
-   should be directed toward answering questions about individual students or whole-class learning.
-   becomes more productive when those questions are specific and the observations are single-minded.
-   should reflect a range of processes and a variety of products.
-   can involve collaboration with student, parents, and colleagues.
-   may be more important to understanding some students and classes than others.

Purves, Rogers, and Soter (1990) discuss an evaluation-of-literature strategy based on observation. Their concern is not to evaluate students' memory of previous "passive" learning but the "processes of thinking, feeling, responding, and imagining they can bring to bear on a new experience" (p. 174). They suggest that the teacher halve the class, present the groups with a new literary selection, ask them to discuss it, and record their discussion through notes, an audiotape, or a videotape. Following the discussion, the teacher and/or the observing students assess the "performance and process" orally or in a written "marking," even playing the tape back. Here are their specific suggestions: "As you listen to the class or the recording, make notes about where you think the students might have checked something, where you think a student did a particularly good job picking up on somebody else's ideas, where you can suggest another example, and so forth" (p. 174).

Rudd (1990) provides a detailed account of her list-keeping strategies as an English teacher. She uses multiple copies of her classroom roster to catalogue such things as a student's implementation of writing skills (use of sensory details or vivid verbs, for example), employment of new vocabulary, misspelled words, and variety of sentence structure. In the spirit of self-directed learning, she advises, "often it is desirable for students to be involved finding the samples themselves," but then urges limiting the number of characteristics to be observed, perhaps even to one. The intention is to use information to focus instruction, not drown the student or teacher in excessive or disconnected data.

ALTERNATIVE GRADING CHOICES

Because few schools in the United States have abolished grades entirely, even teachers who use alternative evaluation strategies wind up having to assign one letter or number to represent student learning. Table 13–3 enumerates the traditional range of grades. To shake the anxiety-producing and

TABLE 13–3
Traditional grading schema

Numerical Range			Letter Grade
95–100	93–100	90–100	A
88–94	85–92	80–89	B
81–87	77–84	70–79	C
75–80	69–76	60–69	D
0–74	0–68	0–59	F

FIGURE 13–9
Alternative grading schemes

A	Excellent	Excellent	G (good)	H (high pass)	/+
B	Good	Shows Improvement	S (satisfactory)	P (pass)	/
C	Fair	Needs Improvement	U (unsatisfactory)	L (low pass)	/−
D	Poor	No Improvement			
F	Fail	Failing	F (fail)	F (fail)	F (fail)

stigmatizing effects of numerical grades or their equivalent letters, some schools have shifted to the alternative systems shown in Figure 13-9. Whatever our attempts to downplay or negotiate around grading's negative consequences, however, grades seem to remain hierarchical and summative. Inertia erodes our best attempts at change. Some systems simplify to pass/fail, but even these are often corrupted into high and low passes. Two of the advantages of such systems—that students are more relaxed about their work and are freed to take greater personal risks with it—are lost as the hierarchical ladder forms itself again. (Credit/No credit systems can avoid these pitfalls and remove the stigma of failure, but in traditional schools they still require a judgment by an authority outside of the student.)

POLARITIES WITHIN EVALUATION

The following 10 polarities contain other choices that teachers can make about how they grade. For clarity, we make these contrasts sharper than they appear in school life. One of Downie's (1967) basic principles about the future of testing is pertinent: "In a democracy every form of appraisal will have critics, which is a spur to change and improvement" (p. 9). After we describe the extremes of our 10 polarities, we invite you to place yourself at some spot along a continuum between each 2. Such a placement between competing claims may spur you to improve both.

Quantitative–Qualitative.   One of the most troubling questions of grading for beginning teachers is "How much should I take the personal lives of my students into consideration in my evaluation?" The quantitative teacher looks at performance objectively, sums scores on graded events, and assigns marks to them. Although the quantitative teacher's strict time lines and standards may send an uncomfortable message to students, they encourage independence and responsibility. Students are asked to manage their own affairs. Knowledge and understanding about a student's private life are not withheld, but the whole class's agenda is the focus. The individual must negotiate around it independently.

The qualitative teacher accepts knowledge about the private lives of students as pertinent to evaluation. Such personal knowledge can be instrumental in encouraging the developing student. Response to the individual student is paramount to the efficient functioning of the whole class. However, just as too little sympathetic awareness of individual students is problematic, so too is involvement with students. For teachers negotiating five classes and 150 students, being as open to the nuances of individual lives as they might want to be is exhausting and complicated. Furthermore, students who are shy, self-sufficient, or distrustful of school authorities can be given less consideration than they deserve. No teacher can be all knowing, and students are not equally accessible.

Personal–Anonymous.   This dichotomy also relates to the matter of judging student responses. In addition, it returns you to the question of omniscience. You can read the responses knowing who wrote them or offer students a measure of privacy. If you prefer the latter, you can let students make codes that they, but not you, can identify. (We have used birthdates and middle initials or social security numbers.) Students often feel a greater sense of fairness in grading when their work is judged anonymously. Even if you intend to have an objective approach to scoring, biases may creep in. With anonymous grading, no prior assumptions or grade stereotypes can be carried from one testing event to the next.

Absolute–Relative.   Another grading dilemma similar to the problem of knowledge about students is that of absolute and relative standards. We can consider relative or absolute standards more broadly in regard to general knowledge or course content. If you work from an open epistemology that does not believe in set and final answers to complex ideas, issues, or texts, you may be open to the many interpretations of "Young Goodman Brown" or be very permissive in the use of the comma. On the other hand, if you hold an unequivocal view about the basic qualities of romanticism or the proper use of *may* and *can,* you might be more rigid about students' literary discussion or written usage.

We also can consider the same polarity in relation to whether grades are established strictly by meeting set criteria (Identifying 9 of 10 quotes from *Macbeth* earns a student an *A.*) or whether the grade assigned is dependent on the performance of the entire group. If seven correct identifications are the best performance in the class, it earns an *A,* not a *C* as it might in an absolute grading system. Seeing the individual's performance with respect to a group's performance (grading on the curve) can be rather sophisticated (as detailed in statistics and tests and measurements courses) or appear to be somewhat quixotic and cavalier (as determined by the charity of the grader). These polar positions also can be referred to as criterion-referenced versus norm-referenced interpretations of performance.

Objective–Subjective.   Many students regard grading as the basic way to label a teacher as either an objective or subjective grader. Students themselves enjoy the comfort of counting on the straightforward, unbiased, public verifiability of the objective test, especially when exam or essay questions are poorly conceived and articulated. In addition, the objectivity brings with it a consoling certainty about what is the right and wrong response. Furthermore, because the objective test tends to challenge the lower mental processes of recall and comprehension, students are not straining to the higher processes of analysis and synthesis. But this exactitude is problematic in English, where certainty in all dimensions of language is evasive and where teachers ask students to operate at the most challenging boundaries of their abilities.

Most teachers and students operate with a more fluid, less exact approach to language and literature, but they realize that open-ended evaluative strategies are difficult. The constructed-response questions of essay tests or long-answer exams are dreaded by students because they are so broad and the teacher's grading of them is so uncertain. Beyond the issue of teacher reliability across many papers is the question of what teachers define as the skill or knowledge that they are evaluating. In having students write about literature, for instance, teachers often are not themselves sure whether they are interested in the writing skills of literary analysis or in the analytical or imaginative skills of literary interpretation. Essay items by definition involve language and writing skills, and thus they handicap the less-able writer, vocabulary user, and speller, and those whose handwriting is poor.

A further dimension of this split is the type of marks that the two poles tend to generate. Most objective grading has the appearance of exactitude and can be quantitatively established: 33 out of 40 correct T/F responses yields an 82.5 percentage. At the other extreme, a very strong essay on nature in Native American chants, an acceptable one on comparisons between Buck's *The Good Earth* and Bertolucci's *The Last Emperor,* and a weak one on Lady Macbeth's metaphors can all come to a *C+* in a qualitative system in which grader reliability is hard to achieve.

Incidental–Cumulative.   Most beginning teachers think of the grading process as assigning just these kinds of quantitative or qualitative marks to each of the tests, papers, or other assignments completed in a term. The grading events most often stand alone, and their sum at the end of a grading period (with various weights assigned to quizzes, tests, class contribution, and long or short projects) comprises the final grade. Beginning teachers often adopt this incidental approach because it is the grading system that they have experienced. When little or no system exists, summing isolated grading events is the system that falls into place. It is further reinforced by the traditional, seemingly commonsensical assigning of an absolute grade to each student product.

The cumulative, or incremental, approach puts all of the grades into a system so that each event is a clear part of a total process. It requires that all assignments be given some weight, and that the sum of those weights equal the grand total, usually 100 or 1,000. It is a planned economy though, not a free market. Because the cumulative approach requires full planning for the term or the year as a necessary precondition for adoption, it is hard to use by those who are teaching a course for the first time or by those who make their plans as they move through the year. It is also alien for those who use their students' styles and experiences to establish their approach to evaluation. But it is an approach that you might find useful as you gain greater confidence and mastery of your classroom. There is a final reckoning, at which point the person with, say, 930 points receives an *A* while another with 870 gets only a *B.* Moreover, the weights for each of the incidents and a knowledge of what part of the total is needed for an *A, B, C, D,* or *F* must be clearly spelled out at the beginning.

The disadvantages of such careful system building are obvious, but strong advantages also argue for its use:

- It avoids the student ego struggles with teachers over whether a paper or test is an *A* or a *B*. The use of numerical weights undercuts that contest.
- It opens the grading process so that mysteries and quixotic obstructions are generally eliminated, or at least diminished.
- It gives students the sense that every effort adds up to a grand total controlled by their own choices rather than by fate.
- It generally encourages the creation of multiple, small, manageable grading events rather than a few overwhelming blockbusters.

The third advantage is especially useful in awarding grades for increments of the extended writing process: Every step that students take is rewarded by a small number of points.

Holistic–Partial.
This dichotomy relates more narrowly to how the teacher reads or grades a test. For essay tests particularly, the teacher has a simple choice between reading each individual student's test all the way through or reading all student responses to the same question and repeating the process through each successive question. Typically, teachers appear to grade each student's entire test, one after the other. A grade is assigned based on the summing of points for each answer or on the teacher's more general impression of quality.

A partial approach has benefits worth considering as an alternative. When you read an entire class response to a single question, you have the advantage of greater clarity about how a student responds to the question because of your focus upon that question and answer. Almost like an assembly-line worker, you economize and clarify the operation by repetition of it. You also do not as easily carry your judgment of the student from one question to the next because of the time interval between questions. (We also reshuffle the pile after each question.) Every response of every student to every question is dealt with in a fresh way.

Independent–Individual.
Independent work places students on different learning tracks of their own making, while individual instruction (programmed instruction) puts all students on the same learning track but with different timetables. With individualized learning, because performance is fixed and only time is variable, evaluation of students occurs at different times, but not necessarily in different forms. Programmed instruction features sameness and objectivity; like the hamburgers at McDonald's and the beds at Holiday Inn, there are no surprises. All student work moves toward a common objective standard, though at differing paces. Assessment of the mastery of these objectives simply requires the teacher to choose from the array of traditional and nontraditional measures.

Independence opens students to choice and invites them to take off in directions of their own choosing. Consequently, an assessment of mastery of content is difficult, and even an assessment of common skills or methodologies (for instance, using the semicolon, varying point of view in a narrative, or identifying rhyme schemes in poetry) is hard. The joy and independence of learning, a general consciousness of language or literature, and the successful completion of chosen tasks might become the most salient features to be evaluated. The idiosyncratic evolutions of free-style student learning will challenge the teacher during assessment, but its possibilities for discovery and growth may make the challenge worth accepting.

Bound–Open.
Embedded in the question of independent versus individual assessment is the question of time. Most of our classrooms are bounded by strict time limitations in their curricula, instruction, and assessment. An open approach might begin with the freedom of time allowed by programmed instruction, but it should run deeper. Bloom's (1968) mastery learning asks teachers to allow students the time they need to do their work well, rather than hustling them onward whether or not they have fully understood their lessons. Such hurry breeds in students and teachers alike a lack of concern for the idea at hand, whether that is constructing simple sentences or contrasting narrative styles in *The Pigman*. Those who are uncertain about the former in the 4th grade will be totally defeated by the latter in the 10th grade.

But an open approach can suggest something more than allowing students to complete a computer-assisted instruction (CAI) program at their own rate. An open classroom allows the time that most of England's elementary schools give children to complete serious, high-quality, unhurried work. English grading relies on a portfolio type of assessment, which does not report 87s or even *A*'s, but contains detailed notes about, for example, the way a student handles narration as opposed to analysis in written composition. In U.S. schools, an open approach could mean more time to do things well and less pressure on tests to spill everything out in one burst. If most testing must be conventionally built on speed, perhaps a part of our grading could be as time-free as possible. Take-home exams or tests that generally take half a period, with the remainder to be used by quick students for silent reading or writing would be useful to both the speedy and the methodical. The extended writing process, of course, signals the switch from 50-minute writing assignments to those that require parts of many days with much time for reflection and sorting things out. A totally open approach to instruction and assessment is hardly conceivable; everything we undertake has finite time limits placed upon it and the most intractable of time constraints—the school year—limits any assignment's ultimate due date.

Formative–Summative.   These terms refer to both the timing and the purpose of testing or evaluation. In timing, formative testing or evaluation is done over time, usually in small increments such as weekly quizzes. Summative testing is done, as the term implies, at the conclusion of instruction; it gives a more summary picture of performance, as with final examinations. In purpose, formative testing monitors student progress and often tests modest instructional objectives. It is used frequently to diagnose individual problems with learning. It is also valuable for questioning students' attitudes toward their work and their engagement in it. If teachers discover negative drifts during the year, they can act to correct them. Sampling student response at the end of a term or year does not yield profitable, course-altering information for that group. Summative testing more often provides information about whether the student has achieved a desired final outcome of instruction. Formative testing has a narrow focus; summative has a wider vision.

Some teachers use formative testing predominantly and even sum such testing for final grading. Others rely more on large, end-of-unit examinations in which students rise or fall on their performance on one day. We employ both for different purposes and in acknowledgement of different student styles. We use formative evaluation to keep track of basic skills or knowledge and to reward those students who try hard and perform best on small, discrete tasks such as quizzes of reading. (We find that it works as both a motivating force—to keep students honest—and as a reward.) We deploy summative examinations to allow students to work at Bloom's higher levels of analysis, synthesis, and evaluation. We are deeply interested in students' work in progress, but we also want students to have the opportunity of making broad kinds of judgments about a larger body of material.

Cooperative–Competitive.   Some teachers work constantly to undermine the competition that seems so basic to our culture, while others assume that competition is both natural and useful and therefore exploit it. Nowhere do students learn competition more readily than in school testing. They quickly see in the elementary and middle grades (before athletics intercedes to introduce physical prowess into the equation) that the rewards schools provide—"grades, honors, recognitions, affection"—are conditioned on individual achievement (Purpel, 1989, p. 35). As testing is established in individual classrooms, schools, systems, states, and our nation, often students are pitted against each other. We erect ladders that move up from failure to success and then arrange students along them. We assume that students arrive at their rungs by their own choices, by the quality of their performance. We fail to acknowledge our own determining part as test constructors of those ladders. We overlook the individual differences of the students whom we expect to climb them. Sadly, we also fail to notice the negative consequences on those who can never progress past the bottom rungs.

But whether we accept competition and hierarchy as inevitable or learned, we can still decide whether to encourage or discourage them. Ways to discourage competition among students and encourage a sense of community purpose in learning range from the construction of group tests to the abandonment of testing altogether. In the former, pairs of students, small groups, and whole classes can be given problems to be solved together. The same mark is given to all members of the group, or individuals can be given their own baseline score with bonus points for the class's or their group's attainment of a specified goal. At the latter end might be a move to portfolio evaluation. But even if the most traditional instruments are used in common ways, teachers can influence a class sense of individual competition versus communal purpose by their professed attitude toward grading. When teachers use grades to punish, cajole, and praise, to single out high achievers and shame low achievers, students become alienated from each other and protective of their own performance. When grading events are treated more casually—high achievers are not publicly extolled, low achievers are not scolded—the corrosive effects of individual competition can be mitigated. Lower achievers also can be praised for specific strengths and successes and the unique contributions that they make to a class. If you provide structured opportunities for expressing multiple intelligences, everyone achieves sometimes.

These dichotomies represent a range of choices that individual teachers can make in developing whole systems, designing questions and assignments, or marking them. Such choices rest within prior decisions about curricula and instructional approaches. We encourage you to make your evaluation consistent with your instruction. We would not expect, for instance, that an exploratory lesson on *The Scarlet Letter* (which asks students in groups to speculate on the moral values of Hester, Dimmesdale, and Chillingworth) be tested by matching or multiple-choice questions. We further encourage your fitting the evaluation strategy to the students before you. As you establish your classroom, you may wish to review this list of polarities and decide which of them will be important to consider seriously. You will want to experiment with some and try different points along these continua to see how you and your students respond. We feel that such wrestling with alternatives is critical to the effectiveness of your teaching and your students' learning. As Downie (1967) reminds us, such struggle spurs us to imagine better possibilities.

Invitation to Reflection 13–3

- Review the ten polar dichotomies and decide where you stand on each of these.

Quantitative	Qualitative
Personal	Anonymous
Absolute	Relative
Objective	Subjective
Incidental	Cumulative
Holistic	Partial
Independent	Individual
Bound	Open
Formative	Summative
Cooperative	Competitive

- Would your former high school and college English teachers fall at different places from you on the continuum?
- Do you find any evaluation possibilities in these 10 that are new to you? If so, which?
- Do you find any evaluation traits about which you feel strongly, and which you hope to incorporate into your own classroom?
- One of William James's Harvard students was the writer Gertrude Stein. Barzun (1983) tells the story of Stein's having gone to too many operas and "finding herself mentally vacant in front of the final in James's course. . . . She addressed James on the blue book, saying she did not feel like writing philosophy that day. As she remembered it after thirty years, the next day, she had from James a postal card: 'I understand perfectly how you feel. I often feel like that myself.' He passed her then, but his sense of justice to others exacted an 'exit' examination [from the university later]" (p. 278). How would you evaluate James as an evaluator?

Keep these alternatives in mind as you observe experienced teachers and note where they fall along these continua. We encourage you to wait 2 years and take another look at this chapter.

All of the contending means of assessment will likely continue to raise questions for you as you become an experienced teacher. We turn now to the more specific challenges for English teachers, who must grade and evaluate performance in reading, writing, speaking, and listening.

EVALUATING KNOWLEDGE AND RESPONSE TO LITERATURE

Many critics deplore the reductive nature of reading and writing tests that tend to concentrate on questions that are testable: questions of content, questions of passive (or remembered) knowledge, and questions with simple answers. They believe that tests of literary knowledge should be tied to our deepest perceptions about student reading and learning. Our teaching purposes should determine our testing, rather than our testing determining our teaching purposes. Purves et al. (1990) explain the dilemma of testing students' knowledge and response to literature. They locate the tension in the act of reading literature. They use a distinction that Rosenblatt makes between reading undertaken to experience a text personally, sensually, and viscerally (aesthetic) and reading undertaken to gain information or instruction (efferent):*

> We have suggested that literary works are not read and talked about as other kinds of texts are read but are to be read differently. Louise Rosenblatt calls this kind of reading aesthetic and contrasts it to the efferent reading that one does with informational texts such as those of social studies and science. The current reading tests only measure efferent reading and by implication signal to students that it is the only kind of reading that is to be valued. (pp. 165–166)

*Britton (1970) uses the terms *poetic* and *transactional* to make the same distinction; Bruner (1986) speaks of "a good story and a well-formed argument" (p. 11).

discover relationships or definitions; the teacher does not have to write plausible distractors; its compression of content allows students to take it quickly and cover a large amount of content. Cautionary guidelines include the following:.

- Make matching items neither tricky nor simplistic.
- Write both columns with clear and parallel structure.
- Avoid lists with longer than 10 entries or students waste time trying to sort out responses.

Some teachers include more options than can be matched to the list of stems to eliminate the confounding problem of one bad answer creating other answers that also must be incorrect.

Multiple Choice.   Multiple-choice questions usually consist of an introductory question, or stem, and four or five statements, one of which best completes that stem. Well-written possible answers, called *distractors,* can engage students in a process of making finer distinctions than can true/false or matching questions. Furthermore, if you analyze the distractors that are most seductive to students, that is, those that many mistakenly choose, you have useful diagnostic information about students' confusions. Cautionary guidelines include the following:

- Write questions that invite application, comparison, analysis, and synthesis.
- Make the distractors parallel in structure and length.
- Write plausible distractors.
- Construct stems and distractors that are simple and compact.
- Avoid distractors that are so close to the correct answer that to choose between them is to split hairs.

    Exercise 13–2 offers you the opportunity to analyze and evaluate a multiple-choice test.

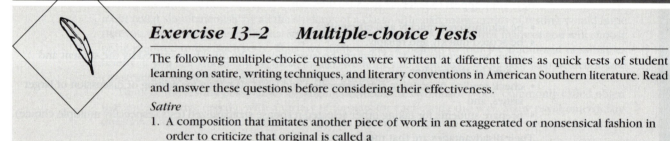

Exercise 13–2   *Multiple-choice Tests*

The following multiple-choice questions were written at different times as quick tests of student learning on satire, writing techniques, and literary conventions in American Southern literature. Read and answer these questions before considering their effectiveness.

Satire

1. A composition that imitates another piece of work in an exaggerated or nonsensical fashion in order to criticize that original is called a
    a. fable
    b. farce
    c. burlesque
    d. parody
    e. comedy
2. A brief tale frequently using animals as characters told to point out a moral is called a
    a. fable
    b. farce
    c. burlesque
    d. comedy
    e. parody
3. The exaggeration or distortion of certain individual (personal) characteristics to produce a comic, grotesque, or ridiculous effect is called
    a. irony
    b. comedy
    c. caricature
    d. farce
    e. innuendo
4. The following lines by La Rouchefoucauld are examples of
    a. invective
    b. epigram
    c. comedy
    d. farce
    e. caricature

"We all have power enough to endure the misfortunes of others."

"In the misfortune of our best friends, we always find something not altogether displeasing."

"We often pardon those who bore us, but we cannot pardon those whom we bore."

5. The following anecdotes of Dorothy Parker are an example of
   a. satire
   b. epigram
   c. caricature
   d. repartee
   e. parody

When a woman told her, "I really can't come to your party, I can't bear fools," Mrs. Parker answered, "That's strange, your mother could."

When told that Clare Boothe Luce was always kind to her inferiors, Mrs. Parker asked, "Where does she find them?"

Writing Technique

1. Honesty is important in writing. A false note will have the effect of
   a. angering the reader
   b. confusing the reader
   c. undermining the reader's confidence in the writer
   d. making the writer appear pedantic
   e. enhancing the thesis perhaps

2. Identify the stylistic device used in the following sentence.
   a. transition
   b. parallel structure
   c. a breezy tone
   d. sentimentality
   e. dialectical language

"None of this improved my character, spurred my ambition, or gave me a deeper understanding of life."

Literary Conventions (in Southern Literature)

1. Freitag's Triangle diagrams the outline of
   a. character
   b. plot
   c. theme
   d. point of view
   e. catastrophe

2. In "Petrified Man," if Eudora Welty had given Mrs. Fletcher the name Mrs. Medusa, we would refer to that naming as
   a. an allusion
   b. a metaphor
   c. a personification
   d. a cliche
   e. an allegory

3. Which of the following literary terms *best* explains how Welty uses Max in relationship to Steve in "Keela, the Outcast Indian Maiden"?
   a. protagonist
   b. antagonist
   c. round
   d. dynamic
   e. foil

- Did these questions follow principles of good multiple-choice construction?
- Did they require students to
  recall?
  analyze?
  understand?
  synthesize?
  apply?
  evaluate?
- Can you envision a teaching situation in which such questions would be helpful?

Review the following multiple-choice questions to see whether you note the difference we are trying to establish between recall and recognition of significant facts and retrieval of trivia.

When Huck visits the Phelps farm, he
a. dresses like a girl
b. helps Tom escape
c. pretends to be Tom
d. turns Jim in to Mr. Phelps

At the Grangerford's funeral, the undertaker returned from the basement
a. with the money in his hands
b. saying a rat was there
c. to have a snort of whiskey
d. after the service was over

In the first question, the distractors contain seeds of other important actions of the story (Huck pretending to be a girl, believing he should turn Jim in as a runaway slave, being overwhelmed once again by Tom's romantic falderal in helping Jim "escape"). The correct answer is a small, yet significant detail: Huck takes on Tom's name and his foolish characteristics during this episode. It is a detail that you would hope any insightful reader would attend to. The second question probably separates a very good memory from a less facile one, but tells you little else about reading and interpretive skills. You can assume that most of the details an author selects are well considered and are thus of some significance, but some are clearly more important than others; they are the ones we need to select. These more significant details are ones that students can infer if they know the work, rather than merely draw out of their memory bank.

A difficult form of multiple-choice question, which presents students with the challenge of making finer discriminations, is one that allows for more than one answer to be correct:

Huck's love of mystery and disguise is suggested by which of the following?
1. He dresses as a girl.
2. He pretends to be a sheriff's deputy.
3. He dresses Jim as an Indian.
4. He pretends to be Tom Sawyer.
The correct response to the preceding question is
a. 1, 2 and 4
b. 1, 2, 3, and 4
c. 1, 2, and 3
d. 1 and 3
e. 4 only

Analogies.   Analogies are another way of asking students to think in terms of relationships of characters, events, places, and objects. Simple analogies can set up three parts of a paradigm and ask students to complete the relationships by selecting one answer from a group of four. Because this format is uncommon and difficult, we recommend that you give students an example and an explanation of why the correct answer is best among the four. A variant of this format centers on relationships, but it asks students to look over a list of paired relationships and select the one that is unlike all the others. An example of this format, Figure 13–11, is taken from a test on 10 adolescent novels: *Home Before Dark, The Princess Bride, Tuck Everlasting, Ordinary People, The Summer of My German Soldier, The Contender, That Was Then, This Is Now, A Hero Ain't Nothin' but a Sandwich, The Chocolate War,* and *House of Stairs.*

CONSTRUCTED-RESPONSE (SUBJECTIVE)

By constructed response, we mean those questions that require students to construct their responses rather than select them. We wish to distinguish a range of such questions between those that offer limited options and those that are more extended.

Limited.   Limited-option questions (short answer and identification or association) have some of the virtues of both selected-response and constructed-response questions. They are

• easy to score,
• quick to take,

FIGURE 13–11
Analogies test on 10 adolescent novels

I. CHARACTER AND THEME

Which relationship or action is unlike that of any other in the group (circle the letter)?

1. a. Ann and Stella
   b. Count Rugen and Westley
   c. Berger and Conrad
   d. Mr. Tuck and Winnie
   e. Ruth and Patty

2. a. Inigo and six-fingered sword
   b. Patty and family ring
   c. Winnie and vial of water
   d. Alfred and alarm wire
   e. Bryon and Charlie's car

3. a. Bryon and Mark's pills
   b. Yellow Suit Man and Music Box
   c. FBI and initialed shirt
   d. Stella and shotgun house

4. a. Butler's wait at detox Center
   b. Stella's move to Maggie's house
   c. Jerry's advice to Goober
   d. Peter's refusal to dance
   e. Calvin's backyard embrace

• not as difficult to construct as good multiple-choice and matching questions, and
• often test a higher level of cognition than selected-response questions do.

Extended questions have a clear advantage of opening a considerable latitude of response to the student; however, issues of scoring fairness and speed arise.

Short Answer. Short-answer questions are in a middle land between clear-cut objective items and subjective essay responses. They are objective enough to call for fairly definite answers yet open enough to challenge more than recall or recognition. Cautionary guidelines include the following:

• Avoid ambiguity.
• Favor a format of questions, rather than of fill in the blank or supply the missing words (so that students have a clearer idea about what is being asked).
• Try to write questions that have only one unique, correct response but that test more than recall.
• Avoid lifting sentences directly from the text.

To guard against encouraging reading for trivial test items, we sometimes ask students to summarize two or three examples of a designated principle or fact. For example, you might ask students to name three examples of false identification in *The Adventures of Huckleberry Finn* or three important references to children in *Macbeth*. This requires a good, working grasp of central issues in the works.

Identification or Association. Identification or association questions, while requiring constructed responses, actually rely strongly on memory because students must supply the missing identity. The stem or descriptor is present, but no identity list is offered. For instance, in assessing students' reading of a play or piece of fiction, a quote is given and students are asked to identify the speaker or even the place, time, and addressee. The answer is indisputable, like those in the four selected-response formats, but the task of answering is more difficult for students, who must recall rather than merely select, and a bit more taxing for teachers, who must grade without simple grading keys.

English teachers commonly use identification of quotes or passages, especially longer excerpts, to check students' knowledge of the work; to query students about any of the elements of fiction, poetry, or drama; or to test broad interpretation. Such passages or excerpts should be representative of or important to the work or the literary element under study; otherwise, students are frustrated and learn to treat testing as a capricious game. One variation on the use of quotes is to ask students to state the central idea or theme among two or three passages. Another is to present in random order a set of five passages that show the linear development of a character such as Huck Finn or Macbeth and ask students to place them in a chronological sequence of development. This order of development might also be used for progression of theme in a longer literary piece. A variant on this strategy involves listing a set of four or five passages, one of which does not carry forward the theme found in the other passages. Students are asked to name the theme embodied in the other four and circle the passage that is not congruent with the others. Cautionary guidelines include the following:

• Make certain that identifications are of significant material.
• Write clear instructions about how students are to respond to that which is being identified.

• Be certain of your testing purpose. If it is to distinguish those who have read a work, for instance, obscure passages are not necessary.

Exercise 13–3 offers you a short-answer test to take and evaluate.

Exercise 13–3   Short-answer Tests

Following is a list of definitions. Write the literary term defined in the space provided.

_____ 1. The context in time and place in which the action of a story occurs.

_____ 2. The central idea or unifying generalization implied or stated by a literary work.

_____ 3. The angle of vision from which a story is told. Another critic defines it as "the physical vantage point" occupied by the narrator in a story and the device by which the writer establishes the "authority" for the fiction.

_____ 4. A character whose distinguishing moral qualities and personal traits are complex and many-sided.

_____ 5. A character whose distinguishing moral qualities and personal traits are one-dimensional.

_____ 6. A character whose essential nature does not change in the course of the story.

_____ 7. A character whose experiences cause a change in attitude, which in turn modifies behavior, so that this character emerges a different person at the conclusion of the work.

_____ 8. The attitudes toward the subject of the story and toward the audience implied in a literary work.

_____ 9. A method of writing that describes the procession of thoughts and sense impressions in a lifelike fashion.

_____ 10. A situation or a use of language that implies some discrepancy or incongruity.

Traditional organization of plot has often been graphed on what is called Freitag's Triangle. Please label each of the points indicated.

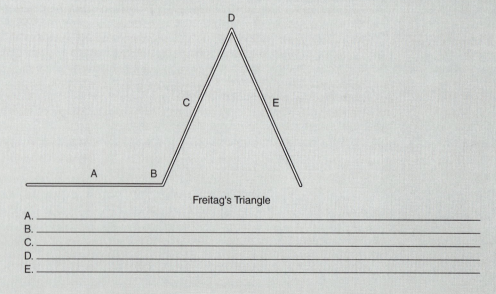

Freitag's Triangle

A. _____
B. _____
C. _____
D. _____
E. _____

• Did taking this test require you to think through literary conventions with anything more than simple recall?
• Can you imagine a classroom context in which it might be useful?

- Did it violate any of the cautions given previously?
- Is it parallel in structure?
- Is it stated clearly?
- Did it operate at Bloom's level of
  knowledge?
  understanding?
  application?
  analysis?
  synthesis?
  evaluation?

Extended.   Extended questions range from the focused to the open. They can be single questions or grouped with two or three other questions from which students can choose to answer a selected number. They can be assigned ahead of the timed testing situation and written (with or without notes) within it or assigned for completion outside of the classroom. Because our bias is toward presenting opportunities for students to construct their own meaning and express their personal understanding, we favor open choices. But some situations (for instance, a curriculum that intends to prepare students for standardized test taking or needs to certify that all students have covered the same material) and some students (those especially who need teacher encouragement or have difficult out-of-school environments for writing) will dictate traditional, in-school, class-long testing.

Regardless of the setup for posing extended questions, they offer the advantages of

- measuring a range of cognitive processes from recall to evaluation,
- inviting students' use of multiple intelligences,
- encouraging students' expression of attitudes and values,
- presenting the possibilities of problem solving or applying knowledge to new situations,
- allowing the possibility of group work, and
- mirroring the kind of organization and expression more typical of adult life.

Focused. Focused questions also ask students to construct rather than select their own responses, but the responses are more elaborate than are those to short-answer and identification questions. The most common college and university testing format is the focused essay question. (It is also common in academic secondary classes.) Students structure their own answers to teacher-made questions, but they usually set forth a central idea and develop it with some detail and at some length. Traditionally, such questions elicit an expository, argumentative, or persuasive essay. Presently, many teachers are moving with greater confidence to more open questions that encourage a greater rhetorical range that encompasses description, narration, and expression.

The focused essay question, for instance, might ask students to respond to a broad idea: gentility in shore communities (*The Adventures of Huckleberry Finn*), ambition and fate (*Macbeth* and *Othello*), the harsh side of nature (Emily Dickinson), or the rootlessness of migrant workers' children (Bridger's *Home Before Dark*). The question requires a knowledge and comprehension of particulars, but at the same time provides a freedom of response that allows individual and creative thinking. Dixon (1984) poses questions that are somewhat similar but offer more freedom of response. A few of his examples follow:

- In Chapter 19 of *Great Expectations:* What do these farewells tell us about the boy Pip at this stage of the novel? Bearing in mind how he develops later, how do you feel about Pip at this point? (Remember, your feelings may vary according to the company.)
- In act 3, scene 2, of *Macbeth:* In what ways do you find Macbeth and Lady Macbeth behaving characteristically, and what do you find unexpected in their behavior, attitudes, and language? (You will need to think back to their earlier scenes together.)
- In Chapter 34 of *Jane Eyre:* What does this scene between St. John Rivers and Jane add to your understanding of him and what he thinks is important in life?

These questions each focus on a very specific incident in the work, but they open up the work and students' responses by asking students to explore the entire work imaginatively in terms of the change undergone by a character.

A further departure still is questions that are based on the text but move away from it. L. H. Willey (personal communication, 1991) has 8th-grade students read *The Diary of Anne Frank* as part of a unit on courage. She then poses a series of questions on *The Diary of Anne Frank* that require students to know the text but then to move imaginatively, speculatively, and personally beyond it:

- Explain why this work is appropriate for this unit.
- Compare and contrast the courage displayed by Anne with the courage displayed by a character in one of the readings (a, b, c).
- Everyone who resided in the Secret Annex died except Otto Frank. Considering the sacrifices, the lack of privacy, the deprivation, and other restrictions, was it worth it to go into hiding for that extra twenty-five months of life?
- Thoroughly describe Anne and Peter's relationship. Then answer this question: If they had survived to live again on the outside, what would have happened to their relationship?

Two primary disadvantages of focused questions concern us. These questions often come in the form of essay assignments, which rely on writing skills that may be tangential to the original evaluative intent. Spelling, vocabulary, grammar, and penmanship may become too instrumental in the essay writing. If writing as a process has been critical to a classroom organization, in-class essay examinations may be confounding because they are timed and thus do not allow for prewriting, rewriting, and editing. Slow writers especially are handicapped in such testing.

A strategy that aids weaker writers with their organization and expression is to pose questions with a built-in structure for the response. Such a question may be quite focused:

Describe one incident in which Huck grows close to Jim and learns from him, and then another in which he is more distant and ruptures their relationship. Give your interpretation of why he acts so differently in the two incidents and explain how this relates to the central intent of the novel.

Some teachers might even place a *1* after the phrase "learns from him," a *2* after the phrase "ruptures their relationship," a *3* after the phrase "the two incidents," and a *4* after the phrase "intent of the novel." The four phrases would create a content outline that would be difficult for many students to construct without such guidance. This format gives students guidelines for their responses, prods them to think about things in terms of relationships, and enables teachers to make better judgments about the quality of the responses. Some latitude is provided, but an enabling structure makes for great progress toward student independence. The answers build on each other so that thought, too, builds to higher levels. The structure also makes it easy for teachers to allot points for nuances of response so the cumulative total for the test recognizes more of the students' understanding of the text. Finally, such a structured question makes key choices for students so they don't have to stew over them.

Scoring is the second disadvantage of focused questions in terms of both teacher time and scorer helpfulness and reliability. (We discuss English teachers' paper load and six scoring alternatives in the next section of this chapter.) Purves (1971) presents excellent guidelines for the constructor of essay questions:

The general rule for the writer of the essay question is . . . to do what he advises his students to do: narrow the topic. He will point his students in the direction he wants them to go, in terms that they can comprehend; he is not putting them in the desert without a compass. It may be that a teacher will want to give an assignment or a test that forces the student to do his own narrowing, particularly as a first assignment to see what sort of focus a class might have, or as an invitation to the class to consider the part of the course that they found most fruitful or relevant. These types of assignments, however, differ from the general purposes of summative evaluation, which will be best served by specific questions. (p. 728)

We add these cautionary guidelines:

- Construct questions that are not too broad, nor too specific, nor too cumbersome.
- Write questions that lead students toward high-level cognitive processes or invite them to use multiple intelligences. Use words such as *compare, contrast, analyze,* and *imagine.*
- Connect the question to the outcome you wish to measure.
- Imagine diverse and creative possibilities for writing.
- Consider asking questions in a way that structures their answer and makes them manageable.
- Consider the time that students will require to answer the question and use only those questions that can be comfortably answered in the allotted time.
- Frame broad, contextual questions to ask "the student to apply the works to the context, rather than the context to the work" (Purves, 1971, p. 728).

Teacher Becky Brown field-tests her essay questions. She constructs her essay topics and then answers them as though she is one of her students. Only then, she says, can she appreciate the hidden difficulties and pitfalls in her questions.

Open. The open test does not present a set of focused prompts for student response, nor is there an expected answer. It provides students more freedom of response than even the most open essay does. Its aim is a creative, idiosyncratic synthesis of the material in question; its method is to create a loose structure in which students operate. For instance, students who have studied Native American writers might be given a culminating "test," in which you tell them to imagine a book about Native American writers, and have them include the following:

1. Title
2. Cover design (rough sketch)
3. Preface (2-3 pages)
4. Table of contents (5-15 chapter titles)
5. Chapter introductions (2 chapters, $\frac{1}{2}$-1 page each)
6. Illustrations: photographs, drawings, paintings (with captions)
7. Notes for the treatment of three pieces
8. Book conclusion about the importance of its contents

You may wish to reverse the order from 8 to 1. Each of the parts of this "test" is working at a progressively more detailed level. Each depends on the other. Students are given choices within a large structure, but they must have a sense of the whole to develop the parts they select. The option of working from 8 to 1 is given because it allows students to develop their generalizations from all of the specifics that they have amassed.

Schaars (1992) suggests an essay question that culminates the study of Thoreau. She credits the idea to Tom Romano (1987, pp. 156-157):

> Through the miracle of 1980s technology, young Henry David Thoreau (same character, personality and principles) has been transported to the present. He is seventeen years old and living in Central Wisconsin. In an essay *describe six things he possesses* that reflect his personality, character, and concerns. Explain what each possession reveals about him. (p. 153)

A 1987 *English Journal* "Our Readers Write" feature asked readers "What's a new and interesting way to test students?" Here are five suggestions that impressed us with their imaginative openness.

Sociograms	Have students think about the relationships among characters in a novel or play and draw sociograms (tables of interpersonal relationships) describing and schematizing those characters. These work especially well in literary pieces with small casts. (Joanne K. A. Peters)
Decision Making	Use the dilemmas of literary works to provide a context in which to reflect on characters outside that work. For instance, in James Hilton's *Lost Horizon*, the characters at the end must decide whether to return to their former civilization or remain in Shangri-La. Have students write about how another character such as Wang Lung from Pearl Buck's *The Good Earth* would react to that situation. (Carl Carlsen)
Talk Shows	Ask students to assume "the hosting duties of their own talk show" and write the "transcript" of a given number of interviews of characters encountered in the course "including a person inside a poem or a poet." The results have been imaginative within a "familiar and comfortable" context. "In almost all transcripts, the dialogue discussed major themes embodied by the characters, and in many cases, the hosts were challenging, asking their character/guests probing questions exploring both sides of a motivation or decision. And, because they were transcribing speech, students used speech patterns and vocabulary appropriate to a chosen character/guest" (p. 72). (Carl Carlsen)
Newspapers	Ask students to write news stories about events in a book. The assignment can be directed to a certain audience—general, sensational, liberal, or conservative—or, we would add, to a specific type of column (for example, editorial page, feature article, obituary, or advice column). (Sharon Snyder)
Children's Books	Have students write "an original story or even a children's story or nursery rhyme as a naturalist like Dreiser or Crane (using any literary philosophy under study) might have, or as told by someone like Holden Caulfield in *The Catcher in the Rye* or McMurphy in *One Flew over the Cuckoo's Nest*" (p. 76). (Sharon Snyder)

Teachers also are devising evaluative opportunities to expand work done by groups of students that exercise the full range of intelligences. *The Council Chronicle* (November, 1991) reported on just such an open assessment, one written and reviewed by NCTE members involved in examining alternative approaches to assessment under the auspices of the New Standards Project of the Learning Research and Development Center (University of Pittsburgh) and the National Center on Education and the Economy (University of Rochester).

Open Assessment Instrument

Imagine that four of the characters from the literature you have read this year have gathered in one place. Work in groups of four. Each group will:

- Choose the four characters and the setting.
- Develop an interesting script that reflects the personality of the characters. The script will deviate from the plots of the works where the characters originally appeared.
- Prepare to perform this script in front of your classmates.
- Consider casting, staging, scenery, costuming, and props.
- Perform your scene for your classmates.
- Evaluate the scenes of other classmates.
- Write a reflective essay about your experiences in this project. (p. 1)

We close this discussion of open assessment with the ideas of Horn (1988), who taught the *Iliad* in a unit on heroes to a reluctant group of students; some were "learning disabled, some [were] foreign students struggling to learn English, some [were] slow learners, some [were] discouraged learners, underachievers, or on the five-year plan" (p. 25). Her imaginative instruction culminated in three evaluative projects.

- She asked students to "cartoon a story strip of *Days of Our Greeks.* Results were graded on completeness of plot, its being turned in on time, and effort."
- She assigned them to "write on one of six essay options ranging from 'Discuss one of the heroes studied in this unit' to 'Write a letter to a personal hero' and 'Imagine that you are a hero in the future. What did you do and why?'"
- And, our personal favorite: Horn wrote the *English Journal* article and then "gave it to small groups . . . to edit and revise. The article was not only a review of the unit but a lesson in editing and a statement to students about their value in the learning situation" (p. 26).

Invitation to Reflection 13–4

- How much of your high school teacher-made evaluation and testing were devoted to the following?

Selected-response: (Objective Tasks)

1. True/False
2. Matching
3. Multiple Choice
4. Analogies

Constructed-response: (Limited Tasks)

1. Short Answer
2. Identification or Association

Constructed-response: (Extended Tasks)

1. Focused (essay questions)
2. Open (holistic possibilities)

- Would your answers differ for your college/university English classes?
- Does any one of these strategies predominate in your memories of high school?
- Which has been the type of evaluation you have preferred for yourself?
- Have you had any teachers who have mixed these strategies?
- Have any of Bloom's cognitive processes or Gardner's multiple intelligences predominated in your experiences of testing? If so, which?
- If you plan to use any of these traditional means of assessment, would you use them differently from how your teachers used them?

EVALUATING WRITING

As with the evaluation of literature, the evaluation of writing needs to be carefully undertaken to assure that it does not undermine the deepest aims of our teaching. Assigning grades itself is dangerous. Mayher (1990) rightly sees the negative consequences when the writer's goal becomes getting the best grade: It "takes the responsibility for choosing how to most effectively compose a piece away from the writer and cedes it to the teacher/grader. Experimentation is therefore restricted, and everyone sticks as carefully as possible to those prestructured genres of antiwriting which have proved themselves the safest paths to good grades" (p. 239). The way those grades are assigned complicates those dangers.

The most common classroom practice in evaluating secondary students' writing is for the teacher to read student papers, mark errors, comment on strengths and weaknesses, and assign a letter grade. Several problems arise from this tradition, beyond the harried and oppressed teacher: Teachers' comments often address only an end product, not the process that preceded it; focus on the narrow, easily graded issues of mechanics (spelling, grammar, and penmanship), rather than on student meaning; justify the grade, rather than respond to the writing; and hinder students' ability to assess their own writing. But what alternatives do we have? Chapters 9, Compelling Writing, and 10, Enabling Writing, addressed some of them, namely, authentic assessment and writing portfolios. We now turn to others.

OUTSIDE THE CLASSROOM

Alternatives have been tried outside the classroom whereby schools, districts, states, and the nation make major educational decisions on the basis of writing evaluation. Early attempts to assess writing on a large scale were based on multiple-choice grammar tests. Reforms of that process have been attempted. Two prominent attempts were in the writing portion of the National Assessment of Educational Progress (NAEP) and in the College Entrance Examination Board's Achievement Test in English Composition. Advanced-placement English literature and composition and English language and composition exams use essays in addition to multiple-choice questions to evaluate the writing skills and literary insights of college-bound students. All three ask students to write for a short time on an assigned topic in a formal testing situation. Graders assemble, determine criteria for grading, test their scoring consistency, and read and score papers holistically. State and school districts have modeled these in developing their own assessment instruments for the purposes of making student placement decisions, of determining student competency, and of evaluating programs and schools. (Myers [1980] wrote a concise guide for constructing such a test—selecting topics, writing directions, scoring, and reporting.) Although these evaluation methods are clearly superior to earlier multiple-choice tests, they still run counter to a student-centered process approach to writing. The genre (essay) is preset, topics are assigned, and the elaborate writing process is constricted; only the final product is evaluated. Dyson and Freedman (1990) observe that "writing for a test has little function for the student writers other than for them to be evaluated" (p. 8).

INSIDE THE CLASSROOM

Although these larger writing tests may well influence your work in the classroom, our major concern is with what you do with your own students. You will remember that in Chapter 9, we expressed our biases for a writing program that is holistic, organic, inclusive, developmental, and foundational—best embodied in a writing process approach. One of the cornerstones for such an approach is the use of student portfolios. We think that the most promising present writing evaluation alternatives rest with portfolio assessment. But having suggested that process for assembling pieces of writing for purposes of evaluation, we still must address how selected pieces might be assessed.

We discuss here six evaluation strategies available to you, some probably familiar from your classroom experiences, and others more hidden in your writing experiences on state and national exams. We do not present them as contestants for your final winning choice, but as viable alternatives given the needs of your students and the aims of your instruction.

1. Crucial-errors summing
2. Rubric scoring
3. Holistic scoring
4. Student, peer, and teacher collaboration
5. Personal-response appraisal
6. Cumulative-process tallying

FIGURE 13–12
Criteria for
manuscript evaluation

NCET					Referee: _____		
ESSAY NO. _____					TITLE: _____		
_____ A. PERTINENCE:	On-Target		Loosely Connected		Largely Tangential		Left Field
	8 7	6	5		4	3	2 1
_____ B. SUBSTANCE:	Very Informative		Interesting		Somewhat Clichéd		Bland
	8 7	6	5		4	3	2 1
_____ C. FORM:	Very Talented		Quite Competent		Somewhat Flawed		Inept
	8 7	6	5		4	3	2 1

_____ TOTAL EVALUATION POINTS
     REJECT   REVISE   PRINT   (Circle One)
REJECTION COMMENTS: _____
_____
_____

REVISION COMMENTS: _____
_____
_____
_____
_____

DATE RECEIVED: _____   DATE MAILED: _____

These six are not always mutually exclusive. Features of each can be merged together, or different strategies can be chosen at different times to meet your instructional (and assessment) aims. As you consider each, evaluate it in terms of your purpose, your style, and your total approach to writing.

Crucial-Errors Summing. In many English classes, writing instruction has been a three-step sequence: classwork on grammar, student writing on assigned topics, and teacher grading of papers by the hour. The old three-step method often centered on surface features as the tool of evaluation: two misspellings, three comma flaws, and a single subject-verb agreement problem could mean a failing composition. Analytical or crucial-errors graders often draw the line after a certain number of errors (usually grammatical or mechanical) in a paper and strive for an error-free text in student writing. Sometimes, analytic-scales teachers enumerate targeted features of composition, each of which has an established weight for grading purposes. The final grade is figured by summing the parts.

Kirby, Liner, and Vinz (1988) acknowledge advantages of this technique in focusing graders as well as writers: "Such guides, when carefully shared and explained to students, can demystify the final grade and highlight strengths and weaknesses in their writings. The guides also ensure that certain surface features in the piece (handwriting, spelling, pronunciation) do not influence the rating of the piece out of proportion to their importance to the piece's effectiveness" (p. 224).

North Carolina's NCTE affiliate journal, *North Carolina English Teacher,* used the rather general set of idea-centered criteria shown in Figure 13-12, by which a panel of referees assessed the value of a manuscript submitted for publication. Interestingly, the referees had an amazing concurrence on their ratings of individual manuscripts. Appendix H contains an analytic scale carefully developed for ETS's SAT essay exam by Diederich and his colleagues. We do not recommend it as your sole writing assessment method, but it is a useful model to be used occasionally.

Some teachers keep individual convention logs, Figure 13-13, which let students see where their errors are most frequent and most flagrant. These logs can allow students to recognize and deal with the conventions over time without becoming so cautious about grammar and usage that little attention is paid to content. They can be kept at the front of a portfolio, placed on file in the classroom, or kept in students' notebooks. Other teachers keep error-count charts for a whole classroom set of papers to track central writing issues that need to be addressed with the whole class.

The adoption of other approaches to writing has brought with it new means of assessment. The surface of any piece of writing is important to communication, but, in the process approach to writing, it represents only the final step in editing and revising, not the central concern. Analytical scoring focuses on problems not specific to the writing assignment at hand. Critics of this means of assessment fear its paralyzing consequences. Diederich (1974) judges its negative effects by the fear and dislike of writing among his remedial college students. He explains their self-disparagement: "All their teachers looked for were mistakes, and there are so many kinds of mistakes in writing that their students despair of ever learning to avoid them" (p. 21). Graves (1986) believes that such avoidance of errors is adverse to risk taking and the cause of bad, not good, writing: "The

FIGURE 13–13
Convention log

Paper # Title Date	1	2	3	4	5	6
Problem areas						
Comma flaws						
Misused semicolons						
Sentence fragments						
Run-on sentences						
Omitted apostrophes						
Lost antecedents						
Dangling modifiers						
Nonparallel construction						
Quotation mark flaw						
Subject-Verb agreement						

biggest misconception is that children learn to write by not making mistakes . . . Putting words on paper involves enormous risk-taking. If the words appear to be a crude form of English, parents and teachers may be tempted to overcorrect. But writing is thinking you have things to say, and having an audience to say them to. Grammar and spelling are not as important as content."

Beyond its crippling effects on the composing process, analytical scoring reduces response to a totaling of countable errors, hardly a nuanced reflection of the paper's merit.

Invitation to Reflection 13–5

Diederich (1974) tells the following story:

Professor Edward Gordon of Yale tells about an examination he once conducted for the College Board. He explained and illustrated the scale of five points that was to be used and had the readers practice using it by grading copies of a set of sample papers.

When the actual grading began, he noticed that one military-looking gentleman—an instructor from West Point—was obviously not using the scale. His grades were all two-digit numbers: 53, 71, 83, and so on.

"How do you get these numbers?" asked Dr. Gordon.

"Well, Dr. Gordon," replied the military gentleman, "I'm too old a dog to learn new tricks like that new-fangled scale you wanted us to use. So I went back to my usual way of grading papers, knowing that you're smart enough to translate my grades into any scale you please. I just count the number of mistakes and subtract that number from 100 percent."

"But what do you call a mistake?" asked Dr. Gordon.

The man's astonishment was obvious. "Why surely, Dr. Gordon, you know what a *mistake* is!" (p. 29)

• What mistake do you see being made here?

Primary-trait Scoring.   Teachers who are not primarily interested in the general writing mechanics of crucial-errors scoring but are still concerned that student writing meet established criteria for a given assignment have turned to primary-trait scoring. This analytical approach identifies the presence or absence of traits required by a particular writing assignment and often joins a concern for writing conventions with an expectation of significant content. The two, the surface and deep structure, can be represented by a set of traits that scorers rate as present or absent.

Table 13–5 is a writing assessment instrument developed by a state educational agency in which traits are articulated for each of several domains. Surprisingly, when the matrix was used by 40 North Carolina Writing Project teachers to evaluate a large set of papers, the intergrader reliability for the rhetorical elements was stronger than those on the conventional features. Such a rubric can help students better define and focus on the many elements that must be mastered to produce fine writing.

Holistic Scoring.   For many teachers, looking at the writing style and mechanics *and* at the conceptual content of a piece is a schizophrenic process. Some teachers compromise by assigning one grade for content and one for form, thus recognizing the importance of both. But in recent years (perhaps encouraged or validated by the College Board's scoring of writing samples on its tests), teachers have been attracted to the idea of seeing writing as a whole, not as the sum of its faltering or successful parts; reading it for a single impression, not for itemized stylistic errors or conceptual blunders; and assigning a total response to it, rather than trying to enumerate the components that give it strength or weakness. Myers (1980) concurs: "Even though one can list all of the characters of a good piece of writing (clarity, coherence, complete sentences, smooth transitions, good spelling and punctuation), the best way to identify a good piece of writing is to ask people to select typical samples which they rate highly" (p. 2). He feels that "the whole of a piece of writing is greater than the sum of its parts" (p. 1).

The procedure for holistic scoring can involve the individual teacher or teams of readers. Neenan (personal communication, 1992) explains that she draws 20 papers randomly from her pile, reads them quickly, constructs her scale based on her impressions of those sample papers, and then begins to read and evaluate deliberately. If two or more teachers work together, usually prior to grading, these readers establish both criteria (which describe the writing features paramount to a particular writing project) and sample anchor papers (which demonstrate what is considered to be high, middle, and low quality). The Advanced Placement (AP) program of the College Board has been conscientious in developing grading standards and rigorous in assuring that the AP readers understand and use them carefully. In fact, 3 to 7 hours of the 5- to 6-day exam reading period are devoted to the readers' review of the standards and to their practice of consistent application of them. As Jensen (1987) reports, the scales themselves are carefully developed to "avoid the problem, on the one hand, of too few points, allowing only coarse distinctions, and, on the other hand, of too many points, requiring overly refined, often meaningless discriminations. Because the standards and their accompanying scales are tailored to the individual questions, they allow each answer to be appropriately ranked" (p. 3).

Kirby et al. (1988) point out that holistic scoring has the advantage of being accomplished "more quickly, more consistently, and more pointedly" (p. 221). It provides significant help with English teachers' paper load as teachers read more rapidly without stopping to mark errors, make suggestions, and explain their responses. Many teachers also report that papers seem fresh to them without the burden of their own extensive note writing. Reader consistency grows from the establishment of effective writing criteria and model anchor papers.

Diederich (1974), who has been deeply involved in implementing this strategy, describes what happens to teachers who have used holistic scoring for 2 years:

> After two years (at most), they move easily and naturally into the use of standard scores as a quicker and easier way to indicate their judgment of the general merit of a paper. We call this "ratings on general impression," but it is no longer a blur: it is a quick summing up of characteristics that determine whether a paper is high, medium, or low in general merit. The teachers also have a common vocabulary for discussing the merits and defects of papers on which their grades disagree. (p. 55)

Diederich tells another story:

> John Stalnaker, long president of the Merit Scholarship Foundation, recalls this incident from his early days as Examiner in English at the University of Chicago. In one of his experiments he had a few hundred papers to grade. He called in four of his most experienced readers and told them, "I want you to grade these papers but not on your regular scale of A to F. I know that you all have

TABLE 13-5 Writing assessment matrix

	Rhetorical Elements			
Assessment	**Quality of Ideas**	**Expression of Ideas**	**Organization of Ideas**	**Maturity of Syntax**
Unacceptable	Operates on a literal level in which the thinking is clichéd and simplistic; the ideas lack soundness or insight; the thought is stale and exhibits no originality; the ideas are not developed in any detail, little or no elaboration of concepts is present.	Cannot communicate ideas; the logic of phrasing is inconsistent and the idea communicated unclear; often awkward or flat word choice; a personality and voice are never established.	Neither states nor implies a point; little or no movement or focus is found in the writing; no structuring features are present; no segmental markers are evident.	Uses only simple sentence structure; has no variety in the sentence patterns.
Weak	Occasionally rises above literal level of clichéd and simplistic thought; the ideas are sound at points and exhibit some insight; the thought is occasionally fresh and original; the ideas are not developed in any detail, little or no elaboration of concepts is present.	Occasionally conveys ideas to audiences other than the self; the logic of the phrasing is often questionable and the idea communicated is somewhat uncertain; word choice is rarely rich or enlivening; a mild sense of personality or voice is evident.	Makes the main idea discernible but it is wholly unstructured; some sense of movement or focus is found in the writing; few or no structuring features are present; no segmental markers are evident.	Typically uses simple sentence structure although there is some use of complex sentence structure with embedded phrases and clauses; has some variety in the sentence patterns.
Satisfactory	Generally rises above the literal level to communicate important ideas; much of the thinking is sound and insightful; the ideas are developed in some detail, some elaboration of concepts is present.	Communicates to audiences other than the self, but not always in a stylistic and sophisticated manner; the logic of the phrasing is most often sound and the idea communicated is generally understood; word choice is at times rich and enlivening; a sense of personality or voice is fairly consistent.	Develops the main idea in an incomplete or loosely structured fashion; a general sense of movement or focus is found in the writing; some structuring elements are present; a few segmental markers are evident.	Often uses complex sentence structures; frequently uses a variety of sentence patterns.
Excellent	Consistently is able to communicate fresh and important ideas in depth; the ideas are sound and insightful; the thought is generally fresh and original; the ideas are developed in great detail, elaboration of concepts is rich.	Consistently is clear and elaborate in communicating ideas in a style acceptable to a literate audience; the logic of the phrasing is rigorous and the idea is communicated clearly; word choice is consistently rich and enlivening; a sense of voice and personality is strongly established throughout the writing.	Fully develops and structures the main idea implicitly or explicitly; a strong sense of movement or focus is found in the writing; structuring elements unify the entire piece of writing; segmental markers are effectively used throughout the writing.	Uses a variety of sentence patterns and sentence structures.

	Conventional Features 1		
Assessment	**Capitalization**	**Spelling**	**Punctuation**
Unacceptable	Fails to apply basic rules of capitalization such as first words in sentences, personal names and the pronoun "I."	Frequently misspells simple common words.	Fails to use end punctuation correctly.
Weak	Applies basic rules of capitalization correctly; often fails to apply other rules of capitalization.	Spells common words correctly; frequently misspells more difficult ones.	Uses end punctuation correctly; rarely uses internal punctuation correctly.
Satisfactory	Correctly applies basic capitalization rules; usually applies other rules correctly.	Rarely misspells even difficult words.	Always uses end punctuation correctly; generally uses internal punctuation correctly.
Excellent	All rules of capitalization are applied correctly.	Spells all words correctly.	Uses all forms of punctuation correctly.

TABLE 13–5 *continued*

	Conventional Features 2	
Assessment	**Usage**	**Vocabulary**
Unacceptable	Constantly makes basic usage errors such as lack of subject-verb agreement, use of double negatives and use of improper verb forms.	Constant misuse of basic words.
Weak	Controls basic usage with frequent problems in less important usage areas such as pronoun antecedents and misplaced modifiers.	Control of basic words; Frequent misuse of more sophisticated language.
Satisfactory	Makes occasional errors in less important usage areas.	Control of basic words and more sophisticated language; occasional misuse of the latter.
Excellent	Has full control of all conventional usage.	Full control of basic words and more sophisticated language.

different ideas about what those letters mean. Just sort these papers into five piles in order of merit. Then mark the highest pile 4, the next pile 3, and so on down to 0."

They agreed to do so, but about a week later they came to his office and said, "We're sorry, John, but we could not do what you wanted. It turned out that there weren't any "4" papers. But we did the best we could. We sorted them into five piles, but we had to mark them 3, 2, 1, 0, 00." (p. 49)

Into which pile should these readers' logic be put?

Student, Peer, and Teacher Collaboration.   Crucial-errors, rubric, and holistic scoring can be done by a classroom teacher acting alone, by groups of teachers, by teachers and students, or by teacher and writer. The most common experience of students is of evaluation done by the single classroom teacher. The AP model is of groups of teachers reading, collaborating, and scoring. Teachers have experimented with involving students (writers' peers or the writers themselves) in writing evaluation and have found that if students have been involved in establishing effective writing criteria, have been trained carefully, and gain some experience, they can be effective readers. Kirby et al. (1988) report that they have "learned the hard way that evaluation by peers must be thoroughly structured and patiently implemented" (p. 222), but they also have learned the advantages of engaging peers in evaluation when such steps are taken:

- Students come to recognize that "the grade represents a reader's estimate of the worth of the piece. A grade is simply a calibrated personal response."
- They become sensitized "to problems in their own papers" and thereby become their own teachers.
- They "use peer papers as creative sources for borrowing ideas, rhetorical and syntactic strategies, and even vocabulary" (p. 230).

Many strategies for such collaboration are possible. Writing process ideas of individual and group conferencing, peer collaboration and review, and small and class workshops are easily adapted for this purpose. We especially like collaborative strategies that involve readers and writers sitting down together to read and discuss the effectiveness of a piece. Beaven (1977) believes that a climate of trust is essential to the developing writer. She quotes Cazden's research (1972), which found that "adults who respond to the content and ideas of the child and carry on a 'conversation,' regardless of the child's grammar or syntax, are reinforcing positive language development, the motivation to talk, the desire to have 'something to say,' and the ability to experiment with language, stretching it to accommodate an expressive need" (p. 137). Beaven discusses kinds of responses that teachers have refined to create that environment of acceptance and trust; these draw on the work of Axline (1964) and Rogers (1961):

- A teacher may ask for more information.
- A teacher may mirror, reflect, or rephrase the student's ideas, perceptions, or feelings.
- A teacher may share with the student times when he or she felt, thought, or behaved in a similar fashion. (p. 139)

Our experience in teaching composition is that the most teachable writing moments occur in the individual discussion between ourselves and one student as we struggle over a composition. Evaluation can be incorporated into such immediate and personal moments if it is done with care. Kirby et al. (1988) "believe that the only consistently helpful and effective evaluation of student writing comes as the two of you sit down with the piece of writing, focusing directly on what's on the page. Extraordinarily successful teachers of writing have one thing in common: they spend very little time in isolation, reading and marking papers, and a great deal of time responding and discussing student writings with the writers themselves" (p. 235).

Personal-response Appraisal. Teachers who have felt that the conventions of writing are less important than the expression of personal thoughts and feelings have tried to diminish the threat of correction. They use free-writing, personal journals, creative writing, and field reporting as ways of starting with personal response. When students focus on what they know and what they are discovering, they are diverted from the paralyzing effects of correctness. They take their eyes off the form when they are coaxed to speak about ideas that matter to them. In a developmental sense, they are starting at home, beginning with Moffett's *I* rather than *It* or even *You.* The caution in school writing to efface themselves and remove the *I* is not lost on them. With this approach the *I* returns and the world at hand—the daily concerns of students—takes precedence.

To switch to this approach is not easy for most students, and one of the impediments is the problem of assessment. Bleich (1975) defines the dilemma in regard to a subjective-response approach to literary study:

> Since we are not dealing with questions of objective truth or falsity, but rather with questions of emotional and social viability, the authority of the teacher is experiential, not evaluative. One cannot set up a standard of response for the class to meet which will not, in application, result in the judgment of the student's character. A student will have real grounds to think he is a "C" person if his emotional responses receive that letter grade. (pp. 105–106)

Clear-cut objective criteria about writing conventions afford teachers an authority that assessing students' objectives responses does not. Teachers who invite self-expression designate criteria for assessment. Some list general criteria such as originality, interest, and clarity and claim that they are not a big departure from real-world judgments about writing. Bleich (1975) discusses the "viable compromise" he worked out "between the evaluative methods demanded by the response process and the need for a letter grade created by competitive admissions policies" (p. 107). Without denying the difficulty and subjectivity of his method, he explains two grading principles that he has worked out for his own classroom: "(1) the amount of work produced by the student, and (2) the seriousness of purpose in the production of that work" (p. 107).

Beaven (1977) discusses a strategy for self-evaluation of writing, a common goal of a personal-response approach. Self-evaluation is consistent with taking one's own thoughts and feelings seriously. It internalizes evaluation and helps students accept responsibility for their own writing. Two practical advantages are that it can be initiated at any time during the stages of writing or the course of a term, and it does not consume large amounts of class time. Beaven's questions that form the basis for her self-evaluation procedures are listed here. She explains that "because students tire of the same questions, teachers need to vary from week to week, adding questions related to the current work of the class" (p. 143).

1. How much time did you spend on this paper?
2. (After the first evaluation) What did you try to improve, or experiment with, on this paper? How successful were you? If you have questions about what you were trying to do, what are they?
3. What are the strengths of your paper? Place a squiggly line beside those passages you feel are very good.
4. What are the weaknesses, if any, of your paper? Place an X beside passages you would like your teacher to correct or revise. Place an X over any punctuation, spelling, usage, etc., where you need help or clarification.
5. What one thing will you do to improve your next piece of writing? Or what kind of experimentation in writing would you like to try? If you would like some information related to what you want to do, write down your questions.
6. (Optional) What grade would you give yourself on this composition? Justify it. (p. 143)

Cumulative-process Tallying. A cumulative process of grading can resemble a performance system in which students get a grade simply by completing an assignment. No evaluative judgments are made about a work's quality, good or bad. Teachers still read and respond to writing, but no error counts are made or holistic scores given. The responsibility for the grade rests solely with the student's willingness to do the assigned work.

The cumulative approach can fit nicely with a process approach to writing. Rather than evaluating the final written product, teachers assign credit to each of the steps (whatever the number) in the writing process. Students are awarded points for their inventing, revising, and peer editing, not just for the final draft. The evaluation of many of these parts of the total process may be straightforward: Points are automatically awarded for completing a particular part. Or, a balance can be struck between points awarded for productivity and those awarded for quality of performance. Newkirk (1990) has suggested an evaluation strategy that assigns grades while maintaining a workshop approach to writing. He suggests that only the students' selections of their best writing should be evaluated for a grade—a "real incentive for revising" (p. 156). He then suggests a combination of quantitative and qualitative evaluation:

> At the end of a marking period a student might be evaluated as follows. All students who complete a satisfactory volume of writing—those who worked regularly and met deadlines—should get a base grade, perhaps a C+. This base grade can go up if the student has made major improvement on a skill identified at the beginning of the marking term or if the quality of the selected pieces of writing is superior.
>
> This system rewards productivity; a student who writes several thousand words in a marking term does not, in my opinion, deserve a D, even if there are substantial difficulties in that writing. The system also rewards quality; excellent writing gets an excellent grade. The system penalizes sloth—and that's the way it should be. (pp. 156–157)

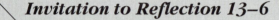

Invitation to Reflection 13–6

Crucial-errors summing	Peer and teacher collaboration
Rubric scoring	Personal-response appraisal
Holistic scoring	Cumulative-process tallying

- In your schooling, which of these evaluative strategies have you experienced?
- Which of them predominated?
- Which kind of writing evaluation did you most enjoy receiving?
- Do you remember any of these strategies that you experienced negatively?
- Recall a personal story about writing evaluation that had a happy ending. Recall one with a sad ending.
- Which of these strategies can you envision using most often in your own high school classroom? Next most often?
- Figure 13–14 contains the written, in-class responses of three 9th-grade students to the prompt "Write about the effect of watching television on young children." Consider how you might evaluate these three using the strategy that you most prefer and the strategy that you least prefer. Do you arrive at different conclusions about the students' work?
- Figure 13–15 is a character sketch written out-of-class by a college-bound senior. Evaluate it with the strategy used by your 12th-grade English teacher. Then consider whether you have discovered any better alternatives to that method.

These six alternatives, or variations of them, offer compromises that allow you to remain true to your best aims in teaching students to write and to your need for supplying a grade to school administrators. We close this discussion with a note on the consequences of writing evaluation on the English teacher—one of those everyday issues that is sometimes overlooked, but that may be of paramount importance to you in your teaching.

One of the fundamental difficulties for English teachers from middle school to senior high school is the paper load. When English teachers face 120 or more students each day, they can easily find themselves buried under five sets of papers each week. Even at 10 minutes each, reading them requires 1,200 minutes, or 20 hours, every week. It is no wonder that many school reforms start with English teachers working carefully with two classes of 20 students each. Such a reduction in teaching load is so expensive that the reform is seldom seriously considered, but it does underscore the problem that English teachers face.

Extended writing-process and writing portfolios have a powerful impact on the problem of English teachers' paper load. A writing workshop structure means that a good part of class time may be

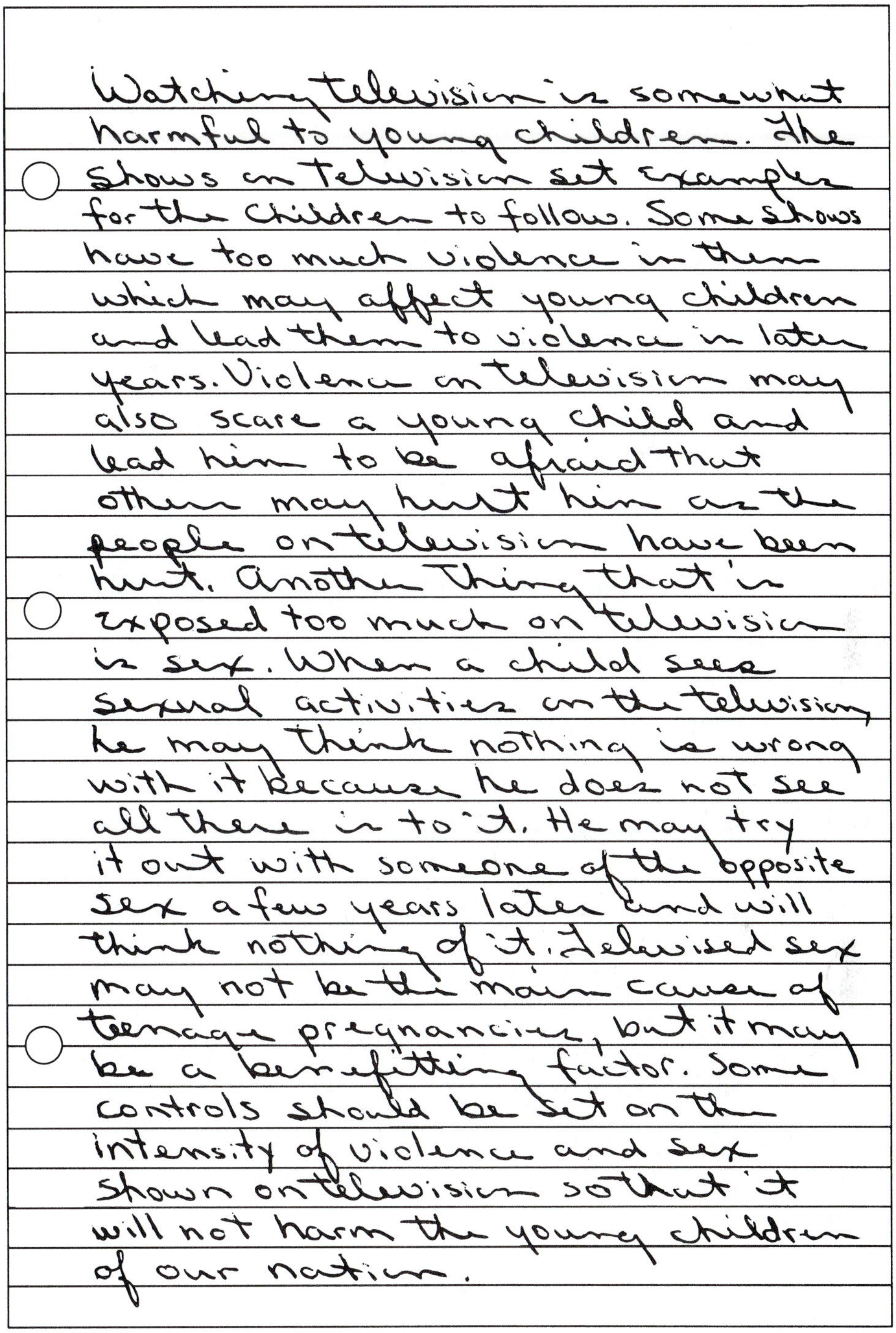

FIGURE 13–14
Student writing samples: the effect of watching television on young children

Watching television is somewhat harmful to young children. The shows on television set examples for the children to follow. Some shows have too much violence in them which may affect young children and lead them to violence in later years. Violence on television may also scare a young child and lead him to be afraid that others may hurt him as the people on television have been hurt. Another thing that is exposed too much on television is sex. When a child sees sexual activities on the television he may think nothing is wrong with it because he does not see all there is to it. He may try it out with someone of the opposite sex a few years later and will think nothing of it. Televised sex may not be the main cause of teenage pregnancies, but it may be a benefitting factor. Some controls should be set on the intensity of violence and sex shown on television so that it will not harm the young children of our nation.

FIGURE 13–14
continued

Watching television is harmful to young children

I think watching television is harmful to young children because young children love to watch television. And when my favorite television show came on they do not move from the television set until they show goes off. Some people like to watch soap propper. The young people seem to be enjoy watching television. If they doing nothing. Some people do not watch television, because some people listen to music. And some young people watch a scare movie on television. And when they go to bed they dream about it. Some people like to watching television but some people don't like to watching television, because they listen to music. And some people do not have they mind on television. Young children have they mind on comic, and cartoon. I believe young children like to watch television, because when something came on like a funny picture they be laugh and having fun watching comic costume on the television.

FIGURE 13–14
continued

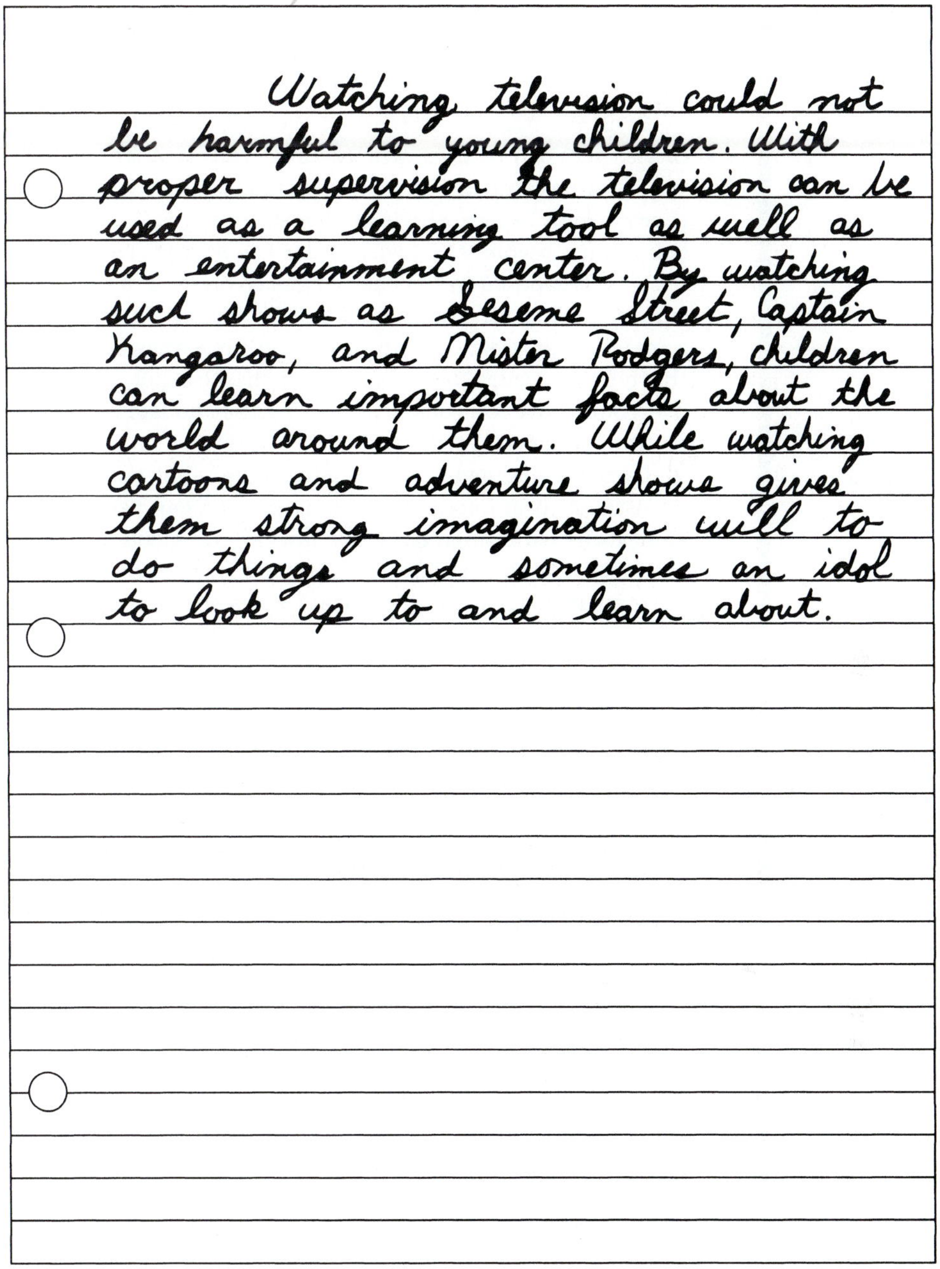

Watching television could not be harmful to young children. With proper supervision the television can be used as a learning tool as well as an entertainment center. By watching such shows as Sesame Street, Captain Kangaroo, and Mister Rodgers, children can learn important facts about the world around them. While watching cartoons and adventure shows gives them strong imagination will to do things and sometimes an idol to look up to and learn about.

FIGURE 13–15
Student writing
sample: character
sketch

SIDNEY CARTON

Of all the many characters in Dicken's novel, <u>A Tale of Two
Cities</u>, there can be none who so drastically changes as Sydney
Carton. Nor can there be one as influential to the story. Finally,
there cannot be one who is such a sorry example of a human
being, then becomes as loving a hero as ever there was. Carton too
is so controversial in that he is once so down and out and then so
caring. So with all this change and contrariety, did Dickens create
a realistic character in Sydney Carton? The answer is yes, for all
this change occurs for love, a power man cannot, and never can,
overcome. Love for Lucie is so strong, that he later trades his life
for that of his rival to Lucie.

Carton's change is obvious and sudden, but nevertheless
realistic. At first Carton is the epitome of a bad person. He is a
sharp-tongued French assistant lawyer and alcoholic who defends
the most wretched and lowly prisoners imaginable. However,
Carton turns out to be the model hero whose immortal last words
are some of the most memorable in literature.

"It is a far, far better thing that I do, than I have ever done;
It is a far, far better rest that I go to, than I have ever known."

He proclaims this as he is about to die in place of his friend and
rival, Charles Darnay, who was imprisoned and sentenced to
death. But through this switch, it is Carton (who looks very much
like Darnay) who will die. Through these last words he shows his
willingness, and even gladness, to die in place of a friend.

Thus, Dickens has masterfully created a change in which an
"unlikely alcoholic" gradually, and believably, progresses into a
dazzling hero. He is a hero who twice risked his freedom and his
life to allow a friend to live and thus a love to continue. The
sacrifice is made more poignant by its involving saving a man to
love the woman whom Carton himself loves.

This character and his change are fundamentally important to
the story in that they allow the main character to live and to
continue his relationship with his mistress. In my eyes, there can
be no greater hero than Carton. Carton has given up his two most
valued things, his love for Lucie and his life, all to allow his friend
to live and love Carton's favorite thing in the world, Lucie.

dedicated to writing. The teacher can then be free during some class time to work with students in conference. More important, each student will spend many more hours on a single paper and thus produce many fewer papers during a term for the teacher to read. When other students have read and responded in the revision stages of the process, they join the teacher as readers and evaluators. Furthermore, writers are challenged to become their own best assessors, with teachers as resources, not judges. Thus, the teacher will respond to fewer papers of higher quality, whereas in the past, teachers were marking many mediocre papers.

In the portfolio approach, all of the students' work has response and revision brought to it, but only a few selected pieces serve as the means of final evaluation. With both strategies, parents, students, and teachers can readily see the progress through the term, but much less out-of-class time is spent grading papers. They also avoid what Kirby et al. (1988) call perhaps the "most seriously damaging habit we get into as 'theme graders' . . . mindlessness. The sheer volume of papers and their frequent drabness have a kind of hypnotic effect that can rob the evaluator not only of objectivity but sensitive and insightful reading. If student papers are important enough to be graded, they deserve the best reading we can possibly give them" (p. 219). What is most important is that students know both how writing will be evaluated and that different means of assessment will be brought to all parts of the writing process.

EVALUATING ORACY

Evaluation of the most fundamental dimensions of language, speaking, and listening is even less discussed and researched than assessment of literature and writing is. Teachers have been hesitant to teach in this area because talking and listening have seemed natural and therefore outside the instructional compass. Furthermore, student talk in classrooms is often considered to be an interruption or intrusion, not part of the learning itself. What is even more confounding is that classrooms neglect talking and listening because they are not easy to evaluate and almost no tests exist to do so. Little has been written about this area of evaluation because oral language has not been taught. As sports announcer Skip Carey would say, it is a "vicious circus."

Traditional oral productions—book reports, brief speeches, debates, oral interpretations, and poetry recitations—have long been used in class to help students learn to "speak on their feet," and these have been traditionally evaluated with the kinds of holistic or analytic instruments used for writing products. Seldom, however, has process been assessed. A federally funded project from the National Basic Skills Improvement Program to our local Winston-Salem/Forsyth County schools expanded those traditional "genres" of speaking and listening. A committee of teachers enumerated oral communication skills needful not simply for occasional speeches, but for everyday life. The project resulted in a book of researched, conceptualized, and tested lessons and activities to help students improve their speaking and listening skills (Barlow & Stankwytch, 1982). Appendix H includes two of their evaluation instruments: The first is an evaluation form for discussion (used by teachers, peers, and students), and the second is its accompanying rating scale. The final evaluation form given in Appendix H is of a talking activity that is rarely addressed in classrooms but is not uncommon in life: announcements.

Instruction in and evaluation of a wider variety of speech acts have had only incidental support in most English classrooms. Particularly overlooked is the active, exploratory talk, which does not report on learning but produces learning. When classrooms are teacher centered and students speak only to clarify the teacher's ideas or to answer the teacher's questions, such exploratory talking seldom occurs. But in classrooms where students are central, talk that grows from questioning, probing, defending one's own position, and narrating experiences becomes essential to the learning of content or language systems and processes. Evaluating such talk is as difficult as separating the filaments from a spider's web to grade the quality of its weaving.

After examining the best theories, research, and practice in the area of oral language development and its evaluation, Harrison (1991) created a set of seven general criteria useful in curricular activities and assessment of oracy.

1. *Articulateness*—Does the student express him/herself with clarity and fluidity? Does he or she speak coherently? Does the speaking or talk make sense?
2. *Effectiveness*—Does the speaker achieve his/her purpose? Does he or she do what he/she sets out to do? For example, if the student is delivering a persuasive speech, is it persuasive? Or, if the student is telling a story, is the telling believable or credible?
3. *Register*—Is the talk appropriate for the particular audience? Does the language used fit the context and the purpose? How well does the student adjust language and delivery to suit the purpose and context? Is the student able to use the very best and exact word where necessary?
4. *Delivery*—How well does the student make use of voice, pitch, tone, volume, eye contact, and body language? Is the voice range too high or too low? Does it reach the listeners? Does the speaker's stance help or hinder his/her communication?
5. *Collaboration*—How well does the speaker relate to others? Is the speaker able to involve and interest the audience? How well does the student function with others in the group? (applicable to group activity) How well does he/she listen to them and how sensitive is he/she to their responses?
6. *Diction*—Does the student use correct speech? Is the diction acceptable? Do the diction or the pronunciations irritate the listener or detract from the effectiveness of the talk?
7. *Fluency*—Does the student overuse stabilizers (*er, mm, you know, sort of, ah, um*)? Does the student speak at a suitable speed, allowing pauses where necessary? Is the student able to elaborate adequately? Is the amount of talk suitable? (especially applicable to dialogues and class discussions)

These seven features of oracy go far beyond what most schools articulate and foster. But further work still needs to focus on the components of each of the "genres" to create an appropriate nomenclature comparable to that used in writing. Of course, much of writing's terminology is well suited for oral production, although many holistic thinkers would rue the day that we dissect speaking. They fear that we would disable students' talking, as we may have their reading and writing, by the close analysis of component parts. The fishbowl conversation of Chapter 3, Developing an Oral Foundation, might provide a model of how talking (formal and informal) is best evaluated: holistically, contextually, non-threateningly, recursively, and as a process (not one product), by listeners (students and teacher) and by the talker.

STANDARDIZED ACHIEVEMENT TESTS

Teachers usually enjoy some autonomy within their own classrooms, but of course those classrooms are not isolated from the wider culture. Whether or not you administer standardized achievement tests or are required to draw from them for your evaluation of students, they will insinuate themselves into your teaching. A quick survey of the construction and purpose of these tests will steady you for meeting them. Standardized achievement tests are developed by publishers or private agencies, such as the Educational Testing Service (ETS), which carefully construct, administer, score, norm, and interpret results. Standardized tests are available to measure aptitude, personality, and other attributes, but schools use them most often to assess the achievement of individual students.

Proponents of standardized tests claim that test items are meticulously prepared and studied for reliability (their consistency of measurement) and validity (the extent to which they measure what and whom they are intended to measure). The value of such tests resides in offering teachers insight into their students within a wider context than the isolated classroom. But Moffett and Wagner (1976) articulate their dangers: "Standardized testing overfocuses on a few, easily testable skills and ignores what is hardest to teach and ultimately most important" (p. 433).

Creators and users of standardized tests operate under a set of strict standards not only for the adequacy of their construction and administration, but also for the appropriateness of their interpretation. Violations of their guidelines appear to occur most often in their being used for purposes other than the assessment of individual students, for instance, certifying completion of a grade, evaluating teachers, accrediting schools, or validating the excellence of school systems. Part of the danger of standardized testing lies with its original strength: the appearance of scientific accuracy and empirical proof. Scores are precise and appear to be infallible. The testing industry is so large, its products so sophisticated, its administration so rigorous, and the interpretation of results so commonplace that the individual teacher finds criticism difficult. Even when test items do not match what is actually taught in school, when the norming groups do not match the students being tested, and when norms are interpreted as standards for all students, teacher criticism is problematic.

How, then, can teachers be responsible to their own classrooms and students, and how can schools profit from the advantages of standardized testing for the purpose of understanding something about individual students, without being overwhelmed by its misuse for other purposes? Moffett and Wagner (1976) suggest a cardinal principle for keeping language arts evaluation sane: "Each party should do his own evaluation" (p. 416). We suggest that you clarify your own possible use of standardized tests for diagnosis of students and reject any potential punitive use of them.

Invitation to Reflection 13–7

- Do you remember being tested by standardized achievement tests during your schooling? How often: never, once, often, or many times?
  Elementary school
  Middle or junior high school
  Secondary school
  College or university
- Did you assume that the purpose of such testing was to measure learning for
  you the student?
  your family?
  your teachers?
  evaluating you?

evaluating themselves?
your school administrators?
your school system?
college or employer applications?
- If you can remember learning the results, can you recall how accurately you felt that they measured what you had learned?
Elementary school
Middle or junior high school
Secondary school
College or university
- Which of the following describes your feelings about taking standardized tests?
Disliked
Preferred classroom tests
Neutral
Liked the different testing environment
Enjoyed the challenge
- Can you tell a personal story about your experience with standardized testing?

CRITIQUE OF TRADITIONAL GRADING

We want to become more specific about our critique of traditional grading. We have struggled to be fairminded in articulating traditional approaches and hopeful in suggesting creative alternatives to them. We discuss here a few final cautions about the dangers of grading in general and the pitfalls for the English teacher in particular.

PEDAGOGICAL DANGERS

Too often, traditional grading compromises the deeper aims of English education. It focuses on the product of learning, not the process, on the adult's need, not the child's, and on teacher control, not student empowerment. It makes little accommodation for the developmental experience of the individual student. It imposes an adult's authority on the personal authority of the child and thereby takes initiative and responsibility from students. Too often, assessment becomes an external rather than an internal event, discouraging self-reliance. Some critics even see grading as subverting the basic aim of schooling. Purpel (1989) writes that grading "is also anti-intellectual in its irrational and arbitrary character, and it is a serious barrier to the true educational process of inquiry, sharing, and dialogue" (p. 120).

PSYCHOMETRIC DANGERS

Testing often invites learning on the most basic level. Moffett and Wagner's (1976) second cardinal principle opened this chapter: "Evaluation should not dictate, distort, or displace what it measures" (p. 416). Often, teachers "teach to the test" and the adage is proven again: "Those who control the tests control the curriculum." Consequently, if a low order of mental activity is being tested, it is the activity that comes to dominate the class. If assessment of reading comprehension extends only to literal recall of plot and character, for instance, students will study that and teachers will teach it. The scope of what is possible in a classroom is restricted and trivialized.

Furthermore, if grading is narrowly conceived, it comes to determine what students will take seriously. If, for instance, a teacher extols the value of class participation to students and yet grades only written quizzes and exams, students quickly devalue their classroom discourse. Even students motivated by a serious interest in the subject matter become calculating and strategic in their study, particularly if they are pushed in other courses.

Finally, the construction of "objective" measures that are fair and valid and "subjective" measures that are reliable and efficiently scored can be done, but only with care, some knowledge, and much time. Few English teachers have that training or time.

PERSONAL DANGERS

On a personal level, grading is problematic because it is most often based on comparative criteria, which leave some students feeling worthless and without dignity. Even those who often score well come to depend on external measures to motivate their action and to validate their worth. Students who consistently fail struggle with self-esteem. They learn to be dependent on the teacher's evaluation of them, rather than on their own evaluation. Because schools are the dominant field of activity through the formative years of students' lives (usually ages 5 through 18), the consequences can be life altering.

Another personal effect of grading students is that they are diverted from intrinsic or personal learning and spend their energies on grades. Purpel (1989) enumerates the consequences: "Students come to worry more about grades than meaning; and both teachers and students respond to these problems by developing techniques (e.g., multiple choice tests, cramming, memorizing) which are at best distracting, and at worse counterproductive to serious learning. The concern for grading produces anxiety, cheating, grade grubbing, and unhealthy competition" (p. 8).

CULTURAL DANGERS

Purpel (1989) sees technical discussions of testing as distractions from the crucial cultural and moral discussions:

> To value grading is to value competition and to accept a society of inequality and a psychology that posits external behavior rather than internal experience as more important. Grading is primarily a technique for promoting particular social, moral, and political goals, and it is those goals which should be debated rather than the technical and misleading questions about the value of essay vs. objective testing or whether to use grade point averages or standardized tests as the basis for college admission. (p. 9)

Our culture tends to structure its thinking around hierarchies, ladders, and pyramids. Greene (1985) observes that teachers "have a habitual tendency to see students in terms of superior and inferior, high up—and lower down—on a scale" (p. 144). She wonders if even Piagetian thought has given legitimacy to hierarchy: "It is simply assumed that development occurs sequentially, that analytic capacities are 'higher' than holistic ones, that the abstract is more worthy than the concrete" (p. 144). Such a ranking makes us tolerate the inevitability of failure in some and success in others. Teachers need to question this basic assumption in our culture.

Invitation to Reflection 13–8

Imagine that you are a first-year teacher in a consolidated rural county high school, the youngest and most inexperienced member of an established faculty. You decide to take some new evaluative ideas into your 11th-grade English classes; namely, you want to set up a process-centered assessment program based primarily on portfolio grading and self-evaluation. Because your students are amazed and then energized by this departure from tradition, a majority of them put considerable time and energy into their work and achieve *A* grades. After the first quarter's grades are reported, the guidance counselor notes the "disproportionate" number of *A*'s, hears from parents of highly competitive students in other classes who wonder about the devaluation of their children's grades, and talks with the principal. The principal also has heard from disgruntled older teachers whose students are either jealous of their peers' good fortune or incredulous that other students are earning *A*'s so easily. The principal values your new instructional approaches but calls you in to talk about your grading. What will you say?

UNIQUE DIFFICULTIES FOR ENGLISH TEACHERS

Beyond these difficulties in evaluation and grading, English teachers have unique, specific burdens. Our field itself, the receptive and creative study of oral and written language, is resistant to narrow measurement. When we define our educative purpose as opening students to the responses and possibilities that are uniquely their own, we falter at the use of grading to measure that personal openness. We find it hard to reduce a novel to a multiple-choice exam, but harder still to reduce the individual response to any criteria- or norm-referenced standard of excellent, good, fair, or unacceptable. The dilemma reminds us of the American composer Charles Ives's reaction to an award for his composing: He said that giving a prize to a composer is like offering a prize to the curate who loves God the most.

Dixon and Stratta (1989) have observed the reductive consequences of the kinds of questions that we pose about literature in classroom discussions, in out-of-class assignments, and on examinations. They find that these questions betray "false assumptions about the act of reading, the kind of knowledge to be derived from literature, and the kinds of writing that help to articulate it" (p. 30). They explain: "To be specific, these exercises assume that you do not create a character in your imagination as you read; that you do not feel sympathy or antipathy to those personae on the screen, that you never test their reality against life as you know it, that you can't read the play as a metaphor for parts of your own life, and that you won't challenge the author's conception of people and society" (p. 26). Because what we aim to teach in the English classroom is complex, measurement of it is a risky business.

CONCLUSION

We must engage in evaluation with resistance to those evaluative acts and attitudes that stymie or harm the individual's making of meaning and with openness to alternative means for expressing understanding. We need also to be clear about the uses of evaluation. Moffett and Wagner (1976) articulate five functions served by language arts evaluation that address each of the constituents of schools. Evaluation should indicate

- to the individual student how effectively he is communicating,
- to the parent how much the student is learning in school,
- to the teacher the needs of the student, for diagnosing and advising,
- to the administrator how good a job the teacher is doing, and
- to all parties how effectively the curriculum and materials reach their goals. (p. 415)

We take each of these seriously and, as we have discussed, feel that different forms of evaluation must address each need. Parents are perhaps the most overlooked of these five. Greene (1985) vividly identifies the range of parents whose particular mindsets come to bear on schools:

> There are middle class parents worried about SATs, insisting on high achievement, whatever the cost. There are poor parents frightened by persisting illiteracy, people who want an exclusive emphasis on the three Rs for the sake of job training and survival in the mainstream. There are academic parents who purport to know more about education than do the teachers; there are zealots who want human relations "experiences" and non-cognitive play; there are fundamentalist parents afraid of certain novels, or of evolutionary theory, or of sex education. It becomes increasingly clear that students, parents, teachers, and the general public have different and competing ideas about how schools should be judged. Their assumptions differ; their values differ with regard to what good schools ought to be. (p. 153)

Greene does not try to provide simple answers to this dilemma. Struggle is inevitable if we attend to those complexities. But we should be anchored in our attention to the student. In the life of the classroom, evaluation is, quite simply, interpretation of the student by the teacher. That interpretation needs to be generous. In fact, we have observed that often the best teachers are those who were not the best students. Their youthful difficulties sensitize them to the feelings of discouragement, anxiety, and shame experienced by their students.

Psychologists G. B. Berenson and Robert Carkhuff (1967) reason that all human encounters work for good or ill. No encounter is neutral. Nowhere is this more true in teaching than in evaluation and grading. To render judgment of process or products too often forecloses on the student's dynamic life processes. We need to recognize the personal and idiosyncratic nature of reading, writing, and speaking and to provide evaluation strategies that give them expression. We should work towards Greene's (1985) hope that "evaluation may some day serve the cause of growth and constant learning" (p. 154).

14

BECOMING A COMPLETE TEACHER

In every lucky life there is one teacher who places [his or her] finger upon our soul.

        William Gibson

We have arrived at the final chapter, and we know that you are anxious to put your ideas to work in the classroom. Calkins (1983) quotes Erikson as saying "We are the teaching species." She goes on to say that "human beings need to teach, not only for the sake of those who need to be taught but for the fulfillment of our identities, and because facts are kept alive by being told, truths by being professed." (p. v). We hope this book has helped you arrive at greater certainty about those facts and truths, where to find them, and how to profess them. But before you launch into the world of real students and actual classrooms, we want you to stop to consider three important concerns that are a part of the context of teaching. All three appear to lie outside the immediate realm of instruction, but each is intimately related to your growth as an English teacher. The first concerns your defining yourself in a setting of other teachers, the second, your building relationships with your students through your connection with their parents and the community, and the third, your developing as a member of your profession.

DEFINING YOURSELF AS A TEACHER

In almost every aspect of your professional life, you will need to work between competing claims that will not allow for easy answers or quick solutions. Like Robert Frost, whose poems acknowledge the rightness of both introspection in snowy fields and movement toward town duties, the virtue of walls and the value of openness, we have to live in the tension between contending possibilities. You will most certainly face some difficult alternatives; we hope you will embrace or resolve them rather than polarize them as being either good or evil.

APPRAISING YOURSELF

At the personal level, you may well waver within yourself, and with your students, colleagues, administrators, and students' parents, between confidence and uncertainty. That confusion often arises from the tension between finding your comfortable teaching style and reaching always to experiment with alternatives. You have much to do in discovering what pedagogy works best for you and your students, but you will also want to enlarge your repertoire. Classroom research can help you see which new directions make sense and what established approaches warrant continued use. But your zest for particular content (the magic realism of Spanish American writers, for example) and modes of discourse (whole-class discussion, perhaps) is also important to recognize and enlarge. In planning, you will need to keep alive this same healthy tension between understanding your course's place in the state, system, and school curricula and establishing learning sequences that depart from those norms. The authorized texts and the adopted curricula may sometimes seem to represent tame conformity, but they also are reservoirs of tested content and practice that may merit a place in the classroom. At the same time, departures that recognize the needs of the particular students you teach and that promote genuine involvement make sense as their complement.

A midground must be struck between working for curricular change and avoiding fads. For example, the questions raised about the canon will have a serious impact on new texts and on the decisions of curriculum committees. Reconsidering what literature we will teach must be undertaken with a consciousness of the integrity and worth of much of the established tradition and the rich and urgent new literature that also deserves to be read. Likewise, computers can be powerful or regressive classroom tools. Videotapes of Shakespearean plays can enliven or deaden. As a new teacher, you are called upon to evaluate these new ideas. Rather than seeing these struggles, these internal dialogues between strong voices, as aberrant, we see them as signs of an alert and critical consciousness at work. Too much self-doubt can, of course, be paralyzing, but too little questioning also can be deadening. You are doing nothing less than composing yourself as a teacher. As Bateson (1990) says of life, "Each of us has worked by improvisation, discovering the shape of our creation along the way, rather than pursuing a vision already defined" (p. 1). You have been brought to teaching by some vision of your own, but all you know for certain of the terms of that actual teaching is that they will be challenging. We acknowledge the legitimate and necessary struggles that are part of the profession when you are aware of your surroundings and awake to yourself.

One teacher's fantasy of dream teaching may remind you of the possibilities of a classroom awakening, as well as of the inevitable challenges and frustrations in achieving it. Even if you don't aspire to a class taking notes and chanting parts of speech, you will recognize this teacher's tenacious dreams. We suggest that you read Edwin Romond's "Dream Teaching" now and later, after you have entered your own classroom and met your own Ernies and Cindys, as a reminder of the shared struggles and hopes of our profession.

Dream Teaching

I am first in line for coffee
and the copier is not broken yet.
This is how dreams begin in teaching high school.

First period the boy who usually carves skulls
into his desk raises his hand instead
to ask about *Macbeth* and, for the first time,
I see his eyes are blue as melting ice.
Then those girls in the back
stop passing notes and start taking them
and I want to marvel at tiny miracles
but still another hand goes up
and Butch the drag racer says he's found the meaning
in that Act III soliloquy. Then more hands join the air

that is now rich with wondering and they moan
at the bell that ends our class and I ask myself,
"How could I have thought of calling in sick today?"

I open my eyes for the next class and no one's late,
not even Ernie who owns his own time zone
and they've all done their homework
that they wave in the air
because everyone wants to go to the board
to underline nouns and each time I turn around
they're looking at me as if I know something they want
and steady as sunrise, they're doing it all right.

At lunch the serpentine food lady discovers smiling
and sneaks me an extra meatball. In the teachers room

we eat like family and for twenty-two minutes
not one of us bitches about anything.

Then the afternoon continues the happiness of hands
wiggling with answers and I feel such a spark
when spike-haired Cindy in the satanic tee shirt
picks the right pronoun and glows like a saint.
And me, I'm up and down the room now, cheering,
cajoling, heating them up like a revival crowd.

I'm living only in exclamatory sentences. They want it all
and I'm thinking, "What drug are we on here?"
Just as Crusher Granorski screams, "Predicate nominatives
are awesome!" the principal walks in
with my check and I almost say, "That's okay,
you can keep it." When the bell sounds
they stand, raise lighted matches
and chant, "Adverbs! Adverbs!"
I drive home petting my plan book.

At night I check the weather without wishing for a blizzard
then sleep in the sweet maze of dreams
where I see every student from years of school days:
boys and girls, sons and daughters who're almost mine,
thousands of them stretching like dominoes into the night
and I call the roll and they sing, "We're all here, Mr. Romond!"
When I pick up my chalk they open their books,
look up, and with eager eyes, ask me to teach them.

Edwin Romond

Invitation to Reflection 14–1

1. Return to the first Invitation to Reflection, 1–1. Are there any impressions of your own schooling that have altered or deepened in the course of your reading this book?
2. Reread and rethink your answer to the last question. Has your sense of the profession of teaching English changed since you first answered that question? Have you changed your sense of why you want to become an English teacher?
3. As you anticipate teaching, where do you feel yourself to be within the tensions we just mentioned?

	Defined, Confident, Established, Traditional	*or*	*Fluid, Open, Experimental, Unknown*
Self:	_____		_____
Teaching Style:	_____		_____
Teaching Content:	_____		_____
Planning:	_____		_____

4. Does our acknowledgement of our sense of necessary struggle unnerve you or relieve you?

Having explored these tensions that you will likely face in the first years of your career in teaching, let us look at a broader scheme in which to view these dichotomies. Years ago, one of us wrote an essay for the *English Journal* (Milner, 1975) that used Ken Kesey's *One Flew Over the Cuckoo's Nest* as a parable for education, pointing out the implications of that book for English classrooms. The response to it was positive, perhaps because other young teachers identified with the use of Kesey's work to challenge traditional methods and philosophy. As we came to understand the profession of teaching more deeply we revised that single vision of education. Our new conceptualization is no longer one-sided and certain; it embraces balance and unity. We believe it is important for you to consider each of 6 levels of education in order to come to an acceptance of the differences that the two sides represent. To understand, if not embrace, the contending poles is a goal that relates to the bridging theme that is central to our book.

Definition. We think that your definition of learning is extremely important. Broadening is a constant theme of this book. Personal growth is a large part of what we hope for our students, but we would not urge you to abandon intellectual growth as a goal either. Texts and lectures may not excite students like film and interaction do, but we have argued, too, that analysis and distance are important dimensions of student growth.

Motivation. The dichotomy attached to motivation is difficult for many people to accept. We are so keyed to goals, rewards, and external regard that the opposite seems hard to sustain for ourselves or our students. We should see that students who have not had easy lives will respond better to immediate rewards and to activities that have intrinsic interest for them. But we have to make peace with those who believe that students will do nothing that is not graded and those who do not care whether students ever take on the responsibility of working for a long-term goal.

Goal. At the level of goals for education, you will be trying to keep alive the fairly new idea that process is central to a true education while still knowing that a grasp of content is a part of what society expects and can most easily see in those whom you teach. Not just parents and school board members, but your own students will judge your course's worth on the grounds of the knowledge that they acquire. As we have said, the AP exams in the last 10 years have given more attention to students' ability to apply skills in reading a poem than in identifying its title or dating it. But The College Board is edging back toward content mastery as the weight of cultural literacy and international competition is felt. In a like manner, in many school districts we see a return to broader survey courses and a move away from the special-topic, intensive issue courses that have been a part of the curriculum for the past 15 years. But after curriculum audits and other conserving tendencies shrink the number of courses offered to make teaching loads more economical today, you will likely see a new yearning for the invigorating special-topic courses that are now being rooted out of the curriculum. You will need to fight for their lives then, just as you may need to agree that the array of courses needs trimming back now. Likewise, you will be caught in a tension between exposing students to the best of our culture and examining it with a critical eye. Both of these goals are compelling; you will never, we hope, resolve that conflict in favor of one at the expense of the other.

Method. The question of classroom methodology is central to how you will operate day by day. The traditional way for teachers to communicate is to present information, but you will feel that tradition as it is being challenged by the constructivist mode: teacher with students, students with other students in small groups, and students with texts and machines that represent the world of ideas and information. The tension between whether students are retaining and digesting or critiquing and discovering knowledge is a natural companion to how you teach. One is the style for you, the teacher; one is the process for those whom you teach. One is built on deduction, the other demands inductive thinking.

Epistemology. The dichotomy of epistemology is connected to that of goal. You will be facing the question of whether to impart to students universal or personal knowledge. You may be evaluated with an instrument built on an epistemology that prizes teachers who see theories as laws and facts as immutable. You may resist this, but you may be equally disturbed by teachers who believe that all knowledge is completely subjective, and all values and generalizations wholly relative. You may have some affinity for both and a revulsion for extreme positions at either pole. You can embrace the bulk of the literary canon and still promote inclusive literature that has obvious pertinence for and presents a challenge to your students. You can plan a course of study in which the central figures and ideas are determined but still allow for the spontaneity of new selections and varied approaches that will ignite your classes.

Philosophy. Finally, we come to philosophy. You may feel that some of the levels of concern are so distant from your personal style and professional method that they won't cause you any tension at all. The tug between a traditional and progressive philosophy, in fact, will guide all that you do. You will, as an English teacher, be aware of the cumulation and continuity of rhetorical and literary history. At the same time, you have to be conscious of the power of the contemporary idiom and the communicative power of the immediate. You know that science is built on throwing away its past, discarding worn-out theories, but you also recognize that Shakespeare does not need to be replaced by a more comprehensive and explanatory literature of today. Or does he? You may be appalled by those who dote on the past and rarely teach a contemporary writer or introduce a current issue as it touches writing in their classes. But you may fear too, as film and computers transform stories and personal responses, that the past will be lost to your students. Modern poets who allude to little outside the contemporary scene and writing that never moves into formal, analytical modes of discourse may trouble you in that both suggest a subtle entrapment in the present world, like that of a contented dog. Neither presents a way to gain a little distance on our lives.

All of these six tensions will capture you in one fashion or another—some you may be aware of or clear about right now. You may sense little goodness in those who relentlessly lecture, or in those who want to teach only relevant material. You may be committed to holistic growth for your students or dedicated to ways of making the beauty of Shakespeare come alive for them. But these worthy polarizations will mellow as you see the worth of those who work at the other end of the spectrum. You will, we hope, reflect on the effectiveness of their work and the depth of their dedication and come to believe that the McMurphys of the world have their dark side and the Big Nurses occasionally stumble into the light.

Invitation to Reflection 14–2

Where would you place yourself on a continuum between these dichotomies?

Classical Education (Big Nurse Learning)		Innovative Learning (McMurphy Learning)
	Level 1: Definition	
Formal _____		_____ Informal
	Level 2: Motivation	
Extrinsic _____		_____ Intrinsic
	Level 3: Goal	
Content _____		_____ Process
	Level 4: Style/Method	
Deductive _____		_____ Inductive
	Level 5: Epistemology	
Universal _____		_____ Personal
	Level 6: Philosophy	
Traditional _____		_____ Progressive

DEFINING YOURSELF IN A PROFESSIONAL CONTEXT

Any self-definition has to begin with a close look at the way we teach and the philosophy that is foundational to that teaching. Beyond that examination lie broader questions of how we see ourselves as part of a profession and how the world sees us as teachers. Nothing says more about that broader self-definition than the issues and concerns of our profession. Many serious issues are out there, but five are paramount: *community support, discipline, class size, funding,* and *attrition.*

Teachers today feel the community's disengagement from the schools. The school-neighborhood connection has nearly been severed, PTAs have withered, and the number of taxpayers with children in schools has been almost cut in half since the 1960s. Discipline is a major problem for teachers that is directly tied to the school-community disconnection and to the societal upheaval that is just now subsiding. The National Center for Educational Statistics (NCES) (1997) reported that "the most satisfied secondary school teachers felt they had more parental support and were less likely to have been threatened by students" (p. 1). Glazer (1997) credits the terrific turnaround in the crime rate in New York City and the rate of teenage murders in Boston to George Kelling's "Broken Windows" theory (p. 29). Kelling provides a plausible explanation for the drop: Small crimes receive swift and certain judgment. Schools might consider these cities's stunning results and move to a similar justice stance.

FIGURE 14–1

National allocation of
school personnel

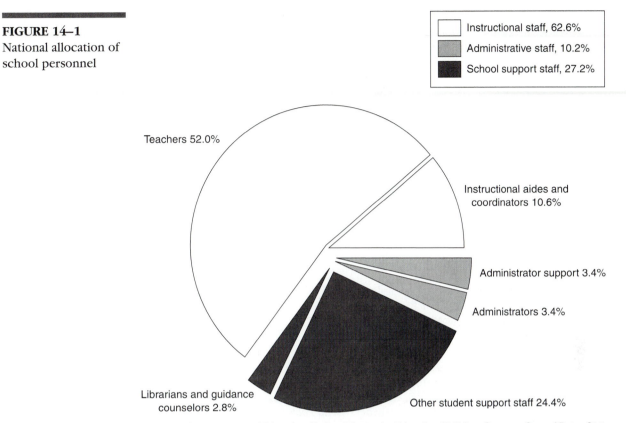

	Instructional staff, 62.6%
	Administrative staff, 10.2%
	School support staff, 27.2%

SOURCE: U.S. Department of Education, National Center for Education Statistics, Common Core of Data, *State Nonfiscal Survey.*

Note: Details may not add to the total due to rounding

Work load is proportional to class size but dropping the average class size by even two students would cost millions at the state level. Moreover, fast-growing states such as California and large urban centers have a student/teacher ratio of 24:1 or worse. The billions of dollars needed to change the ratio dramatically are not likely to be forthcoming, but a solution may reside in the nationwide allocation of school personnel reported by the U.S. Department of Education, Figure 14-1. Other nations (with less heterogeneous populations) employ teachers as almost 75% of their total school staff. If the percentage of teachers in U.S. schools could be raised substantially above the current 52% level, the teacher-student ratio could be improved without huge additional funding. Funding and attrition might appear to be closely related, but the NCES (1997) found that "teacher satisfaction showed a positive though weak relationship with salary and benefits."

Funding is not likely to increase substantially, but allocation of those dollars needs to be shrewder. Attrition is not so much related to salary as it is to issues of autonomy, school support and student behavior. Negative societal forces have an overriding impact on these three important factors; thus, with more positive societal trends, we hope to see improvement in the factors that make teaching a joy rather than a burden. With a greater demand for new teachers and more emphasis on school-based decision making, teacher autonomy has a real chance to flourish. And the NCES (1997) reports that "the teachers with greater autonomy show higher levels of satisfaction than teachers who feel they have less autonomy" (p. 1). The context for teaching may be lightening up a bit.

SCHOOL CRITICS

For many years now, an outspoken group of critics have unrelentingly attacked the public schools by claiming that students' academic performance is lackluster and that discipline is a joke. A vociferous detractor in our state recently said that the high schools award diplomas for 8th-grade work—performance that is equivalent to that of third-world countries. He added that we should once again let adults rather than students run the schools. George Will, who is usually careful with his words, has said that this is the first American generation whose schools are not as good as those that their parents attended. William Bennett, Chester Finn, and Diane Ravich have spent a good part of the last decade thrashing the public schools. In the past several years, Berliner and Biddle (1995), Bracy (1994), and others have returned the fire saying that the myth of failing schools has been manufactured as part of

FIGURE 14–2
What's in and what's out

OUT	IN
Inputs	Outputs
Innate Ability	Effort
Rote Learning	Mastery
Autocratic	Autonomous
Seat Time	Accomplishment
Student as Learner	Student as Worker
Teacher as Lecturer	Teacher as Manager of Instruction
Longevity	Competence
Administrator as Master	Administrator as Servant
Centralized Bureaucracy	Decentralized Management
Technology: Bells and Whistles	Technology: Productivity Enhancer
School Board: Micromangement	School Trustees: Stewardship
Time: Periods, Semesters, Years	Time: Flexible
Schools: Teacher Proof	Schools: Teacher Friendly
Diploma = Seat Time/Age	Diploma = Mastery/Accomplishment
Superintendent = Dictator	Student = Choreographer
Taxpayer	Shareholder
Standardization	Standards
True-and-False Tests	Authentic Assessment
Blue Collar	Professionals
Uniform Salary Schedule	Pay for Scarcity; Pay for Performance
Education: School's Business	Education: Everyone's Business
School = Building	School = Learning

an effort to privatize K–12 education. Popular films have not been a part of any orchestrated effort, but they have, according to Burbach and Figgins (1993), presented negative images of "incompetence and buffoonery" (*Ferris Buller's Day Off* and *The Breakfast Club*) and positive but romantic images of the "youthful idealist" and "tough love teacher" (*Dead Poets Society* and *Stand and Deliver*). Some educators believe that the negativism and the ambivalence are a result of stiff resistance to a paradigm shift from the traditional to a contemporary approach to pedagogy that Doyle and Pimentel (1993) propose, in Figure 14–2.

DEFINING YOURSELF FOR SCHOOLS

As you consider this paradigm, you will naturally reflect on where you stand, where the high school you attended school, and where your future employers might be positioned on this pedagogical split. An immediate test of your stance will come when you interview for a position as an English teacher. You can get a sense of your employers' perspective when you think about the top-10 dilemma questions and the top-10 topics during interviews (as surveyed and reported by Head, 1990, pp. 2–3).

Top Ten Tough or Dilemma Questions	*National Top Ten Interview Topics*
What is your philosophy of education?	Classroom Management
How do you handle discipline in your classroom?	Student Teaching
What are your strengths?	Personal Strengths
What are your weaknesses?	Personal Weaknesses
Describe in detail a lesson you taught.	Hypothetical Situations
How would you develop ( ) skills in your students?	Teaching Style
How would you set up a program in ( )?	Future Plans
What if . . .?	Employment History
Tell me about yourself.	Motivational Theories
Why should I hire you?	

The positions of the 10 interview topics and dilemma questions change from year to year. Most of them are generally used to let prospective teachers define themselves for the interviewers.

This extended look at self-definition includes a recent study that focused on teachers, not structures. Ward (1997) reported that the top teachers at 30 schools of excellence shared four basic characteristics:

- High teaching expectations
- Respect for students and their cultures
- Teaching driven by research and theory
- Classroom experimentation and action research

The first two characteristics speak of these teachers' care for others; the latter two indicate that they are reflective about their practice and their role as teachers.

BUILDING PUBLIC TRUST

As a new teacher, you cannot help thinking about the day-to-day urgencies of teaching: "What will I do Monday?" Developing home-school connections is not likely to be an immediate concern. But those connections provide an essential support on which your classroom teaching will flourish. Conservative and liberal educators and politicians agree on one thing about education: Classrooms that work best have strong bonds with the homes of the students they serve. These bonds are all the more important at a time when homes are fragile and schools are drawing more and more criticism. When over a fourth of our children come from one-parent families, when the population of students that the school serves is racially underrepresented by the teachers who help them learn, when an ever slimmer portion of the taxpaying population has children in public schools, when the parents of some students are little more than children themselves, the odds against strong parental support for teachers' work are very high. At this time, then, the need to build relationships with students' families is all the more important.

Let's review some of the ways in which you can lay this foundation. We suggest three fair and effective ways to relate to parents: *include* them, *inform* them, and *involve* them in all that you do. These three *I*'s are truly basic and can be accomplished with little expenditure of effort yet exceptional profits to you and to your students.

INCLUDE

Many parents have had negative experiences themselves with schools and feel antagonistic or alienated from them. With a new approach, they can become allies instead of aliens. Neil Griffiths, headmaster at Westlea School in Wiltshire, England, begins working with his parents more than a year before their children enter his school. He invites them to come to his school for a meeting and lets them know that he will visit them in their homes if they do not attend. You cannot go that far perhaps, but you can let your parents know what you expect of their sons and daughters and what you plan to accomplish during the school year. This is a beginning point: an oral or written word of welcome, an invitation to become partners, and an agenda for the term. Too much talk with too little action will not impress any parent, but words that lead to action can invite parents to reappraise their relationship to school. If they see useful skills, important knowledge, and personal growth as the end result of your class, the possibilities for a good home-school relationship increase. If, in the attempt to include them, you offer your agenda but also invite parents to express their hopes and fears, the effective potential of your reaching out may rise sharply. If you are able to gather parents together, they can meet you and come to see you as a person. Not only are the chances of their encouragement of their children's efforts in English greater, but also, if you must meet them to discuss an academic problem, they will know you. Without that initial contact, parents can easily become defensive or hostile. In addition to this preliminary letter, meeting, or conference, we recommend that you establish other times when parents can come by to review their children's work or actually visit class for a period. Parent-Teacher-Student Association meetings of scheduled open houses are also times when strong connections can be forged.

INFORM

Periodic *teacher-student-parent conferences* (often held at the end of grading periods) can be very effective means of informing parents of and showing student work (portfolios, writing folders, homework, and tests) and of the curricular agenda for the coming term, especially when you are able to ground talk of the students' progress in concrete particulars. Parents want to see the kind of substantial work that shows the true progress of their children.

Perhaps an even more useful tool for cohesion is *student performance*. Student-conceived, written, and produced presentations can draw on all of the language arts skills. Professionally scripted drama, which can remain inert if it remains on the pages of a textbook, can come alive in student productions. Literature is enlivened for students as classrooms are enlivened for their parents. These productions provide evidence of both student involvement and their recently acquired knowledge.

A less public way to inform parents is to use Tierney's (1990) concept of a class assignment monitor. A log of all out-of-class assignments can be kept by a no-nonsense student whose job description includes providing a record for absent and returning students of exactly what they missed during that time. When parents look at the log, they can see just how much is going on in class and how much congruence exists between a son's or daughter's assessment of the workload and the record of the actual workload.

In addition to telling families about plans for the school year, some teachers send home periodic lists of supplemental readings. If you also ask parents to offer comments and suggestions, you will be both informing them and mitigating the threat of their censoring responses later. This approach becomes even more effective when you include a brief statement about your rationale for choosing the literature and your willingness to discuss any of the texts on the list. Other kinds of lists presented at meetings or in conferences also inform parents of your goals and expectations for your students: lists of skills to be learned, topics to be covered, major due dates to be anticipated. Because the goals, pedagogy, strategies, and content of English education change over time, parents need to become more comfortable with the basic philosophy of your program. When they see little of the activity that was central to their school experience, knowing what is transpiring will assure them that an important kind of learning is taking place. When both your rationale and activities are simply and clearly communicated to parents, they can become allies with you and their children.

INVOLVE

The lines among these three components of strong parent-school connections are not always sharply delineated. Including and informing parents ideally will involve them in the life of the classroom. With some, that involvement might lead to active partnership with the teacher. You will come to imagine ways to initiate and solidify that activity. One of the simplest and least threatening for parents is the role of guest or interviewee. Most adults who are willing to come to class to talk about their lives—vocations, avocations, continued learning, parenting, and life stories—will be able guests to interview. Those with unusual vocations might talk about them or serve as panel members on life work. Parents are more likely to participate if they know that others are involved. (Industry, medical institutions, and public service departments have become more willing to support this kind of partnership with schools.) Another role for a few is actually to teach or talk about fiction, nonfiction, or poetry that they particularly like. Others are willing to volunteer as relief teachers for your occasional times away from the classroom. In each of these approaches, you are supported, the parent is involved, and students are enriched.

An approach that requires less parental time yet still allows parental expression about the work of your class is to survey their opinions. They might be asked about such areas as their language use (idioms, say), reading habits, television viewing or music preferences, and favorite books. Surveys are especially effective when the results of all parental responses are handled anonymously and reported enthusiastically. Tact and common sense are crucial here to protect against awkward self-disclosure. But if you use care, incorporating surveys into the work of the class to enlarge literature is engaging for all: to provide writing ideas, to prompt discussion, or to provide stories for dramatic activities like Choral Reading or Change Agents (Chapter 3).

Another way to involve parents is to use their talents and experience to help as editors of their children's writing. Not all parents are able to write, and some who can don't think of themselves as able writers, but all can help—even by listening and making oral suggestions. Because they attend to content better than to form, parents may be valuable deep-structure revisers. An even larger extension of this approach is used as papers progress through many drafts; such response is freed of the reliability and consistency problems of grading. The parent becomes another active reader. Some schools even pay these paraprofessionals a small stipend.

On another level, parents can be asked to support your goal that students read and write outside of school and beyond the compulsion of assigned texts and topics. You can ask parents to give you 10 minutes of two nights each week to provide a period of uninterrupted, silent, sustained home reading or writing. They might find it a pleasure and a bond, not a tax on their patience and time. For families in which parents are struggling with basic literacy skills themselves, you can try to locate or even develop a program of tutoring.

At the school level, James Comer at Yale and David Perkins at Harvard agree that smart schools are above all else ones that reach out to parents and make the school seem to be an extension of the family. Epstein (1997), at the Center on School, Family and Community Partnership at Johns Hopkins, has identified six important types of cooperation between school and home that can be developed.

1. Parenting: Families must provide for the health and safety of children, and maintain a home environment that encourages learning and good behavior in school.
2. Communicating: Schools must reach out to families with information about school programs and student progress.

3. Volunteering: Schools should create flexible schedules, so more parents can participate, and work to use the talents and interests of parents.
4. Learning at Home: With the guidance and support of teachers, family members can supervise and assist their children at home.
5. Decision-making: Schools can give all parents meaningful roles in the school decision-making process.
6. Collaboration with the Community: Schools can help families gain access to support services offered by other agencies. (p. 4)

The California State Board of Education (1989) has a similar list that goes even further in the direction of parents' taking leadership roles in the schools:

- Include parents and families as leaders and decision-makers in school issues and programs.
- Promote clear, two-way communication between school and family about the instructional programs and children's progress.
- Assist parents, families, and guardians in developing parenting skills and learning techniques to support their children's learning.
- Involve parents and family members, where appropriate, in instructional and support roles at the school.
- Provide access to and coordinate community and support services for children and families.
- Identify and reduce barriers to parent/family involvement.
- Provide professional development for teachers and staff on ways to effectively work with parents and families.
- Provide a written copy of the policy for each parent and/or family and post the policy in the school.

The National PTA (1989) has been more specific in its guidance of teachers and schools. It provides a list of 10 things that parents wish teachers would do.

- Build students' self-esteem by using praise generously and avoiding ridicule and negative public criticism.
- Get to know each child's needs, interests, and special talents, as well as the way each child learns best.
- Communicate often and openly with parents, contacting them immediately when academic or behavioral problems occur and be open and not defensive when discussing these problems.
- Assign homework that helps children learn and advise parents how they can assist their children with this learning.
- Set high academic standards, expecting all students to learn and helping them to do so.
- Care about children, since children learn best when taught by warm, friendly, caring, and enthusiastic teachers.
- Treat all children fairly.
- Enforce a positive discipline code based on clear and fair rules that are established at the beginning of each school year; reinforce positive behavior rather than punish negative behavior.
- Vary teaching methods and make learning fun.
- Encourage parent participation by reaching out to involve parents in their children's education, showing them how they can help their children at home and remembering that parents want to work with teachers to help their children do their best.

All of this adds up to what the U.S. Department of Education calls rebuilding social capital. The responsibility stretches from a welcome at the front door of the school to your thoughtful reflection on students' progress as you listen with their parents or guardians as your students use their portfolios to explain the headway that they have made in their writing over the course of the year. James Comer, the president of the Urban League, and a host of African-American leaders are now marshalling their forces to put out a strong, clear message about the crucial importance of school success for their children. Your action in your classroom, along with the efforts of this coalition, should help to make excellence a reality for all students rather than a hollow one-liner.

The list of ideas for including, informing, and involving parents is as long as your imagination and must be tied to your understanding of your particular circumstances. Exactly what you do is not as important as your communicating to parents that you care about their children, and that you are reaching out to them to promote purposive and successful learning.

Invitation to Reflection 14–3

- How important do you consider the connection between teachers and parents to the learning of the classroom?

    Very Important   *Somewhat Important*   *Important*   *Unimportant*

    To the teacher:
    To the student:
    To the parent:
- Which of the strategies for building public trust appeals to you most?
    Include
    Inform
        Teacher-Student-Parent Conferences
        Student Performance
        Logs of Assignments
        Lists of Supplemental Readings
    Involve
        Guests or Interviewees
        Surveys
        Editors
        Home Reading
- Do you remember your parent or parents coming to your high school? If so, what were the occasions?
- Were they included or involved in the life of your classes?
- Would it have made a difference if they had or had not been?

PROMOTING PROFESSIONAL GROWTH

Thinking about your long-term professional growth may seem quite distant and therefore unimportant to you at this time, but, along with seeing your place in the community of English teachers and making connections with parents, it is an essential indicator of excellence in teaching. You may have heard the old distinction between the teacher who has 20 years of experience and the teacher who has had one year of teaching 20 times. We want you to grow with your years in this profession. In fact, we believe a profession is defined as a community of those who possess a complex body of knowledge and skill that rests on theory, research, and practice and that is constantly tested and refined by experience. Professionals, then, not only understand the universal or the general, but also learn from the particular and the situated. By this definition your growth in teaching becomes proof of your being a professional. We explore seven steps that will promote your growth as an English teacher and as a person who seeks self-knowledge and acts on professional commitments. We list the seven steps to let you see them as a total movement, then we explore each one briefly: goal setting, self-evaluation, peer review, external assessment, action research, guild building, and association linkage.

GOAL SETTING

The first of these steps may be prompted by departmental or schoolwide initiatives, but more likely you will provide your own prompt for setting goals. These can clarify and name specific and/or general areas to explore and accomplish. They can govern curricular directions that you take and instructional choices that you make. They can serve as an index of new measures adopted and areas accomplished toward professional growth. The goals you set may be as personal as working toward a close relationship with a small number of students or as public as increasing the number of attendance days for at-risk students. Some goals may be pedagogical (trying to add two new approaches to literature instruction) or content centered (reading four new young adult novels). The goals may have to do with professional efficiency (reading all short papers within 3 days of their completion) or personal efficacy (leaving every Saturday completely open for a non-school related activity). Such goal setting can enable you to focus your energies, to experiment with new possibilities, and thus to grow professionally. The goals should be few, important, and attainable. You should review them periodically and check out the results at the end of every year. If you can convince your colleagues in the English department to set goals for the entire group, that will be a reinforcement of your own and will lend cohesiveness to the work of the department.

SELF-EVALUATION

Student evaluation provides an important measure of the success of these goals. If you are alert and open, you can sense much about your teaching through informal observation and discussion. But to assure comprehensive and objective assessment, you should let students speak through an evaluation instrument that you devise or select from available ready-made forms. Developing or selecting a form that measures what you think is important about teaching is critical. If you believe that student participation and construction of knowledge are essential, then you need to develop an evaluation form that can measure these accomplishments. Learning about students' perceptions through description is useful too. Asking what they regard as the percentage of class time involved in collaborative writing, say, or asking them to rank the time allotted for talking and listening, reading, writing, and viewing, can enrich your understanding of students' experiences in your classroom. We recommend that your format also provide some space for short responses, open or guided, such as three adjectives to describe the course, two problems with the course, or two topics that should be omitted. Exercise 14–1 prompts you to consider this type of evaluation by examining a form to evaluate both an entire course and its teacher.

Exercise 14–1   Teacher Evaluation Form

Review the following evaluation form and explain its strengths and weaknesses.

Course:

Teacher: Circle your response to the statements below and offer comments where helpful.

Excellent   Good   Average   Below Average   Poor

1. Preparation and Organization of the Subject Matter
         10 9 8 7 6 5 4 3 2 1
   Comment:
2. Intelligence and Insight Brought to Subject Matter
         10 9 8 7 6 5 4 3 2 1
   Comment:
3. Scholarship and Knowledge of the Field of Inquiry
         10 9 8 7 6 5 4 3 2 1
   Comment:
4. Enthusiasm for and Communication of Subject Matter
         10 9 8 7 6 5 4 3 2 1
   Comment:
5. Ability to Stimulate Thought and Provoke Inquiry
         10 9 8 7 6 5 4 3 2 1
   Comment:
6. Sensitivity to and Concern for Student Response
         10 9 8 7 6 5 4 3 2 1
   Comment:
7. Openness to and Reception of Divergent Points of View
         10 9 8 7 6 5 4 3 2 1
   Comment:

8. Accuracy and Fairness of Evaluation of Students

    10 9 8 7 6 5 4 3 2 1

    Comment:

9. Availability for Academic Help and Personal Counsel

    10 9 8 7 6 5 4 3 2 1

    Comment:

10. Adequate Class Time Spent to Cover Course Material

    10 9 8 7 6 5 4 3 2 1

    Comment:

11. General Evaluation of Total Effectiveness as a Teacher

    10 9 8 7 6 5 4 3 2 1

    Comment:

12. General comments:

    Strengths   *Weaknesses*

Two important parts of this process are the students' security and your receptivity. We think that students are most protected and their comments most honest when they are assured full anonymity and when they are assured that grades will be recorded before the evaluations are read. With students thus protected, you will need to protect yourself from disappointment at student evaluations while at the same time opening yourself to listen to their responses, no matter how harsh. One way to elicit thoughtful reflection is to let students know that you will take their perceptions seriously and that you have adapted your teaching to improve it in the ways in which former students have suggested. Ideally, your year's or semester's work with your classes will establish a partnership of learning for which a final evaluation is a natural and promising conclusion, not an occasion for airing gripes and vendettas. If it has not, treating the event seriously may help. You will, of course, need to make your own judgments about students' responses. Some things that they may want are not what is best for the class as you envision it. Some of their remarks may be personal and excessive; they may be borne out of anger or disappointment or out of profound admiration, but they need to be taken seriously. One of our university colleagues assures his own receptivity to student evaluations by waiting a year, just prior to planning for the evaluated course, to read evaluations.

PEER REVIEW

Many schools have established mentor teachers to serve as guides for first-year teachers. If you do not find a mechanism for peer review in place, we strongly recommend that, even in the crowded schedule you will face as a first-year teacher, you try to find an experienced teacher on whom to rely. In actuality, the hard part is not finding time, but establishing trust. We suggest a concrete plan for such a process, an ideal to which you will undoubtedly make personal accommodation.

- Find a partner, someone you like and feel you can learn from.
- Work out a schedule in which you will use part of your planning period once a week to visit the partner's classroom.
- Reciprocally, the partner comes to one of your classes once a week and in brief after-school meetings, gives you impressions of the things you were doing very well. Keep the focus on strengths and capabilities at first, before moving to more problematic observations and questions about the class session. These questions need not imply negative judgments, but rather departures from what was expected or what the partner might have done. The result is greater reflection on diverse ways to accomplish the same learning.
- After four of those sessions, include in the agenda responses about things that the partner might have done differently or accomplished in a different order. This leads to fuller exploration of pedagogy and a more honest sense of differences.
- In the next four sessions, add the exploration of content and method that might have been used but were not. Here, a broader repertoire of method and content is injected, pushing you on to deeper and broader questions of teaching.
- Finally, discuss problems and difficulties in the lesson openly.

The peer review sequence, then, involves a slow progress through

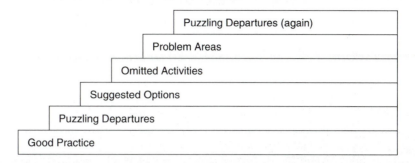

This pace, a slow movement toward a thorough critique, is necessary, or even the sturdiest and most self-confident new teacher will become defensive. The option of taking each of these steps in writing first, before they are taken orally, may help to ease the pain of growth. But when all the steps are taken with a colleague you trust and admire, the time spent will be repaid many times over in terms of what you learn about your teaching. You may not now believe that you can afford that expenditure, but we believe you will not consider using that weekly 30 minutes any other way after completing 10 sessions.

EXTERNAL ASSESSMENT

The kinds of personal assessment of your teaching progress just described will be extremely beneficial to your growth and long-term success as a teacher, but there will be other ways in which you will be evaluated by outsiders that will also have an impact on your career. In the past, external assessments were infrequent and marginal features of the teaching profession, but in these times of public demands for school accountability and competitiveness, you would be naive not to be prepared for encountering many kinds of assessment.

Teaching Portfolios. Teachers in many states are now facing school and individual evaluations based on student-gain scores on standard achievement tests. This is a part of the shift from considering input to considering output (noted in the Doyle-Pimental paradigm shift), but many school leaders complain that the measures of achievement are not authentic and that many confounding and contaminating variables are ignored. An assessment model that responds to those inequities is the teaching portfolio. The teaching portfolio provides a thoughtful means for evaluating ourselves and at the same time presents a solid vehicle for external evaluations. Wolf (1996) explains the process and its merits for teachers at any level. He describes five steps that lend credibility and usefulness to the portfolio.

- Explain your educational philosophy and key principles that underlie your practice.
- Choose specific features of your instructional program to document. Collect a wide range of artifacts, and date and annotate them.
- Collaborate with a mentor and other colleagues to discuss your teaching and your portfolio.
- Assemble your portfolio in a form that others can readily examine.
- Assess the portfolio. Assessment can range from an informal self-assessment to formal scoring. (p. 36).

Wolf also provides a list of contents that lend credibility to a teaching portfolio.

- Background information
    Résumé
    Background information on teacher and teaching context
    Educational philosophy and teaching goals
- Teaching Artifacts and Reflections
- Documentation of an extended teaching activity
    Overview of unit goals and instructional plan
    List of resources used in unit
    Two consecutive lesson plans
    Videotape of teaching
    Student work samples

Evaluation of student work
Reflection commentary by the teacher
Additional units/lessons/student work as appropriate
- Professional Information
   List of professional activities
   Letters of recommendation
   Formal evaluations (p. 35)

These are a part of standard practice in many schools today and are the basis for the certification process of the National Board for Professional Teaching Standards. Both of our teacher education programs require that each graduate prepare an electronic portfolio that includes running commentary on videotapes of instruction, classroom artifacts, and a stated philosophy of education that parallels the structure and requirements of the National Board examination. We believe that this way of demonstrating performance provides a solid account of what a teacher intends to happen in his or her classroom and what does in fact happen. This descriptive account can be used by schools and boards to evaluate, by perspective employers to hire, and by teachers to scrutinize and enlarge their teaching.

GENERAL-KNOWLEDGE TESTS

Some of the major forms of evaluation that are used in the profession today or that are becoming more widespread include both one-time events and those that are administered annually. The teacher achievement tests developed in several states were administered to a teacher only once. They were not based on performance or knowledge about classroom pedagogy, but focused on content knowledge. They set minimal passing scores that teachers had to achieve no matter how long or how successfully they had taught. Some focused on a teacher's specialty area, but most were tests of general knowledge. These tests seemed to be prompted by public perceptions that teachers were not well educated. Some critics blamed this perceived insufficiency on undergraduate education—an overload of professional coursework or poor general education—and others blamed the shift in the population of students entering teaching. Whatever the reason, the tests were used and some very effective teachers suffered.

CLASSROOM PERFORMANCE

A second wave of teacher evaluation has centered on teaching performance, rather than teacher knowledge. It pleased those who felt that the knowledge tests were superficial and reductive, but its instruments created a new set of adversaries. Its critics ranged from classroom teachers to think-tank theorists who assailed its failure to account for the skillful blend of content and pedagogy that astute teachers are able to create. And, while some teacher groups called for a moratorium on such instruments for evaluation of all but novice teachers, other educators defended them as primitive but necessary first steps. Some have said that these instruments need to be balanced with another kind of judgment based on a very different sense of how knowledge is best explored and stored (Milner, 1991). The first list defines what constitutes good teaching for some educators:

- The teacher asks questions and assigns tasks that students handle with a high rate of success.
- The teacher begins the lesson with a review of previous material.
- The teacher summarizes the main point(s) of the lesson at the end of the lesson.

The second list offers a very different set of teaching values.

- The teacher uses words of supposition such as *perhaps, maybe, then again, one wonders, inexplicably, might,* and *possibly* in his or her discourse.
- The teacher actively encourages students to question propositions and theses developed by the teacher and by other students.
- The teacher makes it clear that knowledge is uncertain, that "facts" can change.

Madeline Hunter speaks for the first, Jerome Bruner the second.

Specialty Performance. The National Teacher's Exam (NTE) had for many years been the major paper-and-pencil test for prospective teachers, the gatekeeper for entrance into the classroom for many states. It was akin to the teacher achievement test mentioned earlier, but it also tested pedagogical knowledge. As the Educational Testing Service (ETS) sensed the evolution in evaluation, it began to develop a new test, Praxis, which is more performance centered but provides the content sophistication lacking in the state-developed teacher performance tests. It is discipline specific and makes use of technology to offer an assessment of teaching as authentically as possible. The results have been mixed to date. Most methods teachers support the pedagogy central to the test, but some of the norming procedures in some states have caused real difficulties.

Student Achievement. A recent revolution in evaluation has been toward student performance as the final test of teaching effectiveness. Such a measure doesn't look at philosophy, pedagogy, or even content knowledge; it doesn't care about teaching style or the student-teacher relationship. It evaluates teachers straightforwardly on how well their students achieve. If your students perform well on writing assessments, then you are considered successful. Some states allow the teachers at a particular school to designate a quantifiable dimension of student performance to be evaluated (attendance, for example), and if progress is discernible (the average daily attendance rises), rewards are forthcoming. These evaluations appear at first to have a clear, objective quality about them, but on second glance their defects become more apparent: They often fail to take into account contextual factors, which may radically skew comparisons, and they rely primarily on easily measurable variables. They may not reflect gain scores, for instance, in schools with high-risk students. They may also compromise long-term goals for teaching, such as student attitudes toward the subject at hand. Instead, instruction hammers away at the test, but excludes almost everything else. This approach could eventually turn teachers into assembly-line workers and students into their widgets.

Board Certification. The most promising form of evaluation may be the voluntary kind promoted by the National Board for Professional Teaching Standards. Its model is the Board Examination in medicine, which certifies physicians as specialists in such medical fields as neurology, pediatrics, and pathology. The National Board invites experienced teachers to be examined to qualify for board certification in specialty areas such as middle school language arts (the first area developed). The exam includes various components such as portfolio review, classroom simulation, and a look at content.

Teachers standing for examination have to demonstrate a high level of knowledge, skills, dispositions, and commitments reflected in the five core propositions of the National Board.

- *Teachers are committed to students and their learning.*
  Board-certified teachers are dedicated to making knowledge accessible to all students, act on the belief that all students can learn, treat students equitably, adjust their practice as appropriate, and understand how students develop and learn.
- *Teachers know the subjects they teach and how to teach those subjects to students.*
  Board-certified teachers have a rich understanding of the subject(s) they teach and appreciate how knowledge in their subject is created, organized, linked to other disciplines, and applied to real-world settings.
- *Teachers are responsible for managing and monitoring student learning.*
  Board-certified teachers create, enrich, maintain, and alter instructional settings to capture and sustain the interest of their students and to make the most effective use of time, command a range of generic instructional techniques, know how to engage groups of students to ensure a disciplined learning environment, and understand how to motivate students to learn and how to maintain their interest even in the face of temporary failure.
- *Teachers think systematically about their practice and learn from experience.*
  Board-certified teachers are models of educated persons, exemplifying the virtues they seek to inspire in students—curiosity, tolerance, honesty, fairness, respect for diversity, an appreciation of cultural differences, and the capacities that are prerequisites for intellectual growth.
- *Teachers are members of learning communities.*
  Board-certified teachers contribute to the effectiveness of the school by working collaboratively with other professionals on instructional policy, curriculum development, and staff development and find ways to work collaboratively and creatively with parents. (pp. 6–8)

Some states and a few schools are supporting accomplished teachers who want to earn this national certification. The hope of the enterprise is to bring all of the art and science of teaching together for a rigorous look at best practice.

These three—Praxis as a gatekeeper to beginning practice, the induction period as a passageway for licensure, and the National Board for field certification—form a natural set of steps to full professional standing. If these steps remain meaningful and distinguish those who are truly master teachers in their fields, the profession will be enriched, those who are outstanding will be recognized and rewarded, and excellent teachers will become the mentors of our profession.

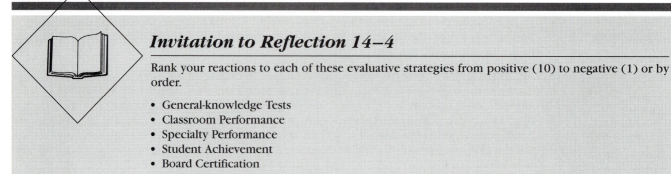

Invitation to Reflection 14–4

Rank your reactions to each of these evaluative strategies from positive (10) to negative (1) or by order.

- General-knowledge Tests
- Classroom Performance
- Specialty Performance
- Student Achievement
- Board Certification

- How do these forms of assessment make you feel about being an English teacher?
- Which ones seem most promising?
- Which seem reductive of teaching? What kind of assessment would seem most helpful for you?
- Which seem to acknowledge the complexity of teaching?
- Which are consistent with your sense of the profession?

ACTION RESEARCH

The act of classroom research is perhaps the most productive, and least used, tool of self-evaluation. It is the tool of growth for excellent teachers. When you teach awareness of language, and self-consciousness about the human condition, it is not surprising that you bring similar antennae into action in your own life. Conventional wisdom tells us that a great spur for learning teaching skills or self-knowledge is a consciousness of classroom difficulties or personal inadequacies.

When teaching skills are learned, say, they enter the teaching repertoire and are used spontaneously. That growth-producing consciousness can be developed through a kind of informal posing of questions about what is going on in your classroom. You may sense, for example, that your students are responding more intensely in their writing when they select their own topics. Because that intensity is important, you may want to make two explorations. You could start with alternating self-selected and assigned topics for a term. Or you might even alternate with two classes, so that one is working in complete freedom one week while the other is given a topic, and the next week reverse the procedure. A second thing you might do is try to define just what you mean by *intensity*. Is it personal identification, revelatory comment, use of the first person pronoun, strong criticism, idiomatic expression, exclamatory phrases, or is it some other criterion you establish? Whatever it may be, it can be used to evaluate the two sets of papers in as objective a manner as possible. By reviewing six sets of papers, you would have a pretty good sense of the relationship between this kind of production of language and the control of topic by the teacher. Once you have come up with a tentative answer, you then may want to see what effect discourse mode (analysis or narrative) has on the same features, or you may want to look at the relationship between intensity and other features that range from control of conventions to syntax maturity.

You may want to be more ethnographic in looking closely at a particular group of students assigned to a long-term project. For instance, does the subject selection of voice differ significantly in the journal writing of males and females? In-depth interviews of the kind Seidman describes can also be used in searching to discover what makes learning most effective in your classroom.

You can develop even more formal designs for your classroom such as the ones a student teacher created when she examined the effectiveness of film and text versions of the same story. She let her students engage the story in its two forms during a regular class period. One class read it; one class saw it. She used adjective checklists and high- and low-level content questions to establish the students' emotional engagement and comprehension of the two versions of the story. Her study was a formal, empirical study, but it did not really violate her teaching style, and it allowed her to gain an insight into a question that had real meaning for her and the teaching community as a whole. The study was particularly meaningful to her and her mentor teacher because he had strong reservations about using film in the English classroom.

Action research is a challenge that more and more young teachers are accepting. Graduates of our teacher education program become involved in ethnographic research on key features of the teaching act. The prospective teachers focus on a particular dimension of teaching such as "Question Types and

Student Response," "The Effect of the Number of Teaching Activities on Student Achievement," "Teacher Control and Release and Student Attention," and "Control of Topic and Audience and Writing Effectiveness." All of these bring greater consciousness to teaching and increase our students' sense of themselves as reflective professionals.

GUILD BUILDING

This is a simple directive for beginning teachers: Join local groups of English teachers who gather to share experiences central to their discipline and the art of teaching it. Members of such collegial associations often work cooperatively on common concerns and become instrumental in influencing administrative decisions about the curriculum. If such a group does not exist in your area, you should consider founding one. If the mechanics such as dues and organization are kept to a minimum, if meetings are regular and focused, and if learning from one another is paramount, the group will flourish. All professionals increasingly realize that continuing education is the cornerstone of their success. Pathologists who do not read and take part in seminars are soon outdated. In the medical profession, the decline of competence is quickly observed by colleagues and even clients, but in our field, where the stakes are not as overtly crucial, English teachers are just as surely approaching professional rigor mortis if they do not create guilds or networks to nourish themselves.

ASSOCIATION LINKAGE

Whereas local guilds are best when their organizational structure is minimal, the complexities of organization are essential and even helpful for national and international professional associations. The National Council of Teachers of English (NCTE) and most state affiliates are huge organizations that have the same function as the local guilds, but they address a broader range of issues and a broader spectrum of English teachers who cannot meet on a regular basis. The executive committees, which deal with the structure and substance of the associations, the committees that focus on crucial and timely issues such as censorship, and the editorial boards that publish the journals and texts that articulate professional issues for those who are rarely able to attend annual meetings are all essential components for perpetuating the life of the organization and the profession it serves. They serve the larger purpose of the group: They nurture individual teachers. They also provide possibilities for service and leadership that allow English teachers to clarify, express, and practice what they believe.

We strongly urge you to take advantage of the tremendous range of resources offered by the National Council of Teachers of English, its state affiliates, and the National Writing Project. Specific professional organizations and their publications address particular interests such as media, reading, and drama. There are many resources available to augment, enliven, and deepen your ideas about teaching. One pleasant discovery for the young teacher is the body of instructional materials surrounding literary works (particularly certain commonly taught classics) that is shared by teachers informally and through the professional literature and meetings. Appendix I lists the associative and periodic resources that we have found to be most valuable.

PROFESSIONAL LEADERSHIP

A cumulation of all of these ways to grow professionally is the act of leadership that begins in the classroom and can extend to the whole profession. Leadership means internal locus of control and personal autonomy. It means teachers moving away from the "boss" qualities that relied on management and control to Glasser's leadership qualities (survival, love, power, fun, and freedom) that promote student autonomy and well-being while increasing achievement (p. 43). Wolfe and Antinarella, in *Deciding to Lead* (1997), describe 15 ways in which English teachers can take the lead in worthwhile reform.

- Don't coerce.
- When asked, help.
- Relate to colleagues as you relate to students.
- Suggest agenda items for faculty gatherings.
- Resist reform strategies you don't believe in.
- Conduct classroom-based research and share it.
- Join a National Writing Project site.
- Don't say "no" to leadership opportunities.
- Promote cross-visitations in teachers' classrooms.

- Get to know influential people who can help.
- Communicate regularly with parents.
- Promote/organize teacher-led seminars.
- Invite nonteaching staff to participate in classrooms.
- Build a reputation as the best listener in your school.
- Work visibly. (pp. 112–116)

Not only is each insightful, but also, the specificity is refreshing and makes the decision to lead all the more possible. The impact of taking any of these leadership roles over the years fashions a growth path that Wolfe and Antinarella see in the careers of all teachers, one that is brought to fruition in the careers of the very best:

> *Emulation/Control:* Highly self-conscious, survival-oriented stage where the teacher is sensitive to his or her every word and action and to students' reactions and does little in the way of profound self-reflection.
> *Experimentation/Discovery:* Initiating conversations with colleagues about professional subjects, reading some professional literature, attending a few professional conferences, analyzing classroom dynamics.
> *Facilitation/Resource:* This stage tends to be philosophy and theory driven, with the teacher as facilitator and resource person, an active learner.
> *Research/Innovation:* Knows how to lead, attract, and win over students to a view of school as a welcoming place, always thinking several shots ahead, able to stand apart from himself or herself and watch with a critical eye what goes on in the classroom, an active researcher. (pp. 96–99)

All of this lies far ahead of you, but as you try on some of the leadership roles in the coming years, you will begin to feel yourself move up the developmental path that Wolfe and Antinarella outline for us.

All of these means of personal growth will not be at your disposal immediately. You will leap into some because you need them and wait on others because you may feel overwrought by the day-to-day pressures of teaching. But the old axiom "an ounce of prevention is worth a pound of cure" is repeated and remembered because it is true. The ounces you give to these elements of professional growth will certainly relieve you from pounds of professional difficulties and the tendency toward burnout. Where there is conscious and supported growth, burnout is less likely. Exercise 14–2 offers you an opportunity to design your own program of parental involvement and course evaluation.

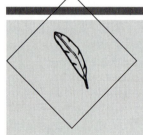

Exercise 14–2   *Designing Evaluation*

You will be teaching an 11th-grade course in American literature and will be required to offer students a list of course requirements and a description of your criteria for evaluation. Come up with a plan for your fall term and a letter to parents that explains your course to them. Also select an evaluation tool for your teaching that makes the most sense given your goals and style.

CONCLUSION

There are many senses in which this book has lived under its title, *Bridging English*. One level on which it has attempted to serve as bridge is between the competing voices within the English profession, those of teachers, researchers, theoreticians, scientists and humanists, pragmatists, and idealists. We have tried to be fair and just to the legitimate claims of many. We have also attempted to span those distances between you as you are now, you as a student in the past, and you as a teacher in the future. William James (1907, 1981) has clarified our sense of how any individual obtains new learning and changes old opinions into new. His description of the process is that the individual "tries to change first this opinion, and then that until at last some new idea comes up which he can graft upon the ancient stock with a minimum disturbance of the latter, and some idea that mediates between the stock and the new experience and runs them into one another." He calls this new truth or idea a "go-between" or a "smoother-over of transitions," which marries old opinions to new facts "so as ever to show a minimum of jolt, a maximum of continuity" (p. 396). As this new truth enters into a person's working knowledge, it too becomes the "old ideas" ready to be challenged and changed in turn. Thus we must always be ready for some new arrangement of our beliefs, and nowhere more than in teaching.

If *Bridging English* has had the role of helping you to new understandings with a "minimum of jolt," it will have been the bridge we hoped. Because despite these many pages of ideas and activities, we believe that you will compose yourself as a teacher as you compose yourself as a person. Bateson's (1990) sense of life as an "improvisatory art" is apt here. We know that after we explain whole-language development, say, or learning theory, reader response criticism, canon challenges, writing process, and portfolio evaluation—all important in themselves—we will only have begun to initiate your entry into teaching. It is in the actual work of the classroom, where you struggle to teach and to learn, that you will become a teacher. To borrow from Henry James's sense of art, we might say that in that classroom you will engage in the teaching art: "a braving of difficulties." Glatthorn (1975) reminded us a quarter century ago that good English teaching does not necessarily involve "a teacher-proof curriculum, an open classroom, or a learning package," but occurs in the act of "an authentic individual who is able to stay real in a very artificial world." Glatthorn says of English teachers with their students; "We teach in our own way, speak with our true voice, search for a deeper self. . . . In our own becoming we touch them and help them come alive again" (p. 39).

APPENDIX A

ERIKSON'S STAGES OF PSYCHOSOCIAL DEVELOPMENT

Age Period	Focal Crisis	Determinants
0–2 years	Trust vs. mistrust	If parents meet the preponderance of the infant's needs, the child develops a stronger sense of trust than of mistrust.
2–4 years	Autonomy vs. shame or doubt	If parents reward the child's successful actions and do not shame his or her failures (say in bowel or bladder control), the child's sense of autonomy will outweigh the sense of shame and doubt.
4–6 years	Initiative vs. guilt	If parents accept the child's curiosity and do not put down the need to know and to question, the child's sense of initiative will outweigh the sense of guilt.
7–12 years	Industry vs. inferiority	If the child encounters more success than failure at home and at school, he or she will have a greater sense of industry than of inferiority.
13–18 years	Identity vs. role diffusion	If the young person can reconcile diverse roles, abilities, and values and see continuity with past and future, the sense of personal identity will not give way to a sense of role diffusion.
19–35 years	Intimacy vs. isolation	With a sufficiently strong sense of personal identity, one can give much of oneself to another person without feeling a loss of identity. The person who cannot do this experiences a sense of loneliness.
35–55 years	Generativity vs. stagnation	The individual who has had children or produced some meaningful work invests much in those children and/or work as continuities of personal identity that will persist when the personal identity no longer does. The person who cannot so invest himself or herself experiences a sense of stagnation, of standing still rather than of growing.
55–	Integrity vs. despair	The individual who has attained a sense of personal identity, intimacy, and generativity can look back upon life as having been well spent and can accept death without regrets. But the individual who reaches old age without having involved himself or herself in other people or work experiences a sense of despair at a life ill spent.

Kohlberg's Stages of Moral Development

Stages	*Characteristics*
PRECONVENTIONAL LEVEL Good or bad, right or wrong, labels are interpreted in terms of physical power. The basic frame of reference for moral decisions is the self.	1. Punishment and Obedience. Physical consequences of an action determine if it's good or bad. Avoidance of punishment is valued. 2. Satisfy one's own needs and sometimes others. "You scratch my back and I'll scratch yours," instead of loyalty, gratitude, and justice. If fairness and sharing are present, they are viewed in terms of one's personal needs.
CONVENTIONAL LEVEL Maintaining expectations of others is valued regardless of consequences. Loyalty to and support of the established order. The concern with self is incorporated into an awareness of groupness.	3. "Good Boy–Nice Girl." Good behavior is that which pleases or helps others and therefore is approved by them. Much conformity to stereotypical images. 4. Law and Order. Authority, fixed rules, and maintaining the social order are valued. Right behavior is doing one's "duty" and showing respect for authority.
POST CONVENTIONAL LEVEL Individual reaches a personal definition of moral values, principles that are valid and applicable apart from authority. Groups and their laws are important, but principles underlie them.	5. Individual Rights. Utilitarian overtones. Awareness of personal values and openness. Other than that which is constitutionally and democratically agreed upon, right is a matter of personal value and opinion. 6. Universal Ethics. Abstract and ethical principles (Golden Rule) not concrete moral codes like the Ten Commandments. Justice, human rights, respect for the dignity of human beings as individuals are valued.

Loevinger's Stages of Ego Development

Stages	*Character Style*
Impulsive	Fear of retaliation, dependent, aggressive, conceptual confusion
Self-Protective	Fear of being caught, manipulative, conceptual cohesion
Conformist	Guilt for rule breaking, superficial niceness, social acceptability, conceptual simplicity
Conscientious	Self-criticism, responsible, self-respect, conceptual complexity
Autonomous	Coping with inner conflict, respect for autonomy, body-psyche integration, increased conceptual complexity
Integrated	Reconciling inner conflict, cherishing of individuality, identity, tolerance of ambiguity

APPENDIX B

BECKY BROWN'S FAVORITE POEMS FOR STUDENT RESPONSES

Poet	*Poem*
Edmund Spenser (1552–1599)	*One day I wrote her name upon the strands*
William Shakespeare (1564–1616)	*Let me not to the marriage of true minds*
	When, in disgrace with fortune and men's eyes
	That time of year thou mayest in me behold
John Donne (1572–1631)	Song: *Go and Catch a Falling Star*
	The Indifferent
	A Valediction: Forbidding Mourning
George Herbert (1593–1633)	*The Pulley*
John Dryden (1631–1700)	*A Song for St. Cecilia's Day*
Alexander Pope (1688–1744)	from *An Essay on Man*
William Blake (1757–1827)	*The Lamb*
	The Tyger
	London
	Infant Sorrow
	The Chimney Sweeper (from *Songs of Innocence*)
	The Chimney Sweeper (from *Songs of Experience*)
William Wordsworth (1770–1850)	*The World is Too Much with Us*
	Anecdote for Fathers
	The Tables Turned
	London, 1802
	Nuns Fret Not at Their Convent's Narrow Room
John Keats (1795–1821)	*To Autumn*
	Bright Star
Elizabeth Barrett Browning (1806–1861)	*How do I love thee?*
Walt Whitman (1819–1892)	*A Noiseless Patient Spider*
Matthew Arnold (1828–1888)	*Dover Beach*
Dante Gabriel Rossetti (1828–1882)	*Sudden Light*
Emily Dickinson (1830–1886)	*There's a Certain Slant of Light,*
	One Need Not Be a Chamber—To Be Haunted
	The Last Night That She Lived
Thomas Hardy (1840–1928)	*The Man He Killed*
Gerard Manley Hopkins (1844–1889)	*Pied Beauty*
A. E. Housman (1859–1936)	*To an Athlete Dying Young*
	When I Was One-and-Twenty
	Loveliest of Trees
William Butler Yeats (1865–1939)	*The Lake Isle of Innisfree*
	The Magi
	When You Are Old

Poet	*Poem*
	Sailing to Byzantium
	Leda and the Swan
Edwin Arlington Robinson (1869–1935)	*Richard Cory*
Robert Frost (1874–1963)	*The Telephone*
	A Considerable Speck
	Mending Wall
	The Objection to Being Stepped On
	"Out, Out—"
	Choose Something Like a Star
Don Marquis (1878–1937)	*The Lesson of the Moth*
Wallace Stevens (1879–1955)	*Thirteen Ways of Looking at a Blackbird*
	The Snow Man
William Carlos Williams (1883–1963)	*Landscape with the Fall of Icarus*
	The Yachts
	Tract
T. S. Eliot (1888–1965)	*Journey of the Magi*
	The Hippopotamus
Camillo Sbarbaro (1888–1967)	*Even If You Weren't My Father*
Edna St. Vincent Millay (1892–1950)	*An Ancient Gesture*
Dorothy Parker (1893–1967)	*Finis*
e. e. cummings (1894–1962)	*somewhere i have never traveled,*
	* gladly beyond*
	when faces called flowers float out
	* of the ground*
	i thank you God for most this amazing
	since feeling is first
Langston Hughes (1902–1967)	*Theme for English B*
Stevie Smith (1902–1971)	*Not Waving but Drowning*
C. Day Lewis (1904–1972)	*Walking Away*
Robert Penn Warren (1905–1989)	*Original Sin: A Short Story*
W. H. Auden (1907–1973)	*Their Lonely Betters*
	Musée des Beaux Arts
	Voltaire at Ferney
Theodore Roethke (1908–1963)	*The Walking*
Elizabeth Bishop (1911–1979)	*One Art*
Josephine Miles (1911–1985)	*Family*
John Berryman (1914–1972)	*Winter Landscape*
William Stafford (1914–)	*At Cove on the Crooked River*
Isabella Gardner (1915–1981)	*Collage of Echoes*
Joseph Langland (1917–)	*Hunters in the Snow: Breughel*
Gwendolyn Brooks (1917–)	*The Bean Eaters*
Lawrence Ferlinghetti (1919–)	*Dog*
May Swenson (1919–1989)	*Bleeding*
Howard Nemerov (1920–)	*Storm Windows*
Richard Wilbur (1921–)	*Advice to a Prophet*
	The Writer
	The Mill
	She
Philip Larkin (1922–1985)	*Aubade*
	Mr. Bleaney
Alan Dugan (1923–)	*Love Song: I and Thou*
Anthony Hecht (1923–)	*More Light! More Light!*
Denise Levertov (1923–)	*Life at War*
	The Secret
A. R. Ammons (1926–)	*Still*
	Reflective
	Terminus
	Reading
	The Role of Society in the Artist

Poet	*Poem*
Robert Bly (1926-)	*Driving to Town Late to Mail a Letter*
Robert Creely (1926-)	*I Know a Man*
	The Rain
Anne Sexton (1928-1974)	*The Farmer's Wife*
John Wakeman (1928-)	*Love in Brooklyn*
Adrienne Rich (1929-)	*Living in Sin*
Guy Snyder (1930-)	*Milton by Firelight*
Sally Buckner (1931-)	*Aunt Maud*
Linda Pastan (1932-)	*Unveiling*
Sylvia Plath (1932-1963)	*The Colossus*
	Words
John Updike (1932-)	*Mosquito*
	Ex-Basketball Player
	The Great Scarf of Birds
Mark Strand (1934-)	*Eating Poetry*
Lois Holt (1935-)	*Southern Style*
Fred Chappell (1936-)	*Second Wind*
John Haines (1936-)	*Foreboding*
	And When the Green Man Comes
	The Tundra
Marge Piercy (1936-)	*If They Come in the Night*
	A Work of Artifice
	For the Young Who Want To
Ishmael Reed (1938-)	*Beware: Do Not Read This Poem*
Emily Herring Wilson (1939-)	*Up-One*
Martha Collins (1940-)	*The Story We Know*
Billy Collins (1941-)	*Schoolsville*
Paul Simon (1942-)	*Richard Cory*
Sharon Olds (1942-)	*The Race*
Nikki Giovanni (1943-)	*Linkage*
Jim Morrison (1943-1971)	*In Russia, the Czar, each year, granted—(from The Lords and New Creatures)*
Kathryn Stripling Byer (1944-)	*Daughter*
Robert Morgan (1944-)	*Catalogue*
William (Billy) Joel (1949-)	*Allentown*
Edward Hirsch (1950-)	*For the Sleepwalkers*
	Execution
Paul Muldoon (1951-)	*Meeting the British*
Kaye Gibbons (1960-)	*Back Roads*
Kate Blackburn*	*Memo to the Caretaker*
Marcia Denius*	*Family Receipts*
Becky Gould Gibson*	*Getting Through*
Marie Howe*	*What the Living Do*
Agnes McDonald*	*Placing Markers*
Merry McDonnell*	*Multiple Listings*

BROWN'S POETRY RESPONSE ASSIGNMENT, 1991–1992

Poetry is unique among the genres we study. Poems demand more than just reading. They want rereading, being read aloud, being memorized, and being understood when you are in different moods. They want your time and energy. They want to become a part of you. Sound a little eerie? Not really.

You have probably studied poetry before. You have probably taken a poem, answered a few questions about it for homework, talked about it in class for 20 minutes, and considered it "done." Not so. Poetry is not like that. It is alive, fluid, breathing, changing, and evolving even as you read this assignment. Why? Because *we* are alive, fluid, breathing, changing, and evolving.

I will give you, therefore, a collection of poems about every four weeks. The collections will be poems that reflect different time periods from early English literature to the present—perhaps from this week's

---

*Dates cannot be found for these authors.

New Yorker. I hope you find that after a while some of these poems stick in your memory, that they are difficult to get rid of, that they stake out a small place for themselves in your imagination. Indeed, I encourage you to memorize a few of these. (I will not test you on that; that is a gift you give yourself.) Read them out loud, read them quickly, read them slowly, and read them when you are in different moods. In other words, give these poems as many chances as possible to claim your attention. Carry them around with you.

Doing the above is the important part of the assignment. But this is a real world we live in, so I must ask you to *do* a couple of things:

(1) Get a spiral-ring notebook with about 90 pages in it. Whenever I give you a collection of poems, write the name of each poem at the top of a page, giving each poem one page. Read all the poems *every week* and write no more than two or three sentences about what the poem says to you on the page designated for that poem. At the end of the four-week period, you should have nearly a full page of responses to the poem. The important aspect of this exercise is that you will have read the poem at least four times in four different moods. Notice how your perceptions of the poem change from week to week. I will check these notebooks at least once a quarter. Stay current. The successful completion of this part of the assignment is an "A."

(2) Every week when you do your responses in your notebook, choose one poem and write a longer response. This response should be about one page in length and should be turned in to me on the day I specify for your class period. (I stagger them so that I can respond appropriately.) I will not take these late. Successful completion of this assignment also will result in an "A." *Put your response in the box provided for it on the book shelf. I do not take them up—class time is valuable. You are responsible for leaving them in the box.*

At the end of the year, you will have accumulated all of these poems as part of your knowledge. This assignment should take no more than 1-2 hours weekly. If I were you, I would set aside a "poetry" evening to do it. Two warnings: Do not get behind on part one of the assignment. You do not know when I will ask to see your notebook. Turn your weekly responses in on time.

BROWN'S EXPLANATION OF HER POETRY ASSIGNMENT'S EVOLUTION

This poetry assignment is still evolving. It has gone through revision after revision over the last 15 years. It was first developed because my students were passively waiting for me to tell them what poems mean. They waited until they heard that before they ventured interacting with themselves. Besides wanting them to become independent learners, I also wanted them to realize that they could read poetry for themselves. I wanted poetry to be *theirs.* By the regular attention to this assignment, students do become comfortable talking about poetry in their own language, and poetry is not relegated to a month's study in the spring, thereby isolating it and making it somehow mysterious.

I like the current revision of the assignment because students are asked to do a brief biography of one of the six poets and find and respond to five poems by that poet. While I've only done this one year, I find it is more successful than the old notebook idea. Only a few students kept the notebook current; most simply changed colors of ink and wrote gibberish about the poems on the night before the notebook was to be checked! It was a good idea that didn't really work for many of my students. The newer assignment is better. Students have to read several poems by a poet before they choose five, and their responses to those chosen poems have more depth than if I had chosen them!

In selecting poems each month, I pick poems that I particularly like or that coordinate well with the other literature we are studying. Introducing these old friends to my students and hearing what they have to say about them continues to teach me wonderful new things.

BROWN'S POETRY RESPONSE ASSIGNMENT, 1997–1998

Poetry is unique among the genres we study. Poems demand more than just reading. They want rereading, being read aloud, being memorized, and being understood when you are in different moods. They want your time and energy. They want to become a part of you. Sound a little eerie? Not really.

You have probably studied poetry before. You have probably taken a poem, answered a few questions about it for homework, talked about it in class for 20 minutes, and considered it "done." Not so. Poetry is not like that. It is alive, fluid, breathing, changing, and evolving even as you read this assignment. Why? Because *we* are alive, fluid, breathing, changing, and evolving.

I will give you, therefore, a collection of six poems about every four weeks. The collections will be poems that reflect different time periods from early English literature to the present—perhaps from this week's *New Yorker.* I hope you find that after a while some of these poems become a part of you, that they are difficult to get rid of, that they stake out a small place for themselves in your imagination. I encourage you to memorize a few. (I will not test you on that; that is a gift you give yourself.) Read them out loud, quickly, slowly, and when you are in different moods. In other words, give these poems as many chances as possible to become a part of you.

Doing the above is the important part of the assignment. But this is a real world we live in, so I must ask you to *do* a couple of things:

(1) Choose one poem every week and write a response. This response should be about one page in length and should be turned in to me on the day that I specify for your class period. (I stagger them so that I can respond appropriately.) **I will not take these late.** Successful completion of this assignment will result in an "A." *You are responsible for leaving them with me as you leave class on the day they are due. I may not ask for them.*

(2) After the second week with these poems, choose one of the poets you would like to get to know better. Do some biographical research on that poet and jot down the pertinent information (you be the judge of what that is—it will vary with the degree of your genuine interest) about him/her. Copy (or make copies) of at least five other poems by this poet and write two or three sentences about why you chose each of them. I may ask that you choose one to present to the class. Turn these in with the fourth poetry response. These will be graded according to the depth of the comments and care you give the assignment.

At the end of the year, you will have accumulated all of these poems and poets as a part of your knowledge. My goal is to introduce you to some "sustaining" poetry—sustaining for both your personal and academic life.

BOOKS ON POETRY AND POETRY TEACHING

Behn, R., & Twichell, C. (Eds.). 1992. *The Practice of Poetry: Writing Exercises from Poets Who Teach.* New York: HarperCollins.

Bizzaro, P. 1993. *Responding to Student Poems: Applications of Critical Theory.* Urbana, IL: NCTE.

Brown, B., & Glass, M. 1991. *Important Words: A Book for Poets and Writers.* Portsmouth, NH: Heinemann.

Brown, R., Hoffman, M., Dushner, M., Lopate, P., & Murphy, S. 1972. *The Whole Word Catalogue, Vol. 1.* New York: Teachers & Writers Collaborative.

Collum, J., & Noethe, S. 1994. *Poetry Everywhere: Teaching Poetry Writing in School and in the Community.* New York: Teachers & Writers Collaborative.

Duke, C., & Jacobsen, S. (Eds.). 1992. *Poets' Perspectives: Reading, Writing, and Teaching Poetry.* Portsmouth, NH: Boynton/Cook Publishers.

Dunning, S., & Stafford, W. 1992. *Getting the Knack: 20 Poetry Writing Exercises.* Urbana, IL: NCTE.

Fagin, L. 1991. *The List Poem: A Guide to Teaching and Writing Catalog Verse.* New York: Teachers & Writers Collaborative.

Grossmann, F. 1991. *Listening to the Bells: Learning to Read Poetry by Writing Poetry.* Portsmouth, NH: Boynton/Cook Publishers.

Heard, G. 1989. *For the Good of the Earth and Sun: Teaching Poetry.* Portsmouth, NH: Heinemann.

Johnson, D. M. 1990. *Word Weaving: A Creative Approach to Teaching and Writing Poetry.* Urbana, IL: NCTE.

Koch, K. 1973. *Rose, Where Did You Get That Red? Teaching Great Poetry to Children.* New York: Random House.

Lies, L. B. 1993. *The Poet's Pen: Writing Poetry with Middle and High School Students.* Englewood, CO: Teacher Ideas Press.

Livingston, M. C. 1984. *Child as Poet: Myth or Reality?* Boston: Horn Books.

Nims, J. F. 1974. *Western Wind: An Introduction to Poetry.* New York: Random House.

Padgett, R. (Ed.). 1987. *The Teachers' and Writers' Handbook of Poetic Forms.* New York: Teachers & Writers Collaborative.

Tsujimoto, J. I. 1988. *Teaching Poetry Writing to Adolescents.* Urbana, IL: NCTE.

Zavatsky, B., & Padgett, R. 1977. *The Whole Word Catalogue, Vol. 2.* New York: Teachers & Writers Collaborative.

Ziegler, A. 1981, 1984. *The Writing Workshop, Vols. 1 & 2.* New York: Teachers & Writers Collaborative.

APPENDIX C

WORKS LISTED ON AP ENGLISH LITERATURE OPEN-ENDED QUESTIONS 1981–1997

The Adventures of Huckleberry Finn, 1982, 1985, 1986, 1987, 1991, 1992, 1994, 1995, 1996
The Age of Innocence, 1997
All My Sons, 1985, 1990
All the Pretty Horses, 1996
An American Tragedy, 1982, 1995
America in the Heart, 1995
Another Country, 1995
Anna Karenina, 1991
Antigone, 1990, 1994
Apprenticeship of Duddy Kravitz, 1959
Antony and Cleopatra, 1991
As I Lay Dying, 1989, 1990, 1994
As You Like It, 1992
The Awakening, 1987, 1988, 1991, 1992, 1995, 1997
The Bear, 1994
Beloved, 1990
Benito Cereno, 1989
Billy Budd, 1981, 1983, 1985
Bleak House, 1994
The Birthday Party, 1989, 1997
Brave New World, 1989
Bless Me, Ultima, 1996, 1997
The Brothers Karamazov, 1990
The Bluest Eye, 1995
Candide, 1996
The Caretaker, 1985
Catch-22, 1982, 1985, 1987, 1989, 1994
Cat's Eye, 1994
The Centaur, 1981
Ceremony, 1994, 1997
The Color Purple, 1991, 1992, 1994, 1996, 1997
Crime and Punishment, 1985, 1991, 1996
Cry, the Beloved Country, 1985, 1987, 1991, 1995, 1996
The Crucible, 1983, 1987
Daisy Miller, 1997
David Copperfield, 1983
Death of a Salesman, 1986, 1988, 1994
The Dead, 1997
Delta Wedding, 1997

The Death of Ivan Ilyich, 1986
Desire Under the Elms, 1981
Dinner at the Homesick Restaurant, 1997
The Diviners, 1995
Doctor Faustus, 1986
A Doll House, 1983, 1987, 1988, 1995
Don Quixote, 1992
The Dollmaker, 1991
An Enemy of the People, 1987
Equus, 1992
Ethan Frome, 1985
Emma, 1996
The Eumenides, 1996
The Fall, 1981
A Farewell to Arms, 1991
Fathers and Sons, 1990
Frankenstein, 1989
The Glass Menagerie, 1990, 1994, 1997
Go Tell It on the Mountain, 1988, 1990
The Grapes of Wrath, 1981, 1985, 1987, 1995
Great Expectations, 1988, 1989, 1992, 1996
The Great Gatsby, 1982, 1983, 1988, 1991, 1992, 1997
Gulliver's Travels, 1987, 1989
The Hairy Ape, 1989
Hamlet, 1988, 1992, 1994, 1997
The Handmaid's Tale, 1992
Hard Times, 1987, 1990
Heart of Darkness, 1991, 1994, 1996
Hedda Gabler, 1992
Henry IV, 1990
The Homecoming, 1990
The House of the Seven Gables, 1989
House Made of Dawn, 1995
The Invisible Man, 1982, 1983, 1985, 1987, 1988, 1989, 1991, 1994, 1995, 1996, 1997
Jane Eyre, 1988, 1991, 1994, 1995, 1996, 1997
J. B., 1981, 1994
Joseph Andrews, 1991
The Joy Luck Club, 1997
Jude the Obscure, 1985, 1987, 1991, 1995
Julius Caesar, 1982, 1997
The Jungle, 1987
King Lear, 1982, 1989, 1990, 1996
The Little Foxes, 1985, 1990
Light in August, 1981, 1982, 1983, 1985, 1995
Long Day's Journey into Night, 1990
Lord of the Flies, 1985, 1992
Lord Jim, 1982, 1986
Love Medicine, 1995
The Lovesong of J. Alfred Prufrock, 1985
Lysistrata, 1987
Macbeth, 1983
Madam Bovary, 1985
Main Street, 1987
Major Barbara, 1996
Man and Superman, 1981
Mansfield Park, 1991
Mayor of Casterbridge, 1993
M. Butterfly, 1995
Medea, 1982, 1992, 1995
The Member of the Wedding, 1997
The Merchant of Venice, 1985, 1991, 1995

The Metamorphosis, 1989
A Midsummer Night's Dream, 1991
Middlemarch, 1995
The Mill on the Floss, 1991, 1992
The Misanthrope, 1992
Miss Lonelyheart, 1989
Moby Dick, 1989, 1994, 1996
Moll Flanders, 1986, 1987, 1995
Mother Courage, 1985, 1987
Mrs. Dalloway, 1994, 1997
Mrs. Warren's Profession, 1987, 1990, 1995
Much Ado About Nothing, 1997
Murder in the Cathedral, 1985, 1995
"My Last Duchess," 1985
Native Son, 1982, 1983, 1985, 1987, 1995
Nineteen Eighty-Four, 1987, 1994
No Exit, 1986
No-Ho Boy, 1995
Notes from Underground, 1989
Obasan, 1994, 1995
The Odyssey, 1986
One Hundred Years of Solitude, 1989
The Optimist's Daughter, 1994
Oresteia, 1990
Othello, 1985, 1988, 1992, 1995
Our Town, 1986, 1996
Pamela, 1986
Paradise Lost, 1985, 1986
A Passage to India, 1988, 1991, 1992
Persuasion, 1990
The Piano Lesson, 1996
Phaedre, 1992
Pnin, 1997
The Power and the Glory, 1995
Portrait of a Lady, 1992, 1996
Portrait of the Artist as a Young Man, 1981, 1986, 1988, 1996
Praisesong for the Widow, 1996
Pride and Prejudice, 1983, 1988, 1992, 1997
The Prime of Miss Jean Brodie, 1990
Pygmalion, 1992
A Raisin in the Sun, 1987, 1990, 1991, 1992, 1994, 1996
The Rape of the Lock, 1981
Redburn, 1987
Romeo and Juliet, 1990, 1992, 1997
Rosencrantz and Guildenstern Are Dead, 1981, 1994
Saint Joan, 1995
The Scarlet Letter, 1983, 1988, 1991
A Separate Peace, 1982
The Shipping News, 1997
Sister Carrie, 1987
Slaughterhouse Five, 1991
Song of Solomon, 1981, 1988, 1996
Sons and Lovers, 1990
The Sound and the Fury, 1986, 1997
The Stone Angel, 1996
The Stranger, 1982, 1986
A Streetcar Named Desire, 1991, 1992
Sula, 1992, 1997
The Sun Also Rises, 1985, 1991, 1995
A Tale of Two Cities, 1982, 1991
Tartuff, 1987

The Tempest, 1996
Tess of the D'Urbervilles, 1982, 1991
Their Eyes Were Watching God, 1988, 1990, 1991, 1996
Things Fall Apart, 1991, 1997
Tom Jones, 1990
To the Lighthouse, 1986, 1988
The Trial, 1989
Tristram Shandy, 1986
Turn of the Screw, 1992, 1994
Twelfth Night, 1985, 1994, 1996
Uncle Tom's Cabin, 1987
Victory, 1983
Volpon, 1983
Waiting for Godot, 1985, 1986, 1989, 1994
The Warden, 1996
Washington Square, 1990
The Waste Land, 1981
Watch on the Rhine, 1987
The Watch That Ends the Night, 1992
Who's Afraid of Virginia Woolf, 1988, 1994
The Wide Sargasso Sea, 1989, 1992
Winter in the Blood, 1995
The Winter's Tale, 1986, 1989
Wise Blood, 1982, 1989, 1995
The Woman Warrior, 1991
Wuthering Heights, 1982, 1983, 1986, 1989, 1990, 1991, 1992, 1996, 1997
The Zoo Story, 1982
Zoot Suit, 1995

READER RESPONSE RESOURCES

Author	Publications	Date
Anderson, Philip and Rubana, Gregory	*Enhancing Aesthetic Reading and Response*	1991
Beach, Richard	*A Teacher's Introduction to Reader-Response Theories*	1993
Berthoff, Ann E.	*The Making of Meaning*	1981
Bleich, David	*Readings and Feelings: An Introduction to Subjective Criticism*	1975
Christenbury, Leila and Kelly, Patricia	*Questioning: A Path to Critical Thinking*	1983
Clifford, John, (Ed.)	*The Experience of Reading: Louise Rosenblatt and Reader-Response Theory*	1990
Cooper, Charles R., (Ed.)	*Researching Response to Literature and the Teaching of Literature*	1985
Corcoran, Bill and Evans, Emrys, (Eds.)	*Readers, Texts, Teachers*	1987
Eco, Umberto	*The Role of the Reader: Explorations in the Semiotics of the Text*	1978
Fish, Stanley E.	*Is There a Text in this Class? The Authority of Interpretive Community*	1980
Holland, Norman	*Five Readers Reading*	1975
Iser, Wolfgang	*The Act of Reading: A Theory of Aesthetic Response*	1978
Karolides, Nicholas, (Ed.)	*Reader Response in the Classroom: Evoking and Interpreting Meaning in Literature*	1992
Langer, Judith, (Ed.)	*Literature Instruction: A Focus on Student Response*	1992
Langer, Judith	*Envisioning Literature: Literary Understanding and Literature Instruction*	1995
Milner, Joseph and Milner, Lucy, (Eds.)	*Passages to Literature: Essays on Teaching in Australia, Canada, England, the United States, and Wales*	1989

Author	*Publications*	*Date*
Nelms, Ben F., (Ed.)	*Literature in the Classroom: Readers, Texts, and Contexts*	1988
Probst, Robert E.	*Response and Analysis: Teaching Literature in Junior and Senior High School*	1988
Protherough, Robert	*Developing Response to Fiction*	1983
Purves, Alan C., Rogers, Theresa, and Soter, Anna O.	*How Porcupines Make Love II: Notes on a Response-Centered Curriculum* (2e)	1990
Purves, Alan C., Foshay, Arthur W., and Hansson, Gunnar	*Literature Education in Ten Countries*	1973
Rosenblatt, Louise	*The Reader, the Text, the Poem: The Transactional Theory of the Literary Work*	1978
Rosenblatt, Louise	*Literature as Exploration* (5e)	1995
Scholes, Robert	*Textual Power: Literacy Theory and the Teaching of English*	1985
Tompkins, Jane P., (Ed.)	*Reader-Response Criticism: From Formalism to Post-Structuralism*	1980
Wilhelm, Jeffrey	*"You Gotta BE the Book:" Teaching Engaged and Reflective Reading with Adolescents*	1997

FICTION BY WOMEN

Alcott, Louisa Mae	*Little Women*	1868
Arnow, Harriette	*The Dollmaker*	1954
Atwood, Margaret	*The Handmaid's Tale*	1986
	Wilderness Tips	1991
Austen, Jane	*Pride and Prejudice*	1813
	Persuasion	1818
Austin, Doris	*After the Garden*	1987
Bambara, Toni Cade	*The Salt Eaters*	1980
Bridgers, Sue Ellen	*Home Before Dark*	1976
Bronte, Anne	*Tenant of Wildfell Hill*	1887
Bronte, Charlotte	*Jane Eyre*	1947
Bronte, Emily	*Wuthering Heights*	1847
Buck, Pearl	*The Good Earth*	1931
Burney, Fanny	*Camilla*	1796
Burns, Olive Ann	*Cold Sassy Tree*	1984
Cather, Willa	*My Antonia*	1918
Chopin, Kate	*The Awakening*	1899
Christie, Agatha	*And Then There Were None*	1940
Cisneros, Sandra	*The House on Mango Street*	1983
Collette	*Gigi*	1995
Davis, Rebecca Harding	*Life in the Iron Mills*	1861
Dinesen, Isak	*Seven Gothic Tales*	1934
Eliot, George	*Middlemarch*	1971
Erdrich, Louise	*Love Medicine*	1984
	Tracks	1988
Freeman, Mary Wilkins	*The Revolt of Mother* in *Selected Stories*	1983
Gibbons, Kaye	*Ellen Foster*	1987
Gilman, Charlotte Perkins	*Herland*	1915
Glasgow, Ellen	*Barren Ground*	1925
Golden, Marita	*A Woman's Place*	1986
Gordimer, Nadine	*July's People*	1981
Gordon, Caroline	*The Collected Stories of Caroline Gordon*	1981
Greene, Bette	*The Summer of My German Solider*	1973
Guy, Rosa	*A Measure of Time*	1983
Head, Bessie	*Maru*	1971
Hulme, Keri	*The Bone People*	1984
Hurston, Zora Neale	*Their Eyes Were Watching God*	1937

Jackson, Shirley	*Come Along with Me*	1968
	The Magic of Shirley Jackson	1966
Jewett, Sarah Orne	*The Country of the Pointed Firs and Other Stories*	1896
Kingsolver, Barbara	*Animal Dreams*	1990
	The Bean Trees	1988
Lee, Harper	*To Kill a Mockingbird*	1960
LeGuin, Ursula	*The Dispossessed*	1974
L'Engle, Madeleine	*A Ring of Endless Light*	1980
Lessing, Doris	*The Summer Before the Dark*	1973
Mansfield, Katherine	*The Garden Party, and Other Stories*	1922
Marshall, Paule	*Praisesong for the Widow*	1983
Mason, Bobbie Ann	*In Country*	1985
McCullers, Carson	*The Member of the Wedding*	1946
McMillian, Terry	*Disappearing Acts*	1989
	Mama	1987
Miller, Sue	*The Good Mother*	1986
Morrison, Toni	*The Bluest Eye*	1969
Naylor, Gloria	*Mama Day*	1988
Oates, Joyce Carol	*The Wheel of Love*	1970
O'Connor, Flannery	*Everything That Rises Must Converge*	1965
	A Good Man Is Hard to Find	1955
Olsen, Tillie	*Tell Me a Riddle*	1961
Paley, Grace	*Enormous Changes at the Last Minute*	1974
Plath, Sylvia	*The Bell Jar*	1963
Porter, Katherine Anne	*Collected Stories*	1967
Proulx, E. Annie	*The Shipping News*	1993
Rhys, Jean	*Wide Sargasso Sea*	1966
Sanders, Dori	*Clover: A Novel*	1990
Sayers, Dorothy	*Gaudy Night*	1935
Shelley, Mary	*Frankenstein*	1818
Silko, Leslie	*Ceremony*	1977
Smiley, Jane	*A Thousand Acres*	1991
	Moo	1995
Smith, Lee	*Family Linens*	1985
Stead, Christina	*The Man Who Loved Children*	1940
Stewart, Mary	*The Hollow Hills*	1973
Stowe, Harriet Beecher	*Uncle Tom's Cabin*	1852
Tan, Amy	*The Joy Luck Club*	1989
Tyler, Anne	*Dinner at the Homesick Restaurant*	1982
	Breathing Lessons	1988
Walker, Alice	*The Color Purple*	1982
Walker, Margaret	*Jubilee*	1965
Welty, Eudora	*Losing Battles*	1970
	Thirteen Stories	1965
West, Jessamyn	*Friendly Persuasion*	1945
Wharton, Edith	*Ethan Frome*	1911
Woolf, Virginia	*Mrs. Dalloway*	1925

AFRICAN AMERICAN WRITERS

	Writer	*Work*

1800–1899

1829	David Walker	*Appeal*
1831	Nat Turner	*The Confessions of Nat Turner*
1845	Frederick Douglass	*Narrative of Frederick Douglass*
1861	Harriet Jacobs	*Incidents in the Life of a Slave Girl*

1900–1929

1904	W. E. B. DuBois	*The Souls of Black Folk*
1912	James Weldon Johnson	*Autobiography of an Ex-Colored Man*
1923	Jean Toomer	*Cane*

	Writer	*Work*

1930s/1940s

1936	Richard Wright	*Uncle Tom's Children*[†]
1937	Zora Neale Hurston	*Their Eyes Were Watching God*
1945	Gwendolyn Brooks	*A Street in Bronzeville*[*]
1947	Countee Cullen	*On These I Stand*[*]

1950s

1950	William Denby	*Bettlecreek*
1952	Ralph Ellison	*Invisible Man*
1953	Gwendolyn Brooks	*Maud Martha*
1953	James Baldwin	*Go Tell It on the Mountain*
1958	Langston Hughes	*The Langston Hughes Reader*
1959	Paule Marshall	*Brown Girl, Brownstones*

1960s

1961	Paule Marshall	*Soul Clap Hands and Sing*[†]
1963	Gordon Parks	*The Learning Tree*
1964	William Melvin Kelly	*Dancers on the Shore*[†]
1966	Margaret Walker	*Jubilee*
1969	James Alan McPherson	*Hue and Cry*[†]
1969	Toni Morrison	*The Bluest Eye*

1970s

1970	Alex Haley and Malcolm X	*The Autobiography of Malcolm X*
1971	Maya Angelou	*I Know Why the Caged Bird Sings*
1972	Toni Cade Bambara	*Gorilla, My Love*[†]
1973	Alice Childress	*A Hero Ain't Nothing but a Sandwich*
1974	Ernest Gaines	*The Autobiography of Miss Jane Pittman*
1974	Albert Murray	*Train Whistle Guitar*
1974	Sharon Bell Mathis	*Listen for the Fig Tree*
1974	Alice Walker	*In Love and Trouble*
1977	Mildred Taylor	*Roll of Thunder Hear My Cry*
1977	James Alan McPherson	*Elbow Room*[†]
1976	Virginia Hamilton	*Arilla Sun Down*
1978	Ernest Gaines	*In My Father's House*

1980s

1980	Anne Moody	*Coming of Age in Mississippi: An Autobiography*
1982	Gloria Naylor	*The Women of Brewster Place: A Novel in Seven Stories*
1982	Alice Walker	*The Color Purple*
1982	Ntozake Shange	*Sassafras, Cypress, and Indigo*
1983	Ernest Gaines	*A Gathering of Old Men*
1983	Paule Marshall	*Praisesong for the Widow*
1984	Andrea Lee	*Sarah Philips*[†]
1984	Virginia Hamilton	*A Little Love*
1984	J. California Cooper	*A Piece of Mine*[†]
1985	Jamaica Kincaid	*Annie John*
1985	Ntozake Shange	*Betsey Brown*
1985	John A. Williams	*The Man Who Cried I Am*
1986	August Wilson	*Fences*

1990s

| 1990 | August Wilson | *Piano Lesson* |
| 1990 | Toni Morrison | *Beloved* |

[*]Collections of Poems
[†]Collections of Short Stories

	Writer	Work
1990	Dori Sanders	*Clover: A Novel*
1990	Charles Johnson	*Middle Passage*
1991	Mary Helen Washington	*Memory of Kin*[†]
1991	J. California Cooper	*Family: A Novel*
1992	Brent Wade	*Company Man: A Novel*
1992	Randall Kenan	*Let the Dead Bury Their Dead and Other Stories*[†]
1993	Gloria Naylor	*Mama Day*
1993	Arthur Ashe	*Days of Grace*
1994	Ernest Gaines	*A Lesson Before Dying*
1994	Alexs Pate	*Losing Absalom*
1995	Yvonne Thornton	*The Ditchdigger's Daughters*
1996	Gloria Naylor	*Children of the Night*[†]

NATIVE AMERICAN WRITERS

Writer	Work	Year
Allen, Paula Gunn	*Woman Who Owned the Shadows*	1983
Dorris, Michael	*Yellow Raft in Blue Water*	1987
Erdrich, Louise	*Baptism of Desire: Poems*	1989
	Beet Queen	1986
	Bingo Palace	1994
	Jacklight (poetry)	1984
Highwater, Jamake	*Anpao: An American Indian Odyssey*	1977
	Many Smokes, Many Moons	1978
Hogan, Lina	*Mean Spirit*	1990
Lesley, Criag	*River Song*	1990
	Winterkill	1990
Momaday, N. Scott	*The Ancient Child: A Novel*	1989
	House Made of Dawn	1969
Neilhardt, John	*Black Elk Speaks*	1932
Owens, Louis	*Sharpest Sight*	1992
Rain, Mary Summer	*Dreamwalker: The Path of Sacred Power*	1993
	Earthway	1992
	Phoenix Rising: No-Eyes Vision of the Changes to Come	1993
	Spirit Song: An Introduction to No-Eyes	1993
Silko, Leslie Marmon	*Ceremony*	1986
	Storyteller	1981
Wall, Steve, and Arden, Harvey	*Wisdom's Daughters: Conversations with Women Elders of Native America*	1993
Welch, James	*Fools Crow*	1986
	The Indian Lawyer	1990
	Winter in the Blood	1974

HISPANIC WRITERS

Writer	Work	Year
Acosta, Oscar	*The Revolt of the Cockroach People*	1973
Allende, Isabel	*The House of the Spirits*	1985
Álvarez, Julia	*How the García Girls Lost Their Accent*	1991
	In the Time of the Butterflies	1994
Anaya, Rudolfo A.	*Bless Me, Última*	1972
Chavez, Denise	*The Last of the Menu Girls*	1986
	The Aquero Sisters	1997
Cisneros, Sandra	*The House on Mango Street*	1983
	Woman Hollering Creek	1991
Eliade, Mircea	*Two Strange Tales*	1986
Fuentes, Carlos	*Old Gringo*	1985
García, Cristina	*Dreaming in Cuban*	1992

[†]Collections of Short Stories

García Márquez, Gabriel	*One Hundred Years of Solitude*	1970
	Leaf Storm, and Other Stories	1979
	No One Writes to the Colonel	1968
	Chronicle of a Death Foretold	1983
Islas, Arturo	*The Rain God*	1984
Lopez-Medina, Sylvia	*Cantora*	1992
Paz, Octavio	*Convergences: Essays on Art and Literature*	1987
	The Monkey Grammarian	1981
Rodriguez, Richard	*Hunger of Memory*	1982
Thurston, Lawrence	*Imagining Argentina*	1989
Vargas Llosa, Mario	*The Storyteller*	1989

ASIAN AMERICAN WRITERS

Chin, Frank	*Donald Duk*	1991
Chan, Jeffrey P., Chin, Frank, Inada, Lawson F., and Wong, Shawn, (Eds.)	*The Big Aiiieeeee!: An Anthology of Chinese-American & Japanese-American Literature*	1974
Criddle, JoAn D.	*To Destroy Is No Loss: The Odyssey of a Cambodian Family*	1987
Guterson, David	*Snow Falling on Cedars*	1994
Kingston, Maxine Hong	*Woman Warrior*	1976
Kogawa, Joy	*Obasan*	1981
Lee, Gus	*China Boy*	1991
Moore, David L.	*Dark Sky, Dark Land: Stories of the Hmong Boy Scouts, Troop 100*	1989
Okada, John and Inada, Lawson F.	*No-No Boy*	1976
Salzman, Mark	*The Laughing Sutra*	1991
Schanberg, Sydney	*Death and Life of Dith Pran*	1985
Tan, Amy	*The Joy Luck Club*	1989
	The Kitchen God's Wife	1991
Watanabe, Sylvia and Bruchac, Carol (Eds.)	*Home to Stay: Asian American Fiction by Women*	1990
Wong Lee, David	*Pangs of Love*	1991
Yamashita, Karen Tei	*Through the Arc of the Rain Forest*	1990
Yep, Laurence	*Dragonwings*	1997

BENEDICT'S RECOMMENDATIONS: YOUNG ADULT FICTION

Adams, Douglas*	*The Hitchhiker's Guide to the Galaxy*	1980	Harmony
Alexander, Lloyd	*Westmark* (One of a series)	1981	Dutton
Anonymous	*Go Ask Alice*	1971	Prentice-Hall
Auel, Jean*	*The Clan of the Cave Bear*	1982	Crown
Baldwin, James	*If Beale Street Could Talk*	1974	Dial
Beagle, Peter S.	*The Last Unicorn*	1968	Ballantine
Blos, Joan	*A Gathering of Days*	1979	Scribner
Blume, Judy	*Forever*	1975	Bradbury
Bond, Nancy	*Another Shore*	1988	Macmillan
Bradford, Richard	*Red Sky at Morning*	1968	Lippincott
Bradshaw, Gillian	*Bearkeeper's Daughter*	1987	Houghton Mifflin
	The Beacon at Alexandria	1986	Houghton Mifflin
Brancato, Robin	*Winning*	1976	Bantam
Bridgers, Sue Ellen	*Home Before Dark*	1976	Knopf
	All Together Now	1979	Bantam
	Permanent Connections	1987	Harper & Row
Brooks, Bruce	*The Moves Make the Man*	1984	Harper & Row

*A group of books which, though originally published for adults, have been read so extensively and profitably by young adults that they appear on young adult reading lists. (Other titles here were also first marketed for an adult audience, but are now read more by young adults than adults and so have moved primarily to a young adult list.)

Brooks, Terry	*The Wishsong of Shannara* (One of a series)	1985	Ballantine
Burns, Olive Ann*	*Cold Sassy Tree*	1984	Ticknor & Fields
Card, Orson Scott	*Ender's Game* (One of a series)	1985	Tor
	Seventh Son (One of a series)	1987	Doherty
Carter, Alden	*Sheila's Dying*	1987	Putnam
	Up Country	1989	Putnam
Childress, Alice	*A Hero Ain't Nothin but a Sandwich*	1973	Coward McCann
	Rainbow Jordan	1981	Coward McCann
Clarke, Arthur C.*	*Rendezvous with Rama*	1973	Harcourt Brace Jovanovich
Cole, Brock	*Celine*	1989	Farrar, Straus & Giroux
	The Goats	1987	Farrar, Straus & Giroux
Conroy, Pat*	*The Great Santini*	1976	Houghton Mifflin
	Lords of Discipline	1980	Bantam
	The Prince of Tides	1986	Houghton Mifflin
Cooper, Susan	*The Dark Is Rising* (One of a series)	1973	Atheneum
Cormier, Robert	*After the First Death*	1979	Pantheon
	Beyond the Chocolate War	1985	Knopf
	The Bumblebee Flies Anyway	1983	Pantheon
	The Chocolate War	1974	Pantheon
Crutcher, Chris	*The Crazy Horse Electric Game*	1987	Greenwillow
	Running Loose	1983	Greenwillow
Davis, Jenny	*Sex Education*	1988	Orchard
Deavers, Julie Reece	*Say Goodnight, Gracie*	1988	Harper & Row
Doherty, Berlie	*White Peak Farm*	1990	Orchard
Duncan, Lois	*Killing Mr. Griffin*	1978	Little, Brown
Edgerton, Clyde*	*The Floatplane Notebook*	1988	Algonquin
	Raney	1985	Algonquin
Fox, Paula	*The Slave Dancer*	1973	Bradbury
Gaines, Ernest	*A Gathering of Old Men*	1983	Knopf
Garden, Nancy	*Annie on My Mind*	1982	Farrar
Golding, William*	*Lord of the Flies*	1955	Coward, McCann & Geoghegan
Greenberg, Joanne	*I Never Promised You a Rose Garden*	1964	Holt, Rinehart, & Winston
	In This Sign	1970	Holt
Greene, Bette	*Summer of My German Soldier*	1973	Dial
Guest, Judith*	*Ordinary People*	1976	Ballantine
Guy, Rosa	*The Disappearance*	1979	Doubleday
	The Friends	1973	Holt
Hadley, Irwin	*Abby, My Love*	1985	Atheneum
Hamilton, Virginia	*Sweet Whispers, Brother Rush*	1982	Philomel
Head, Ann	*Mr. and Mrs. BoJo Jones*	1967	Putnam
Hinton, S. E.	*The Outsiders*	1967	Dell
	Tex	1979	Doubleday
	That Was Then, This Is Now	1971	Dell
Hogan, William	*The Quartzsite Trip*	1980	Avon
Holland, Isabelle	*The Man Without a Face*	1972	Harper
Kerr, M. E.	*Fell*	1987	Harper
	Gentlehands	1978	Harper
	Night Kites	1986	Harper
Kesey, Ken*	*One Flew over the Cuckoo's Nest*	1962	Viking
Keyes, Daniel*	*Flowers for Algernon*	1966	Harcourt
Klaus, Annette Curtis	*Silver Kiss*	1990	Delacorte
Knowles, John	*A Separate Peace*	1959	Macmillan
Lasky, Kathryn	*Beyond the Divide*	1983	Macmillan
LeGuin, Ursula	*A Wizard of Earthsea* (One of a series)	1968	Parnassus
	Enchantress from the Stars	1970	Atheneum

*A group of books which, though originally published for adults, have been read so extensively and profitably by young adults that they appear on young adult reading lists. (Other titles here were also first marketed for an adult audience, but are now read more by young adults than adults and so have moved primarily to a young adult list.)

Lipsyte, Robert	*The Contender*	1967	Harper & Row
	One Fat Summer	1977	Harper & Row
Mahy, Margaret	*The Catalogue of the Universe*	1986	Macmillan
Mathias, Sharon Bell	*Teacup Full of Roses*	1972	Viking
Mazer, Harry	*The Last Mission*	1979	Dell
McCaffrey, Anne	*Dragon Song* (One of a series)	1976	Atheneum
	The Ship Who Sang	1969	Walker
McIntyre, Vonda	*Dreamsnake*	1978	Houghton Mifflin
McKillip, Patricia	*The Forgotten Beasts of Eld*	1974	Atheneum
	The Riddle-Master of Hed (One of a series)	1976	Atheneum
McKinley, Robin	*Beauty*	1978	Harper & Row
	Blue Sword	1982	Greenwillow
	Hero and Crown	1985	Greenwillow
Myers, Walter Dean	*Fallen Angels*	1988	Scholastic
	Hoops	1981	Doubleday
Naylor, Phyllis Reynolds	*The Keeper*	1986	Atheneum
Noonan, Michael	*McKenzie's Boots*	1987	Orchard
O'Brien, Robert	*Z for Zachariah*	1975	Antheneum
Paulsen, Gary	*Hatchet*	1987	Bradbury
Peck, Richard	*Are You in the House Alone?*	1976	Viking
	Remembering the Good Times	1985	Delacorte
Peck, Robert Newton	*A Day No Pigs Would Die*	1973	Knopf
Pierce, Meredith Ann	*The Darkangel* (One of a series)	1982	Little Brown
Portis, Charles*	*True Grit*	1968	Simon & Schuster
Potok, Chaim*	*The Chosen*	1967	Ballantine
Rylant, Cynthia	*A Kindness*	1988	Orchard
Salinger, J. D.*	*Catcher in the Rye*[†]	1951	Little Brown
	Franny and Zooey	1961	Bantam
Sleator, William	*House of Stairs*	1974	Dutton
	Interstellar Pig	1984	Dutton
Strasser, Todd	*Friends Till the End*	1981	Dell
Swarthout, Glendon	*Bless the Beasts and Children*	1970	Pocket
Tan, Amy*	*The Joy Luck Club*	1989	Putnam
	The Kitchen God's Wife	1991	Putnam
Taylor, Mildred D.	*Let the Circle Be Unbroken*	1981	Dial
	Road to Memphis	1990	Dial
	Roll of Thunder, Hear My Cry	1976	Dial
Tolkien, J. R. R.	*The Hobbit*	1966	Houghton Mifflin
	The Lord of the Rings (Trilogy)	1967	Houghton Mifflin
Vinge, Joan D.	*Psion*	1982	Doubleday
Voigt, Cynthia	*Dicey's Song*	1982	Atheneum
	Homecoming	1981	Macmillan
	On Fortune's Wheel	1990	Atheneum
	The Runner	1985	Atheneum
	A Solitary Blue	1983	Atheneum
	Tree by Leaf	1988	Atheneum
Walker, Alice*	*The Color Purple*	1983	Harcourt Brace Jovanovich
West, Jessamyn*	*Massacre at Fall Creek*	1975	Harcourt Brace Jovanovich
Wharton, Wiliam	*A Midnight Clear*	1982	Knopf
White, Robb	*Deathwatch*	1972	Dell
Zindel, Paul	*My Darling, My Hamburger*	1969	Harper & Row
	The Pigman	1968	Harper

*A group of books which, though originally published for adults, have been read so extensively and profitably by young adults that they appear on young adult reading lists. (Other titles here were also first marketed for an adult audience, but are now read more by young adults than adults and so have moved primarily to a young adult list.)

†Donelson and Nilsen (1980) report that in the early 1980s it was still "the most widely censored book in American schools" (p. 164).

HIPPLE'S RECOMMENDATIONS: YOUNG ADULT NOVELS WORTH YOUR ATTENTION

Best Novels of the 1980s*

Gary Paulsen	*Hatchet*	1987
Walter Dean Myers	*Fallen Angels*	1988
Sue Ellen Bridgers	*Permanent Connections*	1987
Katherine Paterson	*Jacob Have I Loved*	1980
Brock Cole	*The Goats*	1987
Cynthia Voigt	*Dicey's Song*	1990
Robert Cormier	*Fade*	1988
Chris Crutcher	*Chinese Handcuffs*	1989

Best Novels of the 1990s**

Aidan Chambers	*The Toll Bridge*	1995	(very bright but very mixed up British teens)
Jan Cheripko	*Imitate the Tiger*	1996	(football and alcohol and how the two don't mix)
Caroline Cooney	*The Face on the Milk Carton*	1990	(a young girl discovers that she may have been kidnapped as a child)
Robert Cormier	*Tunes for Bears to Dance To*	1992	(an anti-Semitic man visits his cruelty on a young boy)
Chris Crutcher	*Ironman*	1995	(a young man's desire to succeed in a triathlon despite his father and his school)
Nancy Garden	*Good Moon Rising*	1996	(two high school lesbians' growing love and conflicts with their peers)
Bette Greene	*The Drowning of Stephan Jones*	1991	(a homophobic incident)
Karen Hesse	*Out of the Dust*	1997	(a teenaged girl confronted with Depression-era dust storms, abject poverty, and her mother's death)
M. E. Kerr	*Deliver Us From Evie*	1994	(a lesbian teenager and the problems her family and community have with her)
Lois Lowry	*The Giver*	1993	(a controlled futuristic society)
Walter Dean Myers	*The Glory Field*	1994	(200 years of African-American history)
Cynthia Voigt	*When She Hollers*	1994	(Honest story of a 17-year-old girl who struggles to survive domestic tyranny)
Virginia Euwer Wolff	*Make Lemonade*	1993	(a welfare mother in an inner city and her babysitter)

*This list ranks the novels that English teachers and English educators surveyed considered the best novels of the 1980s. The full survey is reported in the *English Journal*, November, 1992.

**This list contains novels that Hipple believes will be among those considered the best of the 1990s.

CHESTER'S RECOMMENDATIONS: SCIENCE FICTION

Adams, Douglas	*The Hitchhiker's Guide to the Galaxy*	1985
	Long, Dark Teatime of the Soul	1988
Aldiss, Brian	*Earth Works*	1988
Anderson, Kevin J., Ed.	*War of the Worlds: Global Dispatches***	1997
Anderson, Poul	*Star Fox*	1965
	Polystechnic League	1981
Asimov, Isaac	*Nine Tomorrows**	1969
	*Robot Dreams**	1986
	Caves of Steel	1974
	Foundation	1951
Banister, Manly	*The Conquest of Earth*	1964
Baxter, Stephen	*Flux*	1995
Benford, Gregory, Ed.	*New Hugo Award Winners Vol. IV***	1997
Benford, Gregory and Martin Greenberg, Eds.	*What Might Have Been: Vol. 3: Alternate Wars***	1992
Blish, James	*Earthman, Come Home*	1955
	They Shall Have Stars	1957
Bova, Ben	*Mars*	1993
Bradbury, Ray	*Fahrenheit 451*	1953
Brin, David	*Startide Rising*	1983
Burroughs, Edgar Rice	*A Princess of Mars*	1974
Card, Orson Scott	*Ender's Game*	1992
Claremont, Chris	*Sundower*	1994
Clarke, Arthur C.	*2001: A Space Odyssey*	1968
	*Prelude to Mars**	1965
	*The Nine Billion Names of God**	1967
Crichton, Michael	*Jurassic Park*	1993
Dickson, Gordon R.	*Home from the Shore*	1988
Farmer, Philip Jose	*The Other Log of Phileas Fogg**	1973
Foster, Alan Dean	*With Friends Like These . . .**	1990
	Glory Lane	1987
Greenberg, Martin, Ed.	*Christmas on Ganymede*	1990
	*Issaac's Universe***	1990
Harrison, Harry	*Bill, the Galactic Hero*	1975
Heinlein, Robert	*Beyond This Horizon*	1942
	Starship Troopers	1959
Herbert, Frank	*Dune*	1984
	Direct Descent	1985
	The Dosadi Experiment	1983
Huxley, Aldous	*Brave New World*	1967
Laumer, Keith	*Judson's Eden*	1991
McCaffrey, Anne	*First Fall: The Chronicles of Pern**	1983
	Dragonsdawn	1988
Niven, Larry	*Ringworld*	1970
with Jerry Pournelle	*The Mote in God's Eye*	1974
Norton, Andre	*Starman's Son*	1952
Robinson, Kim Stanley	*Red Mars*	1993
Simak, Clifford	*Time and Again*	1951
	City	1989
	Ring Around the Sun	1969
Sohl, Jerry	*Point Ultimate*	1959
Steele, Allen	*Orbital Decay*	1989
Sturgeon, Theodore	*Voyage to the Bottom of the Sea*	1961

*A collection of the author's stories

**Collections of various authors' stories

Vance, Jack	*Big Planet*	1978
Van Vogt, A. E.	*The Weapon Shops of Isher*	1951
	Voyage of the Space Beagle	1968
Verne, Jules	*20,000 Leagues Under the Sea*	1975
Weber, David	*In Death Ground*	1997
	On Basilisk Station	1993
	Path of the Fury	1992
Wells, H. G.	*War of the Worlds*	1898
Wolfe, Gene	*Endangered Species*	1989

BENEDICT'S RECOMMENDATIONS: MODERN INTERPRETATIONS AND RETELLINGS (REVISIONIST FANTASY AND TWICE-TOLD TALES)

Bradley, Marion Zimmer. *Firebrand.* 1987. (*The Iliad*).
Bradley, Marion Zimmer. *Mist of Avalon.* 1982. (Arthurian legend).
Gadner, John. *Grendel.* 1971. (*Beowulf*).
Lewis, C. S. *Till We Have Faces.* 1956. ("Cupid and Psyche").
McKinley, Robin. *Beauty.* 1978. ("Beauty and the Beast").
McKinley, Robin. *Rose Daughter.* 1997. ("Beauty and the Beast").
Napoli, Donna Jo. *The Magic Circle.* 1993. ("Hansel and Gretel").
Napoli, Donna Jo. *Zel.* 1996. ("Rapunzel").
Stewart, Mary. *The Crystal Cave.* 1984. (Arthurian legend).
Stewart, Mary. *The Hollow Hills.* 1984. (Arthurian legend).
Stewart, Mary. *The Last Enchantment.* 1984. (Arthurian legend).
Sutclif, Rosemary. *The Road to Camlann.* 1994. (Arthurian legend).
Sutclif, Rosemary. *The Sword and the Circle.* 1994. (Arthurian legend).
Sutclif, Rosemary. *Sword at Sunset.* 1987. (Arthurian legend).
White, T. H. *The Once and Future King.* 1958. (Arthurian legend).
Williams, Tad. *Caliban's Hour.* 1994. (*The Tempest*).

ALEXANDER'S RECOMMENDATIONS: JOURNALS, ARTICLES, AND LISTS OF YOUNG ADULT FICTION

The ALAN Review
Booklist
Bulletin for the Center for Children's Books
English Journal
The Journal of Reading
Kirkus Reviews
Horn Book
Language Arts
The New York Times Book Review
The School Library Review
Top of the News
Voice of Youth Advocate
Wilson Library Review

"The Best, the Notable, and the Recommended." 1995. *Emergency Librarian, 22,* 8–15.
    This article includes the American Library Association's 1995 guide to the best children's books and young adult literature. It recommends more than 380 books, various videos and films, and seven computer software programs for all reading skills and age levels.

Monseau, V. R. (1996). *Responding to Young Adult Literature.* Young Adult Literature Series.
    This book focuses on how readers respond to the power of young adult literature. The book describes and discusses the oral and written responses of adolescents and adults to young adult literature. It also explores the significance of this knowledge for the study of literature in the classroom.

Fairbanks, G. and Jaques, T. F. (Eds.). (1995). *Book Beat: A Young Adult Services Manual for Louisiana's Libraries. Face It: Read a Book: Be Somebody.* Baton Rouge: Louisiana State University Press.
    This manual contains information about understanding the nature of young adults and developing a young adult service philosophy for a library. Ideas are provided for programs, activities, and workshops. Bibliographies for young adult collection development are included. Introductory materials include suggestions for a survey of teen users, an assignment alert package for teachers, community resources, and young adult service goals and objectives.

Poe, E. A. (1993). "Twenty-Five Years of Research in Young Adult Literature: Past Perspectives and Future Directions." *Journal of Youth Services in Libraries 7,* **65–73.**

This article describes the history and methodology of a project to compile an annotated bibliography of published critical research on young adult literature. Preliminary findings include recommended book lists, articles by young adult authors, author studies, and topic analyses. Recommendations for future research are included.

Teens' Favorite Books: Young Adults' Choices, 1987–1992. **(1992). Newark, DE: International Reading Association.**

This book provides descriptions of all of the approximately 150 examples of young adult literature that were "Young Adults' Choices" in the yearly voting by teenagers conducted from 1987 to 1992. Each entry in the book includes bibliographic information, an annotation, and the year in which the book was chosen. Entries in the book are grouped by type or genre (adventure, family life, fantasy, friendship, and so on). An author and a title index are included.

Indiana Practitioners' List of Young Adolescent Books. **(1996). Evansville, IN: Middle Grades Reading Network.**

This brochure lists authors and titles of a collection of 554 young adolescent books presented to 40 Indiana colleges and universities. Books listed in the pamphlet were chosen by librarians, consultants, and teachers from five Indiana middle schools. A chart listing contact persons and the location of the collection for each of the 40 colleges or universities is attached.

More Teens' Favorite Books: Young Adults' Choices 1993–1995. **(1996). Newark, DE: International Reading Association.**

This book presents an annotated list of 95 books chosen by adolescents themselves as part of an annual program sponsored by the International Reading Association. Entries are grouped by type or genre of publication to make books of particular interests easy to find.

WORKS ON CENSORSHIP

American Library Association. (1995). *Hit List: Frequently Challenged Young Adult Titles: References to Defend Them.* Chicago, IL: ALA.

Bracken, Harry M. (1994). *Freedom of Speech: Words Are Not Deeds.* Praeger Publishers.

Burress, L., & Jenkinson, E. B. (1982). *The Students' Right to Know.* Urbana, IL: NCTE.

DelFattore, J. (1992). *What Johnny Shouldn't Read: Textbook Censorship in America.* New Haven, CT: Yale University Press.

Garry, P. M. (1993). *An American Paradox: Censorship in a Nation of Free Speech.* Praeger Publishers.

Karolides, N., & Burress, L. (Eds.). (1985). *Celebrating Censored Books!* Racine, WI: Wisconsin Council of Teachers of English.

Moffett, J. (1988). *Storm in the Mountains: A Case Study of Censorship, Conflict, and Consciousness.* Carbondale, IL: Southern Illinois University Press.

National Council of Teachers of English. (1991). *The Students' Right to Read.* Urbana, IL: NCTE.

People for the American Way. (1994). *Attacks on the Freedom to Learn. 1993-1994 Report.* Washington, DC: People for the American Way.*

Shugart, D. (1983). *Rationales for Commonly Challenged/Taught Books.* Enfield, CT: Connecticut Council of Teachers of English.

Zeisel, W. (1993). *Five Hundred Years of Conflict.* New York: New York Public Library.

*Published annually.

APPENDIX D

MEDIA SOURCES
Periodicals

ACT Newsletter (4/yr.)	Action for Children's Television 46 Austin St. Newtonville, Mass. 02160
Booklist (23/yr.)	American Library Association 50 E. Huron St. Chicago, Ill. 60611
Journal of Communication	Annenberg School of Communication University of Pennsylvania Box 13358 Philadelphia, Pa 19104
Media and Methods (9/yr.)	Media and Methods 134 N. 13 St. Philadelphia, Pa. 19107
PSTS (10/yr.)	Prime Time School Television 120 S. LaSalle St. Chicago, Ill. 60603
Scholastic Teacher (monthly)	50 West 44th St. New York, NY 10036
TV Guide (weekly)	Box 400 Radnor, Pa. 19088

DISTRIBUTORS OF VIDEOTAPES, FILMS, AND RECORDED BOOKS

Ambrose Video Publishing, 381 Park Avenue South, Suite 1601, New York, NY 10016, (212)696-3434
Barr Films, 3590 East Foothill Road, Pasadena, CA 91107
Beacon Films, P. O. Box 575, Norwood, MA 02062, (617)762-8011
Benchmark Films, Inc. 145 Scarborough Rd. Briarcliff Manor, NY 10510
Books on Tape, P.O. Box 7900, Newport Beach, CA 92658-9924, 1-800-626-3333
Classroom Video, 9005 Centauris Circle, Burnaby, Vancouver BC V3J7N4, Canada, http: llwww. classroomvideo.com
Coronet/MTI, Film and Video, Distributors of Learning Corporation of America (a Simon and Schuster Company), 108 Wilmot Road, Deerfield, IL 60015
Educational Record Sales, 157 Chambers Street, New York, NY 10007, (212)267-7437
Educational Video, 2688 South La Cienega, Los Angeles, CA 90034
Facets Video, 1517 West Fullerton Avenue, Chicago, IL 60614, (800)331-6197
Films for the Humanities, P. O. Box 2053, Princeton, NJ 08543, (800)257-5126
Films Incorporated, 5547 N. Ravenswood, Chicago, IL 60640-1199
Lannan Literary Video, c/o Small Press Distribution, 1-800-869-7553, MASS.PBS
Merit Audio Visual, P. O. Box 392, New York, NY 10024, (212)267-7437

National Film Board of Canada, 1251 Avenue of the Americas, New York, NY 10020
Novacom Video, P. O. Box 5, Roslyn, NY 11576, (516)883-0020
Phoenix Films & Video, Inc., 468 Park Avenue South, New York, NY 10016
Pyramid Film & Video, Box 1048, Santa Monica, CA 90406
Recorded Books, 270 Shipjack Rd., Prince Frederick, MD 20678, (800)638-1304
Video Distributors, TMW Media, 2321 Abbott Kinney Blvd., Venice, CA 90291
Wombat Productions, 250 West 57th Street, Suite 916, New York, NY 10019
Zenger Video, 10,000 Culver Boulevard, Dept. EV5, P. O. Box 802, Culver City, CA 90232-0802, (800)421-4246

VIDEO SERIES

The Story of English
Host: Robert MacNeil
9 Episodes/60 minutes
Producer: MacNeil-Lehrer-Gannett Productions
Distributor: Films Incorporated
        5547 N. Ravenswood Ave.
        Chicago, IL 60640-1199

The American Short Story Video Series
Stories include such American classics as:
   The Music School, John Updike
   Almos' a Man, Richard Wright
   Bernice Bobs Her Hair, F. Scott Fitzgerald
   Soldier's Home, Ernest Hemingway
   Paul's Case, Willa Cather
Producer: Learning in Focus, Inc.
Distributor: Coronet/MTI Film & Video
        108 Wilmot Rd.
        Deerfield, IL 60015

Bill Moyers: A World of Ideas
Host: Bill Moyers
Producer: Public Affairs Television, Inc.

The Power of Myth
Host: Bill Moyers
6 Interviews/60 minutes each
Producer: Apostrophe S Productions, Inc.
Distributor: Mystic Fire Video
        P. O. Box 30969
        Dept. DL
        New York, NY 10011

American Cinema
Five videocassettes of a 1994 documentary shown on PBS.
An additional cassette with three short segments:
   Film Language
   Writing and Thinking about Film
   Classical Hollywood Style Today
Producer: The Annenberg/CPB Collection
Distributor: The Annenberg/CPB Collection
        P. O. Box 2345
        S. Burlington, VT 05407-2345

Basic Film Terms: A Visual Dictionary
One 14-minute introduction to film language.
Distributor: Pyramid Film and Video
        Box 1048
        Santa Monica, CA 90406-1048

TEASLEY AND WILDER'S 100 GREAT FILMS FOR ADOLESCENTS: ANNOTATED FILMOGRAPHY

10 Best Films About Coming of Age

Alan and Naomi (Sterling Van Wagenen, 1991, PG, 95 min.)
Brighton Beach Memoirs (Gene Saks, 1987, PG-13, 110 min.)
Crooklyn (Spike Lee, 1994, PG-13, 112 min.)
Dark Horse (David Hemmings, 1992, PG, 95 min.)
Empire of the Sun (Steven Spielberg, 1987, PG, 153 min.)
Hope and Glory (Great Britain, John Boorman, 1987, PG-13, 118 min.)
King of the Hill (Steven Soderberg, 1993, PG-13, 102 min.)
The Outside Chance of Maximilian Glick (Canada, Allan A. Goldstein, 1988, G, 92 min.)
This Is My Life (Nora Ephron, 1992, PG, 94 min.)
7 Up (Great Britain, Michael Apted, 1985, NR, 136 min.)

10 Best Films About Families

Breaking Away (Peter Yates, 1979, PG, 100 min.)
Clara's Heart (Robert Mulligan, 1988, PG-13, 108 min.)
The Great Santini (Lewis John Carlino, 1979, PG, 116 min.)
Rich in Love (Bruce Beresford, 1993, PG-13, 105 min.)
A River Runs Through It (Robert Redford, 1992, PG, 123 min.)
Running on Empty (Sidney Lumet, 1988, PG-13, 116 min.)

Unstrung Heroes (Diane Keaton, 1995, PG, 94 min.)
The War (John Avnet, 1995, PG-13, 126 min.)
What's Eating Gilbert Grape? (Lasse Hallstrom, 1993, PG-13, 118 min.)
A World Apart (Chris Menges, 1988, PG, 135 min.)

10 Best Films About Belonging

Addams Family Values (Barry Sonnenfeld, PG-13, 94 min.)
Angus (Patrick Read Johnson, 1995, PG-13, 87 min.)
Housekeeping (Bill Forsyth, 1988, PG, 112 min.)
Lucas (David Seltzer, 1986, PG-13, 100 min.)
Mask (Peter Bogdanovich, 1985, PG-13, 120 min.)
My Bodyguard (Tony Bill, 1980, PG, 96 min.)
Powder (Victor Salva, 1995, PG-13, 112 min.)
Rebel Without a Cause (Nicholas Ray, 1955, NR, 111 min.)
School Ties (Robert Mandel, 1992, PG-13, 110 min.)
Welcome Home, Roxy Carmichael (Jim Abrahams, 1990, PG-13, 98 min.)

10 Best Films About Dreams and Quests

Chariots of Fire (England, Hugh Hudson, 1981, PG, 123 min.)
The Cure (1995, Peter Horton, PG-13, 99 min.)
The Gods Must Be Crazy (Botswana, Jamie Uys, 1981, PG, 108 min.)
Hoop Dreams (Steve James, 1994, PG-13, 176 min.)
Hoosiers (David Anspaugh, 1986, PG, 114 min.)
The Journey of Natty Gann (Jeremy Kagan, 1985, PG, 101 min.)
The Loneliness of the Long-distance Runner, (Great Britain, Tony Richardson, 1962, NR, 104 min.)
Rudy (David Anspaugh, 1993, PG 112 min.)
Stand and Deliver (Ramon Menendez, 1988, PG, 105 min.)
Wild Hearts Can't Be Broken (Steve Miner, 1991, G, 89 min.)

10 Best Films on Love and Romance

Benny and Joon (Jeremiah S. Chechik, 1993, PG, 98 min.)
Clueless (Amy Heckerling, 1995, PG-13, 97 min.)
Gregory's Girl (Scotland, Bill Forsyth, 1981, NR, 87 min.)
The Man in the Moon (Robert Mulligan, 1991, PG-13, 99 min.)
My American Cousin (Canada, Sandy Wilson, 1985, PG, 94 min.)
My Brilliant Career (Australia, Gillian Armstrong, 1979, G, 102 min.)
A Room with a View (James Ivory, 1986, NR, 117 min.)
Sitting in Limbo (Canada, John N. Smith, 1986, PG, 95 min.)
The Umbrellas of Cherbourg (France, Jacques Demy, 1964, NR, 90 min., in French)
The Year My Voice Broke (Australia, John Duigan, 1987, PG-13, 103 min.)

10 Best Films for World Literature Courses

Au Revoir les Enfants (France, Louis Malle, 1987, PG, 104 min., in French)
Gallipoli (Australia, Peter Weir, 1981, PG, 111 min.)
Inner Circle (U.S., [filmed in Russia], Andrei Konchalovsky, 1991, PG-13, 122 min., in English)
The Last Emperor (U.S., [filmed in Beijing], Bernardo Bertolucci, 1987, PG-13, 164 min., in English)
My Life as a Dog (Sweden, Lasse Hallstrom, 1987, NR, 101 min., in Swedish)
Musashi Miyamoto (Samurai I) (Japan, Hiroshi Inagaki, 1954, NR, 92 min., in Japanese)
Pathfinder (Norway, Nils Gaup, 1988, NR, 88 min., in Lapp)
The Return of Martin Guerre (France, Daniel Vigne, 1982, NR, 111 min., in French)
Sarafina! (South Africa, Darrell James Roodt, 1992, PG-13, 98 min.)
Sugar Cane Alley (Martinique, Euzhan Palcy, 1983, NR, 100 min., in French)

10 Best Films for American Literature Courses

The Age of Innocence (Martin Scorsese, 1993, PG, 138 min.)
American Graffiti (George Lucas, 1973, PG, 112 min.)
Citizen Kane (Orson Welles, 1941, NR, 119 min.)
Death of a Salesman (Volker Scholondorff, 1986, NR, 135 min.)
Dr. Strangelove, or How I Learned to Stop Worrying and Love the Bomb (Stanley Kubrick, 1964, NR, 93 min.)
The Grapes of Wrath (John Ford, 1940, NR, 129 min.)

The Little Foxes (William Wyler, 1941, NR, 116 min.)
Malcolm X (Spike Lee, 1992, PG-13, 201 min.)
Roots (Episodel, David Greene, 1977, NR, 99 min.)
1776 (Peter H. Hunt, 1972, G, 141 min.)

10 Best Films of British Literature

Anne of the Thousand Days (Hal B. Wallis, 1969, PG, 145 min.)
Cromwell (Ken Hughes, 1970, G, 139 min.)
The Dead (John Huston, 1987, PG, 82 min.)
Hamlet (Franco Zeffirelli, 1990, PG, 135 min.)
A Man for All Seasons (Fred Zinneman, 1966, G, 120 min.)
Much Ado About Nothing (Kenneth Branagh, 1993, PG-13, 110 min.)
Sense and Sensibility (Ang Lee, 1995, PG, 136 min.)
Tess (Roman Polanski, 1980, PG, 170 min.)
Tom Jones (Tony Richardson, 1963, NR 121 min.)
Wuthering Heights (William Wyler, 1939, NR, 104 min.)

10 Best Films for Genre Study

Westerns
High Noon (Fred Zinneman, 1952, NR, 85 min.)
The Searchers (John Ford, 1956, NR, 119 min.)
Stagecoach (John Ford, 1939, NR, 100 min.)

Detective Films
The Big Sleep (Howard Hawks, 1946, NR, 114 min.)
The Maltese Falcon (John Huston, NR, 101 min.)
Murder, My Sweet (Edward Dmytryk, 1944, NR, 95 min.)

Screwball Comedies
Bringing Up Baby (Howard Hawks, 1938, NR 103 min.)
The Philadelphia Story (George Cukor, 1940, NR, 112 min.)

Gangster Films
Public Enemy (William A. Wellman, 1931, NR, 85 min.)
Scarface (Howard Hawks, 1931, NR, 93 min.)

10 Best Films for Film Study

American Cinema (The Annenberg/CPB Collection, 1994)
Basic Film Terms: A Visual Dictionary (Sheldon Renan, 1970, NR, 14 min.)
The Battleship Potemkin (Russia, Sergei Eisenstein, 1935, NR, 75 min., silent with English titles)
The Birth of a Nation (D.W. Griffith, 1915, NR, 175 min.)
Cinema Paradiso (Italy, Giuseppe Tornatore, 1989, NR, 123 min., in Italian)
The General (Buster Keaton and Clyde Bruckman, 1927, NR, 78 min.)
The Great Train Robbery (Edwin S. Porter, 1903, NR, 10 min.)
Modern Times (Charlie Chaplin, 1937, NR, 87 min.)
Singin' in the Rain (Gene Kelly and Stanley Donen, 1952, NR, 103 min.)
Visions of Light: The Art of Cinematography (Todd McCarthy, Stuart Samuels, and Arnold Glassman, 1993, NR, 95 min.)

APPENDIX E

RECOMMENDED WRITING TEXTBOOKS

Atwell, Nancie	*In the Middle: Writing, Reading, and Learning with Adolescents*	1987	Boynton/Cook
Ballenger, Bruce, and Barry Lane	*Discovering the Writer Within*	1989	Writer's Digest Books
Berthoff, Ann	*The Making of Meaning*	1981	Boynton/Cook
Calkins, Lucy	*The Art of Teaching Writing*	1986	Heinemann
Elbow, Peter, and Belanoff	*A Community of Writers: A Workshop Course in Writing*	1995	McGraw-Hill
Elbow, Peter	*Writing Without Teachers*	1973	Oxford U. Press
Fletcher, Ralph	*Breathing In; Breathing Out: Keeping a Writer's Notebook*	1996	Heinemann
Foster, David	*A Primer for Writing Teachers: Theories, Theorists, Issues, Problems*	1992	Boynton/Cook
Goldberg, Natalie	*Writing Down the Bones: Freeing the Writer Within*	1986	Shabhala
Graves, Donald	*A Fresh Look at Writing*	1994	Heinemann
Graves, Donald	*Writing: Teachers and Children at Work*	1983	Heinemann
Harris, Muriel	*Teaching One-to-One: The Writing Conference*	1987	NCTE
Kirby, Dan and Tom Liner with Ruth Vinz	*Inside Out: Developmental Strategies for Teaching Writing*	1988	Boynton/Cook
Moffett, James	*Teaching the Universe of Discourse*	1983	Boynton/Cook
Murray, Donald	*A Writer Teaches Writing*	1985	Houghton Mifflin
Newkirk, Thomas	*Nuts and Bolts: A Practical Guide to Teaching College Composition*	1993	Boynton/Cook
Rief, Linda	*Seeking Diversity: Language Arts with Adolescents*	1992	Heinemann
Romano, Tom	*Clearing the Way: Working with Teenage Writers*	1987	Heinemann
Romano, Tom	*Writing with Passion: Life Stories, Multiple Genres*	1995	Boynton/Cook
Sloan, Glenna Davis	*Child as Critic*	1991	Teachers College Press
Weaver, Constance	*Teaching Grammar in Context*	1996	Boynton/Cook

APPENDIX F

MEIERS' INDEPENDENT PROJECT FOR ENGLISH: COLLECTING AND WRITING A PERSONAL ANTHOLOGY

1. Find a newspaper report about a subject that especially interests you. Here are some suggestions:

transportation	sports
the future	conservation
work	animals
war	people
new technology	robots
medical developments	computers

2. Keep a note of the date and name of the newspaper in which you found the article.

3. Discuss the article you have chosen with me, and then use it as the first piece in a personal anthology about the subject you have chosen.

4. The collection *must* include the following:
   - a title page
   - An introduction that explains your interest in this subject
   - a table of contents listing, in order, every piece of your collection and the name of the writer of each piece
   - a conclusion (see item 12)
   - 20 different pieces, made up of five short pieces of your own writing, and at least one of each of these kinds of writing:

poems	technical articles
short stories	factual information from various sources
newspaper reports	magazine articles
cartoons	letters
writing by other students	extracts from novels

   - The five pieces of your own writing should include different kinds of writing, too.

5. No photocopied material is to be included. Newspaper articles and cartoons must be cuttings taken directly from the newspaper (note the date and source). All other writing must be copied neatly in your own hand-writing, or on the word processor. (We will try to book the computers during the project.)

6. Marks will be given for presentation—cover, title page, headings, general neatness, illustrations, use of special features such as graphics and calligraphy, etc.

7. You can use looseleaf sheets bound into a special file, a special scrapbook, or a folder with plastic inserts.

8. In assessing your work, special attention will be paid to the accuracy, spelling, punctuation, setting out of dialogue, sentences, and paragraphs.

9. All class time until (due date) will be spent on this project, and you will also need to work at home. Some classes will be booked in the Resource Center.

10. The newspapers in the RC are available as a source of materials. Check with the librarians about those that can be cut up.

11. Report regularly to me on the progress of your anthology, and ask for help whenever you need to. Make sure you check the first draft of your own writing with me.

12. When you have finished making your collection, write a short conclusion expanding what you learned while working on this project.

10 TEXTUAL LEARNING STATIONS: MARK TWAIN'S *THE ADVENTURES OF HUCKLEBERRY FINN*

Each of these stations offers a different approach to the novel's life and ideas. Most will take more than a period to complete by either a single student or a group. Each student will be required to complete 6 of the 10, and none can omit the first station. (More than any other it brings the whole novel together for students.) We'll outline the activity of each station for considering Twain's *The Adventures of Huckleberry Finn.* *

1. River Chart
2. What If . . . Huck Finn?
3. Jim's Diary
4. River Talk—Shore Speak
5. Women's Portraits
6. Scams
7. Aristocracy—Democracy
8. Mark Twain's Humor
9. The Newspaper
10. Religious Professions

1. River Chart

Your first station, River Chart, is the only one that all of you will encounter in your two-week journey into Huck Finn's world.

1. Create a map of Huck's journey from the Widow Douglas's house in Missouri to the Phelps's farm in Arkansas.
2. For every recognizable spot on that river map, draw out a quote from Huck that explains how he feels about one person he encounters there. For instance, you might choose this quote concerning the Widow Douglas.

   That is the way it is with some people. They get down on a thing when they don't know a thing about it. Here she was bothering about Moses, which was no kin to her, an no use to anybody.

3. Tag the quote with your sense of what it says about Huck and his growth as he moves down the river.
4. After other maps are completed, compare your quotes to see how different readers trace the development of the main character, where he is at his best, and where he fails his own sense of himself. (Students who are taught Jane Loevinger's stages of ego development might use these statements to mark Huck's developmental growth.)

2. What If . . . Huck Finn?

(In Chapter 6 we presented a sample portion of an exercise that imaginatively placed Huck in the present. If you used that activity here, you might ask students to work alone and imagine Huck in the contemporary world. Here is another imaginative activity, which leaves Huck in the nineteenth century and asks a group of students to speculate on his journey.)

1. With a small group, brainstorm several pivotal moments in Huck's journey.
2. Discuss these questions about each pivotal moment: What if Huck had decided differently or the event did not take place or was replaced with another event? How might the story have ended?
3. As a group, rewrite Twain's novel by altering a decision or event and telling how the journey would have ended. For example, what if Huck had not gotten the raft back in Chapter 15? What would have happened to Jim?

Because this activity is intended as an explanation of the journey motif, your group's story should indicate how "your" journey influenced the development of Huck's character. Is the Huck at the end of your story the same person as the person Huck is at the end of Twain's story? If not, how is he different and why?

Remember that this story is a group effort and everyone must contribute. Have at least three people serve as secretary during the writing process.

---

*Teacher Jennifer Clark (personal communication, 1992) designed learning stations 2, 8, and 9.

3. Jim's Diary

1. Work alone with a tape recorder to try to capture Jim's responses to his condition as he moves along the river with Huck.
2. Focus on six specific incidents or locales.
3. Gather your thoughts and make a diarylike recording of your feelings about Huck, river society, and the day at hand.

These personal oral utterances should try to capture Jim's "voice," not in its oral dialect as much as in his own unique view of the world. (Remember with sadness that teaching slaves to write was a crime in most states of the Confederacy.)

4. River Talk–Shore Speak

At this station you will have a chance to look at two kinds of language in Twain's dialect-rich book: River Talk and Shore Speak. River Talk is the language Huck uses when he is most touched by nature. We see it early in the text, not when he's on the river, but when he is alone in his room at the Widow Douglas's and says,

> I set down in a chair by the window and tried to think of something cheerful, but it warn't no use. I felt so lonesome I most wished I was dead. The stars were chinning, and the leaves rustled in the woods ever so mournful, and I heard an owl, away off who-whooing about somebody that was dead, and a whippoorwill and a dog crying about somebody that was going to die; and the wind was trying to whisper something to me.

But it comes more often and more deeply when he's on the river alone or with Jim. In contrast, his language is less natural when he's on shore:

> Buck said she could rattle off poetry like nothing. She didn't even have to stop to think. He said she would slap down a line, and if she couldn't find anything to rhyme with it she would just scratch it out and slap down another one, and go ahead.

This language misleads the credulous Huck. The shore folk often incriminate themselves with their own words.

1. Select four pairs of utterance from significant points along the journey downstream representing these two different forms of language.
2. Put them on a chart.

Twain's Words

River Talk	*Shore Speak*
1.	
2.	
3.	
4.	

3. Next, on this same chart, try to decide the difference between the two language styles.

Description of Language Difference

River Talk	*Shore Speak*
1.	
2.	
3.	
4.	

4. Assume the language style of these characters and complete the chart by writing your reaction to the opposite character's language.

Your Imaginative Response

Speak River Talk *About Shore Dwellers*	*Speak Shore Speak* *About Huck*
1.	
2.	
3.	
4.	

(A subset of our exploration of the shore and river voices focuses on Huck's famous dialect. As we go to press, news of scholarship by Shelley Fishkin (1993) is being reported that suggests that Twain modelled Huck's voice on a 10-year-old black servant he called Jimmy. Twain himself said that the models for Huck were a poor white boy from Hannibal, Missouri named Tom Blankenship and his brother Bence. The debate raises the possibilities of another language exercise.

The task is to look at Huck's language very carefully and determine whether it is closer to that of Jim or that of Tom or any of the other white boys in the novel. Look at the vocabulary, syntax, rhythm, and idiom to see how Huck's voice is similar to and different from the novel's white and black characters.)

5. Women's Portraits

1. Select the novel's most interesting female.
2. Project her and Huck or another character into a new scene in the novel.
3. Dramatize this scene in your mind. Study the woman carefully to imagine how she would react in a new situation. Reread the section of the novel where you will insert your vignette.
4. Share your ideas with another student. Discuss with your partner which of your ideas would work best.
5. Develop a written script together, revise, it, rehearse it, and enact it in costume for the whole class.

(After the class has watched them all, discuss the following questions: Which delighted you? Deepened your sense of the novel? Enlarged your sense of the female character? Would your class's collaborative sense of women have been comfortable to Twain or does it reflect a late twentieth-century consciousness?

You can see that this extension of Women's Portraits requires a much longer expenditure of time. More important to its success is a teacher's energy and enthusiasm. Its payoff is equal to its risk, though: to invite students to become creative collaborators with Twain.)

6. Scams

1. List as many scams—tricks, disguises, costumes, playacting—as you can remember in the novel.
2. Compare your list with at least three other classmates'.
3. Review the lists by yourself or with others and come up with two positive and two negative meanings that these acts of foul play and ingenuity may have for Twain's reader.

7. Aristocracy–Democracy

(This station requires a tape recorder and a recorded dramatic reading of speech.)

The Boggs-Sherburn incident is a landmark in Twain's novel. Their clash serves as the focal point for this station.

1. Listen to the spoken tape of Sherburn's speech to the crowd (Chapter 22).
2. Enumerate strategies of rhetoric that Sherburn employs. Name the persuasive technique and illustrate it from the speech.
3. Discuss the effect of his rhetoric on his audience.
4. List scenes in the novel that present the conflict between the natural, unspoiled American person and the restrained, socialized, and tradition-bound citizen.
5. Conclude this station by reflecting on this dilemma, which runs deeply through the entire text. To which of these two groups are you more drawn? Which group can you more easily imagine as being your friends?

8. Mark Twain's Humor

(This station requires two videotape clips, described below.)

This activity explores aspects of Mark Twain's humor. As you participate in this activity, you need to keep in mind these two definitions.

Burlesque—an alteration of content within a given form
Parody—a presentation of content in an altered form

1. Play the clip from *L.A. Story*. Then play the clip from *Hamlet*. If you wish, you can play the clip from *L.A. Story* again.
2. Decide whether the scene from *L.A. Story* is a burlesque or a parody. Write out your answer and explain your reasoning.
3. Now compare the Dukes version of Hamlet's soliloquy with the original text. Underline or note words and phrases that are in both speeches. Allow about 3 minutes for this activity and then play the next clip, which dramatizes this soliloquy.

4. Discuss these questions with others:
   - Is the Duke's version a burlesque or a parody? Why?
   - What do the words *bodkin* and *fardel* mean? Does the Duke preserve the meaning of the speech?
   - What is Huck's reaction to the Duke's rendition? Is this reaction typical of Huck? What is the significance of Huck's response?

9. The Newspaper

Imagine that you work for a newspaper during the year 1885, the year *The Adventures of Huckleberry Finn* was published. Divide the group into editors and reporters. Make certain that you have at least two editors. This exercise is an opportunity to make connections between different kinds of writing.

Reporters: Select an incident in the book that is relatively *brief* and particularly memorable. Imagine that you are a reporter who witnessed the event unobserved. Write an article for the newspaper relating the incident. Remember that this is "Cookbook English" so you should be able to complete this article 10 minutes before the period ends. Be certain to include who, what, where, when, why, and how. Your article should look like an inverted pyramid, with the most important facts first and less important facts coming later in the article. Submit your finished article to the editors.

Editors: While you are waiting for your reporters to return from their assignment, look through the articles taken from an 1885 paper. Select ads and articles that you find especially interesting to include in your newspaper. Do a paste-up of these articles and ads. When the reporters submit their articles, it will be your job to edit them. Explain your revisions (if any) to the reporter. Once all the articles are submitted, work together as a staff (reporters and editors) to cut the articles from the bottom to fit the space.

Discuss the following questions as a group.

- What connections could you make between the novel and the paper?
- Were Mark Twain's views and attitudes representative of the era? Why or why not?

10. Religious Professions

This final station uses Twain's "The War Prayer" as a guide to his regard for his character's religious beliefs.

1. Read Twain's short piece.
2. Pick out three characters in the novel who *appear* to be religious, but may be less than devout.
3. Write down what those characters have said and, beside their words, the secret prayer they may in fact be uttering.

(All private prayers might be collected, read orally by students, and developed into a pastiche of Impious Petitions.)

FOUR TOPICAL LEARNING STATIONS: UTOPIA

The topical learning station may seem to be the stuff of humanities electives or social studies classes: investigations of myths and rituals, utopias, or ambition and identity. In fact, these topics on ideas, which draw students into acts of reading, writing, talking and listening, and material (print and non-print literature) are central to the goals of any expansive English curriculum.

We take the topic of utopias as an example of how stations might be developed to meet the goals of English teachers and the needs of their students. Each of four stations engages students in considering the ideal state: personally, socially, politically, orally and philosophically. Four teams of four to six students explore each. After completing them, each group is responsible for constructing a new utopia station. Each group must then complete two from this set of new stations. They move in graduated steps from the personal and immediate (their school) to the more distant (their culture and politics) to the universal (all life in all cultures). We leave that progression for students to discover for themselves after the total investigation of utopias is completed. The original four stations are

- Draw a School
- Brave New World
- USA II
- Imagine

1. Draw a School

Draw the floor plan for the secondary school of tomorrow within the approximate limits of a school of today. Label the use of its different spaces. Try to imagine not just new architectural possibilities, but new ways of organizing the way we learn in school.

2. Brave New World

Divide into two groups with one or two observers. Choose one of the following two debate topics. Each group should make as strong an argument as possible using a rough debating format: two 5-minute statements (pros, cons) followed by 2-minute rebuttals (cons, pros).

1. Parents should be licensed so as not to inundate society with children whose parents are unprepared to rear productive members of society.
2. Children should be inoculated with mood-stabilizing drugs to eliminate manic and depressive swings (Both the source of psychic distress and, studies show, creativity).

3. USA II

1. Each of you works alone to list five possible major changes that might be made in our government or political system (for example, 6-year presidential terms).
2. Pass your lists around your group so that each list is read by all members.
3. On each list you receive, check those suggestions that are the same as yours. Put a *1* by the suggestion you consider most important.
4. As a whole group, discuss the one or two proposals you would like to present to the whole class. Enumerate good reasons for the proposed changes. Brainstorm all the possible repercussions or results brought on by such a change. What does your chosen reform contribute to a more ideal country?

4. Imagine

Listen to John Lennon's song "Imagine" and discuss the ideal world that he envisions. Does his view of possessions, religion, or government make sense to you? If it does, add a verse about a new topic that is compatible with his ideas. If you don't like his ideas, write verses to a song that satirizes his personal utopia.

DAVIS'S LEARNING CENTERS: FAMILY*

I once created learning centers for high schoolers that allowed students to think about and create responses to various meanings, shapes and forms of "family." I wonder if a similar culminating activity would be helpful for your students.

The set-up included a constellation of four centers through which students moved and worked. The centers included a station in which students wrote a "recipe" for a family. I placed sample recipes and dictionaries and other word sources there. Each student created a sort of poem that combined his/her notion of family "ingredients." The variety of these poems testified to and celebrated (and sometimes lamented, because everyone's notion of "family" isn't positive) the myriad of ways we and literature conceptualized "family."

Another center required students to listen to taped music that suggests various aspects of "family." Carole King's or James Taylor's "You've Got A Friend," Rockapella and the Persuasions' "My Home," and Tracy Chapman's "Behind the Wall" were a few of the pieces to which students listened. After listening, students listed the various images of "family" in each of the songs.

Still another center invited students to make a human knot and to "untie" it by cooperating, listening and acting to untangle it. A description of this activity is in the NEW GAMES book that came out in the eighties. After participating in this exercise, students discussed the qualities required to make the untangling process work—qualities that are vital for the survival of a healthy interactive group (i.e. family).

At the fourth center, I spread a huge canvass (bulletin board paper) on the floor. Around the sheet, I placed many paints, colored pencils, construction paper, etc. for students to use as they created a class collage with their images and/or words of "family."

We used this activity to introduce the unit on family. The experiences provided us with a wide range of ways to conceptualize "family" and so they served as reference points as we discussed various texts about family. This kind of activity could serve as an anticipatory introduction to a unit on family, or it could be a closing, summing up for students.

*Teacher Meg Davis sent us a description of an example of learning centers that she had created and shared with another teacher through NCTE's Listserve. The teacher had asked for ideas about a culminating activity for a unit on family.

APPENDIX G

DEVELOPING A UNIT: WILLIAM SHAKESPEARE

The creative teaching activities that follow were developed by able high school teachers in Indiana, Kentucky, Maryland, and North Carolina.

General

Bringing Oprah to the Classroom. Mary Ann Downs asks students to act as characters, hosts, expert guests, and audience members in a talk-show format. Each student takes on a role based on the literary work being studied. One student is the host/hostess. The panel is made up of students playing the roles of the major characters from the work and "expert" guests. Students in the audience must prepare and ask questions of panelists. Themes for each show range from "Was the assassination of Julius Caesar really in the best interest of Rome?" (*Julius Caesar*) to "Who was to blame for the murder of Duncan?" (*Macbeth*). After reading *Julius Caesar,* for instance, Mudd's panel included Calpurnia, Julius Caesar, Portis, Brutus, Cassius, Casca, and a political analyst. (Some characters appeared posthumously.) Audience members stated their names, told what they were doing when Julius Caesar was assassinated and proceeded with their questions. Panelists had to stay in character and answer the questions based on what they read. Mudd reports that the talk show format serves many purposes. It makes discussion student-centered, assesses the student's understanding of plot and character, and gives students the opportunity to think on their feet.

Shakespeare with Puppets. David Sampson divides students into groups. Each is responsible for condensing a scene to under five minutes. Key scenes and speeches can be abbreviated but not completely cut. Transitional words and phrases can be added but only if necessary. His students create puppets and film their completed work. These puppet shows necessitate a thorough knowledge of the play, critical skills for the editing process, and filming techniques. The class produces a video that can be shown to other classes as well.

Julius Caesar

Julius Caesar Newspaper. An unnamed teacher asks her sophomores to create a "Julius Caesar Newspaper" dated the day of Caesar's assassination. During the course of reading *Julius Caesar,* students write stories relating to the play that correspond to the different sections of a newspaper (editorials, straight news stories, letters to the editor, feature stories on main character, sports stories). Three sample assignments follow.

NEWS STORY: Write a straight news story for a Roman newspaper covering the assassination of Caesar. Be objective (no opinions at all, please) and use third person. Be sure to include who, what, where, why, and how in the article.

LETTER TO THE EDITOR: Write a letter to the editor of a Roman newspaper about an event (from the play, or one you make up). Choose an issue brought up by the event, take a side and argue for your position. Include a complimentary closing and sign it (you may make up a name if you would like).

FEATURE STORY: Write a feature story about a person or an event (real or made up) from the play. It should have a human interest slant, i.e. it ought to tug at the reader's heart. Human interest stories appeal to the emotions: Happy, sad, good, bad, exciting, etc.

Small groups develop layout and pictures for each article. All of the pieces are assembled under a masthead. The paper includes other elements usually found in newspapers such as want ads, personals, advertisements, and advice columns.

Romeo and Juliet

Romeo and Juliet Signaled Suicide. Nancy Nelson's idea was inspired by a local newspaper article critical of teaching *Romeo and Juliet* because it appeared to glamorize teen suicide. To make students aware of the warning signs of a serious teen problem—suicide—and to provide an interesting composition topic for a classic piece of literature, she developed the following activity.

After reading *Romeo and Juliet,* I hand out a list of common warning signs of suicide. We talk about each and how common suicide is for teens today. Then I give the following assignment: Write a four paragraph composition identifying the suicide warning signs in *Romeo and Juliet.* Begin with a general introduction. In the body discuss Romeo's and Juliet's warning signs in separate paragraphs using quotations for support if desired. End with a concluding paragraph.

Common warning signs taken from several different sources in our school library are listed below.

1. Persistent morbid thoughts, dreams, or talk about death or suicide.
2. Changes in grades, appetite, or sleep patterns.
3. Threats of suicide, implied or direct.
4. Isolation, where a formerly active and social person now spends much time alone.
5. Inability or reluctance to express anger or rage, particularly when you would expect such an expression.
6. Giving away of valued possessions.
7. Drug and alcohol addiction or abuse.
8. Severe guilt and shame before the attempt.
9. Helpless or hopeless feelings.
10. Severe depression or despondence.
11. Any of these signs following a serious disruption in the family, school, or social group, especially the loss of a significant person, thing, or condition.

Characters' Values Sort. Katherine Greene developed the following value sort for sophomores studying *Romeo and Juliet.* After students write their individual responses, they are primed for lively small group or whole class discussions.

Paris is in love with Juliet.	T	F
Friar Laurence suggests a valid, sound plan for Juliet to follow.	T	F
Juliet should follow Friar Laurence's advice.	T	F
Juliet should marry Count Paris.	T	F
Lord Capulet's feelings regarding the marriage of his daughter are noble.	T	F
The Nurse meaningfully mourns Juliet's "death."	T	F
Lady and Lord Capulet express genuine remorse at Juliet's "death."	T	F
Friar Laurence's role as a mediator between Juliet, Romeo, and their elders is a good one.	T	F
The apothecary should have sold Romeo the poison.	T	F
Friar John is responsible for the tragedy.	T	F

Macbeth

Macbeth Times. Mary Beth Braker uses a simplified newspaper activity to help students enter *Macbeth* imaginatively. She asks them to assume the roles of reporters traveling with Macduff as he leaves Scotland for England (like the White House reporters who follow the U.S. president on his travels). Write an article for an underground Scottish newspaper opposed to the murderous reign of Macbeth and chronicle the most recent events, including Macduff's flight to England, the police state imposed by the tyrannous Macbeth, the murder of Macduff's family. Come up with a headline and explore the journalistic questions Who, What, Where, When, Why, and How.

Hamlet

Hamlet Questionnaire. Joe Taylor designed an activity to enable students to address many of the universal issues and concerns that will not only pertain to their readings of *Hamlet,* but also to the world in which high school students live today. After students complete a true-false questionnaire, the class spends the next twenty minutes discussing the issues that students are reacting to most vigorously.

True or False

1. It is never right to kill another person.   _____
2. It is better to suffer whatever life brings than to commit suicide.   _____
3. If someone murders your father, you can justify killing that person.   _____
4. There are acceptable reasons for lying to your friends.   _____

5. Our lives are preordained.   _____
6. Leaders usually act in the best interest of their countries.   _____
7. People should never compromise their ideals or beliefs.   _____
8. No cause, political or otherwise, is worth dying for.   _____
9. Sexual passion motivates the behavior of young people more than it
   does the behavior of their parents' generation.   _____
10. It is better to act quickly than to be indecisive.   _____
11. At times it is appropriate to sacrifice yourself for a greater good.   _____
12. Fathers have a different set of expectations for their sons than they do for
    their daughters.   _____
13. It is "unmanly" for men to express their emotions in public.   _____
14. Parents can be optimistic about the world into which they bring their children.   _____

Next Taylor places two of each of the individual statements on the questionnaire into the replica of a human skull. (But, alas poor Yorick, a hat or box will work just fine.) One statement is then labeled "Pro" while the other copy of the same statement is labeled "Con." Students randomly choose the statement they must defend or oppose in class the next day (even though it usually takes two days to complete the point-counterpoint activity). They then prepare a 2–3 minute oral presentation in defense of their position. This presentation will be immediately followed by the student with the opposing point of view. After the pros and cons have been stated, students will take 2–3 minutes to respond. Students are graded on their oral presentations and their written responses to each statement. This same questionnaire can be used as an effective follow-up to reading *Hamlet*. Taylor then has students discuss whether or not their opinions have changed based upon their actual reading of the play.

Creative Projects for Hamlet. Mary Beth Braker assigns these projects for *Hamlet*. Students choose to complete one.

1. Pretend that you are a character *other than Hamlet* in the play (Gertrude, Ophelia, Polonius, Claudius, Laertes, Horatio, Rosencrantz and Guilderstern, etc.) and tell the basic story of the play from your character's *point of view*. Be sure to develop the plot in detail and pay special attention to the relationships your character has with other characters.

2. Write Ophelia's farewell to Hamlet. The correspondence could be in the form of a poem, song, or letter, but it must be composed from Ophelia's point of view and state of mind and must reflect the complicated relationship between Ophelia and Hamlet.

3. As one of the characters in the play, write a letter to either "Dear Abby" or "Ann Landers" expressing your dilemma and asking for advice *and* write the columnist's imaginary reply to your character.

4. Rewrite the ending of the play. You must include the following characters in the final scene: Gertrude, Claudius, Laertes, Horatio, and Hamlet. The only plot requirement is that *only* Claudius dies in the end. You may write this as a play with dialogue and stage directions or as a narrative account of the play's ending.

APPENDIX H

SAT Essay Exam Assessment: Diederich Scale*

1—Poor 2—Weak 3—Average 4—Good 5—Excellent

Reader _____

Quality and development of ideas	1	2	3	4	5
Organization, relevance, movement	1	2	3	4	5

_____ × 5 = _____
Subtotal

Style, flavor, individuality	1	2	3	4	5
Wording and phrasing	1	2	3	4	5

_____ × 3 = _____
Subtotal

Grammar, sentence structure	1	2	3	4	5
Punctuation	1	2	3	4	5
Spelling	1	2	3	4	5
Manuscript form, legibility	1	2	3	4	5

_____ × 1 = _____
Subtotal
Total rate: _____%

How to Interpret This Scale

1. This scale weighs content and organization 50%, aspects of style 30%, and mechanics 20%. The multiplication translates the 40 point scale into a 100 point scale.
2. The ratings for each item range from 1 to 5. Regard 1 as the lowest grade, 3 as the average, and 5 as the highest. Use 2 to designate below-average performance but not marked deficiency and use 4 to designate above-average performance but not marked proficiency. *Reading five randomly selected papers from a set before you attempt to grade the set will help you to form a realistic notion of 1, 3, and 5 performance for that particular assignment.*
3. Observing the following guidelines will also help to assure more uniform and consistent grading.
   a. *Quality and development of ideas.* Grant the writer his choice of subject matter. He was, after all, offered choices dictated by the teacher and should *not* be penalized by the value you place on one choice as compared to another. Look at how well he has supported his subject and *his* point of view or attitude toward the subject.
   b. *Organization, relevance, movement.* A 5 paper will begin with a clear indication of its controlling idea, offer convincing relevant support, and come to a close. A 1 paper begins anywhere and goes nowhere. A 3 paper may be skimpily but relevantly developed or fully developed, but including some irrelevant material.
   c. *Style, flavor, individuality.* Guard against the temptation to give a low score for the use of substandard English. Papers containing substandard English are often rich in flavor and

individuality. Reserve 5 for the truly arresting paper. A single apt, precise, or arresting phrase can move a paper from a 3 to a 4.

d. *Wording and phrasing.* Here is the place to give a low score for impoverished vocabulary and a high one for apt and precise diction and clear phrasing.

e. *Grammar, sentence structure.* Low scores should be given for frequent and varied substandard constructions like errors in agreement between pronoun and antecedent, dangling constructions, subject-verb agreement, etc.

f. *Punctuation.* Again, frequent *and varied* abuses of standard punctuation marks deserve a low score; occasional varied errors in common punctuation marks a middle score; freedom from common errors a high score. Errors in the use of the comma, the apostrophe and end punctuation should be regarded as more serious than errors in the use of the semicolon, quotation marks (especially double quotes), parentheses, and brackets. Regard the mistaken presence or absence of the apostrophe as a punctuation error, not a spelling error.

g. *Spelling.* Give a score of 5 if the writer has misspelled no words; a 4 for one spelling error; a 3 for two spelling errors; a 2 for three spelling errors, and a 1 for four or more errors. This is the only place on the scale where you are to assess spelling. Misspelling the same word is only one error.

h. *Adherence to manuscript from and a clearly readable paper* merits a 5. An unreadable paper without margins and without a proper heading merits a score of 1. Perhaps readers should attempt only a 1, 3, or 5 judgment on this item. Do *not* give a low score for neat cross-outs. (Remember that the students are writing their papers in class and that they have been encouraged not to waste time recopying.) (Quoted in Kirby, Liner, and Vinz [1988], pp. 225–226.)

ORAL COMMUNICATIONS ACTIVITIES LOG[†]

STUDENT NAME _____   GRADE _____

TEACHER NAME _____   COURSE NUMBER _____

SCHOOL _____   DATE OF COURSE ____/____/____

Communication Forms	Month/Day 1 2 3 4 5 6 7 8 9 10 11 12 13 14 15 16 17 18 19 20
Conversation	
Interview	
Formal Discussion	
Dramatization	
Oral Interpretation	
Impromptu	
Prepared Speech	
Giving Directions	
Introductions	
Introducing A Speaker	
Acceptance Speech	
Welcoming Speech	
Storytelling	
Informal Discussion	
Role-Playing	
Telephone Usage	

Total number of days in attendance _____

Total number of days with speaking activities _____

Total number of different forms _____

[†]Permission to reprint these last five exercises given by Francis Snow, Winston-Salem/Forsyth County Schools.

TWO COMMUNICATION INVENTORIES†

Shyness Scale (SS)

Student Name _____   Course No. _____ Grades _____

Teacher Name_____   Date _____

Directions: The following 14 statements refer to talking with other people. If the statement describes you very well, circle "YES." If it somewhat describes you, circle "yes." If you are not sure whether it describes you or not, or if you do not understand the statement, circle, "?". If the statement is a poor description of you, circle "no." If the statement is a very poor description of you, circle, "NO." There are no right or wrong answers. Work quickly; record your first impression.

1. I am a shy person.	YES	yes	?	no	NO
2. Other people think I talk a lot.	YES	yes	?	no	NO
3 I am a very talkative person.	YES	yes	?	no	NO
4. Other people think I am shy.	YES	yes	?	no	NO
5. I talk a lot.	YES	yes	?	no	NO
6. I tend to be very quiet in class.	YES	yes	?	no	NO
7. I don't talk much.	YES	yes	?	no	NO
8. I talk more than most people.	YES	yes	?	no	NO
9. I am a quiet person.	YES	yes	?	no	NO
10. I talk more in a small group (3–6 people) than other people do.	YES	yes	?	no	NO
11. Most people talk more than I do.	YES	yes	?	no	NO
12. Other people think I am very quiet.	YES	yes	?	no	NO
13. I talk more in class than most people do.	YES	yes	?	no	NO
14. Most people are more shy than I am.	YES	yes	?	no	NO

Personal Report of Communication Fear (PRCF)
(Essentially the same directions as above)

1. Talking with someone new scares me.	YES	yes	?	no	NO
2. I look forward to talking in class.	YES	yes	?	no	NO
3. I like standing up and talking to a group of people.	YES	yes	?	no	NO
4. I like to talk when the whole class listens.	YES	yes	?	no	NO
5. Standing up to talk in front of other people scares me.	YES	yes	?	no	NO
6. I like talking to teachers.	YES	yes	?	no	NO
7. I am scared to talk to people.	YES	yes	?	no	NO
8. I like it when it is my turn to talk in class.	YES	yes	?	no	NO
9. I like to talk to new people.	YES	yes	?	no	NO
10. When someone asks me a question, it scares me.	YES	yes	?	no	NO
11. There are a lot of people I am scared to talk to.	YES	yes	?	no	NO
12. I like to talk to people I haven't met before.	YES	yes	?	no	NO
13. I like it when I don't have to talk.	YES	yes	?	no	NO
14. Talking to teachers scares me.	YES	yes	?	no	NO

†Permission to reprint these last five exercises given by Francis Snow, Winston-Salem/Forsyth County Schools.

EVALUATION FORM FOR GROUP DISCUSSION[†]

Teacher Name _____   Course No. _____ Date_____

Group No. _____   Grade _____

Directions: Rate each student on each objective using the following scale:
1 = unsatisfactory; 2 = below average; 3 = average; 4 = above average;
5 = excellent.

NAME _____

OBJECTIVES: The student	Individual Score	Group Average
1. Displays a knowledge of the difference between discussion and debate		
2. Displays a positive attitude toward group		
3. Makes short, frequent, constructive comments		
4. Displays an ability to evaluate information		
5. Stays on the topic		
6. Facilitates group task and interaction		
7. Solicits contributions from others		
8. Displays an awareness of need for order and group leader		
9. Responds directly to comments and follows up ideas		
10. Displays knowledge of summarizing		
Total		
Student Average Across Objectives		

EXPLANATION OF RATINGS USED FOR THE EVALUATION FORM FOR GROUP DISCUSSION[†]

1. Displays a knowledge of the difference between discussion and debate
   (5) Open-minded; gives and solicits ideas to reach best conclusion
   (4) Has definite ideas but honestly tries to understand others
   (3) Tries to sell his own ideas; reluctant to understand others
   (2) Refuses to listen to ideas other than his own or doesn't initiate his own ideas
   (1) Refuses to actively participate
2. Displays a positive attitude toward group
   (5) Encourages others to comment; seeks information; freely contributes
   (4) Gives lots of information but does nothing to encourage others
   (3) Detrimentally slows down process
   (2) Must be prodded to contribute; or makes only destructive comments
   (1) Refuses to participate

[†]Permission to reprint these last five exercises given by Francis Snow, Winston-Salem/Forsyth County Schools.

3. Makes short, frequent, constructive comments
   - (5) Makes short, frequent, constructive comments
   - (4) Frequently gives information but lacks tact dealing with others
   - (3) Monopolizes time
   - (2) Contributes very little and usually only if asked or makes irrelevant comments
   - (1) Refuses to participate

4. Displays an ability to evaluate information
   - (5) Interprets, clarifies, restates, and reflects upon ideas and suggestions; offers solutions
   - (4) Interprets and restates information and recognizes the need for consensus
   - (3) Asks for relevant information
   - (2) Sees only one side
   - (1) Shows no understanding of evaluating information

5. Stays on the topic
   - (5) Knows purpose and pursues it
   - (4) Works on topic but gets too involved in some aspects of the topic
   - (3) Occasionally strays from topic or is occasionally distracted
   - (2) Frequently strays from topic or is frequently distracted
   - *(1) Is inattentive or tries to distract attention

6. Facilitates group task and interaction
   - (5) Makes others feel good about group; works well on task; practices summarizing and consensus taking
   - (4) Makes others feel good; works on task
   - (3) Either makes others feel good or works well on task
   - (2) Must be prodded to contribute
   - (1) Refuses to participate

7. Solicits contributions from others
   - (5) Actively encourages others to participate, asks questions, responds to others
   - (4) Asks for comments but fails to respond verbally and nonverbally
   - (3) Wants others to comment but doesn't know how to get a meaningful response
   - (2) Excludes one or two members
   - (1) Refuses to participate

8. Displays an awareness of need for order and group leader
   - (5) Practices self-control and encourages others to do so *if necessary*
   - (4) Practices self-control but does not encourage others to do so *when necessary*
   - (3) Excitable; uncontrollable urge to participate but is responsive to others
   - (2) Ignores leader's attempts to maintain order and organization and shows lack of awareness of group process
   - (1) Does his own thing; oblivious to group; may be distracting

9. Responds directly to comments and follows up ideas
   - (5) Responds directly to points; analyzes and discusses specific comments
   - (4) Recognizes points of agreement as well as disagreement
   - (3) Student hears only part of what is said; insists on stating his ideas
   - (2) Jumps around from idea to idea without a sense of group direction
   - (1) Refuses to actively participate

10. Displays knowledge of summarizing
    - (5) Helps group by reflecting, summarizing ideas; draws conclusions for group to accept or reject
    - (4) Restates suggestions after the group has discussed them
    - (3) Shows understanding of the mood and attitude of the group
    - (2) Lacks understanding of the group's position
    - (1) Makes no effort to follow the group's development

Note: Tension release in the form of humor is not straying from the topic.

Teacher's Evaluation of Announcements[†]

Name _____

Articulation	precise	clear	careless	inaudible
Volume	regulated	satisfactory	erratic	too high
				too low
Rate	flexible	satisfactory	monotonous	too fast
				too slow
Tone	colorful	average	monotonous	
Juncture	used pauses effectively	used pauses ineffectively	no noticeable use of pauses	
Stress	used emphasis effectively	used emphasis ineffectively	no noticeable use of emphasis	

Content:

1. Organized clearly _____

2. Captured audience attention immediately _____

3. Motivated audience to listen _____

4. Presented complete information _____

5. Presented accurate information _____

Delivery:

6. Looked directly at audience _____

7. Maintained effective posture _____

8. Spoke loudly enough to be heard _____

9. Articulated clearly _____

10. Handled notes well _____

Additional Comments:

[†]Permission to reprint these last five exercises given by Francis Snow, Winston-Salem/Forsyth County Schools.

APPENDIX I

NCTE ORGANIZATIONS AND PERIODICALS FOR THE ENGLISH TEACHER

Organizations

National Council of Teachers of English (NCTE)
1111 Kenyon Road
Urbana, Illinois 61801
Phone: 217-328-3870
Fax: 217-328-9645

NCTE Constituent Organizations and Journals (Published quarterly)

Organization	Journal
Conference on College Composition and Communication (CCCC)	*College Composition and Communication*
Conference on English Education (CEE)	*English Education*
Conference on English Leadership (CEL)	*English Leadership Quarterly*

Professional Journals of the NCTE (Published monthly, September through April)

Title	Intended Readers
English Journal	Teachers of middle, junior, high schools
College English	Teachers of college students
Language Arts	Teachers of elementary schools (kindergarten–eighth grade)
Teaching English in the Two-Year College	Teachers of two-year college students
Research in the Teaching of English	English teachers at all levels: elementary to university

Professional Conventions

Convention	Dates
NCTE Annual Convention	Time: Week preceding Thanksgiving
NCTE Spring Conference	Time: Usually mid-March
Conference on College Composition and Communication	Time: Usually mid-March

NCTE Series

Series	Content
Theory and Research Into Practice (TRIP) (booklets)	This series describes research and then gives examples of practical classroom applications
Ideas Plus, Books One–Ten	This series presents classroom-tested ideas from classroom teachers

EDUCATIONAL PERIODICALS
RECOMMENDED FOR ENGLISH TEACHERS

Educational Leadership
Association for Supervision and Curriculum Development
1250 N. Pitt St.
Alexandria, VA 22314
(703)549-9110
8 issues per year/ISSN 0013-1784

Kappan
Phi Delta Kappa
8th and Union
PO Box 789
Bloomington, IN 47402
(812)339-1156
12 issues per year/ISSN 0031-7217

The Speech Communication Teacher
Speech Communication Association
5105 Backlick Road, Bldg. E
Annandale, VA 22003
(703)750-0533
4 issues per year

Contemporary Education
School of Education
Indiana State University
Terre Haute, IN 47809
4 issues per year/ISSN 0010-7476

Education Digest
Prakken Publications, Inc.
416 Longshore Drive
Ann Arbor, MI 48107
(313)769-1211
8 issues per year/ISSN 0013-127X

Teacher Magazine
Editorial Projects in Education
Suite 250, 4301 Connecticut Ave. N.W.
Washington, DC 20008
(202)364-4114
9 issues per year/ISSN 1046-6193

The New York Times Book Review
229 West 43rd St.
New York, NY 10036
(212)556-1234
52 issues per year/ISSN 0028-7806

The ALAN Review
1111 W. Kenyon Road
Urbana, IL 61801-1096
Published by Assembly on Literature for Adolescents, NCTE

Booklist
50 E. Huron Street
Chicago, IL 60611
Published by American Library Association

Horn Book Magazine
14 Beacon Street
Boston, MA 02108
Published by The Horn Book, Inc.

Journal of Reading
800 Barksdale Road
Box 8139
Newark, DE 19714-8139
Published by International Reading Association

Signal Newsletter
Editorial Offices: English Department
Radford University
Radford, VA 24142
Published by International Reading Association

School Library Journal
249 W. 17th St.
New York, NY 10011
Published by R.R. Bowker Company

Voice of Youth Advocates (VOYA)
PO Box 4167
Metuchen, NJ 08840
Published by Scarecrow Press

REFERENCES

Abbot, M. (1990). Idea exchange: To kill a mockingbird. *North Carolina English Teacher, 47*(2), 16-17.

Abrahamson, R. F., & Carter, B. (1987). Of survival, school, wars, and dreams: Nonfiction that belongs in English classes. *English Journal, 76*(2), 104-109.

Abrahamson, R. F., & Carter, B. (1991). Nonfiction: The missing piece in the middle. *English Journal, 80*(1), 52-58.

Abrams, M. H. (1953). *The mirror and the lamp.* New York: Oxford University Press.

Abse, D., & Abse, J. (Eds.). (1986). *Voices in the gallery.* London: Tate Gallery.

Adams, P. (1987). Writing from reading—"Dependent authorship" as a response. In B. Corcoran & E. Evans (Eds.), *Readers, texts, teachers* (pp. 119-152). Upper Montclair, NJ: Boynton/Cook.

Adams, P. (1989). Imaginative investigations: Some nondiscursive ways of writing in response to novels. In J. O. Milner & L. F. M. Milner (Eds.), *Passages to literature: Essays on teaching in Australia, Canada, England, the United States, and Wales* (pp. 53-75). Urbana, IL: NCTE.

Alexander, J. (1988). Oral communication: A survey of teacher's attitudes. *Use of English* (Vol. 39). Edinburgh: Scottish Academic Press.

Allen, J. (1995). *It's never too late: Leading adolescents to lifelong literacy.* Portsmouth, NH: Heinemann.

Allen, W. (1963). *Reading a novel.* London: Phoenix House, Ltd.

Allen, W. (1980). The Kugelmass episode. *Side effects.* New York: Random House.

Anderson, P. M., & Rubano, G. (1991). *Enhancing aesthetic reading and response.* Urbana, IL: NCTE.

Anderson, S. (1964). *Between the Grimms and "The Group."* Princeton, NJ: Educational Testing Service.

Andrasick, K. D. (1990). *Opening texts: Using writing to teach literature.* Portsmouth, NH: Heinemann.

Anthony, R. J., Johnson, T. D., Mickelson, N. I., & Preece, A. (1991). *Evaluating literacy: A perspective for change.* Portsmouth, NH: Heinemann.

Applebee, A. N. (1974). *Tradition and reform in the teaching of English: A history.* Urbana, IL: NCTE.

Applebee, A. N. (1977). The elaborative choice. In M. Nystrand (Ed.), *Language as a way of knowing.* Toronto: Ontario Institute for Studies in Education.

Applebee, A. N. (1978). *A survey of teaching conditions in English, 1977.* Urbana, IL: NCTE and ERIC/RCS.

Applebee, A. N. (1981). *Writing in the secondary school: English and the content areas.* Urbana, IL: NCTE.

Applebee, A. N. (1984). *Contexts for learning to write: Studies of secondary school instruction.* Norwood, NJ: Ablex.

Applebee, A. N. (1993). *Literature in the secondary school: Studies of curriculum and instruction in the United States.* Urbana, IL: NCTE.

Applebee, A. N. (1996). *Curriculum as conversation: Transforming traditions of teaching and learning.* Chicago: University of Chicago Press.

Applebee, A. N. (1997). Rethinking curriculum in the English language arts. *English Journal, 86*(5), 25-31.

Appleman, D. (1992). "I understood the grief": Theory-based introduction to *Ordinary People.* In N. J. Karolides (Ed.), *Reader response in the classroom: Evoking and interpreting meaning in literature* (pp. 92-101). New York: Longman.

Armstrong, T. (1994). *Multiple intelligences in the classroom.* Alexandria, VA: Association for Supervision and Curriculum Development.

Arnig, G. (1991). National test: "Nay": Nationwide assessment system: "Yea." Princeton, NJ: Educational Testing Service.

Arnold, R. (1987). The hidden life of a drama text. In B. Corcoran & E. Evans (Eds.), *Readers, texts, teachers* (pp. 218-233). Upper Montclair, NJ: Boynton/Cook.

Aronowitz, S. (1977). Mass culture and the eclipse of reason: The implications for pedagogy. *College English, 38*(8), 768-774.

Arrowsmith, W. (1986, Feb. 3). *Liberal education vs. egalitarianism.* The Toqueville Forum, Wake Forest University, Winston-Salem, NC.

Arthur, B. (1973). *Teaching English to speakers of English.* New York: Harcourt Brace Jovanovich.

Athanases, S. Z., Christiano, D., & Lay, E. (1995). Fostering empathy and finding common ground in multiethnic classes. *English Journal, 84*(3), 26-34.

Atwell, N. (1987). *In the middle: Writing, reading, and learning with adolescents.* Upper Montclair, NJ: Boynton/Cook.

Auer, J. (1991). *On teaching speech in elementary and junior high schools.* Bloomington, IN: University of Indiana Press.

Axline, V. (1964). *Dibs: In search of self.* Boston: Houghton Mifflin.

Baker, H. A. (1980). *The journey back: Issues in black literature and criticism.* Chicago: University of Chicago Press.

Baker, R. (1980). Schlemiel. *So this is depravity* (pp. 307-309). New York: Congdon and Lattis.

Baker, R. (1981, April 26). The English mafia. *The New York Times Magazine*, p. 29.

Barker, A. P. (1989). A gradual approach to feminism in the American-literature classroom. *English Journal, 78*(6), 39–44.

Barlow, C., & Stankwytch, C. (1982). *Guidelines for teaching oral communication: English 9–12.* With S. Dahlen, V. Martin, R. Parker, S. Sink, and F. Snow. Winston-Salem/Forsyth County Schools, Winston-Salem, NC.

Barnes, D. (1992). *From communication to curriculum.* (2nd ed.). Portsmouth, NH: Boynton/Cook.

Barnes, D., Britton, J., & Torbe, M. (1990). *Language, learner, and the school.* Portsmouth, NH: Boynton/Cook.

Barth, J. (1968). Lost in the funhouse. In J. Barth (Ed.), *Lost in the funhouse.* New York: Doubleday.

Barzun, J. (1983). *A stroll with William James.* Chicago: University of Chicago Press.

Bateson, M. C. (1990). *Composing a life.* New York: Atlantic Monthly Press.

Bayer, A. S. (1990). *Collaborative-apprenticeship learning: Language and thinking across the curriculum, K-12.* Mountain View, CA: Mayfield.

Beach, R., & Marshall, J. (1991). *Teaching literature in the secondary school.* Orlando: Harcourt Brace & Company.

Beals, T. J. (1998). Between teachers and computers: Does text-checking software really improve student writing? *English Journal, 87*(1), 67–72.

Beaven, M. H. (1977). Individualized goal setting, self-evaluation and peer evaluation. In C. R. Cooper & L. Odell (Eds.), *Evaluating writing: Describing, measuring, judging* (pp. 135–156). Urbana, IL: NCTE.

Beers, J. W. (1980). Developmental strategies of spelling competence in primary school children. In E. H. Henderson & J. W. Beers, *Developmental and cognitive aspects of learning to spell* (pp. 36–45). Newark, DE: IRA.

Beers, J. W., & Henderson, E. H. (1977). A study of developing orthographic concepts among first graders. *Research in the Teaching of English, 11*(2), 133–148.

Belanoff, P., & Dickson, M. (1991). *Portfolios: Process and product.* Portsmouth, NH: Boynton/Cook.

Belgard, M. (1987). Idea exchange: What if . . . Huck Finn? *North Carolina English Teacher, 44*(2), 16–17.

Bencich, C. B. (1996). Writing and teaching. *English Journal, 85*(3), 91–93.

Bennett, B. (1986). *What works. Research about teaching and learning.* Washington, DC: U.S. Department of Education.

Bennett, W. J. (1984). *To reclaim a legacy: A report on the humanities in higher education.* Washington, DC: National Endowment for the Humanities.

Benseler, D. P., & Shultz, R. (1980). Methodological trends in college foreign language. *Modern Language Journal, 64*(1), 88–96.

Berenson, B. G., & Carkhuff, R. R. (1967). *Beyond counseling and therapy.* New York: Holt, Rinehart & Winston.

Berthoff, A. E. (1978). *Forming/thinking/writing.* Upper Montclair, NJ: Boynton/Cook.

Berthoff, A. E. (1981). *The making of meaning: Metaphors, models, and maxims for writing teachers.* Portsmouth, NH: Boynton/Cook.

Bickford, S. (1991). Idea exchange: Huckleberry Finn town meeting. *North Carolina English Teacher, 48*(2), 27–28.

Bigsby, C. W. E. (1980). *The second black renaissance: Essays in black literature.* Westport, CT: Greenwood Press.

Billings, P. (1992). Only a well-digger's teacher. In C. Duke and S. Jacobsen (Eds.), *Poets' perspectives: Reading, writing, and teaching poetry* (pp. 82–87). Portsmouth, NH: Boynton/Cook.

Birk, L. (1996). What's so bad about the lecture? *The Harvard Education Letter, 13*(6), 7–8.

Birkerts, S. (1994). *The Gutenberg elegies.* Winchester, MA: Faber & Faber.

Bissex, G., & Bullock, R. (Eds.). (1987). *Seeing for ourselves: Research by teachers of writing.* Portsmouth, NH: Heinemann.

Black, M. (1997). *Using comics to teach English.* Unpublished master's thesis, Wake Forest University, Winston-Salem.

Blanscet, K. (1988). Themes in stories and songs. In F. A. Kaufmann (Ed.), *Ideas Plus: A collection of practical teaching ideas, book six* (pp. 31–33). Urbana, IL: NCTE.

Bleich, D. (1975). *Readings and feelings: An introduction to subjective criticism.* Urbana, IL: NCTE.

Bleich, D. (1978). *Subjective criticism.* Baltimore: Johns Hopkins University Press.

Bleich, D. (1987). Gender interests in reading and language. In E. Flynn & P. Schweickart (Eds.), *Gender and reading: Essays on readers, texts and contexts* (pp. 234–266). Baltimore: Johns Hopkins University Press.

Block, C. C. (1997). *Teaching the language arts.* Boston: Allyn & Bacon.

Bloom, A. (1987). *The closing of the American mind.* New York: Simon & Schuster.

Bloom, B. S., Englehart, M. D., Furst, E. J., Hill, W. H., & Krathwohl, D. R. (1956). *Taxonomy of educational objectives, handbook I: Cognitive domain.* New York: McKay.

Bloom, B. (1968). Learning for mastery. *Evaluation Comment, 1*(2). Los Angeles: Center for the Study of Evaluation of Instructional Programs.

Bloom, H. (1973). *The anxiety of influence: A theory of poetry.* New York: Oxford University Press.

Bloomfield, M. W., & Newmark, L. (1963). *A linguistic introduction to the history of English.* New York: Alfred A. Knopf.

Book, C., & Galvin, K. (1975). *Instruction in and about small group discussion.* Urbana, IL: ERIC/ACS and SCA. ERIC document Reproduction Service No. ED 113773.

Booksearch. (1988). Magazines in the English classroom. *English Journal, 77*(7), 91–93.

Booksearch. (1989). Using adolescent novels as transitions to literary classics. *English Journal, 78*(3), 82–84.

Booksearch. (1990a). Nonfiction: A link to other lives. *English Journal, 79*(1), 91–95.

Booksearch. (1990b). Magazine and newspaper columns for the English classroom. *English Journal, 79*(2), 79–82.

Booth, W. (1961). *The rhetoric of fiction.* Chicago: University of Chicago Press.

Booth, W. (1979). *Critical understanding: The power and limits of pluralism.* Chicago: University of Chicago Press.

Booth, W. (1988). *The company we keep: An ethics of fiction.* Berkeley: University of California Press.

Bowen, B. (1991). A multi-genre approach to the art of the biographer. *English Journal, 80*(4), 53–54.

Bradbury, R. (1983). *Dandelion wine.* New York: Knopf.

Braddock, R., Jones, R. L., & Schoen, L. (1963). *Research in written composition.* Urbana, IL: NCTE.

Britton, J. (1970). *Language and learning.* Harmondsworth, England: Penguin.

Britton, J. (1986). Talking to learn. In D. Barnes, J. Britton, & M. Torbe (Eds.), *Language, the learner and the school.* Harmondsworth, England: Penguin.

Britton, J., Burgess, T., Martin, N., McLeod, A., & Rosen, H. (1975). *The development of writing abilities: 11-18.* London: Macmillan Education Ltd.

Britzman, D. P. (1991). *Practice makes practice: A critical study of learning to teach.* Albany: State University of New York Press.

Brock, R., & Mirtz, R. (1994). *Small groups in writing workshops.* Urbana, IL: NCTE.

Bromley, K. (1998). *Language arts: Exploring connections.* Boston: Allyn & Bacon.

Brooke, R., Mirtz, R., & Evans, R. (1994). *Small groups in writing workshops: Invitations to a writer's life.* Urbana, IL: NCTE.

Brooks, C. (1947/1968). *The well-wrought urn: Studies in the structure of poetry.* London: Methuen.

Brooks, P. (1973). Mimesis: Grammar and the echoing voice. *College English, 35*(2), 161-168.

Brown, A. L., & Palincsar, A. S. (1989). Guided, cooperative learning and individual knowledge acquisition. In L. B. Resnick (Ed.), *Knowing, learning, and instruction: Essays in honor of Robert Glaser* (pp. 393-451). Hillsdale, NJ: Lawrence-Erlbaum.

Brown, C. R. V. (1992). Contemporary poetry about painting. *English Journal, 81*(1), 41-45.

Brown, D. E. (1983). Films in the English class. *English Journal, 72*(8), 71-72.

Brown, J. R. (1981). *Discovering Shakespeare.* New York: Columbia University Press.

Bruchac, J. (1987). *Survival this way: Interviews with American Indian poets.* Tucson, AZ: Sun Tracks and The University of Arizona Press.

Bruffee, K. A. (1984). Collaborative learning and the conversation of mankind. *College English, 46*(7), 635-652.

Bruner, J. (1966). *Toward a theory of instruction.* Cambridge, MA: Belknap Press of Harvard University.

Bruner, J. (1975). From communication to language: A psychological perspective. *Cognition 3*(3), 255-287.

Bruner, J. (1983). *In search of mind: Essays in autobiography.* New York: Harper & Row.

Bruner, J. (1986). *Actual minds, possible worlds.* Cambridge, MA: Harvard University Press.

Bryson, B. (1990). *The mother tongue: English and how it got that way.* New York: Avon Books.

Bryson, B. (1994). *Made in America: An informal history of the English language in the United States.* New York: William Morrow and Company.

Burbach, H., & Figgins, M. (1993, Sept.). A thematic profile of the images of teachers in film. *Teacher Education Quarterly, 20*(2) 65-75.

Burch, C. B. (1997). Creating a two-tiered portfolio rubric. *English Journal, 86*(1), 55-58.

Burmester, D. (1983). Electronic media: Media probes. *English Journal, 72*(4), 95-97.

Burnett, R. E. (1994). Productive and unproductive conflict in collaboration. In L. Flower, D. L. Wallace, L. Norris, & R. E. Burnett (Eds.), *Making thinking visible: Writing, collaborative planning, and classroom inquiry* (pp. 237-242). Urbana, IL: National Council of Teachers of English.

Caccia, P. (1991). Getting grounded: Putting semantics to work in the classroom. *English Journal, 80*(2), 55-59.

Cage, T., & Rosenfeld, L. B. (1989). Ekphrastic poetry in performance: An examination of audience perceptions of the relationship between poetry and painting. *Text and Performance Quarterly, 9*(3), 199-206.

Cain, B. N. (1989). With worldmaking, planning models matter. *English Education, 21*(1), 5-29.

Caine, R., & Caine, G. (1997). *Education on the edge of possibility.* Alexandria, VA: Association for Supervision and Curriculum Development.

Calkins, L. M. (1983). *Lessons from a child: On the teaching and learning of writing.* Exeter, NH: Heinemann.

Calkins, L. M. (1986). *The art of teaching writing.* Portsmouth, NH: Heinemann.

Calkins, L. M. (1989, Nov.). *Autobiography: The living that surrounds the writing.* Paper presented at the NCTE Annual Convention, Baltimore, MD.

Cameron, R. (1994). Writing to internalize themes in literature. *English Journal, 82*(3), 91-93.

Camp, R. (1990). Thinking together about portfolios. *The Quarterly of the National Writing Project and the Center for the Study of Writing.* Spring, 12-13.

Carey-Webb, A. (1991). Auto/biography of the oppressed: The power of testimonial. *English Journal, 80*(4), 44-47.

Carlson, M. A. Z. (1989). Guidelines for a gender-balanced curriculum in English, grades 7-12. *English Journal, 78*(6), 30-33.

Carney, B. (1996). Process writing and the secondary school reality: A compromise. *English Journal, 85*(6), 28-35.

Carter, B. (1987). *A content analysis of the most frequently circulated information books in three junior high libraries.* Unpublished doctoral dissertation, University of Houston.

Cartwright, C. A., & Cartwright, G. P. (1984). *Developing observation skills* (2nd ed.). New York: McGraw-Hill.

Cazden, C. B. (1972). *Child language and education.* New York: Holt, Rinehart & Winston.

Cazden, C. (1976, Summer). How knowledge about language helps the classroom teacher—or does it: A personal account. *The Urban Review, 9,* 74-90.

Cazden, C. (1979, Nov.). [Keynote speech]. National Council of Teachers of English. Boston, MA.

Cazden, C. B. (1988). *Classroom discourse: The language of teaching and learning.* Portsmouth, NH: Heinemann.

Cazden, C., Cordeiro, P. A., & Giacobbe, M. E. (1985). Spontaneous and scientific concepts: Young children's learning of punctuation. In G. Wells & J. Nicholls (Eds.), *Language and learning: An interactional perspective* (pp. 107-124). Philadelphia: Falmer Press.

CEE Commission on Inservice Education. (1994). Inservice education: Ten principles. *English Education, 26*(2), 125-128.

Chambers, I. (1985). Popular culture, popular knowledge. *One, Two, Three, Four: A Rock and Roll Quarterly,* 1-8.

Cheney, L. V. (1987). *American memory: A report on the humanities in the nation's public schools.* Washington, DC: National Endowment for the Humanities.

Chomsky, C. (1969). *The acquisition of syntax in children from five to ten.* Cambridge, MA: MIT Press.

Chomsky, C. (1972). Write now, read later. In C. Cazden (Ed.), *Language in early childhood education* (pp. 119-126). Washington, DC: National Education Association.

Chomsky, C. (1979). Approaching reading through invented spelling. In L. B. Resnick & P. Weaver (Eds.), *Theory and practice in early reading* (Vol. 2, pp. 43-65). Hillsdale, NJ: Lawrence Erlbaum.

Chomsky, C. (1984). Finding the best language arts software. *Classroom Computer Learning, 4*(6) 61-63.

Chomsky, N. (1957). *Syntactic structures.* The Hague: Mouton.

Chomsky, N. (1968). *Language and mind.* New York: Harcourt, Brace, World.

Christel, M. T. (1988). Idea exchange: *A Tale of Two Cities:* Journal assignment. *North Carolina English Teacher, 46*(1), 19-20.

Christenbury, L. (1994). *Making the journey: Being and becoming a teacher of English language arts.* Portsmouth, NH: Boynton/Cook.

Christenbury, L., & Kelly, P. P. (1983). *Questioning: A path to critical thinking.* Urbana, IL: NCTE.

Christensen, F. (1967). *Notes toward a new rhetoric: Six essays for teachers.* New York: Harper & Row.

Christensen, L. M. (1990). Teaching standard English: Whose standard? *English Journal, 79*(2), 36-40.

Christian, D. (1987, December). Vernacular dialects in U.S. schools. (CN 400-86-0019. *ERIC Digest*).

Ciardi, J. (1959). *How does a poem mean?* Cambridge, MA: Houghton Mifflin.

Cintorino, M. A. (1991). Learning to talk, talking to learn. *English Journal, 80*(7), 69-71.

Clark, C., & Yinger, R. (1979). *Three studies of teacher planning* (Research series No. 55). East Lansing, MI: Institute for Research on Teaching, Michigan State University.

Clark, C., & Elmore, J. (1981). *Teacher planning in the first weeks of school.* (Research Series No. 56). East Lansing, MI: Institute for Research on Teaching, Michigan State University. As reported in J. M. Cooper (Ed.), 1990. *Classroom Teaching Skills.* Lexington, MA: D. C. Heath.

Cobb, M. K. (1985). From oral to written: Origins of a black literary tradition. In C. K. Brooks (Ed.), *Tapping potential: English and language arts for the black learner.* Urbana, IL: NCTE.

Cocteau, J. (1969). Le secret professionel. (1926). In V. Erlich (Ed.), *Russian Formalism: History-Doctrine* (3rd ed.). The Hague.

Coen, R. J. (1997): Ad spending tops 175 billion during robust '96. *Advertising Age, 68*(19).

Coffin, E. (1988). Idea exchange: Microdebates of Benjamin Franklin's moral perfection. *North Carolina English Teacher, 45*(2), 7-8.

Cohen, E. G. (1994). Restructuring the classroom: Conditions for productive small groups. *Review of Educational Research, 64*(1), 1-35.

Coles, R. (1989a). *The call of stories: Teaching and the moral imagination.* Boston: Houghton Mifflin.

Coles, R. (1989b, November 17). Keynote address at National Council of Teachers of English National Convention, Baltimore.

Collette, C., & Johnson, R. (1993) *Common ground: personal writing and public discourse.* New York: HarperCollins.

Collins, K. M., & Collins, J. (1996). Strategic instruction for struggling writers. *English Journal, 85*(6), 54-61.

Collum, J., & Noethe, S. (1994). *Poetry everywhere: Teaching poetry writing in school and in the community.* New York: Teachers & Writers Collaborative.

Coltelli, L. (1990). *Winged words: American Indian writers speak.* Lincoln, NB: University of Nebraska Press.

Combs, W. E. (1977). Sentence-combining practice: Do gains in judgment of writing "quality" persist? *Journal of Educational Research, 70*(6), 318-321.

Conference on College Composition and Communication. (1974). *Students' right to their own language.* (E. Corbett, Ed.). Urbana, IL: NCTE.

Cooke, M. (1989). The humanities in contemporary life or, the bull that could waltz away. In J. O. Milner & L. F. M. Milner (Eds.), *Passages to literature: Essays on teaching in Australia, Canada, England, The United States, and Wales* (pp. 116-124). Urbana, IL: NCTE.

Coon, L. (1991). Planning a poetry unit: The process is the structure. *English Journal, 80*(3), 28-32.

Cooper, C. R. (Ed.). (1985). *Researching response to literature and the teaching of literature: Points of departure.* Norwood, NJ: Ablex.

Coover, R. (1993, Aug. 29). Hyperfiction: Novels for the computer. *New York Times Book Review,* pp. 8-10.

Corcoran, B. (1987). Teachers creating readers. In B. Corcoran & E. Evans (Eds.), *Readers, texts, teachers* (pp. 41-74). Upper Montclair, NJ: Boynton/Cook.

Cordeiro, P. A., Giacobbe, M. E., & Cazden, C. (1983). Apostrophes, quotation marks, and periods: Learning punctuation in the first grade. *Language Arts, 60*(3), 323-332.

Costanzo, W. V. (1987, August). The English teacher as programmer. *Computers and Composition, 4,* 65-76.

Couch, L. L. (1987). "So much depends" . . . on how you begin: A poetry lesson. *English Journal, 76*(7), 29.

The Council Chronicle. (1991). National Council of Teachers of English. *1*(2).

Cox, C. (1987). Film as documentation, social comment, satire, and spoof. *English Journal, 76*(4), 85-87.

Cox, M. (1991). Bards and Beatles: Connecting spontaneity to structure in lesson plans. *English Journal, 80*(3), 33-36.

Crosman, R. (1982). How readers make meaning. *College Literature, 9*(2), 7-15.

Culler, J. (1982). *On deconstruction: Theory and criticism after structuralism.* Ithaca, NY: Cornell University Press.

Cussler, E. B. (1987). Vietnam: An oral history. *English Journal, 76*(7), 66-67.

Dale, H. (1997). *Co-authoring in the classroom.* Urbana, IL: NCTE.

D'Arcy, P. (1977). *Writing across the curriculum: Language for learning.* Exeter, England: Exeter School of Education.

D'Arcy, P. (1989). *Making sense, shaping meaning.* Portsmouth, NH: Boynton/Cook.

Daiches, D. (1956). *Critical approaches to literature.* New York: W. W. Norton.

Davis, B. M. (1989). Feminizing the English curriculum: An international perspective. *English Journal, 78*(6), 45-49.

Davydov, V. (1995). The influence of L. S. Vygotsky on education theory, research, and practice. *Educational Researcher, 24*(3), 12-21.

De Beauvoir, S. (1949). *The second sex* (H. M. Parshley, Trans.). New York: Bantam.

Dellinger, D. (1982). *Out of the heart: How to design writing assignments for high school courses.* Berkeley, CA: National Writing Project, University of California.

Denman, C. (1995). Writers, editors, and readers: Authentic assessment in the newspaper class. *English Journal, 84*(8) 55-57.

de Villeas, J., & de Villeas, P. (1978). *Language acquisition.* Cambridge, MA: Harvard University Press.

Dewey, J. (1933). *How we think* (rev. ed.). Boston: Heath.

Dias, P. (1996). *Reading and responding to poetry: Patterns in the process.* Portsmouth, NH: Boynton/Cook.

Diaute, C. (1986). Physical and cognitive factors in revising. *Research in the Teaching of English, 20*(2), 141-159.

Daiute, C., & Dalton, B. (1988). Let's brighten it up a bit: Collaboration and cognition in writing. In B. A. Rafoth & D. L. Rubin (Eds.), *The social construction of written communication* (pp. 249-269). Norwood, NJ: Ablex.

Diederich, P. (1974). *Measuring growth in English.* Urbana, IL: NCTE.

Dilg, M. A. (1995). The opening of the American mind: Challenges in the cross-cultural teaching of literature. *English Journal, 84*(3), 18-25.

Dilg, M. A. (1997). Why I am a multiculturalist: The power of stories told and untold. *English Journal, 86*(6), 64-69.

Dill, N. L., & Purves, A. C., with Weiss, J., & Foshavy, A. W. (1967). *The teaching of literature.* Report of the United States National Committee, International Literature Project. Unpublished report, Teachers College, Columbia University. Available through National Council of Teachers of English ERIC, ED-039-399.

Dillard, A. (Ed.). (1988). *The Best American Essays 1988.* New York: Ticknor & Fields.

Dillard, A. (1995). Introduction in A. Dillard and C. Conley (Eds.), *Modern American memoirs.* New York: HarperCollins.

Dillon, D., & Hamilton, S. (1985, November). Dimensions of classroom talk. Document drafted at the International Assembly of The National Council of Teachers of English. Philadelphia, PA.

Dilworth, C., & Wilde, P. (1979). Correspondence: A medium rediscovered. In G. Stanford (Ed.), *Activating the passive student.* Urbana, IL: NCTE.

Dittmer, A. E. (1991). Letters: The personal touch in writing. *English Journal, 80*(1), 18-24.

Ditzian, M. (1990). Idea exchange: A child custody hearing: Black Boy. *North Carolina English Teacher, 47*(2), 14-15.

Dixon, J. (1967). *Growth through English.* London: Oxford University Press.

Dixon, J. (1984, November). National faculty lecture for teachers. East Grand Rapids, MI.

Dixon, J., & Stratta, L. (1986). *Writing narrative and beyond.* Ottawa: Canadian Council of Teachers of English.

Dixon, J., & Stratta, L. (1989). Developing responses to character in literature. In J. O. Milner & L. F. M. Milner (Eds.), *Passages to literature: Essays on teaching in Australia, Canada, England, The United States, and Wales* (pp. 25-38). Urbana, IL: NCTE.

Donelson, K. (1997). "Filth" and "Pure Filth" in our schools—censorship of classroom books in the last ten years. *English Journal, 86*(2), 21-25.

Donelson, K. L., & Nilsen, A. P. (1980). *Literature for today's young adults.* Glenview, IL: Scott, Foresman.

Donovan, J. (1985). *Feminist theory: The intellectual traditions of American feminism.* New York: F. Ungar.

Donovan, J. M. (1990). Resurrect the *Dragon Grammaticus. English Journal, 79*(1), 62-65.

Donovan, T., & McClelland, B. (Eds.). (1981). *Eight approaches to teaching composition.* Urbana, IL: NCTE.

Dorney, J. M. (1988). The plain English movement. *English Journal, 77*(3), 49-51.

Downie, N. M. (1967). *Fundamentals of measurement: Techniques and practices* (2nd ed.). New York: Oxford University Press.

Dressel, P. L. (1964). Role of external testing programs in education. *Kansas Studies in Education 14*(2). Lawrence, KS: University of Kansas.

Dreyfuss, H. (1984). *Symbol sourcebook: An authoritative guide to international graphic symbols.* New York: Van Nostran Reinhold.

Dudley, M. (1997). The rise and fall of a statewide assessment system. *English Journal, 86*(1), 15-20.

Duke, C. (1974). *Creative dramatics and English teaching.* Urbana, IL: NCTE.

Duke, C. R., & Jacobsen, S. (Eds.). (1992). *Poets' perspectives: Reading, writing, and teaching poetry.* Portsmouth, NH: Boynton/Cook.

Duke, C. R. (1994). Giving students control over writing assessment. *English Journal, 83*(4), 47-53.

Dunfey, J. (1989). Integrating computers into the language arts curriculum at Lesley College. In C. Selfe (Ed.), *Computers in English and the Language Arts: The challenge of teacher education.* Urbana, IL: NCTE.

Dyson, A. H., & Freedman, S. W. (1990). *On teaching writing: A review of the literature.* Berkeley, CA: Center for the Study of Writing.

Dyson, E. (1997). *Release 2.0: A design for living in the digital age.* New York: Broadway Books.

Eagleton, T. (1983). *Literary theory: An introduction.* Minneapolis, MN: University of Minnesota Press.

Earthman, E. A. (1997). The siren song that keeps us coming back: Multicultural resources for teaching classical mythology. *English Journal, 86*(6), 76-81.

Ebel, R. L. (1982). Proposed solutions to two problems of test construction. *Journal of Educational Measurement, 19*(4), 267-78.

Edwards, V. (1997, Nov. 10). Technology counts. *Education Week,* p. 11.

Eisner, E. W. (1990). *The Enlightened eye: Qualitative inquiry and the enhancement of educational practices.* Upper Saddle River, NJ: Macmillan/Prentice-Hall.

Elbow, P. (1973). *Writing without teachers.* New York: Oxford University Press.

Elbow, P. (1981). *Writing with power.* New York: Oxford University Press.

Elbow, P. (1985). The shifting relationship between speech and writing. *College Composition and Communication, 36*(3), 283-303.

Elbow, P. (1986). *Embracing contraries: Explorations in learning and teaching.* New York: Oxford.

Elbow, P., & Belanoff, P. (1986). Portfolios as a substitute for proficiency examination. *College Composition and Communication, 37*(3), 336-339.

Elbow, P. (1991). Forward. In P. Belanoff & M. Dickson (Eds.),

Portfolios: Process and product. Portsmouth, NH: Boynton/Cook.

Elifson, J. (1977). Teaching to enhance bidialectialism: Some theoretical and practical considerations. *English Education, 9*(1), 11-21.

Eliot, T. S. (1958). *The complete poems and plays: 1909-1950.* New York: Harcourt, Brace.

Elk Grove High School English Staff. (1979). A glossary of poetic terms. *English Journal, 68*(5), 45-46.

Elley, W. B., Barham, I. H., Lamb, H., & Wyllie, M. (1979). *The role of grammar in a secondary school curriculum.* Wellington, NZ: New Zealand Council for Educational Research.

Ellis, W. G. (1987). To tell the truth or at least a little nonfiction. *The ALAN Review, 15*(2), 39-40.

Ellmann, M. (1968). *Thinking about women.* New York: Harcourt Brace Jovanovich.

Emig, J. (1971). *The composing processes of twelfth graders.* Urbana, IL: NCTE.

Emig, J. (1977). Writing as a mode of learning. *College Composition and Communication, 28*(2), 122-128.

Emig, J. (1980). Non-magical thinking: Presenting writing developmentally in schools. In C. H. Fredericksen & J. F. Dominic (Eds.), *Writing process, development and communication, Vol. II* of *Writing: The nature, development and teaching of written communication* (pp. 21-30). Hillsdale, NJ: Lawrence Erlbaum.

English for ages five to sixteen: A national curriculum. (1987). Wales: Department of Education.

Epstein, J. (1997). "Six Types of School-Family-Community Involvement." *The Harvard Education Letter, 13*(5), 4.

Ericson, B. O. (1993). Introducing *To Kill a Mockingbird* with collaborative group reading of related young adult novels. In J. F. Kaywell (Ed.), *Adolescent literature as a complement to the classics* (pp. 1-12). Norwood, MA: Christopher-Gordon Publishers.

Erikson, E. H. (1963). *Childhood and society* (2nd ed.). New York: Norton.

Erikson, E. H. (1968). *Identity: Youth and crisis.* New York: Norton.

Fader, D., & McNeil, E. B. (1968). *Hooked on books: Program and proof.* New York: Putnam.

Farr, J. (1997). New teachers: Becoming a balanced teacher: Idealist goals, realist expectations. *English Journal 86*(6), 106-109.

Fearn, L., & Farnan, N. (1990). *Writing effectively.* Boston, MA: Allyn & Bacon.

Fehlman, R. H. (1987). Quoting films in English class. *English Journal, 76*(5), 84-87.

Ferguson, C. A. (1977). Baby talk as a simplified register. In C. A. Snow & C. A. Ferguson (Eds.), *Talking to children: Language input and requisition.* Cambridge, England: Cambridge University Press.

Fernan, N. (1993, Mar.). Writers workshop. *Middle School Journal, 24*(3), 61-65.

Fish, S. E. (1980). *Is there a text in this class? The authority of interpretive communities.* Cambridge, MA: Harvard University Press.

Fish, S. (1990, July 11). [Untitled lecture]. North Carolina Governor's School. Winston-Salem, NC.

Fishkin, S. (1993). *Huck black? Mark Twain and African-American voices.* Oxford: Oxford University Press.

Flanders, N. A. (1965). *Teacher influence, pupil attitudes and achievement* (Office of Education, Cooperative Research Monograph No. 12). Washington, DC: U.S. Government Printing Office.

Flynn, E. (1985). Gender and reading. In E. Flynn & P. Schweickart (Eds.), *Gender and reading: Essays on readers, texts and contexts* (pp. 267-288). Baltimore: Johns Hopkins University Press.

Forrestal, P. (1990, August). Presentation at the International Federation of Teachers of English (IFTE) Conference, Auckland, NZ.

Forster, E. M. (1927). *Aspects of the novel.* New York: Harcourt Brace & World.

Fowler, J. W. (1981). *Stages of faith: The psychology of human development and the quest for meaning.* San Francisco: Harper & Row.

Fowler, L. J., & Pesante, L. H. (1989). Engaging students with gaps: The whale and the cigar. *English Journal, 78*(8), 28-34.

Francis, W. N. (1958). *The structure of American English.* New York: Ronald Press.

Franza, A. (1984). To make you see: The art of film in the English class. *English Journal, 73*(1), 40-41.

Fraser, K. (1997, Oct. 14). As writers despair, book chains can only exult. *The New York Times.*

Freire, P. (1970). *Pedagogy of the oppressed* (M. B. Ramos, Trans.). New York: Herder & Herder.

Freire, P., & Shor, I. (1987). *A Pedagogy for liberation.* South Hadley, MA: Bergin & Garvey.

Fries, C. C. (1954). *The structure of English: An introduction to the construction of English sentences.* New York: Harcourt Brace.

Fuentes, C. (1992, Oct. 8). Columbus Day address. Wake Forest University. Winston-Salem, N.C.

Fuller, F. (1989). O, reform it altogether. *Virginia English Bulletin, 39*(1), 89-96.

Fulwiler, T. (1987). *Teaching with writing.* Upper Montclair, NJ: Boynton/Cook.

Fulwiler, T., & Young, A. (1982). *Language connections: Writing and reading across the curriculum.* Urbana, IL: NCTE.

Funk, W. (1978). *Word origins and their romantic stories.* New York: Bell.

Gallagher, B. (1988). Film study and the teaching of English: Technology and the future of pedagogy. *English Journal, 77*(7), 58-61.

Gallo, D. R. (1989). Who are the most important YA authors? *The Alan Review, 16*(1), 18-20.

Gambrell, L., & Bales, R. J. (1986). Mental imagery and the comprehension-monitoring performance of fourth and fifth grade readers. *Reading Research Quarterly, 21*(4), 454-464.

Gardner, H. (1983). *Frames of mind.* New York: Basic Books.

Gardner, H. (1984). The seven frames of mind. *Psychology Today, 18*(6), 21-26.

Gardner, H. (1991). *The unschooled mind.* New York: Basic Books.

Gay, G. (1988, August). Designing relevant curricula for diverse learners. *Education and Urban Society, 20*(4), 327-340.

Geisler, E. (1987). A Foxfire introduction to *The Grapes of Wrath.* In F. A. Kaufmann (Ed.), *Ideas plus: A collection of practical teaching ideas, book five* (pp. 40-41). Urbana, IL: NCTE.

Gendernalik, A. L. (1984). I seen it. *English Journal, 73*(8), 42.

Gere, A. R., Fairbanks, C., Howes, A., Roop, L., & Schaafsma, D. (1992). *Language and reflection: An integrated approach to teaching English*. Upper Saddle River, NJ: Macmillan/Prentice-Hall.

Gerbner, G., Gross, L., Morgan, M., & Signorielli, N. (1982). Charting the mainstream: Television's contributions to political orientations. *Journal of Communication, 32*(2), 100–127.

Giacobbe, M. E., & Cazden, C. (1986). *NCTE Research Report*. Spring Conference. Boston.

Giacobbe, M. E. (1982, July 6). *Beginning writing*. Talk presented to the North Carolina Writing Project, Winston-Salem, NC.

Gillard, P. (1994). Insight from the inside: A new perspective on family influences over children's television viewing and its implications for teachers. In J. Milner & C. Pope (Eds.), *Global voices: Culture and identity in the teaching of English* (pp. 68–83). Urbana, IL: NCTE.

Gillespie, J. S. (1991). The life of a seventh grader: Writing a memoir. *English Journal, 80*(4), 57–60.

Gilligan, C. (1982). *In a different voice: psychological theory and women's development*. Cambridge, MA: Harvard University Press.

Gillis, C. (1994). Writing partners: expanding the audiences for student writing. *English Journal, 83*(3), 64–67.

Giroux, H. A. (1992). *Border crossings: Cultural workers and the politics of education*. New York: Routledge.

Giroux, H. A., & Simon, R. I. (1988). Schooling, popular culture, and a pedagogy of possibility. *Journal of Education, 170*(1), 9–26.

Glatthorn, A. (1975). Teacher as person: The search for the authentic. *English Journal, 64*(9), 37–39.

Glatthorn, A. (1988). What schools should teach in the English language arts. *Educational Leadership, 46*(1), 44–50.

Glazer, N. (1997, June). The hard questions: Unsolved mysteries. *The New Republic*, p. 29.

Goebel, B. (1995). Expanding the literary canon and reading the rhetoric of "race." *English Journal, 84*(3), 42–48.

Goldman, R. (1987). Marketing fragrances: Advertising and the production of commodity signs. *Theory, Culture, and Society, 4*(4), 691–725.

Goldstein, R. (1969). *The poetry of rock*. New York: Bantam.

Goldwasser, M. M. (1997). Censorship: It happened to me in southwest Virginia—it could happen to you. *English Journal, 86*(2), 34–42.

Golub, J. (1994). *Activities for an interactive classroom*. Urbana, IL: NCTE.

Golub, J., & Reid, L. (1989). Activities for an "interactive" classroom. *English Journal, 78*(4), 43–48.

Goodlad, J. I. (1984). *A place called school: Prospects for the future*. New York: McGraw-Hill.

Goodman, M. (1980). Proposal writing to RFP specifications. National Humanities Faculty: ETE Summer Institute. Vassar College.

Gorrell, N. (1989). Let found poetry help your students find poetry. *English Journal, 78*(2), 30–34.

Goslin, D. A. (1967). *Teachers and testing*. Hartford, CT: Russell Sage Foundation.

Goswami, D., & Stillman, P. (Eds.). (1987). *Reclaiming the classroom: Teaching research as an agent for change*. Upper Montclair, NJ: Boynton/Cook.

Goswami, D. (1989, Fall/Winter). Assessing assessment. *Bread Loaf News, 20*.

Goswami, D., & Stillman, P. (Eds.). (1987). *Reclaiming the classroom: Teacher research as an agency for change*. Upper Montclair, NJ: Boynton/Cook.

Gould, C. (1987). Josephine Turck Baker, correct English, and the ancestry of pop grammar. *English Journal, 76*(1), 22–27.

Grace, P. (1987). Butterflies. In *Electric city and other stories* (pp. 61–62). Auckland, NZ: Penguin Books.

Graff, G. (1987). *Professing literature: An institutional history*. Chicago: University of Chicago Press.

Grambs, J. D., & Carr, J. C. (1991). *Modern methods in secondary education* (5th ed.). Fort Worth, TX: Holt Rinehart & Winston.

Graves, D. H. (1983a). *Writing: Teachers and children at work*. Exeter, NH: Heinemann.

Graves, D. H. (1983b, Oct.). Keynote speaker at Southeast Regional Meeting of The National Council of Teachers of English, Charleston, SC.

Graves, D. (1986, Jan. 8). Kids learn to write well if they don't fear errors. *USA Today*.

Graves, D. (1991). *The reading/writing teacher's companion: Build a literate classroom*. Portsmouth, NH: Heinemann.

Graves, D. H. (1992). *Helping students learn to read their portfolios*. Portsmouth, NH: Heinemann.

Graves, D. H., & Stuart, V. (1985). *Write from the start: Tapping your child's natural writing ability*. New York: New American Library.

Graves, D. H., & Sunstein, B. (1992). *Portfolio portraits*. Portsmouth, NH: Heinemann.

Greene, M. (1978). *Landscapes of learning*. New York: Teachers College Press.

Greene, M. (1985). Evaluation and dignity. In D. E. Purpel & H. S. Shapiro (Eds.), *Schools and meaning: Essays on the moral nature of schooling*. Lanham, MD: University Press of America.

Greene, M. (1988). *The dialectic of freedom*. New York: Teachers College Press.

Gregory, D. (1998). Letters: Ignoring Canadian literature. *English Journal, 87*(2), 8.

Griffin, C. W. (1989). Teaching Shakespeare on video. *English Journal, 78*(7), 40–43.

Griffiths, N. (1991, April 2). [Untitled lecture]. Winston-Salem Forsyth County Schools. Winston-Salem, NC.

Grimes, M. (1991). Finding hooks to catch reluctant readers. *English Journal, 80*(1), 45–47.

Gross, R. (1967, June 11). Speaking of books: Found poetry. *The New York Times Book Review*.

Grossman, F. (1982). *Getting from here to there: Writing and reading poetry*. Portsmouth, NH: Boynton/Cook.

Grossman, F. (1991). *Listening to the bells: Learning to read poetry by writing poetry*. Portsmouth, NH: Boynton/Cook.

Grossman, P. L. (1990). *The making of a teacher: Teacher knowledge and teacher education*. New York: Teachers College Press.

Guerin, W. L., Labor, E. G., Morgan, L., & Willingham, J. R. (1979). *A handbook of critical approaches to literature* (2nd ed.). New York: Harper & Row.

Guerin, G. R., & Maier, A. S. (1983). *Informal assessment in education*. Palo Alto, CA: Mayfield.

Guilford, D. (1985). Facets: What 1985 classroom teachers should know about women's studies. *English Journal, 74*(3), 24.

Guskey, T. R. (1985). *Implementing mastery learning.* Belmont, CA: Wadsworth.

Haberman, M. (1995). *Star teachers of children in poverty.* West Lafayette, IN: Kappa Delta Pi.

Hahn, J. (1985). Tennis anyone or whose paper is it? *National Writing Project Newsletter,* 5.

Hairston, M. (1981). Not all errors are created equal. *College English, 43,* 794–806.

Hale, S. J. (Ed.). (1856). *The letters of Madame de Sévigné.* New York: Mason Brothers.

Halio, J. L. (1977). Shakespeare's plays as plays. In W. Edens (Ed.), *Teaching Shakespeare.* Princeton, NJ: Princeton University Press.

Halio, J. L. (1988). *Understanding Shakespeare's plays in performance.* Manchester, England: Manchester University Press.

Hall, D. (1987). *To read literature: Fiction, poetry, drama.* (2nd ed.). New York: Holt, Rinehart & Winston.

Halpern, M. (1997). A war that never ends. *The Atlantic Monthly, 278*(3), 19–22.

Hannafin, M., & Land, S. (1997). The foundations and assumptions of technology-enhanced student-centered learning environments. *Instructional Science, 25*(3), 167–200. Norwell, MA: Kluwer Academic Publishers.

Harmston, D. (1988). Impromptu poetry. In F. A. Kaufmann (Ed.), *Ideas plus: A collection of practical teaching ideas, book six* (pp. 55–56). Urbana, IL: NCTE.

Harris, J. (1991). After Dartmouth: Growth and conflict in English. *College English, 53*(6), 631–646.

Harrington-Lueker, D. (1997). Technology works best when it serves clear educational goals. *The Harvard Education Letter 13,* 6.

Harrison, L. R. (1991). *Speaking and listening are much used but little taught: Incorporating oral language instruction into the high school English curriculum.* Unpublished master's thesis. Wake Forest University. Winston-Salem, NC.

Hartwell, P. (1985). Grammar, grammars and the teaching of grammar. *College English, 47*(4), 105–127.

Hasselriis, P. (1991). From Pearl Harbor to Watergate to Kuwait: Language in thought and action. *English Journal, 80*(2), 18–35.

Hawisher, G., & Selfe, C. (1991). *Evolving perspective on computers and composition studies.* Urbana, IL: NCTE.

Hawkey, K. (1995). Learning from peers: The experience of student teachers in school-based teacher education. *Journal of Teacher Education 46,* 175–183.

Hawkins, S. (1984). Teaching the theatre of imagination: The example of Henry IV. *Shakespeare Quarterly* [Special issue], 517–527.

Hawley, R. A. (1979). Teaching as failing. *Phi Delta Kappan 60*(4), 597–600.

Hayakawa, S. I. (1950). Linguistic science and the teaching of composition. *ETC.: A Review of General Semantics,* 7(2), 97–103.

Hayakawa, S. I. (1978). *Language in thought and action* (4th ed.). New York: Harcourt Brace Jovanovich.

Hayakawa, S. K. (1987). Why English should be our official language. *Education Digest, LII*(9), 36–37.

Hayden, C. D., Ed. (1992). *Venture into cultures: A resource book of multicultural materials and programs.* Chicago: American Library Association.

Hayes, J. R., & Tierney, R. J. (1982). Developing readers' knowledge through analogy. *Reading Research Quarterly, 17*(2), 256–280.

Hayn, J. S. (1997, Mar. 7). Another opening, another show: Using reader's theater to enhance composition skills. Presentation at the Annual Conference on Writing and Literature. Lawrence, KS.

Heard, G. (1989). *For the good of the earth and sun: Teaching poetry.* Portsmouth, NH: Heinemann.

Heathcote, D. (1980). *Drama as context.* Upper Montclair, NJ: Boynton/Cook.

Heathcote, D. (1984). *Dorothy Heathcote: Collected writings on drama and education.* (L. Johnson & C. O'Neill, Eds.). London: Hutchinson.

Heilbrun, C. (1979). *Reinventing womanhood.* New York: W. W. Norton & Company.

Heilbrun, C. (1988). *Writing a woman's life.* New York: Ballantine.

Heisenberg, W. (1962). *Physics and philosophy.* New York: Harper & Row.

Heller, D. A. (1996). This world of English: Magnetic poetry. *English Journal, 85*(6), 125–126.

Henry, G. (1974). *Teaching reading as concept development: Emphasis on affective thinking.* Newark, DE: International Reading Association.

Henry, G. (1986). What is the nature of English education? *English Education, 18*(1), 4–41.

Herber, H. L. (1970). *Teaching reading in content areas.* (2nd ed.). Upper Saddle River, NJ: Prentice-Hall.

Herndon, J. (1970). *A survey of modern grammars* (2nd ed.). New York: Holt, Rinehart & Winston.

Herter, R. J. (1991). Writing portfolios: Alternative to testing. *English Journal, 80*(1), 90–91.

Herz, S. K., with D. R. Gallo. (1996). *From Hinton to Hamlet: Building bridges between young adult literature and the classics.* Westport, CT: Greenwood Press.

Higgins, J., & Fowinkle, J. (1993). *The Adventures of Huckleberry Finn,* prejudice, and adolescent literature. In J. F. Kaywell, (Ed.), *Adolescent literature as a complement to the classics* (pp. 37–60). Norwood, MA: Christopher-Gordon Publishers.

Hillocks, G., Jr. (1986). *Research on written composition: New directions for teaching.* Urbana, IL: NCTE.

Hillocks, G., Jr. (1987). Synthesis of research on teaching writing. *Educational Leadership, 44*(8), 71–82.

Hillocks, G., Jr. (1995). *Teaching writing as reflective practice.* New York: Teachers College Press.

Hipple, T. (1989). Have you read . . . ? *English Journal, 78*(8), 79.

Hirsch, E. D., Jr. (1987). *Cultural literacy: What every American needs to know.* New York: Vintage Books.

Hitchcock, G. (Ed.). (1969). *Losers weepers: An anthology of found poems.* San Francisco: Kayak.

Hobble-de-hoy! The word game for geniuses. (1984). E. Seymour (Compiler). Salisbury, CT: Lime Rock Press.

Hodges, R. E. (1982). *Improving spelling and vocabulary in the secondary school.* Urbana, IL: NCTE.

Hogarty, K. (1991). Audit them: Biographies, autobiographies, and other nonfiction. *English Journal, 80*(4), 57–60.

Holden, H. (1994). Turning the page: reading in the DEM. Unpublished paper, Western Carolina University.

Holland, N. N. (1975). *Five readers reading.* New Haven: Yale University Press.

Holland, N. N. (1968). *The dynamics of literary response.* New Haven: Yale University Press.

Hollander, J. (1988). Kitty and bug. In *Harp Lake.* New York: Alfred A. Knopf.

Hollman, M. J. (1989). From art to poetry: "Prance as they dance." *English Journal, 78*(3), 24–27.

Holman, C. H. (1980). *A handbook to literature* (4th ed.). Indianapolis, IN: Bobbs-Merrill.

Holt, J. (1967). *How children fail.* New York: Pitman.

Holt, J. (1969). *The under-achieving school.* New York: Pitman.

Hook, J. N. (1975). *History of the English language.* New York: Ronald Press.

Hook, J. N. (1980). *A long way together.* Urbana, IL: NCTE.

Horn, E. L. (1988). Beware Greeks bearing gifts: Sharing a classic with reluctant twelfth graders. *English Journal, 77*(8), 25–26.

Howe, F. (1982). Feminist scholarship: The extent of the revolution. *Change, 14*(3), 12–20.

Hunt, K. (1965). *Grammatical structures written at three grade levels.* Champaign, IL: NCTE.

Hunter, A. (1996a). A new grammar that has clearly improved writing. *English Journal, 85*(7), 102–107.

Hunter, A. (1996b). A new grammar that has clearly improved writing. *English Journal, 84*(7), 102–107.

Hunter, M. (1976). Teacher competency: Problem, theory, and practice. *Theory into Practice, 15*(2), 162–171.

Hunter, M. (1989). Madeline Hunter in the English classroom. *English Journal, 78*(5), 16–18.

Hutchinson, J., & Suhor, C. (1996). The jazz and poetry connection: A performance guide for teachers and students. *English Journal, 85*(5), 80–85.

Inchautsti, R. (1993). *Spitwad sutras: Classroom teaching as sublime vocation.* Westport, CT: Bergin & Garvey.

Isenberg, J. (1994). *Going by the book: The role of popular classroom chronicles in the professional development of teachers.* Westport, CT: Bergin & Garvey.

Iser, W. (1978). *The act of reading: A theory of aesthetic response.* Baltimore: Johns Hopkins University Press.

Iser, W. (1980). The reading process: A phenomenological approach. In J. P. Thompkins (Ed.), *Reader-response criticism: From formalism to post-structuralism* (pp. 50–69). Baltimore: Johns Hopkins University Press.

James, W. (1907, 1981). What pragmatism means. In O. A. Johnson (Ed.), *The individual and the universe: An introduction to philosophy* (pp. 392–399). New York: Holt, Rinehart & Winston.

Jameson, F. (1983). Postmodernism and the consumer society. In H. Foster (Ed.), *The anti-aesthetic.* Port Townsend, WA: Bay Press.

Jay, G. S. (1991). The end of "American" literature: Toward a multicultural practice. *College English, 53*(3), 264–281.

Jensen, E. (1987). *Grading the advanced placement examination in English language and composition.* Princeton, NJ: College Board Advanced Placement Program.

Jody, M., & Saccardi, M. (1996). *Computer conversations and books on-line.* Urbana, IL: NCTE.

Johannessen, L. R., Kahn, E. A., & Walter, C. C. (1982). *Designing and sequencing prewriting activities.* Urbana, IL: NCTE.

John-Steiner, V. (1987). *Notebooks of the mind: Explorations of thinking.* New York: Harper & Row.

Johnson, B. (1980). *The critical difference: Essays in the contemporary rhetoric of reading.* Baltimore: Johns Hopkins University Press.

Johnson, D. M. (1990). *Word weaving: A creative approach to teaching and writing poetry.* Urbana, IL: NCTE.

Johnson, D. (1990, November). *Fostering collaborative learning in the English curriculum.* Presentation at National Council of Teachers of English Convention, Atlanta, GA.

Johnson, D. (1990). *Telling tales: The pedagogy of promise of African-American literature for youth.* Westpoint, CT: Greenwood Press.

Johnson, D. W., & Johnson, R. T. (1985). The internal dynamics of cooperative learning groups. In R. Slavin, S. Sharan, S. Kagan, R. Hertz-Lazarowitzc, C. Webb, & R. Schuck (Eds.), *Learning to cooperate, cooperating to learn* (pp. 103–124). New York: Plenum.

Johnson, J. (1993). The language of teenagers—Slang. *English Journal, 82*(1), 76.

Johnson, L., & O'Neill, C. (1985). *Dorothy Heathcote: Collected writings on education and drama.* London: Hutchinson.

Johnson, N. J. (1997, Apr. 11). Literature circles in secondary classrooms. Presentation at NCTE's Spring Conference, Charlotte, NC.

Johnson, S. (1986). The biography: Teach it from the inside out. *English Journal, 75*(6), 27–29.

Jones, R. L. (1982, December 27). What's wrong with Black English. *Newsweek,* p. 7.

Judy, S., & Judy, S. (1979). English teachers' literary favorites: The results of a survey. *English Journal, 68*(2), 6–9.

Jung, C. G. (1933). Psychology and literature. In W. S. Dell & C. F. Baynes (Trans.), *Modern man in search of a soul* (pp. 152–172). New York: Harcourt, Brace, & Co.

Kahn, E. A. (1984, June). Lecture to the National Humanities Faculty, Summer Institute, Grand Rapids, MI.

Kahn, E. A., Walter, C. C., & Johannessen, L. R. (1984). *Writing about literature.* Urbana, IL: NCTE.

Kearns, E. A. (1997). Words worth 1,000 pictures: Confronting film censorship. *English Journal, 86*(2), 51–54.

Kell, J. (1995). Teaching ideas: Illustrating imagery. *English Journal, 84*(4), 66–67.

Kellner, D. (1988). Reading images critically: Toward a postmodern pedagogy. *Journal of Education, 170*(3), 31–52.

Kelly, P. (1992). Two reader-response classrooms: Using prereading activity and readers theatre approaches. In N. J. Karolides (Ed.), *Reader response in the classroom: Evoking and interpreting meaning in literature* (pp. 84–91). New York: Longman.

Kelly, P. P. (1993). Reading from a female perspective: Pairing *A Doll House* with *permanent connections.* In J. F. Kaywell (Ed.), *Adolescent literature as a complement to the classics* (pp. 127–142). Norwood, MA: Christopher-Gordon Publishers.

Kennedy, X. J. (1966). *An introduction to poetry.* Boston: Little, Brown.

Kennedy, X. J. (1976). *Literature: An introduction to fiction, poetry, and drama.* Boston: Little, Brown, & Co.

Kernan, A. (1990). *The death of literature.* New Haven: Yale University Press.

Kidder, T. (1989). *Among schoolchildren.* Boston: Houghton Mifflin.

Kimball, S., & Grotewold, S. (1989). The round table: Tell me a story. *English Journal, 78*(7), 76.

Kinneavy, J. (1971). *A theory of discourse.* Upper Saddle River, NJ: Prentice-Hall.

Kirby, D., & Liner, T. (1981). *Inside out.* Upper Montclair, NJ: Boynton/Cook.

Kirby, D., Liner, T., & Vinz, R. (1988). *Inside out: Developmental strategies for teaching writing* (2nd ed.). Portsmouth, NH: Heinemann.

Kirby, D., & Kuykendall, C. (1991). *Mind matters: Teaching for thinking.* Portsmouth, NH: Boynton/Cook.

Kirschenbaum, H., Napier, R., & Simon, S. B. (1971). *"Wad-ja-get?": The grading game in American education.* New York: Hart.

Kirszner, L. G., & Mandell, S. R. (1986). *The Holt handbook.* New York: Holt, Rinehart & Winston.

Klem, E., & Moran, C. (1991). Computers and instructional strategies in the teaching of writing. In Hawisher, G., & Selfe, C. (Eds.), *Evolving perspectives on computers and composition studies.* Urbana, IL: NCTE.

Kliebard, H. M. (1970). The Tyler rationale. *School Review, 78*(2), 259-272. In J. R. Gress & D. E. Purpel (Eds.). 1978. *Curriculum: An introduction to the field* (pp. 256-267). Berkeley, CA: McCutchan.

Kneeshaw, D. (1993). Writing portfolios in secondary school. In K. Yancy (Ed.), *Portfolios in the writing classroom.* Urbana, IL: NCTE.

Knowles, L. (1983). *Encouraging talk.* New York: Methuen.

Knowles, M. T. (1996). The English teacher's Internet resource guide. *English Journal, 85*(8), 91-94.

Knowles, M. T. (1997). Software: More Internet resources for the English teacher. *English Journal, 86*(2), 90-93.

Kohl, H. (1967). *36 Children.* New York: New American Library.

Kohl, H. (1973). *Reading: How to.* New York: Dutton.

Kohlberg, L. (1984). *The psychology of moral development: The nature and validity of moral stages.* San Francisco: Harper & Row.

Kolln, M. (1981). Closing the books on alchemy. *College Composition and Communication, 32*(2), 139-151.

Kolodny, A. (1985). The integrity of memory: Creating a new literary history of the United States. *American Literature, 57*(2), 291-307.

Kopp, S. B. (1973). *If you meet the Buddha on the road, kill him! The pilgrimage of psychotherapy patients.* Ben Lomond, CA: Science and Behavior Books.

Korg, J. (1966). *The force of few words: An introduction to poetry.* New York: Holt, Rinehart & Winston.

Krest, M. (1987). Time on my hands: Handling the paper load. *English Journal, 76*(8), 37-42.

Krest, M. (1990). Adapting the portfolio to meet student needs. *English Journal, 79*(2), 29-34.

Kretzschman, W. A., Jr. (1985). English in the middle ages: The struggle for acceptability. In S. Greenbaum (Ed.), *The English language today* (pp. 20-29). Oxford: Pergamon Press.

Krogness, M. M. (1995). *Just teach me, Mrs. K.: Talking, reading, and writing with resistant adolescent learners.* Portsmouth, NH: Heinemann.

Krueger, C. Y. (1988). *Experiences in composition: A comparison of the Foxfire and writing process methods of teaching composition.* Unpublished master's thesis, Wake Forest University, Winston-Salem, NC.

Kutz, E., & Roskelly, H. (1991). *An unquiet pedagogy: Transforming practice in the English classroom.* Portsmouth, NH: Boynton/Cook.

Labov, W. (1973). The logic of nonstandard English. In J. S. DeStepheno (Ed.), *Language, society and education: A profile of Black English* (pp. 10-44). Worthington, OH: Charles A. Jones.

Labov, W. (1981). *The study of non-standard English.* Urbana, IL: NCTE.

Lacks, C. (1997). The teacher's nightmare: Getting fired for good teaching. *English Journal, 86*(2), 29-33.

LaConte, R. (1980). A literary heritage paradigm for secondary English. In B. J. Mandel (Ed.), *Three Language Arts Curriculum Models.* Urbana, IL: NCTE.

LaFontana, V. R. (1996). Throw away that correcting pen. *English Journal, 85*(6), 71-73.

Laird, C. (1953). *The miracle of language.* Cleveland: World.

Lake, P. (1988). Sexual stereotyping and the English curriculum. *English Journal, 77*(6), 35-38.

Lambert, D. (1976). What is a journal? In K. Macrorie (Ed.), *Writing to be read* (2nd ed.). Rochelle Park, NJ: Hayden.

Langer, S. K. (1958). The cultural importance of the arts. In M. F. Andrews (Ed.), *Aesthetic Form and Education.* Syracuse, NY: Syracuse University Press.

Langer, J. A. (1995). *Envisioning literature: Literary understanding and literature instruction.* New York: Teachers College Press.

Langer, J. A., & Applebee, A. N. (1987). *How writing shapes thinking: A study of teaching and learning.* Urbana, IL: NCTE.

Larson, C. R. (1978). *American Indian fiction.* Albuquerque, NM: University of New Mexico Press.

Larson, R. L. (1974). Students' rights to their own language. *College Composition and Communication* [Special issue], *25,* 1-32.

Laughlin, R. (1993). How do you pronounce *greasy? English Journal, 82*(1), 77.

Lawrence, B. (1995). Teaching ideas: New looks at old literature. *English Journal, 84*(3), 80-82.

Lenneberg, E. H. (1967). *Biological foundations of language.* New York: Wiley.

Lerman, L. (1993, Summer). Toward a process for critical response. *Alternate roots.* Regional Organization of Theatres South.

Lester, J. (1969). *Search for the new land: History of subjective experience.* New York: Dial Press.

Levine, L. W. (1996). *The opening of the American mind: Canons, culture, and history.* Boston: Little, Brown, & Co.

Lewis, C. S. (1961). *An experiment in criticism.* Cambridge, UK: Cambridge University Press.

Lewis, L. J. (1984). Developing critical thinking through media study. *English Journal, 73*(1), 52-53.

Ley, T. C. (1995, Nov. 14). Fostering productive collaborative transactions with poetry. Presentation at the First Combined International Reading Association Regional Conference.

Lincoln, K. (1983). *Native American renaissance.* Berkeley, CA: University of California Press.

Lindemann, E. (1982). *A rhetoric for writing.* (2nd ed.). New York: Oxford University Press.

Linkin, H. K. (1991). The current canon in British romantics studies. *College English, 53*(5), 548-570.

Ling, A. (1990). *Between worlds: Women writers of Chinese ancestry.* New York: Pergamon Press.

Loban, W. (1969). *Teaching literature and language.* New York: Harcourt, Brace & World.

Lockward, D. (1994). Poets on teaching poetry. *English Journal, 83*(5), 65-70.

Loevinger, J. (1976). *Ego development: Conceptions and theories.* San Francisco: Jossey-Bass.

Loevinger, J. (1987). *Paradigms of personality.* New York: Freeman.

Lott, J. G. (1989). Not teaching poetry. *English Journal, 78*(4), 66-68.

Luce-Kapler, R. (1994). Never stepping in the same river twice: Teaching and writing in school. Unpublished master's thesis, University of Alberta, Edmonton.

Luce-Kapler, R. (1996). Narrating the portfolio landscape. *English Journal, 85*(1), 46-49.

Lucking, R., & Stallard, C. (1988). *How computers can help you teach English.* Portland: J. Weston Walch.

Lutz, W. (1989). *Doublespeak.* New York: Harper.

Lynch, J. J., & Evans, B. (1963). *High school English textbooks: A critical examination.* Boston: Little, Brown & Co.

Lynn, S. (1990). A passage into critical theory. *College English, 52*(3), 258-271.

Lytle, S. (1982). Exploring comprehension style: A study of twelfth-grade readers. Unpublished dissertation, Stanford University.

MacKail, J. W. (1970). *The approach to Shakespeare.* New York: AMS Press.

Mackey, M. (1993). Lost in a book: The invisible problems of a learning reader. *English Journal, 83*(1), 65-68.

MacNeil, R. (1988). Listening to our language. *English Journal, 77*(6), 16-21.

MacNeil, R. (1989). *Wordstruck: A memoir.* New York: Viking.

Macrorie, K. (1970). *Uptaught.* New York: Hayden.

Macrorie, K. (1984). *Searching writing.* Portsmouth, NH: Boynton/Cook.

Madden, F. (1989). Using computers in the literature class. In C. Selfe, D. Rodrigues, & W. Oates (Eds.), *Computers in English and the language arts* (pp. 227-241). Urbana, IL: NCTE.

Madden, F. (1987, August). Desperately seeking literary response. *Computers and Composition, 4*, 17-34.

Maimon, E. P., Nodine, B. F., & O'Connor, F. W. (1989). *Thinking, reasoning, and writing.* White Plains, NY: Longman.

Marcus, S. (1986). *Analyzing fiction software: Literature and composition data base for PFS: File.* New York: Scholastic.

Marcus, S. (1987). Computers and English: Future tense . . . future perfect. *English Journal, 76*(5), 88-92.

Marcus, S. (1989). Creating writing activities with the word processor. In C. Selfe, D. Rodrigues, & W. Oates (Eds.), *Computers in English and the language arts* (pp. 241-246). Urbana, IL: NCTE.

Marshall, J. (1991, Dec. 5-6). Presentation at Yale New Haven Teachers Institute: Conference on School-College Collaboration, New Haven, CT.

Martin, J. R. (1985). *Reclaiming a conversation: The ideal of the educated woman.* New Haven: Yale University Press.

Martin, N. (1983). So all talk is significant. In *Mostly about writing: Selected essays.* Upper Montclair, NJ: Boynton/Cook.

Mayer, R. (1979). Can advance organizers influence meaningful learning? *Review of Educational Research, 49*(2), 371-383. Reported in J. D. Grambs, & J. C. Carr, 1991. *Modern Methods in Secondary Education* (5th ed.). Fort Worth, TX: Holt, Rinehart & Winston.

Mayer, Sister J. E. (1988). Neighborhoods: Maya Angelou's "Harlem Hopscotch." *English Journal, 77*(5), 86-88.

Mayher, J. S. (1990). *Uncommon sense: Theoretical practice in language education.* Portsmouth, NH: Boynton/Cook.

McAlexander, P., Dobie, A., & Gregg, N. (1992). *Beyond the "SP" Label.* Urbana, IL: NCTE.

McCarthy, D. (1954). Language development in children. In L. Carmichael (Ed.), *Manual of child psychology* (2nd ed., pp. 492-630). New York: Wiley.

McCaslin, N. (1984). *Creative drama in the classroom* (4th ed.). New York: Longman.

McClaskey, J. (1995). Assessing student learning through multiple intelligences. *English Journal, 84*(8), 56-58.

McCleary, W. (1995). Grammar making a comeback in composition teaching. *Composition Chronicle, 8*(6), 1-4.

McClure, M. F. (1990). Collaborative learning: Teacher's game or students' game? *English Journal, 79*(2), 66-68.

McCollum-Clark, K. (1995). National Council of Teachers of English, corporate philanthropy, and National Education Standards: Challenging the ideologies of English education reform. Unpublished dissertation, University of Pennsylvania, Philadelphia.

McGowen, P. (1997, Mar. 7). Another opening, another show: Using reader's theater to enhance composition skills. Presentation at the Annual Conference on Writing and Literature. Lawrence, KS.

McCrum, R. Cran, W., & MacNeil, R. (1986). *The story of English.* New York: Viking.

McDavid, R. I., Jr. (1985). A linguist to the lay audience. In S. Greenbaum (Ed.), *The English language today* (pp. 280-292). Oxford: Pergamon Press.

McEwan, H. (1992). Five metaphors for English. *English Education, 24*(2), 101-128.

McGlynn, P. D. (1969). The chronology of "A Rose for Emily." *Studies in Short Fiction, 6*(4), 461-462.

McGonigal, E. (1988). Correlative thinking: Writing analogies about literature. *English Journal, 71*(1), 66-67.

McGuire, R. L. (1973). *Passionate attention.* New York: Norton.

McKenzie, B. (1978). *Fiction's journey.* New York: Harcourt Brace Jovanovich.

McLuhan, M. (1957, May). Explorations number seven. A broadcast of the Canadian Broadcasting Corporation.

McLuhan, M. (1964). *Understanding media.* New York: Signet.

McNees, C. (1977). Can one teach each student at his own level? In R. B. Shuman (Ed.), *Questions English teachers ask.* Rochelle Park, NJ: Hayden.

Meiers, M. (1990, Aug.). *Assessing development in English.* Presentation at International Federation of Teachers of English Conference, Auckland, NZ.

Megyer, K. (1996). Reading aloud student writing. *English Journal, 85*(3), 75-76.

Mellon, J. C. (1969). *Transformational sentence combining: A method of enhancing the development of syntactic fluency in English compositions* (NCTE Research Report No. 10). Urbana, IL: NCTE.

Mellon, J. (1975). *National assessment of the teaching of English.* Urbana, IL: NCTE.

Mellown, E. (1986). The use of computers in literary studies: An experimental course. *The Computer Assisted Composition Journal, 1*(1), 55–61.

Meyer, M. (1990). *The Bedford introduction to literature.* (2nd ed.). Boston: St. Martin's Press.

Meyer, J., Youga, J., & Flint-Ferguson, J. (1990). Grammar in context: Why and how. *English Journal, 79*(1), 66–70.

Meyers, G. D. (1993). Three functions of language. *English Journal, 82*(1), 75.

Meyers, J. B. (1993). Where do words come from? *English Journal, 82*(1), 76.

Michael, I., & Swaim, M. (1980). Theoretical bases of communicative approaches to second language teaching and testing. *Applied Linguistics, 1,* 1–47.

Milgram, S., & Shotland, R. L. (1973). *Television and antisocial behavior: Field experiments.* New York: Academic Press.

Mill, J. S. (1989). *On liberty and other writings.* Cambridge, England: Cambridge University Press.

Miller, S. (1991). Planning for spontaneity: Supporting the language of thinking. *English Journal, 80*(3), 51–56.

Milner, J. O. (1975). Ken Kesey's classroom corrective. *English Journal, 64*(7), 34–37.

Milner, J. O. (1976). Right-Left writer: Composition's march to a developmental drummer. *Arizona English Bulletin, 20*(2): 58–62.

Milner, J. O. (1991). Suppositional style and teacher evaluation. *Phi Delta Kappan, 72*(6), 464–467.

Milner, J. O. (1997). Using a flat structure in a hierarchical world. *The Clearing House, 70*(3), 129–135.

Milner, J. O., & Elrod, M. M. (1986). Language reception in three modes. *The Journal of Genetic Psychology, 147*(1), 123–133.

Milner, J. O., & Milner, L. M. (Eds.). (1989). *Passages to literature: Essays on teaching in Australia, Canada, England, the United States, and Wales.* Urbana, IL: NCTE.

Milner, J., & Milner, L. M. (1993). *Bridging English.* Upper Saddle River, NJ: Macmillan/Prentice-Hall.

Milner, J. O., & Richman, C. (1983). *Impulsivity and revision skills.* Presentation at National Council of Teachers of English, Columbus, OH.

Milner, L. F. M. (1986). *A study of the impact of instruction in theories of literary criticism on gifted secondary students.* Unpublished master's thesis, Wake Forest University, Winston-Salem, NC.

Mini Digest of Education Statistics. (1997). Washington, D.C.: National Center for Educational Statistics. Department of Education, OERI. NCES97-541.

Mitchell, D. (1994). Teaching ideas: Putting poetry in its place. *English Journal, 83*(5), 78–80.

Mitchell, D. (1995). Teaching ideas: Bringing literary terms to life. *English Journal, 84*(4), 64–68.

Mitchell, D. (1996). Writing to learn across the curriculum and the English teacher. *English Journal, 85*(5), 93–95.

Mitchell, D. (1997). Teaching ideas: Creating thematic units. *English Journal 86*(5), 80–84.

Moffett, J. (1968). *Teaching the universe of discourse.* Boston: Houghton Mifflin.

Moffett, J. (1981). *Active voice: A program of writing assignments.* Upper Montclair, NJ: Boynton/Cook.

Moffett, J. (1992). *Active voice: A writing program across the curriculum* (2nd ed.). Portsmouth, NH: Boynton/Cook.

Moffett, J., & Wagner, B. J. (1976). *Student-centered language arts and reading, K–13: A handbook for teachers* (2nd ed.). Boston: Houghton Mifflin.

Moffett, J., & Wagner, B. J. (1992). *Student-centered language arts, K–12.* (4th ed.). Portsmouth, NH: Boynton/Cook & Heinemann.

Momaday, N. S. (1966). *House made of dawn.* New York: New American Library.

Mondock, S. (1997). Portfolios—The story behind the story. *English Journal, 86*(1), 59–64.

Monroe, R. (1993). *Writing and thinking with computers.* Urbana, IL: NCTE.

Montgomery, M. (1962). Robert Frost and his use of barriers: Man vs. nature toward God. In J. M. Cox (Ed.), *Robert Frost: A collection of critical essays* (pp. 138–150). Upper Saddle River, NJ: Prentice-Hall.

Moore, L. (1989). One-on-one: Pairing male and female writers. *English Journal, 78*(6), 34–38.

Morine-Dershimer, G. G. (1990). Instructional planning. In J. M. Cooper (Ed.), *Classroom teaching skills* (pp. 18–49). Lexington, MA: Heath.

Morris, B. S. (1989). The television generation: Couch potatoes or informed critics? *English Journal, 78*(8), 35–41.

Morrison, T. (1992). *Playing in the dark: Whiteness and the literary imagination.* Cambridge: Harvard University Press.

Morrow, L. (1997). *Literacy development.* Boston, MA: Allyn & Bacon.

Morse, D. (1972). *Grandfather rock.* New York: Dellacorte Press.

Moyers, B. (1997, Nov. 19). Religion in American life: Reflections from a long-time observer. Speech at Wake Forest University, Winston-Salem, NC.

Muinzer, L. A. (1960, Nov.). Historical linguistics in the classroom. *Illinois English Bulletin, 48*(2).

Muir, K. (1984). The wrong way and the right. *Shakespeare Quarterly* [Special issue], 642–643.

Mura, D. (1988). Strangers in the village. In R. Simonson & S. Walker (Eds.), *The Graywolf annual five: Multicultural literacy* (pp. 135–153). St. Paul, MN: Graywolf Press.

Murphy, G. (1968). *The study of literature in high school.* Waltham, MA: Blaisdell.

Murphy, S., & Smith, M. A. (1990). Talking about portfolios. *The Quarterly 12*(2), 1–3, 24–27.

Murphy, S., & Smith, M. A. (1992). Looking into portfolios. *Portfolios in the writing classroom.* Urbana, IL: NCTE.

Murray, D. M. (1977). Our students will write—If we let them. *North Carolina English Teacher, 30*(1), 1–5.

Murray, D. M. (1980). Writing as process: How writing finds its own meaning. In T. R. Donovan & B. W. McClelland (Eds.), *Eight approaches to teaching composition* (pp. 3–20). Urbana, IL: NCTE.

Murray, D. M. (1982). *Learning by teaching: Selected articles on writing and teaching.* Upper Montclair, NJ: Boynton/Cook.

Murray, D. M. (1985). *A writer teaches writing* (2nd ed.). Boston: Houghton Mifflin.

Myers, K. L. (1988). Twenty (better) questions. *English Journal, 77*(1), 64-65.

Myers, M. (1980). *A procedure for writing assessment and holistic scoring.* Urbana, IL: NCTE.

Myers, M. (1991, Oct.). *How to measure the mind.* A presentation at the Southeastern Regional National Council of Teachers of English Conference, Asheville, NC.

Nagy, W. E. (1988). *Teaching vocabulary to improve reading comprehension.* Urbana, IL: NCTE.

Nash, R. J., & Shiman, D. A. (1974). The English teacher as questioner. *English Journal, 63*(9), 38-44.

Nathanson, S. (1992). Guidelines for using videotape: A checklist for educators. *English Journal, 81*(3), 88-89.

National Board for Professional Teaching Standards. (1994). *What teachers should know and be able to do.* Washington, D.C.

National Council of Teachers of English and International Reading Association. (1996). *Standards for the English language arts.* Urbana, IL and Newark, DE: NCTE and IRA.

Neenan, J. (1989). Idea exchange: Journal entries. *North Carolina English Teacher, 47*(1), 7-8, 12.

Nelms, B. F. (Ed.). (1988). *Literature in the classroom: Readers, texts, and contexts.* Urbana, IL: NCTE.

Nelms, B. F. (1992). Cases: English teachers at work. *English Journal 83*(3), 43.

Nelms, B. F., & Nelms, E. D. (Eds.). (1989). Books for teachers: A new magazine for gifted students—and for their teachers. *English Journal, 78*(2), 91-92.

Nelms, B. F. (1989). EJ survey: What works (ten years later). *English Journal, 78*(5), 81-83.

Nelms, E. D. (1988). Two laureates in April: Lyrics of Wordsworth and Ted Hughes. *English Journal, 77*(4), 23-26.

Nelms, E. D. (Ed.). (1990). Instructional materials: Classroom magazines: A timely alternative to textbooks. *English Journal, 79*(3), 77-78.

Nelms, E. D. (Ed.). (1993). The round table: Mini-lessons on language. *English Journal, 82*(1), 75-77.

Nelson, G. L. (1991). Bringing language back to life: Responding to the new illiteracy. *English Journal, 80*(2), 16-20.

Newkirk, T. (Ed.). (1990). *To compose: Teaching writing in high school and college* (2nd ed.). Portsmouth, NH: Heinemann.

Newlin, L. F. (1984). Shakespeare saved from drowning. *Shakespeare Quarterly* [Special issue], 596-601.

Newmann, F., & Wehlage, G. (1995). *Successful school restructuring.* Madison, WI: Center on Organization and Restructuring of Schools.

Noguchi, R. (1991). *Grammar and the teaching of writing.* Urbana, IL: NCTE.

Noll, E. (1994). The ripple effect of censorship: Silencing in the classroom. *English Journal, 83*(8), 59-64.

Norris, K. (1996). *The Cloister Walk.* New York: The Berkley Publishing Group.

Noskin, D. (1994). The round table: "Can we talk?" *English Journal, 83*(3), 87.

Novello, D. (1977). *The Lazlo letters: The amazing, real-life actual correspondence of Lazlo Toth, American.* New York: Workman.

Nystrand, M., & Gamoran, A. (1991). Instructional discourse, student engagement, and literature achievement. *Research in the Teaching of English, 25*(3), 261-290.

O'Brian, E. J. (1984). Inside Shakespeare: Using performance techniques to achieve traditional goals. *Shakespeare Quarterly* [Special issue], 621-631.

O'Fallon, K. (1977). Varieties of voice: A proposal for dealing with dialect differences in the composition classroom. *Kansas Association of Teachers of English,* 8-15.

O'Hare, F. (1973). *Sentence combining: Improving student writing without formal grammar instruction* (NCTE Research Report No. 15). Urbana, IL: NCTE.

O'Hare, F. (1975). *Sentencecraft.* Lexington, MA: Ginn.

O'Keefe, & Nadel. (1990). Four mat in action. Barrington, IL: Excel.

Oliver, D. W., & Bane, M. J. (1971). Moral education: Is reasoning enough? In C. M. Beck, B. S. Crittenden, & E. V. Sullivan (Eds.), *Moral education: Interdisciplinary approaches.* New York: Newman.

O'Neill, C., & Lambert, A. (1982). *Drama structures: A practical handbook for teachers.* London: Stanley Thornes Publishers Ltd.

Olsen, T. (1978). *Silences.* New York: Delacorte Press.

Orlich, D. C., Harder, R. J., Callahan, R. C., Kauchak, D. P., Pendergrass, R. A., Keogh, A. J., & Gibson, H. (1990). *Teaching strategies: A guide to better instruction.* Lexington: D. C. Heath & Co.

Ornstein, R. (1972). *The psychology of consciousness.* San Francisco: Freeman.

Our readers write. (1987). What's a new and interesting way to test students? *English Journal, 76*(1), 71-76.

Our readers write. (1984). What's an especially good nonfiction book for young readers? *English Journal, 73*(7), 87-88.

Owen, F. (1991). Teaching as a composing process. *English Journal, 80*(3), 57-62.

Packard, V. (1957). *The hidden persuaders.* New York: D. McKay Co.

Palincsar, A. S., & Brown, A. (1984). Reciprocal teaching of comprehension fostering and comprehension monitoring activities. *Cognition and Instruction, 1*(2), 117-125.

Palmer, B. (1990, September). Paper presented at the North Carolina English Teachers' Association Meeting, Wilmington, NC.

Parker, R. P., & Goodkin, V. (1987). *The consequences of writing: Enhancing learning in the disciplines.* Upper Montclair, NJ: Boynton/Cook.

Paz, O. (1956). *The bow and the lyre.* Trans. R. L. C. Simms. Austin: University of Texas Press.

Pearson, M. (1997, June 30). Critical Response Process. Presentation at the North Carolina Governor's School West. Winston-Salem, NC.

Pennac, D. (1994). *Better than life.* Toronto: Coach House Press.

People for the American Way. (1995). *Attacks on the freedom to learn, 1994-1995 Report.*

Perera, C. (1990). *Divergence and convergence in English: A creative tension?* Paper presented at the International Federation of Teachers of English 5th International Congress, Auckland, NZ. August 26.

Perkins, D. (1995). *Outsmarting IQ: The emerging science of learned intelligence.* New York: New York Free Press.

Perrin, R. (1991). When junk mail isn't junk. *English Journal, 80*(1), 30-32.

Perrin, R. (1994). The round table: Whose questions? *English Journal, 83*(3), 89.

Perrine, L. (1978). *Story and structure* (5th ed.). New York: Harcourt Brace Jovanovich.

Perrine, L. (1983). *Literature: Structure, sound, and sense* (4th ed.). San Diego: Harcourt Brace Jovanovich.

Peters, R. L., & Hitchcock, G. (Eds.). (1967). *Pioneers of modern poetry.* San Francisco: Kayak.

Peterson, B. (1987). Why they talk that talk: Language in Appalachian studies. *English Journal, 76*(6), 53–55.

Petruzzella, B. A. (1996). Grammar instruction: What teachers say. *English Journal, 85*(7), 68–72.

Phillips, L. (1989). First impressions: Introducing Monet to Megadeth. *English Journal, 78*(3), 31–33.

Pichaske, D. R. (Ed.). (1972). *Beowulf to Beatles: Approaches to poetry.* New York: Free Press.

Pope, C. (1998, Jan. 21) Connecting students by e-mail. *Technology and Teaching Video Conference.* University of North Carolina General Administration.

Pope, C., & Kutiper, K. L. (Eds.). Instructional materials: Using magazines in the English classroom. *English Journal, 77*(8), 66–68.

Popham, W. J. (1997). The standards movement and the emperor's new clothes. *NAASP Bulletin, 81*(590): 21–25.

Porter, C., & Cleland, J. (1995). *The portfolio as a learning strategy.* Portsmouth, NH: Boynton/Cook.

Portfolio News. (1990). Encinitas, CA: Portfolio Assessment Clearing House. *1*(2).

Postal, P. (1968). Linguistic novelty and the problem of grammar. In R. Jacobs & P. Rosenbaum (Eds.), *English transformational grammar* (pp. 267–289). Boston: Blaisdell.

Postman, N. (1995). *The end of education: Redefining the value of school.* New York: Vintage Books.

Postman, N., & Weingartner, C. (1966). *Linguistics: A revolution in teaching.* New York: Dell.

Postman, N., & Weingartner, C. (1969). *Teaching as a subversive activity.* New York: Dell.

Postman, N. (1979a). *Schools should give children what the media don't.* Times Washington Post News Service.

Postman, N. (1979b). *Teaching as a conserving activity.* New York: Delacorte.

Postman, N. (1985). *Amusing ourselves to death.* New York: Viking.

Pound, E. (1954). A few don'ts. In T. S. Eliot (Ed.). *Literary essays of Ezra Pound* (pp. 3–4). London: Faber & Faber.

Probst, R. E. (1984). *Adolescent literature: Response and analysis.* New York: Merrill/Prentice-Hall.

Probst, R. (1986a). Three relationships in the teaching of literature. *English Journal, 75*(1), 60–68.

Probst, R. (1986b). Mom, Wolfgang and me: Adolescent literature, critical theory and the English classroom. *English Journal, 75*(6), 33–39.

Probst, R. (1988a). *Response and analysis: Teaching literature in junior and senior high school.* Portsmouth, NH: Boynton/Cook.

Probst, R. (1988b). Dialogue with a text. *English Journal, 77*(1), 32–38.

Progoff, I. (1975). *At a journal workshop.* New York: Dialogue House Library.

Protherough, R. (1983). *Developing response to fiction.* Milton Keynes, England: Open University Press.

Prown, J. D. (1982). Mind in matter: An introduction to material culture theory and method. *Winterthur Portfolio, 17*(1), 1–19.

Purcell-Gates, V. (1991). On the outside looking in: A study of remedial-readers' meaning-making while reading literature. *Journal of Reading Behavior, 23*(2), 235–254.

Purpel, D. E. (1989). *The moral and spiritual crisis in education: A curriculum for justice and compassion in education.* Granby, MA: Bergin & Garvey.

Purves, A. (1971). Evaluation of learning in literature. In B. Bloom, J. T. Hastings, & G. F. Madaus (Eds.), *Handbook on formative and summative evaluation of student learning* (pp. 697–766). New York: McGraw-Hill.

Purves, A. (1981). *Reading and literature: American achievement in international perspective.* Urbana, IL: NCTE.

Purves, A. (1986). Commentary on George Henry's "What is the nature of English education?" *English Education, 18*(1), 42–45.

Purves, A., Foshay, A. W., & Hanson, G. (1973). *Literature education in ten countries.* New York: Wiley.

Purves, A., Jordan, S., & Peltz, J. (1996). *Using portfolios in the English classroom.* Norwood, MA: Christopher-Gordon Publishers.

Purves, A., & Monson, D. (1972). *Experiencing children's literature.* Glenview, IL: Scott Foresman.

Purves, A., Quattrini, J., & Sullivan, C. (1995). *Creating the writing portfolio.* Lincolnwood, IL: NTC Publishing Group.

Purves, A., Rogers, T., & Soter, A. O. (1990). *How porcupines make love II: Teaching a response-centered literature curriculum.* New York: Longman.

Pyles, T., & Algeo, J. (1978). *English: An introduction to the language.* New York: Harcourt Brace Jovanovich.

Rabinowitz, P. J. (1987). *Before reading: Narrative conventions and the politics of interpretation.* Ithaca, NY: Cornell University Press.

Radway, J. (1984). *Reading the romance: Women, patriarchy, and popular literature.* Chapel Hill: The University of North Carolina Press.

Raines, P. A. (1996). Writing portfolios: Turning the house into a home. *English Journal, 85*(1), 41–45.

Rakow, S. R. (1991). Young-adult literature for honors students? *English Journal, 80*(1), 48–51.

Randolph, R., Robbins, S., Gere, A. (1994). Writing across institutional boundaries: A K–12 and university collaboration. *English Journal, 83*(3), 68–74.

Raths, J. (1991, May). Lecture to the North Carolina model clinical teaching network. Durham, NC.

Ravitch, D., & Finn, C. (1987). *What do our 17-year-olds know? A report on the first national assessment of history and literature.* New York: Harper & Row.

Ray, J. K. (1985). The ethics of feminism in the literature classroom: A delicate balance. *English Journal, 74*(3), 54–59.

Reed, D. W. (1986). *Children's creative spelling.* London: Routledge & Kegan Paul.

Regina, T. E. (1988). Composing skills and television. *English Journal, 77*(7), 50–52.

Reid, L. (1994). A symposium: Cultivating student expertise. *English Journal, 83*(3), 59.

Reising, R. W., & Wolfe, D. (1983). *Writing for learning.* Portland: J. Weston Walch.

Renwick, M. K. (1994). Real research into the real problems of grammar and usage instruction. *English Journal, 83*(6), 29–32.

Resnick, L. B. (Ed.). (1976). *The nature of intelligence.* Hillsdale, NJ: Lawrence Erlbaum.

Resnick, L. B., & Glaser, R. (1976). Problem solving and intelligence. In L. B. Resnick (Ed.), *The nature of intelligence* (pp. 205-230). Hillsdale, NJ: Lawrence Erlbaum.

Richards, I. A. (1938). *Interpretation in teaching.* New York: Harcourt, Brace.

Rico, G. L. (1983). *Writing the natural way: Using right-brain techniques to release your expressive powers.* Los Angeles: J. P. Tarcher.

Roberts, P. (1956). *Patterns of English.* New York: Harper & Row.

Robbins, S., Brandt, N., Goering, S., Nassif, J., & Wascha, K. (1994). Using portfolio reflections to reform instructional programs and build curriculum. *English Journal, 83*(7), 71-78.

Robinson, M. (1988). Idea exchange: Another *Heart of Darkness, North Carolina English Teacher, 46*(1), 20.

Rogers, C. (1957). The necessary and sufficient conditions of therapeutic personality change. *Journal of Consulting Psychology, 21,* 95-103.

Rogers, C. (1961). *On becoming a person.* Boston: Houghton Mifflin.

Rogers, M. L. (1990). Idea exchange: Writing half a note. *North Carolina English Teacher, 48*(1), 12-14.

Romand, E. (1992). Dream teaching. *English Journal, 80*(4), 96.

Romano, T. (1987). *Clearing the way: Working with teenage writers.* Portsmouth, NH: Heinemann.

Romano, T. (1995). *Writing with passion: life stories, multiple genres.* Portsmouth, NH: Boynton/Cook Heinemann.

Rose, M. (1984). *Writer's block: The cognitive dimension.* Carbondale, IL: Southern Illinois Press.

Rose, M. (1989). *Lives on the boundary: A moving account of the struggles and achievements of America's educationally underprepared.* New York: Penguin.

Rose, P. (1984, March 22). Heroic fantasies, nervous doubts. *New York Times.*

Roseboro, A. J. S. (1994). Student choice/Teacher control: *Braided Lives* in the classroom. *English Journal, 83*(2), 14-18.

Rosenblatt, L. M. (1985). Language, literature, and values. In S. N. Tchudi (Ed.), *Language, schooling and society.* Upper Montclair, NJ: Boynton/Cook.

Rosenblatt, L. M. (1995). *Literature as exploration* (5th ed.). New York: Noble & Noble.

Rosenblatt, L. (1978). *The reader, the text, the poem: The transactional theory of the literary work.* Carbondale, IL: Southern Illinois University Press.

Roszak, T. (1969). *The making of a counter culture: Reflections on a technocratic society and its youthful opposition.* Garden City, NY: Doubleday.

Rothschild, B. (1986, January 8). Kids learn to write well if they don't fear errors. *USA Today.*

Rothwell, D. (1992). Periodic phases of group development. In *In mixed company: Small-group communication* (pp. 55-79). New York: Harcourt Brace Jovanovich.

Roundtable. (1989). Involving students in evaluation. *English Journal, 78*(7), 75-77.

Rouse, J. (1989). In the temple art. *English Journal, 78*(7), 87-88.

Rowe, M. B. (1974). Wait-time and rewards as instructional variables—their influences on language, logic, and fate control: Part one—wait time. *Journal of Research in Science Teaching, 11*(2), 81-94.

Rudd, R. (1990). Idea submitted to Idea Exchange at NCTE Annual Convention, Atlanta, GA.

Ruggiero, V. R. (1988). *Teaching thinking across the curriculum.* New York: Harper & Row.

Russ, J. (1983). *How to suppress women's writing.* Austin, TX: University of Texas Press.

Ruthven, K. K. (1979). *Critical assumptions.* Cambridge, England: Cambridge University Press.

Salomon, G., & Leigh, T. (1984). Predispositions about learning from print and television. *Journal of Communication, 34*(2), 119-135.

Samuels, B. G. (1993). The beast within: Using and abusing power in *Lord of the Flies, The Chocolate War,* and other readings. In J. F. Kaywell (Ed.), *Adolescent literature as a complement to the classics* (pp. 195-214). Norwood, MA: Christopher-Gordon Publishers.

Sanborn, J. (1986). Grammar: Good wine before its time. *English Journal, 75*(3), 72-80.

Sanders, T. E., & Peek, W. W. (1973). *Literature of the American Indian.* Beverly Hills, CA: Glencoe.

Sato, K. (1995). Resources and reviews: Engaging students in poetry. *English Journal, 84*(7), 89-91.

Schaars, M. J. (1992). Hill-climbing with Thoreau: Creating meaningful carryover. In N. J. Karolides (Ed.), *Reader response in the classroom: Evoking and interpreting meaning in literature* (pp. 144-154). New York: Longman.

Schaffer, J. C. (1989). Improving questions: Is anyone out there listening? *English Journal, 78*(4), 40-42.

Scheffler, I. (1967). *Science and subjectivity.* New York: Bobbs-Merrill.

Schneider, D. (1994). The round table: Journaling—a revolution. *English Journal, 83*(3), 88.

Scholes, R. (1985). *Textual power: Literary theory and the teaching of English.* New Haven, CT: Yale University Press.

Scholes, R., Comley, N. R., & Ulmer, G. L. (1988). *Textbook: An introduction to literary language.* New York: St. Martin's Press.

Schorer, M. (1948). Technique as discovery. *The Hudson Review 1*(1), 67-87.

Schroeder, F. E. H. (1966). How to teach a research theme in four not-so-easy lessons. *English Journal, 55*(7), 898-902.

Schwartz, E., & Vockell, E. (1988). *The computer in the English curriculum.* Santa Cruz, CA: Mitchell.

Schwartz, H. (1989). Creating writing activities with the word processor. In C. Selfe, D. Rodriques, & W. Oakes (Eds.), *Computers in English and the language arts* (pp. 197-204). Urbana, IL: NCTE.

Schwartz, J. (1991). Let them assess their own learning. *English Journal, 80*(2), 67-73.

Scott, F. N. (1913). Our problems. *English Journal, 2*(1), 1-10.

Sears, C. (1987). Mood poem. *North Carolina English Teacher, 45*(1), 15-16.

Segel, E. (1986). As the twig is bent . . . : Gender and childhood reading. In E. A. Flynn & P. P. Schweickart (Eds.), *Gender and reading: Essays on readers, texts, and contexts* (pp. 165-186). Baltimore: Johns Hopkins University Press.

Seidman, E. I. (1991). *Interviewing as qualitative research.* New York: Teachers College Press.

Selden, R., & Widdowson, P. (1993). *A reader's guide to contemporary literary theory,* (3rd ed.). Lexington: The University Press of Kentucky.

Shamel, M. T. (1988). Using forms to discover poetry. *North Carolina English Teacher, 20*(2), 1–3.

Shange, N. (1972). *Nappy edges.* New York: St. Martin's Press.

Shange, N. (1978). *Nappy edges: (love's a lil rough/sometimes).* New York: St. Martin's Press.

Shaw, E. (1991). Letters from Vietnam: A film/book combination for a nonfiction course. *English Journal, 80*(1), 25.

Sherwin, J. (1969). *Four problems in teaching English: A critique of research.* Scranton, PA: International Textbook.

Shor, I. (1972). Questions Marxists ask about literature. *College English, 34*(2), 178–179.

Shor, I. (1987). *Critical teaching and everyday life.* Chicago: University of Chicago Press.

Showalter, E. (1971). Women writers and the double standard. In V. Gornick and B. K. Moran (Eds.), *Woman in sexist society: Studies in power and powerlessness.*

Shuman, R. B. (1985). English language in the secondary school. In S. Greenbaum (Ed.), *The English language today* (pp. 315–326). Oxford: Pergamon Press.

Shuman, R. B., & Wolfe, D. (1990). *Teaching English through the arts.* Urbana, IL: NCTE.

Shuy, R. (1982, November 21). *Language and success: Who are the judges?* Paper presented at National Council of Teachers of English Conference, Washington, DC.

Silko, L. M., & Wright, J. (1986). *The delicacy and strength of lace.* Ed. Anne Wright. St. Paul, MN: Graywolf Press.

Sizer, T. R. (1984). *Horace's compromise: The dilemma of the American high school.* Boston: Houghton Mifflin.

Skretta, J. A. (1996). Why debates about teaching grammar and usage 'tweek' me out. *English Journal, 85*(7), 64–67.

Skinner, B. F. (1957). *Verbal behavior.* New York: Appleton, Century, Crofts.

Sledd, J. (1996). Grammar for social awareness in a time of class warfare. *English Journal, 85*(7), 59–63.

Slifkin, J. M. (1997). New teachers: Mixing memory and desire: Some reflections on student teaching and teacher education. *English Journal, 86*(2), 87–89.

Smagorinsky, P. (1991). *Expressions: Multiple intelligences in the English class.* Urbana, IL: NCTE.

Smagorinsky, P., & Fly, P. K. (1994). A new perspective on why small groups do and don't work. *English Journal, 83*(3), 54–58.

Small, R. C. (1972). Teaching the junior novel. *English Journal, 61*(2), 222–229.

Small, R. C. (1977, Winter). The adolescent novel as a working model. *ALAN Newsletter,* p. 4.

Small, R. C. (1992). The literary value of the young adult novel. *Journal of Youth Services in Libraries.* Spring, 227–285.

Smede, S. D. (1995). Flyfishing, portfolios, and authentic writing. *English Journal, 84*(2), 92–94.

Smitherman, G. (1989, Apr. 8). *A three part language program.* National Council of Teachers of English Regional Conference, Charleston, SC.

Smitherman, G. (1990, Apr. 4). Diversity and pluralism in language. Speech delivered at Wake Forest University, Winston-Salem, NC.

Sontag, S. (1967). *Against interpretation.* New York: Dell.

Sorenson, M. (1989). Television: Developing the critical viewer and writer. *English Journal, 78*(8), 42–46.

Spencer, P. (1989). YA novels in the AP classroom: Crutcher meets Camus. *English Journal, 78*(7), 44–46.

Spolin, V. (1967). *Improvisation for the theater.* Evanston, IL: Northwestern University Press.

Squire, J. R. (Ed.). (1968). *Response to literature.* Champaign, IL: NCTE.

Squire, J. R., & Applebee, R. K. (1968). *High school English instruction today.* New York, NY: Appleton-Century Crofts.

Stallman, R. W. (1976). Stephen Crane: a reevaluation. In Bradley, S., Beatty, R., Long, E., & Pizer, D. (Eds.), *The Red Badge of Courage: An authoritative text.* New York: W. W. Norton.

Steinberg, A. (1997). Making school work more like real work. *The Harvard Education Letter, 13*(2). Rutledge, NY.

Stensland, A. L. (1979). *Literature by and about the American Indian: An annotated bibliography* (2nd ed.). Urbana, IL: NCTE.

Stern, D. N. (1977). *The first relationship: Infant and mother.* Cambridge, MA: Harvard University Press.

Sternberg, R. (1997). Technology changes intelligence. *Technos, 16*(2), 12–14.

Stevenson, J. W. (1972). The illusion of research. *English Journal, 61*(7), 1029–1032.

Stewart, W. A. (1964). *Non-standard speech and the teaching of English.* Washington, DC: Center for Applied Linguistics.

Stotsky, S. (1994). Academic guidelines for selecting multiethnic and multicultural literature. *English Journal, 83*(2), 27–34.

Strauss, P. (1993). *Talking poetry: A guide for students, teachers and poets.* Pietermaritzburg, South Africa: University of Natal Press.

Strong, W. (1973). *Sentence combining: A composing book.* New York: Random House.

Strong, W. (1976). Sentence combining: Back to the basics—and beyond. *English Journal, 65*(2), 56, 60–64.

Strong, W. (1981). *Sentence combining and paragraph building.* New York: Random House.

Strong, W. (1986). *Creative approaches to sentence combining.* Urbana, IL: ERIC Clearinghouse on Reading and Communication Skills and National Council of Teachers of English.

Stubbs, B. (1995). Specific strategy instruction to enhance revising and editing skills for the learning disabled. Unpublished master's thesis, Rowan College of New Jersey.

Styan, J. L. (1965). *The dramatic experience.* London: Cambridge University Press.

Styan, J. L. (1980). Teaching through performance: An interview with J. L. Styan. Conducted by Derek Peat. *Shakespeare Quarterly, 31*(2), 142–152.

Suhor, D. (1997). Censorship—When things get hazy. *English Journal, 86*(2), 26–28.

Suhor, C. (1994). National standards in English: What are they? Where does NCTE stand? *English Journal, 83*(8), 25–27.

Suhor, C., & Suhor, B. (1992). *Teaching values in the literature classroom: A debate in print.* Bloomington, IN: NCTE/ERIC.

Summerfield, G. (1982). Literature teaching and some of our responsibilities. In D. Mallick, P. Moss, & I. Hansen (Eds.), *New essays in the teaching of literature.* Norwood, Australia: Australian Association for the Teaching of English.

Swander, H. (1984). In our time: Such audiences we wish him. *Shakespeare Quarterly* [Special issue], 528–540.

Swartz, S. H. (1989). Setting up sense centers. In F. A. Kaufmann (Ed.), *Ideas plus: A collection of practical teaching ideas, book seven* (pp. 32–33). Urbana, IL: NCTE.

Swartz, L. (1988). *Dramathemes: A practical guide for teaching drama.* Marham, Ontario: Pembroke.

Tabbert, R. (1984). Raising the question "Why teach grammar?" *English Journal, 73*(8), 38–42.

Tannen, D. (1984). *Conversational style: Analyzing talk among friends.* Norwood, NJ: Ablex.

Tannen, D. (1990). *You just don't understand: Women and men in conversation.* New York: Ballantine.

Taylor, P. (1970). *How teachers plan their courses.* Slough, England: National Foundation for Education Research in England and Wales.

Taylor, T. E. (1965). Let's get rid of research papers. *English Journal, 54*(2), 126–127.

Tchudi, S., & Mitchell, D. (1989). *Explorations in the teaching of English.* New York: Harper and Row.

Tchudi, S. N., & Tchudi, S. J. (1991). *The English/language arts handbook.* Portsmouth, NH: Boynton/Cook & Heinemann.

Teasley, A., & Wilder, A. (1996, Oct.). 100 great films for adolescents. NCETA Conference, Winston-Salem, NC.

Teasley, A., & Wilder, A. (1997). *Reel conversations: Reading film with young adults.* Portsmouth, NH: Heinemann.

Temple, C., Burris, N., Nathan, R., & Temple, F. (1988). *The beginnings of writing.* Boston: Allyn & Bacon.

Thiesmeyer, E. C., & Thiesmeyer, J. E. (1990). *Editor.* New York: Modern Language Association.

Thoman, E. (1998). Media literacy: A guided tour of selected resources for teaching. *English Journal, 87*(1), 34–37.

Thomas, O. (1965). *Transformational grammar and the teacher of English.* New York: Holt, Rinehart & Winston.

Thompson, N. S. (1988). Media and mind: Imaging as an active process. *English Journal, 77*(7), 47–49.

Tierney, R. (1990, July). *Writing to learn in science.* Lecture at Wake Forest University, Winston-Salem, NC.

Timpson, W. M., & Tobin, D. N. (1982). *Teaching as performing.* Upper Saddle River, NJ: Prentice-Hall.

Tobin, K. (1987). The role of wait time in higher cognitive level learning. *Reviews of Educational Research, 57*(1), 51–67.

Tompkins, G. E. (1990). *Teaching writing: Balancing process and product.* New York: Merrill/Prentice-Hall.

Tompkins, G. (1996). *Literacy for the twenty-first century.* Upper Saddle River, NJ: Prentice-Hall.

Tompkins, J. (Ed.). (1980). *Reader-response criticism: From formalism to post-structuralism.* Baltimore: Johns Hopkins University Press.

Tompkins, J. (1985). *Sensational designs: The cultural work of American fiction, 1790–1860.* New York: Oxford Press.

Trimbur, J. (1985). Collaborative learning and teaching writing. In B. W. McClelland & T. R. Donovan (Eds.), *Perspectives on research and scholarship in composition* (pp. 87–109). New York: MLA.

Tsujimoto, J. I. (1988). *Teaching poetry writing to adolescents.* Urbana, IL: NCTE.

Turner, D. T., & Stanford, B. D. (1971). *Theory and practice in the teaching of literature by Afro-Americans.* Urbana, IL: NCTE.

Turner, M. (1985). Our readers write: Computer software that works. *English Journal, 88*(2), 88.

Tweeten, J. (1988). Odyssey travelogue. *North Carolina English Teacher, 46*(1), 18.

Tyler, R. W. (1975). Specific approaches to curriculum development. In J. Schaffarzick, & D. H. Hampson (Eds.), *Strategies for curriculum development* (pp. 17–33). Berkeley, CA: McCutchan.

U.S. Department of Education. (1998). *Writing framework and specifications for the 1998 National Assessment of Educational Progress.* Washington, D.C.

Velie, A. R. (Ed.). (1979). *American Indian literature: An anthology.* Norman, OK: University of Oklahoma Press.

Veidemanis, G. V. (1988). *Tess of the D'Urbervilles:* What the film left out. *English Journal, 77*(7), 53–57.

Viadero, D. (1997, Oct. 15). Few U.S. schools use technology well, two studies report. *Education Week,* p. 6.

Virginia's Literacy Passport Program: The Literacy Tests. (1994). Richmond, VA: Virginia Department of Education.

Vygotsky, L. S. (1962). *Thought and language* (E. Hanfmann & G. Vakar, Trans.). Cambridge, MA: MIT Press.

Vygotsky, L. S. (1978). In M. Cole, V. John-Steiner, S. Scribner, & E. Souberman (Eds.), *Mind in society: The development of higher psychological processes.* Cambridge, MA: Harvard University Press.

Wagner, B. J. (1976). *Dorothy Heathcote: Drama as a learning medium.* Washington, DC: National Education Association.

Wahlenmayer, C. W. (1991). Ray Charles has been in my classroom. *English Journal, 80*(4), 55–56.

Walker, A. (1982). *The color purple.* New York: Washington Square Press.

Walker, A. (1983). *In search of our mothers' gardens: Womanist prose.* San Diego: Harcourt Brace Jovanovich.

Walker, M. (1997). Authentic assessment in the literature classroom. *English Journal, 86*(1), 69–73.

Walkington, J. W. (1991). Women and power in Henrik Ibsen and Adrienne Rich. *English Journal, 80*(3), 64–68.

Wall, D. (1971). The state of grammar in the state of Iowa. *English Journal, 60*(8), 1127–1130.

Wallace, M. (1988). Invisibility blues. In R. Simonson & S. Walker (Eds.), *Multi-cultural literacy* (pp. 161–172). St. Paul, MN: Graywolf Press.

Ward, W. (1930). *Creative dramatics for the upper grades and junior high school.* New York: Appleton.

Warstler, D., (1997, Apr. 11). Response projects to develop and extend interpretation. Presentation at NCTE's Spring Conference, Charlotte, NC.

Washington, M. H. (1991, Spring). Selected bibliography of African-American literature. *Bread Loaf News,* pp. 5–16.

Watson, G. (1986). *The literary critics: A study of English descriptive criticism.* London: The Hogarth Press.

Weathers, W. (1980). *An alternate style: Options in composition.* Portsmouth, NH: Boynton/Cook.

Weaver, C. (1996). *Teaching grammar in context.* Portsmouth, NH: Heinemann.

Webb, N. (1982). Student interaction and learning in small groups. *Review of Educational Research, 52*(30), 421–445.

Weiner, L. (1997). Designing lesson plans: What new teachers can learn from Moffet and Wagner. *English Journal, 86*(4), 78–79.

Wendt, M. (1990). Bio-poem given to us by Dr. Elizabeth Bowles, University of North Carolina at Greensboro.

West, C. (1982). *Prophesy deliverance! An Afro-American revolutionary Christianity.* Philadelphia: Westminster Press.

What matters most: teaching for America's future. (1996). New York, NY: National Commission on Teaching and America's Future.

Whetsone, C. (1997, Apr. 11). Literature circles in one high school classroom. Presentation at NCTE's Spring Conference, Charlotte, NC.

Whishaw, I. (1994). Translation project: Breaking the "English only" rule. *English Journal, 83*(5), 28-30.

Whitworth, R. (1991). A book for all occasions: Activities for teaching general semantics. *English Journal, 80*(2), 50-54.

Wiersma, W., & Jurs, S. G. (1990). *Educational measurement and testing,* (2nd ed.). Boston: Allyn & Bacon.

Wiggins, G. (1989). A true test: Toward a more authentic and equitable assessment. *Phi Delta Kappan, 70*(9), 703-713.

Wiggins, G. (1997). Work standards: Why we need standards for instruction and assessment design. *NASSP Bulletin, 81*(590), 56-64.

Wigginton, E. (1985). *Sometimes a shining moment.* Garden City, NJ: Anchor Press.

Wilhelm, J. D. (1997). *"You gotta BE the book:" Teaching engaged and reflective reading with adolescents.* Urbana, IL: NCTE.

Wilhelm, J. D. (1998, Februrary 2). *Reading between the lines.* Presentation at Wake Forest University, Winston-Salem, NC.

Wilkinson, A. (1971). *Foundation of language.* Oxford: Oxford University Press.

Will, G. E. (1978). Winston Churchill: In the region of mass effects. In *The pursuit of happiness and other sobering thoughts* (pp. 31-33). New York: Harper & Row.

Williams, J. (1990). *Style: Toward clarity and grace.* Chicago: University of Chicato Press.

Williams, R. (1980). *Problems in materialism and culture.* London: Verso.

Winterowd, W. R. (1975). *Contemporary rhetoric: A conceptual background with readings.* New York: Harcourt Brace Jovanovich.

Winterowd, W. R. (1981). *The contemporary writer.* New York: Harcourt Brace Jovanovich.

Winterowd, W. R., & Murray, P. Y. (1985). *English: Writing and skills* (Teacher's ed.). San Diego, Coronado.

Wiske, M., Niguidula, D., & Shepard, J. (1988). *Collaborative research goes to school: Guided inquiry with computers in classrooms.* Office of Education Research and Improvement. Washington, DC.

Wolf, A. (1990). *Something is going to happen: Poetry alive!* Asheville, NC: IAMBIC Publications.

Wolf, K. (1996). Developing an effective teaching portfolio. *Educational Leadership, 53*(6), 34-37.

Wolfe, D., & Antinarella (1997). *Deciding to lead.* Portsmouth, NH: Heinemann.

Wolfram, W. (1983, Apr.). *Standard English: Demythologizing an American myth.* Lecture at Wake Forest University, Winston-Salem, NC.

Wood, F. (1985). *The asymmetrical brain: Librarians and cowboys.* Paper presented at NC Governor's School, Winston-Salem, NC.

Woolf, V. (1928). Mr. Bennett and Mrs. Brown in *The Hogarth Essays.* In L. Woolf & V. Woolf (Eds.), Garden City, NY.

Woolf, V. (1929). *A room of one's own.* New York: Harcourt Brace & World.

Wootton, M. (Ed.). (1982). *New directions in drama teaching: Studies in secondary school practice.* London: Heinemann.

Wresch, W. (Ed.). (1991). *The English classroom in the computer age: Thirty lesson Plans.* Urbana, IL: NCTE.

Wykoff, G. S., & Shaw, H. (1957). *The Harper handbook of college composition.* New York: Harper.

Yagelski, R. P. (1994). Literature and literacy: Rethinking English as a school subject. *English Journal, 83*(3), 30-36.

Zeeman, K. L. (1997). Grappling with Grendel or what we did when the censors came. *English Journal, 86*(2), 46-49.

Zemelman, S., Daniels, H., & Hyde, A. (1993). *Best practice: New standards for teaching and learning in America's schools.* Portsmouth, NH: Heinemann.

Zimpher, N. (1988). A design for the development of teacher leaders. *Journal of Teacher Education, 39*(1), 53.

Zinsser, W. (Ed.). (1987). *Inventing the truth: The art and craft of memoir.* Boston: Houghton Mifflin.

Zitlow, C. (1995). Young adult literature: Did Patty Bergen write this poem?: Connecting poetry and young adult literature. *English Journal, 84*(1), 110-113.

INDEX